1956

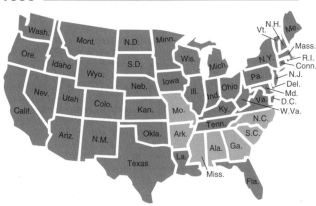

Electoral votes*

Stevenson (D) 74
Eisenhower (R) 457

*An Alabama Democratic elector cast his vote for Walter Jones, making the official count: Eisenhower, 457; Stevenson, 73; Jones, 1.

1960

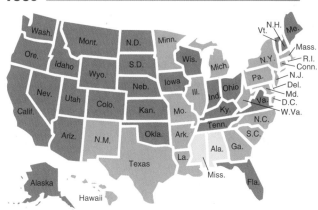

Electoral votes

Kennedy (D) 303
Nixon (R) 219
Byrd (D) 15

1964

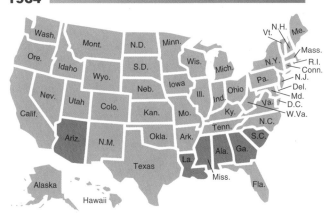

Electoral votes

Johnson (D) 486
Goldwater (R) 52

1968

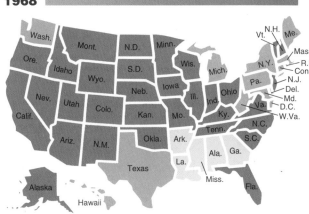

Electoral votes†

Humphrey (D) 191
Nixon (R) 302
Wallace (American Independent) 45

†A North Carolina Republican elector cast his vote for George Wallace, making the official count: Nixon, 301; Humphrey, 191; Wallace, 46.

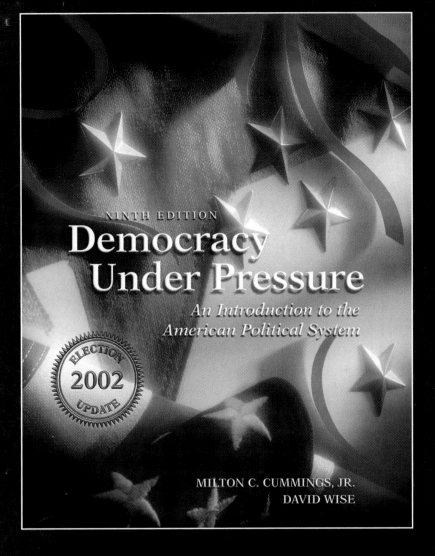

NINTH EDITION

Democracy Under Pressure

An Introduction to the American Political System

MILTON C. CUMMINGS, JR.
DAVID WISE

Democracy Under Pressure
An Introduction to the American Political System
NINTH EDITION

The hallmark of this best-selling textbook for the American Government course has always been its lively narrative and exemplary scholarship. That tradition continues in this new edition, which has been thoroughly streamlined and updated to include the 2002 campaign and election. Greater emphasis has been placed on refining the existing features of the book, providing a broader context for understanding American politics, and on integrating technological resources beyond the textbook itself. These features make it easier than ever before for students to become actively involved in learning about the American political process.

INSPIRE, MOTIVATE, and ENGAGE your students with online access to American Government *as it is* today!

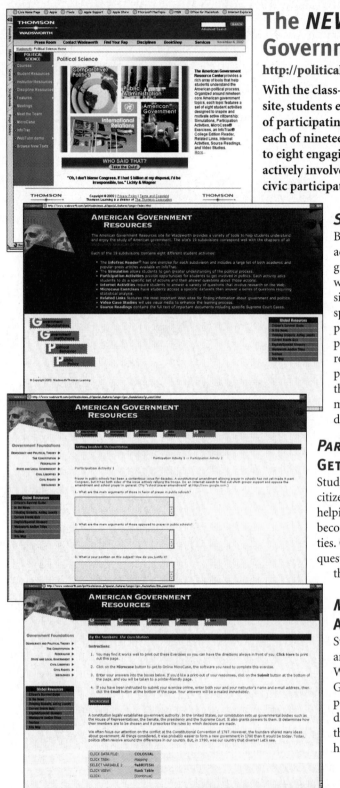

The *NEW* American Government Resource Center

http://politicalscience.wadsworth.com/amgov/

With the class-tested tools included on this exceptional site, students experience the excitement and satisfaction of participating in government and politics. By linking each of nineteen core American government topics to eight engaging types of activities, this new site actively involves students in your course—and in civic participation at the grassroots level!

SIMULATIONS . . . YOU ARE THERE!

By placing the student in the role of political actor, *Simulations* allow students to gain greater understanding of the political process while emphasizing critical thinking and decision-making skills. Class-tested and written specifically for the site to reflect the *current* political environment, simulations are appropriate for individual or group work. Featured roles include: state senator, an adviser to a president who must appoint a new member of the Supreme Court, a lawyer who must determine his clients' rights, an adviser to a presidential candidate, and other political roles.

PARTICIPATION ACTIVITIES . . . GETTING INVOLVED

Students are encouraged to *get involved* in active citizenship by working on a political campaign, helping an interest group, lobbying Congress, and become activists as they participate in these activities. Once the activity is completed, a series of questions about the experience asks students if they feel they *"made a difference."*

MICROCASE® EXERCISES . . . ANALYZING BY THE NUMBERS

Students use actual real-world data to *do* data analysis with these *MicroCase Exercises*. Written specifically for the American Government Resource Center, each exercise presents an issue in American government and directs students to pertinent information through data sets. Accompanying questions help students consider and interpret data.

VIDEO CASE STUDIES . . . OBSERVING AND MAKING DECISIONS

Using visual media to enhance the learning process, these video excerpts—featuring contemporary policy issues—conclude with provocative questions that encourage decision making.

ENRICH your course content with current online material available at the
NEW AMERICAN GOVERNMENT RESOURCE CENTER
http://politicalscience.wadsworth.com/amgov/

INFOTRAC® COLLEGE EDITION READER

Also located at the American Government Resource Center, this reader is updated every semester and organized by core American government topics—featuring exercises that guide students to current articles in the **InfoTrac College Edition** online library. Access to the library is **FREE** when you adopt this text. **See page 9** of this *Preview* for details.

SOURCE READINGS

This section of the Web site contains the full text of important primary and secondary source documents, including Supreme Court Cases. Political and historical contexts are provided.

INTERNET ACTIVITIES

Divided into three groups—"Just the Facts, Please," "Compare and Contrast," and "Exploration"—these activities ask students to answer a variety of questions that involve research on the Web.

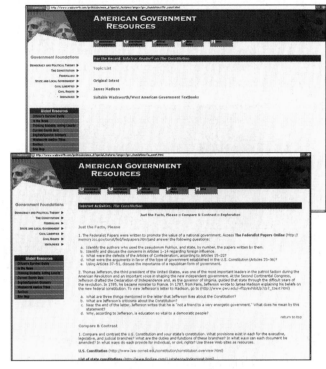

RELATED LINKS

These useful links for each core topic keep readers current and include the most important informational Web sites for government and politics.

 Plus these important resources

Also available . . . a Companion Web Site
AT THE WADSWORTH
POLITICAL SCIENCE RESOURCE CENTER
http://politicalscience.wadsworth.com/cummings9/update/

Designed exclusively for this *Ninth Edition 2002 Election Update*, the book's Companion Web site is fully integrated with the textbook and provides links to major election coverage sites, news sources, political organizations, and other resources related to the American government course. It includes chapter-by-chapter links to the sites referenced in the textbook's Web icons and to other sites directly related to text material. The site provides the glossary from the textbook and the *Instructor's Manual* online as well as a selection of self-assessment questions from the printed *Study Guide*. It also gives students direct access to the Web and new *InfoTrac College Edition* activities provided for each chapter of the book.

RESPECTED!

More than a million students have been introduced to the fundamentals of American government by Milton C. Cummings, Jr. and David Wise.

CURRENT!

Every chapter has been completely updated with coverage and analysis of the 2002 election, as well as the impact of 9/11 and the war on terrorism.

TECHNOLOGICALLY INTEGRATED!

Web icons in every chapter take students to the up-to-the-minute currency of the Internet! This book's robust Companion Web Site takes you and your students beyond the boundaries of the traditional classroom!

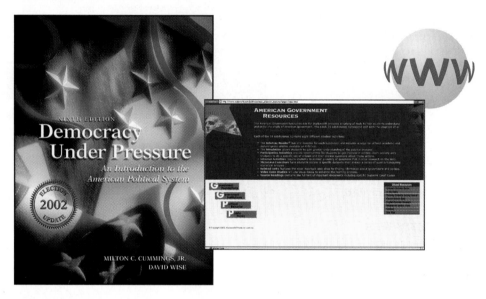

A writing style that engages— combined with exemplary scholarship you can trust!

You'll find it here in this best-selling text that conveys a balanced and realistic sense of our political system, including the historical foundations and current dynamics. In a time of rapid change, the authors continue to focus not only on the very considerable achievements of the American system of government but on its shortcomings too—providing students with a look at the reality as well as the rhetoric of American democracy. Cummings and Wise focus on the gaps, where they exist, between American myths and American realities and the political system's promise and performance.

Democracy Under Pressure: An Introduction to the American Political System, 2002 Election Update succeeds in getting students politically involved and helps motivate them to participate—not just examine—the way democracy responds to the needs and demands of various groups over time. In this new edition, the *Democracy Under Pressure* theme is of particular interest and use as the authors examine the impact and effects of September 11th on the various institutions and policies of American government. With the results of the 2002 congressional election incorporated throughout the book and **FREE** access to *InfoTrac® College Edition* (see page 9), rest assured you and your students are getting the most current information available on American government.

This *LIVELY*, *ENGAGING* book is as *CURRENT* and *TIMELY* as an American Government text can possibly be...

Take a look through the pages of this remarkable text...
on every page, in every discussion, you will find thoughtful analysis and the latest information on the most hotly debated issues facing our nation today.

★ Full coverage of the 2002 congressional elections

★ Exploration of the potential impact of these elections on American politics, government, and the 2004 presidential race

★ Discussion of a wide range of events related to the terrorist attacks of September 11th and the resulting war in Afghanistan, and the long-range war on terrorism

★ Discussion of the general impact of terrorism on foreign policy and domestic security

★ Analysis of the latest economic developments, including the recent recession and recovery, the impact of the September 11th attacks on travel-related industries, the funding of the ongoing war on terrorism, the passage of major tax cuts and their impact on the federal budget, and the general crisis of confidence experienced in the business community as a result of the Enron scandal

★ The latest information on anthrax attacks on the Capitol and elsewhere, violence in the Middle East, campaign finance reform, and the proposed privatization of Social Security

> *I've used just about every text for the introduction to American government course . . . The clarity, style, content, and pedagogy of* Democracy Under Pressure *ranks with the best of them— especially the grace of writing. It is far livelier than one usually finds in such texts.*
> Loch Johnson, University of Georgia, Athens

TOTAL TECHNOLOGY INTEGRATION helps you and your students keep pace with a rapidly changing political landscape

The *Ninth Edition Election Update* **connects your students to its multimedia teaching and learning tools with total integration!** Throughout the book, you'll find Web icons in the margins that direct students to Web sites related to specific topics, issues, or individuals presented in the text.

and that it could rise to more than 300 million after 2015.[17]

According to one study of population patterns in the United States, if the projections of some experts were realized, "we would have close to one billion people in the United States one hundred years from now."[18] Although the authors of the study added that birth control and other factors made it unlikely that such a staggering total will be reached by that time, [they est]imated that the United States could [sustain] a population of a billion without peo[ple bump]ing one another into the oceans.

Online ...y the nation has expanded from a pop-ulation of about 4 million in 1790, and what the future may hold, can be charted with Census Bureau statistics and projections to 2025, as shown in Table 1-1. This dramatic increase in numbers of people—the "population explosion"—is taking place around the world. It raises questions that governments must ponder. Will there be enough food to eat? Enough room to live? Enough oil and water and other natural resources to meet humanity's future needs? Will the environment be destroyed?

Online *For more information about Census Bureau statistics, see:* www.census.gov

An interesting profile of the American public can be sketched with statistics, as presented in Table 1-2, that answer the question "Who are we?" A portrait of national origins can be drawn. The great successive waves of immigration placed a stamp of diversity on America; even third- and fourth-generation Americans may think of themselves as "Irish" or "Italian."[*]

Copyright © Mark Downey/Lucid Images/Picture Quest

An earlier census survey indicated that the ancestry groups of Americans included the following: German, 23.3 percent; Irish, 15.6 percent; English, 13.1 percent; African American, 12 percent; Hispanic, 8.6 percent; Italian, 6.0 percent; French, 4.1 percent; Polish, 4.0 percent; Asian Americans, 2.9 percent; Dutch, 2.5 percent; Scottish, 2.2 percent; and Native American, 0.08 percent.[19] The United States is also a nation of more than 87.4 million Protestants, 61.2 million Catholics, 5.5 million Muslims, 5.3 Eastern Orthodox church members, 4 million Jews, and 1.3 million Hindus.[*]

---
[*]The Census Bureau does not ask the religion of Americans in the decennial census, which is taken every 10 years that end in zero, but religious groups estimate their own membership. These are rounded figures based on *The World Almanac and Book of Facts 2000*, pp. 692–693.

■ TABLE 1-1

Profile of the U.S. Population, 1790–2025

| | Population (in millions) | | | | | | | | | | |
| | Actual | | | | | | | | | Projected | |
	1790	1870	1920	1960	1970	1980	1990	1998		2010	2025
Total population	4	39	106	179	203	226.5	249.4	270.5		297.7	335
Urban	—[*]	10	54	125	149	167	187	NA		NA	NA
Rural	4	29	52	54	54	60	62	NA		NA	NA
Nonwhite	1	5	11	20	25	32	40.7	47.5		58.2	72.8
White	3	34	95	159	178	195	208.7	223		239.5	262.2
	NA	20	25	30	28.1	30	33	35.2		37	38
	NA	7	23	42	53	45	46	53		NA	NA
	NA	—[*]	0.6	3	7	10	13.8	14.7		NA	NA

...sus, and National Center for Education Statistics, Department of Education. Projected totals are the most ...Population figures rounded.

KEY TERMS

public opinion, p. 170
political opinion, p. 171
political socialization, p. 171
reference groups, p. 176
primary groups, p. 176
secondary groups, p. 176

exit polls, p. 178
universe, p. 179
random sample, p. 179
cluster sampling, p. 180
quota sample, p. 180
bandwagon effect, p. 181
political culture, p. 182

CHAPTER HIGHLIGHTS

◆ Public opinion is the expression of attitudes about government and politics. All governments are based, to some extent, on public opinion.
◆ Political socialization is the process by which a person acquires a set of political attitudes and forms opinions about political and social issues.
◆ Many factors influence the opinions people hold. Among the most important are differences in social class, occupation, and income; religion, sex, race, and ethnic factors; sectional and geographic differences; and the views of reference groups. There are two kinds of reference groups: primary groups (such as friends, office associates, or a social club) and secondary groups (such as labor unions or fraternal, professional, or religious groups).
◆ In addition, mass media—television, radio, newspapers, the Internet, online computer service providers, and other media—have a major impact on public opinion.
◆ The qualities of public opinion—direction, intensity, and stability—may be measured by political polls.
◆ Political polls, often useful as a guide to voter sentiment, are a standard part of political campaigns. They measure opinion by taking a random sample of a larger population, or universe. Due to the mathematical law of probability, the results of a poll usually reflect the opinions of the larger group. Although generally reliable, polls are sometimes wrong and do not necessarily predict the outcomes of elections.
◆ In presidential elections, often only a little more than half the people of voting age—and sometimes less than half—bother to vote. In off-year elections for Congress, usually well under half of the voting-age population votes.
◆ Americans have not always sought to express their opinions or to bring about political change through lawful or peaceful means. If the political system fails to respond to the demands placed on it, or if participation is slow to bring about change, individuals or groups may vent their anger against the system in violent ways.
◆ Modern political candidates and leaders are highly attuned to techniques for measuring and influencing public opinion. Political polls, television commercials, Internet Web sites, and professional campaign

managers are all part of the efforts at mass persuasion employed today.
◆ Public opinion in a democracy may be seen as a broad but flexible framework for policy making, setting certain limits within which government may act.

SUGGESTED WEB SITES

http://www.gallup.com
The Gallup Organization
Since 1935 the Gallup Organization has conducted surveys to measure public opinion on various issues. Its polls cover five subject areas: Politics and Elections, Business, Social Issues and Policy, Managing, and Lifestyle.

http://dailynews.yahoo.com/h/zo/nm/
Yahoo! Public Opinion Headlines
Yahoo! and Reuters news service list and provide the text of stories that report public opinion on topics ranging from politics to everyday life.

http://www.msnbc.com
MSNBC Opinions
Provides viewers with opinion articles and transcripts of programs, and allows visitors to the Web site to participate in MSNBC polls and to register their views on a Bulletin Board System (BBS) or through the MSNBC chat room.

SUGGESTED READING

Bennett, Linda, and Bennett, Stephen. *Living with Leviathan: Americans Coming to Terms with Big Government* (University of Kansas Press, 1990) A detailed examination of Americans' changing attitudes toward the expanding role of government in social and economic life.
Bennett, Stephen, and Rademacher, Eric, eds. *After the Boom: The Politics of Generation X* (Rowman & Littlefield, 1997). A series of essays, including several by members of Generation X, examining the social and political thought and behavior of a younger segment of the population that will be increasingly important in the coming years.
Cantril, Albert H., and Cantril, Susan Davis. *Reading Mixed Signals: Ambivalence in American Public Opinion About Government* (Johns Hopkins University Press, 1999) An insightful study of the seemingly paradoxical attitudes toward government in the United States: Americans express distrust for government, and say that its size should be reduced, but when it comes to concrete issues, such as the environment, care for the elderly and young, and health care, they believe that government should be doing more.

190 CHAPTER 6 PUBLIC OPINION

In addition, an **annotated list of significant Web resources** appears at the end of every chapter.

In the helpful *Instructor's Manual*, you'll find **activities based on these Web sites** that encourage students to further explore the chapter's issues.

Preview

The political process, history, and the importance of participation . . .
IT'S ALL HERE IN THE 2002 ELECTION UPDATE

Making a Difference boxes are designed to encourage student participation. These inspiring and insightful boxes provide real-world examples of how individual initiative can change the political process for the better.

MAKING A DIFFERENCE
THE SUPREME COURT RULES FOR BRENDA ROE

After Congress transferred the federal welfare program to the states in 1996, a woman who preferred to be known as "Brenda Roe," to preserve her privacy, moved her family from Oklahoma, where they had received $300 a month in welfare benefits, to California, where the family qualified for $600 a month.

But there was a catch: To discourage people from moving to California to receive higher benefits, the state had passed a law limiting benefits for new residents; for one year they could collect only the same amount they had received in their previous state. About 15 states had enacted such laws, which Congress had allowed in the 1996 law overhauling the welfare system.

Brenda Roe and other families in the same boat sued the state of California. On the face of it, the California law seemed to restrict the right of all Americans to travel and to live where they wish.

The case went all the way to the Supreme Court, where the justices heard arguments early in 1999. It was the first major high court test of the nation's welfare reform law.

The question before the Court was whether a two-tiered benefit policy unfairly hurt needy people who want to move from one state to another.

In oral arguments, California said its program kept down costs and ensured that the state would not become a magnet for poor families. But Justice Ruth Bader Ginsburg suggested the policy violated a fundamental principle "that is the genius of the United States . . . that people can pick their states and states can't pick their people."

"This has grave consequences for [a] family," said Justice Sandra Day O'Connor.

On May 17, 1999, the Supreme Court ruled in the case of *Saenz v. Roe.* It held, 7–2, that states may not limit

welfare benefits for new residents, and it struck down the California law. The Court said a two-tier system violates poor people's right to travel and encroaches on their right to be treated like other residents of their new state.

"Citizens of the United States, whether rich or poor, have the right to choose to be citizens of the state wherein they reside," Justice John Paul Stevens wrote for the court. "The states, however, do not have any right to select their citizens."

The former Oklahoma woman who called herself Brenda Roe had, with the help of the U.S. Supreme Court, won her constitutional right to be treated like other citizens of the state of California. And her victory won those same equal rights for many other needy families struggling to make ends meet.

—Adapted from the *Washington Post,* January 14 and May 18, 1999

Comparing Government boxes provide a broader context for understanding and appreciating the American political system by showing alternative approaches to common processes, institutions, and issues.

Comparing Governments
LIBEL: A TOWN CALLED "SUE"

Because of the constitutional protection of freedom of the press and freedom of expression in the United States, it is often difficult to win a libel suit in American courts. This is especially true if the plaintiff is a public figure. Those who are judged to be public figures must not only prove they were defamed, but also that the offending material was published with knowledge that it was false, or with "reckless disregard" of whether it was false. It is a difficult standard of proof.

In Britain, by contrast, where there has historically been greater concern for preserving public reputations, and less protection for free expression, the burden of proof is not on the plaintiff making the accusa-

often choose to sue in British courts when they can, and London has come to be called "a town called Sue" by international media attorneys.

In her 1993 book *Denying the Holocaust: The Growing Assault on Truth and Memory,* Emory University professor Deborah Lipstadt, an American scholar, denounced British historian David Irving as "one of the most dangerous spokespersons for Holocaust denial," and called him a "Hitler partisan . . . a racist and an antisemite." Irving, who has written admiringly of Hitler and denied the existence of gas chambers at Auschwitz, waited until the book was published in England, and then sued Lipstadt and her publisher.

defense over $3 million, the judge in the case ruled that Lipstadt had been justified in her characterizations of Irving, who had "deliberately misrepresented and manipulated historical evidence" regarding the Holocaust. Because Irving lost, he was required under British law to pay the defendant's legal expenses.

Ironically, it may have been Irving's ability to sue under Britain's plaintiff-friendly libel law which ultimately cost him what had remained of his reputation as a historian of Nazi Germany. "In the U.S., this would have been thrown out of court, but if it had been thrown out, Irving would have been able to say that he never got his day in court," said Ms.

American Past boxes give students the historical context essential for understanding the origin and evolution of the political institutions and controversies we inherit today.

The AMERICAN PAST
THE BILL OF RIGHTS: PRO AND CON

In the political struggle over ratification of the Constitution, the Antifederalists argued that the document was incomplete without an enumeration of the rights of the people:

> People, and very wisely too, like to be express and explicit about their essential rights, and not to be forced to claim them on the precarious . . . tenure of inferences and general principles . . . we discern certain rights, as the freedom of the press, and the trial by jury, which the people of England and of America of course believe to be sacred, and essential to their political happiness. . . .
>
> Perhaps it would be better to enumerate the particular essential rights the people are entitled to. . . . Freedom of the press is a fundamental right, and ought not to be restrained by any taxes, duties, or in any manner whatever. Why should not the people, in adopting a federal constitution, declare this.

—Richard Henry Lee, *Letters from the Federal Farmer*

The Federalists argued that the Constitution as drafted protected the rights of individuals, making a bill of rights unnecessary:

> It has been several times truly remarked that bills of rights are, in their origin, stipulations between kings and their subjects, abridgments of prerogative in favor of privilege, reservations of rights not surrendered to the prince. . . . They have no application to constitutions. . . .
>
> I go further, and affirm that bills of rights . . . are not only unnecessary in the proposed Constitution, but would even be dangerous. They would contain various exceptions to powers not granted; and, on this very account, would afford a colorable pretext to claim more than were granted. For why declare that things shall not be done which there is no power to do? Why, for instance, should it be said that the liberty of the press shall not be restrained, when no power is given by which restrictions may be imposed?

—Alexander Hamilton, *The Federalist,* No. 84

states that "Congress shall make no law" abridging First Amendment freedoms, the Supreme Court has interpreted this to mean that state and local authorities can-

sion, Supreme Court Justice Oliver Wendell Holmes, Jr., had established the classic **clear and present danger test** to define the point at which speech loses First ...dment protection:

> *"I really like the American Past boxes. They are relevant, interesting, sometimes humorous, and always thought-provoking."*
> Pauletta Otis, University of Southern Colorado

TIME-TESTED PEDAGOGY provides students with a learning framework and reinforces true understanding

Your students will find the book's pedagogical tools helpful and easy-to-use! Pedagogy includes:

Key terms in bold-faced type alert students to important topics.

KEY TERMS

federal system, p. 60	enumerated powers, p. 68
federalism, p. 60	
unitary system of government, p. 60	implied powers, p. 68
dual federalism, p. 65	inherent powers, p. 68
cooperative federalism, p. 65	concurrent powers, p. 68
	supremacy clause, p. 72
creative federalism, p. 65	categorical grants, p. 79
new federalism, p. 66	block grants, p. 79
regulatory federalism, p. 66	general purpose grants, p. 79

A bulleted list of chapter highlights helps students organize, synthesize, and review key material from the chapter.

CHAPTER HIGHLIGHTS

✦ The First Amendment to the Constitution protects the freedom of the press. It does so because the supporters of the Bill of Rights understood that the press must be free to report about the activities of the government, and, when necessary, to criticize those in power.

✦ Freedom of the press and freedom of expression are not absolute. Under the Constitution, the Supreme Court has balanced those basic rights against competing needs of society.

✦ Broadly defined, "the media" include TV, the Internet, newspapers, magazines, radio, wire services, books, newsletters, and other published material. Often, as this book does, people use the term "the press" interchangeably with "the media" or "the news media."

✦ The press plays a vital role in a democracy because it is the principal means by which the people learn about the actions and policies of the government. A democracy rests on the consent of the governed, but in order to give their consent in any meaningful way, the governed must be informed.

✦ The press provides a crucial link between the people and the government. It is the essential source of information that helps citizens form opinions about government and politics and decide how to cast their votes in elections.

✦ Until the 20th century, the press consisted only of print media—newspapers, magazines, books, and pamphlets. The press moguls of the 19th century had great influence on American society and on the government. Eventually, sensational reporting in their newspapers became known as "yellow journalism."

✦ In the first decade of the 20th century, long before the modern term "investigative reporting" came into vogue, a group of writers, journalists, and critics known as muckrakers exposed corporate malfeasance and political corruption.

✦ The 20th century brought radio into America's homes. For the first time, it allowed political leaders to speak directly to the voters.

✦ By providing a direct link between political leaders and candidates and voters, television changed the nature of American politics. Television made an enormous impact, not only on the political process, but also on the shape and power of the media. As advertisers poured millions into the TV networks to reach prime-time audiences, inevitably there were fewer advertising dollars invested in print journalism.

✦ Just as television had altered the shape of American politics a half-century earlier, by the year

[...] brought a dramatic new level of [...] to government and the political [...] rmation, census figures, poll [...] hes, legislation, Supreme Court [...] ly unlimited resources of all kinds became available at the click of a mouse button, part of a vast ocean of information that once could only be found in major libraries.

✦ By the year 2000 the shape of the media was changing dramatically. One after another, the giants of the media were joining in multibillion-dollar mergers. The concentration of ownership raised questions about the independence and diversity of the American press.

✦ Radio and television do not enjoy as much freedom as other segments of the press, because, unlike newspapers, broadcast stations are licensed by the Federal Communications Commission. Although broadcast networks are not licensed, the stations they own and operate are. The law requires broadcasters to provide "equal time" to all legally qualified political candidates.

✦ In recent years the Supreme Court has shown increasing concern over pretrial and courtroom publicity that may prejudice the fair trial of a defendant in a criminal case. The right to have a fair trial often conflicts with the First Amendment in another important area—that of confidentiality for reporters and their news sources. The Supreme Court has ruled that reporters must reveal the identity of their sources if the information is needed in a criminal case.

✦ A person defamed by a newspaper or other publication may be able to sue for libel and collect damages because the First Amendment does not protect this form of "free speech." Despite some victories by the press, the threat of libel actions has become a major problem for the news media, publishers, and writers.

✦ Some critics of the press argue that giving widespread coverage to acts of terrorism plays into the hands of the perpetrators, who are seeking publicity. Another argument sometimes voiced is that press coverage can lead to "copycat" acts by others seeking the same notoriety for their deeds or for themselves. The press, however, has a responsibility to report major news events.

✦ The government often attempts to manipulate the press and to manage the news, to put a favorable "spin" on events. It may even mislead the press—and therefore the public—for a variety of reasons. Officials have a vested interest in trying to influence what the press reports, in order to shape public opinion to support administration policies.

✦ The Freedom of Information Act requires federal executive branch and regulatory agencies to make information available to journalists and other persons unless it falls into one of several confidential categories.

✦ Because the press wields great power and influence in American politics it has become a target of criticism. Some critics contend that the press is politically biased. However, poll data suggest that almost

Chapter Highlights **243**

An end-of-chapter list of key terms with page references in every chapter makes it easy to study and review.

Online course builders, a *FREE* online library . . .
EXCEPTIONAL Web-based tools for your classroom

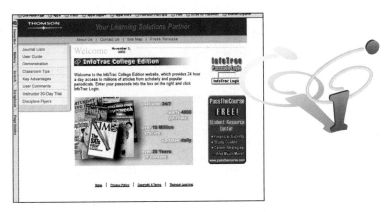

FREE ACCESS TO *INFOTRAC® COLLEGE EDITION!*

A four-month subscription to this extensive online library is **FREE** with every new copy of the book. *InfoTrac College Edition* includes articles from thousands of magazines, newsletters, and such respected journals and periodicals as *American Political Science Review, Foreign Policy, Newsweek,* and *Political Science Quarterly.* These full-length articles (not just excerpts) are updated daily and span 22 years, expertly indexed, and ready to use—24 hours a day, seven days a week! Search words in the margins throughout the **2002 Election Update Edition** direct students to current articles online.

WEBTUTOR™ ADVANTAGE . . .
ONLINE COURSE MANAGEMENT
AND STUDENT TUTORIALS

WebCT: 0-534-25975-8 • Blackboard: 0-534-25976-6

"Out of the box" or customizable, this versatile online tool is filled with pre-loaded, text-specific content, including diagrams and illustrations, as well as Microsoft® *PowerPoint*® files, organized by text chapter. For students, *WebTutor Advantage* offers access to a full array of study tools, including glossary flashcards, practice quizzes, online tutorials, and Web links. Instructors can use *WebTutor Advantage* to provide virtual office hours, post syllabi, set up threaded discussions, and track student progress with the quizzing material.

MYCOURSE 2.0 . . .
OUR NEW ONLINE COURSE
BUILDER! FREE!

Whether you want only the easy-to-use tools to build your site or the content to furnish it, *MyCourse 2.0* offers you the simple solution for a custom course Web site that allows you to assign, track, and report on student progress, load your syllabus, and more. Contact your Thomson/ Wadsworth representative for details.
You can demo *MyCourse 2.0* at
http://mycourse.thomsonlearning.com

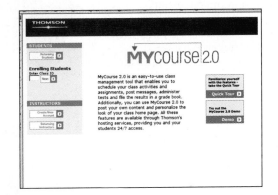

Videos that *SPARK CLASS DISCUSSION* and *LAUNCH LECTURES* . . . Choose from this ever-growing selection

CNN® TODAY: AMERICAN GOVERNMENT VIDEO SERIES

Now you can integrate the up-to-the-minute programming power of CNN and its affiliate networks right into your course. Organized by topics covered in the typical American government course, these 45- to 60-minute videos are divided into clips of three to six minutes in length.

Volume I: 0-534-51944-X • Volume II: 0-534-55362-1
Volume III: 0-534-56957-9

New for 2003! Volume IV: 0-534-58661-9
(includes coverage of the war on terrorism)

AMERICA'S NEW WAR: CNN® LOOKS AT TERRORISM

Free to qualified adopters, this great discussion starter includes 16 two-to-five-minute segments featuring *CNN* news footage, commentator remarks, and speeches dealing with terrorist attacks on U.S targets throughout the world. Topics include: anthrax and biological warfare, new security measures, Osama bin Laden, Al Qaeda, asset freezing, homeland defense, new weapons of terrorism, and the Arab-American response to recent events that have occurred. Ask your Thomson/ Wadsworth representative about our video policy by adoption size. 0-534-16805-1

★ *New!*
VIDEO CASE STUDIES IN AMERICAN GOVERNMENT

Free to adopters, this award-winning video contains 12 video case studies, addressing recent developments in the debate on such policy issues as "Affirmative Action" and "Show Me the Money: Money and the Presidential Campaign." Each case study concludes with questions designed to spark classroom discussion.

0-15-504160-6. An accompanying Instructor's Manual (0-15-504244-0) offers suggestions for use and activities for each case.

WADSWORTH POLITICAL SCIENCE VIDEO LIBRARY

Choose from this library's varied selection of videos to enrich your lectures and extend discussions of text material. Available to qualified adopters. Policy based on adoption size. Please contact your Thomson/ Wadsworth sales representative for details.

Course preparation resources for *INSTRUCTORS*

INSTRUCTOR'S EDITION . . .
featuring the Resource Integration Guide!

The Instructor's Edition of the **Ninth Edition: 2002 Election Update** includes an essential tool for instructors . . . the *Resource Integration Guide*. This guide links every chapter's outline—topic by topic—to instructional ideas and corresponding supplement resources. At a glance, you'll see which specific videos, *PowerPoint*® slides, test questions, and lecture suggestions are appropriate for each key chapter topic. The *Resource Integration Guide* starts on page 14.
0-534-62311-5

INSTRUCTOR'S MANUAL

This manual includes chapter outlines and learning objectives keyed to the *Study Guide* and the textbook, as well as lecture suggestions, video resources, group projects, key points, and key terms. An all-new set of Web activities provides assignments related to the Web icons presented in each chapter of the book. 0-534-62453-7

TEST BANK

by William E. Kelly, Auburn University
The *Test Bank* contains more than 2,400 multiple-choice, true/false, and short-answer essay questions, with page references to the text.
0-534-62452-9

Everything you need to teach the *Voices in Democracy Telecourse*

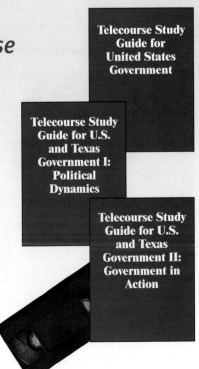

TELECOURSE STUDY GUIDES

Developed specifically to accompany the textbook and video programs for the U.S. Government telecourse and the U.S. and Texas Government telecourse, these study guides serve as the student's tutor through the course, providing assignments, overviews, lesson goals, textbook objectives, video objectives, Web activities, practice test questions and answers that provide feedback to the student before formal testing.
Telecourse Study Guide for United States Government 0-15-507005-3
Telecourse Study Guide for U.S. and Texas Government I:
Political Dynamics 0-15-507006-1
Telecourse Study Guide for U.S. and Texas Government II:
Government in Action 0-15-507012-6

VIDEO TEST BANK TO ACCOMPANY
VOICES IN DEMOCRACY TELECOURSE

This *Video Test Bank* provides multiple-choice questions tied directly to the 26 lessons presented in the *Voices in Democracy Telecourse Videos*. 0-15-503539-8

More tools to help you *PREPARE* and *PRESENT* dynamic, engaging lectures and *TEST* efficiently!

Multimedia Manager for Political Science 2003: A Microsoft® PowerPoint® Link Tool

Turning an everyday lecture into a media event is simple with this combination digital library and presentation tool. *Multimedia Manager's* dual-platform CD-ROM features "ready-to-go" Microsoft® PowerPoint® presentations (which consist of diagrams, charts, tables, and figures Wadsworth political science texts). Just pop in the CD-ROM and you're set!

You can also customize these presentations—pulling images from *Multimedia Manager's* extensive digital library and bringing in your own materials. The program's easy-to-follow wizard guides you at every step along the way.

Cross-platform CD-ROM: 0-534-57120-4

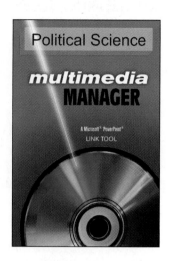

ExamView® Computerized Testing . . . including online testing!

Create, deliver, and customize tests and study guides (both print and online) in minutes with this easy-to-use assessment and tutorial system.

0-534-62451-0

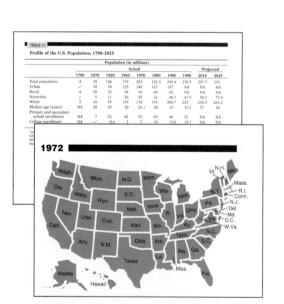

Transparency Acetates for American Government 2003

Illustrate and enhance your lectures with these colorful diagrams, charts, tables, and figures from the text and additional sources. The set contains more than 160 full-color acetates in all. 0-534-58675-9

Transparency Acetates

Over 40 full-color overhead transparencies illustrate concepts from the book. 0-15-507011-8

Handbook of Selected Legislation and Other Documents

ISBN: 0-534-53614-X

Includes excerpts from twelve laws passed by the U.S. Congress that have had a significant impact on American politics.

Handbook of Selected Court Cases

ISBN: 0-534-53613-1

Includes over 30 Supreme Court Cases.

These value-added *RESOURCES* help *STEER STUDENTS* toward *SUCCESS!* You can choose to package any of the resources listed below with each copy of the text.

Study Guide

Prepared by the authors of the textbook, this guide offers learning objectives, definitions, and key points for each chapter. It also includes study exercises and self tests. 0-534-62451-0 To package with the text: 0-534-05258-4

Readings in American Government, Fourth Edition

Edited by Mack C. Shelley, Jamie Swift, and Steffen W. Schmidt
Spark lively debate in your classroom with this on-target reader. Includes more than 60 readings on such topics as diversity on trial, politicians on the Web, campaign reform, and war in cyberspace.
0-534-59269-4 To package with the text: 0-534-26165-5

Critical Thinking and American Government, Second Edition

By Kent M. Brudney, John H. Carver, and Mark E. Weber
This thought-provoking text provides information and exercises that help students hone the skills necessary for interpreting and analyzing American government issues. The exercises correspond to chapter topics in American government texts. 0-15-505848-7 To package with the text: 0-534-26068-3

InfoTrac® College Edition Student Guide for Political Science

This booklet contains 24 pages of guidance to help students get the most benefit from the *InfoTrac® College Edition* database—including log in help, search tips, a search tips quick reference, and a topic list of suggested keyword search terms for political science.
0-534-24728-8 To package with the text: 0-534-04825-0

9-11: The Giant Awakens

By Jeremy Mayer
This brief text focuses on how the American political system, its institutions, and its system of civil liberties and rights are responding to the challenges posed by the September 11th terrorist attacks.
0-534-61659-3 To package with the text: 0-534-42862-2

American Government: Using MicroCase® ExplorIt®, Eighth Edition

By Michael Corbett and Barbara Norrander
Featuring a Windows version of MicroCase Student ExplorIt, this user-friendly workbook/CD-ROM combo makes it easy for students to analyze and learn from real data without getting bogged down in complicated statistical software.
0-534-58785-2 To package with the text: 0-534-26067-5

Election 2002: A Supplement for American Government

By John A. Clark and Brian F. Schaffner, both of Western Michigan University

Election 2002 is an instructionally interesting and unique supplemental 32 page booklet with analysis that includes maps, charts, and graphs. Some factors discussed by the authors are the unpredictable national political climate after September 11th and subsequent economic slowdown, congressional redistricting affecting the outcome of a somewhat contentious yet closely divided legislature and trends and effects of the thirty-two gubernatorial elections that took place across the country.
0-534-59273-2 To package with the text: 0-534-16059-X

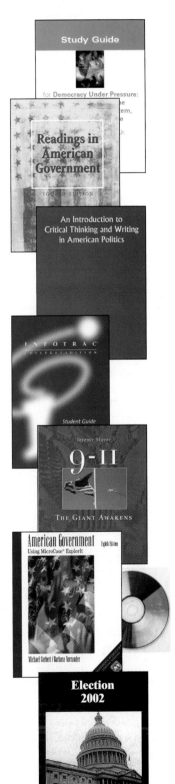

Chapter 1: Government and People

Chapter Outline	Ideas for Instruction	Print Resources	Media & Internet Resources
	Instructor's Manual Chapter 1 • Overview • Learning Objectives • Key Points • Key Terms • Lecture Builders/ Discussion Questions • Chapter Outline • Books • Videos • Web site Activities	**Test Bank** *Chapter 1* Featuring an average of 160 multiple-choice, true-false & short-answer questions. Also available in **ExamView®.** ExamView® **Study Guide** *Chapter 1*	**Web Site** Online chapter quiz and Web links at: http://politicalscience.wadsworth.com **American Government Resources (AGR)** (Democracy and Political Theory) http://politicalscience.wadsworth.com/amgov/ • *InfoTrac College Edition* Exercises • Participation Activities • Internet Activities • *MicroCase* Exercises • Video Case Studies • Simulations • Readings and Links **Multimedia Manager** Chapter 1 Slides
Introduction	**Acetates** CEV-9, CEV-10, CEV-11, CEV-12, DEP-5	**An Introduction to Critical Thinking and Writing in American Politics** Brief booklet that provides critical thinking and overall writing tips for your students	**AGR *InfoTrac College Edition* Exercise** South Africa's Transition to Democracy **AGR *MicroCase* Exercises Democracy and Political Theory** **CNN Today Video Volume 4,** *"Stem Cell Research"* (2:55) *"The American Empire"* (3:03)
The Reciprocal Nature of Democratic Power	**Acetates** PO-8, PO-9, I-1, PP-3, PP-5, PP-6, CT-8		**AGR Internet Activities** Just the Facts: Democratic and Republican Parties **AGR Source Readings** *"Civil Disobedience,"* Henry David Thoreau
What is Government?		**Handbook of Selected Legislation** *The Magna Carta (p. 53)*	**AGR Simulation: *You Are There!*** You are a member of the United States Supreme Court considering the constitutionality of a law banning same sex marriage. **AGR Video Case Studies** Democracy and Political Theory **AGR Source Readings** "The Advantages of Democratic Government" Alexis de Tocqueville
The Concept of a Political System Public Policymaking	**C/W Transparencies** 1, 26 **Acetates** C-3, C-6, C-7, CO-9, B-1, DEP-1	**Corbett/Norrander,** American Government Using MicroCase ExplorIt, Exercise 1, *"One Nation"*	**AGR Participation Exercise** Attend a Local Government Meeting **AGR Internet Activities** Explore the Three Branches of Government
Democratic Government and a Changing Society	**Acetates** D-1, D-2, D-3, D-4, D-5	**Schmidt,** Readings in American Government, Fourth Edition: *"Searching for Democracy"* (p. 7)	**AGR *InfoTrac College Edition* Exercise** Immigration Policy **AGR Participation Exercise** Helping an Interest Group **CNN Today Video Volume 4,** *"Why Hate the Rich?"* (2:21)

Chapter 2: The Constitutional Framework

Chapter Outline	Ideas for Instruction	Print Resources	Media & Internet Resources
The Constitution and the Declaration of Independence	**Instructor's Manual** *Chapter 2* • Overview • Learning Objectives • Key Points • Key Terms • Lecture Builders/ Discussion Questions • Chapter Outline • Books • Videos • Web site Activities	**Test Bank** *Chapter 2* Featuring an average of 160 multiple-choice, true-false, & short-answer questions. Also available in *ExamView*®. **ExamView**® **Study Guide** *Chapter 2*	**Web Site** Online chapter quiz and Web links: **http://politicalscience.wadsworth.com** **American Government Resources (AGR) (Constitution section)** **http://politicalscience.wadsworth.com/ amgov/** • *InfoTrac College Edition* Exercises • Participation Activities • Internet Activities • *MicroCase*® Exercises • Video Case Studies • Simulations • Readings and Links **Multimedia Manager** Chapter 2 Slides
The Political Foundations			**AGR Internet Exercise:** Articles of Confederation
The American Revolution	**Film Suggestions** *1776* *Revolution* *The Patriot*		**AGR** *InfoTrac College Edition* **Exercise:** James Madison **AGR Internet Exercise:** The Federalist Papers
Toward a More Perfect Union	**C/W Transparency 1** **Acetates** C-1, C-2, C-3, C-4, C-5, C-6 **Film Suggestion** *Amistad*		**AGR Simulation:** *You Are There!* You are a delegate to the constitutional convention in Philadelphia in 1787.
America: A Case Study in Nation Building			**AGR** *MicroCase* **Exercise:** The Constitution
The Constitution: A Document "Intended to Endure…"	**C/W Transparency 2** **Acetates** C-7	**Brudney, Culver, Weber,** Critical Thinking and American Government, Second Edition, Chapter 1, *"Governing Principles and Ideologies"*	**AGR** *InfoTrac College Edition* **Exercise:** Original Intent of the Framers **AGR Participation Activity:** School Prayer Amendment **AGR Participation Activity:** Proposed Amendments **CNN Today Video Volume 1** *"First Amendment and the Internet"*

Resource Integration Guide—Make The Connection!

Chapter 3: The Federal System

Chapter Outline	Ideas for Instruction	Print Resources	Media & Internet Resources
Federalism: The Pros and Cons	**Instructor's Manual** *Chapter 3* • Overview • Learning Objectives • Key Points • Key Terms • Lecture Builders/ Discussion Questions • Chapter Outline • Books • Web Site Activities **C/W Transparency** 3	**Test Bank** *Chapter 3* Featuring an average of 160 multiple-choice, true-false & short-answer questions. Also available in ExamView®. ExamView® **Study Guide** *Chapter 3* **Bauer**, Readings and Responses: Chapter 2, *"Federalism"* (p. 15)	**Web Site** Online chapter quiz and Web links at: http://politicalscience.wadsworth.com **American Government Resources (AGR)** (Federalism section) http://politicalscience.wadsworth.com/amgov/ • *InfoTrac College Edition* Exercises • Participation Activities • Internet Activities • *MicroCase* Exercises • Video Case Studies • Simulations • Readings and Links **Multimedia Manager** Chapter 3 Slides
The Checkerboard of Governments The Historical Basis of Federalism	**Acetates** F-1, F-2, F-3, F-4, F-9	**Handbook of Selected Court Cases** *McCulloch v. Maryland*	**AGR Participation Activity** Contact a Member of Congress about a Federalism Issue
The Constitutional Basis of Federalism The Growth of Strong National Government	**Acetates** F-5, F-6	**Handbook of Selected Court Cases** *Gibbons v. Ogden* (p. 53), *Printz v. United States* (p.113)	**AGR Source Readings** *"The Kentucky Resolve"* Thomas Jefferson *"Reply to Hayne"* Daniel Webster
The Impact of Federalism on Government and Politics		**Corbett/Norrander,** American Government Using MicroCase ExplorIt, Exercise 2, *"Federalism: A More Perfect Union"*	**CNN Today Video Volume 2,** "Welfare Reform" **AGR** *InfoTrac College Edition* **Exercise** Welfare Reform **AGR Simulation:** *You Are There!* You are the Attorney General of the United States
Federalism Today	**C/W Transparencies** 4, 5 **Acetates** F-7, F-8, F-9	**Schmidt**, Readings in American Government, Fourth Edition: *"E-Taxes and Federalism"* (p.18) *"The Liberal Rout"* (p. 21) **Brudney, Culver, Weber,** Critical Thinking and American Government, Second Edition, Chapter 2, *"Federalism"*	**CNN Today Video Volume 4,** *"Power, at What Price?"* (1:54) **AGR** *InfoTrac College Edition* **Exercise** States' Rights **AGR** *MicroCase* **Exercises** Federalism **AGR Video Case Studies** Deciding Who Decides
The Future of Federalism			**AGR Participation Activity** Discuss Federalism on the Internet

Chapter 4: Civil Liberties and Citizenship

Chapter Outline	Ideas for Instruction	Print Resources	Media & Internet Resources
Individual Freedom and Society	**Instructor's Manual** *Chapter 4* • Overview • Learning Objectives • Key Points • Key Terms • Lecture Builders/ Discussion Questions • Chapter Outline • Books • Videos • Web site Activities	**Test Bank** *Chapter 4* Featuring an average of 160 multiple-choice, true-false & short-answer questions. Also available in **ExamView®**. **Study Guide** *Chapter 4* **Brudney, Culver, Weber,** Critical Thinking and American Government, Second Edition, Chapter 12, *"Civil Liberties"* **Corbett/Norrander,** American Government Using MicroCase ExplorIt, Exercise 4, *"Civil Liberties"*	**Web Site** Online chapter quiz and Web links at: **http://politicalscience.wadsworth.com** **American Government Resources (AGR)** (Civil Liberties) **http://politicalscience.wadsworth.com/ amgov/** • *InfoTrac College Edition* Exercises • Participation Activities • Internet Activities • *MicroCase* Exercises • Video Case Studies • Simulations • Readings and Links **AGR Internet Activities** Just the Facts, Please **AGR Internet Activities** Explorations **AGR *MicroCase* Exercises** Civil Liberties **AGR Video Case Studies** Gun Control and the Second Amendment
The Bill of Rights: Freedom of Speech		**Schmidt**, Readings in American Government, Fourth Edition: *"Violence, Depravity, and the Movies"* (p. 25)	**CNN Today Video Volume 2,** *"The Internet and Free Speech"* (3:45) **AGR Participation Activity** Freedom of Expression
The Bill of Rights: Freedom of the Press		**Handbook of Selected Court Cases** *New York Times v. United States* (p. 97), *Zurcher v. Stanford Daily* (p. 199)	**CNN Today Video Volume 4,** *"Writer's Rights"* (2:05)
The Bill of Rights: Obscenity and Privacy		**Handbook of Selected Legislation** *The Privacy Act of 1974* (p. 25) **Handbook of Selected Court Cases** *Roe v. Wade* (p.131), *Miller v. California* (p. 87)	**CNN Today Video Volume 2,** *"Physician Assisted Suicide"* (2:45) **CNN Today Video Volume 4,** *"Child Pornography on the Internet"* (2:13) **AGR *InfoTrac College Edition* Exercise** Euthanasia
The Bill of Rights: Freedom of Religion		**Handbook of Selected Court Cases** *Everson v. Board of Education* (p. 35)	**CNN Today Video Volume 2,** *"School Vouchers"* (1:38) **AGR *InfoTrac College Edition* Exercise** Religion in Public Schools **AGR Simulation: *You are There!*** You are a state senator.
The Bill of Rights: Due Process of Law	**Acetates** CRL-1, CRL-2	**Handbook of Selected Court Cases** *Gideon v. Wainwright* (p. 59), *Miranda v. Arizona* (p. 91)	**CNN Today Video Volume 2,** *"The Death Penalty"* (4:23)
Citizenship	**Acetates** D-1, D-8		**CNN Today Video Volume 2,** *"Dual Language Classes"* (1:40) **AGR Internet Activities** Immigration and Naturalization Service

Resource Integration Guide—Make The Connection!

Chapter 5: The Struggle for Equal Rights

Chapter Outline	Ideas for Instruction	Print Resources	Media & Internet Resources
Introduction	**Instructor's Manual** *Chapter 5* • Overview • Learning Objectives • Key Points • Key Terms • Lecture Builders/ Discussion Questions • Chapter Outline • Books • Videos • Web site Activities	**Test Bank** *Chapter 5* Featuring an average of 160 multiple-choice, true-false & short-answer questions. Also available in **ExamView®**. ExamView® **Study Guide** Chapter 5	**Web Site** Online chapter quiz and Web links at: http://politicalscience.wadsworth.com **American Government Resources (AGR)** (Civil Rights) http://politicalscience.wadsworth.com/ amgov/ • *InfoTrac College Edition* Exercises • Participation Activities • Internet Activities • *MicroCase* Exercises • Video Case Studies • Simulations • Readings and Links **Multimedia Manager** Chapter 5 Slides
Some Groups in Profile	**C/W Transparencies** 7, 8, 9 **Acetates** D-2, D-3, D-4, D-5	**Handbook of Selected Court Cases** *Roe v. Wade* (p.131) **Handbook of Selected Legislation** *Seneca Falls Declaration* (p. 75), *The Americans with Disabilities Act,* (p. 33) **Corbett/Norrander,** American Government Using MicroCase ExplorIt, Exercise 5, *"Civil Liberties: Equality"*	**AGR *InfoTrac College Edition* Exercise** Women and the Struggle for Equality **AGR Internet Activities** Just the Facts: Abortion and Women's Rights Compare and Contrast Civil Rights Groups **AGR *MicroCase* Exercises** Civil Rights **AGR Source Readings** *"The Land Was Owned by Our Tribe"* Standing Bear *Bowers v. Hardwick*
Black and White: An American Dilemma	**Acetate** CRL-4	**Brudney, Culver, Weber,** Critical Thinking and American Government, Second Edition, Chapter 11, *"Civil Rights"* Exercise 11.1 – 11.3	**CNN Today Video Volume 4,** *"Racial Profiling"* (2:10) **AGR Participation Exercise** Discuss Human Rights on the Internet Investigate Interest Groups Involved with Civil Rights
The Civil Rights Movement: Freedom Now	**C/W Transparency** 10 **Acetates** D-6, D-7	**Handbook of Selected Court Cases** *Plessy v. Ferguson* (p. 103)	**AGR Simulation: *You Are There!*** You Are a Civil Rights Lawyer **AGR Internet Activities** Visit the On-Line Civil Rights Museum
Affirmative Action: The Supreme Court Rules		**Schmidt**, Readings in American Government, Fourth Edition: *"Why We Must Retain Affirmative Action"* (p. 46) **Handbook of Selected Court Cases** *Adarand Constructors Inc. v. Pena,* (p. 1), *Regents of the University of CA v. Bakke* (p. 119)	**AGR *InfoTrac College Edition* Exercise** Race Relations and Affirmative Action **AGR Video Case Study** Affirmative Action in Higher Education

Chapter 6: Public Opinion

Chapter Outline	Ideas for Instruction	Print Resources	Media & Internet Resources
	Instructor's Manual *Chapter 6* • Overview • Learning Objectives • Key Points • Key Terms • Lecture Builders/ Discussion Questions • Chapter Outline • Books • Videos • Web Site Activities	**Test Bank** *Chapter 6* Featuring an average of 160 multiple-choice, true-false & short-answer questions. Also available in **ExamView**. **Study Guide** *Chapter 6*	**Web Site** Online chapter quiz and Web links at: **http://politicalscience.wadsworth.com** **American Government Resources (AGR) (Public Opinion and Voting)** http://politicalscience.wadsworth.com/ amgov/ • *InfoTrac College Edition* Exercises • Participation Activities • Internet Activities • *MicroCase* Exercises • Video Case Studies • Simulations • Readings and Links **Multimedia Manager** Chapter 6 Slides
What is Public Opinion?	**Acetates** PO-1, PO-2, PO-3 **Film Suggestions** *John Doe* *Fahrenheit 451*	**Brudney, Culver, Weber,** *Critical Thinking and American Government, Second Edition,* Chapter 5, *"Political Socialization and Public Opinion"*	**CNN Today Video Volume 2,** *"Gun Control"* (3:10)
How Public Opinion is Formed **The Qualities of Public Opinion**	**Acetates** PO-4, PO-5, PO-6, PO-7 **Film Suggestions** *Power* *Wag the Dog*	**Corbett/Norrander,** *American Government Using MicroCase ExplorIt, Exercise 6, "Public Opinion and Political Socialization"*	**AGR Participation Activity** You and Political Socialization
Political Polls		**Schmidt,** Readings in American Government, Fourth Edition: *"Polling's Dirty Little Secret: No Response"* (p. 58)	**AGR Internet Activity** Opinion Polls and Polling Organizations **AGR Video Case Studies** *Measuring Public Opinion*
What Americans Believe	**Acetates** PO-10, PO-11	**Handbook of Selected Legislation** *The American's Creed* (p. 79) **Schmidt,** Readings in American Government, Fourth Edition: *"Types of Right: How the Conservatives Break Down"* (p. 71)	**AGR** *MicroCase* **Exercises** Public Opinion and Voting
Political Participation	**C/W Transparencies** 11, 18, 19 **Acetates** CEV-9, CEV-10, PO-8, PO-9	**Corbett/Norrander,** *American Government Using MicroCase ExplorIt, Exercise 8, "Political Participation"*	**AGR Participation Activity** Voting
Mass Opinion in a Democracy		**Schmidt,** Readings in American Government, Fourth Edition: *"Days of Apathy"* (p. 52) **Corbett/Norrander,** *American Government Using MicroCase ExplorIt, Exercise 3, "People: An Interested and Informed Public"*	**AGR Simulation:** *You Are There!* You Are an advisor to the president

Chapter 7: Interest Groups

Chapter Outline	Ideas for Instruction	Print Resources	Media & Internet Resources
	Instructor's Manual *Chapter 7* • Overview • Learning Objectives • Key Points • Key Terms • Lecture Builders/ Discussion Questions • Chapter Outline • Books • Videos • Web Site Activities	**Test Bank** *Chapter 7* Featuring an average of 160 multiple-choice, true-false & short-answer questions. Also available in **ExamView**®. **Study Guide** *Chapter 7*	**Web Site** Online chapter quiz and Web links at: http://politicalscience.wadsworth.com **American Government Resources (AGR) (Interest Groups)** http://politicalscience.wadsworth.com/ amgov/ • *InfoTrac College Edition* Exercises • Participation Activities • Internet Activities • *MicroCase* Exercises • Video Case Studies • Simulations • Readings and Links **Multimedia Manager** Chapter 7 Slides
Who Governs?	**Film Suggestions** *On the Waterfront* *The Insider* *Norma Rae* *Matewan*	**Schmidt**, Readings in American Government, Fourth Edition, *"Congress is a Captive of the Meat Industry"* (p. 61)	**AGR *InfoTrac College Edition* Exercise** The Influence of Interest Groups
Interest Groups at Work	**Acetates** I-1, I-2, I-3, I-4, I-5, I-6, I-7	**Thinking Globally, Acting Locally** *"Interest Groups"* (p. 9) **Thinking Globally, Acting Locally** *"Lobbying"* (p. 13) **Brudney, Culver, Weber,** Critical Thinking and American Government, Second Edition, Chapter 6, *"Interest Groups"* Exercise 11, *"Interest Groups and PACs"*	**CNN Today Video Volume 2,** *"Political Action Committees"* (3:47) *"Music and Video Internet Policy"* (1:30) **AGR *InfoTrac College Edition* Exercise** Lobbying Techniques **AGR Simulation: *You Are There!*** You are an advisor to the head of an Interest Group **AGR Participation Exercise** Support an Interest Group Form Your Own Interest Group **AGR Internet Activities** Just The Facts, Compare and Contrast, Exploration **AGR *MicroCase* Exercises** Interest Groups **AGR Video Case Studies** Interest Groups
Regulating Interest Groups **Interest Groups in the Policy Process**		**Handbook of Selected Court Cases** *Austin v. Michigan Chamber of Commerce* (p. 7), *United States v. Harriss* (p. 167) **Handbook of Selected Legislation** *The Hatch Act of 1939* (p. 1), *The Federal Regulation of Lobbying Act of 1946* (p. 5), *The Federal Election Campaign Act of 1971* (p. 21)	

Chapter 8: The Media and Politics

Chapter Outline	Ideas for Instruction	Print Resources	Media & Internet Resources
Introduction	**Instructor's Manual** *Chapter 8* • Overview • Learning Objectives • Key Points • Key Terms • Lecture Builders/ Discussion Questions • Chapter Outline • Books • Videos • Web site Activities	**Test Bank** *Chapter 8* Featuring an average of 160 multiple-choice, true-false & short-answer questions. Also available in **ExamView®**. **Study Guide** *Chapter 8*	**Web Site** Online chapter quiz and Web links at http://politicalscience.wadsworth.com **American Government Resources (AGR)** (Politics and the Media) http://politicalscience.wadsworth.com/ amgov/ • *InfoTrac* Exercises • Participation Activities • Internet Activities • *MicroCase* Exercises • Video Case Studies • Simulations • Readings and Links **Multimedia Manager** Chapter 8 Slides
A Protected Institution	**Acetates** M-1, M-2, M-3 **Film Suggestions** *Network* *Broadcast News*		**CNN Today Video Volume 2** *"The Internet"* (3:47) **CNN Today Video Volume 4,** *"Music and Video Internet Policy"* (1:30) **AGR Participation Exercise** Improve Local Media Coverage Write a Letter to the Editor **AGR *MicroCase* Exercises** Politics and the Media **AGR Video Case Studies** Politics and the Media
Who Owns the Media?	**Acetates** M-4, M-5	Brudney, Culver, Weber, Chapter 4, *"The Mass Media"*	**AGR Internet Activities** Exploration: *"The Global Media Giants"*
Television and the American Political System	**C/W Transparency** 12 **Acetate M-7**		**AGR Internet Activities** Just the Facts: National Association of Broadcasters and the FCC
The Press: Legal and Constitutional Issues		**Handbook of Selected Court Cases** *Zurcher v. Stanford Daily* (p. 199) and *N.Y. Times v. U.S.* (p. 97) **Schmidt**, Readings in American Government, Fourth Edition: *"Supreme Court's Ruling on Free Speech"* (p. 80) and *"Marketing Violence to Our Children"* (p. 84)	
The Press and the Government **The Press in a Democratic Society**	**C/W Transparency** 13 **Acetate** M-8 **Film Suggestion** *All the President's Men*	Corbett/Norrander, American Government Using MicroCase ExplorIt, Exercise 7, *"The Media"*	**CNN Today Video Volume 4,** *"Writers' Rights"* (2:05) **AGR *InfoTrac* College Edition Exercise** Mass Media Criticism Media Coverage of Political Campaigns **AGR Simulation: *You Are There!*** You Are the President of NBC News **AGR Internet Activities** Compare and Contrast: FAIR

Resource Integration Guide—Make The Connection!

Resource Integration Guide—*Make The Connection!*

Chapter Outline	Ideas for Instruction	Print Resources	Media & Internet Resources
Introduction	**Instructor's Manual** *Chapter 9* • Overview • Learning Objectives • Key Points • Key Terms • Lecture Builders/ Discussion Questions • Chapter Outline • Books • Videos • Web site Activities	**Test Bank** *Chapter 9* Featuring an average of 160 multiple-choice, true-false & short-answer questions. Also available in **ExamView**®. ExamView® **Study Guide** *Chapter 9* **Brudney, Culver, Weber,** Critical Thinking and American Government, Second Edition, Chapter 5, *"Political Parties and Elections"* Exercise 5.4	**Web Site** Online chapter quiz and Web links at: **http://politicalscience.wadsworth.com** **American Government Resources (AGR) (Political Parties)** http://politicalscience.wadsworth.com/ amgov/ • *InfoTrac College Edition* Exercises • Participation Activities • Internet Activities • *MicroCase* Exercises • Video Case Studies • Simulations • Readings and Links **Multimedia Manager** Chapter 9 Slides
What Is a Party? **The Development of American Political Parties**	**Acetates** PP-1, PP-2, PP-10, PP-12	**Thinking Globally, Acting Locally** *"Parties, Elections and Government Service"* (p. 5) **Handbook of Selected Legislation** *The Hatch Act of 1939* (p. 1)	**AGR** *InfoTrac College Edition* **Exercise** Party History
The Two-Party System	**C/W Transparency** 14 **Acetates** PP-3, PP-4, PP-7, PP-8, PP-9, PP-11, PP-13, PP-14, PP-17	**Schmidt**, Readings in American Government, Fourth Edition, *"How the Conservatives Break Down"* (p. 71)	**AGR Participation Activity** Researching and Joining a Political Party **AGR Internet Activity** Exploration: The Green Party Compare and Contrast Political Parties **AGR** *MicroCase* **Exercises** Who Supports Democrats and Republicans
Party Structure	**Acetate** PP-12	**Corbett/Norrander,** Exercise 9, *"Political Parties"*	**AGR Participation Activity** Volunteer for a Party
The National Convention	**Acetates** PP-15, PP-16		**CNN Today Video Volume 3,** *"Green Party"* (2:27) *"Reform Party"* (1:55) **AGR Simulation:** *You Are There!* You Are an Advisor to the Democratic Nominee **AGR Video Case Studies** The National Conventions
Political Parties and Democratic Government **A Look Ahead**	**Acetates** PP-5, PP-6		**CNN Today Video Volume 3,** *"What's the Difference?"* (2:50) **AGR** *InfoTrac College Edition* **Exercise** Social-Policy Differences **AGR Internet Activity** Just the Facts: Candidate Positions **AGR Source Readings** Contract With America

Chapter 10: Political Campaigns and Candidates

Chapter Outline	Ideas for Instruction	Print Resources	Media & Internet Resources
Introduction	**Instructor's Manual** *Chapter 10* • Overview • Learning Objectives • Key Points • Key Terms • Lecture Builders/ Discussion Questions • Chapter Outline • Books • Videos • Web Site Activities	**Test Bank** *Chapter 10* Featuring an average of 160 multiple-choice, true-false & short-answer questions. Also available in **ExamView®**. **Study Guide** *Chapter 10*	**Web Site** Online chapter quiz and Web links at **http://politicalscience.wadsworth.com** **American Government Resources (AGR)** (Campaigns and Elections) **http://politicalscience.wadsworth.com/amgov/** • *InfoTrac College Edition* Exercises • Participation Activities • Internet Activities • *MicroCase* Exercises • Video Case Studies • Simulations • Readings and Links **Multimedia Manager** Chapter 10 Slides
How Campaigns Are Organized	**Acetate** CEV-5 **Film Suggestions** *A Perfect Candidate* *The Candidate* *Running Mates* *Power* *Wag the Dog*		**AGR Participation Exercise** Running for Local Office
Campaign Strategy			**AGR Simulation:** *You Are There!* You are an advisor to a presidential candidate who is facing allegations of past indiscretions
The Issues	**C/W Transparencies** 15, 16		
Campaign Techniques		**Schmidt**, Readings in American Government, Fourth Edition: *"Tremendous Trifles"* (p. 76) **Schmidt**, Readings in American Government, Fourth Edition: *"Politicians Woo Voters on the Web"* (p. 74)	**CNN Today Video Volume 2,** *"Negative Campaign Ads "* (2:45) **AGR Participation Exercise** Help a Candidate Get Elected **AGR Internet Activity** Compare and Contrast: Presidential Debates
Campaign Finance	**C/W Transparency** 17 **Acetates** CEV-6, CEV-16	**Handbook of Selected Legislation** *"The Hatch Act of 1939"* (p. 1), *"The Federal Election Campaign Act of 1971"* (p. 21) **Brudney, Culver, Weber,** Critical Thinking and American Government, Second Edition, Chapter 5, *"Political Parties and Elections"* Exercise 5.5	**AGR** *Infotrac College Edition* **Exercise** Campaign Finance Reform **AGR Internet Activity** Just the Facts: Campaign Spending Compare and Contrast: Campaign Spending **AGR Source Readings** Federal Election Campaign Acts of 1972 and 1974

Resource Integration Guide—Make The Connection!

Chapter 11: Voting Behavior and Elections

Resource Integration Guide—Make The Connection!

Chapter Outline	Ideas for Instruction	Print Resources	Media & Internet Resources
Introduction	**Instructor's Manual** *Chapter 11* • Overview • Learning Objectives • Key Points • Key Terms • Lecture Builders/Discussion Questions • Chapter Outline • Books • Videos • Web site Activities	**Test Bank** *Chapter 11* Featuring an average of 160 multiple-choice, true-false & short-answer questions. Also available in **ExamView®**. **Study Guide** *Chapter 11*	**Web Site** Online chapter quiz and Web links at: **http://politicalscience.wadsworth.com** **American Government Resources (AGR)** (Public Opinion and Voting) (Campaigns and Elections) **http://politicalscience.wadsworth.com/amgov/** • *InfoTrac College Edition* Exercises • Participation Activities • Internet Activities • *MicroCase* Exercises • Video Case Studies • Simulations • Readings and Links **Multimedia Manager** Chapter 11 Slides
Who Votes?	**C/W Transparencies** 18, 19 **Acetate** CEV-10	**Corbett/Norrander,** American Government Using MicroCase ExplorIt, Exercise 10, *"Elections"*	**AGR Participation Exercise** Vote!
How the Voter Decides	**Acetates** CEV-12, CEV-13, CEV-15		
Voting Patterns	**C/W Transparency** 20	**Schmidt**, Readings in American Government, Fourth Edition, *"Days of Apathy"* (p. 52)	
Election 2002: A Case Study	**Acetates** CEV-1, CEV-2, CEV-3, CEV-4	**Clark/Schaffner,** Election 2002 **Brudney, Culver, Weber,** Critical Thinking and American Government, Second Edition, Chapter 5, *"Political Parties and Elections"* Exercise 5.1	**CNN Today Video Volume 3,** All video clips are related to the 2000 elections **AGR *InfoTrac College Edition* Exercise** 2000 Election and *Bush v. Gore* **AGR *MicroCase* Exercises** Characteristics of Voters in the 2000 Election **AGR Source Readings** *Bush v. Gore*
The Electoral System Elections and Democratic Government	**Acetates** CEV-8, CEV-9, CEV-14	**Handbook of Selected Court Cases:** *Reynolds v. Sims* (p. 125), *Baker v. Carr* (p.13) **Handbook of Selected Legislation:** *"The Hatch Act of 1939"* (p. 1), *"The Federal Election Campaign Act of 1971"* (p. 21) **Brudney, Culver, Weber,** Critical Thinking and American Government, Second Edition, Chapter 5, Exercise 5.2 – 5.3 and Chapter 8, Exercise 8.1	**AGR Video Case Studies** Close Calls in Presidential Contests **AGR Source Readings** Federal Election Campaign Acts of 1972 and 1974

24

Chapter 12: The Congress

Chapter Outline	Ideas for Instruction	Print Resources	Media & Internet Resources
Introduction	**Instructor's Manual** *Chapter 12* • Overview • Learning Objectives • Key Points • Key Terms • Lecture Builders/ Discussion Questions • Chapter Outline • Books • Videos • Web site Activities	**Test Bank** *Chapter 12* Featuring an average of 160 multiple-choice, true-false & short-answer questions. Also available in **ExamView** ExamView®. **Study Guide** *Chapter 12*	**Web Site** Online chapter quiz and Web links at: **http://politicalscience.wadsworth.com** **American Government Resources (AGR)** (Congress) **http://politicalscience.wadsworth.com/ amgov/** • *InfoTrac College Edition* Exercises • Participation Activities • Internet Activities • *MicroCase* Exercises • Video Case Studies • Simulations • Readings and Links **Multimedia Manager** Chapter 12 Slides
Congress: Conflict and Controversy **The Varied Roles of Congress**	**Acetates** CO-5, CO-6, CO-7	**Brudney, Culver, Weber,** Critical Thinking and American Government, Second Edition, Chapter 7, *"Congress"*	**AGR Participation Exercise** Enter the Struggle over Congressional Term Limits **AGR Internet Activity** Exploration: 2. Investigate the C-SPAN site Exploration: 3. Qualities of Congressional Campaigns **AGR** *MicroCase* **Exercises** Congress **AGR Video Case Studies** The Cost of Campaigning
The Legislators **The House**	**Acetates** CO-10, CO-11 **Acetates** CO-1, CO-2	**Clark/Schaffner,** Election 2002	**AGR Simulation:** *You Are There!* You Are a Member of Congress **AGR Internet Activity** Just The Facts: Members and Committees
The Party Machinery **The Committee System** **Congressional Reforms**	**Acetates** CO-3, CO-4	**Corbett/Norrander,** American Government Using MicroCase ExplorIt, Exercise 12, *"The Congress"*	**AGR** *InfoTrac College Edition* **Exercise** Shaping Congressional Districts **CNN Today Video Volume 4,** *"Racial Profiling"* (2:10)
Congress and the Budget **A Bill is Passed** **Congressional Ethics**	**Film Suggestions** *Mr. Smith Goes to Washington* **C/W Transparency** 21 **Acetate CO-9**		**AGR Participation Exercise** You Can Lobby Congress **AGR Internet Activity** Exploration: 1. Congressional Budget Office
Congress and the American Political System	**Film Suggestion** *The Seduction of Joe Tynan*	**Schmidt,** Readings in American Government, Fourth Edition: *"Our Unconstitutional Congress"* (p. 91) **Handbook of Selected Court Cases** *U. S. Term Limits v. Thornton* (p. 157), *Wesberry v. Sanders* (p. 189)	**AGR** *InfoTrac College Edition* **Exercise** The Power of Congress **AGR Internet Activity** Exploration: 4. Leadership PACs **AGR Source Readings** *U.S. Term Limits, Inc. v. Ray Thornton*

Resource Integration Guide—Make The Connection!

Resource Integration Guide—*Make The Connection!*

Chapter Outline	Ideas for Instruction	Print Resources	Media & Internet Resources
Introduction	**Instructor's Manual** *Chapter 13* • Overview • Learning Objectives • Key Points • Key Terms • Lecture Builders/ Discussion Questions • Chapter Outline • Books • Videos • Web Site Activities	**Test Bank** *Chapter 13* Featuring an average of 160 multiple-choice, true-false & short-answer questions. Also available in **ExamView**®. **Study Guide** *Chapter 13* **Corbett/Norrander,** American Government Using MicroCase ExplorIt, Exercise 13, *"The Presidency"*	**Web Site** Online chapter quiz and Web links at: **http://politicalscience.wadsworth.com** **American Government Resources (AGR)** (The Presidency) **http://politicalscience.wadsworth.com/amgov/** • *InfoTrac College Edition* Exercises • Participation Activities • Internet Activities • *MicroCase* Exercises • Video Case Studies • Simulations • Readings and Links **Multimedia Manager** Chapter 13 Slides
The Paradox of the Presidency **The American Presidency** **The Expanding Presidency**	**C/W Transparency** 22 **Film Suggestions** *Dave* *The Man*	**Brudney, Culver, Weber,** Critical Thinking and American Government, Second Edition, Chapter 8, *"The Presidency"*	**AGR Participation Exercise** Discuss the President on the Internet Just the Facts: A Quiz and Female Candidates Exploration: Several Exercises **AGR MicroCase Exercises** The Presidency
The Impossible Burden: The Many Roles of the Chief Executive	**Acetates** P-7, P-8, P-9, P-10 **Film Suggestions** *The Missiles of October* *The American President*	**Schmidt,** Readings in American Government, Fourth Edition: *"Emergency Rule Abuse of Power?"* (p. 96)	**AGR Simulation:** *You Are There!* Advise the President on a Supreme Court nominee **AGR Participation Exercise** Contact the President **AGR Source Readings** *"Laws Congress Never Made"* Louis Fisher *William J. Clinton, President of the United States, v. City of New York*
The Tools of Presidential Power	**C/W Transparency** 23 **Acetates** P-2, P-3, P-4, P-5, P-6	**Handbook of Selected Court Cases** *"Sale v. Haitian Centers Council, Inc."* (p. 143) and *Youngstown Sheet and Tube Co. v. Sawyer* (p. 193)	**AGR** *InfoTrac College Edition* **Exercise** Does President Bush Exercise too Much Power? **AGR Video Case Studies** Presidential Style
The Watergate Scandal: A President Resigns **Presidential Impeachment, Disability, and Succession**	**Acetate** P-1	**Schmidt,** Readings in American Government, Fourth Edition: *"Once More Around the Race Track"* (p. 99) **Handbook of Selected Court Cases** *U.S. v. Nixon* (p. 171)	**CNN Today Video Volume 2,** *"Executive Privilege"* (2:38) **AGR Source Readings** *"The Impeachment of President William Jefferson Clinton"* United States Congress
The Splendid Misery: Personality and Style in the White House **The American Presidency: Triumph and Tragedy**	**C/W Transparency** 24 **Acetate** P-11		**AGR** *InfoTrac College Edition* **Exercise** Evaluating Bill Clinton and George W. Bush

Chapter 14: The Bureaucracy

Chapter Outline	Ideas for Instruction	Print Resources	Media & Internet Resources
	Instructor's Manual *Chapter 14* • Overview • Learning Objectives • Key Points • Key Terms • Lecture Builders/ Discussion Questions • Chapter Outline • Books • Videos • Web site Activities	**Test Bank** *Chapter 14* Featuring an average of 160 multiple-choice, true-false & short-answer questions. Also available in **ExamView**®. **ExamView**® **Study Guide** *Chapter 14*	**Web Site** Online chapter quiz and Web links at: **http://politicalscience.wadsworth.com** **American Government Resources (AGR)** (Bureaucracy) **http://politicalscience.wadsworth.com/ amgov/** • *InfoTrac College Edition* Exercises • Participation Activities • Internet Activities • *MicroCase* Exercises • Video Case Studies • Simulations • Readings and Links **Multimedia Manager** Chapter 14 Slides
Introduction **Bureaucracy and the Political Process**	**C/W Transparency** 25 **Acetate** B-12 **Film Suggestions** *1984* *Roger and Me* *Metropolis*	**Schmidt**, Readings in American Government, Fourth Edition: *"American Workers Beware: Big Brother is Watching"* (p. 102)	**AGR Participation Exercise** Discuss Bureaucracy on the Internet **AGR *MicroCase* Exercises** Bureaucracy
The Politics of Bureaucracy	**Film Suggestion** Article 99	**Brudney, Culver, Weber,** Critical Thinking and American Government, Second Edition, Chapter 9, *"Bureaucracy and the Regulatory Process"*	**CNN Today Video Volume 2,** *"Environmental Protection"* (2:56) **AGR Participation Exercise** Interact with a Bureaucratic Agency **AGR Video Case Studies** The Power of Rule-Making
A Profile of the American Bureaucracy	**C/W Transparencies** 26, 27 **Acetates** B-1, B-2, B-3, B-4, B-5, B-6, B-7, B-8, B-9, B-10, B-11	**Handbook of Selected Court Cases** *United States Civil Service Commission v. National Association of Letter Carriers* (p. 177) **Handbook of Selected Legislation** *The Hatch Act of 1939* (p. 1) **Corbett/Norrander,** American Government Using MicroCase ExplorIt, Exercise 4, *"The Bureaucracy"*	**AGR *InfoTrac College Edition* Exercise** Homeland Security Privatization **AGR Simulation: *You Are There!*** You are a bureaucrat desiring promotion **AGR Internet Activity** Just the Facts: Investigate Various Aspects of Government Agencies **AGR Participation Exercise** Explorations: General Services Administration and the "Results Act" **AGR Source Readings** The Pendleton Act The Hatch Act

Resource Integration Guide—Make The Connection!

Resource Integration Guide—*Make The Connection!*

Chapter Outline	Ideas for Instruction	Print Resources	Media & Internet Resources
Introduction	**Instructor's Manual** *Chapter 15* • Overview • Learning Objectives • Key Points • Key Terms • Lecture Builders/Discussion Questions • Chapter Outline • Books • Videos • Web site Activities	**Test Bank** *Chapter 15* Featuring an average of 160 multiple-choice, true-false & short-answer questions. Also available in **ExamView®**. *ExamView®* **Study Guide** *Chapter 15* **Handbook of Selected Court Cases** All cases would serve to familiarize students with the basic format of judicial opinions.	**Web Site** Online chapter quiz and Web links at: http://politicalscience.wadsworth.com **American Government Resources (AGR)** (The Judiciary) http://politicalscience.wadsworth.com/amgov/ • *InfoTrac College Edition* Exercises • Participation Activities • Internet Activities • *MicroCase* Exercises • Video Case Studies • Simulations • Readings and Links **Multimedia Manager** Chapter 15 Slides
The System of Justice **The Law**	**Acetate** CT-2 **Film Suggestion** *Ghosts of Mississippi*		**AGR Participation Exercise** Change the Legal System
The Supreme Court	**Acetates** CT-5, CT-9 **Film Suggestion** *First Monday in October*	**Handbook of Selected Court Cases** *Marbury v. Madison* (p. 79) **Brudney, Culver, Weber,** Critical Thinking and American Government, Second Edition, Chapter 10, *"The Judiciary"* Exercise 10.1 – 10.2 **Corbett/Norrander,** American Government Using MicroCase ExplorIt, Exercise 10, *"The Courts"*	**CNN Today Video Volume 4,** *"Child Pornography on the Internet"* (2:13) **AGR *InfoTrac College Edition* Exercise** Politics and the Courts Just The Facts: The Supreme Court **AGR Internet Activities** Exploration: The Supreme Court, Court Opinions **AGR *MicroCase* Exercises** The Judiciary
The American Court System	**Acetates** CT-1, CT-2, CT-3, CT-4 **Film Suggestion** *And Justice For All*	**Schmidt**, Readings in American Government, Fourth Edition, *"Impeaching Abusive Judges"* (p. 114)	**AGR Participation Exercise** Debate Legal Topics On-Line **AGR Internet Activities** Exploration: The Federal Judiciary, Court Opinions **AGR Video Case Study** Appointments to the Bench **AGR Source Readings** *"The Judiciary Act of 1789"*
Criminal Justice in America **Organized Crime** **Justice and the American Political System**	**C/W Transparencies** 28, 29 **Acetates** CT-2, CT-6, CT-7, CT-8, DEP-2, DEP-3, DEP-4 **Film Suggestions** *Twelve Angry Men* *A Time to Kill* *American Hero* *The Boost*	**Schmidt**, Readings in American Government, Fourth Edition: *"Senseless Sentencing: A Federal Judge Speaks Out"* (p. 111), *"A Sane Drug Policy"* (p. 117) **Brudney, Culver, Weber,** Critical Thinking and American Government, Second Edition, Chapter 10, Exercise 10.3 – 10.5	**CNN Today Video Volume 2,** *"Death Penalty in the U.S."* **AGR *InfoTrac College Edition* Exercise** Supreme Court and Rights of Criminals **AGR Simulation: *You Are There!*** Do you know your rights? **AGR Internet Activities** Just The Facts: Justice Department, FBI, Sentencing Project, Death Penalty

Chapter 16: Foreign Policy

Chapter Outline	Ideas for Instruction	Print Resources	Media & Internet Resources
Introduction	**Instructor's Manual** *Chapter 16* • Overview • Learning Objectives • Key Points • Key Terms • Lecture Builders/ Discussion Questions • Chapter Outline • Books • Videos • Web site Activities	**Test Bank** *Chapter 16* Featuring an average of 160 multiple-choice, true-false & short-answer questions. Also available in **ExamView**®. **ExamView**® **Study Guide** *Chapter 16* **Mayer,** 9-11: The Giant Awakens	**Web Site** Online chapter quiz and Web links at: **http://politicalscience.wadsworth.com** **American Government Resources (AGR)** (Foreign Policy) **http://politicalscience.wadsworth.com/ amgov/** • *InfoTrac College Edition* Exercises • Participation Activities • Internet Activities • *MicroCase* Exercises • Video Case Studies • Simulations • Readings and Links **Multimedia Manager** Chapter 16 Slides
The United States and World Affairs	**C/W Transparency** 30 **Acetate FP-4** **Film Suggestions** *The Testament Saving Private Ryan Born on the Fourth of July*	**Handbook of Selected Legislation** *The Monroe Doctrine (p. 71), The North American Free Trade Agreement of 1993 (p. 41)* **Brudney, Culver, Weber,** Chapter 13, "*Public Policies,*" Exercise 13.3	**CNN Today Video Volume 4,** "*Arafat—Hero or Foe*" (2:53) **AGR Internet Activities Explorations:** Various Exercises **AGR Source Readings** "*The Tonkin Gulf Speech and Resolution*" Lyndon Johnson and the U.S. Congress
How Foreign Policy is Made	**Acetate** FP-7	**Handbook of Selected Legislation** *The Preamble to the Charter of the United Nations (p. 83)*	**AGR Participation Exercise** Support an Interest Group Lobby Congress: Foreign Policy **AGR Internet Activities** Just the Facts: Government Agencies **AGR Simulation: *You Are There!*** *Should the U.S. invade the nation of "Irat"?* **AGR *MicroCase* Exercises** The Public and Foreign Policy
The Defense Establishment **The Military-Industrial Complex**	**C/W Transparency** 31 **Acetates** FP-5, FP-6 **Film Suggestions** *Seven Days in May Fail Safe Crimson Tide*	**Schmidt,** Readings in American Government, Fourth Edition: "*The Myth of the Two Front War*" (p. 143)	**AGR Internet Activities Explorations:** Various Exercises **AGR Video Case Studies** Foreign Policy
America's Role in the 21st Century	**Acetates** FP-1, FP-2, FP-3	**Schmidt,** Readings in American Government, Fourth Edition: "*Using U.S. Troops as Global Cops*" (p. 137), "*Wonder Weapons*" (p. 139) **Brudney, Culver, Weber,** Critical Thinking and American Government, Second Edition, Chapter 13, Exercise 13.2 – 13.4	**CNN Today Video Volume 4,** "*The American Empire*" (3:03) "*Who is Bin-Laden?*" (1:30) "*Are We Prepared?*" (1:59) **AGR *InfoTrac College Edition* Exercise** International Relations: the United States' Future September 11th and American Foreign Policy **AGR Internet Activities Explorations:** Terrorism Exercises

Resource Integration Guide—Make The Connection!

Chapter 17: Government and the Economy

Chapter Outline	Ideas for Instruction	Print Resources	Media & Internet Resources
Introduction	**Instructor's Manual** *Chapter 17* • Overview • Learning Objectives • Key Points • Key Terms • Lecture Builders/ Discussion Questions • Chapter Outline • Books • Videos • Web site Activities	**Test Bank** *Chapter 17* Featuring an average of 160 multiple-choice, true-false & short-answer questions. Also available in **ExamView®**. ExamView® **Study Guide** *Chapter 17*	**Web Site** Online chapter quiz and Web links at: **http://politicalscience.wadsworth.com** **American Government Resources (AGR)** (Economic Policy) **http://politicalscience.wadsworth.com/ amgov/** • *InfoTrac College Edition* Exercises • Participation Activities • Internet Activities • *MicroCase* Exercises • Video Case Studies • Simulations • Readings and Links **Multimedia Manager** Chapter 17 Slides
Managing the Economy	**Film Suggestions** *Barbarians at the Gate* *The Grapes of Wrath* *Rollover* *Wall Street*		**AGR** *InfoTrac College Edition* **Exercise** George W. Bush and the Environment **CNN Today Video Volume 2,** "Environmental Protection"
The Machinery **The American Economy in the 21st Century**	**C/W Transparencies** 32, 33 **Acetates** DEP-5, DEP-6, DEP-7, DEP-8, DEP-9, DEP-19	**Schmidt**, Readings in American Government, Fourth Edition: "Half of Americans Suffer Under a Santa Claus Vision of Government," (p. 125); "What's Really Going On with the Economy" (p. 126) and "Damned if You Do and Damned if You Don't: The New Politics of Global Trade" (p. 129)	**AGR Simulation** Economic Policy **AGR Participation Activity** Lobby Government for Budget Changes **AGR Internet Activities** Just the Facts: Federal Reserve Compare and Contrast: The Dismal Scientist **AGR Internet Activities Exploration:** Federal Budget, Council on Economic Affairs, "Citizen's Guide to the Budget" **AGR** *MicroCase* **Exercises** Economic Policy **AGR Video Case Studies** Economic Policy
			AGR Participation Activity Debate Economic Policy On-Line **AGR Internet Activities Exploration:** Concord Coalition, Economic Policy Institute **CNN Today Video Volume 4,** "Why Hate the Rich?" (2:21) "Music and Video Internet Policy" (1:30) "Profit Recession" (1:48) "DotCom Business Discussion" (2:24) "401K Year-End Analysis" (2:36)

Chapter 18: Promoting the General Welfare

Chapter Outline	Ideas for Instruction	Print Resources	Media & Internet Resources
Introduction	**Instructor's Manual** *Chapter 18* • Overview • Learning Objectives • Key Points • Key Terms • Lecture Builders/ Discussion Questions • Chapter Outline • Books • Videos • Web site Activities	**Test Bank** *Chapter 2* Featuring an average of 160 multiple-choice, true-false & short-answer questions. Also available in **ExamView**®. **Study Guide** *Chapter 18* **Schmidt**, Readings in American Government, Fourth Edition: *"Multiple Choice"* (p. 120)	**Web Site** Online chapter quiz and Web links at: **http://politicalscience.wadsworth.com** **American Government Resources (AGR)** (Public Policy) **http://politicalscience.wadsworth.com/amgov/** • *InfoTrac College Edition* Exercises • Participation Activities • Internet Activities • *MicroCase* Exercises • Video Case Studies • Simulations • Readings and Links **Multimedia Manager** Chapter 18 Slides
Government as Regulator and Promoter		**Brudney, Culver, Weber,** Chapter 13, Exercise 13.1	**AGR *InfoTrac College Edition* Exercise** Deregulation (Economic Policy)
Government as Protector	**Acetates** DEP-10, DEP-11, DEP-12, DEP-13, DEP-14, DEP-15, DEP-16, DEP-17, DEP-18, DEP-19, DEP-20, DEP-21, DEP-22 **Film Suggestions** *Black Board Jungle* *Stand and Deliver*	**Brudney, Culver, Weber,** Critical Thinking and American Government, Second Edition, Chapter 13, Exercise 13.5	**CNN Today Video Volume 2,** *"Environmental Protection"* (3:45) *"Welfare Reform"* (4:35) *"Talks on Tobacco"* (1:30) **AGR *InfoTrac College Edition* Exercise** George W. Bush and the Environment (Economic Policy) **AGR Simulation: *You Are There!*** Amending the Controlled Substances Act **AGR Participation Activity** Affect Social Policy Join an Environmental Policy Interest Group Understanding Social Security **AGR Participation Activity Exploration:** Various Social Welfare Issues and Policies **AGR *MicroCase* Exercises** Social Policy **AGR Video Case Studies** Public Policy **AGR Source Readings** *"Democracy and Education"* John Dewey
Can Government Meet the Challenge?			**AGR *InfoTrac College Edition* Exercise** The Future of Social Security **AGR Participation Activity** The Future of Social Security

Resource Integration Guide—Make The Connection!

Chapter 19: State and Local Government

Chapter Outline	Ideas for Instruction	Print Resources	Media & Internet Resources
Introduction	**Instructor's Manual** *Chapter 19* • Overview • Learning Objectives • Key Points • Key Terms • Lecture Builders/ Discussion Questions • Chapter Outline • Books • Videos • Web site Activities	**Test Bank** *Chapter 19* Featuring an average of 160 multiple-choice, true-false & short-answer questions. Also available in **ExamView**®. ExamView® **Study Guide** *Chapter 19*	**Web Site** Online chapter quiz and Web links at: **http://politicalscience.wadsworth.com** **American Government Resources (AGR)** (State and Local Government) **http://politicalscience.wadsworth.com/amgov/** • *InfoTrac College Edition* Exercises • Participation Activities • Internet Activities • *MicroCase* Exercises • Video Case Studies • Simulations • Readings and Links **Multimedia Manager** Chapter 19 Slides
The States	**C/W Transparencies** 34, 35 **Acetates** SL-1, SL-2, SL-3, SL-4, SL-5, SL-6	**Schmidt**, Readings in American Government, Fourth Edition: *"Grass Roots: The Progress of Medical Marijuana"* (p. 147)	**AGR *InfoTrac College Edition* Exercises** Term Limits **AGR Simulation** State and Local Government **AGR Participation Exercise** Lobby State Government **AGR Internet Activities** Just the Facts: Eleven Different Exercises **AGR Internet Activities** Exploration: Find Your State's Web Site **AGR Video Case Studies** State and Local Government
Local Governments	**Acetate** SL-7	**Schmidt**, Readings in American Government, Fourth Edition: *"True Believers Put Their Necks on the Line"* (p. 149)	**AGR Participation Exercise** Investigate a Commission **AGR Internet Activities Exploration:** Analyze County Governments
Cities and Suburbs: The Metropolitan Dilemma **Exploding Metropolises and America's Future**	**Film Suggestions** *City Hall* *City of Hope* *Turk*		**CNN Today Video Volume 4,** "School Vouchers" (1:38) CNN **CNN Today Video Volume 4,** "Dual Language Classes" (1:40) CNN **AGR *InfoTrac College Edition* Exercises** Federal Mandates

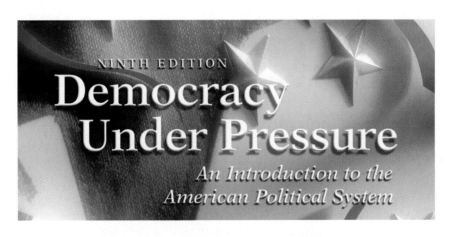

NINTH EDITION

Democracy Under Pressure

*An Introduction to the
American Political System*

2002 ELECTION UPDATE

THOMSON

★ ™

WADSWORTH

Publisher: Clark Baxter
Executive Editor: David Tatom
Development Editor: Stacey Sims
Assistant Editor: Heather Hogan
Editorial Assistant: Dianna Long
Technology Project Manager: Melinda Newfarmer
Marketing Manager: Janise Fry
Marketing Assistant: Mary Ho
Advertising Project Manager: Stacey Purviance
Project Manager, Editorial Production: Ray Crawford
Print/Media Buyer: Judy Inouye

Permissions Editor: Kiely Sexton
Production Service: G & S Typesetters, Inc.
Text Designer: Burl Sloan
Art Editor: Gretchen Otto/G & S Typesetters, Inc.
Photo Researcher: Susan Holtz
Copy Editor: Sam Hurwitt/G & S Typesetters, Inc.
Cover Image: Copyright © Jim Piper—Superstock
Cover Printer: Transcontinental Printing/Louiseville
Compositor: G & S Typesetters, Inc.
Printer: Transcontinental Printing/Louiseville

Printed in Canada
1 2 3 4 5 6 7 07 06 05 04 03

For more information about our products, contact us at:
Thomson Learning Academic Resource Center
1-800-423-0563

For permission to use material from this text, contact us by:
Phone: 1-800-730-2214 **Fax:** 1-800-730-2215
Web: http://www.thomsonrights.com

Library of Congress Control Number: 2002115386

Student Edition with InfoTrac College Edition:
  ISBN 0-534-17362-4
Student Edition without InfoTrac College Edition:
  ISBN 0-534-17380-2
Instructor's Edition: ISBN 0-534-62311-5

Wadsworth/Thomson Learning
10 Davis Drive
Belmont, CA 94002-3098
USA

Asia
Thomson Learning
5 Shenton Way #01-01
UIC Building
Singapore 068808

Australia/New Zealand
Thomson Learning
102 Dodds Street
Southbank, Victoria 3006
Australia

Canada
Nelson
1120 Birchmount Road
Toronto, Ontario M1K 5G4
Canada

Europe/Middle East/Africa
Thomson Learning
High Holborn House
50/51 Bedford Row
London WC1R 4LR
United Kingdom

Latin America
Thomson Learning
Seneca, 53
Colonia Polanco
11560 Mexico D.F.
Mexico

Spain/Portugal
Paraninfo
Calle/Magallanes, 25
28015 Madrid, Spain

Democracy Under Pressure

An Introduction to the American Political System

NINTH EDITION

2002 ELECTION UPDATE

Milton C. Cummings, Jr.
The Johns Hopkins University

David Wise
Author and Political Analyst

THOMSON
™
WADSWORTH

AUSTRALIA • CANADA • MEXICO • SINGAPORE • SPAIN
UNITED KINGDOM • UNITED STATES

ABOUT THE AUTHORS

MILTON C. CUMMINGS, JR. is an award-winning educator who received his undergraduate degree from Swarthmore College in Pennsylvania. After two years of graduate study in England, where he was a Rhodes Scholar at Oxford University, he earned a Ph.D. in political science at Harvard University.

Professor Cummings worked for six years at the Brookings Institution in Washington, D.C., where he did research and writing on American government and politics. He then joined the political science faculty at The Johns Hopkins University in Baltimore, Maryland. For 15 years, he also served as a consultant on NBC News, where he specialized in the network's television coverage of United States congressional elections. He is also a member of the Research Advisory Council of the Center for Arts and Culture.

At Johns Hopkins, Professor Cummings has been honored with numerous awards. These include the George Owen Teaching Award, the Edward H. Griffin Award, and several other citations for outstanding teaching. He has also received fellowships and grants for research from the Social Science Research Council, the National Science Foundation, the Ford Foundation, and the Guggenheim Foundation.

Professor Cummings is the author or editor of an extensive number of scholarly articles and books, including *The Image of the Federal Service; Congressmen and the Electorate; The Patron State: Government and the Arts in Europe, North America, and Japan;* and, of course, *Democracy Under Pressure.*

DAVID WISE is a political writer based in Washington. He is the author or coauthor of ten books on government and politics and is a leading writer on intelligence, espionage, and government secrecy. His articles have appeared in *The New York Times Magazine* and many other major publications.

He is former chief of the Washington bureau of the *New York Herald Tribune* and was a regular weekly commentator on CNN for six years.

A native New Yorker and graduate of Columbia College, he joined the *Herald Tribune* in 1951 and served as the newspaper's White House correspondent before becoming chief of the Washington bureau. He is a former Fellow of the Woodrow Wilson International Center for Scholars in Washington, D.C., and for two years he lectured in political science at the University of California at Santa Barbara.

His recent book, *Spy: The Inside Story of How the FBI's Robert Hanssen Betrayed America* (Random House, 2002), received high praise from reviewers. He is also the author of *Nightmover: How Aldrich Ames Sold the CIA to the KGB for $4.6 Million,* which was excerpted in *TIME* magazine. He is coauthor of *The Invisible Government,* a number-one best-seller about the Central Intelligence Agency that has been widely credited with bringing about a reappraisal of the role of the CIA in a democratic society.

He has received several awards, including, in 1974, the George Polk Memorial Award for his book *The Politics of Lying.* He is married and has two sons.

There is, without doubt, no better experience than revising a college text in government and politics to remind one of the astonishing pace of change that takes place within the American political system.

This revised ninth edition 2002 election update of *Democracy Under Pressure* reflects that rapid pace of change both at home and abroad. Since the publication of the ninth edition two years ago, the nation has experienced the horrors of the 9/11 terrorist attacks on New York and Washington, the war in Afghanistan, the debate over Iraq, a decline in economic conditions, and a sharp drop in the stock market. All of these developments are discussed in this 2002 election update, along with other important changes in American politics and government.

The startling events that occurred in just two years affected the outcome of the congressional elections of 2002, in which control of the Senate and the House of Representatives were at stake. These midterm elections are reported and analyzed in this new edition.

Even before 9/11, the changes in American society and in the political landscape were remarkable. Since the publication of the eighth edition six years ago, America had moved into a new century, survived both the millennium and the impeachment and acquittal of President William Jefferson Clinton, elected a new president in the year 2000, only after a post-election trauma finally settled by the United States Supreme Court, and experienced something like a digital revolution, as the use of the Internet increased exponentially and cell phones, laptop computers, and e-mail became a normal part of the lives of millions of Americans.

The nation's political tides changed as well with the election of George W. Bush as president. The election of Bill Clinton in 1992 had marked an end to 12 years of Republican rule in the White House. At the time, it appeared that the election of a Democratic president and Congress also meant an end to divided government. Yet within two years, the Republicans had rebounded to capture control of both the House and Senate for the first time in 40 years. Then, in 2001, the switch of a single senator returned control of the Senate to the Democrats until the Republican victory in 2002.

By 1996, Clinton, although the Democratic heir to the New Deal of Franklin D. Roosevelt, had moved markedly toward the center. A little more than two months before the election, he signed into law the Republican bill that ended the largest federal welfare program, imposed a work requirement for recipients, and shifted responsibility for welfare to the states. Republicans argued that Clinton was trying to join the GOP.

Then in 1998, the Democrats, instead of losing House seats as would normally be the case in an off-year election, actually gained five seats, and suffered no net loss in the Senate. Not since 1934 and the administration of FDR had the president's party gained seats in a midterm election, a feat the GOP matched in 2002.

In the wake of the Republican losses, the Republican House speaker Newt Gingrich, who had been rebuked by his colleagues over ethical lapses, resigned as speaker and left Congress. Two years later came the extraordinarily close 2000 presidential election campaign as Vice President Al Gore and Governor George W. Bush of Texas battled for the undecided voters in a handful of key states.

The presidential race took place against a background of unprecedented prosperity, even as ordinary Americans, investing in much greater numbers in the stock market, wondered and worried whether the good times would continue to roll. They were concerned as well about the state of the nation's public schools, the high cost of prescription drugs for seniors, and the power of HMOs over the lives of millions of people.

All of these swift currents and shifts in political power are charted in this edition, which also includes a detailed case study of the presidential campaign, an analysis of significant trends in the 2000 elections, and a discussion of the turbulent aftermath, as Vice President Al Gore and George W. Bush battled for Florida's crucial 25 electoral votes—and the White House—a struggle finally brought to an end by the 5–4 decision of the Supreme Court.

As America moved into the 21st century, the world had changed as well. International terrorism posed a new danger to peace and security at home and abroad. A decade earlier, with the collapse of the Soviet Union and the Communist system, the danger of nuclear holocaust had receded. But the United States had been drawn into regional conflicts, from the Middle East to Bosnia and Kosovo. Nuclear proliferation also remained a danger to peace as more nations acquired weapons of mass destruction. NATO had engaged in its first military action when American and allied warplanes bombed Yugoslavia in 1999.

All of these issues, both domestic and international, are explored in this edition, including: the 2000 primary campaigns; the dramatic challenge to George W. Bush by Senator John McCain; the televised presidential debates and the use of television and the Internet in the campaigns; the role of professional campaign managers; and how "soft money," later banned by law, made a mockery of campaign finance laws.

With the publication of this ninth edition 2002 election update, it is more than three decades since *Democracy Under Pressure* first made its appearance. And what extraordinary years they have been: the end of the long war in Vietnam; the Watergate trauma and impeachment inquiry; the resignation and pardon of the president of the United States; the energy crisis; the Carter years; the seizure of American hostages in Iran and in Lebanon; the Soviet invasion of Afghanistan and its withdrawal almost a decade later; the election and reelection of Ronald Reagan, a conservative Republican president pledged to increasing the nation's military strength while cutting a broad range of social programs; the Iran-contra affair; the first George Bush's one-term presidency; his triumph in the Persian Gulf War, forcing Iraq's Saddam Hussein to withdraw from Kuwait; the failed coup attempt against Soviet president Mikhail S. Gorbachev, and, only four months later, Gorbachev's resignation and the end of the Soviet Union—and with it, the end of the Cold War; the rise of Boris N. Yeltsin and then Vladimir Putin as the leader of Russia; that country's first free presidential elections; the continuing search for peace in the Middle East; the assassination of Israel's prime minister, Yitzhak Rabin; in the United States, the advent of domestic terrorism in Oklahoma City; the Clinton scandals, the president's impeachment, trial, and acquittal; and the dramatic economic expansion and prosperity at home, followed by recession and economic difficulties, and the 9/11 terrorist attack on America.

The Ninth Edition, 2002 Election Update

This ninth edition election update of *Democracy Under Pressure* has been revised not only to reflect many of these kaleidoscopic events, but also to focus on the broader trends and on newer interpretations of the American political system.

As in the past, the making of public policy is discussed throughout the book (and particularly in Part Three, "The Policymakers"), and a section introducing the student to policy analysis is included in Chapter 1. This introduction to the policy process follows, in logical progression, the discussion of the concept of a political system.

The many new features, boxes, and Web sites incorporated in this edition, as well as the extensive additional resources available to instructors and students, are described elsewhere, in the special section at the beginning of the book. The Constitution is included, along with the Declaration of Independence, and two essays from *The Federalist*, as well as a list of the presidents of the United States and the votes they received.

Near the start of each subsequent chapter after the introductory one, we have included a key question designed to stimulate critical thinking on the part of the student. In addition, other basic questions about the workings of the American political system are posed near the beginning of each chapter. The book does not, in every case, provide ready answers to those questions, but it raises them for the student's consideration and, if desired, for classroom discussion.

Many new topics and events are also explored in this edition. We discuss and explain the recent series of Supreme Court decisions giving more power to the states within the federal system. Included as well are the historic 7–2 decision upholding the 1966 *Miranda* decision, and other significant Supreme Court decisions, such as the ruling that states may not ban partial-birth abortion, that the Boy Scouts of America have the constitutional right to bar gay members, and that the federal government may place computers and other instructional equipment in parochial schools. We have also expanded our discussion of capital punishment, and the growing reevaluation of the death penalty.

We have revised and expanded our discussion of the many barriers women still face in American society, and of the bias experienced by many minority groups, including African Americans, Hispanic Americans, Asian Americans, gays and lesbians, and disabled persons. We have covered as well the controversy over affirmative action and the plans inaugurated in Florida, Texas, and California to open the state university systems to more students.

Our chapter on public opinion includes a discussion of the controversy over exit polls, the increased percentage of Americans willing to vote for minority candidates for president, and the lack of knowledge of many voters about political matters. Our chapter on the media and politics includes a new discussion of the multibillion-dollar mergers among the media giants, and the potential impact on society. The chapter on political parties reflects how national conventions have to an even greater extent become scripted, controlled, made-for-television events now that the spring primaries in effect choose the nominees long before the conventions ratify them.

The examination of the 2000 presidential campaign and its dramatic aftermath includes extensive data on money and politics, the power of television commercials, and how and why major candidates now vie for time on television talk shows and nighttime comedy hours. The chapter on voting and elections includes new data on Supreme Court decisions affecting the blanket primary and gerrymandered congressional districts, the "gender gap," and new statistics on the correlation between demographics and voting choices.

Our review of Congress has been updated to reflect the changes discussed above, and the growing importance of "holds" placed on legislation or other action in the Senate. The chapter on the presidency includes a detailed case study of President Clinton's difficulties, including the Monica Lewinsky and Paula Jones scandals, the investigation by independent counsel Kenneth W. Starr, and the impeachment drama.

Finally, in the complete, hardcover version of the book, we have revised and expanded the discussion of foreign policy to examine the importance of terrorism, globalization, the role of the United Nations in its peacekeeping missions, the expansion of NATO, the bombing of Kosovo, the renewed violence in the Middle East, and global issues including overpopulation, famine, disease, and ethnic and religious conflicts.

Goals of the Book

As the title of this book indicates, the authors recognize that the American political system is under pressure, that its ability to cope with the problems facing the nation is being questioned by many individuals and groups in our society. In such a time, we continue to believe it useful to provide a book that focuses not only on the very considerable achievements of the American system of government but on its shortcomings too— a book that focuses on the reality as well as the rhetoric of American democracy. We have tried to do this in a textbook designed for today.

In writing this book, we set three goals. First, we believe that a textbook should be lively and stimulating to read. So we have attempted to provide a text that is as clear and readable as possible without sacrificing scholarship or content.

Second, although we present American governmental and political institutions in their historical context, we have sought to relate politics and government to contemporary issues. At the same time, we have attempted to relate those contemporary issues to larger concepts.

Third, as we have indicated, we have attempted to focus on the gaps, where they exist, between American myths and American realities and the political system's promise and its performance. Students and other citizens may not be disillusioned with the principles of American democracy, but they do ask that the political system practice those principles.

In examining the structure and processes of American politics and government, we have tried to ask: How is the political system supposed to work? How does it actually work? What might be done to make it work better? At the same time, the book emphasizes the importance of each individual citizen for the quality of American society and American government. It emphasizes how one person can make a difference. It provides examples of participation in the political process by students and other citizens. It examines the responsibilities as well as the rights of citizens in a democracy.

Acknowledgments

The authors deeply appreciate the assistance of the many people who helped to produce the ninth edition. We must begin with Sarah J. Albertini, who provided outstanding research and editorial assistance throughout the preparation of the revised manuscript for this ninth edition. Her contribution was invaluable, her wizardry on the computer essential to our task, and her dedication and talent unflagging. For this edition, we are grateful as well for the invaluable editorial assistance we received from Professor Matthew C. Price of Texas A&M University, Kingsville.

We also wish to thank our research assistants for previous editions: Norma W. Batchelder and Thomas A. Horne for the first edition (1971), Freda F. Solomon for the second edition (1974), Nancy D. Beers for the third edition (1977), M. J. Rusk-Pierce for the fourth edition (1981), Jessica Tolmach for the fifth edition (1985), Robin G. Colucci for the sixth edition (1989), and Kristin Kenney Williams for the seventh edition (1993) and the eighth edition (1997).

We wish to express our appreciation as well to Justin C. Shaberly, John Quinn Kerrigan, William Rankin, and Conor A. Reidy, who provided additional research assistance for this ninth edition; to Ida Sawyer, who kept our reference files up-to-date; to Geoffrey D. Gray, who helped us on several chapters of the eighth edition; and to John Fox Sullivan, president and publisher of the National Journal.

We are grateful as well to the many persons who gave us the benefit of their advice and assistance along the way. That list is long, and it includes Frederick L. Holborn of the School of Advanced International Studies, The Johns Hopkins University; Dean John R. Kramer of the Tulane University School of Law; Herbert E. Alexander, former director of the Citizens' Research Foundation; Roger H. Davidson of the University of California, Santa Barbara; Walter J. Oleszek of the Congressional Research Service of the Library of Congress; Harry Balfe of Montclair State College; Richard C. Wald, senior vice president, ABC News; Richard M. Scammon, director of the Elections Research Center; Jane E. Kirtley, executive director of the Reporters Committee for Freedom of the Press; Jonathan W. Wise; Christopher J. Wise; Francis J. Lorson, chief deputy clerk, and Daniel Long of the Office of the Reporter, United States Supreme Court; Tony Albertini, of Mediavest; Rich Bond, of The Johns Hopkins University; Caryn Speling of CNN's Public Relations department; Kenneth G. Pankey, Jr., director of the Information Service Project, Knowledge Management Office, National Center for State Courts; Torie Keller, of the International Foundation for Election Systems (IFES); Lawrence W. Hush, of the Office of Management and Budget; Rich Grousset, of the Roper Center for Public Opinion Research; and Maura A. Strausberg, of The Gallup Poll, as well as the many scholars, colleagues, and others whose help was acknowledged in earlier editions and to whom we remain indebted.

A number of professors who are specialists on various aspects of American politics also offered us invaluable chapter-by-chapter comments on the eighth edition that helped us to plan the ninth edition: Rosa Bettencourt, Portland Community College—Sylvania;

Thad L. Beyle, University of North Carolina; John J. Coleman, University of Wisconsin; Anne Costain, University of Colorado—Boulder; Stephen C. Craig, University of Florida; Roger Davidson, then of the University of Maryland; Malcolm Feeley, University of California—Berkeley; Stephen C. Halpern, State University of New York at Buffalo; Jennifer L. Hochschild, Princeton University; William Keefe, University of Pittsburgh; Philip Robbins, formerly of the George Washington University; Francis E. Rourke of The Johns Hopkins University; Harvey L. Schantz of the State University of New York at Plattsburgh; Peter Sederberg, University of South Carolina; and Joseph F. Zimmerman.

The authors are also grateful to a number of additional scholars who read and commented on portions of the previous edition, assisting us greatly as we prepared this new ninth edition: Sean K. Anderson, Idaho State University; John N. Barbour, Angelo State University; Janet Campbell, Mt. Hood Community College; Shirley Castelnuovo, Saddleback College; David Castles, Kilgore College; Brian L. Fife, Indiana University/Purdue University—Fort Wayne; Willie Hamilton, Mount San Jacinto College; Paul Holder, McLennan Community College; Kathleen Holland, Los Angeles City College; Willoughby G. Jarrell, Kennesaw State University; Loch K. Johnson, University of Georgia—Athens; William E. Kelly, Auburn University; John C. Kuzenski, The Citadel; Pauletta Otis, University of Southern Colorado; William J. Parente, University of Scranton; Sharon J. Ridgeway, University of Southwestern Louisiana; David Robinson, University of Houston—Downtown; Rudy Rountree, Brookhaven College; Robert L. Savage, University of Arkansas; Gaye Lynn Scott, Austin Community College; Bert E. Swanson, University of Florida; James Willson-Quayle, George Washington University.

The comments of all these reviewers were consistently helpful. At the same time, responsibility for the final draft, including any errors or shortcomings, is ours.

Finally, we wish to express our thanks to members of the college department of Wadsworth, formerly Harcourt, beginning with David C. Tatom, executive editor in political science, Wadsworth Publishing Company, who supervised this and the previous two editions and whose continuous support and counsel for this project were invaluable; Kathryn M. Stewart, our extraordinarily talented senior project editor; Stacey Sims, our imaginative and creative developmental editor; Michele Gitlin, copyeditor; Julie Guess, assistant to the acquisitions editor, and her successor, Dianna Long; as well as to Charles J. Dierker, senior project editor for the eighth edition and the early chapters of this ninth edition. We shall always owe a special debt of gratitude to the late William A. Pullin, senior editor, who first proposed this project to us and gave it his continued support; to Virginia Joyner, our manuscript editor for the first two editions; to Harry Rinehart, designer for the first four editions; to Joanne D. Daniels, editor for the third and fourth editions; to Drake Bush, our editor for the fifth and sixth editions; and to Bill M. Barnett, senior vice president. For this new edition, we are grateful as well to Susan G. Holtz, who supervised the selection of the many photographs and cartoons, to Shirley Webster, the picture and rights editor who helped coordinate that effort, to Diane Gray, the production manager; to Steven Baker, the proofreader; to Michael O'Neal, the critical reader; and to art director Burl Sloan who applied his creative talents to integrate the whole—type and graphics—into a result that captures in visual form the spirit and purpose of our examination of *Democracy Under Pressure*.

Milton C. Cummings, Jr.
David Wise

CONTENTS IN BRIEF

CONTENTS

Preface   xiii

PART ONE
The American Democracy

CHAPTER 1
Government and People

It was a perfect September day.

The cloudless skies over New York and Washington were bright blue, the sun sparkling. Then, at 8:48 A.M. on September 11, 2001, a Boeing 767 jetliner slammed into the north tower of the World Trade Center in lower Manhattan.

It seemed like a terrible accident until fifteen minutes later when a second jetliner, also heavily laden with fuel, struck the south tower. The world watched in horror on television as smoke billowed from the towers and several people, trapped by flames on the high floors, leaped to their deaths.

In Washington at 9:37 A.M. a third airliner crashed into the Pentagon. In New York at 9:59 A.M. the south tower of the trade center collapsed.

At 10:10 A.M. a fourth jetliner, apparently with the White House as its target, crashed in western Pennsylvania after courageous passengers struggled with the hijackers. Then at 10:28 A.M., the north tower of the trade center collapsed. More than 3,000 persons died, including office workers unable to escape from the two towers, hundreds of firefighters and dozens of police, and all the passengers and crews of the four airliners.

In one hour and forty minutes, America was changed forever. Nineteen hijackers of Middle Eastern origin, fifteen from Saudi Arabia, had carried out the suicide attack on America. Many observers compared it to the Japanese attack on Pearl Harbor on December 7, 1941, that caused the United States to enter the Second World War.

The impact of 9/11, as the terrorists attacks on New York and Washington came to be known, had an enormous and far-reaching effect on America's government and politics, on its foreign and military policies, and on the economy. Few aspects of American life were untouched by the horrific events of those few moments in September.

For the first time, ordinary Americans realized how vulnerable the nation and its infrastructure were to terrorist acts. Its cities, airports, bridges, tunnels, dams, power plants, communications, transportation, and computer networks—all were potential targets.

Osama bin Laden, a wealthy Saudi terrorist, and his Al Qaeda network were quickly pinpointed by Washington as the leader and the organization responsible for the attacks of 9/11. Nine days later, President George W. Bush stood before a joint session of Congress and launched a "war on terror." Any nation "that continues to harbor or support terrorism" would be regarded as a hostile regime, he warned. He denounced the Taliban rulers of Afghanistan, the country where bin Laden and his training camps were based. He was careful to target "Islamic extremism" as the enemy, not Muslims or Arabs in general. He demanded that Afghanistan surrender bin Laden. He also announced the appointment of Pennsylvania governor Tom Ridge to head a new White House Office of Homeland Security.

Only ten months before, Bush, a Republican, had won a disputed presidential election with fewer popular votes than his Democratic rival, Al Gore. When he was

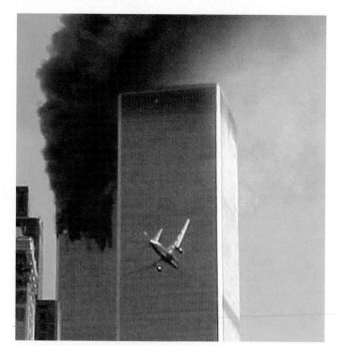

A second jetliner hijacked by terrorists about to crash into the south tower of the World Trade Center in New York City, September 11, 2001.
AP/Wide World

the governor of Texas, he had little experience in foreign policy, and as a candidate, and even later as president, he was lampooned by cartoonists and on *Saturday Night Live* as frivolous and less than brilliant. But that night, in his speech to Congress after the attack on America, he seemed to step into the mantle of the presidency for the first time. He spoke forcefully and well. His approval ratings soared, and it would be almost a year before Democrats dared to criticize his leadership. The country, angry and reeling from the attacks, united behind the president and his war on terrorism.

Even as Bush spoke, U.S. forces were moving into the region around Afghanistan. By early October, American bombers and cruise missiles were pounding that country. Later that month, American special forces, joined by the anti-Taliban Northern Alliance, were fighting inside Afghanistan. By mid-November Kabul, the capital, fell. In December, U.S. warplanes bombed a complex of caves near Tora Bora, in the mountains of eastern Afghanistan where bin Laden was thought to be hiding. By December 16, the war was largely over. Many of the Taliban leaders and Al Qaeda fighters were reported to have fled over the border into Pakistan. Hundreds of Al Qaeda prisoners were captured during the war, but Osama bin Laden was not among them.

President Bush and other senior officials warned, however, that the battle against terrorism would continue and possibly lead to the deployment of American forces to other countries where terrorists were active. A series of threat warnings by the FBI and the Office of Homeland Security reminded Americans of the continuing risk of more attacks against targets in the United States.

October 7, 2001: Terrorist leader Osama bin Laden in a videotaped broadcast praised the September 11 attacks on New York and Washington.
AP/Wide World

By the congressional elections of 2002, the political landscape had changed dramatically in the wake of 9/11. Yet, only two years earlier, the world had seemed a very different place.

In the year 2000, America began a new century as the strongest democracy on the planet. On November 7, its citizens went to the polls to choose a new President of the United States and a new Congress to lead the nation into the future.

But as the dawn broke the next morning, America was stunned to learn that the contest was not over. There was no clear winner because the crucial result in Florida hung in the balance. Nationwide, Vice President Al Gore was ahead of Texas Governor George W. Bush in the popular vote by a thin margin, but Bush was slightly ahead in Florida, where the state's 25 electoral votes would determine who became the next president. Teams of lawyers descended on the Sunshine State, the Democrats demanding a hand recount in four largely Democratic counties. At first, the dispute focused on Palm Beach county, where voters who said they had meant to vote for Gore claimed they were confused by the design of the ballot and punched the wrong hole.

On December 8, Florida's highest court ordered a statewide recount of any votes that the machines had not counted. The Bush camp appealed to the U.S. Supreme Court, which halted the recount. Then in a historic decision on December 12, a bitterly divided Supreme Court ruled 5–4 for Bush, declaring that because the recount lacked uniform standards it was unconstitutional.

Finally, it was official: George W. Bush was the next president of the United States. Bush carried 30 states with 271 electoral votes; Gore won 20 states and the District of Columbia with 267 electoral votes. In the popular vote, however, Gore ran ahead of Bush, 51,003,894 to 50,459,211. Ralph Nader, the Green Party candidate, received 2,834,410 votes, but because he

Senator Joseph I. Lieberman of Connecticut high fives Al Gore in Nashville after his selection in 2000 as the Democratic vice presidential nominee.
Nashville Tennessean/AP/Wide World

did not carry any state, he won no electoral votes. Pat Buchanan, the Reform Party candidate, won 446,743 votes and, like Nader, won no electoral votes.

The Republicans held on to their majority in the House but the Senate was equally divided, with 50 Republicans and 50 Democrats. Only seven months later, however, in May 2001, Senator James M. Jeffords of Vermont switched from the Republican party to the Democratic party, giving the Democrats control of the Senate by one vote until the 2002 midterm election.

The clash between the candidates in the year 2000 was philosophical as well as political. On one side was Al Gore, the modern if more moderate heir to the New Deal tradition established four decades before by President Franklin D. Roosevelt. At the core of that tradition was the belief that government, and particularly the federal government, had a major responsibility for meeting the social and economic needs of the people.

On the other side stood George W. Bush, the namesake and son of the 41st president, George Bush. But unlike several previous Republican presidential candidates, George W. Bush sought to move toward the political center, to reach out to independent voters, and to advocate some of the very programs and policies long identified with the Democrats. Yet there were important differences between the two candidates as well. Bush proposed to sign a bill banning "partial-birth" abortions, and he advocated enforcement of existing gun control laws, rather than enacting new ones. On these issues, Bush reflected the more conservative, traditional stance of the Republican party.

Eight years earlier, in 1992, Bill Clinton, a Democrat, had been elected along with a Democratic Congress. Two years later, however, the Republicans captured both houses of Congress for the first time in forty years. In the powerful speaker of the House,

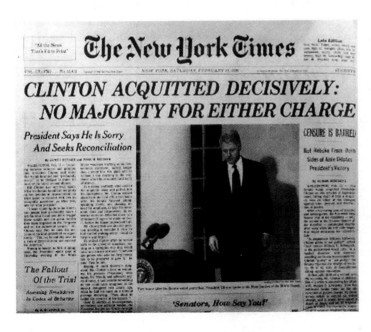

"The House impeached the president. . . . Clinton was found not guilty."
AP/Wide World

November 1989: The Berlin Wall comes down.
Copyright © CORBIS/Reuters/Bettmann

Newt Gingrich, Clinton faced a formidable political foe. But Clinton easily defeated Bob Dole, his presidential GOP opponent, in 1996, and in 1998 the Democrats made surprising gains in the still Republican-controlled House. In the wake of the Republican losses, Gingrich resigned as speaker and left Congress.

But the Clinton administration's 1998 congressional victories were eclipsed a month later when the House impeached the president, accusing him of lying to a federal grand jury about his affair with a young White House intern, Monica Lewinsky, and obstructing justice. Tried by the Senate early in 1999, Clinton was found not guilty by a vote that fell well short of the two-thirds needed to convict. But the many months of scandal had tarnished the president's reputation.

Nevertheless, and despite his personal difficulties, Clinton's approval rating as president remained remarkably high. Voters seemed willing to distinguish between his personal foibles and his performance in office. As a candidate for president in 1992, Clinton had promised

to end the unpopular federal welfare program, and in 1996 he signed a Republican-sponsored bill to restructure the program. He had eliminated the federal budget deficit and transformed it into a huge surplus. Above all, he had presided over an unprecedented period of economic expansion.

Clinton's successor, George W. Bush, led the United States in a new century. The Cold War that had held the world hostage since the end of the Second World War had ended in 1991 when the Soviet Union, the Communist superpower, collapsed. The threat of nuclear war between the U.S. and Russia, which still possessed nuclear missiles, had diminished, but other nations had become nuclear powers, notably India and Pakistan. As a result, the world was not free of the danger of a nuclear conflict. And the risks faced during the years of the Cold War were replaced by the newer peril of terrorist attacks. Political leaders in the U.S. and other Western countries also worried that terrorists might acquire nuclear, biological, or chemical weapons.

At home, millions of Americans, many more than in the past, had invested in the stock market, especially in mutual funds. But by the fall of 2000 a number of major Internet companies had suffered financial setbacks. The "dot-com" firms that had seemed so glamorous only months earlier suddenly seemed a mirage. In the wake of 9/11 the Dow Jones industrial average and the NASDAQ dropped sharply, and in the months that followed many small investors lost the savings they had counted on for their retirement.

Investor confidence was shaken even further by a series of corporate and accounting scandals. First, Enron, a giant Texas-based energy trader, collapsed and the previously-respected accounting firm, Arthur Anderson, Enron's outside auditor, was convicted of obstruction of justice. Other major corporations were revealed to have engaged in questionable practices to inflate earnings, especially the giant telecommunications firm, WorldCom, which had concealed more than $7 billion in expenses. By midsummer of 2002, the corporate scandals had contributed to a steep slide in the stock market.

A dot-com company takes to the skies to advertise.
The News Herald/AP/Wide World

The AMERICAN PAST

GEORGE WASHINGTON: HIS HIGH MIGHTINESS?

When the framers of the Constitution met in Philadelphia in 1787, one of the momentous tasks they faced was to design the executive branch of the government and decide what to call the leader of the new nation:

> During the sessions of the convention, the subject of the presidency caused much disquiet. Persistent rumors were current outside the convention that the establishment of a monarchy was under consideration. The common form of the rumor was that the Bishop of Osnaburgh, the second son of George III, was to be invited to become King of the United States. . . .
>
> There were several of the delegates, conspicuous among whom was [Edmund] Randolph, who distrusted a single executive as savoring of monarchy, and who favored an executive body of three or more. But the convention decided in favor of a single person. . . .
>
> It seems to have been generally accepted . . . that Washington would be the first president of the United States. In 1787 Washington was at the very height of his popularity and so great was the trust in him that no fear was felt regarding the inauguration of the new office. . . .
>
> After the new government was installed, the title which Washington himself was said to have preferred as the most fitting one for his position was "His High Mightiness, the President of the United States and Protector of their Liberties."
>
> —Adapted from Max Farrand, *The Framing of the Constitution of the United States*

Even aside from the scandals, the American corporate culture had undergone vast changes. The traditional belief that workers or managers could toil loyally for one company for all of their careers, and be rewarded with a gold watch and a dependable pension, was proving to be no longer true. Many workers found that their 401(k) retirement plans, heavily invested in stocks, had shrunk disastrously.

Despite economic gains in some industries, there were continuing economic problems as well. In several areas of the country, smokestack industries had declined sharply, resulting in dislocation and hardship for the blue-collar workers who were laid off or dismissed in the steel, automobile, and other plants. Many white-collar employees found themselves out of work as well, sometimes as a result of corporate mergers and dot-com failures.

Globalization—the increasingly interconnected worldwide economy—and trade competition from Asia and other industrialized nations meant that the United States was no longer assured of economic preeminence in the world. Opponents of globalization protested that it led to the exploitation of cheap labor in poor countries and damaged the environment.

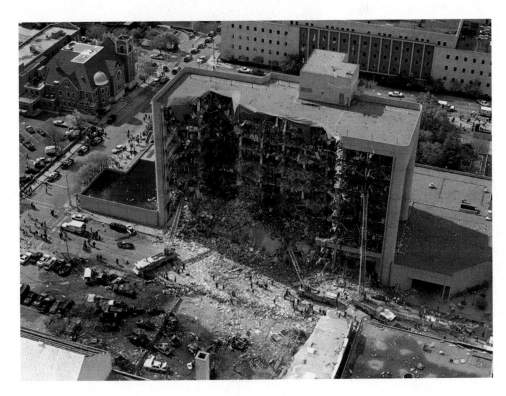

April 19, 1995: the Alfred P. Murrah federal building in Oklahoma City after it was destroyed by a truck bomb that killed 168 persons
AP/Wide World

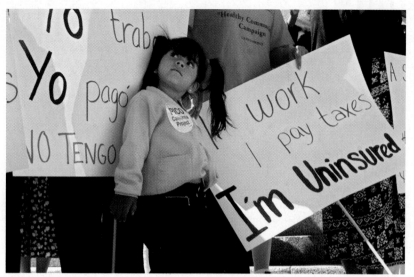
AP/Wide World

Racial divisions, despite outward progress, continued to exist in America. In several cities, for example, what appeared to be racially motivated shootings had cost innocent lives.

Even before September 11, 2001, terrorism, both home-grown and foreign, had come to America. In New York City, Islamic terrorists bombed the World Trade Center in 1993, killing six people and injuring more than 1,000. On April 19, 1995, the federal building in Oklahoma City was destroyed by a truck bomb, killing 168 persons. Two Americans, Timothy McVeigh and Terry Nichols, who had served in the same Army unit, were convicted for that crime and McVeigh was executed. Armed militia groups, although small in number, were deeply suspicious of government. Some of these groups were identified with white supremacist views and spouted hatred over the Internet.

America was grappling as well with a host of domestic challenges, including the rising costs of health care, the growing power of health maintenance organizations (HMOs), the uncertain quality of public education, and the interlocking problems of crime, drugs, poverty, and homelessness—problems often particularly acute in the inner cities.

By the presidential election of 2000, there were other changes in the shape of American politics. That year, and in the election of 1996, hundreds of millions of dollars of unregulated "soft money" flowed into both major parties from corporations, unions, and wealthy donors, and was used to aid candidates indirectly, making a mockery of federal campaign finance laws. As a result, Congress in 2002 passed a new campaign finance law banning contributions of soft money to national political parties and restricting the use of such funds to broadcast "issue ads" in federal elections. Predictably, however, political parties and candidates were scrambling to find new ways to use such funds.

Special-interest groups, often well financed and supporting a single issue, had become powerful ac-

tors in the nation's politics. Often such groups contributed to political candidates through political action committees (PACs), which had grown in number and importance even though a few candidates declined to accept PAC money. Other trends were visible: the nation's political parties appeared to be declining in importance, and public confidence in the institutions of government was relatively low.

Well before the war in Afghanistan, in the post–Cold War era, the United States found itself called upon to intervene in local or regional conflicts or for humanitarian purposes. In the early 1990s, President Clinton sent American troops to Haiti and Bosnia. In 1999 through the NATO alliance, U.S. warplanes bombed Yugoslavia repeatedly for more than two months after that country's armed forces had invaded Kosovo and forced hundreds of thousands of people to flee, mostly into neighboring Albania. Under

Copyright © Robin Layton

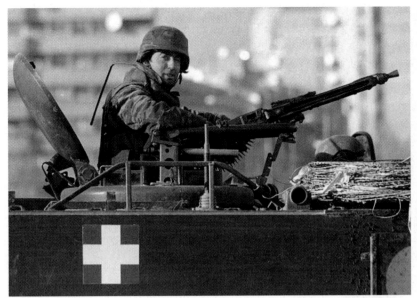

A Greek soldier in Kosovo, part of an international peacekeeping force
AP/Wide World

the Middle East—the Persian Gulf War, the impeachment of President Clinton, and the September 11 terrorist attacks.

The swirling currents of these events had brought change not only to America but to the way Americans perceived their government and their political system. Many voters professed to see little difference between the major parties, and expressed little faith in politicians.

Even before the Reagan-Bush years, many liberals and conservatives alike had questioned the effectiveness of government solutions to some social problems. Five decades earlier, President Franklin D. Roosevelt had ushered in an era of great social reform through federal government programs. John F. Kennedy and Lyndon B. Johnson had followed in his path. But many of the programs of Johnson's "Great Society" had not worked as their architects had envisioned, and in 1980 Reagan successfully assailed the "bureaucracy" and the government in Washington.

pressure of the bombing, then Yugoslav president Slobodan Milosevic signed a peace agreement and allowed international peacekeeping forces to enter Kosovo. As president, Clinton several times brokered attempts to achieve peace between Israel and the Palestinians in the volatile Middle East. President George W. Bush also found himself drawn into diplomatic efforts to bring peace in the region after Israel, responding to repeated suicide bombings of civilians, sent troops and tanks into Palestinian towns.

American influence and military power, while still enormous, did not always seem capable of achieving long-range goals. The first President Bush had dispatched half a million troops to the Persian Gulf; in the brief war fought early in 1991, the American military forced Iraq's dictator, Saddam Hussein, to withdraw from Kuwait. But ten years later, Saddam was still in power in Iraq and the new President Bush called for his removal and with his advisers discussed ways to overthrow him. Unless Saddam disarmed, the U.S. would lead a war against Iraq, Bush warned.

Since the 1960s, America had passed through a long and extraordinarily turbulent period of assassination, civil unrest, war, abuse of presidential power, and economic hardship. The murder of President John F. Kennedy in 1963 had been followed by explosions of anger in the black areas of the nation's cities, the assassination of Dr. Martin Luther King and Robert F. Kennedy, eight years of war in Vietnam, the Watergate scandal—when burglars working for the Republican president's reelection campaign broke into Democratic party headquarters—and the resulting resignation and pardon of Richard Nixon. Then came the seizure in Iran of American hostages, periodic inflation, high unemployment, and economic recession, the Iran-contra scandal—in which President Ronald Reagan's administration sought to trade American arms for hostages in

Copyright © David McCullum/Magnum

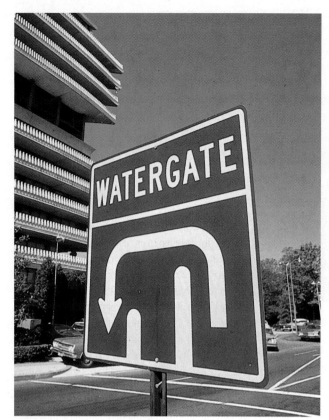

Copyright © Dennis Brack/Black Star

These and other questions will be explored in this book, but first it might be useful to examine the general relationship between people and government in a democratic system.

THE RECIPROCAL NATURE OF DEMOCRATIC POWER

In July 1945 a small group of scientists stood atop a hill near Alamogordo, New Mexico, and watched the first atomic bomb explode in the desert. At that instant the traditional power of government to alter the lives of people took on a terrifying new dimension. With the onset of the nuclear age and the development of intercontinental ballistic missiles (ICBMs), people lived less than 30 minutes away from possible destruction. That is all the time it would take for ICBMs to reach their targets, destroying whole cities and perhaps entire nations. As already noted, with the collapse of the Soviet Union in 1991 and the end of the Cold War, these concerns have diminished considerably, but they have not disappeared. As of 2000 many of the missiles were still in their silos in the United States, Russia, and China. Other powers possessed nuclear weapons, and several smaller countries were trying to acquire them. The threat of a nuclear war between India and Pakistan remained very real.

At the height of the Cold War, when America and the Soviet Union faced each other as hostile superpowers, the president of the United States was often described as a person with his finger "on the nuclear button." The existence of such chilling terminology, and of nuclear weapons, reflects the increasingly complex, technological, computerized nature of the world in which Americans live. As the country has changed through the development of science, technology, and industrialization, government has changed along with it. Government has expanded and grown more complex; it is called on to perform more and more tasks.

There were continuing signs of change. In 1984, Geraldine Ferraro was the Democratic candidate for vice president, the first woman to be nominated for that office by a major political party. In 1996 many persons, white and black, had hoped that former general Colin Powell, an African American, would run for president. In 2000, Joseph I. Lieberman became the first person of Jewish faith to be named to a major party presidential ticket. By that year, more women, more African Americans, and more Hispanics had been elected to Congress and sat in the cabinet and on the Supreme Court.

Beyond the policies of a particular president, broader questions were raised by the problems the nation had experienced over the past four decades.

After more than two hundred years, was the American political system capable of meeting the social and economic needs of the people and preserving the national security? Were crime, violence, and the continuing threat of terrorism changing the quality of life in the United States? Were the nation's institutions gridlocked and too slow to change with the times? Could America's industries remain competitive with those of other nations? At the same time, could Americans preserve the environment? In a multicultural society, with minority groups increasing in numbers, could Americans learn to overcome racial divisions and live in harmony? Was the American democracy still workable, even though it had been subjected to unusual pressures?

Alamogordo, New Mexico, July 1945: The first atomic bomb is tested.
Copyright © CORBIS/Bettmann

The Impact of Government on People

Obviously, government can affect the lives of students or other citizens by sending them overseas to fight in a war in which they may be killed. Less obvious, perhaps, are the ways in which government pervades most aspects of daily life, sometimes down to minute details. For example, the federal government regulates the amount of windshield that the wipers on a car must cover and even the speed of the windshield wipers. (At the fast setting, wipers must go "at least 45 cycles per minute.")[5]

Online *for more information about federal highways, see:* www.fhwa.dot.gov

College students driving to class (perhaps over a highway built largely with federal funds) are expected to observe local traffic regulations. They may have to put a coin in a city parking meter. The classroom in which they sit may have been constructed with a federal grant. Possibly they are attending college with the aid of federal loans or grants. For fiscal year 1999, for example, the government awarded $41.9 billion to assist more than 6 million college undergraduates and graduate students.[6]

Clearly government's impact is real and far-reaching. Americans normally must pay three levels of taxes—local, state, and federal. They attend public schools and perhaps public colleges. They draw unemployment insurance, welfare benefits, Medicare, and Social Security. They must either obey the laws, or pay the penalty of a fine or imprisonment if they break them and are caught and convicted. Their savings accounts and home mortgages are guaranteed by the federal government. Their taxes support the armed forces and police, fire, health, and sanitation departments. To hunt, fish, marry, drive, fly, or build they must have a government license. From birth certificate to death certificate, government accompanies individuals along the way. Even after they die, the government is not through with them. Estate taxes may be collected and wills probated in the courts.

Online *for more information about Social Security, see:* www.ssa.gov

In the United States, "government" is extraordinarily complicated. There are federal, state, and local layers of government, metropolitan areas, commissions, authorities, boards and councils, and quasi-governmental bodies. Many of the units of government overlap. And all affect the lives of individuals.

The Impact of People on Government

Just as government affects people, people affect government. The American system of government is based on the concept that power flows from the people to the

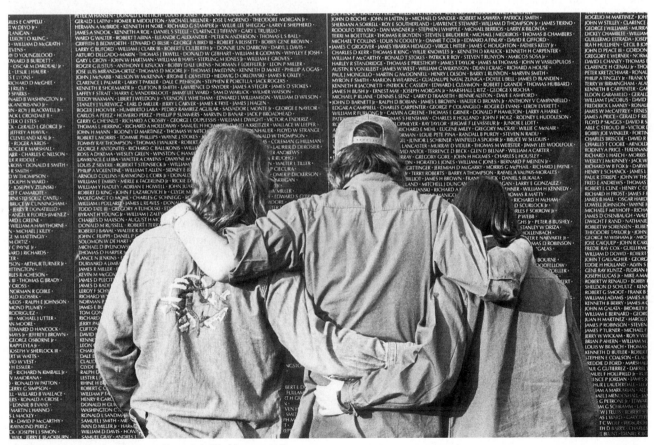

Visitors at the Vietnam Veterans Memorial, Washington, D.C.
D. Gorton/NYT Pictures

government. Jefferson expressed this eloquently when he wrote in the Declaration of Independence that "to secure these rights, Governments are instituted among men, deriving their just powers from the consent of the governed." Abraham Lincoln expressed the same thought in his Gettysburg Address, speaking of "government of the people, by the people, for the people."

These are ideals, statements embodying the principles of democracy. As we note at many points in this book, the principles do not always mesh with the practices. Yet, it remains true that if government in the United States has real and often awesome powers over people, at the same time people—both individuals and the mass of citizens together—can have considerable power over the government.

The reciprocal nature of democratic power is a basic element of the American political system. As V. O. Key, Jr., the distinguished Harvard political scientist, put it: "The power relationship is reciprocal, and the subject may affect the ruler more profoundly than the ruler affects the subject."[7] There are several ways that people influence government.

Voting   The first and most important power of the people in America is the right to vote in free elections to choose those who govern. At regular intervals, the people may, in the classic phrase of Horace Greeley, the 19th-century journalist and politician, "turn the rascals out." The fact that a president, member of Congress, governor, mayor, or school board member may want to stand for reelection influences his or her performance in office. The knowledge of officials that they serve at the pleasure of the voters usually tends to make those officials sensitive to public opinion.

But isn't one person's vote insignificant when millions are cast? Not necessarily. That the individual's vote does matter even in a nation as big as the United States has been illustrated many times in close presidential elections.

Presidents are elected by electoral votes, but these are normally cast by the electors in each state for the candidate who wins the most popular votes in the state.* In 1960 a shift from John F. Kennedy to Richard M. Nixon of only 9,421 voters in Illinois and Missouri would have prevented either candidate from gaining a majority in the electoral college. And in 1968 and 1976, shifts of relatively small numbers of voters in a few states would have changed the outcomes of the presidential elections in those years.

Party Activity   The political party is basic to the American system of government because it provides a vehicle for competition and choice. Without these, "free elections" would be meaningless. Despite an exceptionally strong showing by Ross Perot, an independent can-

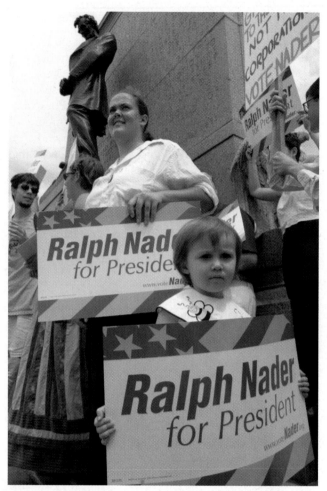

In 2000, consumer advocate Ralph Nader ran as a third-party candidate of the Green Party.
AP/Wide World

didate for president in 1992, for the most part the two-party system has predominated in the United States. Since candidates for public office, even at the presidential level, are usually selected by their parties, people can influence government, and the choice of who governs, by participating in party activities. Whether political campaigns offer meaningful alternatives on the issues depends in part on who is nominated. And that in turn may be influenced by how many people are politically active. Political participation can take many forms, from ringing doorbells to running for local party committees or for public office.

 for more information about the two major political parties, see: www.democrats.org and www.rnc.org

Public Opinion   Candidates and elected officials are sensitive to what the public is thinking. This has been particularly true since the Second World War, when sophisticated methods of political polling and statistical analysis were developed. But citizens do not have to wait around to be polled. They can make their opinion felt in a variety of ways: by voting and partici-

---

*See the description of the electoral college in Chapter 11.

pating in political activities, talking to other people, writing or sending faxes or e-mail to their representatives in Congress, telephoning the members of their city council, writing to their newspapers, or testifying at public hearings. Even by reading the newspapers and watching television news broadcasts (or by not doing those things), people may indirectly influence government. A citizen who carefully follows public issues in the news media and magazines of opinion may help to influence government, since a government is less likely to attempt to mislead when it knows it is dealing with an informed public.

Interest Groups   When people belong to groups that share common attitudes and make these views felt, or when they organize such groups, they may be influencing government. These private associations, or interest groups, may be business and professional organizations, unions, racial and religious groups, or organizations of groups such as farmers or veterans. An interest group does not have to be an organized body. Students, for example, constitute a highly vocal interest group, even when they do not belong to a formal student organization.

Direct Action   At various times in American history, people have sought to influence government by civil disobedience and sometimes by militant or violent action. In the late 1960s and early 1970s, for example, some civil rights leaders and student activists practiced "the politics of confrontation." The idea of direct and often disruptive action to achieve political ends appeared to have grown in part out of the civil rights movement (beginning with peaceful "sit-ins" to desegregate lunch counters in the South) and in part out of the organized opposition to the war in Vietnam. Demonstrations, marches, sit-ins, campus strikes, picketing, and protest characterized those years.

With the end of the war in Vietnam, this type of direct political action diminished considerably, but it has by no means disappeared. Protesters in Seattle disrupted meetings of the World Trade Organization in 1999, to advocate greater protection for the environment and workers. Thousands of people participated in the year 2000 in the "Million Mom March" to call for stronger gun control laws.

Over the years, farmers have demonstrated in Washington for government assistance, and antiabortion groups, peace activists, gay men and women, and others have held rallies on the mall in the nation's capital to

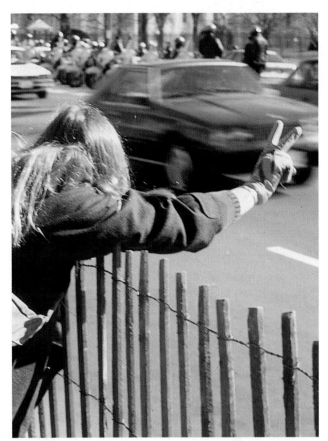

Kristin Kenney Williams

focus attention on their goals. And in the early 1990s, pro-life groups sought to prevent women from having abortions by blocking access to clinics. This tactic was prohibited by a federal law enacted in 1994.

Kathy Brownell

WHAT IS GOVERNMENT?

The words "government," "politics," "power," and "democracy" ought to be clearly defined. The difficulty is that political scientists, philosophers, and kings have never been able to agree entirely on the meanings of these terms.

The ancient Greek philosopher Plato and his pupil Aristotle speculated on their meaning, and the process has continued up to the present day. Bearing in mind that no universal or perfect definitions exist, we can still discuss the words and arrive at a general concept of what they mean.

Government

Even in a primitive society, some form of government exists. A tribal chief emerges with authority over others and makes decisions, perhaps in consultation with the elders of the tribe. The tribal leader is governing.

Government, then, even in a modern industrial state, can be defined on a simple level as the individuals, institutions, and processes that make the rules for society and possess the power to enforce them. But rules for what? To take an example, if private developers wish to acquire a wildlife preserve for commercial use, and environmental groups protest, government may be called on to settle the dispute. In short, government makes rules to decide who gets what of valued things in a society.* It attempts to resolve conflicts among individuals and groups.

David Easton, a political scientist at the University of Chicago, has written:

---

*A definition close to that suggested by the title of Harold D. Lasswell's *Politics: Who Gets What, When, How* (New York: McGraw-Hill, 1936).

Even in the smallest and simplest society someone must intervene in the name of society, with its authority behind him, to decide how differences over valued things are to be resolved.

This authoritative allocation of values is a minimum prerequisite of any society. . . . Every society provides some mechanisms, however rudimentary they may be, for authoritatively resolving differences about the ends that are to be pursued, that is, for deciding who is to get what there is of the desirable things.[8]

Easton's concept has come to be broadly accepted by many scholars today. In highly developed societies the principal mechanism for resolving differences is government. Government makes binding rules for society that determine the distribution of valued things.

Politics

Benjamin Disraeli, the 19th-century British minister and novelist, wrote in *Endymion* that "politics are the possession and distribution of power."

Disraeli's definition of politics comes very close to our definition of government. Disraeli was ahead of his time, for many political scientists today would agree in general with his definition, and they would add that there is little difference between politics and government.

For example, V. O. Key, Jr., equated politics with "the process and practice of ruling" and the "workings of governments generally, their impact on the governed, their manner of operation, the means by which governors attain and retain authority."[9] In other words, **politics** may be defined as the pursuit and exercise of power.

Such a definition might be confusing to those Americans who tend to look at politics as the pursuit of power, and government as the exercise of power. The

HOW BIG IS THE GOVERNMENT?

The federal government:

- Employs 4.2 million full-time civilian, military, and postal workers—close to seven times the number at General Motors, the largest private employer of permanent workers in the United States
- Owns more than 1 million square miles of land—roughly the size of the entire Central Time Zone
- Rents and owns 644 million square feet of offices—enough to fill all the downtown offices in New York, Los Angeles, Chicago, and Houston combined
- Will spend almost $1.6 trillion next year—almost double Japan's [1995] budget

More than one-third of the budget goes to Social Security, Medicare, and Medicaid, and 15 percent is

spent on interest on the national debt. Some of the government's direct obligations include:

- $134.5 billion for salaries
- $2.5 billion for rent
- $271.6 million for office furniture
- $198.3 million for 30-mm or smaller guns
- $34.4 million for tobacco products
- $14 million for brooms, brushes, mops, and sponges

The federal government's recent annual activities include:

- Printing 9.3 billion pieces of currency worth $117.3 trillion
- Housing and feeding 93,708 prisoners

—Adapted from *Washington Post*, May 28, 1995

conventional notion is that people engage in politics to get elected. But, in fact, those who govern are constantly making political decisions. It is very difficult to say where government ends and politics begins. The two terms overlap and intertwine, even if their meanings are not precisely the same.*

Power

Power is the possession of control over others. People have sought for centuries to understand the basis of power, why it exists, and how it is maintained. Authority over others is a tenuous business, as many a deposed South American dictator can attest.

A century ago, Boss Tweed, the leader of Tammany Hall, the Democratic Party machine in New York City, reportedly expressed a simple, cynical philosophy: "The way to have power is to take it." But once acquired, power must be defended against others who desire it. For seven years Nikita Khrushchev appeared to be the unquestioned ruler of the Soviet Union. One day in October 1964, he was summoned back to Moscow from his Black Sea vacation retreat and informed by his colleagues in the Presidium of the Communist Party that he was no longer premier of the Soviet Union. It was reported that those who deposed him changed all the confidential government and party telephone numbers in Moscow, so that Khrushchev could not attempt to rally support among elements still loyal to him.[10] Khrushchev was helpless, cut off from the tremendous power that was his only 24 hours before.

The coup against Khrushchev had its echo more than 25 years later when a group of hard-liners in the Kremlin attempted to overthrow Mikhail Gorbachev in August 1991 while the Soviet leader was vacationing—again at a dacha on the Black Sea. The coup failed, thanks to the intervention of Russia's president, Boris Yeltsin, who mounted a tank to defy the coup plotters. But four months later, Gorbachev resigned, the Soviet Union broke up, and Yeltsin emerged as the most influential leader of the former Soviet republics.

It is a truism that power often destroys those who hold it. Lord Acton, the 19th-century British peer and historian, said that "power tends to corrupt and absolute power corrupts absolutely." The 18th-century French philosopher Montesquieu expressed a similar idea in *The Spirit of the Laws:* "Every man who has power is impelled to abuse it."

As Key has observed, power is not something that can be "poured into a keg, stored, and drawn upon as the need arises."[11] Power, Key notes, is relational—that is, it

William Marcy Tweed, the New York City political leader known as Boss Tweed
Copyright © CORBIS/ Bettmann

involves the interactions between the person who exercises power and those affected by that exercise of power.

If people, even in a primitive state, find it necessary to accept rulers who can authoritatively decide who gets what, then it follows that whoever governs possesses and exercises power in part because of that position. In other words, power follows office. To some extent, we accept the power exercised over us by others because we recognize the need to be governed.

Democracy

Democracy is a word that comes from two Greek roots, *demos,* "the populace," and *kratia,* "rule"—taken together, "rule by the people."† The Greeks used the term to describe the government of Athens and other Greek city-states that flourished in the 5th century B.C. In his famous *Funeral Oration,* Pericles, the Athenian statesman, declared: "Our constitution is named a democracy, because it is in the hands not of the few, but of the many."

All governments make decisions about the distribution of valued things. As was noted earlier, in a democratic government, power, in theory, flows from the people as a whole. This is one of the ideals on which the American democracy was founded. But the United States is too big for every citizen to take part in the deliberations of government, as in ancient Athens, so the distinction is sometimes made that America is a representative democracy, rather than a direct one. Leaders are elected to speak for and represent the people. Thus, the United States can be described as a **republic,** a form of government in which the people are sovereign but their power is exercised by their elected representatives.

---

*Of course, the word "politics" can also refer to a process that occurs in a wide variety of nongovernmental settings—in fact, in every form of social organization where different people, with competing goals and differing objectives, interact. Thus, one sometimes speaks of politics in the local PTA, the politics of a garden club, or the politics in the newsroom of a campus newspaper. In this book, however, we are talking about politics as it is more commonly understood, in its governmental setting.

---

†There are, of course, many possible definitions of the word "democracy." The Greek word *demos* means "the populace," or "the common people"; hence democracy in this sense means government by the mass of people, as distinguished from those with special rank or status.

Government by the people also carries with it the notion of **majority rule,** a concept of government by the people in which everyone is free to vote, but normally whoever gets the most votes wins the election and represents all the people, including those who voted for the losing candidate. But in a system that is truly democratic, minority rights and views are also recognized and protected.

Every schoolchild knows the phrase from the Declaration of Independence: "We hold these truths to be self-evident, that all men are created equal." The concept of **equality**—that all people are of equal worth, even if not of equal ability—is also basic to American democracy. So are basic rights such as freedom of speech, press, religion, and assembly; the right to vote; and the right to dissent from majority opinion. The idea of individual dignity and the importance of each individual is another concept basic to American democracy. And, American government is constitutional—the power of government is limited by a framework of fundamental written law. Under such a government—in theory—the police power of the state should not be used illegally to punish individuals or to repress dissent.

These are the ideals, noble, even beautiful, in their conception. But, this is not always what really happens.

Fred Conrad/NYT Pictures

African Americans and other minorities are still struggling for full equality; the police sometimes have their own views on freedom of assembly; and the government has sometimes committed abuses in the name of national security. In the mid-1970s, for example, congressional investigations disclosed widespread violations of the constitutional rights of individuals by federal intelligence agencies. In the 1980s, the Iran-contra scandal revealed that officials in the White House had acted outside the law in the pursuit of foreign policy objectives.

American democracy is far from perfect. "This is a great country," President John F. Kennedy once declared, "but it must be greater."[12] All citizens have to judge for themselves how far America falls short of fulfilling the principles on which it was founded. Nevertheless, the ideals endure; the goals are there if not always the reality.

THE CONCEPT OF A POLITICAL SYSTEM

In today's electronic world, most people have listened to a stereo. Suppose for a moment that a visitor from outer space dropped in and asked you to describe a stereo system. You might say, "This is a compact disc player. I'm putting this CD in the little drawer that slides back in. This thing with all the knobs and buttons is an amplifier, and these big boxes over here are what we call speakers." Perhaps you might take the trouble to describe the details of each component at some length. At the end of your elaborate explanation, the visitor from space would still not know what a stereo was.

A better way to describe the compact disc player and the other components would be to explain that it is a system for the reproduction of sound, consisting of several parts, each of which performs a separate function and relates to the others. Having said that, you might turn on the power and play some music. Now the visitor would understand.

A Dynamic Approach

In the same way, it is possible either to describe people, government, politics, and power as isolated, static elements, or to look at them as interacting elements in a political system. The concept of a political system may provide a useful framework, or approach, for understanding the total subject matter of this book. Just as in the case of the stereo system, a political system consists of several parts that relate to one another, each of which performs a separate, vital function. If we think in terms of a system, we visualize all the pieces in motion, acting and interacting, dynamic rather than static. In other words, something is happening—just as when the compact disc is playing.

As David Easton says, "We can try to understand political life by viewing each of its aspects piecemeal," or we can "view political life as a system of interrelated activities."* One of the problems of trying to look at a political system is that government and politics do not exist in a vacuum—they are embedded in, and closely related to, many other activities in a society. But it is possible to separate political activity from other kinds of activity, at least for purposes of study.

Just as the CD player is part of a stereo system for the reproduction of sound, a political system also operates for a purpose: It makes the binding, authoritative decisions for society about who gets what.

Inputs, Outputs, and Feedback

We may carry the analogy of a stereo system to a political system even further. A sound system has inputs, outputs, and sometimes a loud whistling noise called feedback. Those are precisely the same terms used by political scientists in talking about a political system.

The **inputs** of a political system are of two kinds: the demands upon, and supports for, the system. **Demands,** as the word indicates, are what people and groups want from the political system, whether it be health care for the aged, loans for college students, equal opportunity for minorities, or higher subsidies for farmers. **Supports** are the attitudes and actions of people that sustain and buttress the system at all levels and allow it to continue to work. They include everything from the patriotism drilled into schoolchildren to public backing for specific government policies.

The **outputs** of a political system are chiefly the binding decisions it makes, whether in the form of laws, regulations, or judicial decisions. Often such decisions reward one segment of society at the expense of another. The millionaire on New York's Park Avenue may be heavily taxed to clothe inner-city children on the South Side of Chicago. Or he may benefit from a tax loophole enacted by Congress. The freeway that runs through a poor urban neighborhood may speed white commuters from the suburbs but dislocate black residents of the inner city. These decisions are "redistributive" measures in that something of value is reallocated by the political system. Sometimes even a decision not to act is an output of a political system. By preserving an existing policy, one group may be rewarded while another group is not.

Feedback in a political system describes the response of the rest of society to the decisions made by the authorities. When those reactions are communicated back to the authorities, they may lead to a fresh round of decisions and new public responses.

---

*David Easton, "An Approach to the Analysis of Political Systems," *World Politics,* vol. 9 (April 1957), pp. 383–384. Our discussion of the concept of a political system relies chiefly on Easton's work, although it should not be read as a literal summary of his approach. For example, the analogy to a stereo system is the authors' own, and Easton's analysis of a political system is both much more detailed and broader in scope than the outline presented here.

The concept of a political system is simply a way of looking at political activity. It is an approach, an analytical tool, rather than a general theory of the type developed to explain the workings of scientific phenomena. It enables us to examine not only the formal structure of political and governmental institutions, but also how these institutions actually work.

PUBLIC POLICYMAKING

There is a tendency in the study of American politics and government to concentrate on the institutions of government, such as the presidency, Congress, and the courts, and on the role of political parties, campaigns, and voters.

The analysis of public policy is another way of looking at government and politics. Instead of examining only institutions, policy analysis looks at what the institutions do.

A **policy** is a course of action decided upon by a government—or by any organization, group, or individual—that usually involves a choice among competing alternatives. When policies are shaped by government officials, the result is called **public policy.**

The analysis of public policy, therefore, focuses on how choices are arrived at and how public policy is made. It also focuses on what happens afterward. How well or badly is a policy carried out? What is its impact in its own policy area? And what effect does it have in other policy areas?

As Robert L. Lineberry has put it, policy analysts "focus, in systems language, on the outputs of the political system and their impact on the political, social, and economic environment."[13]

As Lineberry and other scholars have pointed out, if a problem does not get on the public agenda—the subjects that government policymakers try to deal with—no policy or output will be framed to deal with the problem. "Political issues emerge from contending definitions of a policy problem."[14] Thus, some people feel marijuana should be legalized, but unless a federal or state government acts, its possession and sale remain illegal.

But what happens when an issue does get on the public agenda and results in the creation of a public policy? Sometimes nothing. In 1964 President Lyndon Johnson declared his "war on poverty." A major federal program was launched to try to deal with the problem. But more than three decades later, poverty in America had not been eradicated.

In other words, programs do not always work as intended. "Bills are passed, White House Rose Garden ceremonies held, and gift pens passed around by the president. At that point, when attention has waned, when the television cameras are gone and the reporters no longer present, the other face of policy emerges."[15] This second face of policy analysis, as Lineberry has suggested, is concerned with implementation, impact, and distribution.

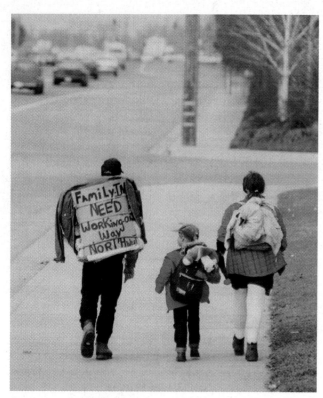

Government "redistributive" policies don't always work. A homeless family in California.
Lodi News Sentinel/AP/Wide World

Implementation is the action, or actions, taken by government to carry out a policy. "When policy is pronounced, the implementation process begins. What happens in it may, over the long run, have far more impact . . . than the intentions of the policy's framers."[16]

The impact of a policy can be measured in terms of its consequences, both in its immediate policy area and in other areas. For example, a government decision to combat inflation by tightening credit and raising interest rates may adversely affect the stock market if investors fear that companies will not be able to borrow enough money to invest in, and expand, their businesses.

Distribution is what occurs when government adopts a public policy that provides, or distributes, benefits to people or groups. Sometimes distribution involves who wins and who loses from a given public policy. When the government builds post offices or maintains national parks, its policies are distributive, and people assume that everyone benefits. But a **redistributive policy** takes something away from one person and gives it to someone else. A Medicaid program that uses taxes collected from more affluent members of society to assist the poor would be an example of such a policy. It is here in the area of redistributive policies that many of the major political battles are fought.

Public policies and policymaking are discussed throughout this book and are the subject, in particular, of Part Four, "Government in Operation."

DEMOCRATIC GOVERNMENT AND A CHANGING SOCIETY

A political system relates to people, and the size of the population affects the outputs of the system. Of equal importance is the qualitative nature of the population: who they are, where they live, how they work, how they spend, how they move about. How the political system works, in other words, is affected to some extent by the surrounding social, economic, and cultural framework. As society changes, the responses of government are likely to change. Government reacts to basic alterations in the nature of a society; it tries to tailor programs and decision making to meet changing needs and demands. Population changes are also important politically; for example, the 2000 census data confirmed that the American population balance had continued to shift from the Northeast to the South and West. As a result, some southern and western states were expected to gain more seats in Congress in 2002.

275 Million Americans

In the year 2000 federal census-takers fanned out across America, counting the population as the Constitution requires every 10 years. By August of that year more than 275 million had been counted, according to Census Bureau estimates. The Census Bureau predicted that by 2010 the total population may reach 297 million people

---

AMERICA IN THE 21ST CENTURY

WASHINGTON, Mar. 13—Fueled by immigration and higher birth rates among Hispanic women, the United States is undergoing a profound demographic shift, and by the middle of the [21st] century only about half of the population will be non-Hispanic whites, the Census Bureau predicted today.

By 2050, the bureau said, immigration patterns and differences in birth rates, combined with an overall slow-down in growth of the country's population, will produce a United States in which 53 percent of the people will be non-Hispanic whites, down from 74 percent today.

In contrast, Hispanic people will make up 24.5 percent of the population, up from the current 10.2 percent, and Asians will make up 8.2 percent, an increase from the current 3.3 percent. The percentage of the black population will remain relatively stable, rising to about 13.6 percent by the year 2050 from the current 12 percent.

The population as a whole will rise to about 394 million from 262 million, an increase of 50 percent, the bureau said.

—*New York Times*, March 14, 1996

and that it could rise to more than 300 million after 2015.[17]

According to one study of population patterns in the United States, if the projections of some experts were realized, "we would have close to one billion people in the United States one hundred years from now."[18] Although the authors of the study added that birth control and other factors made it unlikely that such a staggering total will be reached by that time, they estimated that the United States could support a population of a billion without people pushing one another into the oceans.

How the nation has expanded from a population of about 4 million in 1790, and what the future may hold, can be charted with Census Bureau statistics and projections to 2025, as shown in Table 1-1. This dramatic increase in numbers of people—the "population explosion"—is taking place around the world. It raises questions that governments must ponder. Will there be enough food to eat? Enough room to live? Enough oil and water and other natural resources to meet humanity's future needs? Will the environment be destroyed?

 for more information about Census Bureau statistics, see: www.census.gov

An interesting profile of the American public can be sketched with statistics, as presented in Table 1-2, that answer the question "Who are we?" A portrait of national origins can also be drawn. The great successive waves of immigration placed a stamp of diversity on America; even third- and fourth-generation Americans may think of themselves as "Irish" or "Italian."

Copyright © Mark Downey/Lucid Images/Picture Quest

An earlier census survey indicated that the ancestry groups of Americans included the following: German, 23.3 percent; Irish, 15.6 percent; English, 13.1 percent; African American, 12 percent; Hispanic, 8.6 percent; Italian, 6.0 percent; French, 4.1 percent; Polish, 4.0 percent; Asian Americans, 2.9 percent; Dutch, 2.5 percent; Scottish, 2.2 percent; and Native American, 0.08 percent.[19] The United States is also a nation of more than 87.4 million Protestants, 61.2 million Catholics, 5.5 million Muslims, 5.3 Eastern Orthodox church members, 4 million Jews, and 1.3 million Hindus.*

---

*The Census Bureau does not ask the religion of Americans in the decennial census, which is taken every 10 years that end in zero, but religious groups estimate their own membership. These are rounded figures based on *The World Almanac and Book of Facts 2000*, pp. 692–693.

TABLE 1-1

Profile of the U.S. Population, 1790–2025

	Population (in millions)										
	Actual									Projected	
	1790	**1870**	**1920**	**1960**	**1970**	**1980**	**1990**	**1998**	**2010**	**2025**
Total population	4	39	106	179	203	226.5	249.4	270.5	297.7	335
Urban	—*	10	54	125	149	167	187	NA	NA	NA
Rural	4	29	52	54	54	60	62	NA	NA	NA
Nonwhite	1	5	11	20	25	32	40.7	47.5	58.2	72.8
White	3	34	95	159	178	195	208.7	223	239.5	262.2
Median age (years)	NA	20	25	30	28.1	30	33	35.2	37	38
Primary and secondary school enrollment	NA	7	23	42	53	45	46	53	NA	NA
College enrollment	NA	—*	0.6	3	7	10	13.8	14.7	NA	NA

*Less than 200,000.
NA: Not available.
SOURCES: U.S. Bureau of the Census, and National Center for Education Statistics, Department of Education. Projected totals are the most likely estimates as of July 1, 1998. Population figures rounded.

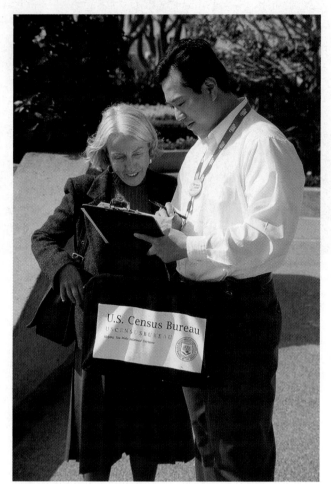

Copyright © Spencer Grant/PhotoEdit

TABLE 1-2

Who Are We?*

138.2 million females
132.0 million males
238.4 million under 5 years
 32.1 million 65 and over
223.0 million white
 47.5 million nonwhite
117.9 million married
 33.0 million divorced or widowed
200.4 million old enough to vote
 14.7 million in college
 53.0 million in primary and secondary schools
131.4 million employed
 65.4 million homeowners

*Data for 1998.
SOURCE: U.S. Bureau of the Census, *Statistical Abstract of the United States: 1999*, pp. 14, 16, 57, 163, 734, 879.

our national life. But as the national origin figures indicate, a majority of Americans stem from other than Anglo-Saxon stock.[20] By midcentury, according to Census Bureau projections, the combined Hispanic, black, Asian American, and American Indian population will outnumber the white population.[21]

Although the accent in America is on youth, the median age of Americans is not 18 or 21 but about 35 and likely to go up because people are living longer.

The Mobile Society

A political system reacts not only to shifts in population totals but also to the movement of people geographically, socially, and economically. For example, farm population

Sometimes, prevailing notions about America's population are incorrect. For example, America is generally thought to be a nation of white Anglo-Saxon Protestants. That group is influential in many areas of

Venice Beach, California: a changing population
Copyright © David Young-Wolff/ PhotoEdit

declined from 30.5 million in 1930 to 4.6 million in 1990.[22] As the nation changed from a predominantly rural to an urban society (see Table 1-1), the political importance of the "farm bloc" decreased.

Americans move about a great deal. According to the Census Bureau, about 16 percent of Americans change their residence each year. In 1964 California sur-passed New York as the most populous state in the Union. As a result, presidential candidates now spend more time than they used to campaigning in California. And in four of the last nine presidential election years (1968, 1972, 1980, and 1984), Californians were elected or reelected president.

During and after the Second World War, as blacks migrated to northern cities, many whites in the central cities moved to the suburbs. All these shifts and changing population patterns affect the American political system. The migration of millions of African American citizens to northern cities resulted in the election of black mayors in several large cities by the mid-1970s and in the election of more African American members of Congress. And the population shift from the cities to the suburbs increased the political power of suburbia. More members of Congress and state legislators now represent suburban areas than in the past, because lawmakers are apportioned according to population.

Technological, Economic, and Social Change

In addition to the population explosion, America has experienced a knowledge explosion. Science and technology, the astonishing growth of the Internet, computers, electronics, and high-speed communications are reshaping society. Americans have split the atom and traveled to the moon and back. We listen for signals

Protest against farm loan policies, Ohio
AP/Wide World

Sony's pet robot dog
AP/Wide World

from other galaxies in outer space and explore the inner space of the human brain. There appear to be no limits to technological potential—except the inability of human beings to control their own nature.

Technological change is soon reflected within the political system. Consider for a moment a single innovation of the electronic age: television. Prior to the Second World War, television did not exist for the mass of Americans. Today, political candidates spend millions of dollars to purchase television time. Presidential nominees may deplore the "packaging" of political candidates by Madison Avenue, but they hire advertising agencies to do just that. Commercials are produced and presidents and candidates sold in the manner of detergents.

A considerable amount of electronic-age technology is the by-product of defense research and development. In his farewell address to the nation in 1961, President Dwight D. Eisenhower, although himself a career soldier, warned of the dangers to liberty and democracy of the **military-industrial complex,** a term now often used to describe the economic and political ties between the military establishment and the defense-aerospace industry. What Eisenhower feared was that the Pentagon and the defense contractors

who produce weapons for the military would gain "unwarranted influence" in the political system.

In the view of economist John Kenneth Galbraith, there already exists a "close fusion of the industrial system with the state," and in time "the line between the two will disappear." As a result of the technological revolution, Galbraith contends, a few hundred huge corporations are shaping the goals of society as a whole.[23] But government, too, exercises great power in the modern industrial state. Government is expected to help prevent either periodic economic recession or depression. Although economists argue over the best methods of managing the economy, they generally agree that the government has the major responsibility in promoting prosperity and full employment.

The past four decades also have been a time of rapid social change in America. At almost every level, wherever one looks, the change is visible—in manners and morals, in civil rights, in the theater, in literature, and in the arts. The change could be seen as well in the continuing emphasis on a youth-oriented culture, and at the same time, the growing concern over problems of the elderly, whose ranks are increasing in numbers.

AP/Wide World

Researchers at George Washington University have forecast possible technological breakthroughs in the 21st century, and one expert listed some of the likely changes to come in the first decade and beyond:

- *Portable Information Devices: The Post-PC World.* Portable information devices combining the computing power of the personal computer, the networking of the Internet, the vivid images of television, and the convenience of the telephone are becoming more and more popular. We estimate that these appliances will be used by 30 percent or more of the population in industrialized nations by 2003 for making telephone calls, sending e-mail, watching video, transmitting documents and data, conferencing, and other forms of computation and communication in general.
- *Fuel-Cell Powered Automobiles.* Today's hybrid cars, which use various combinations of small internal combustion engines and batteries, are simply an intermediate step to an advanced automobile powered by fuel cells. Fuel cells chemically combine hydrogen and oxygen to produce electricity and simple by-products, mainly small amounts of water.
- *Virtual Assistants.* The primary goal of new "dot-com" ventures is no longer profits or market share—it is "eyeballs." Enter the "virtual assistant" (VA) to help you solve . . . problems—in just about the same way a real assistant would. We envision the virtual assistant as a very smart program stored on your PC or portable device that monitors all e-mails, faxes, messages, computer files, and phone calls in order to "learn" all about you and your work. In time, your VA would gain the knowledge to take over routine tasks, such as writing a letter, retrieving a file, making a phone call. . . .
- *Alternate Energy Sources.* Carbon-based fuels—oil, gas, and coal—are likely to continue their dominant role in industrial societies for the foreseeable future. However, wind, geothermal, hydroelectric, solar, biomass, and other alternative energy sources should increase from their present level of 10 percent of all energy used to about 30 percent at the end of this decade. . . .
- *Smart, Mobile Robots.* The robots in factories today will seem primitive compared with the next generation, which will be able to sense their environment, make complex decisions, and learn how to improve their behavior. . . . Authorities working in this field think robots will soon perform more sophisticated factory work, run errands, do household chores, and assist the handicapped.

Top Breakthroughs for the Next Century

- *Advanced Transportation Systems.* Individual vehicles will be replaced by transportation systems: magnetic levitation trains, gliding on a cushion of air at 300 mph and connecting major cities; automated super-highways that take over steering, speed, and braking as cars caravan at 70 mph; and intelligent networks of roadways that monitor traffic flow and direct smart cars toward the least congested routes.
- *Computing with Light.* Scientists estimate that today's computer technology will reach its limit in a decade or so as chip circuits shrink to one molecule wide and can miniaturize no further. What then? . . . Optical computers will be more powerful because they use light—the fastest known force in the universe—rather than electricity.
- *The Coming Biogenetic Payoff.* The enormous investment poured into the biogenetic revolution—1,300 biotech companies employing 100,000 people in the United States alone—is likely to mature and produce unprecedented benefits in a decade or two. Genetic engineering is fraught with risk and social prohibitions, of course. But parents are likely to select major characteristics of their children in about 2012, cloned organs should be used to replace defective ones in about 2020, and genetic therapy is likely to cure most inherited diseases in 2025.
- *Colonizing Our Solar System and Beyond.* We are likely to colonize our solar system over the next few decades. NASA plans several Mars projects, and the GW panel thinks humans will land on the planet about 2022. . . . However, human travel beyond our solar system will probably have to wait until the middle of the 21st century. The nearest star system is four light-years away from Earth.

—Adapted from William E. Halal,
The Futurist, July 1, 2000

Ford Motor Co. displays its concept of a "hybrid electric vehicle."
Ford Motor Co./AP/Wide World

As a result, the political system in 2000 was paying more attention to health care and retirement security for senior citizens.

These social changes have been accompanied by new political concerns. Today, large numbers of people are disturbed about the pollution of the natural environment that has resulted from technological advance. Many American cities are blanketed in smog despite new laws. Some rivers are cleaner as a result of environmental legislation, but many are polluted by industrial and human waste. Across the land, toxic wastes have endangered communities, even forcing the relocation of an entire town, Times Beach, Missouri, in 1983. Pesticides are killing the wildlife in America.[24] Oil spills, from tankers and offshore drilling, and medical waste have fouled beaches. The gasoline engine and power plants and other industries pour smoke and chemicals into the atmosphere. Problems such as acid rain and global warming transcend national boundaries.

It is not only a matter of aesthetics, of preserving the natural beauty of the land. Air and water pollution damage health and upset the delicate balance of nature, the total relationship between human beings and their environment. They raise serious questions about whether humanity will be able to survive the damage it is inflicting on the earth that sustains all life.[*]

The long-range problem of energy resources for the future, and the potential threat to the world's oil supply posed by conflict in the Middle East, underscore the fact

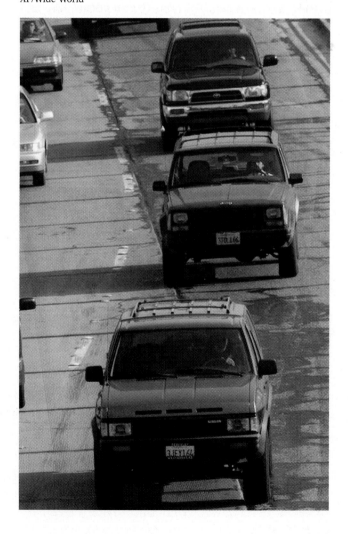

Gas-guzzling SUVs have been popular . . .
AP/Wide World

---

*We examine the problem of environmental pollution in more detail in Chapter 18.

that environmental problems are, in the end, also political problems. They pose for America questions of priorities and values. For example, will people ever be willing to use their cars less or buy smaller cars to conserve energy and reduce pollution? The enormous popularity of gas-guzzling sport utility vehicles (SUVs) suggests otherwise. Do voters favor relaxation of environmental standards to increase the supply of oil and other energy sources? Or to preserve jobs at the expense of endangered species? The environment and energy needs have created conflicting choices for individual citizens, for political leaders, and for society as a whole.

There were many other areas of conflict and change. Back in the 1960s, for example, to any white American who cared to listen, the message of the times was clear: Black Americans would wait no longer to obtain the equality and freedom that are the rights of everyone under the American political system. This was the message preached peacefully by Dr. Martin Luther King, Jr., and expressed violently in the burning black neighborhoods of the nation's cities.

Yet the biggest test of the political system may still lie ahead, in how America adjusts to a population that is becoming increasingly more racially and ethnically diverse. America is no longer just a white society; it is brown and black and other hues. But what, it may be asked, lies at the end of the rainbow? Harmony and understanding, or conflict?

It is not possible to discuss or even list in a few pages all the social, economic, and cultural factors that are influencing the American political system today. Suggested here are simply some of the major changes, currents, and conflicts that have placed enormous pressures on American democracy. In later chapters, these will be taken up in more detail.

The Consent of the Governed

One of the characteristics of a viable political system is that it adapts to change. More than 200 years after its creation, the ability of the American political system to adapt to relentless change, and to cope with recurring political crises, was being tested.

The Vietnam War and the Watergate scandal were followed by a new atmosphere of questioning of presidential power by the public and by Congress. That kind of questioning is appropriate in a democracy. President Kennedy declared, in a speech at Amherst College less than a month before his death in 1963, that "men who create power make an indispensable contribution to the Nation's greatness, but the men who question power make a contribution just as indispensable."[25]

The divisions in American society that had been caused by the war in Vietnam, and the strains placed upon the political system by the trauma of Watergate, the Iran-contra scandal, and the impeachment of President Clinton underscored and renewed a basic truth. The American political system rests on the consent of the governed, but that consent, to be freely given, required that the nation's political leaders earn and merit the trust of the people. At the dawn of the new century, such a bond of trust appeared to offer the best hope for the survival in America of democracy, a system that Winston S. Churchill once described as "the worst form of government except all those other forms that have been tried from time to time."[26]

"Then we agree! We're doing the best job that can be done considering that the country's ungovernable."
Copyright © The New Yorker Collection 1978
Fradon from cartoonbank.com

KEY TERMS

government, p. 14

politics, p. 14

power, p. 15

democracy, p. 15

republic, p. 15

majority rule, p. 16

equality, p. 16

inputs, p. 17

demands, p. 17

supports, p. 17

outputs, p. 17

feedback, p. 17

policy, p. 17

public policy, p. 17

implementation, p. 18

distribution, p. 18

redistributive policy,
p. 18

military-industrial
complex, p. 22

SUGGESTED WEB SITES

www.firstgov.gov
FirstGov
This Web site serves as a single point of entry to every service and department of the federal government. FirstGov is maintained by the U.S. General Services Administration.

www.fedstats.gov
FedStats
The Federal Interagency Council on Statistical Policy maintains this Web site, which allows users to look up any topic and then be connected with the relevant government agency.

www.census.gov
The Census Bureau
The Census Bureau's Web site offers users the decennial censuses of the U.S. population, five-year censuses of state and local governments, and current demographic reports about how Americans live and work.

www.whitehouse.gov
The White House
The official Web site of the White House. Offers presidential speeches, press conferences, interviews, and other documents. Provides links to the personal home pages of the president, the First Lady, and the vice president. Also contains links to the Web sites of departments that make up the cabinet, independent agencies that report to the president, and special presidential commissions.

SUGGESTED READING

Easton, David. *The Political System: An Inquiry into the State of Political Science*, 2nd edition (University of Chicago Press, 1981). (Originally published in 1953.) The first edition was an early statement of the systems approach to the study of politics developed by Easton. See also his *A Framework for Political Analysis* (University of Chicago Press,
1979), and *A Systems Analysis of Political Life* (University of Chicago Press, 1979).

Finer, S. E. *The History of Government from the Earliest Times** (Oxford University Press, 1999). A remarkably comprehensive survey of the varying forms of government that have been established throughout human history, and the efforts that societies have made to control their political institutions. Covers forms of government from ancient Sumeria to the time of the French Revolution.

Galbraith, John Kenneth. *The New Industrial State*, 4th edition* (Houghton Mifflin, 1985). A readable account of changes in the nature and role of the large corporation in the modern state. These changes, Galbraith argues, have had a major effect on political and social life in highly industrialized countries such as the United States.

Grossman, Lawrence K. *The Electronic Republic: Reshaping Democracy in the Information Age** (Penguin, 1996). A useful examination of the growing impact of communications technology on the political process in the United States. The author explores the potential benefits and hazards that emerging media, such as the Internet, hold for American democracy.

Key, V. O., Jr. *Public Opinion and American Democracy* (Philadelphia Book Company, 1961). An important work in which findings about public opinion and mass attitudes toward politics are analyzed in terms of their consequences for the actual workings of government.

Lineberry, Robert L. *American Public Policy: What Government Does and What Difference It Makes* (Harper & Row, 1978). A concise analysis of the making of public policy, its implementation, and its impact. Provides a useful introduction to policy analysis, illustrated by specific case studies.

Nicholas, H. G. *The Nature of American Politics*, 2nd edition* (Oxford University Press, 1986). A survey of major features of the American political system, written by a perceptive English observer. Contains a thoughtful discussion of what the author identifies as the special national style of politics in America.

Schattschneider, Elmer E. *The Semisovereign People* (Harcourt Brace College Publishers, 1975). (Originally published in 1960.) A lively and revealing analysis of the role of American interest groups and political parties in bringing public demands to bear on political officials.

Schneiderman, Jill S., ed. *The Earth around Us* (W. H. Freeman, 2000). A wide-ranging collection of essays by 31 scientists, who discuss the environmental challenges facing the world's citizens now and in the coming years. The essays in this volume were written in tribute to Rachel Carson, who many years ago wrote a highly influential book, *The Sea around Us*.

Tocqueville, Alexis de. *Democracy in America,* 2 vols.[*] Phillips Bradley, ed. (Knopf, 1945). (Available in many editions.) A classic analysis of American political and social life as seen through the eyes of a 19th-century French observer.

Wills, Gary. *A Necessary Evil: A History of American Distrust of Government* (Simon and Schuster, 1999). An insightful analysis of the deeply rooted American tradition of distrust of the national government and its institutions. The author examines the consequences of that distrust for the American political system.

Wilson, Edward O. *The Diversity of Life*[*] (Norton, 1999). A wide-ranging survey of the development of life on earth over the last 4 billion years. Emphasizes the dangers that currently threaten to reduce the number of living species, and argues that it is important to maintain biodiversity.

---

[*]Available in paperback edition.

 Visit http://politicalscience.wadsworth.com/cummings9/update/ for current InfoTrac articles and other student resources related to this chapter.

CHAPTER 2
The Constitutional Framework

Every evening in Washington an unusual ceremony takes place in the great domed Exhibition Hall of the National Archives. There, beneath a gold eagle in the ornate hall, are displayed the Declaration of Independence, the Constitution, and the Bill of Rights. The faded parchments are sealed in protective bronze-and-glass cases containing helium and a small amount of water vapor for preservation.

When the last visitor has left the building, a guard pushes a button. With a great whirring noise, the documents slowly sink into the floor. An electric mechanism gently lowers them into a fireproof, bombproof vault of steel and reinforced concrete 20 feet below. A massive lid clangs shut and the documents are safely put to bed for the night. The whole eerie process takes one minute.

Online for more information about the National Archives & Records Administration see:
http://www.nara.gov

Ideas, of course, cannot be preserved in a vault, but documents can. The documents, and the mystique that surrounds them, are part of what Daniel J. Boorstin has called the "search for symbols."[1] The quest for national identity, in which such symbols play a role, is a continuing process in America.

But the Constitution is much more than a symbol. The Constitution established the basic structure of the American government and a written set of rules to control the conduct of that government; in its own words, the Constitution is "the supreme Law of the Land." As one scholar has noted, "A constitution . . . is not ordinary law, but rather an embodiment of fundamental principles, higher law, law above law."[2] The United States was, in fact, the first nation to have a written constitution. It is a charter that has been continually adapted to new problems, principally through amendment and judicial interpretation by the Supreme Court—changes that often reflect the prevailing political climate.

Yet, the American political system is sometimes attacked for what its critics see as a failure to respond to urgent national problems, such as education, health care, crime, urban decay, poverty, and racial tensions. Nor are the nation's problems only social and economic; some are political and constitutional. The growth of presidential power in the 20th century at times placed great strains on the system of constitutional government. In the 1980s, the Iran-contra affair revealed that a secret foreign policy had been conducted from the White House under President Ronald Reagan, a policy that circumvented laws enacted by Congress. And twice in the 20th century, presidents were the target of impeachment efforts. In 1998 President Bill Clinton was impeached by the House of Representatives after an independent counsel reported he had lied under oath about his sexual involvement with a White House intern. He was tried by the Senate, but not convicted, and he was not removed from office. In 1974, the Watergate scandal resulted in the resignation of President Richard Nixon, under threat of impeachment.

In this chapter we will explore a key question: Is the constitutional framework constructed in 1787 sufficiently flexible to meet the needs of a complex, urban society in the 21st century?

For example, even though the Constitution is reinterpreted by the Supreme Court to meet changed conditions, does that process take place fast enough? Why, for example, did it take nearly one hundred years after the Civil War for the Supreme Court to apply the Constitution to outlaw racial segregation in public schools? Or why did 131 years pass after the nation was founded before the Constitution recognized the right of women to vote?

We will examine other such questions: Who were the framers of the Constitution? What political ideas influenced them? Were they rich men merely interested in protecting their own economic positions? What political bargains were struck by the framers? Why does the United States have a federal system of government, and what does that mean? How did the Supreme Court acquire its power to interpret the Constitution? How does the Constitution affect people's lives today?

THE CONSTITUTION AND THE DECLARATION OF INDEPENDENCE

The Constitution Today

In the spring of the year 2000, the Supreme Court handed down a decision that affected student activities on the campuses of public colleges and universities across America. The justices unanimously ruled that students at state universities and public colleges could be required to pay activity fees that are used to support campus groups whose views the students might oppose.[3]

The case, which presented the Court with a difficult issue under the First Amendment of the Constitution, had begun five years earlier, when Scott Southworth, then an undergraduate at the University of Wisconsin, objected to the $331.50 annual fee the institution charged to provide funds for various college publications and for social, political, and cultural groups. A conservative Christian, Southworth objected in particular to the use of part of his money to support the Lesbian, Gay, Bisexual & Transgender Campus Center. Southworth also complained that his fees were used to support 17 other groups, including the UW Greens, Amnesty International, Students of the National Organization for Women, the International Socialist Organization, Community Action on Latin America, and the Campus Women's Center. "As a conservative Christian," he said, "I don't think I should have to fund these violently partisan, anti-Christian hate groups." The university's position, he argued, was "You either pay for these groups or we will kick you out."[4]

The university responded that the mandatory activity fees were used to ensure a public forum in which diverse student views could be heard. Students, the university argued, could not avoid activity fees any more than they could refuse to pay tuition because some courses might be taught "whose content they disapprove."

 for more information about the Constitution see:
http://www.access.gpo.gov/congress/senate/constitution/toc.html

Alarmed at the possible impact of Southworth's lawsuit, 15 states filed a brief in the Supreme Court defending student funding for a wide range of campus groups, arguing that "these programs further educational goals by fostering 'a marketplace of ideas' . . . [and] exposing students to a variety of viewpoints." Many political, educational, and labor groups also filed "friend of the Court" briefs in the case.

When a federal appeals court in Chicago upheld Southworth's position, the state university appealed. By then, Southworth was a law student at the university. The case was argued in the Supreme Court in the fall of 1999.

The Court's decision was complex because in two earlier cases it had decided that teachers and lawyers cannot be forced to pay dues that would be used by their union or bar association for lobbying and political activities.[5] Furthermore, in a related case in 1995, the Supreme Court had held that universities that disburse student activity fees must subsidize religious as well as secular groups.

That case arose when Ronald W. Rosenberger, a student at the University of Virginia, sought $5,862 from a student activities fund to publish a religious magazine. The school, a state-supported university, refused to pay printing costs for the publication. Without funds, the student-run magazine shut down. Rosenberger sued. The lower federal courts ruled that any contribution of funds to the magazine by the University of Virginia would violate the First Amendment of the Constitution, which contains a barrier against government establishment of religion. But a narrowly divided United States Supreme Court ruled 5–4 that the university had a constitutional obligation to subsidize the Christian magazine.[6] "For the University, by regulation, to cast disapproval on particular viewpoints of its students risks the suppression of free speech and creative inquiry in one of the vital centers for the nation's intellectual life, its college and university campuses," Justice Anthony M. Kennedy, writing for the majority, declared.[7]

In both the Wisconsin and Virginia disputes, students had taken their cases all the way to the Supreme Court. Scott Southworth lost and Ronald Rosenberger won. Both cases had a direct impact on college campuses. And in both instances, the Supreme Court wrote new chapters in the continuing battle over free expression. These cases arose and were decided within the framework of the Constitution.

The Constitution directly affects many other facets of American life and politics. When in 1954 the Supreme Court outlawed officially supported segregation in the public schools, it did so on the grounds that "separate but equal" schools violated the Constitution.[8]

Abortion is another controversial political issue affected by Supreme Court rulings. In 1973, in *Roe* v. *Wade*, the Supreme Court ruled that state laws restricting abortions during the first three months of pregnancy were unconstitutional.[9] (The Court's rulings on abortion are discussed in more detail in Chapter 5.)

As these selected examples illustrate, constitutional government affects the quality of American society here and now, today and tomorrow. Yet it is a story that has been unfolding for more than two centuries; it began, as much as anywhere, in the city of Philadelphia in June 1776.

Scott Southworth
AP Photo/Wisconsin State Journal, Sarah B. Tewes

We Hold These Truths . . .

Early in May 1776, Thomas Jefferson rode down the mountain on horseback from Monticello, his Virginia home, and headed north to take his seat in the Continental Congress at Philadelphia. It had been just over a year since the guns blazed at Lexington and Concord, but the 13 American colonies, although at war, were still under the jurisdiction of the British crown.

Thomas Jefferson
Copyright © Bettmann/CORBIS

At four o'clock the morning of March 4, 1801, a humiliated President Adams left Washington, D.C., to avoid seeing his successor's inauguration. Shortly before noon, President-elect Thomas Jefferson, a month shy of fifty-eight years old, stepped out of Conrad and McMunn's boardinghouse on New Jersey Avenue at C Street and joined an escort of officers of the Alexandria, Virginia, militia and stepped off briskly through the muddy streets of the still-unfinished federal city escorted by District of Columbia marshals and congressmen. Walking to the Capitol, he shunned the splendor of Washington's and Adams's inaugural parades in ceremonial carriages. He wore no elegant suit, no sword as his predecessors had. The Alexandria *Times* reported that "his dress was, as usual, that of a plain citizen without any distinctive badge of office." . . . Jefferson hiked up Capitol Hill, where he had insisted the Capitol be built on higher ground than the President's House to symbolize the preeminence of the people. He acknowledged the cheers of Republicans lining his route. Arriving at the unfinished Capitol, Jefferson strode confidently between ranks of Alexandria riflemen who presented arms as he entered the only finished room, the Senate Chamber. . . . In a single sentence, he declared his program as president: "Peace, commerce and honest friendship with all nations, entangling alliances with none."

—William Sterne Randall,
Thomas Jefferson: A Life

Independence was in the air, however, nourished by the words of an Englishman only recently arrived in America. His name was Thomas Paine, and his pamphlet, *Common Sense*, attacked George III, the British monarch, as the "Royal Brute." Paine's fiery words stirred the colonies.

---

 for more information about the Continental Congress & Constitutional Convention see: http://memory.loc.gov/ammem/bdsds/bdsdhome.html

---

On June 7 Richard Henry Lee, one of Jefferson's fellow delegates from Virginia, introduced a resolution declaring that the colonies "are, and of right ought to be, free and independent States." Four days later, after impassioned debate, the Continental Congress appointed a committee of five, including Jefferson, to "prepare a declaration."

At age 33, Jefferson was already known, in the words of John Adams of Massachusetts, as a man with a "peculiar felicity of expression," and the task of writing the declaration fell to him. Jefferson completed his draft in about two weeks. Sitting in the second-floor parlor of the house of Jacob Graff, Jr., a German bricklayer, Jefferson composed some of the most enduring words in the English language. His draft, edited somewhat by Benjamin Franklin and John Adams, was submitted on June 28.

On July 2 the Continental Congress approved Richard Henry Lee's resolution declaring the colonies free of allegiance to the crown. The Declaration of Independence is not the official act by which Congress severed its ties with Britain. Lee's resolution did that. Rather, the Declaration "was intended as a formal justification of an act already accomplished."[10]

WHAT WAS EDITED OUT OF THE DECLARATION OF INDEPENDENCE

Jefferson's draft of the Declaration of Independence originally included an attack on slavery, and sought to blame that "execrable commerce" on King George III. But the Continental Congress cut the passage out of the final document in deference to the wishes of South Carolina and Georgia, and, Jefferson suspected, those Northerners who profited from carrying slaves in their ships. Had the passage remained in, the Declaration would have included these words:

> He has waged cruel war against human nature itself, violating its most sacred rights of life & liberty in the persons of a distant people who never offended him, captivating & carrying them into slavery in another hemisphere, or to incur miserable death in their transportation thither. This piratical warfare, the opprobrium of *infidel* powers, is the warfare of the *Christian* king of Great Britain. Determined to keep open a market where *Men* should be bought & sold . . . suppressing every legislative attempt to prohibit or to restrain this execrable commerce . . . he is now exciting those very people to rise in arms among us, and to purchase that liberty of which he has deprived them, by murdering the people upon whom he also obtruded.

—Carl L. Becker,
The Declaration of Independence

For two days Congress debated Jefferson's draft, making changes and deletions that Jefferson found painful. No matter; what emerged has withstood the test of time:

> We hold these Truths to be self-evident, that all Men are created equal, that they are endowed by their Creator with certain unalienable Rights, that among these are Life, Liberty, and the pursuit of Happiness—That to secure these Rights, Governments are instituted among Men, deriving their just Powers from the Consent of the Governed, that whenever any Form of Government becomes destructive of these Ends, it is the Right of the People to alter or to abolish it, and to institute new Government. . . .

The Continental Congress approved the Declaration on July 4 and ordered that it be "authenticated and printed." Although the fact is sometimes overlooked, Jefferson and his colleagues produced and signed a treasonable document. They were literally pledging their lives.

Dr. Benjamin Rush of Philadelphia, one of the signers, asked John Adams many years later: "Do you recollect . . . the pensive and awful silence which pervaded the house when we were called up, one after another, to the table of the President of Congress to subscribe what was believed by many at that time to be our own death warrants?"[11]

The solemnity of the moment was breached only once. It is said that Benjamin Harrison of Virginia, whom Adams once described as "an indolent and luxurious heavy gentleman of no use in Congress or committee," turned to Elbridge Gerry of Massachusetts, a skinny, worried-looking colleague, and cackled: "I shall have a great advantage over you, Mr. Gerry, when we are all hung for what we are now doing. From the size and weight of my body I shall die in a few minutes, but from the lightness of your body you will dance in the air an hour or two before you are dead."[12]

THE POLITICAL FOUNDATIONS

Although Jefferson later said he had "turned to neither book nor pamphlet" in writing the Declaration of Independence, he was certainly influenced by the philosophy of John Locke (1632–1704) and others, by his British heritage with its traditional concern for individual rights, and by the colonial political experience itself.

The Influence of John Locke

John Locke advanced the philosophy of **natural rights,** the belief that all people possess certain basic rights that may not be abridged by government. Locke's concept of natural rights was political gospel to most educated Americans in the late 18th century. Jefferson absorbed Locke's writings, and some of the English philosopher's words and phrases emerged verbatim in the Declaration.*

Locke reasoned that human beings were "born free" and possessed certain natural rights when they lived in a state of nature before governments were formed. People contracted among themselves to form a society to protect those rights. All persons, Locke believed, were free, equal, and independent, and no one could be "subjected to the political power of another, without his own consent."[13] These dangerous ideas—dangerous in an age of the divine right of kings—are directly reflected in the language of the Declaration of Independence, written nearly a century later.

---

*For example, the phrase "a long train of abuses."

Jefferson composed the first draft of the Declaration of Independence on this portable writing desk.
Smithsonian Institution

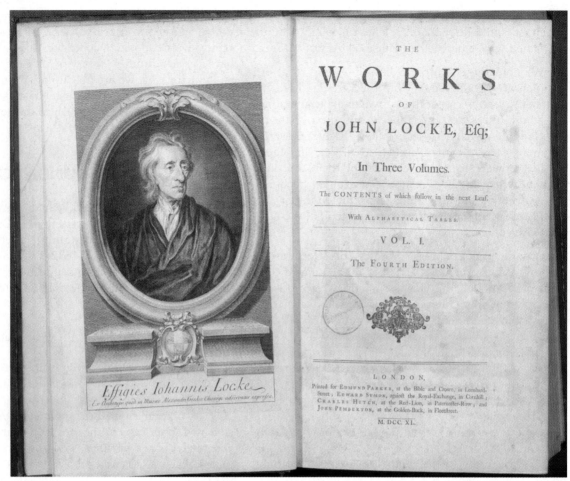

John Locke's philosophy was reflected in the Declaration of Independence.
Copyright © Archivo Inconografico S.A./CORBIS

The English Heritage

The irony of the American Revolution is that the colonists, for the most part, rebelled because they felt they were being deprived of their rights as English citizens. Many of the ideas of the Declaration of Independence, written in 1776, the Constitution, framed in 1787, and the Bill of Rights, added to the Constitution in 1791, evolved from this English heritage. The political and intellectual antecedents of the American system of government included such British legal milestones as the **Magna Carta,** the document issued by King John at Runnymede in 1215, in which the nobles confirmed that the power of the king was not absolute; the Habeas Corpus Act (1679); and the Bill of Rights (1689).

 for more information about the Magna Carta see:
http://www.nara.gov/exhall/charters/magnacarta/magmain.html

From England also came a system of **common law,** the cumulative body of law as expressed in judicial decisions and custom rather than by statute. The men who framed America's government were influenced by the writings of Sir Edward Coke, the great British jurist and champion of common law against the power of the king, and Sir William Blackstone, the Oxford law professor whose *Commentaries on the Laws of England* (1765–1769) is still an important historical work.

But if the ideas embodied in the American system of government are to be found largely in the nation's English heritage, it is also true that American institutions developed to a great extent from colonial foundations. The roots of much of today's governmental structure can be found in the colonial charters.

The Colonial Experience

Even before they landed at Plymouth in 1620, the Pilgrims—a group of English Puritans who had separated from the Church of England—drew up the Mayflower Compact. The Pilgrims had sailed from Holland intending to settle in the area that is now New York City, but landed instead just north of Cape Cod. In the cabin of the *Mayflower,* 41 men signed the compact, declaring that "we . . . doe by these presents solemnly & mutualy in the presence of God, and one of another, covenant & combine our selves togeather into a civill body politick."

The Magna Carta
Copyright © The British Library

The Mayflower Compact, as Samuel Eliot Morison noted, "is justly regarded as a key document in American history. It proves the determination of the small group of English emigrants to live under a rule of law, based on the consent of the people, and to set up their own civil government."[14]

A year earlier at Jamestown, Virginia, a group of settlers had established the first representative assembly in the New World. In 1639, Puritans from the Massachusetts Bay Colony and another group from London framed America's first written constitution, the Fundamental Orders of Connecticut. The Massachusetts Body of Liberties (1641) embodied traditional English rights, such as trial by jury and due process of law (later incorporated into the Constitution and the Bill of Rights).

The political forms established by the Puritans contributed to the formation of representative institutions. Beyond that, Puritanism shaped the American mind and left its indelible stamp on the American character. The English Puritans who came to America were influenced by the teachings of John Calvin, the 16th-century French theologian of the Protestant Reformation. Theirs was a stern code of hard work, sobriety, and intense religious zeal. Even today, with rapidly changing, increasingly liberal sexual and moral codes, Americans do not always seem to be able to enjoy their new freedom entirely. The Puritan heritage is not easily forgotten, a lesson often learned by political leaders caught in sexual indiscretions.

The Colonial Governments The 13 original colonies, some formed as commercial ventures, others as religious havens, all had written charters that set forth their form of government and the rights of the colonists. All had governors (the executive branch), legislatures, and a judiciary.

The eight **royal colonies** were New Hampshire, New York, New Jersey, Virginia, North Carolina, South Carolina, Georgia, and Massachusetts. They were controlled by the king through governors appointed by him. Laws passed by their legislatures were subject to approval of the crown. In the three **proprietary colonies**—Maryland, Delaware, and Pennsylvania— the proprietors (who had obtained their patents from the king) named the governors, subject to the approval of the crown; laws (except in Maryland) also required the crown's approval. Only in the two **charter colonies** of Rhode Island and Connecticut was there genuine self-government. There, freely elected legislatures chose the governors, and laws could not be vetoed by the king.

Except for Pennsylvania, which had a **unicameral legislature,** a legislative body with only one house, the colonial legislatures had two houses. The members of the upper house were appointed by the crown or proprietor (except in Connecticut and Rhode Island, where both houses were elected), and the members of the lower house were elected by the colonists. Appeals from the colonial courts could usually be taken to the Privy Council in London.

Comparing Governments

HAIL, BRITANNIA! BUT IT'S DIFFERENT

Although the new American government created at Philadelphia in 1787 had many features rooted in the British system and legal tradition, the government of Great Britain is significantly different from that of the United States.

Britain is both a parliamentary democracy and a constitutional monarchy. It has no single, formal written constitution like that of the United States. Britain's constitution consists of acts of Parliament, court decisions, traditions, and customs. The hereditary monarch is the head of state, but the powers of the king or queen are largely ceremonial. Real power resides not in Buckingham Palace, but with the prime minister, who is the leader of the majority party in Parliament. The ministers who comprise the British cabinet are normally chosen by the prime minister

from the majority party members elected to Parliament.

Britain's Parliament is the legislative branch, and it is made up of two houses, the House of Commons, whose members are elected to terms of up to five years, and the House of Lords. Members of the House of Lords no longer inherit their posts, as was true for some 800 years prior to 1999, but may now, under one proposal, be appointed or elected. In the United States presidential elections take place every four years in November, but the British prime minister may call for general elections at any time. Britain's judicial branch is headed by a supreme court, but unlike the U.S. Supreme Court, the British high court has no power of judicial review.

Britain has had a predominantly two-party system for most of the past

Queen Elizabeth II opens Parliament.
AP Photo/Max Nash

three centuries. The Conservative (Tory) Party and the Labour Party have been the two strongest parties competing for power in modern times.

The Paradox of Colonial Democracy

Democracy, in the modern sense, did not exist in colonial America. For example, by the 1700s every colony had some type of property qualification for voting. Women and blacks were not considered part of the electorate. In 1765, of the 1,850,000 estimated population of the colonies, 400,000 were blacks, almost all of them slaves. Consequently, "whatever political democracy did exist was a democracy of white, male property owners."[15]

In addition, many white persons were indentured servants during the colonial period. These were English, Scotch-Irish, and western Europeans, including many convicts, who sold their labor for four to seven years in return for passage across the sea.

Even aside from slavery and indentured servitude, there was little social democracy. A tailor in York County, Virginia, in 1674 was punished for racing a horse because "it was contrary to law for a labourer to make a race, being a sport only for gentlemen."[16] In colonial New York, the aristocracy "ruled with condescension and lived in splendor."[17]

Nine of the 13 colonies had an established, official state church. Although the colonists had in many cases fled Europe to find religious freedom, they were often themselves intolerant of religious dissent. The Massachusetts Bay Colony executed four Quakers who

had returned there after being banished for their religious convictions. In Virginia the penalty for breaking the Sabbath for the third time was death.[18] And although the colonial press and pamphleteers developed into a powerful force for liberty, the first newspaper to appear in America, *Publick Occurrences*, was immediately suppressed.[19]

Yet, despite their shortcomings, the colonial governments provided an institutional foundation for what was to come. Certain elements were already visible: separation of powers, constitutional government through written charters, bicameral legislatures, elections, and judicial appeal to London, which foreshadowed the role of the Supreme Court. Equally important, in their relationship with England the colonies became accustomed to the idea of sharing powers with a central government, the basis of the federal system today. It was, in Clinton Rossiter's apt phrase, the "seedtime of the republic."

THE AMERICAN REVOLUTION

"The Revolution," John Adams wrote in 1818, "was effected before the war commenced. The Revolution was in the minds and hearts of the people."[20]

British tax stamps
Copyright © Bettmann/CORBIS

And, in time, the revolt against the British crown brought enormous social and political change, resulting in a new nation based on the idea of freedom and equality. As one constitutional scholar has argued, "That revolution did more than legally create the United States; it transformed American society."[21]

A Growing Sense of Injury

In the eyes of the crown, the American colonies existed chiefly for the economic support of England. Economic conflicts with the mother country, as well as political and social factors, impelled the colonies to revolt.

The British had routed the French from North America and provided military protection to the colonies; England in turn demanded that its subjects in America pay part of the cost. At the same time, the colonies were expected to subordinate themselves to the British economy; ideally they would remain agricultural, develop no industry of their own, and serve as a captive market for British manufactures.

The colonists had no representatives in the British Parliament. They resented and disputed the right of London to raise revenue in America. Whether or not James Otis, the Boston patriot, actually cried, "Taxation without representation is tyranny!"—and there is reason to think he did not—the words reflected popular sentiment in the colonies.*

---

*Otis supposedly uttered his famous line in a speech to the Massachusetts Superior Court in 1761. But as Daniel J. Boorstin points out, the line does not appear in the original notes of the speech taken by John Adams. See Boorstin, *The Americans: The National Experience*, pp. 309, 360–361.

A series of laws designed to give the mother country a tight grip on trade, to restrict colonial exports, and to protect producers in England proved to be the economic stepping stones to revolution. In 1772 Samuel Adams of Massachusetts formed the Committees of Correspondence to unite the colonies against Great Britain. This network provided an invaluable political communications link for the colonies; letters, reports, and decisions of one town or colony could be relayed to the next.

The committees resolved to hold the First Continental Congress, which met in Philadelphia in September 1774. The war began in April 1775. The Second Continental Congress met the following month, and by June 1776 Thomas Jefferson was busily writing in the second-floor parlor of the bricklayer's house in Philadelphia.

The Articles of Confederation (1781–1789)

The Declaration of Independence had proclaimed the colonies "free and independent states." During the war all the colonies adopted new constitutions or at least changed their old charters to eliminate references to the British crown. Seven of the new constitutions contained a bill of rights, but all restricted suffrage in one way or another. All provided for three branches of government, but their dominant features were strong legislatures and weak executives. Governors were elected by the people or by legislatures, and their powers were reduced. For the first time, the colonies began to refer to themselves as "states."

When Richard Henry Lee offered his resolution for independence in June 1776, he also proposed that "a plan

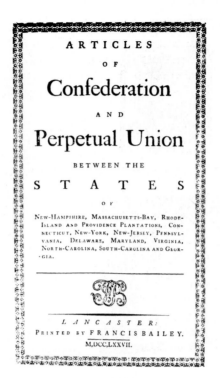

ARTICLES

OF

Confederation

AND

Perpetual Union

BETWEEN THE

STATES

OF

NEW-HAMPSHIRE, MASSACHUSETTS-BAY, RHODE-ISLAND AND PROVIDENCE PLANTATIONS, CONNECTICUT, NEW-YORK, NEW-JERSEY, PENNSYLVANIA, DELAWARE, MARYLAND, VIRGINIA, NORTH-CAROLINA, SOUTH-CAROLINA AND GEORGIA.

LANCASTER:
PRINTED BY FRANCIS BAILEY.
M,DCC,LXXVII.

Culver Pictures

under the Articles was its weakness. Congress, for example, had no power to levy taxes or regulate commerce—the colonies had seen enough of these powers under English rule. Above all, Congress could not enforce even the limited powers it had. The functioning of government under the Articles depended entirely on the goodwill of the states. Because unanimous agreement of the states was required to amend the Articles, but in practice could never be obtained, there was no practical way to increase the powers of the government; the Articles were never amended.

By 1783 the American states had achieved their independence not only from Great Britain but also from each other. They had won their freedom, but they had been unable to form a nation. Yet the Articles did represent the idea of some form of national government, for under them, "Congress waged war, made peace, and kept alive the idea of union when it was at its lowest ebb."[22] As historian Merrill Jensen has emphasized, the Articles "laid foundations for the administration of a central government which were to be expanded but not essentially altered in function for generations to come."[23]

TOWARD A MORE PERFECT UNION

The Background

Under the inadequate government of the Articles of Confederation, the states came close to losing the peace they had won in war. They quarreled among themselves over boundary lines and tariffs. For example, New Jersey farmers had to pay heavy fees to cross the Hudson River to sell their vegetables in New York. With no strong national government to conduct foreign policy, some states even entered into negotiations with foreign powers. General Washington worried that Kentucky might join Spain.[24] There was real concern over possible military intervention by European powers.

By 1786 severe economic depression had left many farmers angry and hungry. Debtor groups demanded that state governments issue paper money. The unrest among farmers and the poor alarmed the upper classes. They feared, in today's terms, a revolution of the left. These political and economic factors, combined with fear of overseas intervention, generated pressure for the creation of a new national government.

Virginia, at the urging of James Madison, had invited all the states to discuss commercial problems at a meeting to be held at Annapolis, Maryland, in September 1786. The Annapolis conference was disappointing. Representatives of only five states turned up. But one of those delegates was Alexander Hamilton, a brilliant 31-year-old New York attorney who was one of a small group of men pushing for a convention to create a stronger government. There had been talk of such a meeting since 1780, when Hamilton wrote to a friend listing the "defects of our present system."[25]

of confederation" be prepared for the colonies. (A **confederation** is a group of independent states or nations that come together for a common purpose and whose central authority is usually limited to defense and foreign relations.) The plan was drawn up by a committee and approved by the Continental Congress in November 1777, a month before George Washington withdrew with his troops for the long, hard winter at Valley Forge. The **Articles of Confederation** (1781–1789) was the written framework for the government of the original 13 states before the Constitution was adopted. The Articles were ratified by the individual states by March 1, 1781, and so were already in effect when the war ended with the surrender of Cornwallis at Yorktown that October. The formal end to hostilities came with the conclusion of the Peace of Paris in February 1783.

But the Articles of Confederation created a national government that was weak and dominated by the states. The Articles really established a "league of friendship" among the states, rather than a national government. No executive branch, no president, no "White House" existed. Instead, Congress, given power to establish executive departments, created five: foreign affairs, finance, navy, war, and post office. Congress had power to declare war, conduct foreign policy, make treaties, ask for—but not demand—revenues from the states, borrow and coin money, equip the navy, and appoint senior officers of the army, which was made up of the state militias. Congress was unicameral, and each state, regardless of size, had only one vote. The most important actions by Congress required the consent of at least nine states. There was no national system of courts.

Although these were not inconsiderable powers, the most significant fact about the government created

Alexander Hamilton
Copyright ©
Bettmann/CORBIS

At Annapolis, Hamilton and Madison persuaded the delegates to call on the states to hold a constitutional convention in Philadelphia in May 1787. In the interim a significant event took place. Late in 1786, angry farmers in western Massachusetts, unable to pay their mortgages or taxes, rallied around Daniel Shays, who had served as a captain in the American Revolution. They were seeking to stop the Massachusetts courts from foreclosing the mortgages on their farms. Armed with pitchforks, the farmers marched on the Springfield arsenal to get weapons. They were defeated by the militia. Fourteen ringleaders were sentenced to death, but all were pardoned or released after serving short prison terms. Daniel Shays escaped to Vermont.

Shays's Rebellion, coming on the eve of the Philadelphia convention, had a tremendous effect on public

opinion. Aristocrats and merchants were thoroughly alarmed at the threat of "mob rule." The British were amused at the American lack of capacity for self-government. The revolt was an important factor in creating the climate for a new beginning at Philadelphia.

The Philadelphia Convention

On February 21, 1787, Congress grudgingly approved the proposed Philadelphia Convention "for the sole and express purpose of revising the Articles of Confederation." Beginning in May, the delegates met and, disregarding Congress's cautious mandate, worked what has been called a "miracle at Philadelphia."[26]

The Delegates Because the story of how a nation was born is in large part a story of people, it might be useful to focus briefly on some of the more prominent delegates who gathered at Philadelphia. First was George Washington, who had commanded the armed forces during the Revolution. A national hero, a man of immense prestige, Washington was probably the only figure who could have successfully presided over the coming struggle in the convention. When Washington arrived in Philadelphia, a crowd gathered and bells rang out. He immediately paid a call on Benjamin Franklin, internationally famous as a scientist, diplomat, and statesman. Then 81 and suffering from gout, Franklin arrived at the sessions in a sedan chair borne by four convicts from the Walnut Street jail. Alexander Hamilton was there as a delegate from New York, but he took surprisingly little part in the important decisions of the convention. From Virginia came James Madison, often called the "Father of the Constitution," who had long advocated a new national government. A tireless notetaker, Madison kept a record of the debates. Without him there would have been no detailed account of the most important political convention in the nation's history.

Gouverneur Morris of Pennsylvania, a colorful man who stumped about on a wooden leg, shatters the image of the delegates as stuffy patriarchs. His wit offended some, but his pen was responsible for the literary style and polish of the final draft of the Constitution. From Massachusetts came Elbridge Gerry and Rufus King, a lawyer with a gift for debating; from South Carolina, John Rutledge, a leading figure of the revolutionary period and later a justice of the Supreme Court, General Charles Cotesworth Pinckney, Oxford-educated war hero

Shays's Rebellion: The aristocrats and merchants were alarmed.
Copyright © Bettmann/CORBIS

George Washington
Granger Collection

Gouverneur Morris
Culver Pictures

and aristocrat, and his second cousin, Charles Pinckney, an ardent nationalist.

Twelve states sent delegates to Philadelphia. Only Rhode Island boycotted the convention; an agrarian party of farmers and debtors controlled the Rhode Island state legislature and feared that a strong national government would limit the party's power. Of the 55 men who gathered at Philadelphia in the Pennsylvania State House (now Independence Hall), 8 had signed the Declaration of Independence, 7 had been chief executives of their states, 33 were lawyers, 8 were businessmen, 6 were planters, and 3 were physicians. About half were college graduates.[27] The delegates, in sum, were generally men of wealth and influence; the Constitution was not drafted by small farmers, artisans, or laborers.

It was a relatively young convention. Jonathan Dayton of New Jersey, at 26, was the youngest delegate. Alexander Hamilton was 32. Charles Pinckney was 29. James Madison was 36. The average age of the delegates was just over 43. (At 81, Franklin pulled the average up.)

The Setting   The convention of 1787 had many of the earmarks of a modern national political convention but for one factor: To preserve their freedom of debate,

Benjamin Franklin
Copyright © The Corcoran
Gallery of Art/CORBIS

the delegates worked in strictest secrecy. The press and public were not allowed in the room. In other respects the setting would be a familiar one today: The weather was intolerably hot and the speeches interminable. And just as in a modern convention, a plush tavern and inn, the Indian Queen, soon became a sort of informal headquarters.

Philadelphia was not a pleasant place 200 years ago. It was a crowded city of open sewers, foul smells, and rotting animal carcasses. The clatter of wagon wheels on the rough cobblestones was so bad that, when the sessions got under way, at the request of the delegates the city spread a load of gravel outside the hall to muffle the noise.

The convention opened on May 14, 1787, but it was not until May 25 that a quorum of delegates from seven states was reached. The delegates gathered in the East Room of the State House, the same chamber where the Declaration of Independence had been signed 11 years before. "Delegates sat at tables covered in green baize—sat and sweated, once the summer sun was up. By noon the air was lifeless, with windows shut for privacy, or intolerable with flies when they were open."[28] For almost four months the stuffy East Room was to be home.

The Great Compromise

On May 29 Edmund Randolph, the 33-year-old governor of Virginia, took the floor to present 15 resolutions that stunned the convention. The resolutions, which Madison strongly influenced and helped to draft, went far beyond mere revision of the Articles—they proposed an entirely new national government under a constitution. Randolph was moving swiftly to make the **Virginia Plan,** as the proposals are known, the main business of the convention.

As John P. Roche has noted, the Virginia Plan "was a political masterstroke. Its consequence was that once business got underway, the framework of discussion was established on Madison's terms. There was no interminable argument over agenda; instead the delegates took the Virginia Resolutions—'just for the purposes of discussion'—as their point of departure."[29] The Virginia Plan called for:

1. A two-house legislature, the lower house chosen by the people and the upper house chosen by the lower. The legislature would have the power to annul any state laws that it found unconstitutional.
2. A "national executive"—the makeup was not specified, so there might have been more than one president under the plan—to be elected by the legislature.
3. A national judiciary to be chosen by the legislature.

The convention debated the Virginia Plan for two weeks. As the debate wore on, the delegates from the smaller states became increasingly alarmed. It had not taken them long to conclude that the more heavily populated states would control the government under the Virginia Plan. "The Virginia Plan," one writer has contended, "would mean nothing less than a second American revolution."[30]

On June 15, William Paterson of New Jersey, a lawyer, "a squat man with a bulbous nose, a receding chin and traces of his native Ireland in his voice,"[31] rose to offer an alternative plan. He argued that the convention had no power to deprive the smaller states of the equality they enjoyed under the Articles of Confederation. Paterson proposed what became known as the **New Jersey Plan,** which called for:

1. Continuation of the Articles of Confederation, including one vote for each state represented in the legislature. Congress would be strengthened so that it could impose taxes and regulate trade, and acts of Congress would become the "supreme law" of the states.
2. An executive of more than one person to be elected by Congress.
3. A Supreme Court, to be appointed by the executive.

The Paterson plan would have merely amended the Articles. The government would have continued as a weak confederation of sovereign states. But many of the delegates at Philadelphia were determined to construct a strong national government, and for this reason the Paterson plan was soon brushed aside. As both the weather and tempers grew warmer, the convention swung back to consideration of the Virginia Plan. But little progress was made.

The fact was that the convention was in danger of breaking up. "I *almost* despair," Washington, presiding over the deadlock, wrote to Hamilton in New York.

The impasse over the makeup of Congress was broken on July 16 when the convention adopted the Great Compromise, often called the **Connecticut Compromise** because it had been proposed by Roger Sherman of that state. As adopted after much debate, the Connecticut Compromise called for:

1. A House of Representatives apportioned by the number of free inhabitants in each state plus three-fifths of the slaves.
2. A Senate, or upper house, consisting of two members from each state, elected by the state legislatures.

The plan broke the deadlock because it protected the small states by guaranteeing that each state would have an equal vote in the Senate. Only in the House, where representation was to be based on population, would the larger states have an advantage.

Catherine Drinker Bowen has suggested that the delegates might never have reached agreement "had not the heat broken." On Monday, July 16, the day the compromise was approved, "Philadelphia was cool after a month of torment; on Friday, a breeze had come in from

AN AMERICAN KING

Charles Pinckney rose . . . to urge a "vigorous executive." He did not say a "President of the United States." It took the Convention a long while to come around to *President.* Always they referred to a chief executive or a national executive, whether plural or single. James Wilson followed Pinckney by moving that the executive consist of a single person; Pinckney seconded him. A sudden silence followed. "A considerable pause," Madison wrote. . . . A single executive! There was menace in the words, some saw monarchy in them. True enough, nine states had each its single executive— a governor or president—but everywhere the local legislature was supreme, looked on as the voice of the people which could control a governor any day. But a single executive for the national government conjured up visions from the past—royal governors who could not be restrained, a crown, ermine, a scepter!

—Catherine Drinker Bowen, *Miracle at Philadelphia*

the northwest. Over the weekend, members could rest and enjoy themselves."[32]

With the large state versus small state controversy resolved by this compromise, the convention named a committee to draft a constitution. Then the convention adjourned for 11 days, and General Washington went fishing.

On August 6 the convention resumed its work. The committee brought in a draft constitution that called for a "congress," made up of a house of representatives and a senate; a "supreme court"; and a "president of the United States of America."

The broad outline of the Constitution as it is today was finally clear. But much work remained:

And so the men of Philadelphia persevered through the hot [summer] days, filling out the details now that the grand design had been set in the Connecticut Compromise, sawing boards to make them fit, as Benjamin Franklin said. Some of the boards required much sanding and smoothing, as the delegates thrashed out irksome but vital aspects of the relations between the national and state governments, the enumerated powers of Congress, the jurisdiction of the courts, the reach of impeachment, the amending clause, and procedures for ratifying the Constitution itself. . . . They deliberated as if the eyes of the world were on them.[33]

The Other Compromises

As debate continued, the convention made other significant compromises. Underlying the agreement to count three-fifths of all slaves in apportioning membership of

Sohm, Chromosohm/Stock Connection/PictureQuest

the House of Representatives was a deep-seated conflict between the mercantile North and the agrarian South, where the economy was based on slave labor. Of the 55 delegates to the convention, at least 25 owned slaves.[34] The men of the North argued that if slaves were to be counted in determining representation in the House, then they must be counted for tax purposes as well. In the end, the South agreed.

The slave trade itself was the subject of another complicated compromise. On August 22 George Mason of Virginia attacked "the infernal traffic" and its evil effect on both individuals and the nation. Slavery, he said, would "bring the judgment of heaven on a Country. As nations can not be rewarded or punished in the next world they must in this. By an inevitable chain of causes & effects providence punishes national sins, by national calamities."[35]

Charles Cotesworth Pinckney of South Carolina warned that his state would not join the Union if the slave trade were prohibited. The issue was settled by an agreement that Congress could not ban the slave trade until 1808. This compromise is contained in Article I of the Constitution, which obliquely refers to slaves as "other persons."*

---

*Acting on President Jefferson's recommendation, Congress did outlaw importation of slaves in 1808. But the illegal slave trade flourished up to the Civil War. Perhaps 250,000 slaves were illegally imported to America between 1808 and 1860. The slavery issue was not settled until the end of the Civil War and the ratification on December 18, 1865, of the Thirteenth Amendment, which declared that "neither slavery nor involuntary servitude, except as a punishment for crime whereof the party shall have been duly convicted, shall exist within the United States."

In yet another compromise, southerners won certain trade concessions. They were worried, with reason, that a northern majority in Congress might pass legislation unfavorable to southern economic interests. Because the South relied almost entirely on exports of its agricultural products, it fought for, and won, an agreement forbidding the imposition of export taxes. Even today, the United States is one of the few nations that cannot tax its exports.

We the People

On September 8 a Committee of Style and Arrangement was named to polish the final draft. Fortunately it included Gouverneur Morris. Morris, probably aided by James Wilson,[36] drafted the final version, adding a new preamble that rivals Jefferson's eloquence in the Declaration of Independence:

> We the People of the United States, in Order to form a more perfect Union, establish Justice, insure domestic Tranquility, provide for the common defence, promote the general Welfare, and secure the Blessings of Liberty to ourselves and our Posterity, do ordain and establish this Constitution for the United States of America.

On September 17 the long task was finished. The day was cool, and the trace of autumn in the air must have reminded the delegates of how long they had labored. Thirty-nine men signed the Constitution that afternoon. Benjamin Franklin had to be helped forward to the table,

FIGURE 2-1

The Government of the United States

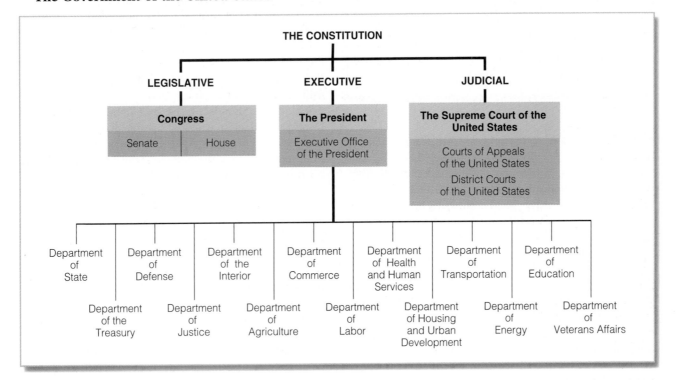

THE CONSTITUTION

LEGISLATIVE | EXECUTIVE | JUDICIAL

Congress
Senate | House

The President
Executive Office of the President

The Supreme Court of the United States
Courts of Appeals of the United States
District Courts of the United States

Department of State

Department of Defense

Department of the Interior

Department of Commerce

Department of Health and Human Services

Department of Transportation

Department of Education

Department of the Treasury

Department of Justice

Department of Agriculture

Department of Labor

Department of Housing and Urban Development

Department of Energy

Department of Veterans Affairs

and it is said that he wept when he signed. According to Madison's notes, while the last members were signing, Franklin observed that often, as he pondered the outcome during the changing moods of the convention, he had looked at the sun painted on the back of Washington's chair and wondered whether it was rising or setting. "But now at length I have the happiness to know," Franklin declared, "that it is a rising and not a setting sun."[37]

The Constitutional Framework

The Constitution was not perfect, but it represented a practical accommodation among conflicting sections and interests achieved at a political convention. And the central fact of the Constitution is that it created the potential for a strong national government where none had existed before, and provided the written framework to control the power and operation of that government. (See Figure 2-1.)

The Federal System The structure of the government created by the Constitution is deceptively simple at first glance, yet endlessly intricate. Article VI declares that the laws passed by Congress "shall be the supreme Law of the Land." This important **supremacy clause** means that federal laws are supreme over any conflicting state laws. But the states also exercise control within their borders over a wide range of activities.

The Constitution thus brought into being a **federal system,** also known as **federalism,** in which the consti-

A REPUBLIC—IF YOU CAN KEEP IT

When the delegates to the Constitutional Convention at Philadelphia ended their long and difficult task in September of 1787, it is said that a lady approached Benjamin Franklin and asked:

"Well, Doctor, what have we got—a republic or a monarchy?"
"A republic," was the reply, "if you can keep it."

—Adapted from "Debates in the Federal Convention in 1787," in *Documents Illustrative of the Formation of the Union of the American States*

tutional powers and functions of government are shared by the national government and the states. Although in the United States a strong national government has evolved over two centuries as the dominant partner, the states retain significant powers of their own. The system of federalism is discussed in detail in Chapter 3.

The National Government The Constitution divided the national government into three branches—legislative, executive, and judicial. It created a government, therefore, based on the principles of **separation of powers** and **checks and balances.** Separation of powers means that each of the three branches is constitutionally equal to and independent of the others. Checks and balances means provisions dividing power among the three constitutionally equal branches of government in the hope of preventing any single branch from becoming too powerful. (In fact, however, the 20th century saw the presidency become the most powerful branch of the federal government, at least in foreign affairs.)

In creating a government based on these ideas, the framers were influenced by the French political philosopher Baron de Montesquieu (1689–1755). In *The Spirit of the Laws*, published in 1748, Montesquieu advocated a separation of powers into legislative, judicial, and executive branches. "When the legislative and executive powers are united in the same person, or in the same body of magistrates, there can be no liberty," he wrote.[38]

Yet the term "separation of powers" is somewhat misleading. Although the Constitution established institutional checks and separated powers, the United States is also a government of shared powers. The branches of the government are separated, but their powers and functions are fused or overlapping. The Constitution provided many ways in which the three branches would interact. For example, although Congress makes the laws, the president submits legislation to it, and he may convene Congress in special session. The president also may veto bills passed by Congress. Clearly, the president is involved in the legislative function.

Similarly, Congress is involved in the executive process in its watchdog role and through its power to create federal executive agencies and to advise on and consent to the appointment of high-level federal officials. Because Congress appropriates money to run the federal government, it may delve deeply, through its committees, into the operations of executive agencies.

Through the process of **judicial review,** the courts decide whether the laws passed by Congress or actions taken by the president—or laws and actions at any level of local or state government—are constitutional. (See Chapter 15 for a detailed discussion of judicial review.) The decisions of the Supreme Court, and other courts, are an important example of the outputs of the political system, because these decisions often determine who gets what in American society. President Woodrow Wilson called the Supreme Court "a kind of Constitutional Convention in continuous session."[39] The president participates in the judicial process through his power to nominate federal judges, including members of the Supreme Court. And Congress can pass laws to overrule Supreme Court decisions.

The notion of three separate-but-equal branches of government was eroded by the pressures of the 20th century. In the past, American presidents have at varying times exercised great powers, as Lincoln did during the Civil War. But in modern times, power, especially military-diplomatic power, has been largely concentrated in the hands of the president. The power of Congress to declare war, for example, has greatly diminished in importance since the Second World War. And in a nuclear attack the president obviously would have no time to consult Congress. But even in the case of protracted conflicts, such as in Korea (1950–1953) and Vietnam (1964–1973), Congress never did declare war. Frustration in Congress over the president's ability to wage war without congressional approval led in 1973 to the passage of the War Powers Resolution, which sets a time limit on the use of combat forces abroad by a president.[40]

In other areas as well, the lines between the three branches of government have become blurred. Today, for example, the complex task of managing the economy has been delegated in part to independent regulatory commissions and agencies that do not fall neatly into any of the three categories—legislative, executive, and judicial—envisioned under the Constitution and in fact exhibit features of all three.

In sum, although the three branches of government are based on separated powers, they also share powers. And among the three branches (as among human beings) there is a never-ending tug-of-war for dominance, a process that Alpheus T. Mason has called "institutionalized tension."[41]

The "Great Silences" of the Constitution Some issues were so difficult and potentially divisive that the framers did not attempt to settle them at all. Because they were trying to construct a political document that stated general principles, they chose to avoid some sensitive problems.

The framers compromised over the vital moral and political issue of whether to abolish the importation of slaves while forming "a more perfect union"; the underlying question of whether to abolish slavery itself was not faced at Philadelphia. Five southern states might not have ratified the Constitution if the framers had abolished the slave trade in 1787. The delegates compromised in order to achieve enough unity to form a new nation, but America paid a high moral and political price. The question of slavery, avoided at Philadelphia, led in time to a bloody civil war. And today, three centuries later, African American men and women are still struggling for the full freedom and equality denied to them by the framers.

The framers also made no explicit statement in the Constitution defining the full scope of the powers of the national government. The history of the Supreme Court is the history of whether the Constitution is to be loosely or strictly interpreted.

Even the Supreme Court's power of judicial review is nowhere expressly provided for in the Constitution (although some scholars argue it is conferred in general terms). "Without some body to act as umpire," Archibald Cox has written, "the several parts must inevitably fall to squabbling and the enterprise launched at Philadelphia break up on the reefs. Yet the Constitution nowhere specifically and explicitly stated who, if anyone, was to have the final word."[42] The power of judicial review, which allows the Supreme Court to declare whether acts of Congress are constitutional, was exercised in several early opinions, but it was not firmly set forth and established until 1803, when the Court ruled in the case of **Marbury v. Madison.**[43] Chief Justice John Marshall, in his historic opinion, argued that, because the Constitution was clearly "superior" to an act of Congress, "It is emphatically the province and duty of the judicial department to say what the law is. . . . A law repugnant to the Constitution is void."

The Constitution says nothing whatever about how candidates for office shall be chosen. The development of political parties, nominating conventions, and primaries all occurred without any formal constitutional provision for them.

Similarly, the cabinet is not specifically established in the Constitution but has evolved through custom, beginning during Washington's first administration. As Richard F. Fenno, Jr., has noted, the cabinet is "an extralegal creation," limited in power as an institution by the very fact that it has no basis in law.[44]

Motives of the Framers   Were the framers of the Constitution selfless patriots who thrust aside all personal interests to save America? Or were they primarily rich men who were afraid of radicals like Daniel Shays? In short, did they form a strong government to protect themselves and their property, or did they act from nobler motives?

John Marshall
Copyright ©
Bettmann/CORBIS

The debate has raged among scholars. Early in the 20th century, the historian Charles A. Beard analyzed in great detail the economic holdings of the framers and concluded that they acted to protect their personal financial interests. The Constitution, said Beard, was "an economic document drawn with superb skill by men whose property interests were immediately at stake."[45]

Later scholars, reacting to Beard, reached opposite conclusions. Forrest McDonald has asserted that of the 55 delegates, "a dozen at the outside, clearly acted according to the dictates of their personal economic interests." He concluded that an "economic interpretation of the Constitution does not work."[46] Similarly, Robert E. Brown has argued it would be unfair to the framers to assume that "property or personal gain was their only motive."[47]

Was It Democratic?   The argument is sometimes advanced that the Constitution was framed to guard against popular democracy and unchecked majority rule. "The evils we experience flow from the excess of democracy," Elbridge Gerry of Massachusetts told the convention.*

The word "democracy" today generally has a favorable, affirmative meaning, but to the framers of the Constitution, it was a term of derision. "Remember," John Adams warned, "democracy never lasts long. It soon wastes, exhausts, and murders itself. There never was a democracy yet that did not commit suicide."[48] The framers preferred the word "republic" to describe what today would be called a democracy.[49]

From a contemporary viewpoint some of the provisions of the Constitution appear highly undemocratic. For example, slavery was permitted to flourish. In addition, because the Constitution leaves voting qualifications to the states, persons without property, women, and many African Americans were long disenfranchised. Until the passage of the Seventeenth Amendment in 1913, senators were elected by state legislatures. The framers had deliberately avoided direct election of senators, for the Senate was seen as a check on the multitudes. Madison assured the convention that the Senate would proceed "with more coolness, with more system, and with more wisdom, than the popular branch." And, of course, the Constitution interposed an electoral college between the voters and the presidency.

But to stress only these aspects of the Constitution would be to overlook the basically representative structure of the government it created—particularly in comparison with other governments that existed in 1787—and the revolutionary heritage of the framers. The Constitution

---

*Bowen, *Miracle at Philadelphia*, p. 45. Elbridge Gerry, Edmund Randolph, and George Mason were the only three framers who refused to sign the Constitution. Much later, Gerry gave his name to a famous but controversial practice. While he was governor of Massachusetts in 1812, the legislature carved up Essex County to give maximum advantage to his party. One of the districts resembled a salamander. From then on, the practice of redrawing voting districts to favor the party in power became known as "gerrymandering." (See Chapter 12.)

In May 1987, as the nationwide celebration of the 200th anniversary of the Constitution approached, Supreme Court Justice Thurgood Marshall broke dramatically with the almost universal acclaim the document had been receiving. Marshall voiced his strong dissent in a speech in Hawaii to a group of lawyers:

> Supreme Court Justice Thurgood Marshall yesterday sharply attacked the Founding Fathers and the planned celebration of the Constitution's bicentennial, urging Americans not to go overboard in praising a document that sanctioned slavery and denied women the right to vote.
>
> Marshall, the Court's only black justice [at that time], said the Constitution was "defective from the start, requiring several amendments, a civil war and momentous social transformation to attain the system of constitutional government, and its respect for the individual freedoms and human rights, we hold as fundamental today." . . .
>
> The preamble's first three words, "we the people," Marshall said, did not include "the majority of American citizens," women and blacks. . . . "The men who gathered in Philadelphia in 1787 could not have envisioned" the "bloody civil war" and amendments that freed slaves and gave blacks the right to vote, followed by the women's suffrage movement that led to the 19th Amendment giving women the right to vote in 1920.
>
> "They could not have imagined, nor would they have accepted, that the document they were drafting would one day be construed by a Supreme Court to which had been appointed a woman and the descendant of an African slave."
>
> —*Washington Post*, May 7, 1987

perhaps originally reflected considerable distrust of popular rule, but it established a balanced institutional framework within which democracy could evolve.

The Fight over Ratification

When the convention had finished its work, a successful outcome was by no means certain. The political contest over ratification of the Constitution lasted for more than two and a half years, from September 1787 until May 29, 1790, when Rhode Island finally joined the Union. But the Constitution went into effect in June 1788 when it was ratified by nine states.

The Articles of Confederation had required that any amendment be approved by Congress and the legislatures of all 13 states. No such unanimity could ever be achieved. In effect this created a box from which the framers could not climb out. So they chose another route—they simply ignored the box and built an entirely new structure. Defending the convention's action, Madison reminded his countrymen of the right of the people, proclaimed in the Declaration of Independence, to alter or abolish their government in ways "most likely to effect their safety and happiness."[50]

Article VII of the Constitution states that "ratification of the Conventions of nine States shall be sufficient for the Establishment of this Constitution." Why conventions and not legislatures? Because the Constitution took power away from the states, the framers reasoned that the state legislatures might not approve it. Second, if the Constitution were approved by popularly elected conventions, it would give the new government a broad base of legitimacy.

The great debate over ratification soon divided the participants into two camps: the **Antifederalists,** who opposed ratification of the Constitution, and the **Federalists,** who supported ratification. Although the debate was vigorous, relatively few people actually participated in the ratification process. The voters could not vote for or against the Constitution. Their choice was confined to selecting delegates to the state ratifying conventions. Only an estimated 160,000 persons voted for delegates to the ratifying conventions, out of a total population of about 4 million.

Some historians tend to pay more attention to the Federalists—because they won—but those opposed to the Constitution had a strong case. The convention, after all, had met in complete secrecy, in a "Dark Conclave," as the Philadelphia *Independent Gazetteer* termed it. What is more, the Constitution, as its opponents argued, was extralegal. The framers had clearly exceeded their mandate from Congress to revise the Articles of Confederation. Above all, the Constitution included no bill of rights to protect individual liberties against the power of the proposed new national government.

The Federalists argued that the states faced anarchy unless they united under a powerful central government. The omission of a bill of rights was difficult to justify, however. The question had not been raised until near the end of the Philadelphia Convention, and the weary delegates were not inclined to open a new debate. Furthermore, many delegates felt that a bill of rights would be superfluous since eight states already had bills of rights. Hamilton argued that "the Constitution is itself . . . a Bill of Rights."[51]

But during the struggle over ratification, the Antifederalists warned that without a bill of rights in the new Constitution, individuals in the states would have no protection against a strong central government. Ultimately, as the price of winning support in the state conventions,

TABLE 2-1

The Ratification of the Constitution

States	Date	Vote in the RatifyingConvention
Delaware	December 7, 1787	Unanimous
Pennsylvania	December 12, 1787	46–32
New Jersey	December 18, 1787	Unanimous
Georgia	January 2, 1788	Unanimous
Connecticut	January 9, 1788	128–40
Massachusetts	February 6, 1788	187–168
Maryland	April 28, 1788	63–11
South Carolina	May 23, 1788	149–73
New Hampshire	June 21, 1788	57–47
Virginia	June 25, 1788	89–79
New York	July 26, 1788	30–27
North Carolina	November 21, 1789	194–77
Rhode Island	May 29, 1790	34–32

the Federalists had to promise to enact a bill of rights as the first order of business under a new government.

Richard Henry Lee's *Letters from the Federal Farmer* was among the most effective of the various Antifederalist attacks circulated among the states. In New York, Hamilton, Madison, and John Jay, writing as "Publius," published more than 80 letters in the press defending the Constitution. Together in book form they are known today as *The Federalist,* the classic work explaining and defending the Constitution.

By January 9, 1788, a little more than three months after the Philadelphia Convention, five states had ratified the Constitution: Delaware, Pennsylvania, New Jersey, Georgia, and Connecticut. Massachusetts, a key and doubtful state, ratified next, thanks to the efforts of Sam Adams and John Hancock. Maryland and South Carolina followed suit, and on June 21, 1788, New Hampshire became the ninth state to ratify.

The Constitution was now in effect, but Virginia and New York were still to be heard from. Without these two powerful states, no union could succeed. Washington, Madison, and Edmund Randolph, who finally decided to support the Constitution that he had not signed, helped to swing Virginia into the Federalist camp four days later. In part because of *The Federalist* papers, New York ratified on July 26 by a narrow margin of three votes. North Carolina finally ratified in 1789 and Rhode Island in 1790. (See Table 2-1.) By that time George Washington was already serving as president of the United States of America.

AMERICA: A CASE STUDY IN NATION BUILDING

"The United States was the first major colony successfully to revolt against colonial rule," Seymour Martin Lipset has written. "In this sense, it was the first 'new nation.'"[52]

The Declaration of Independence and the success of the American Revolution influenced the philosophers and political leaders of the French Revolution. Jefferson's words were translated into many languages, influencing liberals during the 19th century in Germany, Italy, and South America. Even today, the ideas expressed in the Declaration of Independence have relevance in a world in which millions of people are still groping toward political freedom.

Problems of a New Nation

The turmoil that has accompanied the growth of the new countries of Africa and Asia demonstrates that independence does not necessarily bring political maturity and peace. From Vietnam to Zimbabwe, as colonialism has given way to the forces of nationalism, political independence often has been accompanied by political instability and war. The same has proved true in some of the countries of Eastern Europe, notably Yugoslavia, following the collapse of the Soviet Union and its communist system in 1991. Yet America had a successful revolution. And, despite the Civil War, two world wars, the Great Depression, periodic inflation and unemployment, the Vietnam War, Watergate, the Iran-contra affair, the impeachment of two presidents, and other issues that have confronted the nation, it has survived. How did the revolutionary leaders of America carve out an enduring new nation where none had existed before? The process was slow and difficult. As Lipset has observed:

A backward glance into our own past should destroy the notion that the United States proceeded easily toward the establishment of democratic political institutions. In the period which saw the establishment of political legitimacy and party government, it was touch and go whether the complex balance of forces would swing in the direction of a one- or two-party system, or even whether the nation would survive as an entity. It took time to institutionalize values, beliefs, and practices, and there were many incidents that revealed how fragile the commitments to democracy and nationhood really were.[53]

The United States, in other words, went through growing pains similar to those of the new nations of Africa and Asia today. If some contemporary new nations have encountered difficulty in establishing political freedom and democratic procedures, so did America. For example, the Federalists under President John Adams wanted no organized political opposition and used the Alien and Sedition Acts, passed in 1798, to suppress their opponents. At least 70 persons were jailed and fined under the Sedition Act, which made almost any criticism of the government, the president, or Congress a crime. The historical development of the American nation—with all its crises and problems—remains relevant to the emerging nations in today's world.

THE CONSTITUTION: A DOCUMENT "INTENDED TO ENDURE . . ."

The Constitution, Chief Justice Marshall said in *McCulloch* v. *Maryland,* was "intended to endure for ages to come, and consequently to be adapted to the various crises of human affairs."[54] This opinion, delivered in 1819, embodied the principle of loose or **flexible construction** of the Constitution—the concept that the Constitution must be interpreted flexibly to meet changing conditions.

The members of the Supreme Court have generally reflected the times in which they have lived. Successive Supreme Courts have read very different meaning into the language of the Constitution. But the Court is not the only branch of the government that interprets the Constitution. So does Congress when it passes laws. So does the president when he makes decisions and takes actions. In addition, the Constitution has been amended 27 times. The inputs of the American political system have resulted in a continual process of constitutional change. (The Constitution follows the last chapter of this book.)

What It Says

The Legislative Branch Article I of the Constitution vests all legislative powers "in a Congress of the United States, which shall consist of a Senate and House of Representatives." This article spells out the qualifications and method of election of members of the House and Senate. It gives power of impeachment to the House but provides that the Senate shall try impeachment cases. That power has rarely been used; two presidents, Andrew Johnson, in 1868, and Bill Clinton, in 1998, were impeached by the House; both were tried by the Senate, but neither was removed from office. A third president, Richard M. Nixon, resigned in 1974 in the face of threatened impeachment. Article I also empowers the vice president to preside over the Senate with no vote, except in the case of a tie.

Article I provides that all tax legislation must originate in the House. It allows the president to sign or veto a bill and Congress to override his veto by a two-thirds vote of both houses.

Section 8 of this article gives Congress the power to tax, provide for the "general welfare" of the United States, borrow money, regulate commerce (the commerce clause), naturalize citizens, coin money, punish counterfeiters, establish a post office and a copyright and patents system, create lower courts, declare war, maintain armed forces, suppress insurrections and repel invasions, govern the District of Columbia, and make all "necessary and proper laws" (sometimes called the **elastic clause**) to carry out the powers of the Constitution.

Section 9 provides certain basic protections for citizens against acts of Congress. For example, it says that the writ of habeas corpus shall not be suspended unless required by the public safety in cases of rebellion or invasion. One of the most important guarantees of individual liberty, the writ is designed to protect against illegal imprisonment. It requires that a person who is detained be brought before a judge for investigation so that the court may literally, in the Latin meaning, "have the body."

Article I also prohibits Congress or the states from passing a **bill of attainder**—legislation aimed at a particular individual—or an **ex post facto law,** imposing punishment for an act that was not illegal when committed. It provides that only Congress may appropriate money drawn from the Treasury, a provision that is the single most important check on presidential power. The article also outlaws titles of nobility in America.

The Executive Branch Article II states, "The executive Power shall be vested in a President of the United States of America." The framers did not provide for direct popular election of the president. Rather, they established the electoral college, with each state having as many electors as it had representatives and senators. The electors were to choose the president and vice president. Alexander Hamilton argued that by this means the presidency would be filled by "characters preeminent for ability and virtue." The electors, he thought, being "a small number of persons, selected by their fellow-citizens from the general mass, will be most likely to possess the information and discernment requisite."[55]

Under the Constitution, the person with the greatest number of electoral votes would be president and the one with the next highest number would be vice president. The election of 1800 was thrown into the House of Representatives because Jefferson and Aaron Burr, although members of the same party, each received the same number of electoral votes. On the 36th ballot, the House chose Jefferson as president. Afterward, the electoral system was modified by the Twelfth Amendment to provide that electors must vote separately for president and vice president.

The rise of political parties meant that in time the electoral college became largely a rubber stamp. As it works today, the voters in each state choose between slates of electors who usually run under a party label. All the electoral votes of a state normally go to the candidate who wins the popular vote in that state; electors on the winning slate routinely vote for their party's candidates for president and vice president. But the electors do not have to obey the will of the voters. For a variety of reasons (discussed in Chapter 11), there sometimes has been pressure to modify or abolish the electoral college system. However, a proposed constitutional amendment to provide for direct, popular election of the president failed to pass the Senate in 1970 and again in 1979.

The Constitution makes the president commander in chief of the armed forces. It also gives the president the right to make treaties "with the Advice and Consent" of two-thirds of a quorum of the Senate, to appoint ambassadors, judges, and other high officials, subject to Senate approval, and to summon Congress into special session.

The Judiciary Article III states, "The judicial Power of the United States, shall be vested in one supreme Court, and in such inferior Courts" as Congress may establish. It also provides for trial by jury. The Supreme Court's vital right of judicial review of acts of Congress stems from both the supremacy clause of the Constitution (see below) and Article III, which asserts that the judicial power applies to "all Cases . . . arising under this Constitution."

Other Provisions Article IV governs the relations among the states and between the states and the federal government. Article V provides methods for amending the Constitution and for ratifying these amendments. Article VI states that the Constitution, laws, and treaties of the United States "shall be the supreme Law of the Land." This, as noted earlier, is the powerful **supremacy clause** by which laws of Congress prevail over any conflicting state laws. Article VII declares that the Constitution would go into effect when ratified by conventions in nine states.

The Amendment Process

The framers knew that the Constitution might have to be changed to meet future conditions. It had, after all, been created because of the need for change. So they provided

"The executive Power shall be vested in a President of the United States of America."
George Tames/NYT Pictures

two methods of proposing amendments: by a two-thirds vote of both houses of Congress or by a national convention called by Congress at the request of legislatures in two-thirds of the states. (See Figure 2-2.)

Once proposed, an amendment does not take effect unless ratified, either by the legislatures of three-fourths of the states or by special ratifying conventions in three-fourths of the states.

■ **FIGURE 2-2**

Amending the Constitution

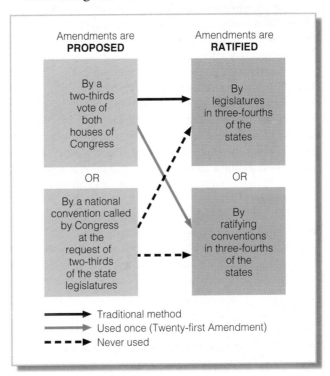

Amendments are **PROPOSED**	Amendments are **RATIFIED**
By a two-thirds vote of both houses of Congress	By legislatures in three-fourths of the states
OR	OR
By a national convention called by Congress at the request of two-thirds of the state legislatures	By ratifying conventions in three-fourths of the states

→ Traditional method
→ Used once (Twenty-first Amendment)
- - -➤ Never used

The Constitution: A Document "Intended to Endure . . ." **49**

No amendment has ever been proposed by the convention method. In the mid-1960s, Senator Everett McKinley Dirksen of Illinois, the Republican Senate leader, encouraged the states to petition Congress to call a constitutional convention to overturn a Supreme Court decision that had forced the reapportionment of state legislatures. Dirksen's campaign came close to success. This led several senators and legal scholars to warn that a constitutional convention might run wild and make sweeping changes in the structure of the federal government, because no precedent exists for setting an agenda of such a convention.

Similar warnings were voiced a decade later when another movement began to call a convention, this time to propose an amendment to require a balanced federal budget. President Jimmy Carter cautioned that such a conclave would be "completely uncontrollable." The effort to persuade the states to call such a convention failed. Nevertheless, the Constitution clearly permits a convention if two-thirds of the state legislatures request it.

Of the 27 amendments ratified by the year 2000, only the Twenty-first Amendment, repealing Prohibition, was ratified by state conventions; the rest were ratified by state legislatures. Some of the amendments add to the Constitution; others supersede or revise the original language of the Constitution.

The Bill of Rights

The amendments to the Constitution fall into three major time periods. The first 12, ratified between 1791 and 1804, were remedial amendments designed to perfect the original instrument. The next three grew out of the great upheaval of the Civil War and were designed to deal with the new position of blacks as free men and women. Amendments in the third group were all passed in the 20th century and deal with a wide range of subjects, in part reflecting more recent pressures toward change in American society.

The first 10 amendments comprise the **Bill of Rights.**[*] The provisions of the first four are: (First Amendment) freedom of religion, speech, press, assembly, and petition; (Second Amendment) the right to bear arms; (Third Amendment) protection against quartering of soldiers in private homes; and (Fourth Amendment) protection against unreasonable search and seizure of people, homes, papers, and effects, and provision for search warrants.

The Fifth Amendment provides that no person can be compelled "to be a witness against himself" or to stand trial twice for the same crime. It also lists other rights of accused persons, including that of indictment by a grand jury for major crimes and the general pro-

vision that no person shall "be deprived of life, liberty, or property, without due process of law." The Sixth Amendment calls for a speedy and public trial by jury in criminal cases and sets forth other protections, including the right to have a lawyer.

The Seventh Amendment provides for jury trial in civil cases, and the Eighth Amendment bars excessive bail or fines, or cruel and unusual punishment. The Ninth Amendment provides that the enumeration of certain rights in the Constitution shall not deny other rights retained by the people, and the Tenth Amendment reserves to the states, or to the people, powers not delegated to the federal government.

These 10 amendments were designed to protect Americans against the power of the *federal* government. Nothing in the Constitution specifically provides that *state* governments also must abide by the provisions of the Bill of Rights. But in interpreting the Fourteenth Amendment, ratified in 1868 after the Civil War, the Supreme Court in the 20th century gradually extended the protection of almost all of the Bill of Rights to apply to the states.

The Later Amendments

The Eleventh Amendment (1795)[56] was added to protect the states from being hauled into federal court by a citizen of another state or by a foreign citizen. In *Chisholm* v. *Georgia*,[†] the Supreme Court had ruled for two South Carolina citizens who had sued the state of Georgia on behalf of a British creditor to recover confiscated property.

The Twelfth Amendment (1804), as already discussed, was adopted after the deadlocked election of 1800. It provided that presidential electors vote separately for president and vice president.

The next three amendments resulted from the Civil War. The Thirteenth Amendment (1865) forbids slavery. It also outlaws involuntary servitude in the United States and its territories except as punishment for a crime. Its purpose was to free the slaves and complete the abolition of slavery in America. Lincoln's Emancipation Proclamation, which was issued during the war,

---

[*]Some scholars regard only the first eight or nine amendments as the Bill of Rights. The first 10 amendments were passed by the 1st Congress on September 25, 1789, and went into effect when ratified by three-fourths of the states on December 15, 1791. The Bill of Rights is discussed in detail in Chapter 4.

[†]*Chisholm* v. *Georgia*, 2 Dallas 419 (1793). However, citizens can sue states in state courts if they are deprived of their rights under the Constitution or federal laws, and states can appeal such cases to the federal courts. *Scheuer* v. *Rhodes*, 416 U.S. 232 (1974); *Maine* v. *Thiboutot*, 448 U.S. 1 (1980).

applied only to areas in rebellion and under Confederate control and therefore did not actually free any slaves.

The Fourteenth Amendment (1868) was adopted to make the former slaves citizens. But it has had other unintended and far-reaching effects. The amendment says that no state "shall abridge the privileges or immunities of citizens"; nor "deprive any person of life, liberty, or property, without due process of law"; nor deny anyone "the equal protection of the laws." The famous "due process" clause of the amendment has been used by the Supreme Court to protect the rights of individuals against the police power of the state in a broad spectrum of cases. The "equal protection of the laws" provision was the basis for the landmark 1954 Supreme Court decision outlawing segregation in public schools.

The Fifteenth Amendment (1870) barred the federal and state governments from denying any citizen the right to vote because of race, color, or previous condition of servitude. It did not, however, prevent some states from disenfranchising blacks by means of restrictive voting requirements, such as literacy tests.

Forty-three years elapsed after the adoption of the Fifteenth Amendment before another was ratified. The Sixteenth Amendment (1913) allowed Congress to pass a graduated individual income tax, in theory based on ability to pay. The tax has been, of course, the largest source of federal revenue.

The Seventeenth Amendment (1913) provided for direct election of senators by the people, instead of by state legislatures.

The Eighteenth Amendment (1919) established Prohibition by outlawing the manufacture, sale, or transportation of alcoholic beverages. It provides a classic instance of a government output doomed to failure because ultimately the input of popular support was lacking. Prohibition led to the era of bathtub gin, "flappers," speakeasies, and bootlegging. It was marked by widespread defiance of the law by otherwise law-abiding citizens and by the rise of organized crime, which quickly moved to meet public demand for illicit liquor. Partly as a result of Prohibition, organized crime remains entrenched in America today, exercising political influence in some areas of the country. Prohibition was repealed in 1933.

The Nineteenth Amendment (1920) guaranteed women the right to vote. Women in many states could vote even before the amendment was proposed, but it provided a constitutional basis for this major expansion of the electorate. Even so, it may seem surprising today that women's suffrage was not constitutionally adopted until 1920, in time for that year's presidential election.

Federal agents destroying barrels of beer during Prohibition
Copyright © Bettmann/CORBIS

Under the Twentieth (or "lame duck") Amendment (1933), the terms of the president and vice president begin on January 20 and the terms of members of Congress on January 3. Prior to that time a president and members of Congress defeated in November would continue in office for four months until March 4 (formerly the date of presidential inaugurations). Injured by the voters, the defeated incumbents sat like "lame ducks."* The amendment also provides alternatives in case of the death of the president-elect before Inauguration Day or in case no president has been chosen.

The Twenty-first Amendment (1933) repealed Prohibition but permitted states to remain "dry" if they so desired.

The Twenty-second Amendment (1951) limits presidents to a maximum of two elected terms. It was proposed after President Franklin D. Roosevelt had won a fourth term in 1944. Before Roosevelt, through hallowed tradition established by George Washington, no president had been elected more than twice.

The Twenty-third Amendment (1961) gives citizens of the District of Columbia the right to vote in presidential elections; they did so for the first time in 1964. When the amendment was adopted, the nation's capital had a population of 800,000—larger than that of 13 of the states.

---

*The phrase apparently originated as London stock exchange slang. It was used to describe a stock jobber or broker who could not make good his losses and would "waddle out of the alley like a lame duck." Abraham Lincoln is sometimes credited with introducing the phrase in America. When a defeated senator called on Lincoln and asked for a job as commissioner of Indian affairs, Lincoln was quoted as saying afterward: "I usually find that a Senator or Representative out of business is a sort of lame duck." See George Stimpson, *A Book about American Politics* (New York: Harper & Row, 1952), pp. 527–528.

The Constitution: A Document "Intended to Endure . . ." **51**

The Nineteenth Amendment,
ratified in 1920, guarantees
women the right to vote.
Granger Collection

The Twenty-fourth Amendment (1964) abolished the poll tax as a prerequisite for voting in federal elections or primaries. It applied only to five southern states that still imposed such a tax, originally a device to keep blacks (and in some cases poor whites) from voting.

The Twenty-fifth Amendment (1967) was spurred by President Dwight D. Eisenhower's 1955 heart attack and by the murder of President John F. Kennedy in Dallas on November 22, 1963. It defines the circumstances in which a vice president may take over the leadership of the country in case of the mental or physical illness or disability of the president. It also requires the president to nominate a vice president, subject to majority approval of Congress, when that office becomes vacant for any reason.*

The Twenty-sixth Amendment (1971) gave persons 18 years of age or older the right to vote in all elections—

---

*The amendment was used for the first time in October 1973 when President Richard Nixon nominated House Republican leader Gerald R. Ford to replace Vice President Spiro T. Agnew, who had resigned. Congress confirmed Ford in December. When Nixon resigned in August 1974, Ford became president, again under the amendment. The amendment was used a third time when President Ford that same month nominated Nelson A. Rockefeller of New York to be vice president. Congress confirmed Rockefeller in December 1974.

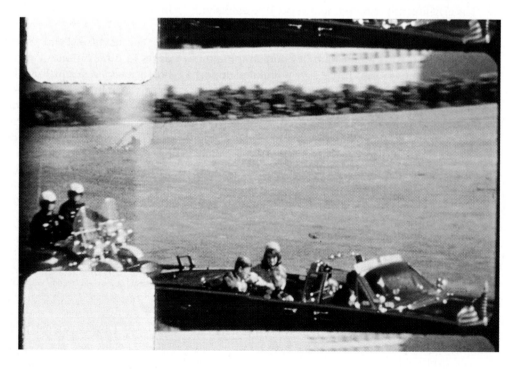

The assassination of
President John F. Kennedy,
November 22, 1963
Smithsonian Institution

MAKING A DIFFERENCE

A STUDENT GETS THE CONSTITUTION AMENDED

In 1789, it bothered James Madison that under the new Constitution he had helped to create, members of Congress could vote to increase their own salaries. They would, he warned, be able "without control to put their hand into the public coffers, to take out money to put in their pockets." There was, Madison said, "a seeming indecorum in such power that leads me to propose a change." Madison proposed an amendment to the Constitution. It said: "No law varying the compensation for the services of the Senators and Representatives shall take effect, until an election of Representatives shall have intervened." The proposed amendment was sent to the states as part of the original Bill of Rights. There it languished; after a century, only seven states had ratified the amendment. Enter Gregory D. Watson, a student of government at the University of Texas in Austin, who came across it in 1982 while researching a paper. Watson made passage of Madison's amendment a personal crusade, and under his prodding, beginning in the mid-eighties, one state legislature after another ratified the proposal. Finally, on May 7, 1992, Michigan became the 38th state to ratify, providing the necessary three-fourths of the states.

Although some scholars argued that the amendment was invalid because of the passage of time, six days later the archivist of the United States pronounced the Twenty-seventh Amendment part of the Constitution. By that time Gregory Watson was an aide to a Democratic state legislator in Texas. "I always knew in my heart of hearts that this day would come," he said.

—Adapted from the *New York Times*, May 8, 1992

---

federal, state, and local. The amendment was proposed by Congress in March 1971 and ratified in June. As a result, 1972 was the first presidential election year in which persons aged 18 through 20 were able to vote in elections at every level of government.

The Twenty-seventh Amendment (1992) prohibited any Congress from voting itself a pay raise; the amendment provides that any vote to increase congressional salaries cannot take effect until after the next Congress is elected. The amendment was first submitted to the states in 1789. Until 1984, only 10 states had ratified the amendment. By the early 1990s, public indignation over congressional pay raises and perquisites led many other states to approve the amendment, and it was ratified in 1992. Some scholars questioned the validity of the amendment, arguing that the states had taken too long to act—203 years. Since 1919, Congress has set deadlines, usually seven years, for states to ratify proposed amendments, but it did not do so in this case.

Several other constitutional amendments have been suggested in recent years. In 1995, for example, the Republican majority in the House passed a proposed constitutional amendment to balance the federal budget, a proposal that was an important part of the party's "Contract with America." However, the measure failed to pass the Republican-controlled Senate. Congress then sought to achieve the same objective over a longer period by enacting legislation requiring the budget to be in balance by 2002.

In 1995, Congress also failed to pass another proposed constitutional amendment to limit the terms of its members to 12 years. That same year the Supreme Court held that the states could not pass laws limiting the terms of members of Congress.[57] That ruling meant that only an amendment to the Constitution could impose congressional term limits.

A proposed amendment designed to guarantee equal rights for women was approved by Congress in 1972 and sent to the states for ratification. "Equality of rights under the law shall not be denied or abridged by the United States or by any State on account of sex," the amendment read. It was proposed to nullify the many state laws that discriminated against women in jobs, business, marriage, and other areas. After an initial burst of support, the Equal Rights Amendment (ERA) ran into increasing difficulty and failed to pass. Although later reintroduced, it was defeated again in 1983.

In 1982 foes of legalized abortion introduced a proposed amendment to the Constitution that would allow states to prohibit abortions. The "pro-life" amendment was designed to overturn a 1973 Supreme Court ruling that legalized abortions. The proposed amendment was defeated in the Senate in 1983.

In 1984, the Senate rejected a proposed constitutional amendment, supported by President Ronald Reagan, to permit organized, spoken prayers in the public schools. The Senate also voted down a proposed constitutional amendment to allow silent prayer in the public schools.

Presidents Reagan, Bush, and Clinton repeatedly urged Congress to enact a constitutional amendment to give presidents the power to veto parts of appropriations bills passed by Congress. The Constitution does not provide for such a line-item veto. In 1996, Congress passed and President Clinton signed legislation to give the president a limited line-item veto over appropriations bills. However, two years later the law was declared unconstitutional by the Supreme Court.[58]

Jesse Nemerofsky

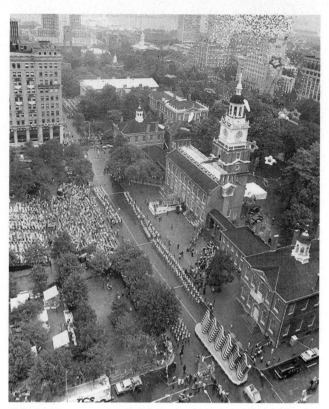

Philadelphia, 1987: the celebration marking the 200th anniversary of the signing of the Constitution
UPI/Archive

A Document for the Living . . .

At 4 P.M. in Philadelphia on September 17, 1987—the moment when, 200 years earlier, the delegates had finished signing their names to the Constitution—former chief justice Warren E. Burger rang a replica of the Liberty Bell. It was a signal for bells to ring throughout Philadelphia, in the capitals of the 50 states, and in United States diplomatic missions around the world.

Philadelphia was bedecked with balloons, flags, and parade floats for the bicentennial celebration. Tall ships sailed the Delaware River. President Reagan spoke at Independence Hall, recalling the convention 200 years before. "In a very real sense it was then, in 1787, that the revolution truly began," he said.

What Alexander Hamilton called "the American drama" had begun its third century. The world of the framers had changed beyond measure. At the outset of this chapter we posed the key question of whether the constitutional framework constructed more than two centuries ago allows for change at a sufficiently rapid pace to meet today's needs. That question lies at the heart of the ongoing political struggle in America. Competing groups can be expected to give different answers to the question. For example, the power of the government to regulate industry in order to protect the environment has expanded greatly under the Constitution. But the logger in Oregon who fears his job is threatened by the law protecting the spotted owl

may have a different view of that expansion of government power than an environmental activist may have. Nevertheless, the process of constitutional change had been foreseen long ago.

"The Constitution belongs to the living and not to the dead," Thomas Jefferson wrote. He added:

> Some men look at constitutions with sanctimonious reverence and deem them like the ark of the covenant, too sacred to be touched. They ascribe to the men of the preceding age a wisdom more than human, and suppose what they did to be beyond amendment. . . . Laws and institutions must go hand in hand with the progress of the human mind. . . . As new discoveries are made, new truths disclosed, and manners and opinions change . . . institutions must advance also, and keep pace with the times.[59]

Through a variety of ways, including amendments and judicial review, the oldest written national constitution in the world remains the vital framework of the American political system. But are constitutional principles enough? Today, many Americans—women and members of minority groups, for example—continue to ask that the nation's institutions fulfill the promise of its ideals, and that principles be translated into reality. Constitutional democracy was born at Philadelphia, but, in a real sense, the work was only begun.

KEY TERMS

CHAPTER HIGHLIGHTS

✦ The Constitution and the Bill of Rights provide the basic framework of American government. The Constitution established the structure of the government and a written set of rules to control the conduct of the government.

✦ A key question is whether that framework constructed in 1787 is sufficiently flexible to meet the needs of a complex, urban society today.

✦ The Declaration of Independence, approved by the Continental Congress on July 4, 1776, proclaimed that "all men are created equal" and that government derived its just powers from "the consent of the governed."

✦ Before the Constitution was framed, a weak central government had been established under the Articles of Confederation.

✦ During the Constitutional Convention of 1787, the Virginia Plan and the New Jersey Plan were debated. The Great Compromise, also called the Connecticut Compromise, was finally adopted as an alternative.

✦ The Great Compromise provided for a House of Representatives based on the population of each state, and a Senate with two members from each state—a solution that satisfied both the large and the small states.

✦ The convention also compromised over the slavery issue by delaying a ban on the importation of slaves until 1808 and by counting three-fifths of all slaves in apportioning the House of Representatives.

✦ The Constitution divided the national government into three branches: legislative, executive, and judicial. The government is based on the principles of separation of powers and checks and balances, even though in practice many powers and functions overlap and are shared.

✦ The Constitution also created a federal system, or federalism, in which the powers and functions of government are shared by the national government and the states. Although in the United States a strong national government has evolved over two centuries as the dominant partner, the states retain significant powers of their own.

✦ The Constitution was ratified in 1788, but only after a long debate and political struggle between the Federalists and the Antifederalists.

✦ In 1791 the states ratified a Bill of Rights intended to protect individuals from the power of the federal government. These first 10 amendments to the Constitution included provisions for freedom of religion, speech, press, assembly, and petition; the right to bear arms; protection against unreasonable search and seizure; the right to due process of law and protection against self-incrimination and double jeopardy; the right to a speedy and public trial by jury in criminal cases; and protection against cruel and unusual punishment.

✦ Through the year 2000, the Constitution had been amended 27 times.

✦ The Supreme Court interprets the Constitution. By exercising judicial review, the Supreme Court decides whether laws passed by Congress or actions by the executive branch—or laws and actions at any level of local, state, and federal government—are constitutional.

SUGGESTED WEB SITES

http://thomas.loc.gov
Thomas—U.S. Congress on the Internet
A comprehensive guide to the current status in Congress of a bill, resolution, or amendment. Includes bills and issues that various congressional committees and subcommittees are considering. The site also includes links to the Web sites of members of Congress.

http://www.supremecourtus.gov
The United States Supreme Court
The official Web site of the U.S. Supreme Court. Opened in April of the year 2000. Contains the full text of the Court's decisions the same day they are released, as well as the Court's calendar, dockets, rules, a visitor's guide, and other information about the Court.

In addition to the Supreme Court's official Web site, there are other Web sites that offer comprehensive coverage of Supreme Court decisions, as well as other information about the Court:

http://www.law.cornell.edu/supct
Cornell Law School—Legal Information Institute Web site
Offers material about cases presented to the U.S. Supreme Court, and whenever possible the full text of decisions, including concurring and dissenting opinions.

http://www.oyez.nwu.edu
The Oyez Project—Northwestern University
Offers synopses and texts of U.S. Supreme Court decisions. Some arguments and decisions are available in Real Audio. Also has a "tour" of the Supreme Court and biographies of current and past justices.

http://www.findlaw.com
FindLaw
FindLaw is a Web portal focused on law and government, providing access to a comprehensive and fast-growing online library of legal resources for anyone with an interest in the law.

http://www.douglass.speech.nwu.edu
Douglass
A growing collection of speeches from the history of the United States.

gopher://wiretap.spies.com/11/Gov/US-History
U.S. Historical Documents
A listing of important documents in U.S. history.

http://lcweb2.loc.gov/ammem/mcchtml/corhome.html
Manuscript Division of the U.S. Library of Congress
A collection of selected documents celebrating the first 100 years of the Manuscript Division of the Library of Congress.

SUGGESTED READING

Bailyn, Bernard. *The Ideological Origins of the American Revolution** (Harvard University Press, 1967). A revealing analysis of the ideas and concepts that were developed by the American colonists and led to their declaration of independence from Great Britain. Bailyn argues that the colonists' political ideas grew out of their experience in America but could also be widely applied in other countries and other times.

Banning, Lance. *The Sacred Fire of Liberty: James Madison and the Founding of the Federal Republic** (Cornell University Press, 1995). A challenging study of the development of the political thought of James Madison from 1780 to 1792. Argues that although Madison supported the creation of a stronger national government in 1787, he was also greatly interested in maintaining effective popular control of that new government.

Casper, Gerhard. *Separating Power: Essays on the Founding Period** (Harvard University Press, 1997). Casper contends that the framers of the Constitution failed to develop fully their principles of constitutional government. As a result, when courts and scholars attempt to interpret the Constitution by turning to the "original intent" of the framers, they may be doomed to failure.

Corwin, Edward S., et al., eds. *The Constitution of the United States of America, Analysis and Interpretation* (U.S. Government Printing Office, 1964). An exposition of the Constitution. See also Corwin, revised by Harold W. Chase and Craig R. Ducat, *The Constitution and What It Means Today,* 14th edition (Princeton University Press, 1978).

Earle, Edward Mead, ed. *The Federalist* (Random House, Modern Library). A classic collection of essays written by Alexander Hamilton, James Madison, and John Jay, prominent supporters of the proposed Constitution during the struggle over ratification. *The Federalist* papers were published in the press under the pseudonym "Publius"; they remain an important exposition of the federal government's structure.

Farrand, Max. *The Framing of the Constitution of the United States** (Yale University Press, 1913). A good general account of the Constitutional Convention by the scholar who compiled in four volumes the basic documentary sources on the convention proceedings.

Kelly, Alfred H., and Harbison, Winfred A. *The American Constitution: Its Origins and Development,* 7th edition* (Norton, 1991). A good general history of American constitutional development beginning with the colonial period.

Ketcham, Ralph. *Framed for Posterity: The Enduring Philosophy of the Constitution* (University Press of Kansas, 1993). A thoughtful and incisive study of the principles embodied in the Constitution. Ketcham concludes that the Constitution reflects general, durable ideas that can be applied by the courts to the problems of today.

Lipset, Seymour Martin. *The First New Nation* (Norton, 1979). An important historical and sociological study of America that seeks to trace the relationship between a nation's values and the development of stable political institutions. Compares the early American experience with that of emerging nations in the 20th century.

Maier, Pauline. *American Scripture: Making the Declaration of Independence** (Knopf, 1997). A fascinating account of how the Declaration of Independence came to be written, and then was reinterpreted by subsequent generations of Americans. Initially, the Declaration of Independence was a justification for rebellion; by the time of Lincoln's Gettysburg Address, through emphasis on the document's proposition that "all men are created equal," it had become a fundamental ideal of the American nation.

Rossiter, Clinton. *1787: The Grand Convention* (Norton, 1987). (Originally published in 1966.) A very readable account of the Philadelphia Convention, the battle for ratification of the Constitution, and the first years of the new republic. Includes interesting observations on the personal characteristics and objectives of the framers of the Constitution.

Rutland, Robert A. *The Birth of the Bill of Rights, 1776–1791*, Bicentennial edition (Northeastern University Press, 1991). (Originally published in 1955.) A study of how Americans came to rely on legal guarantees in an effort to preserve their personal freedom. English common law, colonial charters and statutes, and specific events in the 13 colonies are discussed as important factors that led to the Bill of Rights.

Storing, Herbert J. *What the Anti-Federalists Were For** (University of Chicago Press, 1981). A detailed analysis of the position of the Antifederalists in the struggle over the ratification of the Constitution. Traces how the views of the Antifederalists helped to bring about the enactment of the Bill of Rights.

Wood, Gordon S. *The Creation of the American Republic** (University of North Carolina Press, 1969). A comprehensive analysis of the development of political attitudes and thought in America before the constitutional convention convened in Philadelphia in 1787.

Wood, Gordon S. *The Radicalism of the American Revolution** (Knopf, 1992). A detailed examination of the social, economic, and political forces that led to the creation of democracy in America. Wood argues that the American Revolution was as radical as any in history if measured in terms of the great social changes it produced.

---

*Available in paperback edition.

 Visit http://politicalscience.wadsworth.com/cummings9/update/ for current InfoTrac articles and other student resources related to this chapter.

CHAPTER 3
The Federal System

In Colorado, Montana, Nevada, South Dakota, and half a dozen other states, it is legal to tool along the interstate at 75 miles an hour. In California and Texas, the speed limit is 70. But in New York, New Hampshire, Maryland, and many other states the speed limit is 65. In Hawaii, doing more than 55 can result in a ticket.

Why should there be so many different speed limits in different states? After all, the United States is one country and Congress makes laws that apply to all Americans.

In the case of the varying speed limits, Congress did in fact pass a law—but it allowed the states to make their own rules. At one minute after midnight on December 8, 1995, under the law passed by Congress and signed by President Clinton, the 50 states were free to set their own speed limits on the nation's highways. The 55-mile-per-hour limit that had prevailed on many highways for more than two decades was no longer, in effect, a federal requirement.

Many states passed new laws that increased speed limits to 70 miles per hour or more. Almost immediately, a solid bloc of 10 western states increased their legal speeds to 70 or 75. A total of 26 states had raised their limits within six months after the new law went into effect, and by the year 2000 a total of 29 states had limits of 70 or 75.[1]

The 55-mile-per-hour limit had originally been set in 1974 to save gasoline during an oil embargo imposed by the Arab states. In western states, with wide-open spaces and straight stretches of highway, many motorists chafed under the lower speed limits. The insurance industry, safety, and environmental groups were opposed to higher speeds, however, arguing that the new law would mean 6,400 highway deaths a year in addition to the 41,000 annual fatalities that occurred under the slower speed limits.[2] Some studies have shown that more people are killed at higher speeds.

In addition to repealing the 55-mile-per-hour limit, Congress also removed the penalties that had been imposed on states that did not require motorcycle drivers to wear helmets. On the other hand, the new law required so-called zero tolerance for younger drivers who drink alcohol; it would withhold a portion of federal highway money for states that do not treat minors as driving while intoxicated if their blood alcohol level is 0.02 percent or higher.

How is it that the government in Washington, D.C., could require or repeal speed limits or other highway rules for the 50 states? Congress had done so in 1974 by passing the law that established a national 55-mile-per-hour speed limit. The law barred the release of any federal highway construction funds to states with a speed limit in excess of 55. Because of this provision, every state maintained the lower speed limit.

The controversy over speed limits, and the response by Congress and the president in 1995, were an illustration of a basic fact about government in America: The United States has a federal system of government, in which power is constitutionally shared by a national government and 50 state governments. Within the states, of course, are thousands of local governments—and schools are controlled by localities and independent school districts, operating within standards set by the states.

The constitutional sharing of power by a national government and regional units of government (states, in the case of the United States) characterizes and defines a **federal system,** or **federalism.** The terms "federalism" and "the federal system" are used interchangeably to describe this basic structure of government in the United States. (These terms should not be confused with "the federal government," which simply refers to the national government in Washington.)

In the American federal system each level of government is able to make certain decisions that the other level cannot. For example, only the president can conduct America's relations with other nations; but only a governor, in some states, has the power to reprieve a prisoner on that state's death row.

To say that power in America is shared by the national and state governments may, at first glance, seem merely to be stating the obvious. Yet no principle of American government has been disputed more than federalism. Should that be doubted, one need only recall that more than 500,000 people died during the Civil War settling problems of federalism.

Not every country has a federal system. For example, it used to be said that the French minister of education could, by glancing at the clock in his office, tell at any given moment what book was being read by every schoolchild in France. The tale may be a bit exaggerated, but no official in Washington could even begin to perform the same feat. France has a **unitary system of government.** The nation is divided into administrative units called departments, uniformly administered from Paris. Educational and other policies are set by the central government, even though in recent years France has sought to decentralize a number of government functions. (See Figure 3-1.)

Although the national government in Washington exercises great power, it also shares power with the states. The states, in turn, exercise certain exclusive powers. And,

FIGURE 3-1

Federal and Unitary Systems of Government Compared

Federal System

Overlapping functions

Shared power

Unitary System

Power flows from the national government

National government

Smaller units of government

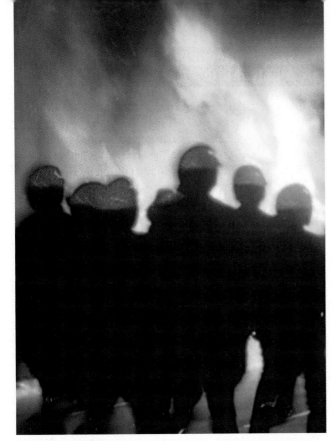

Los Angeles, 1992
Copyright © John Barr/Liaison

at times, the federal system of government created by the Constitution leads to significant conflict.

The rioting that erupted in the streets of Los Angeles in April 1992 provided a dramatic example of that fact. The disorders were triggered when a jury that included no black members in a state court in California acquitted four white police officers in the savage beating of Rodney King, a black motorist. Police in Los Angeles were slow to respond and failed to restore order, so the governor called out the California National Guard. When that, too, appeared inadequate to restore order, the president placed the National Guard under federal authority and dispatched thousands of federal agents and armed troops to the nation's second-largest city. All three layers of government—local, state, and national—were drawn into, and reacted to, the crisis. And all three layers would have to play a role in any long-term solutions to the problems of the nation's inner cities.

The question of how power is to be shared in the federal system is central to the political process in the United States. It is a subject of continuing political debate. It has been reflected in many important decisions of the Supreme Court. The migrant worker in the lettuce fields of California, the West Virginia coal miner, the spouse seeking a Nevada divorce, the murder suspect fighting extradition—these people do not think of their problems in terms of the federal system. Yet the relationship among national, state, and local governments vitally touches their lives. To a considerable extent, federalism affects who wins and who loses as a result of government decisions in American society. It affects the outputs of the political system.

Federalism is one answer to the problem of how to govern a complex nation. Although there are all sorts of institutional arrangements in the 203 nations of the world, governments tend to be either centralized and unitary, or federated. In the 20th century, federalism became a popular style of government. By 1964, one study concluded, "well over half the land mass of the world was ruled by governments that with some justification, however slight, described themselves as federalisms."[3] The list of federal systems includes Switzerland, Canada, Australia, Mexico, India, and Germany.* Unitary systems, in which all power is vested in a central government, include France, Israel, and South Africa.

In this chapter we will explore a key question: How does federalism work in the United States? Many other questions also arise. For example: Who benefits and who loses under the federal system? Does federalism restrict progress in solving national problems? Do the advantages of federalism outweigh the price of fragmented government? Why does the United States have a federal system? What are the problems it has created? What are the consequences of federalism in American politics? In the performance of the states?

FEDERALISM: THE PROS AND CONS

What are the arguments for and against a federal system? (See Table 3-1.) Federalism permits diversity. Since problems and circumstances vary from one community to another, the argument can be made that a number of governments dealing directly with local problems, and accountable to local voters, may perform better than a single, remote bureaucracy. State governments, by this reasoning, may have a better idea than the national government of how to cope with local problems.

Another argument advanced for a federal system of government is that it allows more levels of government, more points of access to the government, and as a result, more opportunities for political participation. A system in which there are multiple points of access to government may offer advantages to individuals or groups seeking benefits from the political system. Americans may vote at frequent intervals for mayors, town council and school board members, governors, other state officials, and, at the national level, members

---

*The former Soviet Union was a federal system. When it broke up in 1991, it was replaced by a Commonwealth of Independent States, a very loose grouping of 11 of the 15 former Soviet republics. Although the future of the Commonwealth was uncertain, it, too, could be roughly characterized as a federal system.

TABLE 3-1

The Federal System

Scholars and political leaders alike have debated the relative merits and drawbacks of federalism since the founding of the republic. Here are some of the major arguments that have been made:

Advantages

Permits diversity and diffusion of power
Local governments can handle local problems better.
More access points for political participation
Protects individual rights against concentrated government power
Fosters experimentation and innovation
Suits a large country with a diverse population

Disadvantages

Makes national unity difficult to achieve and maintain
State governments may resist national policies.
May permit economic inequality and racial discrimination
Law enforcement and justice are uneven.
Smaller units may lack expertise and money.
May promote local dominance by special interests

of the House of Representatives and senators elected from the states.

Some analysts also argue that because power is diffused and fragmented among many different units in a federal system, there is better protection for individual rights than in a highly centralized government.

FEDERALISM UNDER CHALLENGE

Federal assistance to states and localities through grant-in-aid programs, once applauded by respected observers and commentators, has become the object of searching examination. Once regarded as essential institutional innovations, the programs are now criticized for causing bureaucratic nightmares. Once said to be the best hope for social progress, federal involvement is now blamed for increased poverty, escalating medical costs, urban decay, and educational retrogression. What was once accepted as a growing presence has been sharply curtailed, a victim of antigovernment sentiments and pressing budget deficits. . . . Yet federalism works well when national, state, and local governments together take the time to design and implement programs that meet broad social needs not easily addressed by local jurisdictions alone.

—Paul E. Peterson, Barry G. Rabe, and Kenneth K. Wong, *When Federalism Works*

WASHINGTON: COLOR-BLIND IN A BLIZZARD?

While a trivial matter, one example indicates the difficulty of keeping too many strings tied to the center nail, of seeking too much uniformity, or setting one pattern for all of the diverse nation. The state of Wyoming had a slight hassle with the U.S. Bureau of Public Roads over the color of paint to be used to mark the sides and center line of Wyoming highways. Wyoming had painted a solid yellow line to mark the shoulder of the road and an intermittent yellow line for the center. The Bureau of Public Roads said the lines must be standardized with the rest of the country, which meant white lines except in the no-passing stretches. After much haggling Wyoming inevitably gave in, but with a parting comment: "Let them come out here and find one of their white lines during one of our blizzards." The highway engineers had found that in the blowing blizzards of Wyoming's winters, drivers could see yellow lines, but not white ones. In this encounter they learned that yellow lines could not be seen from Washington.

—Terry Sanford, *Storm over the States*

Concentrated power is dangerous, supporters of federalism often maintain.

Advocates of a federal system also stress that the existence of many units of government allows for more experimentation and innovation in solving problems. For example, new social programs are sometimes originated in one state and then adopted in another, or even nationally. Many of the social programs of Franklin D. Roosevelt's New Deal were copied from some of the states, a pattern that was repeated during the 1960s and 1970s. During the Reagan era, when the federal government was trying to cut back spending for social programs, a number of states took the lead in education, economic development, and other important areas. Again in the early 1990s, many states redesigned their welfare programs before the federal government acted to restructure the national welfare system.

In addition, advocates of federalism argue that it is well suited to the United States, a nation covering a large geographic area with a highly diversified population of more than 275 million people.

But critics contend that a federal system also has distinct disadvantages. Federalism may serve as a mask for privilege and economic or racial discrimination.[4] In the past, at least, in some areas of the South and in other sections of the country, the federal system permitted state and local governments to repress blacks. Inequalities may occur when special interests exercise considerable influence on the politics and economy of a state or locality. West Virginia has often been cited as an example. Although the nation's second-leading coal producer, it has long been a relatively poor state, a fact

The AMERICAN PAST

THE STORM OVER McCULLOCH V. MARYLAND

Chief Justice John Marshall secured his place in history with his landmark decision in *McCulloch* v. *Maryland* in 1819. The unanimous ruling by the Supreme Court established the supremacy of the federal government over the states. At the time, however, Marshall was harshly attacked for his opinion:

As soon as [Marshall's critics] recovered from their surprise and dismay, they opened fire from their heaviest batteries upon Marshall and the National Judiciary. The way was prepared for them by a preliminary bombardment in the *Weekly Register* of Hezekiah Niles.

This periodical had now become the most widely read and influential

publication in the country. . . . In the first issue of the *Register*, after Marshall's opinion was delivered, Niles began an attack upon it that was to spread all over the land. "A deadly blow has been struck at the *sovereignty of the states,* and from a quarter so far removed from the people as to be hardly accessible to public opinion," he wrote. . . .

On March 30, [1819] Spencer Roane opened fire in . . . the *Enquirer.* . . . His first article is fair and moderate. . . . In his second article Roane grows vehement, even fiery, and finally exclaims that Virginia "never will *employ force to support her*

doctrines till other measures have entirely failed." . . .

No sooner had copies of the *Enquirer* . . . reached Kentucky than the Republicans of that State declared war on Marshall. . . . Marshall's principles, said the Kentucky correspondent, "must raise an alarm throughout our widely extended empire. . . . The people must rouse from the lap of Delilah and prepare to meet the Philistines. . . . No mind can compass the extent of the encroachments upon State and individual rights which may take place under the principles of this decision."

—Albert J. Beveridge, *The Life of John Marshall*

---

sometimes attributed to its heavy dependence on a single industry. Along with abandoned strip mines, pockets of poverty scar the hillsides; in 1999 West Virginia ranked 49th in the nation in per capita income.[5] Although the energy shortage of the 1970s increased the price of coal and brought greater prosperity to the state, industry pressures tended to keep taxes low. That in turn affected West Virginia's ability to provide social services for its residents. By the 1990s, however, the state had increased taxes and its economy was improving.

Critics also argue that under the federal system, local or special interests—for example, the automobile industry, oil companies, or in the past, the white power structure in the Deep South—have often been able to frustrate efforts to solve national problems like segregated public schools, poverty, pollution, and energy needs. The same local officials whose understanding of local problems is often cited as a benefit of federalism may be in a position to thwart national policies. Government that is "closer to the people" may not serve all the people equally. Nor is it necessarily the case that local governments can solve problems more efficiently; they may lack the national government's skill and money. In fact, because the federal government collects most of the taxes in America, it can be argued that the system of federalism has often left cities and states unable to pay for local services.

Other arguments are sometimes made against a federal system: Its very diversity may make it difficult to achieve and maintain national unity; it can be more difficult and costly to make a complex system work; and law enforcement and justice may be administered unevenly.

The relations between the states and the federal government are thus a source of continuing conflict and controversy in the American political system.

THE CHECKERBOARD OF GOVERNMENTS

Americans sometimes complain that they are being squeezed by high taxes on at least three levels of government—national, state, and local. Depending on where they live, they may be confronted by a bewildering checkerboard of overlapping governments and local districts. One study of the federal system found that a resident of Park Forest, Illinois, paid taxes to 11 governmental units, starting with the United States of America and ending with the South Cook County Mosquito Abatement District.[6] Moreover, states have different laws and rules for dealing with such matters as taxation, criminal justice, education, marriage, and licensing of professions and businesses.

The Census Bureau has counted a total of 87,504 governments in the United States: 3,043 counties; 19,372 municipalities; 16,629 townships; 13,726 school districts; 34,683 special districts (for natural resources, fire protection, housing development, and other services); 50 states; and one national government.[7]

But knowing how many governments exist in America tells little about how the federal system operates—how the various levels of government relate to one another. One way to visualize the system as a whole was suggested by Morton Grodzins:

The Checkerboard of Governments **63**

The federal system is not accurately symbolized by a neat layer cake of three distinct and separate planes. A far more realistic symbol is that of the marble cake. Wherever you slice through it you reveal an inseparable mixture of differently colored ingredients. There is no neat horizontal stratification. Vertical and diagonal lines almost obliterate the horizontal ones, and in some places there are unexpected whirls and an imperceptible merging of colors, so that it is difficult to tell where one ends and the other begins. So it is with federal, state, and local responsibilities in the chaotic marble cake of American government.[8]

Cooperation—and Tension

Is the American federal system essentially cooperative—or is it competitive? In fact, federalism can be seen both as a rivalry between the states and Washington and as a partnership. A system of 87,504 governments could not operate without a substantial measure of cooperation, but a great tension is built into the system as well.

In 1975, for example, New York City was in deep financial trouble; there was a real possibility that the city would default on its bonds. The administration of President Gerald R. Ford at first declined to help, then relented, and Congress passed a bill providing billions in federal loan guarantees for the city. Ultimately, the federal government, and New York State, did not permit the nation's biggest metropolis to go broke, but the political struggle over aid to New York City was protracted and bitter.

There have been other dramatic examples of tension within the federal system. Several times in the 1950s and 1960s the president of the United States deployed armed federal troops in states experiencing civil disorders. In 1957 President Dwight D. Eisenhower

sent troops into Little Rock, Arkansas, to enforce court-ordered integration of the previously all-white Central High School.

In the fall of 1962 two men were killed on the campus of the University of Mississippi at Oxford during rioting over the admission of James H. Meredith, a black student. President John F. Kennedy deployed 16,000 federal troops in Mississippi to enroll Meredith and protect him as he attended classes. In June 1963 Governor George Wallace carried out a campaign pledge to "stand in the schoolhouse door" to try to prevent two black students from entering the University of Alabama. Wallace backed down after President Kennedy federalized the state's National Guard to enforce the order of a federal court.

"A great tension is built into the system . . .": federal troops on guard at Central High School in Little Rock, Arkansas, September 1957

Copyright © CORBIS/UPI/Bettmann

1963: Alabama Gov. George C. Wallace tries to prevent two black students from entering the University of Alabama.
AP/Wide World

In 1967, President Lyndon B. Johnson dispatched 4,700 federal paratroopers to quell racial disorders in Detroit; and in 1992, President George Bush sent 4,500 troops and 1,000 federal law enforcement agents to Los Angeles after rioting broke out there.

Although presidents tend to use the rhetoric of cooperation when they talk about federal-state relations, there is clearly an underlying tension among competing levels of government. Sometimes the tensions arise from social issues, as in the armed confrontations over racial desegregation. Often, as in the case of the bailout of New York City, they are rooted in disagreements over how tax revenues should be shared or used.

Political and ideological tensions arise as well—between those who look to the federal government to solve major national social and economic problems, and those who tend to see the government in Washington as a threat to individual liberty and initiative and regard the states as a bulwark against expanding federal power.

The Changing Federal Framework

The federal system has been viewed differently at various times. During much of the 19th century and until 1937, although the states and the national government cooperated in several areas—such as the construction of dams, and the housing of prisoners—the concept of **dual federalism** prevailed. In this view, the federal government and the states were seen as competing power centers, with the Supreme Court as referee. During this era, the Supreme Court saw itself as an umpire between two competing power centers—the states and the federal government—each with its own responsibilities.

This orthodox view of the federal system prevailed until the New Deal of Franklin D. Roosevelt. During the 1930s the Roosevelt administration responded to the Great Depression with a series of laws establishing social-welfare and public works programs. In 1937 the Supreme Court began holding more of these programs constitutional. With the federal government thrust into a position of expanded power, a new view of federalism emerged, that of **cooperative federalism.** In this view, the various levels of government are seen as related parts of a single governmental system, characterized more by cooperation and shared functions than by conflict and competition. For example, the federal government provides most of the money to build major highways, but the program is administered by state and local governments. Some scholars have argued that, historically, the American federal system has always been characterized by such shared functions at the federal, state, and local levels.[9]

One student of the federal system, Michael D. Reagan, has suggested that it no longer makes sense to think of federalism "as a wall separating the national and state levels of government." Rather, he maintains, extensive federal financial aid to the states created *"a nationally dominated system of shared power and shared functions."*[10]

President Johnson used the term **creative federalism** to describe his own view of the relationship between Washington and the states. During his administration,

1935: President Franklin D. Roosevelt signs the Social Security Act.
Copyright © CORBIS/UPI/Bettmann

Smog in Houston: a target of regulatory federalism
Copyright © Jeff Greenberg/PhotoEdit

Congress enacted Great Society legislation that further expanded the role of the federal government. President Nixon launched what he termed the **new federalism,** designed to return federal tax money to state and local governments.

In recent years yet another concept, that of **regulatory federalism,** has emerged as a new description of the changing pattern of federal-state relations. Under this concept, the federal government has set requirements for the states through federal laws and regulations. The federal programs are then implemented by state and local governments. (The concept of regulatory federalism is discussed in greater detail later in this chapter.)

Beginning in the 1960s, a series of federal laws dealing with the environment and a broad range of other concerns imposed various requirements on the states. An example was the 1974 law mentioned at the opening of this chapter, since repealed, barring the release of any federal highway construction funds to states with speed limits over 55 miles per hour.[11]

The Clean Air Act of 1970 set federal air quality standards for the whole country, and required states that wished to regulate air quality to draft plans to enforce the federal standards. To a lesser extent, similar requirements were contained in the 1990 amendments to the act.

During the 1980s, President Reagan proposed a broad restructuring of federal-state relations. He asked that the welfare and other social programs costing billions of dollars be shifted to the states, with the federal government in return paying the states' share. Congress did not approve the plan.

Political scientist Donald F. Kettl has contended that Reagan's promise to relax federal rules and return more power to state governments was in reality "a Trojan horse . . . to disguise budget cuts." Reagan, he concluded, left the federal system "even more entangled in regulation and the problems that accompany it."[12]

TROUBLED WATERS: THE SECOND BATTLE OF NEW ORLEANS

NEW ORLEANS—Twelve Mile Point is just above the Huey P. Long Bridge on the Mississippi River. The river is 2,000 feet wide there, very deep and a main thoroughfare of one of the last independent breeds of riverboat kings.

Twelve Mile Point is also where a 600-foot cargo ship collided with a tug towing eight barges on a moonless evening in October 1986. No one was injured, but the collision set off one of the greatest river battles between the locals and the federals since Mark Twain plied these waters on the eve of the Civil War.

The ship was piloted by Capt. Robert M. (Mickey) Karr. . . . Why Karr had trouble at Twelve Mile Point has been debated at length, and the debate has escalated into a war between the National Transportation Safety Board (NTSB) and river pilots about states' rights.

The pilots handle ship traffic on the 143-mile stretch of the river between New Orleans and Baton Rouge, through a thicket of oil refineries, past such old sugar plantations as White Hall and a place known as Kamikaze Alley, named because of the erratic maneuvering sometimes required when a huge barge fleet moored there.

"Piloting is an art, it's not a science," [Capt. Martin] Gould said after NTSB probers returned to Washington. "The government can't treat it from a scientific approach. If they do, they're making a mistake."

This kind of mood about accident investigations extends throughout piloting, in part because river pilots have remained independent of federal regulation since 1851, when the Supreme Court, in deciding a Philadelphia case, ruled that the states should regulate pilots. Since then, the Coast Guard has tried to gain jurisdiction but has never succeeded. The Coast Guard investigates all marine accidents but has no jurisdiction on the Mississippi River, a state waterway. Therefore, its recommendations have no teeth.

The pilots said the dispute is a matter of principle. To them, it is about an abuse of power by a federal agency, despite the fact that NTSB recommendations are not binding. "This is America," Gould said. "I have a hell of a hard time understanding how Washington could allow these people to have that kind of power."

—Washington Post, January 2, 1988

The relationship between Washington and the states became an intense political issue once more during the Clinton administration after the Republicans came to power in Congress following the 1994 elections. The Republican-controlled Congress sought, wherever possible, to shift power away from Washington to the states.

In 1996, Congress passed and President Clinton signed a law that ended Aid to Families with Dependent Children (AFDC), the largest federal welfare program which assisted poor families. The law turned the program over to the states and compelled states that receive federal funds to require recipients in state welfare programs to find work within two years. Under the law, the federal government provides block grants to help finance state welfare programs.

Because regulatory federalism resulted in federal laws that required states to meet certain standards, but often provided no money to help the states comply, many governors and other state and local officials complained that such "unfunded mandates" were placing them under severe financial strain. Laws imposing standards on the states, the governors argued, should be accompanied by the necessary funds.

One often-cited example of the problem is the city of Columbus, Ohio, which faced costs of $1 billion to comply with the Clean Water Act and the Safe Drinking Water Act. Health officials in Columbus estimated the federal laws would cost each household an additional $685 a year throughout the 1990s. New York City officials estimated that it would cost $1.3 billion to modify elevators in subways to accommodate disabled persons under federal law, again with no help from the federal government.

One of the goals of the Republican "Contract with America," a list of legislative objectives of the Republican-controlled Congress elected in 1994, was to restrict such unfunded mandates. Congress passed a law to accomplish this and in March of 1995 President Clinton signed the Unfunded Mandates Reform Act. The law required Congress to fund mandates placed on the states unless a majority of the House and Senate voted not to do so. The law, however, applied only to new mandates and not to such past legislation as the Clean Air Act, the Clean Water Act, and the Motor Voter Act.

Many of these changes over the decades in the patterns and language of federalism reflect the fact that the United States has to a great extent become a national society. People may demand more power for the states and localities, but they also often look to Washington to solve problems. Today, for example, most people expect the federal government—not their

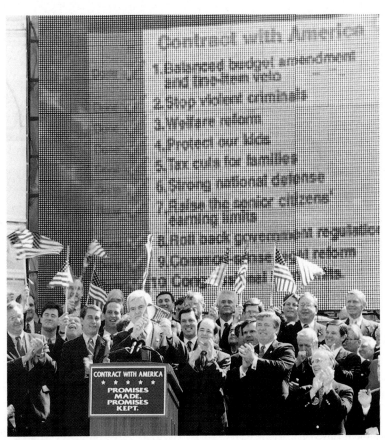

1995: In Washington, Newt Gingrich, then the House Speaker, leads House Republicans in celebrating the party's "Contract with America."
Mike Theiler/Reuters/Archive Photos

mayor or town council members—to deal with large-scale periodic economic difficulties, such as inflation and unemployment. But the need for solutions to major national problems has not resolved the larger question of how to make a federal system work. As one study viewed the problem:

> The basic dilemma . . . is how to achieve goals and objectives that are established by the national government, through the action of other governments, state and local, that are legally independent and politically may be hostile. Those state and local governments are subject to no federal discipline except through the granting or denial of federal aid. And that is not very useful, because to deny the funds is in effect to veto the national objective itself.[13]

THE HISTORICAL BASIS OF FEDERALISM

"A Middle Ground"

In April 1787, a month before the Constitutional Convention opened at Philadelphia, James Madison set forth his thoughts on the structure of a new government in a letter addressed to George Washington.

for more information about the Constitutional Convention and the Founding Fathers' views on federalism, see: http://lcweb2.loc.gov/const/ccongquery.html

Madison argued that while the states could not each be completely independent, the creation of "one simple republic" would be "unattainable." Madison wrote: "I have sought for a middle ground which may at once support a due supremacy of the national authority, and not exclude the local authorities wherever they can be subordinately useful."[14]

Essentially, Madison had forecast the balanced structure that emerged from a compromise five months later. The bargain struck at Philadelphia in 1787 was a federal bargain. The Constitutional Convention created the concept of the American federal system, with its sharing of power by the states and the national government. The delegates to the convention agreed to give up some of the states' independence in order to achieve enough unity to create a nation. Yet America probably got a federal system of government because no stronger national government would have been acceptable to the framers or to the states.

There are a number of reasons why a stronger central government would have been unacceptable. First, public opinion in the states almost certainly would not have permitted adoption of a unitary form of government. Loyalty to the states was strong. The Articles of Confederation showed just about how far people had been willing to go in the direction of a central government prior to 1787—which was not very far. The diversity of the American people, regional interests, even the state of technology—transportation was slow and great distances separated the colonies—all militated against the establishment of a central government stronger than the one framed at Philadelphia. Finally, federalism was seen as an effective device for limiting national power by distributing authority between the states and the national government.

A Tool for Nation Building

The collapse of European colonial empires since the Second World War confronted successful rebels in Africa and Asia with an urgent problem: how to organize their new nations. William H. Riker has suggested that large emerging nations face two alternatives: They can unite under a central government, in which case they have "merely exchanged one imperial master for a lesser one"; or they can join "in some kind of federation, which preserves at least the semblance of political self-control." He added, "In this sense, federalism is the main alternative to empire as a technique of aggregating large areas under one government."[15]

The framework of federalism in the United States first permitted a disunited people to find a basis for political union, and then allowed room for the development of a sense of national identity. As a result, "The United States of America" is not only the name of a country—to an extent, it is also a description of its formal governmental structure.

THE CONSTITUTIONAL BASIS OF FEDERALISM

Federal Powers: Enumerated, Implied, Inherent, and Concurrent

The Constitution established the framework for the American federal system. Certain **enumerated powers** are specifically granted to the three branches of the federal government under the Constitution. Congress, for example, has the power to coin money; the president is commander in chief of the armed forces.

In addition, the Supreme Court has held that the national government also has broad **implied powers** that flow from its enumerated powers and the "elastic clause" of the Constitution, which gives Congress power to make all laws "necessary and proper" to carry out its enumerated powers. For example, the right of the United States to establish a national banking system is an implied power flowing from its enumerated power to collect taxes and regulate commerce.[16]

The Supreme Court also has held that the national government has **inherent powers** that it may exercise simply because it exists as a government. One of the most important inherent powers is the right to conduct foreign relations. Because the United States does not exist in a vacuum, it must, as a practical matter, deal with other countries, even though the Constitution does not spell this out. The Court made clear in the *Curtiss-Wright* case that the "war power" of the United States government is an inherent power. It said, "The power to declare and wage war, to conclude peace, to make treaties, to maintain diplomatic relations with other sovereignties, if they had never been mentioned in the Constitution, would have vested in the federal government as necessary concomitants of nationality."[17]

Finally, the federal government and the states also have certain **concurrent powers,** which they exercise independently. The power to tax, for example, is enjoyed by both the federal and state governments. Of course, a state cannot exercise a power that belongs only to the federal government under the Constitution, nor can a state take actions that conflict with federal law.

These various powers are complex concepts. They developed slowly as the nation grew and found it necessary to adapt the Constitution to changing conditions.

The Supreme Court as Umpire

The Supreme Court serves as an arbiter in questions of state versus national power. The federal system could not function efficiently without an umpire.

The Court's attitude has changed radically over the decades; sometimes the Court has supported states' rights, and sometimes it has supported expanded federal power. But in every period, the Court has served as a major arena in which important conflicts are settled within the federal framework.

McCulloch _v._ Maryland   The most important of these Supreme Court decisions was that of Chief Justice John Marshall in _McCulloch_ v. _Maryland_ in 1819. His ruling established the doctrine of implied powers and gave the federal government sanction to take giant steps beyond the literal language of the Constitution.

James W. McCulloch might otherwise not have gone down in American history. But as it happened he was cashier of the Baltimore branch of the National Bank of the United States, which had been established by Congress. The National Bank had failed to prevent a business panic and economic depression in 1819, and some of its branches were managed by what can only be termed crooks. As a result, several states, including Maryland, tried to force the banks out of their states. Maryland slapped an annual tax of $15,000 on the National Bank. McCulloch refused to pay, setting the stage for the great courtroom battle of the day. Daniel Webster argued for the bank, and Luther Martin, attorney general of Maryland, for his state.

The first question answered by Marshall in his opinion for a unanimous Court was the basic question of whether Congress had power to incorporate a bank. Marshall laid down a classic definition of national sovereignty and broad constitutional construction:

"Congress . . . has the power to coin money."
AP/Wide World

"The government of the Union . . . is emphatically and truly a government of the people. In form and substance it emanates from them. Its powers are granted by them, and are to be exercised directly on them, and for their benefit."[18]

Marshall conceded that the Constitution divided sovereignty between the states and the national government but said that "the government of the Union, though limited in its powers, is supreme within its sphere of action." Although the power to charter a bank was not among the enumerated powers of Congress in the Constitution, he said, it could be inferred from the "necessary and proper" clause. In short, Congress had "implied powers." Even the Tenth Amendment, reserving certain powers to the states or the people, Marshall argued, did not prohibit the exercise of these implied powers.

"Let the end be legitimate," Marshall wrote, "let it be within the scope of the Constitution, and all means which are appropriate, which are plainly adapted to that end, which are not prohibited, but consist with the letter and spirit of the Constitution, are constitutional." Congress, Marshall said, had the right to legislate with a "vast mass of incidental powers which must be involved in the Constitution, if that instrument be not a splendid bauble."

On the second question of whether Maryland had the right to tax the National Bank, Marshall ruled against the state, for "the power to tax involves the power to destroy." No state, he said, possessed that right because this implied that the federal government depended on the will of the states. Marshall ruled the Maryland law unconstitutional.

Thus, at an early stage in the nation's history, Marshall established the key concepts of implied powers, broad construction of the Constitution, and national supremacy. More than 100 years would pass before these powers were exercised fully, but the decision laid the basis for the future growth of national power.

The Division of Federal and State Power

Under the Tenth Amendment, "The powers not delegated to the United States by the Constitution, nor prohibited by it to the States, are reserved to the States respectively, or to the people."

At first glance, this amendment might seem to limit the federal government to powers specifically enumerated

Chief Justice John Marshall: "Let the end be legitimate."
Copyright © CORBIS/Bettmann

After the First World War the Supreme Court struck down laws dealing with child labor. Here, children toil as coal miners in Pennsylvania.
AP/Wide World

and "delegated" to the federal government by the Constitution. But in deciding *McCulloch* v. *Maryland*, Chief Justice Marshall emphasized that the Tenth Amendment (unlike the Articles of Confederation) does not use the word "expressly" before the word "delegated."

This omission was not accidental. In 1789, during the debate on the first 10 amendments, James Madison and others blocked the attempt of states' rights advocates to limit federal powers to those "expressly" delegated.[19] During the debate, Madison objected to insertion of the key word "because it was impossible to confine a Government to the exercise of express powers; there must necessarily be admitted powers by implication, unless the Constitution descended to recount every minutia."[20]

The Supreme Court that followed the Marshall Court took a much narrower view of the powers of the federal government. Under Roger B. Taney, who served as chief justice from 1836 to 1864, the Court invoked the Tenth Amendment to protect the powers of the states. And in 1871 the Supreme Court ruled that the amendment meant that the federal government could not tax the salaries of state officials, a decision the Court later overruled.[21]

For two decades after the First World War, the Court invoked the Tenth Amendment to invalidate a series of federal laws dealing with child labor and regulating industry and agriculture. And in 1935 the Court

cited the amendment in declaring unconstitutional the National Industrial Recovery Act, a major piece of New Deal legislation designed to reduce unemployment.[22]

But in the watershed year of 1937, the Court swung around and upheld the Social Security program and the National Labor Relations Act as valid exercises of federal power.[23] And in 1941 it specifically rejected the argument that the Constitution in any way limited the power of the federal government to regulate interstate commerce. The decision upheld the Fair Labor Standards Act. Speaking for the Court, Chief Justice Harlan Fiske Stone called the Tenth Amendment "a truism that all is retained which has not been surrendered."[24]

Thus, more than 120 years after *McCulloch* v. *Maryland*, the Supreme Court swung back to John Marshall's view of the Constitution as an instrument that gave the federal government broad powers over the states and the nation. In the years that followed, however, the Supreme Court zig-zagged again. In 1976, the Court struck down a federal law extending federal minimum-wage and maximum-hour provisions to 3.4 million state and municipal workers.[25] But in 1983 the Court ruled that a federal law prohibiting age discrimination in employment protected Bill Crump, a supervisor for the Wyoming Game and Fish Department, who had been forced to retire at age 55.[26]

In 1985, the Supreme Court reversed its 1976 decision by holding, 5–4, that federal minimum-wage standards covered public transit workers.[27] The landmark case, *Garcia* v. *San Antonio Metropolitan Transit Authority*, confirmed the federal government's power to regulate the states.

A decade later, the pendulum swung in a completely opposite direction, when the Supreme Court sharply limited the power of the federal government to

Culver Pictures

intervene in state and local law enforcement.[28] The decision restricted the power of Congress, established in the Constitution, to regulate interstate commerce. Congress, the Court ruled 5–4, had exceeded its authority when it passed a law making it a federal crime to carry a gun within 1,000 feet of a school.

The decision struck down the Gun-Free School Zones Act of 1990. Now the Court had begun to reverse the trend of its decisions supporting federal power that had begun in 1937. Beginning in the mid-1990s, the Court, under Chief Justice William H. Rehnquist, handed down a series of decisions greatly strengthening states' rights against the power of the federal government.

In 1996, for example, the Supreme Court ruled that Congress could not require the states to negotiate over gambling casinos with Indian tribes.[29] In rapid succession, the Court invalidated a key section of the Brady gun control law that had required local sheriffs to check the backgrounds of gun buyers;[30] declared states immune from lawsuits by their employees for violation of federal

labor laws;[31] and, despite its earlier ruling for Bill Crump, the Wyoming game and fish supervisor, it held that states could not, after all, be sued by their employees under the federal age discrimination law.[32] And it struck down a key provision of the Violence Against Women Act of 1994, holding that Congress had exceeded its powers under the Constitution when it passed that law.[33] The trend continued in 2002 when the Supreme Court in *Federal Maritime Commission* v. *South Carolina Ports Authority* expanded state power by ruling that states did not have to answer private complaints before federal agencies.[34] The case arose when a cruise line complained to the Federal Maritime Commission that the port of Charleston, South Carolina, had denied a berth to one of its ships, the *Tropic Sea.* The Court's 5–4 ruling expanded the scope of the Eleventh Amendment to the Constitution, which bars private lawsuits against the states.

Many advocates of increasing the power of the states continue to rely on the Tenth Amendment as the constitutional foundation for their argument. In

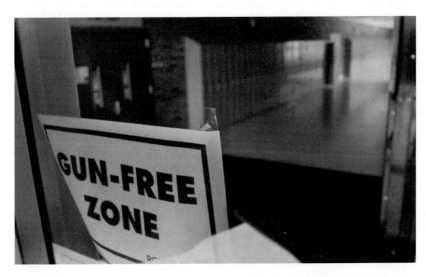

The Supreme Court invalidated a federal law banning guns within 1,000 feet of a school.
AP/Wide World

Christy Brzonkala reported she was raped by two football players at her college. The Supreme Court ruled she could not sue them in federal court.
AP/Wide World

general, they see the Constitution as the result of a compact among the states. It may also be argued, however, that the national government represents the people, and that sovereignty rests not with the states but with "we the people," who created the Constitution and approved it.

Restrictions on the States The **supremacy clause** of the Constitution (Article VI, Paragraph 2) makes it clear that the Constitution, and the laws and treaties of the United States made under it, are "the supreme Law of the Land" and prevail over any conflicting state constitutions or laws.

In addition, the Constitution places many restrictions on the states: They are forbidden to make treaties, coin money, pass bills of attainder or ex post facto laws, impair contracts, grant titles of nobility, tax imports or exports, keep troops or warships in peacetime, engage in war (unless invaded), or make interstate compacts without congressional approval. Much of the Bill of Rights, as interpreted by the Supreme Court, and the Fourteenth and Fifteenth Amendments place additional restrictions on the states.

Local governments derive their powers from the states and are subject to the same constitutional restrictions as are the states. If a state cannot do something, neither can a locality, since "in a strictly legal sense . . . all local governments in the United States are creatures of their respective states."[35]

Although the Constitution is supreme, under the American federal system, it should be noted again, each level of government possesses certain powers to make decisions that other levels cannot.

Federal Obligations to the States The Constitution (in Article IV) defines the relations of the federal government to the states. For example, the United States must guarantee to every state "a republican form of government." In addition, the federal government must protect the states against invasion and against domestic violence on request of the governor or legislature. Presidents have on several occasions intervened in the states with force either at the invitation of, or over the objections of, the governor.

Congress may admit new states to the Union, but the Constitution does not spell out any ground rules for their admission. In practice, when a territory has desired statehood, it has applied to Congress, which has passed an "enabling act" allowing the people of the territory to frame a constitution. If Congress approved the constitution, it passed a joint resolution recognizing the new state. (If in the future Congress should admit another state, it could follow this procedure or could adopt a new one.) As the frontier expanded westward, Congress steadily admitted new states until 1912, when New Mexico and Arizona, the last contiguous continental territories, became states. The 48 states became 50 in 1959 with the admission of Alaska and Hawaii—the only states of the Union that do not border on another state.

Interstate Relations Article IV of the Constitution also requires the states to observe certain rules in their dealings with one another.

First, states are required to give "full faith and credit" to the laws, records, and court decisions of another state. In practice, this simply means, for example, that a judgment obtained in a state court in a civil (not a criminal) case must be recognized by the courts of another state. If, for example, a person in New York loses a lawsuit and moves to California to avoid paying the judgment, the courts there will enforce the New York decision.

Sometimes, however, states fail to meet their obligations to one another. For example, a couple legally married in one state might not be legally married in another. In the famed *Williams* v. *North Carolina* cases[36]—the dispute went up to the Supreme Court twice—a man and a woman left their respective spouses in North Carolina, went to Nevada, got six-week divorces, and married each

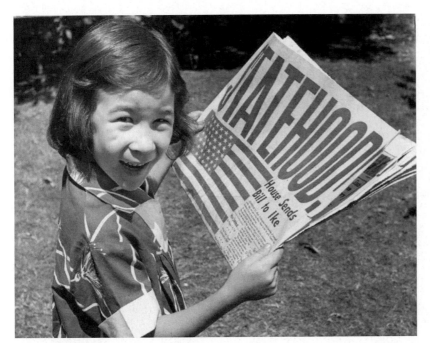

Hawaii celebrated statehood in 1959.
Hawaii State Archives/AP/Wide World

One famous example arose in the Scottsboro cases, which began in 1931 when nine black youths were pulled off a freight train in Alabama by a white mob and accused, on the basis of very flimsy evidence, of raping two young white women. There was considerable doubt that the crime had even been committed. In 1932, the Supreme Court reversed death sentences imposed on seven of the defendants, ruling that they had been denied adequate counsel,[37] but all drew long prison terms. Three years later, the Supreme Court again reversed the death sentences of two of the defendants because blacks had been excluded from the jury.[38] In 1948 one defendant, Haywood Patterson, escaped from an Alabama prison and fled north. He was later arrested in Detroit by the FBI, and the state of Alabama demanded his return. Governor G. Mennen Williams of Michigan refused to send him back to Alabama.[†]

other. When they returned home, the state of North Carolina successfully prosecuted them for bigamy, convictions that were upheld when the case reached the Supreme Court the second time.[*]

Second, the Constitution provides that the citizens of each state are entitled to "all privileges and immunities" of citizens in other states. As interpreted by the Supreme Court, this hazy provision has come to mean, in principle, that one state may not discriminate against citizens of another. But in practice, states do discriminate against persons who are not legal residents. For example, a state university often charges higher tuition fees to out-of-state students. For fishing and hunting licenses, nonresidents of a state must often pay much higher fees than residents pay.

Finally, the Constitution provides for the return of fugitives who flee across state lines to escape justice. A state may request the governor of another state to return fugitives, and normally the governor will comply with such a request. But in several instances in the past, northern governors refused to surrender blacks who had escaped from chain gangs or prisons in the South.

 Online *for more information about the Scottsboro cases, see:*
www.law.umkc.edu/faculty/projects/ftrials/scottsboro/
scottsb.html

[†]Patterson was convicted in 1951 of stabbing a man in a barroom brawl, sent to prison for manslaughter, and died there soon afterward. The other Scottsboro prisoners were freed on parole by 1950. Clarence Norris, believed to be the last survivor of the nine original defendants, was finally pardoned by the state of Alabama in 1976.

The states set their own marriage rules. Stacey Jolles, left, and Nina Beck, with their son, Seth, were joined in a civil union in Vermont in March 2000.
AP/Wide World

---

[*]Despite the confusion of the divorce laws, the situation had improved somewhat since an earlier landmark case, *Haddock v. Haddock,* 201 U.S. 562 (1906). In the words of one constitutional scholar: "The upshot [of that Supreme Court decision] was a situation in which a man and a woman, when both were in Connecticut, were divorced; when both were in New York, were married; and when the one was in Connecticut and the other in New York, the former was divorced and the latter married," in Edward S. Corwin et al., eds., *The Constitution of the United States of America, Analysis and Interpretation* (Washington, D.C.: U.S. Government Printing Office, 1964), p. 750.

Alabama, 1933: The defendants in the controversial Scottsboro case received long prison terms.
Copyright © CORBIS/UPI/Bettmann

Interstate Compacts The Constitution permits the states to make agreements with one another with the approval of Congress. These interstate compacts were of minor importance until the 20th century, but the spread of metropolitan areas—and metropolitan problems—across state borders and the increasing complexity of modern life have brought new significance to the agreements.

The Port Authority of New York and New Jersey was created by an interstate compact between the two states and approved by Congress in 1921. The powerful and quasi-independent authority operates, among other things, John F. Kennedy International Airport and La Guardia Airport in New York and Newark Airport in New Jersey. It also controls and runs the bridges and tunnels leading into Manhattan, and the world's largest bus terminal, near Times Square. Air and water pollution, pest control, toll bridges, and transportation are matters on which states have entered into agreements with one another, with varying degrees of success. A state often enters into several interstate compacts that deal with these and other regional concerns.

THE GROWTH OF STRONG NATIONAL GOVERNMENT

The late Senator Everett McKinley Dirksen of Illinois, a legislator noted for his Shakespearean delivery and dramatic flair, once predicted sadly that the way things were going, "The only people interested in state boundaries will be Rand McNally."[39]

This may be an exaggerated view of trends in the American federal system—especially in the light of the series of recent Supreme Court decisions favoring the states—but Dirksen's remark reflected the fact that, overall, the national government has gained increased power in relation to the states. The formal structure of American government has changed very little since 1787, but the balance of power within the system has changed markedly.

The Rise of Big Government

A century ago, the federal government did not provide Social Security, medical insurance for millions of citizens, vast aid to public and private education, or billions of dollars in welfare payments to the states. Nor did it have independent regulatory agencies to watch over various segments of the economy.

As American society has grown more complex, as population has surged, the national government's managerial task has enlarged. People demand more services and government has grown bigger in the process. Six cabinet departments—Housing and Urban Development, Transportation, Energy, Health and Human Services, Education, and Veterans Affairs—have been created since 1965.

The power to tax and spend for the general welfare is a function of the national government that expanded

A dinner party in Dallas . . .
Copyright © Topham/Image Works

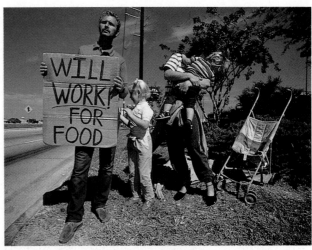

. . . and a homeless family in California.
Copyright © Dan Ford Connolly

enormously in the 20th century. The government's role in the regulation of interstate and foreign commerce has also increased.

Much of the growth of big government and of federal social-welfare programs took place under Democratic presidents, during the New Deal in the 1930s and during Lyndon Johnson's Great Society in the 1960s. Although conservatives attacked these programs as "handouts" that create dependence on government, the major programs were so well established that the Republican presidents elected in the 1980s were not able to abolish them. President Reagan, for example, came into office in 1981 determined to make substantial cuts in federal spending in the field of social welfare. He had repeatedly pledged to do so in his campaign for the presidency.

And during the Reagan Administration there were indeed billions of dollars in cuts in domestic spending—in social-welfare and food programs designed to assist the poor as well as in a broad range of other programs aimed at helping low-income families, including Medicaid, housing subsidies, and student loans. Together, these spending cuts came to be known popularly as "the Reagan revolution."

But how big were the reductions in domestic spending? The Reagan White House claimed it had reduced federal domestic programs by $232 billion during the administration's first four years, compared to projected spending by the previous Democratic administration.[40] But in the public debate over budget cuts there was "confusion as to exactly what had been accomplished."[41] In part, this was because federal spending actually increased in many of the programs that the Reagan administration claimed it had cut. In most cases, the "cuts" were reductions in what might have been spent.

Nevertheless, the Reagan program did have a measurable impact on government spending and on the outputs of the political system. The budget cuts "landed heavily on the poor and near poor. Education and training, community development, welfare, nutri-

tion, housing assistance and other antipoverty programs suffered most."[42]

And the rich got richer. According to one survey of incomes by the Congressional Budget Office, for the 2.5 million people in the top 1 percent in America, incomes rose by about 75 percent between 1980 and 1990, to an average of more than $500,000 a year.[43]

After the Republicans captured Congress in 1994 there were new attempts, led by House Speaker Newt Gingrich, to dismantle or modify social programs and to shift control over them to the states. That effort achieved a major goal in 1996 when Congress passed, and President Clinton signed into law, the bill shifting the federal welfare program to the states.

These political struggles revolve around the basic question of how power should be shared or divided in the federal system. The role of the federal government, particularly in the field of social-welfare programs, will undoubtedly continue to be debated in America. Although a particular administration or Congress may reduce the share of the pie allocated to social programs, the pie itself—the federal budget—keeps growing. Even as the states take on more responsibilities, many Americans still tend to look to the national government to solve national problems.

Big Government and Foreign Policy

The responsibility of the federal government for the conduct of foreign affairs in the nuclear age has increased the size of the national government. In fiscal 2001, for example, the budget request for national defense was more than $306 billion, a substantial 16.7 percent of the total federal budget, and, except for Social Security, the largest single item.[44] The State Department, the Central Intelligence Agency, the National Security Agency, and related agencies have expanded along with the Pentagon.

With the collapse of the Soviet Union in 1991, the military threat to the United States had diminished

"The defense budget remained high. . . ." An Air Force F-117 stealth fighter plane
DOD/Woodfin Camp & Associates

dramatically, but the defense budget remained high. Defense industries and military bases provided jobs for many Americans and enjoyed strong support in Congress, where members are sensitive to the concerns of their districts. Partly as a result, the so-called "peace dividend"—the funds allocated to national defense that might be spent on domestic needs because of the end of the Cold War—seemed elusive.

THE IMPACT OF FEDERALISM ON GOVERNMENT AND POLITICS

America's government institutions and its political system developed within a framework of federalism, and they reflect that fact. Federalism has also placed its stamp on a broad range of informal activities in American society, including the operations of many private groups.

Federalism and Government

The nature of representation in Congress reflects the impact of federalism. Each state, no matter how small, has two senators who represent the constituents of their state. Members of the House represent districts within the states, but they also constitute an informal delegation from their states. Senators and representatives, when elected, must reside in the states they represent. In the event of a deadlock in the electoral college, the House of Representatives votes by state to select the president, with each state having one vote.

Federalism also affects the court system. State and local courts exist side by side with federal courts in the United States and handle the vast majority of cases. But even the federal district courts and circuit courts are organized along geographic lines that take into account state boundaries. And, under the custom of "senatorial courtesy," before the president appoints a federal district or circuit court judge, the White House privately submits the name to the senators representing the home state of the nominee. If the state has a senator from the same party as the president, and that senator objects, the name is usually dropped.*

Many powerful interest groups are in a sense federations of state associations and groups. This is true, for example, of the American Medical Association, the American Bar Association, and to some extent the American Federation of Labor–Congress of Industrial Organizations (AFL-CIO).

Federalism and American Politics

When Governor George W. Bush of Texas sought the Republican presidential nomination in 2000, his first big test came in the Iowa caucuses in January. Bush won in Iowa, but lost to his most serious challenger, Senator John McCain of Arizona, in the New Hampshire primary on February 1. A number of primary victories on "Super Tuesday" in early March, including California, Ohio, and New York, assured Bush of his party's nomination.

Today, as a rule, the victory of a national political candidate is achieved long before it is ratified by the delegates in a noisy convention hall in the heat of July or August. Often, the candidate's eventual triumph gains its first momentum in the snows of New Hampshire in February. But other key primary states also may play an important role; in 1992 Bill Clinton's victories in Illinois, New York, and Pennsylvania helped to secure his position as the front-runner for the Democratic presidential nomination.

As the primary contests illustrate dramatically, federalism affects party politics in the United States. National political parties are organized along federal lines. The United States has no national party system such as that in Britain, for example. Rather, a federation of 50 state parties is precariously held together by a national committee between presidential nominating conventions.

The governors' chairs in the 50 states are political prizes. As a result, 50 centers of political power in the states compete with the locus of national power in Washington.

 for more information about the National Governors' Association, see:
www.nga.org

---

*As the system of senatorial courtesy has operated in recent years, some presidents have notified both home-state senators of potential nominees, even when one or more senator does not belong to the president's party. However, in practice, only an objection by a member of the president's party is likely to affect a nomination.

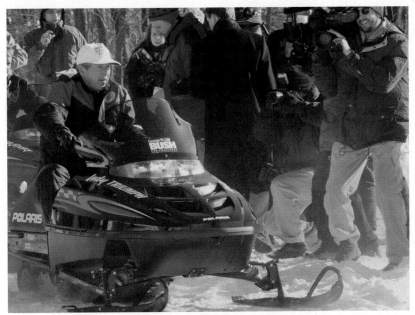

Republican presidential candidate George W. Bush tries out a snowmobile in New Hampshire during that state's primary campaign in January 2000.
AP/Wide World

Although state political parties constitute basic political units in the United States, state political systems vary greatly. In some states, such as New York, there is lively competition between Democrats and Republicans. Other states have often been dominated by one party. The makeup of the electorate in the states may differ from that of the nation as a whole. For example, proportionately, there are fewer Democrats in Kansas and Nebraska than in the national electorate.

State governments also vary in what they do and in the quality of their performance. How good are the schools in a state? Does the state have effective programs in the fields of health services, penology, welfare, law enforcement, and pollution control? As anyone who has driven across America knows, some states just look (and are) wealthier; they have better state roads, for example. Some have adopted innovative social programs that have led the way for other states and the federal government.

To a party out of power nationally, the existence of state political machinery takes on special importance. By building up state parties and demonstrating leadership ability on the state level, the "out party" may consolidate its position and prepare for the next national election. Often a strong governor or a former governor will emerge as a contender for the party's presidential nomination.

Policy Outcomes in the States   Inasmuch as state governments do vary in quality, does the nature of a political system in a state affect the types of public policies adopted in the state? In other words, does the

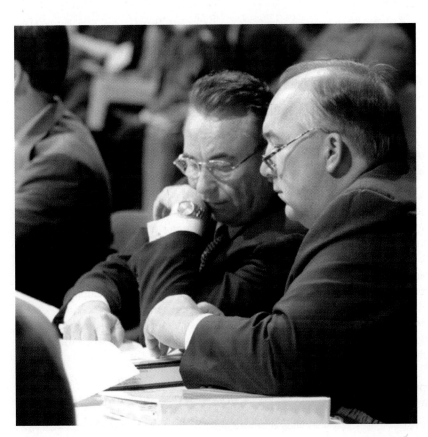

State governors may play important political roles. Gov. Tommy G. Thompson, R., Wisconsin, confers with Gov. John Engler, R., Michigan.
Courtesy National Governor's Association

MAKING A DIFFERENCE
THE SUPREME COURT RULES FOR BRENDA ROE

After Congress transferred the federal welfare program to the states in 1996, a woman who preferred to be known as "Brenda Roe," to preserve her privacy, moved her family from Oklahoma, where they had received $300 a month in welfare benefits, to California, where the family qualified for $600 a month.

But there was a catch: To discourage people from moving to California to receive higher benefits, the state had passed a law limiting benefits for new residents; for one year they could collect only the same amount they had received in their previous state. About 15 states had enacted such laws, which Congress had allowed in the 1996 law overhauling the welfare system.

Brenda Roe and other families in the same boat sued the state of California. On the face of it, the California law seemed to restrict the right of all Americans to travel and to live where they wish.

The case went all the way to the Supreme Court, where the justices heard arguments early in 1999. It was the first major high court test of the nation's welfare reform law.

The question before the Court was whether a two-tiered benefit policy unfairly hurt needy people who want to move from one state to another.

In oral arguments, California said its program kept down costs and ensured that the state would not become a magnet for poor families. But Justice Ruth Bader Ginsburg suggested the policy violated a fundamental principle "that is the genius of the United States . . . that people can pick their states and states can't pick their people."

"This has grave consequences for [a] family," said Justice Sandra Day O'Connor.

On May 17, 1999, the Supreme Court ruled in the case of *Saenz* v. *Roe*. It held, 7–2, that states may not limit

welfare benefits for new residents, and it struck down the California law. The Court said a two-tier system violates poor people's right to travel and encroaches on their right to be treated like other residents of their new state.

"Citizens of the United States, whether rich or poor, have the right to choose to be citizens of the state wherein they reside," Justice John Paul Stevens wrote for the court. "The states, however, do not have any right to select their citizens."

The former Oklahoma woman who called herself Brenda Roe had, with the help of the U.S. Supreme Court, won her constitutional right to be treated like other citizens of the state of California. And her victory won those same equal rights for many other needy families struggling to make ends meet.

—Adapted from the *Washington Post*, January 14 and May 18, 1999

---

politics of a state make a difference in the lives of the people of that state?

Political scientists have done a good deal of research on this question, and their answers have varied. One analysis suggested that states with active two-party competition were more likely to enact broad

social-welfare programs because both parties would compete for the votes of a state's "have-nots."[45]

Later studies found that socioeconomic factors (whether a state was rich or poor in per capita income), rather than political factors, seemed to account for most of the differences in state welfare expenditures and for

---

TOGA! TOGA! FROM *ANIMAL HOUSE* TO THE STATEHOUSE

WASHINGTON, July 25—In a scene straight out of *Animal House*, the Massachusetts House of Representatives mixed the low art of late-night partying with the serious business of writing the government's budget for the coming year. They guzzled beer and snoozed in back offices. They chanted "Toga! Toga!" on the House floor, according to witnesses, while staffers took turns voting in the place of members missing from the chamber.

Amid the rowdiness that closed out this year's annual budget deliberations, the House quietly tucked into a spending bill language that would gut an ethics law enacted years earlier.

Such frat-house antics might not be typical in the gilded chambers of America's state legislatures, but

attempts to weaken ethics laws that govern the conduct of legislators are becoming commonplace. In recent years, lawmakers in at least a dozen states have dismantled the strongest provisions of ethics laws or prevented passage of new, tougher ones. They have stranded ethics-related bills in committees, driven truck-size loopholes through disclosure laws already on the books, and chipped away at the power of watchdog agencies.

The result: The measures for holding some state lawmakers accountable are eroding at a time when the influence of legislatures is growing.

—Robert Moore, *The Public I, An Investigative Report of the Center for Public Integrity*, 1999 differences in spending, taxing, and services among the states.[46] But another study concluded that if taxing and spending in a state were measured in terms of their redistributive impact—who gets what and who pays for it—then the politics of the state was considerably more important than its economics. Lower socioeconomic groups did fare better, for example, in states with certain political characteristics, such as higher levels of political participation.[47] Additional studies have suggested that other variables, besides politics and economics, may affect the policies of a state government. Religion, demographic factors, and in particular the actions of bureaucrats and the organization of a state government's bureaucracy may all play important roles.[48]

The fact that America has a federal system directly affects people's lives because the quality of the services provided by the states in which people live varies greatly. Not only the structure and performance of government but the whole political process is federalized.

FEDERALISM TODAY

The Budget of the United States Government, Fiscal Year 2001 is a black-and-white-covered volume the size of a telephone book and two inches thick. To the nonexpert, it seems a bewildering mass of statistics and gobbledygook, filled with phrases such as "object classification" and "unobligated balance lapsing."

 Online for more information about the U.S. government budget, see: *http://w3.access.gpo.gov/usbudget*

Buried in the budget's somewhat mysterious statistics are figures that add up to a substantial total of federal aid to state and local governments. For fiscal 2001, the amount was estimated at $305.6 billion.[49] The following figures show the sharp increase in federal aid to state and local governments since 1950:

1950: $ 2.3 billion	1985: $105.9 billion
1960: $ 7.0 billion	1990: $135.3 billion
1970: $24.1 billion	1995: $225.0 billion
1980: $91.4 billion	2001 estimate: $305.6 billion

Any analysis of American government must take into account the huge sums of money flowing from people and corporations in the states, to Washington in the form of taxes, and back out again in the form of federal aid. It is here that federalism moves from the realm of theory into practical meaning in terms of dollars and cents.

The federal government channels money to states and local communities in three ways:

Categorical grants, also known as grants-in-aid, are earmarked for specific purposes only, such as Medicaid, pollution control, schools, or hospitals, for example.

Block grants are for general use in a broad area, such as community development.

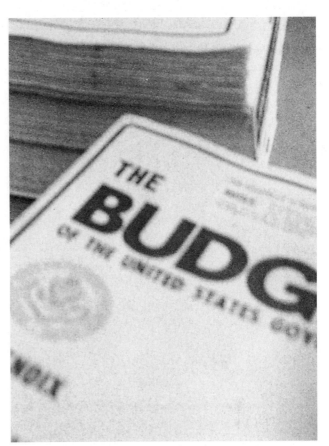

General purpose grants, the smallest category, may be used by states and localities mostly as they wish.

By far the largest amount of federal aid comes in the form of categorical grants. Block grants rank next, and then general purpose aid. (See Figure 3-2.) As discussed earlier, after the Republicans won control of Congress in 1994 they tried to shift money away from categorical grants and into block grants that would give the states substantially more power in deciding how to spend the money. One example was the bill passed by Congress in 1996 to revamp the welfare system; it ended federal "entitlements" to poor families with children and turned money over to the states instead, in the form of block grants. The measure, as noted earlier in the chapter, was signed into law by President Clinton.

Categorical Grants

In fiscal 2001, as in previous years, the great bulk of federal aid to states and local communities came in the form of categorical grants-in-aid. A categorical grant is "money paid or furnished to state or local governments to be used for specific purposes"[50] in ways spelled out by law or administrative regulations. There are hundreds of such separate grant programs administered by various federal agencies. Not surprisingly, many state and local officials have complained that the maze of federal grants-in-aid creates a burdensome amount of paperwork for them.

FIGURE 3-2

The Federal Aid Pipeline: 1995 Grants to States and Localities

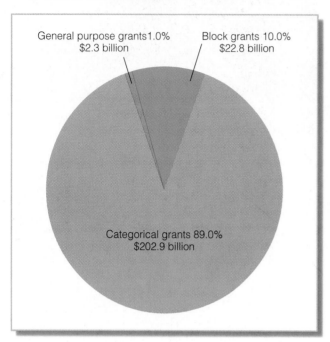

General purpose grants 1.0%
$2.3 billion

Block grants 10.0%
$22.8 billion

Categorical grants 89.0%
$202.9 billion

Typical categorical grants have been in the fields of education, pollution control, highways, conservation, and recreation. The Medicaid and Food Stamp programs are examples of two very large categorical grants.

The federal government distributes most aid under formulas that take into account the needs of the states; for example, grants for education are based on the number of low-income children, and grants for social services are based on population. To be eligible for federal aid, the state and local governments must sometimes meet matching requirements. That is, Washington requires the recipients to put up some of their own funds in order to get the federal money. When local governments and states match federal money, they sometimes do so according to a formula that takes into account their ability to pay. Under the formula, poor states pay less than rich states. For most programs, however, all states pay the same matching share.

It is in the administration of federal grants that the gears of national, state, and local governments mesh or collide. Federal fiscal aid is the primary means by which local, state, and federal governments interre-

late. In dealing with such programs as education or welfare services, mayors, governors, and lesser officials communicate with one another and with administrators and legislators in Washington. Because of these aid programs, the lines of the federal system criss-cross, linking various levels of government that must cope with common problems from pollution to poverty.

The result is both cooperation and conflict. For example, cities and states collaborate in a wide range of programs such as law enforcement and highway planning. But as a group, mayors tend to distrust state governments; they argue that the states are receiving too large a share of federal revenues at a time when the cities are desperate for funds.

Block Grants

In addition to categorical grants, since the 1960s aid to the states and local communities has also flowed from Washington in the form of block grants. These grants are used "within a broad functional area largely at the recipient's discretion."[51] Among the major block grants typically included in the federal budget are programs for community development, social services, health care, employment and training, and education.

Revenue Sharing: The End of the Experiment

Between 1972 and 1986, the federal government turned over $83 billion in federal tax monies to state and local governments to spend at will under a program known

"It's too bad you can't get federal matching funds, whatever they are."

as general revenue sharing. The program was controversial—critics feared that local governments might use the money to build golf courses instead of health clinics, and some did. Revenue sharing proved very popular with local communities. However, many members of Congress objected to appropriating federal funds without controlling how the money was spent and the program was ended.

Where the Money Goes

How was the estimated $305.6 billion total in federal aid to the states spent in fiscal 2001? Federal budget estimates show that almost all of it was allocated to eight major categories: health; income security; education, training, employment, and social services; transportation; community and regional development; natural resources and the environment; general government; and agriculture, in that order. (Figure 3-3 and Table 3-2 show where the money goes.)

Fiscal Headaches in the Federal System As state and local authorities have argued, state and local spending has increased at an even faster rate than federal spending. Yet the federal government collects 81 percent of the most important "growth" tax—the income tax, more than four times as much as states collect from income taxes.[52] These revenues from federal individual and corporate income taxes directly reflect economic growth, providing the federal government with increased tax receipts in an expanding economy. By contrast, local governments rely mainly on real estate taxes, and state governments depend heavily on sales taxes; both of these sources of revenue tend to grow less rapidly than the economy as a whole. Although more states were taxing

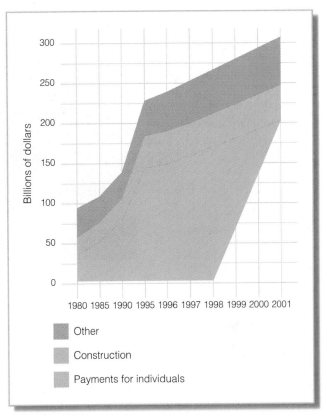

FIGURE 3-3

Federal Grants to State and Local Governments, 1980–2001

- Other
- Construction
- Payments for individuals

SOURCE: Adapted from *Analytical Perspectives, Budget of the United States Government, Fiscal Year 2001* (Washington, D.C.: U.S. Government Printing Office, 2000), p. 241. Construction grants are for highways, airports, mass transit, community development, and other facilities. Other grants are for education, training, employment, and social services. Figures for 1999–2001 are estimated.

TABLE 3-2

Where the Money Goes: Federal Grants to State and Local Governments, by Function, 2001 (in billions of dollars)

Percent	Category	Total	Major Items
43.7	Health	$133.4	Medical assistance
22.0	Income security	67.2	Unemployment compensation, retirement, and welfare-to-work
15.3	Education, training, employment, and social services	46.8	Aid to elementary and secondary schools, job training, and foster care
11.2	Transportation	34.3	Highways
2.7	Community and regional renewal	8.2	Housing and urban development
1.6	Natural resources and environment	5.0	Construction of sewage treatment plants
0.7	General government	2.2	Collection of taxes
0.3	Agriculture	0.8	Crop insurance; animal and plant health programs
2.5	Other	7.6	National defense, energy, veterans' benefits, and administration of justice
Total 100		$305.6	

SOURCE: Adapted from *Analytical Perspectives, Budget of the United States Government, Fiscal Year 2001* (Washington, D.C.: U.S. Government Printing Office, 2000), p. 246. Figures and percentages are estimated and rounded.

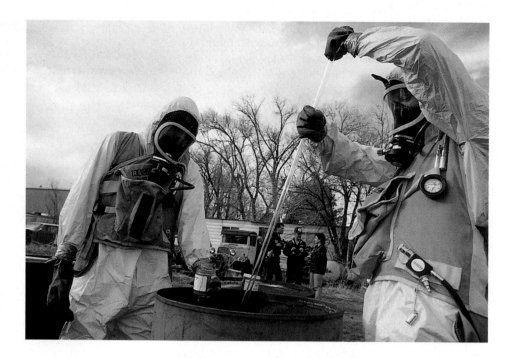

Environmental Protection Agency workers measuring toxic waste in Denver
Copyright © A. Ramey/PhotoEdit

personal income by the year 2000, there were still seven states that did not.*

Regulatory Federalism

Beginning in the 1960s and continuing to the present, a series of federal laws have imposed strict standards on state and local governments. The Clean Water Act, for example, required cities to spend nearly $120 billion to build wastewater treatment plants. As discussed earlier in this chapter, the growth of such federal programs aimed at, or implemented by, state and local governments has been termed regulatory federalism.[53]

Legislation with this kind of impact on state and local governments includes the 1964 Civil Rights Act, the 1965 Highway Beautification Act, the 1970 Occupational Safety and Health Act, as well as many other laws dealing with clean air and water, endangered species, education, employment, and persons with disabilities.

Some of these laws apply directly to the states or local governments. The Equal Employment Opportunity Act of 1972, for example, bars job discrimination by states or localities on the basis of race, religion, sex, and national origin.

Other laws cut across all federal programs. The 1964 Civil Rights Act, for instance, prohibits discrimination under any program that receives federal money. Other laws "cross over" and impose rules in one area of government activity to influence policy in another area; the 1974 law, later repealed, holding back federal highway funds for states that refused to adopt and enforce the

nationwide speed limits set by Congress is one such example. Another was the 1984 law withholding up to 10 percent of federal highway funds from states with a drinking age under 21. And finally, some laws, such as

Copyright © Bob Daemmrich/Stock, Boston

---

*States with no federal income tax in 1999 were Alaska, Florida, Nevada, South Dakota, Texas, Washington, and Wyoming.

Clean Air Act of 1970 and its later amendments, set standards for the states.

Many of these federal laws were passed to meet national goals, such as providing cleaner air and water. And often, those goals were supported by states and communities. But the complex federal requirements contained in these laws, and the extensive paperwork that goes with them, have given rise to intergovernmental tensions and to a continuing debate over the nature of regulatory federalism.

As discussed earlier in this chapter, in 1995 Congress passed a law curbing "unfunded mandates." For any new legislation, the law obliged Congress to fund requirements placed on the states by the federal government unless a majority of the House and Senate voted not to do so.

THE FUTURE OF FEDERALISM

Clearly, the shape of relations among Washington, the statehouses, and city halls has changed considerably over time and continues to be characterized by both conflict and cooperation.

But new ideas have been introduced into the mix. The state of Minnesota, for example, has dramatically modified state and local fiscal relations. Minnesota revamped its system of school aid to ensure equal funds for students throughout the state, regardless of the wealth of the school districts where they lived.

By the mid 1990s two-thirds of the states and the District of Columbia had adopted a "circuit breaker" system of property tax relief for low-income homeowners and for the aged. Persons in these categories, below certain income ceilings, were guaranteed property tax reductions.

LaTanya Brown's life changed when she enrolled in a welfare-to-work program in Hampton, Virginia. She landed a job as a pharmacy technician.
AP/Wide World

The vast problems of metropolitan areas provide one of the greatest challenges to the American federal system. Some efforts have been made at new approaches. For example, increasing attention has been paid to solving problems on a metropolitan areawide basis. Many communities, especially in urban areas, have ignored traditional political jurisdictional lines to pool their efforts in attacking common problems (such as pollution) that respect no political boundaries, and in planning to take advantage of federal grants. Some federal legislation has been designed to assist and encourage areawide solutions to urban problems.

Yet serious dislocations and new problems of regulatory federalism continue to plague the federal system. Many critics of the federal structure question whether states are willing or able to meet their responsibilities. By contrast, defenders of the states have noted that most of the successful programs of the New Deal "had been anticipated, by experiment and practice, on the state level or by private institutions."[54]

In the 1990s, when the pendulum swung against such programs, the states were once again ahead of Congress. In 1995, as Congress and the president deadlocked over welfare reform, many states, including Wisconsin, California, and Michigan, were already testing new programs that required most welfare recipients to work or that limited the length of time that benefits were paid. In 1996, President Clinton endorsed the Wisconsin plan. Soon after, he signed the law turning over the largest federal welfare program to the states.

The booming economy of the 1990s was dramatically reflected in the states, virtually all of which were enjoying strong financial health. By 1998, a majority of the states had cut a total of $7 billion in taxes, more than at any time in the past, despite a projected loss of tax revenues from the sale of goods over the Internet.[55] The economic expansion that had brought unprecedented prosperity to many Americans might not last indefinitely, however. There were substantial underlying tensions and conflicts in the federal system, even as the Supreme Court grappled with the proper balance of power between the states and the national government.

The problems that confronted America in the 21st century continued to raise the fundamental question of whether a federal system born in compromise more than two centuries ago can adapt itself to the needs of a technological, urban society in an age of onrushing change.

KEY TERMS

federal system, p. 60
federalism, p. 60
unitary system of
    government, p. 60
dual federalism, p. 65
cooperative federalism,
    p. 65
creative federalism, p. 65
new federalism, p. 66
regulatory federalism,
    p. 66

enumerated powers,
    p. 68
implied powers, p. 68
inherent powers, p. 68
concurrent powers, p. 68
supremacy clause, p. 72
categorical grants, p. 79
block grants, p. 79
general purpose grants,
    p. 79

CHAPTER HIGHLIGHTS

✦ The United States has a federal system of government, in which power is constitutionally shared by a national government and 50 state governments.

✦ The terms "federalism" and "the federal system" are used interchangeably to describe this basic structure of government in the United States.

✦ The federal system has been viewed differently at various times. Until 1937 the concept of dual federalism prevailed—the federal government and the states were seen as competing power centers, with the Supreme Court as referee.

✦ Then, as the federal government's power expanded, the concept of cooperative federalism emerged, with the various levels of government seen as related parts of a single governmental system, characterized more by cooperation and shared functions than by conflict and competition.

✦ In recent years another concept, that of regulatory federalism has emerged, under which the federal government has set requirements for the states through federal laws and regulations.

✦ The Constitution established the framework for the American federal system. Certain enumerated powers are specifically granted to the three branches of the federal government under the Constitution.

✦ The Supreme Court has held that the national government also has broad implied powers that flow from its enumerated powers and the elastic clause of the Constitution, which gives Congress power to make all laws "necessary and proper" to carry out its enumerated powers.

✦ The Supreme Court also has held that the national government has inherent powers that it may exercise simply because it exists as a government.

✦ The federal government and the states also have certain concurrent powers, which they exercise independently.

✦ The supremacy clause of the Constitution (Article VI, Paragraph 2) makes it clear that the Constitution, and the laws and treaties of the United States made under it, are "the supreme Law of the Land" and prevail over any conflicting state constitutions or laws.

✦ The federal government channels money to states and local communities in three ways: categorical grants, block grants and general purpose grants.

SUGGESTED WEB SITES

www.whitehouse.gov/omb/index.html
The Office of Management and Budget
The Office of Management and Budget (OMB) controls the administration of the federal budget. OMB's site includes links to the current and previous budgets, OMB bulletins, legislative information, and other budget information.

www.jamesmadison.org
The James Madison Institute
The James Madison Institute is a public policy research organization dedicated to the principles of federalism. The site offers access to the quarterly publication of *The Journal of the James Madison Institute*, the monthly newsletter *The Madison Messenger*, and excerpts from current books and studies.

www.min.net/~kala/fed
U.S. Federalism Site
Developed by a George Washington University graduate student, the U.S. Federalism Site offers various definitions of federalism, perspectives on federalism, and links to federalism resources.

www.vote-smart.org/index.phtml
Federalism from Project Vote Smart
Project Vote Smart, a nonprofit, nonpartisan Web site, researches issues affecting voters and people running for office. Go to Issue Links in the left-hand frame, then to Federalism/States Rights. The federalism section offers historical background on federalism and philosophical perspectives on this topic.

www.closeup.org/federal.htm
Close Up Foundation on Federalism
The Close Up Foundation, a nonprofit, nonpartisan citizenship education organization, offers a time line of federalism and links to historical documents, outside analysis, government Web sites, and media resources.

SUGGESTED READING

Beer, Samuel H. *To Make a Nation: The Rediscovery of American Federalism** (The Belknap Press of Harvard University Press, 1993). An illuminating study of the various theories of federalism that have been advocated in America. The author emphasizes the practical consequences those theories have had for American politics and government.

Bowman, Ann O'M., and Kearney, Richard C. *The Resurgence of the States* (Prentice Hall, 1986). A survey of salient trends in state government and politics in the United States. Argues that by the mid-1980s most state governments had been revitalized, and that the states continue to be highly important institutions in the American system of government.

Conlan, Timothy. *From New Federalism to Devolution: Twenty-five Years of Intergovernmental Reform** (The Brookings Institution, 1998). An account of three waves of reform efforts, from 1969 to 1995, aimed at limiting the power of the national government and shifting many of its responsibilities to the states.

Davis, S. Rufus. *The Federal Principle: A Journey through Time in Quest of Meaning* (University of California Press, 1978). An examination of the history of federalism from the Hellenic age through the 20th century. Contains an interesting analysis of the American model of federalism created at the Constitutional Convention of 1787.

Derthick, Martha. *Between State and Nation: Regional Organizations of the United States** (The Brookings Institution, 1974). An analysis of the theory and actual operation of regional organizations in the American federal system. The Appalachian Regional Commission, the Tennessee Valley Authority, and the Delaware River Basin Commission are among the regional organizations discussed.

Donahue, John. *Disunited States* (Basic Books, 1997). An examination of the push for the decentralization of governmental power, and the transferring of certain programs from the federal government to the states. The author argues that there are many functions which Washington can perform more effectively than state governments.

Elazar, Daniel J. *American Federalism: A View from the States*, 3rd edition (Harper & Row, 1984). A good general treatment of American federalism. The book emphasizes some of the problems and areas of controversy in contemporary intergovernmental relationships, and traces the historical roots of cooperation and shared functions among the various layers of government in the federal system.

Grodzins, Morton. *The American System* (Transaction Books, 1983). (Edited by Daniel J. Elazar.) A comprehensive analysis of American federalism by a leading authority on the subject.

Hovey, Harold A. *The Devolution Revolution: Can the States Afford Devolution?** (The Century Foundation, 1998). An analysis of the effort to shift programs away from the national government to the states, and the economic constraints which states face in meeting those new responsibilities.

Kincaid, John. *American Federalism: The Third Century* (The Annals of the American Academy of Political and Social Science, Vol. 509, May 1990). A valuable survey of trends in the American federal system. Stresses the complicated relationships among the national government, state governments, and local governments in the United States.

Peterson, Paul E. *The Price of Federalism** (The Brookings Institution, 1995). A thoughtful assessment of how the federal system actually worked in the United States in the 1990s. The author evaluates both the strengths and the weaknesses of contemporary American federalism.

Reagan, Michael D., and Sanzone, John G. *The New Federalism*, 2nd edition* (Oxford University Press, 1981). An excellent study of the pattern of federalism in the United States. The book questions traditional definitions of a federal system and examines the development of federal grants-in-aid, the limited ability of state governments to finance public services, and the dominant role of the federal government in the American federal system.

Riker, William H. *Federalism: Origin, Operation, Significance* (Little, Brown, 1964). An historical and comparative analysis of federalism. Riker examines with great clarity the conditions that give rise to federalism and maintain it. He is sharply critical of certain aspects of American federalism and argues that historically it permitted the oppression of blacks.

Walker, David B. *The Rebirth of Federalism*, 2nd edition* (Seven Bridges Press, 1999). A detailed analysis of the conflicting tendencies—some toward a state-centered system and some toward a nation-centered system—that could be found in the United States in the 1990s. The author proposes an "agenda for reform," which includes reallocating some programs and responsibilities among the different levels of government.

Wheare, K. C. *Federal Government*, 4th edition (Greenwood Press, 1980). (Originally published in 1963.) A perceptive comparative analysis of federal governmental systems. Based primarily on a comprehensive examination of the workings of federalism in Australia, Canada, Switzerland, and the United States.

Zimmerman, Joseph F. *Interstate Relations: The Neglected Dimension of Federalism** (Praeger, 1996). A useful examination of the evolving relationship between states, from preconstitutional trade disputes to their contemporary struggle against the centralization of power.

*Available in paperback edition.

 Visit http://politicalscience.wadsworth.com/cummings9/update/ for current InfoTrac articles and other student resources related to this chapter.

CHAPTER 4

Civil Liberties and Citizenship

As America moved into the 21st century, the Internet had brought enormous changes in the lives of millions of people. The growth of the global electronic network meant that anyone with a computer, a mouse, and a modem was connected to the world. A high school student in Colorado could access a database in London; a lobsterman in Maine could chat with a rancher in Australia.

The world had suddenly become a much smaller place. The Internet had brought a revolution in the way people acquired information, purchased goods and services online, invested, and communicated with one another through e-mail and chat rooms. But the enormous flow of data across fiber-optic cables into people's homes created problems that could not have been foreseen by the framers of the Constitution.

For the Internet was more than a vast electronic shopping mall; it was also a powerful medium of communication. The First Amendment to the Constitution provides for freedom of speech and freedom of the press. But many parents of young children and other citizens objected to the constant barrage of e-mail and the many Web sites offering sexual content. Did Congress have a responsibility to regulate the Internet in order to bar pornographic material? If it did so, would that not violate the freedom of speech protected by the First Amendment?

PROTECTING THE INTERNET

In 1996, Congress passed the Communications Decency Act, a law that sought to protect children from "indecent" material on the Internet. A year later, the Supreme Court struck down the law as a violation of the First Amendment, the provision of the Constitution that protects freedom of speech. Following are excerpts from the Court's ruling:

> The statute abridges "the freedom of speech" protected by the First Amendment. . . . It is true that we have repeatedly recognized the governmental interest in protecting children from harmful materials. But that interest does not justify an unnecessarily broad suppression of speech addressed to adults. As we have explained, the Government may not "reduc[e] the adult population to . . . only what is fit for children." . . . The general, undefined terms "indecent" and "patently offensive" cover large amounts of nonpornographic material with serious educational or other value. . . . Under the CDA [Communications Decency Act], a parent allowing her 17 year old to use the family computer to obtain information on the Internet that she, in her parental judgment, deems appropriate could face a lengthy prison term. . . . The interest in encouraging freedom of expression in a democratic society outweighs any theoretical but unproven benefit of censorship.
>
> —*Reno* v. *American Civil Liberties Union* (1997)

THE INTERNET VERSUS THE FIRST AMENDMENT

As we try to make sense of the school massacre in Littleton, Colo., we suddenly find ourselves swept up in a national debate about whether the Internet, with its dazzling array of interactive mayhem and violence, is partly to blame.

Should the Internet be available to anyone, of any age, with a computer and a telephone connection? Many who have long wanted to muzzle the Internet are making symbols of Eric Harris and Dylan Klebold, who used the Internet to play violent computer games and promote their racist views. . . .

The point to remember is that basic constitutional principles do not arise and disappear as each new technology comes on the scene. . . . The same First Amendment that safeguards the right of Nazis to march through Skokie protects the right of an adult to put virtual machine guns aimed at lifelike human targets on his or her computer screen.

At the same time, Internet speech doesn't have more constitutional protection than speech disseminated in a more old-fashioned and limited manner. In particular, direct threats or other messages that by their very utterance cause harm receive no more protection on the Internet than anyplace else. Releasing a computer virus through E-mail deserves no greater immunity than crying "Fire" in a crowded theater.

—Laurence H. Tribe, *New York Times*, April 28, 1999

And who would define what was pornography and what was an acceptable expression of human sexuality?

Concerned parents and religious conservatives argued that even if consenting adults had a right to transmit or view such material, children did not. They expressed dismay at images of bondage, bestiality, and child-molesting freely transmitted across the Internet.

In 1996, Congress passed and President Clinton signed a telecommunications law containing penalties of up to $250,000 for individuals (and twice that for companies) who "knowingly" transmit material "indecent to minors" over computer networks available to children. The law, the Communications Decency Act, was immediately challenged by civil liberties groups, which argued that it was an unconstitutional infringement on freedom of speech.

In 1997, the Supreme Court struck down the law, 7–2, as unconstitutional, declaring it was too vague and would restrict information available to adults in the name of protecting children.[1] It was a landmark decision, because for the first time, the Supreme Court had ruled that the free speech provision of the First Amendment applied to cyberspace. Justice John Paul Stevens, who wrote the majority opinion upholding an earlier decision of a federal appeals court, noted that under the law a parent "who sent his 17-year-old college freshman information on birth control via e-mail" could land in jail.[2]

The debate over whether and how to regulate "cyber-porn" brought into sharp focus the complex problem of how fundamental constitutional rights can be preserved when they collide with other societal values. A father who believes strongly in free speech may still object equally strongly if his 8-year-old daughter turns on her computer and sees a woman having sex with a horse.

Similar demands to censor the Internet arose after two students in Littleton, Colorado, Eric Harris and Dylan Klebold, shot and killed 12 classmates and a teacher, wounded more than 30 other people, and then took their own lives at Columbine High School, in April 1999. The shooters had played violent computer games, and Harris had spewed hatred and violence on his Web site and discussed the pipe bombs he had built and exploded. Some critics blamed the Internet, as well as violence on television and in the movies, for inspiring the killings. But others argued that censorship would infringe on the First Amendment and would not prevent violence.

In this chapter we will explore a key question: In the American democracy, how should the rights of the individual be balanced against those of society as a whole?

It is a question that often confronts the Supreme Court, as well as the other branches of the government. In deciding cases under the Bill of Rights, the Supreme Court frequently has the difficult task of attempting to balance competing constitutional principles. The issues raised in this process are many and complex. For example, should freedom of the press and freedom of expression be absolute rights under the First Amendment? What if free speech conflicts with the rights of others? Should prayer be allowed in public schools? What does the law say now about government wiretapping and "bugging"? What are the legal rights of student demonstrators? Can police search your home or car without a warrant? Will the Constitution's Bill of Rights be of any help to you if you are arrested by state or local police? These are some of the additional questions to be explored in this chapter.

Police search for illegal drugs at a home in Fort Lauderdale, Florida.
Copyright © Steve Starr/Stock, Boston/PictureQuest

INDIVIDUAL FREEDOM AND SOCIETY

Civil liberties are the fundamental rights of a free society that are protected by the Bill of Rights. The Supreme Court's decisions in the area of civil liberties and individual rights often illustrate the tension between liberty and order in a free society. Freedom is not absolute, for as Supreme Court Justice Oliver Wendell Holmes, Jr., once said, "The right to swing my fist ends where the other man's nose begins." But the proper balance in a democracy between the rights of an individual and the rights of society as a whole can never be resolved to everyone's satisfaction. The rights of the individual should not always be viewed as competing with those of the community; in a free society, the fullest freedom of expression for the individual also may serve the interests of society as a whole.

The 19th-century British philosopher John Stuart Mill advanced the classic argument for diversity of opinion in his treatise *On Liberty:* "Though the silenced opinion be an error, it may, and very commonly does, contain a portion of truth; and since the general or prevailing opinion on any subject is rarely or never the whole truth, it is only by the collision of adverse opinions that the remainder of the truth has any chance of being supplied."[3] In American society, the Supreme Court is the mechanism called upon to resolve conflicts between liberty and order, between the rights of the

---

LIBERTY AND JUSTICE FOR ALL?

"The way they say it, it's as if there is liberty and justice, but there isn't."

Twelve-year-old Mary Frain, sitting pensively on a wooden rocker in her Jamaica, Queens, home, gave this explanation yesterday as one of her reasons for objecting to the daily Pledge of Allegiance to the flag in school.

The crank calls and angry letters have almost disappeared from the life of the introverted seventh grader who, with a classmate, Susan Keller, won a federal court decision on Dec. 10 permitting students in city schools to remain in their seats during the flag-saluting ceremony. Because of the pressure, Susan Keller soon transferred to another school. But Mary still refuses to stand in the morning when most of the children in her honors class at Junior High School 217 at 85th Avenue and 148th Street stand to recite the pledge.

At home, following a quick lunch, the youngster discussed the impact of the court case on her life.

"Like when we walked along the halls, the kids used to call us commies. We had phone calls. One was obscene. Some just laughed or breathed when you picked it up. But it's dying down now. . . ." Mary persisted, she said, because of strong objections to the wording of the pledge.

"Liberty and justice for all?" she said. "That's not true . . . for the blacks and poor whites. The poor have to live in cold miserable places. And it's obvious that blacks are oppressed."

The girl would compromise her position if the pledge were rephrased to be spoken as a "goal." "Like if when you say it you're making a vow to make it liberty and justice for all," she explained.

—*New York Times,* January 31, 1970

individual and the rights of the many. In doing so, the Court operates within the framework of what James Monroe called that "polar star, and great support of American liberty," the Bill of Rights.

THE BILL OF RIGHTS

The first 10 amendments to the Constitution constitute the **Bill of Rights.**[4] These vital protections were omitted from the Constitution as drafted in 1787. (See Chapter 2.) The supporters of the Constitution, it will be recalled, promised to pass a Bill of Rights in part so that they might win the struggle over ratification.

Although the Bill of Rights is the fundamental charter of American liberties, it is the Supreme Court that ultimately decides how those rights shall be defined and applied. The Supreme Court does not operate in a vacuum. Its nine justices are human beings and actors in the drama of their time. As former chief justice Earl Warren once declared, "Our judges are not monks or scientists, but participants in the living stream of our national life."[5] Individual liberties may depend not only on what the Court says in particular cases but on what the political system will tolerate in any given era.

Although the Bill of Rights was passed to guard against abuses by the new *federal* government, the Supreme Court has ruled over the years, case by case, that virtually all the safeguards of the Bill of Rights apply as well to *state* and *local* governments and agencies.

Alpheus T. Mason, a leading constitutional scholar, observed that the fundamental rights of a free society gained "no greater moral sanctity" by being written into the Constitution, "but individuals could thereafter look to courts for their protection. Rights formerly natural became civil."[6]

Freedom of Speech

"Congress shall make no law respecting an establishment of religion, or prohibiting the free exercise thereof; or abridging the freedom of speech, or of the press; or the right of the people peaceably to assemble, and to petition the Government for a redress of grievances."

These 45 words are the **First Amendment** of the Constitution. Along with due process of law and other constitutional protections, these words set forth basic American freedoms. As Justice Benjamin N. Cardozo once wrote, freedom of thought and of speech is "the matrix, the indispensable condition, of nearly every other form of freedom."[7] (Although the Constitution

DON'T TINKER WITH THE BILL OF RIGHTS

Mitch McConnell, a Republican senator from Kentucky, is a strong conservative on most issues. But he opposed a proposed constitutional amendment prohibiting flag desecration. The Senate rejected the amendment in 1995:

It is hard to believe that burning a flag can be considered "speech." But a majority of the (Supreme) court has found this despicable behavior to be "political expression," protected by the First Amendment. So, advocates of a new constitutional amendment banning flag-burning argue that it's the only way we can protect the flag and punish flag-burners.

Those who burn the flag deserve our contempt, but they should not provoke us to tamper with the First Amendment. After all, among the values the American flag symbolizes is free speech, even those ideas with which we disagree. While we revere the flag for the values and history it represents, we cannot worship the flag as an end unto itself. And we cannot coerce people to respect the flag in the manner in which we know it deserves to be respected. . . .

As conservatives, we should be skeptical of tinkering with the Bill of Rights and restricting freedom even in the cause of patriotism.

—Mitch McConnell, *Washington Post,*
December 5, 1995

"PUT THIS ON – YOU'RE OBVIOUSLY NOT COVERED BY THE FIRST AMENDMENT"

In the political struggle over ratification of the Constitution, the Antifederalists argued that the document was incomplete without an enumeration of the rights of the people:

> People, and very wisely too, like to be express and explicit about their essential rights, and not to be forced to claim them on the precarious . . . tenure of inferences and general principles . . . we discern certain rights, as the freedom of the press, and the trial by jury, which the people of England and of America of course believe to be sacred, and essential to their political happiness. . . .
>
> Perhaps it would be better to enumerate the particular essential rights the people are entitled to. . . . Freedom of the press is a fundamental right, and ought not to be restrained by any taxes, duties, or in any manner whatever. Why should not the people, in adopting a federal constitution, declare this.

—Richard Henry Lee, *Letters from the Federal Farmer*

The Federalists argued that the Constitution as drafted protected the rights of individuals, making a bill of rights unnecessary:

> It has been several times truly remarked that bills of rights are, in their origin, stipulations between kings and their subjects, abridgments of prerogative in favor of privilege, reservations of rights not surrendered to the prince. . . . They have no application to constitutions. . . .
>
> I go further, and affirm that bills of rights . . . are not only unnecessary in the proposed Constitution, but would even be dangerous. They would contain various exceptions to powers not granted; and, on this very account, would afford a colorable pretext to claim more than were granted. For why declare that things shall not be done which there is no power to do? Why, for instance, should it be said that the liberty of the press shall not be restrained, when no power is given by which restrictions may be imposed?

—Alexander Hamilton, *The Federalist*, No. 84

---

states that "Congress shall make no law" abridging First Amendment freedoms, the Supreme Court has interpreted this to mean that state and local authorities cannot do so, either.)

Yet the courts have frequently placed limits on speech. Several types of expression do not enjoy constitutional immunity from government regulation. These include fraudulent advertising, obscenity (which courts have had vast difficulty in defining), child pornography, libel, and, in some cases, street oratory. The Supreme Court, for example, has ruled that police are justified in arresting a sidewalk speaker if he is too effective in stirring his audience.[8] Three decades before that deci-

sion, Supreme Court Justice Oliver Wendell Holmes, Jr., had established the classic **clear and present danger test** to define the point at which speech loses First Amendment protection:

> The most stringent protection of free speech would not protect a man in falsely shouting fire in a theater and causing a panic. . . . The question in every case is whether the words used are used in such circumstances and are of such a nature as to create a clear and present danger that they will bring about the substantive evils that Congress has a right to prevent.[9]

In reconciling the requirement of free speech with other social rights and needs, the Supreme Court often has tried to draw a line between "expression" and "action." But that is not always an easy matter. In the major draft-card-burning case, in 1968, David P. O'Brien had argued that when he burned his draft card to protest the Vietnam War, his action was "symbolic speech" protected by the Constitution. But the Court rejected this argument, 7–1. Chief Justice Warren, in his majority opinion, declared: "We cannot accept the view that an apparently limitless variety of conduct can be labeled 'speech.'"[10]

On the other hand, the Supreme Court has ruled that neither the states nor Congress may prohibit the burning of an American flag, even though many persons find that form of free expression deeply offensive. The emotionally charged issue of flag-burning first came before the Court after Gregory Lee Johnson, a protester at the 1984

Justice Oliver Wendell Holmes, Jr.
Culver Pictures

Protesters burning the flag in Chicago
Copyright © Bob Kusel/SIPA

Republican National Convention in Dallas, doused an American flag with kerosene and set it on fire while dozens of demonstrators chanted, "America, the red, white and blue, we spit on you." He was convicted of violating the Texas flag desecration law, fined $2,000, and sentenced to one year in prison. When the case reached the Supreme Court, the justices ruled, 5–4, that the Texas law and all federal and state laws protecting the flag violated the right of freedom of speech, contained in the First Amendment to the Constitution.[11]

Justice William J. Brennan, Jr., writing for the majority, said, "If there is a bedrock principle underlying the First Amendment, it is that the Government may not prohibit the expression of an idea simply because society finds the idea itself offensive or disagreeable. . . ."

Across the land, outraged citizens attacked the court for defending flag burners. Congress enacted a federal law barring flag-burning. But the Supreme Court, again by a vote of 5–4, struck down the new federal law, which had been used to prosecute flag burners in two cases.[12]

In an earlier case, the Supreme Court struck down a Massachusetts law under which Valarie Goguen had been arrested and sentenced to six months in jail for wearing an American flag patch on the seat of his blue jeans.[13]

In 1987, the Court held, 5–4, that public employees could not be fired for exercising their constitutional rights of free speech. The case arose in 1981 when Ardith McPherson, a clerk-typist employed by the county government in Houston, Texas, heard of the assassination attempt against President Reagan. McPherson, who is African American, speculated to a friend that the presi-

dent might have been shot by a black person angered by the administration's cuts in welfare and social programs. She added: "If they go for him again, I hope they get him." A passing supervisor overheard the remark and McPherson was fired, although she said the comment was not serious. Justice Thurgood Marshall, writing for the Court majority, said that the remark, taken in context, was "political speech" for which, under the Constitution, Ardith McPherson could not be fired.[14]

In 1991, the Supreme Court struck down a New York State law that was designed to prevent criminals from profiting from books or movies about their crimes. The Court ruled that the law violated the First Amendment because it restricted a certain kind of speech, writing about one's own criminal conduct. The case concerned Henry Hill, a Mafia figure whose story was told in the book *Wiseguy* and the movie *GoodFellas*.[15]

In 1987 the Supreme Court ruled that the First Amendment protects the right of individuals "verbally to oppose or challenge police action." It struck down as unconstitutionally overbroad a city law in Houston that allowed the police to arrest almost anyone who might annoy them while they were on official business.[16]

On the other hand, the Supreme Court has ruled, in effect, that some rock music is too loud. In 1989, it upheld a New York City noise-control ordinance governing rock concerts in Central Park.[17]

The First Amendment, Hate Crime Laws, and Campus Speech Codes In 1992 the Supreme Court unanimously ruled unconstitutional a St. Paul, Minnesota, hate crime law that had sought to prohibit speech or action aimed at persons because of their race, religion, or gender.[18] The case arose when a 17-year-old white high school dropout was arrested for burning a cross on the lawn of a black couple. Although it found the cross-burning "reprehensible," the Court said the city law violated the First Amendment because it prohibited only certain kinds of speech on a selective basis.

The Supreme Court decision had a noticeable impact on college campuses, where, in some cases, administrators had established speech codes prohibiting students from making racist or sexist remarks. The codes were created because many minority students felt threatened by hateful expressions and derogatory remarks and actions by some of their fellow students.

"I was shocked, hurt, and angry," Kenya Welch, a black senior at Clemson University, in South Carolina, told a Senate committee in 1992, as she described events on campus—a blackface homecoming skit, white students wearing Ku Klux Klan sheets for Halloween, and a group of white men who called her "nigger."[19] William Schendel, a gay student at Indiana University, said he was jeered every night by students screaming, "Faggot!"[20]

In the wake of the Supreme Court's decision in the Minnesota case, the University of Wisconsin repealed its speech code, acknowledging that it may have violated

CHINA CRACKS DOWN ON THE FALUN GONG

Many of the nations of the world do not permit political dissent. Their citizens do not have the protection of a written provision, similar to the First Amendment of the U.S. Constitution, that allows freedom of speech and expression. In China in 1999, for example, the authorities dealt harshly with a group whose millions of members were regarded as a threat to the government:

BEIJING, Dec. 26—Three men and a woman accused of being top leaders of the Falun Gong spiritual movement outlawed by the Chinese government last summer were given prison sentences today ranging up to 18 years.

The severe sentences, issued by a Beijing court after a one-day trial, and their prominent announcement on national television tonight were clearly intended to show the authorities' determination to crush Falun Gong. Two of the sentences, for 18 years in one case and 16 years in another, were harsher than any given to leaders of . . . any other democracy advocate [in China] in the last several years.

Promising good health and spiritual salvation, the Falun Gong movement gained millions of enthusiastic followers since its founding in 1992. It was officially condemned and outlawed as an "evil cult" in July after it held unauthorized demonstrations, including one by 10,000 people who surrounded the communist leaders' compound in Beijing in April.

That silent demonstration, and the evident appeal of Falun Gong across society and even among members of the Communist Party, seems to have touched a raw nerve in the secretive leadership. . . .

A dynamic offshoot of Chinese qigong, which is said to harness invisible forces to promote health and well-being, Falun Gong has been popular among retirees and middle-aged women, who gathered in urban parks to practice its slow, meditative exercises. But the membership of officials and party members was a sign of the broad appeal that so frightened the national leadership.

—*New York Times,*
December 27, 1999

---

students' First Amendment rights. Wisconsin's code had barred slurs against a person's race, religion, sexual orientation, disability, or ancestry. Other colleges also abandoned their speech codes, but controversy continued on campuses over ways to deal with inflammatory speech directed at ethnic or other groups.

In 1993, a year after the Minnesota decision, however, the Supreme Court ruled unanimously that states may impose longer prison terms and stiffer fines on people convicted of hate crimes without violating the First Amendment's protection of free speech.[21] In that case, a black defendant was convicted of urging a group of youths to beat up a white passerby. The Court ruled that a judge, in imposing a sentence, could consider whether a defendant was motivated by racial or religious prejudice.

The First Amendment and Student Rights The Supreme Court has ruled that students do not lose their constitutional right of free expression simply because they are in school.

The case that brought about this decision arose during the Vietnam War, when the Court decided that a 13-year-old Iowa girl, Mary Beth Tinker, could not be suspended from her junior high school for wearing a black armband to class in protest against the war. "In our system," the Court held, "state-operated schools may not be enclaves of totalitarianism. School officials do not possess absolute authority over their students."[22] In winning the fight for her constitutional rights, Mary Beth Tinker had made a much broader point for all students in America, for the Court concluded: "It can hardly be argued that either students or teachers shed their constitutional rights to freedom of speech or expression at the schoolhouse gate."

But the Supreme Court also has made it clear that student rights to free expression are not unlimited. In 1983, Matthew Fraser, a 17-year-old high school student near Tacoma, Washington, gave a speech on behalf of a candidate for the student government. In it, he described his friend as "a man who is firm—he's firm in his pants . . . his character is firm . . . a man who will go to the very end, even the climax, for each and every one of you." The school suspended Matthew Fraser for disruptive conduct. In 1986, the Supreme Court ruled in favor of the school officials, holding, 7–2, that students may be suspended for using "vulgar and offensive" language.[23]

And in 1988, in a major decision on student rights, the Supreme Court upheld, 5–3, the power of school administrators to censor a high school newspaper, student plays, and other activities in certain circumstances.[24] The case arose when a high school principal in a St. Louis, Missouri, suburb removed from *Spectrum*, the student newspaper, articles on teenage pregnancy and the effect of divorce on children. The newspaper was

MAKING A DIFFERENCE

"THE POWER OF THE FIRST AMENDMENT"

On March 10, 1999, George Dohrmann, a sports reporter for the *St. Paul Pioneer Press,* wrote a story that began: "At least 20 men's basketball players at the University of Minnesota had research papers, take-home exams or other course work done for them during a five-year period." The article said that four former players had confirmed that the class work was prepared for them.

The story capped three months of interviews and fact-gathering. It appeared in the *Pioneer Press* on the eve of the Golden Gophers' appearance in the 1999 NCAA men's basketball tournament. The timing caused tremors throughout Minnesota and beyond. Gov. Jesse Ventura called the newspaper "despicable," and hundreds of readers canceled their subscriptions.

The university launched its own investigation, which led to the exit of coach Clem Haskins and the resignation of men's athletic director Mark Dienhart. Among other sanctions, the university cut back on men's basketball scholarships, restricted recruitment efforts, and returned money earned from the team's participation in three previous NCAA championship tournaments.

A year later, on April 10, 2000, cheers and champagne filled the *St. Paul Pioneer Press* newsroom as the newspaper learned that George Dohrmann had won the Pulitzer Prize, journalism's most coveted award.

After the announcement, Dohrmann wiped away tears as he was surrounded by his colleagues in the sixth-floor newsroom in downtown St. Paul.

"I'm a big believer that if you cover the college sports beat, you also cover the police blotter and the courtrooms," said Dohrmann. "This was my first run as the lead guy on something like this. (The editors) never laughed at me, never told me to shut up. They just trusted me and were totally supportive."

Mark Yudof, president of the University of Minnesota, called the award "deserved" and said Dohrmann's work was "a piece of outstanding investigative journalism."

"I used to teach the First Amendment," President Yudof said. "The story," he added, vindicated "the . . . power of the First Amendment."

—Adapted from the *St. Paul Pioneer Press,* April 11, 2000

---

published as part of a journalism class. The Court ruled that where an activity was part of classwork, schools have broad powers of censorship. Justice William Brennan, in a sharp dissent, argued that the First Amendment did not permit school officials to act as "thought police."[25]

The right of students to read books in the school library has been supported by the Supreme Court. Steven Pico, a student at a high school in Levittown, Long Island, a suburb of New York City, sued the Island Trees school district when nine books, including Desmond Morris's *The Naked Ape,* were removed from the library shelves after objections by some members of the community. The Court, ruling that the First Amendment limits the power of a school board to ban books, declared: "Our Constitution does not permit the official suppression of ideas."[26] Despite the Court's decision, however, censorship of books in public schools, sometimes under pressure from conservative or liberal groups, has continued.[27]

Preferred Freedoms and the Balancing Test

Different philosophies, often identified with particular justices, have emerged as the Supreme Court has struggled with problems of freedom of expression.

For example, Justices Hugo Black and William O. Douglas established themselves as advocates of the **absolute position.** Black argued that "there are 'absolutes' in our Bill of Rights"[28] that cannot be diluted by judicial decisions. He maintained, for instance, that

obscenity and libel are forms of speech and therefore cannot be constitutionally limited. But a majority of the Court took the position that the rights of the First Amendment must be "balanced" against the competing needs of the community to preserve order and to preserve the state. This position was championed by Justice Felix Frankfurter and others. The majority of the Supreme Court has thus adhered to the **balancing test,** the view that First Amendment rights must be weighed against the competing needs of the community to preserve order.

In performing this delicate balancing act, however, some members of the Court have argued that the basic freedoms should take precedence over other needs. Thus, Justice Harlan Fiske Stone argued that the Constitution had placed freedom of speech and religion "in a preferred position."[29]

Despite these mixed views, the Supreme Court, while reluctant to narrow the scope of basic liberties, has generally not hesitated to balance such freedoms against other constitutional requirements.

Freedom of the Press

Closely tied to free speech, and protected as well by the First Amendment, is freedom of the press. However, the courts do not always rule in favor of the press, despite the First Amendment. In a number of cases, courts have ruled against the news media. For example, the Supreme Court has sometimes required journalists to reveal sources, and some reporters have gone to jail rather than to obey court orders to do so. The Supreme Court has permitted individuals to sue the press for libel; recognized the right of privacy; banned the publication of "obscene" material; supported the right of public schools to censor student newspapers; and upheld the power of the government to regulate radio and television. Again, the Supreme Court has balanced the First Amendment's language protecting freedom of the press against the competing needs of society. The role of the press in the American political system is explored in depth in Chapter 8.

Obscenity

Long before the Internet, with its many Web sites devoted to pornography, most large American cities and many smaller communities had X-rated movie houses, showing endless varieties of sexual intercourse, in color. Explicit videotapes could be rented or purchased for home viewing. In books, magazines, films, and on television, human sexuality was described and depicted, often in graphic terms.

All this seemed a far cry from an earlier time, when the books of Edgar Rice Burroughs were almost removed from a Downey, California, elementary school library because of persistent reports that Tarzan and Jane were unmarried. (When it was established that the jungle king and his mate were in fact husband and wife, the books were left on the shelves.)

Today, changing standards of public morality have resulted in freer acceptance of sex in art, literature, and motion pictures by some—but certainly not all—segments of the public. In 1957 in *Roth* v. *United States,* the Supreme Court held for the first time that "obscenity is not within the area of constitutionally protected speech or press."[30] Justice William J. Brennan, Jr., ruled for the Court that material that is "utterly without redeeming social importance" is not protected by the Constitution. Brennan went on to give his definition of obscene matter: "whether to the average person, applying contemporary community standards, the dominant theme of the material taken as a whole appeals to prurient interest."*

The Court, however, has had continued difficulty in defining obscenity. D. H. Lawrence, whose book *Lady Chatterley's Lover* was banned in the United States from 1928 until 1959, once said: "What is pornography to one man is the laughter of genius to another."[31]

Justice Potter Stewart, concurring in one Supreme Court decision, said he would not attempt to define hard-core pornography, "but I know it when I see it."[32]

The practical effect of these cases was to remove almost all restrictions on content of books and movies as long as the slightest "social value" could be demonstrated. Then, in 1973, came the landmark case of *Miller* v. *California,* which set new standards for defining obscenity.[33] Chief Justice Burger, who wrote the majority opinion in the 5–4 decision, explained that the case began

---

Webster's New International Dictionary defines "prurient" as "itching, longing; uneasy with desire, or longing; or persons, having itching, morbid, or lascivious longings; or desire, curiosity, or propensity, lewd."

"No one could claim that Judge Walker doesn't approach these obscenity hearings with an open mind."
Drawing by Stevenson. Copyright © 1969 *New Yorker* Magazine, Inc. www.cartoonbank.com

when unsolicited mail arrived at a restaurant in Newport Beach, California. The envelope, "opened by the manager of the restaurant and his mother," included an advertising brochure for a book titled *Sex Orgies Illustrated*.

In the *Miller* ruling, the Court set a new three-part test for judging works dealing with sexual conduct:

1. Whether the average person, "applying contemporary community standards," would find that the work, taken as a whole, "appeals to prurient interest."
2. Whether the work depicts "in a patently offensive way" sexual conduct prohibited by state law.
3. Whether the work as a whole "lacks serious literary, artistic, political, or scientific value."

The Court seemed to rule, in effect, that local communities should be permitted to set their own standards. Justice Burger wrote: "It is neither realistic nor constitutionally sound to read the First Amendment as requiring that the people of Maine or Mississippi accept public depiction of conduct found tolerable in Las Vegas or New York City."[34] But in a series of subsequent decisions, the Supreme Court made it clear that there were limits to the right of communities to ban material as obscene. And in 1987 the Court shifted away from the

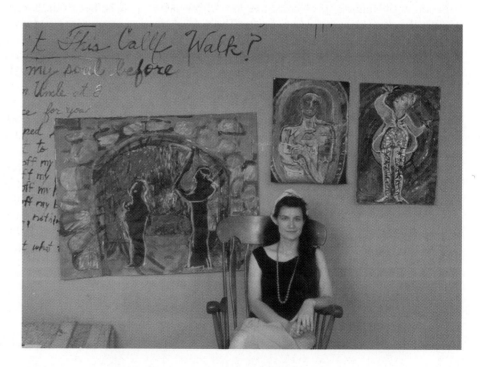

Performance artist Karen Finley
Copyright © Larry Barnes/Black Star
Publishing/PictureQuest

"community standards" yardstick by ruling that the social value of a work must be judged from the standpoint of a "reasonable person," not the entire community.[35]

Even earlier, the Supreme Court's decisions had demonstrated that the *Miller* ruling did not give communities free reign to censor sexually explicit works. The Court held that local juries did not have "unbridled discretion" under the *Miller* case to declare what was obscene.[36]

But the Supreme Court has ruled that the First Amendment does not protect nude dancing; it held in 1991 that states may prohibit such entertainment. The case had been brought by the owners of the Kitty Kat Lounge, an adult club in South Bend, Indiana, featuring live performances.[37]

Again in the year 2000, the Court reaffirmed that states and local communities may ban nude dancing and require dancers to wear "pasties and G-strings."[38] It upheld an Erie, Pennsylvania, ordinance that had been challenged by the owner of an establishment known as Kandyland.

The Court struck down an attempt by Congress to ban the "dial-a-porn" industry, ruling that a part of a law barring "indecent" speech on the telephone was unconstitutional.[39] On the other hand, the Court upheld the conviction of William Hamling, who had published an illustrated version of the report of the President's Commission on Obscenity and Pornography.[40]

In 1982 the Supreme Court held that child pornography is not a category of speech protected by the Constitution. It ruled that works visually depicting sexual conduct by children could be banned by state law, even though the material might not meet the legal test of obscenity under the *Miller* case.[41]

And in 1998 the Court upheld, 8–1, a law passed by Congress allowing the National Endowment for the Arts to consider "general standards of decency and values of the American public" in giving taxpayer money to the arts.[42] Four performance artists, including Karen Finley, who was noted for smearing her nude body with chocolate, had challenged the law.

 for more information about the National Endowment for the Arts, see: arts.endow.gov

Privacy

Although not specifically provided for in the Constitution, the "right" to privacy has been recognized to a considerable extent by the courts. Justice Louis Brandeis wrote that the makers of the Constitution sought to give Americans "the right to be let alone . . . the right most valued by civilized men."[43]

Today that right has been defined and protected by a series of Supreme Court decisions and by legislation. Nevertheless, in the age of the Internet, computerized data banks, and sophisticated surveillance techniques, the right of individuals to be free of intrusion into their

PRIVACY: THE SECRET ZONE

Generally speaking, the concept of a right to privacy attempts to draw a line between the individual and the collective, between self and society. It seeks to assure the individual a zone in which to be an individual, not a member of the community. In that zone he can think his own thoughts, have his own secrets, live his own life, reveal only what he wants to the outside world. The right of privacy, in short, establishes an area excluded from the collective life, not governed by the rules of collective living. It is based upon premises of individualism, that the society exists to promote the worth and the dignity of the individual. It is contrary to the theories of total commitment to the state, to society, or to any part thereof.

—Thomas I. Emerson,
The System of Freedom of Expression

privacy remains a subject of continuing concern and conflict. The government, corporations, credit firms, the press, insurance companies, schools, banks, and other institutions have all, to some degree, been accused of infringing on privacy. Because visitors to Web sites can be tracked and may be asked to provide personal information, privacy on the Internet has become a volatile issue.

The concept of a right of privacy was first given expression by the Supreme Court in the 1965 case of *Griswold* v. *Connecticut*.[44] The head of the state's Planned Parenthood League, along with a physician who was also a professor at Yale Medical School, prescribed contraceptives and provided birth control information to married couples. They were convicted and fined under a state law prohibiting the use of contraceptives. In *Griswold*, however, the Supreme Court ruled that guarantees in the Bill of Rights cast "penumbras," or shadows, that may encompass other rights not specifically mentioned. "Various guarantees create zones of privacy," the Court said. The police must be kept out of the bedroom, the Court added, citing "a right of privacy older than the Bill of Rights."

In other cases, the Supreme Court, in the past, at least, has reiterated the right to privacy in very clear language. In the controversial case of *Roe* v. *Wade*, for example, the justices ruled that the concept of privacy included the right to a legal abortion. "The Constitution does not explicitly mention any right of privacy," the Court declared. But "the Court has recognized that a right of personal privacy, or a guarantee of certain areas or zones of privacy, does exist under the Constitution."[45]

And in yet another decision, the Court ruled that Robert Eli Stanley, a Georgia resident, had the right to watch pornographic movies in his own home.[46] The case arose when police with a warrant searched Stanley's home for evidence of bookmaking activity, found three

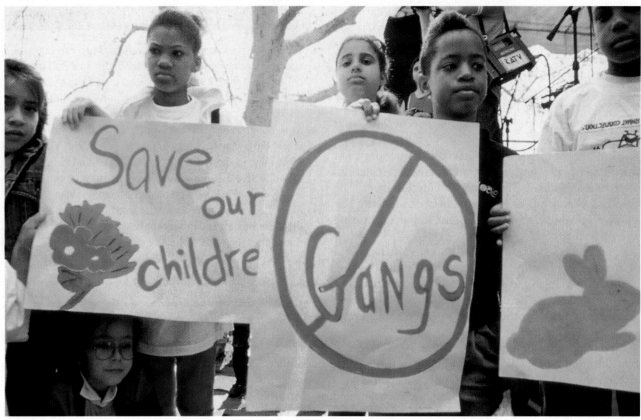

Copyright © Joe Sohm/Image Works

reels of 8-millimeter film, and viewed them on a projector in Stanley's living room.

What if the right of the press to report the news under the First Amendment conflicts with the individual's right to be left alone? Sometimes the Supreme Court has sided with the individual, sometimes with the press.

After a construction worker in West Virginia died when a bridge collapsed, a Cleveland newspaper referred to his family as "hillbillies." The Court upheld a $60,000 judgment against the paper for invasion of privacy.[47] But in a Georgia case, the Court ruled in favor of a television station that broadcast the name of a young woman who had been raped and killed by six teenage boys. The victim's father sued the station, but the Court said his privacy had not been invaded because the broadcaster had obtained his daughter's name from public court records.[48]

Congress has passed a series of laws relating to personal privacy. The Privacy Act of 1974 gives individuals a degree of control over government files maintained about them. The Fair Credit Reporting Act (1970) regulates credit agencies, department stores, and banks. And the Family Education Rights and Privacy Act (1974) gives parents and then students who are 18 years old or over or in college the right to see school records and instructional materials.*

---

*Under the law, the right of access to school records transfers from parents to students who turn 18 or attend college. But parents who declare their children as dependents still have the right to access student records.

Freedom of Assembly

In addition to protecting free speech, the First Amendment protects the right of the people "peaceably to assemble." The Supreme Court has held this right to be "equally fundamental" to the right of free speech and free press.[49] It ruled in 1897 that a city can require a permit for the "use of public grounds."[50] But a city, in requiring licenses for parades, demonstrations, and sound trucks, must do so in the interest of controlling traffic and regulating the use of public streets and parks; it cannot—in theory—exercise its licensing power to suppress free speech.[51] The legitimate responsibility of public officials and police to control traffic or prevent a demonstration from growing into a riot is sometimes used as a device to suppress free speech because there is a thin, and not always readily distinguishable, line between crowd control and thought control.

In 1977 the heavily Jewish suburb of Skokie, Illinois, passed three ordinances designed to prevent a march there by the American Nazi Party, an anti-Semitic group. Emotions ran high in Skokie, the home of several thousand survivors of Hitler's Nazi regime. Jews who had lived through the Holocaust were understandably angry at the prospect of homegrown Nazis marching in the streets of America. The American Civil Liberties Union (ACLU), although a liberal group strongly opposed to the Nazis, went into court to defend the Nazis' right to march. Leaders of the Nazis ultimately called off plans to demonstrate in Skokie. In

AP/Wide World

1978 the Supreme Court let stand a lower court ruling that Skokie's ordinances had violated the constitutional guarantees of free speech.[52]

 for more information about the ACLU, see: www.aclu.org

But in 1995 the Supreme Court ruled, 9–0, that private sponsors of Boston's St. Patrick's Day parade had a constitutional right to exclude marchers who identified themselves as gay and lesbian.[53] The Court said that a parade, even though it takes place in a public place, is a form of private expression. As a result, the Court held, the sponsors could not be forced by state law to include marchers who carried an unwanted message.

In 1983 the Supreme Court permitted people to picket and to display flags and signs on the sidewalk outside the Supreme Court itself. The case was brought by two persons who had been asked to leave when they picketed the Court.[54]

Freedom of Religion

President Jefferson wrote in 1802 that the freedom of religion clause of the First Amendment was designed to build "a wall of separation between Church and State."* The wall still stands, but in several areas the Supreme Court has modified its contours.

Many of the American colonies were settled by groups seeking religious freedom but who were themselves intolerant of religious dissent. Gradually, however, religious tolerance increased. When the Bill of Rights was passed, its first words were: "Congress shall make no law respecting an establishment of religion, or prohibiting the free exercise thereof."

The Free Exercise Clause   The **free exercise clause** of the First Amendment protects the right of individuals to worship or believe as they wish, or to hold no religious beliefs. It also means that people cannot be compelled by government to act contrary to their religious beliefs, unless religious conduct collides with valid laws. In that difficult area, the courts have had to try to resolve the conflict between the demands of religion and the demands of law.

For example, in a number of instances the Supreme Court has attempted to define the grounds that may be invoked by conscientious objectors to military service. Ever since the draft began during the Civil War, the law has provided some form of exemption for those whose religious beliefs would not permit them to serve in the armed forces. In 1965 the Supreme Court ruled that a "sincere and meaningful" objection to war on religious grounds did not require a belief in a Supreme Being.[55]

Then, in June 1970, with the war in Vietnam still in progress, the Court extended this protection to persons opposed to war for reasons of conscience. It ruled that Elliott Ashton Welsh II, a 29-year-old computer engineer from Los Angeles, could not be imprisoned for his refusal on ethical and moral grounds to serve in the armed forces. Welsh—and therefore other young Americans—the Court ruled, did not have to base his

---

*Jefferson used the now-famous phrase in a letter to a group of Baptists in Danbury, Connecticut. See Saul K. Padover, ed., *The Complete Jefferson* (New York: Duell, Sloan & Pearce, 1943), pp. 518–519.

refusal on a belief in God or religious training. The government must exempt from military service, the Court declared, "all those whose consciences, spurred by deeply held moral, ethical, or religious beliefs, would give them no rest or peace if they allowed themselves to become part of an instrument of war."[56] The draft law, the Supreme Court ruled, did not require military service by "those who hold strong beliefs about our domestic and foreign affairs or even those whose conscientious objection to participation in all wars is founded to a substantial extent upon considerations of public policy."[57] But a year later the Court held that the draft law and the Constitution did not permit conscientious objection to particular wars.[58]

In a series of flag-salute cases, the Court initially ruled in 1940 that children of Jehovah's Witnesses could not be excused from saluting the American flag on religious grounds.[59] But three years later the Court reversed itself and decided in favor of Walter Barnett, also a member of the Jehovah's Witnesses, whose seven children had been expelled from West Virginia schools for refusing to salute the flag. Justice Robert H. Jackson, speaking for the Court, held that "the flag salute is a form of utterance" protected by the First Amendment. "If there is any fixed star in our constitutional constellation," Jackson said, "it is that no official, high or petty, can prescribe what shall be orthodox in politics, nationalism, religion or other matters of opinion."[60] Because the Court's decision rested on the free speech clause, it protects anyone who refuses to salute the flag for whatever reason. The Supreme Court also ruled that members of the Amish church could not be forced to send their children to school beyond the eighth grade.[61] And it held that a state could not deny unemployment compensation to a member of the Seventh-Day Adventist church who refused to take a job that required her to work on the Sabbath.[62]

Although peyote, a variety of cactus containing the hallucinogenic drug mescaline, is a narcotic under California law, the California Supreme Court ruled that the state could not prohibit the religious use of the drug by the Navajo Indians.[63]

The California case did not reach the U.S. Supreme Court, but in 1990, the Court upheld an Oregon law that banned the use of peyote in religious ceremonies.[64] Despite the Supreme Court's decision, individual states could decide whether or not to outlaw the religious use of the hallucinogen.*

Not every religious practice is protected by the First Amendment, however. During the 19th century the Supreme Court outlawed polygamy.[65] Although George Reynolds proved that as a Mormon he was required to have more than one wife, the Supreme Court sustained his conviction. The Court ruled that religious conduct could not violate the law, adding, rather gruesomely: "Suppose one believed that human sacrifices were a necessary part of religious worship?"

The Supreme Court has, however, permitted animal sacrifice as part of a religion. In Florida, some 70,000 persons practice Santería, an Afro-Cuban religion in which goats, chickens, sheep, pigeons, and turtles are killed. The city of Hialeah passed a law forbidding the practice. In 1993, the Supreme Court ruled unanimously that the

---

*After the Supreme Court's 1990 ruling, Oregon enacted a new law permitting the religious use of peyote. At the time of the Court's decision, federal law and 24 states, many with large American Indian populations, did permit the sacramental use of peyote.

A Santería priest in Hialeah, Florida
Copyright © Bill Gentile/SIPA

ban was unconstitutional because it violated the religious freedom of the followers of the Santería religion.[66]

But the Supreme Court does not permit racial discrimination based on religious beliefs. It has denied tax-exempt status to schools that practice such discrimination.[67]

And in an important decision in 1997, the Court struck down the Religious Freedom Restoration Act, which sought to give churches protection from government laws and actions that "substantially burden" religion.[68] When a Catholic church near San Antonio, Texas, was refused a building permit to enlarge its structure, the church challenged the city under the 1993 federal law. Beyond invalidating the law, the Court's decision reminded Congress that it cannot poach on the judicial branch's responsibilities or intrude upon the powers of the states within the federal system.

The Establishment Clause   The **establishment clause** of the First Amendment means, in the words of Justice Hugo Black, that "neither a state nor the federal government can set up a church. Neither can pass laws that aid one religion, aid all religions, or prefer one religion over another."[69]

Despite the constitutional separation between church and state, religion has always been a significant factor in American life. Since 1865 U.S. coins have borne the motto "In God We Trust"; many presidential speeches end with a reference to the Almighty; public meetings often open with invocations and close with benedictions; and a chaplain opens the daily sessions of Congress. The pledge of allegiance that school children recite contains the phrase "one nation under God," and when a federal appeals court ruled in 2002 that these words violated the separation of church and state, it set off a storm of protest. The next day, the ruling was stayed by one of the judges who had issued it.

In 1984 the Supreme Court narrowly upheld the right of cities to include the nativity scene as part of an official Christmas display.[70] In this and other cases, the Court has held that not every expression of religion in a public forum violates the First Amendment's establishment clause.

Yet hardly any subject generates more emotion than church-state relations. In 1962 the Supreme Court outlawed officially composed prayers in the public schools.[71] The initial school prayer case arose after the Board of Regents of New York State composed a "nondenominational" prayer that it recommended local school boards adopt.[72] The parents of 10 children in New Hyde Park, New York, objected and went to court. In ruling the prayer unconstitutional, Justice Hugo Black, speaking for the Court, declared that the First Amendment means "that in this country it is no part of the business of government to compose official prayers for any group of the American people to recite as part of a religious program carried on by government."[73] In 1963 the Court outlawed daily Bible reading and recitation of the Lord's Prayer in public schools.[74] These decisions by the Court brought down a tremendous storm of protest upon its marble pillars. Some school districts openly defied the rulings.

Another major constitutional argument over church-state relations centers on the question of whether, and to what extent, the government can aid church-related schools. Many students attend such schools. In 1996, for example, more than 2.6 million students, about 5.5 percent of the nation's 48 million schoolchildren, were enrolled in Roman Catholic schools.[75]

In 1947 the Supreme Court ruled as constitutional a New Jersey statute under which the parents of both public and parochial students were reimbursed by the local school district for the fares paid by their children to get to school on public buses.[76] This was the celebrated *Everson* case. The fare payments, the Court held, did no

Parochial school children praying in classroom
Copyright © Jack Kurtz/Impact Visuals/PictureQuest

more than "help parents get their children, regardless of their religion," safely to and from school.

In 1960 John F. Kennedy became the first Roman Catholic to be elected president. Politically, it would have been awkward for him to propose federal aid to church-supported schools, and he did not do so.

Congress in 1965, during President Lyndon Johnson's administration, passed the first general bill authorizing federal aid to elementary and secondary schools. It provided aid, through the states, to children in both public and church-supported schools. By emphasizing assistance to children in low-income areas, it avoided much of the religious controversy that had surrounded previous attempts to pass an education bill.

Since the *Everson* case in 1947, more than two-thirds of the states have enacted various kinds of aid to parochial schools, ranging from free lunches to driver education programs. Some of these programs have been upheld. For example, the Supreme Court upheld a "released time" program allowing public school students to attend religious classes outside of school.[77]

In 1971, however, the Supreme Court declared unconstitutional certain state programs of direct aid to parochial schools.* The result was to severely limit state aid to church-affiliated schools throughout the nation. But in 1997 the Court overturned one of its own precedents and ruled that public schools may send teachers into parochial schools to teach remedial classes to low-achieving students from low-income families.[78]

And three years later, in 2000, the Supreme court moved further down the road toward assisting religious schools when it held, 6–3, that federal funds could be used to put computers and other "instructional equipment" in parochial school classrooms.[79] Under the federal program, money for this purpose had been distributed to both public and private schools since 1965.[80]

In interpreting the establishment clause, the Supreme Court has sometimes permitted religious-oriented extracurricular activities. In 1985, for example, Bridget Mergens, a senior at a high school in Omaha, Nebraska, was denied permission to organize a Christian Bible study group at the school. Although the school already had other extracurricular activities—a chess club and a scuba diving club, for example—the principal said the Bible group would violate the Constitution's establishment clause.

Mergens took her case to court. She contended that she had as much right to study the Bible before or after classes as to learn how to play chess or scuba dive. The Supreme Court ruled, 8–1, for Mergens.[81] And the Court

has upheld the use of government funds to pay for a sign language interpreter to accompany a deaf student to a parochial school.[82]

But the Court has ruled that prayers may not be included in public school graduation ceremonies.[83] The case arose when a rabbi in Providence gave a nondenominational invocation and benediction at a high school graduation ceremony. Daniel Weisman, whose daughter Deborah was among the graduates, filed suit, claiming that the prayer violated the Constitution's prohibition on the "establishment" of religion. The Supreme Court agreed. In a 5–4 decision, it ruled that the First Amendment did not permit prayers at graduation ceremonies. Such prayers, the Court reasoned, coerced students to participate in a religious activity—or miss their graduation. No school, the Court held, "can persuade or compel a student to participate in a religious exercise. That is being done here, and it is forbidden by the Establishment Clause of the First Amendment."

And in the year 2000 the Court ruled, 6–3, that the constitutional separation of church and state did not permit prayer at high school football games.[84] Under the First Amendment, the government "may not coerce anyone" to support or participate in religion, the Court held. The decision struck down a Texas school district's policy that allowed student-led prayers before football games.[85]

In June 2002, the Court in a landmark 5–4 ruling upheld the use of public money for school vouchers to send children to religious and other private schools.* The decision approved the program in Cleveland, where about 3,700 of the district's 75,000 children used vouchers of up to $2,250 to attend private schools. Almost all of the children were enrolled in religious schools.

For this reason, school vouchers remained a controversial issue. Advocates argued that vouchers would give low-income students the same opportunities as more affluent students. Opponents contended that vouchers violated the constitutional separation of church and state and in addition would weaken the public school system by drawing the best students away and reducing budgets. The National Education Association, the teachers' union, led the opponents of vouchers. The Supreme Court ruling in the Cleveland case did not end the debate over "school choice," because the battle would likely continue in the states and in local communities.

Although it has restricted aid to religious primary and secondary schools, the Supreme Court has approved some forms of government aid to church-related private colleges and universities.[86] In deciding cases that relate to freedom of religion under the First Amendment, the Supreme Court has always faced a dilemma, because the two clauses of the amendment in a sense clash with each other. That is, in protecting the rights of a particular religious group to engage in the free exercise of its faith, the Court might be viewed as

---

*Lemon v. Kurtzman, the Pennsylvania case, and Earley v. DiCenso and Robinson v. DiCenso, the Rhode Island cases, all 403 U.S. 602 (1971). In *Lemon*, the Court set forth a three-pronged test to determine if a given practice was constitutional or if it violated the separation of church and state: whether it had a secular purpose, whether it had the principal effect of advancing or inhibiting religion, and whether it complied with the "excessive government entanglement" standard the Court had cited in *Walz v. Tax Commission of the City of New York*, 397 U.S. 664 (1970).

*Zelman v. Simmons-Harris, No. 00-1751, June 2002.

The Supreme Court said "no": school prayer at a high school football game in Texas
Copyright © Bob Daemmrich/Stock, Boston/PictureQuest

favoring a religion in violation of the establishment clause. Recognizing this dilemma, the Court has attempted to exercise what it has called a "benevolent neutrality" in order to protect freedom of religion without sponsorship of a particular faith.

Loyalty and Security

Should those who would destroy the Bill of Rights enjoy its protection? This dilemma was at the heart of a great public debate that began with the end of the Second World War. In this area two constitutional principles clashed: the right to individual freedom of expression and the government's responsibility to protect national security.

Today, years after the collapse of the Soviet Union in 1991, it might be hard for many Americans to understand the political atmosphere that prevailed in the United States half a century ago. The emergence of the Soviet Union as a rival power to the United States, the onset of the Cold War, and the division of the world during the 1950s into two armed nuclear camps created fear of communism at home and generated pressures to curb dissent and root Communists or "radicals" out of government posts.

Some political leaders, notably Senator Joseph R. McCarthy, a Wisconsin Republican, exploited public concern for political benefit. During the early 1950s McCarthy's freewheeling investigations of alleged Communists in the State Department and other agencies injured many innocent persons, destroyed careers, and created a widespread climate of fear in the federal government and in the nation. Few dared to raise their voices against him. When he attacked the Army in 1954, a series of public hearings exposed McCarthy's methods to the blinding light of television and led to his censure by the Senate later that year. After that, McCarthy lost influence; he died in 1957.

Senator Joseph R. McCarthy
Copyright © Phillips/Black Star

In the 1990s, with the end of the Cold War, documents became available to historians, both in the United States and in the former Soviet Union, that shed additional light on the identities of certain Soviet agents and sympathizers who had worked inside the government in Washington decades earlier. But in the view of most analysts and historians, the new information did not justify McCarthy's scattershot approach or the unfair accusations that his name came to symbolize in the 1950s.

During the Cold War era, two opposing views crystallized in the Court and within American society. One view was that a nation, like an individual, has the right to self-preservation; it must take action against internal enemies, and it need not wait until the threat is carried out, for that may be too late. The other view was that the First Amendment guarantees free speech for everyone, that if Americans have confidence in the democratic system they need not fear other ideologies or the clash of ideas.

The effort to suppress dissent did not begin with "McCarthyism." As early as 1798, the Alien and Sedition Acts had provided a maximum fine of $2,000 and two years in prison for "malicious writing" against the government of President John Adams. The first person to be convicted under the acts was Matthew Lyon, a Vermont congressman whose "crime" was to accuse President Adams of "a continual grasp for power . . . an unbounded thirst for ridiculous pomp, foolish adulation and selfish avarice." After Jefferson became president in 1801, the various Alien and Sedition Acts were repealed or permitted to expire.

In 1940 Congress passed the Smith Act, which made it unlawful for any person to advocate overthrowing the government "by force or violence." In 1951 the Supreme Court upheld the constitutionality of the Smith Act and the conspiracy conviction of 11 Communist Party leaders.[87] In later decisions, however, the Supreme Court severely restricted the use of the act.[88]

After the outbreak of the Korean War, Congress passed the Internal Security Act of 1950, known as the McCarran Act. It required Communist "front" organizations to register with the attorney general. The Supreme Court held that the Communist Party could be compelled to register under the McCarran Act, but it was never actually forced to do so.[89] And the Court ruled that to require individual Communists to register would violate the Fifth Amendment.[90]

As the postwar years have shown, however, freedom of expression has varied sharply with the political climate; even a "fixed star" may be viewed through a very different telescope in each decade.

Due Process of Law

"The history of liberty," Justice Felix Frankfurter once wrote, "is largely the history of the observance of procedural safeguards."[91] A nation may have an enlightened system of government, but if the rights of individuals are abused, then the system falls short of its goals.

The Fifth and Fourteenth Amendments to the Constitution provide for **due process of law,** a phrase designed to protect the individual against the arbitrary power of the state. Sometimes the distinction is made between *substantive due process* (laws must be reasonable) and *procedural due process* (laws must be administered in a fair manner).

Until 1937 the Supreme Court used the concept of substantive due process to protect the "liberty" of businesses against regulation by Congress and the states. It adopted the view that laws regulating industry must be reasonable. After 1937, the Court abandoned substantive due process as it upheld laws passed by Congress during the New Deal to regulate business. In so doing, the Court took the view that economic regulation was the responsibility of Congress and the legislatures, not of the judicial branch. But in the area of civil rights, civil liberties, and privacy, the Court has continued to apply substantive due process.

Searches and Seizures   Due process begins at home, for the right of individuals to "be secure in their persons, houses, papers, and effects, against unreasonable searches and seizures" is spelled out in the Fourth Amendment and marks a fundamental difference between a free and a totalitarian society.

The Fourth Amendment also provides important protections against the government. In the United States, as a general principle, police are not authorized to search a home without a search warrant signed by a judicial officer and issued on "probable cause" to believe that the materials to be seized are in the place to be searched.

In 1999, for example, the Supreme Court ruled unanimously in two cases that police who allowed journalists and television cameras into people's homes to witness and record searches or arrests violated the Fourth Amendment.[92] In one of these cases, police in Rockville, Maryland, searching for a man who was a parole violator, took along a *Washington Post* reporter and photographer and raided the home of the man's parents, who were asleep. Police pinned the man's father to the floor with a gun to his head. He wore only boxer shorts; his wife wore a sheer nightgown.[93] In a companion case, 21 armed officers, accompanied by a TV crew from CNN, descended on the Montana home of a 72-year-old man with emphysema who was suspected of poisoning eagles.[94] The Court's decision in these two cases curbed but did not end the popular television programs that show police making dramatic arrests, because it did not apply to situations where journalists ride along with police to videotape action that takes place on the street or in other public places.

 for more information about CNN, see: **www.cnn.com**

Until 1980, police could lawfully enter a home without a warrant to make a valid arrest, and they could conduct a limited search at the same time. But in April

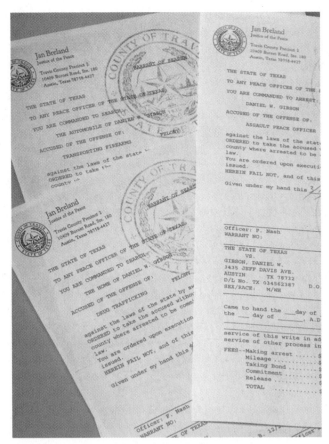

Search warrants issued in Travis County, Texas
Copyright © Bob Daemmrich/Stock, Boston/PictureQuest

of that year, the Supreme Court ruled that the Fourth Amendment prohibited police from entering a home without a warrant to make a routine arrest.[95] Police must obtain a warrant except in emergency circumstances, the Court held. Justice John Paul Stevens ruled, in effect, that a family's home is its castle: "The Fourth Amendment has drawn a firm line at the entrance to the house. Absent exigent circumstances, that threshold may not reasonably be crossed without a warrant."[96] The decision invalidated the laws of 23 states. But police with a search warrant do not have to knock and announce their presence before entering a house if there is a probability of violence or immediate destruction of evidence.[97]

In 1969 the Supreme Court ruled that police lacking a search warrant could not ransack a home in the course of making a lawful arrest but must confine their search to the suspect and the immediate surroundings.[98] The decision overturned the conviction of Ted Steven Chimel of California, who had been serving a five-years-to-life term for stealing rare coins—which police found after searching his home without a search warrant.

Although the Constitution is designed to protect against unreasonable government intrusion, in actual practice constitutional principles are sometimes violated. Two innocent families in Collinsville, Illinois, found that out when federal narcotics agents kicked in the doors of their homes, terrorized them at gunpoint, and ransacked their houses in a drug raid based on false information.

The agents had no search or arrest warrants. Subsequent investigations disclosed that dozens of other such raids, sometimes fatal to the victims, had been carried out by federal, state, and local narcotics agents.[99]

These violations of the Fourth Amendment rights of individuals are an unpleasant example of the gap between promise and performance in the American political system. Sometimes the outputs of the system violate the constitutional rights that distinguish the American democracy from authoritarian regimes. Although such episodes may be infrequent, they demonstrate that the system does not always function the way it was designed.

During the Nixon administration, it was disclosed that agents employed by the White House had burglarized the office of a psychiatrist who had treated Daniel Ellsberg, a former government official who leaked the Pentagon Papers, a secret history of the Vietnam War, to the news media. This was in addition to the illegal entry into the Democrats' Watergate headquarters by burglars working for President Nixon's campaign. It also was disclosed that Nixon himself had approved for a time a plan that included "surreptitious entry" into the homes or offices of persons suspected by the government of being a threat to internal security—even though the president had been warned, in writing, that this was "clearly illegal" and "amounts to burglary." In 1975 the FBI admitted it had conducted hundreds of illegal break-ins against dissident groups and individuals.[100]

Although the Bill of Rights was designed to guard against government misdeeds against individuals, public school students are not afforded the same Fourth Amendment protections as are other citizens. One case involved a 14-year-old girl whose purse was opened by a school official who found marijuana, a pipe, and letters indicating the student sold marijuana. The Court ruled, 6–3, that school officials do not need a warrant, or "probable cause" to believe a crime has taken place, in order to search students, only "reasonable grounds" to conduct a search.[101] In 1995 the Supreme Court held, 6–3, that public schools could require student athletes to submit to random drug testing.[102] The Court held that testing student athletes for drugs was reasonable. It ruled that students' rights under the Fourth Amendment were outweighed by a school's interest in deterring drug use. In 2002, the Supreme Court expanded its ruling to allow random drug testing of public school students engaged in a wide range of "competitive" activities, including cheerleading.*

Automobiles have less protection against search and seizure than do homes. Under Supreme Court rulings, police may search an automobile without a warrant if they have probable cause to believe it contains illegal articles, and also may search any containers and packages found in such a car, even in a locked trunk.[103] "When a legitimate search is underway," the Court held, police could not be expected to make "nice distinctions . . . between glove compartments, upholstered seats, trunks and wrapped packages."[104] And police may search the

---

Board of Education v. Earls, No. 01-332 (2002).

"Automobiles have less protection. . . ."
Port Authority police officers in New York City search a car for drugs.
Copyright © Craig Filipacchi/Liaison

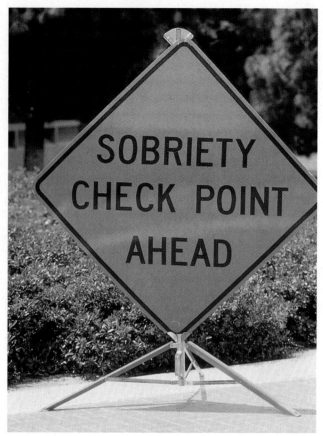

Copyright © Phil McCarten/PhotoEdit

personal belongings of passengers in a car whose driver is suspected of breaking the law, even though the passengers themselves are not suspected of a crime.[105]

Police who stop a car for a traffic violation may order the occupants to get out.[106] And the Court has also ruled that police may search a car and its contents if they have lawfully arrested its occupants.[107] That case arose in New York State when Roger Belton and three friends were stopped by a state trooper for speeding. The officer smelled burnt marijuana and saw an envelope on the floor marked "Supergold." He arrested all four people and, while searching Belton's jacket, found cocaine. The Court ruled the search was justified because it was limited to an area where a suspect might reach for a weapon or evidence.[108] But police may not search a car merely because the driver was speeding.[109]

The Supreme Court has also ruled that police may stop drivers at roadside checkpoints to see if they are intoxicated.[110] That decision, in 1990, was the first in which the Court has upheld the right of police, in enforcing the law, to detain individuals without any suspicion of wrongdoing. Until then, some basis for police action was required.

For example, in the landmark case of *Terry* v. *Ohio*, the Supreme Court ruled that police may stop and frisk a suspect on the street without a warrant if they are reasonably suspicious that the person is armed or dangerous.[111] A police officer also may stop and frisk a criminal suspect on the basis of an informant's tip that the officer considers to be reliable.[112] And police may arrest someone in a public place without a warrant on proba-

ble cause that the person has committed a crime.[113] The overwhelming majority of arrests in the United States are, in fact, made *without* a warrant.

The Court has ruled, 5–4, for example, that if someone flees at the mere sight of the police, that act may be suspicious enough to justify a stop-and-frisk search.[114] But it has also ruled that a person may not be stopped and searched simply because police receive an anonymous tip that the suspect is carrying a gun.[115]

Cherished constitutional principles are usually established in cases involving criminals and other people who are not pillars of the community. In 1957 Cleveland police, with no search warrant, barged into the house of a woman named Dollree Mapp. They did not find the fugitive or the betting slips they were after but seized some "lewd and lascivious books and pictures." She was tried and convicted for possession of these items. But the Supreme Court ruled in 1961 that a state could not prosecute a person with unconstitutionally seized evidence, a decision that protected not only Dollree Mapp but every American.[116]

The Supreme Court had long held that the federal government could not use illegally seized evidence in court, a principle known as the **exclusionary rule**.[117] The *Mapp* case meant that the states, too, were subject to this rule. Over the years, however, the Court backed away from its earlier decisions about illegally seized evidence, creating enough exceptions to the exclusionary rule that

Police may stop and frisk suspects without a warrant. Here, members of an East Los Angeles street gang are searched for weapons.
Copyright © A. Ramey/Woodfin Camp

criminal defendants could no longer count on it to protect them in every instance.

In a series of cases over several years, the Burger Court substantially narrowed the exclusionary rule. It held that a witness before a grand jury could not refuse to answer questions based on evidence seized unlawfully.[118] Later, Justice William J. Brennan, Jr., warned in a dissent that the rule faced "slow strangulation."[119] And the Court curtailed the power of federal courts to overturn state court convictions because of illegally seized evidence.[120]

The trend continued. In 1983 the Supreme Court ruled in an Illinois drug case in which police had arrested a couple on an anonymous tip and, armed with a search warrant, seized 350 pounds of marijuana in their home and car. The Court, in deciding against the defendants, held that judges who issue warrants do not have to decide if the anonymous tips are true and instead should exercise "common sense."[121] And the Court ruled that evidence obtained illegally may be admitted at a trial if the evidence would "inevitably" have been discovered lawfully.[122]

In 1984, the Supreme Court for the first time created a "good faith" exception to the rule, permitting courts to consider illegally seized evidence in some cases when police reasonably believed that their search was constitutional, even when their search warrants turned out to be flawed.[123] The Court's 6–3 decision was immediately

Dollree Mapp
AP/Wide World

hailed by conservatives, who contended that the exclusionary rule had interfered with law enforcement.

In still another case, after the fatal beating of a woman in Roxbury, Massachusetts, police searched the home of her friend Osborne Sheppard and found incriminating evidence, which was used to convict him of murder. Later, it turned out that police had used the wrong form in filling out the search warrant. The Supreme Court ruled against the defendant.[124] And in 1987 the Court held that evidence seized improperly as the result of "honest mistakes" by police may be used at trial.[125]

However, because courts still can and do suppress evidence seized illegally, police, in many although certainly not all cases, have become more cautious and careful in conducting searches. As a result, the exclusionary rule, however weakened, still serves to protect citizens against violations of the Fourth Amendment.

Sometimes Congress passes legislation that attempts to overturn or modify Supreme Court decisions. That happened in the case of police searches of newsrooms. In a controversial 1978 decision, the Supreme Court had permitted police to search newspaper offices and seize evidence of a crime, even though the newspaper was an innocent third party not suspected of any wrongdoing.[126] The case began in 1971 on the campus of Stanford University. A group of antiwar demonstrators attacked police, two of whom were seriously injured. The university newspaper, the *Stanford Daily*, published photographs of the incident. The next day, armed with a warrant, police swooped down on the paper's newsroom and searched its photo labs, filing cabinets, desks, and wastepaper baskets. The Supreme Court ruled that the First Amendment does not bar newsroom searches for criminal evidence.

 for more information about the Stanford Daily, see:
daily.stanford.org

In the aftermath of the Stanford case, sheriff's deputies and other law enforcement officials raided a television station newsroom in Boise, Idaho, in 1980, searching for and seizing videotapes of a prison riot. The local prosecutor said he needed the tapes to identify the riot leaders. Reacting to these incidents, Congress enacted a law barring most such newsroom searches. The law, the Privacy Protection Act of 1980, ordinarily requires federal, state, and local authorities to use subpoenas, rather than searches, in seeking evidence from journalists, authors, scholars, and others who write for publication.

The Uninvited Ear In the technological age, the right of privacy has been threatened by highly sophisticated wiretapping and eavesdropping devices.

In Washington practically anyone of importance assumes, or at least jokes, that his or her telephone is tapped. (One leading columnist would begin his telephone conversations: "Hello, everybody.") As a Senate committee has demonstrated, even the olive in a martini may be an electronic "bug," a tiny transmitter that broadcasts con-

THE CONSTITUTION PROTECTS TELEPHONE BOOTHS

The Fourth Amendment protects people, not places. . . . No less than an individual in a business office, in a friend's apartment, or in a taxicab, a person in a telephone booth may rely upon the protection of the Fourth Amendment.

One who occupies it, shuts the door behind him, and pays the toll that permits him to place a call, is surely entitled to assume that the words he utters into the mouthpiece will not be broadcast to the world.

—Justice Potter Stewart,
in *Katz* v. *United States* (1967)

versations. With infrared light, persons in a room may be photographed through the wall of an adjoining room. Infrared light also may be used to pick up speech as far away as 34 miles. A person who swallows a "radio pill" becomes for a time a human broadcasting station, emitting signals that enable an investigator to follow the subject from some distance away.[127]

Modern technology has made possible a new form of government intrusion into the private lives of individuals, a threat that Justice Potter Stewart had called the "uninvited ear." Many prosecutors and law enforcement officials insist that wiretapping and electronic bugs are essential tools in cases involving espionage, kidnapping, and organized crime. Other observers believe that such devices inevitably will be abused by government authorities and result in the violation of constitutional liberties.

Despite Justice Holmes's denunciation of wiretapping as "dirty business," the Supreme Court for almost 40 years (1928–1967) held that the practice did not violate the Fourth Amendment.[128] But the Federal Communications Act of 1934 outlawed wiretapping, and three years later the Supreme Court held that wiretap evidence could not be used in federal courts.[129] Finally, in 1967, the Court caught up with modern technology by ruling that a conversation was tangible and could be seized electronically. Thus, placing a bug or tap did not have to involve physical trespass to violate the Fourth Amendment, the Court ruled, and police therefore could not eavesdrop without a court warrant. The case involved Charles Katz, a Los Angeles gambler who made interstate telephone calls to bookmakers from a public phone booth to bet on college basketball games. Unknown to Katz, the FBI had taped a microphone to the top of his favorite phone booth on Sunset Boulevard. Because the FBI had no warrant, the Supreme Court held that Katz's constitutional rights had been violated and threw out his conviction.[130]

Technology creates continuing dilemmas for the Supreme Court's justices. Cordless telephones came into widespread use in the 1980s, but conversations over those phones can often be overheard. Unbeknownst to the Scott Tyler family of Dixon, Iowa, their nearby neighbors, Sandra and Rich Berodt, were listening to their conversations, mistakenly concluded that they were dealing in cocaine, and called the sheriff's office. The Tylers' conversations were then taped, and based in part on what was overheard, Scott Tyler was charged with stealing $35,000 in merchandise from his company, convicted, and jailed for four months. The Tylers sued the Berodts for listening in on their conversations. But the Supreme Court let stand a lower court decision that the Tylers had no "reasonable expectation of privacy" when they used their cordless phone.[131] The Fourth Amendment may protect telephone booths, but it does not protect cordless phones.

When public concern over crime increases, so do pressures to employ wiretaps and bugs. In the late 1960s "law and order" became a growing political issue. In 1968 Congress passed the Omnibus Crime Control and Safe Streets Act permitting court-authorized wiretapping and bugging by federal, state, and local authorities in a wide variety of cases, and the use of such evidence in trials.

In 1969, when the Nixon administration came to power, the Justice Department claimed it had the authority, even without court approval, to tap and bug domestic groups it considered to be a threat to internal security. However, the Supreme Court ruled, in an 8–0 decision, that this highly controversial policy violated the Fourth Amendment of the Constitution.*

President Nixon, in a supposed effort to plug news "leaks" and protect "national security," authorized FBI wiretaps of a total of 17 White House aides, other officials, and news reporters. Warrantless wiretapping and bugging had taken place under other presidents as well, including Lyndon Johnson and John F. Kennedy. In 1978 Congress passed the Foreign Intelligence Surveillance Act (FISA), which, for the first time, required a court order even for wiretapping and bugging in national security investigations. The law also established a special, seven-judge court to issue such warrants. The only exception in the law permits the government to eavesdrop on the communications of foreign powers without a warrant. The special court did not appear to be any great obstacle to government wiretapping, however. As of the end of 1998, the panel of rotating judges to whom

requests come had approved 12,941 wiretapping applications and had rejected only one.[132]

Because the 1968 Omnibus Crime Control Act required police to obtain court warrants to eavesdrop in domestic criminal investigations, the two laws, taken together, prohibit virtually all electronic surveillance without a warrant. But in 1979 the Supreme Court held that a break-in by government agents to plant a court-authorized bug is constitutional; it said that Congress had not ruled out "covert entry" to carry out electronic surveillance.[133]

Rights of the Accused   "Due process of law" may mean little to average Americans—unless and until they are arrested. This is because most of the important procedural safeguards provided by the Constitution, as interpreted by the Supreme Court, concern the rights of accused persons.

Before anyone may be brought to trial for a serious federal crime, there must be a grand jury **indictment**, a finding that enough evidence exists to warrant a criminal trial. The Constitution does not require states to use grand juries; in most state cases, in place of an indictment, to bring a person to trial officials file a **criminal information**, a statement presented to the court by a prosecutor charging a person with a crime. The Bill of Rights entitles suspects or defendants to be represented by a lawyer; to be informed of their legal rights and of the charges against them; to have a speedy and public trial by jury; to summon witnesses to testify in their behalf; to cross-examine prosecution witnesses; and to refuse to testify against themselves. In addition, they may not be held in excessive bail, or subjected to cruel and unusual punishment or to double jeopardy for the same offense. These rights are contained in the Fifth through Eighth Amendments.

As far back as 1957, the Court had laid down the *Mallory* rule, requiring that a suspect in a federal case be arraigned without unnecessary delay.[134] Under Chief Justice Earl Warren, the Supreme Court, in a series of split decisions in the mid-1960s, greatly strengthened the rights of accused persons, particularly in the period immediately following arrest. It is in the station-house stage that police traditionally attempt to extract a confession from suspects. It is also the very time at which accused persons may be most disoriented, frightened, and uncertain of their rights. The Court came under severe political attack for these decisions, which many law enforcement authorities argued would hamper their ability to fight crime.

The Warren Court rulings came at a time of rising violence and unrest in America. Many citizens, worried about "law and order," focused their criticism on the Supreme Court and on the judicial system, which was often accused of "coddling" criminals. Supporters of the Warren Court decisions and of civil liberties argued that there is no better test of a democracy than the procedural safeguards it erects to protect accused persons from the police power of the state.

United States v. United States District Court for the Eastern District of Michigan, 407 U.S. 297 (1972). In this case, sometimes also known as the *Keith* case, the Supreme Court did not address itself to the question of whether the president had power to order electronic surveillance against foreign intelligence activities or agents.

A landmark case of the Warren era began in Chicago in 1960 when police arrested Danny Escobedo, a laborer suspected of murdering his brother-in-law. Under interrogation he asked to see his lawyer, but the request was refused. During the long night at police headquarters, Danny Escobedo confessed. In 1964, by a vote of 5–4, the Supreme Court reversed his conviction, freeing him after four and a half years in prison. The Court ruled that under the Sixth Amendment, a suspect is entitled to counsel even during police interrogation once "the process shifts from investigatory to accusatory."[135] Nor can the government use incriminating statements made by a suspect to an informer imprisoned with him or her before a trial; the Supreme Court has ruled that use of such evidence deprives the suspect of the right to have an attorney present, unless the incriminating statements concern a separate crime for which the prisoner has not been indicted.[136]

***The Battle over* Miranda**   In 1966, the Supreme Court, in the case of *Miranda* v. *Arizona*, required that suspects in police custody be advised of their rights before they are interrogated. These **Miranda warnings** ("You have the right to remain silent. . . . Anything you say may be used against you in a court of law. . . . You have the right to an attorney. . . .") became familiar to generations of television viewers of crime shows. The Supreme Court's decision greatly expanded the protection granted to suspects. In March 1963 Ernesto A. Miranda, an indigent 23-year-old man, described by the Court as mentally disturbed, was arrested 10 days after the kidnapping and rape of an 18-year-old woman near Phoenix, Arizona. The woman picked Miranda out of a police lineup, and after two hours of interrogation—during which he was not told of his right to silence and a lawyer—he confessed. The Supreme Court struck down Miranda's conviction; in a controversial 5–4 decision, the Court ruled that the Fifth Amendment's protection against self-incrimination requires that suspects be clearly informed of their rights before they are asked any questions by police.

 for more information about Miranda warnings, see: www.courttv.com/legalhelp/lawguide/criminal/91.html

Chief Justice Warren ruled for the narrow majority that statements made by accused persons may not be used against them in court unless strict procedures are followed: "Prior to any questioning, the person must be warned that he has a right to remain silent, that any statement he does make may be used against him, and that he has a right to the presence of an attorney, either retained or appointed."[137] Although a defendant may knowingly waive these rights, Warren ruled, he cannot be questioned further if at any point he asks to see a lawyer or indicates "in any manner" that he does not wish to be interrogated.

The chief justice, declaring that Miranda went to "the roots of our concepts of American criminal

Ernesto Miranda after his arrest on parole violations
Arizona Republic

jurisprudence," argued eloquently that the "compelling atmosphere" of a "menacing police interrogation" was designed to intimidate suspects, break their will, and lead to an involuntary confession in violation of the Fifth Amendment. That is why, he concluded, "procedural safeguards" must be observed in the police station. In a strong dissent Justice John Harlan said: "It's obviously going to mean a gradual disappearance of confessions as a legitimate tool of law enforcement." After the decision many police began carrying "Miranda cards" to read suspects their rights.

With the election of President Nixon in 1968, the era of the Warren Court ended. In 1969 Nixon named a new chief justice, Warren E. Burger. Within four years, Nixon had appointed three more Supreme Court justices who were, as a group, generally more conservative than their predecessors. Particularly in the area of criminal justice, the pendulum gradually began to swing back from the liberal philosophy of the Warren Court.

In 1971 the Burger Court handed down a decision that greatly narrowed the scope of the *Miranda* ruling. The Court held that if a statement were made by a suspect without proper *Miranda* warnings, it still could be used to discredit his or her testimony at a trial.* In a series of

---

Harris v. *New York*, 401 U.S. 222 (1971). The defendant claimed at his trial that he had sold baking soda, not heroin, to an undercover narcotics agent. The prosecution then read a statement the defendant had made, without police warnings, just after his arrest, admitting the sale and making no mention of baking soda.

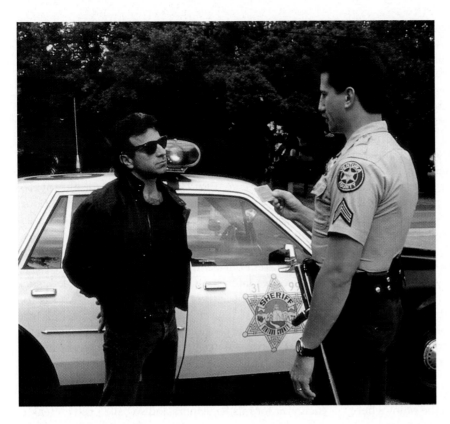

Reading Miranda rights to a suspect in California
Copyright © Laima Druskis/Photo Researchers

decisions, the Supreme Court retreated even further from Miranda.[138] For example, it held that even after suspects exercise the right to remain silent about one crime, they still can be questioned about another.[139] Despite these rulings, in 1976 the Burger Court did reinforce the *Miranda* decision by holding that silence by suspects after being advised of their *Miranda* rights could not later be used against them.[140] However, in 1980 the Court ruled that if a defendant took the stand at a trial, he or she could be questioned about pre-arrest silence.[141]

In 1977 the Burger Court, in a grisly Iowa murder case, reaffirmed the right of counsel provided by the Sixth Amendment. The suspect, Robert Anthony Williams, with no lawyer present, led police to the body after a detective drew him into conversation about the crime during a long automobile ride. The Supreme Court, by a 5–4 margin, reversed the conviction.[142] But when the same defendant was found guilty at a second trial, the Supreme Court upheld his conviction, ruling that the body would have been discovered even without the help of Williams.

The Court also appeared to permit the use of subtle psychology on suspects unless police were aware that their actions or words were "reasonably likely" to make a suspect confess.[143] The case arose when Thomas Innis, a murder suspect, led police to a hidden weapon after officers remarked that it would be too bad if a child "would pick up the gun and maybe kill herself." The Court said that this was not the sort of "interrogation" forbidden by *Miranda*.

And in 1984, in another retreat from Miranda, the Supreme Court held that where "public safety" is endan-

gered, police can question suspects without advising them of their rights.[144]

In 1985 President Reagan's attorney general, Edwin Meese III, publicly attacked the Supreme Court's *Miranda* decision as "infamous" and wrong.[145] And the Court, under Chief Justice William H. Rehnquist, whom President Reagan appointed in 1986, continued to narrow the scope of suspects' rights.[146]

Ernesto Miranda was stabbed to death in a barroom quarrel in Phoenix, Arizona, on February 1, 1976. Fernando Rodriguez Zamora was arrested on a murder charge for allegedly handing the knife to the assailant, who fled. The police read Zamora his rights. They used a "*Miranda* card."

More than three decades after the *Miranda* ruling, a new controversy arose. In 1968, Congress had passed major crime legislation including a section that attempted to overturn the Supreme Court's *Miranda* decision. However, Congress does not have power to overturn an interpretation of the Constitution by the Supreme Court; that can only be done by a constitutional amendment. But Congress does have power to modify Supreme Court decisions if the Court's ruling does not address a basic constitutional issue.

Little attention was paid to Section 3501 of the Congress's 1968 legislation until Paul Cassell, a conservative law professor at the University of Utah and a former Justice Department official, began a crusade to challenge *Miranda*. Cassell maintained that many crimes went unpunished because suspects, once warned, declined to confess. He argued that the Supreme Court had not said the warnings set forth in *Miranda* were required by the Constitution, and that the overlooked Section 3501 of the crime law had therefore invalidated the decision. As a test case, Cassell chose the interrogation by the FBI in 1997 of Charles Thomas Dickerson, who was suspected of robbing a bank in Alexandria, Virginia. Although he was warned of his rights, Dickerson claimed the warning had been given after he confessed. In 1999, the Court of Appeals in Richmond, Virginia, the most conservative of the federal appeals courts, sided with Dickerson. The Supreme Court agreed to hear the case.

In late June of the year 2000, in a landmark decision, the Supreme Court voted, 7–2, to reaffirm its 1966 *Miranda* decision, ruling that the warnings police must give to criminal defendants are in fact required by the Constitution.[147]

In its majority opinion, written by Chief Justice Rehnquist, the Court declared: "We hold that *Miranda*, being a constitutional decision of this court, may not be in effect overruled by an act of Congress, and we decline to overrule Miranda ourselves."

The Court added that "Miranda has become embedded in routine police practice to the point where the warnings have become part of our national culture." Those words were a significant reminder that in interpreting the Constitution, the Court considers not only legal arguments but the political currents and attitudes of the larger society of which it is so important a part.

The Right to Counsel The right of an indigent defendant to have a lawyer in a state court might seem basic, but in fact it was not established by the Supreme Court until 1963 in the celebrated case of *Gideon* v. *Wainwright*.[148]

Clarence Earl Gideon
Copyright © Flip
Schulke/Black Star

Clarence Earl Gideon petitioned the Supreme Court in 1962 from the Florida State Prison at Raiford, where he was serving a five-year term for allegedly breaking into a poolroom in Panama City, Florida, and stealing some beer, wine, and coins from a cigarette machine and a jukebox. A drifter, a man whose life had had more than the normal share of disasters, Gideon nevertheless had one idea fixed firmly in his mind—that the Constitution of the United States entitled him to a fair trial. And this, he insisted in his petition, he had not received. Clarence Earl Gideon had not been provided with a lawyer by the court. In 1942 the Supreme Court had ruled that the right of counsel was not a "fundamental right," essential to a fair trial in a state court, and that it was not guaranteed by the due process clause of the Fourteenth Amendment.[149] But in *Gideon*, two decades later, the Court changed its mind. Justice Black declared for the majority: A person "who is too poor to hire a lawyer cannot be assured a fair trial unless counsel is provided for him." A few months later, Gideon won a new trial and this time—with the help of a lawyer—he was acquitted.

The landmark *Gideon* decision left open a question of vital importance to millions of poor persons arrested each year for misdemeanors and so-called petty offenses, crimes carrying maximum penalties of six months in jail. Because Gideon had been convicted of a felony, the decision in his case did not clarify whether defendants accused of lesser offenses also were entitled to free counsel. Then in 1972 the Supreme Court overruled the conviction of Jon Richard Argersinger, a Tallahassee, Florida, gas station attendant who had not been offered an attorney when he pleaded guilty to carrying a concealed weapon, a misdemeanor.[150] The decision meant that no persons—unless they voluntarily give up their right to a lawyer—may be sentenced to jail for any offense, no matter how minor, unless they have been represented by an attorney at their trial.

It should be noted, of course, that the concept of due process is not limited under the Constitution to protecting the rights of criminal defendants. It applies, in varying degrees, in civil proceedings as well. In administrative actions related to welfare benefits, education, licensing, zoning, and many other areas, states and the federal government must observe due process. However, individuals or groups in such administrative proceedings and civil cases are not afforded the same strict protections of due process as are followed in a courtroom for defendants whose liberty is at stake. A local school board, for example, may hold a public hearing, but it is not obliged to follow the same rules as a court of law in a criminal case.

An Expanding Umbrella of Rights

The Bill of Rights was passed as a bulwark against the new *federal* government. It did not apply to the *states*.

Congress, in fact, rejected a proposal by James Madison to prohibit the states from interfering with basic liberties.

Because America has a federal system of government, this created a paradox: The same constitutional rights established under the federal government were often meaningless within a state. It was as though the Bill of Rights were a ticket valid for travel on a high-speed train but no good for local commuting. Not until 1925 did the Supreme Court systematically begin to apply the Bill of Rights to the states. By 1970 the process was virtually complete. But even today, there is no written provision in the Constitution requiring the states to observe the Bill of Rights.

In 1833 the Supreme Court ruled in *Barron* v. *Baltimore* that the provisions of the Bill of Rights did not apply to the state governments and "this Court cannot so apply them."[151] Near the end of the Civil War, Congress passed the Fourteenth Amendment, which for the first time provided that "No State shall . . . deprive any person of life, liberty, or property, without due process of law." Did Congress thereby mean to "incorporate" the entire Bill of Rights into the Fourteenth Amendment and apply the Bill of Rights to the states? The argument never has been settled, but the point—thanks to the decisions of the Supreme Court in the 20th century—is rapidly becoming moot.

In the *Gitlow* case in 1925, the Court held that freedom of speech and press were among the "fundamental personal rights" protected by the Fourteenth Amendment from abridgment by the states.[152] The Court thus began a process of **selective incorporation** of the Bill of Rights by applying most of its provisions to the states under the Fourteenth Amendment. Two years later, the Court confirmed that freedom of speech was locked in under the Fourteenth Amendment.[153] In 1931 freedom of the press was specifically applied to the states.[154] In 1932, the Court partially incorporated the Sixth Amendment by requiring that a defendant in a capital case be represented by a lawyer.[155] Two years later, it applied freedom of religion to the states.[156] In 1937 freedom of assembly was held to apply to the states.[157]

Later that same year came the landmark incorporation decision of *Palko* v. *Connecticut*.[158] Frank Palko had been sentenced to life imprisonment for killing two policemen. Under an unusual Connecticut statute, the state could appeal and did; a new trial resulted in a death sentence. Palko appealed to the Supreme Court, contending that the second trial had placed him in double jeopardy, in violation of the Fifth Amendment. Justice Benjamin Cardozo ruled that the Fourteenth Amendment did require the states to abide by the Bill of Rights where the rights at stake were so fundamental that "neither liberty nor justice would exist if they were sacrificed." But, Cardozo added, although procedural rights such as the immunity against double jeopardy were important, "they are not of the very essence of a scheme of ordered liberty," and therefore not binding

to the states. The distinction was not helpful to Frank Palko; he was executed.

In 1947 the *Everson* case incorporated the principle of separation of church and state, and in 1961 *Mapp* established that the Fourth Amendment applied to the states. In 1962 the Court carried the Eighth Amendment's protection against cruel and unusual punishment to the states, and it further extended this protection in 1972 when it held that capital punishment as then administered constituted cruel and unusual punishment in violation of the Eighth Amendment.[159] In rapid succession, other rights were applied to the states: the Fifth Amendment's protection against self-incrimination;[160] and the Sixth Amendment's rights to counsel,[161] to a speedy trial,[162] to confrontation of an accused person by the witnesses against him,[163] to compulsory process for obtaining witnesses,[164] and to trial by jury in all serious criminal cases.[165]

In 1969, on Earl Warren's final day as chief justice, the Court, in *Benton* v. *Maryland*,[166] finally applied the Fifth Amendment's prohibition of double jeopardy to the states; it ruled that John Dalmer Benton should not have been tried twice for larceny. The Court thus overruled Justice Cardozo's decision in the *Palko* case.

The process of incorporation had in effect come full circle in the 32 years between *Palko* and *Benton*. Of the portions of the Bill of Rights that could apply to the states, almost every significant provision—with the exception of the Fifth Amendment's right to indictment by grand jury for major crimes—had been applied.* Thus, through the slow and shifting process of selective incorporation, the Supreme Court has brought the states almost entirely under the protective umbrella of the Bill of Rights.

Balancing Liberty and Order

At a time when democracy is under pressure, when the American political system is being tested to determine whether it can meet the problems of an urbanized, complex, and changing society and the impact of economic globalization, the Bill of Rights is more important than ever.

The Bill of Rights and the Supreme Court remain a buffer between popular emotion and constitutional principle. For it is precisely in times of stress that fundamental liberties require the most protection. As

---

*The Supreme Court, in *Hurtado* v. *California*, 110 U.S. 516 (1884), and later cases, declined to apply to the states the requirement of a grand jury indictment. Four other provisions of the Bill of Rights have not been incorporated to apply to the states—these have not been tested at the Supreme Court level. They are the right to a jury trial in civil cases where the amount in dispute exceeds $20 (Seventh Amendment); the ban on "excessive bail" and "fines" (Eighth Amendment); the right of the people "to keep and bear arms" (Second Amendment); and the ban on peacetime quartering of soldiers in private homes (Third Amendment). See Henry J. Abraham and Barbara A. Perry, *Freedom and the Court: Civil Rights and Liberties in the United States*, 7th ed. (New York: Oxford University Press, 1998), pp. 87–91.

Justice Robert H. Jackson put it so eloquently, freedom to differ over "things that do not matter much" is a "mere shadow" of freedom. "The test of its substance is the right to differ as to things that touch the heart of the existing order."[167]

Although the Supreme Court may at times be more zealous than other institutions in protecting civil liberties, it is by no means insensitive to public pressure. As John P. Frank has noted: "The dominant lesson of our history . . . is that courts love liberty most when it is under pressure least."[168] It is not enough, therefore, to leave the protection of fundamental liberties to the courts. Public support for civil liberties is a vital factor in the preservation of those liberties.

It is in the field of civil liberties and civil rights that some of the most sensitive demands and supports (inputs) are fed into the political system. For example, in weighing the rights of defendants versus the suppression of crime by society, the federal government is making some highly important allocations of values (outputs). And in Supreme Court decisions on topics such as abortion, the rights of suspects, capital punishment, and school prayer, the public reaction (feedback) is formidable.

In applying the First Amendment and in balancing the claims of individual rights versus those of society, the Supreme Court generally moved during the 1960s in the direction of freer expression, reflecting the attitudes of a more permissive society. However, the Warren Court's decisions on the rights of defendants collided with a public alarmed about crime. In the 1970s, under Chief Justice Warren Burger, the Court became more conservative. The Rehnquist Court in some, but by no means all, decisions expanded the rights of free expression and of the press even as it continued, in many instances, to limit the rights of criminal defendants.

As always, the Court was charting new waters against a background of strong public sentiment. The delicate balance between liberty and order is constantly shifting, from issue to issue and from one decade to the next. Even with the Constitution as ballast, this will always be so.

CITIZENSHIP

Who Is a Citizen?

Although the Constitution as framed in 1787 uses the phrase "citizen of the United States," the term was not defined until the adoption of the Fourteenth Amendment in 1868. It provides that: "All persons born or naturalized in the United States . . . are citizens of the United States and of the State wherein they reside."

The amendment rests on the principle of **jus soli** ("right of soil"), which confers citizenship by place of birth. Congress by law has also adopted the principle of **jus sanguinis** ("right of blood"), under which the citizenship of a child is determined by that of the parents. All persons born in the United States, except for the children of high-ranking foreign diplomats, are citizens. But in addition, children born abroad of American parents, or even of one American parent, may become citizens if they and their parents meet the complex and varying legal requirements.

An immigrant who wishes to become a citizen may become "naturalized" after residing in the United States continuously for five years, or three years in the case of the spouse of a citizen. Applicants must be able to read, write, and speak English and demonstrate knowledge of the history, principles, and form of government of the United States. The oath of citizenship is administered by a federal judge, but the processing of applications for citizenship is handled by the Immigration and Naturalization Service (INS) of the Department of Justice. Children under age 18 of naturalized citizens normally derive their American citizenship from their parents. Generally speaking, naturalized citizens enjoy the same rights as native-born Americans, although no naturalized citizen may be elected president or vice president.

Loss of Citizenship

It is sometimes believed that persons lose their citizenship if imprisoned for a year and a day, but this is not so; the laws of most of the 50 states deprive persons convicted of certain crimes of the right to vote, but no state may deprive Americans, native-born or naturalized, of their citizenship. In general, the Supreme Court has barred congressional attempts to deprive natural-born Americans of their citizenship as punishment for crimes. For example, the Court has ruled that desertion from the armed forces during wartime is not grounds for deprivation of citizenship, because that penalty would constitute "cruel and unusual punishment," forbidden by the Eighth Amendment,[169] and it struck down a law that provided automatic loss of citizenship for leaving the country in wartime to evade the draft.[170] As a result, the young men who went to live in Canada during the late 1960s to avoid military service in the Vietnam War did not lose their citizenship. In January 1977 President Jimmy Carter granted a blanket pardon to most Vietnam draft evaders.

The Supreme Court has held that naturalized citizens enjoy the same rights as native-born Americans.[171] It voided a law that said naturalized persons lost their citizenship for living three years in their country of national origin.

And in 1967, in the landmark case of *Afroyim* v. *Rusk*, the Court ruled that Congress had no power to take away American citizenship unless it is freely renounced.[172] Specifically, the Court held that Beys Afroyim, a natural-

Naturalization ceremony, California
Copyright © Porter Gifford/Liaison

ized American, could not be deprived of citizenship for voting in an election in Israel.

A Nation of Immigrants

In the 1920s, Congress imposed a "national origins" system of quotas to curb the wave of immigration that followed the First World War. Opponents of the national origins quota system argued that it was based on racial prejudice and designed to give preference to white, northern Europeans over immigrants from southern and eastern Europe. For example, in 1965, before the system was changed, the quota for all countries totaled 158,503. Of this, 108,931 (70 percent) was allotted to three countries—Great Britain, Ireland, and Germany. Italy, where thousands of young people desired to come to the United States, had a quota of 5,666. India had a quota of 100, as did most of the Asian and African nations. (From 1917 until 1952, Chinese and all other Asians were completely excluded.)

The Immigration Act of 1965 abolished the national origins quota system and substituted a new annual ceiling that Congress in 1980 set at 270,000 a year. The law also permitted a varying number of refugees to enter each year above that total.

By the mid-1980s, Congress was struggling to cope with problems created by the increasing flow of immigrants who entered the United States illegally, particularly from south of the border. In 1986 Congress passed a major immigration bill designed to reduce the flow of undocumented immigrants by punishing employers who knowingly hired them. The law also granted legal status to those who had arrived before January 1, 1982. The law did little to slow down the tide of undocumented aliens, however. Government and civilian demographers estimated that there were about 5 million persons in the country illegally.[173] Some analysts put the figure much higher.

In 1990, Congress enacted a comprehensive revision of the immigration laws, setting a new annual ceiling of 675,000 immigrants beginning in 1995. The new law gave preference to relatives of U.S. citizens and was also designed to allow more Europeans to immigrate to America and to attract professionals, scientists, executives, and workers with special skills. It also eliminated the provisions of the McCarran-Walter Act of 1952 that had excluded people from entering the United States because of their political beliefs or ideology. In 1991, the State Department began a three-year lottery program to allow 40,000 immigrants annually from Ireland and

A highway sign on Interstate 5 near San Diego, California, warns motorists to watch out for undocumented immigrants darting across the road. Many have been killed at this spot at night.

Copyright © Bart Bartholomew/ Black Star

other countries from which immigration had been reduced when the national origins system was abolished in 1965. Beginning in 1995, under the annual ceiling 55,000 immigrants have been admitted each year from various countries, also by lottery.

In addition to immigrants who arrive under the annual ceiling, refugees may be admitted if they are granted political asylum. The Refugee Act of 1980 defined those who may claim political asylum as persons with "a well-founded fear of persecution" based on race, religion, nationality, or their political opinions. Washington interpreted the law narrowly, to bar those whom it claimed were simply seeking better economic conditions.

By the early 1990s, America had tightened the restrictions on political refugees seeking asylum on its shores. A decade earlier, thousands of Cuban and Haitian refugees who streamed into Florida by boat in 1980 were admitted outside any quotas and given special status. Vietnamese "boat people" who escaped from Vietnam during the same period were admitted to the United States under the parole authority of the attorney general.

But by 1992, thousands of Haitian refugees who had tried to escape their country by boat were forcibly turned back by the Coast Guard under a policy begun by President Bush and continued by President Clinton. In 1993, the Supreme Court, by a vote of 8–1, upheld Clinton's policy of intercepting Haitian refugees at sea and returning them to their homeland without any hearing on whether they should be granted political asylum.[174] Under a 1995 agreement with Cuba, the United States began returning Cuban refugees who were intercepted in boats by the Coast Guard on their hazardous journey toward Florida. Under the accord, Havana agreed it

would take no action against the migrants for leaving Cuba. But intercepted Cubans who could demonstrate a well-founded fear of persecution in their country could be resettled to other countries rather than being forced to return home.

Not all immigrants seek to become citizens, of course. Persons living abroad can apply for an immigrant visa, and if approved they are granted legal permanent residence when they arrive in the United States. They then receive "green cards," alien registration cards, permitting them to work. Foreign students, certain undocumented immigrants, and temporary workers already in this country can also apply for legal permanent residence. There were about 10.5 million legal permanent residents in the United States in the 1990s.[175]

The Supreme Court has considerably enlarged the rights of legal immigrants by providing them with access, equal to that of citizens, to welfare benefits, Medicaid, and the right to practice law (although not to state employment as troopers or teachers).[176] And the children of undocumented aliens have the same right to attend public schools as the children of citizens.[177]

By the mid-1990s, however, a political backlash had developed against immigrants who crossed the nation's borders and entered the United States illegally. The sentiment was particularly high in states such as California, Texas, and Florida, which had a high influx of undocumented immigrants.

In California, the Republican governor, Pete Wilson, found a responsive audience for his anti-immigration crusade. Wilson argued that the state was spending more than $3 billion a year on education, health care, and prisons for undocumented immigrants. He supported Proposition 187, a measure to deny government welfare and other benefits to per-

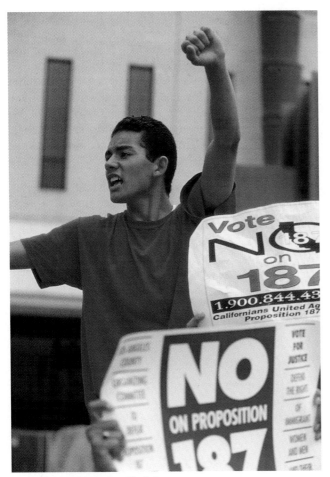

Copyright © Todd Bigelow/Black Star

issues, whether they dissent from established policy or support it, they are participating in the democratic process. Their opinions and actions are inputs to the political system. Freedom to dissent is an important aspect of democracy. In fact, it may be argued that one of the most important responsibilities Americans have is to exercise the rights protected by the Constitution, including those of free speech and dissent.

Voting in elections, participating in political party activity and community programs, forming and expressing political opinions, either singly or through groups—all are necessary to the workings of a healthy political system.

Many Americans, however, lament that the system is not responsive enough to their interests. They complain that politicians are only interested in getting reelected and lining their own pockets. Often, they are right. But sometimes those who feel this way fail to take as simple a step as registering to vote. Frequently it does seem that the political system is slow to respond to pressures for change, and that ordinary citizens have no way to express themselves to influence political leaders. Yet, at times, individual citizens have shown that it is not only possible to "fight City Hall" but, occasionally, to win.

In Los Angeles three decades ago, a social worker named John Serrano, the son of a Mexican shoemaker, was told by a principal to get his children out of the barrio of East Los Angeles and into a better school "if you want to give them a chance." Serrano took the advice and moved out to a suburb, but he did not forget the encounter. It seemed to him unjust that schools in a poor Mexican American neighborhood should be worse than those in wealthier neighborhoods. He joined forces with John E. Coons, a University of California law professor who had been opposing inequalities in public school funding. Serrano, with the parents of a group of other Los Angeles schoolchildren, signed a complaint and went to court. The Supreme Court of the State of California ruled that John Serrano was right, that a system of financing public schools through local property taxes "invidiously discriminates" against the poor because it makes the quality of a child's schooling depend on where the child lives.

The implications of the California decision were dramatic. Over time, it has gradually led to a sweeping change in the way public schools are financed across America.

Except for Hawaii, where the state finances school costs, every state relies heavily on real estate taxes to pay for public schools. However, in the wake of the Serrano case, dozens of lawsuits were filed in other states to try to bring about a change. The effort received a temporary setback in 1973, when the U.S. Supreme Court ruled in a similar case in Texas.[178] The Court held, 5–4, that the Texas system did not violate the Fourteenth Amendment "merely because the burdens

sons in the state illegally. The voters of California overwhelmingly approved the proposition in 1994. But in 1995 a federal district court declared the major provisions of Proposition 187 unconstitutional. The state, the court ruled, could not deny education, health, and welfare services to undocumented immigrants. To do so, the court reasoned, would amount to a state scheme to control immigration, a power granted to the federal government under the Constitution.

In 1999, Governor Gray Davis, Wilson's Democratic successor, agreed that certain remaining provisions of the proposition would not be implemented, and the court approved that decision. Supporters of Proposition 187 sought to place it on the ballot in the year 2000 as an amendment to the state's constitution.

Change, Citizen Action, and Dissent

The Bill of Rights is really a list of promises by the government to the people. There is no similar list of constitutional obligations of the people to the government. Nevertheless, for a democracy to work, citizens must be willing to participate in the political process. When Americans work for a better environment, support political candidates, or speak out or organize on public or benefits . . . fall unevenly depending upon the relative wealth of the political subdivisions in which citizens live." Despite the Supreme Court's ruling, John Serrano's lawsuit had set in motion forces that could not be stopped. Many states adopted alternative methods of school financing as a result of the California decision. In 1989, for example, the Texas Supreme Court unanimously ruled that the state's system would have to be changed because of "glaring disparities" between rich and poor school districts.[179]

By the year 2000, some 48 states had modified the way they financed public schools, in order to provide some help to poorer districts.[180] In 41 states, state programs have been established to guarantee all pupils a minimum level of school funding.[181] The United States Supreme Court's ruling had slowed down the momentum of change, but pressures for equality of school district financing continued. In California, and in America, John Serrano had demonstrated that sometimes, at least, one citizen can make a difference.

KEY TERMS

CHAPTER HIGHLIGHTS

✦ The Bill of Rights, the first 10 amendments to the Constitution, is the fundamental charter of American liberty.

✦ In a democratic society, freedom is not absolute. In the American political system, the Supreme Court is the mechanism called upon to resolve conflicts between liberty and order and between the rights of the individual and the rights of society. The Court operates within the framework of the Bill of Rights.

✦ The First Amendment is designed to protect freedom of religion, speech, press, assembly, and petition.

✦ The Supreme Court has limited the freedom of expression and freedom of the press in various ways. It has sometimes required journalists to reveal sources; permitted individuals to sue the press for libel; recognized the right of privacy; banned "obscene" material; and upheld the power of the government to regulate radio and television.

✦ The First Amendment has two clauses protecting freedom of religion. The free exercise clause protects the right of individuals to worship or believe as they wish, or to hold no religious beliefs. The establishment clause provides that "Congress shall make no law respecting an establishment of religion."

✦ The Fourth Amendment protects the right of individuals to "be secure in their persons, houses, papers, and effects, against unreasonable searches and seizures." In the United States, as a general principle, police are not authorized to search a home without a search warrant signed by a judicial officer and issued on probable cause that the materials to be seized are in the place to be searched.

✦ The right of privacy, or what Justice Brandeis called "the right to be left alone," has been defined and protected by a series of Supreme Court decisions and legislation. In the 1973 case *Roe* v. *Wade,* the Court held that the concept of privacy included the right to a legal abortion.

✦ In the electronic age, the right of privacy has been threatened by sophisticated wiretapping and eavesdropping devices. However, Congress has passed laws requiring court warrants for electronic surveillance in domestic criminal cases and in national security cases.

✦ The Fifth and Fourteenth Amendments to the Constitution provide for "due process of law," a phrase designed to protect the individual against the arbitrary power of the state. The Bill of Rights entitles suspects or defendants to be represented by a lawyer; to be informed of the charges against them; to have a speedy and public trial by jury; to summon witnesses to testify in their behalf; to cross-examine prosecution witnesses; and to refuse to testify against themselves.

✦ The Fifth through Eighth Amendments also protect the accused from being held in excessive bail, or subjected to cruel and unusual punishment, or being tried twice for the same offense.

✦ The rights of the accused were strengthened by the cases *Gideon* v. *Wainwright* (1963), *Escobedo* v. *Illinois* (1964), and *Miranda* v. *Arizona* (1966). *Miranda* held that suspects must be clearly informed of their rights—including the right to be silent and the right to a lawyer—before they are asked any questions by the police. In the year 2000, the Supreme Court, in *Dickerson* v. *United States,* rejected a challenge to the *Miranda* decision.

✦ The Bill of Rights was passed as a safeguard against the new federal government. It did not apply to the states. But between 1925 and 1970, through the process of selective incorporation, the Supreme Court brought states and local governments almost entirely under the Bill of Rights.

✦ Under the Fourteenth Amendment, anyone born or naturalized in the United States is a citizen. The Supreme Court has held that Congress may not take away a person's citizenship unless it is freely renounced.

SUGGESTED WEB SITES

www.aclu.org

American Civil Liberties Union

The ACLU is a nonpartisan, nonprofit public interest organization devoted exclusively to protecting the basic civil liberties of all Americans and extending them to groups that have traditionally been denied them. The ACLU seeks to do this in three ways—through litigation, legislation, and education.

www.freedomforum.org

Freedom Forum

The Freedom Forum is a nonpartisan, international foundation dedicated to the freedoms covered by the First Amendment.

www.ins.usdoj.gov

Immigration and Naturalization Service

The INS, a division of the Department of Justice, oversees immigration to the United States. The INS also regulates permanent and temporary immigration to the United States. Additionally, the INS oversees the U.S. Border Patrol, which covers more than 8,000 miles of international boundaries.

www.nnirr.org
National Network for Immigrant and Refugee Rights
The NNIRR is a national organization composed of local coalitions and immigrant, refugee, community, religious, civil rights, and labor organizations and activists. The goals of NNIRR are to promote a just immigration and refugee policy in the United States and to defend and expand the rights of all immigrants and refugees, regardless of immigration status.

http://www.supremecourtus.gov
The United States Supreme Court
The official Web site of the U.S. Supreme Court. Opened in April of the year 2000. Contains the full text of the Court's decisions the same day they are released, as well as the Court's calendar, dockets, rules, a visitor's guide, and other information about the Court.

www.wlf.org
Washington Legal Foundation
The WLF advocates for free enterprise principles, limited government, property rights, and reform of the civil and criminal justice system. Litigation, publication of legal studies, and education are the ways the WLF tries to achieve its goals.

SUGGESTED READING

Abraham, Henry J., and Perry, Barbara A. *Freedom and the Court: Civil Rights and Liberties in the United States,* 7th edition* (Oxford University Press, 1998). A detailed examination of the Bill of Rights. Analyzes how the Supreme Court, through decisions in specific cases, has gradually enlarged the area of constitutional freedom in the United States.

Berns, Walter. *Freedom, Virtue, and the First Amendment* (Greenwood Press, 1969). (Originally published in 1957.) A provocative analysis that takes sharp issue with some of the major court decisions designed to protect freedom of expression in the United States.

Blanchard, Margaret. *Revolutionary Sparks: Freedom of Expression in Modern America* (Oxford University Press, 1992). A broad historical overview of the evolution of free expression in the United States.

Fiss, Owen M. *The Irony of Free Speech* (Harvard University Press, 1996). The author, an eminent legal scholar, argues that unfettered freedom of speech can actually diminish liberty, and that certain types of expression—such as hate speech and pornography—should be restricted.

Hentoff, Nat. *The First Freedom: The Tumultuous History of Free Speech in America* (Delacorte Press, 1980). A lively, clearly written analysis of the history of the First Amendment. Contains a detailed discussion of leading Supreme Court cases involving free speech, freedom of the press, and freedom of religion.

Hentoff, Nat. *Living the Bill of Rights: How to Be an Authentic American** (HarperCollins, 1998). A spirited argument in favor of maximum respect for individual liberties in public and private life, by a leading defender of civil liberties. According to Hentoff, unless Americans know and embrace the Bill of Rights, "the future of the nation as a strongly functioning constitutional democracy will be at risk."

Jackson, Robert H. *The Supreme Court in the American System of Government* (Harvard University Press, 1955). A very useful general discussion of the Supreme Court's role in the American political system. Jackson was an associate justice of the Supreme Court.

Lewis, Anthony. *Make No Law: The Sullivan Case and the First Amendment** (Random House, 1991). A highly readable account of a landmark Supreme Court case on freedom of the press. The case involved a 1960 libel suit brought by an Alabama public official against the *New York Times,* and the outcome redefined the boundaries of the First Amendment by allowing the press to report on public officials with much greater freedom.

Lewis, Anthony. *Gideon's Trumpet** (Random House, 1989). (Originally published in 1964.) A detailed and readable account of the Supreme Court case that established the right of a poor man to have a lawyer when charged with a serious criminal offense in a state court. Sheds light on the role of the Court in safeguarding the rights of defendants.

Mason, Alpheus T. *The Supreme Court: Palladium of Freedom** (University of Michigan Press, 1962). A concise discussion of the Supreme Court's place in the American political system by a distinguished scholar of constitutional law. Emphasizes the Bill of Rights and the Court's role in protecting minority views.

Matsuda, Mari J.; Lawrence, Charles R., III; Delgado, Richard; and Crenshaw, Kimberlè Williams. *Words That Wound: Critical Race Theory, Assaultive Speech, and the First Amendment** (Westview Press, 1993). A vigorous presentation of the case for measures such as "speech codes" on American college campuses.

McCloskey, Robert G. *The American Supreme Court,* 2nd edition* (University of Chicago Press, 1994). (Revised by Sanford Levinson.) This book, an unusually perceptive analysis of the role of the Supreme Court in the American political system, contains the full text of chapters from a book that the late Robert McCloskey originally published in 1960. To these, Levinson has added two new concluding chapters extending McCloskey's analytical framework into the 1990s.

Mill, John Stuart. *On Liberty** (Broadview Press, 1999). (Originally published in 1859.) A classic examination of the problem of balancing individual rights and the rights of the community.

The Supreme Court and Individual Rights, 3rd edition* (Congressional Quarterly, 1999). A useful survey of the impact of Supreme Court decisions on individual rights. Focuses on First Amendment rights and the guarantees of political participation, due process, and equal protection.

White, G. Edward. *Justice Oliver Wendell Holmes: Law and the Inner Self* (Oxford University Press, 1993). A readable and absorbing biography, rich in historical detail and psychological insights, of the Supreme Court justice whom the author has called the "best known judge in American history."

*Available in paperback edition.

 Visit http://politicalscience.wadsworth.com/cummings9/update/ for current InfoTrac articles and other student resources related to this chapter.

CHAPTER 5
The Struggle for Equal Rights

On the night of June 7, 1998, in Jasper, Texas, James Byrd, Jr., was beaten, chained to a pickup truck by three men, and dragged two miles to his death. His head and arm were found a mile from the rest of his body. Four months later, in Laramie, Wyoming, Matthew Shepard, a 21-year-old college student, was badly beaten, tied to a fence on the prairie, and left for dead. He was found the next morning and taken to a hospital but died five days later.

Both crimes horrified the nation. In both cases, the victims were apparently singled out and killed because they were different. Byrd was an African American, and his murderers were white; two were white supremacists. Matthew Shepard was gay.

Although these are extreme examples of brutal crimes, many members of minority groups in America face discrimination—sometimes subtle, sometimes blatant—in their everyday lives. It is a truth well known to those who experience it, whether faced by the Hispanic newcomer struggling for a foothold in American society, or the woman executive who hits the "glass ceiling" that blocks her further ascent on the corporate ladder.

America, to be sure, is a multicultural society, made up of many groups with distinct ethnic, racial, and religious identities. Early in the 20th century there was a popular notion that immigrants should be rapidly assimilated into American society, into "the melting pot." Even that controversial concept, however, reflects a basic truth—that the United States is a land of astonishing diversity. Yet, the rights proclaimed in the Declaration of Independence and those set forth in the legal language of the Constitution are not enjoyed equally by all Americans. For many minority groups, the equality promised by these fundamental American charters has been an elusive goal rather than an achieved fact, a vision of a possible future rather than a description of the often bleak present.

Although progress has been made in reducing inequalities among diverse groups, there are continuing racial divisions in American society, as well as racial tensions, sometimes accompanied by violence. At times the images on television are horrifying, as when police in Los Angeles were captured on videotape clubbing an African American man whom they had stopped after a car chase. These images may not be typical, and they may even give a distorted picture of America to the world. But they are nonetheless real and cannot be ignored or wished away.

Despite the civil rights laws enacted by Congress in the 1960s and decisions of the Supreme Court, even today many of the more than 35 million African Americans do not enjoy full social and economic equality. About one out of four blacks in the United States is poor—by official definition of the federal government—as opposed to about one out of 10 whites.* (See Figure 5-1.) African Americans, it is true, have made some economic gains in recent years. For example, half of black families earn more than $26,000 a year.[1] But at the same time, the gap in income levels and living standards has widened between the growing African American middle class and the millions of blacks still below the poverty line. Economic gains registered by some African Americans were little comfort to the unemployed black youth in the inner city, or even to a middle-class black family seeking to move into a hostile white suburb.

In America today, the infant mortality rate for African American children is more than twice as high as it is for whites.[2] Among young black males, homicide is the leading cause of death.[3] Nearly one out of three African American men in their twenties is in prison, on parole, or on probation.[4] Black males have a 29 percent chance of serving time in prison at some point in their lives; white males have a 4 percent chance.[5]

In 2000, as the new decade began, the rate of black unemployment was 8.2 percent, more than double that

*Adapted from U.S. Bureau of the Census, Current Population Reports, *Poverty in the United States, 1998*, series P60-207, September 1999, pp. v, vi, 1. The poverty level for a family of four in 1998 was defined by the federal government as an annual income of less than $16,530.

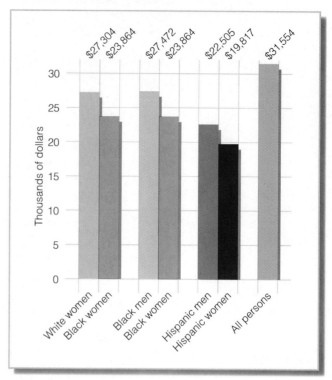

FIGURE 5-1

Median Income of Selected Minorities in the United States, 1998

SOURCE: U.S. Bureau of the Census.

of whites.[6] And the median income of black families was only somewhat more than half that of white families.[7]

This statistical portrait does not sketch in the daily indignities, the rebuffs, the humiliations, and defeats that many African Americans may face. And despite substantial changes for the better in recent years, the African American citizen in many cases remains on the outside of American society, looking in. It is true that black income, political power, education, and employment opportunities have increased since the civil rights movement of the 1960s, especially for the black middle class. But William Julius Wilson and other scholars have suggested that, even with the gains of the civil rights movement, conditions have actually deteriorated for blacks in the inner cities.[8]

An African American still has a greater chance than a white American of being born in a poor neighborhood and of living in crowded, substandard housing. If an African American youth does not succumb to rats, crime, cocaine, heroin, drive-by shootings, gang warfare, AIDS, and other soul-destroying forces of the ghetto, perhaps he or she will obtain work when the economy is strong. But the work may be menial and low-paying. Black families may have to buy shoddy merchandise at high credit rates from neighborhood merchants. The food at the local chain

The earliest memory of my life is of an incident which occurred when I was three-and-a-half years old in Holly Springs, Mississippi. My father was registrar and professor of religion and philosophy at Rust College, a Negro Methodist institution there.

One hot summer day, my mother and I walked from the college campus to the town square, a distance of maybe half a mile. I remember it as clearly as though it were a few weeks ago. I held her finger tightly as we kicked up the red dust on the unpaved streets leading to the downtown area. When we reached the square she did her shopping and we headed for home. Like any other three-and-a-half-year-old on a hot day, I got thirsty.

"Mother," I said, "I want a Coke." She replied that we could not get Cokes there and I would have to wait until we got home where there was lots of Coke in the icebox.

"But I want my Coke now," I insisted. She was just as insistent that we could not get a Coke now. "Do as I tell you," she said, "wait 'til we get home; you can have a Coke with plenty of ice."

"There's a little boy going into a store!" I exclaimed as I spied another child who was a little bigger than I. "I bet he's going to get a Coke." So I pulled my mother by the finger until we stood in front of what I recall as a drugstore looking through the closed screen doors. Surely enough, the other lad had climbed upon a stool at the counter and was already sipping a soft drink.

"But I told you you can't get a Coke in there," she said. "Why can't I?" I asked again. The answer was the same, "You just can't." I then inquired with complete puzzlement, "Well, why can he?" Her quiet answer thundered in my ears. "He's white."

We walked home in silence under the pitiless glare of the Mississippi sun. Once we were home she threw herself across the bed and wept. I walked out on the front porch and sat on the steps alone with my three-and-a-half-year-old thoughts.

—James Farmer, former national director of CORE, in *Esquire*, May 1969

---

supermarket—if any large chains operate branches in the neighborhood at all—may be of poorer quality and priced higher than the same items at the chain's branches in white neighborhoods. If an African American man or woman raises a family, the children may face the same bleak future, continuing the cycle of poverty and despair.

In some communities police engage in "racial profiling." In those localities black Americans have a greater chance of being stopped by police while driving or even walking down the street.

Even if a black youth gets a job as a skilled worker, or goes to college and enters a profession, his or her troubles are not necessarily over. On moving to a white neighborhood, black families may encounter hostility and ostracism. In the best of economic circumstances, African American parents still must face the problem of explaining to their children the divisions in American society between white and black.

But it is not only African Americans who are struggling for equal rights in the United States. For the more than 2 million American Indians, the rhetoric of equality has a particularly ironic sound. Often living in poverty, with an unemployment rate on the reservations about 12 times the national average, the first Americans are outcasts in a land that once was theirs.

The nation's Hispanic community, the second-largest minority group in the United States, is another major segment of the population that has been denied full equality in American society. The term "Hispanic" usually includes Mexican Americans—by far the largest group—as well as Puerto Ricans, Cubans, and persons of Central or South American or other Spanish origin. The Census Bureau reported in 1999 that there were 31 million Hispanics in the United States, including undocumented immigrants.[9] More than half of the total number of Hispanics—56 percent—were born in the United States.[10] During the 1990s, the Hispanic population grew by 9.1 million, more than any other group. By 2005, the Census Bureau has estimated, Hispanics will comprise the nation's largest minority group, exceeding the black population.[11]

 Online *for more information about The Census Bureau, see: www.census.gov*

According to the Census Bureau, there were 18.8 million Mexican Americans in the United States. Although Mexican Americans make up a sizable population bloc in five southwestern states, they are underrepresented politically. Many are migrant workers living in abysmal conditions.

Puerto Ricans, all of whom are American citizens, form another important segment of the Hispanic community. Yet many of the approximately 3.1 million Americans of Puerto Rican background who live on the mainland suffer discrimination and poverty and are locked in the barrios, or slums, of the great cities.

Asian Americans have often been the targets of hostility and bias, sometimes by other ethnic groups. The more than 11 million Asian Americans are now the third-largest minority in the nation, ranking in size right after African Americans and Hispanics.

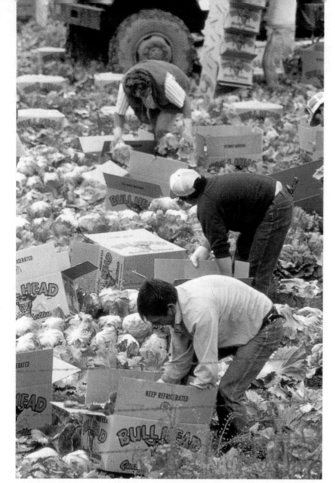

Lettuce pickers, San Joaquin Valley, California
Copyright © Chromosohm/Sohm/Photo Researchers

The women's liberation movement that emerged as an important social and political force during the 1970s reflected the growing awareness that women, although constituting a majority of the population, were, in effect, another "minority group." Discrimination based on sex is built into many public and private institutions.

Some indication of the problem may be seen in the gap in earnings between men and women. In 1998, for example, the median income of men was $34,199, while that of women was $25,362.[12]

Gay men and women, although gradually gaining acceptance in many American communities, still face formidable obstacles, ranging from subtle bias in the workplace to physical violence on the streets. Gay and lesbian voters, however, have become an important political force in a number of communities, and nationally.

The 54 million Americans with disabilities comprise another group whose rights, until recently, were often neglected. And many other minorities also have suffered discrimination. Jews have been widely accepted in many areas of American society but are still unwelcome in some private clubs, in the executive suites of some corporations, and in some residential areas. Until Al Gore chose Senator Joseph I. Lieberman as his vice-presidential running mate in the 2000 presidential campaign, no Jew had ever run for that office or for president as a major-party candidate. Prejudice against Catholics was a major issue in John F. Kennedy's 1960 presidential campaign. Italian Americans are often the victims of subtle discrimination because of the stereotype, reinforced by movies and television, that they are members of, or somehow linked to, organized crime. Arab Americans and other groups are still victims of racial slurs and discrimination. And discrimination is not limited to ethnic or religious minorities. Older Americans may face discrimination when they seek employment or in other ways. Children and persons with AIDS also have sometimes been deprived of their rights.

All these inequalities cast a shadow over the ideals and the future of America. Racial polarization has been reflected in the nation's political issues and alignments.

"You'll just love the way he handles."
Copyright The New Yorker Collection from cartoonbank.com

For example, as African Americans and other minority groups pressed for greater equality and opportunity, white blue-collar workers in many cases reacted with hostility. Blacks and Hispanics migrating outward from the inner city frequently moved into white ethnic neighborhoods. White factory or construction workers who had saved their money to buy modest houses in such neighborhoods often felt that their property values, their schools—and perhaps their jobs—were threatened by the newcomers. Ugly racial incidents sometimes resulted. Social tension and racial protests put continuing pressure on American institutions.

There is a great irony in all this, because, if present demographic trends continue, whites in the United States might become a minority sometime near the middle of the 21st century. By 2060, according to Census Bureau projections, it seems likely that the combined Hispanic, black, Asian American, and American Indian population will outnumber the white population.[13] When and if that happens, the struggle for minority rights will take on a rather different meaning.

By the 1990s, the increasing use of the term "multiculturalism" among many scholars, political leaders, and members of the news media reflected the fact that America was made up of many different groups of diverse backgrounds and cultures. But as these groups vied for the political and economic power that had often been denied to them, critics raised the question of whether there might be serious disadvantages for America in all of this—a danger that the country might fragment into many separate ethnic groups and lose its national identity and unity.

Nevertheless, in a society marked by diversity, the problems remained. In this chapter we will be exploring a key question: Will the nation support programs that try to deal with some of the causes of racial inequality—poverty, hunger, discrimination, powerlessness, and unemployment—or will the public support substantial cuts in the government programs created to alleviate these problems? In 1996, for example, Congress passed and President Clinton signed a law ending the federal welfare program and shifting it to the states. Underlying the political debate over social programs, of course, were deeper questions about the proper role, size, and reach of government.

A number of additional issues arise in any discussion of civil rights. What steps has government taken to ensure the rights of minorities? What is the history of the struggle for equal rights in America? How did the civil rights movement of the 1960s evolve? How have government and private institutions contributed to discrimination? Can African Americans and other minority groups achieve integration only at the cost of losing their ethnic and cultural identity? Does the emphasis on multiculturalism in American society weaken national unity? These are some of the problems we will explore in examining the continuing struggle for equality in America.

SOME GROUPS IN PROFILE

American Indians

Who is an American Indian? Because there is no accepted demographic definition, an American Indian is whoever tells the census-taker he or she is one. (In the 1990s, the term "Native American" was preferred by some individuals and tribal groups who found "Indian" objectionable.* As of the year 2000, however, the federal government still maintained a Bureau of Indian Affairs, which used the term "Indians."† Groups representing American Indians and Native Americans generally expressed no preference for one term over the other and regarded them as interchangeable.) According to the Census Bureau, there were 2.4 million American Indians, Aleuts, and Eskimos in the United States at the end of the 20th century.[14] (The Eskimos and Aleuts of Alaska are two culturally distinct groups and prefer the term "Alaska Natives.") An estimated 1.5 million American Indians live on or near reservations.[15]

 for more information about the Bureau of Indian Affairs, see: www.doi.gov/bureau-indian-affairs.html

Native Americans are American citizens (Congress conferred citizenship on all Indians in 1924), and there is no requirement that Native Americans live on a reservation, an area of land "reserved" for their use and held in trust by the federal government. There are 333 reservations in 33 states, varying in size from California settlements of only a few acres to the 16-million-acre Navajo reservation spreading through Arizona, New Mexico, and Utah.

The federal government spends more than $9 billion a year on aid to Native Americans.[16] But the Bureau of Indian Affairs does not have responsibility for assisting those who are living off the reservation, of whom almost one-third live in poverty.[17] And the plight of Native Americans living on the reservation is little better.

WHITE AMERICA KEEPS ITS PROMISE

They made us many promises, more than I can remember, but they never kept but one; they promised to take our land, and they took it.

—Anonymous American Indian

---

*The term "Indians" reflected the widespread belief in the time of Columbus that the peoples who lived in North America before the Europeans arrived inhabited the outer edge of the Indies, or what is now known as Asia.
†The term "Native Americans" initially applied to American Indians and Alaska Natives. Over time, however, the term has been expanded in some usage to include all native peoples of the United States and its territories, including native Hawaiians, Chamorros, and American Samoans. Source: Bureau of Indian Affairs, U.S. Department of the Interior.

Few reservations can support their populations; unemployment among Native Americans averages 49 percent on the reservations, and almost a third of those who do find work earn below the poverty level.[18] Many live in shacks, adobe huts, even abandoned automobiles. Incidence of illness and disease is significantly higher among Native Americans than among the white population; and the rate of drug-related deaths among American Indians was 18 percent higher than for other groups.[19] Unsanitary housing, unsafe water, and malnutrition all contribute to ill health among Native Americans. The percentage of Native Americans who graduate from college is less than half that of the total U.S. population.[20] The suicide rate among Native Americans is higher than that of all Americans, and among Native Americans age 15 to 24 it is more than twice as high as the national average.[21] Although the rate of deaths from alcoholism among Native Americans has decreased in recent years, it is more than five times as high as the national average.[22] In recent years some American Indians have prospered by operating gambling casinos, but their wealth did not change the dismal conditions in which the majority lived.

"Some have prospered." Indian gambling casino near Albuquerque, New Mexico
AP/Wide World

The federal government has been deeply involved in the history of the white man's broken promises to the Native Americans. Until 1871 the government treated Indian tribes as separate, sovereign nations. After that, the government stopped making treaties with the tribes and adopted a policy of breaking down the tribal structure. The Dawes Act of 1887 divided reservations into

Budnick/Woodfin Camp

John Running/Stock, Boston

SACAGAWEA: HONORING AN AMERICAN INDIAN WOMAN

In the year 2000, Sacagawea, the young American Indian woman who acted as interpreter for the Lewis and Clark expedition (1803–1806), was honored on the new one-dollar coin.

The daughter of a Shoshone Indian chief, Sacagawea was kidnapped by the Hidatsa Indians as a young girl. She became one of two wives to Toussaint Charbonneau, a French Canadian trader who won her in a bet with the Indians. When Charbonneau signed on with Meriwether Lewis and William Clark, Sacagawea, although just 15 years old and six months pregnant, was enlisted as interpreter. She was the only woman to accompany the 33 members of the permanent party to the Pacific Ocean and back.

In the late summer of 1805, the Americans were running low on food, and were without fresh horses. With Sacagawea's help, they crossed the Continental Divide at Lemhi Pass. They then encountered a band of 60 Shoshone warriors who could have wiped them out easily, ending the expedition. But Sacagawea recognized their chief, Cameahwait, as her long-lost brother, and recognized another Shoshone, Jumping Fish, as a girl she had not seen since the kidnapping.

For her services on the expedition, Sacagawea was given nothing, though her husband received $500 and 320 acres of land. Six years after the expedition, Sacagawea gave birth to a daughter, Lisette. On December 23, 1812, Sacagawea died of an illness at age 25. Eight months after her death, William Clark legally adopted her two children.

On July 23, 1999, one dozen special 22-karat gold versions of the Sacagawea coin traveled aboard the space shuttle *Columbia,* and were later donated to several museums.

The captain of the spacecraft was Eileen Collins, the first woman to command a space shuttle.

In January 2000, the new dollar coins were sent to the Federal Reserve and began circulation.

—Adapted from *New York Times,* October 26, 1999; PBS Online, "Lewis and Clark: The Journey of the Corps of Discovery"; and the U.S. Mint, "The Birth of the Golden Dollar Coin: A Timeline"

The golden dollar issued in 1999 honors Sacagawea, the young Shoshone Indian woman who acted as interpreter for Lewis and Clark.
Kearney Hub/AP/Wide World

small allotments, but the land not distributed to individuals was put up for public sale. Between 1887 and 1934, some 90 million acres were removed from tribal hands in one way or another. When a 1934 federal law ended the practice of breaking up the reservations, the tribes regained some of their vitality.

In 1953 Congress adopted a policy declaration designed to end the special trustee relationship between the federal government and Native Americans. This policy of "forced termination" was almost unanimously opposed by Native Americans, who feared that without federal protection their lands and cultural identity would vanish. Finally in 1974 Congress ended the policy of forced termination and gave Native American tribes control over federal programs on their reservations.

In recent decades, a number of Indian tribes have had some success in recovering lands taken by the

Steve Kelley/San Diego Union Tribune

The Second Battle of Wounded Knee, 1973
UPI/Bettmann/CORBIS

government. For example, under a law passed by Congress in 1980, the federal government agreed to pay Indian claimants in Maine $84 million and return 300,000 acres as compensation for 12.5 million acres of land originally taken. Later that year, 60,000 Sioux were awarded $122.5 million by the U.S. Supreme Court in compensation for 7 million acres taken by Congress in the Black Hills.[23]

Beset by poverty, disease, illiteracy, substandard housing, and the threat of forced cultural assimilation, American Indians felt they had long overdue claims on the American political system. Beginning in the 1960s, Native Americans added their voices to the protests of other minorities. In 1972 several hundred Native Americans went to Washington and occupied the Bureau of Indian Affairs (BIA). The protesters arrived in a caravan they called "The Trail of Broken Treaties."

In 1973, 200 armed supporters of the American Indian Movement (AIM) seized the tiny village of Wounded Knee on the Pine Ridge Indian Reservation in South Dakota. The militants had chosen their target carefully and with a shrewd understanding of modern mass communications; Wounded Knee was the site of the massacre of at least 153 Sioux by the U.S. Army in 1890, and it was named in the title of a best-selling book published in 1970.[24] The occupation stirred national attention and attracted network television coverage. For 70 days, U.S. marshals surrounded the village; although the marshals were determined to avoid another mas-

sacre, two Native American supporters were killed in exchanges of gunfire, and one federal agent was paralyzed. After more than two months, the militants surrendered under a peace agreement. The second battle of Wounded Knee was over, but the broader problems faced by Native Americans remained.

Hispanic Americans

Like Native Americans, Americans of Hispanic origin must contend with the twin problems of discrimination and poverty. Of the total Hispanic American population of 31 million, almost two-thirds, or 18.8 million, are Mexican Americans. (See Figure 5-2.) Most Mexican Americans live in five states of the South and West, where they are the largest minority group. (See Table 5-1.) California has the largest Mexican American population, followed by Texas. Other Mexican Americans are concentrated in New Mexico, Arizona, and Colorado.

According to one Census Bureau study, more than 25 percent of all Hispanics were living in poverty—compared to a national average of 12.7 percent. The median income for Hispanics was $21,161 a year.[25] Unemployment was substantially higher than among the rest of the population. A little more than half of adult Mexican Americans had completed high school, much lower than the rate for the nation as a whole.[26]

Between 1951 and 1964, hundreds of thousands of Mexican migrant laborers entered the United States

FIGURE 5-2

Hispanic Americans, 1999

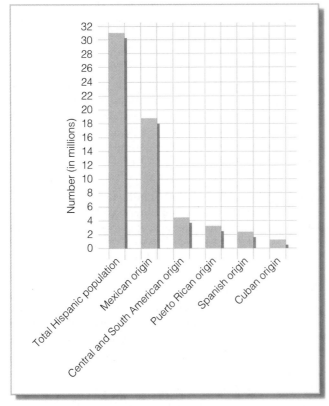

Number (in millions)

Total Hispanic population
Mexican origin
Central and South American origin
Puerto Rican origin
Spanish origin
Cuban origin

SOURCE: U.S. Bureau of the Census.

TABLE 5-1

Number of Hispanic Americans in the South and the West, 1995

State	Number of Hispanics
California	9,143,000
Texas	5,260,000
Arizona	853,000
New Mexico	686,000
Colorado	511,000

SOURCE: U.S. Bureau of the Census. Figures are rounded projections.

temporarily as farm workers under the *bracero* program enacted by Congress. Millions of others have entered the country illegally to join the ranks of the migrants.

Many migrants, whether legal or not, live and work under the most difficult conditions. They perform backbreaking stoop labor in the fields under the hot sun, risking injury from insecticides used to protect the crops. Often they must live in shacks without electricity or running water, their health endangered by open sewage and other unsanitary conditions. Migrant Mexican American workers have a life expectancy much shorter than the national average, and a much higher birth rate and infant mortality rate.

Farm workers are not covered by the National Labor Relations Act, and they have encountered great obstacles

"WHAT IS THE WORTH OF A MAN?"

In 1979 Cesar Chavez led a strike by his United Farm Workers against the lettuce growers of California. On February 9, in the Imperial Valley, Rufino Contreras, a young lettuce worker taking part in the strike, was shot to death during a clash between pickets and nonunion workers. He left a widow and two young children. Two foremen and an equipment operator, all employees of the owner of the farm where Contreras died, were charged with murder, but the case was later dismissed.

Reporter Laurie Becklund of the *Los Angeles Times* attended the funeral and filed this account:

CALEXICO—Rufino Contreras, the 27-year-old lettuce picker who was shot to death on Saturday, was buried here Wednesday morning after an outdoor mariachi funeral mass in which he was mourned as a martyr by more than 7000 United Farm Workers of America members and their families.

"Rufino is not dead," UFW President Cesar Chavez said in his eulogy. "Wherever farm workers organize, stand up for their rights and strike for justice, Rufino Contreras is with them."

Sitting in . . . the front row of a flower-filled shrine where the Mass was celebrated was Rosa Contreras, the young man's widow. . . . Clutching her 5-year-old son to her, she seemed oblivious to the labor leader's words.

"Mis hijos," she said time after time, leaning her head back and moaning, tears running down her thin, youthful face. "My children, children of my heart. Where is their father; where are you, Fino?"

"What is the worth of a man?" Chavez asked during his eulogy. "Rufino and his father and his brother together gave the company 20 years of their labor. . . ." The cries of Contreras's young widow could be heard throughout the eulogy. . . . She grabbed hold of [her son] and cried into his shoulder as if he were a man.

Her other child, Nancy Berenice, 4, smiled when she saw her mother. She did not know she was supposed to cry.

—*Los Angeles Times*, February 15, 1979

Cesar Chavez
AP/Wide World

in organizing labor unions. In 1970 Cesar Chavez and his United Farm Workers won a five-year strike against grape growers in central California. Chavez's effort, aided by a nationwide boycott of table grapes by consumers in sympathy with the strike, helped focus national attention on *La Causa*, as the grape workers called their movement, and on *La Raza*, the Mexican Americans themselves. In 1975 California passed legislation generally providing for farm workers the same rights held by union members in other industries. It was the only such law in the nation recognizing the right of farm workers to bargain collectively. The landmark farm labor bill was a victory for Chavez.

During the 1960s, Chavez had emerged as an extraordinary figure, a quiet and determined man who became a symbol of the Chicanos (as many Mexican Americans call themselves). Chavez's childhood reads like a passage in John Steinbeck's Depression-era novel, *The Grapes of Wrath*. His parents were Mexican migrant workers. Following the seasons, the family traveled back and forth between California's Imperial and San Joaquin Valleys. By the time Chavez finished the eighth grade he had attended 37 schools. Eventually the family settled in a slum neighborhood near San Jose called by its residents Sal Si Puedes ("get out if you can"). Chavez began organizing the United Farm Workers (UFW) in 1962; within six years, the union had 17,000 members. But by the early 1980s, Chavez and his union faced a variety of problems, and the UFW had lost some of its power.

Cesar Chavez died in the spring of 1993. An estimated 25,000 farm workers and their supporters took part in the three-mile funeral procession in Delano, in California's Central Valley. Chavez did not live to see it, but in 1996, after a struggle of nearly 18 years with lettuce growers in California's Salinas Valley, the UFW signed a contract with one of the nation's largest growers, Red Coach lettuce.

The percentage of Hispanics, including Mexican Americans, in the general population is not reflected in the makeup of Congress. In California, for example, where Hispanic Americans constitute about 25 percent of the population, only 9 percent, or five of the 54 members of the state's congressional delegation in the year 2000, were Hispanic Americans: Xavier Becerra, Matthew G. Martinez, Lucille Roybal-Allard, Loretta Sanchez, and Grace Flores Napolitano.

Hispanics have joined the ranks of other minority groups fighting for full equality in American society. Mexican Americans have served as governor of New Mexico, and in 1986 Bob Martinez was elected as Florida's first governor of Hispanic descent. By the year 2000 there were 20 Hispanic members of Congress, and an Hispanic American, Bill Richardson, was serving in the cabinet as Secretary of Energy. In the nation, 4,966 Hispanics had been elected to public office.[27]

Mexican Americans and other Hispanics have registered additional political gains, electing mayors in recent years in Austin, Denver, Miami, Santa Fe, and San Antonio. In addition, the number of Hispanic state legislators increased by more than half from 1984 to 1999 in Texas, California, New Mexico, Arizona, Colorado, Florida, Illinois, and New York.[28] But many Mexican Americans, desiring to preserve their own identity, have not felt the need to participate in American politics. "We are another country," said Miguel Garcia of East Los Angeles. "We have our own culture, our own language. We feel different from the rest of America."[29] Yet, when Hispanic Americans have organized politically, they often have made their voices heard. In Parlier, California, a small town near Fresno, the local council refused to appoint a Mexican American chief of police. In response, the Hispanic community organized, defeated three members of the council, and elected as mayor Andrew Benitez, a 22-year-old Mexican American.[30]

Hispanic voters have become a powerful force in elections on a national scale as well, courted by presidential, congressional, and gubernatorial candidates. And as the 21st century began, Hispanics were having an increasing impact on American culture and life in other ways—from baseball stars such as Sammy Sosa and Orlando Hernandez to singer Ricky Martin. In New York, Miami, Texas, and California, as well as other places, life in America had taken on a Latin beat.

Undocumented Immigrants Although the precise number of undocumented immigrants in the United States is not known, government and private demographers have estimated that as many as 5 million or more persons are in the country illegally.[31] The majority are Mexicans or other Latin Americans. The Census Bureau has estimated that about 78 percent of all undocumented persons are Hispanic.[32]

Some employers, particularly growers and farm owners in California and Texas, have hired undocumented workers as a source of cheap labor. Labor unions and some other groups, however, have argued that undocumented persons in the United States under-

BELL GARDENS, CALIF., Dec. 29—The problem with Bell Gardens, a city official said not long ago, is that "we just have too many people."

With that in mind, the City Council passed a zoning ordinance last year to control population density. But the five-member City Council was all white, while almost 90 percent of the 42,000 people squeezed into the 2.5 square miles of this gritty industrial suburb were Hispanic. The residents, most of them recent arrivals from Mexico, saw the Council's move as an attempt to drive them from their low-cost homes. Several hundred existing housing units would be affected by the ordinance.

So the immigrant population of Bell Gardens rose up and seized political power, registering voters, drawing up petitions and ousting the white mayor and three other white City Council members in a special election earlier this month.

Local politicians were stunned. . . . "They didn't think we could do it," said Josefina Macias, a school attendance assistant who was a leader of the recall movement. "We've awakened the community. They were just asleep. This sends a message to our people everywhere that they can take hold of their government."

—*New York Times*, December 30, 1991

Ricky Martin singing "Livin' la Vida Loca" on NBC's Today *show*
AP/Wide World

mine minimum wage, health, and safety laws and other benefits enjoyed by American workers. The Supreme Court has ruled that states can bar the employment of persons who are in the United States illegally.[33] But the Court declared unconstitutional a Texas law barring the children of undocumented persons, most of them Mexicans, from attending public schools.[34] As noted in Chapter 4, in 1994 California voters approved Proposition 187, a measure to deny government welfare and other benefits to persons in the state illegally, but a federal district court declared its major provisions unconstitutional, and in 1999 Governor Gray Davis agreed that certain remaining provisions of the proposition would not be implemented.

In 1986, as also discussed in Chapter 4, Congress passed a bill designed to reduce the flow of undocumented immigrants by punishing employers who knowingly hired them. The law has proved largely ineffective. Undocumented immigrants have continued to flow across the border, and many have obtained false identity papers, which are inexpensive and easily available.

Puerto Ricans Puerto Rico has commonwealth status and Puerto Ricans are American citizens, with a nonvoting resident commissioner in the U.S. House of Representatives. As Americans, Puerto Ricans living on the island use U.S. currency, mail, and courts and may receive U.S. welfare benefits and food stamps. They pay no federal taxes unless they move to the mainland. Islanders cannot vote in national elections, but in 1980, for the first time, they were able to vote in primaries to express their presidential preference and to select delegates to the Democratic and Republican national conventions. Puerto Ricans sing their own national anthem, have their own flag, and are Spanish-speaking.

Yet many of the island's residents who come to the mainland seeking a better life encounter not only a language barrier but economic and racial discrimination as well. Puerto Ricans who migrate to the mainland frequently settle in cities. If the newcomers find employment, it may be in unskilled, low-paying jobs in hotels, restaurants, and factories. Often forced to live in substandard housing, Puerto Ricans sometimes face hostility from inner-city blacks who regard them as an economic threat.

The population of Puerto Rico was 3.8 million in 1997; about 3.1 million more persons of Puerto Rican origin lived in the continental United States.[35] About 900,000 lived in New York City, and there were large Puerto Rican communities in Chicago; Philadelphia; Newark, New Jersey; and Bridgeport and Hartford, Connecticut. The median income of Puerto Rican families was a little more than half that of other Americans, and the unemployment rate often much higher.

New York, 2000: cheering the Puerto Rican Day Parade
AP/Wide World

United States. The number of Asian Americans more than doubled during the 1980s. By 2000, Asian Americans constituted about 4 percent of the population and were the third largest minority, after African Americans (about 13 percent) and Hispanics (12 percent).

In July 2000, Norman Y. Mineta, a former member of the House of Representatives from California's Silicon Valley, became the first Asian American to serve in the cabinet when he was named by President Clinton as Secretary of Commerce. Mineta, a Japanese American who served as a Democratic representative for 21 years, was sent to an internment camp as a boy during the Second World War.

The largest group of Asian Americans were persons of Chinese heritage, who comprised almost 23 percent of the total, followed by Filipino Americans and Japanese Americans. (See Table 5-2.) California, the nation's fastest-growing state, had 39 percent of all Asian Americans. Although many persons of Chinese, Japanese, and other Asian descent live in California and other western states, there has been a rapid increase in the Asian population in New York and Texas. The increase has resulted in some surprising statistics. For example, there were more Asian Americans in New York (694,000) than in Hawaii (685,000).[36]

Among Asian nations, immigration from Vietnam, India, and South Korea increased at the fastest rate. Although the stereotype of the Korean grocer or Asian retail store owner had some basis in fact, it was also true that Asian Americans included a successful professional

On the island itself, a continuing debate over Puerto Rico's political status has focused on three choices: continuing as a commonwealth; statehood; or independence. The commonwealth status for Puerto Rico was established in 1952 under Luis Muñoz Marin's Popular Democratic Party. In 1967 a majority of voters in Puerto Rico voted to continue commonwealth status. The New Progressive Party, which came to power in 1992, favors statehood, but in 1993, by a narrow margin, Puerto Ricans again chose to have their island remain a commonwealth; and in another referendum in 1998, statehood once more failed to win a majority.

Few Puerto Ricans favor outright independence. One group that does, the Puerto Rican Armed Forces of National Liberation (FALN), was blamed for 130 bombings in the United States in the 1970s and 1980s that killed six people and wounded dozens of others. In 1979 President Carter freed four Puerto Rican nationalists who had served long prison terms after attempting to assassinate President Truman and shooting at members of Congress on the floor of the U.S. House of Representatives in 1950. In 1999, President Clinton granted clemency to 11 Puerto Rican nationalists who had served prison terms of almost 20 years but had not themselves been convicted of crimes that caused injuries or loss of life.

Like other minority groups, Puerto Ricans in the United States have evidenced growing cultural pride and political awareness in recent years. In several cities, Puerto Rican citizen groups have organized to work for such goals as better education and employment.

Asian Americans

The estimated 11.2 million Asian Americans in the year 2000 made up a rapidly growing minority group in the

TABLE 5-2

Asian Americans in the United States, 1990

Asians or Pacific Islanders, by Group	Number	Percent
Chinese	1,645,472	22.6
Filipino	1,406,770	19.3
Japanese	847,562	11.7
Asian Indian	815,447	11.2
Korean	798,849	11.0
Vietnamese	614,547	8.4
Hawaiian	211,014	2.9
Samoan	62,964	0.9
Guamanian	49,345	0.7
Other Asian or Pacific Islander	821,692	11.3
Total	7,273,662	100.0

SOURCE: Data provided by the U.S. Bureau of the Census.

In 1848, Elizabeth Cady Stanton and Lucretia Mott invited approximately 100 men and women to Stanton's hometown of Seneca Falls, New York, for a meeting on women's rights. The Seneca Falls convention launched the women's suffrage movement in America.

"We are assembled to protest against a form of government existing without the consent of the governed," Stanton began, "to declare our right to be free as man is free, to be represented in the government which we are taxed to support, to have such disgraceful laws as give man the power to chastise and imprison his wife, to take the wages which she earns, the property which she inherits, and, in case of separation, the children of her love; laws which make her the mere dependent on his bounty . . .

forever erased from our statute books. . . . We now demand our right to vote according to the declaration of the government under which we live."

Stanton's moving words spurred the convention to pass the Declaration of Sentiments, modeled after Jefferson's Declaration of Independence written 72 years earlier, but with one big difference: "We hold these truths to be self-evident; that all men *and women* are created equal . . ." (italics added).

It was another 72 years before the Nineteenth Amendment, which gave women the right to vote, was ratified. Thus, 144 years after Jefferson's words were written, America finally accepted the principle that freedom was for everyone—both men and women.

class of scientists, engineers, and physicians. The rapid increase in the numbers of Asian Americans has had a continuing political and cultural impact, not only in California, but in many other areas of the country as well.

Women

As the 2000 elections approached, Elizabeth Dole, a former cabinet secretary, campaigned for a time for the Republican presidential nomination. Madeleine K. Albright, the highest-ranking member of the Clinton cabinet, served as secretary of state, and Janet Reno was the attorney general. Two women sat as associate justices of the U.S. Supreme Court, and 67 women were members of Congress.[37] The governor and four highest officials of the state of Arizona were women, as were hundreds of state legislators. Women served as generals in the armed forces and as astronauts exploring outer space.

None of this seems remarkable in today's world, and yet a few short decades ago, the path to these accomplishments was not open to most women. Sex discrimination is far from eradicated in American society—women still bump up against the invisible "glass ceiling" in much of the corporate world, for example— but increasingly, women have achieved the rights, responsibilities, and power long denied to them by a male-dominated culture.

In many arenas, the change in the role of women has been dramatic. When President Clinton sent American military forces into Bosnia in 1995 as part of a NATO effort to bring peace to the former Yugoslavia, television viewers were not surprised to see women among the troops.

Only a few years earlier, however, the presence of women in full camouflage gear was not taken for granted. In 1991, the United States was at war in the Persian Gulf. For the first time, the images that flashed across the television screens in American living rooms showed women

as well as men risking their lives in that war. More than 35,000 women served in the war; 15 died, and two were taken prisoner.* The nightly news showed pictures of Army Major Marie Rossi, who was killed when her helicopter went down in Saudi Arabia, and Army Specialist Melissa Rathbun-Nealy, who was taken prisoner by the Iraqis but released unharmed after the war.

When the conflict began, women were officially barred from combat, even though, as a practical matter, they were exposed to the hazards of war. After the war ended, Congress voted to relax the restrictions somewhat by letting women in the Air Force and Navy fly combat missions. But many women in the military, and civilians as well, remained angered by the broader, more general ban on the use of women in combat. In 1999, 195,000 women were on active duty in the military, making up more than 12 percent of the 1.6 million total personnel in the armed services.[38]

The role of women in American politics has also changed rapidly. In 1984, Geraldine Ferraro, a 48-year-old member of Congress from New York, accepted the Democratic nomination for vice president at San Francisco. The cheering delegates at the national convention and the millions who watched on television knew they were witness to an historic moment. For the first time, a major party had selected a woman for the second highest office in the land. Walter F. Mondale, the Democratic presidential nominee, had chosen the Queens Democrat several days before in a move that electrified the nation and gave his campaign new momentum for a time.

The Mondale-Ferraro ticket was defeated by President Reagan and Vice President George Bush. But today, women occupy high office in all three branches of the government. In the year 2000, as noted earlier,

---

*Of the total of 15 dead, 4 were killed by enemy action—including 3 women who died when an Iraqi Scud missile hit their barracks—and 11 died in accidents or of natural causes.

two women, Sandra Day O'Connor and Ruth Bader Ginsburg, sat on the Supreme Court, and four women served in the cabinet. Women comprised almost 23 percent of state legislators and served as mayors in 192 larger cities.[39] Of the nation's 100 biggest cities, 16 had female mayors.[40] And in 2000, for the first time in history, a First Lady, Hillary Clinton, ran for national office as a candidate for the U.S. Senate in New York and won.

Much of the progress toward equal rights and full participation in American society achieved by women in recent decades can be credited to the women's liberation movement. The movement, which began in the 1970s, changed the way that Americans think and act about the role of women in the family and in society. Many women combined careers and child-rearing, and by the 1990s the two-income family in which both husband and wife worked was as common as it had been rare a few decades earlier.

Although the organized effort to end sex discrimination was generally known as women's liberation, or the women's movement, it encompassed many groups. And it drew support from many people of both sexes who were not actively engaged in the women's liberation movement but agreed with the objective of full equality for women.

Yet the gains made by women on the political front could hardly conceal the barriers faced by women in almost every aspect of American society and the glaring economic inequalities between men and women. How many women were chief executive officers of the top 500 American corporations, for example? The answer in the year 2000 was dismaying: three.[*] The "glass ceiling" was not easily shattered.

Despite impressive advances, American women still struggle for equality in the marketplace. The median income of women is only 73 percent of that of men. The stereotype of the female office worker as a secretary is all too real. In 1998, the 63.7 million women workers in the United States made up 46.3 percent of the labor force, yet women held 76 percent of all clerical jobs.[†] These statistics reflect the fact that many companies do not promote women to executive-level jobs. And even when women are hired in professional and executive positions, they earn considerably less than their male counterparts. (See Figure 5-3.) On the other hand, more women are entering the prestigious professions of law and medicine; beginning in the 1970s, the number of women graduating from medical and law schools rose dramatically, from 1,500 in 1970 to 23,981 in 1997.[41]

Carleton Fiorina became Hewlett-Packard's president and CEO in 1999.
AP/Wide World

One of the most significant social developments of the past two decades has been the dramatic increase in the number of employed women, who since 1980 have outnumbered those at home. By the year 2000, more than 60 percent of adult American women were employed. (See Figure 5-4.) By comparison, in 1970, only about 41 percent held jobs outside the home.[42]

Clearly, and despite the continuing barriers, American women, if they so choose, are no longer limited to home, kitchen, and children (even though some television commercials persist in showing stereotyped women comparing laundry detergents and floor waxes). As Carol A. Whitehurst has suggested, "Women, today, seldom think in terms of career versus marriage, but instead believe that they can successfully combine the two. As an increased number of women enter the labor force and the time spent on motherhood shortens, careers become more attractive to women, and old negative images of women with careers begin to decline."[43]

Women dividing their lives between career and home, however, may feel under pressure to excel in both. Still, many career women today are managing to spend more time at home with their children, by working part-time, for example. Others choose to leave the work force entirely. At the same time, many men are taking more responsibility for child-rearing than was the case in the past.

In June 1983 Sally K. Ride, a 32-year-old physicist from Encino, California, became the first American

---

[*]Adapted from the *Los Angeles Times*, November 12, 1999, p. 3C. In February 2000, the only female CEOs of companies on the *Fortune* 500 list of major American corporations were Carleton S. Fiorina of Hewlett-Packard; Andrea Jung of Avon; and Marion Sandler, co-CEO with her husband of Golden West Financial.
[†]Adapted from U.S. Bureau of the Census, Current Population Reports, *Money Income in the United States: 1998*, series P60-206, September 1999, pp. x–xi; and U.S. Bureau of Labor Statistics, *Bulletin 2307*, and U.S. Bureau of Labor Statistics, *Employment Earnings*, January issues. By the year 2000, the proportion of women in the workforce had increased to 60.1 percent. (See Figure 5-4.)

FIGURE 5-3

The Earnings Gap: Why Women Complain

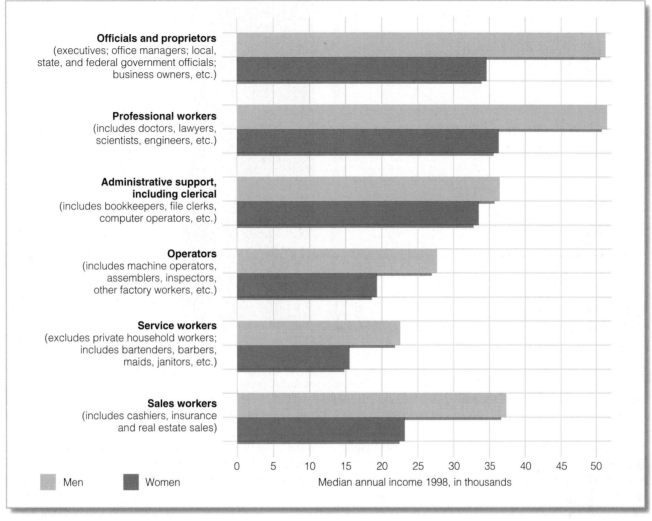

Officials and proprietors
(executives; office managers; local, state, and federal government officials; business owners, etc.)

Professional workers
(includes doctors, lawyers, scientists, engineers, etc.)

Administrative support, including clerical
(includes bookkeepers, file clerks, computer operators, etc.)

Operators
(includes machine operators, assemblers, inspectors, other factory workers, etc.)

Service workers
(excludes private household workers; includes bartenders, barbers, maids, janitors, etc.)

Sales workers
(includes cashiers, insurance and real estate sales)

Men   Women

Median annual income 1998, in thousands

SOURCE: U.S. Bureau of the Census.

woman to travel in outer space. She was a crew member of the space shuttle *Challenger* on a successful six-day mission. In January 1986 astronaut Judith A. Resnick died tragically with five other astronauts and Christa McAuliffe, a New Hampshire schoolteacher, when the *Challenger* blew up shortly after launch. In October 1984, Dr. Kathryn D. Sullivan became the first American woman to walk in space. In 1992, Mae Jemison flew aboard the shuttle *Endeavour,* becoming the first African American woman in space. And in 1999, Eileen Collins, an Air Force lieutenant colonel, became the first woman to command a space shuttle mission. With Collins at the controls, the space shuttle *Columbia* successfully completed its mission to launch an X-ray telescope in space.

Despite these gains for women in some areas, the Constitution does not specifically guarantee equal rights for women. For more than a decade, the women's

Ann Telnaes/Reprinted with special permission King Features Syndicate

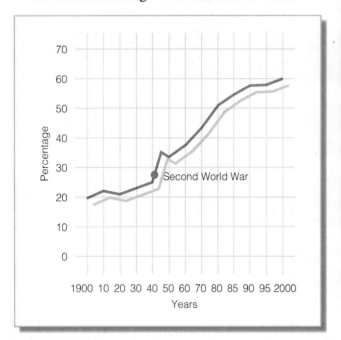

FIGURE 5-4

How Many Women Work: The Percentage of Women over Age 16 in the Labor Force

SOURCE: U.S. Bureau of the Census.

Mae Jemison, the first black woman in space, on the way to the launch pad, 1992
AP/Wide World

movement struggled but failed to pass a constitutional amendment to secure those rights.

In 1972, Congress proposed such an amendment to eliminate discrimination against women. The Equal Rights Amendment (ERA) said simply: "Equality of rights under the law shall not be denied or abridged by the United States or by any state on account of sex." The Equal Rights Amendment was aimed at state laws that discriminate against women in such areas as marriage, property ownership, and employment.

The battle over the ERA represented a philosophical conflict between the more traditional concept of the role of women and the modern view of women as both liberated and fully equal. In 1982, the amendment fell three states short of the 38 necessary to win ratification. By the year 2000, however, 16 states had equal rights provisions in their constitutions.

In 1972, Congress enacted a law barring discrimination because of a person's sex by schools and colleges that receive federal funds. As a result of the law, Title IX of the Education Amendments of 1972, many schools improved their athletic programs for women. In 1984, however, the Supreme Court ruled that the law applied only to the specific departments or programs that received federal money, not to the educational institution as a whole.[44] This narrower view of the law had been supported by the Reagan Administration, reversing the policy of three previous administrations. In 1988 Congress, over President Reagan's veto, passed a law to undo the Supreme Court decision. As a result, federal antidiscrimination laws once again applied to an entire institution if any department or program receives federal funds.

Laws benefiting women were to some extent a reflection of the growth of the feminist movement. The women's movement, one study concluded, "has developed a sophisticated organizational structure and has established itself as a significant presence in national policy making."[45] Feminists, the same study suggested, had an important impact on the adoption of Title IX, as well as on the passage of other laws providing equal credit opportunities for women and extending disability benefits to pregnant women.[46]

The role of women in the military, as noted earlier, has changed dramatically in recent years. In 1981 the Supreme Court ruled that the government may exclude women from the military draft and registration for it: "The Constitution requires that Congress treat similarly situated persons similarly, not that it engage in gestures of superficial equality."[47]

More than half of the first women who graduated from the U.S. Military Academy at West Point were assigned to combat branches at their own request. They were barred by law, however, from assignments likely to involve close combat.[48]

Two major groups represent women's rights: the National Women's Political Caucus and the National Organization for Women. The National Women's Political Caucus, founded in 1971, has helped to increase the number of female delegates to the national party conventions as well as the total of women elected to public office. It emphasizes political goals, including the election and appointment of more women to public

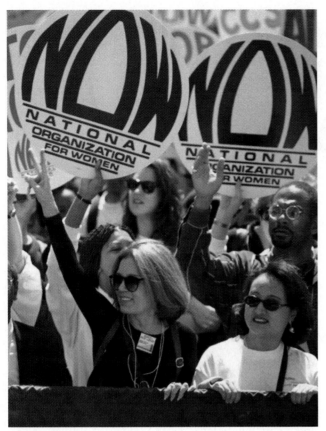

AP/Wide World

office. The number of women holding public office has increased noticeably since the women's movement began. Yet, in the history of the United States through the year 2000, just 197 women had served in Congress, compared to more than 12,000 men.[49]

 for more information about the women's groups listed above, see: www.nwpc.org and www.now.org

Four women were named to cabinet posts by President Clinton, including Janet Reno, the first woman to serve as attorney general; Madeleine K. Albright, the first woman to serve as secretary of state; Alexis M. Herman, secretary of labor; and Donna E. Shalala, appointed to head Health and Human Services. Twenty-one of the highest-ranking officials of the Justice Department under Reno were women. Other recent presidents all named women to their cabinets. In the year 2000 three women—Christine Todd Whitman of New Jersey, Jane Dee Hull of Arizona, and Jeanne Shaheen of New Hampshire—were governors of their states. The number of women in state legislatures grew from 305 (4.1 percent) in 1969 to 1,669 (22.5 percent) in 2000.[50]

The National Organization for Women (NOW), founded in 1966, shares some of the political aims of the National Women's Political Caucus but places more emphasis on other issues affecting women. NOW, with about 500,000 members, has worked to improve employment opportunities for women, defended abortion rights,

the rights of lesbians, and supported the reform of laws dealing with women. Its goals include gaining equality for women, stopping violence against women, and ending discrimination based on sexual orientation or race.

Many issues sometimes seen as primarily affecting women are not really "women's issues" at all, but concern the entire society. One example is the issue of sexual harassment, which dramatically came to the attention of millions of Americans in the fall of 1991 when the Senate Judiciary Committee was considering the nomination to the Supreme Court of Judge Clarence Thomas. Anita Hill, a 35-year-old law professor at the University of Oklahoma and a former aide to Thomas, stunned the nation with her graphic testimony accusing Thomas of sexual harassment. According to Hill, Thomas spoke to her about pornographic materials, sex organs, and sexual acts and repeatedly asked to date her. Thomas denied all of Hill's charges, accused the committee of conducting a televised, "high-tech lynching," and was eventually confirmed by the panel and then by the full Senate, 52–48.

Senators and television viewers were left puzzled as to whether Thomas or his accuser was telling the truth, but there was no doubt that the hearings had sensitized many American men to an issue that they had not taken seriously before. One poll taken at the time reported that 53 percent of men said they had engaged in behavior that women might interpret as sexual harassment; the same survey reported that 38 percent of women felt they had been subjected to sexual harassment at work.[51] The Senate hearings had a noticeable political effect as well. Many women were outraged at the treatment of Hill by several white male senators. As a result, more women participated in the 1992 elections, both as campaign workers and as candidates.

In 1993, the Supreme Court ruled unanimously that a woman suing her employer for sexual harassment does not have to show that she suffered severe psychological injury in order to collect damages.[52] Teresa Harris, who worked for a trucking company in Nashville, Tennessee, quit her job and sued the company, charging that her boss, Charles Hardy, called her a "dumb-ass woman," suggested they repair to a Holiday Inn "to negotiate your raise," and asked female workers to retrieve coins from his front pants pocket. In her majority opinion, Justice Sandra Day O'Connor ruled for Harris, saying that the 1964 Civil Rights Act prohibited that kind of "hostile or abusive working environment."[53]

If women face sexual harassment in the workplace, it is also true that they may be subject to physical abuse at home. In one poll, 22 percent of women questioned in the United States, which would be equal to 24 million women if projected to the adult female population, said they have been physically abused by their husbands or partners.[54]

Abortion   Probably no issue divides American society today as sharply as the controversy over abortion. For three decades, abortion has been a politically volatile social issue. On one side are a majority of pro-choice women and men who support the right of a woman to have an abortion to terminate a pregnancy. Many women feel that state regulation of pregnancies violates their right of privacy. Pro-choice groups, such as the Planned Parenthood Federation of America, argue that women have the right to control their reproductive systems and to make decisions about their own bodies.

The pro-life Americans—including many women—strongly disagree. Legalized abortion has been deplored by the Roman Catholic Church; many Americans feel abortions are a form of murder and violate the rights of unborn children. To an extent, therefore, the moral and legal arguments revolve around the question of when life begins. The antiabortion forces argue that life begins at the moment of conception, but that view has not been accepted by the pro-choice forces or by the U.S. Supreme Court.

In 1973 a Supreme Court decision gave dramatic evidence of the shifting social attitudes in America and the concerns of the women's movement. In the landmark case of *Roe* v. *Wade*, the Court ruled 7–2 that no state may interfere with a woman's right to have an abortion during the first three months of pregnancy.[*] The decision in effect struck down laws restricting abortion in 46 states. Reaffirming its decision in 1983, the Supreme Court invalidated various state laws designed to make it more difficult to obtain legal abortions.[55] Again in 1986 the Supreme Court narrowly reaffirmed *Roe* v. *Wade*, voting 5–4 to strike down a Pennsylvania law that discouraged abortions.[56] A year later, the Court invalidated an Illinois law that would have required teenagers to notify their parents before having abortions.[57]

The continued political opposition to legalized abortion, however, along with a decided conservative shift in the makeup of the Supreme Court, combined to create a climate in which the future of a woman's right to legal abortion was in doubt. In 1989, the Supreme Court in a Missouri case, *Webster* v. *Reproductive Health Services*, ruled 5–4 that states may impose sharp restrictions on abortions.[58] Although it stopped short of overturning *Roe* v. *Wade*, the Court held that states could regulate abortions at any stage of pregnancy, including the first three

By permission of Mike Luckovich, Creators Syndicate

months. "For today, at least," Justice Harry A. Blackmun said in a dissent, "the law of abortion stands undisturbed. . . . But the signs are evident and very ominous, and a chill wind blows."[59]

Later Supreme Court decisions seemed to march in the same antiabortion direction. In 1990, the Court ruled in cases from Minnesota and Ohio that states may require teenage girls to notify both parents before having an abortion.[60]

In 1992, however, a narrowly divided Court reaffirmed, 5–4, the constitutional right to an abortion that it had first established in *Roe* v. *Wade*.[61] At the same time, it upheld parts of a Pennsylvania law that had imposed restrictions on abortion and had made it compulsory for minors to get the advance consent of one parent or a judge. Although the Court upheld most of the restrictions in the Pennsylvania law, it struck down a requirement that a woman notify her husband before having an abortion. The majority opinion held that "an entire generation" had come of age relying on the liberty of women to make reproductive choices. For the Court to overrule its own decision in *Roe* v. *Wade* under political pressure, the opinion said, would damage the public confidence in the Court, the "legitimacy" on which the Court's power rests.[62]

In a separate opinion, Justice Blackmun joined the majority in upholding the essential principles of *Roe* v. *Wade*, the decision he had written almost two decades before. There had been little reason to hope that abortion rights would survive, he said. "But now, just when so many expected the darkness to fall, the flame has grown bright."[63]

The Supreme Court's 1973 guidelines in *Roe* v. *Wade* severely limited the power of a state government to regulate abortions. During the first three months, or first

---

[*]*Roe* v. *Wade*, 410 U.S. 113 (1973); *Doe* v. *Bolton*, 410 U.S. 179 (1973). In 1995, Norma McCorvey, the woman known as "Jane Roe," whose case led to the *Roe* v. *Wade* Supreme Court decision, announced that she had been baptized, had switched sides on the abortion issue, and had joined the antiabortion group Operation Rescue.

Opponents had made so-called partial-birth abortion a national political issue by widely publicizing the graphic details of the procedure, in an effort to enlist public support against it. But abortion has been a volatile political issue ever since the Supreme Court decision in *Roe* v. *Wade* three decades ago. As a result of that decision, the National Right to Life Committee was formed. This committee and other pro-life groups became a powerful force in a number of political campaigns, where they opposed candidates who favor legalized abortion.

Although abortions became legal after *Roe* v. *Wade*, the Supreme Court's decision did not settle the question of who should pay for abortions. Congress in 1976 had passed a controversial amendment sponsored by Representative Henry J. Hyde, an Illinois Republican. The Hyde amendment banned federal Medicaid payments for abortions, even those medically necessary, except in cases of rape or incest or when the mother's life was "endangered." In 1980 the Supreme Court, by a vote of 5–4, upheld the Hyde amendment.[65] The result was that poor women could no longer count on the government paying for abortions; Medicaid had been paying for an estimated 300,000 abortions a year.

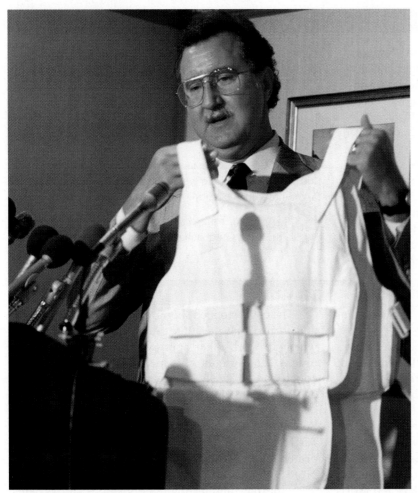

Dr. Brian Finkel displays a bulletproof vest like the one he wears when entering or leaving his abortion clinic in Phoenix, Arizona.
Barry Thumma/AP/Wide World

trimester, of a pregnancy, the decision was up to the woman and her physician. During the last six months, the state could regulate abortion procedures, but only during the last 10 weeks could a state ban abortions (except when abortion is necessary to preserve the life or health of the mother). The Court reasoned that a child born during the last 10 weeks of normal pregnancy is presumed to be capable of survival. In the wake of the Supreme Court's decision, medical authorities have estimated that about 1.5 million abortions are performed each year in the United States.

In 2000, the Supreme Court decided one of the most controversial aspects of abortion rights when it struck down a Nebraska law that barred a procedure sometimes used in abortions in the second trimester of pregnancy.[64] Supporters of abortion rights called the procedure a "late-term" abortion; opponents called it "partial-birth" abortion, because in the procedure the fetus is drawn partially out of the uterus, the skull collapsed, and its contents suctioned. The Nebraska law, like those in other states, applied to abortions of fetuses that cannot live outside the womb—that is, during about the first 24 weeks of pregnancy.

In the meantime, antiabortion groups remained highly vocal and in some cases highly militant. In Wichita, Kansas, in 1991, pro-life activists of Operation Rescue caused turmoil for 46 days by attempting to block the entrances to abortion clinics, a tactic designed to discourage women from entering. Antiabortion activists adopted the same strategy in several larger cities. Pro-choice activists attempted to keep the entrances to the clinics open.

Within a few years, militance had turned to violence. There have been hundreds of incidents of bombings, arson, vandalism, and death threats directed at clinics where women could have their pregnancies terminated. In 1993, David Gunn, a doctor who worked for an abortion clinic in Pensacola, Florida, was shot three times in the back and killed, the first physician to be murdered as a result of violence against abortion clinics. His assailant was sentenced to life in prison. In 1994, President Clinton signed a law barring antiabortion demonstrators from blocking access to clinics or threatening patients. But two months later, another doctor and his unarmed escort, a retired Air Force officer, were murdered outside another abortion clinic in Pensacola. Their killer was sentenced to death. And later that year, a gunman attacked two abortion clinics in Brookline, Massachusetts, killing two staff workers and wounding five other people. The

Norma McCorvey, a slight, green-eyed carnival worker known as "Pixie" to her friends, became pregnant one night in 1969. McCorvey, then 21, did not want the baby. The product of a broken home in Dallas, she was a high school dropout, a bride and mother at 16, a divorcee within a year, a troubled and impoverished young woman who considered herself one of life's losers.

Her pregnancy set off a social revolution.

Under the pseudonym of Jane Roe, her case, *Roe* v. *Wade,* became the landmark 1973 Supreme Court decision overturning antiabortion laws in Texas and in other states, one of the most controversial and hotly debated in history.

Few court decisions have had a more immediate impact on such a personal aspect of American life.

According to the Alan Guttmacher Institute, a research affiliate of the Planned Parenthood Federation of America:

• An estimated 28 million legal abortions have been performed in the United States from 1973 to 1992.

• The number of abortions performed annually grew from 744,600 in 1973 to 1.5 million in 1992.

In 1995, Jane Roe announced a change of heart and left the abortion clinic where she had worked and became a volunteer for Operation Rescue, an antiabortion group.

—Adapted from *Washington Post,* January 23, 1983; the Alan Guttmacher Institute, *Facts in Brief,* 1995; and *Time,* August 21, 1995

gunman was sentenced to life and after two years in prison committed suicide.

But the killings did not end. In October 1998, Dr. Barnett Slepian was standing with his wife and son in the kitchen of his home in Amherst, New York, a suburb of Buffalo, when a sniper shot him fatally through an undraped window. Slepian had performed abortions at a Buffalo clinic despite several death threats. Authorities found a high-powered rifle buried in the woods behind the physician's home and linked it to James C. Kopp, an antiabortion extremist, who was indicted for the murder in 1999 but remained a fugitive on the FBI's Ten Most Wanted list.

Gay Rights

In December 1999, the Supreme Court of Vermont ruled that gay couples are entitled to the same benefits and protections that the state grants to heterosexual married couples.[66]

The court stopped short of legalizing gay marriages, and turned that question over to the state legislature, which in April 2000 approved a law allowing "civil unions." In Vermont, this meant that a gay or lesbian couple can be legally joined in a ceremony that creates a same-sex marriage in everything but name.

The language of the decision of the Vermont Supreme Court had far-reaching implications. Chief Justice Jeffrey Amestoy wrote that guaranteeing equal protection for homosexual couples who seek "legal protection and security for their avowed commitment to an intimate and lasting relationship is simply, when all is said and done, . . . a recognition of our common humanity."[67]

According to a study by researchers at the University of Chicago, 2.8 percent of American men and 1.4 percent of American women identify themselves as homosexual or bisexual. In addition, 9.1 percent of men and 4.3 percent of women reported they have had some homosexual experience.[68] But estimates of the size of the gay

On June 29, 1992, the last Monday of its term, the Supreme Court reaffirmed, 5–4, the essential principles of *Roe* v. *Wade,* its 1973 decision establishing the constitutional right of women to have abortions in the early stages of pregnancy. At the same time, the Court upheld most restrictions on abortion contained in a Pennsylvania law. Following are excerpts from the majority opinion:

Our obligation is to define the liberty of all, not to mandate our own moral code. . . . These matters, involving the most intimate and personal choices a person may make in a lifetime, choices central to personal dignity and autonomy, are central to the liberty protected by the Fourteenth Amendment. At the heart of liberty is the right to define one's own concept of

existence, of meaning, of the universe, and of the mystery of human life. . . .

An entire generation has come of age free to assume *Roe*'s concept of liberty in defining the capacity of women to act in society, and to make reproductive decisions. . . . A decision to overrule *Roe*'s essential holding under the existing circumstances would address error, if error there was, at the cost of both profound and unnecessary damage to the Court's legitimacy, and to the Nation's commitment to the rule of law. It is therefore imperative to adhere to the essence of *Roe*'s original decision, and we do so today.

—*Planned Parenthood of Southeastern Pennsylvania* v. *Casey,* 1992

R. Taylor/Sygma

population vary; an earlier study based on data from the Kinsey Institute for Sex Research concluded that about 20 percent of American men had such experience at some time in their lives.[69] Although no one knows the size of the gay population in the United States, it is certainly in the millions.

Like other minority groups, gay men and lesbian women often have been discriminated against in jobs and other areas. Some of this stems from a long-standing general bias against gays by many individuals; in other cases, discrimination is fueled by the opposition of conservative or religious groups who feel that homosexuality violates moral or religious precepts.

According to poll data, 59 percent of the public have said they believe homosexual behavior is "morally wrong."[70] In recent years, however, changing public attitudes, the increased political power of gays, and the willingness of more gay men and women to express their sexual preferences openly—to "come out of the closet"—have given this minority a greater degree of visibility and acceptance in American society.

There has in fact been a pronounced shift in public attitudes. A majority of Americans support equal rights for gays in employment, housing, and job protection.[71] And the revulsion at violence directed at gays, such as the murder of Matthew Shepard, is shared even by many people who do not approve of the gay lifestyle.

A poll conducted by the Gallup organization in 1999 found that 83 percent of all Americans favored equal job opportunities for homosexuals.[72] A January 2000 poll found that 41 percent of Americans thought it acceptable for gay persons to serve openly in the armed forces. More than half of those polled, 54 percent, thought gay persons should be hired as elementary school teachers. Exactly half, 50 percent, believed that homosexual relations between consenting adults should be legal.[73] In an earlier Gallup poll, however, 66 percent of Americans had said they would not vote for a homosexual for president.[74]

As a result of court decisions, legislative action, and changing public perceptions of homosexuals, many jurisdictions have protected gay rights. By the year 2000, some 163 communities—including New York, San Francisco, Boston, Detroit, Los Angeles, and Washington, D.C.—had passed local laws or taken executive action to protect gay rights in employment, housing, and other

TAMMY BALDWIN MAKES HISTORY

Tammy Baldwin (D-Wis.) is one of the rare House freshmen who's already made her mark on American history.

The citizens of Madison, Wisconsin made Baldwin the first openly gay person to win a seat in Congress (Reps. Barney Frank [D-Mass.] and Jim Kolbe [R-Ariz.] told voters after they were already in office.) She is also the first woman Wisconsin has sent to the House of Representatives.

Unlike other firsts—the first African American, first Asian American—Baldwin does not have the luxury of flaunting her unique identity. Instead, she has to be a new kind of ground breaker, out to prove she can make what's special about her disappear.

She's aware some of her constituents fear she'll morph into a single-issue automaton, obsessed with pushing the gay rights agenda. As a state legislator she did support civil rights for gays and lesbians, but as one among many different issues. "They'll be able to watch what I do," Baldwin said. "I feel very

comfortable they'll find I represent a broad cross section of values."

But she knows most of her constituents are not hanging rainbow flags on the porch and would not want to see their representative marching at gay pride events around the country. She knows, in other words, that, like much of America, many of Madison's citizens are uneasy with the fact that their congresswoman is gay. Her challenge is now to avoid triggering fears like the ones the men and women in the Madison focus group expressed, and slowly change the stereotype.

"It's pretty simple," Baldwin said. "The more people who have the opportunity to know and work with openly gay and lesbian people, the more acceptance and tolerance there will be."

—Adapted from *Washington Post* and Congresswoman Tammy Baldwin's biography on www.house.gov/baldwin/biography.html

areas. Twenty-five counties, 19 states—including California, New York, Illinois, Michigan, Ohio, Pennsylvania, Massachusetts, Wisconsin, and Connecticut—and the District of Columbia had taken similar action.[75]

It was much different a little more than a decade earlier. In 1986, the Supreme Court ruled 5–4 that the Constitution does not protect homosexual relations between consenting adults, even in the privacy of their homes.[76] The Court did so in upholding a Georgia law that prohibited oral or anal sex. The justices did not rule whether the same law could be applied to heterosexuals. The case arose when Michael Hardwick, a gay bartender in Atlanta, failed to pay a ticket for drinking in public. A police officer with a warrant was admitted to Hardwick's home and found Hardwick in his bedroom, having sex with another man. Hardwick was arrested for violating the Georgia sodomy law.

Before the Supreme Court's ruling, 25 states, including California, Illinois, Ohio, and New York, had removed criminal sanctions from private sex acts by consenting adults. Yet the laws concerning gays were uneven, varying greatly from state to state.

In 1992, voters in Colorado approved an amendment to the state constitution that barred local governments from passing laws to protect gays from housing and job discrimination. In 1996, in a major victory for gay rights, the Supreme Court, by a vote of 6–3, struck down the amendment as unconstitutional.[77] The decision opened the way for local governments in Colorado and elsewhere to pass laws prohibiting discrimination against gays and lesbians.

In his majority opinion, Justice Anthony M. Kennedy wrote: "We must conclude that Amendment 2 classifies homosexuals . . . to make them unequal to everyone else. This Colorado cannot do. A state cannot so deem a class of persons a stranger to its laws." He ruled that the Colorado amendment violated the Fourteenth Amendment of the U.S. Constitution, which provides that no state may deny any person equal protection of the laws.

On the other hand, in the year 2000, the Supreme Court ruled 5–4 that a private group, the Boy Scouts of America, had a constitutional right to ban gay members.[78] In the majority opinion of Chief Justice William H. Rehnquist, the Court held that the Boy Scouts believed gay conduct was "inconsistent with the values it seeks to instill in its youth member."[79] The case had been brought by James Dale, a scoutmaster in new Jersey who had been expelled by the Boy Scouts.

Congress has at times acted to protect the rights of gay persons. It was the crisis over acquired immune deficiency syndrome (AIDS) that led to the first major congressional action benefiting gays. The disease devastated the homosexual community—although it was by no means limited to gays, since the virus that causes AIDS could be transmitted not only by sexual contact between homosexuals but also by heterosexual sex, blood transfusions, needles used by drug addicts, and

by infected pregnant mothers to their babies.[*] Prodded by gay activists, in 1988 Congress passed its first comprehensive AIDS legislation. The $1 billion package included funds for research, new drugs, home health care for AIDS patients, and anonymous testing. Similar bills, with larger dollar amounts, were enacted in later years.

In October 1987, more than 200,000 gay men and women from across the nation gathered on the mall in Washington, the scene of many political protests. They carried signs that read "Get Ready for the Gay 90s," "Dyke from Ohio," and "Condoms, Not Condemnation." They had come to march for an end to discrimination against homosexuals and for more funds to fight AIDS.

Under the Civil Service Reform Act of 1978, most federal agencies cannot discriminate against homosexuals in their hiring practices, but for many years the Federal Bureau of Investigation, the Central Intelligence Agency, and other "sensitive" government agencies could as a rule dismiss or refuse to hire gay persons. In 1995, however, President Clinton signed an executive order prohibiting the denial of security clearances "solely on the basis of the sexual orientation of the employee." The order had a dramatic impact; in June 2000, a gay pride ceremony was held at CIA headquarters in Langley, Virginia, attended by some 100 gay employees of the intelligence agency, and by workers from the National Security Agency, the nation's code agency, as well.[80]

The armed forces have exercised the right to dismiss or exclude homosexuals. In 1992, as a candidate for president, Bill Clinton pledged to end the ban on gay persons in the military. After his election as president, however, strong opposition by the military and by Senator Sam Nunn of Georgia, then chairman of the Senate Armed Services Committee, forced Clinton to modify his stand. What emerged was a policy of "don't ask, don't tell." Under this policy, homosexuals were permitted to remain in the armed forces if they did not disclose their sexual orientation by statements or behavior.

In the past, federal law had permitted the Immigration and Naturalization Service to bar gay persons from the United States. In 1980, however, the Justice Department ruled that homosexual aliens would not be barred unless they made a voluntary declaration of their homosexuality. The law barring foreign homosexuals from entering the United States was passed four decades ago, long before the American Psychiatric Association, in 1973, removed homosexuality from its list of mental disorders and urged that gays be given the same legal protections as other citizens.

---

[*]As of 1998, the AIDS epidemic in the United States had exceeded 600,000 cases. Of that total, more than 400,000 persons had died. More than 60,000 heterosexual AIDS cases had been reported. By that time, it was estimated that there were between 600,000 and 900,000 Americans carrying the AIDS virus. Data from U.S. Centers for Disease Control and Prevention.

In many cities and states, political leaders could ignore gay power only at their own peril. In San Francisco, with its large gay population, no mayor can be expected to win election without the support of members of the gay community. In New York, Denver, Houston, Austin, and Washington, D.C., gays have become an important political force. In 1980, a political action committee, the Human Rights Campaign, was formed to help elect officials who support gay rights.

 for more information about the Human Rights Campaign, see: www.hrc.org

Disabled Americans

Until relatively recently, the estimated 54 million[81] Americans with disabilities were a kind of invisible minority, their rights of equal treatment and equal access more often than not overlooked or neglected.

A person in a wheelchair has as much need to enter a shopping mall or a restaurant as anyone else; but often no ramp has been available, and a set of stairs difficult or impossible to navigate blocks the way. In employment, transportation, access to other public facilities, and in other ways, the disabled have been disadvantaged.

In 1990, Congress acted to remove these everyday barriers to a normal life for persons with disabilities. The Americans with Disabilities Act, enacted in that year and signed into law by President George Bush, was the most significant antidiscrimination law since the 1964 Civil Rights Act. The act defines disabled persons as anyone with "a physical or mental impairment that substantially limits one or more of the major life activities." The law, with provisions to take effect over a period of years, bans discrimination against such persons in employment, public accommodations, transportation, and telecommunications. Under the law, employers of more than 15 persons cannot refuse to hire qualified disabled persons. New buses, taxis, trains, hotels, restaurants, stores, schools, parks, museums, movie and other theaters, as well as auditoriums, doctors' offices, and health clubs must be accessible to disabled persons. Banks must lower ATM machines to accommodate persons in wheelchairs, and restaurants must provide menus in Braille for the blind or visually impaired. Public and other telephones, to the extent possible, must allow hearing- or voice-impaired persons to place and receive calls. In every aspect, the law sought to accommodate the rights of disabled Americans far beyond what had ever been done before.

BLACK AND WHITE: AN AMERICAN DILEMMA

On March 3, 1991, officers of the Los Angeles Police Department cornered a 25-year-old motorist, Rodney G. King, after a wild automobile chase. Police said he had been speeding. As officers surrounded King, four of them beat him repeatedly with their metal batons and kicked him. He was clubbed more than 50 times and shocked with a Taser electric stun gun as he lay near his car. Fifteen officers stood by and witnessed the savage beating but did not intervene.

Unknown to the police, a resident of a nearby apartment building turned on his video camera and recorded the scene. In millions of homes on television news broadcasts, and later in a courtroom in California, the videotape was played again and again. Rodney King's skull was fractured in at least nine places. He suffered many other injuries, including a shattered eye socket, a fractured cheekbone, and a broken leg.

Rodney King was black. The four officers who beat him were white. All four were later tried for assault with

Bob Daemmrich/Image Works

Rodney King is seen being beaten by Los Angeles police on the famous videotape.
Rob Crandall

a deadly weapon and excessive use of force, and two were also charged with falsifying police reports. In their defense, the officers contended that King had aggressively resisted arrest. On April 29, 1992, all four were acquitted of state charges by a jury that included no blacks in suburban Simi Valley, the community where the trial was held.

Within a few hours of the verdict, the predominantly black area of South Central Los Angeles erupted in violent anger. Some people were dragged from their vehicles and beaten as television crews in helicopters videotaped the riots.* More than 3,700 fires were set, and many stores were looted. In three nights of destruction, more than 50 persons died, most of them black and Hispanic, and more than 2,300 were injured. Close to 14,000 persons were arrested.

The violence spread to other parts of Los Angeles and to other cities. Los Angeles Mayor Tom Bradley declared a curfew, and California Governor Pete Wilson called out the National Guard. The city of the angels was turned into a virtual war zone. A pall of dark smoke hung over the city, closing all but one runway at Los Angeles International Airport. Freeways were clogged as thousands of frightened residents fled the city. Most businesses and offices shut down.

On the third day, President Bush sent in 1,000 federal law enforcement agents and ordered 4,500 federal troops to stand by; some later joined the National Guard in patrolling the streets. The president spoke to the nation on television, with a plea for racial harmony and a promise to restore law and order. Rodney King, whose terrible beating had begun it all, also went on television with an emotional plea for peace. "People," he said, "I just want to say, can we all get along? Can we get along?"[82]

Gradually, the violence diminished, but the scars remained.

The nation was shaken to the core by the terrible events in Los Angeles. Because the videotaped evidence had seemed clear, millions of persons, black and white, were baffled by the jury's decision. President Bush said he had been "stunned" by the verdict. Few Americans condoned the violence, even if they understood the emotions that had fueled it. Some political leaders called for social programs to get at the root causes of poverty and hopelessness. Democrats pummeled Republicans for neglecting urban problems during the Reagan and Bush administrations.

In Washington, the Justice Department began an investigation of the King beating. In 1993, two of the police officers were convicted in federal court of violating King's civil rights, and sent to prison. The two other officers were acquitted. In 1994, a jury in Los Angeles ordered the city to pay Rodney King $3.8 million in damages in compensation for the beating.

---

*Millions of people saw a white truck driver, Reginald O. Denny, pulled from his truck and beaten. In 1993, Damian M. Williams was sentenced to eight years in prison for felony mayhem in the attack on Denny.

Los Angeles riots, 1992
David Butow/Black Star

If not for the damning videotape, would Americans have ever known about the attack on Rodney King? Obviously not. The fact that a motorist, even one who was breaking the law by speeding, could be treated this way by police in the nation's second-largest city shocked many white Americans. It might have come as less of a shock to those African Americans who had personal experience with the racial prejudice that still existed among individuals in many segments of American society, including, in some cases, the police.

The issue of police prejudice and of racial divisions among Americans arose dramatically again at the 1995 trial of O. J. Simpson, the former pro-football star accused of murdering his ex-wife, Nicole Brown Simpson, and her friend, Ronald Goldman, in 1994 in the affluent Brentwood section of Los Angeles. During the trial, detective Mark Fuhrman testified he found a "bloody glove" at Simpson's estate on the night of the murders that matched one at the crime scene, so his testimony was crucial to the prosecution's case. But it later developed that Fuhrman, in a series of taped interviews, had used racial epithets in speaking of African Americans, although he had denied that on the witness stand. He had also boasted of planting evidence in other cases. The disclosures were shocking; racism had entered the courtroom of Judge Lance Ito and race became a key part of the Simpson defense. When Simpson was acquitted in October, the attitudes of the public toward the verdict reflected the continuing racial divisions in America. In a survey taken a few days before the jurors' decision, 77 percent of whites thought Simpson was guilty and 72 percent of blacks thought he was not.[83]

But violence among whites and blacks, burning cities, and sensational trials in a sense divert attention from the everyday reality of prejudice faced by many members of minority groups. Perhaps no white man or woman can ever fully comprehend what it is like to be born with black skin in America. In his prophetic 1963 book *The Fire Next Time*, author James Baldwin wrote:

Long before the Negro child perceives this difference, and even long before he understands it, he has begun to react to it, he has begun to be controlled by it. . . . He must be "good" not only in order to please his parents and not only to avoid being punished by them; behind their authority stands another, nameless and impersonal, infinitely harder to please, and bottomlessly cruel. And this filters into the child's consciousness through his parents' tone of voice as he is being exhorted, punished, or loved; in the sudden, uncontrollable note of fear heard in his mother's or his father's voice when he

MAKING A DIFFERENCE
"THERE WAS DAYS I ATE BEANS"

OAKLAND, CALIF.—In 1987, real estate agent Oral Lee Brown walked into a class of first graders in a blighted neighborhood and made a promise: If the students stayed in school and graduated, Mrs. Brown would pay for their college.

This fall, she made good, sending 19 students off to the colleges of their choice. When Mrs. Brown, who was making about $45,000 a year selling working-class homes, offered to shepherd a group of first graders through college, "I almost fell through the floor," said Yolanda Peeks, then the principal of Brookfield Elementary.

Getting the group of kids into college took more than good intentions.

There were monthly meetings with parents, weekly meetings with students, lunches on school playgrounds.

Sometimes there was trouble. The children of Brookfield went to class with all the problems of their neighborhood. On the tough streets of Oakland, drugs, gangs, and poverty take a lot of kids out of school.

"There's been times that I went home, put down my purse, went upstairs and got in bed and cried myself to sleep and said, 'I'm never going back,'" Mrs. Brown said. "I'd wake up the next morning and I was the first one there."

But how could one woman who makes $45,000 a year selling real

estate pay for 19 college educations? Paying for the dream wasn't easy. Mrs. Brown, who is widowed and has two grown daughters, found $10,000 every year to put into a trust fund. "There was days I ate beans," she said. She also started a foundation that raised more money.

In four years she plans to attend 10 different college graduations. "When my babies walk across the stage," she said, "then they can just lay me down and let me die."

—Adapted from the Associated Press, November 16, 1999; and Roger O'Neil on *NBC Nightly News with Tom Brokaw,* December 23, 1999

---

has strayed beyond some particular boundary. He does not know what the boundary is, and he can get no explanation of it.[84]

Another writer, Ralph Ellison, argued that the black adult was unseen by the white world. "I am an invisible man," he wrote. "I am a man of substance, of flesh and bone, fiber and liquids—and I might even be said to possess a mind. I am invisible, understand, simply because people refuse to see me."[85]

Ellison wrote those words in 1952. If African American men and women in America are visible today, it is because a revolution in civil rights has taken place since that time. Yet black Americans still have not been able to reach the goal of full equality in American society.

It is paradoxical, and tragic as well, that a nation founded on the principle that all people are created equal should have "a race problem." This is the paradox that the Swedish sociologist Gunnar Myrdal termed the "American Dilemma" in his classic study more than half a century ago.[86] "The American Dilemma," Myrdal wrote, ". . . is the ever-raging conflict between, on the one hand, the valuations preserved on the general plane which we shall call the 'American Creed,' where the American thinks, talks, and acts under the influence of high national and Christian precepts, and on the other hand . . . group prejudice against particular persons or types of people."[87]

Author Charles E. Silberman has argued that in one sense, "Myrdal was wrong. The tragedy of race relations in the United States is that there is no American Dilemma. White Americans are not torn and tortured by

the conflict between their devotion to the American creed and their actual behavior. . . . What troubles them is not that justice is being denied, but that when racial conflicts erupt their peace is . . . shattered and their business interrupted."[88]

The tension between black and white Americans is not only a problem for the African American still seeking a rightful place in society but also a problem for all citizens, a moral contradiction that strikes at the roots of American democracy. Two decades after Myrdal had summarized his views, and again in 1992, the "fire next time" predicted by James Baldwin visited American cities in the form of racial disorders, and social conflict remained a continuing threat to the nation's future.

By the 1980s a substantial black middle class had emerged in the United States, and black incomes were growing. But this created even deeper divisions among blacks. William Julius Wilson has suggested that economic class, rather than race, may have become more important in determining the status of blacks in America: "As the black middle class rides on the wave of political and social changes . . . the black underclass falls behind."[89] Other scholars have disagreed with Wilson's interpretation, arguing that "the biggest problem that black Americans face is that they are in a country that has historically oppressed black people because they are black."[90] Wilson himself later said he might avoid the use of the term "underclass" in the future because it enabled some analysts to blame the poor for their plight.

The unprecedented migration of blacks from the South to northern cities after the Second World War helped to create explosive ghetto conditions in those cities. And the poverty of the inner city continued to exist in the midst of what is, for many Americans, an affluent society. Blacks, Silberman noted, are "an economic as well as a racial minority." No matter how "assimilated" the black American is, because of his skin color "he cannot lose himself in the crowd. He remains . . . an alien in his own land."[91]

THE HISTORICAL BACKGROUND

The African American

Unlike most other immigrants, who came to these shores seeking freedom, African Americans came in slavery. Theirs was a forced immigration. While Irish Americans, Italian Americans, and other Americans might regard their forebears' country of national origin with pride, until the 1960s few black Americans identified with African culture. In part this was because black Americans absorbed the whites' concept of Africa as a land of jungles and savages. Only in recent years have substantial numbers of scholars explored the distinctive history and culture of West Africa.

It was there, south of the Sahara along the coast of West Africa, that most of the slaves brought to America were captured, to be transported across the sea under cruel conditions. The slaves, chained together and lying on their backs, were packed in layers between the decks in spaces that sometimes measured less than two feet. Often, only a third survived the voyage "and loss of half

was not at all unusual."[92] It was not surprising that the slaves sometimes mutinied aboard ship.

No one knows how many slaves were brought to North and South America and the West Indies between the 16th and the mid-19th centuries, but the figure has been estimated at 15 million. It easily may have been twice that.

An African American Heritage

In the 1950s a white or black child reading an American history textbook scarcely would have realized that African Americans were a significant part of the American past. Beginning in the 1960s, however, interest in the cultural heritage of African Americans was accompanied by new studies of the role of blacks in the nation's history.

Perhaps the first person to fall in the American Revolution was a black man, Crispus Attucks. A 47-year-old runaway slave, later a sailor, he was the first of five men killed by British soldiers in the Boston Massacre of 1770, five years before the Revolutionary War began.[93] African Americans took part in the battles of Lexington, Concord, and Bunker Hill; they were with George Washington at Valley Forge. About 5,000 blacks served in the Continental Army. During the Civil War, 186,000 blacks served in the Union ranks and blacks fought in later wars, including World War II, Korea, and Vietnam.

Black explorers, soldiers, scientists, poets, writers, educators, public officials—the list of such men and women who made individual contributions is long and distinguished; moreover, blacks as a group have contributed to the culture of America and have participated in its historical development. Yet from the start, the role

A total of 186,000 African Americans served in the Union Army during the Civil War.
Copyright © Bettmann/CORBIS

of African Americans was overlooked or neglected. "We hold these truths to be self-evident," the Declaration of Independence says, "that all men are created equal." But that soaring language was not meant to include the African American, who was recognized by the framers at Philadelphia as only "three-fifths" of a person. The American Dilemma, even as the republic began, was engraved in the new nation's Constitution but had scarcely touched its conscience.

Dred Scott, Reconstruction, and "Jim Crow"

Citizens of a state automatically are citizens of the United States under the Constitution. Until after the Civil War, however, this in reality referred only to free white persons. The citizenship status of free blacks—there were almost 100,000 in the early 1800s—remained a subject of political dispute. The Supreme Court ruled on the question in the famous **Dred Scott decision** of 1857.

Dred Scott was a slave who had lived in the North for four years. Antislavery forces sought to bring Scott's case before the Supreme Court on the grounds that his residence on free soil had made him a free man. To sue for freedom, Scott first had to prove he was a citizen. But Chief Justice Roger B. Taney ruled that Dred Scott and other black Americans "are not included, and were not intended to be included, under the word 'citizens' in the Constitution."[94]

It took a civil war and a constitutional amendment to reverse Taney's decision. In 1865, eight months after the surrender of Robert E. Lee's army at Appomattox, the states ratified the Thirteenth Amendment, abolishing slavery. The Fourteenth Amendment, ratified in 1868, reversed the *Dred Scott* decision by making citizens of the freed slaves. The Fifteenth Amendment, ratified in 1870, was designed to give former slaves the right to vote.

Dred Scott
National Archives

During the Reconstruction era (1863–1877), Congress passed a series of civil rights measures. Two laws enacted in 1870 make it a crime for police to violate a person's civil rights or for anyone to conspire to do so. The statutes were seldom invoked until the 1960s, when the federal government used them to prosecute and convict police in brutality cases in which local authorities had failed to act or the offenders had received light sentences. Of the laws passed during Reconstruction, the last, the Civil Rights Act of 1875, was the strongest. The law was aimed at providing equal public accommodations for blacks. But this postwar trend toward equality was short-lived. In the *Civil Rights Cases* of 1883, the Supreme Court struck down the 1875 Civil Rights Act, decreeing that the Fourteenth Amendment protected citizens from infringement of their rights by the states but not by private individuals. Discrimination by one citizen against another was a private affair, the Court held.

Thus, less than two decades after the Civil War, the Supreme Court had seriously weakened the Fourteenth Amendment and neutralized the efforts of Congress to pass civil rights laws to protect black citizens. The Court decisions were also a sign of what was to come.

After 1883 the atmosphere was ripe for the rise of segregation and of **Jim Crow laws** designed to segregate black and white Americans and give legal recognition to discrimination.[*]

Segregation, the separation of black and white Americans by race, became the new way of life in the South. Jim Crow laws were accompanied by lynchings and terror for African Americans.[†]

Plessy v. Ferguson

In 1896 the Supreme Court put its seal of approval on racial segregation in America. The great constitutional test of legal discrimination began on a June day in 1892, when Homer Adolph Plessy bought a ticket in New Orleans, boarded an East Louisiana Railroad train, and took his seat—in a coach reserved for whites. He was asked to move, but he refused and was arrested.

Plessy was chosen for this test by opponents of the state's Jim Crow railroad law, which required equal but separate accommodations for white and black passengers. The Supreme Court ruled in 1896 that the Louisiana statute did not violate the Fourteenth Amendment.

Yet *Plessy* v. *Ferguson* is remembered as well for the ringing dissent of a single justice, a former slaveholder from Kentucky, John Marshall Harlan. Shocked by the activities of the Ku Klux Klan, Harlan had become a champion of civil rights for blacks. And he declared: "Our Constitution is color-blind, and neither knows nor tolerates classes among citizens. . . . The thin disguise of 'equal' accommodations for passengers in railroad coaches will not mislead any one, nor atone for the wrong this day done."[95]

Despite Harlan's eloquent dissent, the doctrine of "separate but equal" remained the law of the land for 58 years, until 1954, when the Supreme Court finally ruled that it had no place in American life.

The Case of Linda Carol Brown

In the city of Topeka, Kansas, more than half a century after *Plessy*, Oliver Brown, a black man and a welder by trade, was disturbed by the fact that his 8-year-old daughter, Linda Carol, attended an elementary school 21 blocks from her home. Only black students attended the school, for Topeka elementary schools were segregated by local option under state law. To go the 21 blocks to Monroe Elementary School, Linda Carol caught a school bus at 7:40 A.M. The difficulty was that the bus arrived at the school at 8:30 A.M., but the doors of the school did not open until 9 A.M. Often, it meant that the children had to wait outside in the cold. To get home in the afternoon, she

had to walk past the railroad tracks and cross a dangerous intersection. Oliver Brown tried to enroll his children at Sumner Elementary School, which was only seven blocks from the Brown home. He was unable to do so. Sumner was a school for white children. With the help of the National Association for the Advancement of Colored People (NAACP), Oliver Brown took his case to court.

Brown v. Board of Education

On May 17, 1954, Chief Justice Earl Warren delivered the unanimous opinion of the Supreme Court in the case of ***Brown* v. *Board of Education of Topeka, Kansas,*** ruling that racial segregation in public schools violates the Fourteenth Amendment's requirement of equal protection of the laws for all persons. The issue before the Supreme Court was very simple: The Fourteenth Amendment guarantees equal protection of the laws. The plaintiffs argued that segregated schools were not and could never be equal, and were therefore unconstitutional.

Chief Justice Warren asked: "Does segregation of children in public schools solely on the basis of race, even though the physical facilities and other 'tangible' factors may be equal, deprive the children of the minority group of equal educational opportunities? We believe that it does." Such segregation of children, the chief justice added, "may affect their hearts and minds in a way unlikely ever to be undone. . . . We conclude that in the field of public education the doctrine 'separate but equal' has no place. Separate educational facilities are inherently unequal. Therefore, we hold that the plaintiffs . . . are, by reason of the segregation complained of, deprived of the equal protection of the laws guaranteed by the Fourteenth Amendment."[96]

The Supreme Court did not attempt in 1954 to enforce its decision. The Court, as Justice Robert Jackson pointed out, "is dependent upon the political branches for the execution of its mandates, for it has no physical force at its command."[97]

Much of the South reacted to *Brown* by adopting a policy of massive resistance. How, then, would the Court's ruling be implemented? A year later, in May 1955, the Supreme Court itself addressed the problem, unanimously ordering local school authorities to comply with the decision "with all deliberate speed."[98] But compliance was very slow, and in some instances there were direct armed confrontations between federal and state power.

Little Rock, Oxford, and Alabama

In September 1957 nine black children attempted to enter the all-white Central High School in Little Rock, Arkansas, under a federal court order. Governor Orval Faubus called out the National Guard to block integration of the school, but the troops were withdrawn by direction of the court. The black students braved a screaming mob of whites. President Dwight Eisenhower

---

[*]In 1832 Thomas D. "Daddy" Rice, a blackface minstrel, had introduced a song and dance about a slave named Jim Crow ("Weel a-bout and turn a-bout/And . . . jump Jim Crow"), and the term came to be applied to the antiblack laws of the 1890s.
[†]There were about 100 lynchings a year in the 1880s and 1890s; 161 lynchings took place in 1892.

reluctantly dispatched federal paratroopers to Little Rock to quell the violence. Central High was integrated.

Violence continued to flare in the South during the Kennedy administration. After James Meredith, a black student, enrolled in the University of Mississippi at Oxford in 1962, two men were killed and several injured in the rioting that took place on the campus. President Kennedy dispatched federal marshals and ordered 16,000 troops to restore peace and protect Meredith. The following year, Alabama Governor George Wallace attempted to block the enrollment of two black students at the University of Alabama at Tuscaloosa. Wallace backed down only after Kennedy federalized the Alabama National Guard.

The School Decision: Aftermath

Fifteen years after the *Brown* decision, only 20 percent of black students in the South attended integrated public schools. Faced with continued defiance, the Supreme Court ruled unanimously in October 1969 that school districts must end segregation "at once" and operate integrated systems "now and hereafter."[99] Through federal court rulings and the efforts of the federal government in working with local school boards, the pattern gradually changed. But even as more schools became integrated, the question of public school desegregation, in the North as well as in the South, remained a volatile issue.

And in Topeka, Kansas, where it had all begun, a federal judge in 1979 reopened the *Brown* case after a group of parents complained that, 25 years later, the city's schools were still segregated. Among the group of parents who filed the complaint was Linda Carol Brown, now the mother of two children in the Topeka public school system. In 1987 a federal district court ruled that the school district, although not totally integrated, was in compliance with the law.

The Busing Controversy

In September 1999, a federal judge in Charlotte, North Carolina, ruled that busing of public school children was no longer necessary to prevent discrimination against black students.[100] A year later, a federal appeals court overturned that decision, requiring continued desegregation of schools in the city where busing had begun three decades earlier.

In 1971, in a case that arose in Charlotte, the Supreme Court had ruled unanimously that in some circumstances the Constitution required busing of school children to achieve desegregation.[101] By the mid-1970s the familiar yellow school bus had become the symbol of a deeply divisive political and social issue in the United States. But the Court did not require busing in every case. For instance, it struck down plans to bus children to desegregate schools in some cities, while it upheld a busing plan in Boston, the scene of prolonged violence over busing in the mid-1970s.

Although millions of public school children rode school buses every weekday in the United States, many parents, both white and black, objected to busing to

UPI/Bettmann/CORBIS

achieve desegregation. White parents often opposed the busing of their children into largely black, inner-city schools. A number of parents, black and white, objected to long bus rides into unfamiliar neighborhoods for their children.

As the issue continued to trouble the nation, some black educators concluded that a high-quality education did not depend on busing and desegregation. Wilson Riles, the superintendent of education in California, rejected the idea "that a black child can't learn unless he is sitting next to a white child."[102]

In the cities of the North, school segregation often has been the result not of law but of de facto segregation—residential patterns that created black neighborhoods and, along with them, black schools. The 1954 *Brown* decision did not deal with de facto segregation, but the issue was involved in a case in Denver decided by the Supreme Court in 1973.[103] The Court ruled that Denver had to desegregate its school system; the decision in effect warned the North that it could not operate deliberately segregated schools by manipulating school boundaries, any more than the South could.

Rosa Parks: Her courage made her a symbol of the civil rights movement.
Copyright © Bettmann/CORBIS

For a time, the Supreme Court continued to approve busing plans in other cities. In 1991, however, the Supreme Court ruled, 5–3, in an Oklahoma City case that busing need not continue once a school district had made good faith efforts to end racial segregation.[104] Later decisions of the Supreme Court and lower federal courts made it easier for school districts to be released from desegregation orders and busing. The critics argued that neighborhood schools, even if predominantly white or minority, were favored by a majority of parents. Some black leaders concluded that the goal should be improvement of majority black schools, rather than integration.

More than four decades after the *Brown* decision, most minority students still attended segregated schools across the nation. In 1999, for example, 69 percent of blacks students attended predominantly minority schools.[105] It was clear in the years following *Brown* that racial problems were not confined to any one section of the nation.

THE CIVIL RIGHTS MOVEMENT: FREEDOM NOW

The Montgomery Bus Boycott

On the evening of December 1, 1955, Rosa Parks, a 43-year-old seamstress, boarded a bus in Montgomery, Alabama, as she did every working day to return home from her job at a downtown department store. When half a dozen whites got on at a bus stop, the driver asked black passengers near the front of the bus to give up their seats to the whites and move to the rear. Three other black passengers got up; Rosa Parks did not. She was arrested and fined $10, but her quiet refusal launched a boycott of the bus line by a black population that had had enough. It was a remarkable year-long protest, and it catapulted to national fame the 27-year-old Baptist minister who led it. His name was Dr. Martin Luther King, Jr.

During the boycott, King went to jail and his home was bombed, but he won. The boycott ended in November 1956 as a result of a federal court injunction prohibiting segregation of buses in Montgomery. The victory set the pattern for other boycotts and for direct action throughout the South.

King, who led the civil rights movement and remained its symbolic head until his assassination in 1968, was an apostle of nonviolence, an eloquent man who attempted, with some success, to stir the American conscience. King grew up in comfortable middle-class surroundings in Atlanta, where his father was pastor of the Ebenezer Baptist Church. It was in Atlanta in 1957, following the Montgomery boycott, that King formed the Southern Christian Leadership Conference (SCLC) as a vehicle for his philosophy of nonviolent change, which had been influenced by the teachings of Gandhi.

Until then, the principal black organization in the United States had been the NAACP, which stressed legal

MARTIN LUTHER KING'S MORAL THEATER

When the antiabortion mothers march around the Capitol, when the farmers jam the streets with their tractors, they are, consciously or otherwise, imitating the moral theater Martin Luther King staged for the mass audience of television. Sometimes it works, and often it doesn't, but a range of political strategies, now regarded as orthodox and acceptable, was considered outrageous [and] sometimes illegal when King introduced it.

—*Washington Post*, April 2, 1978

The police dogs of Birmingham, 1963
AP/Wide World

action in the courts as the road to progress. It was a lawyer's approach, and it had won many important struggles. King's battleground was the streets rather than the courts, and he sought through nonviolent confrontation to dramatize the issue of civil rights for the nation and the world.

The civil rights movement came of age at a time when many blacks were growing impatient with the slow pace of "gradual" change. Their desire was for "freedom now"—rather than at some unspecified time in the future.

Sit-Ins and Freedom Rides

In February 1960 four black college students in Greensboro, North Carolina, sat down at a lunch counter at Woolworth's and asked politely for cups of coffee. They were refused service. They continued to sit for the rest of the morning. They came back the next day, and the next. Soon other students, white and black, joined them. They were spattered with mustard and ketchup and spat upon and cursed by whites. But at Greensboro the sit-in movement was born.

It spread to seven other states. The new tactics were a success. Within six months, not only the Woolworth's in Greensboro but hundreds of lunch counters throughout the South were serving blacks. In 1961 the sit-in technique was adapted to test segregation on interstate buses and in bus terminals. Black and white Freedom Riders rode into Alabama, where they were beaten, slashed with chains, and stoned by whites. One bus was burned. But the Freedom Riders succeeded in publicizing the fact that segregation on interstate transportation, although outlawed by the Supreme Court, was still a reality.[106]

Birmingham and the Dream

In the spring of 1963, Dr. King organized demonstrations against segregation in industrial Birmingham, Alabama. When arrests failed to stop the demonstrators,

the authorities used high-pressure fire hoses, police dogs, and cattle prods. The demonstrators sang "We Shall Overcome" and continued to march. Photographs of police dogs attacking demonstrators on orders of Birmingham Police Commissioner Eugene "Bull" Connor went out on the news wires. Another photograph showed police kneeling on a black woman and pinning her to the sidewalk. The scenes outraged much of the nation and the world.

Late in August, King led a massive, peaceful "March on Washington for Jobs and Freedom." Some 200,000 Americans, black and white, jammed the mall between the Lincoln Memorial and the Washington Monument. The nationally televised, orderly demonstration had a powerful effect on the nation, but even more powerful were the words of Dr. King, who articulated the vision of what America could be and might become:

I have a dream that one day this nation will rise up and live out the true meaning of its creed. . . . I have a dream . . . that my four little children will one day live in a nation where they will not be judged by the color of their skin but by the content of their character. . . . So let freedom ring. . . . From every mountainside, let freedom ring . . . to speed up that day when all of God's children, black and white men, Jews and Gentiles, Protestants and Catholics, will be able to join hands and sing

154 CHAPTER 5 THE STRUGGLE FOR EQUAL RIGHTS

Dr. Martin Luther King, Jr., at the March on Washington, August 1963: "I have a dream. . . ."
Ebony Magazine

lation since 1875. It created the Commission on Civil Rights and strengthened the civil rights section of the Justice Department. However, the law proved to be of limited value in protecting civil rights.

The Civil Rights Act of 1964

In 1963 President Kennedy proposed a comprehensive civil rights bill. After Kennedy's assassination in November of that year, the House acted, but southerners in the Senate staged a 57-day filibuster. In June 1964 the Senate invoked cloture to cut off debate—the first time it had ever done so on a civil rights bill—and passed the measure. On July 2 President Lyndon Johnson signed the Civil Rights Act of 1964 into law. The principal provisions were designed to:

in the words of that old Negro spiritual, "Free at last! Free at last! Thank God Almighty, we are free at last!"[107]

Eighteen days later in Birmingham, a bomb was thrown into the Sixteenth Street Baptist Church on a Sunday morning. Four black girls attending Bible class died in the explosion. But from the agony of Birmingham that summer, from the impressive March on Washington, and from the powerful words of Dr. King, there emerged the strongest civil rights legislation since Reconstruction.

The Legislative Breakthrough

During the Eisenhower administration, Congress had passed the Civil Rights Act of 1957, the first such legis-

1. Prohibit racial or religious discrimination in public accommodations that affect interstate commerce, including hotels, motels, restaurants, cafeterias, lunch counters, gas stations, movie houses, theaters, and sports arenas.
2. Prohibit discrimination because of race, color, sex, religion, or national origin by employers or labor unions.
3. Bar voting registrars from adopting different standards for white and black applicants.
4. Permit the attorney general to bring suit to enforce desegregation of public accommodations, and allow individuals to sue for their rights under the act.

Denise McNair, 11; Carole Robertson, 14: Addie Mae Collins, 14; and Cynthia Dianne Wesley, 14, were all killed in the 1963 bombing of the Sixteenth Street Baptist Church in Birmingham, Alabama.
AP/Wide World

5. Permit the executive branch of the federal government to halt the flow of funds to public or private programs that practice discrimination.
6. Extend the life of the Civil Rights Commission, create a Community Relations Service to conciliate racial disputes, and an Equal Employment Opportunity Commission to enforce the fair employment section of the act.

The 1964 act did not cover violence directed at black Americans or at civil rights workers, white or black. Two days after President Johnson signed the bill into law, the bodies of three young civil rights workers—two of them from the North—were found in a shallow grave near Philadelphia, Mississippi.* In a civil rights act passed in 1968, Congress provided criminal penalties for injuring or interfering with civil rights workers or any persons exercising their civil rights; under the law, if the injury results in death, the maximum penalty is life imprisonment. The 1968 law also made it a federal offense to cross state lines with intent to incite a riot.

At the same time, Congress passed the Fair Housing Act, the first federal open housing law in the 20th century. It prohibited discrimination in the rental or sale of all privately owned single-family houses rented or sold through real estate agents or brokers.

The Voting Rights Act of 1965 During the Reconstruction era, state governments in the South were controlled by northern radical Republicans. After the white South regained control of its governments, particularly in the 1890s and thereafter, blacks were systematically denied the right to vote. What the Ku Klux Klan could not accomplish by intimidation, a broad range of other obstacles did. **Literacy tests,** designed to test a voter's ability to read and write, were rigged to keep black voters from the polls. Other barriers included the all-

---

*In 1967 seven men were convicted of conspiracy against the slain civil rights workers under an 1870 federal statute. Because the murders of the rights workers did not constitute a federal crime, the conspiracy statute was the only weapon available to the Justice Department. The seven, including an Imperial Wizard of the Ku Klux Klan and the deputy sheriff of Neshoba County, were given prison sentences ranging from 3 to 10 years.

white primary (which rested on the theory, rejected by the Supreme Court in 1944, that political parties were private clubs); the **poll tax,** a tax on voting used to keep poor voters from participating in elections; and **gerrymandering** of election districts, redrawing lines to favor one party or group over another. All were attempts to keep black voters in the South from gaining political power and challenging or changing the existing order. In short, the Fifteenth Amendment was being systematically flouted.

Only 12 percent of blacks of voting age were registered in the 11 southern states in 1948. Although the figure rose substantially in later years, in the mid-1960s it was still far below the 73.2 percent white registration in the same states.[108] (See Table 5-3.)

In Dallas County, Alabama, exactly 335 blacks out of a black population of 15,115 were registered to vote at the start of 1965. Martin Luther King chose Selma, the county seat, as the place where he would dramatize the voting rights issue. Dr. King called for a 50-mile march from Selma to Montgomery, the state capital. State troopers acting under orders of Governor Wallace used tear gas, whips, and night sticks to break up the march. President Johnson federalized the National Guard, and the march resumed under protection of the troops. Through the heat, the mud, and the rain, their

---

TABLE 5-3

Voter Registration in the South before and after the Voting Rights Act of 1965

Percent of Voting-Age Population Registered							
	1964	1972	1980	1986	1992	1994	1996
Black	43.3	56.6	60.0	64.0	63.9	58.3	64.7
White	73.2	67.8	68.4	65.3	70.1	64.2	67.0

SOURCES: Congressional Quarterly; *The Voting Rights Act: Ten Years After,* Report of the U.S. Commission on Civil Rights (Washington, D.C.: U.S. Government Printing Office, 1975), p. 43; and U.S. Bureau of the Census.

March on Montgomery, Alabama, 1965
James Karales/DPI

ranks swelling in numbers and in pride, the marchers walked on until, joined by Dr. King, they reached the steps of the Alabama capitol building.

In the midst of the struggle that began in Selma, and before the marchers had finally reached Montgomery, President Johnson went on nationwide television to address a special joint session of Congress and to urge new legislation to assure black Americans the right to vote. Then, in a dramatic moment, the president from Texas invoked the song and the slogan of the civil rights movement. "And we shall overcome," he said slowly. Thunderous applause greeted the remark, and Congress responded to Johnson's appeal with a second landmark civil rights measure.

The Voting Rights Act of 1965, passed after the Senate once again imposed cloture to crush a filibuster, covered six southern states—Alabama, Georgia, Louisiana, Mississippi, South Carolina, and Virginia—as well as parts of North Carolina and three other states. Through an automatic "triggering" formula, the act suspended literacy tests in areas where less than half the voting-age population had registered for, or had actually voted in, the 1964 election. It gave the federal government power to appoint examiners to require enrollment of qualified voters in such areas. Even outside of such areas, the attorney general could go into federal court to seek the appointment of examiners.

The effect of the Voting Rights Act was immediate. Within two years, black registration increased by almost 1.3 million in the 11 states of the South. In Mississippi, black registration jumped from 6.7 percent of eligible voters to 59.8 percent.[109] Figure 5-5 shows increases in the number of registered black voters for seven southern states.

At the same time, black registration drives in some southern states following passage of the Voting Rights Act also spurred new white registration. As a result, despite the percentage increase in black registration, in actual numbers, there were more new white voters in those states than new black voters.

In 1970 the Voting Rights Act (which would otherwise have expired that year) was extended for five years and its scope broadened to include areas of California, Oregon, four New England states, and parts of New York City. In 1975 Congress extended the act for seven more years and broadened its basic provisions to protect language minorities—Spanish-speaking Americans, Native Americans, Asians, and Alaska Natives. The revised law covered about a dozen more states. Literacy and character tests were permanently banned throughout the nation. Then, in 1982, Congress extended the Voting Rights Act for 25 years. This assured Americans that the protections built into the act would remain law through 2007.

The Voting Rights Act encouraged blacks to run for office, and many did. By 1984, registration and turnout of black voters nationwide was a major theme of Rev. Jesse L. Jackson's campaign for the Democratic presidential nomination. Even before that, blacks in large numbers were registering to vote.

Only 4.4 million blacks had voted in 1966. In 1988, some 10.1 million blacks voted.[110] In that year, Jackson emerged as a serious contender in the race for the Democratic presidential nomination. His enormous appeal and support among black voters was the most dramatic illustration of how the Voting Rights Act, and the increased participation of blacks in elections, had influenced the shape of politics in America in little more than two decades. In 1996, the number of African American voters rose again, to 11.4 million.[111]

In the early 1990s, after prodding by the Justice Department, about two dozen majority-black congressional districts were drawn in the South to conform to

FIGURE 5-5

Increase of Black Voter Registration in the Seven Southern States Covered by the 1965 Voting Rights Act

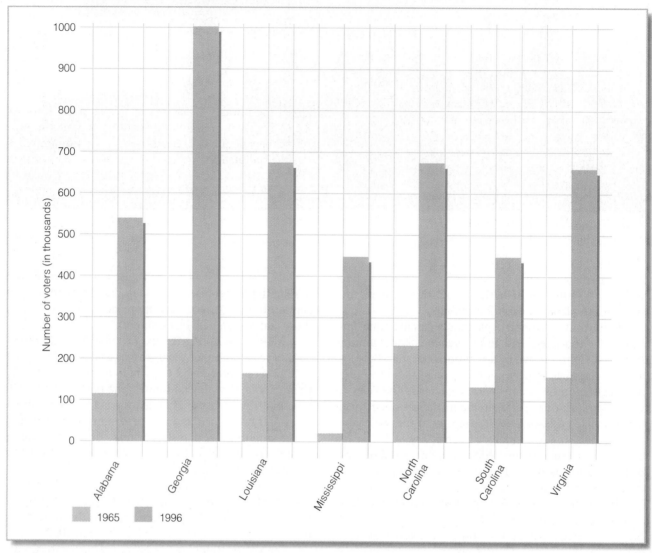

1965   1996

SOURCE: U.S. Bureau of the Census.

the Voting Rights Act and to make possible the election of more African American representatives in Congress. Some of the districts were oddly shaped in order to achieve that goal. Although the redistricting resulted in the election of more blacks and Hispanics, the changes created a dilemma for the Supreme Court, which grappled with the question of whether the new districts were constitutional.

In 1993, the Supreme Court, in a 5–4 decision in a North Carolina case, ruled that districts drawn with "bizarre" shapes that cannot be attributed to anything other than an effort to separate voters on the basis of race are unconstitutional unless "narrowly tailored" to serve a "compelling state interest."[112] The opinion, written by Justice Sandra Day O'Connor, created turmoil in the South. Federal district courts declared unconstitu-

tional congressional districts in Texas, Louisiana, and Georgia. In 1995, the Supreme Court, by a 5–4 vote, struck down the Georgia redistricting plan.[113] A year later, the Court invalidated four predominantly black and Hispanic congressional districts as unconstitutional—three in Texas and one in North Carolina—because they were based on race.[114]

The Court's view in these cases was set forth in Justice Anthony M. Kennedy's majority opinion in the Georgia redistricting case. He wrote: "When the state assigns voters on the basis of race, it engages in the offensive and demeaning assumption that voters of a particular race, because of their race, think alike, share the same political interests, and will prefer the same candidates at the polls." Writing for the dissenting justices, Ruth Bader Ginsburg argued that the specially drawn districts were necessary to "protect minority voters," and she referred to "generations of rank discrimination against African Americans, as citizens and voters."

The Urban Riots

Even as the major civil rights laws of the mid-1960s were taking effect, black protest in America entered a new phase. The great expectations aroused by the civil rights movement and legislative action by Congress had brought no visible change of status to the millions of blacks in the inner city. Frustration and poverty characterized the ghettos. Combined with summer heat and police incidents, the mixture proved volatile and tragic.

Los Angeles was sweltering in a heat wave on the night of August 11, 1965, when a white highway patrolman stopped a young black driver for speeding and arrested him. A crowd gathered, more police arrived, and trouble flared. By the time the police had left, the residents of Watts, the city's black ghetto, were in an angry mood. Two days after the incident, arson, looting, and shooting broke out. The Watts riot had begun. Cries of "Burn, baby, burn!" filled the air. When it was all over, 34 persons were dead, more than 1,000 had been injured, and $35 million in damage had been done.

The Watts explosion was the most dramatic event in a pattern of major violence that was to afflict dozens of American cities. After the assassination of Martin Luther King in April 1968 outbreaks occurred in Washington, D.C., and more than 100 other cities. More than 13,000 troops were dispatched to Washington, where rioters had set fires only a few blocks from the White House. For 12 days, armed troops occupied the capital of the United States.

During a major riot in Detroit in 1967, President Johnson went on nationwide television to plead for calm and to announce the appointment of a commission on civil disorders. The commission reported in March 1968:

> Our nation is moving toward two societies, one black, one white—separate and unequal. . . . Certain fundamental matters are clear. Of these the most fundamental is the racial attitude and behavior of white Americans toward black Americans. . . . Race prejudice has shaped our history decisively; it now threatens to affect our future. White racism is essentially responsible for the explosive mixture which has been accumulating in our cities since the end of World War II.[115]

To meet these problems, the commission recommended a national effort to eliminate racial barriers in employment, education, and housing and to create jobs. The commission's findings were controversial—many Americans disagreed with the emphasis on white racism as the cause of the urban riots. Few could disagree, however, with the gravity of the problems underscored by the explosions in the cities in the 1960s and in 1992.

Black Power, Black Pride

During the late 1960s, advocates of direct, militant action had to a considerable extent drowned out the voices of moderate black leaders. Black Power advocates and members of the militant Black Panthers often found it easier to capture the attention of the public and the press than did the moderates. And the assassination of Martin Luther King and other leaders committed to nonviolence weakened the position of the moderates.

Stokely Carmichael, a black leader who had popularized the phrase "Black Power," defined the term as "a call for black people in this country to unite, to recognize their heritage, to build a sense of community."[116] A common theme of Black Power was the need for African Americans to exercise political control of their communities. Economically, the term was tied to the creation of independent, black-owned and black-operated businesses. Spiritually, it meant racial pride; it also gave rise to slogans such as "Black is beautiful" and to an emphasis on "soul" and "soul brothers." Black Panthers and police were killed in a series of shootings in several cities. The most widely publicized case took place in 1969, when Chicago police raided an apartment before dawn, allegedly in a search for weapons, and shot to death Fred Hampton, chairman of the Illinois Black Panther party.[117]

Although militants had for a time commanded an audience, most black Americans sought full social and economic equality and dignity within the system rather than apart from it. Along with many white Americans, they still believed in Martin Luther King's dream.

In October 1995, Louis Farrakhan, the controversial leader of the Nation of Islam, organized the "Million Man March" that gathered on the mall in Washington to emphasize once again the themes of racial pride and responsibility. Because Farrakhan's rhetoric was often inflammatory and sometimes anti-Semitic, President Clinton distanced himself from Farrakhan. Many groups, including the NAACP, opposed the march because of its organizer. But for the hundreds of thousands of men who came together peacefully in Washington, the march was an impressive demonstration that emphasized personal responsibility, black pride, and unity.

AFFIRMATIVE ACTION: THE SUPREME COURT RULES

The civil rights movement and the legislation enacted in the 1960s did not settle a larger constitutional question: Was **affirmative action**—programs of government, universities, and business, designed to favor minorities and remedy past discrimination—constitutional?

Supporters of affirmative action argue that black Americans, unlike other ethnic groups, have faced greater barriers to achieving equality. Studies of ethnic patterns have noted that other nationality groups, as members of the white majority, have been more easily assimilated into American society.

John F. Kennedy, in an executive order issued in 1961, was the first president to call for affirmative action by the government. The order prohibited discrimination by contractors who received federal money and instructed them to hire and promote members of minority groups.

The Civil Rights Act of 1964 barred discrimination by universities or others who received federal assistance. The act also outlawed discrimination by employers or unions. Many universities, employers, and unions went a step further and established affirmative action programs that gave preference in admissions or jobs to minorities. The programs were based on the theory that members of these groups were disadvantaged as a result of past discrimination. Merely guaranteeing minorities equal opportunity, it was argued, would not solve the problem, because members of such groups often would be at a disadvantage when competing with whites who had not suffered discrimination. Advocates of affirmative action, therefore, pressed for positive steps to aid minorities to compensate for the past and bring about equality of opportunity and equality of results.

Bakke and *Weber:* The Battle Is Joined

Opponents of affirmative-action programs argued that the programs were a form of "reverse discrimination" against whites. Because the Fourteenth Amendment to the Constitution extended equal protection of the laws to everyone, and because the 1964 Civil Rights Act outlawed any form of discrimination, were programs unconstitutional if they favored a black or a Hispanic over a white person?

As with many constitutional questions, these arguments and counterarguments ebbed and flowed and eventually focused on the case of one person—a white man named Allan Paul Bakke. Bakke graduated from college in 1963 with an engineering degree and a 3.51 grade-point average. He joined the Marines, served in Vietnam, and later went to work on the moon program for the National Aeronautics and Space Administration (NASA). But what he wanted most was to be a doctor. Nights and weekends, he was a hospital volunteer.

In 1973 and 1974 Bakke applied to the medical school of the University of California at Davis. He did not get in. Davis had a special admissions program that reserved 16 out of 100 places in the medical school each year for minorities. In both years, minority students were admitted with much lower scores than Bakke's. Bakke sued. He contended that he had been excluded on the basis of his race in violation of the Constitution and the 1964 act.

In June 1978, the U.S. Supreme Court, by a vote of 5–4, ordered Bakke admitted to the medical school at Davis. At the same time, the Court upheld the right of

AFFIRMATIVE ACTION WINS THE GOLD IN ATLANTA

ATLANTA, June 9—All across America, affirmative action has been chased into retreat by lawmakers and judges. But here in Atlanta, the private corporation that is staging this summer's Olympic Games has awarded almost a third of its $387 million in construction and vending contracts to companies owned primarily by minorities and women.

Experts on affirmative action say such numbers are unheard-of in the private sector. But to city leaders, the commitment to minority participation is a reflection of a political reality so entrenched that it has come to be known as "the Atlanta way." . . .

"Everybody who is a person of color in this country has benefited from affirmative action," said Mayor Bill Campbell, the third black to lead a city that is now 67 percent black. "There's not been anybody who's gotten into a college on their own, nobody who's gotten a job on their own, no one who's prospered as a businessman or businesswoman on their own without affirmative action.

"The sad truth in this country, the sad truth even in the city of Atlanta, is that without our affirmative-action programs, our minority businesses would wither."

—*New York Times*, June 10, 1996

universities to give preference to blacks and other minorities as long as they do not use rigid racial "quotas" such as the one used at Davis.

The majority based its decision not on the 1964 law, but on the Fourteenth Amendment's guarantee of equal protection of the laws. Associate Justice Lewis F. Powell, Jr., who provided the swing vote in the case, delivered the majority opinion: "Preferring members of any one group for no reason other than race or ethnic origin is discrimination for its own sake. This the Constitution forbids." At the same time, Powell said, flexible admission programs, such as Harvard's, that "take race into account" but do not set a "fixed number of places" for minorities, were constitutional.[118]

In September, Bakke, by then 38, married, and the father of two young children, entered the medical school at Davis, California. He graduated in 1982 and became an anesthesiologist at a hospital in Minnesota.

The *Bakke* decision left unsettled the question of affirmative action in employment. But a year later, the Supreme Court ruled in the case of Brian Weber, a blue-collar worker in a small town in Louisiana, who suddenly found himself in the vortex of a major constitutional test. Weber, a 32-year-old white man, was employed as a lab technician for the Kaiser Aluminum and Chemical Corporation.

Weber applied and was rejected for a training program that would lead to higher pay. The program set aside half the jobs for black workers. Several of the blacks selected had less seniority than Weber, who took his case to the Supreme Court and lost. The Court ruled 5–2 that the 1964 Civil Rights Act was designed to help minorities and not to prohibit private affirmative action programs.[119] Then in 1980 the Supreme Court ruled that Congress could constitutionally require that 10 percent of federal public works contracts be awarded to minority-owned business firms in order to remedy past discrimination.[120]

In 1987, in its broadest endorsement of affirmative action to date, the Court ruled that employers may promote women and minorities ahead of white men, even when there is no evidence of prior discrimination.[121] It did so in the case of Diane Joyce, who had been a road repair worker in Santa Clara, California.

In 1995, however, in a Colorado highway construction case, the Supreme Court cast some doubt on the constitutionality of federal affirmative action programs that award contracts or other benefits to help minorities.[122] An Hispanic-owned company, Gonzales Construction, received a contract to build guardrails on a federal highway in the San Juan National Forest. A white contractor submitted a lower bid but lost the job. In its 5–4 decision, the Supreme Court ruled that federal affirmative action programs must be "narrowly tailored" to be constitutional.[123]

The Supreme Court often reflects the political environment of the times. In the wake of the Republican capture of Congress in 1994, the concept of affirmative action no longer enjoyed the same political support that it once had. The old arguments that such programs amounted to "reverse discrimination" against whites resurfaced and affirmative action programs fell under increased pressure.

In California in 1995, the regents of the university system banned affirmative action in admissions. In 1996, California voters approved Proposition 209, which banned race or gender preferences in public hiring, contracting, and education. In 1999, however, as an alternative, Gray Davis, the state's Democratic governor, initiated a program of admission to the University of California, starting in 2001, for the top 4 percent of graduates in each high school.

In 1996, a federal appeals court ruled unconstitutional the affirmative action program at the University of Texas. The "racial preferences" given by the university's law school benefited blacks and Mexican Americans, the court said, "to the detriment of whites and nonpreferred minorities."[124] The U.S. Supreme Court let the decision stand, leaving the status of such programs at other universities unclear. But a state law passed in Texas in 1997 and supported by Governor George W. Bush substituted a program that guaranteed admission to the state university system of all students who graduated in the top 10 percent of their high school class.

In 1998, voters in the state of Washington banned state-sponsored affirmative action programs. Two years later, Florida governor Jeb Bush was defending his One Florida plan, modeled after the one in Texas, his brother's state, that guaranteed admission to a state university to the top 20 percent of high school graduates. Although many affirmative action programs remained in place, their future was uncertain.

EQUAL RIGHTS: A BALANCE SHEET

In 1995, millions of Americans, both white and black, were hoping that Colin L. Powell, the retired Army general who had been chairman of the Joint Chiefs of Staff, would seek the 1996 presidential nomination. Enthusiastic crowds turned out in cities from coast to coast as Powell traveled to promote his autobiography. When he announced soon afterward that he would not be a candidate for president in 1996, his supporters were deeply disappointed. But the fact that an African American, the son of poor immigrants from Jamaica, enjoyed such widespread support was a milestone in itself.

It proved as nothing else had that at long last, and despite the nation's troubled history of race relations, the color of a person's skin was no longer a barrier to seeking the highest office in the land.

For example, in the year 2000 there were 39 African Americans in Congress, and 8,800 others in elective offices throughout the nation.* Three African Americans served in the cabinet, and another sat on the Supreme Court.[125] General Powell, a black man, had held the highest military post in the nation. There were 445 black mayors, including in such large cities as Detroit, San Francisco, Dallas, Memphis, Denver, and Washington, D.C.[126] A decade earlier, L. Douglas Wilder, the grandson of slaves, had served as governor of Virginia, the country's first elected African American governor. Rev. Jesse Jackson, a black, had twice run for the Democratic presidential nomination and gained the support of a substantial number of white voters. And Martin Luther King Day is a federal holiday observed on the third Monday in January in every state.

The American political system, in the civil rights legislation passed in the mid-1960s, had demonstrated its ability to respond to peaceful pressures for change. Black voters in the South, who came to the polls in increasing numbers, were better protected by federal law. Public accommodations were finally, by federal law, open to all Americans. And the nation had become aware that millions of black Americans would no longer wait.

But these gains reflected only part of the picture. The urban ghettos still existed. Fewer than 2 percent of all

---

*All 39 African Americans in Congress were serving in the House; 38 were Democrats, and one was a Republican. Data provided by the Congressional Black Caucus. Total for black elected officials, as of January 1998, from the Joint Center for Political and Economic of Studies.

elected officials were black. In jobs, housing, education, and income, the black man or woman still sat, figuratively, in the back of the bus.

Other minority groups as well were not sharing equally in the benefits of American society. Women earned only 73 cents for every dollar that men earned. Hispanic Americans and Native Americans, as we have seen, lagged far behind society as a whole by every economic yardstick.

While inequalities remained between whites and blacks, there were some signs of change. The number of successful black-owned businesses had increased along with the size of the black middle class.

America today is a multicultural society, a land of diversity, and, often, conflict among groups. Some see danger in diversity, and a loss of national identity. The liberal historian Arthur M. Schlesinger, Jr., for example, has warned that the emphasis on ethnic differences may fragment the nation. What Schlesinger termed the "cult of ethnicity" could, in his view, divide the country into "separate ethnic and racial communities."[127]

Despite that danger, in the year 2000 the need remained to remedy the persistent inequalities that mocked the ideals of American society. Although minorities had registered political and economic gains, serious racial divisions persisted, and substantial numbers of blacks, Hispanics, Native Americans, and other groups remained outside the mainstream of American affluence.

A century after the Civil War, many Americans were still struggling for equality and justice. In 1963, in an address to the nation about civil rights for blacks, President Kennedy declared: "This is not a sectional issue. . . . We are confronted primarily with a moral issue. It is as old as the scriptures and is as clear as the American Constitution." America, he said, "will not be fully free until all its citizens are free."[128]

How America responds to this moral issue in the 21st century might well decide its future. The continued struggle for equality for all Americans remains a great domestic challenge, testing the nation's political system and the minds and hearts of the American people.

KEY TERMS

CHAPTER HIGHLIGHTS

✦ Many of the more than 35 million African Americans do not enjoy full social and economic equality. About one out of four blacks in the United States is poor—by official definition of the federal government—as opposed to about one out of 10 whites.

✦ Native Americans are among the most disadvantaged of all minorities. Unemployment among Native Americans on the reservations is high, life expectancy low. Many live in shacks, adobe huts, and abandoned automobiles.

✦ The nation's Hispanic community—which includes Mexican Americans, Central and South Americans, Puerto Ricans, persons of Spanish origin, and Cubans—constitutes another group that struggles with discrimination and poverty. More than 25 percent of all Hispanics were living in poverty—compared to a national average of 12.7 percent.

✦ Although the precise number of undocumented immigrants in the United States is not known, government and private demographers have estimated that as many as 5 million or more persons are in the country illegally. Some employers, particularly growers and farm owners in California and Texas, have hired undocumented workers as a source of cheap labor.

✦ The estimated 11.2 million Asian Americans in the year 2000 made up a rapidly growing minority group in the United States. The number of Asian Americans more than doubled during the 1980s. By the mid-1990s, Asian Americans constituted the third-largest minority, after African Americans and Hispanics.

✦ Women, although constituting a majority of the population, are, in effect, another "minority group." In 1998 the median income of men was $35,345 while that of women was $25,862. The median income of women is only 73 percent of that of men.

✦ The women's liberation movement can be credited with much of the progress made by women toward equal rights and full participation in American society. Women have proved they can combine careers and child-rearing; by the 1990s, the two-income family in which both husband and wife worked was as common as it had been rare a few decades earlier.

✦ The number of women holding public office has increased substantially since the women's movement began. As of 2000, four women served in the cabinet, 67 women were members of Congress, there were three women governors, and women comprised almost 22.5 percent of state legislators.

✦ In 1973, the Supreme Court ruled in *Roe* v. *Wade* that no state may interfere with a woman's right to have an abortion during the first three months of pregnancy. In the year 2000, the Supreme Court decided one of the most controversial aspects of abortion rights when it struck down a Nebraska law that barred a procedure sometimes used in abortions in the second trimester of pregnancy. Supporters of abortion rights called the procedure a "late-term" abortion; opponents called it "partial birth" abortion.

✦ The controversy over abortion has turned violent in recent years. A number of doctors who performed abortions have been murdered, and there have been hundreds of incidents of bombings, arson, vandalism, and death threats directed at clinics where women could have their pregnancies terminated.

✦ By the year 2000, some 163 communities—including New York, San Francisco, Boston, Detroit, Los Angeles, and Washington, D.C.—had passed local laws or taken executive action to protect gay rights in employment, housing, and other areas. In December 1999, the Supreme Court of Vermont ruled that gay couples are entitled to the same benefits and protections that the state grants to heterosexual married couples.

✦ Until relatively recently, the estimated 54 million Americans with disabilities were a kind of invisible minority, their rights of equal treatment and equal access more often than not overlooked or neglected. In 1990, Congress acted to remove these everyday barriers to a normal life by passing the Americans with Disabilities Act, the most significant antidiscrimination law since the 1964 Civil Rights Act.

✦ Unlike most other immigrants who came to these shores seeking freedom, African Americans came as slaves. In the *Dred Scott* decision (1857), the Supreme Court ruled that blacks were not citizens under the Constitution. The decision was later reversed by the Fourteenth Amendment, which in 1868 made citizens of the freed slaves.

✦ The Supreme Court ruled in *Plessy* v. *Ferguson* (1896) that a state law requiring equal but separate accommodations for white and black railroad passengers did not violate the Fourteenth Amendment. This doctrine of "separate but equal" remained the law of the land until 1954, when Chief Justice Earl Warren delivered the unanimous decision of the Supreme Court in the historic school desegregation case of *Brown* v. *Board of Education of Topeka, Kansas*. The justices ruled that school segregation violated the Fourteenth Amendment's requirement of equal protection of the law for individuals. Yet, nearly five decades later, public school segregation still exists in many cities across the nation.

♦ Dr. Martin Luther King, Jr., a black minister, led the civil rights movement that began in the 1950s. Largely in response to that movement, several important civil rights bills were enacted by Congress in the mid-1960s. The Civil Rights Act of 1964 prohibited racial or religious discrimination in public accommodations. The Voting Rights Act of 1965 suspended literacy tests in southern counties in which blacks were being denied the right to vote. The 1965 law was later amended to apply to other minorities as well, and to states in the North and West.

♦ Protests by minority groups in the inner cities of America have sometimes turned violent. The riots of the 1960s were repeated in Los Angeles in 1992 after a jury that included no African Americans acquitted four white police officers on trial for the beating of Rodney G. King, a black motorist.

♦ In the wake of the civil rights movement, affirmative action programs were established to give preference in university admissions or jobs to minorities. The programs were based on the theory that members of these groups were entitled to special preference because they were disadvantaged as a result of past discrimination. Opponents of affirmative action argued that such programs were a form of reverse discrimination against whites.

♦ In the year 2000 there were 39 African Americans in Congress, and 8,800 others in elective offices throughout the nation. Three African Americans served in the cabinet, and another sat on the Supreme Court. General Colin Powell, a black man, had held the highest military post in the nation. There were 445 black mayors, including mayors in such large cities as Detroit, San Francisco, Dallas, Memphis, Denver, and Washington, D.C. Some economic gains had been registered by blacks by the 1990s. However, the median income for black families was only somewhat more than half that of white families.

♦ Despite political and economic gains by African Americans, serious racial divisions persisted, and substantial numbers of blacks, Hispanics, Native Americans, and other groups remained outside the mainstream of American affluence.

SUGGESTED WEB SITES

www.naacp.org
National Association for the Advancement of Colored People
The NAACP is the oldest and largest civil rights organization in the United States. Its principal goal is to work for the political, educational, social, and economic equality of blacks and other minority groups in the United States.

http://thekingcenter.com
Martin Luther King, Jr., Center for Nonviolent Social Change
The King Center works to carry forward the legacy of Dr. Martin Luther King, Jr., through research, education, and training in the principles, philosophy, and methods of nonviolence.

www.now.org
National Organization for Women
NOW is the largest feminist organization in the nation, with more than 500,000 contributing members. It seeks to protect the rights of women and end inequality based on sex. It engages in lobbying, grass-roots political organizing, and litigation.

www.naral.org
National Abortion and Reproductive Rights Action League
NARAL is a pro-choice group that advocates reproductive freedom for women through abortion or birth control. NARAL's activities include research and legal work, policy reports, public education campaigns, and leadership training for grass-roots activists.

www.all.org
American Life League
The American Life League is a pro-life group that advocates the view that human life begins at conception. ALL is opposed to the use of birth control and believes that abortions should be prohibited in all cases, with no exceptions.

www.hrc.org
Human Rights Campaign
The Human Rights Campaign, the largest national lesbian and gay political organization, advocates equal rights for lesbians and gays. HRC lobbies on gay, lesbian, and AIDS issues, participates in election campaigns, and organizes volunteers.

www.nod.org
National Organization on Disability
NOD advocates the full and equal participation of America's 54 million men, women, and children with disabilities in all aspects of life. Lists resources and links for people interested in disabilities or who are disabled.

www.latinoweb.com
Latino Web
Latino Web seeks to bring Latino people together by providing Web links that relate to the concerns of Hispanics in the United States.

www-personal.umich.edu/~lwu/asian.html
Asian American Resources
The Asian American Resource Center lists Web sites that cover a wide variety of Asian American interests and concerns.

www.doi.gov/bureau-indian-affairs.html
Bureau of Indian Affairs
The BIA, a division of the U.S. Department of the
Interior, was created to assist Indians and Alaska
Natives. Includes data about both groups.

SUGGESTED READING

Baldwin, James. *The Fire Next Time* (Dial Press, 1963).
An examination of the status of blacks in America
by a leading black writer. Baldwin argues for "total
liberation" of blacks and maintains that blacks are
the key to America's future.

Barker, Lucius J., and Jones, Mack H. *African-Americans
and the American Political System,* 3rd edition*
(Prentice Hall, 1994). A comprehensive analysis
of how blacks have fared in the American political
system. Includes discussions of how Congress, the
courts, the presidency, and political parties have
responded to the problems faced by African
Americans.

Brown, Dee. *Bury My Heart at Wounded Knee**
(Holt, Rinehart and Winston, 1970). A powerful,
detailed, and highly readable account of how
Native Americans were driven from their villages
and hunting grounds, often brutally, by white
Americans as the frontier was pushed westward.
The book, which became a national best-seller,
contains excellent descriptions of major American
Indian chiefs and tribal leaders.

Carmichael, Stokely, and Hamilton, Charles V. *Black
Power** (Random House, 1967). The political
definition of Black Power. Carmichael, the black
leader who popularized the term, and Hamilton,
a political scientist, urged black Americans to
seek community control and use other such
political tools.

Edsall, Thomas Byrne, with Edsall, Mary D. *Chain
Reaction: The Impact of Race, Rights, and Taxes
on American Politics** (Norton, 1991). A study of
the rise to power of the presidential wing of the
Republican Party from 1968 to 1988. Argues that
during this period the Republicans were able to
forge a new coalition of voters, and to win five
out of six presidential elections, by capitalizing
on the twin issues of race and taxes.

Ellison, Ralph. *Invisible Man** (Modern Library, 1992).
(Originally published in 1952.) In this novel a black
writer describes the identity problem of blacks in a
white society. The "invisible man" cannot be seen,
Ellison argued, because whites refuse to acknowledge his existence.

Franklin, John Hope. *From Slavery to Freedom,* 7th edition* (McGraw-Hill, 1994). A classic study of black
history in America written by a distinguished black
historian.

Jaynes, Gerald David, and Williams, Robin M., Jr.
A Common Destiny: Blacks and American Society
(National Academy Press, 1989). A comprehensive
review, sponsored by the National Research
Council, of the position of African Americans in
American society since the Second World War.
Emphasizes political participation, employment
and income, family patterns, education, health,
crime and the criminal justice system, and the
important role of social, political, and religious
institutions within the black community.

Jordan, Winthrop D. *White over Black: American
Attitudes toward the Negro, 1550–1812** (University
of North Carolina Press, 1968). A detailed examination of the attitudes of whites toward blacks
during the first two centuries of slavery in North
America. The book draws extensively on newspaper accounts, speeches, pamphlets, letters, and
court records of the day.

McClain, Paula D., and Stewart, Joseph Jr. *Can We
All Get Along? Racial and Ethnic Minorities in
American Politics,* 2nd edition (Westview Press,
1998). A useful and readable introduction to the
experiences of primarily four ethnic groups in
the United States (African Americans, Native
Americans, Asian Americans, and Latinos),
and their efforts to achieve full social, economic, and political representation within the
American system.

McGlen, Nancy E., and O'Connor, Karen. *Women,
Politics and American Society,* 2nd edition*
(Prentice Hall, 1998). An analysis of the changing
roles of women in American society, and their
growing political activity and influence.

Meier, August, and Rudwick, Elliott M. *From
Plantation to Ghetto,* 3rd edition* (Hill and Wang,
1976). A history of blacks in America with emphasis on black protest movements, particularly in the
20th century. Includes a discussion of the African
heritage of American blacks.

Myrdal, Gunnar. *An American Dilemma: The Negro
Problem and Modern Democracy** (Transaction,
1996). (Originally published in 1944.) A classic
study of race relations in the United States until
the time of the Second World War. Traces the
history of blacks in America and stresses the
gap between the American creed of equality for
all and the actual treatment African Americans
have received. This book, by an eminent Swedish
sociologist, has had a major influence on
American thought about race relations.

O'Connor, Karen. *No Neutral Ground: Abortion Politics
in an Age of Absolutes** (Westview Press, 1996).
A study of one of the most intractable issues of
our time. O'Connor examines the factors that have
made abortion so politically incendiary, and so
resistant to political compromise.

Rosales, Francisco A. *Chicano! The History of the Mexican American Civil Rights Movement* (Arte Publico Press, 1996). A thoughtful account of the history of Mexican-Americans, from the effects of the war with Mexico, to the Hispanic civil rights movement of the 1960s and 1970s, and the challenges still facing America's fastest-growing ethnic group.

Schlesinger, Arthur M., Jr. *The Disuniting of America: Reflections on a Multicultural Society,* 2nd revised edition* (Norton, 1998). An essay on America as a multicultural nation. The author argues that too much emphasis on the culture of separate ethnic groups will result in a fragmented society that loses its sense of national unity and American identity.

Sniderman, Paul M., and Carmines, Edward G. *Reaching beyond Race* (Harvard University Press, 1997). The authors use polling data to show that racial intolerance has diminished in the United States, and suggest that politicians could build multiracial coalitions by appealing to "moral principles that reach beyond race."

Sniderman, Paul M. and Piazza, Thomas. *The Scar of Race** (Harvard University Press, 1993). Drawing upon the results of several broad surveys, the authors conclude that the racial attitudes of white Americans have evolved since the 1960s, due in large part to the role of education in combating racism.

Thernstrom, Abigail, and Thernstrom, Stephen. *America in Black and White: One Nation, Indivisible** (Simon & Schuster, 1997). An impressive historical overview of the black struggle for equal rights in the 20th century. The authors credit the reforms accomplished by the civil rights movement as having had significant impact upon the quality of life for black Americans, while maintaining that there is much yet to be accomplished on race relations in the United States.

Woodward, C. Vann. *The Strange Career of Jim Crow,* 3rd revised edition* (Oxford University Press, 1974). A classic study of the establishment and consequences of segregation laws in the South after the Civil War.

_____

*Available in paperback edition.

 Visit http://politicalscience.wadsworth.com/cummings9/update/ for current InfoTrac articles and other student resources related to this chapter.

PART TWO
Politics
and People

CHAPTER 6
Public Opinion

When Marie Antoinette, according to legend, responded to the bread shortage in France by remarking, "Let them eat cake," she was showing an unwise disregard for public opinion. In due course, her head was cut off on the guillotine.

After President Lyndon B. Johnson sent half a million men to fight in Vietnam, he discovered that public opinion had turned against him. In 1968, he announced that he would not run for president again and retired to his ranch in Texas.

When his successor, Richard Nixon, became entangled in the Watergate scandal, his popularity dropped almost 40 percentage points, the House Judiciary Committee voted to impeach him, and in 1974 he resigned.

Online *for more information about the House Judiciary Committee, see:* www.house.gov/judiciary

In 1998, when President Clinton wagged his finger at the TV cameras and denied that he had had "sexual relations" with White House intern Monica Lewinsky, his approval rating in the polls remained high, even after he admitted months later that his relationship with the intern had been "inappropriate" and the salacious details were recounted at great length in a report by independent counsel Kenneth Starr. Clinton was impeached by the House of Representatives in December. Although acquitted by the Senate in February 1999, he never fully recovered the stature he had enjoyed before the scandal.*

Yet if the public recognized flaws in Clinton's character, public opinion also played a major role in saving him from being convicted in the Senate and removed from office. A Gallup poll taken during the trial reported that only 33 percent of the public wanted their senators to vote to convict the president; 64 percent favored a vote against conviction.[3]

In 2001, in the immediate aftermath of the September 11 terrorist attacks on New York and Washington, President George W. Bush's approval rating rose for a time to an extraordinary 90 percent.† The increase reflected a surge of public support for the leader of the nation at a perilous moment in the wake of his strong response to the attacks.

All governments are based, to some extent, on public opinion. Even dictators must pay some attention to public opinion—if only in order to repress it. In a democracy, public opinion is often described as a controlling force. "Public opinion stands out, in the United States," the English statesman James Bryce wrote, "as the great source of power, the master of servants who tremble before it."[4] But in fact, the relationship of public opinion and government is elusive and difficult to define, since political leaders help shape public opinion and are in turn influenced by it.

In this chapter we will explore a key question: What is the role of public opinion in the American democracy?

Many related issues grow out of this central question: Who is the public? What is public opinion? Does a person's opinion matter? Do political candidates and leaders manipulate public opinion? What role do the mass media play in the formation of public opinion? Should government leaders try to follow public opinion or their own judgment? What influence should, or does, public opinion have on government? On policymaking? These are questions that continue to divide philosophers, politicians, pollsters, and political scientists.

---

*A poll taken during the Senate trial reflected Clinton's problem; it found that only 24 percent of those questioned believed Clinton to be "honest and trustworthy." Gallup poll, "Clinton Personal Characteristics," January 15–17, 1999.
†Gallup/USA Today/CNN Poll, reported in *The New York Times*, September 24, 2001, p. B6.

WHAT IS PUBLIC OPINION?

Although people often speak about opinions held by "the public," the phrase is not very useful because there are few questions on which every citizen has an opinion. The concept of special publics was developed by political scientists "to describe those segments of the public with views about particular issues."[5] In short, there are many publics.

What is opinion and when does it become public opinion? People have opinions on many subjects—music, fashions, and movies, for example. Sometimes such views are loosely referred to as "public opinion." For political scientists, however, only opinions about public matters constitute public opinion.

Public opinion may thus be defined as the expression of attitudes about government and politics.

Public opinion would mean little if it had no effect. Many political scientists, therefore, talk about public opinion as a process of interaction between the people and the government. V. O. Key, Jr., for example, defined public opinion as "those opinions held by private persons which governments find it prudent to heed."[6] Floyd Allport conceived of public opinion as enough people expressing themselves so strongly for or against something that their views are likely to affect government action.[7] And W. Lance Bennett has suggested that public opinion is situational, because the people who hold and express opinions are constantly changing, as do the issues and conditions to which the public responds.[8]

In the language of a political system (discussed in Chapter 1), public opinion can be thought of as one of the inputs of the system that may affect the outputs, or

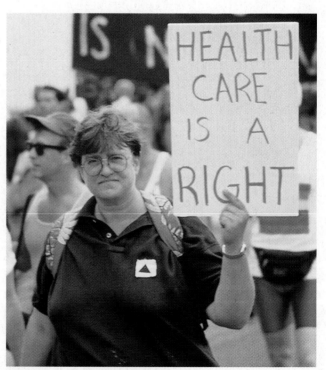

Copyright © Robert W. Ginn/PhotoEdit

The AMERICAN PAST

AND THE WINNER IS . . . HARRY TRUMAN

In 1948, President Harry S Truman, a Democrat, defeated Governor Thomas E. Dewey of New York, the Republican candidate, despite public opinion polls that reported Dewey far in the lead.

The polls everywhere overwhelmingly provided reassurance that Dewey's strategy was right. Even in the farm belt both the Gallup and *Des Moines Register* polls indicated a Republican landslide. . . . In Cleveland Truman made a rollicking speech, comparing the current polls with the *Literary Digest* poll of 1936, which indicated that Roosevelt would lose to Landon, who in the end carried only Maine and Vermont. "These polls that the Republican candidate is putting out are like sleeping pills designed to lull the voters into sleeping on Election Day," Truman said. "You might call them sleeping polls. . . . My friends, we are going to win this election." . . .

Truman went home to Independence. The final polls were published. The final columns on the election were written for the newspapers. . . . *Changing Times,* published by the Kiplinger organization, featured on its cover "What Dewey Will Do." Government would remain large and expensive under President Dewey, the *Wall Street Journal* reported. . . . The *New York Times* foresaw a Dewey victory with 345 electoral votes.

In their final versions the Gallup poll gave Dewey an edge of 49.5 to 44.5 and the Crossley poll 51 to 42.

By the time the polling places had closed in the East on Election Night Republican fat cats, the men in dinner jackets, the women in evening gowns and jewels, were waiting in line to get into the impending Dewey victory celebration in the ballroom of the Hotel Roosevelt in New York. . . . With three Secret Service men—James J. Rowley, chief of the White House detail, Henry Nicholson, and Frank J. Barry—Truman had slipped away by car and headed for The Elms, a hotel at Excelsior Springs, Missouri, thirty-two miles northeast of Kansas City. When he arrived he had a Turkish bath, then went up to his suite and dined alone on a ham sandwich and a glass of buttermilk. . . .

By three or four in the morning bewilderment and disgust had fallen over the Roosevelt ballroom. . . . Dewey went to bed for a couple of hours of sleep. . . . The telephone rang in the Secret Service agents' suite in Excelsior Springs. . . . Illinois had gone for Truman. Rowley, Nicholson, and Barry could not resist telling the president. When they entered his room he woke up, squinting without his glasses. "That's it," he said when they gave him the word.

"Now let's go back to sleep, and we'll go downtown tomorrow early and wait for the telegram from the other fellow," he said. On second thought he added: "Well, boys, we'll have one and then we'll all go to sleep." He got the bottle of bourbon off the dresser. "I'll pour the first one," he said.

—Robert J. Donovan, *Conflict and Crisis: The Presidency of Harry S Truman 1945–1948*

---

binding decisions, of the government. However, government officials try very hard to shape and manipulate public opinion to support their policies; to the extent that they succeed in this effort, public opinion also may be thought of as an output of the political system.

Private opinions become public—provided they are expressed—when they relate to government and politics. Not all privately held opinions about government and politics are expressed publicly, however; because of pressures for conformity, people may sometimes find it more prudent to keep their views private.[9] The phrase **political opinion** is sometimes used to refer to opinions on political issues—a choice among candidates or parties, for example.

HOW PUBLIC OPINION IS FORMED

Walter Lippmann, in his classic study of public opinion, observed that each individual, in viewing distant events, tends to form a "picture inside his head of the world beyond his reach."[10] And, Lippmann noted, these mental snapshots do not always correspond with reality. How do individuals form their opinions about government and politics? As might be expected, the answer is as varied as the range of opinions people hold. The views of a 60-year-old white dairy farmer in Wisconsin may vary sharply from those of an African American youth in South Central Los Angeles. We know this instinctively. But why may their opinions differ? A person's political background, and such factors as the influence of family and schools, certainly play a part. So do such variables as age, social class, income, religion, sex, ethnic background, geography, group membership, and political party preference.

Political Socialization: The Family and the Schools

Over the years, a person acquires a set of political attitudes and forms opinions about political and social issues. In other words, a person undergoes **political socialization.**

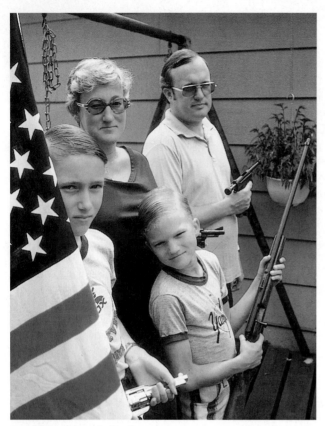

A well-armed Georgia family
Copyright © Jerome Delay/Liaison

The family may play a significant role in this process. In the view of Robert E. Lane, the family "incubates" political attitudes and opinions.[11] And the "crucial period" of a child's political, social, and psychological development is between the ages of 9 and 13.[12]

Through watching television programs, and in various other ways, children acquire rudimentary ideas about politics at an early age. For example, 63 percent of fourth graders questioned in one study identified with a political party. Almost every one of the children interviewed thought of party affiliation as a family characteristic: "All I know is we're not Republicans."[13] Children may acquire not only party preferences by listening to their parents, but "an orientation toward politics" and a set of "basic values and outlooks, which in turn may affect the individual's views on political issues long after he has left the family fold."[14] Although children may later come to hold views different from those of their parents, party loyalty tends to be passed on from one generation to the next.

How then to explain the students who protested the Vietnam war on college campuses in the 1970s, even though in some cases their parents may have supported the war? The answer is that children, obviously, do not always follow the political leanings of their parents and may even come to hold completely opposite views. That should not be surprising. A family is a group, and its

influence on political attitudes may tend to diminish as children grow older and come into contact with other groups. A classic study of Bennington College students during the 1930s illustrates the point. Bennington had always been a very liberal college with a politically liberal faculty. During the Great Depression, however, "the families that could afford to send their daughters to an expensive private college tended to be conservative Republicans. The result was that women whose parents identified with the Republican party . . . were exposed to a faculty who were by and large Roosevelt Democrats. With each year of residence at the college, each successive class of students became more liberal and identified more strongly with Franklin D. Roosevelt than the class behind it."[15]

These and similar findings have led some political scientists to question the long-established emphasis on the family as the primary political influence on children. After studying a national sample of high school seniors, M. Kent Jennings and Richard G. Niemi concluded that the political "similarity between students and their parents was often modest."[16]

Elementary schools also play a part in the political socialization of children. Every country indoctrinates its schoolchildren with the basic values of its political system. American children salute the flag in school, sing patriotic songs, such as "America the Beautiful," learn about George Washington's cherry tree (an invention of a literary charlatan named Parson Weems), and acquire some understanding of democracy and majority rule. In junior high or high school they are required to take "civics" courses.

But the extent of the influence of schools on opinion formation also has been questioned. The same study that found a divergence in views between parents and older children also reported that in high school, "Students gravitated toward the opinions of their friends more so than toward those of their social studies teachers."[17]

The political socialization of students continues in college—as the Bennington study suggests—and not only in the political science courses they may take. They also learn from the political environment on the campus. The high degree of political involvement, conflict, and controversy that characterized many American campuses in the 1960s and early 1970s, during the war in Vietnam, obviously had some influence on the political opinions of college students, whether or not they participated personally in the protest demonstrations.

While the gradual process of political socialization may have some general effect on the opinions people hold, a number of sociological and psychological factors also may have an influence on public opinion. Whether a person is young or old, rich or poor, farmer or city dweller, or westerner or southerner may affect the opinions he or she holds. This can be measured by taking almost any controversial public issue and analyzing the findings of public opinion polls. For example, in 1999, the Gallup poll asked people whether they approved of legalized gambling. The results varied with age. Nearly two-thirds, 63 percent, of adults approved, but only a little over half, 52 percent, of young teenagers thought it was a good idea.[18]

In an earlier survey, only 32 percent of those interviewed said abortion should be legal in all circumstances, but among college graduates, 48 percent said abortion should always be legal.[19] In other words, a much higher proportion of college graduates favored legal abortion. On any issue—from legalizing pot to affirmative action—opinions often vary with such factors. Which factors are more important than others varies with the individual, and their relative significance is difficult to measure with precision. But a number can be identified.

Social Class

Differences in social class, occupation, and income do appear to affect people's opinions on public matters. For example, one study indicates that people who identify with the working class are more likely to favor federal social-welfare programs than are people who identify with the middle class.[20] Another survey found that community leaders were more tolerant of atheists and nonconformists than were people of lower social and economic status.[21] And income levels may affect opinions; one Gallup poll showed that 70 percent of people with annual incomes less than $20,000 favored distributing condoms in high schools to prevent AIDS, compared with a lower proportion, 59 percent, of people with incomes above $50,000.[22]

One study of political learning suggests that children brought up in homes of lower economic status are taught to accept authority more readily than children reared in upper-class homes. This study found that upper-class children are therefore more likely to criticize political authority, that they receive more political information from their parents, and that they are more likely to become politically active.[23]

Religion, Sex, and Ethnic Factors

Religion, sex, race, and ethnic background also may influence the opinions people hold. To appeal to voters from ethnic groups, political parties in New York and other large cities customarily run a "balanced ticket"—one that includes an Irish candidate, an Italian candidate, and a Jewish candidate. In a primary election for mayor of New York City years ago, the victorious Democratic candidate, Mario Procaccino, repeatedly emphasized that he was once an immigrant boy from Bisaccia, Italy. In a sentence that reached artistic perfection in its wide-ranging ethnic appeal, he told the crowds: "I couldn't get a job on Wall Street because my name was Procaccino and I was a Catholic, and my father was a shoemaker right in the heart of black Harlem."

Although Americans like to think they form their opinions without reference to race, creed, sex, or color, studies of their political behavior have demonstrated that this has not been the case in years past. (See Table 6-1.) For example, no Catholic was elected president until 1960, when John F. Kennedy defeated Richard M. Nixon. But in public opinion polls today, Americans say they are much more willing to accept members of minority groups or women as political leaders.

There may be a gap, however, between how people say they will vote and their actual behavior in the voting booth. In 1988, for example, Jesse L. Jackson, an African American candidate, won several important Democratic presidential primaries and caucuses and demonstrated substantial strength among white voters. But many party

TABLE 6-1

How Race, Religion, and Sex Influence Voter Attitudes
Nationwide surveys taken by the Gallup poll have shown that voter prejudice against blacks, Jews, Catholics, and women in politics has declined dramatically in recent years.

Beginning in 1958, the Gallup poll asked voters whether they would vote for a black for president. Following are the answers received in selected years:

	Yes	No	No Opinion
1958	38%	53%	9%
1965	59	34	7
1969	67	23	10
1978	77	18	5
1983	77	16	7
1987	79	13	8
1997	93	4	3
1999	95	4	1

(Continued on next page)

TABLE 6-1

How Race, Religion, and Sex Influence Voter Attitudes *(continued)*

Voters also were asked whether they would vote for a Jew for president. Following are the answers received in selected years:

	Yes	No	No Opinion
1937	46%	46%	8%
1958	62	28	10
1969	86	8	6
1978	82	12	6
1983	88	7	5
1987	89	6	5
1997	NA*	NA	NA
1999	92	6	5

Voters also were asked whether they would vote for a Catholic for president. Following are the answers received in selected years:

	Yes	No	No Opinion
1937	64%	28%	8%
1958	68	25	7
1969	88	8	4
1978	91	4	5
1983	92	5	3
1987	NA	NA	NA
1997	NA	NA	NA
1999	94	4	2

Voters also were asked whether they would vote for a woman for president. Following are the answers received in selected years:

	Yes	No	No Opinion
1937	31%	65%	4%
1958	52	44	4
1969	54	39	7
1978	76	19	5
1983	80	16	4
1987	82	12	6
1997	NA	NA	NA
1999	92	7	1

Voters also were asked whether they would vote for a homosexual for president. Following are the answers received:

	Yes	No	No Opinion
1983	29%	64%	7%
1987	NA	NA	NA
1997	NA	NA	NA
1999	59	37	4

*NA: Not available.

SOURCES: Adapted from *The Gallup Poll: Public Opinion 1935–1971*, vols. 1–3 (New York: Random House, 1972); *Gallup Opinion Index*, March 1976, p. 20, and November 1978, p. 26; *Gallup Report*, September 1983, pp. 9–14, and July 1987, no. 262, pp. 16–20; and the Gallup Organization, *Poll Releases*, "Americans Today Much More Accepting of a Woman, Black, Catholic, or Jew as President," March 29, 1999, pp. 3–6, online at <www.gallup.com/poll/release/pr990329.asp>.

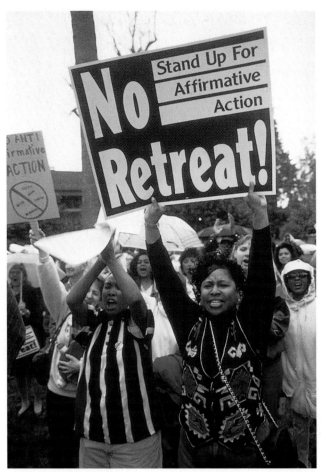
Copyright © Lou Dematteis

Jews may support aid to Israel, and Catholics may oppose the use of federal funds for abortions for the poor. Similarly, ethnic identification may help to shape public opinion on certain issues—Americans of Italian descent may be offended by the depiction of fictional gangsters with Italian names on publicly licensed television stations; African Americans may favor stronger legislation aimed at preventing housing discrimination.

Geographic Factors

People's opinions are sometimes related to where they live. Democrats have traditionally been more numerous in the big cities of the North; Republicans have been stronger in the Plains States, most of the Rocky Mountain States, in rural areas, and in the suburbs. Yet sectional and geographic differences among Americans are often exaggerated; on some broad questions of foreign policy, for example, sectional variations are likely to be minimal. And, on many issues, differences in outlook between the cities and suburbs have replaced the old sectional divisions. Whether people come from an urban or rural background may be more significant today than their geographic roots.

Group Influence

Although the shape of a person's opinions on public questions is initially influenced by the family, in later life other groups, friends, associates, and peers also influence individual views. In numerous experiments psychologists have discovered that people tend to go along with the decision of a group even when it contradicts accepted standards of morality and behavior. In a classic and controversial experiment at Yale University, Stanley Milgram placed subjects in groups of four, three of whom were secretly Milgram's assistants. The one unwitting subject was told to administer powerful electric shocks to the person serving as the "learner" in the experiment whenever the "learner" made an error in performing a laboratory task. In fact, no electricity was being administered, but the subject did not know that, and the "learner" shouted, moaned, and screamed as the supposed voltage became higher. The results were surprising: Egged on by their colleagues, 85 percent of the subjects administered shocks beyond what they believed would be 120 volts, and 17.5 percent went all the way to the maximum, a shock of 450 volts.[*]

On occasion, group influence may even prevent the expression of opinion. Almost everyone has been in a situation at one time or another in which he or she

leaders and voters said at the time that they felt a black person could not be elected president. Jackson did not receive the nomination.

By the mid-1990s, however, the hesitation about nominating a black candidate for the nation's highest office appeared to have diminished substantially. As noted in Chapter 5, former General Colin Powell, an African American, enjoyed enthusiastic support among many white and black voters when for several months he flirted with the possibility of entering the 1996 presidential race. By 1999, only 4 percent of Americans said they would not vote for a black presidential candidate; the overwhelming majority, 95 percent, said they would. (See Table 6-1.)

A voter's religious or ethnic background may affect party preference or political leanings. For example, in the 1996 presidential election, according to the Gallup poll, 55 percent of Catholics voted for President Clinton, the Democratic nominee, but only 35 percent voted for his Republican opponent, Robert Dole. Among Protestants the vote went the other way: 50 percent for Dole to 44 percent for Clinton.[24] In another survey, Jewish and black voters questioned were more inclined to support governmental social-welfare programs than were other groups.[25]

Religious affiliation may also affect public opinion on specific issues—Quakers may favor disarmament,

---
[*]Stanley Milgram, "Group Pressure and Action against a Person," *Journal of Abnormal and Social Psychology*, vol. 69 (1964), pp. 137–143. In a somewhat similar experiment, Solomon Asch, a psychologist at Swarthmore College, placed subjects among groups of college students whose members, unknown to the subjects, deliberately responded incorrectly when they were asked to match up black lines of varying lengths on white cards. Influenced by the group's false judgments, the subjects gave incorrect answers 37 percent of the time. S. E. Asch, *Psychology Monograph*, vol. 70, no. 416 (1956).

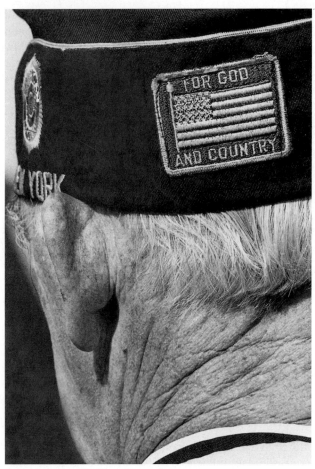

Copyright © Ray Ellis/Photo Researchers

"The Late Show"

Rush Limbaugh: Talk radio may have helped the Republican Party capture Congress in 1994.
Antonin Kratochvil/DOT Pictures

hesitates to express a political opinion because those listening might disagree or even be hostile. The author Mark Twain said he would expose to the world "only my trimmed and perfumed and carefully barbered public opinions and conceal carefully, cautiously, wisely, my private ones."[26] An individual who expresses an opinion is vulnerable, because "social groups can punish him for failing to toe the line."[27] If a view seems too risky to express, an individual may keep it private. But if public opinion changes, people may voice previously hidden feelings.[28]

Various types of groups may influence people. Groups whose views serve as guidelines to an individual's opinion are known as **reference groups.** There are two types of reference groups. Groups that people come into face-to-face contact with in everyday life—friends, office associates, or a social club—are known as **primary groups,** since their influence is direct. **Secondary groups,** as the term implies, may be more remote. These are organizations or groups of people such as labor unions or fraternal, professional, or religious groups.

Mass Media

In the television age, the images that flash into people's living rooms obviously have a major impact on public opinion. So do newspapers, magazines, radio, the Internet, online computer service providers and publications, and other media that bring news about government and politics to the public.

For example, talk radio, with a large audience, especially among more conservative voters, was credited by many observers with helping the Republican Party capture control of Congress in 1994. In election year 2000, many viewers watched televised events such as the closely fought presidential primary campaigns, the debates among the candidates, and the drama of election night on November 7. Political candidates appeared on televised talk shows, running the gamut from *Meet the Press* to Jay Leno and David Letterman. It is reasonable to assume that the opinions formed by many voters about these events were influenced by what they saw on television and absorbed through other media.

Online *for more information about the TV shows listed above, see:*
www.msnbc.com/news/meetpress_front.asp;
www.nbc.com/tonightshow; and www.cbs.com/lateshow

In the year 2000, as in previous recent presidential elections, voters were bombarded by political commercials. Candidates who could outspend their opponents to buy television time for commercials often enjoyed an advantage. The broadcast and cable networks provided extensive coverage of the spring primaries, the party nominating conventions in July and August, the general election campaign, and the results flowing in from across the nation on election night. The impact of mass media on the formation of public opinion is discussed in greater detail in Chapter 8.

Party Identification

In any campaign, voters are influenced by a candidate's personality and appearance and by the nature of the issues that arise. But how they vote and what they think about public issues may also be closely linked to their political party affiliation. Political scientists distinguish, therefore, among voters' views of candidates, voters' attitudes on issues, and their party identification.[29]

As an example of how party identification may relate to opinions, a 1999 Gallup poll reported that 22 percent of Republicans favored the legalization of marijuana, compared to 27 percent of Democrats and 37 percent of independents.[30] And party identification clearly was a major factor in public opinion about the impeachment of President Clinton. In a 1998 poll, 73 percent of Republicans but only 12 percent of Democrats approved of the decision of the House of Representatives to impeach the president.[31]

There is evidence, however, that party ties are becoming somewhat less important; the number of Americans who consider themselves political independents has increased in recent years. The loosening of party loyalties was dramatically illustrated during the 2000 presidential election campaign. Early on, Texas Governor George W. Bush was widely regarded as the front-runner for the Republican presidential nomination. His bandwagon was briefly slowed in February, however, when Senator John McCain of

Senator John McCain attracted many independent voters during the 2000 presidential primaries.
AP/Wide World

Arizona won the Michigan primary. Polls showed that 45 percent of those who voted for McCain in Michigan were independents, and 29 percent were Democrats.[32] Despite the willingness of voters to cross party lines to support candidates they like, more than 60 percent of all adult Americans identify with one of the two major parties.

THE QUALITIES OF PUBLIC OPINION

Public opinion has identifiable qualities. Like pictures, public opinions may be sharp or fuzzy, general or detailed—and they may fade. In analyzing the qualities of opinions, political scientists speak of direction, intensity, and stability.

There was a time when political scientists would describe people as being either "for" or "against" something. But after the Second World War, when public opinion polling evolved into a more exact science, pollsters and analysts discovered that simple "yes" or "no" answers sometimes masked wide gradations in opinion

PEANUTS CHARLES M. SCHULZ

Copyright © 1999 United Feature Syndicate, Inc.

"Grayson is a liberal in social matters, a conservative in economic matters, and a homicidal psychopath in political matters."

on a given subject. In other words, it is possible to measure opinions in *direction* along a scale.[33] Thus people speak of liberals and radicals as being "to the left" and conservatives "to the right," with moderates "in the center." If radical political opinions are thought of as being at one end of a line and conservative at the other end, the opinion of one individual may be located at a given point along the line. One person may favor a government program of health care for everyone; another may prefer that federal health programs be limited to the aged, children, and the needy; and a third person may favor wholly private health care.

Public opinion varies in *intensity* as well as direction. A person may have mild opinions or more deeply felt views. An automobile owner may be only mildly in sympathy with attempts to reduce gasoline consumption by holding down the speed limit. By contrast, a pro-life antiabortion activist may hold very strong opinions. Robert E. Lane and David O. Sears have suggested that there may be "something congenial" about extreme views and intensity of opinion "which suggests a mutual support."[34] That is, people well to the left or right may hold their political opinions more fiercely than others.

Another quality of public opinion is its degree of *stability*. Opinions change—sometimes slowly, sometimes rapidly and unpredictably—in response to new events or personalities. For example, in the early 1990s public opinion about President Bush fluctuated widely, rising to great heights during the Persian Gulf War early in 1991 and then plunging downward when the econo-

my faltered. These sharp variations in voter attitudes can be recorded with some degree of precision. Public opinion may be measured and its qualities analyzed. The measuring tool is the political poll.

POLITICAL POLLS

Today, virtually all presidential candidates rely on advice from a poll-taker. And on Election Day, even before the votes are counted, **exit polls** of citizens leaving the voting booth may prove a reliable indicator of the final result.

The data gathered by political polls are not always reliable, however. In 1948 the Gallup and Roper polls wrongly predicted that Governor Thomas E. Dewey of New York, the Republican candidate, would defeat President Harry S Truman.* Dewey lost. "I never paid any attention to polls myself," Truman later wrote in his typically direct style.[35]

The art of political polling has come a long way since 1948, and the margin of error has been greatly reduced. But polls may still be wrong or in conflict with one another. For example, several polls just before the 1988 New Hampshire presidential primary showed Republican George Bush, then the vice president, and

---

*Truman was given just the letter "S" as a middle name. It was a compromise by his parents to honor his paternal grandfather, Anderson Shippe Truman, and his maternal grandfather, Solomon Young, both of whom had names beginning with that letter. Since the "S" was a name and not an initial, Truman himself usually did not include the period, but it is considered correct with or without the period.

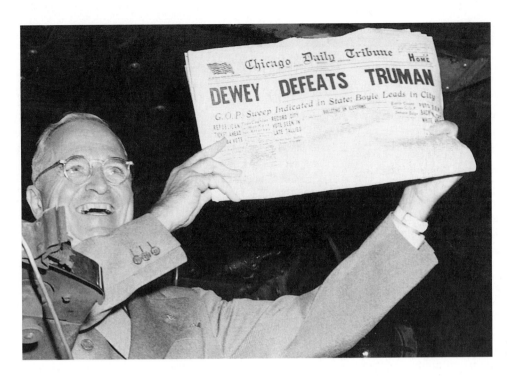

1948: A victorious President Truman holds up an erroneous newspaper headline.
Copyright © CORBIS/UPI/Bettmann

Senator Bob Dole in a dead heat. But the final Gallup poll showed Dole ahead by 8 points. In the actual vote in New Hampshire, Bush defeated his rival by 9 percentage points, a 17-point error for Gallup.[36]

Even when polls are accurate, they may be so swiftly overtaken by events as to appear to be misleading. During the campaign for the Republican presidential nomination in the year 2000, polls reported George W. Bush and John McCain in a close race in the New Hampshire primary. But in the election on February 1, McCain scored a sweeping victory, beating Bush 48 percent to 30 percent.[37]

Despite some well-publicized errors, however, political polls are substantially accurate more often than not, and frequently are useful as a guide to voter sentiment. Politicians are convinced of their value. For example, one Democratic senator described the heavy reliance on polls by the Clinton White House: "They just poll the daylights out of everything from every angle. . . . I've never been to the White House without hearing the staff and even the president talk about polls."[38]

Today, polls—before, during, and even after Election Day—are a standard part of political campaigns. In a presidential election year, millions of dollars are paid to the more than 200 polling organizations in the United States.*

---

*Major political polling organizations include the American Institute of Public Opinion (the Gallup poll), Louis Harris & Associates, Inc. (the Harris survey), and Zogby International, all of which publish their findings in newspapers and magazines. A number of pollsters also take private polls for political clients. In addition, there are many smaller state and regional polls, as well as polls conducted by newspapers and television networks.

How Polls Work

A political polling organization may question only 1,500 people, or even fewer, to measure public opinion on a given issue or to determine which candidate leads in a campaign.[†] Many people find it difficult to accept the idea that public opinion in an entire nation may be measured from such a small sample. Behind some of the skepticism is the belief that each individual is unique, and that his or her thoughts cannot be so neatly categorized. If only 1,500 Americans are polled in a population of 275 million, each person questioned is, in effect, "speaking for" 183,333 people. How, it may be asked, can the views of one individual represent the opinions of so many fellow citizens?

The answer lies in the mathematical law of probability. Toss a coin 1,000 times, and it will come up heads about 500 times. The same principle of probability is used by insurance companies in computing life expectancy. And it is used by poll-takers in measuring opinion. Because the group to be measured, known as the population or the **universe,** is usually too large to be polled individually on every issue, the poll-taker selects at random a sample of the population. The **random sample** is a group of people, chosen by poll-takers, that is representative of the universe being polled. A random sample is sometimes also called a probability sample.

But the random sample must be carefully chosen and must be representative of the universe being polled.

---

†The Gallup poll normally uses a national sample of 1,000 persons. Louis Harris interviews 1,250 people.

COUNTING THE BEANS

The federal government's Crop Reporting Board, among its various duties, must count the number of soybeans in America. It can't, so it takes a random sample. The results are closely guarded, so that speculators in the commodities markets cannot profit from advance information. The following news story describes how the board works:

> WASHINGTON—The Agriculture Department's Crop Reporting Board . . . works primarily for the nation's farmers, who decide how much to plant, or breed, based on the board's predictions. . . .
>
> Across the United States, the board employs 3,500 part-time "enumerators," as they are called. . . . The enumerators might be assigned to estimate the soybean crop. They cannot count every bean, so instead they select random-sample plots and use probability tables, much the way opinion pollsters do, to predict a total. . . .
>
> For the soybean crop, enumerators in several states pick out sample plots three feet long and two rows wide. Then they get down on all fours and, yes, they count the beans. . . .
>
> The results of all those bean counts, top-secret totals that cannot be discussed on pain of going to jail, are sent to Washington, where they are locked into a safe at the Crop Reporting Board.
>
> —*New York Times*, February 20, 1984

When the *Literary Digest* polled owners of automobiles and telephones in 1936—a time when many Americans had neither—it was not sampling a representative group of Americans. As a result, its prediction that Franklin Roosevelt would lose the presidential election proved incorrect. If the sample is of sufficient size and properly selected at random, the law of probability will operate, and the results will usually be accurate within a 3 to 4 percent margin of error.

One way to conceptualize the principles involved in polling is to think of a huge jar of white marbles to which a smaller number of yellow marbles are added. Suppose the jar is thoroughly shaken so that all the marbles are completely mixed together. If a scoop is used to remove enough of the marbles, the sample should contain the same proportion of yellow to white marbles as exists in the entire jar.

Take another example. Suppose that one out of every four Americans has blue eyes. For the same rea-son that a flipped coin comes up heads half the time, or the same percentage of yellow marbles can be scooped from the jar each time, the probability is that a random sample will catch in its net the same percentage of blue-eyed persons as exists in the whole population. Using this technique, the number of blue-eyed Americans can be estimated from a random sample. Similarly, the number of Americans who support abortion or who oppose capital punishment can be estimated from a random sample.

But a true random sample of the entire United States would be very difficult (and very expensive) to conduct. A survey researcher would, in theory, have to have a list of everyone in the population, and then select at random the names of people to be questioned. To simplify the task, most polling organizations use **cluster sampling**—interviewing several people from the same neighborhood. As long as the geographic areas are chosen at random, the clustering will usually not result in an unacceptable margin of error.[39]

Poll-takers often combine the cluster technique with the selection, in a series of stages or steps, of geographic areas to be polled, with each unit selected becoming successively smaller. For example, in pinpointing the location for an interview, the pollster might start by selecting regions of the country, and then choose counties or other smaller areas at random within those regions. From there, still selecting at random, the researcher would scale down to a city, a neighborhood, a precinct, a block of houses, an apartment building, and then one apartment, where the actual interview would take place. The desirable size of the sample does not depend very much on the size of the population being measured, and beyond a certain point, increasing the number of persons polled reduces the sampling error only slightly.

A less reliable method of polling is based on the **quota sample,** a method of polling in which interview-

"That's the worst set of opinions I've heard in my entire life."
Copyright © The New Yorker Collection 1993 Weber from cartoonbank.com. All rights reserved.

Reprinted with special permission of King Features Syndicate

ers are instructed to question members of a particular group in proportion to their percentage in the population as a whole. For example, an organization that wanted to test ethnic opinion would instruct its staff to interview African Americans, Italians, Jews, Poles, Hispanics, and so on, in proportion to their percentage in the population as a whole. Under this method the interviewer has considerable discretion in the choice of persons selected to be questioned. The poll-taker might select only well-dressed or cooperative individuals, thus skewing the results. Therefore, quota sampling is less useful than random sampling as a method of measuring political opinion.

The method of selecting the sample is not the only factor that may affect the reliability of a poll. The way in which questions are phrased, the personality of the interviewer, and the manner in which poll data are interpreted may all affect the result.[40] A Gallup poll completed two days before the 1996 election showed 6 percent "undecided"—a fairly normal percentage of persons in this flexible category.[41] How this undecided vote is interpreted and allocated can drastically affect the accuracy of a political poll.

There is another problem that increasingly plagues poll-takers. A lot of people don't want to be bothered to respond to surveys. A decade ago, typically half the people approached responded to polls. Today, the response rate, according to poll-takers, may fall as low as 20 percent in some cases. That means that perhaps 8 out of 10 people interviewed may refuse to answer.[42]

Political polls do not necessarily predict the outcome of an election. A poll only measures opinion at the moment the survey is taken. It is a snapshot of the electorate at that instant, not necessarily a prediction of how voters may feel later. A poll taken a few days before an election, for example, will not always match the vote on Election Day. In 1992, a Gallup poll taken during a three-day period immediately before the presidential election reported Bill Clinton ahead by six points more than his actual margin of victory.[43]

An intriguing question often raised is whether there is a danger that political polls themselves may create a

bandwagon effect and influence the outcome of an election. Do some voters or convention delegates, out of a desire to be with the winner, jump on the bandwagon of the candidate who is leading in the polls?

Whether or not a bandwagon effect really exists has been debated by political scientists for some time. For example, Bernard Hennessy found "little evidence" of such an effect, arguing that indifferent voters would not care who won or even remember poll results, and concerned voters would not cast their ballot for a candidate simply because of a poll.[44]

But other scholars have suggested that indeed there may be a bandwagon effect. As already noted, people often compare their views to the dominant public opinion before speaking out. Elisabeth Noelle-Neumann argues that there exists a "spiral process which prompts . . . individuals to perceive the changes in opinion and to follow suit."[45]

During past presidential elections, the television networks were criticized for projecting the outcome before the voting booths had closed in California. The networks based their predictions either on mathematical projections of early returns or on exit polls. Critics of this practice argued that such early "calls" of an election would discourage some potential voters from bothering to cast their ballots at all.

In 1985, the networks in testimony to Congress individually agreed not to release exit polls too early. But no joint agreement among the networks was reached until 1990. It remained in force after 1993, when the networks and the Associated Press formed the Voter News Service (VNS) to report election returns. The members of VNS agreed not to release exit polls until a majority of polling places had closed in each state. On election night 2000 the television networks initially called Florida for Gore, based on exit polls. Then the networks awarded the state to Bush, only to retract that call hours later.

And holding back exit polls has proved difficult in the age of the Internet. During the key Michigan primary in February 2000, *Slate*, an online magazine, released numbers correctly predicting that John McCain would defeat George W. Bush. The magazine trumpeted the

MAKING A DIFFERENCE

THE "PUSH-POLL" HADN'T COUNTED ON DONNA DUREN

Donna Duren, a resident of Spartanburg, South Carolina, heard only at the last minute that Senator John McCain of Arizona, who was then seeking the Republican presidential nomination, was in town. It was February 2000 and at the time, McCain was locked in a hard-fought primary battle in South Carolina with Texas Governor George W. Bush. Duren, an admirer of Senator McCain, rushed over to the auditorium on the campus of the University of South Carolina.

"He talked about teaching our children, at home and in the community, ethics and values and morals and integrity," she recalled. "That really touched a chord with me. I have a 14-year-old boy, Chris. Something in his speech moved me to speak.

"My son is interested in aviation and in Senator McCain's story, his tenacity in the Hanoi Hilton when he was a prisoner of war in Vietnam. He kind of idolizes Senator McCain. He saw him as a role model, a positive person to emulate."

The day before McCain's speech, someone who claimed to be conducting a poll had called the Duren household. Duren's son had answered the phone. Chris kept telling the caller that he was only 14, but the man continued to talk to him anyway, asking "questions" that unsettled Chris.

At the McCain rally the next day, Donna Duren got up. "I was so nervous. I never stood up before, I never participated in a town meeting. I got up and after a minute I realized the cameras were on me. I was so nervous."

She told McCain about the call to her son. "I don't know who called him. I don't know who's responsible. But he was so upset when he came upstairs and he said, 'Mom, someone told me that Senator McCain is a cheat and a liar and a fraud.' And he was almost in tears. I was so livid last night I couldn't sleep." Her complaint made the national news on television and was widely reported in the press.

Chris Duren had been the target of a "push-poll," a practice some-

times used in political campaigns. Under the guise of conducting an independent survey, a caller poses as a legitimate poll-taker, but asks "questions" that are really statements designed to smear or discredit the opposition candidate.

Questioned by reporters, George W. Bush denied any knowledge of the type of call described by Duren. "If anybody in my campaign has done that, they're going to be fired," he said.

Most voters had never heard the term "push-poll" before. Now, thanks to one courageous mother in South Carolina, millions of voters might be wary of such calls, and some candidates or their supporters might even hesitate to employ that tactic in the future. To an extent, at least, Donna Duren may have helped to change how political campaigns are conducted in America.

—Based on a telephone interview by the authors with Donna Duren, February 24, 2000

---

exit poll data under the headline, "Git Yer Early Exit Poll Numbers Here!"[46]

 Online *for more information about* Slate, *see:* slate.msn.com

Polls may affect elections in other ways. For example, a candidate may need to make a strong early showing in the polls in order to attract and raise the money needed to campaign, and especially to buy television ads. Many contributors want to back a winner; favorable polls can help to bring in the dollars.

On the other hand, if the polls suggest that a candidate is running behind, supporters of that candidate may be more inclined to vote. Conversely, if the candidate's rating in the polls is high, some potential supporters may become complacent and stay home on Election Day. Such theories, based on present evidence, are debatable, but the possible effect of polls on voting is a subject that merits further exploration. In any event, polls today are a permanent part of the political landscape and an important tool of the "new politics."

WHAT AMERICANS BELIEVE

Do Americans agree on anything? Some people say that there is an underlying consensus in America, a basic agreement among its citizens on fundamental democratic values and processes, that permits democracy to flourish. Some political scientists speak of a nation's **political culture,** a set of fundamental beliefs about how government and politics should be conducted. Most Americans, for example, believe that—unlike in many other countries—the military in the United States should be subordinate to the elected civilian leaders. And Americans agree that whoever loses an election should leave office.

But the supposed underlying consensus in America often melts away on closer examination.

For example, Americans say they believe in fair play and justice, but they do not necessarily stick by those principles when their own interests are threatened. White homeowners may know that it is "fair" for a black family to buy the house next door, but they may

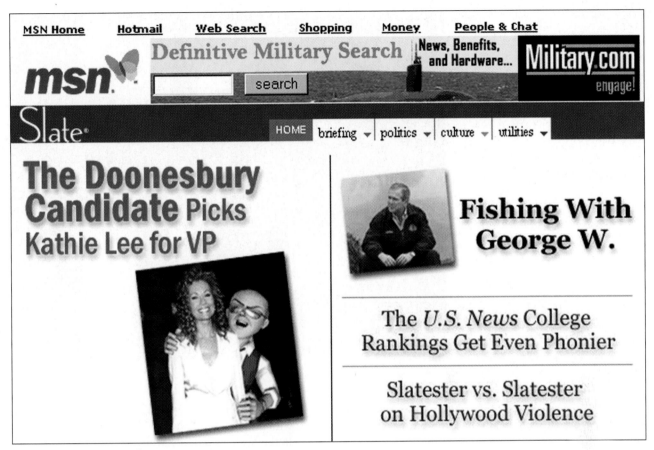

Slate *published the exit polls. . . .*

oppose the sale if they believe that the value of their property would go down if the neighborhood becomes racially mixed.

On the whole, Americans seem to be pragmatic, approaching each issue as it comes up and judging it on its merits. Most Americans, though, do not have a fixed, coherent set of political beliefs. People may have clear preferences on specific issues, but often their convictions are not interrelated. A voter who is liberal on one issue may be conservative on another. For example, one study found that a majority of Americans thought that "the Federal Government should act to meet public needs" in such fields as education, medical care, public housing, urban renewal, unemployment, and poverty.[47] But when the same Americans were asked questions about their general concepts of the proper role of government, they were "pronouncedly conservative." A clear majority agreed with this statement: "We should rely much more on individual initiative and not so much on governmental welfare programs."[48] On some issues, in short, Americans seem to have a split personality.

Why should Americans hold such seemingly contradictory opinions? One explanation may lie in the competing fundamental values of individualism and equality that observers such as Alexis de Tocqueville saw in America as far back as the early 19th century. The belief in "rugged individualism" may cause some Americans to complain about "welfare chiselers." The belief in equality may explain why the same individuals favor government social programs.[49]

Some political research has suggested that the pattern of beliefs in America is changing and that voters are becoming more aware of political issues and thinking about them more coherently. One study, *The Changing American Voter*, found "long-term tendencies of the public to move in one direction or another" on the issues.[50] Since the 1960s, the study found, voters have begun to evaluate candidates and parties more in terms of their issue positions, with this being reflected to some extent by how citizens vote.[51] "The role of party has declined as a guide to the vote," the study reported. "And, as party has declined in importance, the role of issues appears to have risen."[52]

POLITICAL PARTICIPATION

One way people can influence government is through the force of public opinion. An even more direct way people can make their opinions felt is by voting. Yet, one of the more surprising facts about America is that

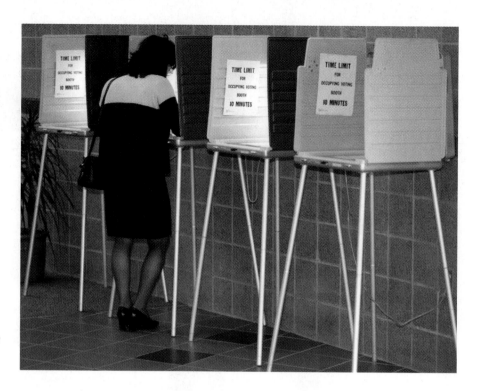

Not everybody votes: a polling place in Orlando in 2000
AP/Wide World

in presidential elections, often only a little more than half the people of voting age—and sometimes less than half—bother to vote.

In 1996 the Census Bureau estimated that 196,507,000 Americans were old enough to vote. Of that total, 129,498,000 registered to vote. Of these, 96,278,000 actually cast ballots for president on Election Day, November 3. That means 49 percent of the population of voting age actually voted.[53]

In off-year, nonpresidential elections, usually well under half of the voting-age population goes to the polls to vote for senators and representatives. In 1970, for example, 43.5 percent cast ballots for candidates for the House. In 1974 only 35.9 percent voted in House races. For 1978 the figure was down to 34.9 percent. It rose to 38.0 percent in 1982, then dropped to 33.5 percent in 1986. There was no significant change in 1990, with 33.1 percent voting in House races. In 1994, 36 percent voted in House races.[54] In 1998, the figure dropped to 32.9 percent.[55]

These figures, not uncommon for American elections, raise important questions about the nature of "government by the people." "Every regime lives on a body of dogma, self-justification, glorification and propaganda about itself," E. E. Schattschneider has written.

In the United States, this body of dogma and tradition centers about democracy. The hero of the system is the voter who is commonly described as the ultimate source of all authority. The fact that something like forty million adult Americans are so unresponsive to the regime that they do not trouble to vote is the single most truly remarkable

fact about it. . . . What kind of system is this in which only a little more than half of us participate? Is the system actually what we have been brought up to think it is?[56]

Some people do not vote because they may feel the system holds no benefits for them, or because they feel there is no difference between the candidates. For some, therefore, not voting may be a form of protest. Others are nonvoters because they are apathetic about politics and political issues.

Americans not only fail to participate fully in the political system, it has been argued, but they also are often poorly informed about government and many public issues. One study found only 26 percent of the American public to be well informed on specific questions dealing with international affairs (such as the identity of four major world leaders).[57]

Public knowledge about many specific questions concerning domestic politics is equally limited. A January 2000 Gallup poll reported that 66 percent of Americans were able to name Regis Philbin as the host of the television quiz show *Who Wants to Be a Millionaire?* but only 6 percent knew that the speaker of the House of Representatives was Dennis Hastert.[58] Another survey revealed that only half of those questioned knew that there are 100 U.S. Senators or that the first 10 amendments to the Constitution are usually called the Bill of Rights.[59] Another poll showed that 4 in 10 Americans could not name the vice president of the United States. Almost half of those surveyed did not know that the Supreme Court has the final word on whether a law is constitutional.[60]

FIGURE 6-1

Confidence in Institutions: Percentage of Americans Who Have a "Great Deal" or "Quite a Lot" of Confidence in Major U.S. Institutions

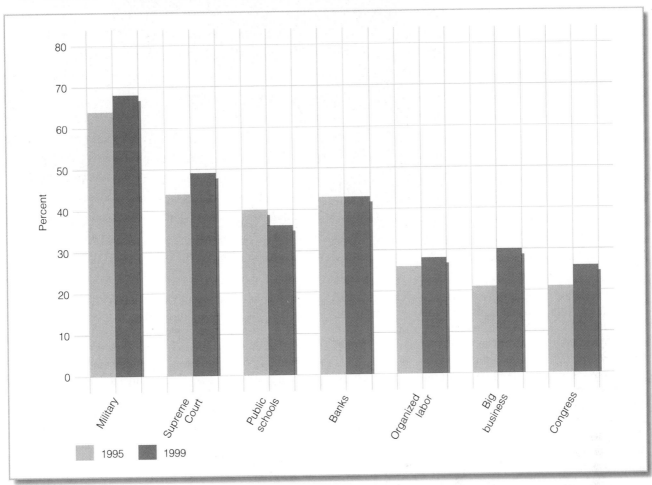

SOURCE: The Gallup Organization, *Gallup Social and Economic Indicators*, "Confidence in Institutions," June 25–27, 1999, pp. 1–2, online at <http://www.gallup.com/poll/indicators/indconfidence.asp>.

Online *for more information on Gallup polls, see:*
www.gallup.com

In a Gallup poll of college seniors, 24 percent of the students did not know that Franklin Roosevelt was president during the Second World War, 23 percent thought that Soviet ruler Joseph Stalin coined the phrase "Iron Curtain" (it was British statesman Winston Churchill), and two-thirds thought that the words "government of the people, by the people, for the people shall not perish from the earth" appear in the U.S. Constitution, rather than Lincoln's Gettysburg Address.[61]

Schattschneider has concluded, "An amazingly large number of people do not seem to know very much about what is going on."[62] One effect of the lack of public knowledge is that government officials have wider latitude in making policy decisions, because they may assume that the public will neither know nor

care very much about the results of those decisions. In other words, at least on some issues, bureaucrats who are confident of public ignorance or lack of interest may not worry about adverse reaction to their decisions—the outputs of the political system—or about possible feedback.

On the other hand, ignorance about political matters is not always the fault of the public. The government, in an effort to place its policies in the best possible light, sometimes issues misleading information or engages in outright deception.[63] For example, the Kennedy administration initially denied that CIA-supported exiles had invaded Cuba in 1961; the Johnson administration suppressed crucial information about events in the Tonkin Gulf in 1964; and in 1983 the Reagan White House denied that American military forces had invaded or planned to invade the Caribbean island of Grenada even as the troops prepared to land.

American soldiers prepare to invade Grenada.
Copyright © CORBIS/Bettmann

Later, President Reagan ordered that his dealings with Iran, in an effort to trade arms for American hostages, be hidden from Congress and the public. And President Clinton misled the nation about his adulterous affair with a young White House intern.

Some scholars challenge the traditional assumption that many voters are politically ignorant. They suggest that the degree of information possessed by the public is "situational"—that is, it may vary from one election to another. For example, when differences between candidates are sharper, the public seems to absorb more information. "Voters can take stands, perceive party differences, and vote on the basis of them. But whether they do or not depends heavily on the candidate and the parties."[64]

Violence and Politics

On the afternoon of March 30, 1981, as President Reagan left the Washington Hilton Hotel, John W. Hinckley, Jr., fired a .22-caliber revolver at him, seriously wounding the president and three other persons. A Secret Service man pushed Reagan into his limousine, and he was taken to the hospital, where surgeons removed a bullet from his lung. Reagan recovered from his wounds. His 25-year-old assailant, tried and found not guilty by reason of insanity, was committed to a mental hospital for an indefinite period.

As the television networks played and replayed the videotape of that moment when the president was shot, it seemed all too familiar. Assassination and violence have loomed over the political landscape several times in recent years.

Democracy operates on the premise that at least a substantial number of citizens will participate peacefully in the political system. The "consent of the governed" implies that public opinion plays a role in the political process. But if the system fails to respond to the demands placed upon it, or if participation is slow to bring change, individuals or groups may vent their anger against the system in violent ways. Or unbalanced persons, acting out of personal frustration, may choose political targets.

Sometimes the violence is viewed as a form of political or social protest, such as the rioting that broke out in Los Angeles in April 1992 after a jury with no black members acquitted four white police officers in the beating of a black motorist, Rodney G. King. At other times, organized groups, such as the Weather Underground in the 1960s or the Puerto Rican nationalists, have engaged in bombings for stated political ends. And all too often in American history, deranged assassins have struck at political leaders.

The United States has had a violent past, for Americans have not always sought to bring about political change through lawful or peaceful means. The American Revolution, the Civil War, the settling of the frontier, racial lynchings, and the Ku Klux Klan are some examples. Clearly, assassination and violence are not new forms of American political behavior. Four presidents have been assassinated—Lincoln, Garfield, McKinley, and Kennedy—and serious attempts have been made against the lives of six others—Jackson, Theodore Roosevelt, Franklin Roosevelt, Truman, Ford, and Reagan. In addition, a Colorado man was convicted in 1995 of attempting to assassinate President Clinton after firing an assault rifle at the front of the White House from the sidewalk on Pennsylvania Avenue. That means that by the year 2000, an astonishing one-quarter of all American presidents had been murdered or targeted.

Secret Service agents moments after assassination attempt on President Reagan, March 30, 1981, Washington, D.C.
AP/Wide World

Political assassination and violence occurred with tragic frequency during the 1960s. The assassinations of President Kennedy in 1963; of his brother Robert Kennedy, a presidential candidate, in 1968; and of Dr. Martin Luther King, Jr., also in 1968, all dramatically affected the political process. So did racial violence in the cities.

The Warren Commission, the presidential panel that studied President Kennedy's assassination, concluded that it had been carried out by Lee Harvey Oswald, who "acted alone," a finding challenged in many books and in the popular 1991 film *JFK* by those who contend that shots were fired by more than one person and that Kennedy was the victim of a conspiracy. Similar conspiracy theories circulated for many years after the assassination of President Lincoln in 1865. But most assassinations in American history appear to have been the acts of unbalanced persons venting their rage and frustration on the national leader. Such purposeless acts differ in motivation from a planned assassination by conspirators or terrorists. Planned assassinations may be viewed as an attempt to go outside the political system. They are not a form of "participation" in the political system, but rather a rejection of that system.

As a presidential study panel reported, "Assassination, especially when the victim is a president, strikes at the heart of the democratic process. It enables one man

to nullify the will of the people in a single, savage act. It touches the lives of all the people of the nation."[65]

MASS OPINION IN A DEMOCRACY

Suppose the president of the United States could push a button every morning and receive, along with the morning's toast and coffee, a printout summarizing the precise state of public opinion on a given spectrum of issues during the preceding 24 hours. And suppose the president tried to tailor the administration's policies to this computerized intelligence. Would that be good or bad?

Good, one person might respond. After all, democracy is supposed to be government "by the people," and if the government knows just what the people are thinking, the president can act in accordance with the popular will. Bad, another might answer. The president is elected to exercise his or her judgment and lead the nation, not follow the shifting winds of public opinion. After all, if the people are not satisfied with a president's leadership and decisions, they can elect a new one every four years.

Both arguments have merit. A president or a member of Congress usually tries to lead and shape public opinion and at the same time to follow it. No president can ignore public opinion during the four years between elections. But if our hypothetical president did try to rule according to computer printouts,

"Damn it, Turner, you were supposed to orchestrate public opinion!"

it would soon become apparent that there was no way to please everybody. The president also would discover that if the policies suggested by the poll data failed to work, those policies and the president would soon become highly unpopular.

Nevertheless, modern political candidates and leaders are highly attuned to techniques for measuring and influencing public opinion. Ross Perot, a billionaire Texas businessman, made his fortune in the computer industry and was fascinated with the idea of using technology to interact with the voters. When he ran for president in 1992, Perot said that if elected he would not raise taxes unless electronic consultation with the public persuaded him that there was a "grass-roots consensus" to do so.[66]

Critics of "government by e-mail" argue that a president who merely responds to the public whim would have abdicated his leadership, and that electronic responses would come only from the more politically active citizens, a group that would not be representative of the entire electorate.

Political polls, television commercials, and professional campaign managers are all part of the efforts at mass persuasion employed today. (These techniques are discussed in detail in Chapter 10.) Political leaders often attempt to "manage" public opinion or to manipulate it in their favor by using such techniques and by the conscious use of symbols. For example, when a president addresses the nation on television in a military crisis, the dramatic format of the Oval Office of the White House and a nationwide television address are symbols of his

power, designed to engender public support. When the president travels to make a speech, the presidential seal goes with him, and an aide unobtrusively hangs it on the rostrum just before the chief executive appears. Ronald Reagan, a veteran movie actor, used his polished skills as a performer to good advantage on television, both as a campaigner and as president.

Public officials, political candidates, professional campaign consultants, media advisers, and government information officers customarily engage in political persuasion designed to influence or even manipulate the electorate. Indeed, as Dan Nimmo has suggested, "The political communicator not seeking to persuade others to his views is more rare than the whooping crane."[67]

Although leaders may court public opinion, it remains an elusive concept. The truth is that the role of public opinion in a democracy has always been difficult to define. The people, Walter Lippmann argued, "can elect the government. They can remove it. They can approve or disapprove its performance. But they cannot administer the government. They cannot themselves perform. . . . A mass cannot govern."[68]

Certainly the public does not possess nearly so much information as the president, who daily receives a massive flow of intelligence from all over the globe to aid him in his decision making. On the other hand, as E. E. Schattschneider has pointed out, "nobody knows enough to run the government. Presidents, senators, governors, judges, professors, doctors of philosophy, editors, and the like are only a little less ignorant than the rest of us."[69]

The unstated premise of opinion polls, Schattschneider adds, is that "the people really do decide what the government does on something like a day-to-day basis."[70] Obviously, that is rarely the case. It is reasonable to assume, however, that presidents and legislators, because they hope to be reelected, do take public opinion into consideration in reaching major policy decisions. In addition, they try to influence public opinion to win support for the decisions they have made.

Public opinion in a democracy, then, may be seen as a broad but flexible framework for policy making, setting certain limits within which government may act. As V. O. Key, Jr., has observed, "Unless mass views have some place in the shaping of policy, all the talk about democracy is nonsense."[71]

KEY TERMS

CHAPTER HIGHLIGHTS

✦ Public opinion is the expression of attitudes about government and politics. All governments are based, to some extent, on public opinion.

✦ Political socialization is the process by which a person acquires a set of political attitudes and forms opinions about political and social issues.

✦ Many factors influence the opinions people hold. Among the most important are differences in social class, occupation, and income; religion, sex, race, and ethnic factors; sectional and geographic differences; and the views of reference groups. There are two kinds of reference groups: primary groups (such as friends, office associates, or a social club) and secondary groups (such as labor unions or fraternal, professional, or religious groups).

✦ In addition, mass media—television, radio, newspapers, the Internet, online computer service providers, and other media—have a major impact on public opinion.

✦ The qualities of public opinion—direction, intensity, and stability—may be measured by political polls.

✦ Political polls, often useful as a guide to voter sentiment, are a standard part of political campaigns. They measure opinion by taking a random sample of a larger population, or universe. Due to the mathematical law of probability, the results of a poll usually reflect the opinions of the larger group. Although generally reliable, polls are sometimes wrong and do not necessarily predict the outcomes of elections.

✦ In presidential elections, often only a little more than half the people of voting age—and sometimes less than half—bother to vote. In off-year elections for Congress, usually well under half of the voting-age population votes.

✦ Americans have not always sought to express their opinions or to bring about political change through lawful or peaceful means. If the political system fails to respond to the demands placed on it, or if participation is slow to bring about change, individuals or groups may vent their anger against the system in violent ways.

✦ Modern political candidates and leaders are highly attuned to techniques for measuring and influencing public opinion. Political polls, television commercials, Internet Web sites, and professional campaign managers are all part of the efforts at mass persuasion employed today.

✦ Public opinion in a democracy may be seen as a broad but flexible framework for policy making, setting certain limits within which government may act.

SUGGESTED WEB SITES

http://www.gallup.com
The Gallup Organization
Since 1935 the Gallup Organization has conducted surveys to measure public opinion on various issues. Its polls cover five subject areas: Politics and Elections, Business, Social Issues and Policy, Managing, and Lifestyle.

http://dailynews.yahoo.com/h/zo/nm/
Yahoo! Public Opinion Headlines
Yahoo! and Reuters news service list and provide the text of stories that report public opinion on topics ranging from politics to everyday life.

http://www.msnbc.com
MSNBC Opinions
Provides viewers with opinion articles and transcripts of programs, and allows visitors to the Web site to participate in MSNBC polls and to register their views on a Bulletin Board System (BBS) or through the MSNBC chat room.

SUGGESTED READING

Bennett, Linda, and Bennett, Stephen. *Living with Leviathan: Americans Coming to Terms with Big Government* (University of Kansas Press, 1990) A detailed examination of Americans' changing attitudes toward the expanding role of government in social and economic life.

Bennett, Stephen, and Rademacher, Eric, eds. *After the Boom: The Politics of Generation X* (Rowman & Littlefield, 1997). A series of essays, including several by members of Generation X, examining the social and political thought and behavior of a younger segment of the population that will be increasingly important in the coming years.

Cantril, Albert H., and Cantril, Susan Davis. *Reading Mixed Signals: Ambivalence in American Public Opinion About Government** (Johns Hopkins University Press, 1999) An insightful study of the seemingly paradoxical attitudes toward government in the United States: Americans express distrust for government, and say that its size should be reduced, but when it comes to concrete issues, such as the environment, care for the elderly and young, and health care, they believe that government should be doing more.

DelliCarpini, Michael X., and Keeter, Scott. *What Americans Know About politics and Why It Matters** (Yale University Press, 1996). A scholarly analysis, spanning half a century, of Americans' levels of political information. The authors conclude that whites and upper-income citizens are more likely to be politically informed, and argue that this has broad consequences for the distribution of political power.

Erikson, Robert S. *American Public Opinion: Its Origins, Content and Impact** (Allyn & Bacon, 2000). A useful introduction to the field of public opinion research and analysis. The author examines influences upon public opinion, the process of opinion formation, and the importance of public opinion for democratic government.

Glynn, Carroll J., et al. *Public Opinion: Politics, Communication and Social Process* (Westview Press, 1998). A collection of readable essays on the formulation of mass opinion, its measurement, and its impact upon politicians and the political process.

Shafer, Byron E., and Claggett, William J.M. *The Two Majorities: The Issue Context of Modern American Politics* (Johns Hopkins University Press, 1995). A detailed study of Americans' attitudes toward issues. The authors argue that on a cluster of economic and social insurance issues, the public prefers the Democratic Party's position; but on issues related to cultural values, civil liberties, and national defense, the public normally prefers the Republican Party's positions.

Stimson, James A. *Public Opinion in America: Moods, Cycles and Swings** (Westview, 1999). The author uses polling data to support the view that American public opinion goes through regular, cyclical fluctuations between conservatism and liberalism.

Zaller, James. *The Nature and Origins of Mass Opinion** (Oxford University Press, 1992). An illuminating exploration of how citizens acquire political information, and how public opinion is formed.

---

*Available in paperback edition.

 Visit http://politicalscience.wadsworth.com/cummings9/update/ for current InfoTrac articles and other student resources related to this chapter.

CHAPTER 7
Interest Groups

In 1997, the tobacco industry, beset by lawsuits by state attorneys general and private individuals, reached a multibillion-dollar settlement that required approval by Congress. At first, the tobacco companies favored the deal because it would have ended what threatened to be continuous and very costly lawsuits by the states and individual smokers. Many antismoking activists opposed the deal as too favorable to Big Tobacco. In the first six months after the tentative settlement was negotiated, the tobacco giants spent $15.8 million to hire an astonishing 186 lobbyists to press their case with lawmakers and government regulators in Washington. Of these, 37 were company lobbyists, and 149 were outside lawyers and lobbyists.[1] In addition, during the same six-month period the tobacco industry gave $1.9 million to political party committees and $587,000 to candidates.[2]

When the proposal was modified by the Senate in 1998 in ways that the companies opposed, the industry turned against it. The number of lobbyists for the tobacco interests—now working against the legislation—increased dramatically. The $368.5 billion tobacco deal collapsed. Later that year the industry and the states reached a much more limited settlement.

Although the large number of lobbyists hired by Big Tobacco was unusual, the industry's effort was not. Congress and the executive branch are the targets of similar efforts by all sorts of groups, not only big corporations but also organizations representing older Americans, gun owners, labor unions, trial lawyers, teachers, and other special interests.

The millions of dollars spent every year on influencing Congress and government officials in Washington raise a basic question about the nature of democracy: Do the people really rule, through their elected officials and representatives? Or do powerful groups with deep pockets full of money control government policies and determine what laws get passed? Who is really in charge?

WHO GOVERNS?

Who governs in a democracy? Three answers are possible. It can be said that "the people" govern through political leaders nominated as candidates of political parties (or running as independents) and elected by the voters.

Another view is that a "power elite," a "power structure," or an "establishment" actually runs things. This was the view advanced more than four decades ago by sociologist C. Wright Mills in *The Power Elite*. Mills argued that a small group, "possessors of power, wealth and celebrity," occupies the key positions in American society.[3] This theory holds that elites rule, that power is held by the few and not by the masses. Many other social scientists have interpreted American society in terms of elite theory.[4] And "the establishment" is an expression

that is sometimes used to describe elite power. Political writer Richard H. Rovere, in a semihumorous vein, once described the "American Establishment" as a loose coalition of leaders of finance, business, the professions, and the universities, who hold power and influence in the United States regardless of what administration occupies the White House.[5]

Although elites do exist in almost every field of human activity, many scholars reject the concept that a single economic and social elite wields ultimate political power. In his classic study of community power in New Haven, Connecticut, Robert A. Dahl provided a third answer to the question of "Who governs?" He examined several specific public issues and traced the process by which decisions were made on those issues. He concluded that the city's economic and social "notables" did not run New Haven. Some individuals and groups were particularly influential in the making of one type of decision—educational policy, for example. But in other policy areas, different individuals and groups often played the most important role. The city was dominated by many sets of leaders: "It was, in short, a pluralist system."[6]

Other scholars have criticized Dahl's approach on the grounds that the wielders of power cannot always be identified by examining key decisions. For example, truly powerful persons might prevent certain issues from ever reaching the public arena.[7] On such issues, those favoring the status quo are the winners, because no decisions are made that might lead to change. In short, the power to set the agenda, to determine which public policy questions will be debated or even considered, may prove at least as important as the power to decide on the issues themselves.

Actor Charlton Heston, president of the National Rifle Association, brandishes a gun at the NRA annual convention in May 2000.
AP/Wide World

Nevertheless, the pluralist character of American democracy is widely, although not universally, recognized. **Pluralism** is a system in which many conflicting groups within the community have access to government officials and compete with one another in an effort to influence policy decisions.

Pluralism supposes that many individuals are active in groups and associations to advance their interests, and that these multiple interests and memberships may overlap and often conflict. For example, the same person who favors new school construction as a member of the PTA may oppose higher taxes as a member of a neighborhood association. However, many groups have been badly underrepresented or left out of the pluralist system. Minorities, the poor, migrant workers, consumers, and others who do not belong to organized interest groups do not always fare well in a pluralist society. And many Americans do not join groups. Moreover, a case may be made that some interest groups can become too powerful; a classic example often cited is the National Rifle Association, which for years has opposed gun control legislation favored by a majority of Americans.

It has been argued that pluralism really consists of competing groups of elites, so that even a pluralist system falls far short of the classic democratic model. Some scholars who contend that America is ruled by the few are critical of elite power and argue that the political system must be opened up to give more people access to it. Other scholars claim that only elites are dedicated to democratic principles and that the masses of citizens have little allegiance to freedom, the right of dissent, First Amendment values, or equal opportunity. But this latter view diminishes the importance of the ordinary voter and citizen and reflects little confidence in representative democracy.

To an extent, the debate over whether America is an elite or pluralist democracy may pose the question in terms that are too rigid. As with most things, there is a mix. Elites do exercise power in and out of government, but competing groups also play an important role. And the voters retain the ultimate power of replacing elected leaders—from the school board member to the president of the United States.

INTEREST GROUPS AT WORK

Interest groups are private groups that attempt to influence the government to respond to the shared attitudes of their members.

Public opinion, as noted in Chapter 6, is the expression of attitudes on public questions. When people organize to express attitudes held in common and to influence the government to respond to those attitudes, they become members of interest groups.

When one group wins, another may lose. David B. Truman has pointed out that interest groups may make "certain claims upon other groups in the society" by acting through "the institutions of government."[8]

Concern over the potential power of private groups is even older than the republic; James Madison warned of the "mischiefs of faction" in his famous essay, *The Federalist,* No. 10." But Madison also recognized that reconciling the competing interests of various groups was what legislation was all about, and "involves the spirit of party and faction in the necessary and ordinary operations of the government."[9] (The text of *The Federalist,* No. 10," appears in the Appendix of this book, on pages A-14–A-16.)

President Woodrow Wilson argued that government should act as a sort of referee among interest groups to protect the public. "The business of government," he said, "is to organize the common interest against the special interests."[10]

An anti-smoking interest group put up this billboard in Nashville, Tennessee.
AP/Tennessean/Wide World

In the 19th century, political cartoonists were fond of drawing potbellied men in top hats and striped pants to represent Big Business. In the early 20th century, muckrakers—journalists such as Lincoln Steffens, who exposed business misconduct—assailed oil, steel, and railroad barons, calling them members of interest groups in league against the public welfare. Partly as a result of this muckraking tradition, many people tend to regard all interest groups as evil, business-dominated organizations plotting against the common good. And it is true that some powerful interest groups, employing well-paid lobbyists in Washington, often bring about legislation that benefits corporate America, sometimes at the expense of the broader public. But it is also true that today many other interest groups champion consumers, the environment, campaign finance reform, or other causes that benefit the public as a whole.

Many political scientists now consider interest groups a normal and vital part of the political process, conveyors of the demands and supports fed into the political system. In other words, interest groups provide many of the important inputs of the political system. Whether such groups are called "interest groups," "pressure groups," or "lobbies"—and there is some disagreement over which label is best—their purpose is much the same: to influence government policies and actions. The historian Clinton Rossiter has observed: "We call them 'interest groups' when we are feeling clinical, 'pressure groups' when we are feeling critical, and 'lobbies' when we are watching them at work in our fifty-one capitals."[11] These groups should not be confused with political parties, which also seek to influence government but by electing candidates to office. As noted in Chapter 1, the members of some interest groups—college students, for example—may not even be formally organized as a group.

Who Belongs?

The tendency of Americans to come together in groups was noticed in the early 19th century by a remarkably perceptive French observer, Alexis de Tocqueville. "In no country of the world," he observed, "has the principle of association been more successfully used or applied to a greater multitude of objects than in America."[12]

There are more than 100,000 clubs and associations in the United States. Not everyone belongs to a group, however. In America, "more than one-third of the population has no formal group association."[13] And nearly half of those who do belong to groups are affiliated with social, fraternal, or church-connected organizations that may have little relation to politics.[14] Not all organizations are interested in influencing government, so only a minority of Americans belong to interest groups. One survey reported that only 31 percent of the population belonged to groups that sometimes take a stand on housing, better government, school problems, or other public issues.[15] That well over one-third of Americans belong to

no groups at all raises basic questions about pluralist democracy that will be discussed later in this chapter.

How They Operate

Although interest groups vary tremendously in size, goals, budget, and scope of interest, they often employ the same techniques to accomplish their objectives. The following examples illustrate some of these techniques.

Several years ago, the Federal Trade Commission proposed a set of rules designed to protect people who buy used cars. The rules would have required the dealers to reveal to a buyer any major defects in a car. The nation's used-car dealers, led by the National Automobile Dealers Association, mounted a massive lobbying campaign in Congress to overturn the FTC proposal. According to Ralph Nader's Congress Watch, the auto dealers' group gave campaign contributions of $770,000 to members of the House.

Online   *for more information about Ralph Nader's Congress Watch, see:* www.citizen.org/congress

Congress voted to kill the rules that would have helped car buyers know what they were buying. "This says a lot about the contamination of the political arena by campaign contributions," said Representative Toby Moffett, Democrat of Connecticut.[16] Another opponent of the congressional action, Representative Barbara A. Mikulski, a Maryland Democrat who was later elected to the Senate, said the rules would have protected car buyers from gypsy dealers such as "Happy Harry and Smiling Sam." She added: "People should know if they're getting a car in reasonable condition or a four-wheel-drive lemon."[17]

It was a blatant but effective case of lobbying by an industry group. It won, and the consumers lost.

But if the used-car dealers triumphed, it was consumers who won in another battle a few years later, in New York State, when beer prices rose as much as 31 per-

SEVEN RULES FOR THE SUCCESSFUL LOBBYIST

From extensive comments by lobbyists and their targets, Lester W. Milbrath drew up the following list of guidelines for Washington's lobbyists:

1. Be pleasant and non-offensive
2. Convince the official that it is important for him to listen
3. Be well prepared and well informed
4. Be personally convinced
5. Be succinct, well organized, and direct
6. Use the soft sell
7. Leave a short written summary of the case

    —Lester W. Milbrath, *The Washington Lobbyists*

cent. The reason: Brewers ordered their distributors to carve out exclusive territories and avoid competition with other distributors—competition that would have meant lower prices. In Washington, senators who had received substantial contributions from the beer industry introduced legislation to exempt such practices nationwide from provisions of the federal antitrust laws. Consumer activists, working with the states, defeated the measure, saving the nation's beer drinkers from higher prices, if not from larger waistlines.[18]

Lobbying One of the most powerful techniques of interest groups is **lobbying,** communication with legislators or other government officials to try to influence their decisions. Originally, the term "lobby-agent" was used to describe someone who waited in the lobbies of government buildings to buttonhole lawmakers. The term "lobbying" dates back to the 1600s in England, where the large antechamber near the floor of the House of Commons was called the "lobby." In the United States, the term first came into use in the New York state capital at Albany and was being used in Washington by the early 1830s.

The term "Washington lobbyist" is not always complimentary. Lobbyists and the interest groups they represent are often the target of attacks by political candidates during campaigns. But lobbying is not necessarily harmful, or incompatible with democracy, since groups, no less than individuals, have a right to express their views.

Although the word "lobbying" is often applied to mean direct contact with lawmakers, in its broadest sense lobbying is not confined to efforts to influence the legislative branch. Lobbyists also seek to influence officials of the executive branch, regulatory agencies, and sometimes the courts. And lobbyists spend much of their time monitoring events in Washington, in order to alert their clients to government actions or plans that may affect them.

One way that lobbyists influence officials is simple: They get to know them. By paying visits to members of Congress and government officials, by attending hearings of congressional committees, government agencies, and regulatory commissions, and by forming friendships with staff members and bureaucrats, lobbyists make their presence felt. Lester Milbrath found that more than half the Washington lobbyists thought the personal presentation of viewpoints was the most effective way of reaching members of Congress.[19] Senators and representatives are busy people; often the lobbyists' chief value is that in support of their arguments they present carefully researched background material that may help a member of Congress decide how to vote on a complex bill.

Agriculture lobbyists in Washington waiting to buttonhole Senators in the Capitol
Copyright © David Burnett/Contact Press Images/PictureQuest

"MONEY DOES TALK"—THE TAB FOR WASHINGTON LOBBYING: $1.42 BILLION

WASHINGTON, July 28—The capital of the United States is a city with no real industry except for politics and influence, and so huge sums of money are paid to lobbyists trying to influence politicians. Last year $1.42 billion was spent in that endeavor, a research group said today.

That total was a 13 percent increase over the $1.26 billion that lobbyists were paid in 1997, said the group, the Center for Responsive Politics. If all the money had been spent on Capitol Hill, it would have worked out to $2.7 million earmarked to persuading each of the 535 lawmakers on a host of issues, the center said.

Of course, not all was spent on Capitol Hill; much was spent trying to persuade various regulatory agencies and other offices of the executive branch, the center's communications director, Paul Hendrie, pointed out.

The $1.42 billion was paid to lobbyists by airplane manufacturers, bankers, doctors and lawyers, drug companies, hospitals, universities, Indian tribes—in short, by just about any person or any institution that has business before the Federal Government.

"There's certainly nothing inherently illegitimate about any of these interests' having their voices heard," Mr. Hendrie emphasized. "We don't think so, either," said Tom McMahon, a spokesman for Cassidy & Associates, which took in $19.9 million in fees last year. . . .

Still, Mr. Hendrie said, the huge sums spent on lobbying are cause for concern. "People who don't have the money to spend are not going to speak with as loud a voice," he said. "Money does talk."

—David Stout, *New York Times,* July 29, 1999

How lobbyists are viewed often depends on whose interests are at stake. When reporters asked President Harry S Truman whether he would oppose lobbyists who worked for his programs, he replied with a twinkle: "We probably wouldn't call those people lobbyists. We would call them citizens appearing in the public interest."[20]

Money: The Lobbyist's Tool In 1998, some 50 of the nation's top lobbyists posed for a group photograph in *Washingtonian* magazine, a glossy publication well read in the capital. The photograph accompanied an article titled "Show Me the Money!"

The phrase might well be the motto for one of the most affluent groups in Washington, the lobbyists and lawyers who represent large corporations and industry groups and other clients seeking to influence the government. Lobbyists and their firms are paid millions of dollars a year, and in turn, they contribute generously to political candidates and parties.

The magazine group photo was published despite the fact that one of the capital's most publicized lobbyists, Michael K. Deaver, a former White House deputy chief of staff, got into trouble when he appeared on the cover of *Time* magazine 12 years earlier. The cover photograph of Deaver showed him telephoning someone from his richly appointed limousine, alongside the headlines "Who's This Man Calling?" and "Influence Peddling in Washington." Deaver had set up his own lobbying firm in Washington when he left the White House in 1985. Foreign governments, defense contractors, corporations, and others seeking access to the center of power flocked to hire Deaver at fees ranging into millions of dollars.

Federal law prohibits former government employees from appearing before their former agencies to represent clients for a period of two years after leaving government

service. Deaver was summoned to testify to Congress and explain his lucrative activities. In 1987, a federal jury convicted Deaver of lying to Congress and to a grand jury about his lobbying. He was fined $100,000 and sentenced to three years' probation. It did not seem to inhibit his continued success as a lobbyist.

In 1998, one top law firm—Verner, Liipfert, Bernhard, McPherson and Hand—reported that it earned $19 million in lobbying fees the previous year, the largest amount reported by any firm. Bob Dole, the Republican presidential candidate in 1996, joined the law firm after his defeat. In an appearance on the *Late Show with David Letterman* he criticized President Clinton for his policy toward Taiwan. What viewers did not know was that Verner, Liipfert represents Taiwan.

Former Texas governor Ann Richards entered the ranks of Washington lobbyists.
AP/Wide World

Former Senate majority leader George J. Mitchell, of Maine, joined the Washington law firm with the highest earnings from lobbying.
AP/Wide World

The firm also hired prominent Democrats, including Ann Richards, the former governor of Texas, and George J. Mitchell, the former Senate majority leader.[21]

Although a great deal of lobbying is directed at Congress, sometimes even a president is lobbied. For example, during the Nixon Administration, America's dairy industry wanted the price supports for milk raised. The dairy industry group agreed to contribute campaign funds to the president. In due course, the attorney for the largest of the milk cooperatives, the Associated Milk Producers, Inc. (AMPI), delivered a satchel containing $100,000 in cash to the president's lawyer. The milk producers later pledged to contribute $2 million to Nixon in the 1972 presidential campaign. Soon afterward, the president invited the dairy leaders to the White House, posed for pictures with them, and thanked them for their political support.

The dairy industry won a large price increase. Later, however, the secretary of agriculture ruled against any further price increases. John Connally of Texas, secretary of the treasury and a supporter of the dairy industry, warned the president that a veto of legislation to raise prices might cost him six farm states in the election.[22]

Nixon met with the dairy leaders again. He decided to increase milk prices—provided the milk producers kept their $2 million campaign pledge. The secretary of agriculture reversed himself and announced that milk prices would be increased after all. With a satchel full of cash and a promise of $2 million, lobbyists for a powerful industry had directly influenced the president of the United States.[23]

The success of the dairy industry in winning price increases worth more than $300 million is a dramatic illustration of how lobbying by interest groups can affect—even reverse—public policy. In the policy-making process, interest groups play a key role. In this instance, an input of hard cash resulted in the output the milk industry wanted.

As this case demonstrated, money is often a useful tool for the lobbyist. The public often thinks of the lobbyist as someone who hands out money to buy the votes of legislators. That may happen. A direct bribe, however, is a violation of federal law. Under a 1962 statute, a person who bribes a member of Congress, or a member of Congress who takes "anything of value" in exchange for a vote, may be fined $20,000 and imprisoned up to 15 years. The language of the statute is broad enough to cover any kind of valuable favor, not just money. Bribery is illegal and risky, and there are better, legal ways to channel money to legislators. For example, lobbyists are expected to purchase tickets or whole tables of tickets to fund-raising dinners for political parties and candidates. And of course lobbyists and their clients can—and do—contribute to political campaigns.

Until Congress passed a law in 1995 to regulate the practice, lobbyists might, without regard to the cost, take a senator to lunch at an expensive restaurant in Washington, arrange a weekend on a yacht, or provide a free trip to a plush resort; Christmas might bring a legislator a ham, a case of Scotch, or a pair of gold cuff links. The new law placed limits on these practices, but did not eliminate them; according to one report, at the Capital Grille, an expensive restaurant not far from the Capitol building, "lobbyists flaunt their clients and their expensive tastes with brass name plaques on private wine lockers."[24]

In the summer of 2000, a group of top lobbyists invested in, and opened, their own restaurant in Washington, complete with discreet private dining rooms to entertain members of Congress. Appropriately, the restaurant was called the Caucus Room. But lunches, fine wines, and small favors are only relatively minor props in the drama of influencing lawmakers. Many members of Congress are practicing lawyers, insurance agents, bankers, and business executives. For example, in 1998, some 217 members—or about two-fifths—of the

Tobacco industry executives testify to Congress. The industry spent millions on Washington lobbyists.
AP/Wide World

106th Congress were lawyers. It is not difficult for interest groups with nationwide chapters and members to channel legal or insurance fees or bank loans to members of Congress. Unless such payments can be shown to be outright bribes, they are legal; in any event, they are difficult to trace.

For the most part, lobbyists for interest groups are able to exert influence by means of campaign contributions and fund-raising. The American Medical Association (AMA), representing more than 293,000 physicians, residents, and medical students, is an example of a highly active interest group that has spent millions of dollars opposing national health insurance and other medical legislation. The American Medical Association Political Action Committee (AMPAC), the AMA's political arm, contributed $2.3 million to congressional candidates in the 1998 election.

Online *for more information about the American Medical Association, see:*
www.ama-assn.org

Many large interest groups are deeply involved in politics. For example, the AFL-CIO's Committee on Political Education (COPE) contributes money to candidates, runs voter-registration drives, publicly endorses candidates, publishes their voting records for union members, and often provides volunteers to assist in political campaigns. COPE contributed $1.1 million to candidates for Congress in the 1998 election. Although ostensibly nonpartisan, COPE in fact has mainly aided Democrats, just as the AMA is Republican oriented.

As these examples illustrate, large amounts of money flow to political leaders and candidates from interest groups and corporations maneuvering to influence public policy. When George W. Bush, a former businessman in the oil industry, began his quest for the 2000 Republican presidential nomination, he received more than $1.42 million dollars from various oil and gas companies to

support his campaign in the spring primaries. In contrast, Al Gore, his Democratic rival, received only $84,750 from those sources. Gore, on the other hand, got $806,690 from the entertainment industry during the same period, about $200,000 more than Hollywood gave to Bush.[25]

Hollywood is a source of campaign money for both major political parties. Here Al Gore follows actor Leonardo DiCaprio at an "Earth Day 2000" rally in Washington.
AP/Wide World

A small class of men . . . arose at the time of our Civil War and suddenly swept into power.

The members of this new ruling class were generally, and quite aptly, called "barons," "kings," "empire builders," or even "emperors." They were aggressive men, as were the first feudal barons; sometimes they were lawless; in important crises, nearly all of them tended to act without moral principles. . . .

While busy carving up the country into baronies the captains of industry worked also with unremitting vigilance in the field of political action [penetrating] into the highest assemblies of the country: the Congress, the Senate, and even sometimes the President's cabinet. . . .

Instead of outright bribery, highly subtle methods of distributing rewards to political friends came into play. In the Pacific Railway Investigation of 1887, [Collis P.] Huntington stated candidly that he was opposed to giving politicians free liquor and cigars too open-handedly. And where [Thomas A.] Scott or [Jay] Gould gave free passes on all the roads touching Washington, Huntington organized huge "junketing parties" on private trains at a cost of tens of thousands of dollars, by which politicians, their families and journalists might go on exhilarating excursions through his broad territories.

In time, all of the captains of industry found it greatly to their advantage to use the system of the hired "lobbyist," a type of professional public agent who had flourished from the earliest days of the republic, but who came to assume a tremendously important and confidential role in the last quarter of the nineteenth century. All the "interests," banks, railways, mines, steel, munitions and war materials, ended by having their specialized go-betweens or lobbies.

[On] May 8, 1890, a young Republican prosecuting attorney in Ohio, with the enthusiasm of an amateur, began a suit to annul the charter of the Standard Oil Company. At once Mark Hanna wrote him the letter which contained the famous line: "You have been in politics long enough to know that no man in public office owes the public anything."

—Adapted from Matthew Josephson, *The Robber Barons: The Great American Capitalists 1861–1901*

As vice president, Gore also enjoyed the benefit of large contributions from corporations and individuals, to make improvements in his official residence that were not paid for by the government—including a billiard table, a hot tub, and landscaping. Some of the large corporations that gave $10,000 each to beautify the Gore residence included Bell Atlantic, Coca-Cola, MCI WorldCom, Time Warner, General Motors, and Microsoft. "There is a small group of people making an investment in the vice president's residence for access and influence and it's largely out of public view," said Peter Eisner, the managing director of the Center for Public Integrity, a nonprofit group advocating campaign finance reform. "For donors, this is a better deal than giving to the campaign."[26]

Despite their money and influence, Washington lobbyists do not always fit their popular image as glamorous figures who entertain powerful senators and dine at the best places. As most lobbyists are quick to point out, much of their work consists of solid research, long hours of committee hearings, and conversations with lawmakers in their offices. Whatever their technique, lobbyists—and their dollars—have a substantial influence on political decision making.

Mass Propaganda and Grass-Roots Pressure

One of the ways in which interest groups try to influence public opinion in order to influence government is through mass-publicity campaigns. Using television, magazine, and newspaper advertising, and direct mailings to the general public and specialized audiences, interest groups seek to create a favorable climate for their goals.

With the aid of a public relations firm, an interest group can use all the latest techniques of Madison Avenue. But it takes a great deal of money to influence public opinion enough to create a response from government, and only affluent interest groups can afford programs aimed at the manipulation of mass public opinion.[27]

A classic example of an apparently successful campaign by an affluent group was the publicity campaign of the American Automobile Association (AAA) against a bill that would have allowed bigger trucks on the nation's roads. The AAA ran newspaper advertisements showing a triple-trailer truck with a huge boar's head devouring the highway as John Q. Motorist sat helplessly by, trapped in a monstrous traffic jam. The ad urged that the bill be defeated for reasons of safety and "because of the irreparable damage bigger trucks will do to our highways and bridges." With the public alarmed and the nation's bridges in apparent danger of imminent collapse, Congress abandoned the trucking bill.[28]

 Online for more information about the American Automobile Association, see: www.aaa.com

Evangelical Christian groups have organized grass-roots pressure in political campaigns. Here Republican presidential candidate George W. Bush and wife, Laura, join hands at Bob Jones University in February 2000.
AP/Wide World

In addition to such mass-propaganda campaigns, many interest groups approach some members of the public directly to try to create various forms of grass-roots pressure that will affect government. To influence senators, for example, an interest group might persuade powerful bankers in the senators' states to telephone them in Washington. Lobbyists may ask close friends of the senators to get in touch with them. Or lobbyists may try to get great numbers of legislators' constituents to write, fax, or e-mail them.

Both mass propaganda and grass-roots pressure have been employed by highly organized evangelical Christian groups in political campaigns in recent years. In the 2000 Republican presidential primary race, for example, the support for George W. Bush by Pat Robertson and other evangelical Christians became a major campaign issue.

Today, many interest groups use computerized mailing lists to contact their members and supporters; the National Rifle Association (NRA), an aggressive group opposed to gun control, reportedly can barrage Congress with a half-million letters on 72 hours' notice. The NRA has 3.5 million members, a budget of $120 million, and a full-time staff of almost 500 persons; in 1998 it contributed $1.6 million to almost 300 Senate and House candidates.[29]

Members of Congress are well aware that interest groups may be behind a sudden flood of letters, e-mails, or faxes on a pending bill. In addition, legislators know that, since most people do not write letters to their representatives in Congress, the mail they receive reflects the feelings of only a small percentage of their constituents. One study showed that only 17 percent of the general public writes letters to members of Congress.[30]

Nevertheless, grass-roots pressure remains a popular form of trying to influence government, in part because interest groups, never certain which techniques are the most effective, tend to try them all.

And now, with the enormous growth of the Internet, it is easier than ever for lobbyists to organize a seemingly grass-roots campaign in which citizens bombard their lawmakers with thousands of e-mails. When those computer messages bear the names of constituents, legislators are likely to pay attention.

The Washington Lawyers: Access to the Powerful

Members of prestigious Washington law firms are among the capital's most effective lobbyists. Often, large corporations pay big fees to Washington lawyers, not only for their expert knowledge of how the bureaucracy works, but also for their political access and friends inside the government and in Congress.

In 1994, Pearl Jam, the Seattle-based grunge band, filed a complaint with the Justice Department alleging that the Ticketmaster company had a monopoly on ticket sales in violation of federal antitrust laws. Other bands and consumer groups joined with Pearl Jam in an alliance designed to open up ticket sales and lower the prices. Ticketmaster fought back. It opened a Washington "government relations" office and hired not one but five powerful lobbyist, public relations, and law firms to represent it. A little over a year later, the Justice Department announced that it had ended its antitrust investigation of Ticketmaster. It would not elaborate on its announcement. But Pearl Jam had lost.[31]

On more than one occasion, Washington lawyers have been able to orchestrate the passage of legislation designed to help their clients: "The lawyer's historic role was that of advising clients how to comply with the law. The Washington lawyer's present role is that of advising clients how to make laws, and to make the most of them."[32] Often government lawyers leave to join Washington law firms, where they are highly paid to find the loopholes in the very laws they formerly enforced. This sort of "revolving door" is a common practice in the nation's capital.

For several decades until the 1990s, one of the most renowned of Washington lawyers was Clark M. Clifford, who served in the cabinet and as an adviser to Democratic presidents. Aware of his stature, bureaucrats and members of Congress tended to return his telephone calls, giving Clifford the kind of political clout that corporate clients want—and pay large fees to obtain. President Kennedy, who received a good deal of free advice from Clifford, once joked: "All he asked in return was that we advertise his law firm on the backs of one-dollar bills."[33]

Public Interest Groups

Corporate lawyers and lobbyists have sometimes faced a new kind of opponent in recent years. Since the 1960s, public interest groups and public interest lawyers have also waged successful battles to influence public policy. In the fields of the environment, consumer protection,

Pearl Jam in concert. Ticketmaster's Washington lobbyists called the tune.
John Mead/Star File Photo

health, minority rights, campaign finance reform, and many other areas, these public interest groups have brought class action and other lawsuits, lobbied Congress, and through the powerful weapon of publicity, added new issues to the government agenda.

One such public interest group is Common Cause, a national citizens' lobby with more than 250,000 members. Common Cause received major credit for passage of the election reform laws of the 1970s. But the laws proved ineffective, and Common Cause has continued to do battle for campaign finance reform.

The best-known public interest lobbyist, Ralph Nader, heads a network of lawyers, lobbyists, and political analysts working in more than 20 organizations. Among the Nader-affiliated public interest groups are Public Citizen, an umbrella organization that includes Congress

WHO LOBBIES FOR THE POOR?

The poor are powerless because they are a minority of the population, are often difficult to organize, and are not even a homogeneous group with similar interests that could be organized into an effective pressure group. . . .

Although every citizen is urged to be active in the affairs of his community and nation, in actual practice participation is almost entirely limited to organized interest groups or lobbies who want something from government.

As a result, legislation tends to favor the interests of the organized: of businessmen, not consumers, even though the latter are a vast majority; of landlords, not tenants; doctors, not patients. . . . While the American political structure often satisfies the majority, it also creates outvoted minorities who can be tyrannized and repressed by majority rule, such as the poor and the black, students, migrant workers and many others.

—Herbert J. Gans, "We Won't End the Urban Crisis until We End Majority Rule," the *New York Times Magazine*, August 3, 1969

Ralph Nader
Copyright © Franklin Wing/Stock, Boston

Each year, *Fortune* magazine ranks groups and associations that have the most power and political clout in Washington, based on a survey of more than 2,700 persons, including members of Congress, their staffs, and White House officials. Here are the top 10 on *Fortune*'s list:

1. American Association of Retired Persons
2. National Rifle Association
3. National Federation of Independent Business
4. American Israel Public Affairs Committee
5. AFL-CIO
6. Association of Trial Lawyers of America
7. Chamber of Commerce
8. National Right to Life Committee
9. National Education Association
10. National Restaurant Association

—*Fortune*, December 6, 1999

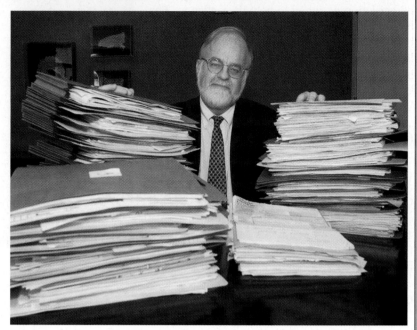

John Rother, chief lobbyist for the American Association of Retired Persons (AARP)
AP/Wide World

Watch, which concentrates on consumer affairs, the environment, transportation, congressional reform, and other legislation; the Critical Mass Energy Project, which monitors nuclear power; the Health Research Group, which works to improve medical care and food and drug safety; and the Freedom of Information Clearinghouse, which seeks to obtain government records under the Freedom of Information Act. In addition, there are other Nader groups, including the Center for Study of Responsive Law, a clearinghouse for studies and reports by Nader task forces; the Center for Auto Safety; and the Public Interest Research Groups (PIRGs) in several states. The PIRGs enlist students and other citizens in a variety of public interest and consumer projects.

Web page of Congress Watch, part of Ralph Nader's Public Citizen
Courtesy Public Citizen

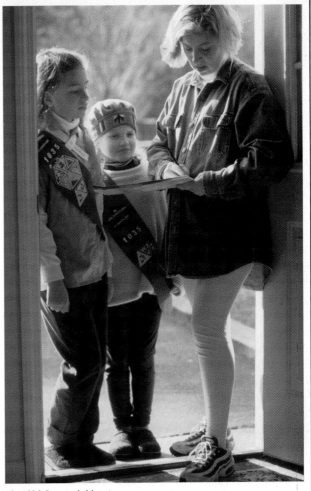
In addition to lobbying and working for consumers, the Nader organizations have produced a number of studies and books, including reports on land use, air pollution, corporate power, and many other subjects. Nader's activities are financed by foundations, income from the sale of books, membership dues, contributions from the public, and Nader's own funds, earned in lecturing and writing. In 2000, Nader ran as a presidential candidate on the Green Party ticket. After four decades as the nation's best-known public interest lobbyist, Nader and his organization are somewhat less powerful today, but his record of accomplishment as an interest group leader remains unchallenged.

Single-Issue Groups

In recent years, the single-issue interest group has become an increasingly significant phenomenon on the political scene. These groups concentrate on lobbying for or against a particular issue, often with devastating effect.

The National Right to Life Committee and the National Rifle Association are examples of single-issue lobbies that have campaigned for such specific issues as ending legalized abortions and blocking gun control legislation. Beyond lobbying on the issues, such groups may also influence election results.

Sometimes, however, public opinion counters even the most effective single-issue lobbying groups. Early in the year 2000, President Clinton pushed hard for trigger locks to prevent children from firing guns, and for closing the loophole that allowed sales of firearms at gun shows without requiring a background check of the purchaser. In a television commercial, Charlton Heston, the movie actor who was president of the NRA, suggested Clinton was a liar; and a high official of the association even asserted that the president did not mind "a certain level of killing to further his political agenda" because it might help the White House to gain public support for gun control.[34]

Smith & Wesson agreed to equip its guns with trigger locks. This revolver has a cable-type lock.
AP/Wide World

But the NRA's public relations barrage proved to be ill-timed. Less than a year earlier, a dozen students and a teacher had been shot to death in the Columbine High School massacre in Littleton, Colorado, and in February 2000 a 6-year-old boy shot and killed a 6-year-old girl in a classroom in Michigan. The public was shocked by the killings—and in mid-March, Smith & Wesson, the nation's largest handgun manufacturer, agreed to equip its guns with trigger locks and hidden serial numbers, and to allow its dealers to take part only in gun shows where background checks were required for sales. True, Smith & Wesson acted in exchange for ending some lawsuits that had threatened to put it out of business, but the gunmaker's decision gave the appearance of bowing to public opinion and was immediately assailed by the NRA as a "sellout" and a "surrender."[35]

Political Action Committees

Often, single-issue lobbies work through **political action committees,** or **PACs** (pronounced "packs"), which are sometimes independent organizations but are more often the political arms of corporations, labor unions, or interest groups established to contribute to candidates or to work for general political goals. (See Tables 7-1 and 7-2.)

Several factors account for the growth of PACs. The Federal Election Campaign Act of 1974 permitted unions and corporations to establish political committees that could contribute up to $5,000 to each candidate in a primary or general election. The law was immediately challenged by Senator James Buckley of New York. In 1976, in the case of *Buckley* v. *Valeo*, the Supreme Court upheld many of the law's provisions. But the Court ruled unconstitutional a provision of the law that had placed limits on **independent expenditures,** funds spent for or against a candidate by committees not formally connected to the candidate's campaign and without coordination with the campaign.[36]

The Supreme Court's decision—and a 1975 ruling of the Federal Election Commission allowing the Sun Oil Company to set up a PAC—opened the way for vastly increased expenditures by PACs in political campaigns. These may range from bumper stickers and buttons to television spots endorsing a candidate. Even though direct contributions by a PAC to a federal candidate are still limited to $5,000 in each election, the number of political action committees is so large that PAC contributions totaled $220 million in the 1998 congressional campaigns.[37]

"SHORTER THAN THEIR SHOTGUNS": THE NRA STARTS THEM YOUNG

Thirty-one hunters in camouflage pants and orange vests gathered just after dawn on a recent Saturday morning at a state preserve . . . sipping from steaming cups, munching doughnuts and talking about barrel gauges and bird dogs.

It was a quintessential fall scene, except that the cups contained cocoa, not coffee, and these hunters were boys and girls, many just under 10 years old and some shorter than their shotguns. . . .

It was Take a Kid Pheasant Hunting Day, an event run since 1996 by the New Jersey Division of Fish, Game and Wildlife and partly paid for by the National Rifle Association Foundation, an arm of the gun lobby.

Shooting programs for children are nothing new; the N.R.A. and private clubs have had them for generations. . . . But the New Jersey pheasant shoot was an example of a newer and growing phenomenon: public wildlife agencies and the gun lobbies working hand in hand to promote hunting among children. . . .

New Jersey game officials say they are happy to accept the money.

—*New York Times,* November 17, 1999

Copyright © CORBIS/Reuters NewMedia Inc.

WHAT DO I DO? THIS CONGRESSMAN SAYS HE ALREADY SOLD HIS SOUL TO A POLITICAL ACTION COMMITTEE.

Supreme Court decisions also have encouraged corporate political activity. In 1978 the Court overturned a Massachusetts law that prohibited corporations from spending money to influence the outcome of public referenda. The Court ruled that the state law violated the corporation's First Amendment rights.[38] In 1980 the Supreme Court ruled that a public utility could include statements on controversial political issues along with its monthly bills.[39]

A Harvard University study prepared for Congress identified other reasons for the growth of PACs. The study gave as one reason the changes in the federal election laws that have made it more difficult to raise campaign funds from individuals. And the study suggested that the decline in the power of political parties has forced candidates to turn to interest groups for money.[40]

Undoubtedly the publicity given to PACs in recent years has encouraged the formation of even more such committees. Changes in the structure of Congress may have also contributed. In the 1970s Congress reduced the power of its committee chairmen; as a result, power became fragmented among hundreds of subcommittees, each of which is cultivated by various lobbyists.

As the Harvard study noted, "PAC money is interested money."[41] That is, the PACs often give contributions to committee chairpersons with specific legislative outcomes in mind. Interest groups clearly try to put their money where it will have the most influence; for example, in 1998, PACs representing the banking industry gave members of the House Banking Committee just over $1.73 million.[42]

One analysis of political spending suggested that PAC contributions follow an "investment pattern," aimed at strengthening the group's long-term influence with members of Congress.[43] That pattern is reflected in the top-heavy support by PACs for incumbents. In 1998,

TABLE 7-1

PACs: The Top 10

These 10 political action committees gave the most to candidates in the 1998 congressional campaigns.

Political Action Committee	Amount Contributed (in millions)
Realtors Political Action Committee	$2.47
Association of Trial Lawyers of America Political Action Committee	2.43
American Federation of State, County & Municipal Employees—PEOPLE, Qualified	2.37
American Medical Association Political Action Committee	2.34
Democratic Republican Independent Voter Education Committee	2.18
Dealers Election Action Committee of the National Automobile Dealers Association	2.11
UAW-V-CAP (UAW Voluntary Community Action Program)	1.92
International Brotherhood of Electrical Workers Committee on Political Education	1.88
National Education Association Political Action Committee	1.85
BUILD Political Action Committee of the National Association of Home Builders	1.81

SOURCE: Data provided by the Federal Election Commission, June 1999.

PACs: The Top 10 Corporate PACs

These 10 political action committees, created by various corporations, gave the most to candidates in the 1998 congressional campaigns.

Political Action Committee	Amount Contributed (in thousands)
United Parcel Service of America Inc. Political Action Group (UPSPAC)	$1,527
Lockheed Martin Employees Political Action Committee	1,043
Federal Express Corporation Political Action Committee (FEPAC)	996
Union Pacific Corp. Fund For Effective Government	831
Philip Morris Companies Inc. Political Action Committee (PHIL-PAC)	789
Bell Atlantic Corporation Political Action Committee	783
AT&T Corp. Political Action Committee (AT&T PAC)	772
SBC Communications Inc. Employee Federal Political Action Committee (SBC EMPAC)	761
Bank One Corporation PAC	668
General Electric Company Political Action Committee	663

SOURCE: Data provided by the Federal Election Commission, June 1999.

for example, members of Congress received 78 percent of all PAC contributions, compared to only 10 percent received by challengers.[44]

In 1974 there were 608 PACs. By January 2000 there were more than 3,800.[45] Beyond question, the explosive growth and influence of political action committees, often tied to single-issue lobbying, is having a significant, controversial, and sometimes disturbing influence on politics and policy in America.

REGULATING INTEREST GROUPS

Public concern over lobbying abuses led Congress, beginning early in the 20th century, to try to impose legal controls on interest groups. Not until 1946, however, did Congress pass a general bill that attempted to control lobbying.

The Federal Regulation of Lobbying Act of 1946 required individuals and groups to register with the clerk of the House and the secretary of the Senate if they solicit or collect money or any other thing of value "to be used principally to aid . . . the passage or defeat of any legislation by the Congress of the United States." In 1954 the Supreme Court narrowed the scope of the act by ruling that it applied only to lobbyists who communicated directly with members of Congress and not to grass-roots lobbying aimed at the public.[46] Because of this decision and the loose wording of the statute, many interest groups simply did not register on the grounds that lobbying was not their "principal purpose." Moreover, although the law contained penalties, it had no enforcement provision. As a result, there were few prosecutions after its enactment in 1946.

In 1991, the General Accounting Office (GAO), which serves as a watchdog for Congress, reported that it had studied 13,500 entries in *Washington Representatives*, a book that lists lobbyists and consultants. The GAO found that only 3,700 had registered.[47] Of the estimated 60,000 to 80,000 lobbyists active in Washington, only about 6,000 had registered.[48]

 for more information about the General Accounting Office, see: www.gao.gov

In sum, the Lobbying Act did not effectively regulate lobbying of Congress. And, of course, it did not apply at all to lobbying of the executive branch or the independent regulatory commissions. Another loophole in an earlier law, the Foreign Agents Registration Act, exempted lawyers representing foreign clients. In the years that followed 1946, Congress periodically considered bills to strengthen the regulation of lobbying. Finally, in 1995, a new bill to regulate lobbyists passed both houses of Congress and was signed by President Clinton.

Under the law, lobbyists must register with the clerk of the House and the secretary of the Senate, report who their clients are, what agencies or branches of Congress were lobbied, and how much they were paid. In an effort to tighten the rules, the new law defines lobbyists as people who spend at least 20 percent of their time in that activity. And under the new law, most lawyers representing foreign clients are no longer exempt. Moreover, the law restricted gifts to lawmakers beginning in 1996. Under the law and rules adopted by Congress, senators, representatives, and employees of the legislative branch can accept only gifts worth less than $50, except for home-state products and foodstuffs, and minor items such as T-shirts. Yet despite the improvements and the increased disclosure requirements, there was a major loophole in the 1995 law: It did not apply to grass-roots lobbying, which comprises efforts by interest groups to generate phone calls, faxes, e-mails, and letters in support of, or in opposition to, a bill or program.

MAKING A DIFFERENCE

A WATCHDOG IN THE CORRIDORS OF POWER

Charles Lewis was asleep in a hotel room when the telephone rang at 8:15 A.M. If you're going to be awakened by a call that early when you're on vacation in Southern California, it ought to be good.

And it was: He had been granted $275,000 by the John D. and Catherine T. MacArthur Foundation as one of 29 MacArthur fellows.

Lewis runs a nonprofit, nonpartisan research organization that began as little more than a post office box in May 1990 but now occupies 4,400 square feet in downtown Washington, D.C. With a full-time staff of 24 and a $2 million annual budget, the center has carved out a prominent niche in Washington's watchdog subculture.

Lewis, soft-spoken and boyish, hardly looks the part of scourge of the lobbying world. A Delaware native, he did some part-time work for the home-state papers, then came to Washington to get a master's degree from the Johns Hopkins University School of Advanced International Studies.

Lewis came up with the idea for the Center for Public Integrity in 1989, during a long, ruminative pool game with Alejandro Benes, now the center's managing director. "I was basically frustrated," says Lewis, who was then a producer at *60 Minutes,* and who resembles the mild-mannered reporter Clark Kent. "I felt that the press had arrived on the scene late in a spate of scandals—Iran-contra, the savings-and-loan scandal. What if we were unfettered by time and space? What if you had your own journalistic utopia?"

The center's diverse portfolio has included investigations into airline safety, the Forest Service, and the chemical industry. Its first report, in 1990, disclosed that nearly half of White House trade officials since 1974 had registered—or their firms had registered—as representatives of foreign governments and corporations.

The center's 1996 book, *The Buying of the President,* was the first detailed history of the financial support behind the major presidential contenders. And in August 1996, a study by Lewis's group disclosed the use of White House sleep-overs as a perk for fat-cat donors. Much later, after the Democratic fund-raising scandal broke, the mainstream news media forced the White House to acknowledge that the Lincoln Bedroom was one of the top rewards for big contributors.

Perhaps the greatest thing about winning a MacArthur fellowship is that the award carries no restrictions or instructions. It's like getting lucky in Las Vegas.

"Everyone has given me their theory on what I should do with it," Lewis says.

Like take a sabbatical. Or go off somewhere and write fiction.

"But I'll probably do nothing dramatic or wild," he adds. "I'll probably pay off my bills and my child's tuition."

—Adapted from the *Washington Post,* June 2, 1998; the *New Yorker,* March 25, 1996; and the *National Journal,* March 13, 1993

INTEREST GROUPS AND THE POLICY PROCESS

The view persists in American politics that interest groups are undemocratic and that they work for narrow goals against the general welfare. Some do. But an interest group like Common Cause represents no narrow economic interest; it works on a wide spectrum of issues to promote its conception of "the public welfare." So have the organizations formed by consumer advocate Ralph Nader. It may be more realistic to view interest groups simply as one part of the total political process. Citizens have every right under the Constitution to organize to influence their government. Interest groups compete for the government's attention and action—but so do individual voters, political parties, and the press.

On many major issues, there are likely to be interest groups arrayed on opposite sides. Those who accept democratic pluralism and the politics of interest groups believe that out of these conflicting pressures some degree of balance may be achieved, at least much of the time.

Interest groups perform certain functions in the American political system that cannot be performed as well through the conventional structures of government, which are based largely on geographic representation.

The kind of *representation* that interest groups provide supplements the representation provided by Congress. Interest groups may also permit the *resolution of intergroup conflicts*. In collective bargaining, for example, differences between two powerful interest groups—management and labor—are resolved. Interest groups also perform a *watchdog* function; they can sound the alarm when new government policies threaten to injure the interests of their members. Finally, interest groups perform the function of *idea initiating;* that is, they generate new ideas that may become government programs. So important are these functions, Lester Milbrath concluded, that "if we had no lobby groups and lobbyists we would probably have to invent them."[49]

Some very serious criticisms can be leveled at interest groups, however. Perhaps the most comprehensive criticism of interest-group politics was formulated by Theodore J. Lowi.[50] Lowi questions the assumption of many scholars and political leaders that the interest-group process in a pluralist society provides a desirable, or satisfactory, way for the government system to work.

What are the effects of interest groups on public policy formation? Lowi argues that there is no assurance that the "pulling and hauling among competing interests" will result in policy decisions that are adequate to meet the social and political problems facing the United States. In Lowi's view, interest-group pluralism has not resulted in "strong, positive government" but in "impotent government" that can "neither plan nor achieve justice."[51] For example, if business groups succeed in weakening environmental legislation, the interests of the larger public may be diminished.

As we have seen, most Americans do not belong to interest groups. Those who do belong tend to come from the better-educated, middle- or upper-class backgrounds that produce citizens with a high degree of political motivation. "The flaw in the pluralist heaven," E. E. Schattschneider has observed, "is that the heavenly chorus sings with a strong upper-class accent. Probably about 90 percent of the people cannot get into the pressure system."[52]

Some of the voter disenchantment with government and political candidates that was visible in recent presidential election years might be attributed, at least in part, to the feeling of many ordinary voters that they had been left out of the political system. And disadvantaged groups—the poor, inner-city blacks, Hispanics, migrant workers—often lack the money to organize to advance their interests. Interest-group politics, in other words, is biased against minorities and in favor of business organizations and other affluent groups.

The ordinary consumer is not as well represented in interest-group politics as are manufacturers. Americans who drive to work in a costly but possibly unsafe car, who are assailed by noisy commercials, who swim at a beach polluted by oil or chemical effluents, who inhale pesticides and smog, and who eat food enhanced with dangerous additives may be forgiven if they wonder what interest group represents them.

There are hundreds of business groups represented in Washington, but a much smaller number of consumer organizations. One reason is that the interest of consumers is so general that it does not lend itself to organized expression as readily as the narrower interest of a special group, such as physicians or truckers. And as Mancur Olson, Jr., pointed out, unless the number of individuals in a group is very small, or unless there is coercion or some special incentive to make individuals work together in their mutual interest, many people will not organize or act to achieve common or group interests through the political process.[53]

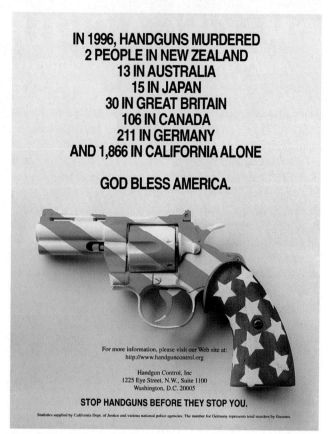

IN 1996, HANDGUNS MURDERED
2 PEOPLE IN NEW ZEALAND
13 IN AUSTRALIA
15 IN JAPAN
30 IN GREAT BRITAIN
106 IN CANADA
211 IN GERMANY
AND 1,866 IN CALIFORNIA ALONE

GOD BLESS AMERICA.

For more information, please visit our Web site at:
http://www.handguncontrol.org
Handgun Control, Inc
1225 Eye Street, N.W., Suite 1100
Washington, D.C. 20005
STOP HANDGUNS BEFORE THEY STOP YOU.
Statistics supplied by California Dept. of Justice and various national police agencies. The number for Germany represents total murders by firearms.

Courtesy Handgun Control, Inc.

Even organized, active interest groups do not represent all they claim to represent. The leaders of an interest group tend to formulate policy positions for the group as a whole. Consequently, the public stance of an interest group often represents the views of an oligarchy rather than the views of the rank and file. The American Medical Association, for example, is more conservative than are many of its 293,000 members. Moreover, more than half of the nation's 650,000 physicians do not even belong to the AMA.

Despite all their flaws, interest groups do supplement formal channels of representation and allow for the expression of public opinion in an organized manner. But if American democracy is to become more responsive to the needs of its people, the nation's legislators must find new ways to heed the voice of ordinary citizens—consumers, the poor, minorities, and the powerless—groups that are much less likely to have a steel-and-glass office building and a team of registered lobbyists to speak for them in Washington.

KEY TERMS

pluralism, p. 195
interest groups, p. 195
lobbying, p. 197

political action committees
  (PACs), p. 206
independent expenditures,
  p. 206

CHAPTER HIGHLIGHTS

✦ Interest groups are private groups that attempt to influence the government to respond to the shared attitudes of their members.

✦ Public opinion, as noted in Chapter 6, is the expression of attitudes on public questions. When people organize to express attitudes held in common and to influence the government to respond to those attitudes, they become members of interest groups.

✦ One of the most powerful techniques of interest groups is lobbying—communication with legislators or other government officials to try to influence their decisions.

✦ One of the ways in which interest groups try to influence public opinion in order to influence government is through mass-publicity campaigns. Using television, magazine, and newspaper advertising, as well as direct mailings to the general public and specialized audiences, interest groups seek to create a favorable climate for their goals.

✦ In recent years, the single-issue interest group has become an increasingly significant phenomenon on the political scene. These groups concentrate on lobbying for or against a particular issue.

✦ Often, single-issue lobbies work through political action committees (PACs), which are sometimes independent organizations, but are more often the political arms of corporations, labor unions, or interest groups established to contribute to candidates or to work for general political goals.

✦ The Federal Regulation of Lobbying Act of 1946 required individuals and groups to register with the clerk of the House and the secretary of the Senate if they solicit or collect money or any other thing of value "to be used principally to aid . . . the passage or defeat of any legislation by the Congress of the United States." The law did not prove effective.

✦ In 1954 the Supreme Court narrowed the scope of the act by ruling that it applied only to lobbyists who communicated directly with members of Congress and not to grass-roots lobbying aimed at the public.

✦ In 1995, a new bill to regulate lobbyists passed both houses of Congress and was signed by President Clinton. Under the law, lobbyists must register with the clerk of the House and the secretary of the Senate, report who their clients are, what agencies or branches of Congress were lobbied, and how much they were paid. In an effort to tighten the rules, the new law defines lobbyists as people who spend at least 20 percent of their time in that activity.

✦ Despite the improvements and the increased disclosure requirements, there was a major loophole in the 1995 law: It did not apply to grass-roots lobbying, which comprises efforts by interest groups to generate phone calls, faxes, e-mails, and letters in support of, or in opposition to, a bill or program.

✦ Interest groups perform certain functions in the American political system that cannot be performed as well through the conventional structures of government, which are based largely on geographic representation.

✦ Most Americans do not belong to interest groups. Those who do tend to come from the better-educated, middle- or upper-class backgrounds that produce citizens with a high degree of political motivation.

✦ Some of the voter disenchantment with government and political candidates that was visible in recent presidential election years might be attributed, at least in part, to the feeling of many ordinary voters that they had been left out of the political system. And disadvantaged groups often lack the money to organize to advance their interests. Interest-group politics, in other words, is biased against minorities and in favor of business organizations and other affluent groups.

SUGGESTED WEB SITES

http://www.opensecrets.org/home/index.asp
The Center for Responsive Politics
A nonpartisan, nonprofit organization that tracks money in politics and its effects on public policy and elections. Contains extensive data about lobbyists, soft money contributions, PACs, presidential and congressional races, and political donors.

www.publicintegrity.org
The Center for Public Integrity
A nonprofit center dedicated to government accountability, ethics, and campaign finance reform. The center's research accessible from the Internet includes selected reports, newsletters, and databases.

www.commoncause.org
Common Cause
A nonprofit, nonpartisan organization that promotes government accountability. Visitors to the Web site can research soft money contributions to the Republican and Democratic parties by donor name, donor location, or industry, as well as news about a wide range of government agencies and topics.

www.publiccitizen.org
Public Citizen
Founded by Ralph Nader in 1971, Public Citizen calls itself "the consumer's eyes and ears in Washington."

Its searchable database includes information about auto safety, congressional voting, and First Amendment issues, as well as the organization's publications.

www.fec.gov
Federal Election Commission
The branch of the federal government that oversees federal elections. The Web site contains a citizens' guide to elections, including current rules for upcoming campaigns, how to support a candidate, and FEC publications.

SUGGESTED READING

Berry, Jeffrey M. *The Interest Group Society,* 3rd edition* (HarperCollins, 1997). An examination of the role of "factions" in American politics and society. Berry argues that interest groups are essential to democracy, and can play a positive role in American politics.

Berry, Jeffrey M. *Lobbying for the People* (Princeton University Press, 1977). A useful and readable analysis of the political and organizational behavior of public interest groups. Using case studies, Berry profiles in detail the activities and strategies of two public interest lobbying organizations.

Baumgartner, Frank, and Leech, Beth L. *Basic Interests: The Importance of Groups in Politics and Political Science* (Princeton University Press, 1998). A scholarly survey of the important role that interest groups have played in the American political process, and as the subjects of research by political scientists.

Cigler, Allan J., and Loomis, Burdett A., eds. *Interest Group Politics,* 5th edition* (CQ Press, 1998). A wide-ranging and informative set of essays on interest-group behavior in the 1990s.

Costain, Anne M., and McFarland, Andrew S., eds. *Social Movements and American Political Institutions* (Rowman and Littlefield, 1998). A useful collection of essays on a number of grass-roots movements in the United States, including Protestant fundamentalists, and coalitions advocating issues for women, protection of the environment, and civil rights.

Dahl, Robert A. *Who Governs?* (Yale University Press, 1961). An influential and detailed exploration of the nature of political power, based on a study of political decision making in New Haven, Connecticut. Dahl maintains that there is a pluralism of power—rather than a single "power elite"—in the United States.

Heinz, John P., Laumann, Edward O., Nelson, Robert L., and Salisbury, Robert H. *The Hollow Core: Private Interests in National Policymaking* (Harvard University Press, 1993). A comprehensive and important survey of interest-group activities in the nation's capital. The study draws upon a large number of personal interviews of both interest-group representatives and the government officials whom they attempt to influence.

Kollman, Ken. *Outside Lobbying: Public Opinion and Interest Group Strategies* (Princeton University Press, 1998). A detailed analysis, drawing upon numerous examples and case studies, of the various ways that interest group leaders in Washington attempt to involve the general public in an effort to influence public policy.

Lowi, Theodore J. *The End of Liberalism: The Second Republic of the United States,* 2nd edition* (Norton, 1979). A stimulating analysis of the theory and practice of interest-group politics in the United States. Lowi is strongly critical of the consequences of the interest-group bargaining process as it has developed since the New Deal.

Mills, C. Wright. *The Power Elite* (Oxford University Press, 1956). One of the best-known statements of the view that there is a unified "power elite" in the United States. In Mills's view, wealth, prestige, and power in America are concentrated in the hands of a hierarchy of corporate, government, and military leaders.

Olson, Mancur, Jr. *The Logic of Collective Action: Public Goods and the Theory of Groups,* revised edition (Harvard University Press, 1971). An important analysis of the role of groups in the American political process. Based on an application of economic analysis to the relationships between individual self-interest and group membership and activity. Examines the consequences these relationships have for politics.

Putnam, Robert. *Bowling Alone: The Collapse and Revival of American Community* (Simon & Schuster, 2000). An influential analysis of community in the United States. The author amasses a large body of research to support his contention that Americans are increasingly disconnected from social institutions, and that this isolation threatens to erode American civil society.

Schlozman, Kay Lehman, and Tierney, John T. *Organized Interests and American Democracy* (Harper & Row, 1986). A comprehensive overview of interest groups in the United States. Among other topics, the book discusses how and why interest groups are formed, their rapid growth in the 1960s and 1970s, and their impact on the political system as a whole.

Truman, David B. *The Governmental Process,* 2nd edition* (Knopf, 1971). An influential study of interest groups in the United States. Develops and modifies a general theory of groups and applies it to American politics.

Walker, Jack L. *Mobilizing Interest Groups in America** (University of Michigan Press, 1991). A thoughtful and valuable analysis of the role of interest groups in the American political system.

Wilcox, Clyde. *God's Warriors* (Johns Hopkins University Press, 1992). A readable account of the religious right in America, and the political role it played during the 20th century.

Woliver, Laura. *From Outrage to Action: The Politics of Grass-Roots Dissent* (University of Illinois Press, 1993). Discusses how grass-roots groups organize and what factors may influence their success or failure. Includes a number of interesting case studies of grass-roots political movements.

---

*Available in paperback edition.

 Visit http://politicalscience.wadsworth.com/cummings9/update/ for current InfoTrac articles and other student resources related to this chapter.

CHAPTER 8
The Media and Politics

On Thanksgiving Day 1999, fishermen found Elián González, a young Cuban boy, lashed to an inner tube in the waters off Fort Lauderdale, Florida. Fourteen people had set off in a small motorboat to make the hazardous trip from Cuba; Elián's mother and 10 others drowned when the boat sank.

What had begun as a tragedy of people attempting to escape the oppressive regime of Fidel Castro, Cuba's leader, quickly developed into a long-running media and political circus. Elián moved in with his great-uncle and other relatives in Miami. Castro and Elián's father in Cuba demanded the return of the boy; the highly vocal Cuban American community in Miami insisted he remain with his relatives in the United States.

Mass demonstrations, orchestrated by Castro, were staged in Havana. The Miami Cubans organized demonstrations of their own, and clashed with police. The Justice Department and a federal court ruled that Elián should be returned to his father. Miami's mayor announced he would not assist federal officials if they came for the boy. Some Cubans in Florida believed Elián's survival was a religious miracle, or that he had been spared to bring freedom to Cuba.

The six-year-old child was showered with gifts, taken to Disney World, interviewed by Diane Sawyer on ABC television, and made the subject, night after night, of extensive coverage on television and in newspapers and magazines. Elián González was big news—so big that on the day his father arrived in Washington to try to reclaim his son, CBS's Dan Rather led the network's evening news broadcast with an interview with President Clinton about Elián. Attorney General Janet Reno flew to Miami, intervening personally to try to resolve the crisis.

The drama of the Cuban child even became caught up in presidential politics in 2000. Vice President Al Gore, assured of the Democratic presidential nomination, and with an eye on Florida's 25 electoral votes, broke with the Clinton administration and urged Congress to pass a law granting permanent residence status to Elián and his father and family. Gore's move upset many Democrats and a few days later he appeared on NBC's *Today Show* and seemed to modify his position, indicating that the boy should be allowed to return to Cuba with his father.

George W. Bush, Gore's Republican rival, attacked the vice president for inconsistency and proclaimed that Elián should be given U.S. citizenship. Both candidates, of course, were hoping to capture Florida, a key southern state with a large Cuban emigré population, in the 2000 presidential election.

Finally at 5:10 A.M. on April 22, there were more dramatic television pictures as armed federal agents, some wearing masks, goggles, and flak jackets, broke into the home of the Miami relatives and seized Elián, who was flown to Washington and reunited with his father, Juan Miguel González. A little more than five hours later, President Clinton appeared before TV cameras on the White House lawn to support the action ordered by Janet Reno. A disturbing photograph of a federal agent with a huge automatic weapon, an MP-5 submachine gun, and a frightened Elián was flashed around the world by the media; it was partly countered by a photograph, released later in the day by the father's lawyer, of the grinning, happy child in his father's arms.

The following month the Supreme Court rejected a final appeal by the Miami relatives to keep the boy in the United States, and on June 28, Elián and his father flew home to Cuba on a private plane. The long drama was over.

But the hoopla and the protracted struggle over Elián's future was a dramatic example of the power of television and the intersection between media and politics. Elián's story was highly visual, from the demonstrations and marches, to Elián playing in his backyard in Miami. It was a good TV story, and the broadcast and cable networks played it for all it was worth. As a result, Gore, Bush, Clinton, assorted members of Congress, and many other political leaders felt they had to take a position in the controversy.

As the Elián story demonstrated once again, technology, especially television, has changed the face of America and its politics. The framers of the Constitution and the Bill of Rights could not have conceived of instant mass communication via TV, let alone the development of the Internet. They could not have predicted a computer network linking the entire world. But if the framers could not foresee the technological changes, they understood the importance of a free press in a democratic system.

As discussed in Chapter 4, however, freedom of the press and freedom of expression are not absolute. Under the Constitution, the Supreme Court has balanced those basic rights against competing needs of society. For example, the press can be sued for libel or for invasion of privacy, or can be prosecuted if it publishes material deemed "obscene" by the courts. And television and radio are subject to regulation by the federal government.

Broadly defined, "the media" include TV, the Internet, newspapers, magazines, radio, wire services, books, and newsletters and other published material. Often, people use the term "the press" interchangeably with "the media" or "the news media." Sometimes, however, they may use the term "the press" more narrowly to refer only to newspapers. In our discussion, we use "the press" in its broadest meaning, to include both print and electronic media.

In this chapter, we will explore a key question: How do the press, the government, and politics interact in the American political system today? Other issues flow from this basic question. For example: Why does the First Amendment of the Constitution protect a free press in America? Has the press grown too powerful? Has television distorted the political process, allowing the candidates with the most money to buy more commercials and win elections? Can government manipulate and manage the news to mislead the voters? Is the press biased? Is tabloid journalism driving out responsible reporting? These and many related questions will be explored.

A PROTECTED INSTITUTION

The First Amendment to the Constitution protects the freedom of the press. It does so because the supporters of the Bill of Rights understood that the press must be free to report about the activities of the government, and, when necessary, to criticize those in power. By contrast, totalitarian systems are usually characterized by censorship and control of the press by the government.

The press plays a vital role in a democracy because it is the principal means by which the people learn about the actions and policies of the government. A democracy rests on the consent of the governed—but in order to give their consent in any meaningful way, the governed must be informed. And a free press remains the major source of information about government and politics. For example, in developing political opinions or in choosing among candidates, most voters rely on the news media—television, newspapers, the Internet, radio, magazines—for their information.

Perhaps no one has explained the special role of the press more eloquently than Supreme Court Justice Hugo Black, in his opinion on the majority side in the famous Pentagon Papers case. He wrote: "The press was protected so that it could bare the secrets of government and inform the people."[1]

The press, in sum, provides a crucial link between the people and the government. It is the essential source of information that helps citizens to form opinions about government and politics and to decide how to cast their votes in elections.

As noted in Chapter 2, freedom of the press was not included in the original draft of the Constitution. But in order to win the struggle for ratification, the framers of the Constitution promised to add a Bill of Rights providing for freedom of the press, speech, religion, and assembly.

In a real sense, then, a free press, free expression, and freedom of thought were the price of nationhood. Having rid themselves of British rule, the new Americans insisted that these hard-won freedoms be spelled out in the basic law of the land, the Constitution. And they were.

The Development of the American Press

Until the 20th century, of course, the press consisted only of print media—newspapers, magazines, books, and pamphlets. The press moguls of the 19th century—men like William Randolph Hearst, owner of the *New York Journal*, and Joseph Pulitzer, publisher of the *New York World*—had great influence on American society and on the government. Hearst beat the drums for a militant foreign policy and helped to whip up public opinion in favor of the Spanish-American War of 1898. Hearst sent the celebrated artist, Frederic Remington, to Cuba. Remington complained that there was no fighting and wanted to come home. Hearst cabled back: "You furnish the pictures and I'll furnish the war."[2] The *Journal* and the *World* outdid each other in reporting alleged Spanish atrocities in Cuba and demanding that the United States intervene. Their sensational reporting became known as "yellow journalism."*

In the first decade of the 20th century, long before the modern term "investigative reporting" came into vogue, a group of writers, journalists, and critics known as **muckrakers** exposed corporate malfeasance and political corruption. They included Lincoln Steffens, who publicized municipal corruption, Ida Tarbell, who

William Randolph Hearst
Culver Pictures

investigated the Standard Oil Company, and Upton Sinclair, whose novel *The Jungle* exposed unsanitary conditions in the meatpacking industry.

The 1920s brought radio into America's homes. For the first time, it allowed political leaders to speak directly to the voters. On March 12, 1933, President Franklin D. Roosevelt delivered the first of what became known as his "fireside chats" on radio, informing citizens that the banks—which had been closed to avoid a panic during the Depression—would reopen the next day.

In 1948, the Democratic National Convention at Philadelphia that nominated Harry Truman for president was televised. Now, presidents could be seen as they spoke to their fellow Americans in their living rooms. Dwight D. Eisenhower allowed his presidential press conferences to be filmed, edited, and then released to the public. Then on January 25, 1961, John F. Kennedy held the first live, televised presidential news conference. Other presidents who followed him have done the same. Typically, presidents also use television to address the nation from the Oval Office in times of crisis.

By providing a direct visual link between political leaders and candidates and the voters, television changed the nature of American politics. Television has had an enormous impact, not only on the political process, but also on the shape and power of the media. With advertisers pouring millions into the TV networks

---

*The phrase had its origin in the battle between the two papers over the rights to publish a popular comic strip known as "The Yellow Kid."

Franklin D. Roosevelt delivers a "fireside chat" in 1938.
Copyright © CORBIS/Bettmann

to reach prime-time audiences, inevitably there were fewer advertising dollars invested in print journalism.

Although movies are not usually thought of as part of the news media, films are an important part of the nation's political culture and may sometimes have more influence than the press. Oliver Stone's *JFK* suggested that government complicity—and various dark conspiracies—were somehow behind the assassination of President Kennedy; although it did not pretend to be a factual documentary, it added fuel to the controversy. The film *A Civil Action* focused on corporate pollution. *The Insider*, star-

ring Al Pacino, criticized the celebrated Mike Wallace and the CBS program *60 Minutes*. And *Erin Brockovich*, a huge box-office hit featuring Julia Roberts, dramatized the issue of groundwater contamination.

The Internet

Just as television had altered the shape of American politics a half-century earlier, by the year 2000 the Internet had brought a dramatic new level of technological change to government and the political process. The White House

1961: President Kennedy in the first presidential press conference broadcast live on television
Copyright © CORBIS/UPI/Bettmann

"On the Internet, nobody knows you're a dog."

and virtually every federal agency each had its own Web site, as did political candidates and parties.

The Internet had its origins in ARPANET, a computer network established in 1969 by the Defense Department to enable research scientists to communicate. In the early 1990s, Congress enacted legislation that expanded the government's computer network and opened it up to commercial networks. In 1994, Netscape released its first browser (software to access the World Wide Web), and the following year, Microsoft released Internet Explorer, its own browser. By the start of the 21st century, there were about 100 million people using the Internet in the United States, a number that was expected to double within three years. Worldwide, some 240 million persons were connected to the Internet. That figure was expected to soar to 600 million by 2003.[3]

As the Internet rapidly expanded, political information, census figures, poll data, the texts of speeches, legislation, Supreme Court decisions, and virtually unlimited resources of all kinds became available at the click of a mouse button, part of a vast ocean of information that once could only be found in major libraries. Television networks, cable networks, and newspapers soon began posting breaking news on their Web sites, instantly accessible to anyone, anywhere in the world, with a computer or other electronic device linked to the Internet. News on the Internet was not limited to that posted by major networks and news organizations. There were hundreds of Internet journalists, as well as a number of online magazines, or "zines," of which *Salon* was the best known. To a great extent, the world had become a global electronic village.

JOURNALISTS USE THE INTERNET, TOO

Some say the Internet poses a threat to print journalists. But, according to a study by Middleberg & Associates, a public relations and marketing agency, print journalists themselves may be among those benefiting most from the Internet.

In a 1999 survey of managing editors and business editors at 1,509 daily newspapers and 2,500 magazines . . . 73 percent said they went online at least once a day, compared with 48 percent in 1998. The new level was the highest percentage-point increase since the survey was first conducted in 1994. That year, only 17 percent of the respondents went online daily.

The study also found trends in the way print journalists use the Internet. In 1999, the most popular use was research. . . . Ninety percent of respondents used the Internet to research articles or as a reference source . . . 83 percent used the Internet for e-mail. . . . In 1999, more than half said they used e-mail at least occasionally to communicate with readers.

Print publications are adapting to new media as well. In 1999, 67 percent of newspapers with Web sites used a common newsroom for Web and print operations. . . . And 40 percent of the respondents said their publications allowed their Web sites to report information before its appearance in their newspaper or magazines.

—*New York Times*, March 20, 2000

A Salon Web page

This artwork first appeared in Salon.com at http://www.Salon.com. An online version remains in the Salon archives. Reprinted with permission.

The AMERICAN PAST
MY LAI: A REPORTER UNCOVERS A MASSACRE

What happened at My Lai is now well known. C Company, First Battalion, Twentieth Infantry, Eleventh Brigade, America Division, entered the village of My Lai on March 16, 1968, and killed between ninety and 130 men, women, and children. Acting, the men said later, under orders from the platoon commander, Lieutenant William L. Calley, Jr., they gathered the villagers into groups and "wasted" them with automatic-weapons fire. Anyone who survived was then picked off. . . .

The army began a full-scale investigation on April 23, 1969, and in September, only days before he was due to be discharged from the army, Lieutenant Calley was charged with the murder of 109 "Oriental human beings." . . .

This fact was made public in a small item, of fewer than a hundred words, put out from Fort Benning, Georgia, by the Associated Press on September 6. The item did not say how many murders Calley had been charged with, and it gave no indication of the circumstances. It is not surprising, therefore, that not a single newspaper or broadcasting station called the AP to ask for more information. . . . That might have been the end of the matter had it not been for a free-lance reporter called Seymour Hersh.

Hersh, then aged thirty-two, had covered the Pentagon in 1966–67 for the Associated Press. . . . It took Hersh two days and twenty-five telephone calls to find out that the civilians numbered 109, and to sense that the story warranted a lot more effort and would require more money than he had. He telephoned Jim Boyd, of the Fund for Investigative Journalism, in Washington, and was promised $1,000. He then flew to Fort Benning and, after an amazing run-around, finally found Calley and on November 11 interviewed him at length. The problem now was where to publish the story. . . . Hersh turned to a little-known Washington agency, the Dispatch News Service, started only a few months earlier by his neighbor, David Obst, aged twenty-three. Obst telephoned some fifty newspapers, offering the story for $100 if it was used. Subsequently, thirty-six of the fifty—including *The Times* of London, the *San Francisco Chronicle*, the *Boston Globe*, and the *St. Louis Post-Dispatch*—ran the story. It was first printed on November 13. . . . Seymour Hersh won a Pulitzer Prize.

—Phillip Knightley, *The First Casualty*

Pulitzer-prize winning journalist and author Seymour M. Hersh exposed the My Lai massacre.
AP/Wide World

Newspapers

A farmer in Nebraska and an attorney in Manhattan may both read newspapers, but the treatment of news about government and politics may be very different in the pages they read. The New Yorker probably reads the *New York Times*, which places heavy emphasis on national and international news gathered by its own reporters. The Nebraskan may read a small-town daily that concentrates on crop reports, wheat prices, and local events and that relies on the wire services for sketchy reports about national and world events.

There are a number of excellent newspapers in the United States. A partial list would include the *New York Times*, the *Washington Post*, the *Los Angeles Times*, the *Wall Street Journal*, the *Dallas Morning News*, the *Boston Globe*, the *Chicago Tribune*, and the *Baltimore Sun*. But for most Americans, who live outside the circulation area of such publications, the outstanding fact about their newspaper is often not its excellence but how limited is its coverage of national and world news.

Online

for more information about the newspapers listed above, see:
www.washingtonpost.com; www.latimes.com; www.wsj.com; www.dallasnews.com; www.boston.com/globe; www.chicagotribune.com; and www.sunspot.net

The movement of Americans from the cities to the suburbs after the Second World War made it difficult for many newspapers, even prestigious ones in large cities, to hold onto their urban readers. The advent of CNN and cable television in the 1980s made further inroads on newspaper circulation. As a result of all these factors, the newspaper industry has been shrinking steadily.

In 1909 there were 2,600 dailies in the United States. By 1955 there were 1,785, by 1986 only 1,657, by 1994 only 1,538, and by 1998 only 1,498.[4] As a result, more and more cities have no competing newspapers—either there is only one daily newspaper or else all the papers are controlled by one owner. By 1999, only 49 cities had competing daily newspapers. New York City, for example, had eight major newspapers in 1948 and just three in 2000.

The loss of newspapers has been accompanied by concentration in the hands of a few owners and the rise of newspaper groups or chains. For readers, the lack of competition may affect the nature of the stories that are published. For example, if a mayor is corrupt but enjoys the support of the city's single newspaper publisher, there is much less likelihood of an exposé than there would be if a rival newspaper existed.

On the other hand, as the number of newspapers has declined, the number of electronic information sources has increased. There were 2,429 television and 12,853 radio stations in the United States in 1999, more than double the number of two decades earlier. National Public Radio (NPR) provides a wide range of programming that often deals with political and social issues. As already noted, cable television programming has expanded dramatically. And millions of people have access to information on the Internet.

Magazines

Citizens who feel that their local newspaper and broadcast outlets fail to provide them with enough news on public issues may, of course, subscribe to a weekly news-

magazine. Only a small percentage of the population does so, however.

The circulation of *Time* is 4,122,699; *Newsweek* is 3,147,497; and *U.S. News & World Report* is 2,195,668. Smaller magazines that comment on public affairs have relatively tiny circulations and are usually struggling to survive. For example, as of 1999, the circulation of *Atlantic Monthly* was 460,121; *Harper's* 212,661; *Mother Jones*, an alternative magazine often highly critical of the government, 150,941; *National Review*, a conservative journal, 150,144; and *New Republic* 95,713.[5]

 for more information about the magazines listed above, see: www.newsweek.com; www.usnews.com; www.theatlantic.com; www.harpers.org; www.motherjones.com; www.nationalreview.com; and www.tnr.com

WHO OWNS THE MEDIA?

By the year 2000, as America began a new century, the shape of the media was changing dramatically. One after another, like large fish gobbling up smaller ones—and sometimes the other way around—the giants of the media were joining in multibillion-dollar mergers.

The pace of change was breathtaking. As an example of the enormous impact of the Internet, America Online, with more than 20 million subscribers, bought Time Warner, becoming the world's biggest media company, with a market value of $342 billion. Time Warner had already bought CNN, the Cable News Network, four years earlier. Federal regulators approved the merger, which meant that AOL owned *Time* magazine, Warner Brothers, CNN, HBO, and Netscape.

Only a few months earlier, Viacom—the company that owned Paramount Pictures (the makers of *Titanic*), Blockbuster, MTV, and book publisher Simon & Schuster had bought CBS. NBC was already owned by General Electric; and in 1995 the Walt Disney Company purchased ABC, which meant that the three major networks were no longer independent.

The mergers were also taking place in the print world. In March 2000, for example, the *Chicago Tribune*'s parent company bought the *Los Angeles Times*. And cable and telecommunications companies were joining forces in the competition to bring high-speed Internet connections to consumers and businesses.

The extraordinary concentration of ownership raised questions about the independence and diversity of the American press. Would ABC be as quick to report the news if a story reflected adversely on Disney? Would NBC expose General Electric if one of its plants was a polluter? Would *Time* magazine be inclined to write anything unfavorable about Steve Case, the billionaire chairman of AOL? Moreover, some analysts believed that the mergers would ultimately mean less competition, more entertainment, less news, and perhaps a tendency to be less responsive to the public. In the days when many big cities had more than one newspaper, for example, the competition

John Carpenter, left, an IRS employee, became the first million-dollar winner on the popular game show Who Wants to Be a Millionaire? He was quizzed by host Regis Philbin.
ABC/AP/Wide World

often resulted in a greater flow of news to the readers. The giant media mergers could also result in a few powerful corporate chiefs pushing their own political views, and reaching a huge audience.

Whatever the future impact of these mergers, the creation of mega-entertainment, information, television, and Internet giants was a reflection of the rapid change brought by the new technology. As the AOL–Time Warner deal illustrated, the new media were buying up the old.

TELEVISION AND THE AMERICAN POLITICAL SYSTEM

With more than 200 million television sets in American homes, the potential for creating an informed public through TV is vast. But it is only a potential; the reality often falls short.

Entertainment is the economic heart of the television industry, and news and public affairs programs occupy only a small part of the broadcast day. True, the cable channel C-SPAN broadcasts the proceedings of the House and Senate, CNN provides full coverage of important events, and public television often carries serious programming about political issues and public policy. But in prime time, the after-dinner hours when millions of Americans are home watching TV, sitcoms, sports, and game shows rule. Entertainment programs such as these, or so-called reality television shows like CBS's Survivor, draw the largest audiences. Advertisers want to sell cars, cruises, and deodorants, and they know that comedy, crime programs, and quiz shows are more likely to achieve that end than, say, a documentary about the high cost of health care.

The six major broadcast networks—CBS, NBC, ABC, Fox, UPN, and The WB—occupy a leading position in the industry. But in recent years CNN, the Cable

News Network, has taken its place alongside them. In the 1980s and 1990s, cable television grew rapidly, reaching more than 65 million homes, or 76 percent of all households with television, by 1999.[6]

Even so, a substantial share of all television revenue goes to the six broadcast networks and the 86 TV stations they own.* Advertising on the six broadcast networks exceeds $12 billion a year.[7] The networks sell popular packaged shows to affiliates across the nation and charge large fees for airing sponsors' commercials during prime time.

The networks command huge fees to enable advertisers to reach large television audiences. In 2000, for example, ABC charged $350,000 per minute of commercial time on Who Wants to Be a Millionaire?, its top-rated game show.[8] For Super Bowl XXXIV, in January 2000, ABC charged some advertisers as much as $2 million for a 30-second commercial.

Audience rating figures are the controlling statistics in the broadcast industry. As already noted, news programs are not as profitable as popular mass-entertainment shows. Still, television is not totally the mindless "wasteland" that one critic once called it.[9] The three older networks—CBS, NBC, and ABC—have evening television news programs that reach a combined total audience of almost 28 million persons each night. (See Figure 8-1.) Other news programs reach millions of viewers on CNN, which broadcasts news 24 hours a day; on the Public Broadcasting System (PBS); over C-SPAN; and on other cable and satellite systems.

Magazine-style news programs, such as 60 Minutes, Dateline, and 20/20, have increased in number in recent years, and they sometimes broadcast stories about politics and government. In addition to news programs, Sunday panel shows such as Meet the Press air political issues, and the commercial networks and public television broadcast a wide range of news documentaries. The networks and many local stations maintain their own news staffs.

Because television reaches millions of homes, news programs and live broadcasts of major events can have a strong influence on public opinion. Television may help to shape or change public opinion, or it may reinforce existing public attitudes.

The searing images in 2001 of the World Trade Center hit by airliners and then collapsing helped to build public support for the Bush administration's war on terrorism. In 1999, there was extensive TV coverage of the bombing of Yugoslavia by U.S. and NATO warplanes, and of the plight of the Muslim refugees who

---

*Data as of March 2000. Before February 1996, television networks or companies were limited in the number of TV stations they could own. The telecommunications bill signed into law that month lifted the restriction, provided the stations belonging to one owner did not reach more than 35 percent of U.S. households.

FIGURE 8-1

Audiences Reached by Leading Media

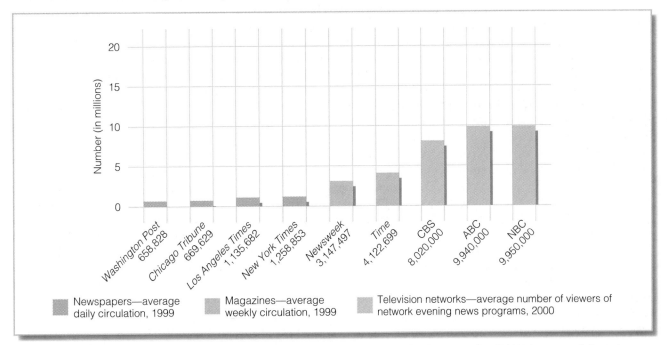

SOURCES: Audit Bureau of Circulations, average paid circulation for the six-month period ending September 30,1999 (newspapers); December 31, 1999 (magazines); and Mediavest as of April 2000.

fled Kosovo to Albania, where they lived in open fields in the mud, cold, and rain. Because of television, the public could hardly ignore the human suffering of the refugees and the Serbian targets of the NATO bombs. In an earlier era, news reports and television pictures of the fighting in Vietnam brought that conflict into American living rooms night after night and were a major factor in swinging public opinion against the war.

During the war in the Persian Gulf in February 1991 and the unsuccessful coup against Soviet leader Mikhail Gorbachev in August of that year, not only the public but even high government officials relied on CNN to bring them minute-by-minute developments. When American planes bombed Baghdad, Iraq, during the Persian Gulf War, viewers watching Peter Arnett on CNN could see it happening. Indeed, in a foreign policy crisis, CNN often brings the news to Washington faster than the government's secure communications channels.

Television has a major impact during presidential election years, when viewers are bombarded with political commercials, many of them negative—attacking opponents—during the primary and general election campaigns. The commercials, even negative ones, do provide information to the voters, although the information is nearly always distorted in favor of the candidate who is paying for the TV ad. In addition, candidates vie to appear on televised talk shows, the networks' morning shows, and even the late-night entertainment programs.

Television provides extensive coverage of the primaries, the national conventions, and the campaigns. More than 90 million people have viewed some of the televised debates among the candidates in presidential election years. Television coverage of hearings and political debates, and the extensive cable and public TV coverage of the national conventions, conveys an immediacy and has an impact that no other medium can approach.

And candidates have often used television to try to defuse a threatened scandal in the midst of a campaign. Near the start of the 1992 presidential election year, for example, Gennifer Flowers, a former lounge singer, claimed in the *Star*, a supermarket tabloid, that she had

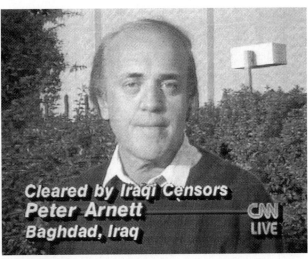

Cleared by Iraqi Censors
Peter Arnett
Baghdad, Iraq
CNN LIVE

Television and the American Political System **223**

engaged in a 12-year affair with Governor Bill Clinton. In an appearance on *60 Minutes* with his wife, Hillary, Clinton denied Flowers's allegations but conceded marital "wrongdoing." Clinton's effective use of television helped to defuse an issue that for a time threatened to derail his presidential ambitions. Six years later, in a deposition in a civil lawsuit, Clinton reportedly acknowledged one sexual encounter with Flowers in 1977 when he was governor of Arkansas.[10]

In the 2000 presidential primaries, millionaire publisher Steve Forbes spent about $32 million—a large chunk of his personal fortune, much of it on television commercials—in his second unsuccessful quest for the Republican presidential nomination. Four years earlier, with unlimited money and access to TV, Forbes, who had no political or government experience, had become a force in the Republican campaign almost overnight. Although there is a danger that a candidate with unlimited money will "buy" an election by saturating the airwaves with political commercials, that does not necessarily happen. Forbes did not win the Republican nomination either in 1996 or 2000. (The issue of money and television in political campaigns is discussed in detail in Chapter 10.)

Television and Radio: A Limited Freedom

Radio and television do not enjoy as much freedom as other segments of the press, because, unlike newspapers, broadcast stations are licensed by the Federal Communications Commission (FCC). Although broadcast networks are not licensed, the stations they own and operate are.

---

 for more information about Federal Communications Commission see:
www.fcc.gov

The FCC does not directly regulate news broadcasts, but stations are required to operate in "the public interest." For example, the Federal Communications Act requires broadcasters to provide **equal time** to all legally qualified political candidates. Under the rule, candidates must be given equal opportunity, if they can afford it, to buy air time for commercials if their opponents have run ads. However, the requirement does not apply to news broadcasts, interviews, and documentaries, nor does it mean that stations must include fringe candidates in televised presidential or other political debates, because debates are considered news.

Stations that ignore the FCC's rules could have their licenses revoked, although the commission has seldom exercised its power to do so. Potentially, however, the federal government has powerful leverage over the operations of the broadcasting industry.

Why is the government able to regulate broadcasters but not the written press? The reason most often advanced is that the broadcast spectrum has a limited number of spaces, and that stations would overlap and interfere with one another if the government did not regulate them. As the Supreme Court has stated, "Unlike other modes of expression, radio (and television) is not available to all."[11] This scarcity theory has been criticized because, in fact, there are more broadcasting stations than newspapers in the United States. And later technology such as the rapid growth of cable television and satellite broadcasts have opened up even more outlets to the public.[12] Indeed, in 1994 the Supreme Court, recognizing technological change, ruled that cable television is entitled to nearly the same constitutional protection as newspapers and magazines.[13]

The First Amendment clearly protects the written press. But the Constitution did not anticipate the invention of television. The result "is a major paradox: TV news, which has the greatest impact on the public, is the most vulnerable and least protected."[14]

In 1969 the Supreme Court specifically rejected the claim of the broadcasting industry that the free press provisions of the First Amendment protected it from government regulation of programs. The Court did so in upholding the FCC's "fairness doctrine," later abolished,

Television has less First Amendment protection than print media. . . . Here TV satellite trucks are clustered outside the White House at the height of the Monica Lewinsky scandal.
AP/Wide World

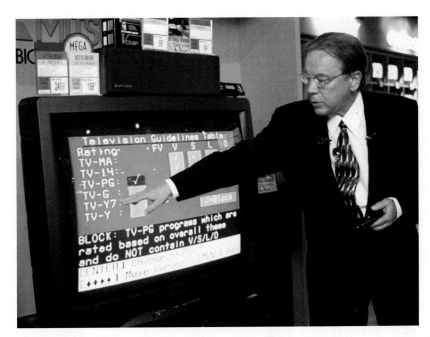

The V-chip allows parents to block television programs they do not want their children to view.
AP/Wide World

that required radio and television broadcasters to present all sides of important public issues.[15] In 1987, the FCC abandoned the fairness doctrine on the grounds that it unconstitutionally restricted the First Amendment rights of broadcasters.

Although the Supreme Court has declined to extend full freedom of the press to broadcasters, it has held that the First Amendment protects the right of broadcasters to report news events.[16] In 1978, however, the Supreme Court ruled in the "seven dirty words" case that the government has the right to prohibit the broadcasting of "patently offensive" language.[17] That case began at 2 P.M. one afternoon in New York City, when a station owned by the Pacifica Foundation broadcast a monologue by comedian George Carlin called "Filthy Words." In it, Carlin gave a detailed analysis of "the words you couldn't say on the public airwaves . . . the ones you definitely wouldn't say, ever." Soon after, a man wrote to the FCC complaining that he heard the broadcast while driving with his young son. The FCC reprimanded the station but later indicated it would permit such broadcasts only at times of the day "when children most likely" would not be listening or watching. It therefore prohibited "indecent speech" over the airwaves between 6 A.M. and 8 P.M.

By the 1996 presidential election year, violence and sex on television, in movies, and in popular music had become a much-debated social issue. Opinion polls showed many voters were concerned over this issue and fearful that the nation had lost its moral compass. Conservatives in particular argued that children and others exposed to a steady diet of TV violence might come to accept violent behavior as normal. In addition, critics contended that violence on television led to crime and violence in society. Many of these same arguments were voiced again after the killings at Columbine High School in Littleton, Colorado, in 1999.

In an effort to give parents more control over what their children watch on television, Congress early in 1996 included a provision in the Telecommunications Reform Act requiring manufacturers to include a "V-chip" in most new television sets. President Clinton signed the measure into law. The chip was designed to allow parents to block out programs that they did not want their children to view.

THE PRESS: LEGAL AND CONSTITUTIONAL ISSUES

Prior Restraint

The strong tradition of a free press in the United States rests on the principle, rooted in English common law, that normally there must be no governmental **prior restraint** of the press—the censoring of news stories by the government prior to publication. The Supreme Court dealt with this issue seven decades ago, when it ruled that a Minneapolis weekly newspaper could not be suppressed because of articles attacking city officials as "corrupt" and "grafters."[18] The Court held that even "miscreant purveyors of scandal" were protected from prior restraint by the First Amendment. But the Court said that the press might be censored in advance by the government in "exceptional cases" relating to national security—during wartime, for example—and it gave as one illustration a news story that might report the sailing date of a troopship.[19]

In 1971 the federal government, claiming that national security was endangered, tried to stop the *New York Times* from continuing to publish a series based on a secret history of the Vietnam War—the so-called Pentagon Papers. For 15 days, the federal

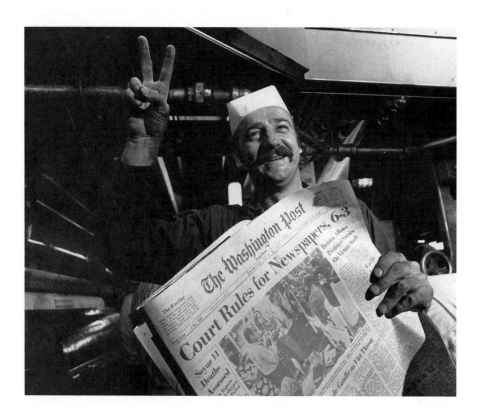

The Pentagon Papers: A Washington Post *printer reacts to the Supreme Court's decision.*
Copyright © CORBIS/UPI/Bettmann

courts restrained publication. Finally, the Supreme Court ruled 6–3 that the *Times* and other newspapers that had been restrained were free to publish.[20] "In the First Amendment," Justice Black wrote in the Pentagon Papers case, "the Founding Fathers gave the free press the protection it must have to fulfill its essential role in our democracy. The press was to serve the governed, not the governors."[21]

The Supreme Court made it clear in 1990, however, that it will not, in every instance, prohibit censorship. It voted 7–2 to let stand a lower court order that barred CNN from broadcasting tape recordings of conversations between Manuel Antonio Noriega, Panama's deposed dictator, and his lawyer.[22]

More often, however, the press has triumphed in the continuing tension between official secrecy and the First Amendment. One of the most dramatic cases took place two decades ago in the city of Milwaukee, Wisconsin.

The Progressive *and the H-Bomb*   In March 1979, in Milwaukee, Federal District Court Judge Robert W. Warren issued an order restraining *The Progressive* magazine from publishing an article on how the hydrogen bomb works. The U.S. government claimed that the article would help other countries to build thermonuclear bombs, bringing civilization "one step closer to its potential destruction in a nuclear holocaust."

The magazine, a liberal monthly journal of opinion, countered that the article disclosed no secrets. According to the magazine, the writer, Howard Morland, had been given no access to classified data and had pieced the story together by interviewing scientists and touring

nuclear plants with the knowledge and permission of the government.

The First Amendment to the Constitution, on its face, might seem to prohibit the government from censoring an article in advance—even an article about the hydrogen bomb. The amendment states that "Congress shall make no law . . . abridging the freedom . . . of the press." But the Supreme Court, the ultimate arbiter of what the Constitution means, has always balanced the First Amendment against other social needs and other parts of the Constitution.

And so Judge Warren, in barring publication of the article, ruled that a hydrogen bomb, if used, would not leave people alive to enjoy their rights under the First Amendment. "You can't speak freely when you're dead," he said.[23]

"Since you have already been convicted by the media, I imagine we can wrap this up pretty quickly."

As the *Progressive* case unfolded, additional facts emerged. A government physicist stated that the magazine article contained no information that could not be learned from the diagrams published by the *Encyclopedia Americana* with an article by Dr. Edward Teller, a physicist known as the "father of the H-bomb."

The *Progressive* appealed, but the U.S. Supreme Court declined to intervene. Then the government dropped its suit because a newspaper in Madison, Wisconsin, had published the very facts the government was trying to suppress. In November 1979, *The Progressive* finally published the Morland article.[24] But for six months the federal government had succeeded in imposing prior restraint on the press.

Despite the outcomes in the *Progressive* case and the Pentagon Papers case, the larger issue remained

unresolved as the 21st century began. The press is protected by the First Amendment, but how far that protection extends is not clear. In the case of the Noriega tapes, for instance, a television network was prohibited from airing material. These battles illustrate one facet of the continuing struggle between the press and the government in American democracy.

As these cases show, freedom of the press is a relative term, applied differently by the Supreme Court at different times. For example, the Court has ruled unanimously that it is unconstitutional to compel a newspaper to provide free space for a political candidate to reply to editorial criticism.[25] The Court thereby rejected the argument that the First Amendment requires citizen "access" to newspapers to present differing viewpoints. But while the Court has usually protected the press under the First Amendment, it also has placed limitations on freedom of the press in several areas.

Free Press and Fair Trial

When basic rights collide, the Supreme Court may be called upon to act as a referee. In recent years the Supreme Court has shown increasing concern over pretrial and courtroom publicity that may prejudice the fair trial of a defendant in a criminal case. The issue brings into direct conflict two basic principles of the Bill of Rights—the right of an accused person to have a fair trial and the right of freedom of the press.

In 1981 the Supreme Court ruled that states could permit trials to be televised. The use of television has continued to raise questions, however. Do cameras in the courtroom affect the right of a defendant to a fair trial? As of 1999, although 48 states allowed cameras in the courtroom, television and cameras were barred from most federal courts, including the Supreme Court. In the words of Supreme Court Justice David H. Souter, "The day you see a camera come into our courtroom, it's

Cameras in the courtroom: Can the defendant receive a fair trial?

The Press: Legal and Constitutional Issues **227**

A crush of reporters surround Stephen Jones, defense attorney for Timothy McVeigh, who was convicted of blowing up the federal building in Oklahoma City.
AP/Wide World

going to roll over my dead body."[26] In 1996, however, federal appeals courts were given the option of televising appellate arguments. Even in the states that allow cameras, judges can exercise their discretion to bar them. And in the wake of the much-televised O. J. Simpson murder trial, many judges did so.

The trial of the former football star, who was accused of killing his former wife and a young man, ended in his acquittal in 1995, as an enormous audience of 150 million people watched the verdict on television. The trial itself was carried live by CNN and Court TV and was covered extensively by the television networks, which often led their evening news broadcasts with the day's events in the Los Angeles courtroom. Comedian Jay Leno frequently commented on the trial on *The Tonight Show*, and as a regular feature he brought out "the dancing Itos," a black-robed male troupe whose members were made up to resemble the trial judge, Lance Ito. The lawyers for both sides became instant celebrities.

Critics of courtroom television have argued that television contributes to a circuslike atmosphere that may reduce the defendant's chance of getting a fair trial. They contend that lawyers play to the cameras, which may increase the length, and cost, of the trial. On the other hand, televised trials permit ordinary citizens, who may never have been in a courtroom, to learn how the legal system operates. And because trials must be open to the public, it can also be argued that television is merely an extension of that principle, bringing the courtroom proceedings to a larger audience.

Closely related to the controversy over cameras in the courtroom is the issue of pretrial publicity. In 1966 the Supreme Court reversed the conviction of a Cleveland, Ohio, osteopath found guilty of bludgeoning his wife to death, ruling that the defendant's constitu-

tional rights had been prejudiced by publicity that gave the trial the "atmosphere of a 'Roman holiday' for the news media."[27] Similar excessive publicity influenced the 1966 decision of the Texas Court of Criminal Appeals to reverse the conviction of Jack Ruby for the murder of Lee Harvey Oswald, the accused assassin of President Kennedy. (However, before Ruby could be retried, he died of illness in January 1967.)

Sometimes, defense lawyers seek to avoid the effects of pretrial publicity by seeking a change of venue—requesting that a trial be moved to another city where the defendant's alleged crime was less publicized. Again, in the age of instant communication, that remedy may often be meaningless.

After a truck bomb blew up the federal building in Oklahoma City on the morning of April 19, 1995, killing 168 people, Timothy McVeigh was arrested as the prime suspect. In the hope of finding impartial jurors, his lawyers succeeded in having the trial moved from the scene of the tragedy to Denver. But in the television era it is unlikely that most people in Colorado were any less aware of the bombing than the citizens of Oklahoma, since the terrorist act was widely publicized in America and all over the world. McVeigh was convicted and sentenced to death.

Although the Supreme Court has recognized the dangers of excessive courtroom publicity, it ruled 7–1 that trials must be open to the public and the press except in the most unusual circumstances. "We hold that the right to attend criminal trials is implicit in the guarantees of the First Amendment," the Court declared.[28]

Confidentiality: Shielding Reporters and Their Sources

The right to have a fair trial often conflicts with the First Amendment in another important area—that of confidentiality for reporters and their news sources.

Journalists argue that they must offer confidential sources complete anonymity, particularly in the case of investigative reporting, when disclosure of the name of a source might lead to reprisals against that person. But what if a news reporter has information vital to the defense in a criminal trial, or which the government needs in order to prove its case? Do reporters have the "privilege" under the First Amendment of refusing to surrender such evidence? The Supreme Court has said no.

In a 1972 decision, the Court explored the question of whether reporters have the constitutional right to protect their sources. Specifically, the Court ruled that the First Amendment did not exempt news reporters from appearing and testifying before state and federal grand juries. The decision came in the case of Earl

Caldwell, a reporter for the *New York Times,* and in two related cases.[29] Caldwell had declined to appear before a federal grand jury to testify about the Black Panthers in the San Francisco area. He argued that merely appearing would destroy his relationship of trust with his confidential news sources. But the Supreme Court said that the investigation by a grand jury of possible crimes was of greater importance to the public than the protection of news sources. The courts had generally taken this position even before the Supreme Court ruled. But some reporters have gone to jail rather than reveal their sources, and many members of the press feel that compelling reporters to testify abridges their First Amendment rights.*

By 1999, some 31 states and the District of Columbia had passed **shield laws** designed to protect reporters from revealing their sources. And Congress had made periodic efforts to enact a federal immunity law for journalists. But many journalists preferred no legislation, arguing that a shield law, even though well intentioned, would violate the First Amendment by defining—and thus limiting—reporters' rights.

Libel

A person defamed by a newspaper or other publication may be able to sue for libel and collect damages because the First Amendment does not protect this form of "free speech." Libel is a published or broadcast report that exposes a person to public contempt or injures the person's reputation. For example, some years ago a New York newspaper suggested that one Stanislaus Zbyszko, a wrestler, was built along the general lines of a gorilla.

New York Times *reporter Earl Caldwell testifies to a House subcommittee.*
Copyright © CORBIS/Bettmann

Near the article, it ran a picture of a particularly hideous-looking anthropoid. The New York State courts held this to be libelous.[30]

Truth has always been an absolute defense in libel cases. That is, if a publication can show that a story is true, the person claiming to have been libeled cannot recover damages. More recently, under the *New York Times* rule, the Supreme Court has made it almost impossible to libel a public official, unless the statement is made with "actual malice"—that is, "with knowledge that it was false or with reckless disregard of whether it was false or not."† Ruling against Alabama officials who had brought a libel suit against the *Times,* the Supreme Court held in 1964 that in a free society "debate on public issues should be uninhibited, robust and wide-open, and . . . may well include vehement . . . attacks on government officials."[31] Later Court decisions expanded the *New York Times* rule to include not only officials but "public figures" such as political candidates and persons involved in events of general or public interest.[32]

But the Supreme Court has greatly narrowed its definition of a public figure. For example, the Court ruled in favor of Mrs. Russell A. Firestone and against *Time* magazine, which inaccurately reported that her husband

---

*Earl Caldwell did not go to jail, because the term of the federal grand jury seeking his testimony had expired by the time the Supreme Court ruled.

†In the Supreme Court's decision, the word "malice" is not used in its commonly understood meaning of "ill will."

REPORTERS' SOURCES: THE JUSTICES DISAGREE

The issue in these cases is whether requiring newsmen to appear and testify before state or federal grand juries abridges the freedom of speech and press guaranteed by the First Amendment. We hold that it does not. . . .

Citizens generally are not constitutionally immune from grand jury subpoenas; and neither the First Amendment nor other constitutional provision protects the average citizen from disclosing to a grand jury information that he has received in confidence. . . .

We are asked . . . to grant newsmen a testimonial privilege that other citizens do not enjoy. This we decline to do.

—Justice Byron R. White in
United States v. *Caldwell* (1972)

The Court's crabbed view of the First Amendment reflects a disturbing insensitivity to the critical role of an independent press in our society. . . . The Court in these cases holds that a newsman has no First Amendment right to protect his sources when called before a grand jury. The Court thus invites state and federal authorities to undermine the historic independence of the press by attempting to annex the journalistic profession as an investigative arm of government.

—Justice Potter Stewart, dissenting in
United States v. *Caldwell*

Comparing Governments

LIBEL: A TOWN CALLED "SUE"

Because of the constitutional protection of freedom of the press and freedom of expression in the United States, it is often difficult to win a libel suit in American courts. This is especially true if the plaintiff is a public figure. Those who are judged to be public figures must not only prove they were defamed, but also that the offending material was published with knowledge that it was false, or with "reckless disregard" of whether it was false. It is a difficult standard of proof.

In Britain, by contrast, where there has historically been greater concern for preserving public reputations, and less protection for free expression, the burden of proof is not on the plaintiff making the accusation, but on the person being accused of libel. The statement in question is presumed to be false, and it is the legal responsibility of the defendant to prove it is true.

Because it is so much easier to win a libel suit in Britain, plaintiffs often choose to sue in British courts when they can, and London has come to be called "a town called Sue" by international media attorneys.

In her 1993 book *Denying the Holocaust: The Growing Assault on Truth and Memory,* Emory University professor Deborah Lipstadt, an American scholar, denounced British historian David Irving as "one of the most dangerous spokespersons for Holocaust denial," and called him a "Hitler partisan . . . a racist and an antisemite." Irving, who has written admiringly of Hitler and denied the existence of gas chambers at Auschwitz, waited until the book was published in England, and then sued Lipstadt and her publisher, Penguin books, for libel in the British courts. Under British libel law, it was Lipstadt's responsibility to show that the accusations she had made against Irving were true. After a trial that lasted five years, involved dozens of expert witnesses, and cost the defense over $3 million, the judge in the case ruled that Lipstadt had been justified in her characterizations of Irving, who had "deliberately misrepresented and manipulated historical evidence" regarding the Holocaust. Because Irving lost, he was required under British law to pay the defendant's legal expenses.

Ironically, it may have been Irving's ability to sue under Britain's plaintiff-friendly libel law which ultimately cost him what had remained of his reputation as a historian of Nazi Germany. "In the U.S., this would have been thrown out of court, but if it had been thrown out, Irving would have been able to say that he never got his day in court," said Ms. Lipstadt after the trial. "I thought, 'This British law is making me jump through hoops.' But he was the one who was stripped naked."

—*Washington Post,* April 12, 2000; *New York Times,* July 22, 2000

---

had been granted a divorce on grounds of adultery (although the judge did note that some of her reported but unsubstantiated extramarital escapades "would have made Dr. Freud's hair curl"). Despite the extensive publicity surrounding the divorce, the Court ruled that Mrs. Firestone was not a public figure.[33]

The Supreme Court's position has left the press vulnerable to libel suits by persons who might—or might not—be considered public figures. The Court narrowed the definition of a public figure even further in 1979. Senator William Proxmire, a Wisconsin Democrat, gave one of his derisive "Golden Fleece" awards to a scientist who had received a half-million dollars in federal funds to study aggression in monkeys. The purpose of the study was to help select crew members for submarines and spacecraft. Proxmire charged in a Senate speech and in news releases and newsletters that the scientist, Ronald R. Hutchinson, had "made a monkey out of the American taxpayer." Hutchinson sued the senator for libel. The Supreme Court said the scientist had not become a public figure by accepting federal funds, and it ruled that while the Constitution protected Proxmire's speeches in the Senate, his press release describing the monkey research was not immune.[34]

Similarly, the Court has ruled that a private person does not automatically become a public figure "just by becoming involved in . . . a matter that attracts public attention."[35] But the Supreme Court permitted a libel award against a novelist, when it let stand a $75,000 judgment against the author of *Touching,* a novel about nude encounter groups.[36] The suit had been brought by a California psychologist who said he was the recognizable model for one of the characters in the book.

In a widely publicized case, General William C. Westmoreland, the former U.S. military commander in Vietnam, sued CBS for $120 million because in a documentary broadcast it had charged that a "conspiracy" existed within the highest levels of the American military to conceal the strength of the communist enemy during the war in Vietnam. In 1985, after the trial had gone on for almost five months, Westmoreland, faced with strong testimony against him and mounting legal bills, dropped the lawsuit.

In 1988, the Supreme Court overturned a $200,000 award to Jerry Falwell for "emotional distress," which the conservative television evangelist claimed he had suffered when *Hustler* magazine published a parody that portrayed Falwell as a drunk having sex with his

Jerry Falwell: The Supreme Court ruled for Hustler.
Copyright © CORBIS/ Bettmann

mother in an outhouse. Although the Court found that the parody was "doubtless gross and repugnant in the eyes of most," it ruled that a public figure was not protected against satire or political cartoons, however "outrageous" or offensive.[37] On the other hand, the Supreme Court has held that expressions of opinion, such as those in a newspaper column, may be libelous if false and defamatory.[38]

In 1991, the Supreme Court dealt with the knotty problem of whether, and to what extent, reporters may alter quotations of persons they interview. The case arose when Jeffrey Masson, director of the Sigmund Freud archives, claimed that quotes attributed to him by journalist Janet Malcolm in the *New Yorker* magazine had been altered or fabricated, which the writer denied. The Court ruled that even "deliberate alteration" of quotes is not grounds for libel unless the alteration resulted "in a material change in the meaning" of the statement.[39]

Despite some victories by the press, the threat of libel actions has become a major problem for the news media, publishers, and writers. In a number of cases, multimillion-dollar damages have been awarded by juries to plaintiffs in libel cases. Most of these big awards were later overturned or reduced by the courts, but some First Amendment students argue that large punitive damages and legal costs in libel cases inhibit press freedom.

Corporations have gone into court to battle the press on other legal grounds as well. In 1992, ABC television broadcast a report charging that Food Lion, the supermarket chain, had sold outdated beef in its stores. Two ABC employees had lied to get jobs with Food Lion for the network's inside report. A jury awarded Food Lion $5.5 million in damages, later reduced by an appeals court to a mere two dollars. But the message to the media was clear; news organizations might pay a price if they engage in fraud even to expose shoddy practices.

Similarly, in 1998 the *Cincinnati Enquirer* paid $10 million to avoid a lawsuit by Chiquita Brands International after the newspaper accused the banana company of bribing foreign officials and carelessly using pesticides that harmed the health of hundreds of workers and others. The newspaper said it acted because its series of articles was apparently based on voice-mail messages stolen from Chiquita by the *Enquirer*'s reporter. Although the banana firm denied the charges, the newspaper said it had no reason to believe the stories themselves were fabricated.

The Press and Terrorism

As Americans discovered in the 1990s, modern urban societies are tempting targets for terrorists. In 1993 Islamic terrorists bombed the World Trade Center in New York, an attack that killed six people and injured more than 1,000. Other terrorists were arrested before they could carry out their plans to blow up bridges, tunnels, and the United Nations headquarters in Manhattan. Then in April 1995 came the bombing of the federal building in Oklahoma City, killing 168 persons.

Some critics of the press argue that giving widespread coverage to such events, or to the school shootings in Littleton, Colorado, and other locales, plays into the hands of the perpetrators, who are seeking publicity for their violent acts. Another argument sometimes voiced is that press coverage can lead to "copycat" acts by others seeking the same notoriety for their deeds or for themselves. The press, however, has a responsibility to report major news events. It could hardly fail to do so in the case of an act of terrorism such as occurred in Oklahoma City, an attack that caused great carnage and shocked the entire nation. The press, after all, is a mirror held up to society. It may sometimes influence events, but it also has the responsibility to report what happens.

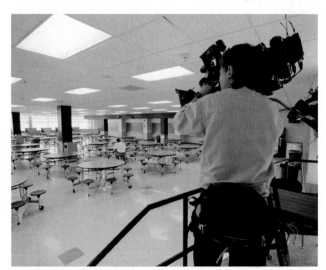

The cafeteria at Columbine High School, Littleton, Colorado, a year after the carnage that killed 12 students and a teacher
Copyright © Reuters NewMedia Inc./CORBIS

At the same time, critics argue that the press does not always exercise restraint in situations where it might do so and still report the news. Is it really necessary, for example, for news helicopters to provide extensive live coverage of high-speed car chases or shootouts on Los Angeles freeways? To news directors making snap decisions under pressure, there are no easy answers to such questions.

A second, more difficult issue is whether the press should, in some instances, agree to the demands of terrorists in order to try to save human life. In 1995, two major newspapers faced this very dilemma in the Unabomber case. For 17 years, an unknown terrorist had sent bombs in the mail. His devices killed three persons and wounded 23 others. From his writings, it appeared that the person whom the FBI called the Unabomber—because his targets included universities and airlines—harbored a deep grudge against the effects of technology on society and against college graduates, scientists, and computer researchers. Then, in 1995, he offered to halt the killings if the *New York Times* or another national publication would print his 35,000-word essay. The *Washington Post*, in cooperation with the *Times*, did so. Critics said that there was

no assurance the Unabomber would keep his word and that the press had opened itself to blackmail by terrorists. A majority of the nation's editors, however, agreed with the decision to publish; they contended that with human lives at stake, there was little choice but to do so.

As it turned out, publication of the manifesto led to the arrest of the suspected Unabomber, Theodore J. Kaczynski. His brother, David, suspicious that some of his sibling's writings resembled the manifesto, notified the authorities. In April 1996, the FBI arrested Theodore Kaczynski at his remote mountain cabin in Montana. Inside, they found a bomb and bomb-making materials. He was tried, pleaded guilty, and sentenced to life in prison.

THE PRESS AND THE GOVERNMENT

Like heavyweight boxers circling each other warily in the ring, the press and the government are adversaries who need each other.

The government often attempts to manipulate the press and to manage the news, to put a favorable "spin" on events. Officials have a vested interest in trying to influence what the press reports, in order to shape public opinion to support administration policies.

Although the press is powerful, so are political leaders. Presidents are well aware that their actions and words tend to dominate the news. They know that the press is obliged to report what they say and do and that the news that presidents generate has a strong influence on public opinion.

The press relies on the government as a crucial source of information. At the same time, the press serves a watchdog function. It is on the alert for stories about incompetence, waste, or outright corruption in the same government it cultivates for information.

To an extent, therefore, the press and government have a relationship that is at once adversarial and mutually dependent. Politicians want to get reelected, and they communicate with the voters for the most part through the press; the press in turn wants to report the news. Sometimes those two forces collide. Yet, each side needs the other.

The public, in turn, relies on the press for its information about government, but is often critical of both. Out of the three-way interaction among the press, the government, and the voters, public opinion emerges and plays its key role in the political process.

News Leaks and "Backgrounders"

Officials at every level of government frequently "leak" stories to the press, divulging information on condition that the officials remain anonymous. The motives for such leaks vary greatly. For instance, a political leader may be launching a "trial balloon," an idea for a new

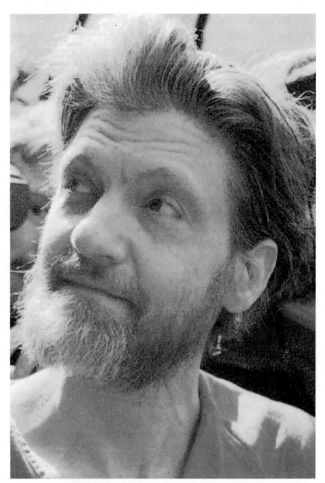

Unabomber Theodore Kaczynski after his arrest by FBI agents in Montana, April 1996
AP/Wide World

policy or program, in order to test public reaction. If the reaction is unfavorable, the administration can deny the program was ever even contemplated. Or a story may be leaked to attack a political opponent in a campaign, to undermine or embarrass an opponent, or to increase public support and sympathy for a political leader. The military services have leaked "secrets" about other countries' weaponry to inflate their own budgets.

But another kind of leak, the unofficial leak at a lower level, often plagues presidents and other political leaders. In Washington, for example, presidents—infuriated by some disclosure or other in the press—have periodically called in the Federal Bureau of Investigation to try to find the source of the leak. President Reagan once said he had "thought of the guillotine" for leakers. But the culprits are almost never uncovered.

During the lengthy investigation by Independent Counsel Kenneth Starr of President Clinton's relationship with Monica Lewinsky, a White House intern, the press reported continually on the progress of the probe, often quoting sources "close to" Starr. Later, Starr confirmed in an interview with editor Steven Brill that he and an assistant had in fact briefed reporters from major news organizations.[40]

There is a great deal of hypocrisy surrounding the periodic outcries over leaks; the same officials who order lie detector tests for government employees to try to stop leaking of classified information may turn around and invite a correspondent to lunch to reveal similar information. And when high officials, including presidents, leave office, they often write books and, in effect, sell secrets to the public in their memoirs.

Although disclosures of information are often deplored by high officials, neither government nor the

Independent counsel Kenneth Starr was a source of news leaks about his investigation of President Clinton.
AP/Wide World

news media could really operate without the institution of the news leak. For the press, one astute observer has commented, the leak is "its lifeline to unauthorized truth."[41]

When a leak takes place in a group setting, it is known as a "backgrounder." Officials in Washington often meet reporters to discuss government policies and plans with the mutual understanding that the information can be attributed only to unnamed "officials" or sometimes not attributed to any source at all.

Max Frankel, when he was chief of the Washington Bureau of the *New York Times,* filed an affidavit in the Pentagon Papers case explaining that officials and reporters "regularly make use of so-called classified, secret, and top secret information. . . . Without the use of 'secrets' . . . there could be no adequate diplomatic, military, and political reporting of the kind our people take for granted, either abroad or in Washington."

SPINNING THE MEDIA

spin—deliberate shading of news perception; attempted control of political reaction.

As a verb meaning "to whirl," *spin* dates back to Old English; by the 1950s, the verb also meant "to deceive," perhaps based on "to spin a yarn." . . . As a current noun, *spin* means "twist" or "interpretation." . . .

During the 1984 presidential campaign, *spin* entered the political lexicon with the phrase *spin doctor.* A *New York Times* editorial on October 21, 1984, commented on the televising of presidential debates:

Tonight at about 9:30, seconds after the Reagan-Mondale debate ends, a bazaar will suddenly materialize in the press room. . . . A dozen men in good suits

and women in silk dresses will circulate smoothly among the reporters, spouting confident opinions. They won't be just press agents trying to impart a favorable spin to a routine release. They'll be the Spin Doctors, senior advisors to the candidates.

Four days after its first print appearance, *spin doctor* was lowercased and defined by Elisabeth Bumiller in the *Washington Post:* "the advisers who talk to reporters and try to put their own spin, or analysis, on the story."

Spin terms have spun several derivatives, from *spin control* by *spin doctors* or *spinmeisters* who have formed a *spin patrol* operating in an area called *spin valley.*

—William Safire, *Safire's New Political Dictionary*

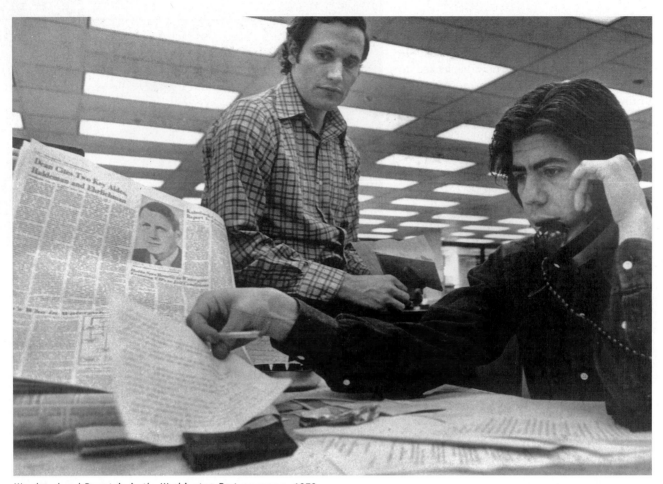

Woodward and Bernstein in the Washington Post *newsroom, 1973*
Copyright © CORBIS/ Bettmann

The *Times* correspondent cited several instances when he had been given secret information: "I remember President Johnson, standing beside me, waist-deep in his Texas swimming pool, recounting for more than an hour his conversation the day before . . . with Prime Minister Kosygin of the Soviet Union . . . for my 'background' information, and subsequent though not immediate use in print. . . . This is the coin of our business and of the officials with whom we regularly deal. . . . The government hides what it can . . . and the press pries out what it can. . . . Each side in this 'game' regularly 'wins' and 'loses' a round or two."[42]

Investigative Reporting

Because the government is such a major source of news, the press is sometimes criticized for relying too much on press releases and "official sources," ranging all the way from the local police chief, to the mayor or governor, to the president's press secretary. The press has been faulted for becoming dependent on these sources instead of digging deeper.

But, especially over the past three decades, the press has shown that it often does dig deeply, investigating a wide range of alleged improprieties both inside the government and in the private sector. The importance of investigative reporting—which relies in part on confidentiality of sources—was dramatically illustrated during the Watergate affair, when reporters Bob Woodward and Carl Bernstein of the *Washington Post* uncovered many details of the break-in at Democratic Party headquarters by burglars employed by the president's campaign, and the cover-up of that crime by the Nixon administration.

In the wake of Watergate, Americans became much more aware of the role of investigative reporting. Although the practice has led to some abuses and considerable criticism, one Gallup poll reported that almost four out of five Americans, or 79 percent, favored investigative reporting, and only 18 percent disapproved.[43]

In recent years, magazine-style television programs on all the networks, modeled after CBS's *60 Minutes*, have broadcast aggressive investigative reports. Many newspapers have continued to publish such stories as well.

Press critics contend that in some cases, the news media carry investigative reporting too far, damaging reputations of corporations, officials, or other individuals in an overzealous effort to expose wrongdoing and win journalism prizes. Some of this criticism comes from officials who are themselves the target of press scrutiny.

MAKING A DIFFERENCE
REPORTING RADIOACTIVE SECRETS

Few journalists look for important stories in seemingly boring places. Eileen Welsome, a reporter for the *Albuquerque Tribune*, possesses the relentless curiosity often deemed necessary for any journalist to achieve greatness. In 1987 that curiosity launched her, then an obscure reporter at a medium-sized New Mexico newspaper, on a quest that would pit her against the U.S. national security and medical power structures.

The story Welsome originally intended to pursue revolved around efforts by the U.S. Air Force to clean up hazardous waste sites throughout the nation. It could be important, sure, but pretty much routine. It was only while studying a dense government report on that topic that Welsome noticed an unexpected local angle: several dumps at Kirtland Air Force Base in Albuquerque.

Buried in those dumps, according to the report, were radioactive animal carcasses. Welsome just visited the base, read dry technical papers there for hours, and decided there was not enough material for a story. Just as she was about to leave, she noticed a footnote describing a human plutonium experiment.

"The information jolted me deeply," Welsome writes. "One minute I was reading about dogs that had been injected with large amounts of plutonium and had subsequently developed radiation sickness and tumors. Suddenly there was this reference to a human experiment. I wondered if the people had experienced the same agonizing deaths as the animals."

Nobody within the government or the medical world wanted to tell Welsome the names of the participants, or much else either, so she chipped away at the puzzle in stolen moments from her regular newspaper stories. She tracked down technical reports, talked to scientists, and used the Freedom of Information Act to ask the U.S. Department of Energy for documents.

As the information trickled in, Welsome learned that 18 people had been injected with plutonium. She started a file for each of the nameless 18 and developed a sketchy profile listing gender, race, date of birth, and the hospitals that originally admitted each person for treatment of a specific disease. These same hospitals administered the plutonium injections, perhaps without the full knowledge of the patients.

Years passed, and she continued to search. Many, perhaps most, beat and general assignment reporters would have given up in discouragement, worn down by the bureaucracy. Not Welsome.

Then Welsome decided to systematically review all the information she had collected in 1992. Two words on a page jumped out at her, words that had failed to register previously. The document said that a government scientist had written "to a physician in Italy, Texas, about contacting patient CAL-3."

"Italy, Texas" were the two words that provided a clue. Based on her painstakingly constructed profile, Welsome knew patient CAL-3 was an African American man who would be about 80 if still alive. She knew he

had been injected with plutonium on July 18, 1947, in a San Francisco hospital where he was apparently being treated for bone cancer.

Looking at a Texas map, Welsome learned that Italy was a small town near Dallas. Welsome started by calling city hall, and she described the man to the clerk who answered the telephone. That would be Elmer Allen, the clerk said without hesitation. He had died a year ago. The clerk gave Welsome the telephone number of Allen's widow, still living in Italy.

Welsome traveled to Texas, talked to Allen's widow and daughter, and then started concentrating on the bigger story. The *Albuquerque Tribune* articles in November 1993 received little attention outside New Mexico until Secretary of Energy Hazel O'Leary held a news conference on December 7, 1993.

She expressed her shock at learning about the experimentation, then promised a new departmental policy of openness. President Bill Clinton followed up by directing other federal agencies to release information about the matter and by appointing an advisory committee on human radiation experiments.

In 1994, Eileen Welsome won the Pulitzer Prize for National Reporting for her articles about the Americans who had been used without their knowledge in the government's secret human plutonium experiments.

—Adapted from Steve Weinberg, "Persistence Pays Off," *IPI Report, The International Journalism Magazine,* First Quarter 2000

But there have also been some instances of unfair investigative reporting. In 1993, for example, NBC was embarrassed, and issued an apology to General Motors, after the network's popular magazine show, *Dateline,* rigged explosions in the gasoline tanks of GM pickup trucks to show how some had blown up on impact, posing a serious safety problem. The problem was real

enough, but the network, in attempting to illustrate it on film, had seriously overstepped the line.

According to one study, two-thirds of the public think journalists "are too focused on the misdeeds and failings of public figures."[44] And almost as many members of the public, 60 percent, think that both national and local news media are "more adversarial than they should be."[45] It is not a perception shared by journalists, however; about two-thirds of journalists in the national and local media did not feel that the press is too adversarial.[46]

Freedom of Information

Freedom of the press is diminished if the news media are unable to obtain information from official agencies of government. Beginning in 1955, Congressman John E. Moss, a California Democrat, pushed for legislation to force the federal government to make more information available to the press and public. As a result, the Freedom of Information Act was signed into law by President Johnson in 1966.

The **Freedom of Information Act** requires federal executive branch and regulatory agencies to make information available to journalists, scholars, and the public unless it falls into one of several confidential categories. Exempted from disclosure, for example, are national security information, personnel files, investigatory records, and the "internal" documents of an agency. The law provides that individuals can go into federal district court to force compliance by the government.

The law was strengthened in 1974 with a number of amendments. One permits federal courts to review whether documents withheld by the government on grounds of national security were properly classified in the first place; another provision requires the government to respond within 10 days to persons who make requests. But the responses are merely acknowledgments that a request has been received; the actual material may not be released—if at all—for months or years. The law, however, has resulted in the release of considerable amounts of information to the public. Nonetheless, a House subcommittee noted that "foot dragging by the federal bureaucracy" had hindered the release of information under the act.[47] Often, federal agencies have refused to release meaningful information under the act unless citizens go into federal court and sue, an expensive and time-consuming process.

While encouraging a greater flow of government information to the public through the Freedom of Information Act, Congress also has responded to demands for tighter control over federal files on individuals. The Privacy Act of 1974 provides that the government may not make public its files about an individual—such as medical, financial, criminal, or employment records—without that person's written consent. The privacy law also generally gives citizens the right of access to information about themselves in government files.

In the field of national security and foreign policy, government secrecy is supported by a formal security classification system. Under executive orders issued by every president since Truman in 1951, thousands of officials can stamp documents Top Secret, Secret, or Confidential if, in their judgment, disclosure would jeopardize national security. Under this system, millions of government documents are classified every year.

Beginning with President Kennedy, most presidents have issued executive orders providing that at least some secret documents be automatically declassified after a certain number of years.

In 1980 the Supreme Court ruled that CIA employees who sign secrecy agreements were not free to publish books about their experiences without prior agency approval.[48] The Court ruled that Frank W. Snepp, III, a former CIA officer in Vietnam, had to give the government the royalties earned from his book *Decent Interval*, even though it contained no classified information. The Court declined to consider Snepp's argument that the secrecy agreement he had signed violated his First Amendment rights.

The Press as Target

Inevitably, a free press that investigates and reports on the government will itself become a target of government attacks. Because the press wields great power and influence in American politics, it has become a target for such attacks, not only by government officials but by many private citizens, organizations, and other critics.

When a bomb went off in Atlanta during the summer Olympics in 1996, killing one person and injuring more than 100 others, Richard Jewell, a security guard at Olympic Park, fell under suspicion. Jewell had discovered the knapsack containing the device and had helped to move people away from the bomb, but his name was leaked to the press as a suspect. A media frenzy resulted, amid speculation that Jewell had planted the device in order to "discover" it so that his action might help him obtain a job in law enforcement. The FBI interrogated Jewell, who was finally and officially removed as a suspect three months later. He settled a threatened libel lawsuit against NBC for an undisclosed amount of money, and sued the parent corporation of the *Atlanta Journal-Constitution* over the newspaper's coverage. The performance of both the FBI and the news media in the controversy was widely criticized.

In an earlier time, under President Nixon, criticism of the news media was encouraged by various government actions and by attacks on the press by high administration officials. In a celebrated speech in November 1969, Vice President Spiro T. Agnew assailed "a small band of network commentators and self-appointed analysts" who had discussed a televised address to the nation by President Nixon.[49] A week later, Agnew attacked the *Washington Post* and the *New York Times*.

Possibly some of these government pressures on the press were designed to divert public attention from the question of the government's own truthfulness; the Nixon administration in time became ensnared in scandals that led to the resignation of both Nixon and Agnew. At the same time, pressures on the press also

After the news media publicized security guard Richard Jewell as a suspect in the 1996 bombing of Olympic Park in Atlanta, Jewell sued.
AP/Wide World

seemed designed to persuade the news media to temper their criticism and present news about the government in a more favorable light.

In this respect, the television networks are potentially in a vulnerable position, because they are composed of stations licensed by the federal government. Jeb Stuart Magruder, while an assistant to President Nixon, suggested in a memo that the administration could "get the media" by such tactics as threatening IRS investigations of news organizations.

During the Watergate episode, however, there was wide recognition of the fact that the press, and particularly the *Washington Post,* had played a significant role in uncovering the massive abuse of power by the Nixon White House. The disclosures by the press helped to shape public opinion and were one factor among many leading to Nixon's resignation as president.

Although the press is sometimes attacked by government officials, it is also true that presidents and other political leaders are often cautious in their criticism of the news media, because they recognize the power of the press to influence public opinion.

Criticism of the press is not limited to government officials, however. As poll data show, the public has a low level of confidence in the press. (For example, see Table 8-1.) Some critics attribute hostility toward the press partly to the fact that several correspondents in Washington have become media "stars" who appear on weekly political talk shows and command huge speaking fees from the very industries and groups they may cover. And one correspondent, Sam Donaldson, "whose base pay from ABC is approximately $2 million per year," claimed "nearly $97,000 in sheep and mohair subsidies" from the federal government for ranches he owned in New Mexico.[50] Another ABC star, *Nightline*'s Ted Koppel,

A VICE PRESIDENT ATTACKS THE PRESS

In November of 1969 network analysts criticized an address by President Nixon in which the president defended his policy to end the Vietnam War. Ten days later, Vice President Spiro T. Agnew flew to Des Moines, Iowa, and delivered a famous speech blasting the news media:

The purpose of my remarks tonight is to focus your attention on this little group of men who not only enjoy a right of instant rebuttal to every presidential address, but . . . wield a free hand in selecting, presenting and interpreting the great issues of our Nation [on the evening newscasts]. . . . These commentators and producers live and work in the geographical and intellectual confines of Washington, D.C., and New York City. . . . [They] draw their political and social views

from the same sources. Worse, they talk constantly to one another, thereby providing artificial reinforcement to their shared viewpoints. . . .

The American people would rightly not tolerate this kind of concentration of power in government.

Is it not fair and relevant to question its concentration in the hands of a tiny and closed fraternity of privileged men, elected by no one, and enjoying a monopoly sanctioned and licensed by government?

The views of this fraternity do not represent the views of America.

—Quoted in John Anthony Maltese, *Spin Control:*
The White House Office of Communications
and the Management of Presidential News

TABLE 8-1

The Public Views the Press

Does the press go too far in pursuing the truth?	Should journalists be licensed like doctors?
Yes: 49%	Yes: 41%
No: 36%	No: 50%
Overall, what is your opinion of the news media?	Hostage at gunpoint on live TV: Should a station broadcast?
Favorable: 45.5%	Yes: 22%
Unfavorable: 44.6%	No: 74%
Other: 10.0%	
From where do you get most of your news?	Would you watch?
Television: 49.5%	Yes: 59%
Newspaper: 25.5%	No: 38%
Radio: 11.0%	
Newsmagazine: 5.0%	Should executions be shown on television?
Internet: 4.9%	Yes: 20%
Other: 4.1%	No: 76%
Should journalists covering politics have to reveal their own leanings?	Would you watch?
Yes: 48%	Yes: 21%
No: 45%	No: 65%

SOURCE: Frank Luntz, *Brill's Content*, March 2000, pp. 74–79, 114.

reportedly charges $50,000 per speech.[51] One critic of the large speaking fees earned by some journalists declared: "The bluntest way to criticize journalists on the lecture trail is to say, simply, that they are corrupt."[52] At the very least, acceptance of large speaking fees may open up journalists to charges of possible conflict of interest.

Some of the hostility to the press probably stems from the perception that it wields too much power. A Harris poll taken early in the year 2000 reported that 77 percent of the public thought the press had "too much" power, and only 8 percent thought the press had "too little" power.[53] Asked by a Roper survey whether a president or the news media had more influence on events,

ABC's Sam Donaldson: Many media stars lecture for large fees.
Timothy White/ABC

73 percent answered "the news media," and only 18 percent chose "the president."[54] And despite the First Amendment, a remarkable 53 percent of respondents in a 1999 poll thought the press had "too much . . . freedom to do what it wants."[55]

Some critics of the news media have suggested that the press should involve itself in "civic journalism"— that it should use its power and influence to encourage voters and communities to become more involved in politics. As one example, advocates of this approach have suggested, a newspaper might poll its readers and urge political candidates to comment on issues that voters say they are concerned about. But others strongly reject this type of activist role for news organizations, arguing that the press should not try to shape events or join forces to pressure candidates to discuss particular issues. Many editors and journalists contend that the job of the press is to report the news. (See Table 8-2.)

Is the Press Biased? Some critics contend that the press is biased, unfair, or inaccurate in its reporting of public issues. Some of this type of criticism stems from conservatives who feel the press is too "liberal." Even among the general public, only 13 percent of those questioned in one poll had a "great deal" of confidence in the press; 54 percent had "only some" confidence.[56] On the other hand, public confidence was low for many major institutions, including Congress, business, and organized labor.

TABLE 8-2

The Press Views Itself

National journalists and news media executives were asked in the following survey to say whether they agreed with various criticisms of the press.

Criticism	% Who Agree
Reporting full of errors	40
News organizations are moving too far into entertainment	74*
Distinction between reporting and commentary blurred	69
Too adversarial	34
Too little attention to complex issues	71
Out of touch with the public	57

*News staff; for management the figure was 65%.
SOURCE: The Pew Research Center for the People and the Press, data for 1999, online at <www.people-press.org>.

In another survey conducted early in 2000, some 32 percent of respondents said they saw "a great deal" of political bias in news coverage, and 37 percent saw "a fair amount" of bias.[57] On the other hand, the perception of political bias lies partly in the eye of the beholder; a Gallup poll taken during the Senate impeachment trial of President Clinton reported that 63 percent of Republicans thought the media was biased in favor of Clinton, but 48 percent of Democrats thought the press was biased against the president.[58]

What are the political views of members of the press? In one study, only 2 percent of the national and local press considered themselves "very liberal," and only 1 percent of both groups said they were "very conservative." While 22 percent of the national and 14 percent of the local press characterized themselves as "liberal," the overwhelming majority—64 percent—of both the national and local news media called themselves "moderates." Four percent of the national press and 17 percent of local press described themselves as "conservative." Among talk radio hosts, however, a significantly higher number, 36 percent, described themselves as "conservative" or "very conservative."[59] (Also see Figure 8-2.) Conservative talk radio hosts such as Rush Limbaugh have a large

FIGURE 8-2

The Politics of the Press: How Reporters and Broadcasters Describe Themselves

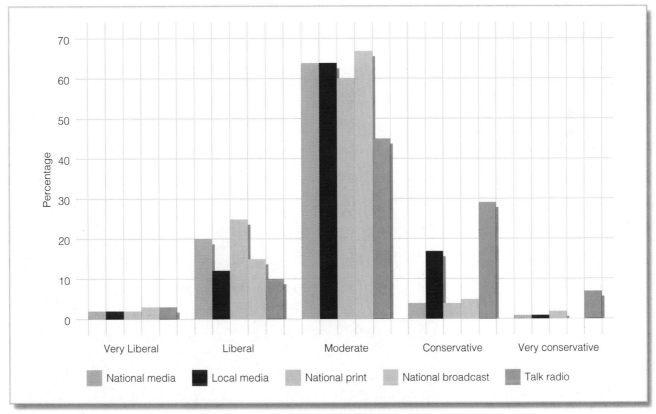

SOURCE: Adapted from *The People, the Press & Their Leaders, 1995* (Washington, D.C.: The Times Mirror Center for the People & the Press, 1995), p. 115.

following and at times their views have had considerable political impact.

One survey of political party identification among reporters showed that 44.4 percent identified themselves as Democrats, 34.4 percent as Republicans, and 16.3 percent as independents.[60]

Critics of the news media argue that bias in reporting is not simply a question of party identification among journalists; conservatives argue that the media are culturally liberal, in favor of gay rights, against religion, pro-abortion, permissive about pornography, and closer to the views of liberal or moderate Supreme Court justices, rather than to conservatives such as Chief Justice William H. Rehnquist or Justices Clarence Thomas and Antonin Scalia.

Measuring the political or cultural views or party affiliations of members of the press, however, tells only part of the story. A more relevant question—the real test—is whether "news *as reported to the public* is biased."[61] The focus on the economic, social, and political background or personal beliefs of members of the press implies that reporters' politics will always necessarily be reflected in their stories. But members of the press, like doctors, social scientists, judges, and many other people, are daily called upon to make "objective" judgments. While complete "objectivity" may not be possible, most news reporters strive for accuracy even if they do not always achieve it.

And if reporters in Washington are biased in favor of Democrats, as conservatives often claim, it is difficult to explain why presidents Kennedy and Johnson, both Democrats, complained bitterly about their treatment in the press. The long-running Whitewater affair, a constant irritant to President Clinton, a Democrat, was first brought to public attention in 1992 by the *New York Times*, often considered the most prominent liberal paper in the country. In its editorials, the *Times* consistently accused both the president and his wife, Hillary, of delay in turning over documents to the independent prosecutor and to Congress and of evading questions about the scandal. And the press provided extensive coverage of Clinton's troubles over Monica Lewinsky and the charges by two other women, Kathleen Willey and Paula Jones, who claimed he had made improper sexual advances against them.

Some critics of the press have suggested that the media failed to report the sexual indiscretions of President Kennedy because he was a Democrat and well-liked by many reporters. However, in the 1960s, by common consent, correspondents as a rule did not write about the private lives of public figures. It was another era. If a reporter wrote about Kennedy's affairs, his publisher in those years would almost certainly have declined to print the story. Moreover, there is a big difference between reporters being "aware" of a president's sexual liaisons, as many were, and being able to prove it. No responsible reporter would write a story based on mere rumor.

Times have changed; with the increased openness about sexual matters in society today, the press had no hesitation in reporting about the sexual activities of President Clinton. But there was another crucial difference; the two women made highly public charges against the president, and one, Paula Jones, sued him in federal court for sexual harassment. The Lewinsky affair was investigated by independent Counsel Kenneth W. Starr,

NBC's Andrea Mitchell asks President Clinton a question at a White House press conference.
Copyright © Paul Conklin/PhotoEdit

who filed a 445-page report containing explicit sexual details. These were legitimate, dramatic news stories, and the press reported them.

Government Misinformation and the Press

Sometimes the government does not tell the truth to the press. It may mislead the press—and therefore the public—for a variety of reasons, for example: to put a favorable "spin" on the news, to cover up wrongdoing, to conceal a foreign policy maneuver, or to protect a military or intelligence operation.

The Eisenhower administration lied when it denied at first that the CIA's U-2 spy plane had deliberately flown over the Soviet Union. The Kennedy administration falsely said it had not intervened in Cuba at the time of the Bay of Pigs invasion by CIA-supported exiles. Lyndon Johnson persuaded Congress to support the war in Vietnam by making public a misleading account of an attack on American warships in the Tonkin Gulf. Nixon lied about Watergate. Clinton lied about his affair with Monica Lewinsky.

When the government puts out misleading information and that fact becomes known, it almost inevitably lowers public confidence in government. During the Johnson administration, the difference between the government's actions and its words became known as the "credibility gap."

Sometimes, as noted above, the government misleads the public in order to protect an intelligence operation. Closely related to this practice is the issue of whether the Central Intelligence Agency may use journalistic "cover" for espionage—that is, to employ spies posing as "journalists" or to recruit real journalists to gather intelligence.

Until 1977, the CIA was free to do both. In that year, the CIA banned the practice—after it was exposed by a Senate investigating committee—but with a loophole that allowed the CIA director to approve exceptions to the rule. Most journalists are opposed to the practice, because if some CIA officers pose as reporters or some journalists work as spies, then all American reporters could be suspect, and at risk, in many parts of the world.

During the 1990s there was concern among law enforcement authorities and the public about the apparent increase in the number of right-wing armed "militia" groups in the United States. The militias harbored a deep distrust of government, especially the federal government, which its members viewed as a threat to their safety and freedom. Whether this distrust of the government is related to the fact that the government has not always been truthful in its public statements is difficult to measure. But certainly suspicion of political leaders is fueled when they release information that is later revealed to be untrue or misleading.

The Press and the Military

Special problems arise when the press attempts to cover a war. Here, the desire of the news media for information may collide with the military's responsibility to protect the security of its troops and its battle plans. For example, strict censorship was imposed by the government on the press during the Second World War.

The military may also impose restrictions for another reason: to present its actions—and government policy—in the best possible light. During the Vietnam War, the military and the White House constantly reassured the public that the United States was winning the war. But a small group of reporters in

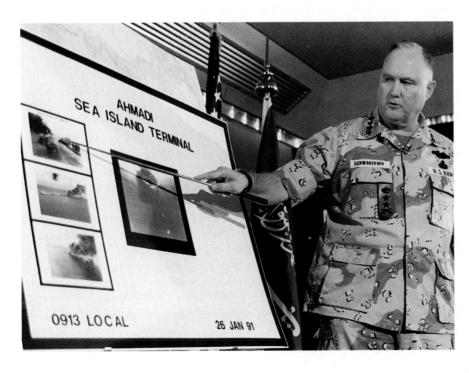

General H. Norman Schwarzkopf briefs the media during the Persian Gulf War.
AP/Wide World

On the anniversary of Iraq's invasion of Kuwait, many journalists described also falling in defeat to the U.S. Government due to censorship and Pentagon propaganda.

Painful examples abound, including buying into exaggerated figures on Iraqi troop strength, inflating the success and significance of "smart bombs" and Patriot missiles and hiding the thousands of Iraqi dead by confining reporters and camera crews to press pools that—with few exceptions—never got to the scene of actual fighting. Overall, Americans got a more realistic view of the war from a few journalists who remained in Baghdad (and who were widely denounced for it!) than they did from the press corralled far from the battlefield.

—John R. MacArthur, in an Op-Ed article,
New York Times, July 27, 1992

Vietnam wrote stories that contradicted official policy and presented a much more realistic picture of the quagmire from which the United States eventually retreated.

Often, in military operations, the press is confined to "pools," in which a few designated reporters are allowed to visit a particular area and are then expected to brief the rest of the press. This practice prevailed during the Persian Gulf War in 1991, when combat reporting was limited to small pools of correspondents whose movements were restricted and controlled by the military.

After the war, Secretary of State James Baker declared, perhaps only half in jest: "The Gulf War was quite a victory. But who could not be moved by the sight of that poor demoralized rabble—outwitted, outflanked, outmaneuvered by the U.S. military. But I think, given time, the press will bounce back."[62]

In the wake of the Gulf War, a new set of rules was drawn up in negotiations between the Pentagon and representatives of the press. The new regulations provided that pools would be used only when necessary and for brief periods. The Pentagon agreed to honor "open and independent reporting" in future wars. However, the military refused to drop its requirements that it review all stories filed from the battle zone before publication.

THE PRESS IN A DEMOCRATIC SOCIETY

As we have seen, there are considerable pressures on the American press. The rapid expansion of television has resulted in a struggle for survival by many newspapers.

The growth of cable TV, in turn, has placed economic pressures on the television networks. Media mergers have created economic giants and raised questions about the independence of news organizations subject to control by their corporate masters.

Exploding changes in technology and the rise of the Internet and online services have already had an impact on how news is gathered and presented to the public. The future will undoubtedly bring even more changes. Newspapers may be printed on home computers, to take one example, instead of being delivered to the front door; television sets as small as wristwatches may become as common as cellular phones. And those phones, originally used only for voice communication, are now often capable of surfing the Internet. The whole future of the communications industry is one of rapid change.

The increased popularity of tabloid-style television news programs and talk shows has had a discernible impact on broadcast news. Television news has adapted to this trend by packaging information in ways designed to "entertain" viewers. And the news divisions of the TV networks are under constant pressure to cut back their budgets, as more money is poured into sitcoms and other light fare.

The press is a business. Publishers and broadcasters may speak of their responsibility to inform the public and of their special role in the political system under the First Amendment. But they also keep a close eye on the bottom line. If they fail to make a profit, they may go under.

Despite its shortcomings—the lack of high-quality newspapers in many communities, for example—a free press in the United States is essential to the functioning of the American democracy and a vital link between the public and the government.

Public opinion is formed on the basis of what the news media present to the public. Democratic government rests broadly on public opinion and presupposes a fairly well-informed public. (The role of the press in political campaigns is discussed in Chapter 10, and the relationship between the president and the press is discussed in Chapter 13.)

Aside from its role of informing the general public, the American press, particularly the high-quality newspapers, magazines, and television news programs, does an excellent job of informing those who are politically aware—politicians, opinion leaders, political scientists, lawyers, journalists, college students, and others who are attuned to politics.

There is nothing about democracy that guarantees an alert, educated public. Like voting and other forms of political participation, knowledge of public affairs—the basis of intelligent public opinion—is largely up to the individual. Information about public affairs, however, is available to those who want it. It is gathered, published, broadcast, and posted online by the nation's free press, operating under the protection of the U.S. Constitution.

KEY TERMS

muckrakers, p. 217
equal time, p. 224
prior restraint, p. 225

shield laws, p. 229
Freedom of Information
Act, p. 236

CHAPTER HIGHLIGHTS

✦ The First Amendment to the Constitution protects the freedom of the press. It does so because the supporters of the Bill of Rights understood that the press must be free to report about the activities of the government, and, when necessary, to criticize those in power.

✦ Freedom of the press and freedom of expression are not absolute. Under the Constitution, the Supreme Court has balanced those basic rights against competing needs of society.

✦ Broadly defined, "the media" include TV, the Internet, newspapers, magazines, radio, wire services, books, newsletters, and other published material. Often, as this book does, people use the term "the press" interchangeably with "the media" or "the news media."

✦ The press plays a vital role in a democracy because it is the principal means by which the people learn about the actions and policies of the government. A democracy rests on the consent of the governed, but in order to give their consent in any meaningful way, the governed must be informed.

✦ The press provides a crucial link between the people and the government. It is the essential source of information that helps citizens form opinions about government and politics and decide how to cast their votes in elections.

✦ Until the 20th century, the press consisted only of print media—newspapers, magazines, books, and pamphlets. The press moguls of the 19th century had great influence on American society and on the government. Eventually, sensational reporting in their newspapers became known as "yellow journalism."

✦ In the first decade of the 20th century, long before the modern term "investigative reporting" came into vogue, a group of writers, journalists, and critics known as muckrakers exposed corporate malfeasance and political corruption.

✦ The 20th century brought radio into America's homes. For the first time, it allowed political leaders to speak directly to the voters.

✦ By providing a direct link between political leaders and candidates and voters, television changed the nature of American politics. Television made an enormous impact, not only on the political process, but also on the shape and power of the media. As advertisers poured millions into the TV networks to reach prime-time audiences, inevitably there were fewer advertising dollars invested in print journalism.

✦ Just as television had altered the shape of American politics a half-century earlier, by the year 2000 the Internet had brought a dramatic new level of technological change to government and the political process. Political information, census figures, poll data, the text of speeches, legislation, Supreme Court decisions, and virtually unlimited resources of all kinds became available at the click of a mouse button, part of a vast ocean of information that once could only be found in major libraries.

✦ By the year 2000 the shape of the media was changing dramatically. One after another, the giants of the media were joining in multibillion-dollar mergers. The concentration of ownership raised questions about the independence and diversity of the American press.

✦ Radio and television do not enjoy as much freedom as other segments of the press, because, unlike newspapers, broadcast stations are licensed by the Federal Communications Commission. Although broadcast networks are not licensed, the stations they own and operate are. The law requires broadcasters to provide "equal time" to all legally qualified political candidates.

✦ In recent years the Supreme Court has shown increasing concern over pretrial and courtroom publicity that may prejudice the fair trial of a defendant in a criminal case. The right to have a fair trial often conflicts with the First Amendment in another important area—that of confidentiality for reporters and their news sources. The Supreme Court has ruled that reporters must reveal the identity of their sources if the information is needed in a criminal case.

✦ A person defamed by a newspaper or other publication may be able to sue for libel and collect damages because the First Amendment does not protect this form of "free speech." Despite some victories by the press, the threat of libel actions has become a major problem for the news media, publishers, and writers.

✦ Some critics of the press argue that giving widespread coverage to acts of terrorism plays into the hands of the perpetrators, who are seeking publicity. Another argument sometimes voiced is that press coverage can lead to "copycat" acts by others seeking the same notoriety for their deeds or for themselves. The press, however, has a responsibility to report major news events.

✦ The government often attempts to manipulate the press and to manage the news, to put a favorable "spin" on events. It may even mislead the press—and therefore the public—for a variety of reasons. Officials have a vested interest in trying to influence what the press reports, in order to shape public opinion to support administration policies.

✦ The Freedom of Information Act requires federal executive branch and regulatory agencies to make information available to journalists and other persons unless it falls into one of several confidential categories.

✦ Because the press wields great power and influence in American politics it has become a target of criticism. Some critics contend that the press is politically biased. However, poll data suggest that almost two-thirds of the members of the press consider themselves moderate, rather than liberal or conservative.

✦ Exploding changes in technology, and the rise of the Internet and online computer services, has already had an impact on how news is gathered and presented to the public.

SUGGESTED WEB SITES

www.freedomforum.org
Freedom Forum
Freedom Forum is a nonpartisan, international foundation that provides information about the freedoms covered by the First Amendment, including freedom of the press and freedom of speech.

http://www.pbs.org/mediamatters/index.shtml
Media Matters
Media Matters examines important and current topics in journalism. Included are polls, videos, and an in-depth look at such topics as what the media report and why, the future of the media, and common media practices.

www.newseum.com
Newseum
The Internet version of news museums located in New York City and Washington, D.C. This Web site offers exhibits that focus on the past, present, and future of the news business.

www.journalism.org/concern.html
Committee of Concerned Journalists
A consortium of reporters, editors, producers, publishers, owners, and academics. Visitors can read reports, studies, essays, and articles about the future of journalism.

www.cjr.org
Columbia Journalism Review
This Web site is the online version of *Columbia Journalism Review,* a magazine that covers issues affecting the media. Resources on the site include lists of which corporations own the media; special reports on the issues involved in covering controversial topics such as AIDS, tobacco, mental health care, and money and politics; and links to other journalism Web sites.

SUGGESTED READING

Barber, James David. *The Pulse of Politics: Electing Presidents in the Media Age** (Transaction Publications, 1992). An interesting study of presidential campaigns and presidencies in the 20th century. Emphasizes the role played by journalists and the news media in presidential politics.

Bennett, W. Lance, and Paletz, David L. *Taken by Storm: The Media, Public Opinion, and U.S. Foreign Policy in the Gulf War** (University of Chicago Press, 1994). An illuminating series of essays by academic specialists and journalists analyzing the performance of the press and of the government during the Persian Gulf War.

Entman, Robert M. *Democracy without Citizens: Media and the Decay of American Politics** (Oxford University Press, 1989). A searching critique of American journalism and its role in the political process. Argues that the way the media operate almost compels politicians to be demagogues.

Fallows, James. *Breaking the News: How the Media Undermine American Democracy** (Pantheon Books, 1996). A highly critical view of the press by a Washington writer. Fallows criticizes journalists for such practices as emphasizing political strategies and personalities over issues and for accepting large speaking fees from business and other interest groups.

Frankel, Max. *The Times of My Life: And My Life with the* Times (Random House, 1999). A fascinating autobiography by the reporter who became the executive editor of the *New York Times.* Provides revealing insights into the politics and conflicts inside the world's most prestigious newspaper.

Graber, Doris A. *Mass Media and American Politics,* 5th edition* (CQ Press, 1996). A comprehensive survey of the role of the mass media in American politics. Stresses the impact that the media have on citizens' attitudes and perceptions, and argues that the mass media are exerting a growing influence on social values and public policy.

Graber, Doris A. *Media Power in Politics,* 4th edition* (CQ Press, 2000). A summary of the history of the mass media. Emphasizes the ability of the media to shape the political agenda.

Hersh, Seymour M. *My Lai 4: A Report on the Massacre and Its Aftermath* (Random House, 1970). A detailed reconstruction by a leading investigative journalist of the events that led to the murder of more than 100 civilians in a South Vietnam village by American troops in 1968. Hersh's account of the My Lai massacre earned him the 1970 Pulitzer Prize for international reporting.

Knightley, Phillip. *The First Casualty** (Harcourt Brace Jovanovich, 1975). A lively examination, by a British author and journalist, of the major wars of the 19th and 20th centuries and the correspondents who covered them.

Maltese, John Anthony. *Spin Control: The White House Office of Communications and the Management of Presidential News,* 2nd edition (University of North Carolina Press, 1994). A detailed study of how the White House Office of Communications has attempted to control the public agenda by making presidential news. Contains examples from five presidential administrations, beginning with the presidency of Richard Nixon.

Paletz, David L., and Entman, Robert M. *Media Power Politics** (Macmillan, 1981). A wide-ranging examination of the role of the mass media in American politics. Argues that the media have a major impact on what happens in the political arena.

Sabato, Larry J. *Feeding Frenzy: How Attack Journalism Has Transformed American Politics* (Free Press, 1991). A forceful argument, by a leading political scientist, that the media have become increasingly focused on sensational news stories, to the detriment of substantive news. Sabato maintains that the growing interest in scandal and in politicians' private lives has detracted from the level of political debate, and has made politics less civil.

Sanford, Bruce. *Don't Shoot the Messenger: How Our Growing Hatred of the Media Threatens Free Speech for All of Us* (Free Press, 1999). A thoughtful analysis, by a respected First Amendment attorney, of the growing public distrust of the mass media. The author suggests that this public cynicism undermines the impact of journalists' efforts to expose corruption.

---

*Available in paperback.

 Visit http://politicalscience.wadsworth.com/cummings9/update/ for current InfoTrac articles and other student resources related to this chapter.

CHAPTER 9
Political Parties

When Vice President Al Gore stood before the cheering national convention delegates in Los Angeles in August 2000 and accepted their nomination, the Democratic Party was far from confident of victory in November.

Although Bill Clinton had proved a popular president, he had been impeached and was entangled in scandal for much of his time in the White House. Could the vice president free himself of this taint? He was, after all, the number two man in the Clinton Administration. Moreover, Gore had his own problems—he had visited a Buddhist temple in California, a controversial event that produced thousands of dollars in contributions to the 1996 Clinton-Gore campaign, and he had made fund-raising calls from his office in the White House.

Finally, Gore himself might joke about his wooden speaking style and lack of charisma, but that, too, might have been a problem for a presidential candidate on the hustings. Initially, at least, Texas Governor George W. Bush, who had been nominated by the Republicans two weeks earlier in Philadelphia, was ahead in all the polls and seemed more at ease as a candidate. But Gore surprised even his own supporters by bounding down the aisle of the Democratic convention, high-fiving the delegates, giving a vigorous speech, and then enthusiastically kissing his wife, Tipper, as millions watched on television in some amazement.

The candidate seemed transformed—at least he had, to a great extent, shed his robotic image before a huge television audience.

Gore's performance gave him the "convention bounce"—the gain in the polls that a candidate often enjoys after a national convention—that the Democrats had hoped to achieve. By early September, less than a month later, Gore had moved ahead of Bush in several public opinion polls, although by early October, when they met in their first televised debate, the polls showed them about even.

Gore was helped in September by the fact that the Bush campaign seemed to stall and go into a defensive mode in the face of the Gore upswing. Bush quarreled over accepting the three televised debates with Gore proposed by the bipartisan Commission on Presidential Debates. On September 8, Bush termed himself an "underdog." After rejecting the commission's plan, Bush reversed himself and agreed to the panel's three scheduled debates and a fourth between the vice presidential candidates.

There were good statistical reasons as well for Bush and his advisers to be concerned. By the year 2000, as had been true for many years in the past, there were more people in America who called themselves Democrats than there were people who identified with the Republicans. But the gap between the two parties had narrowed; the number of people who identified themselves as Republicans had increased during the 1980s. In addition, more than a third of the voters called themselves independents.* And sizable numbers of blue-collar and middle-class Democrats had crossed party lines and voted for Ronald Reagan in 1980 and 1984.

Beyond the candidates' maneuvering over tax cuts, Social Security, and health care, the 2000 campaign offered voters a choice between competing political philosophies. Although—as often happens—both major-party candidates tended to move toward the center during elections, there were still marked differences between the Democratic and Republican Parties and their nominees.

In this chapter, we will explore a key question: Do political parties still perform a useful role in the American democratic system? A number of related questions may also be asked. Have the parties been eclipsed by powerful interest groups? Has the influence of television commercials become more important than party loyalties? Are political parties truly responsive and responsible instruments of democracy? Do they offer a genuine choice on the major issues facing the nation? Are parties elitist organizations controlled by a few leaders and closed to outsiders? Are national conventions—which

have increasingly become carefully scripted television extravaganzas—still useful tools of representative government? In discussing the role, history, organization, and performance of American political parties, we shall explore all of these questions.

WHAT IS A PARTY?

"As there are many roads to Rome and many ways to skin a cat," Frank J. Sorauf has written, "there are also many ways to look at a political party."[1] A political party is a group of men and women meeting in a small community in Connecticut to nominate a candidate for town council. It is a group of ward heelers in Chicago turning out to cheer at a political rally. It is the officials and supporters of the party in the 50 states. It is congressional leaders having a private breakfast at the White House with the president to discuss the administration's legislative proposals. It is the delegates to a national political convention exploding in a frenzy of noise, emotion, confetti, and balloons after the name of their candidate for president is placed in nomination—even though, in recent years, the convention's choice had been determined months earlier in the spring primaries. It is the party's national committee, chosen by the convention. It is the millions who vote on Election Day.

As Sorauf has concluded, the nature of a political party is somewhat in "the eye of the beholder."[2] There are the *voters*, a majority of whom consider themselves Democrats or Republicans; the *party leaders outside of government*, who frequently control the party machinery and sometimes have important power bases; the *party activists*, who ring doorbells, serve as delegates to county, state, and national conventions, and perform the day-to-day, grass-roots work of politics; and finally, the *party leaders in the government*, including the president, the leaders in Congress, and party leaders in state and local governments.

When someone speaks of "the Democratic Party" or "the Republican Party," that person may really mean any of these diverse elements—or all of them. Because a political party is made up of so many groups and individuals, it is difficult to define in a shorthand way. But, in very general terms, a **major political party** is a broadly based coalition that attempts to gain control of the government by winning elections, in order to exercise power and reward its members.

Today, political parties are less powerful than in the past, as party allegiances among voters have declined and as competing groups—political action committees, professional campaign managers, and interest groups—have increasingly come to share many of the traditional roles of parties. Nevertheless, political parties continue to perform vital functions in the American political system.

The best way to look at political parties is not in terms of what they are, but in terms of what they do. One of the major problems of government is managing the

---

*Among eligible voters, 28 percent identified themselves as Republicans, 34 percent said they were Democrats, and the largest bloc, 38 percent, called themselves Independents. The Gallup Organization, *Poll Releases*, "Independents Rank as Largest U.S. Political Group," April 1999, online at <www.gallup.com/poll/releases/pr990409c.asp>.

transfer of power. In totalitarian governments, power, once seized, is seldom peacefully relinquished. Usually the change comes unexpectedly. A democracy, however, provides orderly institutional arrangements for the transfer of power.

In normal circumstances in the United States, a candidate for president, running as the nominee of a political party, is elected every four years and serves one or two terms. American political parties thus perform "an essential function in the management of succession to power."[3] They serve as a vehicle for choice, offering the electorate competing candidates for public office, and often, alternative policies. The element of choice is absolutely vital to democratic government. Where voters cannot choose, there is no democracy. The parties operate the machinery of choice: nominations, campaigns, and elections.

Within the framework of a political system (the concept discussed in Chapter 1), political parties help to mobilize the demands and supports that are fed into the system, and participate as well in the authoritative decision making, or outputs, of the government.

In a presidential election, the party in power traditionally defends its record and attacks its opponents, while the party out of power suggests that it is time for a change. That is exactly what happened in the 2000 presidential election between the two major-party candidates, Texas Governor George W. Bush and Vice President Al Gore, who represented the party that had been in power for almost eight years.

By seeking to mobilize mass opinion behind their slogans and policies, political parties channel public support for, or against, the government. In so doing, they normally serve as an essential bridge between the people and the government. They provide a powerful means for the public's voice to be heard—and politicians must listen if they wish to survive in office. Parties thus help to hold officials accountable to the voters. They also help to recruit candidates for public office.

Because a political party consists of people expressing attitudes about government, it might seem to fit the definition of an interest group. But a political party runs candidates for public office. It is therefore much more comprehensive than an interest group. Instead of seeking only to influence government, often on a narrow range of issues, a major party attempts to win elections and gain control of the government.

The major political parties try to form "winning coalitions" by maneuvering "to create combinations powerful enough to govern."[4] In the process, they may serve to reconcile the interests of conflicting groups in society. The political party can fill the natural role of broker or mediator among interest groups, organized or not, because in order to win elections it usually tries to appeal broadly to many groups of voters.

Parties also play a key role in the governmental process. When the Clinton Administration succeeded the Bush Administration in January 1993, Washington real estate agents were happy; it meant that Republicans would be selling their houses and Democrats would be buying them. After a presidential election, the White House staff, the cabinet, and the more important policy makers and officials of the various executive branch departments are for the most part appointed from the president's party. To the victors belong the White House limousines.

Political parties play a vital role in the legislative branch as well. The president appeals to party loyalty through the party's legislative leaders in order to get his programs through Congress (although he may face a Congress controlled by the opposition party, as President Clinton did after the 1994 congressional elections). And both major parties have "whips" in Congress—legislative leaders who are responsible for rounding up their party's members for important votes.

Because political parties are involved in the governmental process, they serve to link different parts of the government: The president communicates with party leaders in Congress; the two houses of Congress communicate in part through party leaders; and relationships among the national, state, and local governments depend to a considerable degree on ties among partisan officials and leaders.

The Republicans met in a huge box-like structure called the "Wigwam" in Chicago in May and drew up a platform opposing the extension of slavery . . . and upholding the Union. . . . The chief contenders for the Republican nomination were William H. Seward of New York and Abraham Lincoln of Illinois. . . .

Lincoln decided to stay in Springfield, Illinois, during the Chicago convention. . . . His managers went to Chicago with only Illinois in the bag, but did everything they could think of to build up support for their man in other state delegations. They hired two Chicagoans, whose shouts, it was said, could be heard above the howling of the most violent tempest on Lake Michigan, to lead the cheers whenever Lincoln's name was mentioned in the convention. They also packed the Wigwam with "Lincoln shouters." . . . "We are going to have Indiana for Old Abe, sure," said another just before the balloting. "How did you get it?" someone asked. "By the Lord," he was told, "we promised them everything they asked."

After nailing down Indiana, Lincoln's managers went after Pennsylvania, with fifty-six delegates ready to vote for Simon Cameron, a favorite son, on the first ballot, but open to other candidates after that. . . . Jesse Dubois telegraphed Lincoln to tell him they could win the Keystone State if they promised Cameron the Treasury Department. "I authorize no bargain," Lincoln wired back, "and will be bound by none." "Damn Lincoln!" exclaimed Dubois. "Lincoln ain't here," broke in [Judge David] Davis impatiently, ". . . we will go ahead as if we hadn't heard from him, and he must ratify it." . . . About midnight Joseph Medill ran into Judge Davis in a hotel lobby just after he left the Pennsylvania delegation. "How will they vote?" he asked. "Damned if we haven't gotten them," exulted Davis. "How did you get them?" asked Medill. "By paying the price," replied Davis and revealed they had agreed to make Cameron Secretary of the Treasury. Medill expressed some consternation. "Oh, what's the difference," cried Davis

airily, "We are after a bigger thing than that; we want the Presidency, and the Treasury is not a great stake to pay for it." . . . Lincoln reluctantly made Cameron Secretary of War (not Treasury) after the election but he proved so incompetent he had to be replaced in a few months.

When Lincoln received the Republican nomination in Chicago, a friend of his at once wired the news to Springfield: "Abe, we did it. Glory to God!" The telegraph operator in Springfield wrote on a scrap of paper, "Mr. Lincoln, you are nominated on the third ballot," and gave it to a boy who ran to the office of the *State Journal* where Lincoln was awaiting the news with some friends. Lincoln took the message, read it aloud quietly, and, as his friends started cheering, put it in his vest pocket and said thoughtfully: "There's a little woman down at our house would like to hear this. I'll go down and tell her."

—Paul F. Boller, Jr., *Presidential Campaigns*

In sum, political parties perform vital functions in the American political system. They (1) manage the transfer of power, (2) offer a choice of rival candidates and programs to the voters, (3) serve as a bridge between government and people by helping to hold elected officials accountable to the voters, (4) help to recruit candidates for office, (5) may serve to reconcile conflicting interests in society, (6) staff the government and help to run it, and (7) link various branches and levels of government.

THE DEVELOPMENT OF AMERICAN POLITICAL PARTIES

The framers of the Constitution created the delicately balanced machinery of the federal government and provided for regular elections of a president and Congress, but they said not a word about political parties. The reason was simple: In the modern sense, they did not exist.

Yet James Madison, the "father of the Constitution," foresaw that Americans would group together in factions. In *The Federalist*, No. 10, he predicted that the task of regulating conflicting economic interests would involve "the spirit of party and faction in the necessary and ordinary operation of the government."

In his farewell address, George Washington warned against "the baneful effects of the spirit of party." His vice president, John Adams, had declared: "There is nothing I dread so much as the division of the Republic into two great parties, each under its leader."[5] Yet the American party system began to take just such a shape in the 1790s during Washington's administration.

Federalists and Democratic-Republicans

The Federalist Party, organized by Alexander Hamilton, Washington's secretary of the treasury, was the first national political party in the United States. The Federalists stood for strong central government, and

These political buttons for George Washington were intended to be sewn on clothing.
Steve Laschever/University of Hartford Collection

their appeal was to banking, commercial, and financial interests.

Thomas Jefferson built a rival coalition that became known as the Republican Party, or Democratic-Republicans.* It was primarily an agrarian party of small farmers, debtors, southern planters, and frontiersmen. Being a practical politician, Jefferson sought to expand his coalition; in 1791 he made a famous trip to New York

---

*The name tends to be confusing to anyone attempting to trace the origins of the American party system. Today's Democratic Party, the oldest political party in the world, claims the Jeffersonian Republican, or Democratic-Republican, Party as its political and spiritual ancestor, a fact that Democratic orators remind us of endlessly and annually at Jefferson-Jackson Day dinners. Today's Republican Party invokes Abraham Lincoln, not Jefferson.

Ralph E. Becker Collection/Smithsonian Institution

State, allegedly on a "butterfly hunting" expedition, but actually to form an alliance with Aaron Burr and the Sons of Tammany, the political organization that was to dominate New York City. In the partnership of rural America and the cities, the Democratic Party was born.

Jefferson's triumph in the election of 1800 inaugurated a 28-year period of ascendancy by the Jeffersonian Democratic-Republicans. In fact, the Federalists never again tried for the presidency after 1816 when James Monroe, the Democratic-Republican candidate, was elected overwhelmingly. Monroe's victory launched the brief Era of Good Feelings, in which there was little partisan activity.

Democrats and Whigs

By 1824 the Democratic-Republicans had split into several factions and the first phase of party government in the United States came to an end. The election in 1828 of Andrew Jackson, the hero of the War of 1812, opened a new era of two-party rivalry, this time between Democrats and Whigs. Jacksonian democracy soon came to symbolize popular rule and the aspirations of the common man.

The rival Whigs, led by Henry Clay, William Henry Harrison, and Daniel Webster, were a coalition of bankers, merchants, and southern planters held together precariously by their mutual distaste for Jacksonian democracy. The Whigs won two presidential elections between 1840 and 1854, and the two-party system flourished.† As Clinton Rossiter has noted, "Out of the conflict of Democrats and Whigs emerged the American political system—complete with such features as two major parties, a sprinkle of third parties, national nominating conventions, state and local bosses, patronage, popular campaigning, and the presidency as the focus of politics."[6]

---

†Four Whig presidents occupied the White House. Only two were elected, however—William Henry Harrison in 1840 and Zachary Taylor in 1848. Both died in office and were succeeded by their vice presidents, John Tyler and Millard Fillmore.

Indiana Historical Society

Duke University Special Collections Library

During the 1850s, the increasingly divisive issue of slavery caused the Democratic Party to split between North and South. The Whigs, crushed by Democrat Franklin Pierce's landslide victory in 1852, were equally demoralized. The nation was about to be torn apart by civil war, and the major political parties, like the Union itself, were disintegrating.

Democrats and Republicans

The Republican Party was born in 1854 as a party of protest against the extension of slavery into the territories. The Kansas-Nebraska Act, passed that year, permitted slavery to move westward with the frontier and aroused discontent in the North and West.

In February 1854, a group of Whigs, Free-Soilers, and antislavery Democrats gathered in a church at Ripon, Wisconsin, to recommend the creation of a new party to fight the further expansion of slavery.* The name "Republican Party" was suggested at the meeting. The political organization that resulted from the meeting replaced the Whigs as the rival party of the Democrats, but it was a new party and not merely the Whigs masquerading under another label.

The first Republican presidential candidate, John C. Fremont, the "Pathfinder of the Rockies," was unable to find the trail that led to the White House in the election of 1856. But in 1860 the Republicans nominated Abraham Lincoln. By that time, the Democratic Party was so badly divided over the issue of slavery that its northern and southern wings each nominated separate candidates for president. A fourth candidate ran as the nominee of the Constitutional Union Party. The four-way split enabled Lincoln to win with only 39.8 percent of the popular vote.

His election was a rare fusion of the man and the times. Lincoln preserved the Union; in the process, he ensured the future of the Republican Party. By rejecting slavery, the Republicans had automatically become a sectional party, representing the North and West. And

North and West meant Union, emancipation, and victory. The Democrats and the South meant slavery, secession, and defeat. Having been on the losing side of the bloody and tragic Civil War, the Democrats were a long time in recovering; the party was trapped and tangled in the folds of the Confederate flag.

For 25 years after 1860, the Republicans consolidated their strength and ruled America, becoming known

Ralph E. Becker Collection/Smithsonian Institution

---

*The party birthplace is also claimed by Jackson, Michigan, where the Republicans held their first state convention five months later.

252 **CHAPTER 9** **POLITICAL PARTIES**

Ralph E. Becker Collection/Smithsonian Institution

Stanley King Collection/Smithsonian Institution

by the 1870s as the Grand Old Party, a term later shortened to GOP. But by 1876 the Democrats had recovered sufficiently to give the Republicans a spirited, two-party competition for two decades. Twice, in 1884 and 1892, the Democrats elected Grover Cleveland as president.

America was changing. After the Civil War, the nation gradually became industrialized; railroad tracks pushed westward, spanning the continent; immigrants from Europe poured in. As the rail and steel barons amassed great fortunes, small farmers found themselves squeezed economically and outnumbered by workers. Agrarian discontent was reflected in the rise of minor parties like the Grangers, the Greenbackers, and the Populists.

The Populists, or People's Party, were a protest party of western farmers. In 1892 their presidential candidate, James B. Weaver, showed surprising strength. By 1896 the spirit of populism had captured the Democratic Party, which nominated William Jennings Bryan for president. Bryan, running on a "free silver" platform,* lost to Republican William McKinley, who defended the gold standard and conservative fiscal policies. The election resulted in a major realignment of the parties, from which the Republicans emerged stronger than ever as a coalition of eastern business interests, urban workers, midwestern farmers, and New England Yankees.

Theodore Roosevelt held the coalition together while he was president from 1901 to 1909, but his attempt to move the Grand Old Party in a more progressive direction alarmed its conservative business wing. In 1912 the Republican Party split apart. The conservative wing renominated William Howard Taft, who had been Roosevelt's handpicked successor. The other wing, the Progressive ("Bull Moose") Party, nominated

Roosevelt. The Republican split resulted in victory for Woodrow Wilson, the Democratic nominee.

Wilson's two terms proved to be a short Democratic interlude. A nation weary of the First World War chose to "return to normalcy" in the 1920s with the Republican administrations of Warren G. Harding and Calvin Coolidge, two of the less distinguished presidents to occupy that office. Big Business dominated; it was the era of the Teapot Dome scandal, flappers, bathtub gin, and the Prohibition "speakeasy." In 1928 Republican Herbert Hoover defeated Al Smith, the first Roman Catholic nominee of a major party. A year later, the stock market crash and the onset of the Great Depression dealt the Republican Party a blow comparable to the effect of the Civil War on the Democrats.

The result of these events was the election of Franklin D. Roosevelt in 1932, the New Deal, and 20 years of uninterrupted Democratic rule under Roosevelt and his successor, Harry S Truman. Roosevelt put together a new, grand coalition composed of the South, the big cities of the North, labor, immigrants, blacks, and other minority groups.

In 1952, in the midst of the Korean War, the Republicans nominated General Dwight D. Eisenhower and recaptured the presidency. But the Eisenhower magic could not be transferred to Richard Nixon, who narrowly lost the presidency to John F. Kennedy in 1960. Kennedy's "New Frontier" seemingly opened a new era of Democratic supremacy—but he was assassinated in 1963. In 1964 Barry Goldwater, a conservative from Arizona, captured control of the GOP from its long-dominant and more liberal eastern, internationalist wing. The result was Republican disaster. Lyndon Johnson, who had succeeded to the presidency after Kennedy's death, was elected in his own right with 61.1 percent of the total vote—the greatest share of the popular vote in history.

But American political parties have extraordinary resiliency: "Each one is a citadel that can withstand the impact of even the most disastrous national landslide and thus provide elements of obstinacy and stability in

---

*During the 1890s there was a populist call for the "free" or unlimited coinage of silver, which was seen as a remedy for the economic troubles of debtors and farmers who were suffering under tight monetary policies.

A 1980 campaign button advertising President Carter and his wife, Rosalyn
Smithsonian Institution

the two-party pattern."[7] The Republican Party survived the Goldwater debacle. It regrouped around Richard Nixon, who accurately gauged the temper of the nation in 1968. Lyndon Johnson, unable to hold the Democratic coalition together in the face of war and urban riots, did not choose to run for reelection. With the Democrats divided into at least three camps, Nixon triumphed, restoring the Republican Party to power and demonstrating anew the strength of the American two-party system. Nixon's landslide victory in 1972 was an even more dramatic illustration of the point—a triumph soon overshadowed by the scandal of Watergate, the resignation of Vice President Spiro Agnew, and Nixon's own resignation in 1974 on the brink of impeachment.

Then in 1976 Jimmy Carter, starting from a very modest political base as the former governor of Georgia, captured the Democratic nomination, succeeded in reunifying the Democratic Party, and went on to win the White House in a very close race against the incumbent, Gerald R. Ford, who had been vice president and then became president when Nixon resigned. The Democrats controlled both Congress, where they maintained their majority, and the executive branch. Yet, only six years after Nixon's resignation, the Republican Party surged back to power in 1980, capturing the White House under Ronald Reagan and gaining control of the Senate for the first time in more than a quarter of a century. Reagan's landslide victory in 1984 consolidated Republican control of the presidency.

This ability of American political parties to survive adversity and rise again rests in part on the fact that many areas of the country and many congressional districts are dominated by one party; even when a party is defeated nationally, it will still have durable pockets of power across the nation. This remains true despite the spread of two-party politics to more states in recent years. For example, Reagan carried 49 states in winning reelection to the presidency in 1984, and his party kept

control of the Senate, but the Democrats retained 34 of the state governorships and continued to control the House of Representatives.

The Democrats recaptured control of the Senate in 1986. As a result, President Bush, a Republican, faced a Congress with both houses controlled by the Democrats during his four years in office. The election in 1992 of a Democratic president, Bill Clinton, and a Democratic Congress brought to a close 12 years of Republican control of the White House. Only two years later, the Republicans captured both houses of Congress, demonstrating once again the ability of American political parties to regroup and return to power.

THE TWO-PARTY SYSTEM

Under the two-party system that has prevailed during most of the nation's history, winning nomination by one of the two major parties is at least half the battle for some candidates. In areas where one party dominates, it is equivalent to election. Throughout most of the nation's history, two major political parties have been arrayed against each other. The Democrats, in one guise or another, have endured. During successive eras they have been challenged by the Federalists, the Whigs, and the Republicans. Minor or third parties have joined the struggle, with greater or lesser effect, but the main battle has been, historically, a two-party affair. As Allan P. Sindler has observed, "From 1828 to the present with few exceptions the two parties together have persistently polled upward of 90 percent of the national popular vote—that is, there has been little multi-partyism."[8]

In 1968 George Wallace formed the American Independent Party and ran for president outside the two-party framework. He received 13.5 percent of the popular vote. Although a substantial showing for a minor-party candidate, it was nowhere near enough to win. In 1976 Eugene McCarthy, an independent candidate, received less than 1 percent of the popular vote. In 1980 Representative John B. Anderson, an Illinois Republican, won a place on the ballot in every state as an independent and waged a vigorous campaign for president. But he received only 6.6 percent of the popular vote and no electoral votes.

In 1992, Ross Perot, who also ran as an independent, made the strongest showing of any candidate who was not a major-party nominee since Theodore Roosevelt ran as the head of the Progressive ("Bull Moose") Party in 1912. Unlike most minor-party and independent candidates, Perot did not run short of funds to advertise his candidacy in the closing weeks of the campaign. A successful businessman and a billionaire, Perot financed most of his campaign with his own money.

With more than 19 million votes (19 percent), Perot was a major factor in the 1992 campaign, and in most states his presence on the ballot drew votes from both Clinton and Bush. In all, about one in five voters chose Perot, the independent. Perot's strong showing as an outsider may have reflected the fact that America's major parties were weaker in 1992 than they had been in earlier years. It may also have reflected voter discontent with the established political parties and political leaders. Again in 1996, Perot entered the presidential race, this time as the candidate of his own party, the Reform Party. But in 1996, Perot had lost much of the appeal that he had enjoyed as a newcomer and a fresh voice four years earlier.

In the year 2000, the first presidential election of the new millennium, the two major-party candidates received the overwhelming majority of the votes. There were other contenders, however. After a raucous convention between two competing factions, conservative Pat Buchanan was nominated by what was left of Perot's Reform Party. Ralph Nader's Green Party enjoyed the support of many environmental and consumer-oriented activists, but Nader also was not a serious contender for the White House. Nader's critics, however, charged that he might jeopardize Al Gore's election by siphoning votes away from the Democratic ticket.

The Roots of Dualism

In the states and in many local communities, one party may dominate, as the Democrats did for decades in the so-called Solid South and the Republicans did in Kansas and Vermont. But on the whole, America has been a two-party nation. Why this should be so is a subject of mild dispute because there is no wholly satisfactory answer. Among the explanations that have been offered are the influence of tradition and history, the structure of the U.S. electoral system, and ideological patterns among the electorate.

Tradition and History   The debate over ratification of the Constitution split the country into two groups. Dualism, therefore, is as old as the nation itself. And, once established, human institutions tend to perpetuate their original form. To some extent, Americans accept the two-party system because it has almost always been there.

The Electoral System   Many features of the American political system appear to be compatible with the existence of two major parties. In the United States, the single-member district system prevails in federal elections. For example, only one member of Congress may be elected from a congressional district, no matter how many candidates run—it is a case of winner-take-all. The same is true of a presidential election; normally in each state the candidate who receives the most popular votes wins all of the state's electoral votes. Under such a system, minor parties lacking a strong geographical base have little chance of poaching on the

Smithsonian Institution

two-party preserve. They tend to lose and, having lost, to disappear.[*] (By contrast, a system of proportional representation with multimember districts, as in Italy, encourages the existence of many parties by allotting seats to competing parties according to the percentage of votes that they win.)

Other aspects of the electoral system also work against third parties. For example, state election laws often make it difficult for third parties to get on the ballot. The nation's basic political and legal structure, in other words, favors the two-party system.

Patterns of Belief   A majority of voters stand somewhere near the middle ground on many issues of American politics. Ideological differences among Americans in the past have normally not been strong enough to produce a broad range of established minor parties

---

[*]The two parties need not be the same in all areas of the country, however. In some states, historically, minor parties have competed successfully with one of the two major national parties. For example, in Minnesota during the 1920s and 1930s, the Farmer-Labor Party—not the Democratic Party—was the chief competitor of the Republican Party in state and congressional elections. Since a merger in 1944, the Democratic-Farmer-Labor Party has been the principal rival to the Republicans in Minnesota. In 1998, Jesse Ventura was elected governor of Minnesota as a candidate of the Reform Party.

Comparing Governments

THE UNITED STATES AND ITALY: STABILITY OR CHOICE?

In the American "winner-take-all" political system, congressional candidates who receive the most votes in their district win the election. In practice, this has meant that, in nearly all elections, voters choose between the candidates of the only two parties with a real chance of winning office—the Republicans and the Democrats. With just two parties normally competing for power, it is inevitable that one or the other will gain majority control in each house of Congress, and one party has often controlled both.

Italy's multiparty system, by contrast, uses proportional representation, and Italian political parties are able to secure seats in the Parliament by winning just a small percentage of the vote. Italian voters are faced with a choice of more than a dozen political parties. With votes divided among so many parties, however, it is rare for any single party to win the majority required to establish a government in the parliamentary system. Instead, coalition governments are formed, consisting of several different parties joined in a single governing alliance.

But those coalitions are politically fragile, because they require the cooperation of parties that often have different agendas and constituencies. In fact, through mid-2000 there had been 58 such coalition governments in Italy since the end of the Second World War, an average life expectancy of only 11 months for each government.

On May 21, 2000, Italians held a national referendum in an attempt to reform the unstable system. The referendum was designed to move Italy closer to a two-party system. It called for the elimination of proportional representation. The measure was opposed by the smaller political parties, which feared they would disappear under the proposed new system.

Only a third of eligible voters cast their ballots, far less than the 50.1 percent turnout required for approval. The low turnout mainly reflected most Italians' disgust with politics as usual. The failure to win approval for a change in the electoral system means that it is likely that Italy's political instability will continue.

—Adapted from the *New York Times*, May 22, 2000

representing widely varying shades of political opinion, as is the case in many nations in western Europe.

Democrats and Republicans: Is There a Difference?

As noted earlier, American presidential candidates generally try to make very broad-based appeals. Although there are more Democratic than Republican voters in America, neither party enjoys the support of a majority of the electorate, and both must therefore look outside their own ranks for victory. To put together a winning coalition, a presidential candidate usually appeals to the great mass of voters in the ideological center. As a result, in some elections it may appear that there is very little difference between the two major parties. Because both parties woo the same voters, it is not surprising that, to an extent, they look alike. But they have important differences as well.

A classic study of national convention delegates found that the opinions of Democratic and Republican leaders diverged sharply on many important issues. What is more, these opinions were found to conform to party images: Republican leaders identified with "business, free enterprise, and economic conservatism in general," and Democrats were friendly "toward labor and toward government regulation of the economy." Differences of opinion among party leaders were found to be much sharper than the differences of opinion among ordinary members of the rank and file of the two parties.[9]

A more recent survey of party leaders, conducted in 2000, also found pronounced differences between the attitudes of Democratic and Republican leaders. For example, among delegates to the 2000 Democratic National Convention, 83 percent favored "programs . . . to help minorities get ahead in order to make up for past discrimination." But among delegates to the Republican National Convention that year, only 29 percent favored affirmative action.[10] And 73 percent of Democratic delegates thought the "government should do more to solve national problems." But among delegates to the Republican convention, only 4 percent agreed with that statement.[11]

The Decline of Party Loyalties and Party Influence

The fading of party loyalties among many voters has been one of the most visible features of contemporary American politics. Beginning in 1974, about a third of the voters described themselves as independents. Only about two-thirds of the voters called themselves Republicans or Democrats.[12]

As Everett Carll Ladd, Jr., observed: "A growing section of the electorate has become relatively weakly tied to political parties and open to change in preference depending upon its reading of current performance."[13] As he also noted, "all measures lead to the same conclusion. There has been a long-term decline of party allegiance."[14] Political scientist Martin P. Wattenberg has made the point even more strongly: "Once the central guiding forces in American electoral behavior, the parties are now perceived with almost complete indifference by a large proportion of the population."[15]

Of course, candidates and issues, not just party affiliations, influence voters. But the diminishing influence of parties is a significant change from the past. One observer, Austin Ranney, has suggested that something approaching a "no-party system" has emerged in presidential politics.[16] In 1984, for example, the Republican candidate, President Reagan, won more than 58 percent of the vote even though less than one-third of the electorate described themselves as Republicans. In 1992, nearly one out of five voters cast their ballots for Ross Perot, who represented no party.

Various reasons have been suggested for the decline of party ties: a more educated electorate, less dependent on parties for guidance; an increase in "split-ticket" voting by persons who may, for example, vote for a Republican candidate for president and a Democrat for governor; the increasing importance of television and the news media generally; and the breaking up of the old loyalties and alignments within the major parties.[17]

In addition, as already noted, political parties themselves have become less powerful. Other groups such as political action committees, professional campaign managers, and interest groups have taken over some of the functions of parties. Interest groups today provide much of the money that is used to finance election campaigns.

"How would you like me to answer that question? As a member of my ethnic group, educational class, income group, or religious category?"

Moreover, urban political machines have declined. And candidates no longer rely on parties to run their campaigns to the extent that was true in the past. As Frank J. Sorauf has observed, "All the campaign assets [candidates] once received from the party organizations and their workers—skills, information, pulse readings, manpower, exposure—they now can get from pollsters, the media, public relations people, volunteer workers, or even by 'renting a party' in the form of a campaign management firm."[18] The "fairly primitive campaign skills" of parties "have been superseded by a new campaign technology, and more and more they are finding themselves among the technologically unemployed."[19]

Despite the fading of party loyalties and influence, however, political parties in America have by no means become extinct. And even though the number of unaffiliated voters has increased, the combined total of Americans who call themselves Democrats or Republicans is still greater than those who say they are independents.

The Democrats

One way to perceive the differences between the two major parties is to examine their images. In the public's imagination, the "typical" Democrat lives in a big city in the North. He or she is a member of a minority or ethnic group—an African American, a Hispanic American, a Jew, a Pole, or an Italian, for example. The imaginary Democrat drinks beer, belongs to a labor union, works on an assembly line, goes bowling, and has a relatively low income.

Genus Republican's habitat, by contrast, is the hedge-trimmed suburbs. The imaginary Republican lives in a split-level house with a picture window, commutes to the city, and belongs to a country club that has no members from minority groups. The male of the species is very likely a white Protestant. He drinks martinis and eats white bread. His wife drives a BMW. He owns his own company or is a corporate executive. He golfs on weekends. He is rich, or at least comfortable, equally at home in the boardroom or the locker room. That, at any rate, is the popular image.

Like any caricature, these portraits are greatly overdrawn and not necessarily accurate. For example, one study of shifts in the American electorate concluded that the Democrats' base "has changed somewhat from the New Deal era. . . . They have lost ground among some of their old constituencies, such as trade unionists, big-city whites, and Southern whites; while they have made up for such losses with gains among the upper-middle class." The study suggested that the Republicans have "lost their grip on the American establishment, most notably among young men and women of relative privilege."[20] Republicans could no longer count on the automatic support of this affluent group; in the last three presidential elections, both parties battled for the support of "yuppies"—young, upwardly mobile professionals with substantial incomes.

Still, the image of each party and of individual Democrats and Republicans, at least to an extent, mirrors reality: Studies have shown that the Democrats usually, although not always, enjoy greater voter support from labor, African Americans, Jews, ethnic minorities, young people, those who have not attended college and who have lower incomes, and those who live in the cities. Republicans are more likely to be white, suburban, Protestant, rural, wealthy, older, college educated, and professionals or business executives. "Republicans tend to see themselves as middle class, and Democrats are much more apt to consider themselves as working class."[21]

Online for more information about the Democratic Party, see: www.dnc.org

Many of these patterns are changing, however. For example, in the 1992 presidential election, "Catholics . . . a mainstay of earlier Democratic coalitions, continued . . . their long drift away from decisive Democratic loyalties."[22] This was particularly true among young white Catholics. One exit poll reported that 42 percent of white Catholics under age 30 identified themselves as Republicans.[23] And one-quarter of Hispanic Americans, usually thought to be a Democratic constituency, voted Republican in that year.[24]

Nevertheless, whether a person identifies with the Democratic Party or the Republican Party may be related to socioeconomic factors. For example, one survey found that half of the people interviewed with low incomes considered themselves Democrats, but only about 26 percent of this group thought of themselves as Republicans. (See Table 9-1.) Moreover, in recent years the Republicans have often suffered from a distinct "gender gap"—more women have tended to vote for Democrats than for Republicans. In 1996, for example, 54 percent of women but only 44 percent of men voted for Clinton.[25]

And Democrats, political scientist Jo Freeman has observed, believe in "the inclusion of all relevant groups and viewpoints," while Republicans, in Freeman's view,

see themselves as "insiders who represent the core of American society and are the carriers of its fundamental values."[26] Perhaps partly in response to such perceptions, in the 2000 presidential race, George W. Bush, the Republican nominee, frequently asserted that the Republicans were a party of "inclusion," with room for all Americans.

Since 1932, in most presidential elections, the Democratic Party has, in spirit, been the party of Franklin D. Roosevelt. The vast social-welfare programs launched by the New Deal changed the face of America and gave the Democratic Party an identity that persisted for many years. Truman's "Fair Deal," Kennedy's "New Frontier," and Johnson's "Great Society" were all patterned on Roosevelt's New Deal. All sought to harness federal funds and federal energies to solve national problems. Clinton, elected in 1992 as a self-described "New Democrat," moved to a more centrist position. But in the 1996 presidential election, Clinton supported many federal government programs that were opposed by his Republican opponent, Bob Dole. In the 2000 presidential election, the Democratic candidate, Al Gore, proposed to pay for prescription drugs for seniors through the existing Medicare program; his Republican opponent favored a plan that involved private insurance companies as well as the government.

Despite the success of Roosevelt's grand coalition, the Democratic Party continues to display some of the characteristics of a bivalve, with two distinct halves. The southern or more moderate wing of the party differs significantly from the northern, urban, more liberal wing. Normally, the overriding desire for power and electoral victory is the muscle that holds the two halves together. Sometimes the muscle fails. For example, in 1948 southern Democrats walked out of the national convention over the civil rights issue.

For decades the Democrats could count on the 11 states of the Old Confederacy as a solid Democratic bloc. But no longer. Today, the South is a two-party battleground, and one in which the Republicans often have the upper hand. In 1972, for the first time, the

TABLE 9-1

Income and Party Identification

Income	Democratic	Republicans	Independents
Less than $15,000	41%	17%	35%
$15,000–$19,999	35	22	40
$20,000–$29,999	33	25	40
$30,000–$49,999	29	35	33
$50,000–$74,999	30	29	39
$75,000 and over	28	40	30

SOURCE: The Roper Center for Public Opinion Research, University of Connecticut, Storrs, Conn., July 16–18, 1999. Totals do not add up to 100% because the respondents either volunteered another party affiliation or declined to answer the question: "In politics, as of today, do you consider yourself a Republican, a Democrat, or an Independent?"

Ralph E. Becker Collection/Smithsonian Institution

southern states voted solidly for a Republican, Richard Nixon. In the South in 1980, Jimmy Carter, the Democratic nominee, carried only his home state of Georgia against his Republican opponent, Ronald Reagan. In 1984, Walter Mondale, the Democratic candidate for president, carried not a single state in the South, as happened again in 1988, when Massachusetts Governor Michael Dukakis was the Democratic nominee. Governor Bill Clinton of Arkansas, a Democrat and a southerner, carried only four southern states when he won the presidency in 1992 and when he was reelected in 1996. Between 1952 and 2000, every Republican presidential candidate won some southern electoral votes. (See Table 9-2.)

TABLE 9-2

The Growth of Republican Strength in the South, 1950–1998

Year	U.S. Representatives		U.S. Senators		Governors		States Voting for Presidential Nominee	
	D	R	D	R	D	R	D	R
1950	103	2	22	0	11	0		
1952	100	6	22	0	11	0	7	4
1954	99	7	22	0	11	0		
1956	99	7	22	0	11	0	6	5
1958	99	7	22	0	11	0		
1960	99	7	22	0	11	0	7	3*
1962	95	11	21	1	11	0		
1964	89	17	21	1	11	0	6	5
1966	83	23	19	3	9	2		
1968	80	26	18	4	9	2	1	5†
1970	79	27	16(1)‡	5	9	2		
1972	74	34	14(1)‡	7	8	3	0	11
1974	81	27	15(1)‡	6	8	3		
1976	82	26	16(1)‡	5	9	2	10	1
1978	77	31	15(1)‡	6	8	3		
1980	69	39	11(1)‡	10	6	5	1	10
1982	82	34	11	11	9	2		
1984	73	43	12	10	9	2	0	11
1986	77	39	16	6	6	5		
1988	78	38	14	8	6	5	0	11
1990	77	39	15	7	8	3		
1992	77	48	14	8	8	3	4	7
1994	61	64	9	13	5	6		
1996	55	70	6	16	5	6	4	7
1998	54	71	8	14	4	7		

NOTE: The 11 states of the South are Alabama, Arkansas, Florida, Georgia, Louisiana, Mississippi, North Carolina, South Carolina, Tennessee, Texas, and Virginia.
*The eight Mississippi electors voted for Harry Byrd.
†George Wallace won five states on the American Independent ticket.
‡Harry Byrd, Jr., was elected in Virginia in 1970 and 1976 as an Independent.
SOURCES: House, governor, and president figures in Congressional Quarterly, *Politics in America 1945–1966* (Washington, D.C.: Congressional Quarterly Service, 1967), pp. 101, 123, 117–121. Senate figures in Richard Scammon, *America Votes 7* (Washington, D.C.: Governmental Affairs Institute, 1968), pp. 12, 31, 74, 82, 147, 205, 289, 357, 371, 379, 404. Data since 1968 from Congressional Quarterly, *Weekly Reports; The New York Times;* and *The Almanac of American Politics 2000.*

In political campaigns, Republicans like to label the Democrats as "spenders." On the whole, Democrats have been more willing to appropriate federal funds for social action. As a result of this political reality, the Democratic Party since 1933 has been the party of Social Security, the Tennessee Valley Authority, Medicare, and federal aid to education. It has, in short, often been the party of social innovation.

In addition to differences of substance, the two parties show perceptible differences in style. "I don't belong to any organized party," the humorist Will Rogers once quipped. "I'm a Democrat."[27] Democrats do tend to be uninhibited and occasionally raucous, fighting among themselves; Republicans are normally more sedate.

Of course, these differences do not always hold true. In 2000, for example, the Democrats gathered in unusual harmony to nominate Al Gore, the vice president and the accepted front-runner. Twelve years earlier, in 1988, it was the Republican convention, thrown into turmoil by the controversy surrounding George Bush's choice of Senator Dan Quayle for vice president, that provided unexpected color and excitement. More often, however, it is the Democrats who brawl and squabble.

"A gathering of Democrats is more sweaty, disorderly, offhand, and rowdy than a gathering of Republicans," Clinton Rossiter has noted. "A gathering of Republicans is more respectable, sober, purposeful, and businesslike than a gathering of Democrats."[28] The Democratic donkey brays, snorts, kicks up its heels, balks, fusses, and is a very different animal in appearance, substance, and temperament from the Republican elephant. Today, of course, both parties' national conventions tend to be scripted and carefully manicured for television; in the era of the sound bite, the donkey and the elephant rarely bray or trumpet.

The Republicans

In describing the Republican Party, Theodore H. White once wrote: "Two moods color its thinking. One is the old Protestant-Puritan ethic of the small towns of America. . . . The other is the philosophy of private enterprise, the sense that the individual, as man or corporation, can build swifter and better for common good than big government. From middle-class America the Republicans get their votes; from the executive leadership and from the families of the great enterprises they get their funds."[29]

Despite the success of the Republicans in five out of the six presidential elections between 1968 and 1988, since the New Deal the Republican Party has, in terms of party identification, enjoyed the support of only a minority of American voters; people who identify themselves as Democrats have, in recent decades, outnumbered people who say they are Republicans. In the face of the party identification figures, the Republican Party's constant task is to broaden its popular appeal and turn its minority into a majority, or at least a plurality. The Republican Party won the presidency in 1980, 1984, and 1988 precisely because it was able to attract large numbers of Democrats and independents.

Online *for more information about the Republican Party, see: www.rnc.org*

The familiar Democratic charge that "the Republican Party is the party of Big Business" is partially accurate, just as it is true that, nationally, the Democrats have traditionally been the party of organized labor. The preference of business for the Republican Party may be measured by analyzing campaign contributions. For example, in the year 2000, corporations and business executives contributed $113.2 million to the national Republican Party and a smaller amount, $87 million, to the Democratic Party.[30]

During the Eisenhower years, federal regulatory agencies were markedly friendly to the broadcasting networks, airlines, and other businesses they were supposedly regulating. It can be argued that "it does make a difference to the television industry, the railroads, or

"Yes, son, we're Republicans."
Cartoon by Richter copyright © 1991 The New Yorker Collection from cartoonbank.com. All rights reserved.

Bill Snead

the stock exchanges whether Democrats or Republicans have a majority in the independent commissions."[31]

Like the Democrats, the Republicans have a split personality. The scar left when Theodore Roosevelt bolted the party in 1912 has never entirely healed; in modern times the battle of Republican conservatives (the political heirs of William Howard Taft) against Republican liberal-moderates (the heirs of Theodore Roosevelt) has continued, although in muted form during the strongly conservative Reagan years.

The struggle broke out in 1952 in the convention battle between Senator Robert A. Taft of Ohio (the son of William Howard Taft) and General Eisenhower, who was backed by the eastern liberals. Then, in 1964, Goldwater and the conservative wing won control of the party from the Eastern Establishment led by Nelson Rockefeller.

Again in 1976 the split was reflected in the battle between President Ford and Ronald Reagan for the party's presidential nomination, the most serious challenge to a Republican president from within his own party since the revolt against William Howard Taft. Despite Ford's nomination in 1976, the right wing of the Republican Party remained a strong force within the GOP and recaptured the White House in 1980, with Ronald Reagan as their standard-bearer.

The traditional split surfaced again during the vote on the impeachment of President Clinton in 1999. Five moderate Republicans from the northeast broke ranks with their party to vote against both articles of impeachment.

In the 1980s and 1990s, the Republican Party also often drew support from conservative Christian religious groups. In 1988, a former television evangelist, Pat Robertson, challenged Vice President George Bush in the Republican primary elections. In 1996 the Christian Coalition, the most prominent of the religious right groups, supported Bob Dole, the Republican candidate.

Although fundamentalist religious groups varied in their methods and goals, they shared common social views. "The New Right is generally concerned with what is seen as the breakdown of family, community, religion, and traditional morality in American life," sociologist Jerome L. Himmelstein has written. "Abortion, . . . affirmative action, sexual permissiveness, drugs, prohibitions on school prayer, the secular curriculum in public schools, and many similar things are opposed on the grounds that they contribute to . . . social breakdown and moral decay."[32]

Minor Parties and Independent Candidates

Minor parties have been active throughout most of the nation's history, from the Anti-Masons of the 1830s and the Barnburners of the 1840s, to the Know-Nothings of the 1850s, the Greenbackers of the 1880s, the Populists of the 1890s, the Progressives of the 1920s, and the American Independents in 1968. (See Figure 9-1.)

In 1968 the third-party movement of Alabama's George Wallace scared major-party supporters because of the possibility that Wallace would carry enough states to prevent either major-party candidate from gaining a majority of electoral votes. Wallace would then have been in a position to bargain with his electoral votes, or to throw the outcome into the House of Representatives. (The electoral college machinery is discussed in Chapter 11.)

Although Wallace appeared on the ballot in every state, usually as the candidate of the American Independent Party, he carried only five southern states; his 46 electoral votes were not enough to deadlock the presidential election. His 13.5 percent of the popular vote was considerably less than the 21.1 percent received by the Know-Nothings* in 1856, the 27.4 percent polled by Theodore Roosevelt's Progressive ("Bull Moose") Party in 1912, or the 16.6 percent received by Robert La Follette's Progressives in 1924. In 1972 John G. Schmitz, the candidate of the American Independent Party, received more than a million votes, or 1.4 percent of the popular vote.

In recent years, several candidates have run for the presidency as independents, without bothering to organize a third party. In 1992, Ross Perot, a billionaire, accepted no federal funds and invested an estimated $63.4 million of his own money in his independent campaign, which relied heavily on television. Although Perot's final share of the vote—19 percent—was very large, he did not carry a single state. In 1996, when Perot again ran for president, this time as the candidate of the Reform Party, he accepted $29 million in federal campaign funds.

 for more information about the Reform Party, see: www.reform-party-usa.org *or* www.reformparty.org

---

*The anti-Catholic, anti-Irish Native American Party was so secretive that its members pretended ignorance of party affairs; as a result editor Horace Greeley dubbed it the Know-Nothing Party.

FIGURE 9-1

Minor-Party and Independent Vote, 1880–1996

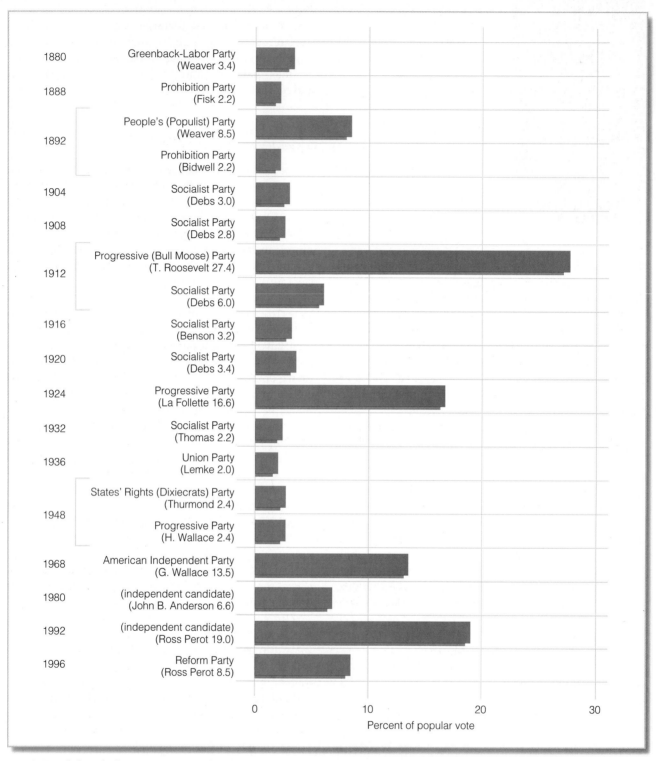

NOTE: Includes only those minor parties and independent candidates for president that polled 2 percent or more of the popular vote.
SOURCES: Neal R. Peirce, *The People's President* (New York: Simon & Schuster, 1968), pp. 305–307, reprinted by permission of Simon & Schuster; Donald B. Cole, *Handbook of American History* (New York: Harcourt Brace Jovanovich, 1968), pp. 304–305; *Politics in America*, 4th ed. (Washington, D.C.: Congressional Quarterly, 1971), p. 91; *New York Times*, January 6, 1981, p. A14; *Washington Post*, November 5, 1992, p. A26; and *New York Times*, November 7, 1996, p. B5.

Other independent candidates for president have been much less well funded than Perot, and they have polled a much smaller share of the vote. In 1980 independent candidate John B. Anderson, like Perot in 1992, did not carry a single state. But with 6.6 percent of the popular vote, Anderson did better than have many others, including Eugene McCarthy, who received less than 1 percent of the popular vote in 1976.

V. O. Key, Jr., has suggested that minor parties fall into two broad categories: "those formed to propagate a particular doctrine," and "transient third-party movements" that briefly appear on the American scene and then disappear. The Prohibition Party and the Socialist Party are examples of doctrinal parties that "have been kept alive over long periods by little bands of dedicated souls."[33] Among the transient third-party movements, Key perceived two types: parties of economic protest, such as the Populists, the Greenbackers, and the Progressives of 1924; and "secessionist parties" that have split off from one of the major parties, such as the Progressives in 1912 and the Dixiecrats in 1948.

Sometimes minor parties have a strong nativist streak. Just as the Wallace campaign played upon white fears of African Americans, more than a century ago the Know-Nothings, or Native American Party, exploited fear of Irish immigrants and other "foreigners." The party platform in 1856, when Millard Fillmore ran as the Know-Nothing candidate, warned: "Americans must rule America."

In certain states minor parties have gained a powerful position. The Liberal Party and the Conservative Party in New York have sometimes held the balance of power in elections in that state. Nationally, however, minor parties have never consistently enjoyed much power or influence. On some occasions they have influenced the policies of the major parties—as when Populism captured the Democratic Party in 1896.

"One of the persistent qualities of the American two-party system," one analyst concluded, "is the way in which one of the major parties moves almost instinctively to absorb (and thus be somewhat reshaped by) the most challenging third party of the time. In any case, it is a notable fact that no third party in America has ever risen to become a major party, and that no major party has ever fallen to become a third party."[34]

PARTY STRUCTURE

One could draw a neat organizational chart of a major political party, with the national chairperson and national committee at the top of the pyramid, and state and local party machinery arrayed below. The chart would be technically correct but highly misleading. In fact, the national party exists more on paper than in reality, in theory more than in fact.

American political parties are decentralized and only loosely organized. Rather than as a pyramid, with all power flowing from the top down, party structure "may be more accurately described as a system of layers of organization. Each successive layer—county or city, state, national—has an independent concern about elections in its geographical jurisdiction."[35]

National Political Parties

Leadership of a national political party is somewhat like a sports trophy that a team may win and retain for a time but must eventually return so that it may be awarded to a new team. Thus, President Bush led the Republican Party in 1992, but after his defeat, he was obliged to give up control of the party machinery. Four years later, it belonged to Bob Dole. In 1992, Bill Clinton's capture of the Democratic presidential nomination and his election in November put the Democratic Party organization firmly in the hands of Clinton supporters.

On paper, the party's quadrennial **national convention** is the source of all authority within the party. The convention nominates the party's candidates for president and vice president; it writes a platform, settles disputes, writes rules, and elects the members of the national committee.

The **national chairperson,** the head of a national political party, is formally elected by the members of the national committee. In practice he or she is chosen or retained by the party's presidential nominee at the end of the national convention.

Between conventions, the **national committee** of each major political party is the governing body of the party. Members of the national committee are chosen in the states and formally elected by the party's national convention.

In the past, national committees have sometimes been little more than the permanent offices in Washington that house the national chairperson and the staff. More recently, the national committees of both parties have become more active between presidential elections. Between elections, the chief functions of the national committee staff are public relations, patronage, research, and fund-raising.

As a rule, presidential nominees either largely ignore the machinery of the national committee and build a personal organization to run their campaign, or they take over the national committee machinery and make it their own. In theory, the national chairperson's main job is to manage the presidential campaign; in practice, however, the candidate's real campaign manager is seldom the party chairperson.

Independent of the national committees, and serving as further evidence of the decentralization of American party politics, are the congressional leaders of each party, elected by their colleagues, and the congressional and senatorial campaign committees. Both major parties have campaign committees in the House and Senate; their members are chosen by party members in each branch of Congress. The congressional committees

Los Angeles, August 2000: Al Gore, the Democratic nominee for president, addresses delegates at the party's national convention.
AP/Wide World

channel money, speakers, advice, and assistance to party members who are up for election.

In both the Republican and Democratic parties, there is often a good deal of conflict between the party leaders in Congress and the leaders of the more presidentially oriented national party organization, a built-in tension often reflected in rivalry and jealousy between the congressional campaign committees and the national committee.

State and Local Parties

Party organization and election laws vary tremendously in the states, with the result that one can find kaleidoscopic variety in almost any given phase of American politics below the national level. Just as the national party in power is controlled by the president, the state party is often dominated by the governor. In the case of some large northern industrial states, the mayor of a large city may wield considerable influence. On the other hand, the state party may be led by a party chairperson who is not obligated to, and was elected without, the support of the incumbent governor. And, of course, a state chairperson may head a party that is out of power and does not control the governor's office.[36] Some state party organizations are the fiefdom of a single party boss—either an elected official or a party leader

outside government. But this is less often the case today than in the past.

Political scientist David R. Mayhew has classified a number of states as having "traditional party organizations" that are independent, long entrenched, and highly organized; that seek to nominate candidates to a wide range of public offices; and that offer jobs and other tangible rewards to their followers. But he notes that within other state parties there is "persistent factionalism" in which two or more party organizations "commonly operate in the same party in the same city or county, normally competing against each other in primaries for a broad range of offices."[37]

Republicans or Democrats may consistently dominate within a state, or power may be divided between the two parties. But even within a party, there are great variations from state to state. The Democratic Party in Alabama is very different from the one in Michigan. In both parties, liberals may control one state, conservatives or moderates another. And these local differences tend to make American political parties decentralized, fragmented, and weak.

State politics often reflect geographic cleavages. In New York the Democratic Party traditionally controls New York City, while Republicans dominate "upstate," in areas outside the city. In Illinois the Democrats, strong in Chicago's Cook County, must often contend with a heavy downstate Republican vote. In Michigan, Democrats are strong in Detroit, but Republicans dominate many other areas of the state.

The state parties are bound together within the national political party by a mutual desire to have a "winner" at the head of the national ticket. Often, although not always, a strong presidential candidate will sweep state and local candidates into office on his coattails.

The layer of party organization below that of the national committees is the state committees. Like national committee members, members of the state committees are chosen in many different ways, including county conventions and direct primaries.

At the grass-roots of each major political party is a third layer of party organization, consisting of the county committees, county chairpersons, district leaders, precinct or ward captains, and party workers. The local party organization is held together in part by the paste of patronage—the rewarding of party faithfuls with government jobs. The old-style, big-city political machines depended almost entirely on patronage; even today a substantial portion of party workers may be found on town, city, and county payrolls.

Although big-city machines still exist, the cigar-chomping, derby-hatted political "boss" of the late 19th and early 20th centuries has in most areas enjoyed his last hurrah. At one time, Frank Hague, the Democratic boss of Jersey City, could blatantly declare: "I am the law." Edward J. Flynn, the boss of the Bronx, could rise to considerable power within the national Democratic Party. Carmine De Sapio, the leader of Tammany Hall, was able to dominate New York City politics in the 1950s. But as Frank J. Sorauf has suggested: "The defeat of Carmine De Sapio and the Tammany tiger by the reformers in the fall of 1961 may stand as one of the great turning points in American politics."[38] Chicago's mayor Richard J. Daley, for many years a power in national Democratic politics, drew substantial support from the city's business community. He gave them what they wanted—"a new downtown area, an expressway, . . . confidence in the city's economic future"—and in the process made it almost impossible for Republican candidates to find any support among business leaders.[39] Daley, often described as the last of the big-city bosses, died in 1976.

The urban machines drew their power from the vast waves of immigrants to America's cities. The machines offered all sorts of help to these newcomers—from food baskets to city jobs. In return, all the boss demanded was the newcomer's vote. Each ward captain knew precisely how many votes he could deliver—the captain who did not would soon find that he was no longer a municipal inspector of sewers. Since the 1930s, Social Security, welfare payments, food stamps, unemployment benefits, and general prosperity have cut the ground out from under the city machines: The social services formerly provided by the party clubhouse now flow from the impersonal bureaucracy in Washington and from the

THE OLD POLITICS—MACHINE STYLE

George Washington (Boss) Plunkitt, a political leader in New York City at the turn of the 20th century, explained his philosophy for attracting votes:

What holds your grip on your district is to go right down among the poor families and help them in the different ways they need help. I've got a regular system for this. If there's a fire in Ninth, Tenth, or Eleventh Avenue, for example, any hour of the day or night, I'm usually there with some of my election district captains as soon as the fire engines. If a family is burned out I don't ask whether they are Republicans or Democrats; and I don't refer them to the Charity Organization Society, which would investigate their case in a month or two and decide they were worthy of help about the time they are dead from starvation. I just get quarters for them, buy clothes for them if their clothes were burned up, and fix them up til they get things runnin' again. It's philanthropy, but it's politics, too—mighty good politics. Who can tell how many votes one of these fires brings me?

—Boss Plunkitt, in William L. Riordon, *Plunkitt of Tammany Hall*

states. And the establishment of the direct primary and internal party reforms have, in some cases, impaired the power of the bosses to control nominations.

However, the local party can still sometimes find a city job for a loyal worker, for "the power to hire is still an important power resource."[40] And urban machines can help the poor deal with complex city bureaucracies.[41] Or a city machine can award municipal construction contracts to party activists or financial contributors. But people participate in politics at the grass-roots level today for a variety of reasons, not only for economic motives. The woman in Ohio who telephoned her neighbors and urged them to vote for George W. Bush in 2000 may have wanted to feel that she was personally participating in the election of a president. The volunteers who rang doorbells for Gore that year did so in many cases for the sheer excitement of being involved in a political campaign. The suburban man who serves as a precinct captain may be active in politics because he enjoys the added prestige that he acquires in the eyes of his neighbors. (He is the person who can get a new streetlight installed or the potholes filled in.) He may even be a party worker because he likes to attend the party's national convention as a delegate every four years.

Increasingly, two new kinds of activists are taking part in American politics at various levels, including service as delegates to national conventions. These are the issue activists—persons committed to a particular

TABLE 9-3

Political Participation

	1964	1968	1972	1976	1978	1980	1982	1984	1986	1988	1992	1996
Do you belong to any political club or organization?	4%	3%	*	*	*	3%	3%	4%	*	4%	*	*
Did you give any money or buy tickets or do anything to help the campaign for one of the parties or candidates?	11%	12%	10%	9%	13%	8%	*	7%	10%	9%	11%	9%
Did you go to any political meetings, rallies, dinners, or things like that?	8%	14%	9%	6%	10%	8%	9%	4%	7%	7%	8%	6%
Did you do any other work for one of the parties or candidates?	5%	5%	5%	4%	6%	4%	6%	4%	3%	3%	3%	3%
Did you wear a campaign button or put a campaign bumper sticker on your car?	17%	15%	14%	8%	9%	7%	8%	9%	7%	*	*	*

*Data not available.
SOURCES: Survey Research Center/Center for Political Studies, University of Michigan, in William H. Flanigan and Nancy H. Zingale, *Political Behavior of the American Electorate*, 4th ed. (Boston: Allyn and Bacon, 1979), p. 163. Reprinted with permission. Data for 1978 through 1982 and for campaign buttons and bumper stickers from the American National Election Studies, National Election Studies, Institute for Social Research, University of Michigan. Data for 1984 through 1996 from the Survey Research Center/Center for Political Studies/National Election Studies, in William H. Flanigan and Nancy H. Zingale, *Political Behavior of the American Electorate*, 8th ed. (Washington, D.C.: CQ Press, 1994), p. 13; and 9th ed., p. 16.

issue, such as civil rights or women's rights—and activists who work in the organizations of political candidates. These new breeds are, to some extent at least, replacing the "ward heelers" and party regulars of yesteryear.

The number of political activists at any level is fairly small, however. Perhaps only about 10 percent of the population could be classified as "politically involved." (See Table 9-3.) If we apply the percentages shown in the table for 1996 to the 1996 voting-age population of 193,651,000, we find that in round numbers 17.4 million Americans spent money to help the campaign for one of the parties or candidates, 11.6 million attended political gatherings or functions, and 5.8 million did political work for parties or candidates.[42]

THE NATIONAL CONVENTION

Such is the influence of television on American politics that by 1996 and again in 2000, both major-party national nominating conventions were carefully controlled, made-for-television entertainment, designed by professional TV producers to appeal to prime-time audiences. And in 2000, the conventions were wired as well for Internet viewers. Visitors to convention Web sites could select the main speakers on the podium or they could zoom in on the floor to see what was happening in a particular state delegation.

Gone are the days of gavel-to-gavel coverage by the major television networks, when the national conventions would often provide real drama as candidates for the presidential nomination vied for support of the delegates. Beginning in 1992, the networks cut back on their

convention coverage. By 1996 and 2000, the major network broadcasts were limited on most nights to an hour or two of prime time, although public television and the cable networks still provided much fuller coverage, and C-SPAN viewers could watch the proceedings gavel-to-gavel. The change was not solely the result of television, of course. The conventions themselves have, for the most part, become tame spectacles emphasizing platitudes, balloons, and confetti.

As one political analysis has put it, "One of the lessons of recent presidential elections is that national conventions are declining in importance as decision-making bodies. . . . National conventions no longer pick presidential nominees; they merely ratify the work of primaries and caucuses."[43] This is true because, as a rule, the preconvention campaigns and the primary elections are now decisive. By the time the conventions come along, the only battles are usually over the platform.

What the voters see of the conventions on TV is carefully managed, both by the parties and the networks. Listen to Bill Greener, the manager of the 1996 Republican National Convention at San Diego, talking about the constraints imposed on him by the television networks:

We don't make the rules to the game. We are dealing with the rules. And the rules are: You get an hour and don't forget in that hour we have got our commercials to air and our station breaks, and don't forget that we need time to showcase our talent . . . and even before we think about going to the podium we have got to establish the presence of our anchor and our four floor correspondents, and don't forget that

SAN DIEGO, Aug. 14—In the high-security zone back-stage at the Republican National Convention, in Trailer 22, Margaret Tutwiler and her squad of six are on the phones with producers at all of the big TV networks. Their mission: to deliver the faces of women, minorities or young people that Tutwiler hopes will change her party's image.

About 50 yards away, inside another trailer, CBS News President Andrew Heyward has spotted a face on a tiny monitor that sends him shooting up from his seat.

"That's Lesley! With him!" he shouts.

CBS floor reporter Lesley Stahl has poked her way to within earshot of Jack Kemp, who at this second is striding onto the convention floor for the first time.

Instantly, director Eric Shapiro cuts to the camera focused on Stahl and Kemp. Not two seconds later, the network audio captures Stahl's two-sentence interview with the vice presidential candidate. In the CBS trailer,

Heyward and Lane Venardos, who runs the convention coverage, throw their fists in the air in celebration.

"Excellent, Lesley, excellent!" Venardos exults into his headset.

Inside these impossibly crammed trailers shoehorned into the dank loading docks behind the red, white and blue stage, the cultures of Washington political strategists and New York TV producers clash in a nightly frenzy of decisions. . . .

Five seconds before 10 P.M. EDT, director Shapiro says, "Here we go, guys, there's no turning back. Cue Dan. Zoom in."

"Keynote night at the convention," anchor Dan Rather says, and the Campaign '96 animation dances across the screen.

—*Washington Post,* August 15, 1996

after that we are going to take a commercial break, and then we are going back to the anchor, and then we might take what you've got going at the podium. And that's just the way it is.[44]

Actually, the networks' rules are only part of the story. The political parties themselves now block out the convention proceedings down to the minute. For example, at the Republican convention in 1996, one account summarized the script of a segment this way: "Call to Order . . . from 05:00 to 05:01, followed by the Introduction of Colors . . . at 05:01 to 05:02, followed by the Presentation of the Colors by San Diego Joint Scouting Color Guard from 05:02 to 05:04 . . . ending applause from 05:21 to 05:24." Another event, running

from 05:16 to 05:18, was described as "Ending Applause and Spotlight Sequentially on Each of Six American Dream Murals with Main Street Americans Moving to Positions Behind Podium."[45]

Nor are convention speakers always allowed to say what is on their minds. At the Republican convention in 1996, for example, Governor William Weld of Massachusetts bowed out as a prime-time speaker after party officials objected to his plan to talk about abortion; he favored a pro-choice position in opposition to the party platform.

Yet for all of the control now exercised over the conventions, television has brought American politics into the living room, and these events still provide a chance for millions of viewers to watch the candidates

Three Michigan delegates show their support for Al Gore at the 2000 Democratic National Convention in Los Angeles.
Bob Riha, Jr./Newsmakers

The National Convention   **267**

With the increasing importance of presidential primaries, national conventions are today much less important in the process of selecting a presidential nominee. The conventions today normally ratify the decisions of the voters in the party primaries. But the colorful atmosphere of party conventions in the past was captured in this vivid word picture by one observer more than half a century ago:

The national nominating convention is something unknown to the Constitution and undreamed of by the founding fathers. It is an American invention, as native to the U.S.A. as corn pone or apple pie. A Democratic or a Republican national nominating convention, once it gets going, emits sounds and lights that never were on land or sea. . . . At different hours of the day or night, it has something of the painted and tinselled and tired gaiety of a four-ring circus, something of the juvenile inebriety and synthetic fraternal sentiment of a class reunion, something of the tub-thumping frenzy of a backwoods camp meeting. . . . What goes on beneath the surface and behind locked doors is something both realistic and important. For it is here, unexposed to the public eye, that the deals and bargains, the necessary compromises are arranged—compromises designed to satisfy as well as possible all of the divergent elements within the party.

—Carl Becker, "The Will of the People,"
Yale Review, March 1945

deliver their acceptance speeches. Some of the hoopla, speeches, and interviews at the presidential nominating conventions are still interesting. And actually, viewers at home have a better and closer view of a national convention than the delegates. Network and cable television reporters roam the convention floor interviewing political leaders. In darkened rooms just off the convention floor, TV directors follow the action on glowing monitors. They bark crisp orders; the camera cuts to correspondents on the floor. The latest gossip, the newest rumor, is fed back to millions of American homes.

True, the television viewer will miss the sense of being in the convention hall, the actual feel of the crowd, the vast size of the amphitheater. On the other hand, viewers can sit back in the comfort of home and watch the Democrats and Republicans choose their candidates for the most powerful office in the world.

As noted, in most recent conventions the delegates have merely ratified what has been a foregone conclusion for weeks or months. Do the delegates have meaningful power and independent judgment, or are they robots legally bound to vote for the winner of their state's primary? Are some of them puppets taking orders from political bosses? Would it perhaps be better, after all, to watch a late movie? The answers to these questions depend entirely on what convention, what delegation, and which delegates one has in mind. Depending on the year and the circumstances, one can actually answer "yes" or "no" to each question. Although many of the convention proceedings draw a relatively small television audience, the acceptance speech by a presidential nominee, usually on the last night of the convention, normally draws a large audience of many millions of people.

The national convention has been roundly denounced as a carnival and a bore, and vigorously defended as the most practical method of choosing political candidates in a democracy. It may be all three.

Today, Nelson W. Polsby has observed, "National conventions survive primarily as spectacle. . . . More and more conventions are designed as entertainment, although . . . they may still conduct business of great importance to the future of the party."[46]

In 1996, the only drama at the Democratic convention in Chicago was the tabloid disclosure that Dick Morris, President Clinton's chief political adviser, had engaged in a dalliance with an expensive prostitute. In 2000, both major-party conventions took place with no unexpected developments, major street protests, or awkward revelations in the news media.

Nevertheless, the national conventions of both major parties can play an important role in rallying voter support for their party's candidates. In 2000, Vice President Al Gore came out of the Democratic National Convention in Los Angeles with a "convention bounce" and momentum that placed his opponent, George W. Bush, on the defensive for several weeks.

Nominating a Presidential Candidate

National party conventions, today greatly diminished in importance, normally take place over four days in July or August. The convention city is often hot and overcrowded; delegates spend long hours waiting for elevators and attempting to do such ordinarily simple things as ordering breakfast in a hotel coffee shop or getting through to someone on the telephone. If there is competition for the nomination—and that has not been the case in recent years—rumors may fly of deals and of switches by key delegations. There are press conferences, television interviews, parades, bands, and other forms of confusion and diversion. In 2000, large corporations set up hospitality suites, or provided cars for bigwigs, or threw lavish parties that doubled as fund-raisers for members of Congress attending the conventions.

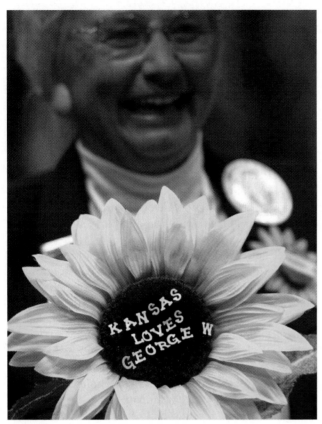

AP/Wide World

The convention, on its first day, normally hears the report of its credentials committee, the body that decides which delegates shall be seated. Sometimes, rival delegations claim to represent the party in a state, or one faction may charge irregularities in the selection of delegates. The credentials committee must decide these disputes, subject always to the approval of the convention. In the evening, the keynote speaker fills the air with the customary rhetoric. A good keynote speech stirs the delegates and sets the tone for the rest of the convention; it may also catapult the speaker into national prominence, possibly as a contender for the party's nomination in the future.

On the second day the party platform is debated and voted on. On the third day the nominations and balloting for the presidential nominee usually begin. Traditionally, a candidate's name is not mentioned until the very end of the nominating speech. ("I give you the name of the next president of the United States!") The name is a signal for a carefully planned, "spontaneous" demonstration on the floor, often employing professional demonstrators and organized to the split second by experts armed with noisemakers, walkie-talkies, and stopwatches.

Then the roll of states is called in alphabetical order for the balloting. In both parties, the candidate who wins a simple majority of the convention votes is nominated. In the past, when sometimes there were contests for the nomination, front-runners attempted to win on the first ballot. Today, however, delegates do not expect to vote more than once; 1952 was the last year in which a major-party presidential nomination was not settled on the first ballot.

It is the traditional privilege of the presidential nominee to select the vice presidential nominee.* The convention nominates the vice presidential candidate, who delivers an acceptance speech. On the fourth day the presidential candidate delivers his acceptance speech. The presidential and vice presidential candidates make their climactic appearance with their families before the cheering delegates and the television audience. This moment of high personal and political

---

*In 1956 Adlai Stevenson, the nominee of the Democratic National Convention, threw open the choice of a vice presidential candidate to the delegates. In the floor balloting, Senator Estes Kefauver of Tennessee narrowly defeated Senator John F. Kennedy of Massachusetts to become Stevenson's running mate.

Delegates at the 2000 Democratic National Convention display their support for Vice President Al Gore.

Copyright © Michael Newman/PhotoEdit

The National Convention **269**

drama underscores the fact that a national convention also serves the function of a party pep rally, generating enthusiasm for the ticket and, in effect, kicking off the presidential campaign.

Beneath the hoopla and the ballyhoo of a national party convention, some serious business has taken place. At times, differences on issues within the party have been publicly aired. And a major political party has produced its nominees for the highest offices in the land.

The Delegates

Who are the few thousand men and women formally entitled to select the presidential nominees of the two major parties? In general, they represent a cross section of the party, but a generally affluent cross section, since the cost of travel to a convention city, and of hotels and meals, mounts up to hundreds of dollars. The delegates usually include governors, senators, members of Congress, mayors, state legislators, state party officials, candidates for local, state, and federal offices, and activists and contributors at the grass-roots level.

Delegates to national party conventions are chosen by a variety of methods. A majority of states select dele-gations in presidential primaries, in which voters in one or both parties select all or some convention delegates. In the remaining states, delegates are chosen by other methods, including state conventions, party caucuses, and state committees.

Because of reforms instituted by the Democratic Party, its 1972 national convention included for the first time substantial numbers of women, African Americans, youths, and Spanish-speaking delegates. Until that year, in some states, members of those groups were systematically excluded from Democratic Party delegations to national conventions. (See Table 9-4.) Both major parties apportion delegates under complicated formulas based on population and party strength within each state.

Delegates who are chosen by state and local party organizations are sometimes under the control of party leaders. But the growth of primaries and caucuses that choose delegates pledged to vote for a particular candidate has greatly reduced the power of party leaders to control national conventions. By 1980, however, many Democrats felt that grass-roots party reform had gone too far. A party commission recommended new rules designed to give party regulars—officeholders and party officials—more power to nominate a presidential candi-

AP/Wide World

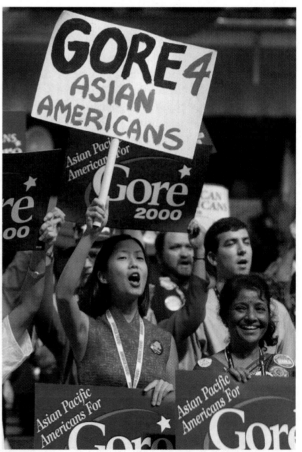

AP/Wide World

Some junior high school students aspire to be astronauts or rock stars. Thomas Santaniello wanted to be in politics. At the Democratic National Convention in Los Angeles in 2000, he achieved his dream.

At 17, Tom Santaniello was the youngest delegate at the Democratic convention. And he was not even old enough to vote.

"I've kind of been preparing for this since about the eighth grade," said the South Carolina delegate.

Santaniello got involved in politics when he had to write a letter to a famous person for a junior high

school English class. He wrote to Senator Ernest Hollings, Democrat of South Carolina, who responded, urging him to get involved in local politics.

Santaniello attended his first precinct caucus in his hometown of Spartanburg in 1996 and immersed himself in local Democratic Party politics. He took part in several campaigns, holding candidate signs on street corners and driving senior citizens to polling places.

But those chores were nothing like the personal campaign he undertook early in 2000. He began writing

letters and making phone calls, urging Democrats to send a youth representative to the national convention.

The campaign paid off. Santaniello was one of two delegates elected from South Carolina's 4th Congressional District.

"A dream come true," he said.

After the convention, Santaniello heads to Furman University where he plans to major in—what else?—political science.

—Adapted from the Associated Press, August 15, 2000; and Gannett News Service, August 15, 2000

date. At the party's national convention in 2000 at Los Angeles, for example, 13 percent of the delegates identified themselves as politicians, a number larger than any other group.[47]

| TABLE 9-4 |

Delegates, by Selected Groups, to the Democratic National Convention, 1968–2000

Year	Women	African Americans	Youth*
1968	13%	5.5%	4%
1972	38	15	21
1976	34	9	14.8
1980	49.9	14.9	NA
1984	50	18	8
1988	49	21	5
1992	49.7	17	4
1996	57	21	4†
2000	58	19	NA

*Ages 18 to 30.
†Ages 18 to 29.
SOURCES: *The Party Reformed*, Final Report of the Committee on Party Structure and Delegate Selection (Washington, D.C.: Democratic National Committee, July 7, 1972), pp. 7–8; *New York Times*, July 12, 1976, p. C5; 1980 data from Democratic National Committee; 1984 data from *New York Times*, July 15, 1984, p. 26; 1988 data from *Washington Post*, July 12, 1988, p. A27; 1992 data from *Washington Post*, July 12, 1992, p. A13, and the Democratic National Committee; 1996 data from *Washington Post*, August 25, 1996, p. M4; 2000 data from *New York Times*, August 14, 2000, p. A17.

From Smoke-Filled Rooms to the Television Age

The national nominating convention evolved slowly in American politics. Until 1824, nominations for president were made by party caucus in Congress. As a presidential aspirant that year, Andrew Jackson knew he did not have enough strength in the congressional caucus to gain the nomination, so his supporters boycotted the caucus. The Tennessee legislature nominated Jackson, who received the most popular and electoral votes. But no candidate received a majority of the electoral votes, and the selection of a president fell to the House of Representatives. Jackson lost when the House chose John Quincy Adams. Jackson's efforts, however, successfully dethroned "King Caucus"; for the election of 1832, presidential candidates of all political parties were nominated by national conventions for the first time.

The early conventions provided no surprises, but in 1844, on the eighth ballot, the Democrats chose James K. Polk, a "dark horse"—a term used to describe a candidate who is thought to have only an outside chance of gaining the nomination. Polk won the election and proved an able president. Polk's nomination "marked the coming of age of the convention as an institution capable of creating as well as of ratifying consensus within the party."[*]

The phrase "smoke-filled room," often used to describe the selection of a candidate by political bosses operating in secret, grew out of the 1920 GOP convention. There, a group of Republican leaders met in Suite

---

*V. O. Key, Jr., *Politics, Parties, and Pressure Groups*, 5th ed. (New York: Crowell, 1964), p. 398. Polk was, in fact, the first "dark horse" to be nominated for president by a national political convention.

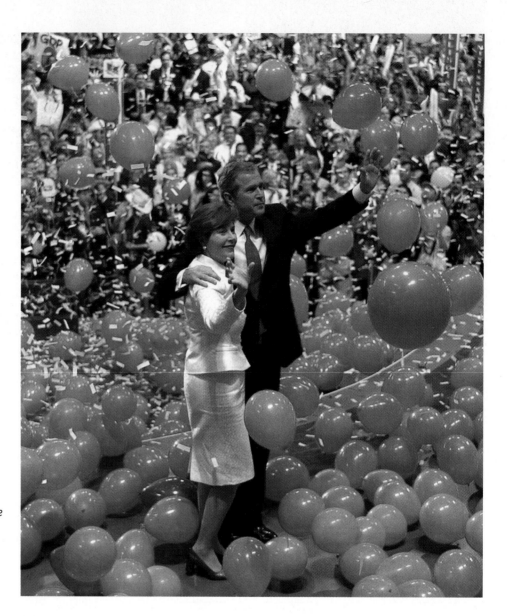

Philadelphia, August 2000: George W. Bush and his wife, Laura, acknowledge the cheers of the delegates at the Republican National Convention that nominated him for president.
AP/Wide World

404 of Chicago's Blackstone Hotel and ended a convention stalemate by selecting Warren G. Harding of Marion, Ohio, who looked like a president but was otherwise a mediocre chief executive.

Harding died in office in 1923 and his vice president, Calvin Coolidge of Vermont, succeeded to the presidency. A year later, in the historic Democratic National Convention of 1924, the delegates were deadlocked and split between supporters of Alfred E. Smith, the Roman Catholic governor of New York, and William Gibbs McAdoo of California, President Woodrow Wilson's secretary of the treasury and son-in-law. Finally, on the 103rd ballot, the convention nominated John W. Davis, a New York lawyer and former ambassador to Great Britain, as the Democratic standard-bearer. It was the longest convention ever held, but all to no avail. The Republicans nominated President Coolidge, a man of so few words that he was known as "Silent Cal," and the Progressive Party nominated Senator Robert M.

"Fighting Bob" La Follette of Wisconsin. Coolidge, who was identified with prosperity, won.

Franklin D. Roosevelt led the field at the Democratic National Convention in 1932, but he was not nominated until the fourth ballot. In 1940, with the galleries chanting "We want Willkie," the Republicans nominated Wendell L. Willkie, a Wall Street lawyer and a true dark horse. The Taft-Eisenhower convention battle in 1952 reflected the greatest split in the Republican Party since 1912.

Since 1960, however, national conventions have filled more of a ratifying function than a selective one. The power of party leaders and bosses, which had been very strong in national conventions for more than a century, was ebbing. (See Table 9-5.)

As a result of the intense press coverage now given to presidential primaries and to preconvention campaigning, one or another candidate has tended to gain a clear lead in the minds of the public, in the political

William Safire, in his authoritative political dictionary, tracked down the origin of a famous phrase in American politics, born at the 1920 Republican National Convention in Chicago:

> **smoke-filled room:** A place of political intrigue and chicanery, where candidates are selected by party bosses in cigar-chewing sessions.

This sinister phrase is usually attributed to Harry Daugherty, an Ohio Republican who supported Senator Warren Harding for the party's presidential candidacy. Daugherty sensed that the two best-known candidates, General Leonard Wood and Governor Frank Lowden of Illinois, would start off with almost equal support. "The convention will be deadlocked," Daugherty is quoted as having said, "and after the other candidates have gone their limit, some twelve or fifteen men, worn out and bleary-eyed for lack of sleep, will sit down about two o'clock in the morning, around a table in a smoke-filled room in some hotel and decide the nomination. When that time comes, Harding will be selected."

Daugherty later denied having said any such thing. . . . But William Allen White, editor of the *Emporia Gazette* and a respected Republican figure, corroborated the Daugherty prediction. A story filed at 5 A.M. on June 12, 1920, by Associated Press reporter Kirke Simpson, led off with the words "Harding of Ohio was chosen by a group of men in a smoke-filled room early today as Republican candidate for President."

—William Safire, *Safire's New Political Dictionary: The Definitive Guide to the New Language of Politics*

---

polls, and often, within the rank and file of the party well before the convention. "News accounts of nominating campaigns play up the competition, reporting the campaign as if it were a game or a sporting event," one observer has noted. "The metaphor of choice is a horse race. The news focuses on favorites, dark horses, and also-rans, on candidates neck-and-neck, gaining ground, or running far behind."[48]

National conventions nominate candidates for president who go before the voters every four years. But most Americans do not participate in selecting the convention delegates who make this crucial choice. In 1996, for example, 10.8 million people voted in the Democratic primaries and 14.1 million in the Republican primaries, for a total of 24.9 million people, or only about 13 percent of the total number of Americans of voting age.

TABLE 9-5

Development of the System for Nominating Presidential Candidates in the United States, 1790s–2000

Year	System Used to Nominate Presidential Candidates	Key Features	Consequences
1790s–1824	Congressional caucus	Presidential nominees are selected by a party's legislators in Congress.	Selection of the presidential nominee is controlled by the congressional wing of the party.
1831–1908	"Classic" convention system	Presidential nominees are selected by the party convention. Convention delegates are chosen by party leaders and party organizations.	Party leaders and "party bosses" retain maximum power to control nomination.
1912–1968	"Mixed" convention system	Some convention delegates are chosen in presidential primaries, where rank-and-file party members vote for delegates pledged to particular candidates. Most delegates are still chosen by party leaders and party organizations.	Convention still "decides." Party leaders and "party bosses" continue to be very influential.
1972 to present	The age of presidential primaries	Most delegates are selected in presidential primaries. Delegates are pledged to particular candidates.	Decision is usually made before the convention meets. Convention no longer decides.

AP/Wide World

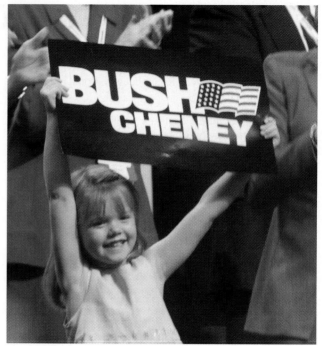

AP/Wide World

Moreover, a leading political scientist has concluded that those who do vote in the presidential primaries are "quite unrepresentative" of the party identifiers who do not participate.[49] Even fewer people choose the delegates who are selected in ways other than the primaries. Most people, for example, have never attended a district or state party convention where delegates are chosen.

The Future of the Convention System

From time to time various proposals have been made to revamp the national nominating convention or even replace it with some presumably more representative or more dignified procedure. One of the proposals has been for a national presidential primary, in which the voters could directly choose the presidential candidates of the major parties.

The plan has some possible drawbacks, however: Critics have argued that there is no assurance that voters in a national primary would be representative of party rank-and-file members; that if too many candidates enter the primary, the candidate who wins the most votes might be one who enjoyed intense but limited support, and who could not, therefore, win a general election; or, no single candidate might receive a majority of the votes, forcing a runoff. In that case, the candidate who initially led the field might lose.[50] Moreover, a national presidential primary might work against lesser-known candidates who benefit from a nominating process that is spread out over several months, allowing them to gain

greater public recognition. And, it has been contended, a national primary would further weaken American political parties by bypassing party organizations, while increasing the power of the news media to influence the electoral process.[51]

Nelson W. Polsby has suggested that political parties deserve a continuing role in the selection of presidential nominees, for "no better institutions have evolved to conduct nominating politics."[52] Moreover, Polsby argues, political parties, because of their varied roles, are "crucial for the proper general functioning of the political system."[53]

In any event, the convention system, having survived since 1832, is not likely to disappear in the television age. Nor is it at all clear that the national convention should be replaced.

The conventions may no longer, as a rule, be an arena for political struggle, nor do they have the excitement of years past. But they still serve a purpose. They choose the nominees for president and vice president, they provide a forum for the voters to see the candidates in action as they deliver their acceptance speeches, they may unify the party, and they may also generate voter interest in the fall elections.

POLITICAL PARTIES AND DEMOCRATIC GOVERNMENT

At best, Americans have always had a somewhat ambivalent attitude toward politics and politicians. "Politics," Clinton Rossiter has noted, "is sin, and politicians, if not sinners, are pretty suspicious fellows."[54]

In 1952 General Eisenhower enjoyed the support of many voters who believed that he was "above politics" or "not a politician." The same was true of Ronald Reagan when he ran for governor of California for the first time in 1966, in a campaign that emphasized his nonprofessional political status.

Among many voters, the image of the politician as an unprincipled opportunist persists. The initial reaction of many Americans to the Watergate scandal was not shock at the illegal acts committed by the Nixon Administration but the view that "they all do it."

Because political parties are vital to the functioning of American democracy, it is somewhat paradoxical that politics and politicians—especially with their access to the image-making resources of Madison Avenue—do not enjoy greater prestige.

The truth about politics and its practitioners may lie somewhere between Aristotle's view that "the good of man" is the object of politics and the classic statement of Simon Cameron, the Republican boss of Pennsylvania, that "an honest politician is one who, when he is bought, will stay bought."

Possibly, Americans would have a more generous view of the craft of politics if it were more widely understood that parties and democracy are mutually depend-

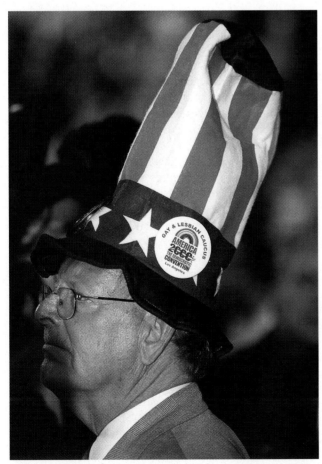

A delegate displays patriotic headgear at the 2000 Democratic National Convention.
Copyright © Jonathan Nourok/PhotoEdit

ent. Competition among political parties is the essence of democracy. Political parties in America, as we have seen, provide a vehicle of political choice. They also manage the transfer of power, help to hold politicians accountable to the voters, recruit candidates, staff and link branches of the government, and may sometimes resolve social conflict.

The rest of the world also has a vital stake in the politics of American democracy; certainly the party nominee chosen by the electorate to be president has greater power than any other world leader. How an American president uses that power, including the nuclear weapons under his control, is of direct concern to all other nations, as well as to the voters at home.

The "brokerage" role of political parties in mediating among interest groups (whether such groups are organized or not) and in resolving social conflict is of tremendous importance in a democracy under pressure. Both major political parties try to form a broad base by appealing to diverse groups in society. As a result, when one party loses power and another wins the presidency, the change tends to be accepted, or at least tolerated, by the voters. At the same time, the party out of power plays a valuable role as the opposition party, offering alternative programs in Congress and serving as a rallying point for its followers. The "out party" keeps alive the possibility of change for another four years. In these ways parties help to keep conflict manageable, for if substantial numbers of voters violently opposed the election results, the political system could not work.

A Choice, Not an Echo?

In his classic complaint about the similarity of American political parties, James Bryce concluded that "neither party has any principles, any distinctive tenets." The similarities of American parties are often lamented, but, as noted earlier, there are significant differences as well.

Some of these differences can be measured by comparing contrasting party platforms in presidential elections. Although the conventional view is that platforms are "meaningless," Gerald M. Pomper has concluded that platforms in fact "are reasonably meaningful indications of the party's intentions" and serve to identify the parties with "certain policies."[55]

Moreover—as surprising as it might be to many people—in a majority of cases, Pomper concluded, political parties actually carry out the promises contained in their platforms. Analyzing 1,795 platform pledges over a 10-year period, Pomper determined that "almost two-thirds" of these promises were fulfilled.[56]

Although it is true that American parties are not sharply ideological, it is also true that many American voters have not been sharply ideological. The argument is often made that major parties should offer a more pronounced choice on issues, not merely a choice between candidates; but it is by no means clear that extreme polarization of the parties on issues that divide American society is desirable. "The difference between Democrats and Republicans," Max Lerner has observed, "while it is more than the difference between Tweedledum and Tweedledee, is not such as to split the society itself or invite civil conflict. . . . The choices between the two are usually substantial choices but not desperate ones."[57]

Are Parties Accountable to the Voters?

When Americans go to the polls, they do not elect parties; they elect officials who usually run as the candidates of political parties. By its very nature, the American political system holds these officials accountable to the voters while holding the parties only indirectly accountable.

The most frequent criticism of the American party system is that the parties are not "responsible" to the electorate, that there is no way to make them keep the promises outlined in their platforms, and that, in any event, they lack the internal discipline to whip their programs through Congress.[58] One difficulty is that party platforms "are written for use in presidential campaigns, yet they consist mainly of proposals for legislation that will be meaningless unless there is congressional action."[59] Yet, as Gerald Pomper has noted, political parties often do carry out platform pledges.

In a parliamentary system of government, such as that in Great Britain, political parties are more closely linked to the popular will because the voters choose a majority party that is responsible for the conduct of both

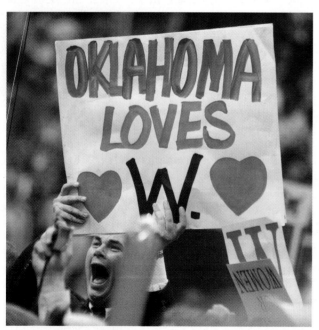

AP/Wide World

the executive and legislative branches of government. Because few critics of the American party system advocate parliamentary government for the United States, party accountability in America is likely to remain a matter of degree.

Many political scientists do not agree on the need for or desirability of greater party responsibility. For example, party cohesion strong enough to pass programs in Congress could only be achieved by reducing the importance and independence of individual legislators. But advocates of strong, responsible parties point to several ways that party responsibility can be strengthened, short of adopting the British system of parliamentary government—for example, attempting to achieve greater discipline within parties by rewarding cooperative members with campaign funds, and electing the chairpersons of congressional committees on the basis of party loyalty rather than seniority.

To an extent, however, a measure of party responsibility already exists. When American parties embark on courses of action that displease large numbers of voters, the voters may retaliate. In 1964 Barry Goldwater, the Republican candidate, was the "hawk" who advocated "total victory" over communism. President Lyndon Johnson, on the other hand, presented himself as a "dove," promising: "We are not about to send American

Al Gore, right, his vice-presidential choice, Sen. Joseph I. Lieberman, and their wives at the Democratic National Convention in 2000.
AP/Wide World

boys nine or ten thousand miles away from home to do what Asian boys ought to be doing for themselves."[60] In less than a year, however, Johnson was sending combat troops to Vietnam. Many of his supporters felt misled; it turned out that they had voted for a "dove" and elected a "hawk." But in the election of 1968, Johnson found it prudent not to run again, and the nation sent a Republican to the White House. That election, and others, provide evidence that a measure of accountability is not wholly lacking in American politics.

A LOOK AHEAD

Attempting to predict the future of American political parties is a perilous business. Like life itself, politics is often unpredictable; those who had forecast the eclipse of the Republican Party in 1964 were required to watch the elephant ride into the White House in 1968 and again in 1972. Although similar predictions of Republican doom were heard after Nixon's resignation over the Watergate scandal in 1974, the GOP with Ronald Reagan as its candidate won the presidential elections of 1980 and 1984, and, with George Bush, won in 1988. And the Democrats, whose prospects seemed bleak at the outset of the 1992 campaign, triumphed in November. Two years later, the Republicans, seemingly humbled by Clinton's victory, won control of Congress.

One fact seems clear: Over a period of time, political parties must respond to the pressures for, or against, change, or pay the price of defeat. And it seems likely that minor parties of the right and left will periodically continue to arise. Possibly, more "nonparty" candidates will seek the presidency, as did Ross Perot in 1992. Yet, in one form or another, the two-party system has flourished since the beginning of the republic.

The increased importance of television and of preconvention campaigns makes the last-minute selection of an unknown candidate by a national convention far less likely than in the past. Candidates will probably continue to rely more on television, which can reach millions of people, than on old-fashioned stump campaigning. Political commercials, "attack ads," and professional campaign managers who are skilled in media techniques now play a major role in campaigns. So too do political polls.

Political parties mirror the society in which they function. If government can be made more responsive to the public, political parties may play a vital part in that process, for they are uniquely situated to translate the hopes of the American people into action by the American government.

KEY TERMS

major political party,
  p. 248

national chairperson,
  p. 263

national convention, p. 263

national committee, p. 263

CHAPTER HIGHLIGHTS

✦ A major political party is a broadly based coalition that attempts to gain control of the government by winning elections, in order to exercise power and reward its members.

✦ In the United States, the two-party system has prevailed during most of the nation's history.

✦ Today, political parties are less powerful than in the past, as party allegiances among voters have declined and as competing groups—political action committees, professional campaign managers, and interest groups—have increasingly come to share many of the traditional roles of parties.

✦ Political parties perform vital functions in the American political system. They (1) manage the transfer of power, (2) offer a choice of rival candidates and programs to the voters, (3) serve as a bridge between government and people by helping to hold elected officials accountable to the voters, (4) help to recruit candidates for office, (5) may serve to reconcile conflicting interests in society, (6) staff the government and help to run it, and (7) link various branches and levels of government.

✦ The fading of party loyalties among many voters has been one of the most visible features of American politics in recent years. Beginning in 1974, about a third of the voters described themselves as independents. Only about two-thirds of the voters called themselves Republicans or Democrats.

✦ Various reasons have been suggested for the decline of party ties: a more educated electorate, less dependent on parties for guidance; an increase in "split-ticket" voting; the increasing importance of television and the news media; and the breaking up of the old loyalties and alignments within the major parties.

✦ Studies have shown that the Democrats usually, although not always, enjoy greater voter support from labor, minorities, young people, those who have not attended college and who have lower incomes, and those who live in the cities. Republicans are more likely to be white, suburban, rural, wealthy, older, college educated, and professionals or business executives.

✦ There are also philosophical and ideological differences between the parties. Democrats tend to believe more in the ability of government to solve problems than do Republicans.

✦ Although presidential candidates are nominated by national political party conventions, in recent years the convention's choice has been determined months earlier by the results of the spring primaries. The increased importance of television and of preconvention campaigns makes the last-minute selection of an unknown candidate by a national convention far less likely than in the past.

✦ On paper, the party's quadrennial national convention is the source of all authority within the party. The convention nominates the party's candidates for president and vice president; it writes a platform, settles disputes, writes rules, and elects the members of the national committee.

✦ Over a period of time, political parties must respond to the pressures for, or against, change—or pay the price of defeat. And it seems likely that minor parties of the right and left will periodically continue to arise.

SUGGESTED WEB SITES

The Web sites listed below include political party home pages that provide data about party platforms, information about candidates, and advice about how to become involved in politics:

www.dnc.org
Democratic Party

www.greenparty.org
Green Party

www.lp.org
Libertarian Party

www.reform-party-usa.org or **www.reformparty.org**
Reform Party

www.rnc.org
Republican Party

www.vote-smart.org
Project Vote Smart
Project Vote Smart, a nonprofit, nonpartisan Web site, researches issues affecting voters and people running for office.

www.grassroots.com
Grassroots.com
Grassroots.com is a nonpartisan Web site that allows users to look up their representatives in local, state, and federal government offices. Also includes information about issues that may affect elections.

SUGGESTED READING

Aldrich, John. *Why Parties? The Origin and Transformation of Political Parties in America** (University of Chicago Press, 1995). An insightful examination of the role of political parties. According to the author, parties fulfill three basic functions: they help organize the selection of candidates for public office, they mobilize the electorate, and they play a vital role in the policymaking process.

Bartels, Larry M. *Presidential Primaries and the Dynamics of Public Choice** (Princeton University Press, 1988). An illuminating analysis of how the present system for nominating presidential candidates works.

Beck, Paul Allen, and Sorauf, Frank J. *Party Politics in America*, 8th edition* (Longman, 1998). A comprehensive analysis of American political parties. Examines party organization, the behavior of party supporters in the electorate, the role of parties in elections, and the impact of parties on government.

Crotty, William J., and Jacobson, Gary C. *American Parties in Decline*, 2nd edition (HarperCollins, 1984). A revealing analysis of the diminishing influence and importance of political parties in the electorate, in election campaigns, and in Congress.

David, Paul T.; Goldman, Ralph M.; and Bain, Richard C. *The Politics of National Party Conventions*, revised edition (Peter Smith, 1987). A detailed examination of the historical development of national party conventions. Stresses the functions that the national conventions have performed in the American party system.

Duverger, Maurice. *Political Parties: Their Organization and Activity in the Modern State*, 3rd edition (Methuen, 1964). An influential comparative analysis of political parties in a number of countries. Among other topics, Duverger, a French political scientist, examines the nature of party organization in different types of parties. He also explores the relationship between a country's electoral system and the type of party system that flourishes there.

Epstein, Leon D. *Political Parties in the American Mold** (University of Wisconsin Press, 1986). A thoughtful analysis of the historical development and operation of political parties in America.

Epstein, Leon D. *Political Parties in Western Democracies** (Transaction Books, 1980). A useful comparative study of political parties in various countries, with special emphasis on those in Great Britain and the United States. Examines the historical development of parties, recruitment of party leaders, and the contribution of the parties to governing.

Fiorina, Morris. *Divided Government*, 2nd edition* (Allyn and Bacon, 1995). A thoughtful analysis of a phenomenon that was once rare in American politics, but has become increasingly common.

Green, John C., ed. *The State of the Parties** (Rowman & Littlefield, 1998). A readable and wide-ranging collection of essays on the evolving role of political parties in elections and governance.

Keefe, William J., ed. *Political Parties and Public Policy in America*, 8th edition* (Congressional Quarterly, 1998). A useful introduction to the historical development, political functions, and current status of parties in the American political system.

Key, V. O., Jr. *Politics, Parties, and Pressure Groups*, 5th edition (Crowell, 1964). A comprehensive analysis of political parties and interest groups. Examines the nature of the American party system, party structure and procedures, the relations between parties and the voters, and the impact of parties on government.

Magleby, David B., ed. *Outside Money: Soft Money and Issue Advocacy in the 1998 Congressional Elections** (University Press of America, 2000). A valuable collection of essays, including seven different case studies, on the growing role of soft money in American politics.

Mayer, William G., ed. *In Pursuit of the White House 2000: How We Choose Our Presidential Nominees** (Chatham House, 2000). A comprehensive examination of the intricate process by which American presidential candidates are nominated.

Mayhew, David R. *Placing Parties in American Politics** (Princeton University Press, 1986). A thoughtful and detailed analysis of the American party structure on the state level. Points out that although some states have strong, unified party organizations, in other states parties are much weaker.

Mazmanian, Daniel A. *Third Parties in Presidential Elections* (The Brookings Institution, 1974). A comprehensive examination of American third parties: the conditions that cause them to arise, the factors that impede their success, and their role in the American party system.

Polsby, Nelson W. *Consequences of Party Reform** (Oxford University Press, 1983). A study of reforms in the presidential nominating system and of changes in the way that campaigns and parties are financed. Analyzes the results of these reforms and evaluates proposals for further change.

Ranney, Austin. *Curing the Mischiefs of Faction: Party Reform in America* (University of California Press, 1975). A thoughtful analysis of the theory and practice of party reform in the United States. Emphasizes three main periods when major changes were made in American party institutions: 1820–1840, 1890–1920, and 1956–1974.

Wattenberg, Martin P. *The Decline of American Political Parties, 1952–1996** (Harvard University Press, 1998). A concise study of the diminishing importance of political parties and the growing impact of candidate images in American elections. Argues that voters have become indifferent to parties because of an increasing belief that parties no longer play a significant role in the governing process.

---

*Available in paperback edition.

 Visit http://politicalscience.wadsworth.com/cummings9/update/ for current InfoTrac articles and other student resources related to this chapter.

CHAPTER 10
Political Campaigns and Candidates

Americans watching television one night in the year 2000 saw an interesting 30-second commercial. It was not an advertisement for a detergent, a toothpaste, or a breakfast cereal. Rather, it sought to attack the Democratic candidate for president of the United States, Al Gore, and sell the voters on the Republican candidate, George W. Bush.

It was mid-September, after Labor Day, and the campaigns had gotten under way in earnest. Vice President Al Gore had made headlines with the surprise selection of his running mate—Senator Joseph I. Lieberman of Connecticut, who had assailed President Clinton over the Lewinsky scandal. Gore, hammering away on the issues, had seemed to place Bush on the defensive. Bush had committed some gaffes on the campaign trail; his own running mate, Richard B. Cheney, had not proved to be an electrifying speaker; and some polls showed Gore pulling ahead.

It was time, the Bush strategists decided, to meet Gore head-on over the issues. In the commercial, a female announcer intoned: "Al Gore's prescription plan forces seniors into a government-run HMO. Governor Bush gives seniors a choice. Gore says he's for school accountability, but requires no real testing.

Voice over: Al Gore's prescription plan forces seniors into a government-run H.M.O. Governor Bush gives seniors a choice. Gore says he's for school accountability, but requires no real testing.

Courtesy www.georgebush.com

Governor Bush requires tests and holds schools accountable for results. Gore's targeted tax cuts leave out 50 million people—half of all taxpayers.

Under Bush, every taxpayer gets a tax cut and no family pays more than one-third of their income to Washington. Governor Bush has real plans that work for real people.

Governor Bush requires tests and holds schools accountable for results. Gore's targeted tax cuts leave out 50 million people—half of all taxpayers. Under Bush, every taxpayer gets a tax cut."[1]

The television screen showed a smiling young man and woman, dressed in T-shirts and obviously designed to look like the Average American Taxpayer, as the words "GOVERNOR BUSH: Tax Cut For Every Taxpayer" were displayed.

Like most political commercials, this one was only partly true. As an analysis by the *New York Times* pointed out, Gore's prescription drug plan for seniors was voluntary, and did not involve HMOs, which are unpopular. Gore as well as Bush proposed testing for schoolchildren, although Bush's plan called for more tests covering more grades. Bush's tax-cut plan would benefit all income brackets, but would cost more than twice as much as Gore's plan to give "targeted" tax breaks for specific purposes such as college education and child care.

Few viewers would know these details, however, and objectivity is not the point of political commercials. They are designed to sell a product—in this case a candidate—and get people to "buy" that product in the voting booth. In that sense, political commercials have the same goal as croaking frogs in a beer commercial or a Chihuahua selling tacos. And they are effective, or candidates would not spend a large portion of their total budget on television commercials. "As a general rule, a campaign should spend 50 to 80 percent of its budget" on TV commercials, according to political consultants.[2]

Television commercials are an important aspect of modern political campaigns. Candidates at the presidential level and below now routinely advertise their wares in this fashion—or snipe at their opponents. For a moment, through the medium of television, Bush's message had been seen by millions of viewers.

Nor are commercials the only way that candidates use television to reach the voters. In 2000 the presidential candidates appeared, to an even greater extent than in any past campaign, on the major television talk and entertainment shows.

George Bush planted a large kiss on Oprah Winfrey as he appeared on her program in September. It was a forum that allowed him to show off his sense of humor and considerable personal charm, and not incidentally to try to appeal to the millions of women who make up the largest portion of her audience. A few nights later Jay Leno began spouting praise for Al Gore, then pretended to be surprised when the man holding the large cue cards containing those words turned out to be—Al Gore.

Oprah, Leno, David Letterman, Larry King—all welcomed the presidential candidates, who clowned around and sought to show the voters their "human side." One might have trouble visualizing George Washington or John Adams on Oprah or Leno, but then, times and technology have changed.

This sort of thing did not begin in 2000. During the 1992 presidential campaign, all three major candidates—Bill Clinton, President George Bush, and Texas businessman Ross Perot—also appeared on the talk show circuit. Clinton, wearing dark glasses and looking like one of the

Republican candidate George W. Bush demonstrates his affection for Oprah Winfrey—and her large audience of women viewers.
AP/Wide World

"Blues Brothers," even played the saxophone one night on the *Arsenio Hall Show*. President Bush went on CNN's *Larry King Live* to question Clinton's patriotism and attack Clinton's participation in demonstrations against the Vietnam War while a student in England. Ross Perot appeared so often on the *Today* show that he became almost as familiar to viewers as Katie Couric and the other stars of that program. Perot, in fact, based almost his entire campaign on television appearances and commercials. Again in 1996, the candidates—Clinton, Bob Dole, his Republican challenger, and Perot—were familiar faces on television.

Jay Leno and Democratic candidate Al Gore ham it up on NBC's Tonight Show *during the 2000 presidential campaign.*
AP/Wide World

It is not surprising in the television age that candidates for political office try to sell themselves and their ideas on TV. Once nominated, candidates must appeal to the voters. And television offers the surest means of reaching the largest number of people.

As a result, television has dramatically changed American political campaigns since 1948. The day is long past when a William McKinley could campaign from his front porch in Canton, Ohio. Today's candidates hire an advertising agency or a special team of consultants to prepare television spots—commercials that may air for ten seconds or longer.

The candidates may debate their opponents on television, as the two major presidential rivals did in 1960, 1976, and every election since then. They may appear in carefully staged, televised question-and-answer sessions designed to display their warm personalities and firm grasp of the issues. Or they may buy an expensive half-hour of prime television time for a sincere talk to the American people.

As the candidates whirl around the country, their campaign appearances in each state are tailored for the statewide and local evening television news broadcasts, and, if possible, the nightly network news programs that reach a national audience. Their speeches on the campaign trail often include "sound bites"—colorful turns of phrase, or sharp words for their rivals—that they hope will make the evening news. Television, in short, is an essential part of a modern political campaign.

In 2000, the candidates campaigned on the Internet as well. All offered Web sites that featured the latest speeches, news, and pronouncements of the presidential campaign. Not only Gore and Bush, but also Pat Buchanan, the candidate of the Reform Party, and Ralph Nader, the nominee of the Green Party, had their own Web sites, as did a number of rival candidates in the spring primaries. Several candidates used their Web sites to raise money and recruit volunteers.

Some candidates, particularly Buchanan in the 1996 Republican primaries, relied heavily on talk radio to get out their message. Because many talk radio hosts and their listeners tend to be conservative, Buchanan had a ready-made audience.

For every candidate, between nomination and election there stands the campaign. In American politics, the campaign is the battleground of power. Victory may depend on how well the battle is fought, for often a third or more of the voters decide how to vote during the campaign. Mostly because of the wide use of television, campaigns are expensive: In 1996 candidates for president and Congress spent $2.1 billion, a figure that rose to an estimated $3 billion in 2000.[3]

In this chapter, we will explore a key question about political campaigns: In the era of electronic mass media, television commercials, and "image" makers, can the voters make a reasonable choice for themselves and for the nation?

Other related questions may be asked as well. Will the candidate with the best image—the most attractive

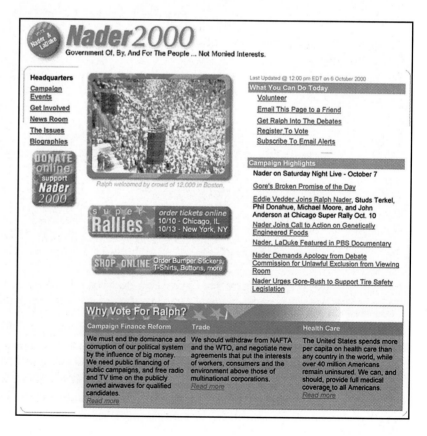

Web site of Ralph Nader, the presidential candidate of the Green Party, October 2000.

The AMERICAN PAST

TIPPECANOE AND TYLER TOO

Indiana Historical Society

Campaign songs, particularly in the 19th century, were an important way to appeal to the voters in the pretelevision age. Perhaps the most famous was the song that publicized "Tippecanoe and Tyler too," the slogan of the Whigs in the presidential election of 1840. William Henry Harrison, the Whig candidate, had defeated the Indians loyal to Chief Tecumseh in the Battle of Tippecanoe in the Indiana Territory in 1811. His vice presidential running mate was John Tyler. The Democrats renominated incumbent Martin Van Buren of New York as their presidential candidate—the "little Van" referred to in the Whig song, which was written by Alexander Coffman Ross, a jeweler and amateur clarinetist from Zanesville, Ohio. To the tune of a minstrel number, "Little Pigs," the song went like this:

What's the cause of this commotion,
Motion, motion, motion,
Our country through?
It is the ball a-rolling on,
For Tippecanoe and Tyler too,
For Tippecanoe and Tyler too,
And with them we'll beat little Van,
Van, Van is a used up man;
And with them we'll beat little Van.

Harrison won the election, but he refused to wear a coat at his inauguration despite the cold and the stormy weather. He caught pneumonia and died a month later. Tyler became president.

—Irwin Silber,
Songs America Voted By

appearance, the cleverest television advisers and consultants, the smoothest packaging—win the election?

Furthermore, political candidates do not always have equal financial and creative resources. Does the candidate with the most money always win? Should one candidate enjoy a financial advantage over another in a democracy? If not, what can be done about it? Do political polls influence the voters and affect the outcome of elections?

These questions have no easy answers. And yet, however imperfect campaigns may be, however raucous and divisive, they are a vital part of the American political system. Campaigns, in the words of the historian Henry Adams, are "the dance of democracy."

HOW CAMPAIGNS ARE ORGANIZED

Campaigns are organized chaos. On a national level, large numbers of people—professionals and volunteers—are thrown together for a relatively short period of time to mount an incredibly complex effort to elect a president. The candidate is rather like someone in the eye of a hurricane: jetting around the country—stumping, speechmaking, and handshaking—besieged by the crowds and camera crews, the press and the voters, local politicians and aides. The candidate may arise at 5 A.M. and not get to sleep until 2 A.M. the next morning, with a dozen cities and thousands of miles traversed in the interim. Physically exhausted, hands cut and bruised from the crowds, the candidate is expected to keep smiling throughout and to remain alert—ready to respond instantly to any new issue or crisis. In some remote cornfield of Iowa, a TV reporter may ask for comment on a sudden and complicated development in the Middle East. The candidate worries that an inappropriate word or phrase might cost the election. An assassin may lurk in the hotel kitchen. The news media are ready to pounce on any mistake. In the jet age, the pressures on the candidate are constant and cruel.

The candidate, flying from one appearance to the next at 500 miles per hour, obviously must have an elaborate campaign organization with a headquarters staff to plan and coordinate the total effort. Ultimate success may depend on many variables—the candidate's charisma, smile and appearance, television makeup, advertising agency, and experience; the issues, the number of registered Democrats and Republicans, a sudden foreign policy crisis, an ill-advised remark, even the weather on Election Day. But not the least of these factors is the quality of the candidate's campaign organization.

A presidential candidate must have a campaign manager and a small group of top-level aides to give overall direction to the campaign. The candidate may hire a professional political consultant as well. There has to be someone in charge of fund-raising, for a national

How Campaigns Are Organized **285**

Voter Canvass. A volunteer often says something like this: "Hello, I'm (Name), a neighbor of yours, and I'm here to tell you about (Name), who's a candidate for (Office). He is running for office because he believes (Vision). Can (Name) count on your vote on Election Day, (Date)?"

The best time of day to canvass is when people are home. . . . Don't be afraid to walk during the dinner hour since it may be the only time to find people at home. Keep the visit short and cordial—apologize if you interrupt dinner. Never enter a person's home—you're not a salesman. When the person comes to the door, take a step back so you're less threatening to the voter. Notice children, if they're present; it makes a great impression and wins votes from parents. . . . Skip places that have dogs (Avoid potential bites!). Stick to sidewalks and driveways rather than cutting across lawns.

Television. If your event is outside, note the location of the sun before selecting the podium site. The sun should never be behind the speaker nor directly in the speaker's eyes. . . . Make-up is appropriate. Most women already wear make-up to avoid reflections; men should use a little light powder or pancake make-up, close to their natural skin tone, to minimize shine and hide any five o'clock shadow. . . . Avoid flashy, distracting clothing. Men should avoid plaids and narrowly striped shirts; women should avoid layers of jewelry and necklines with no place to anchor a clip microphone.

Dealing with Reporters. Contrary to many people's opinion, reporters are just like everybody else. . . . *Don't treat reporters like the enemy.* . . . Most reporters try to be fair. Our evaluation of what's fair or unfair is made through tinted glass: as Republican partisans we're not the most objective people ourselves. . . . *Don't feed the media material you know they won't use.* If you "cry wolf" too many times, the media will start to ignore you altogether. . . . Be honest and accurate. . . . Lying will get you in trouble. . . . If all else fails, respond with a simple "no comment." . . . Remember: NEVER TELL A REPORTER SOMETHING YOU DON'T WANT REPORTED. If the story is juicy enough, "off-the-record" has no meaning.

Speeches. *Greet the audience visually.* Wave like Ronald Reagan. Walk like an Olympic athlete. . . . *Save and polish your applause lines.* Applause lines are like diamonds. Formed under pressure, cut and polished until they shine.

Newspaper. A coordinated letter-to-the-editor program, run by a volunteer, can be another effective way to communicate your message.

Communications Basics. *Don't feel compelled to respond to a reporter's exact question.* . . . The basic rule is:

campaign costs millions of dollars; a media team to handle advertising and television; a press secretary; representatives to handle advance details of personal appearances; speechwriters; regional and state coordinators; and citizens' groups to enlist volunteer support. And the campaign staff must attempt to coordinate the work of national, state, and local party organizations so that there is a unified effort at all levels.

When a presidential candidate is victorious, key staff members often move into the White House or into other high positions in the government. In 1992, for example, Bill Clinton's campaign was run by a

Cornell Capa/Magnum

A reporter can ask any question he wants; you can answer any question you want. . . . Don't exaggerate resumé items. Every single item contained in a campaign biography must be the truth, the whole truth, and nothing but the truth. Failure to follow this rule will mean likely defeat.

Phone Banks. Cold-call prospecting is a telemarketing program which has been proven to produce a good list of prospective donors and at the same time make enough money to cover phone bank expenses. . . . The script you use will depend on whether you're calling as follow-up to a direct mail piece, making a cold-call prospect call, calling to enhance an event, or as a boiler-room operation.

Graphics. What guidelines should I follow when designing a logo? *Use credible colors.* Traditional campaign colors, such as dark blue, red, green and burgundy invoke trust. . . . Avoid using pink—it's too feminine.

Fundraising. It is important that the decoration chairman be well acquainted with novelty/florist/gift shops in the area, so that "freebies" can be arranged. . . . Flowers, as we all know, are not cheap. . . .

Get-Out-the-Vote. What activities can be implemented on Election Day?

1. *Victory Squads.* Victory squads are teams of volunteers who actually knock on the doors of favorable voters and urge them to vote. . . . Each team has a car and driver that can take the voter to the polls while a volunteer babysits or watches the house.

2. *Sign Waving.* In some states, it has become standard for volunteers (and sometimes candidates) to wave signs at key intersections to rouse interest. . . . Since there's no way to differentiate Republican cars from Democrat cars, it's best to do this activity in or around Republican areas. Be careful you don't cause accidents. Attractive young people may get the attention of drivers but can also be traffic hazards. . . .

To ensure an honest vote, you'll want to be sure only qualified voters cast their ballots on Election Day. . . . While most problems are with machine malfunctions, the practice of "voting dead people and vacant lots" is still all too prevalent. Therefore, it's important that Republican volunteers be visible in each precinct to help avoid voter fraud.

What Should I [the Candidate] Do on Election Day? Take time to have dinner with your family and friends. Election night has a habit of being the longest night of the year; rest and collect your thoughts. Prepare your remarks for a victory speech.

—Republican National Committee, *Campaign Encyclopedia*

Texas Governor George W. Bush works the crowd at Westchester, Pennsylvania during the 2000 presidential race.
AP/Wide World

Campaign Planning. You need to have a strategy in mind. . . . Creating a positive image, proving your candidate is a good person—often a necessary strategy element. Proving the opponent is a bad person, based on creating a negative image of the opponent.

Campaign Message in the Plan. Repeat, repeat, repeat. An average voter is bombarded with millions of pieces of information every day. The few dozen pieces of information you get through during the campaign must be consistent and reinforcing. . . . Remember: the image, like the message, is not just what comes out of the candidate's mouth. A candidate who does not pay child support will have a bad image and message about kids, no matter what he or she says about day care.

Research. In essence, opposition research—more appropriately thought of as *comparative research*—is the means by which you find the nuggets of information that support your campaign's message and bring the point home to voters.

Educational History. Verify the [opposition] candidate's degree and graduation date with the school registrar or alumni association; if possible, get his or her grade point average.

Military Service & Draft Records. Did the [opposition] candidate serve when and where he says he did? Did the candidate get any special treatment, or have a family member pull strings to get a deferment? What was his draft status during the Vietnam War?

Country Club Memberships/Fraternal Organizations. Does the club or group to which [the opposition] candidate belongs discriminate against women or minorities? Has it been involved in any scandals or lawsuits?

Hobbies. A candidate's love of golf, yachting, or polo might come to symbolize her elitism in a blue-collar community.

Associates/Friends. Is your opponent close with any known felons or other questionable characters? Find out about the company he keeps.

Direct Mail. Direct mail writers are always thirsty for spicy rhetoric and interesting statistics. Research that's a bit too hot for your press secretary to use may in fact make for great copy for a fundraising letter.

Working with Reporters: On Background. . . . if you spend any length of time talking to reporters, expect to get burned—expect it, shrug it off, and move on. It's happened to everybody and it will be forgotten by the next crisis.

Vice President Al Gore, the Democratic presidential nominee, exhorts supporters in Moline, Illinois during the 2000 campaign.
AP/Wide World

What to Outlet: Beyond Just Paper. Web sites, while now an essential campaign tool, should be tailored to the people likely to access them. In San Jose, California, where net penetration is high, it's worth spending time on a good, credible web site; but in areas where people can't even make a local call for Internet access, you might focus the bulk of your attention elsewhere. Beyond paper—and beyond the web—there are gimmicks. . . . In long campaigns, the press becomes fascinated with gimmicks. So don't call that musty room your research office: call it your rapid response war room (unnerving your opponents in the process). Don't write just a written report on ethical misdeeds—paste it up on the wall and call it the Wall of Shame.

Budget. Every day you learn something new about your expenses—your opponent has placed an early TV buy . . . your volunteers are eating pizza at an alarming rate.

Candidate Rhythms. Here's a basic but often forgotten point: Candidates are people, too. They have families and kids and likes and dislikes and certain rhythms that have to be recognized, unless you don't mind getting your head torn off several times a day by a candidate who's exhausted, missed his/her kid's big recital/birthday/ball game, etc.

Thinking Visually. One campaign sent their candidate to an urban development site, but the shot showed the candidate talking in front of a pornographic video store. Pay attention to what is immediately behind your candidate's head. It sounds silly, but that's the shot TV will use when the candidate is talking.

Appropriate Furniture. You can only sit on a crate for so long. Don't expect volunteers to submit to a torture test. Have enough chairs and tables (donated from unions, old campaigns or volunteers) for them to get the job done. . . .

Election Day Legal Team. Unfortunately, Republican voter intimidation operations have made Election Day legal teams a necessity. The Republican Party has a history of discouraging voting among traditional Democratic groups. The methods employed range from fake sample ballots, signs at polling places threatening arrest and armed guards at polling places, to simply allowing the machinery of election to break down. The campaign has to be prepared to contest Election Day problems in court.

—Democratic National Committee,
campaign training manuals

group of political operatives, many of them relatively young and unknown, who had been recruited by the Arkansas governor. His campaign chairman was Mickey Kantor, 52, a Los Angeles lawyer long active in Democratic politics, who later became Clinton's secretary of commerce. The communications director, George Stephanopoulos, 31, like Clinton a former Rhodes scholar, was in charge of the candidate's traveling staff and often appeared on television as a Clinton spokesperson. He became a senior White House adviser after Clinton won the presidency but later left to join ABC News. James Carville, an unconventional, behind-the-scenes campaign operative in ragged blue jeans, who grew up in a small town in Louisiana's Cajun country, was perhaps Clinton's most important political adviser. He chose not to join the administration, however.

An incumbent president who runs for reelection normally enjoys certain advantages. He may benefit from the trappings of his high office, and from the aura of the presidency that surrounds him. He may award lucrative defense contracts to plants in key states that he needs to win for reelection. With the elaborate communications systems available aboard Air Force One and everywhere else that he moves, and with a huge White House staff to support his campaign, a president almost inevitably has the logistical edge over a rival.

A president's campaign appearances, even more than the challenger's, are carefully planned. Several days before a presidential appearance in a town or city, the Secret Service checks over locations for security, and the political advance staff determines the best way to display the crowds for the TV cameras, the most pleasing backdrops, and other details—all designed to maximize the political benefit to the chief executive. It should be noted, however, that the advantages of incumbency do not guarantee reelection, as Gerald Ford, Jimmy Carter, and George Bush all discovered. All told, through the year 2000, 10 incumbent presidents had been defeated in general-election contests.

Presidents running for reelection attempt to exploit many of the benefits of incumbency. In 1996, President Clinton, running for reelection, journeyed to the United Nations in September to sign the Comprehensive Nuclear Test Ban Treaty aimed at barring all nuclear tests in the air, underground, at sea, or in outer space. Television and newspapers carried photos of Clinton signing the treaty and looking like a world statesman. During the campaign, as president, Clinton was able to sign bills in the White House Rose Garden, another photo opportunity that his opponent, Bob Dole, could not match. Clinton even signed a bill preserving land for a national monument against the spectacular backdrop of the Grand Canyon.

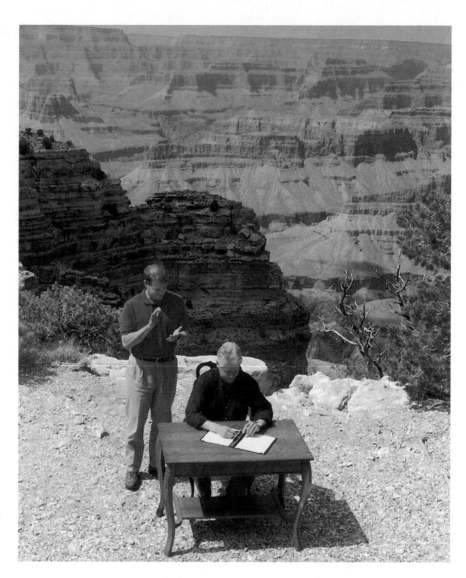

". . . the advantage of incumbency."
With the Grand Canyon as a backdrop,
and accompanied by Vice President Gore,
President Clinton—running for reelection
in 1996—signs a document setting aside
canyon land in Utah as a national
monument.
AP/Wide World

CAMPAIGN STRATEGY

Aiming for the Undecided

Studies have shown that many voters, more than half in recent decades, are committed to one candidate or another in advance of the campaign. Nevertheless, a large group of voters, often one-third or more, make their decision during the campaign. (See Table 10-1.)

Nelson W. Polsby and Aaron B. Wildavsky, in a study of presidential elections, contended that, for the majority of citizens in America, "campaigns do not function so much to change minds as to reinforce previous convictions."[4] Even so, when a third or more of the people make up their minds during a campaign, their votes may well determine the outcome. For example, if 100 million votes are cast in a presidential election, one-third, or 33 million votes, is a sizable bloc by any standard.

The undecided voters may hold the key to victory in close elections. Since some two-thirds of all American voters identify with one of the two major parties,

political candidates try to preserve their party base—to hold on to their natural constituency—while winning over voters from the other party, independents, and the undecided.

Although some poll data suggest that political campaigns do not influence the choice of a majority of voters, political analysts have concluded that campaigns may influence "a small but crucial proportion of the electorate. . . . Clearly, professional politicians drive themselves and their organizations toward influencing every undecided voter in the expectation that they are the key to providing, or maintaining, the winning margin."[5]

And a number of scholars have disagreed with the view that campaigns have minimal influence on voters. Dan Nimmo and Robert L. Savage have argued that "there is a close relationship between candidate images and voting behavior."[6] They concluded that although candidates' images usually emerge early in a campaign and remain about the same, those images can and do change during campaigns. As examples, they cite John F. Kennedy in 1960 and Hubert Humphrey in

TABLE 10-1

Presidential Elections: When the Voter Decides

	1948	1952	1956	1960	1964	1968	1972	1976	1980	1984	1988	1992	1996
Decided how to vote													
Knew all along	41	32	45	25	18	21	33	20	20	30	15	19	27
When candidate announced	NA	4	15	6	23	14	11	14	20	22	17	21	23
During conventions	31	32	19	31	25	24	18	21	18	18	29	14	13
Post-convention	15	21	12	26	21	19	24	22	15	17	22	22	17
Last 2 weeks of campaign	10	9	7	9	9	14	8	17	17	10	12	17	12
Election Day	3	2	2	3	4	7	5	7	9	4	5	8	7

SOURCE: Data provided by University of Michigan, Institute for Social Research, Center for Political Studies, American National Election Studies.

1968, whose images improved as their campaigns progressed.[7] In arguing that "campaigns make a difference," Nimmo and Savage emphasized that this is particularly true for independent voters, who are more likely than other voters to shift their impressions of the candidates during campaigns.[8]

Nimmo and others view political campaigns as "a process of communication" in which voters do not respond automatically on the basis of their socioeconomic backgrounds or party loyalties. Rather, Nimmo contends, voters tend to "construct" their own individual view of the campaign; they arrive at a decision by interpreting the symbols offered to them, often by drawing upon their own experience.[9]

Norman H. Nie, Sidney Verba, and John R. Petrocik argue in *The Changing American Voter* that campaigns may affect voting because "the public responds to the political stimuli offered it." The behavior of voters, they concluded, is influenced not only by psychological and sociological factors, "but also by the issues of the day and by the way in which candidates present those issues."[10]

Similarly, Walter DeVries and Lance Tarrance concluded that in many elections the outcome is determined by "ticket-splitters." They define a ticket-splitter as a voter likely "to be basically a Republican or Democrat, but one who occasionally splits off to vote for a candidate of another party."[11] To convince the ticket-splitters, DeVries and Tarrance contend, candidates must use campaigns to communicate their views on the issues.[12]

Increasingly, in campaigns today the strategists for the candidates "target" certain groups of voters. Some of these targets are geographic; for instance, a candidate may select specific states for special effort. In September 2000, for example, the Bush campaign ran

SHOULD YOU BE A CANDIDATE?

Before the campaign can begin, there must be a candidate. And that job is not easy, as the following excerpt from a Republican Party manual suggests:

The person who cannot answer virtually all of the following questions in the affirmative should not be running.

1. Does your family fully support your candidacy? Are they prepared to assume much more responsibility at home and put in extra time campaigning? Can they tolerate the verbal abuse you may receive and long hours you will spend away from home? Will your children accept and understand your frequent absence from home?

2. Can you afford to run? Can you expect enough contributions to keep out of serious personal debt? Is your business in good hands while you campaign?

If you are employed, do you have a job to go back to in the event you lose?

3. Can your personal background stand intensive scrutiny? Are you fully prepared to have the public know about your debts, personal and organizational associations, past relationships with members of the opposite sex, family background, sources of income, health history, partners, etc.?

4. Are you strong enough physically and emotionally to stand up to the rigors of a tough campaign? Can your health tolerate long hours, poor food, erratic rest, continuing pressure, rejection and frustration? Most important, could your ego tolerate a loss if it should come?

—"Candidate Recruitment," Republican National Committee campaign manual

"I'm going to do a flip-flop on Africa. Can you make it look good?"

Reform Party candidate Ross Perot campaigning, 1996
AP/Wide World

a commercial in 17 states mocking Al Gore's controversial appearance at a Buddhist temple in 1996. The visit resulted in campaign contributions, ostensibly by the monks. Or, strategists may target specific categories of voters, such as white southerners, young voters, African Americans, Hispanics, or other demographic groups.

Which Road to the White House?

Long before aspiring presidential candidates can get into a general-election campaign, they must, as a rule, enter the bruising arena of the primaries. In 2000, Texas Governor George W. Bush and Vice President Al Gore each won primaries in California, New York, and several other states on "Super Tuesday," March 8, that assured both men of nomination by their parties.

Conversely, former President Ford's decision not to enter the primaries in 1980 may have been the decisive factor in his failure to win the Republican nomination. However, the candidate who wins the most primaries does not necessarily gain the nomination. In 1984 Walter Mondale actually won fewer primaries than Senator Gary Hart of Colorado—11 to Hart's 16. But it was Mondale who got the party's nomination.

For relatively unknown political candidates, the primary route may prove an attractive means of demonstrating their strength and gaining nationwide exposure in the media. For example, Jimmy Carter was not widely known in 1976, and his primary election victories that year were essential to his successful campaign for the Democratic presidential nomination. In 1980 George Bush, whose son ran for president 20 years later, lost several key primaries to Ronald Reagan. But the fact that Bush also won some primaries may have

helped to persuade Reagan to select him as his vice presidential running mate.

Even for a presidential aspirant who is far out in front, entering the primaries is almost always necessary in order to win the nomination. Today, virtually all candidates feel compelled to take the primary route.

One presidential candidate who found another way to gain the public's attention was Ross Perot, the Texas businessman who disdained the primaries in 1992 but captured an enormous amount of free TV time and media attention by challenging the major-party candidates. Perot built an organization of "volunteers," many of them paid, but did not run on a party label that year.

With preconvention campaigns so crucial, most candidates find it necessary to have a well-financed campaign organization already in operation long before the national convention. In recent presidential elections, the preconvention campaign organizations of major-party candidates have been hardly distinguishable in size from those of major-party nominees in a general election.

Where and How to Campaign

Once nominated, candidates must decide how and where their precious time (and money) can be most profitably spent. Typically, candidates tend to spend more time campaigning in pivotal states such as New

President Theodore Roosevelt campaigning
Harvard University Library/Theodore Roosevelt Collection

York, California, Pennsylvania, Illinois, Ohio, and Michigan. Their strategists know that the contest normally will be won or lost in the populous states with big electoral votes.

But the candidate who logs the most miles on the campaign trail may not harvest the most votes. In 1960 Richard Nixon pledged to become the first candidate to take his presidential campaign to all 50 states. He did so, but at great physical and political cost, as he lost to John F. Kennedy. By contrast, in 1968 Nixon moved at a relatively serene pace that preserved his physical energies. He concentrated on 10 populous "battleground states," on those states in the South that might be captured from George Wallace, and on the border states.[13] This time, Nixon won.

Television has, of course, influenced the pattern of political campaigning. Aside from the advantage offered by television in reaching large numbers of voters, it also can reduce the risk to the safety of the candidate. In light of the assassinations of President John F. Kennedy and his brother, Senator Robert F. Kennedy, the attempt on the life of George Wallace, the two attempts against President Ford, and the attack on President Reagan in which he was seriously wounded, precautions would seem sensible. Yet candidates are under great pressure to mingle with the voters and to show themselves in person: "Rightly or wrongly, presidential candidates judge that they must be personally seen by audiences throughout the country, through such rituals as motorcades,

Robert F. Kennedy campaigning in Detroit, 1968
Copyright © Andrew Sacks

shopping center rallies and whistle-stop campaigns."[14] After Robert Kennedy was fatally shot during the preconvention campaign of 1968, President Johnson assigned Secret Service agents to all the candidates, a practice that Congress speedily made law.*

Political candidates also worry about timing in a campaign. Generally speaking, candidates attempt to gear their campaign to a climactic windup in the last two weeks. Often in the final weeks of a presidential campaign, the airwaves are saturated with a "media blitz" of TV commercials.

Political campaigns help to weld political parties together. For instance, campaign rallies and personal appearances by the candidate generate enthusiasm among partisan workers and volunteers. Candidates are concerned about maintaining their momentum and a certain level of excitement, not only with the voters, but for the sake of their own party organization as well.

The President as Candidate

Although presidents have been defeated when they ran for reelection, an incumbent at least starts out with a great potential advantage over an opponent in a presi-

_____

*The law authorizes Secret Service protection, unless declined, for "major presidential or vice presidential candidates." The secretary of the treasury, after consultation with an advisory committee that includes leaders of Congress, decides who qualifies as a candidate under this definition. The law does not specifically provide protection for preconvention candidates, but the precedent was set in 1968 when the Secret Service guarded a total of 12 candidates: six presidential candidates before the conventions and six party nominees (for president and vice president).

dential campaign. As noted earlier, not only do the prestige and power of the office follow the president on the hustings, but all the visible trappings go along as well: Air Force One, the gleaming presidential jet, lands for an airport rally, the band plays "Hail to the Chief," and the voters are enveloped by the aura and mystique of the presidency. Just before a president speaks, an aide hangs a portable presidential seal on the lectern.

Aside from prestige, an incumbent president already has a huge organized staff and all the advantages of White House communications and other facilities, including extensive arrangements for handling the press. And he may be able to dominate the news by taking actions as president that are carefully timed for maximum political advantage.

Some of the perquisites of office may also help a vice president who is a candidate for the presidency. For example, both Vice President George Bush in 1988 and Vice President Al Gore in 2000 were able to fly on Air Force Two as they campaigned around the country. The candidates were required to reimburse the government for their air travel costs, however.

An incumbent president can also use the power of his office as he campaigns. For example, in presidential election years when an incumbent is running, large federal grants may flow to states in which key primaries will take place. In other words, a president may use the levers of bureaucracy in an attempt to win votes. He may also seize on a foreign policy crisis to gain political advantage and display his leadership as commander in chief.

SEVEN TIPS FOR VICE PRESIDENTIAL HOPEFULS

When presidential nominees look for running mates, it's hardly love at first sight. The vetting process that's used today would confound political matchmakers of years ago.

Now small, volunteer armies of lawyers, accountants, former law enforcement officials, and even private eyes, comb through almost every detail of a prospective vice presidential candidate's life. The advent of computerized databases that are searchable from desktops has increased the speed at which vetting teams can go about their task. . . .

There are some things vice presidential wanna-bes can do to improve their chances of being chosen.

1. Get your FBI file now. It's not uncommon for the presidential nominee to ask for a peek, but if you wait until then to request a copy, it might not arrive on time. If you're a run-of-the-mill elected official, chances are your file is less than 500 pages, small by FBI standards.
2. Get a major outside accounting firm to go over your back tax returns.
3. Get a medical checkup. If you haven't been to the doctor for a while, better go for a comprehensive physical. . . . Health questions are common.

4. Raise your visibility. Now's the time to give a few big policy speeches. Chat up your friends in the national press corps or make some new ones. Some favorable press clips can help you get on the long list, which is the first step to getting on the short list.
5. Don't treat the vetter like hired help. The vetter may be the only individual that the presidential nominee talks to who's had an in-depth look at all the contenders on the short list. Comparisons are inevitable.
6. Don't hold anything back. If there's dirt out there, do the dishing yourself. Make an honest inventory of your vulnerabilities before you meet with your vetter. This will be your opportunity to explain and put potential problems in context.
7. Don't apply pressure in public. It's OK for your allies in the interest-group community to lobby on your behalf. Indeed, it may help your cause. But make sure they do it in private.

—*National Journal*, April 29, 2000

In the midst of the 1996 presidential election campaign, when Iraq's brutal dictator Saddam Hussein moved his troops north into Kurdish territory and then threatened American aircraft, President Clinton responded with two cruise missile attacks. In addition he ordered an impressive display of American military might—including aircraft carriers, bombers, fighter planes, and ground troops—into the Persian Gulf region. Not only was Bob Dole helpless to do anything about Clinton's actions as commander in chief, but he was forced to adopt a largely bipartisan position, giving qualified support to Clinton, because criticizing the president during a foreign policy crisis, even a mini-crisis, is not considered good form.

On the other hand, an unexpected foreign policy crisis in the middle of an election campaign can cause political problems for the president. In 1996, growing tensions between Palestinians and Israel erupted in September into violent firefights that resulted in the deaths of dozens of Palestinians and many Israelis. Because Clinton had invested his own prestige in the Middle East peace process, the violence was not a welcome foreign policy development in the midst of the presidential campaign.

At considerable political risk, Clinton invited the prime minister of Israel, Benjamin Netanyahu, and the Palestinian leader, Yasir Arafat, to confer with him in Washington. Had Clinton not acted he would have opened himself to criticism by his opponent, Bob Dole, for failing to exercise leadership. But if the meetings failed to reduce tensions, Clinton would also face criticism. Netanyahu and Arafat met and talked, shook hands, and agreed to keep talking when they returned home. Clinton was able to take some credit for getting the warring parties to sit down together. Dole accused Clinton of conducting "photo-op foreign policy."[15]

Sometimes, an incumbent president may be in such a strong position that he will decide to restrict his campaigning, allow the dignity of his office to work for him, and, in effect, campaign from the White House. He may adopt the "lofty, nonpartisan pose."[16] It does not always work, however. In 1976 President Ford attempted for a time to campaign from the White House, but when Carter accused him of trying to "hide in the Rose Garden," he soon took to the campaign trail.

THE ISSUES

Political candidates in most cases develop a central theme for their campaign. Sometimes it emerges as the battle progresses, or it may be conceived well in advance. Candidates attempt to choose their terrain and stay "on message," staking out certain issues that they believe will give them the advantage over their opponents.

But to a great extent the campaign theme is shaped by the candidate's status—candidate of the "out party,"

incumbent president, or political heir to an incumbent. For example, in 1988, Vice President Bush defended the record of the Reagan-Bush administration, which had occupied the White House for almost eight years, and offered himself to the voters as the logical heir to a generally popular president, Ronald Reagan. Bush won. By 1992, however, the economy was in shambles and a younger and more charismatic Democratic opponent, Bill Clinton, took a commanding lead in the early polls and went on to win the election.

But even a popular president cannot always transfer his appeal to a successor. As Polsby and Wildavsky noted, "One of the most difficult positions for a candidate is to try to succeed a President of his own party. . . . No matter how hard he tries to avoid it he is stuck with the record made by the President of his own party."[17] And a vice president attempting to succeed the president sometimes "faces the worst of all possible worlds. He suffers from the disadvantages . . . of having to defend an existing record. . . . He cannot attack the administration in office without alienating the president and selling his own party short, and he cannot claim he has experience in the presidential office. It may be difficult for him to defend a record he did not make and may not wholly care for. His is the most difficult strategic problem of all the candidates."[18]

There is evidence, in fact, that some incumbent presidents are a bit reluctant to expend their prestige on behalf of the heir apparent—who may not always want

President Johnson and Vice President Hubert Humphrey
AP/Wide World

their help. In 1968, for example, President Johnson's attitude toward Vice President Hubert Humphrey, the Democratic nominee, seemed ambivalent at first, although in the end he publicly supported him. But Humphrey lost the election.

In much of the 2000 campaign, President Clinton kept a relatively low profile, lest the personal scandals that had enveloped him impair Vice President Al Gore's own quest for the White House. At the Democratic National Convention, Gore had pointedly drawn a line between himself and Clinton by declaring: "I stand here tonight as my own man."

Negative Campaigning

Sometimes, the substantive issues in a campaign become submerged as the candidates devote more time to attacking each other than to discussing policies and programs. In 1996, both major-party candidates, Clinton and Dole, pledged at the outset to abstain from personal attacks. Almost immediately, however, both began airing harsh TV commercials about each other. Clinton ran a commercial that accused Dole of "quitting" the Senate. Dole in turn aired a commercial that showed Clinton in a 1992 appearance on MTV joking, in answer to a question, that if he were to revisit his youth and again attempt to smoke marijuana, this time he would try to inhale.

It was no better in 2000. The same Bush commercial that showed Gore nodding to a bowing Buddhist monk also quoted Gore as announcing on *Larry King Live:* "I took the initiative in creating the Internet." The Typical American Housewife featured in the commercial watches the Gore claim on her kitchen TV and says: "Yeah, and I invented the remote control, too. Another round of this, and I'll sell my television."[19]

When a Bush commercial attacked the Clinton-Gore record on education, the Gore campaign struck back with a commercial that said: "Bush's Texas record? 45th in the nation in SAT scores, an accountability system so full of cheating it's under investigation; Texas ranked the 48th worst state in America to raise a child. On the issue of education, America deserves a real debate, not more negative ads from George W. Bush. Al Gore is ready. Is George W?"[20]

Mudslinging and charges of corruption are common in campaigns. Under the unwritten rules governing the seamier side of American politics, a candidate may attempt to "get something" on an opponent. The information might not be publicized, however, if the other side possesses equally damaging information, or if it is believed that the opponent can successfully cry "smear." Because mudslinging, rumors, and scandals presumably influence some voters, their use in political campaigns persists. It is often near the end of a campaign that a candidate's supporters try to leak such stories to the news media to damage a rival.

Bread-and-Butter Issues

Peace and pocketbook issues have tended to dominate presidential campaigns. On domestic issues, the Democrats can point to a wide range of social legislation passed during Democratic administrations. Not all of these programs have worked equally well, and one, the federal welfare program, was widely criticized and ultimately restructured with the agreement of a Democratic president, Bill Clinton. Nevertheless, Democratic candidates since the New Deal have been able to campaign on the party's efforts toward achieving social progress at home. And, perhaps remembering that the Great

Vice President Al Gore's controversial visit to a Buddhist temple in California in 1996 was used in a television commercial by his Republican opponent in 2000.
AP/Wide World

FIGURE 10-1

Political Party Rated Best for Prosperity

"Which political party—the Republican or Democratic—will do a better job of keeping the country prosperous?"

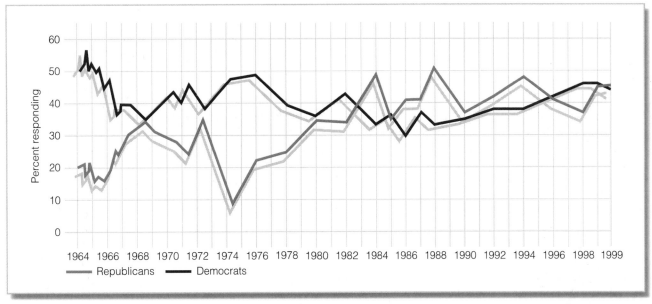

SOURCES: *Gallup Opinion Index*, Report no. 106 (April 1974), p. 21; Report no. 135 (October 1976), p. 5; Report no. 159 (October 1978), p. 21; Report no. 181 (September 1980), p.8; Report no. 223 (April 1984), pp. 18–19; and Gallup poll news release (September 23, 1984). Data for 1985 through 1999 provided by the Gallup Organization.

Depression began in 1929 under a Republican president, voters have, in some years, tended to associate prosperity with Democrats. (See Figure 10-1.)

Bread-and-butter issues do not always work for the Democrats, however. In 1980, for example, double-digit inflation and continued high unemployment made the economy one domestic issue that President Carter preferred not to emphasize. It proved to be, in fact, one of the weakest issues for the Democratic incumbent, who lost.

By 1992, with the economy troubled and unemployment high, the Democrats had regained a powerful domestic issue for the presidential campaign, an issue, perhaps more than any other, that helped the party and its candidate, Bill Clinton, to recapture the White House. In 2000, the booming economy that had developed during the Clinton-Gore administration made it more of a challenge for George W. Bush to persuade the voters it was time for a change.

Foreign Policy Issues

In the area of foreign affairs, the Republicans often have had an advantage. (See Figure 10-2.) Because the Democrats were in power during the First World War, the Second World War, Korea, and Vietnam, the Republicans frequently have been able to tag the Democrats, fairly or not, as the "war party." Richard Nixon in 1968 was able to promise new leadership to bring an end to the war in Vietnam. Although Nixon did not succeed in ending the American combat role in the Vietnam War until more than two months after his reelection in 1972, his trips to Beijing and Moscow earlier that year, and the appearance of progress toward a Vietnam peace agreement during the campaign, once again provided the Republican candidate with an advantage in the area of foreign policy.

In 1992 President Bush, the Republican candidate, emphasized that the Cold War had ended during his administration, and that the danger of nuclear annihilation had receded. And he reminded the voters that Iraq and its dictator, Saddam Hussein, had been forced to retreat from Kuwait in the Persian Gulf War. The Democrats sought to counter Bush's claims of foreign policy successes by charging that he had not disclosed his role in the Iran-contra scandal, that his administration had secretly helped to arm Iraq, and that Saddam Hussein was still in power despite the Gulf War.

Although presidents customarily present foreign policy decisions in lofty terms unrelated to their election prospects, the truth is that foreign affairs and domestic politics are closely intertwined. It means that, in making foreign policy choices, presidents often have one eye on potential voter reaction at election time. This was well illustrated by a remark made by President Bush early in 1992 as he campaigned in the New Hampshire presidential primary: "If I'd listened to the leader of the United States Senate, George Mitchell,

Political Party Rated Best for Peace

"Looking ahead for the next few years, which political party do you think would be more likely to keep the United States out of war—the Republican or the Democratic Party?"

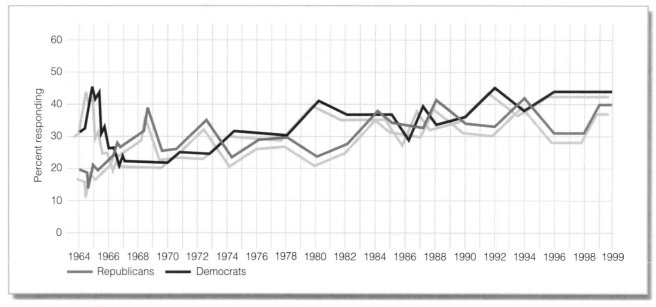

NOTE: Prior to 1992, the question was phrased, ". . . keep the United States out of World War III . . ."
SOURCES: *Gallup Opinion Index,* Report no. 106 (April 1974), p. 19; Report no. 135 (October 1976), p. 6; Report no. 159 (October 1978), p. 22; Report no. 181 (September 1980), p. 7; Report no. 223 (April 1984), pp. 18–19; and Gallup poll news release (September 23, 1984). Data for 1985–1999 provided by the Gallup Organization.

Saddam Hussein would be in Saudi Arabia and you'd be paying twenty bucks a gallon for gasoline. Now try that one on for size."[21]

The Imponderables

A sudden foreign policy crisis, a personal scandal, a chance remark—these are among the many imponderables that may affect voter attitudes in political campaigns.

In 1884, when Grover Cleveland was the Democratic nominee, his Republican opponents chanted: "Ma, Ma, where's my Pa? Gone to the White House, ha, ha, ha." The slogan was a gleeful reference to the illegitimate child that Cleveland was accused of fathering.* It was soon overshadowed, however, by another slogan.

---

*During the campaign, the story broke in a Buffalo, New York, newspaper under the headline: "A Terrible Tale—A Dark Chapter in a Public Man's History." Ten years earlier, Maria Crofts Halpin, an attractive widow, had given birth to a son, whom she named Oscar Folsom Cleveland, charging Cleveland with the baby's paternity. Cleveland said he was not certain that he was the boy's father, but he had assumed full responsibility for supporting the child. When the scandal broke, he telegraphed his friends in Buffalo: "Tell the truth." Because of his open attitude, Cleveland managed to minimize the damage to his presidential campaign. After Cleveland's election, the Democrats celebrated their first presidential victory in 28 years by singing: "Hurrah for Maria,/Hurrah for the kid./We voted for Grover,/And we're damned glad we did!"

A few days before the election, a Protestant minister supporting James G. Blaine, the Republican candidate, referred to the Democrats as the party of "rum, Romanism, and rebellion." The insult to Roman Catholics may have cost Blaine New York State and thereby the election.

In 1948 Thomas Dewey's campaign train, the "Victory Special," lurched backward into the crowd while the Republican nominee was orating at Beaucoup, Illinois. "Well, that's the first lunatic I've had for an engineer," snapped Dewey. The remark was widely publicized and did not sit well with the railroad unions. Overnight, "Lunatic Engineers for Truman" and other similar groups sprang up to plague the Republican candidate along the right-of-way traveled by the "Victory Special."

In 1952 Richard Nixon's place as vice presidential candidate on the Republican ticket was endangered when newspapers reported the existence of the "Nixon fund," some $18,000 contributed by a group of California businessmen to meet Nixon's political expenses as a U.S. senator. Nixon went on nationwide television and, in his famed "Checkers" speech, defended his use of the $18,000 fund, listed his personal finances, noted that his wife Pat wore a "respectable Republican cloth coat," and announced that, come what may, his family intended to keep a black-and-white cocker spaniel named Checkers, which had been given to his

"BE SURE TO CRY SCANDAL!"

The following is an excerpt from a publication of the Republican National Committee that advised GOP candidates on campaign techniques:

Researching Scandals in the Democratic Party. With proper research and publicity, exposure of scandals can serve as a public service and as a source of votes. . . . Most scandals evolve from "tips," usually coming from newsmen, victims of the "scandal," public reports such as those of the State Auditor, or abused factions within or on the fringes of the wrongdoer's organization. . . .

Publicizing the Scandal. A "believable" springboard from which to break the scandal must be found. A newsman, a disenchanted insider, or a local prosecutor are possible means for breaking the scandal to the public.

Once the public has been informed that a scandal in fact does exist, it must be kept continually aware that its trust has been violated. . . . Question the principles of the opposition at every opportunity—at public gatherings as well as in the press. In other words, take advantage of every possible form of publicity—and be sure to cry, SCANDAL!

—Republican National Committee, *Research Techniques for Republican Campaigns*

Richard M. Nixon delivering his "Checkers" speech on television, 1952
Copyright © UPI/Bettmann/CORBIS

two children.* Although the speech was a patently emotional appeal for which Nixon was often assailed by later critics, it turned the tide of public opinion and impressed General Eisenhower, the Republican presidential nominee. Nixon stayed on the ticket.

Perhaps the most startling and disturbing surprise development of any modern presidential campaign occurred in June 1972, when five men, wearing surgical rubber gloves and carrying electronic eavesdropping equipment, were arrested inside the Washington headquarters of the Democratic National Committee in the Watergate building. One of the men, James W. McCord, Jr., a former CIA agent, turned out to be director of security for President Nixon's campaign organization. Three weeks before the election, a federal grand jury in Washington indicted the five men plus two former White House aides, E. Howard Hunt, Jr., and

G. Gordon Liddy, on charges of burglary, illegal wiretapping, and bugging.

The case immediately raised a host of questions about who had sent the men on their espionage mission to the Democratic headquarters. The White House and President Nixon repeatedly denied involvement. But one of the Watergate defendants, it developed, had $89,000 in his bank account that had been delivered to the Republican campaign committee and "laundered" through Mexico to disguise its origin.

The charges of espionage and financial irregularities, however, seemed to have little impact on the voters in the 1972 election.[†] The Watergate case and the issue of political espionage began to grow into a major scandal only well after the presidential election campaign. Early in 1973, five of the defendants pleaded guilty, and two others were convicted by a federal jury. Within months, the scandal had reached the president; several

---

[†]A Gallup poll published in October showed that 52 percent of the voters had heard of the Watergate scandal, but only about a third were able to recite the key facts of the situation. Eight out of 10 persons who knew about the incident said it was not a strong reason for voting for Nixon's Democratic opponent, Senator George McGovern. Source: Gallup poll, *Washington Post*, October 8, 1972, p. A5.

RONALD ZIEGLER ON WATERGATE

White House spokesman Ronald L. Ziegler told reporters in Florida with the President that he would not comment on "a third-rate burglary attempt." In addition, Ziegler said that "certain elements may try to stretch this beyond what it is."

—*Washington Post*, June 20, 1972

---

*Checkers died in September 1964, and is buried at Westhampton, Long Island. He was not the first canine to gain fame in a presidential campaign. Running for a fourth term in 1944, Franklin D. Roosevelt ridiculed the Republicans for charging that he had sent a destroyer to fetch his dog: "The Republican leaders have not been content to make personal attacks upon me—or my wife, or my sons—they now include my little dog, Fala. . . . I am accustomed to hearing malicious falsehoods about myself but I think I have a right to object to libelous statements about my dog." See Robert E. Sherwood, *Roosevelt and Hopkins* (New York: Harper & Row, 1948), p. 821.

THE WHITE HOUSE
WASHINGTON

August 9, 1974

Dear Mr. Secretary:

I hereby resign the Office of President of the
United States.

Sincerely,

[signature: Richard Nixon]

11.35 AM

HK

The Honorable Henry A. Kissinger
The Secretary of State
Washington, D. C. 20520

*"His presidency shattered": The Watergate scandal led
President Nixon to resign two years later.*
The White House/AP/Wide World

of his top aides resigned and some went to prison. A year later, facing certain impeachment, Nixon resigned in disgrace, his presidency shattered less than two years after his landslide reelection.

In 1984 a joke by President Reagan at the start of the presidential campaign caused him some embarrassment. Preparing for his weekly radio broadcast, Reagan was asked for a "voice check" by technicians. The president replied: "My fellow Americans, I'm pleased to tell you today that I've signed legislation that would outlaw Russia forever. We begin bombing in five minutes." The remark was not broadcast, but it was recorded by two networks and became public, arousing a storm of controversy. The comment was denounced by the Soviet Union, criticized by Walter Mondale, the Democratic candidate, and apparently triggered a partial Soviet military alert.[22]

At the very start of the 1992 presidential election year, Gennifer Flowers, a former lounge singer, claimed in the *Star*, a supermarket tabloid, that she had engaged in a 12-year affair with Governor Bill Clinton. In an appearance with his wife, Hillary, on the CBS television program *60 Minutes*, Clinton denied Flowers's allegations but conceded marital "wrongdoing." For a time, however, the charges of infidelity threatened to derail Clinton's presidential hopes. Afterward, Clinton's sup-

porters worried about what they termed "the bimbo factor"—fearing that one or more other supposed lovers would surface during the campaign. Much later, under siege by the Lewinsky scandal, Clinton testified in a deposition in the Paula Jones lawsuit that he had once had a sexual encounter with Flowers, but he did not admit to a 12-year relationship.[23]

The Republicans experienced some unexpected gaffes as well in 1992, thanks to Vice President Dan Quayle. In a speech upholding "family values," Quayle caused a nationwide uproar when he attacked Murphy Brown, a popular fictional television character, for having a baby as a single, unmarried mother. Not long afterward, Quayle visited a school in Trenton, New Jersey, and coached a 12-year-old student, William Figueroa, to add an "e" to the word "potato." Political cartoonists had a field day. The schoolboy, an instant celebrity, appeared on the David Letterman show. The principal got a call from the Potato Museum in Great Falls, Virginia. "Potatoe" T-shirts sprouted on college campuses.

Ross Perot was moving up rapidly in the polls after he reentered the race in October 1992 when, nine days before the election, he dropped a bombshell. Perot charged that President Bush's campaign had engaged in "dirty tricks" and had planned to leak a fake, computer-generated photograph to embarrass his daughter and had also planned to disrupt her church wedding. According to news reports, Perot believed that the supposed photograph would have depicted his daughter, Carolyn, in a sexual pose with another woman.

Perot offered no proof of his charges, which were based in part on information from a man long regarded by the news media as a fabricator of bizarre tales of intrigue. Bush's press secretary labeled the allegations "crazy," compared Perot to people who believe in UFOs, and called the independent candidate "paranoid."[24] Perot's bizarre and unsupported claims raised questions about his temperament and fitness for the presidency in the minds of some voters.

In 1996, Dole fell off a platform in Chico, California, when a railing gave way as he was shaking hands with the crowd. A picture of the Republican candidate lying on the ground, grimacing in pain, made some newspaper front pages. Dole got to his feet quickly and made light of the episode. But there was speculation in the press that the minor incident was somehow symbolic of his presidential campaign.

In the 2000 campaign, George W. Bush was preparing to speak at a rally in Naperville, Illinois, when he was caught by an open microphone as he pointed out a *New York Times* reporter, Adam Clymer, whom he described as a "major league [expletive]."[25] His running-mate, Dick Cheney, dutifully chimed in, "Oh, yeah. He is, big time."[26] Because Bush had promised, if elected, to restore "dignity" to the Oval Office, the remark appeared to contradict his public pledge and the image he was trying to project to the voters.

But Al Gore was embarrassed when he told an audience in Tallahassee, Florida, that his mother-in-law paid $108 a month for the same arthritis medicine that for his dog cost only $37.80. While it was true that Gore had both a mother-in-law and a dog, and they did take human and animal versions of the same drug, the dollar figures he cited, his campaign was forced to admit, came from a House study of drug prices.[27] Bush charged that Gore was "misleading" the voters, and the Bush camp put out a press release entitled "Gore Makes Things Up."[28]

Incidents of this sort may be trivial, but they can leave their mark on a campaign. Voters may tend to remember them long after they have forgotten the details of a weighty policy address by a candidate dealing with health care or some other important issue.

World crises that erupt suddenly during a campaign are still another category of imponderables that may affect voter decisions. In general, foreign policy crises tend to help the party in power because of voter reluctance to "change horses in midstream." The Tonkin Gulf crisis of 1964, many details of which are disputed, created an atmosphere of wartime tension that, in the short run, may have benefited the election campaign of President Johnson. On the other hand, a foreign crisis that leads to a war, as in Korea or Vietnam, or that

KEEP ON SMILING: JOHN McCAIN, BOB DOLE'S CHESHIRE CAT

As Bob Dole, the Republican candidate for president, prepared for his first debate with President Clinton in 1996, his advisers tried to make sure that he remembered to smile a lot, according to the following news account:

> Dole and his staff . . . were afraid that he would come across as too dour and old, and they made every effort to protect against those perceptions. In the final rehearsal, his wife, Elizabeth, sat behind the cameras and chirped, "Your smile looks great on the monitor, Bob!"—words she hoped her husband would replay in his mind as he stood at the podium at Bushnell Hall.
>
> To reinforce that notion, the Dole camp planted their smile specialist, Sen. John McCain (R-Ariz.) in a prime seat inside the hall with the sole mission of beaming so broadly that the senator might notice the crescent flash of whiteness in the audience. McCain performed the same Cheshire cat role during a crucial debate in the South Carolina primary; Dole looked out, saw his Senate pal giving it the ear-to-ear and—so the legend goes—loosened up and won the debate.

> —*Washington Post*, October 7, 1996

damages the prestige of the country, such as the seizure of American hostages in Iran, may, in the long run, erode the strength of the party in power and lead to retribution at the polls.

CAMPAIGN TECHNIQUES

Television and Politics

In September 2000, as the presidential race grew in intensity, the Republican National Committee sponsored a television commercial attacking Al Gore's plan to provide prescription drug benefits for senior citizens. Suddenly the word "RATS," in huge capital letters, flashed on the screen, so quickly that most viewers could not have seen it. But if the commercial was replayed and slowed down, there it was.

Were George W. Bush's supporters trying to characterize the Gore campaign? "It's absurd to think it was intentional," a Bush aide said, "it was an editing mistake." Other Bush advisers explained it was part of the word "bureaucrats." Alex Castellanos, a veteran media consultant, whose firm produced the commercial, chuckled and said the word RATS was an error. Bush himself went on *Good Morning America* and denied there was "a plot to try to put subliminal messages into people's minds."[29]

"Ten, nine, eight, seven . . ."   six, five, four, three . . .   two, one . . .

These are the stakes. To make a world in   or to go into the dark. We must either   The stakes are too high for you to stay
which all of God's children can live . . .   love each other or we must die. . . .   home."

With permission of Doyle, Dane, Bernbach, Inc./photos courtesy Tony Schwartz

The controversy might have seemed amusing, but it was just another reflection of the enormous importance of television in political campaigns. Nor was it the first controversial TV ad to make headlines during a campaign. Perhaps the most famous commercial aired in 1964 during the presidential contest between Barry Goldwater, the Republican candidate, and Lyndon Johnson, the Democratic incumbent.

The little girl in that television commercial stood in a field of daisies, plucking the petals and counting, as birds chirped in the background. Then, as the little girl reached number 10, a doomsday voice began a countdown. When the voice reached zero, there was a rumbling explosion and a huge mushroom cloud filled the screen. As it billowed upward, President Johnson's voice boomed out: "These are the stakes. To make a world in which all of God's children can live or to go into the dark. We must either love each other or we must die." A message was then flashed on the screen reading: "Vote for President Johnson on November 3."

Millions of Americans saw the famous "Daisy Girl" commercial during the 1964 campaign, even though it was shown only once before being withdrawn because of the controversy it created. To many it seemed to suggest that Barry Goldwater, the Republican candidate, might lead the nation into nuclear war. As Theodore White noted, "The film mentioned neither Goldwater nor the Republicans specifically—but the shriek of Republican indignation fastened the bomb message on them more tightly than any calculation could have expected."[30]

The marriage of television and politics took place in 1948, the first year in which a small but significant number of Americans tuned in to parts of the national nominating conventions.* Because fewer than 200,000 homes had television sets in 1948, however, the real impact of the new medium was not felt until the 1952 and 1956 Eisenhower-Stevenson campaigns. By 1956 almost 35 million homes had television sets. In 1960, of America's 53 million households, 46.6 million, or 88 percent, had sets. By this time, television was playing a central role in presidential campaigns.

The Presidential Debates   It was in 1960 that the major-party candidates were first able to reach vast audiences in a series of televised debates. Congress made the debates possible. Under Section 315 of the Federal Communications Act, broadcasters are required to provide "equal time" to all legally qualified candidates. The networks argued that if the major-party candidates debated on television, this equal-time provision would force the networks to give time to minor-party candidates as well. Congress suspended the equal-time provision in 1960, clearing the way for four debates between Senator John F. Kennedy and Vice President Richard Nixon, his Republican opponent. Most observers believed that the debates helped Kennedy win the election, in part because

---

*1948 was not the first year in which the national conventions were televised. But because very few people owned television sets in the 1940s, fewer than 100,000 persons saw broadcasts of the 1940 and 1944 conventions.

John F. Kennedy and Richard M. Nixon in a televised debate, 1960
CBS Photo

Nixon looked pale and haggard in the first debate and wore "Lazy Shave" powder as makeup. By contrast, Kennedy, looking tanned and vigorous, presented a much more telegenic image to the public.

The millions of voters watching the first debate may have remembered little of what the candidates said, but they noticed that Nixon did not look as pleasing as Kennedy. As White put it, "Probably no picture in American politics tells a better story . . . than that famous shot of the camera on the vice president as he half slouched, his 'Lazy Shave' powder faintly streaked with sweat, his eyes exaggerated hollows of blackness, his jaw, jowls, and face drooping with strain."[31]

 for more about the 1960 presidential debates, see: www.debates.org/pages/debhis60.html

Sixteen years went by before another televised presidential debate took place. In 1976, the debates between President Ford, the Republican incumbent, and Jimmy Carter, his Democratic challenger, were credited by some analysts with providing Carter's narrow margin of victory.*

As president, Ford was better known than Carter at the start of the 1976 campaign, and thus in theory had more to lose by debating his opponent. Normally, an incumbent president, or the better known of two candidates, has little incentive to debate an opponent; the television exposure only serves to help his rival become better known. But Ford, behind by 33 points in the polls, sought to regain the initiative by challenging his opponent to debate, and Carter accepted.[†]

Carter benefited from Ford's erroneous pronouncement in the second debate that the Soviet Union did not dominate Eastern Europe.

 for more about the 1976 presidential debates, see: www.debates.org/pages/debhis76.html

Again in 1980, voters watched the candidates debate. The main debate took place between President Carter, now the incumbent, and former governor Ronald Reagan of California. Both candidates performed well, but Reagan gained ground by displaying an affable, apparently relaxed manner, thereby offsetting Carter's previous warnings that the Republican nominee was an aggressive hawk who might lead the country into a

---

*Although Congress did not suspend the equal-time provision again in 1976, the debates were made possible by a 1975 FCC ruling that debates could be broadcast as long as they were not sponsored by the networks or held in a television studio, and were telecast in their entirety. In 1983, the FCC eased the rules for presidential debates even further, holding that broadcasters could stage political debates in their studios as "bona fide news events." The ruling applied to political debates in campaigns at any level, from school board to president.

---

†The Democrats nominated Carter on July 14. The Gallup poll of July 16–26 showed Carter leading Ford, 62 to 29 percent, with 9 percent undecided. Source: *Gallup Opinion Index*, Report no. 134, September 1976, p. 8.

military adventure. Reagan hammered away at the faltering economy of 1980. Near the end of the 90-minute debate, he urged voters to ask themselves: "Are you better off than you were four years ago? Is it easier for you to go and buy things in the stores than it was four years ago?"[32] It was an effective sales pitch. Polls showed that Reagan had won the debate.

 for more about the 1980 presidential debates, see: www.debates.org/pages/debhis80.html

In 1984, the public again had a chance to view the major-party candidates in televised debates, this time between President Reagan and his Democratic opponent, Walter Mondale. In 1987, before the next presidential election, a bipartisan Commission on Presidential Debates, a nongovernmental group, was established by the two major parties to schedule presidential debates in future elections.

 for more about the 1984 presidential debates, see: www.debates.org/pages/debhis84.html

In 1988, Vice President Bush and Governor Michael Dukakis of Massachusetts debated twice on television. In the vice presidential debate, Senator Dan Quayle, the Republican candidate, seemed uncertain when asked repeatedly what he would do if, as vice president, he suddenly became president. A majority of voters thought Senator Lloyd Bentsen of Texas, the Democratic candidate, had bested his rival. At one point, when Quayle compared his experience in Congress to that of John F. Kennedy, Bentsen snapped: "Senator, I served with Jack Kennedy. I knew Jack Kennedy. Jack Kennedy was a friend of mine. Senator, you're no Jack Kennedy."[33] The retort became famous and entered the nation's political lore. A CBS poll reported Bentsen the winner by more than 2 to 1.[34]

 for more about the 1988 presidential debates, see: www.debates.org/pages/debhis88.html

Although Bill Clinton challenged President Bush to a series of televised debates in 1992, Bush at first refused, citing differences over the format of the debates. By declining to debate, Bush found himself on the defensive for several days. The Clinton camp had taken to dressing volunteers in chicken suits to heckle the president at campaign stops, implying he was afraid to face his Democratic opponent. The giant fowl were known as "Chicken George," and they appeared to greatly annoy the president. At an appearance in the Midwest, Bush got into an argument with one of the chickens, accusing the bird of polluting the Arkansas River.

Then Bush, who was lagging in the polls, countered by suddenly challenging Clinton to debate. Both camps finally agreed on three presidential debates plus one vice presidential debate, all sandwiched into a nine-day period in mid-October. Because Ross Perot had jumped back into the race, he was invited to take part.

In the first debate, Bush emphasized his experience and argued that the economy was not as bad as Clinton said it was. However, Bush failed in his effort to catch up with Clinton. The unexpected star of the evening was Perot, whose biting, homespun comments and humor contrasted with the more ponderous arguments of the two major-party candidates. Asked how, if elected, he planned to get his program passed by Congress, Perot

SPIN CONTROL: "CALL AND PRAISE THE PRESIDENT'S PERFORMANCE"

After every televised presidential debate, members of the candidates' staffs—so-called "spin doctors"—circulate among the news media to try to persuade reporters that their candidate won, or at least did not lose. The staffers try to put a favorable "spin," or twist, on events to help their candidate. The spin doctors' marching orders are supposed to be confidential, but in 1992, by mistake some copies of the Bush-Quayle instructions for action after the October 15 debate were faxed to the news media. Here are some excerpts:

Call your local political reporter and give the spin. Don't wait for him or her to call you—call ASAP. Remember, they are under a tight deadline due to the hour of the debate. *It is vital that you call right away and give your reaction.*

If there are any talk-radio shows on the air, call and praise the president's performance. Please use the talking points. It is imperative that all surrogates are giving the same message. . . . Issue a news release declaring the president the winner.

The instructions include these "talking points":

Tonight was a clear win, a big win for the president. Bill Clinton came in a cautious and weak third place. . . . The president forcefully stated that character is a key issue in this campaign. The person the American people choose to be president must be of unquestioned character and integrity. President Bush is known for his strength of character. . . .

Tonight the president asked the key issue in this campaign. If a major domestic or international crisis breaks out, who is it you trust to solve the crisis and get the job done? The answer is George Bush.

—*Washington Post,* October 17, 1992

replied: "Now, all these fellows with thousand-dollar suits and alligator shoes running up and down the halls of Congress that make policy now—the lobbyists, the PAC guys, the foreign lobbyists, and what-have-you—they'll be over there in the Smithsonian, you know, because we're going to get rid of them, and the Congress will be listening to the people."[35]

In the second presidential debate that year Bush attacked Clinton for taking "different positions" on issues and said: "You can't turn the White House into the Waffle House." The debate did nothing to help Bush close the gap in the opinion polls. President Bush was more forceful in the last debate and during the final two weeks of the campaign he narrowed the gap in the polls, gaining ground on his Democratic rival.

 for more about the 1992 presidential debates, see:
www.debates.org/pages/debhis92.html

But it was not enough; Clinton was elected president, and reelected in 1996, when he debated Bob Dole, the Republican candidate, on television.

 for more about the 1996 presidential debates, see:
www.debates.org/pages/debhis96.html

In 2000, Texas Governor George W. Bush at first agreed to only one of the debates proposed by the bipartisan commission, saying he wanted the other two debates with Al Gore to take place on *Meet the Press* and *Larry King Live*. Criticized for his stance, Bush reversed course and accepted the three debates organized by the commission. The debates took place in October in Boston; Winston-Salem, North Carolina; and St. Louis. The vice presidential candidates, Joseph Lieberman and Dick Cheney, debated at a college in Danville, Kentucky. Because polls on the eve of the first presidential debate on October 3 indicated that both the popular vote and the electoral vote might be close, the presidential debates took on especial importance in 2000.

In one sense, it may be unfair to the candidates and the voters for so much to depend on the impression that the presidential office-seekers make in one or more 90-minute televised debates. Candidates often misstate some facts, which many viewers at home probably do not realize. On the other hand, the televised debates give millions of voters an opportunity they would not otherwise have to watch the candidates in action, to hear and contrast their views on a wide range of domestic and foreign issues, and to make judgments about each candidate's style and character.

Studies of the effect of televised debates on elections have reached varying conclusions. To an extent, some studies suggest, viewers see what they wish to see; that is, their perception of the candidates and issues hews closely to their "original voting preference."[36] But other studies suggest that debates may have "a measurable direct influence on the outcome of the election."[37]

In 2000, as in all recent presidential election years, the tradition of televised debates had given the voters a

Al Gore and George W. Bush during their first televised debate in Boston, October 3, 2000.
MSNBC/AP/Wide World

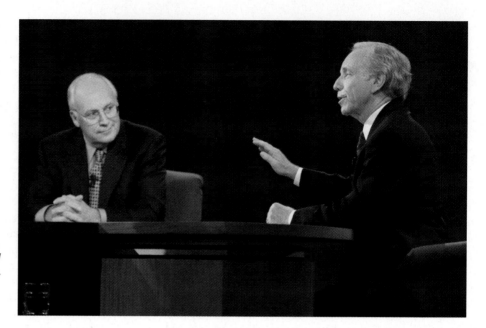

Republican vice-presidential candidate Dick Cheney, left, appears unconvinced by a point made by Joseph Lieberman, his Democratic opponent during their 2000 televised debate.
AP/Wide World

chance to see the candidates interact, and the debates may have helped the viewers to make their own choice about who was best qualified to lead the nation as president of the United States.

Madison Avenue: The Packaging of the President

By the year 2000 there were more than 224 million television sets in about 100 million homes in America; 99.4 percent of all homes with electricity in the United States had televisions—more than had bathtubs or telephones. The ability of political candidates to reach greater numbers of voters through television was reflected in a dramatic rise in campaign spending for commercials. In 1972, $10.8 million was spent for political broadcasts at the presidential level. In subsequent years, the cost increased greatly. Spending for television advertising by candidates at all levels is even higher, of course, amounting to $300 million in 1992.[38] Four years later, in 1996, the total had jumped to more than $400 million. By 2000, an estimated $665 million was spent on television commercials.[39]

The increasing use of television and Madison Avenue advertising techniques has raised the question

of whether political candidates can be merchandised and packaged like toothpaste. To some extent the answer must be yes; many of the advertising executives who handle political accounts think in just those terms.

As a professional actor for most of his adult life, President Reagan enjoyed an added advantage on television. "Reagan," the *Washington Post* reported in 1980, ". . . calls upon his actor's training to get misty on cue, near the end of his talks. . . . His Sunday night closer was an anecdote . . . about looking into the faces of young people in Kansas City and feeling all warm and lumpy about it."[40]

Besides praising the candidate, television ads often jab at opponents. This kind of **negative advertising**—political commercials that strongly attack a rival candidate—is a technique that has become increasingly popular in political campaigns. In 1982 the Republican Senate candidate in Tennessee, Robin Beard, tried to portray his opponent, Senator Jim Sasser, as "soft" on Fidel Castro. In Beard's television commercial, an actor made up to look like Castro lit his cigar with an American bill and sneeringly said, "Muchas gracias, Señor Sasser."[41]

In 1984, several of President Reagan's commercials portrayed happy Americans in various everyday activi-

NON SEQUITUR WILEY

ties—going to work, raising flags, getting married, painting a picket fence. "It's morning again in America," a syrupy-voiced announcer intoned, "and under the leadership of President Reagan, our country is prouder . . . and stronger . . . and better." The commercials were primarily designed to win votes for Reagan by making Americans feel good about themselves.

In 1988, one of President Bush's commercials became notorious. Bush's Democratic opponent was Massachusetts governor Michael Dukakis. Aimed at the Massachusetts prison-furlough program, the commercial showed a group of inmates streaming through a revolving door. As Massachusetts crime statistics flashed on the screen, an announcer attacked Dukakis's "revolving door prison policy [that] gave weekend furloughs to first-degree murderers not eligible for parole. While out, many committed other crimes like kidnapping and rape, and many are still at large."[42] To underscore the point, Bush partisans enlisted the aid of a Maryland man who, with his fiancée, had been brutally assaulted by a Massachusetts convict, Willie Horton, a murderer who was out on a furlough. The man, and a woman whose brother had been slain by the same convict, made a number of campaign appearances in California, a key state in presidential elections.

In addition, a conservative, pro-Bush political action committee aired television commercials featuring a photograph of Horton and linking him to Dukakis. Because Horton was African American, the Dukakis camp charged that the Republicans were injecting racism into the campaign, an accusation that Bush denied. So effective was the commercial that the name "Willie Horton" entered the political lexicon and became synonymous with negative, attack commercials. The "Willie Horton" commercial was credited with helping Bush win the election.

The appearance of Bush on a boat in Boston harbor, charging that the Massachusetts governor's own seaport was one of the most polluted in the nation, was another television image that stuck with the voters. Somehow, when Dukakis tried the same tactic, it didn't work. He rode in an Army tank, wearing a helmet, to emphasize his commitment to a strong national defense—a campaign appearance that appeared silly and contrived to many viewers.

Television ads can, demonstrably, make the difference in the outcome of some elections:

For example, in 1984, Senator Walter Huddleston (D.-Ky) was forty-six points ahead in the polls and appeared headed for relatively easy reelection to a third term until the campaign of his opponent was ignited and the voters' interest captured by a series of imaginative campaign ads. These ads sought to portray the incumbent as a man who shirked his senatorial duties and obligations to his constituents by taking junkets to plush vacation spots at government expense. His challenger's television ads

showed bloodhounds on the seemingly elusive senator's trail first at the Capitol, where he was nowhere to be found, and then at a posh Caribbean resort, where his trace was discovered. By the end of the campaign, Senator Huddleston had seen his comfortable lead disappear and on Election Night Kentucky had a new senator, Republican Mitch McConnell.[43]

What is the impact of television in a political campaign? Thomas E. Patterson and Robert D. McClure have argued that the "nightly network newscasts of ABC, CBS, and NBC present a distorted picture of a presidential election campaign. These newscasts pay only limited attention to major election issues. These newscasts almost entirely avoid discussion of the candidates' qualifications for the Presidency. Instead . . . [they] devote most of their election coverage to the trivia of political campaigning that make for flashy pictures. Hecklers, crowds, motorcades, balloons, rallies, and gossip—these are the regular subjects of network campaign stories."[44]

In a study of the effect of television on voters in Summit County, Ohio, Harold Mendelsohn and Garrett J. O'Keefe found that persons who made up their minds late in a campaign were more likely than others to be influenced by television commercials. Similarly, they reported that "switchers," those who changed their minds during the course of a campaign, were more likely to be influenced by commercials.[45]

The impact of television on American politics should not be underestimated, but it is easy to exaggerate the influence of Madison Avenue and commercials. The idea that a few advertising executives in New York can manipulate the mass of voters ignores other important factors—such as party identification or the voters' personal economic circumstances—that affect how people cast their ballots.

In 1992, for example, in the midst of a recession, the millions of dollars spent by the Bush-Quayle campaign on television commercials did not, in the end, persuade enough voters to reelect the president and vice president.

With the increased importance of television, however, there is at least a danger that a candidate with more money, more skilled media advisers, or a better television style will enjoy a substantial advantage over a rival. Under federal election laws the two major-party presidential candidates in 2000 and other recent elections accepted public funding and were held, in theory, to equal spending levels. But huge loopholes in the laws allowed these rules to be circumvented, and there was no such restriction in congressional and state campaigns.

Moreover, with access to an audience of millions of voters through television, a political candidate may be tempted to display an image that masks the real person, to present the issues in capsulized, simplistic form, and to become a performer rather than a leader. But the candidate who goes too far in this direction takes the risk that the voters may see through the slickness and, in effect, switch channels—by voting for the opposing candidate. And even the cleverest media advisers must work within the existing political framework; their advertising campaigns are limited by the issues that seem important to the voters, by campaign spending laws, by party loyalties, and by the strengths and weaknesses of their client, the candidate. There are, in short, limits to the ability of Madison Avenue to package and sell a candidate.

Professional Campaign Managers

During the 1996 presidential campaign, before scandal forced him to resign, Dick Morris exercised a strong influence behind the scenes on President Clinton's political strategy. It was Morris who was reported to have persuaded Clinton to sign the Republican bill that ended the largest federal welfare program. The Democratic Party's liberal wing was angered at this departure from the principles of the New Deal, but Morris had his eye on Election Day. And he was aware, as was the president, that many voters were unhappy with the existing program and supported the bill because it required welfare recipients to work within two years and limited lifetime benefits to five years.

Four years earlier, James Carville, a Washington political consultant, gained national recognition when he served as a key behind-the-scenes adviser to Clinton, then governor of Arkansas and the Democratic candidate for president. During the campaign, a reporter asked Carville to assess his job. He replied: "Let's say you ask a politician what time it is. Some pols will tell you the time. Some will tell you how to build a clock.

Bill Clinton will tell you how to build a Swiss village. The consultant's job is to say: 'Governor, just tell them it's time for a change.'"[46]

Today, and for the past four decades, political consultants and professional campaign managers have been part of almost every major campaign. When Representative John B. Anderson of Illinois decided to run for president in 1980, he hired David Garth, a professional campaign manager with a reputation for a high degree of success.

A colorful, cigar-smoking New Yorker, Garth at one point scribbled a note on a sign-up sheet at Anderson headquarters in Washington. The sheet encouraged campaign workers to enter an upcoming softball game.

"It is a superb vision of America, all right, but I can't remember which candidate projected it."

"We don't have time for softball," Garth wrote. "We're playing hardball."[47]

Garth was quick to defend his craft against critics who argue that professional campaign managers manipulate the voters. "What is not manipulation?" he asked. "One of the great stupidities is that somehow what we do is manipulation, which it is, and that nothing else is. . . . When Roosevelt sat down to discuss his next fireside chat did they say 'You go ahead and say just what you think is right'? What I'm trying to say is, what happens behind the scenes hasn't changed in politics."[48]

At all levels of politics, candidates turn to professional campaign managers and consultants. The firms earn large fees for their varied services, which include advertising, public relations, research on issues, public opinion sampling, creating Web sites, organizing focus groups to test voter reaction, fund-raising, telephone solicitations, computer analysis, and speech writing.

As Larry Sabato has pointed out, however, the importance of campaign consultants can be overstated: "In most elections the new campaign techniques, and the consultants themselves, probably do not make the difference between winning and losing, although they make some difference and in at least a few cases can convincingly be given credit or blame for the margin of victory or defeat." But because consultants are often treated favorably in the press, and are skilled at self-promotion, "the perception is that consultants and technology make the difference in a greater percentage of elections than they likely do."[49]

Sabato suggests that members of the press, who value consultants as key sources of information, tend to treat them "with kid gloves."[50] And he adds: "Political consultants and the new campaign technology may be producing a whole generation of office-holders far more skilled at running for office than in the art of governing. Who can forget Robert Redford as a newly elected, media-produced U.S. senator at the end of the film *The Candidate* asking pathetically, 'Now what do I do?'"[51]

In the spring of 1965, when Ronald Reagan was thinking about running for governor of California, he approached the Spencer-Roberts political management firm to see whether it would handle his campaign. Such was the reputation of the California firm that aspirants for political office sought out Spencer-Roberts

CREATING THE REAGAN MYTH

In the midst of another presidential campaign, three experienced political strategists sat in a highly confidential meeting and mapped Ronald Reagan's way to a landslide victory. . . .

The meeting was run by Stuart Spencer, the California political consultant who almost 20 years earlier helped transform Ronald Reagan from a B-grade movie actor into the governor of California, and who is now providing similar services to Republican vice-presidential nominee, Sen. Dan Quayle. Spencer . . . consented to have the discussion taped so that an internal memo could be drafted. The result is a series of recordings that allow the listener to be virtually a fly on the wall in the innermost sanctum of the campaign. . . .

As the June 30, 1984, meeting began, the strategists had already sensed that something crucial was missing. "The problem," Spencer told the others, "is we've been talking to everybody at the White House over the past few days—and the Reagan administration fired all its bullets very early and very successfully in the first two years. All their plans, all their priorities, all their programs. They've run out of ammunition. The most striking thing I discovered is that they don't have a goddam thing in the pipeline. They don't have an idea."

[Robert] Teeter concurred. "Days digging around, and we found nothing," he said. "This is a national election. We've got to find something to say." . . .

Spencer suggested that perhaps they could have Reagan say something about "acid rain and all that stuff," since he was vulnerable on environmental issues. But [Kenneth] Khachigian threw up another red flag. "We're better off without it. If you get the old man going on it, he does 'killer trees,'" he warned, referring to Reagan's embarrassing assertion in 1980 that trees caused pollution. . . .

The three men had no doubt that Reagan would agree to their campaign strategy, even though he hadn't helped draft it. The president's political career was in many ways the product of a revolution in American politics which, well before 1984, had turned campaigns into sophisticated marketing operations run by experts more professional than the candidates themselves. Reagan supplied the broad vision and vocal cords. But from the start, Spencer's consulting firm had done the coaching and packaging, marketing him brilliantly to the most media-oriented state in the country and, later, to the most media-oriented nation in the world. . . .

"The President was never really involved in any of the planning or strategy of the campaign," conceded his campaign manager, Edward J. Rollins. . . . "The truth of the matter is that Ronald Reagan is the perfect candidate. He does whatever you want him to do. And he does it superbly well."

—*Washington Post*, September 18, 1988, adapted from Jane Mayer and Doyle McManus, *Landslide: The Unmaking of the President, 1984–1988* rather than vice versa. George Christopher, the former mayor of San Francisco, had also approached Spencer-Roberts. After meeting with Reagan, the political management firm "accepted" him, rather than Christopher, as a client.[52]

Spencer-Roberts managed Reagan's successful campaign against incumbent governor Edmund "Pat" Brown. Because Reagan was an actor, some voters believed that he was simply playing the part of a candidate and memorizing his speeches. Spencer-Roberts advised Reagan to hold question-and-answer periods after each of his speeches to demonstrate to the voters that he had a real grasp of the issues. The firm's advice helped to elect Reagan as governor, his first step on the road to the presidency.

From its beginnings in California in the 1930s, campaign management rapidly grew to the status of a profitable nationwide industry. Some firms handle only Republican candidates, and others specialize in managing Democrats. Almost inevitably, public relations firms that have branched out into campaign management have evolved from technicians giving advice on press releases to strategists helping candidates make major campaign policy decisions. As Stanley Kelley, Jr., accurately predicted: "It is hard to see why the same trends which have brought the public relations man into political life will not also push him upward in political decision-making. His services are valuable because effective use of the mass media is one of the roads to power in contemporary society, and it is difficult clearly to separate strategic and tactical considerations in that use."[53]

One political scientist, Dan Nimmo, has contended that the use of professional campaign managers raises disturbing questions about American politics. The campaign consultants, he has observed, tend to approach elections as "contests of personalities" rather than choices between political parties or principles. And, he warns, the professional image makers "can make a candidate appear to be what he is not."[54]

The Polls

Public opinion polls, as pointed out in Chapter 6, are widely used in political campaigns, not only by the news media, but by the candidates themselves. Political candidates are always concerned about their standing in the polls published by the press, but the use of public opinion surveys has become much more sophisticated than a simple comparison of the relative standing of competing candidates. Politicians may order a confidential poll to be taken well before a campaign in order to gauge their potential strength and may decide whether to run on the basis of the findings.

Once candidates are committed to running in a primary or running in a general-election campaign, they may commission private polls to test voter sentiment.

The results then assist them in identifying the issues and planning their campaign strategy. After the campaign is under way, additional private polls are taken to measure the success of the candidate's personal appeal and handling of the issues; both the candidate's style and positions on the issues may be adjusted accordingly. If elected, officials may rely on polls to measure voter reaction to their performance in office.

Political leaders often complain about polls, but almost all candidates rely on them. After Ronald Reagan was first elected president in 1980, it was revealed that during his campaign he had employed a highly sophisticated, computerized polling system. With fresh data flowing in constantly from national-sample interviews and surveys in 20 states, Reagan's staff was able to track shifts in opinion among the electorate, and to take action based on the information. As his chief poll-taker, Richard Wirthlin described it, "Tracking allows you to watch a campaign almost the same way you watch a movie."[55]

In 1988, Dukakis trailed President Bush in the polls during the fall campaign. "The business of polls is really having a terrible effect. . . . It's terrible," Dukakis complained in Ohio in mid-October, after a *Wall Street Journal*/NBC News poll showed Bush ahead by 17 points.[56] The Democratic nominee argued that matters had reached the point where "polls drive the process."[57]

In 1992, it was Bush's turn to complain about the polls, which showed him trailing Clinton during the entire general-election campaign. In the week after the final televised debate, Bush—modeling himself on Harry Truman—took a whistle-stop train tour through three southern states. He told the crowd gathered along the tracks: "Don't believe these crazy polls. Don't believe these nutty pollsters. Don't let these guys tell you what you think. You have a debate, you see what you think, and then two seconds later some crackpot comes on and tells you what you think. We don't need that in the United States."[58] Bush lost.

But whether polls influence voters and affect election outcomes is not entirely clear. It might also be argued that polls are merely a mirror reflecting public opinion at a given moment. And candidates who are leading in the polls also may worry that their supporters will be less inclined to bother to vote. (For further discussion of the possible effect of polls on elections, see Chapter 6.)

There is a close interrelationship among the various tools and techniques of modern politics. The images that candidates try to project on television may be tailored to advice provided by professional campaign managers, who in turn rely on polls that they have taken or commissioned. Many of these expensive, interlocking, and highly professionalized services were relatively new in the campaigns of the 1960s; today they are taken for granted.

The News Media

After he lost the California governor's race in 1962, Richard Nixon held a famous news conference in which he declared: "You won't have Nixon to kick around any more, because, gentlemen, this is my last press conference." The press, Nixon added, should recognize "that they have a right and a responsibility, if they're against a candidate, to give him the shaft, but also recognize if they give him the shaft, put one lonely reporter on the campaign who will report what the candidate says now and then."[59]

Nixon was exhausted and upset when he made these remarks, but his comments reflected his feelings after the 1960 presidential campaign and the 1962 California contest that he had been treated unfairly by the press. The complaint was not a new one; in 1807 President Jefferson had lamented "the falsehoods of a licentious press."

Modern candidates for political office can ill afford to ignore the press. In 1960, a mutual hostility developed between the press and Nixon, who allowed himself to be interviewed by only a few favored correspondents. By contrast, John F. Kennedy and his staff cultivated the friendship of the reporters assigned to his campaign, and a friendly atmosphere prevailed on his press plane. Eight years later, Nixon ran for president again, this time successfully. Determined not to repeat his earlier mistake, Nixon in 1968 paid great personal attention to the creature comforts of the reporters traveling with him; his staff was available to the press and conspicuously affable.[60]

But sometimes campaign staffs try to shield their candidates from the press, to avoid news conferences where a candidate may say something embarrassing. In the 2000 campaign, reporters complained that it was difficult to get close enough to ask Al Gore questions; his advisers carefully controlled access to the candidate, the better to shape his image for the voters.

In most presidential election years, more newspapers have endorsed Republican presidential candidates than Democratic candidates in their editorials. "Democratic candidates probably have to work a little harder at cultivating good relations [with the press] in order to help counteract the editorial slant of most papers. But Republicans have to work harder to win the sympathies of reporters of liberal tendency who dominate the national press corps, one study asserted."[61]

No doubt personal bias does color reporting at times. However, it is also true that the personal politics of news reporters may not be reflected in their stories, because many news reporters attempt to adhere to professional standards of fairness in covering the candidates. For example, despite charges by the Nixon Administration that reporters have a Democratic and liberal bias, it was the intense coverage of Senator Thomas F. Eagleton's medical history—perhaps more than any other factor—

that forced him to resign from the Democratic ticket in 1972. The highly publicized Eagleton story was helpful to Nixon and very damaging to George McGovern's campaign for president.

Again in 1984, the supposedly liberal press intensely scrutinized the finances of Geraldine Ferraro, the Democratic vice presidential candidate, and her husband. The

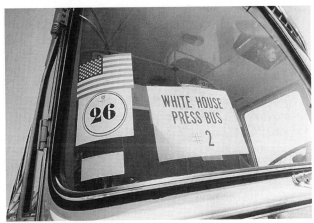

Copyright © Dennis Brack/Black Star

Average length of candidate statement on evening network TV news:

42.3 seconds

1968
Copyright © UPI/Bettmann/Corbis

9.8 seconds

1988
AP/Wide World

7.3 seconds

1992
AP/Wide World

SOURCE: Data for 1992 cover first six months of the year. *Washington Post*, June 21, 1992.

controversy bogged down the Mondale-Ferraro campaign for weeks in its crucial early stages. And in 1992, the press spent more time on the question of whether Clinton told the truth about his draft status while a student during the Vietnam War than it did, until just before the election, on the question of whether Bush told the truth about the extent of his involvement in the Iran-contra scandal while vice president.

And as noted in Chapter 8, the tangled Whitewater story, a continuous source of embarrassment to the Clintons, was first brought to public attention in 1992 by the *New York Times*, usually regarded as the most prominent liberal paper in the country. It was not until September 2000, in the last months of Clinton's presidency, that a special prosecutor closed the Whitewater investigation, announcing there was "insufficient" evidence to bring charges against Clinton or his wife, Hillary Rodham Clinton.

National political correspondents and columnists play an influential role in interpreting political developments and even in recruiting candidates. Speculation in the press about who may or may not become a candidate,

THE CAMPAIGN: "SOME KIND OF A CROSS-COUNTRY RACE"

Reporters and candidates live at a breakneck pace during presidential campaigns. A sense of the hectic nature of life on the campaign trail was captured by author Timothy Crouse in a conversation with reporter James Doyle of the *Washington Star:*

Doyle was slouching in an armchair by the picture window of his bedroom, dead tired from a week on the road. . . . He took a gulp of beer and looked out the window at the sun setting on the river.

"A lot of people," he said, "look at this coverage as if it were some kind of a cross-country race—you gotta get two paragraphs in when he stops at Indianapolis and two more when he stops at Newark. If you do it that way, without making any meaning out of it, it is going to come out like some crazy disjointed trip across the country.

"The problem is, if you try to write every day, you get caught up in sheer exhaustion. It's as simple as that. You do it by rote, because that's all you've got the energy for. It's the lack of sleep, the keeping up with deadlines, the disorientation from all this flying around—your mind just goes blank after a while. When it comes time to write the story, all you can do is just kind of a level job of stumbling through the day's events. I don't think I know how to cover a campaign."

—Timothy Crouse, *The Boys on the Bus*

and published stories analyzing the relative strengths and abilities of rival contenders, may affect what happens at the conventions and on Election Day.

In contrast, editorial support of political candidates by newspapers has a less demonstrable effect on the outcome of presidential campaigns. (See Table 10-2.) During the New Deal years, Roosevelt was consistently opposed by one-half to two-thirds of the nation's daily newspapers; Harry Truman in 1948 and John Kennedy in 1960 were endorsed by only 15 percent of the daily papers, but both won. So did Jimmy Carter in 1976, with endorsements from only 12 percent of the daily papers. Of course, an endorsement from a prestigious paper such as the *New York Times* carries more weight than the endorsement of smaller dailies.

Despite the importance of television in politics and campaigns, daily newspapers in the United States have a circulation of about 56 million, and the impressions that voters receive in political campaigns are formed in part by what they read. As a result, candidates must include the written press in their calculations of campaign techniques and strategy, even if they rely on television for direct mass appeal to the electorate.

CAMPAIGN FINANCE

When Abraham Lincoln ran for Congress in 1846, it cost him 75 cents: "I made the canvass on my own horse; my entertainment, being at the houses of friends, cost me nothing; and my only outlay was 75¢ for a barrel of cider, which some farm-hands insisted I should treat to."[62]

Clearly, times have changed. (See Figure 10-3.) The immense cost of American political campaigns can be seen at a glance from the following figures, which represent total spending at all levels in presidential years since 1972:

$425 million in 1972

$540 million in 1976

$1.2 billion in 1980

$1.8 billion in 1984

$2.7 billion in 1988

$3.2 billion in 1992

$4.2 billion in 1996

$5.5 billion in 2000[63]

By the presidential election of 1976, the nature of political spending in the United States had been significantly reshaped by Watergate, Congress, and the Supreme Court. For the first time, under the Federal Election Campaign Act amendments of 1974 and 1976, both major candidates, Jimmy Carter and Gerald Ford, financed their 1976 election campaigns with federal funds. Major-party presidential candidates have since continued to use federal funds.

In 1992, President Bush and Bill Clinton each received $55.2 million in public funds.[64] Ross Perot, a billionaire, emphasized that he was spending his own money to pay for his campaign, and he accepted no federal funds. During the campaign he spent $63.4 million of his personal fortune to seek the presidency, which made him the single largest self-contributor in American history.[*]

In the 2000 election campaign, George W. Bush and Al Gore each accepted $67.5 million in public funds for the general election campaign. In addition to the federal money provided to the major candidates and parties for the national conventions and

---

Political Division of Daily Newspapers in Presidential Elections, 1932–1996

Year	Republican	Democratic	Independent or Neutral
1932	55.5%	38.7%	5.8%
1936	60.4	34.5	5.1
1940	66.3	20.1	13.6
1944	60.1	22.0	17.9
1948	65.2	15.4	19.4
1952	67.3	14.5	18.2
1956	59.0	17.0	24.0
1960	54.0	15.0	31.0
1964	34.7	42.4	22.9
1968*	60.8	14.0	24.0
1972	71.4	5.3	23.3
1976	62.0	12.0	26.0
1980†	42.2	12.0	42.0
1984	57.7	9.4	32.7
1988	31.2	13.3	55.4
1992‡	14.9	18.3	66.8
1996§	18.7	10.9	69.9

NOTE: Figures represent percentages of total number of papers replying to questionnaires. The number responding varied from year to year.
*George Wallace had the support of 1.2 percent.
†John Anderson had the support of 3.8 percent.
‡Ross Perot had the support of 0.12 percent.
§Other, 0.5 percent.
SOURCES: Data for 1932–1960 from William B. Dickinson, Jr., "Politicians and the Press," in Richard M. Boeckel, ed., *Editorial Research Reports*, vol. 2, no. 2 (September 2, 1964), p. 659. Data for 1964–1996 from *Editor & Publisher*, October 31, 1964; November 2, 1968; November 4, 1972; October 30, 1976; November 1, 1980; November 3, 1984; November 5, 1988; November 7, 1992; and October 26, 1996.

---

*Perot also received $5 million in 1992 from private contributions, so he spent a total of $68.3 million. Because he received 19.7 million votes, the cost per vote was $3.46. Source: Herbert E. Alexander and Anthony Corrado, *Financing the 1992 Election* (Armonk, N.Y.: Sharpe, 1995), p. 128.

Major-Party Campaign Spending in Presidential Elections, 1956–2000

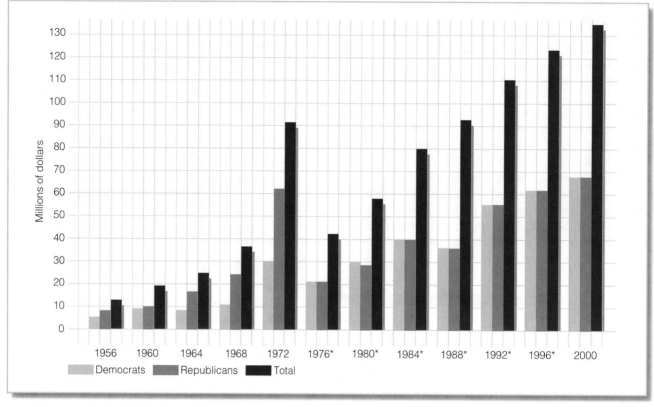

NOTE: Figures are for the postconvention campaigns.
*Both major-party presidential candidates accepted public funding in 1976, 1980, 1984, 1988, 1992, 1996, and 2000. Totals for those years reflect total federal funding for such candidates under the Federal Election Campaign Act amendments of 1974.
SOURCES: Herbert E. Alexander, *Financing Politics: Money, Elections, and Political Reform*, 3rd ed. (Washington, D.C.: CQ Press, 1984), p. 7. Data for 1984, 1988, 1992, 1996, and 2000 provided by the Federal Election Commission. In 1992, in addition to the totals that include the full spending by major-party national committees shown above, independent candidate Ross Perot spent $68.4 million to finance his presidential campaign. In 1996, Perot received $29.1 million in federal funds when he ran as a candidate of his Reform Party.

the general election, some candidates in primary elections may receive federal money. Those who raise the $100,000 necessary to qualify to receive federal dollars are also eligible to receive matching funds from the government to help pay for some of the costs of their primary election campaigns.

In 2000, George W. Bush declined federal money in his Republican primary campaign, relying instead on his own highly successful fund-raising efforts—which also meant he was not subject to federal restrictions on how much he could spend. With the large donations to Bush that poured in, he spent $80.9 million on the primaries, almost twice the $48.4 million spent by Al Gore in the Democratic primaries.[65]

The most significant feature of the federal campaign spending laws enacted in the 1970s was that they had utterly failed to control the size of contributions and spending in political campaigns.

The goals of these laws were simple: First, limit political contributions so that wealthy individuals, corporations, or interest groups do not exercise undue

influence on the politicians to whom they give money. Second, limit the amount that candidates can spend so that all compete on a level playing field, thereby denying an advantage to a wealthy candidate.

But loopholes in the law, court decisions, and new patterns of financing campaigns all combined to undermine the effectiveness of the election law. Efforts at reform might eventually succeed—but laws are made by lawmakers, the very people who have the least incentive to control the money flowing into their campaigns.

As Larry J. Sabato, a political scientist who has studied efforts at campaign reform, put it bluntly: "This is all about self-preservation and survival. . . . It may be a rotten system, but it has one redeeming feature—it elected you."[66]

The presidential election of 1976 was the first in which the law sought to provide effective limits on the size of contributions to candidates. In 1972 Max Palevsky, a California millionaire, gave almost $320,000 to George McGovern, the Democratic candidate. In 1976 he could give only $1,000 to Jimmy

Carter. The conclusion that might logically be drawn is that a candidate who receives a $1,000 contribution will feel less obligated to the donor than one who receives $320,000. And that result is what the new law was designed to achieve. But, as will be seen, the loopholes that developed greatly weakened the effectiveness of the law.

By the 1988 presidential campaign, so-called "soft money" and "independent expenditures" on behalf of the presidential candidates totaled as much or more than the funds allotted under the Federal Election Campaign Act. These two types of campaign spending amounted to a huge gap in the law. By the presidential election of 2000, soft money expenditures by the two major parties far exceeded the spending by their presidential candidates, who had accepted federal funds subject to a cap.

Soft money, until the law was changed in 2002, described the unregulated campaign funds from corporations, unions, and wealthy donors, that were not subject to the limits of federal law. The campaign finance law passed in 2002 banned contributions of soft money to national political parties.

Even before the new law went into effect after the 2002 congressional elections, the two major political parties had created new organizations to accept the continuing flow of soft money. And more soft money was being shifted to the state parties.

The 2002 campaign finance law capped a long effort by senators John McCain, the Arizona Republican, and Russell D. Feingold, a Wisconsin Democrat. In addition to banning gifts of soft money to national political parties, the law prohibited the use of such funds to broadcast "issue ads" that mentioned a specific candidate if the ads ran within 60 days of a general election or 30 days before a primary. The law did allow limited contributions of soft money to state parties for voting and registration drives.

The new law also doubled the amount that individuals can give to a candidate from $1,000 to $2,000.

Until the law was changed in 2002, many critics argued that the unrestricted use of soft money was illegal. Others called it "the loophole that ate the law," because political committees could not only accept large donations but did not have to make them public.[67]

The 2002 campaign finance law was immediately challenged by a group of senators, led by Mitch McConnell, a Kentucky Republican, who argued that restrictions on campaign contributions violated the First Amendment's protection of freedom of speech. Ultimately, that argument was expected to be decided by the Supreme Court.

Independent expenditures are funds spent for or against a candidate by committees not formally connected to a candidate and without coordination with the campaign. The groups that raise and distribute these funds are not subject to federal spending regulations.

These gigantic loopholes in the law undercut the post-Watergate efforts at reform. Big contributors in corporations and both parties were making contributions of $100,000 or more, gifts to party or "independent" committees that would be illegal if made to the candidates directly.

Many millions in soft money contributions poured into the Republican and Democratic Senate and House campaign committees in 2000. The money came from business, individuals, and labor unions. Once again, "fat cats"—big contributors—and special interests were influencing election campaigns.

Four years earlier, in 1996, another issue, that of foreign contributions, arose in the closing weeks of the presidential campaign when it was disclosed that almost $1 million had been given to the Democratic Party by donors linked to a wealthy Indonesian family and their conglomerate, the Lippo Group. One Indonesian couple, permanent residents of the United States at the time, gave $450,000. The Republican candidate, Bob Dole, seized on the issue and used it to attack Bill Clinton and to call for reform of the campaign finance laws. The Dole camp raised the question of what the Indonesians might have expected from the Clinton Administration in return for their largesse.

In the 2000 Republican primary race Senator John McCain of Arizona, who challenged George W. Bush,

SOFT MONEY

Copyright © 2000 Herblock in the *Washington Post*

made campaign finance reform the centerpiece of his unsuccessful quest for his party's nomination. McCain lost his primary bid. With Senator Russell D. Feingold, a Wisconsin Democrat, McCain had sponsored a campaign finance reform bill to outlaw soft money contributions in political campaigns. The measure had been rejected five times by the Senate since it was first introduced in 1995.

Money in election campaigns is a subject cloaked by a good deal of secrecy, and a vast amount of confusion. Even before the passage of the 1974 law, Congress over the years had attempted to control the sources, amounts, and reporting of campaign expenditures. But it was not until after the Watergate scandal that the political climate was favorable for the first comprehensive attempt to regulate campaign finance. As mentioned earlier in this chapter and discussed in more detail in Chapter 13, that scandal had begun when, in 1972, burglars, employed by President Nixon's reelection campaign, broke into the Democratic Party headquarters in the Watergate office building in Washington. The burglary and cover-up, Nixon's resignation to avoid impeachment, and the widespread financial abuses in his 1972 campaign that were revealed by the Senate Watergate committee and by the press increased sentiment for public financing of elections and related reforms. The result was passage of the Federal Election Campaign Act amendments of 1974.

Despite the law, no politician or political scientist would accept the officially reported campaign spending figures as fully reflecting actual political campaign costs. Of the iceberg that is campaign finance, only a portion shows above the surface. Partly as a result, an atmosphere of public cynicism and mistrust has tended to surround the subject of money and politics. Voter attitudes on the subject are reflected in such statements as: "Money wins elections," "Politicians can be bought," or "Politics is a rich man's game."

Money is important. It did not, however, win the Democratic nomination for Averell Harriman in 1956, nor did it put Nelson Rockefeller in the White House in three attempts in the 1960s—and neither man lacked money. Since the Second World War, the Republicans have generally spent more than the Democrats on national campaigns. Therefore, if money alone had determined the result of presidential elections, the Democrats could not have won. There are, in other words, some limits to the influence of money in elections.

Regulating Campaign Finance

Despite the glaring defects of the 1974 legislation, that law and others enacted in the 1970s at least attempted to strengthen the regulation of campaign spending in federal elections. The previous patchwork of federal legislation had also sought to require disclosure of gifts and expenditures, and to limit spending, but the laws had fallen far short of achieving these goals. Most states have campaign financial reporting laws, but they vary greatly and few are stringent.

The Federal Election Campaign Act of 1971 required disclosure of the names of all persons giving more than $100 to a federal campaign, placed limits on what candidates could spend, and repealed the Corrupt Practices Act of 1925, which had failed to limit political spending and did not apply to primary elections. In addition, the law repealed certain provisions of the Hatch Act of 1940, which had sought to limit political contributions and spending in federal elections. These provisions, however, had been evaded in actual practice by various subterfuges.

As far back as 1907, Congress prohibited corporations from contributing to candidates for office in federal elections. The Taft-Hartley Act of 1947 bars gifts by labor unions or corporations to federal election campaigns. But the law did not stop unions or corporations from financing political campaigns; they simply set up separate political arms to make campaign contributions, such as the AFL-CIO Committee on Political Education (COPE), and BIPAC, the Business-Industrial Political Action Committee.

Beginning in 1973, Congress provided that taxpayers could specify a small amount of each person's federal income taxes—$3 by the year 2000—to go into a campaign fund to be distributed among the candidates in the next presidential election. The "checkoff law" was designed to provide public financing of presidential campaigns in order to free political parties of dependence on private contributions. Beginning in 1974, this option was included on the standard income tax forms to make it more convenient for taxpayers.

The Federal Rules The 1974 amendments to the Federal Election Campaign Act rewrote the laws of campaign finance. The law was modified by the Supreme Court in *Buckley* v. *Valeo*, an important ruling in January 1976 that opened the way to independent expenditures.[68] Amendments enacted later that year and in 1979 made further changes, as did the campaign finance law of 2002. The law as of 2002 provided as follows:

Contribution limits. Individuals may give up to $2,000 to federal candidates in primary elections and general elections; individuals may also give up to $95,000 over two years, distributed among candidates, party committees, or political action committees (PACs), such as those sponsored by corporations or labor unions. (These limits will be indexed to increase with inflation.)

Public financing. Presidential—but not Senate or House—candidates may accept federal money to pay for primaries or general elections, as did both major-party candidates in 1996. In 2000, both major party candidates accepted funds for the general election funds, but Bush did not take matching funds during the primary elections. To qualify for public funds in the primaries, a candidate must raise at least $5,000 in each of twenty states in contributions of up to $1,000, for an overall total of $100,000. In addition, public funds may be used to help each major political party to finance its national convention.

Spending limits. Presidential candidates who accept federal funds are limited to spending the amount they receive—$67.5 million each for Gore and Bush in 2000. Candidates who receive federal funds in the general election can accept no private contributions. For each candidate in the presidential primaries who accepted federal funds, the spending limit in 2000 for the primary elections was $40.5 million from both private contributions and federal matching funds.* In 2004, the Federal Election Commission estimated that these amounts would increase, perhaps to about $45 million for candidates in the primaries, and about $75 million for candidates in the general election.

Disclosure. Candidates must file periodic reports with the government disclosing the names and addresses of all donors of more than $200 and listing all expenditures of more than $200.

Federal Election Commission. The law created a bipartisan, six-member Federal Election Commission (reconstituted after the Supreme Court decision) to enforce the campaign finance laws and administer the public financing machinery.

The 1974 law had sought to limit campaign expenditures in all federal elections and to restrict individual spending by candidates or their families. But two years later, in *Buckley* v. *Valeo*, the Supreme Court ruled that these limits, in general, restricted freedom of expression and it struck them down—except for presidential candidates who accept public financing. The Court upheld the limits on contributions, ruling that this imposed less of a burden on free expression.

The Supreme Court's decision in *Buckley* v. *Valeo* opened the way for wealthy candidates to spend vast amounts of their own money in their campaigns. The ruling also permitted independent expenditures to be made by committees not formally connected with a candidate. This opened up one part of the enormous loophole in the law discussed earlier in this chapter.

As political writer Elizabeth Drew has noted, "The law that established public financing of Presidential campaigns was intended to remove the role of private money from Presidential contests, but great rivers of private money, much of it untraceable, still flow into them." That is because the "'independent' committees working on a Presidential candidate's behalf . . . are independent in name only."[69]

In addition, a second Supreme Court ruling in 1996 further diminished the reach of the 1974 amendments to the federal campaign finance law. The Court held, 7–2, that state and national political parties may spend unlimited amounts on congressional campaigns as long as the party and the candidate are not working together.[70] The 1974 law had imposed strict limits on such party spending. But under the Supreme Court's ruling in a Colorado case, the parties are able, for example, to pay for commercials that specifically urge voters to vote for or against a candidate. The decision came early enough to enable the parties to spend such funds for the first time in the 1996 congressional campaigns.

How Much Does It Cost?

In many districts it costs several hundred thousand dollars to run for Congress; and some candidates for the House spend several million dollars in the hope of being sent to Washington by the voters. The $1 million threshold in a House race was crossed for the first time in 1978 by Carter Burden, a wealthy candidate in Manhattan's "silk stocking" district, who lost, and Robert L. Livingston, a Louisiana Republican, who won.[71] In 1990, there were 11 candidates for the House who spent $1 million or more.[72] By 1994, the number had increased to 48.[73] By the year 2000, $1 million for a House race no longer seemed all that unusual; for example, James F. Humphreys, a Democratic candidate for a House seat in West Virginia, had spent $3.5 million even before the fall campaign got under way.[74]

To run for the U.S. Senate, candidates may spend even more staggering amounts. In 1988, the average cost of Senate campaigns was almost $4 million.[75] But the cost of Senate races keeps spiraling upward; in 1990 Senator Jesse Helms, the North Carolina Republican, spent $17.8 million to win reelection.[76] In California in 1994, Michael Huffington, a Republican, spent $28 million of his own money in an unsuccessful attempt to defeat Senator Dianne Feinstein, a Democrat, in the most expensive Senate race ever up to that time.[77] Feinstein won by only 2 percent of the vote. Oliver North, the central figure of the Iran-contra scandal, spent $21 million on his unsuccessful Virginia Senate campaign in 1994 to unseat the Democratic incumbent, Charles S. Robb.[78]

---

*The 1976 amendments to the Federal Election Campaign Act contained an escalator clause keyed to the cost-of-living index, allowing the amount of public funds received by candidates to increase with inflation. In addition, major and minor party candidates who accept public funds may spend up to $50,000 of their own money on the campaign.

Hillary Rodham Clinton and a well-known supporter during her campaign for the U.S. Senate in New York in 2000.
AP/Wide World

In the 2000 elections, Jon S. Corzine, a Wall Street millionaire, spent $35.5 million to win the Democratic nomination for the U.S. Senate in New Jersey.[79] By late September, in a closely watched Senate race in New York, Hillary Rodham Clinton, the Democratic candidate, had spent $14.6 million and her Republican opponent, Rep. Rick A. Lazio, a latecomer to the race after New York City mayor Rudolph W. Giuliani pulled out, had spent $9.4 million.[80] Hillary Clinton won.

Gubernatorial races also often prove to be very expensive. In 1980, Jay Rockefeller, a member of one of America's wealthiest families and heir to the Standard Oil fortune, spent about $12 million in winning reelection as governor of West Virginia. Almost all of the money was his own.[81] By 1990, the average total cost of gubernatorial campaigns was $10 million.[82]

The Jay Rockefeller campaign was a dramatic example of the enormous financial resources that may be utilized by a wealthy candidate, although it paled beside Ross Perot's spending in his campaign for president in 1992. On the other hand, the candidate who spends the most does not always win. "Money also can turn off voters," Herbert E. Alexander has noted. "Wealthy candidates can create a backlash among the electorate."[83]

Running for president is vastly more expensive than running for Congress (although the cost per voter in congressional races is often comparable or sometimes even greater than in presidential campaigns). The cost of nominating and electing a president has increased steadily. The presidential election of 1980, including the preconvention campaigns and the national conventions, cost about $275 million. The figure rose to $325 million in 1984, and to about $500 million in 1988. In 1992, the cost of the presidential race was $550 million.[84] In 1996 it had increased to $700 million.[85] By 2000, it had reached an estimated $1 billion.[86]

Although presidential candidates have been accepting public funds to finance their campaigns, as already noted, as much or more private, soft money may be contributed to presidential campaigns through state and local party committees, independent expenditures, and other categories.

Individuals, corporations, and labor unions have channeled money to state parties for voter registration and get-out-the-vote drives, compilation of lists of target voters, promotion of entire party slates, and other "party-building" activities—the soft money permitted under amendments to the 1974 law.[87] The soft money also has been used for partisan advertising, primarily TV commercials, and even though it must be spent at the state level, considerable benefit may be gained by the party's presidential candidate.[88]

Alexander Heard, author of a number of authoritative studies of campaign finance, has concluded that money is particularly important in "the shadow land of our politics" where it is decided who shall be a nominee of a political party: "Cash is far more significant in the nominating process than in determining the outcome of elections."[89]

Where Does the Money Go?

Today, radio and television costs are by far the biggest single item in campaign spending at the presidential level and in many congressional contests. The cost of TV commercials is the chief reason that presidential candidates take time to appear at fund-raisers even in the midst of barnstorming around the country to win votes. Indeed, Al Gore and Joseph Lieberman were criticized in the 2000 election for first attacking Hollywood for peddling violence to children, and warning the entertainment industry that it might be subject to government regulation—and then soliciting money from movie and television moguls at a fund-raising appearance in Los Angeles.

Candidates' political committees also spend money on other forms of publicity and advertising. They must pay for polls and data processing, printing costs, telephone bills, headquarters costs, and salaries of party workers. A great deal of money is spent on Election Day to pay poll workers, to provide transportation to get the voters to the polls—and, sometimes, illicitly, to pay voters. Alexander Heard has estimated that Election Day spending accounts for "as much as one-eighth of the total election bill in the United States."[90]

Where Does the Money Come From?

By the 1980s, long before Al Gore and George W. Bush battled for the White House in 2000, **political action committees (PACs)** had become a powerful and controversial source of campaign money. PACs are independent organizations, or more often, political arms of corporations, unions, or interest groups. (See Chapter 7 for a detailed discussion of PACs and single-issue groups.) PAC spending in all 1984 campaigns at the federal level totaled $113 million. That total increased to $140 million in 1986, to $159 million in 1988 and again in 1990, $189 million in 1992, $190 million in 1994, $217.8 million in 1996, and $219.9 million in 1998.[91]

PACs tend to give to candidates already serving in Congress (and who therefore have a better chance of winning), not to their challengers. "PACs have tended to move away from ideology and instead have become incumbent-oriented. . . . Three out of four PAC dollars in 1988 went to incumbents of both parties."[92]

By 2000, the number of PACs had increased rapidly to 3,706, up from 2,279 two decades earlier.[93] The growth of PACs was due, in part, to the 1976 Supreme Court decision permitting independent expenditures in political campaigns by groups not formally connected with a candidate.[94] PACs often contribute to political campaigns because they hope a candidate will support legislation that will benefit a specific industry, union, or interest group. Elizabeth Drew has suggested that PAC money in turn has led candidates "to solicit and accept money from those most able to provide it, and to adjust their behavior in office to the need for money—and the fear that a challenger might be able to obtain more."[95]

The reasons why people give money to campaigns vary widely. Some contributors simply believe in a party or a candidate and wish to express their support. Others give because they do expect some tangible benefit or reward from the winning candidate. Others hope to buy access to a public official; for some who long for social recognition, an invitation to a White House dinner may be reward enough.[96]

Some of America's wealthiest families have contributed heavily to political campaigns. The bulk of the contributions from these families—whose wealth is rooted in oil, steel, autos, railroads, and other large industries—went to the Republican Party. Although the contribution limits in the 1974 act have reduced the influence of individual donors, wealthy individuals and families can still contribute substantially to congressional and presidential candidates, because the law permits an aggregate contribution of $25,000 a year by each person. And the federal law does not apply in state or local elections, where wealthy individuals can make their presence felt.

September, 2000: With a Houston oil refinery as a backdrop, Democratic vice-presidential candidate Joseph Lieberman attacks Texas Governor George W. Bush's environmental record and ties to the oil industry.
AP/Wide World

MAKING A DIFFERENCE

"WAKE UP, AMERICA"

She is 90 and has arthritis, emphysema, a bunion on her big left toe, and a steel brace supporting her back. However, Doris "Granny D" Haddock completed a 14-month, 3,200-mile walk across America for campaign finance reform. The passion that drove this great-grandmother was sparked after her weekly women's club discussed campaign finance reform.

"I believe very strongly that democracy is threatened by illegal money that corporations, unions and wealthy men are giving to political candidates," said Haddock, who retired in 1972 as an executive secretary at a shoe firm.

The Dublin, N.H., woman scolded lawmakers for turning "this temple of our fair republic into a bawdy house where anything and everything is done for a price."

"Along my 3,000 miles through the heart of America . . . did I meet anyone who thought that their voice as an equal citizen counts for much in the corrupt halls of Washington? No, I did not. Did I meet anyone who felt anger or pain over this? I did indeed, and I watched them shake with rage sometimes when they spoke, and I saw tears well up in their eyes," she said.

When her son Jim first heard about his mother's plan to walk across the nation, he placed her on a "Herculean" training program. She walked 10 miles a day, practiced carrying a 25-pound backpack and slept on the ground.

"If your mother is 88 years old with emphysema and arthritis, you're not just going to say, 'Have a good time,'" her son said. "I'm proud of her."

Not once has Haddock missed a meal or slept on the floor. Friends and strangers have given her shelter and motels have let her stay for free.

Haddock began her trip in Pasadena, California, on January 1, 1999, and arrived in Washington, D.C., on February 29, 2000. Three members of Congress aided Granny D as she climbed the east steps of the Capitol, saying they wanted to support her on the final leg of her trip because of her extraordinary efforts to draw attention to an issue they've championed for years.

As she arrived at the Capitol, Granny D had this to say: "Wake up, America, recognize what is happening to your country and do something about it."

—Adapted from *USA Today*, February 29, 2000; the Associated Press, March 1, 2000; and *Los Angeles Times*, March 1, 2000

Both major parties rely on a variety of sources to raise money: PAC contributions, individual contributions from the public, $100-a-plate and $1,000-a-plate dinners, direct mail and Internet solicitation, televised appeals, contributions from members of labor unions and corporation executives, and corporate advertising in convention programs and political booklets.

An unadvertised source of campaign funds is the underworld. In some communities, close ties exist between organized crime and politics. Elected officials may take graft to protect criminal operations, and sometimes the payoffs take the form of campaign contributions. Heard has guessed that perhaps "15 percent of political campaign expenditures at state and local levels" comes from the underworld.[97]

Campaigns, Money, and Democracy

The reforms in election laws during the 1970s sought, however unsuccessfully, to limit contributions, to provide meaningful public disclosure of campaign gifts and spending (in place of laws that invited evasion), to broaden the base of campaign giving, and to provide public funding for part of the costs of presidential campaigns. The reforms were based on the belief that candidates should not have to depend on big contributors to whom they might become obligated and that roughly equal resources should be available to candidates for public office.

The case for this reform effort was compelling, because inadequate controls only served to reinforce

"Senator, according to this report, you're marked for defeat by the A.D.A., the National Rifle Association, the A.F.L.-C.I.O., the N.A.M., the Sierra Club, Planned Parenthood, the World Student Christian Federation, the Clamshell Alliance . . ."

voter cynicism about politics. But the growth and influence of soft money and independent expenditures have mocked these reforms. Because of the rivers of soft money flowing into political campaigns, and the failure of the 1974 law to control political spending, there were continuing pressures for meaningful reform. But there was also strong resistance from many members of Congress, corporations, and interest groups.

Clearly, special interest money from PACs has achieved undue influence in the electoral process. In 1988, Michael Dukakis refused to accept PAC money in the primary election campaigns. Almost eight years earlier, President Carter, in his farewell address to the nation, warned that single-issue groups and special interest organizations had become "a disturbing factor in American political life."[98]

As presidential candidates have relied more on public funding, PAC money has been diverted elsewhere. In 1992, as in previous campaigns, millions of dollars in special interest money that might otherwise have gone into the presidential campaign was funneled into congressional races through political action committees.

The growth and power of the PACs helped to undermine the reforms of the federal election laws. Various suggestions have been made for controlling PACs, plugging loopholes in the law, and, above all, banning soft money contributions. Some analysts also have suggested that public financing, available since 1976 in presidential campaigns, be extended to congressional campaigns.

Glaring loopholes in the law and the fact that some candidates have unequal financial resources tend to undermine public confidence in the American political process. And campaigns are a vital part of that process, for, within limits, they give the voters a chance to decide who shall govern.

KEY TERMS

CHAPTER HIGHLIGHTS

✦ For every candidate, between nomination and election there stands the campaign. In American politics, the campaign is the battleground of power.

✦ Campaigns are organized chaos. On a national level, large numbers of people—professionals and volunteers—are thrown together for a relatively short period of time to mount an incredibly complex effort to elect a president.

✦ Studies have shown that many voters, more than half in recent decades, are committed to one candidate or another in advance of the campaign. Nevertheless, a large group of voters, often one-third or more, make their decision during the campaign.

✦ Long before they can get into a general-election campaign, aspiring presidential candidates must, as a rule, enter the bruising arena of the primaries.

✦ Political candidates in most cases develop a central theme for their campaign. Sometimes, the substantive issues in a campaign become submerged as the candidates devote more time to attacking each other than to discussing policies and programs.

✦ Television is an essential part of a modern political campaign. Candidates normally spend much of their budgets on TV commercials. In all recent presidential elections, the major-party candidates have also debated each other on television. In 2000, the candidates appeared on talk and entertainment shows and campaigned on the Internet as well. All offered Web sites that featured the latest speeches, news, and pronouncements of the presidential campaign.

✦ Public opinion polls are widely used in political campaigns, not only by the news media, but by the candidates themselves.

✦ At all levels of politics, candidates have turned to professional campaign managers and consultants. The firms earn large fees for their varied services, which include advertising, public relations, research on issues, public opinion sampling, creating Web sites, fund-raising, telephone solicitations, computer analysis, and speech writing.

✦ In 1976 for the first time, under the Federal Election Campaign Act amendments of 1974 and 1976, both major candidates—Jimmy Carter and Gerald Ford—financed their election campaigns with federal funds. Major-party presidential candidates have since continued to accept federal funds.

✦ By 1996, however, the most significant feature of the federal campaign spending laws was that they had utterly failed to control the size of contributions and spending in political campaigns. And the growth and influence of soft money and independent expenditures mocked the reforms of the 1970s. But Congress in 2002 banned gifts of soft money to national political parties. The new law also prohibited the use of such funds to broadcast "issue ads" for a specific candidate within 60 days of a general election.

✦ Political action committees (PACs) are a powerful and controversial source of campaign money.

✦ Loopholes in the federal election law and the fact that some candidates have unequal financial resources tend to undermine public confidence in the American political process.

SUGGESTED WEB SITES

http://www.opensecrets.org
The Center for Responsive Politics
A nonpartisan, nonprofit organization that tracks money in politics and its effects on public policy and elections. Contains extensive data about lobbyists, soft money contributions, PACs, presidential and congressional races, and political donors.

www.publicintegrity.org
The Center for Public Integrity
A nonprofit center dedicated to government accountability, ethics, and campaign finance reform. The center's research accessible from the Internet includes selected reports, newsletters, and databases.

www.commoncause.org
Common Cause
A nonprofit, nonpartisan organization that promotes government accountability. Visitors to the Web site can research soft money contributions to the Republican and Democratic Parties by donor name, donor location, or industry, as well as news about a wide range of government agencies and topics.

www.fec.gov
Federal Election Commission
This is the branch of the federal government that oversees federal elections. The Web site contains a citizens' guide to elections, including current rules for upcoming campaigns, how to support a candidate, and FEC publications.

SUGGESTED READING

Barber, James David. *The Pulse of Politics: Electing Presidents in the Media Age* (Transaction Publications, 1992). A valuable study of presidential campaigns and presidencies in the 20th century.

Emphasizes the role played by journalists and the news media in presidential politics.

Bailey, Michael A., ed. *Campaigns and Elections: Contemporary Case Studies* (CQ Press, 1999). A readable collection of election case studies, drawn from *Campaign and Elections* magazine, offering an insider perspective on national, state, and local campaigns.

Bennett, W. Lance. *The Governing Crisis: Media, Money, and Marketing in American Elections,* 2nd edition* (St. Martin's, 1996). A trenchant critique of the conduct and content of recent presidential election campaigns. Includes several proposals for improving the quality of the national debate.

Bibby, John F. *Politics, Parties, and Elections in America,* 4th edition* (Nelson-Hall, 2000). An overview of the role of the Republican and Democratic Parties in recruiting leaders, nominating candidates, and contesting elections. Argues that political parties are still a strong force in American elections even though many voters do not vote for the candidate of their party.

Drew, Elizabeth. *The Corruption of American Politics** (Carol Publishing, 1999). A critical examination of campaign finance. Drew, a long-time Washington journalist, argues that the incessant demands of fund-raising have eroded the quality of American politics and politicians over the past generation.

Heard, Alexander. *The Costs of Democracy** (University of North Carolina Press, 1967). (Originally published in 1960.) A comprehensive and useful analysis of the relationships between money and politics. Examines the motives for campaign contributions, who contributes, techniques for raising money, past efforts to regulate campaign financing, and some of the political consequences of various campaign financing practices. Makes specific policy recommendations.

Jamieson, Kathleen Hall. *Dirty Politics: Deception, Distraction, and Democracy** (Oxford University Press, 1992). A careful analysis of deceptive television ads and other manipulative practices used in modern election contests. Argues that the news media focus too much attention on the polls and the candidates' campaign strategies and give too little attention to the candidates' proposals.

Maisel, Louis Sandy. *Parties and Elections in America: The Electoral Process,* 3rd edition* (Rowman & Littlefield, 1999). An excellent general analysis of how election campaigns are conducted in America. The author was himself a major-party candidate for the U.S. House of Representatives.

Patterson, Thomas E. *Out of Order** (Vintage Books, 1994). A detailed study of the influence of the mass media in presidential elections. The author argues that the media, and especially television, have replaced political parties as the main factor in screening and selecting potential presidential candidates.

Polsby, Nelson W., and Wildavsky, Aaron B. *Presidential Elections,* 10th edition* (Chatham House, 1999). An excellent, concise analysis of the basic strategic considerations affecting the conduct of presidential election campaigns.

Sabato, Larry J. *The Rise of Political Consultants: New Ways of Winning Elections** (Basic Books, 1981). A lively discussion of the role of professional political consultants, whose wide-ranging services have become a familiar part of modern election campaigns. Discusses the new campaign technology and the problems that have accompanied the rise of consultants.

Sorauf, Frank J. *Inside Campaign Finance: Myths and Realities* (Yale University Press, 1992). A comprehensive examination of the American system for financing election campaigns. Questions that are explored include: Who gives money for election campaigns? How much do they give? Why do people give? And, what are the consequences of the current financing system for American politics?

Thurber, James A., and Nelson, Candice J., eds. *Campaigns and Elections American Style** (Westview Press, 1995). A useful collection of essays on what it takes to enter and win elections in America today.

Troy, Gil. *See How They Ran: The Changing Role of the Presidential Candidate,* revised and expanded edition* (Harvard University Press, 1996). A survey of how presidential candidates—from George Washington to Bill Clinton—have campaigned for the office. Emphasizes campaign tactics and strategies, and how they have changed over time.

Wayne, Stephen J. *The Road to the White House 2000: The Politics of Presidential Elections** (St. Martin's, 2000). A clearly written analysis of the strategy and tactics of winning the American presidency. Includes sections on campaign finance, delegate selection, national conventions, the media, and voting.

White, Theodore H. *The Making of the President, 1960* (Atheneum, 1961); *The Making of the President, 1964* (Atheneum, 1965); *The Making of the President, 1968* (Atheneum, 1969); and *The Making of the President, 1972* (Atheneum, 1973). Colorful, detailed accounts of American presidential campaigns, set against the background of the social and cultural forces at work in American society. White, a leading political analyst, had access to many of the political figures he wrote about.

*Available in paperback edition.

 Visit http://politicalscience.wadsworth.com/cummings9/update/ for current InfoTrac articles and other student resources related to this chapter.

CHAPTER 11
Voting Behavior and Elections

There comes a moment in every campaign when the bands are silent and the cheering stops. The candidate has given the last speech, made the last promise, answered the last question from reporters, smiled at the red light on the television camera for the last time. There is nothing left to do but to board the campaign plane and fly home to await the verdict of the voters.

There is a certain majesty and mystery in this moment, for until the votes are counted, no one—not the candidates, the voters, the poll-takers, the news reporters, not even the computers blinking and buzzing in the control centers of the television networks—knows what the precise outcome will be. And in the extraordinary presidential election of 2000, the suspense lasted for weeks after Election Day; nobody knew who had won.

In a democracy, the people choose who shall govern, and that choice is expressed in the voting booth. Although the right to vote is basic to the American political system, it is not as common elsewhere as might be thought. Only about half of the world's countries hold regular free elections in which the people may choose among rival candidates.

Chapter 1 examined the reciprocal nature of power in a democracy: Government makes authoritative, binding decisions about who gets what in society, but derives its power from the people. People may influence government in a number of ways—by taking part in political activity, by the opinions they hold, by belonging to interest groups, by direct action. But a fundamental way that people influence government is through the ballot box; voting is a very powerful input in the political system.

For example, as the presidential election of 1992 demonstrated, one of the most potent weapons of popular control in a democracy is the ability of the electorate to remove a party from power. In that year, Bill Clinton of Arkansas, the Democratic challenger, defeated the Republican incumbent, President George Bush.

In the federal system that exists in the United States, the voters choose at all levels of government. In a presidential year, for instance, the voters select many of the nation's more than 500,000 local, state, and federal elected officials, including the president and vice president, 435 members of the House, one-third of the Senate, and 11 state governors.

American voters normally may choose among two or more competing candidates for the same office. In a democracy, voting is an act of choice among alternative candidates, parties, and, depending on the election, alternative policies.

Under a democratic form of government, then, the voter is theoretically supreme. Yet, as we have seen, there is often a gap between democratic theory and practice. For example, candidates for public office—at least below the presidential level—may compete with vastly unequal financial resources. TV commercials may attempt to manipulate the voters and create "images" of candidates, rather than informing the electorate. What the voters perceive may be distorted if one side or the other engages in unethical campaign practices or "dirty tricks." Some voters may be unenthusiastic about the nominees of both major parties and may believe that their choice is between the lesser of two evils. In some years, they may choose to support a minor-party or independent candidate. Or they may easily come to feel that, for them, voting is a waste of time.

FIGURE 11-1

Voter Participation in Presidential and House Elections, 1960–2000

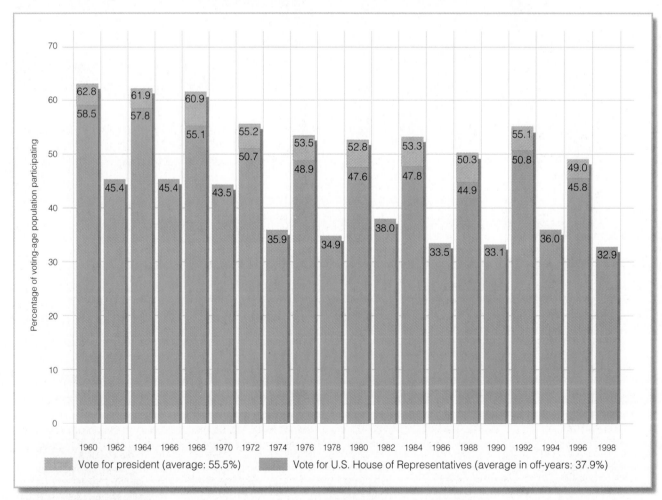

SOURCE: Data provided by U.S. Bureau of the Census, *Statistical Abstract of the United States: 1999*, p. 301.

In this chapter we will explore a key question: What are the consequences of voting and elections in a democratic society? We will also examine a number of related questions. Do enough people vote? Why do large numbers of people fail to vote? How do voters make up their minds? What do elections mean in a democracy—do voters speak in a voice that can be understood by those whom they elect? Do their votes influence government policies? In other words, do elections make a difference in terms of who gets what, when, and how?

WHO VOTES?

The voter may have the final say in the United States—but how many people vote? To those who hold an idealized view of representative democracy, the statistics are bound to be disappointing. In some elections there are as many nonvoters as voters.

The Voter

Almost half or more of the Americans of voting age have voted for president in each election since 1928. But in nonpresidential election years, considerably less than half have bothered to vote for members of Congress. In the 10 off-year congressional elections since 1962, an average of only 37.9 percent voted for members of the House of Representatives. By contrast, in the 10 presidential elections from 1960 through 1996, an average of 55.5 percent cast their ballots for president. During these elections, voter turnout declined in every presidential year but two;

the 1996 turnout—49 percent—was the lowest since 1924. In 1992, however, the voter turnout for president increased substantially—from 50.3 percent in 1988 to 55.1 percent four years later. (See Figure 11-1.)

Although 20th-century Americans have made great technological progress, their forebears in the horse-and-buggy era scored much higher in voting participation. A much larger proportion of voters took part in presidential elections in the 1890s than in recent years. In the election of 1896, for example, almost 80 percent of the eligible voters cast their ballots. The drop in turnout since then is often attributed to the fact that the adoption of women's suffrage in 1920 brought into the electorate a large new group unaccustomed to voting. But the decline in voter participation had begun well before then. After voter turnout dipped to a low point in the early 1920s, it moved to generally higher levels in 1928 and in subsequent elections. (See Figure 11-2.) Despite this trend, voting participation in the United States is substantially lower than it is in many other countries of the world, including Great Britain, Germany, France, and Canada. (See Table 11-1.) Because other nations calculate voter turnout in varying ways, however, the comparison with the United States is not precise.

Socioeconomic Factors   It is clear that who votes varies with factors of geography, age, sex, education, ethnic background, religion, income, social class, and occupation. This does not necessarily mean that people vote or do not vote because of such social, demographic, and economic factors; it merely means that these factors often coincide with higher or lower voting participation.[1]

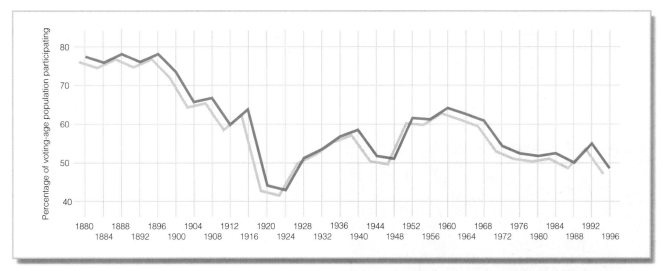

■ FIGURE 11-2

Voter Participation in Presidential Elections, 1880–1996

SOURCES: Figures for 1880 to 1916 in Robert E. Lane, *Political Life* (New York: Free Press, 1965), p. 20. Reprinted with permission of Macmillan Publishing Co., Inc., from *Political Life* by Robert E. Lane. Copyright 1959 by The Free Press. Figures for 1920 to 1948 in *Statistical Abstract of the United States: 1969*, p. 368. Data for 1952 to 1980 from *Statistical Abstract of the United States: 1984*, p. 262. Data for 1984 from *Washington Post*, January 8, 1985, p. A3. Data for 1988 from *New York Times*, November 13, 1988, p. 32. Data for 1992 provided by the Committee for the Study of the American Electorate, Washington, D.C. Data for 1996 from U.S. Bureau of the Census, *Statistical Abstract of the United States: 1999*, p. 301.

Voter Participation in Other Countries

Nation	Election Year	Turnout
Australia*	1998	96%
Belgium*	1999	95
Canada	1997	67
France	1997	68
Germany	1998	82
Great Britain	1997	72
Greece	2000	75
India	1998	62
Ireland	1997	66
Netherlands	1998	73
New Zealand†	1999	90
Portugal	1999	62
Russia	2000	69
Switzerland	1999	43

*Compulsory registration and voting.
†Compulsory registration.
NOTE: Turnout for Russia is for the country's presidential election. Data for all other countries are for elections for the national legislature.
SOURCES: *Facts on File;* International Foundation for Election Systems; British Information Service; and the Irish Embassy.

For example, regional differences in voter participation may be associated with social and economic factors in those areas, the degree of two-party competition, and, in some cases, differences in the election laws governing registration and voting.

Middle-aged people vote more than the young or the very old. Although some college students and young people take an active part in election campaigns, poll data indicate that nearly half of Americans between the ages of 18 and 24 did not register to vote in 1996.[2] In the past, studies showed that voting and political participation increase slowly with age, peak in the mid-forties and fifties, and decline after age 60.[3]

During the first several decades after the women's suffrage amendment was ratified in 1920, men voted

Copyright © Rebecca Cooney/NYT Pictures

more than women. By 1996, however, the percent of women who turned out to vote was about 2 percent higher than that of men.[4] Because there are more women than men in the United States, in absolute numbers there are likely to be more women than men voters in future elections. Sandra Baxter and Marjorie Lansing concluded in a 1980 study: "A major shift has occurred in the voting balance in the last decade: more women than men have gone to the polls to vote for president."[5]

College graduates vote substantially more than people with high school or grade school educations. One survey found that 80.4 percent of college-educated Americans reported that they voted in the 1996 presidential election, whereas only 62.2 percent of those with four years of high school and 40.7 percent of those with grade school educations said they voted.[6] Education seems to cause the greatest variation in voter turnout of all the factors.[7]

Income, education, social class, and occupation are closely related; the higher the level in all these categories, the more likely a person is to vote. (See Table 11-2.)

Jews vote more than Catholics, and Catholics vote more than Protestants. Churchgoers are more likely to vote than nonchurchgoers, a phenomenon perhaps associated with the willingness of the churchgoer to participate in organized activity and the inclination of some religious groups to get involved in politics. African

Voter Turnout by Group and Region, 1996

Voting Groups	Percent Voting
College graduate	80.4%
65 years and older	77.0
45–64 years old	73.5
1–3 years college	72.9
Midwest	71.6
White	67.7
Female	67.3
35–44 years old	66.5
South	65.9
Northeast	64.7
Male	64.4
African American	63.5
High school graduate	62.2
West	60.8
25–34 years old	56.9
Unemployed	52.5
21–24 years old	51.2
Some high school education	47.9
18–20 years old	45.6
8 years school or less	40.7
Hispanics	35.7

SOURCE: Data provided by U.S. Bureau of the Census, *Statistical Abstract of the United States: 1999,* p. 300.

The AMERICAN PAST

SUSAN B. ANTHONY AND THE BATTLE FOR WOMEN'S SUFFRAGE

In 1920, the nineteenth amendment to the Constitution guaranteed women the right to vote. But the struggle for women's suffrage had begun in 1848. For many years, the leader of that battle was Susan B. Anthony. The following account tells of her attempt to influence the Republican convention of 1880 to recognize the rights of women in the party's platform. Anthony described her plans in a letter to one of her followers:

"I want the rousingest rallying cry ever put on paper—first, to call women by the thousand to Chicago; and second, to get every one who can not go there to send a postal card to the mass convention, saying she wants the Republicans to put [an] Amendment pledge in their platform. Don't you see that if we could have a mass meeting of 2,000 or 3,000 earnest women, June 2, and then receive 10,000 postals from women all over the country, what a tremendous influence we could bring to bear on the Republican convention, June 3? We can get Farwell Hall for $40 a day, and I think would do well to engage it for the 2d and 3d, then we could make it our headquarters—sleep in it even, if we couldn't get any other places. . . ."

The mass meeting opened in Farwell Hall, Chicago, June 1, the day before the Republican convention, with delegates from twenty-six States, and continued in session three days. . . . The audience numbered 3,000 and the enthusiasm was unprecedented in all the records of this movement. . . .

The Chicago press gave very satisfactory reports of this meeting, but the *Springfield Republic* was vulgar and abusive, called the ladies "withered beldames," "cats on the back roof," and advised them to "go home and attend to their children, if they had any, and if not, to engage in that same occupation as soon as they could regularly do so."

The charge being so often made that the leaders of the suffrage movement were a lot of old maids and childless wives, Miss Anthony prepared a list showing that sixteen of the most prominent were the mothers of sixty-six children. Of the pioneers she herself was the only one who never married.

—Ida Husted Harper, *The Life and Work of Susan B. Anthony*

Americans vote less often than whites—but historically African American voters in the South were often prevented from voting by legal subterfuge, violence, or intimidation. As was noted in Chapter 5, the number of black registered voters in the South increased dramatically after passage of the Voting Rights Act of 1965.

Voter Attitudes Voter turnout does vary with demographic and social differences, but other research has identified additional factors that seem to influence participation at the polls. This research has focused on voter attitudes.

For example, a strong Democrat or a rock-ribbed Republican is more likely to get out and vote than a citizen whose party loyalties are casual. The higher the *intensity of partisan preference*, therefore, the more likely it is that the person will vote. Similarly, the *degree of interest* that people have in the campaign and their *concern over the election outcome* appear to be related to whether they vote. If people think the election is close, they are more likely to vote, because they may believe that their votes will count. And, if people think they can understand and influence politics, they are more likely to vote than are those who regard politics and government as distant and complicated. The greater a person's *sense of political effectiveness*, in other words, the greater the chance that he or she will vote. Americans, moreover, are indoctrinated with the importance of voting

long before they are old enough to do so. Thus the voter's *sense of civic duty* also bears on whether he or she goes to the polls.[8]

The Nonvoter

Some 35 to 45 percent or more of Americans do not vote in presidential elections. Who are they? Why don't they vote? The preceding discussion indicated that the nonvoter is more likely to be less educated, rural, nonwhite, very young or very old, a person "whose emotional investment in politics . . . is on the average much less than that of the voter."[9] Although a rough portrait of the nonvoter can be sketched in these terms, the picture does not explain why he or she does not vote.

As noted earlier, about 49 percent of the voting-age population—or 96.3 million people—voted in the 1996 election. However, millions of Americans of voting age did not. After an earlier election, in 1988, the *New York Times*/CBS News poll released the following breakdown of nonvoters and the reasons they gave for not voting (with the percentages from the sample projected into numbers of people):

33.8 million were not registered

11.9 million did not like the candidates

11.9 million were too busy, had to work, or had problems getting child care

5.5 million chose not to vote

3.6 million did not care or were not interested

3.6 million had just moved and had not met the residence requirements

2.7 million were sick or their child was sick

1.8 million thought their vote did not matter

1.8 million had never voted

0.9 million thought the voting process too complicated

0.9 million had no transportation

0.9 million were out of town

6.3 million mentioned a variety of other reasons[10]

Even taking into account the fact that some people had good reasons for not voting, a nation with some 91.6 million persons who do not turn out in a presidential election would seem to fall somewhat short of the idealized model of popular democracy. But some political scientists believe that what might work in a simple, agrarian society does not apply in a modern, highly industrialized society like the United States today.[11] The harassed parent with five young children may well find it difficult to get to the polls on Election Day. Most people spend more time worrying about money, sex, illness, crime, the high cost of living, automobile repairs, and a host of other things than they do worrying about politics.

So if we ask whether enough people vote in the United States, we must also ask: How much is enough? A turnout of 50 to 60 percent in a presidential election may not meet the classic standards of democracy, but it may be the best that can be expected in the United States today. In any event, it is reality; it is what we have.

One overall pattern that emerges from all the data about the voter and the nonvoter in the United States is that those who are more advantageously situated in the social system vote more than the "have-nots," or less advantaged. If members of all social groups in the United States voted in equal proportions, candidates might have to offer programs that appealed more to the disadvantaged groups, many of whose members do not now come to the polls. In short, if everybody voted, the candidates and policies of the American political system might be somewhat different from what they are today.

HOW THE VOTER DECIDES

We have an idea who votes and who does not. The next question is: Why do people vote the way they do? How people make up their minds to vote for one candidate instead of another is obviously of great interest to politicians, campaign managers, advertising executives, and pollsters. But the question also has much broader implications for all citizens and for democratic government; the kind of society in which we live depends in part on whether voters flip a coin in the voting booth or choose on a somewhat more rational basis—satisfac-

tion or dissatisfaction with the incumbent administration, for example.

Although American voters have been extensively analyzed, we still do not know precisely why they behave the way they do. We do not know which of many factors ultimately will cause a person to stay home or to vote for one candidate or party instead of another. To say, for example, that many Catholics are Democrats does not mean a person is a Democrat because he or she is a Catholic. And, although party loyalty appears to be related to voting habits, we do not know, for example, that a Vermont farmer votes Republican *because* he identifies with the Republican Party. Psychologists know that it is extremely difficult to judge people's motives from their behavior; even asking voters to explain their actions may not produce satisfactory answers.

So there are limits to the ability of political scientists to interpret the behavior of voters. Even allowing for these limits, however, a great deal has been learned about voting habits in recent decades.

Two basic approaches have been followed in studying how the voters decide:

1. *Sociological method.* This approach focuses on the social and economic background of the voters— their income, class, ethnic group, education, and similar factors—and attempts to relate these factors to how they vote.
2. *Psychological method.* This approach attempts to go beyond socioeconomic factors and find out what is going on inside the minds of the voters, to measure their perceptions of parties, candidates, and issues.

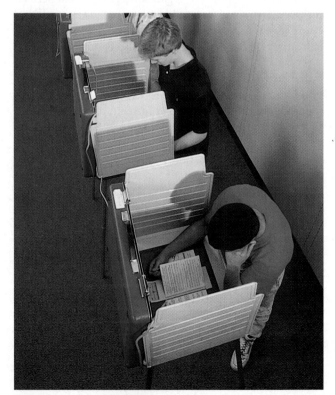

This second approach is based on the premise that how the voter responds depends less on static factors, such as social class, than on dynamic changing factors of issues and politics. In short, voting behavior may change as the issues and candidates change.

The difference between these two approaches is not as great as it might seem at first glance: How the voters currently perceive the issues may well be shaped by their social and economic backgrounds. The social psychologists who followed the second approach beginning in the 1950s built on the foundations laid by the political sociologists in the 1940s.

The Sociological Factors

In the first of two classic voter studies, 600 residents of Erie County, Ohio, were interviewed during the 1940 presidential election.[12] The study found a pattern that has been repeated over and over again in American national elections. Wealthier people usually voted Republican, and poorer people voted Democratic: "Different social characteristics, different votes."[13]

But the voter is a member of several groups simultaneously. Sometimes the claims of one group conflict with those of another. For example, the study concluded that rich people were more likely to vote Republican, Catholics were more likely to vote Democratic. What of wealthy Catholics? Such persons are said to be "cross-pressured" because their social affiliations are pulling them in opposite directions. The study found that these voters were more likely than others to delay their decision and change their minds during a campaign. In 1948 the same research method was used in a study of how 1,000 voters in Elmira, New York, made up their minds during the Truman-Dewey campaign.[14] This more detailed study also concluded that social class influenced voting behavior.

Today, however, many of the more recent voter analyses, whether following the sociological or the psychological approach, are based on national rather than local poll data. From these various studies, it is possible to draw a picture of the American voter in terms of his or her social class and other sociological factors. (A breakdown of how different groups have voted in presidential elections is summarized in Table 11-3.)

Social Class, Income, and Occupation Upper-class and middle-class voters are more likely to vote Republican than are voters of lower economic and social status, who tend to be Democrats. The vote of union members has usually gone Democratic.

Professional and business people have been more likely to support Republicans than Democrats. For example, with the exception of 1964—when Republicans in droves deserted Goldwater for Johnson—business and professional people voted heavily Republican in the seven elections from 1960 to 1984. (See Table 11-3.) Among

persons in the highest income brackets, Republican candidates usually draw more votes than do Democrats. In a 1996 survey, for example, the one income group where Bob Dole had a substantial lead over Bill Clinton was among voters with an annual family income of $75,000 or more.*

Education In 1996 Bill Clinton received 47 percent of the votes of college graduates, compared to 45 percent voting for Dole. In the past, however, college graduates have tended to vote for Republicans rather than Democrats. A majority of college-educated voters were in the ranks of the GOP during the elections of Kennedy, Nixon, and Reagan, and during Vice President George Bush's 1988 race for the presidency. Although Nixon averaged 43.4 percent of the popular vote in 1968, he received 54 percent of the votes of college graduates; by contrast, only 33 percent of voters with a grade school education voted for Nixon. (See Table 11-3.) In 1996, Clinton, who received 49.2 percent of the total popular vote, was supported by 58 percent of voters with a grade school education.

Religion and Ethnic Background In a 1992 survey, 59.5 percent of Jews and 41.8 percent of Catholics, but only 36 percent of Protestants, said they considered themselves Democrats.[15] In 1960, Jews, Catholics, and Protestants voted 81, 78, and 38 percent, respectively, for Kennedy. Because Kennedy was the first Roman Catholic to be elected president, the 1960 election was carefully analyzed to assess the effect of his religion on the result. The Michigan Survey Research Center concluded that Kennedy won a "bonus" from Catholics of 4.3 percent of the two-party vote (2.9 million votes) but lost 6.5 percent (4.4 million votes) from Protestant Democrats and independents. His religion cost him a net loss of 2.2 percent, or 1.5 million popular votes.[16] On the other hand, the heavy Catholic vote in big northern industrial states probably helped him win in the electoral college.[17] It cannot be demonstrated, however, that Kennedy won because he was a Catholic.

Various studies have shown that voters of Irish, Italian, Polish, East European, and Slavic descent often favor Democrats, although President Reagan made strong gains among several of these groups in 1980 and 1984. Black Americans, who generally had voted Republican until the New Deal, shifted away from the party of Lincoln to give approximately 94 percent of their votes to the Democrats in 1964. And in the next eight presidential elections from 1968 to 1996, the support among nonwhites for the Democratic presidential nominee never dropped below 77 percent. In a 1996 survey, Clinton received 84 percent of the vote from African Americans.[18]

---

*In this high-income group, Bob Dole received 50 percent of the votes of those polled, while Bill Clinton received 42 percent, and Ross Perot received 7 percent. Exit polls conducted by Voter News Service, *National Journal*, November 9, 1996, p. 2407.

TABLE 11-3

Votes by Groups in Presidential Elections, 1960–1996

	1960 Dem.	1960 Rep.	1964 Dem.	1964 Rep.	1968 Dem.	1968 Rep.	1968 Wallace	1972 Dem.	1972 Rep.	1976* Dem.	1976* Rep.	1976* McCarthy
National	50.1%	49.9%	61.3%	38.7%	43%	43.4%	13.6%	38%	62%	50%	48%	1%
Men	52	48	60	40	41	43	16	37	63	53	45	1
Women	49	51	62	38	45	43	12	38	62	48	51	†
White	49	51	59	41	38	47	15	32	68	46	52	1
Nonwhite	68	32	94	6	85	12	3	87	13	85	15	†
College education	39	61	52	48	37	54	9	37	63	42	55	2
High school education	52	48	62	38	42	43	15	34	66	54	46	†
Grade school education	55	45	66	34	52	33	15	49	51	58	41	1
Professional and business people	42	58	54	46	34	56	10	31	69	42	56	1
White-collar workers	48	52	57	43	41	47	12	36	64	50	48	2
Manual workers	60	40	71	29	50	35	15	43	57	58	41	1
Union members	65	35	73	27	56	29	15	46	54	63	36	1
Farmers	48	52	53	47	29	51	20	‡	‡	‡	‡	‡
Under 30	54	46	64	36	47	38	15	48	52	53	45	1
30–49 years	54	46	63	37	44	41	15	33	67	48	49	2
Over 49	46	54	59	41	41	47	12	36	64	52	48	†
Protestants	38	62	55	45	35	49	16	30	70	46	53	†
Catholics	78	22	76	24	59	33	8	48	52	57	42	1
Republicans	5	95	20	80	9	86	14	5	95	9	91	†
Democrats	84	16	87	13	74	12	14	67	33	82	18	†
Independents	43	57	56	44	31	44	25	31	69	38	57	4

*Figures for some groups do not add to 100 percent because of the vote for other minor-party candidates.
†Less than 1 percent.
‡Not available.

Primary Groups In addition to conventional social groups, voters are influenced by personal contacts with much smaller "primary" groups, such as families, coworkers, and friends. Sometimes these influences may change a voter's mind. However, because people of similar social background tend to associate with one another, primary groups often merely reinforce the political views that are already held by the voter.

Geography In general, the Democrats still draw their strength from the big cities of the North and East. Voters in rural areas in the North are more likely to be Republicans. Until the 1960s, at least, Democrats normally ran strongly in the South. But the Democrats can no longer count on the South in presidential contests. In 1972, for example, President Nixon polled 71 percent of the popular vote in the South, and for the first time since Reconstruction, the Republican presidential ticket carried all 11 states of the Old Confederacy. In 1976 the

Democratic candidate, Jimmy Carter, was a former governor of the Deep South state of Georgia, and he carried every southern state except Virginia. But in 1980 Republican Ronald Reagan polled 51 percent of the popular vote in the South and won 10 southern states. And in 1984, Reagan won every state in the South by a decisive margin; he also polled 62.4 percent of the popular vote in the region.[19] This trend continued when George Bush won every southern state in 1988 and polled 58.7 percent of the vote in the South.

In 1992 the Democrats nominated a pair of southerners for president and for vice president, and this time the presidential race in the South was much closer. The Clinton-Gore Democratic ticket received 41.5 percent of the popular vote in the region, while Bush and Quayle won 42.7 percent for the Republicans, and Ross Perot and James B. Stockdale polled 15.8 percent. Clinton carried four states in the South in 1992; the remaining seven went to Bush. Two years later, in the midterm

	1980				1984		1988		1992			1996		
	Dem.	Rep.	Anderson	Other	Dem.	Rep.	Dem.	Rep.	Dem.	Rep.	Perot	Dem.	Rep.	Perot
	41%	50.8%	6.6%	1.4%	41%	59%	46%	54%	43.2%	37.8%	19.0%	50.0%	41.0%	9.0%
	38	53	7	2	36	64	44	56	41	37	22	45	44	11
	44	49	6	1	45	55	48	52	46	38	16	54	39	7
	36	56	7	1	34	66	41	59	39	41	20	46	45	9
	86	10	2	2	87	13	82	18	77	11	12	82	12	6
	35	53	10	2	39	61	43	57	43	40	17	47	45	8
	43	51	5	1	43	57	46	54	40	38	22	52	34	14
	54	42	3	1	51	49	56	44	56	28	16	58	27	15
	33	55	10	2	34	66	‡	‡	‡	‡	‡	‡	‡	‡
	‡	‡	‡	‡	47	53	‡	‡	‡	‡	‡	‡	‡	‡
	48	46	5	1	46	54	‡	‡	‡	‡	‡	‡	‡	‡
	50	43	5	2	52	48	‡	‡	‡	‡	‡	‡	‡	‡
	31	61	7	1	‡	‡	‡	‡	‡	‡	‡	‡	‡	‡
	47	41	11	1	40	60	37	63	40	37	23	54	30	16
	38	52	8	2	40	60	45	55	42	37	21	49	41	10
	41	54	4	1	41	59	49	51	46	39	15	50	45	5
	39	54	6	1	39	61	36	64	41	41	18	44	50	6
	46	47	6	1	39	61	51	49	47	35	18	55	35	10
	8	86	5	1	4	96	7	93	7	77	16	10	85	5
	69	26	4	1	79	21	85	15	82	8	10	90	6	4
	29	55	14	2	33	67	43	57	39	30	31	48	33	19

SOURCE: Data provided by the Gallup poll.

elections of 1994, the Republican Party made big gains in southern congressional races. For the first time since Reconstruction, Republican candidates for the House of Representatives decisively outpolled their Democratic opponents in the popular vote in the South. In 2000, both major parties nominated a candidate from a southern state to head their presidential ticket.

The suburbs, originally Republican strongholds after the Second World War, are today more a mixture of Democrats and Republicans. Democratic strength has grown in suburbia as lower- and middle-class whites and many blacks have left the cities, but Republicans still dominate many suburbs.

Sex Until 1980, in most presidential elections, whether voters were men or women did not seem to have a significant influence on how they voted.[20] In 1980, however, it was different. The election that year provided the most striking example of a difference in voting behavior between men and women since voter polls began in the 1930s. In 1980 men voted for Ronald Reagan over Jimmy Carter by a dramatic margin of 15 percentage points or more. By contrast, women—perhaps because they perceived Reagan as being more likely to engage in a military adventure than Carter—split their votes more evenly between the two candidates.* (Virtually all surveys on the subject have shown that women are substantially less likely than men to favor military action.[21])

At the beginning of 1984, some Republican electoral strategists were worried that this "gender gap" might seriously hamper President Reagan in his bid for reelection. But when Reagan won his sweeping victory in November 1984, women voters as well as the men gave him a solid reelection margin. There was still a substantial difference

---

*The Gallup poll data in Table 11-3 indicated that Reagan ran 15 percentage points ahead of Carter among men. The ABC News exit poll, based on interviews of 9,341 voters leaving voting precincts on Election Day, reported that Reagan's margin over Carter was 19 percentage points among men. Both the Gallup poll and the ABC News exit poll found that among women who were interviewed, Reagan ran 5 percentage points ahead of Carter.

in the voting preferences of men and women in 1984, however. Reagan won the votes of 64 percent of the men, compared with 55 percent of women. In 1996 there again was a gender gap in the vote for president. The polls indicated that Clinton and Dole ran almost even among male voters. Among women who voted, by contrast, Clinton's lead was sizable—54 percent to 39 percent. (See Table 11-3.) The 1980, 1984, and 1996 elections all suggested that men and women may vote differently—when the images and issue positions of the candidates coincide with differences in political attitudes between men and women. In the 2000 presidential election, both George W. Bush and Al Gore campaigned for the votes of women—which perhaps explains why both made a point of appearing on Oprah Winfrey's television program, with its large audience of women.

Age   In most national elections since 1960, younger voters were more likely to vote Democratic than Republican. Older voters seemed to find the GOP attractive. From 1960 to 1980, the Democrats consistently got a higher percentage of the vote from those under age 30 than from voters 50 and older. In 1984, however, this pattern changed. During the 1984 campaign, many observers noted that Ronald Reagan, the oldest person ever to serve as president, was showing surprising strength among the nation's youngest voters. And the final returns confirmed this trend. Reagan, the Republican, ran as strongly among voters under 30 (60 percent) as among the older age groups. After his election in 1992 Bill Clinton became America's third-youngest president. Clinton led George Bush by 47 percent to 31 percent among voters who were under age 25, but his lead was only 3 percent among voters in their fifties.[22]

In the 1996 presidential election, the Dole campaign was concerned about their candidate's age—at 73, Bob Dole was the oldest major-party nominee to seek a first term in the White House. Dole's advisers worried about whether Dole's age would diminish his appeal to the voters, and especially to younger voters. And Dole did run far behind Clinton among voters under 30; Clinton received 53 percent of those votes, to 34 percent for Dole.[23]

The Psychological Factors

It would be wrong to give too much weight to sociological factors in determining how voters behave. To do so would be to ignore the very important question of people's changing attitudes toward politics. After the Second World War, a group of scholars at the University of Michigan conducted new studies of voting behavior, concentrating on the psychology of voting—on how individuals perceive and evaluate politics.

The Michigan researchers noted that social characteristics of the population change only slowly over a period of time. The percentage of Catholics or Jews in the United States does not change overnight, for example. Yet the electorate may behave very differently from one election to the next. Long-term factors such as social class did not seem adequate to explain such sudden shifts; candidates and issues, which change in the short term, provided a more likely explanation: "It seemed clear that the key to the finer dynamics of political behavior lay in the reactions of the electorate to these changes in the political scene."[24]

In measuring voter attitudes, the Michigan electoral analysts identified three powerful factors: *party identification, candidates,* and *issues.*

Party Identification   Many Americans display persistent loyalties to the Democratic or Republican Party. Voters may form an attachment to one party or the other and often do not change. Most national elections have taken place within the framework of this basic division in the electorate. However, in the 1992 election year, many voters, dissatisfied with the candidates and platforms of the major parties, turned their loyalties to independent candidate Ross Perot.

Since the late 1930s there have been substantially more Democrats than Republicans in the United States in

Democratic presidential candidate Al Gore high-fives Oprah Winfrey during the 2000 election campaign.
AP/Harpo Productions, Inc./Wide World

most presidential election years. (See Table 11-4.) In fact, in 1964, 1976, and 1980, Democrats outnumbered Republicans by more than 2 to 1. By 1984 this Democratic advantage in party identification had narrowed considerably. The Gallup poll reported that between 1980 and 1984 the number of voters who called themselves Democrats dropped by 6 percentage points, while the number of Republicans increased by 6 percentage points. And other polls in 1984 reported that the gap between Republicans and Democrats was only 2 or 3 percentage points. By 1988, however, Democrats outnumbered Republicans by 43 to 29 percent. By a decade later, the Democrats' advantage over the Republicans in party identification had narrowed further. In 1999, 34 percent of the electorate considered themselves to be Democrats, compared to 28 percent who said they were Republicans. And a very large group—38 percent—called themselves independents.

Although party identification remains a key factor in American politics, it may be growing somewhat less important. As far back as the 1972 presidential election, according to the University of Michigan election analysts, "issues were at least equally as important as party identification" as an explanation of the vote.[25] Moreover, as shown in Table 11-4, the number of people who identified with either of the two major parties dropped from 80 percent in 1940 to 62 percent in 1999, as the number of independents rose from 20 to 38 percent. And in most elections since the Second World War, there also has been extensive ticket-splitting by many voters. As explained in Chapter 10, a ticket-splitter is a voter who votes for candidates of more than one party in the same election. For example, a person may vote for a Republican presidential candidate and a Democratic senator or representative. In 1988 Bush won by a sizable margin despite the Democratic advantage in party identification.

The Candidates   Between 1952 and 1992 the GOP won 7 of the 11 presidential elections that were held. How was this possible, given the higher percentage of those who identify with the Democratic Party?

The answer is that although people may identify with a party, and frequently vote for its candidates, they do not always vote that way. Short-term factors, such as changes in candidates or issues, may cause enough voters to switch from the party they normally favor to have a decisive impact on the outcome of the election. In 1952 and 1956 Dwight Eisenhower, the Republican candidate, easily defeated Adlai Stevenson, a Democrat. Eisenhower's personal appeal, his smile, his image as an outstanding military hero of the Second World War, and—in the second election—his popularity as president all helped to offset normal party loyalties.

Clearly, the personal impression a candidate makes on the voters may have a powerful influence on the election returns. Thus, dour Calvin Coolidge looked like he had been "weaned on a pickle." Thomas E. Dewey, in the classic phrase of Alice Roosevelt Longworth, resembled "the bridegroom on a wedding cake." Nixon in 1968

TABLE 11-4

Party Identification among the American Electorate, 1940–1999

Year	Percentage of Voters Identifying Themselves as:		
	Democrats	**Republicans**	**Independents**
1940	42%	38%	20%
1950	45	33	22
1960	47	30	23
1964	53	25	22
1966	48	27	25
1968	46	27	27
1970	45	29	26
1972	43	28	29
1974	44	23	33
1976	46	22	32
1980	47	23	30
1984	41	29	30
1986	40	30	30
1988	43	29	28
1990	40	32	28
1992	38	29	33
1994	39	28	33
1996	35	30	35
1998	34	29	37
1999	34	28	38

SOURCE: Data provided by Gallup poll.

remained "Tricky Dick" to many strong Democratic partisans. Humphrey "talked too much." Ford struck many voters as "well-meaning but dull." Carter was often seen as "decent but ineffective." Ronald Reagan, particularly during his highly successful 1984 reelection campaign, was a "leader who inspired confidence" for many voters. In 1988 George Bush, for a time at least, had difficulty overcoming his image as a rich "Ivy League" patrician who was ill at ease among the common folk. In 1992 and 1996, Bill Clinton, not yet tarred by scandal, was seen favorably by many voters as "an ordinary guy" who wolfed donuts and enjoyed mingling with the people. In 1996 Bob Dole was often viewed as a solid, capable legislator, but also by some as dull, "too old," and painfully laconic. And at least early in the 2000 campaign, voters perceived Al Gore as "stiff" and "wooden." George W. Bush, by contrast, was seen as more at ease with rank-and-file voters, but was ridiculed on late-night television for his occasional tangled syntax and mispronounced words. Appearance, personality, and popularity of the candidates obviously bear some relation to the number of votes they receive.

The Issues   Two central questions should be asked about the role issues play in a political campaign: Do voters vote according to their opinions about public issues? If so, do their policy preferences later affect the direction of the government? Both points will be discussed later in this chapter. For now, it is enough to note that a voter must be aware of the existence of an issue and must have an opinion about it if he or she is to be directly motivated by it.*

If an issue is to have a direct effect on an individual's voting behavior, a voter must not only recognize the issue and have a minimum degree of feeling about it, but he or she also must come to think that one candidate or the other is closer to his or her own position. Research shows, however, that human beings are sometimes highly selective in accepting political messages. If they do not happen to be tuned in to the proper "wave length," the messages may be received only as so much noise. Increasing the volume may only make the voter flick the "off" switch. Like mechanisms that control the body's blood pressure and temperature, this mental fuse "seems to protect the individual citizen from too strenuous an overload of incoming information."[26] In some elections, even among voters who do hold opinions on public issues, only 40 to 60 percent can perceive differences between the parties on those issues.[27]

On certain major issues, or on issues that affect them directly, the voters do seem to "tune in" and form definite party preferences. It was noted in Chapter 10 that, in some years, many people have tended to associate prosperity with Democrats while others have thought the Republicans were more likely to keep the peace.

When one group of voters is directly affected by a political issue, its members may listen carefully to the political debate. For example, in 1964 Barry Goldwater voted against the first major civil rights bill since Reconstruction. Partly because black voters seemed to know in general where Goldwater stood on civil rights, they turned out in unprecedented numbers to vote for his Democratic opponent, Lyndon Johnson.

Moreover, issues may be more important in some elections than in others. Research by Norman H. Nie, Sidney Verba, and John R. Petrocik suggests that substantial "issue voting" took place during the elections of 1964, 1968, and 1972. Issues such as the Vietnam War, race, and several controversial social issues sharply divided the voters during those election years.[28] In 1980, however, the public's evaluation of the candidates played a very important role.[29]

In 1996, one survey found 21 percent of those polled said that the "economy/jobs" was one of the issues that mattered most in deciding how to vote. Among that sizable bloc of voters, 61 percent voted for Clinton, compared to 27 percent who supported Dole and 10 percent who voted for Perot. In addition, among the one-sixth of the voters who said that "Medicare, Social Security" was important in deciding how to vote, 67 percent voted for Clinton.[30]

---

*Issues also may have an *indirect* effect on voters. For example, if a candidate takes a position pleasing to labor union leaders, the union leaders may work enthusiastically on a voter registration drive among union members. That in turn may result in more votes for the candidate.

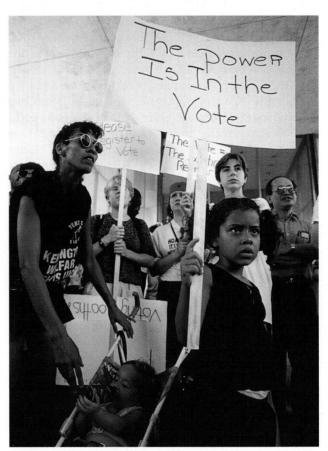

Nicole Bengiveno/USN&WR

Retrospective Voting

The relative importance of candidates, issues, and party identification thus appears to vary from election year to election year. But in most elections another factor also seems to be at work—many voters appear to make up their minds by looking back at what has happened under the country's current political leadership and making a rough judgment about their leaders' performance in office. Morris P. Fiorina and other political scientists have explored this concept of retrospective voting. Fiorina points out that citizens "typically have one comparatively hard bit of data: they know what life has been like during the incumbent's administration." He explains:

> They need *not* know the precise economic or foreign policies of the incumbent administration in order to see or feel the *results* of those policies. And is it not reasonable to base voting decisions on results as well as intentions? In order to ascertain whether the incumbents have performed poorly or well, citizens need only calculate the changes in their own welfare. If jobs have been lost in a recession, something is wrong. If sons have died in foreign rice paddies, something is wrong. If polluters foul food, water, or air, something is wrong. And to the extent that citizens vote on the basis of such judgments, elections do not signal the direction in

which society should move so much as they convey an evaluation of where society has been. Rather than a prospective decision, the voting decision can be more of a retrospective decision.[31]

Rational Choice

In addition to such factors as social class, income, party identification, and retrospective voting, some political scientists emphasize "rational choice"—the concept that individuals engage in political behavior, such as voting, to serve their own best interests.

For example, Morris P. Fiorina has argued: "The central premise of the [rational choice] approach . . . is that behavior is purposive. Political behavior is not solely the product of psychological drives, socialization, or organizational norms. Rather individuals have goals they try to achieve, acting as rationally as their knowledge, resources, and the situation permit."[32]

VOTING PATTERNS

Although the act of voting represents an individual decision, the result of an election is a group decision. On Election Day as the sun moves westward across the continent's four time zones, the tides and patterns of electoral choice are already beginning to form. The polls have closed in the East as voters in California, elsewhere along the Pacific Coast, and in Hawaii are still casting their ballots.* The results from the first precincts in New England trickle in, then more, and in time, the decision takes shape much as a photograph gains definition in the developing trays of a darkroom.

Sometimes the resulting picture is sharp, quickly seen, and its meaning clear; other times it is as blurred as an impressionist painting. Yet the trained eye analyzing the results of American elections can detect patterns and trends, interrelationships, currents, sectional nuances, and sometimes national meaning.

Control

For national political parties, the prize is control of the presidency. But party success or failure is measured in terms of states won or lost. Broad voting patterns on the national level can easily be seen by comparing political maps in presidential years, such as those found inside the front and back covers of this book. Some political results are geographically dramatic—for example, Lyndon Johnson's 1964 landslide, in which the map is predominantly Democratic except for a cluster of states in the Deep South and Arizona. Ronald Reagan's strong

electoral victory in 1984 also covered nearly every part of the map; the Democrats that year carried only one state, Walter Mondale's Minnesota, and the District of Columbia. By contrast, GOP bedrock strength in parts of the Midwest is illustrated by the maps of the elections of 1940, 1944, and 1948; in each case the Plains states are a Republican island in a Democratic sea.

In 1996, when the Democrats' Bill Clinton won a solid victory over Bob Dole, the Democratic tide spread over most regions of the country. But there were still a sizable number of states that Dole carried—concentrated mainly in a belt of territory in the center of the country running from Texas northward to the Canadian border, in the Southeast, and in the Rocky Mountain section of the West.

Coalitions

The broad outline of the national vote can be shown on a map, but much that is politically significant is less visible. Electoral victories are built not merely on simple geographic foundations; they also are formed by alliances of segments of the electorate and of interest groups, and by unorganized masses of voters who coalesce behind the winner. Politicians and political scientists are interested, therefore, in coalitions of voters.

Roosevelt's New Deal brought together a coalition of the South, the urban North, minority groups, and labor unions. Nixon's winning coalition in 1968 included part of the South, most of the Midwest, the West, whites, Protestants, businesspeople, and white-collar workers. Long-term trends in American politics can be traced by analyzing the makeup of winning and losing coalitions.

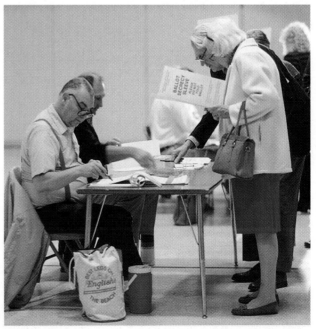

Archaubault/USN&WR

---

*In the past, sometimes the major television networks projected the winner of a presidential race before the polls had closed in the West. In 1980 President Carter conceded while the polls were still open in California, Oregon, Washington, Alaska, and Hawaii.

Congress

In analyzing these alignments, however, congressional as well as presidential voting patterns should be considered. Although, as will be shown, the two are often linked, in most presidential elections since the New Deal days, the Democratic Party has been stronger in congressional elections than in contests for the presidency. In the period from 1932 to 1992, Republican presidential nominees were elected to seven four-year terms in the White House. Yet during that same period, the Republicans won full control of Congress for a total of only four years (1947–1948 and 1953–1954). In presidential election years from the late 1940s through 1992, the Democratic presidential nominee received fewer votes than the total vote polled by Democratic candidates for the House of Representatives in every presidential election except 1964. And in 1992 Ross Perot won more than 19 million votes as an independent candidate for president, in an election in which all the Senate races and all but one of the 435 seats in the House of Representatives were won by a Democrat or a Republican.

Then, in 1994, the Republican Party brought about a dramatic change in the balance of power in congressional elections, winning control of the House of Representatives for the first time in 40 years, and also winning a majority in the Senate. The GOP gained House seats in all major regions of the country in 1994, but its gains were particularly large in the South, the Midwest, and the West. The change in the South was especially striking. There, in 1994, for the first time since Reconstruction, more Republicans than Democrats were elected to the U.S. House of Representatives.[*]

---

[*]In the 11 states of the former Confederacy, the Republicans won 64 U.S. House seats in November 1994. The Democrats won 61 seats. See Milton C. Cummings, Jr., "Political Change since the New Deal: The 1992 Presidential Election in Historical Perspective," in Harvey L. Schantz, ed., *American Presidential Elections: Process, Policy, and Political Change* (Albany: State University of New York Press, 1996), pp. 56–57, 59.

FIGURE 11-3

Presidential and House Vote, 1928–1996

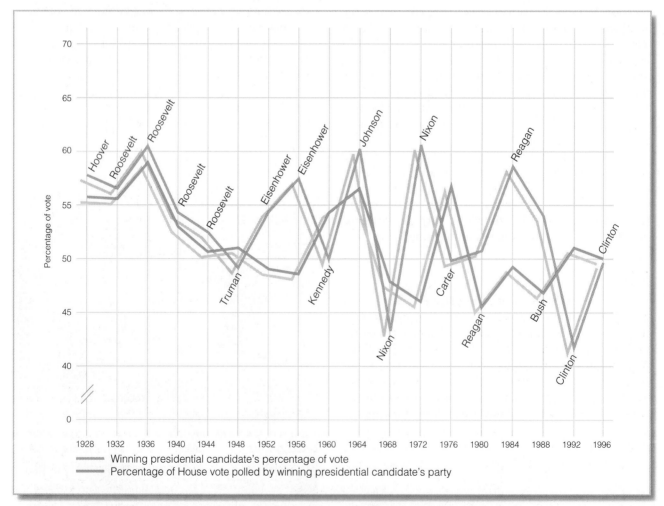

Winning presidential candidate's percentage of vote
Percentage of House vote polled by winning presidential candidate's party

SOURCES: Congressional Quarterly, *Politics in America* (Washington, D.C.: Congressional Quarterly, May 1969), p. 41. Reprinted with permission. Data for 1972 and later from Congressional Quarterly, *Weekly Reports.* Data for 1996 House vote from *New York Times,* November 7, 1996, p. B3.

Coattails

The entire House of Representatives and one-third of the Senate are elected every two years. In a presidential election year, the vote for president may affect the vote for Congress and also can have an effect on state and local offices, although there are signs that in recent years the impact of the presidential vote on contests for other offices may be lessening.

The interrelationship between the vote for president and for members of the House is illustrated in Figure 11-3. Some individual members of Congress are strong enough to withstand the tides of presidential voting, but at times a president has been able to carry into office with him a majority of his own party in the House.

The fortunes of presidential and senatorial candidates are also sometimes linked, especially in the more competitive two-party states. In the 20th century,

TABLE 11-5

Major-Party Lineup: Winning Presidential Candidate and Congress, 1932–2000

Election Year*	President and Party		Congress	House D R	Senate D R	President's Popular Vote Percentage
1932	Roosevelt	D	D	313–117	59–36	57.4%
1934	Roosevelt	D	D	322–103	69–25	
1936	Roosevelt	D	D	333–89	75–17	60.8
1938	Roosevelt	D	D	262–169	69–23	
1940	Roosevelt	D	D	267–162	66–28	54.7
1942	Roosevelt	D	D	222–209	57–38	
1944	Roosevelt	D	D	243–190	57–38	53.4
1946	Truman	D	R	188–246	45–51	
1948	Truman	D	D	263–171	54–42	49.6
1950	Truman	D	D	234–199	48–47	
1952	Eisenhower	R	R	213–221	47–48	55.1
1954	Eisenhower	R	D	232–203	48–47	
1956	Eisenhower	R	D	234–201	49–47	57.4
1958	Eisenhower	R	D	283–154	66–34	
1960	Kennedy	D	D	263–174	64–36	49.5
1962	Kennedy	D	D	259–176	68–32	
1964	Johnson	D	D	295–140	67–33	61.1
1966	Johnson	D	D	248–187	64–36	
1968	Nixon	R	D	243–192	58–42	43.4
1970	Nixon	R	D	255–180	54–44†	
1972	Nixon	R	D	243–192	56–42	60.7
1974	Ford	R	D	291–144	60–37‡	
1976	Carter	D	D	292–143	61–38	50.0
1978	Carter	D	D	277–158	58–41	
1980	Reagan	R	D/R	243–192	46–53	50.8
1982	Reagan	R	D/R	269–166	46–54	
1984	Reagan	R	D/R	253–182	47–53	58.8
1986	Reagan	R	D	258–177	55–45	
1988	Bush	R	D	260–175	55–45	53.9
1990	Bush	R	D	267–167§	56–44	
1992	Clinton	D	D	259–175§	57–43	43.2
1994	Clinton	D	R	203–231§	47–53	
1996	Clinton	D	R	207–227	45–55	49.2
1998	Clinton	D	R	211–223	45–55	
2000	Bush	R	R	212–221	50–50**	47.9

NOTE: Does not include independents and minor parties.

*Presidential years appear in boldface.

†Harry Byrd, Jr., of Virginia was elected as an independent and is therefore not included in this and subsequent totals until his retirement in 1982. However, he received committee assignments as a Democrat. Also in 1970, James Buckley was elected as a Conservative from New York. He generally voted Republican but is not included in this table. In 1976 he was defeated.

‡The total became Democrats 61, Republicans 37, after a disputed Senate contest in New Hampshire was won by the Democratic candidate in a special election in September 1975.

§After the 1990, 1992, 1994, 1996, and 1998 elections, there was one independent in the House.

**In May 2001 Senator James A. Jeffords, a Vermont Republican, switched to independent, giving Democrats control of the Senate 50–49.

SOURCES: Adapted from Congressional Quarterly, *Politics in America* (Washington, D.C.: Congressional Quarterly, 1979), pp. 120–121; Congressional Quarterly, *Weekly Reports;* and *National Journal.*

TABLE 11-6

Midterm Loss in House of Representatives of Party in Control of Presidency, 1922–2002

Size of Loss (average 30 seats)	Net Number of Seats Lost or Gained Since Previous Election	Year	Incumbent President
Massive	−75	1922	Harding
	−71	1938	Roosevelt
	−55	1946	Truman
	−53	1994	Clinton
	−49	1930	Hoover
	−48*	1974	Ford
Above average	−47	1958	Eisenhower
	−47	1966	Johnson
	−45	1942	Roosevelt
	−29	1950	Truman
	−26	1982	Reagan
	−18	1954	Eisenhower
	−12†	1970	Nixon
Below average	−12	1978	Carter
	−10	1926	Coolidge
	−8	1990	Bush
	−5	1986	Reagan
	−4	1962	Kennedy
	+5	1998	Clinton
	+5	2002	Bush
	+9	1934	Roosevelt

*Republicans lost five House seats in special elections in 1974; their net loss on Election Day in 1974 was 43 seats.
†Republicans lost three House seats in special elections in 1969; their net loss on Election Day in 1970 was nine seats.
SOURCE: Adapted from Congressional Quarterly, *Weekly Reports*.

however, four presidents were elected along with a Congress controlled by the opposition party in both wings of the Capitol—Eisenhower in 1956, Nixon in 1968 and 1972, George Bush in 1988, and Clinton in 1996. (See Table 11-5.) The 1980 and 1984 elections left the Republicans in control of the Senate and the presidency, but the Democrats remained the majority party in the House. In 1992 the Democrats took control of both the executive and legislative branches for the first time in 12 years, but, as noted, they lost the House and the Senate just two years later.

As Table 11-6 shows, the president's party generally loses strength in midterm congressional elections. In off-year elections since 1920, the party in power has lost an average of 30 seats in the House; in some of those election years, the party's losses were well above average, as in 1922 and 1938. Occasionally, the party in power may actually gain a few seats, as in 1934, or suffer only minor losses, as in 1962 and 1990. In 1998, the Democrats gained five seats in the House, and held on to the same number of seats as before in the elections for the U.S. Senate. It was the first time since 1934 that the president's party gained seats in a midterm election.

Why the voters normally reduce the strength of the party of the president they elected two years earlier has

been the subject of considerable scholarly research. It is clear that substantially fewer voters turn out in off-years. (See Figure 11-1.) Angus Campbell has suggested that in presidential elections that stimulate a high degree of public interest, the normally "less involved peripheral voters" tend to turn out and vote for the winner, as do many independents and people who switch from the opposing party. In the midterm elections, the peripheral voters tend to drop out, and many independents and party switchers move back to their usual positions. The result is a decline in the proportion of the vote for the president's party.[33] Barbara Hinckley, in an analysis of midterm House results from 1954 through 1966, found that the "midterm loss was concentrated" in marginal House districts where the president ran ahead of his party's winning congressional candidate in the preceding election.[34] In the ensuing off-year election, when the party's presidential nominee was not heading the ticket, these members of Congress were particularly vulnerable to defeat.

But why are the midterm losses of the president's party sometimes very large and sometimes quite small? Edward R. Tufte has suggested that such variations are related to two factors: "The vote cast in midterm congressional elections is a referendum on the performance of the president and his administration's management of the economy." The size of the midterm loss, Tufte added, "is substantially smaller if the President has a high level of approval, or if the economy is performing well, or both."[35]

Nevertheless, the kind of campaigns that individual House candidates run in local congressional districts also shape the midterm verdict. In 1982, for example, near the bottom of a severe recession, the approval rating in the polls for President Reagan, a Republican, was 42 percent. Republican House candidates took great pains to demonstrate their independence from the Reagan Administration's economic policies, and Republican strategists targeted their campaign contributions into districts where GOP House incumbents faced close races. In November, Republicans lost 26 seats in the House—the second-largest midterm loss for a president in his first term in the 20th century. Nevertheless, as Thomas Mann and Norman Ornstein have argued, "the losses [in 1982] would have been much deeper had national economic conditions alone determined the net shift in House seats."[36]

Although the "coattail" effect in presidential voting exists, it can be overstated. In 1984, for example, the Republicans made a net gain of only 14 seats in the House of Representatives and actually lost strength in the Senate—despite the Reagan landslide in the presidential voting. The absence of presidential coattails was seen again in 1988 when the Republican Party lost seats in the House, despite the election of George Bush. And in most elections, many candidates of the party that loses nationally are able to survive. This is because voters are selective: Some do not vote for all candidates on the ballot; others pick and choose and split their tickets. At times the coattail effect may work in reverse, as when a local candidate pulls a larger vote than the national ticket.[37]

Sometimes, candidates for governor may ride into the statehouse on a sufficiently long presidential coattail, for there may be a relationship between national and state election results in presidential election years. "The great tides of presidential politics," V. O. Key, Jr., observed, "tend to engulf the affairs of states and often to determine the results of state elections."[38]

One reason for the relationship between presidential and gubernatorial voting is that many voters find it convenient to vote a straight party ticket by making a single mark or pulling a single lever (in states where they are permitted to do so). Even so, ticket-splitting between candidates for president and governor is common, particularly in states where there is strong two-party rivalry.

Moreover, three-fourths of the gubernatorial races cannot be directly affected by the presidential campaign. A large number of states have scheduled gubernatorial elections in off-years to insulate themselves from the tides of national presidential politics. (See Table 11-7.) In 2000, a presidential year, 11 governors were elected, but in 2002, a midterm election, 36 governors' races were

TABLE 11-7

Party Control of Governorships, 1946–2000

After Elections of*	Democrats	Republicans
1946	23	25
1948	30	18
1950	23	25
1952	18	30
1954	27	21
1956	28	20
1958	35	14
1960	34	16
1962	34	16
1964	33	17
1966	25	25
1968	19	31
1970	29	21
1972	31	19
1974	36	13†
1976	37	12†
1978	32	18
1980	27	23
1982	35	15
1984	34	16
1986	26	24
1988	28	22
1990	28	20†
1992	30	18†
1994	19	30†
1996	17	32†
1998	17	31†
2000	19	29†

*Presidential years appear in boldface.
†After the 1974, 1976, 1994, 1996, and 1998 elections, there was an independent governor in Maine. After the 1990 and 1992 elections, independents held the governorship in Alaska and Connecticut. The Reform Party won the governorship of Minnesota in 1998. After 2000 there was one independent and one Reform Party governor.
SOURCES: Congressional Quarterly, *Politics in America* (Washington, D.C.: Congressional Quarterly, 1969), p. 69; Congressional Quarterly, *Weekly Reports; National Journal;* and *The World Almanac and Book of Facts 1996,* p. 99.

TABLE 11-8

How the States Elect Governors (through 2002)

Two-Year Term	
Election in even-numbered years	2
Four-Year Term	
Election in presidential years	9
Election in even-numbered years at midterm	34
Election in odd-numbered years	5
Total, all states	**50**

SOURCE: Data provided by the National Governors Association.

scheduled. (See Table 11-8.) This separation of gubernatorial and presidential races may help candidates of the party that is out of power nationally.*

 Online for more information about the gubernatorial issues, see: www.nga.org

ELECTION 2000: A CASE STUDY

In the extraordinarily close, disputed election of 2000 the Republican nominee, Texas Governor George W. Bush, defeated Vice President Al Gore, his Democratic opponent. Bush's victory came after a tumultuous and divisive post-election legal and political struggle to determine who won Florida's 25 electoral votes—and, with them, the presidency. Bush carried 30 of the 50 states and won 271 electoral votes to 266 for Al Gore. But for many suspenseful days that stretched into weeks, the nation and the world did not know who would be the next president of the United States. The outcome marked the return of the Republican Party to power in the White House after eight years of Democratic rule. The results were:

	Popular Vote*	Electoral Vote	Percentage
George W. Bush (R)	50,456,169	271	47.9%
Al Gore (D)	50,996,116	266	48.4
Ralph Nader (Green)	2,831,066	0	2.7
Pat Buchanan (Reform)	447,798	0	0.4
Others	595,176	0	0.6
Totals	105,326,325	537	100.0%

*Totals as of December 22, 2000, The Associated Press.

The Democrats

As the Democrats awaited the presidential year of 2000, they realized that four factors could have a powerful effect on their party's prospects.

First, who would the Democrats nominate for president? Under the Twenty-second Amendment, President Bill Clinton, a Democrat, was barred from running for a third term. It was almost universally assumed that his vice president, Al Gore, would seek the presidency; but would other Democrats give Gore a fight for the nomination?

Second, how popular—or unpopular—would the Clinton administration be in 2000? The greater the president's approval rating in the polls, it was assumed, the better the chances might be that another Democrat could be elected to succeed him.

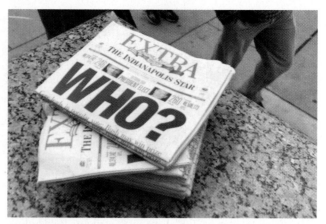

November 8, 2000: The Indianapolis Star got it right.
AP/Wide World

Third, how would the American economy be performing by the summer and fall of 2000? If the bouyant economy continued to do well (see Table 11-9), the chances of a Democratic victory would be increased. But if the economy began to falter, the Democrats would lose what they hoped would be one of their strongest campaign assets.

Finally, would the Democratic cause be hurt by the third-party candidacy of Ralph Nader, running again on the Green Party ticket? In 1996, Nader had run in some

TABLE 11-9

Annual Rates of Inflation and Unemployment in the United States, 1980–2000

	Inflation	Unemployment
1980	13.5%	7.1%
1981	10.4	7.6
1982	6.1	9.7
1983	3.2	9.6
1984	4.3	7.4
1985	3.6	7.1
1986	1.9	6.9
1987	3.6	6.1
1988	4.4	5.5
1989	4.6	5.3
1990	5.4	5.6
1991	4.2	6.8
1992	3.0	7.5
1993	3.0	6.9
1994	2.6	6.1
1995	2.8	5.6
1996	3.3	5.4
1997	1.7	4.9
1998	1.6	4.5
1999	2.7	4.2
2000*	3.4	4.0

*2000 figures are averaged for the first 10 months of the year.
SOURCE: U.S. Bureau of Labor Statistics.

---

*In 1942 only 10 states with four-year gubernatorial terms scheduled their election for governor midway through the president's term. By 1962 the number of such states stood at 20; for 1990 it was 34. Adapted from Congressional Quarterly, *Politics in America* (Washington, D.C.: Congressional Quarterly, May 1969), pp. 148–155; and Congressional Quarterly, *Weekly Reports.*

Vice President Al Gore on the campaign trail in Atlanta during the 2000 presidential race.
AP/Wide World

states and had polled 685,000 votes—many of them, it was believed, votes that otherwise would have gone to the Democratic presidential ticket. In a close presidential contest in 2000, Democrats reasoned, a new and more vigorous candidacy by Ralph Nader might hurt their party severely.

As expected, Vice President Al Gore announced in June 1999 that he would seek the Democratic nomination. The most prominent Democrat to challenge Gore was Bill Bradley, a former senator from New Jersey and onetime professional basketball star, who had served for 18 years in the Senate.

In December, Bradley announced that he would make a major effort to win the Democratic caucuses in Iowa. On January 24, Gore scored a decisive victory in Iowa, winning the Democratic caucuses by a margin of 2 to 1. Eight days later, Gore won a fiercely contested and narrow victory over Bradley in New Hampshire, by 76,527 votes to 70,295.

After those twin defeats in Iowa and New Hampshire, much of the energy seemed to go out of the Bradley campaign. Five weeks later, on Super Tuesday, March 7, 2000, when Democratic primaries were held in 13 states, Gore won them all. Two days later, on March 9, Bradley announced that he was suspending his campaign. The race for the Democratic nomination was over.[39]

The Republicans

In June 1999, nearly a year and a half before the 2000 election, George W. Bush, the governor of Texas and the son of former President George Bush, announced his candidacy for the Republican nomination. That same month, Senator John McCain of Arizona also declared that he was a candidate. Senator McCain was well known as the cosponsor of the McCain-Feingold campaign finance reform bill.

But Governor Bush quickly emerged as the front-runner for the Republican nomination. By December

1999, he had amassed a record-setting $67 million in campaign funds and had won early endorsements from a large number of Republican members of Congress, governors, and conservative leaders.[40] In fact, Bush's early political strength and the enormous amount of money that had poured in to his campaign forced close to half of the potential Republican field out of the race well before the primaries began.

Senator McCain announced that he would not campaign actively in Iowa. Instead, he concentrated his energies in New Hampshire, criss-crossing the state in a bus labeled "The Straight Talk Express," and appearing at more than 100 town meetings. When the voters of New Hampshire went to the polls on February 1, they gave John McCain a stunning victory over Bush. McCain defeated the Texas governor by 19 percentage points.[41]

McCain's victory in New Hampshire was followed by an upswing of support for the Arizona senator in other states. But it was also clear that the Bush supporters were better organized and better financed than McCain's in many parts of the country. Bush won the crucial South Carolina primary on February 19—the first Republican primary in the South. And on Super Tuesday, March 7, although McCain won in four more New England states, Bush was the winner in eight states, including three states—Ohio, New York, and California—that would send large delegations to the Republican convention. Two days after Super Tuesday, Senator McCain announced: "I am no longer an active candidate for my party's nomination for president." The battle for the Republican nomination, like the Democratic contest, was effectively over.[42]

April to July 2000, and the Republican and Democratic Conventions

In the relatively quiet period after April, each party prepared for its national convention. Throughout these months, to the distress of Democratic partisans, Bush

Texas Governor George W. Bush looking for votes on a college campus in Charleston, South Carolina in 2000.
AP/Wide World

generally ran ahead of Gore in the public opinion polls. Bush led by 6 percentage points in the Gallup poll at the end of April, and in late July his lead was even greater. (See Table 11-10.) On July 25, Bush announced that his choice for his vice presidential running mate was Dick Cheney, a former member of Congress with extensive experience in Washington who had served on the White House staff and in the cabinet.

The harmonious Republican National Convention in Philadelphia (July 31–August 3) was a great success for the GOP. And the four days were capped by a strong performance by Bush himself in his acceptance speech. When the Republican convention was over, Bush led Gore in the polls by 54 to 37 percent. (See Table 11-10.)

The Democrats now made plans to launch a counterattack, at their own convention in Los Angeles on August 14–17. But as the Democrats began to gather on the West Coast that month, they faced a major strategic problem. Democrats realized that their candidate, Al Gore, would have to overcome a special challenge in the fall campaign. Gore had been President Clinton's hand-picked choice for vice president, and had served in the Clinton administration for eight years. Despite Clinton's impeachment in 1998 and his much publicized relationship with Monica Lewinsky, Clinton's job approval ratings in the polls remained high—unusually high for an American president nearing the end of his second term. (See Table 11-11.) But when prospective voters were asked whether they approved of President Clinton's "personal behavior," they said they disapproved by a margin of 2 to 1.* There were both pluses—and minuses—for Gore in being closely associated with Clinton.

As the opening day of the Democratic National Convention approached, Vice President Gore sought to distance himself from Clinton. In a dramatic move, Gore chose Senator Joseph Lieberman of Connecticut as his vice presidential running mate. Lieberman had been the most prominent Democrat to speak out and criticize Clinton during the Monica Lewinsky scandal, declaring on the Senate floor: "Such behavior is not just inappropriate, it is immoral."[43] Lieberman was also the first Jewish candidate to be selected for a major-party presidential ticket.

Just as the Republicans had two weeks earlier, the Democrats seemed to get a "convention bounce" in the polls from the viewers' response to the televised convention proceedings.

The first Gallup poll taken after the Democratic convention reported that Gore was now 1 percentage point ahead of Bush; allowing for sampling error, the race was a toss-up. And two weeks after that, following the Labor Day weekend, the traditional starting point for a fall general election campaign, the Gallup poll reported that Gore still held a modest lead over Bush. (See Table 11-10.)

Ralph Nader and Pat Buchanan

As Bush and Gore prepared to do battle in the autumn of 2000, two other presidential candidacies attracted intense interest and attention among campaign strategists. One was Pat Buchanan, a conservative commentator and former aide to President Nixon, who emerged as the new standard-bearer of the Reform Party that Ross Perot had led in 1996. The other was consumer advocate Ralph Nader, the candidate of the Green Party.

In April, Buchanan was drawing 4 percent of the total vote in the Gallup poll, the same percentage as Nader had. (See Table 11-10.) Many observers assumed that a large number of those Buchanan votes might go to

---

*On November 4–7, 1999, when a national sample of the U.S. public was polled, 28 percent of those interviewed said that they "approved" of President Clinton's personal behavior, and 61 percent "disapproved." A similar poll taken October 17–18, 2000, found that 30 percent "approved" of Clinton's personal behavior, and 60 percent "disapproved." See Voter.com, online at <www.voter.com>.

Bush, if Buchanan were not on the ballot. But Buchanan was forced to suspend active campaigning for a time while he underwent major surgery. And after midsummer, virtually every national poll reported his voter support at 1 percent or less. Perhaps the most important aspect of the Buchanan candidacy was that it was Buchanan—not Perot—who was running on the Reform Party ticket in 2000. Perot had received nearly 8 million votes when he ran for president in 1996. Although Perot was not on the ballot in the year 2000, the election outcome might be greatly influenced by the votes of those former Perot supporters.

In contrast to the fading electoral appeal of Pat Buchanan, voter support for Ralph Nader was more persistent. In the Gallup polls it peaked at 6 percent in early June and still stood at 4 or 5 percent in the final two pre-election polls. (See Table 11-10.) It was widely assumed that Nader cut into Gore's voter support more than Bush's; and during the closing weeks of the campaign Gore spent considerable time trying to persuade

prospective Nader voters to switch their support to the Democratic presidential ticket.

The General Election Campaign

As the Labor Day weekend came to a close, there were just 9 weeks remaining until Election Day. As it turned out, those 9 weeks seemed to break almost evenly into three distinct phases. The first three weeks were dominated by a "debate over the debates," as the Bush campaign and the Gore campaign argued over the character and the timing of the proposed presidential and vice presidential televised debates. During the next three weeks, attention focused on the debates themselves—and on the voters' response to what they saw and heard. The final three weeks were a sprint to the finish, as both candidates campaigned frantically to motivate their own supporters to turn out and vote. Both Bush and Gore concentrated their efforts on states where the race was close.

TABLE 11-10

Voter Support for Bush, Gore, Nader, and Buchanan: The Gallup Poll's Four-Way Trial Heats between April and Election Eve, 2000

Date of Interviews	For Bush	For Gore	For Nader	For Buchanan	For Others; Don't know
April 28–30, 2000	47%	41%	4%	4%	4%
June 6–7, 2000	46%	41%	6%	2%	5%
July 25–26, 2000	50%	39%	4%	1%	6%
Republican National Convention (July 31–August 3)					
August 4–5, 2000	54%	37%	4%	1%	4%
August 11–12, 2000	55%	39%	2%	1%	3%
Democratic National Convention (August 14–17)					
August 18–19, 2000	46%	47%	3%	2%	2%
September 5–7, 2000	43%	46%	3%	1%	7%
"Debate over the Debates" (first half of September)					
September 18–20, 2000	41%	51%	3%	1%	4%
October 1–3, 2000	41%	49%	2%	1%	7%
First Presidential Debate (October 3)					
October 5–7, 2000	49%	41%	4%	1%	5%
October 8–10, 2000	45%	45%	2%	1%	7%
Second presidential debate (October 11)					
October 13–15, 2000	47%	44%	3%	1%	5%
Third presidential debate (October 17)					
October 18–20, 2000	51%	40%	4%	1%	4%
October 22–24, 2000	48%	43%	3%	1%	5%
November 1–3, 2000	47%	43%	5%	0%	5%
November 5–6, 2000	47%	45%	4%	1%	3%
Election Results	00%	00%	00%	0%	0%

SOURCE: Data provided by the Gallup poll.

TABLE 11-11

President Clinton's Job Rating, 1996–2000*

Date of Interviews	Approve	Disapprove	No Opinion
Clinton reelected with 49% of the vote (November 1996)			
Clinton's second inauguration (January 1997)			
November 21–24, 1996	58%	35%	7%
January 30–February 2, 1997	60%	31%	9%
November 21–23, 1997	61%	30%	9%
Monica Lewinsky scandal becomes public;			
Clinton denies having had sexual relations with Lewinsky (January 1998)			
February 13–15, 1998	66%	30%	4%
July 7–8, 1998	61%	34%	5%
Clinton addresses the American people; reports that he did			
have a relationship with Lewinsky that was "inappropriate" (August 1998)			
September 11–12, 1998	63%	34%	3%
Kenneth Starr, independent counsel, submits report to Congress			
with details of the Clinton-Lewinsky relationship;			
report asserts that Clinton had obstructed justice (September 1998)			
October 9–12, 1998	65%	32%	3%
Midterm congressional elections; Democrats gain seats in House,			
and do not lose strength in the Senate (November 3, 1998)			
November 13–15, 1998	66%	31%	3%
House votes to impeach President Clinton (December 19, 1998)			
December 19–20, 1998	73%	25%	2%
Trial of Clinton begins in the Senate (January 1999)			
January 22–24, 1999	69%	29%	2%
February 9, 1999	70%	27%	3%
Senate votes not to convict Clinton (February 12, 1999)			
February 19–21, 1999	66%	30%	4%
July 13–14, 1999	59%	37%	4%
January 17–19, 2000	62%	35%	7%
Clinton's final State of the Union address (January 2000)			
February 4–6, 2000	62%	33%	4%
May 5–7, 2000	57%	36%	7%
Republican National Convention (July 2000)			
Democratic National Convention (August 2000)			
August 29–September 5, 2000	62%	35%	3%
October 6–9, 2000	58%	37%	5%

*Responses to the question: "Do you approve or disapprove of the way Bill Clinton is handling his job as president?"
SOURCE: Data provided by the Gallup poll.

Going into the fall campaign, Gore had had more experience than Bush in high-pressure nationally televised debates. Some observers therefore assumed that Gore would perform better than Bush in a series of formal debates on television. The nonpartisan Commission on Presidential Debates, a group that had conducted debates in previous presidential elections, proposed that there should be four debates from October 3 to October 17—three between the two major-party presidential candidates, and one featuring the two candidates for vice president. Nader and Buchanan, to their great distress, were excluded by the commission from the presidential debates.

Vice President Gore said that he was prepared to participate in all of the presidential debates proposed by the commission. Governor Bush, however, was initially reluctant to agree to the commission plan. His representatives argued instead for different, more informal

Consumer advocate Ralph Nader, campaigning for president on the Green Party ticket in 2000
AP/Wide World

formats, suggesting one debate moderated by NBC's Tim Russert, and another with CNN's Larry King.[44] As the controversial "debate over the debates" dragged on during the first part of September, Democrats began to charge that Bush was afraid to debate Gore. In the end Bush agreed to participate in three debates on the dates the commission had originally proposed—October 3, 11, and 17. The Bush camp also agreed to a vice presidential debate on October 5. In one of the first Gallup polls taken after the debate controversy ended, covering the period September 18–20, Gore had opened up a sizable lead over Bush. Gore now led the Texas governor by 10 percentage points. (See Table 11-10.)

The first debate between Bush and Gore took place in Boston with an estimated television audience of 50 million viewers.[45] The two candidates seemed to battle fairly evenly as they discussed the issues; but many viewers disliked Gore's debating style.[46] Some criticized him for interrupting and being too aggressive, and others felt he did not show proper respect for his opponent, sometimes sighing audibly at Bush's remarks. The Gallup poll taken in a three-day period shortly after the first debate suggested that the relative strength of the two candidates in the electorate had been reversed. Bush now led Gore by 8 percentage points. In addition, voter support for the man who wasn't there in the debate, Ralph Nader, had doubled. (See Table 11-10.)

In the days that followed, it was clear that the Republicans were heartened by their candidate's showing in the first debate, and that Gore was startled and shaken by the public response to his debate performance. In the second debate, held at Wake Forest University in Winston-Salem, North Carolina, on October 11, a subdued Gore changed his debate tactics and attempted to be conciliatory, saying six times of Bush's comments, "I agree." Many observers regarded Gore's performance

in the second debate as weak, and a national post-debate poll reported that 47 percent of those interviewed felt Bush had "won" the debate. Only 31 percent said that Gore had won.[47]

The third and final presidential debate was held in St. Louis on October 17, amid somber and dramatic circumstances. Missouri's popular Democratic Governor Mel Carnahan, who was his party's candidate for the U.S. Senate, had been killed in a plane crash the previous evening. Many observers felt that Gore's performance was better in this third debate than it had been in the first two; but the Gallup tracking polls taken during the three days that followed suggested that Bush still held the lead. He was now running ahead of Gore by 11 points. (See Table 11-10.) If Gore had won the "debate over the debates" in September, it seemed clear that overall, Bush had won the debates themselves in October.

In the final three weeks before Election Day, both campaigns appeared to adjust—and readjust—their schedules several times in response to the rapidly changing dynamics of the race. Governor Bush made several visits to Oregon and Washington, states once assumed to be safely in Gore's column but where a large expected vote for Nader had now tightened the race. Gore spent considerable time in a cluster of closely contested states, pleading with potential Nader voters not to "waste their vote" and arguing that a vote for Nader was in effect a vote for Bush. Nader continued to campaign actively, hoping to win at least 5 percent of the total vote so that the Green Party would qualify for federal campaign funds in the next presidential election in 2004. And both major parties concentrated on "GOTV" drives, efforts to "get out the vote" of their core supporters.

In the final two days before the balloting, both Gore and Bush spent much of their time campaigning in Florida, a state that both parties regarded as crucial. Most

"And now with a rebuttal . . ."

of the national polls still had Bush slightly ahead of Gore. Those same polls suggested, however, that Gore had narrowed the gap during the final days of the campaign.

By midday on Election Day, there were reports of heavy turnouts in some of the states where the race was thought to be closest; and, for only the second time in the nation's history, more than 100 million Americans were going to the polls.

As the American people sat down before their television sets that evening to watch their votes be counted, it is doubtful that many of them were prepared for the tumultuous events that followed. Beginning at 7:47 P.M. EST, the major television networks declared that Gore had carried the crucial state of Florida, with 25 electoral votes. Soon afterward, Michigan and Pennsylvania, two closely watched states with sizable electoral votes, were also called for Gore. It began to look as though Gore would win. Then, at 9:54 P.M., the television networks started to retract their previous award of Florida to Gore. The Sunshine State, they now said, was "too close to call." And Bush was winning several states that the Democrats had hoped to carry, including New Hampshire, Missouri, West Virginia, Arkansas, and, most startling of all, Vice President Gore's home state of Tennessee.[48]

At 2:18 A.M., EST, on Wednesday, the networks declared that Bush had won Florida after all, which now made Bush the next president of the United States.[49] Gore telephoned Bush from Nashville to concede the election, and congratulated the Texas governor on his victory. But soon after, as Gore was on his way by motorcade to make a concession speech to his supporters, his aides learned that Bush's lead in Florida was dwindling fast.

At 3:30 A.M. EST, Gore telephoned Bush and in a second, tense conversation he retracted his concession. At 4:04 A.M. the networks reported that Florida had swung back into the "undecided" column.[50] The long wait for a definitive result in Florida had begun.

By Wednesday, November 8, county elections supervisors in Florida began to recount the votes, as required by state law in a close election. As the recount proceeded, Bush's initial lead of 1,700 votes over Gore began to shrink.

There was immediate controversy over the form of the ballot used in some precincts in Palm Beach County. Democrats argued that the "butterfly" layout of the ballot—with the names of the presidential candidates on both the left and right sides—was not only confusing but also potentially illegal according to Florida law, and that it caused hundreds of citizens who wished to vote for Gore to punch the hole next to Buchanan's name instead. Buchanan himself agreed that many of the votes that he had received in the county had been intended for Gore. Republicans, however, pointed out that the ballot had been designed and approved by a Democratic Party official.

But the major controversy between the two parties centered on a tiny piece of paper known as a "chad." As Americans soon learned, a chad was the bit of paper that normally fell out when a ballot was punched by the voter with a stylus. Sometimes, however, voters failed to punch the ballot all the way through. A tiny dangling piece of paper—a "hanging chad"—may remain and can fall back to fill the hole in the card. Or a weak punch of the ballot may leave only an indentation, known as a "dimpled chad." Voting machines read such ballots as not having cast any vote. Democrats argued that they had lost a substantial number of votes intended for Gore. They demanded a hand recount of the ballots in four largely Democratic counties, in order to identify those votes.

On Saturday, November 11, election officials began a slow hand count in some precincts in South Florida. That same day, the Bush campaign filed suit in a federal district court to try to block the manual recounts. They argued that a manual recount is open to human error and subjective judgments that are not present in a machine count.

Two days later, however, the federal court ruled against the Republicans. Bush now led by about 300 votes in the unofficial tally; but, for the moment at least, the manual recount would proceed.

On Wednesday, November 15, the Florida secretary of state, Katherine Harris, a Republican and co-chair of the Bush campaign in Florida, made an announcement. She said that once the absentee ballots were in, she would certify the results of the presidential race on Saturday, November 18, without including any additional votes from the hand recounts because, she maintained, those tallies would arrive too late under Florida law.

On Thursday, November 16, the Republicans lost their bid to halt the manual recount of the vote. The Florida Supreme Court ruled that the hand counting could continue; but the court left open the question of whether the results of those hand counts would have to be included in the final statewide vote tally.

On Friday, November 17, the Florida Supreme Court ordered Secretary of State Harris not to certify the election results until the Court could hear arguments from both sides on Monday, November 20. On Saturday, November 18, after the overseas ballots had been counted, Bush had a 930-vote lead statewide. Palm Beach and Broward Counties continued their manual counts; and Miami-Dade County decided that it would begin its hand count on Monday.

On November 20, Gore's attorneys, led by David Boies, a prominent trial lawyer, urged the Florida Supreme Court to allow recounts to proceed and to require Katherine Harris to include the results of the recounts in the final state tally. Bush's lawyers argued that the deadline for including the recounts had passed and that it was unfair to recount votes only in selected Democratic counties.

Shortly before 10 P.M. on November 21, the court announced its unanimous decision: It allowed the recounts to continue for 5 days and ordered Harris to include the results when she certified the election. Rejecting the Republican argument that recounts by hand were unreliable, the court declared: "Although error cannot be completely eliminated in any tabulation of the ballots, our society has not yet gone so far as to place blind faith in machines. In almost all endeavors, including elections, humans routinely correct the errors of machines."

The very next day, however, the Gore camp was dealt an unexpected setback when, as Republican demonstrators chanted noisily outside, election officials in Miami-Dade County stopped their hand recount, declaring that it could not be completed by the deadline set by the court. At the same time, Bush's lawyers appealed to the U.S. Supreme Court to overturn the ruling of the Florida high court. On November 24, the U.S. Supreme Court agreed to hear the case.

At 7:30 P.M. EST on Sunday night, November 26, the Florida secretary of state, Katherine Harris, officially certified the election results, which showed Bush now in the lead over Gore by 537 votes out of nearly 6 million votes cast. However, Harris rejected the partial tally submitted by weary Palm Beach election officials, who had been unable to complete their hand recount by the 5 P.M. deadline. The television networks broke into their regular programming to cover Harris's announcement in the state capitol in Tallahassee. "I hereby declare Governor George W. Bush the winner of Florida's 25 electoral votes," she said to the cheers of Bush supporters gathered outside.

On Monday, November 27, Gore's attorneys filed a lawsuit in Tallahassee, the Florida state capital, contesting the results in Miami-Dade, where the recount had

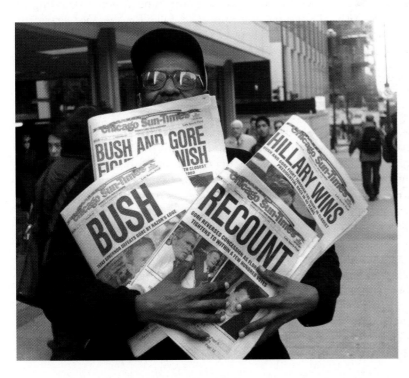

The morning after: Headlines on four editions of the Chicago Sun-Times *on November 8, 2000, reflect the confused result of the election.*
AP/Wide World

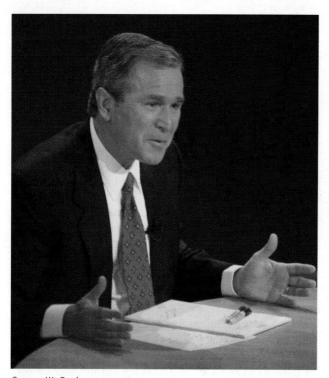

George W. Bush . . .
AP/Wide World

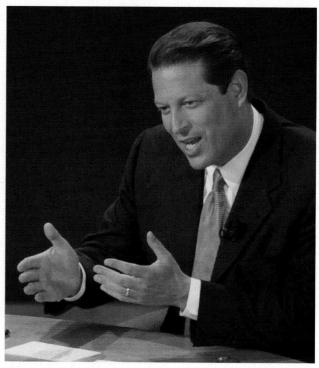

. . . and Al Gore during their second televised debate, October 11, 2000
AP/Wide World

been halted, in Palm Beach, where the recount was rejected, and in tiny Nassau county in northern Florida, where there had been confusion in the vote count. Gore's supporters argued that a recount in Miami-Dade alone, where almost 700,000 people had voted, might—had it not been halted—have provided Gore the margin of victory in the state. That night, with millions of Americans back home after the long Thanksgiving weekend, Gore addressed the voters on television with a sea of American flags displayed behind him. In a democracy, Gore said, it was essential that every vote be counted. "That is all we have asked since Election Day—a complete count of all the votes cast in Florida. . . .We haven't had that yet."

The political framework for the struggle was clear: Bush had all but declared himself the next president of the United States. Gore was saying, in effect, not so fast—there are still votes to be counted. Since Gore led by more than 500,000 votes in the national popular vote, the vice president felt he had the moral authority to continue the fight. But the clock was ticking; December 12 was the deadline for Florida to designate the electors who would meet to vote for president and vice president on December 18, as other electors would do in state capitals throughout the country. And opinion polls showed that many members of the American public wanted the election settled.

On December 4, the U.S. Supreme Court—avoiding any definitive ruling in the presidential election dispute—sent the recount case back to the Florida Supreme Court,

asking that court to clarify the basis of its November 21 decision that had allowed the hand recounts to continue. That same afternoon, a state court in Tallahassee emphatically rejected Gore's plea to order the recounts resumed. Gore's lawyers immediately appealed to the Florida Supreme Court.

Friday, December 8, was a day of high drama as the Florida Supreme Court handed down its ruling on Gore's recount appeal. It held for the Vice President, ordering recounts of "undervotes"—ballots on which machines had not registered a vote—in all 67 Florida counties. The Court also restored certain disputed votes to Gore, reducing Bush's lead to 154 votes statewide. The Bush lawyers immediately appealed to the U.S. Supreme Court.

Less than 24 hours later, on Saturday afternoon, another thunderbolt: by a 5–4 vote, a split U.S. Supreme Court issued a stay that stopped the recount in Florida that was already underway. On Monday, December 11, the Court heard arguments from both sides.

Just before 10 P.M. December 12, on a freezing night in Washington, a rancorous, bitterly divided United States Supreme Court handed down its unsigned decision in the historic case of *Bush* v. *Gore.* By a vote of 5–4, the Court reversed the Florida high court, holding that because there were no uniform standards for inspecting ballots in a statewide recount, it could not be done without violating the constitutional requirements "of equal protection and due process" of law "to protect the fundamental right of each voter" in Florida.

In a stinging dissent, Justices John Paul Stevens, Ruth Bador Ginsburg, and Stephen G. Breyer warned: "Although we may never know with complete certainty the identity of the winner of this year's presidential election, the identity of the loser is perfectly clear. It is the nation's confidence in the judge as an impartial guardian of the rule of law."

But the Supreme Court majority, by ruling for George W. Bush, had settled the election. The next night, Vice President Al Gore conceded in a televised address to the nation. An hour later, President-elect Bush went on television with a call for national reconciliation. At last, the historic election of 2000 was over.

Despite the long, divisive post-election struggle, several noteworthy features of the voting patterns of 2000 were clear:

1. More than 105.3 million voters went to the polls. The number of people who voted was up by about 9 million from the presidential election of 1996; and the percentage of the voting age population who voted—approximately 51 percent—was about 2.2 percentage points higher than the 48.8 percent who voted in 1996. The overall gain in the turnout was only moderate; but in some of the states that were closely contested—including Florida and Michigan—voter turnout increased sharply.

2. George W. Bush's share of the total popular vote was 47.9 percent. He received 539,947 fewer popular votes than Gore; and Bush thus became the third American president since the Civil War to win the presidency while losing the popular vote. The other two were Rutherford B. Hayes in 1876 and Benjamin Harrison in 1888.

3. Ralph Nader and the Green Party polled 2,831,066 votes. Nader's 2.7 percent of the total vote was far short of the 5 percent he needed for the Green Party to qualify for federal campaign matching funds in 2004. But in Florida and New Hampshire, states with 29 electoral votes that went to Bush, Nader's vote total was far larger than the margin by which Gore lost those states.

4. Pat Buchanan made a weak showing. He received 447,798 votes (0.4 percent) on the Reform Party ticket—an enormous drop from the vote the Reform Party received in 1996 when Ross Perot headed the party's ticket (8.2 million votes).

5. One of the most striking features of the 2000 election was the continuation of the "gender gap"—the tendency of women and men to vote differently in the presidential race. Among men, Bush led Gore 53 to 42 percent. Women favored Gore over Bush 54 percent to 43 percent. (See Table 11-12.)

6. Voters' evaluations of their own economic circumstances were strongly reflected in the returns. Half of the voters reported that their family's financial situation was better in 2000 than it had been in 1996. Among that large group of voters, Gore led

Bush by 61 to 36 percent. Among voters who said that their family's situation was worse or was the same in 2000, however, Bush polled 60 percent or more of the vote. (See Table 11-12.)

7. There was a pronounced sectional pattern in the voting returns. Gore ran well ahead of Bush in nearly all of the Northeast, and led by somewhat smaller margins in most areas along the West Coast. Except in Florida, Bush ran well ahead of Gore throughout the South; and Bush also had a substantial lead in the Plains States and in most of the Rocky Mountain States. In the Midwest, the vote totals of the two candidates were very close.

8. Former supporters of Ross Perot provided a vitally important element of Bush's electoral strength. More than 6 million persons who had voted for Perot in 1996 voted again in 2000. Among those former Perot voters, Bush led Gore by 64 to 27 percent. In other words, some 4 million former Perot supporters cast their ballots for Bush, compared with less than 2 million who voted for Gore.

9. The 11 contests for governor in 2000 left the Democrats with a net gain of one governorship. But there were still 29 Republican governors, compared with 19 Democratic governors. Two governors were independents.

10. In the battle for control of the House of Representatives, the Republicans repulsed a major Democratic effort to win control of the House. Democrats made a net gain of just one or two House seats, leaving the Republicans with a narrow majority of 221 to 212. In addition, two independents were elected to the House.[51]

11. In the contests for the U.S. Senate, the Democrats made a net gain of four Senate seats, with the result that the chamber was evenly divided, with 50 Republicans and 50 Democrats. This close outcome promised another spirited battle for control of the Senate in the midterm elections of 2002.

12. Overall, the elections of 2000 left the United States with an exceptionally close balance of power between Democrats and Republicans. The stage was set for a continuation of the struggle for ascendancy between the two parties. And that battle was sure to be intensified when the states began to draw new congressional district boundary lines for the House of Representatives in 2001.

Although the election was finally over, many larger questions remained. Until November 7, 2000, very few people had realized the horse-and-buggy nature of the voting process in America—or the great variation in the way that elections have been run in the nation's 3000 counties in the 50 states. Some areas used machines, others ballots that were punched or marked by hand. The reason for this patchwork quilt of voting systems was money: most counties had small budgets and spent little on election equipment.

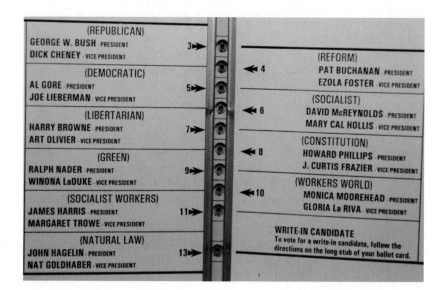

The controversial ballot in Palm Beach County, Florida. Democrats argued that because of its design, some Gore supporters mistakenly voted for Pat Buchanan.
AP/Wide World

The remarkably close election reminded Americans that the winner of the popular vote may not win in the electoral college. Although there were calls to abolish the electoral college, some observers warned that direct election of the president might, in a close election, lead to even more demands for recounts in several states.

In the 2000 election, the legal battles over the vote in Florida also illustrated just how complex the electoral system is, with power divided and shared among the states and the federal government. The battle for Florida involved a complicated mix of state and federal statutes and provisions of the U.S. Constitution, all coming into play, as well as conflicts between the state courts and the legislature, and the state and federal courts. Perhaps the basic lesson of the 2000 election was this: when the electorate is closely divided, there may be enormous difficulties—and enormous pressures—within the political system to determine who won.

ELECTIONS 2002: A CASE STUDY

The contest for the presidency in 2000 had hardly been settled before political leaders in both major parties began to plan for the midterm elections that would be held two years later. The normal pattern has been for the party of the president to lose seats in both houses of Congress in midterm general elections. Until 2002, the president's party had gained seats in both the House and Senate only once since 1902. But at the end of 2001, each party controlled one house of Congress by such a narrow margin that both Republicans and Democrats were determined to spare no effort to increase their strength in November 2002.

The parties' leaders knew that two broad factors could have a major impact on the midterm election results. First, how popular or unpopular would President Bush and his administration be by the fall of 2002? In previous midterm elections, when the incumbent president's popularity was low (as measured by the public's assessment of his job performance), his party usually sustained substantial losses in the House and Senate. When the incumbent president's job rating was high, his party usually lost seats but did better in the midterm congressional races.

The state of the economy was a second broad factor that both parties believed could be important in 2002. If the economy appeared to be performing poorly, most observers concluded, that would give the Democrats economic issues on which to attack their Republican opponents. As it turned out, however, by the summer and fall of 2002, a host of new issues had arisen which few people had anticipated in January 2001.

When President Bush assumed office that month, he had narrow Republican majorities—and Republican committee chairs—to work with in both the House and the Senate. He soon submitted an ambitious legislative program to the Congress, and some of his proposals, most notably a major tax cut, were enacted into law. In May 2001, however, the Republican Senator from Vermont, James M. Jeffords, stunned his Republican colleagues by leaving their party and becoming an independent. This switch gave the Democrats a one-seat edge over the Republicans and control of the Senate and the committee chairmanships. With the Democrats now in the majority, President Bush found it considerably harder to move the more controversial parts of his legislative program through Congress.

During his first half year in office, President Bush's job rating from the American public was more positive than negative, but not spectacularly high. In early September 2001, for example, 51 percent of the American public said they approved of "the way George W. Bush" was "handling his job as president," while 39 percent said that they "disapproved."

Then came September 11, and the horrifying terrorist attacks on New York and Washington that destroyed

With members of the news media watching through the window, Palm Beach County's election officials conduct a hand recount of the paper ballots in the 2000 election.
AP/Wide World

the World Trade Center and seriously damaged the Pentagon. In the days and weeks that followed, President Bush and his administration developed America's response to this unprecedented threat to the nation's security; and the public rallied to the support of their chief executive. President Bush's popularity and job ratings rose to heights almost never before attained by an American president—hovering for several months in the 85 to 90 percent range.[52]

During the first weeks after the September 11 attack on America, President Bush also enjoyed broad, bipartisan support in Congress. For both Democrats and Republicans, the emphasis was on national unity in the face of a common foe. But during the second session of the 107th Congress in 2002, large areas of disagreement opened up between the president and the Democratic-controlled Senate. There were battles over the president's nominations for federal judgeships, over energy policy—particularly an administration proposal for more oil drilling in Alaska—over how to finance prescription drug costs for senior citizens, and over the precise form that a proposed Homeland Security cabinet department should take. Above all, there were differences about the president's assertions that the United States might have to go to war with Iraq if it became clear that Saddam Hussein was building an arsenal of nuclear and other weapons of mass destruction. On a number of these and other policy issues, Democrats blocked the Bush administration's proposals in the Senate.

The Setting

When the 2002 election year began, there were 34 U.S. Senate seats (out of a hundred) to be filled in the November general elections. Of these, the Democrats had 14 Senate seats to defend; and the Republicans had 20. In all 14 of the Democratic seats, the incumbent senator announced plans to seek reelection. But in four

states that had Republican senators—Texas, North Carolina, South Carolina, and Tennessee—the incumbent announced that he would not be running for reelection. And in New Hampshire, the incumbent Republican senator, Bob Smith, was defeated in his party's primary.

The Bush administration thus faced a double challenge: to help recruit strong new candidates to defend five seats which their party already controlled, and to encourage strong Republican candidates to challenge the Democratic incumbents in states where there was a good chance for the Republicans to gain a seat. Democrats, by contrast, concentrated their efforts on defending the 14 seats they already had. They also tried to encourage strong candidates to run in the three or four states where they thought that their party had a good chance to gain a seat. Between ten and twelve of the 34 Senate races—close to a third—were thought to be capable of going either way.

In the House of Representatives, the strategic situation was markedly different. There were 435 House seats to be filled, but less than a tenth of those seats—40 at most—were considered to be competitive. In 78 of the nation's House districts, one of the major parties conceded the race in advance and did not even run a candidate.

This low number of competitive House races prevailed in part because of the way the political landscape of the House had been substantially altered by redistricting, the redrawing of congressional district boundary lines following the national census of 2000. In most states, redistricting was done by the state legislature, with the approval of the governor.

In some states where one party controlled both the governorship and both houses of the state legislature, the dominant party pushed through sweeping redistricting plans designed to benefit its candidates in the 2002 congressional elections. This was done by Republicans in Pennsylvania and Michigan and by Democrats

TABLE 11-12

How Groups Voted in 2000

	Gore	Bush	Nader
All (100%)	48%	48%	2%
Men (48%)	42	53	3
Women (52%)	54	43	2
Whites (82%)	42	54	3
Blacks (10%)	90	8	1
Hispanics (4%)	67	31	2
Asian (2%)	54	41	4
Married (65%)	44	53	2
Unmarried (35%)	57	38	4
Didn't complete high school (5%)	59	39	1
High school graduate (21%)	48	49	1
Some college (32%)	45	51	3
College graduate (24%)	45	51	3
Postgraduate (18%)	52	44	3
Age			
18–29 (17%)	48	46	5
30–44 (33%)	48	49	2
45–59 (28%)	48	49	2
60 and up (23%)	51	47	2
Family income:			
Less than $15,000 (7%)	57	37	4
$15,000–29,999 (16%)	54	41	3
$30,000–49,999 (24%)	49	48	2
$50,000 or over (53%)	45	52	2
White Protestants (47%)	34	63	2
Catholics (26%)	49	47	2
Jews (4%)	79	19	1
Family financial situation compared with 1996:			
Better (50%)	61	36	2
Worse (11%)	35	60	3
About the same (38%)	33	63	4
Democrats (39%)	86	11	2
Republicans (35%)	8	91	1
Independents (27%)	45	47	6
Liberals (20%)	80	13	6
Moderates (50%)	52	44	2
Conservatives (29%)	17	81	1
1996 votes:			
Clinton (46%)	82	15	2
Dole (31%)	7	91	1
Perot (6%)	27	64	7
First-time voters (9%)	52	43	4
Union households (26%)	59	37	3

SOURCE: *New York Times*, November 12, 2000, section 4, p. 4.

in Georgia and Maryland. In other states controlled by one party, however, party leaders redistricted in a way that protected the incumbents of both parties. In California, for example, the Democrats took this approach rather than gamble on creating new districts

that might turn out to be less safe for some Democratic members of Congress.

The net effect of the redistricting was to leave only a relatively small number of the nation's 435 House districts truly competitive. Thus, the possibility of large net gains in the House—for either party—was severely limited.

Thirty-six of the nation's 50 governorships also were to be filled in 2002, and well over half of the seats in the state legislatures. When the election year began, Republicans controlled 27 governorships, and 21 were held by Democrats. Two governors were independents. Many of the races for governor were close, and the Democrats hoped to win enough gubernatorial contests to control a majority of the 50 states for the first time since 1994.

The Election Campaign

In a real sense, the 2002 fall campaign began almost a year earlier, as both parties began to recruit candidates and raise money for their campaigns. In late March 2002, President Bush began an extensive series of fundraising trips that took him to all parts of the country, and eventually these efforts by the president produced $140 million for Republicans.[53] By campaign's end, Republicans were able to outspend Democrats by a substantial margin.

Many Democratic candidates sought to make the sluggish performance of the economy the central issue of their campaign. And a Gallup poll in October found that when voters were given a list of six issues and asked to say which issue was "MOST important," 25 percent chose "economic conditions." But another 25 percent said that "the possibility of war with Iraq" was most important; and 14 percent said that "terrorism" was the key issue.[54]

In the final weeks of the Senate campaigns, there were two startling events. At the end of September, Senator Robert B. Torricelli, a Democrat from New Jersey, withdrew from the race. His poll numbers had been dropping sharply amid charges that he had accepted improper gifts from a campaign contributor. And on October 25, while campaigning in his home state, Senator Paul D. Wellstone, a Democrat from Minnesota, was killed in the crash of a small plane, along with his wife and daughter, three members of his staff, and the plane's two pilots. Democrats in New Jersey picked former Senator Frank R. Lautenberg to run as Torricelli's replacement; and in Minnesota, Democrats selected Walter Mondale, who had been the Democratic candidate for president in 1984, to replace Wellstone.

During October President Bush began the most active midterm campaigning for his party's candidates ever undertaken by an American president. This effort culminated in a dramatic final swing that took the president to 17 cities in 15 states in the last five days before the election. Everywhere he went, the president asked voters to send him more supporters in Congress. In St. Louis, where he was campaigning for former Representative Jim Talent, who was challenging Democratic Senator Jean Carnahan, the president said he was looking for "some allies"—people "whose vote we can count on to do the right thing to make sure this country is strong and safe and a better place."[55] And, in almost every speech, he drew cheers from the crowd by ending with an attack on Saddam Hussein. The Iraqi dictator, President Bush insisted, had connections to the Al Qaeda terrorist network and was a threat to the United States. The president also said that he himself would lead a coalition to disarm Saddam if the United Nations was unwilling to do so.[56]

During the final weekend before Election Day, there were some signs that public support was moving toward the Republicans, particularly among those most likely to vote.[57] Even so, most observers were expecting an extremely close election result. "The correct analysis on the Sunday before this election is, 'Who knows?'" said Newt Gingrich, the former speaker of the House of Representatives and the architect of the Republican takeover of the House in 1994. "This is the least decided election in my lifetime."[58]

The Results

When the returns began to roll in on Election Night, however, it soon became clear that the Republicans were doing unusually well for a party that controlled the White House at midterm. The GOP made a net gain of five House seats, solidifying its control of the House of Representatives. Late returns confirmed that Senator Carnahan had lost in Missouri, and that a Republican, Norm Coleman, had defeated Walter Mondale in Minnesota. The Republican party had made a net gain of two Senate seats and would again be the majority party in the Senate. Only in the races for governor, where the Democrats made a net gain of three, was there much good news for Democrats.[59]

Several noteworthy features marked the voting patterns of 2002:

1. About 78.7 million voters went to the polls. According to the Committee for the Study of the American Electorate, there was a turnout of 39.3 percent of all citizens of voting age—an increase in turnout of 1.7 percent from the last midterm election in 1998. In some traditionally Democratic counties turnout dropped, however; but in two states which had closely contested races for the U.S. Senate—Minnesota and South Dakota—the turnout exceeded 60 percent.[60]

2. Independent and minor-party candidates were weaker than they had been in 1998 and 2000. The two governors who were independents were each replaced by a major-party governor.

3. Democrats lost key Senate races in several different regions of the country. The Democrats failed to pick up a seat they had hoped to win in the Northeast (New Hampshire) and in the West (Colorado). And they lost Senate seats they had previously controlled in the South (Georgia), the Border States (Missouri), and in the Midwest (Minnesota).

4. One Senate contest, in Louisiana, was decided in a runoff election in December 2002. But the election results on November 5 assured that the Republicans would control the Senate with at least 51 seats. Senator Jeffords of Vermont, who had caucused with the Democrats in 2002, remained an independent.

5. In the battle for control of the House of Representatives, the Republicans' net gain of five House seats marked the first time the GOP had gained strength in the House since 1994. The results left the Republicans with a majority of 228 to 206, pending some final vote recounts. In addition, one independent was elected to the House.

6. The new drawing of congressional district boundary lines apparently left the House of Representatives with even fewer genuinely competitive districts than before. As noted, seventy-eight candidates ran without major-party opposition. And, according to the Center for Voting and Democracy, the average winning candidate received more than 70 percent of the vote. In only 75 of the 435 House races was the margin of victory less than 20 points.[61]

7. Republicans made some major gains in the South. They elected two and possibly three governors in states in the Deep South that previously had Democratic chief executives. The GOP's victory in Georgia was the first time that state had elected a Republican governor in 130 years.

8. The Democrats fared better in other races for governor. Nationwide, in the 36 contests for governor in 2002, the Democrats made a net gain of at least three, winning in major states including Pennsylvania, Michigan, Illinois, and California. But there were still at least 25 Republican governors, compared with 24 Democratic governors, with one race undecided.

9. The results of contests for the state legislatures provided perhaps the clearest evidence that 2002 was a Republican year. The GOP made a net gain of about 200 state legislative seats, and the Republicans wrested control of one house of the state legislature from the Democrats in five states. The Republican Party thus ran counter to an historic trend; since 1938, the president's party had lost an average of 350 seats in every midterm election. When the newly elected state legislators assumed office, the Republicans held more than half of the

nation's 7,382 state legislative seats for the first time since 1952.[62]

10. Perhaps the most important point of all about the 2002 elections was that they left the Republican Party in control of two main branches of the national government—the legislative branch and the executive branch. For a time, at least, there would be no more divided government, less "partisan gridlock," and fewer excuses for legislative or executive inaction. For the first time in eight years—except for a brief, four-month period in early 2001—the White House and Congress would be controlled by the same party. How well the Republicans were perceived as governing would go a long way toward determining how their party would fare in 2004 and beyond.

THE ELECTORAL SYSTEM

The act of choice performed by the American voter on Election Day takes place within a legal and structural framework that strongly influences the result. The electoral system in the United States is not neutral—it affects the dynamics of voting all along the way. Before voters can step into the voting booths, they must meet a number of legal requirements. The candidates whose names appear on the ballot must have qualified under state law. The form of the ballot may influence voters' decisions—if they are allowed to make a single mark or pull a single lever, for example, they are more likely to vote a straight party ticket than if they must make several marks or pull many levers to vote that way. How their votes count in a presidential election is controlled by custom, state law, and the Constitution, for all three affect the workings of the electoral college. In short, the structure, details, and workings of the electoral system affect the people's choice.

Suffrage

The Constitution provides for popular election of members of the House of Representatives, a provision extended to the election of senators by the Seventeenth Amendment, ratified in 1913. In electing a president, the voters in each state actually choose electors, who meet in December of the election year and cast their ballots for a chief executive. (See the discussion about the electoral college later in this chapter.)

Voting is a basic right provided for by the Constitution. Under the Fourteenth Amendment, it is one of the privileges and immunities of national citizenship that the states may not abridge and that Congress has the power to protect by federal legislation. For example, in 1970 Congress limited state residence requirements for voting in presidential elections. The states, however, set many requirements for voting. State laws in part govern the machinery of choice—residence and other voting

requirements, registration, primaries, and the form of the ballot. And state laws regulate political parties.

Until the age of Andrew Jackson, voting was generally restricted to men who owned property and paid taxes. Since then, suffrage has gradually been broadened. Most states lifted property requirements in the early 19th century. In 1869 Wyoming became the first state to enact women's suffrage, and three other western states did so in the 1890s. In 1917 the suffragettes began marching in front of the White House; they were arrested and jailed. In 1919 Congress passed the Nineteenth Amendment, making it unconstitutional to deny any citizen the right to vote on account of sex. The amendment was ratified by the states in time for women to vote in the presidential election of 1920.

The long struggle of African Americans for the right to vote is described in Chapter 5. As we have seen, even though the Fifteenth Amendment specifically gave black citizens the right to vote, it was circumvented when the South regained political control of its state governments following Reconstruction. Poll taxes, all-white primaries, phony literacy tests, intimidation, and violence were all effective in disenfranchising blacks in the South. In 1964 the Twenty-fourth Amendment eliminated the last vestiges of the poll tax in federal elections.* But blacks still faced many of the other barriers to voting; only 44 percent of voting-age black citizens in the South voted in the 1964 presidential election. The Voting Rights Act of 1965, which was extended in 1970, 1975, and in 1982 to the year 2007, sought to throw the mantle of federal protection around these voters. It was followed by a dramatic increase in blacks voting in the South.

Residence Requirements   When Congress extended the Voting Rights Act in 1970, it included a provision permitting voters in every state to vote in presidential elections after living in the state for 30 days. This uniform federal standard was designed to override state residence requirements, some of which had prevented millions of persons from voting for president. The Voting Rights Act also required states to permit absentee registration and voting. Subsequently, the Supreme Court ruled that states may not require residence of more than 30 days to vote in federal, state, and local elections,[63] although in 1973 the Court modified this standard to permit a state residency requirement of 50 days, at least in state and local elections.[64] But neither case changed the 30-day maximum residence requirements for voting in presidential elections.

---

*Only five southern states still imposed a poll tax as a requirement for voting in federal elections when the Twenty-fourth Amendment went into effect on January 23, 1964. Under the Voting Rights Act of 1965, the U.S. attorney general filed lawsuits against four of the 27 states still imposing poll taxes in state and local elections. In 1966 the U.S. Supreme Court ruled in *Harper v. Virginia State Board of Elections* (383 U.S. 633) that any state poll tax violated the Fourteenth Amendment. The decision outlawed the use of poll taxes at any level of election.

Suffragettes marching to the White House, 1917
AP/Wide World

Literacy and Character Tests Historically, literacy tests were used to keep recent immigrants and blacks from voting. The Voting Rights Act of 1965 suspended literacy tests in the six southern states and all or part of four other states where less than half the voting-age population had registered or voted in the 1964 election. The law also suspended in those areas tests requiring voters to prove "good moral character."

Later amendments to the Voting Rights Act extended the ban against literacy and character tests to all states.

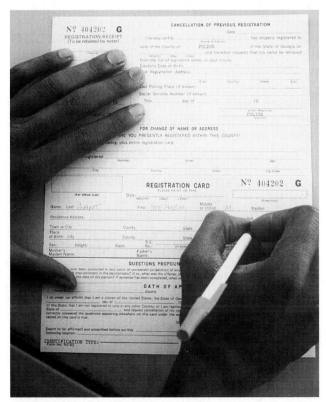

Copyright © Thomas England/Photo Researchers

Prior to passage of the law, 12 states—including California and New York—still listed literacy as a requirement for voting. Two states, Idaho and Connecticut, had "good character" tests. Under Idaho law, prostitutes, their customers and madams, bigamists, persons of Chinese or Mongolian descent, and persons who "lewdly or lasciviously cohabit together"[65] were banned from voting. And Connecticut had a law on its books requiring that voters be of "good moral character."

Although these anachronistic character tests were suspended along with literacy tests by the 1970 amendments to the Voting Rights Act, a number of states retained on the statute books other odd barriers to voting. The laws of nine states, for example, disqualified paupers, and Louisiana law disqualified parents of illegitimate children. The laws of seven states disqualified persons engaging in duels. Such oddities were not affected by the Voting Rights Act or its various extensions, but they were generally not enforced by the states anyway.

Most states bar mentally incompetent persons and inmates of prisons from voting. Persons convicted of certain types of crimes lose the right to vote under the laws of 46 states and the District of Columbia. Some states restore the right to vote on release from prison, or after a set number of years of imprisonment, or by executive or legislative clemency.

 for more information about voting rights, see:
www.usdoj.gov:80/crt/voting/intro/intro_a.htm

Age Requirements In the late 1960s, with young Americans fighting and dying in Vietnam—but denied the right to vote—pressure to lower the voting age to 18 built up rapidly. After November 1970 eight states had lowered their legal voting age to below 21. In all other states, however, the minimum voting age was 21.

Exercise
your right to vote.
BE A VOTER!

In 1970 Congress, by statute, lowered the voting age to 18 in all elections, but later that year the Supreme Court ruled that Congress had power to do so only in *federal* elections.[66] The result was confusion. In 1971 Congress passed, and the necessary three-fourths of the states ratified, a constitutional amendment lowering the voting age to 18 in all elections.

The Twenty-sixth Amendment enfranchised 10.5 million persons between the ages of 18 and 21 in time to vote in the 1972 presidential election. Many political observers reasoned that the addition of so large a group of young voters could have an impact on the political system. But the lower voting age did not result in dramatic political change, in part because younger voters traditionally have had a low rate of turnout. In fact, in the first election in which all persons aged 18 through 20 could vote (1972), fewer than half (48 percent) voted.[67] In 1996, about 10 percent of the total vote for president was cast by persons age 18 through 24.[68]

Citizenship Requirements Only U.S. citizens can vote in U.S. elections. This was not always the case, however. In the 19th century, 22 states and territories gave aliens the right to vote; the last state to abolish alien voting was Arkansas, in 1926. As a result, the presidential election of 1928 was the first in which only U.S. citizens

could cast ballots. More than 10 million U.S. residents reported that they could not vote in 1988 because they were not American citizens.

The Nominating Process: Primaries and Conventions

Voting requirements restrict the number of people who can step into the voting booth. The nominating process restricts choice, since the voter is effectively limited to those candidates nominated by parties or running as independents and placed on the ballot. (Write-in votes, where permitted, seldom elect anyone.)

State laws govern the nominating process and the selection of party leaders. Although the Constitution provides for election of members of Congress and the president, it makes no direct mention of how they shall be nominated and placed on the ballot. In the 19th century, candidates for public office were chosen by backroom caucuses of politicians or by local or state conventions. The abuses of that manner of selection led to demands for reform. By 1915 two-thirds of the states had some kind of law providing for primary elections to choose candidates for the general elections. Today every state has provisions for primary elections to choose some candidates who run in statewide contests. Party officials also may be chosen in primaries.

Currently most states hold direct primaries to nominate candidates for the House and Senate. In a handful of other states, nominations are by convention, party committee, or by a combination of methods. In states using primaries, the most common form is the **closed primary,** in which only registered members of a party or persons declaring their affiliation with a party can vote. About 20 states use the **open primary,** in which any voter may participate and vote for one political party's slate of candidates.

In recent years, four states—Alaska, California, Louisiana, and Washington—used the **blanket primary,** a system in which any registered voters are able to vote for candidates from more than one party. A voter, for example, could vote for a Democratic nominee for the U.S. Senate, and for a Republican gubernatorial nominee. In 2000, however, the U.S. Supreme Court ruled against California's blanket primary system, declaring that it violated the constitutional right to freedom of association by forcing political parties to allow nonmembers to choose a party's candidates.[69] The Court's decision struck down the blanket primary in Alaska and Washington, as well as California, but left intact a somewhat different "nonpartisan" version of the blanket primary in Louisiana. Political party leaders have usually opposed the blanket primary, arguing that it weakens party identification and loyalty.

Political parties still hold conventions to nominate candidates for president and vice president. Delegates to these conventions are usually, but not always, selected in presidential primaries. In 1996, 34 states and the District

MAKING A DIFFERENCE

ROCK THE VOTE: EMPOWERING YOUNG AMERICANS

Only 33 percent of 18- to 21-year-olds voted in the 1988 presidential election. That low turnout continued a steady decline that began in 1971, when the Twenty-sixth Amendment lowered the voting age to 18.

That was the situation in 1991 when Patrick Lippert, a Los Angeles political activist, became executive director and later president of Rock the Vote, an organization founded in 1990 by record industry executives to counter efforts at censorship. When Lippert joined, he expanded the focus of the nonpartisan organization's goals to include the political empowerment of young Americans.

Lippert's political work began in California in the early 1980s, when the Minnesota native volunteered as an activist to help organize the entertainment community around progressive causes. At the helm of Rock the Vote, he was credited with an 18 percent increase in turnout by 18- to 24-year-old voters in 1992. He was helped by music videos on MTV produced for Rock the Vote

and featuring Madonna and rapper Ice-T. In her video, Madonna wraps herself in the American flag and cries out "Vote!" to the music of her hit song, "Vogue." In his video, Ice-T intones: "We're youth, we have to change things."

Lippert seemed an unlikely candidate to awaken the slumbering political conscience of twenty-something rock and rollers; he didn't own a stereo and rarely watched MTV. Yet, Lippert stirred a potent mix of celebrity and politics that sent young Americans to the polls in record numbers. His passion and sharp political sense won him a special place at the intersection of entertainment and politics. Lippert was one of the few people that both stodgy legislators and outlaw rock stars could trust.

Besides increasing young voter participation Rock the Vote also played a key role in congressional passage of the "motor voter" bill, a law that added millions of persons to the voter rolls by allowing people to

register to vote when they receive or renew their driver's licenses. He was invited to the White House by President Clinton for the bill-signing ceremony. For his work, Lippert was honored with many awards, including the Congressional Arts Caucus Award.

Patrick Lippert wrote in the *Los Angeles Times* Opinion section: "For a democracy to be truly realized, all citizens eligible to vote must exercise their constitutional right. For this reason, until this happens, Rock the Vote is committed to registering America's youth on college campuses, in high schools and at record stores and concerts."

On July 13, 1993, Patrick Lippert died from complications due to AIDS. He was 35 years old. Until the end, he was devoted to his cause. In lieu of flowers, he had asked that any memorial donations be made to Rock the Vote.

—Adapted from the *Los Angeles Times, Time, Rolling Stone,* and Rock the Vote

---

of Columbia held Democratic presidential primaries, and 41 states plus the District of Columbia and Puerto Rico held Republican presidential primaries, in which voters in one or both parties chose all or some convention delegates. Other states chose delegates to national nominating conventions by different methods, including selection by state conventions, party caucuses, and party committees. But because most of the large states held presidential primaries in 1996, about three-fourths of the delegates to the national conventions were selected in presidential primaries in that year.

Voter Registration

The old Tammany Hall slogan, "Vote Early and Vote Often," still brings nostalgic smiles to the faces of some political leaders in New York. But the use of "repeaters" to vote more than once, and of "tombstone voters" (using the names of deceased voters) and similar devices, is made much more difficult—although by no means impossible—by modern systems of voter registration.

Before voters can vote, they must register. Under state laws, when voters register, their names are entered on a list of people qualified to vote. They may, if they wish, declare their party affiliation when they register. On Election Day, the registration list may be checked for each voter who comes to the polling place to ensure that he or she is qualified to cast a ballot.

Permanent registration, under which the voter registers only once in his or her district, prevails in all but a few states. **Periodic registration,** under which the voter must register every year or at other stated intervals, is used in a very small number of states.

Like other forms of election machinery, registration procedures can affect the political result. For example, Idaho has used roving canvassers to remind people to register to vote, and the turnout has consistently been higher than the national average. No doubt other factors are at work in Idaho, but, as a presidential commission concluded: "The average American is far more likely to vote if few barriers stand between him and registration."[70]

I know every man, woman, and child in the Fifteenth District, except them that's been born this summer—and I know some of them, too. I know what they like and what they don't like, what they are strong at and what they are weak in, and I reach them by approachin' at the right side.

For instance, here's how I gather in the young men. I hear of a young feller that's proud of his voice, thinks he can sing fine. I ask him to come around to Washington Hall and join our Glee Club. He comes and sings, and he's a follower of Plunkitt for life. Another young feller gains a reputation as a baseball player in a vacant lot. I bring him into our baseball club. That fixes him. You'll find him workin' for my ticket at the polls next election day. . . . I don't trouble them with political arguments. I just study human nature and act accordin'.

—Boss Plunkitt, in William L. Riordon,
Plunkitt of Tammany Hall

A basic factor affecting registration and voting in the United States is that an American who wishes to register usually must take the initiative and appear in person at the local registration office. (In Great Britain and a number of European countries, the government takes the initiative in attempting to register eligible voters.) In more recent years, however, some attempts have been made to make it easier to register in the United States. In some states, potential voters may register at tables set up in stores, or with citizen registrars or party volunteers who go from door to door seeking new voters.

Online *for more information about voter registration, see:*
www.lwv.org/voter/index.html

In 1993, Congress passed and President Clinton signed a "motor voter" bill, which was designed to make it easier for people to register to vote. The law required states to allow people to register when they applied for a driver's license or when they visited public assistance agencies or military recruitment offices.[71]

The law, which went into effect in January 1995, was challenged in court by Governor Pete Wilson of California, as well as by public officials in six other states. Governor Wilson argued that the law would cost California an additional $18 million to administer beyond the federal funding contained in the legislation. He also argued that the law infringed on rights of the states that Wilson claimed were guaranteed by the Tenth Amendment to the Constitution.[72]

In January 1996, however, the Supreme Court refused to hear Governor Wilson's challenge to the "motor voter" law. In 1995, the first full year that the law was in effect, an estimated 11 million additional people registered to vote.[73]

Ballots

The secret (so-called Australian) ballot was not adopted by every state in the United States until 1950. Early in American history the voter often orally announced his vote at the polling place. After the Civil War, this method was replaced by ballots printed by each political party; since the ballots were often of different colors, it was easy to tell how someone voted. Concern over voter intimidation and fraud led to pressure for secret ballots printed by public authorities. By 1900 a substantial number of states had adopted the secret ballot. This ballot has two chief forms:

1. The **party-column ballot,** or Indiana ballot, lists the candidates of each party in a row or column, beside or under the party emblem. In most cases, the voter can make one mark at the top of the column, or pull one lever, and thus vote for all the party's candidates for various offices. This ballot encourages straight-ticket voting.

2. The **office-column ballot,** or Massachusetts ballot, groups candidates according to the office for which they are running—all the presidential can-

"People of North Dakota! Or possibly South Dakota!"

"Good God! He's giving the white-collar voters' speech to the blue collars."

didates of all the parties appear in one column or row, for example.

Research has demonstrated that the form of the ballot may influence the vote. Among independent voters, one study found that a party-column ballot increased straight-ticket voting by 60 percent.[74]

The first voting machine was used in 1892 by the city of Lockport, New York. By 1990 more than half the states used machines statewide or in most areas.

Although states have long permitted voting by mail for persons out of town on Election Day, a growing number of states have tried additional strategies to increase voter turnout and to decrease the cost of conducting elections. Some states now allow voting by mail, even for persons who may be at home on Election Day. Other states permit early voting weeks before Election Day. By 1998, some 21 states permitted either mail balloting or early voting, and a few, such as Arizona and Colorado, allowed both.[75]

In January 1996, Oregon allowed all of its registered voters to vote by mail in an election for the U.S. Senate; the election was held to fill the Senate seat vacated by Republican Senator Bob Packwood. Under this method, voters did not have to go in person to a polling place. Ballots were mailed to registered voters on January 10 and had to be mailed back (or dropped off at specified locations) by 8 P.M. on January 30.[76] When the ballots were counted, Democratic Congressman Ron Wyden defeated his Republican opponent, Gordon Smith, and became the first U.S. senator to be elected by mail ballots.[77]

In 2000, following a statewide referendum, Oregon went to an all-mail ballot, in which every vote in state-wide elections would be cast through the mail. Advocates of the new system argued that it would improve voter participation. Critics worried that it would increase election fraud.[78]

Counting the Votes

On Election Night the results in each state are tabulated by state and local election officials and reported to the nation through the Voter News Service, a cooperative pool of the three major television networks, CNN, and the Associated Press (AP) and United Press International (UPI), the two major wire services.

The drama of Election Night is in a sense entirely artificial. As the night wears on, one candidate may appear to lead, then fall behind, and perhaps forge ahead again. Actually, once the polls close, the popular vote result is already recorded inside the ballot boxes and voting machines.

In recent years the nation has no longer had to wait until the votes actually were counted to know the results of some elections, because the television networks have developed systems of projecting the vote with the aid of computers. In 1996 the three major broadcast networks promised not to call the presidential winner until the polls had closed in enough states to guarantee the 270 electoral votes needed for victory. "That happened at 9 P.M. Eastern Standard Time, when the polls closed in Minnesota, New Mexico, New York, Rhode Island, and Wisconsin. Moments later, all three networks announced President Clinton's victory."[79] But in the 2000 presidential election, the vote projections led to an embarrassing disaster for the major television networks. First, the networks called Florida for Vice President Gore, only to retract that news two hours later. Early the next morning, the networks awarded Florida to Bush, then retracted that as well. As it turned out, the gap between the two candidates in Florida was razor thin.

The computerized vote-projection systems are based on exit polls and on the analysis of key precincts that are chosen at random from each state. Past election data about the sample precincts are coded and stored in the computers and compared with actual returns as they come in on Election Night. As the computer processes the data flowing in, it is able to make a statistical forecast of the probable outcome. In 1980 a number of western Democratic candidates as well as other political leaders complained sharply when the television networks declared Reagan the projected winner early in the evening, and President Carter conceded at 8:50 P.M. EST. These events, coming while the polls were still open on the West Coast, they argued, discouraged many potential voters from voting. Again in 1984, the television networks declared President Reagan the winner before the polls had closed on the West Coast.

In 1992, in order to deflect criticism, the television networks agreed that they would not project the winner in a state until the majority of the polls had closed in that state.

Fraud

With so much at stake on Election Night, it is not surprising that from time to time there are charges of voting fraud, even in presidential elections.

In 1960, after John Kennedy's narrow popular-vote victory over Richard Nixon, some Republicans charged that there had been election frauds in Cook County, Illinois, and in Texas. If Kennedy had failed to carry these two states, Nixon would have won in the electoral college. Kennedy carried Illinois by a mere 8,858 votes, but his margin in Texas was much larger, 46,257 votes. Nixon considered, but decided not to ask for, an investigation or a recount.[80]

It may well be that in the age of the computer, some form of electronic voting system will be developed so votes can be recorded and tallied quickly with a minimal possibility of tampering.

The Electoral College

The Constitution does not provide for the popular election of the president. Instead, it provides that each state "shall appoint, in such manner as the legislature thereof may direct," electors equal in number to the representatives and senators that the state has in Congress. Instead of voting directly for president, an American, in casting his or her ballot, votes for a slate of electors that is normally pledged to the presidential candidate of the voter's choice.

Many voters are unaware that they are voting for electors because their names do not even appear on the ballot in about two-thirds of the states. The slate of electors that receives the most votes meets in the state capital in December of a presidential election year and casts its ballots. Each state sends the results to Washington, where the electoral votes are officially counted in a joint session of Congress early in January. The candidate with a majority of the electoral votes is elected president. (In 2000, as in every presidential election since 1964, there were a total of 538 members of the **electoral college;** 270 electoral votes were required to win the presidency.) If no one receives a majority, the House of Representatives must choose the president from among the three candidates with the largest number of electoral votes, with each state delegation in the House having one vote. Members of the electoral college also vote for vice president in a separate balloting procedure. If no candidate for vice president receives a majority of the electoral votes, the Senate must choose the vice president from one of the two candidates with the most electoral votes.[*]

 Online *for more information about the electoral college, see:* *http://gi.grolier.com/presidents/ea/side/elecollg.html*

---

*The House chose the president twice: after the election of 1800, when it elected Jefferson, and following the election of 1824, when it elected John Quincy Adams. The Senate chose the vice president only once, when it elected Richard M. Johnson of Kentucky in 1837. In the case of a tie in the presidential balloting in the House that is not resolved by Inauguration Day, January 20, the vice president-elect becomes acting president. Since the Senate chooses the vice president in the event of an electoral vote deadlock, the Senate, in effect, would select the new president on Inauguration Day; if no president or vice president has been selected by January 20, the presidency would go to the speaker of the House, or next to the President Pro Tempore of the Senate, or down through all the cabinet posts under the Presidential Succession Act.
†In fact, in 1969 Maine changed its system of choosing presidential electors; under a state law passed that year, two electors are chosen at large and two are chosen from Maine's two congressional districts. Nebraska adopted a similar system. Other states elect their presidential electors on a statewide basis.

Custom, not the Constitution, is the reason electors are chosen in each state by popular vote. In the first four presidential elections, state legislatures chose the electors in most cases. South Carolina was the last state to switch to popular election, in 1860. Although there is hardly any possibility that a state would discontinue the popular election of electors, legally, a state may select them any way it wishes.†

The framers of the Constitution had great difficulty in agreeing on the best way to elect the president. Some favored direct election by all of the voters, but others thought this would give an advantage to the more populous states. The provision for presidential electors represented a compromise between the big and little states. For, "only a few delegates to the Constitutional Convention felt that American democracy had matured sufficiently for the choice of the President to be entrusted directly to the People."[81]

Over the decades, the electoral college has been severely criticized as an old-fashioned device standing between the people and their choice of a president. The criticism may be summarized as follows:

1. The "winner-take-all" feature of the electoral college means that if a candidate carries a state by even one popular vote, he wins all the state's electoral votes, distorting the will of the voters because the minority votes cast within a state count for nothing. As a result, a president may be elected who has lost the total popular vote. This actually happened in the elections of John Quincy Adams in 1824, Rutherford B. Hayes in 1876, Benjamin Harrison in 1888, and George W. Bush in 2000.

2. The system, with its winner-take-all feature, gives an advantage to the populous states that have many electoral votes, and to the members of minority groups that constitute powerful voting blocs within those states. At the same time, very small states are overrepresented because every state has a minimum of three electoral votes.

3. Electors are not bound by the U.S. Constitution to vote for the candidate to whom they are pledged. In 2000, in 26 states and the District of Columbia electors were bound by state law or pledges to vote for their party's candidate, although most legal scholars believed those statutes were unconstitutional; 24 states had no such laws. Through 1996, 12 electors had failed to vote for the candidate to whom they were pledged.

In 1968 major-party supporters feared that George Wallace would receive enough electoral votes to deprive Nixon or Humphrey of a majority; the third-party candidate then might be in a position to win concessions in return for his electoral votes, or force the election into the House of Representatives, where he might strike further bargains.

The closeness of the 2000 election, and the lengthy post-election dispute over Florida's 25 electoral votes,

created new pressures for electoral college reform. Past debates had centered on plans to award each candidate electoral votes in proportion to his share of the popular vote within each state. In the 1960s, the idea of direct election of the president gained in popularity. It seemed closest to the principle of "one person, one vote" enunciated by the Supreme Court.

Ralph E. Becker Collection/Smithsonian Institution

Proposals for Direct Election of the President

In September 1969 the House passed a proposed constitutional amendment to abolish the electoral college and substitute direct election of the president and vice president. Under the amendment, if no candidate received 40 percent of the popular vote, a runoff election would be held between the top two presidential candidates. The amendment did not pass but many similar proposals were put forward after the 2000 post-election crisis.

One reason the 1969 amendment did not pass was a widespread reluctance, in and out of Congress, to change a fundamental aspect of the American political system. There were also a number of specific objections. Critics argued that it would encourage the growth of splinter parties. The result, they warned, could be fragmentation of American politics and destruction of the two-party system.[82] And the two-party system, these critics have contended, is a vital instrument in resolving social conflict and managing the transfer of power.

Those opposed to direct election also argued that the electoral college is compatible with the federal system and that direct election would (1) increase the temptation for fraud in vote counting, leading to prolonged recounts and chaos, (2) rob minority groups of their influence in big electoral-vote states, and (3) tempt states to ease voter qualification standards in order to fatten the voter rolls.

One Person, One Vote

During the 1960s the Supreme Court ruled in a series of reapportionment decisions that each person's vote should be worth as much as another's. Yet the decisions were controversial, for they upset the balance of political power between urban and rural areas in the United States. The result was a concerted but unsuccessful effort in Congress and the states to amend the Constitution to overturn the Supreme Court rulings.

The State Legislatures All votes are equal when each member of a legislative body represents the same number of people. In the United States, however, successive waves of immigration and the subsequent growth of the cities resulted in glaring inequalities in the population of urban and rural state legislative districts by the turn of the 20th century. The 1920 census showed that for the first time more Americans lived in urban than in rural areas. The rural state legislators, representing sparsely populated districts, passed state laws to maintain their advantage over the cities. By 1960, in every state the largest legislative district was at least twice as populous as the smallest district.

In Tennessee that year, the smallest district in the lower house had a population of 3,400 and the largest had 79,000. Obviously, the people in the biggest district were not equally represented with the voters in the smallest. Because the legislature had refused to do anything about it, a group of urban residents, including a county judge named Charles W. Baker, sued Joe C. Carr, Tennessee's secretary of state. The case went to the U.S. Supreme Court, which in 1946 had refused to consider a case involving malapportionment in Illinois (*Colgrove* v. *Green*). Justice Felix Frankfurter, in that earlier opinion, ruled that the Supreme Court "ought not to enter this political thicket."[83]

But in 1962, in *Baker* v. *Carr,* the Supreme Court ruled in favor of the voters who had challenged the established order in Tennessee.[84] In 1964, in *Reynolds* v. *Sims,* the Supreme Court made it clear that the Fourteenth Amendment required that seats in *both* houses of a state legislature be based on population. Second, the Court ruled that although legislative districts might not be drawn with "mathematical exactness or precision," they must be based "substantially" on population.[85] The Court had laid down the principle of "one person, one vote."

The reapportionment decisions had an immediate effect on the political map of America. The legislature of Oregon had reapportioned on the basis of population in 1961; between the *Baker* v. *Carr* ruling in 1962 and 1970, the other 49 states took similar steps.

Congressional Districts It was not just the state legislatures that were malapportioned prior to the mid-1960s. Although the average congressional House district had a population of 410,000 in the 1960s, the actual population of these districts varied greatly. For example, in Georgia, one rural district had 272,000 people, but the 5th Congressional District (Atlanta and its suburbs) numbered 823,000 people. In 1964, in the case of *Wesberry* v. *Sanders*,[86] the Supreme Court ruled that this disparity in the size of Georgia's congressional districts violated the Constitution. As a result, the states were required to redraw the boundaries of their congressional districts to conform to the Court's ruling.

The Supreme Court's reapportionment decisions left open the question of how much the population of state legislative and congressional districts might vary from one another without violating the principle of "one person, one vote." In a series of decisions the Court shifted ground as it grappled with this difficult question, eventually ruling that deviations as high as 10 percent in state legislative districts were too small to merit attention by the courts.[87]

Under the Constitution and federal law, Congress determines the total size of the House of Representatives, which grew from 65 members in 1790 to 435 in 1912. Congress has kept the House membership at 435 since then, although it could change that semipermanent figure.* After each 10-year census, federal law requires that the number of representatives for each state be reapportioned on the basis of population. If a state gains or loses members of Congress, the state legislature redistricts by drawing new boundary lines for its House districts.† In 1972, for example, California gained a total of five seats as a result of the 1970 census, making its House delegation the largest in the nation. Previously, New York's was the largest. Again, after the 1980 and 1990 censuses, California, Florida, and Texas gained seats, and New York, Pennsylvania, Ohio, and Illinois lost seats. The average population of House districts had risen to about 607,000 by the time of the 1996 elections.

As a result of the reapportionment revolution of the 1960s, rural areas had been expected to lose power to the cities. But because of the population exodus from the cities, the suburbs have proven to be the areas that gained the most from reapportionment of state legislatures and congressional districts. As far back as 1965 an official of the National Municipal League noted that almost half of the big cities in the United States had less population than their suburbs: "No center city contains the necessary 50 percent of the people to dominate the state. . . . The U.S. is an urban nation, but it is not a big-city nation. The suburbs own the future."[88]

Because the suburbs have grown much faster than the nation as a whole, in the 1970s, for the first time, there were more members of the House of Representatives from the suburbs than from the cities. And since then, this trend has continued. (See Table 11-13.) As the political battle shifts to the suburbs, Gerald M. Pomper has predicted: "Suburban power will influence the way both politics and government are conducted."[89]

Following the 1990 census, state legislatures created a number of congressional districts in which the majority of the population was black or Hispanic. The lines of these new districts, subject to approval by the Justice Department, were drawn to conform with judicial interpretations of the Voting Rights Act requiring that minority voters have the maximum opportunity to elect minority members to Congress. Thirteen new African Americans and six new Hispanic Americans were elected to the House in these newly created districts in 1992. Also elected that year was Carol Moseley-Braun of Illinois, who became the first African American woman and the first African American Democrat to serve in the Senate. In all, there were 17 Hispanic Americans and 38 African American members at the start of the 103rd Congress in January 1993. Two years later, when the new 104th Congress convened, there were 17 Hispanic American

| TABLE 11-13 |

Suburban, Central City, and Rural Congressional Districts in the United States House of Representatives, 1962–1992

	1962	1966	1974	1986	1992
Metropolitan districts	254	264	305	347	351
Central city	106	110	109	98	86
Suburban	92	98	132	167	196
Mixed metropolitan	56	56	64	82	69
Rural districts	181	171	130	88	84
Total	435	435	435	435	435

SOURCES: Data for 1962–1974 provided by Richard Lehne, "Suburban Foundations of the New Congress," *Annals of the American Academy of Political and Social Science*, November 1975, p. 143; and analysis extended for 1986 and 1992 by Harvey L. Schantz, State University of New York, Plattsburgh.

---

*The membership of the House increased only briefly, to 436 in early 1959 and to 437 from late 1959 through 1962, as a result of the admission to statehood of Alaska and Hawaii.
†In some instances the new lines have been drawn by federal courts.

members and 40 African Americans. By the 106th Congress, there were 39 African Americans and 20 Hispanic Americans, all in the House of Representatives.[90]

As noted in Chapter 5, the Supreme Court in 1993 and 1995 ruled that congressional districts that had been specifically drawn to contain a majority of black voters were open to challenge on the grounds that they were unconstitutional. On June 13, 1996, in two 5–4 decisions, the Court went a step further, as it invalidated two districts in Texas and one in North Carolina with black majorities, and another district with a majority of Hispanic voters in Houston, Texas.[91] (See Figure 11-4.)

All of the affected districts were oddly shaped rather than compact—the 12th Congressional District in North Carolina, for example, followed a narrow, winding course along 160 miles of Interstate Highway 85, in the central part of the state. The two decisions of the Court totaled 189 pages, and Justice Sandra Day O'Connor's opinion in the Texas case included a detailed analysis of the challenged districts.[92] "Significant deviations from traditional districting principles, such as the bizarre shape and noncompactness demonstrated by the districts here, cause constitutional harm insofar as they convey the message that political identity is, or should be, predominantly racial," Justice O'Connor declared.[93]

The two decisions suggested that the high court was likely to examine on a case-by-case basis districts in which minority group voters predominated. The decisions also suggested that additional congressional districts, as well as districts drawn to increase minority representation in state and local legislative bodies, would be scrutinized by the court.[94]

Following the Supreme Court's decisions and the redrawing of the congressional districts' boundary lines, one question remained: Would the black candidates who had won in the gerrymandered districts be able to retain their seats now that they had to run in districts where white voters were in the majority? The answer, to the surprise of many observers, was yes. In 1996, all five of the black members of Congress running in redrawn districts were reelected. All of the redrawn districts were in southern states; and all five of the districts had white majorities. For some observers, the victories of these black congressional candidates were evidence of changing racial attitudes in the South; for others, they were proof of the power of incumbency.[95]

ELECTIONS AND DEMOCRATIC GOVERNMENT

Who won the election? In the United States, with its federal system, the question must be asked on all levels—national (the president, Congress), state (the governor and state legislatures), and local (county and city governments). Since candidates of both major parties win these offices, the outcome of American elections is mixed. Which party won or lost is not always as simple as it might appear. In 1984, for example, Reagan, a Republican, won by a landslide in the presidential election and the GOP won a majority in the Senate. But the Democrats retained control of the House of Representatives and a majority of the nation's statehouses and state legislatures. Yet there are differences in elections; the voice of the voter speaks more clearly in some years than in others.

Types of Elections

V. O. Key, Jr., has suggested three broad types of presidential elections.[96] A *landslide for the out-party* "expresses

---

FIGURE 11-4

Irregular House Districts
The Supreme Court ruled in 1996 that four congressional districts, one in North Carolina and three in Texas, were unconstitutional.

"The Untouchable Incumbent. Incumbents . . . evolved in the manner of the porcupine. They grew longer and longer quills."
Drawing by Jeff MacNelly from *A Political Bestiary* by Eugene J. McCarthy and James J. Kilpatrick, McGraw-Hill, Inc. Reprinted by permission.

clearly a lack of confidence in those who have been in charge of affairs." Some observers felt that the defeat of President George Bush in 1992 was fundamentally an election of this type. In other election years, however, the voters may approve an incumbent administration in a vote of confidence that amounts to a *reaffirmation of support.* Moreover, both in elections that oust the party in power and in those that produce a reaffirmation of support, people appear to be engaged in retrospective voting—looking back and making a judgment on the way things have gone and the kind of government they have had during their political leaders' time in office.

A third type of election, a *realignment,* may return the party that controls the presidency to power, but with the support of a new coalition of voters. (There also may be a major realignment when the president's party loses control of the White House.) When the realignment within the electorate is "both sharp and durable," Key suggests that a "critical" election has taken place, one that results in "profound readjustments" in political power.[97]

Angus Campbell and his associates have classified presidential elections in somewhat similar fashion: They relate the election returns to the basic pattern of party identification. They speak of **maintaining elections,** which reflect the standing party identification of the voters; of **deviating elections,** in which the majority

party (according to party identification) is defeated in a temporary reversal; and of **realigning elections,** which may lead to a basic shift in the party identification of the electorate.[98]

The Meaning of Elections

Much of the discussion in this chapter has focused on the wide variety of reasons, sociological and psychological, that may cause different voters to vote for the same political candidate. Regardless of these individual reasons, the overall election verdicts have broad meaning for the political system as a whole.

First of all, elections decide which individuals shall govern. Who wins can make a difference—in the political philosophy and caliber of those appointed to the Supreme Court by the president and approved by Congress, to take but one example.

Second, elections can have important consequences for the broad direction of public policy. Naturally, many specific questions are not settled by elections, but 1936 was rather clearly a broad approval of the New Deal, just as 1964 was a repudiation of conservative Republicanism in that year. The series of four Democratic presidential victories from 1936 to 1948 ("maintaining elections" in Angus Campbell's terminology, "reaffirmations of support" in Key's classification) served to ensure that most of the policy innovations of the New Deal would become established public programs.

The voice of the people is not always so clear. The meaning of a particular election, the "mandate" of the people to the president on specific issues, may be subject to varying interpretations. As we have noted, many different people vote for the same candidate for different reasons; this candidate, once elected, may make decisions that cause some of the voters to feel misled. For example, in 1964 Americans voted for a president who seemed to promise, among other things, to avoid an Asian war, but did not.* In the presidential election of 1968 some voters retaliated by voting Republican.

It is also true that issues may be warped and facts concealed from the public in campaign debate, so that people may cast their votes on the basis of inadequate information. For example, during the 1972 campaign, President Nixon, his press secretary, and spokespersons for the president's election committee all repeatedly denied responsibility for the burglary and bugging of the Democrats' Watergate headquarters. In the summer of 1973 Senate hearings disclosed in great detail the involvement of high government officials in the incident and in subsequent attempts to cover it up. And in the 1976 presidential election, Watergate, which had occurred during a Republican administration, worked to Gerald Ford's

---

*See Chapter 9. At the start of the 1964 campaign there were 16,000 American troops in Vietnam as "advisers." Three months after his election in 1964, President Johnson ordered the bombing of North Vietnam. By June 1965, U.S. troops were admittedly fighting, not advising. By 1968 more than 500,000 American troops were in Vietnam. The last U.S. forces were pulled out by President Nixon in March 1973.

disadvantage.* Ford, the Republican incumbent, lost to Carter, the Democratic challenger.

To summarize, elections leave elected officials with a great deal of flexibility in governing. Yet elections also often set broad guidelines within which decision makers must stay—or risk reprisal by the voters.

Continuity and Change

It is true that most American elections have tended to be fundamentally centrist, or middle-of-the-road in character. Parties and candidates have competed for the center ground in American politics because that is where the parties believed the biggest bloc of voters were.† For this reason candidates do not as a rule endorse radical programs of social change. Yet the New Deal marked a considerable departure in government's approach to America's problems. Since 1932 government has intervened in the social and economic order to an unprecedented extent. Even President Reagan's conservative approach and extensive budget cuts did not fundamentally alter the major social role played by the federal government. Its role as economic regulator has been approved by many voters in elections for five decades. At the same time, on many public issues, the coming to power of the Reagan Administration did change the terms of the debate over social policy in America. Moreover, the Republican Party's capture of both the House and the Senate in 1994 was followed by a serious challenge within Congress to a number of long-established domestic programs and enactment of a law that ended the largest federally run welfare program. Elections do at times set broad parameters for change.

"The people," Key has observed, "may not be able to govern themselves but they can, through an elec-

toral uprising, throw the old crowd out and demand a new order, without necessarily being capable of specifying exactly what it shall be. An election of this type may amount, if not to revolution, to its functional equivalent."[99]

Besides establishing a framework for change, elections also provide continuity and a sense of political community, for they are links in a chain that bind one generation of voters to the next. Every four years the voters come together in an act of decision that is influenced by the past and present, but designed to shape the future.

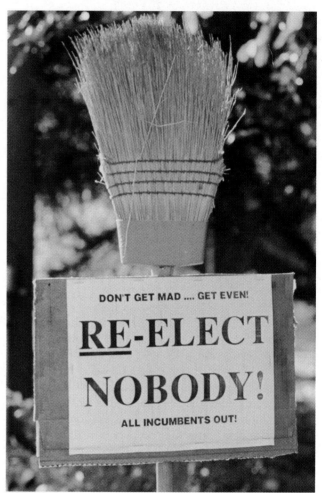

AP/Wide World

---

*On Election Day 1976, CBS News interviewed 14,836 persons as they left the polls. Those who voted for Jimmy Carter were given a list of 10 possible issues and asked to check as many as three that "led you to vote for Jimmy Carter." By far the largest group—49 percent—checked "Restoring trust in government." One in five checked "Watergate and the pardon." See *National Journal,* November 6, 1976, p. 1588.
†For a detailed statement of the view that elections are won and lost "in the center," see Richard M. Scammon and Ben J. Wattenberg, *The Real Majority* (New York: Coward-McCann, 1971).

KEY TERMS

CHAPTER HIGHLIGHTS

♦ In a democracy, the people choose who shall govern, and that choice is expressed in the voting booth. The right to vote is basic to the American political system.

♦ In the federal system that exists in the United States, the voters choose at all levels of government.

♦ One overall pattern that emerges from all the data about the voter and the nonvoter in the United States is that those who are more advantageously situated in the social system vote more than the "have-nots," or less advantaged.

✦ Although American voters have been extensively analyzed, we still do not know precisely why they behave the way they do. We do not know which of many factors ultimately causes a person to stay home or to vote for one candidate or party instead of another.

✦ Although party identification remains a key factor in American politics, it may be growing somewhat less important.

✦ In most elections since the Second World War, there also has been extensive ticket-splitting by many voters.

✦ For national political parties, the prize is control of the presidency. But party success or failure is measured in terms of states won or lost. Broad voting patterns on the national level can easily be seen by comparing political maps in presidential years, such as those found inside the front and back covers of this book.

✦ The entire House of Representatives and one-third of the Senate are elected every two years. In a presidential election year, the vote for president may affect the vote for Congress and also can have an effect on state and local offices, although there are signs that in recent years the impact of the presidential vote on contests for other offices may be lessening.

✦ Voting requirements restrict the number of people who can step into the voting booth. The nominating process restricts choice, because the voter is effectively limited to those candidates nominated by parties or running as independents and placed on the ballot.

✦ State laws govern the nominating process and the selection of party leaders. Although the Constitution provides for election of members of Congress and the president, it makes no direct mention of how they shall be nominated and placed on the ballot.

✦ In states using primaries, the most common form is the closed primary. About 20 states use the open primary.

✦ Permanent registration prevails in all but a few states. Periodic registration is used in a very small number of states.

✦ The secret (so-called Australian) ballot was not adopted by every state in the United States until 1950. Concern over voter intimidation and fraud led to pressure for secret ballots printed by public authorities. This ballot has two chief forms, the party-column ballot, or Indiana ballot, and the office-column ballot, or Massachusetts ballot.

✦ The Constitution does not provide for the popular election of the president. Instead, it provides that each state "shall appoint, in such manner as the legislature thereof may direct," electors equal in number to the representatives and senators that each state has in Congress. The electors form the electoral college.

✦ Instead of voting directly for president, an American, in casting his or her ballot, votes for a slate

of electors that is normally pledged to the presidential candidate of the voter's choice.

✦ In the early 1960s, the Supreme Court made it clear that the Fourteenth Amendment required that seats in both houses of a state legislature and congressional districts be based on population. The Court had laid down the principle of "one person, one vote."

✦ Most American elections have tended to be fundamentally centrist, or middle-of-the-road in character. Parties and candidates have competed for the center ground in American politics because that is where the parties have believed the biggest bloc of voters may be found.

✦ In 2000, George W. Bush won the contest for president of the United States. He became president in January 2001. Bush carried 30 states with 271 electoral votes; Gore won 20 states and the District of Columbia with 267 electoral votes. In the popular vote, however, Gore ran ahead of Bush, 50,996,116 to 50,456,169.

✦ In the midterm elections of 2002, the Republican Party did considerably better than the president's party usually does at midterm. Republicans increased their majority in the House of Representatives and captured control of the Senate from the Democrats.

SUGGESTED WEB SITES

www.rockthevote.org
Rock the Vote
Nonpartisan organization that is dedicated to educating young Americans about the importance of voting and the issues facing them as voters. Includes links to register to vote and education about important issues.

www.vanishingvoter.org
Vanishing Voter Project
The Vanishing Voter Project, a project of the Harvard University Kennedy School of government, includes weekly polls of the electorate and voter involvement index.

www.gallup.com
The Gallup Organization
Since 1935, the Gallup Organization has conducted surveys to measure public opinion on various issues. Its polls cover five subject areas: Politics & Elections, Business, Social Issues & Policy, Managing, and Lifestyle.

SUGGESTED READING

Berelson, Bernard R.; Lazarsfeld, Paul F.; and McPhee, William N. *Voting: A Study of Opinion Formation in a Presidential Campaign** (University of Chicago Press, 1954). An influential study of how voters decide for whom they will vote. Based on interviews with about 1,000 residents of Elmira, New York, during the Truman-Dewey presidential contest of 1948.

Campbell, Angus; Converse, Philip E.; Miller, Warren E.; and Stokes, Donald E. *The American Voter* (University of Chicago Press, 1986). (Originally published in 1960 and an abridged paperback in 1964.) A landmark study of voting behavior, based on interviews with national samples of the American electorate.

Conway, M. Margaret. *Political Participation in the United States*, 3rd revised edition* (CQ Press, 2000). A comprehensive analysis of patterns of political participation. The author examines who gets involved in politics, for what reasons, and with what effects.

Fiorina, Morris, P. *Retrospective Voting in American National Elections* (Yale University Press, 1981). An important analysis of voting behavior. Emphasizes that many voters make a rough judgment about the performance of the incumbent administration, and then cast their votes accordingly.

Flanigan, William H., and Zingale, Nancy. *Political Behavior of the American Electorate*, 9th edition* (CQ Press, 1999). A concise analysis and summary of research on how and why Americans vote.

Jacobson, Gary C. *The Politics of Congressional Elections*, 4th edition* (HarperCollins, 1997). A comprehensive, general analysis of congressional elections. Focuses on the candidates, their campaigns, the voters, and the relationship between national politics and congressional elections.

Key, V. O., Jr. *The Responsible Electorate*ern* (The Belknap Press of Harvard University Press, 1966). An examination of American voting behavior in presidential elections, based primarily on analyses of Gallup poll data from 1936 to 1960. Key argues that the voters' views on issues and government policy are quite closely related to how they vote in such elections.

Key, V. O., Jr. *Southern Politics in State and Nation*, 2nd edition* (University of Tennessee Press, 1984). (Originally published in 1949.) A landmark study of the politics of the South. Analyzes why the Democratic Party dominated that region for nearly three generations after the Civil War, and what the political consequences were.

Lazarsfeld, Paul F.; Berelson, Bernard; and Gaudet, Hazel. *The People's Choice: How the Voter Makes Up His Mind in a Presidential Campaign*, 3rd edition (Columbia University Press, 1968). (Originally published in 1944.) A classic in the study of voting behavior, based on a series of interviews with potential voters in Erie County, Ohio, during the Roosevelt-Willkie presidential contest of 1940. The book stresses the relationship between the voters' socioeconomic status and how they voted.

Nelson, Michael, ed. *The Elections of 1996** (CQ Press, 1996). Informative analysis of the 1992 elections. Includes essays on the strategies of the presidential candidates and the elections for Congress.

Nie, Norman H.; Verba, Sidney; and Petrocik, John R. *The Changing American Voter*, enlarged edition (Harvard University Press, 1979). An important sequel to the classic 1960 study, *The American Voter*, based primarily on public opinion polls from 1956 to 1973. The authors conclude that, compared with the 1950s, issues were more visible and had a greater effect on voting in the elections from 1964 through 1972.

Page, Benjamin I, and Shapiro, Robert Y. *The Rational Public: Fifty Years of Trends in Americans' Policy Preferences** (University of Chicago Press, 1994). A comprehensive analysis of Americans' political attitudes from the 1930s to the 1980s.

Peirce, Neal R., and Longley, Lawrence D. *The Electoral College Primer 2000** (Yale University Press, 2000). A detailed study of the history of the electoral college and its effects in past presidential elections. Presents the case for abolishing the electoral college and electing presidents directly by popular vote.

Scammon, Richard M., and Wattenberg, Ben J. *The Real Majority* (Coward-McCann, 1970). A lively analysis of political attitudes and voting patterns. Argues that the majority of American voters are "unyoung, unpoor, and unblack," and contends that candidates who take moderate positions on issues—close to the "political center"—are more likely to be elected than candidates who take more extreme positions.

Schantz, Harvey L., ed. *American Presidential Elections: Process, Policy, and Political Change** (State University of New York Press, 1996). A comparative analysis of the 52 U.S. presidential elections held between 1788 and 1992. Emphasizes the basic patterns of presidential elections, and traces the impact of various types of presidential elections on public policy and American society.

Sundquist, James L. *Dynamics of the Party System: Alignment and Realignment of Political Parties in the United States*, revised edition* (The Brookings Institution, 1983). A comprehensive historical analysis of the relative electoral strength of America's political parties over a 150-year period.

Traugott, Michael W., and Lavrakas, Paul J. *The Voter's Guide to Election Polls*, 2nd edition* (Chatham House, 2000). A concise, readable guide for understanding public opinion polls. Examines how surveys are conducted, common problems facing pollsters, and the interpretation of survey results.

---

*Available in paperback edition.

 Visit http://politicalscience.wadsworth.com/cummings9/update/ for current InfoTrac articles and other student resources related to this chapter.

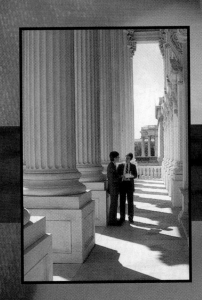

PART THREE

The Policymakers

CHAPTER 12
The Congress

In the fall of the year 2000, relations between the Republican-controlled Congress and Bill Clinton, the Democratic president, were marked by gridlock and conflict, the pattern that had prevailed for much of the previous six years.

Less than two years earlier, Congress had impeached but then acquitted the president over his actions in the Monica Lewinsky scandal. It was only the second time in U.S. history that a president had been impeached. And in the fall of 2000, in the midst of the presidential and congressional election campaigns, many members of the 106th Congress were concentrating more on reelection than on legislation.

Despite the strong partisan differences between the Democratic president and the Republican-controlled Congress in September 2000, only weeks before the election the legislators and the White House reached agreement on a sweeping $12 billion plan to conserve America's wilderness areas, parks, and wildlife. President Clinton signed the bill into law on October 11.

The measure was a compromise; many environmental groups had pushed for a broader $45 billion plan over 15 years. The plan that emerged allocated $12 billion over six years, and the money was to be set aside in a special conservation fund, similar to the Highway Trust Fund. It would be used to buy land for national parks and monuments and for grants to cities for parks and green space; to buy and maintain historic sites, such as Civil War battlefields; and to establish wildlife refuges.[1]

The conservation bill was a rare example of bipartisanship during the Clinton years, notable more as an exception than the rule. In 1992, Bill Clinton, a Democrat, had been elected president, along with a Senate and House controlled by his party. But only two years later, in 1994, for the first time in 40 years the voters of America chose a Congress in which both houses were controlled by the Republican Party.

From 1994 through 2000 the president faced a Congress led by the opposition. The Republican victory in the congressional elections of 1994 was the worst first-term loss for a president since Herbert Hoover had occupied the White House more than half a century before. In just two years, Clinton's political world had been turned upside down.

Or so it seemed. The Republican victory catapulted Newt Gingrich, the new Republican speaker of the House, to the forefront of national attention. The news media could not write enough about the powerful new figure on the political stage, the outspoken representative from the northern suburbs of Atlanta, Georgia.

But nothing is certain in life or in politics. In the months that followed the 1994 election, the Republican-controlled Congress fell short of its legislative goals. Twice, in 1995 and in early 1996, the federal government had to shut down when Congress and the president could not agree on a budget. In the battle of the budget, the public blamed the Republican Congress more than the Democratic president. And in 1997 Gingrich was reprimanded by the House for ethics violations and fined $300,000.

Then in the elections of 1998, the Democrats gained five seats in the House, and suffered no net loss in the Senate. Not since 1934 had the president's party gained seats in a midterm election. In the wake of this poor Republican showing and his rebuke by the House, Gingrich resigned as speaker and left Congress.

Against this background, in this chapter we will explore a key question: Can Congress meet the needs of

SENATOR RUDMAN: "THIS ISN'T MUCH FUN"

In March 1992, Warren B. Rudman, a Republican senator from New Hampshire, announced that he would not seek a third term. Rudman later described why he left Congress:

The Republican Party I grew up with was starting to vanish: the party of Eisenhower, Taft, Dirksen and Baker, men who believed in a strong defense and less government, and who didn't think you could solve every problem by passing a law. If someone had told me in the 1960s that one day I would serve in a Republican Party that opposed abortion rights—which the Supreme Court had endorsed—advocated prayer in the schools, and talked about government-inspired "family values," I would have thought he was crazy.

To me the essence of conservatism is just the opposite: Government should not intrude in anything as personal as the decision to have a child, it should not be championing prayer or religion, and family values should come from families and religious institutions, not from politically inspired, Washington-based moralists. . . .

I thought the essence of good government was reconciling divergent views with compromises that served the country's interests. But that's not how movement conservatives or far-left liberals operate. The spirit of civility and compromise was drying up. By the 1990s, many nights I would go home and shake my head and

think, We're not getting a hell of a lot done here. And then I would think, This isn't much fun. . . .

I kept my decision a secret from everyone except my family and a few close friends. . . . On December 28, 1992, while most of my staff was on vacation, I went to my Senate office for the last time, to pack up all my photographs and personal belongings and have them shipped back to New Hampshire. . . . I turned to Marion Phelan, my longtime aide, and said, "I never carved my name in the Daniel Webster desk," and we headed for the Senate floor.

Each senator has a desk, the old-fashioned kind with tops that lift up like those that once were used in schoolrooms. By tradition each senator carves his name inside his desk, and the senior New Hampshire senator has the special privilege of carving his name in Daniel Webster's desk because, although Webster represented Massachusetts, he was a New Hampshireman.

The Senate wasn't in session, so Marion could go onto the floor with me. We took a chisel and other tools I'd need to do the job right. Several of the Capitol Police came over to watch as I lifted the top of the desk and started to work. When I finished carving my name in the desk, I shook hands with everyone and made my exit.

—Warren B. Rudman, the *Washington Post Magazine*, April 21, 1996 the American people in the 21st century? Can it legislate when there is "divided government," with one party in control of the White House and the opposition party in control of Congress?

A number of closely related questions arise: Is Congress an outmoded institution, hobbled by powerful special interests? Because senators and representatives are normally concerned about getting reelected—and because campaigns are increasingly costly—are members too easily influenced by campaign contributions from business or labor? Are too many members of Congress insensitive to ethical standards? How well does Congress represent the voters, and should its members lead or follow public opinion? What is the role of Congress in the American political system as a whole? How well does it perform that role?

CONGRESS: CONFLICT AND CONTROVERSY

Congress is a big tent. And as in a circus, all sorts of balancing acts, distractions, and acrobatics are going on simultaneously under the Big Top. This should not be surprising. Most of the conflicts and pressures in the political system as a whole are reflected in the institution of Congress.

At its best, Congress can enact far-reaching and vital legislation that affects people's lives for the better—as, for example, when it passes laws and appropriations dealing with health care, education, and cancer or AIDS research. It doesn't always act in this fashion, however. Individual lawmakers often succeed in pushing through **pork-barrel legislation,** bills that benefit their home districts, or powerful corporate contributors, with sometimes wasteful or unnecessary public works or other projects.

Congress is a much-criticized institution, often attacked for failure to act, obstructionist rules, low ethical standards, and a variety of other imperfections. As an institution, it is seldom held in high esteem by the voters.

To take one example, for more than 20 years, until the enactment of Medicare in 1965, Congress declined to pass health care legislation for the elderly. Yet the need for such help was clear enough: In March 1965, a few months before passage of Medicare, the median income of Americans aged 65 and over was $1,355 a year.[2] Obviously, on such incomes most older Americans were unable to afford adequate health care in the face of rising medical costs.

Wolf von dem Busche

The Kansas-Nebraska Act of 1854, which opened up the territories to slavery if their residents voted for it, prompted heated—and ultimately violent—debates in Congress between pro- and antislavery legislators:

> Charles Sumner, a scholar and a radical lawyer, senator from Massachusetts as the result of a political deal, had begun to rival William H. Seward as the spokesman of antislavery sentiment. His handsome features and oratorical talent caused him to be compared with [Senator John C.] Calhoun; but he had none of Calhoun's restraint. He was one of those fortunately rare and rarely fortunate persons who are not only thick-skinned themselves but assume that everyone else is. In a turgid oration on 19 May 1856, "The Crime against Kansas," he exhausted the vocabulary of vituperation. The elderly and moderate Senator Butler of South Carolina he described as a Don Quixote whose Dulcinea was "the harlot slavery," and Stephen A. Douglas as Sancho Panza, "the squire of slavery, ready to do its humiliating offices." The tone of this speech was so nasty that it would probably have ended Sumner's political career, had not "Southern chivalry" demanded physical chastisement. Three days after its delivery a South Carolina congressman [Preston Brooks], a distant cousin of Senator Butler, passed up the opportunity to attack Sumner on the steps of the Capitol . . . then, with a stout stick, beat him senseless when sitting helplessly at his desk in the Senate chamber. The assailant was praised by the Southern press and presented by admirers with suitably inscribed sticks. Sumner, badly injured, returned to his seat only at intervals for the next three years; but he was now a hero and martyr in the North.
>
> —Samuel Eliot Morison, *The Oxford History of the American People*

What is more, the public supported such legislation; a Gallup poll in 1962 showed 69 percent in favor of Medicare.[3] By 1940 every West European country had some form of government health insurance. Yet the United States, the richest country in the world, had failed to act. A powerful interest group, the American Medical Association, fought Medicare as "socialized medicine," and for two decades Congress would not be moved.

Nor was Medicare an isolated example. President Kennedy was killed by gunfire in 1963, his brother Robert in 1968, and Martin Luther King, Jr., that same year. While campaigning for the Democratic presidential nomination, Alabama Governor George Wallace was shot and severely wounded in 1972. In 1981, President Reagan was shot and seriously wounded after only a little more than two months in office. The 1990s brought a wave of school shootings, some by very young children. Despite the hue and cry for gun control after each tragedy, Congress, under pressure from the gun lobby, enacted only limited gun control legislation to deal with this major national problem.

In the three decades since Robert Kennedy's assassination, an estimated 733,000 persons have been killed by handguns in the United States.[4] In the nation's cities—including the capital, Washington, D.C.—"drive-by" shootings, often drug related, have become commonplace among inner-city youths. Finally, in 1993 Congress enacted and President Clinton signed the Brady Bill to restrict handgun purchases. In 1994, Congress banned 19 types of semiautomatic assault weapons.

Yet despite bipartisan efforts like these, too often Congress has seemed caught in a "gridlock," unable to act. This has been especially true during periods of divided government, when a Democratic president has faced a Republican-controlled Congress, or vice versa.

GUNS AND VIOLENCE: "A PUBLIC HEALTH EMERGENCY"

WASHINGTON, June 9—Gunshot wounds are the second-leading cause of death among all high-school-age children in the United States, and they are increasing faster than any other cause in that age group among both whites and blacks, according to Federal statistics published today.

One third of high school students say they have easy access to handguns, and six percent of them say they bring handguns to school. About six percent of high school students say they actually own handguns, and among those about one third have fired them at someone.

General owners of handguns give as their chief reason for owning one "protection from crime," but gun owners kill themselves and family members 43 times as often as they shoot down a criminal at home. . . .

The studies overall, said Dr. [George] Lundberg, "paint a grotesque picture of a society steeped in violence, especially by firearms, with such ubiquity and prevalence as to be seemingly accepted as inevitable." It is not inevitable, he said, adding, "Violence in America is a public health emergency."

—*New York Times*, June 10, 1992

MAKING A DIFFERENCE

FOR CAROLYN McCARTHY, "THE ROAD IS ALWAYS LONG"

AP/Wide World

It all started for Carolyn McCarthy on December 7, 1993, when a deranged gunman opened fire with a 9-mm pistol on a Long Island Rail Road commuter train and killed six people, including her husband Dennis, and wounded 19 others, including her son Kevin.

The Long Island Rail Road massacre transformed Carolyn McCarthy into an advocate of gun control. Before it thrust her into the media spotlight, McCarthy was a Republican whose idea of political involvement was volunteering to pick up litter at the local beach. But when her congressman, Dan Frisa, voted in 1996 to repeal an assault weapons ban, she became incensed. When local party officials squelched her inquiries about mounting a primary challenge to Frisa, she gave up her GOP registration and launched a Democratic campaign to unseat him.

She raised more than $1 million and outspent Frisa. Frisa seemed at a loss for an effective response to Mc-Carthy, and in the final days of the campaign, he did a disappearing act, shunning appearances and interviews. McCarthy rolled to victory by 17 per-

centage points, taking 57 percent of the vote. She was reelected in 1998.

Drawing on more than 30 years' experience as a licensed practical nurse, McCarthy has worked on health-related bills. And as one who struggled with learning disabilities as a child, she has spoken for more federal aid for school districts to cope with the costs of educating learning-disabled children.

But make no mistake: Gun control legislation is her raison d'être on Capitol Hill. More than three-fifths of her substantive floor speeches so far in the 106th Congress have been on gun control matters or on issues arising from the Long Island shooting.

She often becomes teary-eyed when discussing gun control, a reminder to all how deeply personal the issue remains. She told the *New York Daily News* that her Long Island colleague, Republican Peter T. King, had urged her to try not to take politics so personally, but she finds that impossible.

Colleagues in the House say she has evolved from being a symbol to being an effective legislator as well. "She has the passion, the moral

authority and the know-how to get things through," says Rep. Rosa DeLauro, Democrat of Connecticut.

Even opponents find her difficult to counter.

"I think Carolyn McCarthy is a very sincere, dedicated advocate for gun control unlike a number of other advocates," says the National Rifle Association's chief lobbyist, Jim Baker.

"The road is always long but I have faith," she says.

—Adapted from the Associated Press; and *Congressional Quarterly 50: 50 Ways to Do the Job of Congress*

But is all of the criticism leveled at Congress entirely fair? Many political scientists who have studied the operation of Congress have concluded that Congress does a fairly good job on the whole. Those who defend Congress argue that it is a generally representative assembly that broadly mirrors the desires of the people. If it fails to act "fast enough" to meet social needs, perhaps it is because the people do not want it to act any faster. And one may ask: How fast is fast enough?

Congress to an extent, at least, reflects the diversity of American society. And often when Congress is divided on an issue and fails to act, it is because the country is divided on that issue. Ralph K. Huitt, a leading student of the congressional process, noted that at one time much criticism of Congress as being "obstructive" came from liberals who complained that presidents such as Truman and Kennedy had encountered obstacles to their liberal programs.[5]

THE VARIED ROLES OF CONGRESS

Congress plays a central and crucial role in the political system by making laws, the general rules that govern American society. It is called upon to deal with all of the major issues confronting the nation—the economy, the tax structure, protection of the environment, and many other problems. No less than the president, Congress, by legislating, makes and implements national policy.

Most of the controversy over how well or how badly Congress performs focuses on this lawmaking function. But Congress plays other important roles. It has several nonlegislative functions: It proposes amendments to the Constitution; it may declare war; it can impeach and try the president or other civil officers of the United States, including judges; it may rule on presidential disability; it regulates the conduct of its members, and can punish, censure, or expel them; and it has power to decide

Copyright © George Tames/NYT Pictures

closely questioned at appropriations hearings, Congress is exercising its supervisory powers. The power of the purse, which the Constitution grants to Congress, carries with it the power to monitor how well the money is spent. For this purpose Congress conducts investigations and holds hearings. These are ostensibly tied to a legislative purpose, but often they serve a broader function of focusing public attention on specific social problems.

For example, in the year 2000 a House committee investigated when it became apparent that some Firestone tires were defective, resulting in tread separation and causing fatal accidents, most involving Ford Explorers. The committee hauled in Firestone and Ford executives to testify, as well as the federal officials responsible for auto safety.

During the early 1950s, Senator Joseph R. McCarthy achieved formidable personal political power by using the Senate's investigatory function to conduct "witch hunts" in search of alleged Communists in government. McCarthy succeeded in creating an atmosphere of fear in which the rights of witnesses were frequently violated. In the 1990s, with the end of the Cold War, documents became available indicating that some Soviet agents had indeed worked inside the government in Washington, but that hardly justified McCarthy's abuses of power.

Congressional investigations also have been used to publicize risks to consumers, the problems of American policy during the war in Vietnam, the tragedy of hunger in the midst of plenty, the political corruption of Watergate, the violation of individual rights by government intelligence agencies, and the conduct of a secret foreign policy in the Iran-contra scandal.

Perhaps even more important than some of these formal roles is the function of Congress in "legitimizing" the outputs of the political system. People are more likely to accept the policy decisions of a political system if major decisions are made by representative institu-

whether a prospective member has been properly elected or should be seated. The House may choose the president in the event of electoral deadlock. The Senate approves or rejects treaties and presidential appointments, and, through the unwritten custom of **senatorial courtesy,** individual senators who belong to the same political party as the president exercise an informal veto power over presidential appointments in their states.

In addition, Congress oversees and supervises the operations of the executive branch and the independent regulatory agencies. For example, when bureaucrats are

"Perhaps the witness would care to reconsider his answer to the last question?"
Copyright © The New Yorker Collection 1979
Stevenson from cartoonbank.com

tions. Congress, therefore, at times plays a key role in the resolution of conflict in American society. As in the case of all political institutions, Congress is subject to external pressures by organized interest groups, unorganized public opinion, the press, and individual constituents. Not every problem can be solved by passing a law. But in responding to social needs with legislation, Congress can at least help to ease the friction points.

In thus managing conflict (or making conflict manageable), Congress helps to integrate various groups and interests within the community by acting, to some extent, as a referee. However, as was noted in Chapter 7, not all groups in a pluralistic society have equal power. And highly organized, well-financed, single-issue lobbies may exercise an influence out of proportion to their number of supporters. Disadvantaged groups—the poor and African Americans, for example—may find it more difficult to influence Congress than does the oil industry. Consequently, in resolving conflict, Congress may still leave many groups unsatisfied.

Yet Congress does provide one of several points of access to the political system for many individuals and groups. The inputs, in the form of demands and supports by segments of the community, are transformed by Congress through the legislative process into policy outputs and binding decisions for all of society.

But Congress is more than just a machine for making decisions. It is also a group of 535 men and women, and who they are is worth examining in some detail, for it may affect what they do.

THE LEGISLATORS

Portrait of a Lawmaker

When the 106th Congress convened in January 1999, the average age of House members was 52 and of senators, 58. In part, the age level of Congress is higher than the average American because of constitutional restrictions: A member of the House must be at least 25 (and a citizen for seven years) and a senator must be at least 30 (and a citizen for nine years). In part, of course, it is explained by the fact that senators and representatives usually do not achieve their office without considerable prior experience in politics or other fields.

More than half the nation's population are women, but only 12.5 percent, or 67 members, of the 106th Congress were women. Nine women served in the Senate: Barbara Boxer and Dianne Feinstein, California Democrats; Susan Collins and Olympia J. Snowe, Maine Republicans; Kay Bailey Hutchison, a Texas Republican; Blanche Lambert Lincoln, an Arkansas Democrat; Mary Landrieu, a Louisiana Democrat; Barbara A. Mikulski, a Maryland Democrat; and Patty Murray, a Washington Democrat.[6]

The 106th Congress had 39 African American members and 20 Hispanic members, all in the House of Representatives. There were five Asians and Pacific Islanders in the House, and two in the Senate. Congress had only one Native American, Senator Ben Nighthorse Campbell, a Colorado Republican.[7]

In many other respects, the socioeconomic makeup of Congress is not representative of the general population. For example, 217 out of 535 members, or about 40 percent of the 106th Congress, were lawyers. In the population as a whole, lawyers compose only 0.7 percent of the labor force. Other major occupational groups of members of Congress were: business or banking, 184; education, 99; farmers and ranchers, 28; journalism, 17; medical profession, 15; and law enforcement, 10. Among the members, 23 had Ph.D. degrees, and six were Rhodes scholars.[8] The 106th Congress also included three professional athletes, two actors/entertainers, one winery owner, and a former CIA officer.[9] As Roger Davidson has suggested, however, representatives "are recruited almost wholly from the same relatively high-status occupations."[10]

Although America is a highly urbanized society, Congress historically has been predominantly Main Street and rural. However, this is much less true today, since many members represent city and suburban districts. Congress is also mostly Protestant; for example, of the members of the 106th Congress, a majority listed their religion as Protestants of various denominations; there were also 150 Catholics, and 34 Jews.[11] If one were to draw a portrait of a typical member of Congress, that person might turn out to be about 54, male, white, Protestant, and a lawyer.

How significant is it that in many ways Congress is not literally a cross section of America? Obviously, Congress does not have to be an exact model of the population in order to represent its constituents. Nor is it entirely surprising that lawyers are overrepresented in a body that makes laws. Yet it is not hard to see how some blacks, other minorities, women, blue-collar workers, the poor, and members of underrepresented socioeconomic groups in general may feel left out of a system that produces a predominantly white, male, Protestant, and upper-middle-class national legislature.

The Life of a Legislator

"It is true that we just don't have much time to legislate around here."[12] The complaint was voiced by a Republican congressman who participated in a series of roundtable discussions about life on Capitol Hill. It could easily have come from almost any one of the 100 senators or 435 members of the House. There are so many demands on members of Congress that lawmakers soon discover they cannot possibly do all that is expected of them. One House member attempted some years ago to list all the aspects of his job. Only a sample is quoted here: "A Congressman has become an expanded messenger boy, an employment agency . . . wardheeler . . . kisser of babies, recoverer of lost luggage . . . contributor to good causes—cornerstone layer . . . bridge dedicator, ship christener."[13]

Although members of Congress differ in how they choose to allocate their time, it is constituents who elect legislators, and most of those elected spend a fair portion of their day trying to take care of their constituents' problems. Many lawmakers bounce back and forth between Washington and their districts like Ping-Pong balls.

As of 2000, members of the House and Senate received salaries of $141,300 a year, plus funds to hire a staff (senators from populous states are permitted to hire more assistants), and certain other allowances for office supplies, telephone calls, and travel, as well as the franking privilege for their official mail. Although the basic salary and benefits are considerable, members of Congress also have substantial expenses—many maintain residences both in Washington and their hometowns, for example.

The mail and e-mail pour in from constituents and must, somehow, be answered. Because the volume of mail is so great, many lawmakers use computers to churn out personalized form letters. Thanks to the franking privilege, members of Congress are entitled to send mail to constituents without charge by putting their frank, or mark, on the envelope. A 1973 law restricts use of the frank to official business and forbids its use to solicit votes or money, or for mass mailings 60 days before an election. Even so, the privilege is widely abused by members who are simply puffing their accomplishments. As one observer put it, "with the coming of the computer, the swift creation of sophisticated mailing lists and laser devices capable of printing individualized letters at the speed of 20,000 lines a minute, there is almost no limit to the letters that members can now generate."[14] In fiscal 1994, members of Congress sent 363 million pieces of franked mail, almost two letters for every adult American, at a cost of $53 million.[15]

Controversy over the franking privilege led to reforms in the 1990s. The major change required members to pay mailing costs as part of their office budgets, "which forces tradeoffs between mail and other expenditures, such as travel or staff."[16] In addition, the new rules limit the amount of mail that members can send out to their constituents.

Computers enable senators and representatives to target specialized groups with their mailings. In addition, almost all members of Congress have e-mail addresses, and their own Web page as well. All of this technology has increased the advantages that incumbents enjoy over their challengers, who do not have free mailing privileges. Staff members and legislators, however, defend their use of the mail as "outreach programs" designed to keep members of Congress in close touch with their constituents.

Not all of the incoming mail is friendly, of course. But few senators and representatives dare to reply to abusive letters as Congressman John Steven McGroarty of California once did. He wrote to a constituent: "One

of the countless drawbacks of being in Congress is that I am compelled to receive impertinent letters from a jackass like you in which you say I promised to have the Sierra Madre mountains reforested and I have been in Congress two months and haven't done it. Will you please take two running jumps and go to hell."[17]

On a typical day, a member of Congress may spend an hour reading mail, making calls, dictating memos, then rush off to a 10 A.M. committee meeting, eat lunch (if there is time), dash to the floor for a vote, and then return to a committee hearing. Perhaps late in the afternoon the member manages to get back to the office, where a group of constituents is waiting. A powerful interest group (a labor union or business association, for example) has invited the member to one or more cocktail receptions, and he or she must dutifully put in an appearance, have a drink, and chew on a rubbery shrimp before getting home for dinner—that is, on the nights not spent at a dinner in some hotel banquet hall. And some nights members must remain on Capitol Hill; for the past several years, the House has held afternoon legislative sessions on Wednesdays that often last into the late evening. Members spend many weekends in their home state or district, flying there to march in the Veterans Day parade or listen to constituents' woes. All of this can be difficult for the family of a representative or senator.

A 1993 congressional survey asked a sample of representatives and senators how they allocated their time. More than two-thirds responded that they spent a "great deal" of their time meeting with constituents in their home districts. Just under half said they spent a "great deal" of time attending committee meetings. A smaller proportion of members said they spent a "great deal" of time speaking with lobbyists and government officials about legislative issues, studying legislation, working with informal groups of colleagues, and attending floor debate or watching it on television.[18]

Although members of Congress do spend much of their time handling problems of constituents, 77 percent of House members questioned in one study listed legislative work as their most time-consuming job; only 16 percent listed "Errand Boy; lawyer for constituents."[19]

"We're like automatons," one senator said. "We spend our time walking in tunnels to go to the floor to vote."[20]

Members of Congress must choose among alternative roles open to them—whether, for example, to concentrate on working for the interests of their districts, on seeking to become party leaders, on running for higher office, on specializing in a committee, or on seizing an issue that may bring them national recognition.

The Image of the Legislator

Congress and its individual members enjoy a rather mixed public image. In recent years, voters have had a generally negative view of Congress, although this was not always the case. Voter attitudes toward Congress

A legislator's work is never done, as seen this series of photographs of Representative Scott McInnis, Republican of Colorado.

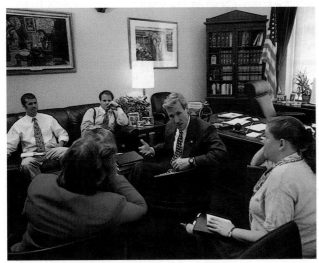

A member of Congress must confer with staff . . .
Copyright © Chris Kleponis/Zuma Press

communicate with the voters . . .
Copyright © Chris Kleponis/Zuma Press

attend committee meetings . . .
Copyright © Chris Kleponis/Zuma Press

participate in community functions . . .
Courtesy office of Scott McInnis

fluctuate markedly. For example, in 1965, after Congress passed landmark Great Society legislation, 64 percent of the public rated its performance "excellent" to "pretty good."[21] (See Table 12-1.) By the year 2000, however, the percentage of those who had confidence in Congress was low; only 24 percent of the public said they had "a great deal" or "quite a lot" of confidence in Congress.[22]

Low public confidence in Congress was reflected in demands to limit the terms of senators and representatives. In 1992, voters in 14 states approved term limits for members of both houses of Congress. However, in 1995 the U.S. Supreme Court ruled that the states could not pass laws limiting the terms of members of Congress.[23] As a result of that decision, only an amendment to the Constitution could impose congressional term limits.

There is a paradox in public attitudes toward the legislative branch: Public opinion of Congress as a whole may be negative, but individual lawmakers are often popular and frequently reelected. For example, 71 percent of those surveyed in one poll were critical of Congress, but only 30 percent were critical of their own representative.[24] And since the Second World War,

TABLE 12-1

Public Attitudes toward Congress, 1965–2000

	Approve	Disapprove	Don't Know
1965	64%	26%	10%
1967	38	55	7
1968	46	46	8
1969	34	54	12
1970	34	54	12
1971	26	63	11
1974	38	54	8
1978	34	63	3
1982	29	54	17
1987	42	49	9
1990	24	68	8
1991	32	53	15
1992	19	78	3
1993	24	65	11
1994	23	70	7
1995	38	53	9
1996	39	49	12
1997	39	52	9
1998	42	52	6
1999	37	56	7
2000	39	52	7

SOURCES: Louis Harris; the *Washington Post;* and the Gallup poll.

through 1996, some 92 percent of House members and 78 percent of senators who sought reelection were victorious.[25] As Richard F. Fenno, Jr., has asked: "How come we love our Congressmen so much more than our Congress?"[26]

Representation: The Legislators and Their Constituents

Should members of Congress lead or follow the opinions of their constituents? The question poses the classic dilemma of legislators, mixing as it does the problems of the proper nature of representation in a democracy with practical considerations of the lawmaker's self-interest and desire for reelection.

One answer was provided by Edmund Burke, the 18th-century British statesman, in his famous speech to the voters of Bristol, who had just sent him to Parliament. As Burke defined the relationship of a representative to his constituents: "Their wishes ought to have great weight with him; their opinion high respect. . . . But his unbiased opinion, his mature judgment, his enlightened conscience, he ought not to sacrifice to you. . . . Your representative owes you, not his industry only, but his judgment."[27] Parliament, Burke contended, was an assembly of one nation, and local interests must bow to the general, national interest.

The Burkean concept of the legislator as **trustee** for the people, the belief that legislators should act according to their conscience, clashes with the concept of the representative as **instructed delegate,** the idea that legislators should automatically mirror the will of the majority of their constituents. (Burke encountered political difficulties with his own constituents; those who cite his independence as a role model for legislators seldom note that six years after his speech, he withdrew as the member from Bristol.)

On the other hand, members of Congress who attempted faithfully to follow opinion in their districts would soon discover that it was very difficult to measure opinion accurately. They would face the practical problem of how to go about it. And they would find that on some issues many voters had no strong opinions.

Copyright © Jake McGuire/Washington Stock Photo

Despite these hurdles, members do try, of course, to gauge the thinking back home. They rely on conversations with friends, party leaders, and journalists in their states or districts; the mail, particularly personal letters; local newspapers; and political polls published in their states. Some lawmakers have turned to professional polling organizations for help. Others have mailed questionnaires to the voters. But such mail "polls" may be taken not so much to gauge constituency thinking as to promote legislators by flattering their constituents with a questionnaire.[28]

Even when opinions can be discerned and measured, the members are aware that a constituency is made up of competing interests and is in actuality several constituencies. Often they could please one group only at the expense of offending another.

A large proportion of House and Senate members, therefore, reject the role solely of trustee or solely of instructed delegate. Instead they try to combine the two by exercising their own judgment and representing constituency views. As Roger Davidson has suggested, "Many congressmen observe that their problem is one of balancing the one role against the other."[29] In interviews with 87 members of the House of Representatives, Davidson found that almost half, by far the largest group of respondents, sought to blend the trustee and delegate conceptions.[30]

Davidson and his colleague Walter J. Oleszek have emphasized the dual nature of Congress. On the one hand, they note, Congress is an institution that makes laws and public policy. But, equally important, it is also a representative body of 535 men and women who must constantly relate to their home districts and constituents in order to be reelected. Thus, "there are really two Congresses."[31]

Sometimes a member of Congress faces the dilemma of local versus national interest. Constituents may feel foreign aid is a waste of money, but the legislator may decide it is in the best interests of the United States and vote accordingly. Often, however, local interests are put first—that is where the voters are. And some members of Congress feel that their first obligation is to the constituency that elected them.

Political scientists have studied the process of how legislators make up their minds on an issue. David R. Mayhew has suggested that the "electoral connection," the relationship between members of Congress and their constituents, profoundly influences congressional behavior. "United States congressmen are interested in getting reelected," Mayhew emphasizes, and that basic fact, he adds, influences the kinds of activities congressmen find it "electorally useful to engage in."[32] And Richard F. Fenno, Jr., has emphasized that the reelection prospects of members of Congress depend greatly on their "home style"—the way they present themselves to constituents back in the district.[33]

Aage R. Clausen has concluded that members of Congress generally vote according to their known policy positions and display substantial stability and continuity in their voting patterns.[34] Donald R. Matthews and James A. Stimson have reported that when members of Congress must cast a vote on a complex issue about which their knowledge is limited, they search "for cues provided by trusted colleagues" who may possess more information about the legislation in question.[35]

To an extent the dilemma faced by the members of Congress may be artificial. One major study of constituent influence discovered that average voters know little about their representative's activities—a finding that contrasted with the view of most members of Congress, who regard their voting record as important to their reelection.[36] Approximately half the voters surveyed in one House election year said they had heard *nothing* about either the incumbent or the opposing candidate. The study, based on interviews with both members of Congress and voters, also indicated that, although legislators tend to think that the views of their constituents match their own, there is often a gap between the actual opinions of constituents and the member's perception of their views.[37]

THE HOUSE

Although Congress is one branch of the federal government, the House and Senate are distinct institutions, each with its own rules and traditions and each jealous of its own powers and prerogatives. (See Table 12-2.)

■ TABLE 12-2	
Major Differences between the House and Senate	

House	Senate
Larger (435 members)	Smaller (100 members)
Shorter term of office (2 years)	Longer term of office (6 years)
Less flexible rules	More flexible rules
Narrower constituency	Broader, more varied constituency
Policy specialists	Policy generalists
Power less evenly distributed	Power more evenly distributed
Less prestige	More prestige
More expeditious in floor debate	Less expeditious in floor debate
Less reliance on staff	More reliance on staff
Less press and media coverage	More press and media coverage
More partisan	Less partisan

SOURCE: Adapted from Walter J. Oleszek, *Congressional Procedures and the Policy Process*, 4th ed. (Washington, D.C.: CQ Press, 1996), p. 26.

One basic difference, of course, was established by the Constitution, which provided two-year terms for members of the House and staggered six-year terms for senators. The result is that all members of the House, but only one-third of the Senate, must face the voters every other year.

Online for more information about the U.S. House of Representatives, see: www.house.gov

Because the House has 435 members compared to 100 in the Senate, the House is a more formal institution with stricter rules and procedures. For example, the Senate permits unlimited debate most of the time, but representatives in the House may be limited to speaking for five minutes or less during debate.

And because there are so many representatives, they generally enjoy less prestige than senators. At Washington dinner parties where protocol is observed, House members sit below the salt, ranking three places down the table from their Senate colleagues. (House members are outranked not only by senators, but also by governors and former vice presidents.[38]) In the television age, some senators, especially those who are presidential aspirants, have become celebrities, instantly recognizable to the spectators in the galleries. By contrast, visitors in the House galleries find it difficult to pick out their own representative, let alone any other.

A survey in the year 2000 reported that less than half of Americans—just 47 percent—could name their representative in Congress.[39] While the figure is somewhat

Copyright © Dennis Brack/Black Star

low, it does not give the whole picture. Although many voters cannot *remember* the name of their own representative, a much higher percentage can *recognize* the name from those on a list. In a selected group of congressional districts, "virtually all voters recognized the name of the incumbent when they heard it," and "most had a positive or negative response."[40]

Despite its size, the House has achieved a stability of tenure and a role never envisioned by the Founding Fathers. The men who framed the Constitution distrusted unchecked popular rule, and provided an indirectly elected Senate to restrain the more egalitarian House of Representatives (the Seventeenth Amendment in 1913 provided for the direct election of the Senate). As Gouverneur Morris put it: "The second branch [the Senate] ought to be a check on the first [the House]. . . . The first branch, originating from the people, will ever be subject to precipitancy, changeability, and excess. . . . The second branch ought to be composed of men of great and established property—an aristocracy. . . . Such an aristocratic body will keep down the turbulency of democracy."[41]

Ironically, the House and Senate have on some issues exchanged places in terms of these expectations of the framers. One reason is that House seats are safer. A commonly cited standard for a "safe" congressional district is one in which the winner receives 55 percent of the vote or more. Less than that is considered "marginal." And House elections have shown a pattern of what David Mayhew has called "vanishing marginals."[42] That is, the percentage of congressional districts that are unsafe and marginal is relatively low.

Morris P. Fiorina has suggested one possible explanation for these "vanishing marginals." He contends that "the Washington System" (discussed in Chapter 14) may be responsible. Under it, members of Congress create new bureaucracies in the executive branch and then gain credit by helping constituents deal with the complex rules issued by the new agencies. Representatives from marginal districts, Fiorina contends, have increasingly found it possible to base their reelection on such casework for constituents and on "procuring the pork."[43]

Senate seats are less safe; often a third of those running are elected with less than 55 percent of the vote. Since Senate races often tend to be close, there is a greater possibility of dramatic shifts in party strength in the Senate. Because members of the House are more likely to come from safe districts than their colleagues in the Senate, the House has sometimes been less responsive than the Senate to pressures for change in the status quo. Senators have statewide constituencies that are frequently dominated by urban areas with powerful labor and minority-group vote blocs; as a result, the Senate at times has proved to be the more "liberal" branch of Congress.[44] When the Republicans captured both houses of Congress in 1994, for example, the House, with its 73 freshman Republicans, was decidedly the more strongly conservative branch.

In an angry election year, when the worst name a politician can be called is "incumbent," Rep. Steny H. Hoyer (D-Md.) has found something good about that awful condition. In fact, Hoyer has come up with millions of good things.

There's the $10 million Hoyer wedged into the federal budget for a new aircraft testing facility at Patuxent River Naval Air Station. There's the $5 million for research on airplane ejection seats at Indian Head Naval Surface Warfare Center. And there's the $2 million for a new day-care center there.

Those projects have three things in common. They are in southern Maryland, three largely rural counties that the state legislature placed in Hoyer's district earlier this year. They are included in the House's defense appropriations bill at least in part because of Hoyer's lobbying. And they offer solid proof that, even at a time when voters seem eager to throw the bums out, being one of the bums ain't all bad.

Hoyer, the House's fourth-ranking Democrat and a senior member of the Appropriations Committee, is dramatically demonstrating to his new constituents the art of pork-barrel politics. He unabashedly declares that one man's pork is another man's national priority.

"'Pork' is an epithet that applies to projects that are not in one's district," Hoyer says. "It's politics. I'm trying to represent my area as effectively as I can. And I plead guilty to representing my area very effectively."

—*Washington Post*, July 5, 1992

Despite the relative safety of House seats, there has been a dramatic turnover in the membership of the House over the past decade. For example, a majority of the members of the 104th Congress, which convened in January 1995, had been elected in the 1990s.[45] Some members, tired of constituent pressures and election campaigns every two years, have quit. Others, of course, have been defeated.

Power in the House: The Leadership

In the House, the **speaker** is the presiding officer and the most powerful member. The position of speaker is provided for in the Constitution ("The House of Representatives shall chuse their Speaker and other Officers").

The speaker has a number of official powers: to preside over the House, to recognize or ignore members who wish to speak, to appoint the chair and his party's members of the Rules Committee, to appoint members of special or select committees that conduct special investigations, to refer bills to one or more committees, and to exercise other procedural controls.

Much of the speaker's real power, however, stems from the combination of these formal duties with that of political leader of the majority party in the House. Technically, the speaker is elected by the House, with each party offering a candidate. In practice, the speaker is chosen at the start of each Congress by a caucus, or meeting, of the majority party. Because in the past, at least, the formal voting in the House has been strictly along party lines, the majority party's candidate for speaker has automatically won.

Historically, the speaker exercised great power until 1910, when the rules were revised to strip much of the speaker's formal power, including the right to appoint members to committees of the House. But a speaker with a strong personality and great legislative skill can still exert broad influence in the House, as Newt Gingrich did briefly, and as Sam Rayburn of Texas demonstrated when he held that post for 17 of the 21 years between 1940 and 1961. Over bourbon and branch water in a small room in the Capitol, Rayburn and his intimates would plan strategy for the House and swap political stories in an informal institution known as the "Board of Education."[46] Today, the speaker remains a key figure, exercising more formal powers than at any time since 1910.

For 10 years, until he retired in 1987, Thomas P. "Tip" O'Neill, Jr., of Massachusetts reigned as speaker, and he made a considerable impact on both Congress and the nation. As a member of the House, he had succeeded John F. Kennedy. He became majority leader in 1972 and speaker in 1977. O'Neill, a huge barrel-chested man with a thatch of shaggy white hair and a booming, easy laugh, proved to be a colorful speaker. He looked exactly like what he was—an old-time Irish politician from Boston. But he was more than that. Early in his career as a House leader, he was called upon to take actions of historic importance for the nation. As majority leader, O'Neill played a key role in the decision to hold the impeachment hearings that became an important factor in Richard M. Nixon's decision to resign as president in 1974.

O'Neill's successor was Representative Jim Wright, a Texas Democrat from Fort Worth. He was able to guide a good deal of legislation through Congress, but was controversial from the start. A pugnacious, often quick-tempered man, he did not hesitate to plunge into turbulent political waters. By 1988, Wright found himself under serious criticism over a book that earned him $55,000 in royalties and had been published by a Texas supporter who received $250,000 from the Wright election campaign committee. As criticism of Wright mounted, the House Ethics Committee voted to investigate the speaker. Wright resigned in 1989 after the committee charged him with violating House rules.

The House then chose Representative Thomas S. Foley, a liberal Democrat from Spokane, Washington, as the new speaker. Six-foot-four, white-haired and distinguished-looking, Foley was a mild-mannered congressional veteran with a low-key personality.

Then, following the election of 1994, Newt Gingrich of Georgia became the Republican speaker of the House. Gray-haired, stocky, and combative, Gingrich became almost as familiar to the public as the president. It was Gingrich who had brought the ethics charges against Jim Wright.

Ironically, Gingrich himself became a subject of controversy over his own book deal, for which he had agreed to accept a $4.5 million advance from the publisher. Because of criticism that he was exploiting his position as speaker, Gingrich backed down and instead accepted normal royalties on the book's sales. Gingrich was also criticized for his actions as head of GOPAC, the political action committee he had headed that was a powerful force in the Republican congressional triumph in 1994. It was in the wake of these charges that Gingrich was investigated by the House Ethics committee and by an outside counsel. The committee concluded that Gingrich had violated federal tax law and misled the committee, which led to his reprimand and fine by the full House.

Aggressive and quick to attack his opponents, Gingrich was unpopular with the public. When he protested in a fit of pique that he had been snubbed by the president when traveling on Air Force One, cartoonists and critics had a field day with what seemed to many to be a trivial complaint.

To an extent greater than any recent modern speaker, Gingrich "took command of the House as few leaders before him. Not only did he set the nation's agenda when he assumed the speakership, functioning as the House's chief executive officer . . . he bypassed the custom of seniority to handpick loyalists to chair committees crucial to the success of the Republican agenda."[47]

After Gingrich resigned as speaker and left Congress, the House chose Dennis Hastert, a six-term conservative Republican from rural Illinois to succeed him. Hastert's quiet style was just the opposite of Gingrich's bombast.

The speaker has two chief assistants, the majority leader and the majority whip, both elected by the party caucus. The majority leader is the party's floor leader and a key strategist. Together with the speaker and the members of the House Rules Committee, the majority leader schedules debate and negotiates with committee chairs and party members on procedural matters. The majority **whip,** along with a number of deputy whips, is responsible for rounding up party members for important votes and counting noses. (The term "whip" comes from "whipper-in," the person assigned in English fox hunts to keep the hounds from straying.) In 2000, for example, the majority whip was Tom DeLay, a Texas

Republican from Houston, who was so effective in his job that he earned the nickname "The Hammer." The minority party also elects a minority leader, a minority whip, and deputy whips. Rep. Richard A. Gephardt, a Democrat from Missouri first elected to Congress in 1976, became majority leader in 1989 and minority leader after 1994 when the Republicans gained control of the House. In those posts, he became a nationally known spokesperson for his party.

The Rules Committee

The House Committee on Rules exercises considerable control over what bills are brought to the floor. Most major legislation cannot be debated without a special rule from the Rules Committee that limits the time for floor debate and the extent to which a bill may be amended. The whole House must adopt each special rule before it goes into effect.[48]

In 1961 President Kennedy and Speaker Sam Rayburn barely won a fight to enlarge the House Rules Committee and thus curb the power of its conservative chairman. Democrats at that time controlled the House, but a coalition of southern Democrats and Republicans frequently succeeded in blocking passage of liberal legislation. In the 1961 change, the committee's size was increased, and the new members were chosen for their support of the administration's position on controversial bills.[49] By the 1970s, the Rules Committee was no longer a bottleneck to legislation. The most important change made during the early 1970s empowered the speaker of the House to nominate all majority-party members of the Rules Committee. Since then, as a result, the committee has operated as an arm of the leadership of the political party in control of the House.

The Legislative Labyrinth: The House in Action

The basic power structure of the House, then, consists of the speaker, the floor leaders and whips of the two major parties, the Rules Committee, and the chairs of the 19 standing committees. How these individuals and committees interact powerfully affects the fate of legislation. But the business of making laws is also governed by a complicated, even Byzantine, set of rules and procedures. Although most citizens are not familiar with them, these procedures can affect policy outcomes. Whether a bill is steered through the legislative labyrinth or gets lost along the way often depends on how the rules and procedures are applied.

About 5 percent of all bills and joint resolutions introduced in Congress become public law. In the 104th Congress (1995–1997), for example, 6,808 public bills and joint resolutions were introduced but only 333 became public law.[50]

After a bill is introduced by a House member, it is referred to a committee by the speaker. Often the choice is limited by the jurisdictions of the standing committees, but when jurisdictions overlap or when new kinds of legislation are introduced, the speaker may have considerable discretion in deciding where to assign a bill.

Only about 16 percent of bills get out of committee in the House. The committee chair may assign the measure to one of the 87 subcommittees of the standing committees. If the bill is reported out of committee, it is placed on one of five calendars, or lists of business eligible for House floor consideration. The various House calendars and the kinds of bills referred to them are shown in Table 12-3.

On two days a week any bill may be debated under a procedure called "suspension of the rules." About half of the bills passed by the House are enacted under this procedure; only 40 minutes of debate is permitted, with no floor amendments, and a two-thirds vote is required for passage. Some noncontroversial bills in the House are passed by unanimous consent.

A quorum consisting of a majority of the House, 218 members, is required for general debate. When the House is considering legislation that deals with taxes and spending, however, it sits as a **Committee of the Whole,**

■ **TABLE 12-3**

Regulating Legislative Traffic:
The House Calendars

Union

Bills that directly or indirectly appropriate money or raise revenue are placed on the Union Calendar.

House

Bills that do not appropriate money or raise revenue go on the House Calendar. Most bills go either to the Union Calendar or House Calendar.

Private

Bills that affect specific individuals and deal with private matters, such as claims against the government, immigration, or land titles, are placed on the Private Calendar and are called on the first and, with the speaker's approval, third Tuesdays of each month.

Corrections*

Noncontroversial bills that have been favorably reported by committees, but which may require changes, may be placed by the speaker on the Corrections Calendar and debated on the second and fourth Tuesdays of each month.

Discharge

Motions to force a bill out of committee are placed on the Discharge Calendar if they receive the necessary 218 signatures from House members. The procedure is rarely successful.

*The Corrections Calendar was created in 1995 after the Republicans won control of the House. It replaced the Consent Calendar, which had seldom been used in recent years.

---

a device that allows the House to conduct its business with fewer restrictions on debate and a quorum of only 100 members.

Until 1971, one kind of vote in the Committee of the Whole allowed members to file down the aisle to be counted, so that their constituents usually had no way of knowing how their representative had voted. Growing pressures for reform led the House in 1970 to provide—if enough representatives demand them—**recorded votes,** in which the position of each member is noted and published in the *Congressional Record.* Under this procedure, members vote electronically. Sometimes the House uses a voice vote, in which members shout "aye" or "no" and the chair decides the result. Or a member may demand a division or standing vote, in which members for or against a bill stand up for a head count.

The system of electronic voting was installed in the House in 1973. Under it, when an electronic vote is taken, members insert a plastic identification card in one of 44 voting stations on the floor and press one of three buttons. If the member votes "yes," a green light appears on a display board over the speaker's head; for "no," a red light appears, and for "present," an amber light. The use of electronic voting has greatly reduced the time needed for recorded votes; under the old system, the clerk called the roll and each member present had to answer by name. The changes in voting procedure in the Committee of the Whole and the inauguration of electronic voting in the House itself have greatly increased the number of on-the-record votes by representatives.

Supporters or opponents of a bill sometimes request recorded votes as a delaying tactic to gain time to round up their forces. Often, however, such votes are demanded to place members on the spot; in a roll-call vote each representative's position must become a matter of public record. Some interest groups regularly rate the records of members on the basis of their roll-call votes. Constituents may not pay much attention to how representatives vote, but opponents in an election campaign may use legislators' roll-call votes on key issues against them.

When debate is concluded in the Committee of the Whole, the House may vote on final passage. On rare occasions, the House may vote instead to send the bill back to its committee of origin (thereby killing it permanently), or it may send the bill back to the committee with instructions to make further changes in the bill (thereby delaying it temporarily).

Televising Congress

In March 1979, amid much controversy, the House began live television and radio broadcasts of floor debate. The Senate permitted televising of its deliberations starting in 1986. The broadcasts from both chambers are carried gavel-to-gavel over the nonprofit C-SPAN network by 6,500 cable television systems in all 50 states, with a potential audience of 77 million households as of the year

2000.* In addition, excerpts are sometimes carried by local stations and the major networks.

 for more information about the C-SPAN network, see: www.cspan.org

When the television coverage began, there were dire predictions that publicity-seeking members would engage in ham acting and long-winded oratory. Although some members did play to the cameras, a majority of House members reported they were satisfied with the results. Nevertheless, the opportunity to posture for audiences at home has lengthened House sessions. "There are an awful lot of added speeches that we wouldn't have without television," Speaker O'Neill once complained.[51]

Not all members of the public have been impressed by watching Congress on television. "The results of government in action are disgusting enough without having to have it aired," a woman in Winston-Salem, North Carolina, wrote to the House. But a man in Chelsea, Massachusetts, wrote: "This has given me much more knowledge of the manner in which the laws of this great nation are devised, debated, amended and finally resolved."[52]

Many viewers do not know, however, that television in the House operates under restrictions. The cameras are operated by employees of the House, not by the cable networks. And under the rules set by the speaker, the cameras are not permitted to pan around the floor and show members yawning, sleeping, or fidgeting. Most of the time, during regular floor debate, the cameras must focus on the person speaking. However, occasionally the reaction of a member to the debate is shown. The cameras also show members when they file into the chamber and vote.

The Senate, after resisting television for many years, finally voted in 1986 to permit the deliberations on the Senate floor to be televised. Since the 1950s, Senate committee meetings, particularly important investigations that attracted widespread public interest, have often been televised.

THE SENATE

The Senate may not be "the most exclusive club in the world" nor a "rich man's club," although it has been called both. But it certainly has both the atmosphere and appearance of a club. Its membership is relatively small; its quarters are ornate and gilded; its ways are slow. In 2000, there were 30 millionaires in the Senate.[53] And with good reason; the growing costs of Senate campaigns, and legal limits on contributions by individuals, means that rich candidates and incumbents may spend

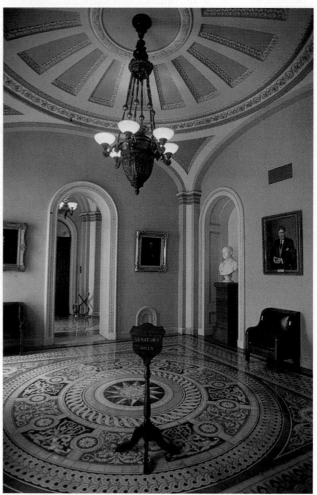

Copyright © Paul Conklin

millions of dollars of their personal fortunes to finance their own campaigns.

 for more information about the U.S. Senate, see: www.senate.gov

But the folkways and customs of the Senate have changed markedly since the days, four decades ago, when William S. White, then Senate correspondent of the *New York Times*, wrote of the "Inner Club" run by southerners.[54] Around the same period, Donald Matthews, a political scientist, described the Senate's "unwritten rules of the game, its norms of conduct." The freshman senator, Matthews wrote, was expected to serve a silent apprenticeship, to be one of the Senate "work horses" rather than one of the "show horses," to develop a legislative specialty, pay homage to the institution, and observe its folkways.[55] At the time, these included the elaborate courtesy with which senators, even bitter enemies, customarily addressed each other on the floor.

A decade later Nelson W. Polsby argued that "the role of the Senate in the political system has changed over the last 20 years," decreasing the importance of Senate norms. He contended that television, with its ability to publicize individual senators, had made the

---

*Data provided by C-SPAN, online at <www.cspan.org/about/company/>. C-SPAN carries proceedings of the House and presidential campaigns. A second cable network, C-SPAN2, televises Senate proceedings. Both C-SPAN channels also carry public affairs programming.

Senate "an incubator of presidential hopefuls" and eroded the significance of its rules of behavior.[56] And Ralph K. Huitt observed that the Senate has always had a place for "mavericks" and "independents."[57]

Today, newcomers to the Senate often speak up and speak out, sometimes gaining national recognition very rapidly. Many of the old ways have faded. As political scientist Barbara Sinclair has noted, senators now seek "broad involvement across multiple issues and arenas."[58] She adds: "In the contemporary Senate, freshmen are not expected to remain on the sidelines, nor even to be restrained in their participation in committee or on the floor."[59] Thus, a "new Senate style" has emerged, replacing the old behavior.[60] Although courtesy is still observed in floor debate, "it seems to be breached more often than it used to be."[61] For example, during one Senate debate, Senator Lowell Weicker of Connecticut suggested that his Republican colleague, John Heinz of Pennsylvania, was "an idiot."[62] It is not unknown for senators to yell at each other on the Senate floor; the sedate solons of yesteryear might not recognize the old club today.

Political scientists Robert L. Peabody, Norman J. Ornstein, and David W. Rohde have also analyzed the decline of folkways and norms in the Senate. The emergence of the Senate as "a major breeding ground for presidential candidates," they suggest, has affected the behavior of "a wider circle of senators." For example, when Senator John F. Kennedy set his sights on the presidency, he spoke out on a variety of subjects "beyond the jurisdictions of his original committee assignments." Kennedy was contributing to the decline of the silent apprenticeship as a Senate norm. Soon other senators with presidential ambitions began to speak out, adding to "the breakdown of apprenticeship."[63]

As more senators run for president, they can be expected to ignore the norm of "legislative work," the authors argue. And the tradition that senators should specialize in certain subjects has been weakened by the need for presidential contenders to be generalists, with a wide knowledge of public policy questions.[64]

Another reason that senators today are more vocal even as newcomers is that they have become much more vulnerable to electoral challenges. In a sense, they must begin working for reelection from day one. To the public, "senators are right out front as visible targets for the expression of voter dissatisfaction."[65]

THE SENATE: ARM-WAVING AND SCREAMING MATCHES

Long viewed as the more dignified and cautious body of Congress, the Senate now finds itself mired in partisan, sand-lot warfare more typical of the House of Representatives.

The past few weeks in the Senate have been marked by an arm-waving screaming match between the Republican and Democratic leaders and a series of threats and counter-threats over spending bills that must be passed before the November election. The Senate has passed only a handful of significant bills this year, leaving things like increasing the minimum wage and cracking down on juvenile crime still in limbo. . . .

The vitriol and partisanship between the two parties has reached new heights, casting a shadow on the Senate's reputation, or at least its self-image, for careful deliberation and effectiveness.

Republicans say that the Democrats, rather than pushing for consensus, are behaving more like their rowdy counterparts in the House. All too often, Republicans argue, Democrats cavalierly slow things on the floor by attaching irrelevant amendments to important bills and by threatening filibusters so they can portray the Republicans as "do-nothing" senators in an election year.

"The last couple of weeks before we went out has been the most obstructionist I've ever seen them," said Senator Trent Lott of Mississippi, the majority leader, referring to Democratic senators. "I don't think it's in anybody's best interest for the Senate to be balled up with obstructionism on either side."

For their part, Democrats say the Republicans have effectively gagged them and stifled thorough, deliberative discussion. They want Mr. Lott to loosen his hold and permit the Democrats to debate such issues as managed health care, gun control and the minimum wage. Until that happens, they say, they will continue to engage in parliamentary tactics.

Senator Tom Daschle of South Dakota, the Democratic leader, lamented Mr. Lott's style of running the Senate, arguing that denying the minority the chance to vote on its agenda has hurt the overall institution.

"This has been probably the most damaging to the Senate institutionally that I can recall," Mr. Daschle said today, referring to Mr. Lott's method of limiting debate and refusing amendments. "If this practice continues, there really won't be any difference in how the Senate and House function." . . .

"We have always been free to talk, always free to offer amendments," said Senator Daniel Patrick Moynihan, Democrat of New York.

But Mr. Moynihan said he worried that those freedoms might vanish, with the imposition of time limits and other restrictions like those in the House.

"The Senate," he said, "was never meant to be that."

—*New York Times*, June 7, 2000

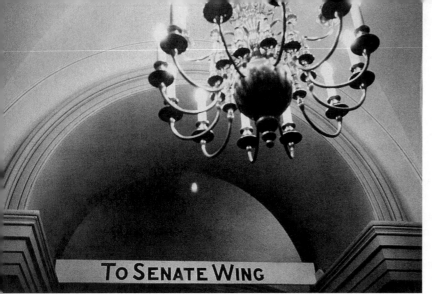

Wolf von dem Busche

Power in the Senate: The Leadership

Just as the speaker is elected by the House, the Senate elects a President Pro Tempore, who occasionally presides in the absence of the vice president. Although the office is provided for in the Constitution, it has little formal power.

The closest parallel to the speaker is the Senate majority leader, who is the most powerful elected leader of the Senate—although, as in most political offices, a great deal depends on the person and political circumstances. Lyndon Johnson, the Democratic Senate leader from 1953 to 1960, was widely regarded as an extraordinarily skillful and powerful floor leader. Johnson's power to persuade was formidable. A big man, he towered over most other senators as, on occasion, he subjected them to "The Treatment"—a prolonged exercise in face-to-face persuasion that combined elements of a police "third degree" with Johnson's flair for dramatic acting.

In addition to his powerful personality, Johnson had several tangible tools at his disposal. He could assist a senator in getting legislation passed; he controlled committee assignments; and, above all, he built an intelligence system known as "the Johnson Network." At its heart was Bobby Baker, "a country boy from Pickens, South Carolina, who had come to Washington as a teenaged Senate page" and whom Johnson made his top assistant.* Baker knew how to count noses; because Johnson was well informed of sentiment in the Senate, he was able to anticipate the outcome of close votes. The effect was cumulative, for after a while "it was taken for granted that 'Lyndon's got the votes.'"[66]

*Rowland Evans and Robert Novak, *Lyndon B. Johnson: The Exercise of Power* (New York: New American Library, 1966), pp. 68, 99. When it later developed that Bobby Baker had used his Senate position to amass a personal fortune, the scandal became an issue in the 1964 presidential election campaign and embarrassed Lyndon Johnson, who by then was president. Baker was convicted in 1967 of income tax evasion, theft, and conspiracy to defraud the federal government and served sixteen months in prison.

Through his network, Johnson came to know the strengths and weaknesses of each senator, and he used that knowledge to further his goals; his was a highly personal leadership.

In contrast, Johnson's successor as majority leader, soft-spoken Mike Mansfield of Montana, did not attempt to exercise power in the way that Johnson had. When Mansfield was accused of not providing sufficient leadership for the Senate, he declared: "I am neither a circus ringmaster, the master of ceremonies of a Senate nightclub, a tamer of Senate lions, or a wheeler and dealer."[67] When Mansfield retired from the Senate in January 1977, Robert C. Byrd of West Virginia was elected the majority leader.

Byrd, who rose from rural poverty in the hills of West Virginia, played country music on his fiddle for the voters and even released a record album. Extremely hardworking, Byrd, when he served as majority leader, concentrated more on making the Senate work than on influencing legislation ideologically.[68]

Senator George J. Mitchell of Maine succeeded Byrd in 1988. He grew up in Waterville, Maine, in modest circumstances; his father was a janitor at Colby College and his mother was a Lebanese immigrant. As majority leader, Mitchell projected an image of calm and confidence.

Before Bob Dole of Kansas left the Senate in 1996 to campaign for the presidency, he served as the Republican majority leader. He was defeated that year by President Clinton, who was reelected to a second term.

When George W. Bush, a Republican, was inaugurated in 2001, he could look forward to working with a

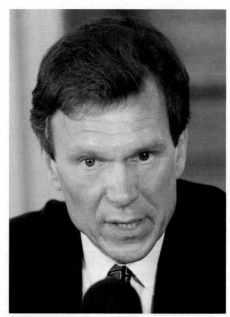

Tom Daschle, Democrat of South Dakota, became the Senate minority leader after the 2002 election.
AP/Wide World

Trent Lott, Republican of Mississippi, became the Senate majority leader.
Copyright © Ficara/Sygma

Republican Congress. His party controlled the House, and although the Senate was divided 50–50, Republicans effectively were in control, because in case of a deadlock, Vice President Dick Cheney, a Republican, would cast the tie-breaking vote.

But after only four months, in a dramatic move, Senator James M. Jeffords of Vermont, a moderate, left the Republican party and became an independent. That gave control of the Senate to the Democrats by a razor-thin margin, 50–49. Overnight, the Senate minority leader, Thomas A. Daschle of South Dakota, found himself the majority leader. Although he operated in a low-key style, he became much more visible on television and was soon seen as a potential Democratic presidential candidate in 2004. The sudden shift in the Senate gave Democrats the chairs of all the committees and subcommittees and control of the legislative agenda. Trent Lott of Mississippi, who had been the majority leader until Jeffords' move, became the Senate minority leader. Lott became majority leader again after the GOP regained control of the Senate in 2002.

The Senate majority and minority leaders represent their party in the Senate. But they may not represent majority sentiment in their party nationally.

The Senate in Action

Unlike the House, with its complex procedures, calendars, and tight restrictions on debate, the Senate is more informal and less bound by rules. In part this is because the Senate is smaller than the House.

Senate bills appear on only one legislative calendar, and they are usually called up by unanimous consent. Since a single senator may object to this procedure, the majority leader, in conducting floor business, consults with the minority leader across the aisle on most major matters to avoid objections. A separate, second Senate calendar is used to schedule debate on treaties and nominations.

The Senate does not have electronic voting as the House does; instead, the clerk calls the roll, reading out the name of each senator. The yes or no vote of each member is checked off by the clerk on a printed form and the tally is announced.

The Filibuster

Most of the time, the Senate allows unlimited debate. Because of this, a single senator, or a group of senators, may stage a **filibuster** to talk a bill to death.* Usually, the filibuster is employed to defeat a bill by tying up the Senate so long that the measure will never come to a vote. But a number of factors, including the 1975 rule change making it easier to cut off debate, have combined to diminish the importance of the filibuster as a weapon to block legislation.

The traditional filibuster, of the kind staged by the actor James Stewart in the classic 1939 movie *Mr. Smith Goes to Washington,* is rarely seen now. Rather, the mere threat of a filibuster, or "extended debate," may be enough to bring about compromise on a bill. Or senators may invoke various points of order and other procedural rules to tie up the Senate without actually making a long speech.

Today, senators more often can delay or even kill floor action on legislation or other Senate matters simply by asking their party leaders not to schedule them—an informal tactic known as a **hold.** This maneuver can effectively stall action on bills or a nomination for an ambassador or other administration official whose appointment requires senate confirmation. Until 1999, when the rules were changed, senators could place holds on legislation or nominations in secret; since that year, they must identify themselves.

To conduct an old-style filibuster, all that senators must do is remain on their feet and keep talking. For the first three hours, their comments must relate to the subject of the debate, but after that, they may, if they wish, read the telephone book. The record for such marathon performances by a single senator was set by Senator Strom Thurmond of South Carolina, who spoke against the Civil Rights Act of 1957 for 24 hours and 18 minutes.

Although filibusters have often been used by southern conservatives, northerners and liberals have used them, too. For example, northern liberals filibustered in the early 1970s against funds for the Vietnam War and extension of the military draft.

---

*The word "filibuster" originally meant a privateer or pirate, and its origin in American politics is not certain. See William Safire, *Safire's New Political Dictionary* (New York: Random House, 1993), p. 245.

"Listen, pal! I didn't spend seven million bucks to get here so I could yield the floor to you."

NIGHT OF THE FILIBUSTER

For nine days in September 1977, Senators James Abourezk of South Dakota and Howard M. Metzenbaum of Ohio staged a filibuster against a gas deregulation bill that was part of President Carter's energy package. The filibuster included an all-night session, described in this newspaper account:

The usually decorous Senate chamber was not very dignified early Wednesday morning as senators jumped up from folding cots every half hour or so to answer yet another roll-call vote demanded by Metzenbaum and Abourezk.

Under normal circumstances, senators wear ties and jackets on the Senate floor, but Wednesday some removed their ties and left their shirt-tails hanging out over their trousers. Sen. Ernest F. Hollings (D-S.C.) showed up in a jogging costume.

Shoeless, Sen. Barry Goldwater (R-Ariz.) padded onto the floor in his socks and asked, "Isn't it time to go home?"

Sen. Robert J. Dole (R-Kan.) said the Senate was looking ridiculous and quoted a tourist who had remarked to him Wednesday, "I'm so happy the Senate is open because the zoo is closed."

—*Los Angeles Times,* September 29, 1977

A group filibuster may go on for many days or even months. When one senator tires, he or she merely "yields" to a fresher colleague, who takes over. To counter these tactics, the Senate may meet round-the-clock in the hope of wearing down the filibusterers. But the senators conducting the filibuster may retaliate by suggesting the absence of a quorum (51 senators). Such a demand voiced at, say, 4 A.M. is inconvenient for other senators. So, senators attempting to break the filibuster set up cots in the halls and straggle in to answer the roll; then they try to go back to sleep.

Today, however, more often than not, the Senate permits "gentleman's filibusters" that run from 9 A.M. to 5 P.M. and allow senators to get home in time for dinner. This was not always the case. Donald A. Ritchie, the associate historian of the Senate, recalled the days when senators such as Huey Long, the Louisiana Democrat, would take the floor for marathon filibusters. "He used to read recipes for gumbo and for pot liquor and greens, the Bible and Shakespeare," Ritchie said.[69]

Under Rule XXII of the Senate, a filibuster may be ended if three-fifths of the entire Senate (60 members) vote for **cloture.*** Cloture is difficult to impose. From 1919 through 1998, it was voted only 169 times in 490 attempts.[70] Furthermore, even when cloture is invoked

---

*To cut off debate on changes in Senate rules, a vote of two-thirds of the senators present is still required.

to cut off debate, senators may stage a post-cloture fili-buster until the final vote. Since 1986, when the Senate allowed its debates to be televised, post-cloture fili-busters have been limited to 30 hours.

One of the most dramatic—some thought comic—episodes surrounding a filibuster took place early in 1988, when Senate Republicans tried to block a Demo-cratic bill to limit the cost of Senate campaigns. Senator Robert C. Byrd invoked a rule to compel the attendance of senators in the chamber. He ordered the sergeant-at-arms to arrest any senators who could be found and bring them to the floor. The sergeant-at-arms and a posse of Capitol police began scouring the buildings: "They spotted Sen. Steven D. Symms (R-Idaho), but he fled before they could apprehend him."[71] Then the police "forced their way into the office of Sen. Bob Packwood (R-Ore.), arrested him and car-ried him feet-first into the Senate chamber in a flam-boyant climax to a bitter all-night filibuster."[72] Angry Republicans accused the Democrats of turning the Senate into a "banana republic." The Democrats failed in their effort to invoke cloture to end the filibuster, and the bill was set aside.

THE PARTY MACHINERY

Senate and House Republicans and Democrats are organized along party lines for both political and leg-islative purposes. As noted earlier, in the House and Senate, the leader of each party is assisted by a whip, and several deputy whips, to round up members for key votes.

In addition, the party conference (or caucus, in the case of House Democrats) consists of all the members of that party in each branch of Congress. The party con-ferences elect leaders, who assume the title of majority or minority leader, depending on which party controls the House and Senate.

In addition, the policy committees of each party provide a forum for discussion of party positions on legislative issues. In both the House and Senate, there is active competition among members for assignment to choice committees. In the House, the Republicans and Democrats each have a Steering Committee that makes committee assignments. In the Senate, this task is per-formed by the Republican Committee on Committees and for the Democrats by the Steering and Coordination Committee.

Finally, the major parties in both houses have con-gressional campaign committees that funnel contribu-tions and other assistance to their party's candidates for Congress.

THE COMMITTEE SYSTEM

Committees and subcommittees are where Congress does most of its work. Policies are shaped, interest groups heard, and legislation hammered out.

Long before Woodrow Wilson became president, he described what he called "government by the chairmen of the Standing Committees of Congress." Wilson saw congressional committees as "little legislatures," and added that the House sat "not for serious discussion, but to sanction the conclusions of its Committees" as rapidly as possible. "Congress in its committee-rooms," Wilson concluded, "is Congress at work."[73]

The growth of the modern presidency has modified the Wilsonian view of the power of Congress and its com-mittees. The committees are, nevertheless, vital centers of congressional activity.

The **standing committees** of Congress are the per-manent committees that consider bills and conduct hear-ings and investigations. In the 106th Congress there were 17 standing committees of the Senate and 19 standing committees of the House. (The 36 standing committees of Congress are listed in Table 12-4.)

The standing committees constitute the heart of the committee system. At times, Congress also creates spe-cial committees or select committees to conduct special investigations. In addition, there are **joint committees** of the House and Senate dealing with such subjects as the economy and taxes.

PEANUTS CHARLES M. SCHULZ

TABLE 12-4

Standing Committees of the 106th Congress

Senate Committees	House Committees
Agriculture, Nutrition and Forestry	Agriculture
Appropriations	Appropriations
Armed Services	Armed Services
Banking, Housing and Urban Affairs	Banking and Financial Services
Budget	Budget
Commerce, Science, and Transportation	Commerce
Energy and Natural Resources	Education and the Workforce
Environment and Public Works	Government Reform
Finance	House Administration
Foreign Relations	International Relations
Governmental Affairs	Judiciary
Health, Education, Labor and Pensions	Resources
Indian Affairs	Rules
Judiciary	Science
Rules and Administration	Small Business
Small Business	Standards of Official Conduct
Veterans' Affairs	Transportation and Infrastructure
	Veterans' Affairs
	Ways and Means

Committee Chairs

The party that controls the House or Senate selects the chairs and the party's members of the standing committees for that body. Most committee chairs still achieve their power and position by the **seniority system.** Until modified and reformed in the 1970s, that system automatically resulted in the selection as committee chair of the member of the majority party in Congress who had the longest continuous service on a particular committee. Today, in both the Senate and the House, members can no longer count on length of service to promote them automatically to committee chairs.

Beginning in the early 1970s, both Democrats and Republicans in the House passed reforms that allowed party members to vote by secret ballot to select committee chairs and ranking minority members. In the Senate, both parties also provided for election of committee chairs and ranking minority members.

Republican members of Senate committees select their chairs, when Republicans control the Senate, or ranking members when they do not, subject to approval by the party conference. Senate Democrats vote as a group for committee chairs or ranking members.

Until the reforms of the seniority system (sometimes assailed as "the senility system") were adopted, no aspect of Congress had been criticized more often. The system has not been entirely abandoned, however, since older members usually are selected as committee chairs.

Despite the reforms, as of 2000 the seniority principle had been set aside only rarely in the House. However, Speaker Gingrich passed over three senior Republicans in the House when he approved chairs in the 104th Congress. Seniority is even stronger in the Senate, although Senate and House Republicans adopted a party rule limiting chairs to six years of service. Even so, seniority is still the leading factor in choosing committee chairs in Congress.

The chief argument against seniority has been that it bestows power not necessarily on the most qualified, but on the longest-lived. In the past, for example, the seniority system resulted in the selection of many older, conservative southern Democrats who had been reelected from safe districts.

But the same seniority system that historically benefited southerners also has rewarded those northerners and liberals who are regularly returned to Capitol Hill. In 1992, for example, when the Democrats controlled Congress, there were four African American chairs of House standing committees.

Committee chairs still wield considerable influence. They schedule meetings, decide what bills will be taken up, and usually control the hiring and firing of the majority committee staff. In some cases a committee chair can pigeonhole a bill simply by refusing to hold hearings. But, today, chairs must also pay attention to the views of the majority party and its leaders.

Members of the House and Senate are assigned to committees by the party machinery discussed earlier in this chapter. By tradition, each party is usually allotted seats on committees roughly in proportion to its strength in each house of Congress.

Members are rarely assigned to committees solely on the basis of seniority, although they are ranked by seniority once they are on a committee. Various factors are taken into account in making committee assignments, including the party standing of members, willingness to vote with the leadership, geographical balance, the number of available vacancies, the interests of the legislators' districts, and whether the assignment will help their reelection. Certain committees are more important than others. In the House, members compete for places on Appropriations, Rules, and Ways and Means. In the Senate, particularly desirable committees include Appropriations, Finance, Foreign Relations, and Armed Services.

In recent years, there has been a trend toward greater democracy within some of the committees. Rules have been adopted by some committees giving rank-and-file members a greater voice in committee operations and providing for regularly scheduled meetings.

The House Judiciary Committee, with Chairman Henry J. Hyde, Republican of Illinois, presiding, hears testimony that led to the impeachment of President Clinton in December, 1998.
Copyright © Wally McNamee/CORBIS

The Subcommittees

The 36 chairs of the standing committees of the House and Senate still wield substantial power. Yet here, too, Congress has changed. As Anthony King has observed, "by the late 1970s, committee chairmen, although still very influential people, had lost much of their former power. They felt bound to defer to the other members of the committee; much of the committees' work had been devolved onto subcommittees, often chaired by junior, even freshman, congressmen, and senators."[74]

As a result of these changes, Congress had become somewhat decentralized. "The most striking feature of congressional organization is decentralization," Samuel C. Patterson observed, and "congressional government by subcommittee" increased in the 1970s.[75] The pendulum began to swing back toward greater centralization in the 1980s, however. When the Republicans won control of Congress in 1994, they reduced the number of subcommittees and curtailed the authority of subcommittee chairs. As a result, the heads of the standing committees once again exercised considerable power. Congress became a more centralized body.

The subcommittee explosion and subsequent contraction can be clearly traced by studying the subcommittee totals in the House over the past three and a half decades. In 1951 there were only 69 subcommittees in the House; by 1992 it had reached 135—an increase since 1951 of 96 percent. By the year 2000, however, the number of House subcommittees had dropped to 87. The number of Senate subcommittees had also declined, to 69. Thus, the power of the subcommittees has varied with the times.

The Committees at Work

Committees perform the valuable functions of division of labor and specialization in Congress. No member of the House or Senate could hope to know the details of all 6,808 bills introduced, for example, in the 104th Congress (1995–1997).[*] For that reason, senators and representatives tend to rely on the expert knowledge that members of committees may acquire. If a committee has approved a bill, other members generally assume that the committee has considered the legislation carefully, applied its expertise, and made the right decision. That is why Congress, for the most part, approves the decisions of its committees.

As a result of the committee system, members of Congress specialize in various fields. Sometimes they become more knowledgeable in their areas than the bureaucrats in the executive branch. Finally, many scholars argue that a legislative body should have some forum where members of competing parties can resolve their differences. Committees serve this purpose; they are natural arenas for political bargaining and legislative compromise.

Not all committees are alike. Richard F. Fenno, Jr., has identified a number of factors that may affect a committee's degree of independence, influence in Congress, and success in managing legislation. Fenno found five key variables in committee behavior: *Member goals* reflect the benefits desired by each committee member; for instance, those serving on the Senate Armed Services Committee may be primarily interested in improving their own chances of reelection by getting new military bases for their districts. *Environmental constraints* are the outside influences that affect a committee—primarily the other members of the House, the executive branch, client groups, and the two major political parties. *Strategic premises* are the basic rules of the game for a committee—the Appropriations Committees often try to reduce presidential budget

---

[*]It should be noted that many of the bills introduced were either private bills for the benefit of individuals or duplicates of other bills. A public law applies to whole classes of citizens.

requests, for example, and thus appear more responsible with taxpayers' money. *Decision-making processes* are the internal rules for each committee. Finally, *decisions of committees* vary; the Appropriations Committees, for example, generally do cut the president's budget, but the Armed Services Committee tends to respond to the president's wishes.[76]

Congressional Investigations

Although committees basically process legislation, they perform other tasks, such as educating the public on important issues through hearings and investigations. In 1973 the Senate Select Committee on Presidential Campaign Activities began its far-reaching inquiries into the Watergate affair. Those hearings revealed that President Nixon had tape-recorded his White House conversations, a disclosure that precipitated the legal confrontation between the president and the courts over access to the tapes.

More than anything that had gone before, the Watergate hearings revealed the inside workings of the executive branch at that time. The hearings demonstrated the tremendous power of a congressional investigation, particularly a televised Senate investigation, to focus the nation's attention on its political process. In 1974, the hearings were followed by the House Judiciary Committee's impeachment investigation and Nixon's resignation.

Again, in 1987, the televised hearings on the Iran-contra scandal were viewed by millions of Americans and revealed a great deal of information about the secret foreign policies of the Reagan Administration.

For 250 hours, the committee and a House panel had taken testimony from witnesses who unfolded a tale of how President Reagan's administration had secretly sold arms to Iran to try to free American hostages in the Middle East, then siphoned off the profits to the contra rebels in Nicaragua. Somehow, even more millions of dollars had also ended up in the Swiss bank accounts of the private individuals involved.

Marine Lt. Col. Oliver L. North, who ran the secret operation from the White House, had, briefly, captured the imagination of the American public; he wore his uniform when he testified and was perceived by many viewers as a hero. But he admitted to the congressional committees that he had misled Congress and shredded key documents. Rear Adm. John M. Poindexter, the president's national security adviser, also said he had destroyed evidence to save the president embarrassment.

Then it was time for Senator Daniel K. Inouye, the chairman of the Senate committee investigating the Iran-contra affair, to deliver his closing remarks to the television cameras and the American people. "The story has now been told," Inouye said. "I see it as a chilling story, a story of deceit and duplicity and the arrogant disregard of the rule of law. . . . Vigilance abroad does not require us to abandon our ideals or the rule of law at home. On the contrary, without our principles and without our ideals, we have little that is special or worthy to defend."[77]

Some congressional investigations, such as those conducted by Senator Joseph R. McCarthy, have tram-

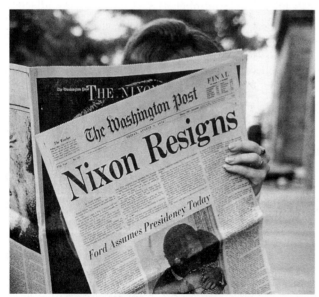

IRAN-CONTRA: "DISDAIN FOR THE LAW"

The common ingredients of the Iran and Contra policies were secrecy, deception, and disdain for the law. . . . [Marine Lt. Col. Oliver L.] North admitted that he and other officials lied repeatedly to Congress and to the American people about the Contra covert action and Iran arms sales, and that he altered and destroyed official documents. . . .

Secrecy became an obsession. Congress was never informed of the Iran or the Contra covert actions, notwithstanding the requirement in the law that Congress be notified of all covert actions in a "timely fashion." . . .

The President's N.S.C. staff secretly diverted millions of dollars in profits from the Iran arms sales to the Contras, but the President said he did not know about it and [Vice Adm. John M.] Poindexter claimed he did not tell him.

The Chairman of the Joint Chiefs of Staff was not informed of the Iran arms sales, nor was he ever consulted regarding the impact of such sales on the Iran-Iraq war or on U.S. military readiness.

The Secretary of State was not informed of the millions of dollars in Contra contributions solicited by the N.S.C. staff from foreign governments with which the State Department deals each day. Congress was told almost nothing—and what it was told was false.

—Report of the Congressional Committees
Investigating the Iran-Contra Affair, 1987

Congressional investigating committees air public issues. Here, Public Citizen president Joan Claybrook testifies to a Senate committee in 2000 about the Firestone tire recall.
Copyright © AFP/CORBIS

pled on individual rights. But a series of Supreme Court decisions, starting in 1957, has attempted to give some protection to witnesses before committees. For example, the Supreme Court has ruled that Congress has no power to "expose for the sake of exposure" and that questions asked by a congressional investigating committee must be relevant to its legislative purpose.[78] On the other hand, the Supreme Court has ruled that witnesses cannot refuse under the First Amendment to answer questions about their political beliefs if the questions are pertinent to the committee's legislative purpose.[79] Of course, witnesses before a committee can invoke the Fifth Amendment on the grounds that their answers might tend to incriminate them. But many people infer that witnesses who invoke this constitutional privilege are guilty of something, and the witnesses may lose their jobs or suffer other social penalties as a result.

Congressional Staffs

Congress has become a bureaucracy. In recent years, the number of people on the congressional payroll has increased enormously. In addition to staff members on their office payrolls, senators and representatives have large committee and subcommittee staffs to serve them. Office staffs are likely to concentrate on legislative and constituent services, whereas on the committees, staff members draft and analyze bills, coordinate with officials in the executive branch, and prepare for hearings. In 1957 congressional staffs totaled 4,489 workers. By the year 2000 the figure had increased to approximately 24,000.[80]

Although congressional staff members have been criticized for having too much influence, one study concluded that members of the staff "do much of the congressional work and . . . in many instances, this work could not be done without staff."[81] The staffs have grown

because of "a greater congressional workload" and the desire of senators and representatives to have "the assistance of skilled experts."[82]

Staff members on some key committees wield power almost comparable to that of White House staff members. Along with the explosion in congressional staff there has been a corresponding increase in cost. Between 1970 and 1998 the cost of running the legislative branch rose from $361 million to $2.3 billion.*

In addition to their staffs, members of Congress have several legislative support agencies that help them do their jobs. The Congressional Research Service of the Library of Congress provides quick answers and long-range studies on a wide range of issues and has computerized databases available to members and their staffs. The General Accounting Office (GAO) serves as an important watchdog into waste or fraud in the bureaucracy and conducts investigations at the request of congressional committees. The Congressional Budget Office provides Congress with an independent analysis of the president's budget and economic assumptions.

CONGRESSIONAL REFORMS

Congress has reformed and modernized its procedures in recent decades and has opened up most of its committee meetings. As noted, until the mid-1970s, under the workings of the seniority system, those members of Congress with longest continuous service on a committee automatically became heads of committees. The seniority system

---

*Ornstein, Mann, and Malbin, *Vital Statistics on Congress 1999–2000*, pp. 127, 140–142. The total includes money for the Library of Congress, the General Accounting Office, and other units of the legislative branch. The actual cost of running the House and Senate was $1.2 billion in 1998, or about half the total.

was criticized for rewarding age, rather than merit, and for concentrating too much power in the hands of a few old, often conservative, committee chairs who were accountable to no one. That is no longer true.

In the late 1950s, the established Democratic leadership of the House faced challenges from party liberals. A number of the liberals banded together in 1959 in an informal organization known as the Democratic Study Group. In 1973 House reformers, led by members of the Democratic Study Group, succeeded in achieving a number of changes in Democratic Party rules in the House. These included modification of the seniority system, opening up more bills to floor amendment, and new provisions to limit committee secrecy. Because the selection of committee chairs is no longer automatic, they now must be much more responsive to the wishes of other members of their committee and to other legislators.

Then early in 1975 the House and Senate made a number of significant internal reforms. In the House, Democrats, finally departing from the seniority system, ousted three committee chairmen and granted more power to subcommittees and increased their staffs. The Senate changed its rules to make it easier to end debate; and Senate Democrats, too, modified the seniority system for the selection of committee chairs. Other changes and reforms modernized and liberalized the more restrictive procedures of both houses.

Although committee chairs are now elected by their party colleagues, they still tend to be the older members with longer years of service. It may be argued, however, that to some degree an internal system that places substantial power in the hands of individual committee and subcommittee chairs is necessary for Congress to function at all. Richard F. Fenno, Jr., studying the House of Representatives, noted that a body of 435 people "must process a workload that is enormous, enormously complicated and enormously consequential. . . . To meet the more general problems, the House has developed a division of labor—a system of standing committees."[83] And the workload of Congress, measured by hours in session and the number of committee meetings, has increased dramatically since Fenno's study.[84]

Congress also has sometimes been assailed in the past, although less frequently today, for rules and procedures designed to block rather than facilitate the passage of legislation. Nor does Congress always get its work done on time. On several occasions, for example, it has failed to act on the federal budget in time for the government to meet its payroll. When that happens, Congress has usually resorted to "continuing resolutions" to fund the departments and keep federal workers on the job. When it does not act to do so, the government has temporarily shut down.

But Richard Fenno concluded that the House enjoys stability as a result of "internal processes which have served to keep the institution from tearing itself apart while engaged in the business of decision making." For example, it is generally assumed that members will not "pursue internal conflicts to the point where the effectiveness of the House is impaired."[85]

In short, the House operates under a set of rules that may be necessary for system maintenance—that is, to keep a diverse, unwieldy institution functioning. From this basic premise has flowed the defense of such congressional procedures as the committee system and the tradition of elaborate courtesy that senators normally, although certainly not always, display in addressing one another on the floor.

A case may even be made for some of the other procedures of Congress that are often condemned. Much of the earlier criticism of Congress originated with liberals and activists who were impatient for the national legislature to get on with the business of meeting social needs. Some analysts argue that congressional procedures may protect the country in a crisis against hasty or misguided action that could result from bowing to popular emotion.

In the field of foreign affairs, Congress has often been criticized for yielding too much power to the president. Under the Kennedy, Johnson, and Nixon administrations, the United States engaged in a major, divisive military conflict in Vietnam, although Congress never declared war. The War Powers Resolution, passed in 1973, was an important attempt by Congress to reassert its authority. In the two and a half decades since the resolution was passed, however, the law has not effectively restricted the president's military power. In the Persian Gulf, for example, President Bush embarked on a major war against Iraq in 1991 without a declaration of war by Congress.

As congressional investigations in the mid-1970s revealed, Congress—and the executive branch—failed to exercise proper control over the activities of the federal intelligence agencies. Although intelligence committees were established in the House and Senate in the wake of those investigations, they have performed their task of overseeing the intelligence agencies with mixed results.

But if Congress sometimes fails to monitor executive agencies, to an extent that is perhaps underemphasized Congress innovates and initiates, sometimes on matters of great importance. And since the passage of the Congressional Budget and Impoundment Control Act of 1974, Congress has taken a greater role in the entire budget process—the way in which the government decides how its money is spent.

Congress has been criticized in the past for being unrepresentative. However, the abuses of malapportionment in the makeup of the House have been declared unconstitutional by the Supreme Court. As a result, the ideal of equal representation in terms of population is coming closer to being a reality. (Even though congressional districts now must be nearly equal, the problem remains of how the district lines should be drawn. Where these lines are drawn by state legislatures for political advantage, in order to favor one party or group over another, the process is known as **gerrymandering.**)

CONGRESS AND THE BUDGET

In preparing the government's annual budget, Congress acts in two stages. First, it passes **authorizations** for spending, laws that recommend levels of funding for federal programs. Then it enacts **appropriations bills,** separate legislation that allows the money to be spent.*

Before Congress passed the Congressional Budget and Impoundment Control Act of 1974, it was hard for members to keep track of the dollar total of the various appropriations bills it passed. Certain programs were favored by members of Congress, and, partly as a result, the lawmakers proved unable to control federal spending. Conflict over the budget on the one hand, and soaring costs on the other, were the twin factors that helped to bring about passage of the 1974 act.[86] The new law required Congress to adopt budget resolutions each year setting target figures for total spending. The act also created a House Budget Committee, a Senate Budget Committee, and a Congressional Budget Office within Congress to provide the experts, the computers, and the data needed by the members. Moreover, the law established a timetable for Congress and its committees to act on spending bills. This schedule was an attempt to give Congress time to evaluate the president's budget and to choose among competing programs.

Later legislation revised the timetable for the budget process. On October 1, the federal fiscal year begins, running until the following September 30. On more than one occasion, however, Congress has failed to meet the October 1 deadline and has been forced to enact stopgap measures to keep the government operating. Deadlock in the battle of the budget resulted in two government shutdowns in late 1995 and early 1996.

In 1990, Congress again tackled the huge federal deficit that then existed and revised the budget process once more. The new procedures emerged in the wake of a power struggle between President Bush and Congress. In the process Bush reneged on his 1988 campaign promise—"read my lips, no new taxes"—and agreed to $164 billion in new taxes over five years as part of a compromise that included spending limits. Bush's retraction of his promise not to raise taxes may have contributed to his defeat by Bill Clinton two years later.

The complex new legislation, known as the Budget Enforcement Act of 1990, set caps on appropriations for domestic, international, and defense programs. It placed such mandatory spending programs as Medicare on a pay-as-you-go basis. Under the law's new timetables for the budget process, the president's budget request is due the first Monday in February each year. As before, Congress is required to adopt a budget resolution by April 15, and the fiscal year begins on October 1.

Many members of Congress have complained that the procedural demands of the budget act have proved burdensome. On the other hand, the new process has "helped Congress overcome its image of fiscal irresponsibility."[87] And the creation of the Congressional Budget Office meant that Congress no longer had to rely on the executive branch for fiscal facts and figures.

These changes have shifted more power to Congress in dealing with the federal budget. Allen Schick, a student of the congressional budget process, concluded that the 1974 law gave Congress the tools it needs to manage conflict over the budget, if it has the will to do so.[88] At the same time, the new budget procedure "concentrates enormous power in the Budget Committees."[89]

A BILL IS PASSED

All of the institutions, people, and procedures we have discussed in this chapter—the formal organization of Congress, the party leadership, the floor maneuvering, the committee system, staff work—bear some relationship to whether a bill will make its way into law. To do so, it must cross hurdles every step of the way.

The formal route that a bill must follow is shown in Figure 12-1. Any member may introduce a bill. (Some legislation is introduced as a "joint resolution," which becomes law in the same manner as a bill.†) After a bill is introduced in either the House or the Senate, or both, it is referred to a committee, which may hold hearings or assign the bill to a subcommittee. Hearings are almost always open to the public. They may be closed by an open vote of the committee, but this normally occurs only when national security or classified information is being discussed. After receiving the subcommittee's recommendations, the full committee meets to decide what action to take on the bill. It may do nothing, or it may rewrite the bill completely, or it may report out the original bill to the House or Senate, with or without amendments. A written report, often with minority views, accompanies the bill from committee.‡ The bill is placed on one of the House calendars or the Senate calendar to await floor action.

If a bill is passed by one house, it is sent to the other chamber, which may pass the bill as is, send it to committee, or ignore it and continue to press its own version of the legislation. If there are major differences in the final bill passed by each house, one house may ask for a conference. The presiding officer of each

---

*When funds are actually spent, they are called "outlays."

†There are two other kinds of congressional resolutions. A "simple" resolution is passed by one branch of Congress and relates to matters entirely within the jurisdiction of that house. A "concurrent" resolution must be passed by both houses. Neither a simple nor a concurrent resolution goes to the president for his signature and neither has the force of law.

‡The minority section of the report sets forth the views of those opposed to the majority recommendation of the committee. Typically, but not always, the minority view is signed primarily by members of the committee who belong to the minority party in that house of Congress.

FIGURE 12-1

How a Bill Becomes Law

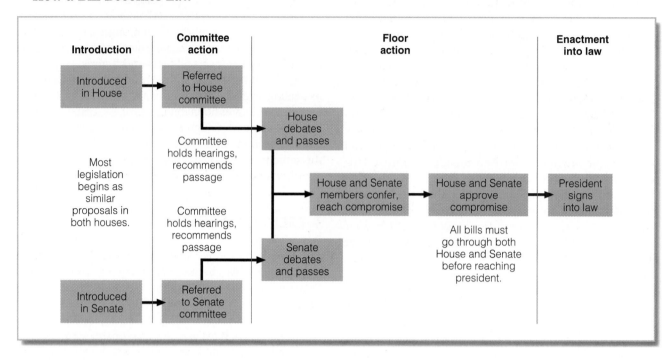

house names a conference committee composed of members of the standing committees or subcommittees that have considered the bill. The selection of members to serve on the conference committee may influence whether any legislation emerges, or the nature of the legislation that is reported out. The conferees attempt to iron out disagreements and reconcile the two versions. Usually, they reach some form of agreement and report back to their respective houses. But agreement is not always reached, or it may be reached only after important changes in the legislation are made. Each house then approves or rejects the conference report. If both houses approve, the final version is signed by the speaker and the president pro tempore of the Senate and is sent to the president, who may sign the bill into law, let it become law without his signature, or veto or pocket veto the bill, as described in Chapter 13. If Congress overrides a presidential veto by a two-thirds vote in both houses, the bill becomes law without the president's signature.

Legislative Vetoes

In recent decades, Congress has enacted many laws containing a legislative veto over acts of the executive branch. A **legislative veto,** as the term suggests, is a provision of law in which Congress asserts the power to override or strike down an action by the executive branch. Presidents have consistently opposed such provisions as being unconstitutional, and in 1983 the Supreme Court agreed. In the landmark *Chadha* case, the Court ruled 7–2 that the legislative veto violated the constitu-

tional requirement of separation of powers among the branches of the government.[90]

But the Court's decision, although historic, left a great deal of uncertainty in its wake. One of the most important legislative vetoes is contained in the War Powers Resolution, which Congress passed in 1973 to limit the president's authority to commit troops to combat overseas. Many constitutional scholars thought it unlikely that any president would directly challenge Congress over the war powers law.

And despite the Court's decision, Congress has continued to pass laws containing legislative veto provisions. Both Congress and the president, however, have found it convenient to compromise rather than fight over the issue.

Even after Congress enacts a law, it can continue to influence the executive branch in ways other than legislative vetoes. It controls spending authority, it oversees the executive branch agencies, it can enact new legislation to strengthen or modify earlier laws, and it can conduct congressional investigations.

CONGRESSIONAL ETHICS

Congress, it is true, has been tarnished by scandal and by the questionable ethics and activities of some of its members. Some members of Congress travel abroad on "junkets" for dubious legislative purposes. Some have relatives on their office payroll. Many have accepted speaking fees from lobbyists. However, since 1991, members of the House and Senate have been prohibited from accepting fees for articles or speeches. And in 1995,

"You've been around here longer than I have. What are 'congressional ethics'?"

Congress passed a law restricting its members from accepting gifts or free lunches from lobbyists.

In 1991, the American public was outraged at disclosures that members of the House of Representatives had written 8,331 bad checks on the private bank maintained for members. But unlike checks written by ordinary citizens who overdraw their accounts, those written by the representatives did not bounce, but were honored by the bank. Some legislators had written hundreds of bad checks totaling hundreds of thousands of dollars.

The House bank scandal focused attention on other "perks" or privileges enjoyed by representatives and senators, including their own dining rooms, hideaway offices, health facilities, medical services, barber shops, and a cut-rate store. On top of the check scandal, irregularities were uncovered in the House Post Office. These disclosures came soon after widespread publicity about "the Keating 5," five senators accused of intervening on behalf of Charles H. Keating, Jr., a big contributor to their campaigns who was eventually imprisoned for his role in the scandal that surrounded the collapse of many of the nation's savings and loan institutions.

All of these scandals have contributed to voter disillusionment with politics and politicians. But it is not only the voters who became disenchanted with the process—many members of Congress, including some who retired, also expressed frustration with their own jobs and complained of the difficulty of getting anything done on Capitol Hill.

Since 1970, more than 30 members of Congress have been the subject of criminal charges. Several members were prosecuted for allegedly using their influence as legislators in return for bribes. Representative Dan Rostenkowski, an Illinois Democrat, the chairman of the House Ways and Means Committee and one of the most powerful members of Congress, pleaded guilty to mail fraud in 1996 and was sentenced to 17 months in prison. He had put people on the payroll who did little or no work, and used office funds to buy gifts for friends and supporters. As noted earlier, two speakers of the House, Jim Wright and Newt Gingrich, were disciplined by their colleagues and resigned from Congress.

Yet scandal and dishonesty among members of Congress are the exception and not the rule. The majority of senators and representatives are both hardworking and honest. Not every lawmaker junkets to the French Riviera at the taxpayers' expense—and if the Senate produced Warren Harding, whose presidency was tarnished by the Teapot Dome scandal, it also produced Robert A. Taft, Hubert H. Humphrey, and John F. Kennedy. In fact, four out of five presidents elected between 1948 and 1972, and every presidential nominee of a major party between 1960 and 1972, had served in the U.S. Senate. In recent years, although state governors—such as Jimmy Carter, Ronald Reagan, Michael Dukakis, Bill Clinton, and George W. Bush—have played a prominent role as presidential candidates, Congress remains an important source of political leaders. In 1992, the Republican candidate for reelection was President George Bush, a former member of the House of Representatives; the Republican nominee for vice president was former Senator Dan Quayle of Indiana, and the Democratic candidate for vice president was the junior senator from Tennessee, Al Gore. In 1996, the Republican nominee for president was Bob Dole, the former majority leader of the Senate. And in 2000, Vice President Gore was his party's presidential nominee.

CONGRESS AND THE AMERICAN POLITICAL SYSTEM

Congress is a major battleground of American democracy. But in attempting to manage the external demands placed on it, Congress often finds itself caught among the crosscurrents of a restless and rapidly changing society.

Programs enacted by Congress may not fit together as a coherent whole. This policy fragmentation is particularly visible in the House, where bills on major subjects such as energy and health are sometimes referred to well over a dozen committees and subcommittees. The House has sometimes created temporary ad hoc committees to deal with energy and welfare reform. These temporary arrangements are symptoms of "the difficulties the House has in attempting to come to grips with major policy questions that cut across the dispersive power structure of subcommittee governments."[91]

"I'm sorry, sir, Congressman Clayborne isn't in at the moment. He's doing two to five for mail fraud."

On the other hand, the Congressional Budget and Impoundment Control Act of 1974 and its successors represented major efforts by Congress to adopt a more coherent approach to federal spending. "Most important," it has been noted, "budget reform forced Congress to confront the budgetary consequences of its own actions."[92]

For many years, Congress failed to exercise a leadership role in the field of foreign policy; it tended to defer to the president in the exercise of its war powers. One result was Vietnam: the longest war in American history, fought without a declaration of war by Congress. But starting in 1973, Congress began to try to reassert its power in the field of foreign policy. It ended the bombing of Cambodia, enacted the War Powers Resolution, and ordered the Central Intelligence Agency to report to Congress on covert operations. In recent years, however, Congress has not sought to exercise much influence over foreign policy.

Some scholars have argued that the American political system is not designed to cope with change, that the checks and balances embedded in the Constitution, combined with differences between the president and Congress, make the legislative branch unable to act. Others have criticized the procedures of Congress itself.

Certainly there is still room for reform in Congress. The behavior of some members who violate ethical standards casts a cloud over all members. For many years Congress showed little desire to institute reforms. Its prevailing attitude was reflected by the late senator Everett Dirksen, who, when asked about prospects for a reform measure, replied: "Ha, ha, ha; and I might add, ho, ho, ho."

In the wake of scandals, however, both the House and Senate established ethics committees, and in 1968 both houses adopted weak codes of conduct for their members. In 1977 the House and Senate strengthened their ethics codes, requiring financial disclosure by members and limiting outside earned income. As noted earlier, beginning in 1991, members of the House and Senate could no longer accept fees for speeches or articles, and in 1995 Congress set limits on the value of gifts that members of both houses may receive.

In the 1970s, both the Democrats and the Republicans modified the seniority system and adopted many other important reforms. The changes in the seniority system—such as the election of committee chairs by the majority party members—have altered power relationships by making chairs more responsive to the majority sentiment in their party and more representative of the country as a whole. Committee chairs now have to seek the support of their colleagues to ensure their reelection as chairs—a major departure from the autocratic ways of the past.

In addition, as already noted, Congress does more than approve legislation. At times it does innovate and initiate, and it serves to give a measure of legitimacy to the process of rule-making for society. Many of the innovative measures that a president finally adopts as his own have first been proposed by individual legislators.

There are times when Congress seems to be still operating in the 19th century. But at other times it is perhaps slow to act because the consensus in the country that Congress needs to act and to innovate is slow to develop. To a great extent, Congress reflects the pluralism that characterizes the American political system as a whole. A powerful argument can be made that Congress does act when the people demand it, their voice is clear, and the need unmistakable. E. E. Schattschneider has described American government as a political system "in which the struggle for democracy is still going on."[93] Viewed in that context, Congress is neither ideal nor obsolete, but rather an enduring arena for political conflict and a crucible for democratic change.

KEY TERMS

pork-barrel legislation,
    p. 375
senatorial courtesy, p. 378
trustee, p. 382
instructed delegate, p. 382
speaker, p. 385
whip, p. 386
Committee of the Whole,
    p. 387
recorded votes, p. 387
filibuster, p. 391

hold, p. 391
cloture, p. 392
standing committees,
    p. 393
joint committees, p. 393
seniority system, p. 394
gerrymandering, p. 398
authorizations, p. 399
appropriations bills,
    p. 399
legislative veto, p. 400

CHAPTER HIGHLIGHTS

✦ Congress plays a central and crucial role in the political system by making laws, the general rules that govern American society.

✦ In part, the age level of Congress is higher than the average American because of constitutional restrictions: A member of the House must be at least 25 (and a citizen for seven years) and a senator must be at least 30 (and a citizen for nine years).

✦ Although Congress comprises a single branch of the federal government, the House and Senate are distinct institutions, each with its own rules and traditions and each jealous of its own powers and prerogatives.

✦ One basic difference between the House and Senate was established by the Constitution, which provided two-year terms for members of the House and staggered six-year terms for senators.

✦ In the House, the speaker is the presiding officer and the most powerful member. The position of speaker is provided for in the Constitution. The basic power structure of the House consists of the speaker, the floor leaders and whips of the two major parties, the Rules Committee, and the chairs of the standing committees.

✦ In March 1979, amid much controversy, the House began live television and radio broadcasts of floor debate. The Senate permitted televising of its deliberations starting in 1986. The broadcasts from both chambers are carried gavel-to-gavel over the nonprofit C-SPAN network by 6,500 cable television systems in all 50 states, with a potential audience of 77 million households as of the year 2000.

✦ The Senate majority leader is the most powerful elected leader of the Senate. Most of the time, the Senate allows unlimited debate. Because of this, a single senator, or a group of senators, may stage a filibuster to talk a bill to death, although the device is now rarely used.

✦ Today, senators more often delay or even kill floor action on legislation or other Senate matters simply by asking their party leaders not to schedule them, an informal tactic known as a hold.

✦ Under Rule XXII of the Senate, a filibuster may be ended if three-fifths of the entire Senate (60 members) vote for cloture.

✦ Although committees of the House and Senate basically process legislation, they perform other tasks, such as educating the public on important issues through hearings and investigations.

✦ The party that controls the House or Senate selects the committee chairs and their party's members of the standing committees for that body. Most committee chairs still achieve their power and position by the seniority system.

✦ In preparing the government's annual budget, Congress acts in two stages. First, it passes authorizations, laws that recommend levels of funding for federal programs. Then it enacts appropriations bills, separate legislation that allows the money to be spent.

✦ Even though congressional districts now must be nearly equal in size, the problem remains of how the district lines should be drawn. If these lines are drawn by state legislatures for political advantage, in order to favor one party or group over another, the process is known as gerrymandering.

✦ In the wake of scandals, both the House and Senate established ethics committees, and in 1968 both houses adopted weak codes of conduct for their members. In 1977 the House and Senate strengthened their ethics codes, requiring financial disclosure by members and limiting outside earned income. Beginning in 1991, members of the House and Senate could no longer accept fees for speeches or articles, and in 1995 Congress set limits on the value of gifts that members of both houses may receive.

✦ To a great extent, Congress reflects the pluralism that characterizes the American political system as a whole. A powerful argument can be made that Congress does act when the people demand it, their voice is clear, and the need unmistakable.

SUGGESTED WEB SITES

www.senate.gov   **www.house.gov**
The Senate   *The House of Representatives*
The official Web sites of the U.S. Senate and House of Representatives. The sites include a list of members of Congress and ways to contact them via e-mail, their Web site, office phone numbers, and mailing addresses. Also includes home pages for House and Senate committees.

http://thomas.loc.gov
Thomas—U.S. Congress on the Internet
A comprehensive guide to the current status in Congress of a bill, resolution, or amendment. Includes bills and issues that various congressional committees and subcommittees are considering. The site also includes links to the Web sites of members of Congress.

www.cspan.org
C-SPAN
The Web site companion to the C-SPAN cable television channels. The site includes video and audio clips of Congress, interviews and debates, sorted by subject, and allows visitors to watch or listen to C-SPAN live on the Web site. Additional information about current events and special topics in American history are available.

SUGGESTED READING

Barone, Michael, and Ujifusa, Grant. *The Almanac of American Politics 2000,** published biennially (Crown, 1999). A comprehensive guide to political leaders at the local, state, and national levels. Includes political profiles of the governors, members of Congress, their constituencies, their voting records on major issues, and ratings from various interest groups.

Congressional Quarterly, *Weekly Report* and annual *Almanac* (Congressional Quarterly, Inc.). A detailed and very useful report on American politics, with emphasis on Congress and current legislation. Published weekly, with an annual almanac that contains much of the material from the weekly reports.

Davidson, Roger H., and Oleszek, Walter J. *Congress and Its Members,* 6th edition* (CQ Press, 1998). An outstanding general introduction to Congress and to the men and women who are elected to serve. Includes the changes instituted by the Republicans after their party won control of Congress in 1994.

Dodd, Lawrence C., and Oppenheimer, Bruce I. *Congress Reconsidered,* 6th edition* (CQ Press, 1997). A useful collection of essays analyzing the evolving institutions and folkways of Congress, and the effects of the "Republican revolution" of 1994.

Fenno, Richard F., Jr. *Congressmen in Committees* (Little, Brown, 1973). A valuable comparative analysis of how congressional committees make decisions. Based on a detailed examination of six committees in the House of Representatives and their six Senate counterparts.

Fenno, Richard F., Jr. *Home Style** (Addison-Wesley, 1997). A thoughtful analysis of a very important aspect of the political behavior of House members—their relationships with the constituents in their home districts.

Fiorina, Morris P. *Congress: Keystone of the Washington Establishment** (Yale University Press, 1989). A lively and interesting discussion of how Congress creates new bureaucracies in Washington and then gains credit at home by helping voters to deal with those agencies. The author argues that House seats are safer as a result.

Glaser, James M. *Race, Campaign Politics, and the Realignment in the South** (Yale University Press, 1996). An insightful analysis of the political transformation under way in southern states. The author explores why Republican presidential candidates have run strongly in the South during recent years, while Democrats have held their own in southern congressional elections.

Herrnson, Paul S. *Congressional Elections: Campaigning at Home and in Washington,* 3rd edition* (CQ Press, 2000). A detailed study, based on hundreds of interviews, of what it takes to run a successful congressional campaign.

King, David C. *Turf Wars: How Congressional Committees Claim Jurisdiction** (University of Chicago Press, 1997). A thoughtful examination of the struggle for power among committees in Congress. King shows how members of Congress may gain political advantage by having legislative authority over certain policy areas, and describes the tug-of-war among members of Congress for slots on desirable committees.

Loomis, Burdett A. *Contemporary Congress,* 3rd edition* (St Martin's, 1999). A useful overview of policy-making in the modern Congress.

Mayhew, David R. *Congress: The Electoral Connection** (Yale University Press, 1974). A stimulating analysis of congressional behavior. Argues that the basic motivation of members of Congress is to win reelection and traces the effects this has on a member's legislative behavior and the way Congress makes policy.

Oleszek, Walter J. *Congressional Procedures and the Policy Process,* 4th edition* (CQ Press, 1996). An extremely useful, clearly written examination of the rules and procedures in the Senate and the House of Representatives. Describes the congressional legislative process in detail, from the introduction of a bill to final presidential action.

Ornstein, Norman J., Mann, Thomas E., and Malbin, Michael J. *Vital Statistics on Congress 1999–2000** (AEI Press, 2000). A comprehensive summary of today's Congress—its membership, political orientation, and performance. Includes numerous historical tables and figures illustrating congressional elections, committees, voting patterns, budget, and campaign finance.

Peabody, Robert L., and Polsby, Nelson W., eds. *New Perspectives on the House of Representatives,* 4th revised edition* (Johns Hopkins University Press, 1992). A useful series of articles on various aspects of the House, including specific congressional committees, leadership contests, and legislative-executive relations.

Polsby, Nelson W. *Congress and the Presidency,* 4th edition (Prentice Hall, 1986). A concise, readable analysis of the legislative and executive branches of government. Polsby makes useful observations on the Senate and House of Representatives as distinct political institutions and traces the budgetary process in the executive branch and Congress.

Sinclair, Barbara. *The Transformation of the U.S. Senate** (Johns Hopkins University Press, 1989). A perceptive analysis of how and why Senate norms have been transformed in recent decades. Argues that senatorial folkways have changed because senators are now rewarded for broad involvement in multiple issues and policy arenas.

Smith, Steven S., and Deering, Christopher J. *Committees in Congress,* 3rd edition (Congressional Quarterly, 1997). A detailed analysis of the dynamics of congressional committees. Argues that over the past two decades, for a variety of reasons, committees of Congress have become less powerful and less autonomous.

Sundquist, James L. *The Decline and Resurgence of Congress** (The Brookings Institution, 1981).

A major study that focuses on the efforts made by Congress in the early 1970s to recapture some of the powers it had lost to the presidency. Discusses the expansion of congressional staff, procedural changes, the strengthening of legislative oversight, and reforms in the congressional budget process.

Wilson, Woodrow. *Congressional Government: A Study in American Politics** (Peter Smith, 1973). (Originally published in 1885.) A classic study of congressional government in the late 19th century by a scholar who later became president of the United States. Stresses the separation of powers in the American political system, the importance of congressional committees and committee chairs, and what Wilson viewed as the dominance of congressional power over that of the president in that era.

*Available in paperback edition

Visit http://politicalscience.wadsworth.com/cummings9/update/ for current InfoTrac articles and other student resources related to this chapter.

CHAPTER 13
The President

As the 43rd president of the United States was inaugurated in January 2001, the nation would not soon forget his predecessor, Bill Clinton. His eight years in the White House were a kind of roller-coaster ride through the American political landscape.

Clinton was the first Democratic president to be elected for two terms since Franklin D. Roosevelt. He was only the second president ever to be impeached, but like the first, Andrew Johnson, he was not convicted or removed from office. He was brilliantly articulate, a Rhodes scholar at Oxford, and a resourceful political leader. Yet, in sworn testimony and in public statements, he misled the nation about his sexual liaison with a young White House intern, Monica Lewinsky, a scandal that sadly tarnished his legacy. Although millions of voters disapproved of his personal behavior and felt it had brought disgrace to his high office, his approval ratings in the polls remained extraordinarily high. For the nation had enjoyed unprecedented prosperity and a booming economy during his years in office, and the enormous budget deficits to which the voters had become accustomed turned into a huge surplus. Americans seemed willing, perhaps for the first time, to make a distinction between a president's personal life and his public performance.

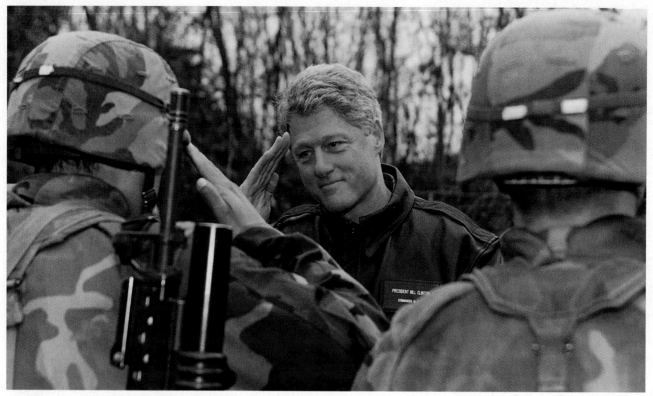

President Clinton reviewing U.S. troops in Bosnia
AP/Wide World

It was as though in his own person, Clinton embodied the peaks and valleys, the contradictions and contrasts, and the paradox of the presidency itself. At the very least, he reminded the American public that the president is also a human being, subject to all the failings, foibles, and weaknesses of the human spirit.*

THE PARADOX OF THE PRESIDENCY

The American presidency is a place of paradox. It is an office of enormous contrasts, of great power—and great limits. Over the past several decades, a number of factors and events have altered the public's perception of the presidency.

Although once viewed as extraordinarily powerful, the presidency more recently has seemed an institution of uncertain power. President Clinton, a Democrat, could not force the Republican-controlled Congress to accept the budget he proposed in 1996. Two years later, as the Lewinsky scandal intensified, Congress impeached him. President Kennedy was assassinated

in 1963, and his four immediate successors left office under adverse circumstances: President Johnson, harshly criticized over the war in Vietnam, chose not to run again; President Nixon was forced to resign because of the Watergate scandal; Presidents Ford and Carter were defeated. Less than three months after his first inauguration, President Reagan was wounded in an assassination attempt. And in 1992 President Bush failed in his bid for reelection.

Of the 10 presidents who have served since the Second World War, only four—Dwight Eisenhower, Richard Nixon, Ronald Reagan, and Bill Clinton—were elected twice, and Nixon, who resigned to avoid impeachment, failed to complete his second term.

Reagan was a popular chief executive, but his public approval eroded midway into his second term. His image was diminished by the disclosure that he had approved a secret foreign policy, allowing the sale of arms to Iran, and that—without the knowledge of the

---

*Franklin D. Roosevelt had an extramarital relationship with a close female friend, and another admired president, John F. Kennedy, had several mistresses. The difference was that their affairs did not become public knowledge until long after their presidencies; Clinton's became headline news while he still occupied the White House.

> ### A PRESIDENT VIEWS HIS POWER
>
> Power? The only power I've got is nuclear—and I can't use that.
>
> —Lyndon Johnson, quoted in Hugh Sidey, *A Very Personal Presidency*

American people—millions of dollars in profits had been diverted to the contra rebels in Central America who were seeking to overthrow the government of Nicaragua. It was revealed that secret operations, many of them illegal, were being run out of the White House by Marine Lt. Col. Oliver L. North and concealed from Congress and the public.

Reagan's political heir, Vice President George Bush, was elected president in 1988. Bush's popularity, extraordinarily high after the Persian Gulf War early in 1991, dropped dramatically by the time he began his campaign for reelection in 1992 amid voter discontent and economic recession. (See Figure 13-1.)

Why has presidential power sometimes appeared so fragile? Perhaps one reason was that many of the problems faced by presidents have become more difficult to manage. Bush's problems in managing the economy were compounded by his most famous campaign promise. As a candidate for president in 1988, he had proclaimed to the Republican National Convention, "Read my lips, no new taxes." The delegates cheered wildly. But two years later, he broke that celebrated pledge, agreed to raise taxes by $165 billion over five years, and thereby lost the trust of many voters.

In the wake of presidential scandals and public skepticism, some observers have asked whether any chief executive, however able, can manage the nation's problems. Yet only a few decades ago, in the early 1970s, many commentators and some voters had been concerned with a different problem. They worried about the expansion of presidential power and the emergence of what the historian Arthur M. Schlesinger, Jr., termed "the imperial Presidency."[1] Particularly in the area of foreign and military policy, Schlesinger and others contended, the presidency had exceeded constitutional bounds and usurped congressional war powers.

The growth of the power of the presidency, many of these historians noted, was accompanied by excessive reverence for the person of the president, a phenomenon that one scholar called "the Sun King complex."[2] As Schlesinger viewed the problem, "the age of the imperial Presidency had in time produced the idea that run-of-the-mill politicians, brought by fortuity to the White House, must be treated thereafter as if they had become superior and perhaps godlike beings."[3] Similarly, Thomas E. Cronin criticized the "textbook Presidency," the creation, he argued, of political scientists, journalists, and others who endow the chief executive with a "halo." Cronin perceived a "cult of the Presidency," in which the occupant of the White House becomes "benevolent, omnipotent, omniscient."[4]

Yet, against the background of Bill Clinton's weakened presidency, and the relentless pursuit of Clinton by independent counsel Kenneth W. Starr, Schlesinger himself wrote that the imperial presidency no longer existed. The "protracted crisis" from the beginning of the Second World War to the breakup of the Soviet Union in 1991, Schlesinger argued, "came close to institutionalizing the imperial Presidency." In other words, danger from abroad had fueled presidential power. With the fall of the Soviet system, Schlesinger wrote, "the imperial Presidency collapsed."[5]

Even as the presidency was being criticized in the 1970s for an excess of power, it was simultaneously

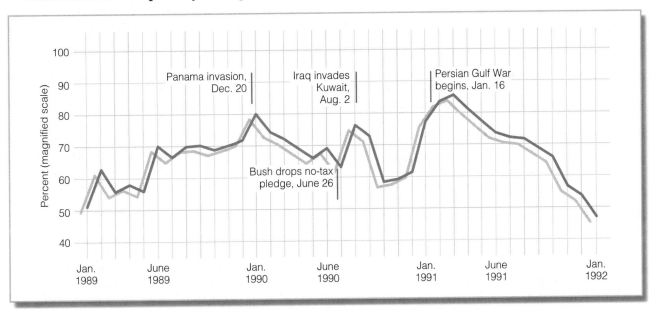

FIGURE 13-1

President Bush's Popularity during Times of Crisis

SOURCE: Data provided by Gallup poll. Respondents were asked: "Do you approve or disapprove of the way George Bush is handling his job as president?"

Andrew Jackson was the People's President, and it seemed fitting that on the day of his inauguration in 1829 the doors of the White House should be opened to the common man. At the reception, food and drink vanished as soon as they were served; glassware, china, and furniture were shattered by the boisterous mob. The new President, astonished and trapped, was finally rescued by friends who locked arms, formed a flying wedge, and led Jackson out. Since then, Presidents have under-standably preferred to entertain only invited guests. Their problem has been to do so in a way that is dignified and elegant yet does not appear excessively lavish. Jefferson, who believed in democratic informality, was criticized for wearing "yarn stockings and slippers down at the heels" while receiving the British ambassador; Martin Van Buren, on the other hand, was denied reelection in 1840 partly because the sumptuous banquets he gave offended many voters. For modern Presidents the solution has been to provide the proper formality and pomp at state dinners at the White House, and to demonstrate their informality by inviting dignitaries to their own homes. Thus F.D.R. served hot dogs to the king of England at Hyde Park, and Lyndon Johnson entertained the chancellor of Germany at a barbecue on his ranch.

—Marcus Cunliffe and the editors of *American Heritage, The American Heritage History of the Presidency*

---

perceived as having been weakened by the Vietnam War and the Watergate scandal. Both of those traumatic events diminished public trust in the institution of the presidency, and—some analysts believed—diminished the actual power of that office as well.

Any discussion of the modern presidency is inevitably colored by Watergate. To some extent, that scandal may have resulted from political and institutional factors—among them the growth of presidential power in the 20th century, increasing government secrecy, a lack of government credibility, a burgeoning national security bureaucracy, and the use of intelligence agencies and techniques in domestic politics. Many of the same factors were responsible for the Iran-contra scandal, which began unfolding more than a decade later in 1986 under President Reagan.

President Clinton, in turn, was impeached, and for most of his presidency was dogged by the Whitewater affair, which centered chiefly on events that had taken place in Arkansas before he occupied the White House—his participation with his wife, Hillary, in a real estate development, their ties to a failed savings and loan association, and Mrs. Clinton's legal work for the bank. Clinton also was sued by Paula Corbin Jones, who charged he had sexually harassed her in a hotel room in 1991 when he was governor of Arkansas and she was an employee of the state. That lawsuit in turn led to the disclosure of Clinton's entanglement with Monica Lewinsky.

Long before Bill Clinton's problems, Congress, in the wake of Vietnam and Watergate, moved in the early 1970s to reassert its power within the political system. It enacted the **War Powers Resolution,** a law passed in 1973 in an effort to set a time limit on a president's use of combat forces abroad. Congress imposed other restrictions on the president in the foreign policy and military fields, and it created a new structure to deal with the federal budget—an action designed to permit Congress to share power with the president over the budget process and the establishment of national priorities.

Congress reached new levels of assertiveness after the Republicans captured both houses in 1994 and Representative Newt Gingrich of Georgia was elected speaker of the House. In 1995 and early 1996, the government shut down twice, throwing hundreds of thousands of federal employees out of work, because President Clinton and the Republican Congress could not agree on a budget.

The opposing perceptions of the presidency—either as an office grown too powerful, or one in danger of being weakened by a reassertive Congress—leave unresolved the question of how the presidency can be controlled without so reducing its powers that the president cannot manage national problems and lead the nation. "The American democracy," Schlesinger has suggested, "must discover a middle ground between making the President a czar and making him a puppet. . . . We need a strong Presidency—but a strong Presidency *within the Constitution*."[6]

In this chapter we will explore a key question: In the light of the nation's experience over recent decades, has the presidency grown too powerful, or too weak? Other questions flow from this central issue. For example, are there enough checks on presidential power? Does a president have enough control over the bureaucracy and policy formation, and enough influence with Congress, to solve the nation's problems? Can any president govern? Are the public's expectations of presidential performance so high that any president is doomed to failure from the start? Is the press so determined to find scandal in high places that every president will be tarred and feathered by the news media?

THE AMERICAN PRESIDENCY

The day before he took the oath of office as 35th president of the United States, John F. Kennedy called on President Eisenhower at the White House. "There are no easy matters that will ever come to you as President," Eisenhower told the younger man. "If they are easy, they will be settled at a lower level."[7]

The president is not merely the symbolic and actual leader of more than 270 million Americans, sworn to "preserve, protect and defend" the Constitution, but also a world leader, whose decisions may affect the future of the more than 6 billion inhabitants of the globe.

Yet the presidency is an office of both power and limits—that is the paradox of the modern presidency, discussed at the start of this chapter. The core of the dilemma is that the technology of the nuclear age and the growth of government in a modern industrial society have combined to concentrate great power in the hands of a chief executive in some policy areas, while restricting his options in others. For example, the president's power to use military force without a declaration of war by Congress was demonstrated during the 1960s

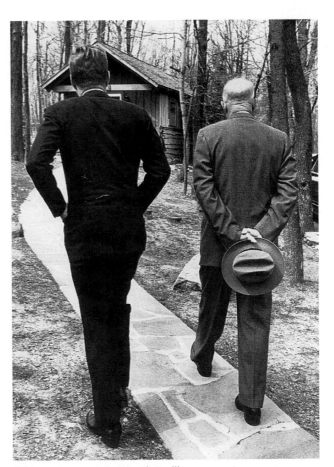

"There are no easy matters that will ever come to you as President. . . ." President Kennedy (left) is visited by former President Eisenhower at Camp David, Maryland.
George Tames/NYT Pictures

in Southeast Asia, in the Persian Gulf in 1991 when President Bush took the country to war against Iraq, and in Yugoslavia in 1999 when U.S. warplanes led the NATO bombing attacks on Serbia to force Yugoslav president Slobodan Milosevic to withdraw his troops from Kosovo. Yet, the Constitution provides that only Congress can declare war.

When in 1973, over President Nixon's veto, Congress enacted a law designed to recapture its war powers, that effort did not effectively limit presidential power. Even before the Persian Gulf War, President Bush had ordered the military into Panama in 1989. The invasion ousted dictator Manuel Noriega, who was arrested, taken to Miami, tried, convicted of drug trafficking, and sentenced to 40 years in prison. Bush dispatched U.S. forces to Somalia in 1992 as part of a United Nations peacekeeping force. President Reagan sent the marines to Lebanon in 1982, dispatched military forces to invade and capture the Caribbean island of Grenada in 1983, bombed Libya in 1986, sent the Navy into the Persian Gulf in 1987 to protect Kuwaiti ships from attacks by Iran, and during much of his presidency waged a covert war against the leftist government of Nicaragua. President Clinton sent military forces to Haiti and Bosnia, and bombed Iraq and

The American Presidency **411**

Yugoslavia. In none of these instances did the War Powers Resolution restrict presidential power.

But these actions all took place abroad. Presidential power at home may be more limited. For example, although President Nixon was able to continue the war in Vietnam for five years and invade and bomb Cambodia, in the domestic sphere he could not get Congress to pass his plan to reform the welfare system.

Other presidents have faced the same dilemma. A president was able to bring the nation to the brink of nuclear disaster in the Cuban Missile Crisis of 1962, or involve America in war in the Persian Gulf in 1991, almost entirely by his own decisions and actions. The president's sheer military power, which he exercises as commander in chief, remains formidable. Yet the president may not be able to get a health care reform bill through Congress or strengthen the Social Security system.

The Institution, the Person

The presidency is both an institution and a person. The institution is the office created by the Constitution, custom, cumulative federal law since 1789, and the gradual growth of formal and informal tools of presidential power. The person is a human being, powerful yet vulnerable, compassionate or vain, ordinary or extraordinary. To the institution, the president brings the imprint of his personality and style. Under the Twenty-second Amendment, the incumbent must normally change at least once every eight years.* The presidency is, then, both highly institutionalized and highly personal.

George Washington assumed the office feeling not unlike "a culprit who is going to the place of his execution." William Howard Taft thought it "the loneliest place in the world." Harry Truman declared that "being a President is like riding a tiger. A man has to keep on riding or be swallowed." Warren Harding thought the White House "a prison." Lyndon Johnson spoke of "the awesome power, and the immense fragility of executive authority." Jimmy Carter called it "the most difficult job, maybe, on earth." Ronald Reagan complained that "you live in a fishbowl." George Bush observed, "You have to have a fairly thick skin."

Bill Clinton, however, musing about the presidency in his final months in office, insisted he enjoyed the job, despite his troubles. "Some people who have been in this position," he said, ". . . talk about what a terrible burden it is, and how the White House is the crown jewel of the federal penal system, and how they can't wait to get out of there. . . . Frankly, most of those guys didn't have a tougher time than I've had there—and I don't know what in the heck they're talking about."[8] A few weeks earlier he told a gathering in the White

The presidency is both an institution and a person.
Copyright © CORBIS UPI/Bettmann

House East Room: "You've just got to show up every day and do your best."[9]

The strands of power have come together in the person and the institution of the modern presidency. When the president speaks to the nation, millions listen. His words are instantly transmitted around the globe by satellite and high-speed communications. When he pulls his beagle's ears, as Lyndon Johnson did, the bark of dog lovers is heard around the world. If he cancels a subscription to a newspaper, as John Kennedy did, a thousand thunderous editorials denounce him. When he says he does not like broccoli, as George Bush revealed, crates of the vegetable are shipped to the White House by indignant growers. Is his kitten ill? His chef disloyal? Does he carry his own garment bag aboard the plane? Does he dye his hair? Does he eat too much fast food? Does his wife consult astrologers? Does she have imaginary conversations with celebrated figures from the past? No detail in the life of a modern president (and these are real examples) escapes the eyes of the media, which provide such information to a public apparently hungry for more.

Public disclosure of intimate details of a president's life is not limited to the press, revelations of scandal, or the literary endeavors of White House cooks, seamstresses, and bottle-washers. His own distinguished,

---

*Under the Twenty-second Amendment, a vice president who succeeded to the presidency for less than two years could run, and if elected, serve as president for two more full terms. Thus, the same person could conceivably be president for almost 10 years.

high-level staff assistants may be secret diarists, scribbling away at night for the sake of posterity and the best-seller lists. Indeed, presidents themselves write books, not only for money but to give their own version of events and, they hope, to secure their place in history. Truman, Eisenhower, Johnson, Nixon, Ford, Carter, and Reagan all published memoirs after they left the White House.

The intense public interest in the person and office of the president is a reflection of how the job of chief executive became magnified in the 20th century. The immense pressures on the human being who occupies the office of president have intensified because the institution of the presidency has evolved and grown with the nation.

THE EXPANDING PRESIDENCY

"We Never Once Thought of a King"

The framers of the Constitution who met at Philadelphia toiled in the greatest secrecy. No television cameras invaded their privacy in 1787. Yet even in that preelectronic age, the framers felt it necessary to issue a press release (their only one) to counteract rumors that were circulating around the country. The statement was leaked to the *Pennsylvania Herald* in August: "Tho' we cannot, affirmatively, tell you what we are doing; we can, negatively, tell you what we are not doing—we never once thought of a king."[10] (Alexander Hamilton, however, did propose a virtual monarchy in the form of a lifetime chief executive, but his plan won no support.)

The colonists who made the American Revolution were, perhaps understandably, prejudiced against kings. At the same time, the difficulties encountered under the Articles of Confederation had exposed the shortcomings of legislative government and demonstrated the need for a strong executive. But how strong?

James Wilson and Gouverneur Morris championed a single powerful chief executive, and James Madison eventually adopted that view. Many of the framers considered legislatures to be dangerously radical; the blessings of liberty could best be enjoyed, they felt, if popular government was checked by a strong executive branch that could protect wealth, private property, and business. Support for a powerful single president was by no means unanimous, however; some of the framers had specifically proposed a plural executive, and some wanted the president to be chosen by Congress. The framers, as Thomas E. Cronin has observed, knew that the American presidency is always a "potentially dangerous institution. . . . The framers wanted a more authoritative and decisive national government, yet they were keenly aware that the American people were not about to accept too much centralized power vested in a single person."[11]

Out of the debates at Philadelphia emerged the basic structure of the presidency as we know it today: a single president who headed one of three separate branches of government and was elected independently for a four-year term. The great authority given to the president by the framers was limited by the separation of powers among the three branches of government, by the checks and balances engraved in the Constitution, by the federal system, and, in time, by other informal controls generally unforeseen in 1787—the rise of political parties and mass media, for example.

The Growth of the American Presidency

"I prefer to supervise the whole operations of the government myself . . . and this makes my duties very great," President James Polk wrote in his diary in 1848.[12]

So great had those duties become in the 20th century that by fiscal 2001 the president proposed an estimated federal budget of more than $2 trillion and presided over a bureaucracy of 2.7 million civilians and 2.6 million members of the armed forces. He would not have dreamed of attempting to "supervise the whole operations of the government" by himself.

Great crises and great presidents have contributed to the growth of the presidency since 1789. George Washington, Andrew Jackson, Abraham Lincoln, Theodore Roosevelt, Woodrow Wilson, and Franklin Roosevelt all placed their personal stamp on the presidency. When a president strengthens and reshapes the institution, the change may endure even after he leaves. The modern presidency, for example, is rooted in the style of Franklin D. Roosevelt.

Although presidents and events have played a decisive role in the development of the presidency, several

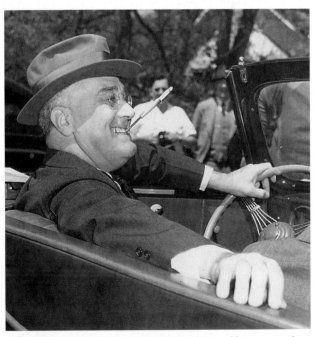

Franklin D. Roosevelt influenced the modern presidency more than any other chief executive.
AP/Wide World

The Expanding Presidency **413**

Of course I miss it. . . . President Nixon said to me, "How did you feel when you weren't President any more?" And I said, "I don't know whether you'll understand this now or not, but you certainly will later. I sat there on that platform and waited for you to stand up and raise your right hand and take the oath of office, and I think the most pleasant words . . . that ever came into my ears were 'So help me God' that you repeated after that oath. Because at that time I no longer had the fear that I was the man that could make the mistake of involving the world in war, that I was no longer the man that would have to carry the terrifying responsibility of protecting the lives of this country and maybe the entire world, unleashing the horrors of some of our great power if I felt that that was required. But that now I could ride back down that avenue, being concerned about what happened, being alarmed about what might happen, but just really knowing that I wasn't going to be the cause of it." . . . The real horror was to be sleeping soundly about three-thirty or four or five o'clock in the morning and have the telephone ring and the operator say, "Sorry to wake you, Mr. President." . . . There's just a second between the time the operator got me on the line until she could get . . . Mr. Bundy in the Situation Room, or maybe . . . Secretary McNamara. . . . And we went through the horrors of hell that thirty seconds or minute or two minutes. Had we hit a Russian ship? Had an accident occurred? We have another *Pueblo?* Someone made a mistake—were we at war? Well, those experiences are gone.

—Lyndon B. Johnson, excerpts from a CBS television news special, "LBJ: Why I Chose Not to Run," December 27, 1969

broad historical factors have combined to create a powerful chief executive today.

The Nuclear Age and the End of the Cold War For more than four decades after the end of the Second World War, the United States and the Soviet Union lived under the terrible shadow of nuclear war. Each possessed nuclear missiles that could destroy the other country in half an hour or less; given the time factor, the president, rather than Congress, of necessity became the one who had to decide whether to use such hideous, and ultimately irrational, weapons. (As Clinton Rossiter noted, the next wartime president "may well be our last."[13])

In 1991, the collapse of the Soviet Union and the breakup of the communist central government into 15 separate nations marked the formal end to the **Cold War** (1945–1991), the period after the Second World War marked by rivalry and tension between the two nuclear superpowers, the United States and the communist government of the Soviet Union. Although both sides were moving to cut strategic weapons drastically, the United States and Russia in the year 2000 still possessed long-range missiles with powerful nuclear warheads. At least six other countries were nuclear powers, and a number of Third World nations were attempting to develop nuclear arms. Despite the disintegration of the Soviet Union, the world was still a volatile place, and the president continued to control the "nuclear button."

In sum, the constitutional power of Congress to declare war was eroded in the last half of the 20th cen-

Copyright © Steve Kelly/*Union-Tribune*

tury by the power of the president to use nuclear weapons, to commit U.S. forces to meet sudden crises, and to fight so-called limited wars. Even in a changed world, the president remains the dominant figure in responding to crisis with military force.

Foreign Affairs The president, under the Constitution, has the prime responsibility for conducting the foreign affairs of the United States. From its isolationism before the Second World War, the United States emerged in the postwar period as one of the two major world powers. During the Eisenhower administration, when John Foster Dulles exercised a powerful influence as secretary of state, the United States adhered to the principle of collective security to "contain" communism and entered into a series of military alliances with other nations for this purpose.

The wisdom of the role of the United States as a "world policeman" was seriously questioned in the 1960s and 1970s, when the United States became bogged down in the Vietnam War. By 1980, following the hostage crisis in Iran and Soviet intervention in Afghanistan, some of the post-Vietnam emphasis on détente and disarmament had given way to a renewed concern over national security and military strength. And in that year, and again in 1984, the voters in the presidential election chose Ronald Reagan, who increased defense spending and emphasized military preparedness. President Bush committed American forces to two wars between 1989 and 1991, while proclaiming a "new world order." President Clinton sent American troops to Haiti and Bosnia, launched missiles and bombs against Iraq, and ordered American NATO warplanes to bomb Yugoslavia during the crisis in Kosovo in 1999. Because the United States remains one of the most powerful nations, the president is inevitably a world leader as well as a national leader.

Domestic Affairs The great increase in presidential power in the 20th century took place in the domestic field as much as in foreign affairs. Franklin Roosevelt's New Deal, as Edward S. Corwin pointed out, brought "social acceptance of the idea that government should be active and reformist, rather than simply protective of the established order of things."[14]

This concept of a large, activist government as the engine of social progress was dramatically challenged by House Speaker Newt Gingrich and other leaders of the Republican-controlled Congress elected in 1994. They supported an agenda to reduce government's role in the lives of Americans, to cut the rate of growth of social programs, and to turn more power back to the states. With the political winds blowing strongly against the traditional Democratic, New Deal philosophy, even President Clinton could announce in 1996: "The era of big government is over."[15] But after the Democrats made surprising gains in the House of Representatives in the 1998 off-year elections, Gingrich quit as speaker and left Congress, and the public seemed less enchanted with his philosophy.

The years after the New Deal brought a tremendous growth of government as manager. As a result, the president today directs a huge bureaucracy. Although political leaders may continue to argue over the nature and extent of Washington's role, modern government is expected to deal with social problems, from racial discrimination to health care, and the president is at the center of the debate. Nor have Republican presidents necessarily been successful in turning back the tide of big government, try as they might. President Nixon cut back and dismantled some federal programs, but the federal budget increased substantially during his presidency. Ronald Reagan, too, attacked the bureaucracy in his 1980 campaign, but its size increased during his eight years in office. Reagan cut back or limited spending in a number of federal domestic areas, but he did not change such established major programs as Social Security, Medicare, or Medicaid. Nor did President Bush, his successor, attempt to tinker with these basic programs, on which millions of Americans depend.

The Mass Media Television and the other news media have helped to magnify the person and the institution of the presidency. (The relationship between the president and the press is discussed later in this chapter.) All the major television and radio networks, newspapers, magazines, and wire services have correspondents assigned full-time to covering the president. These "White House regulars" accompany the chief executive wherever he travels, sending out a steady flow of news about his activities.

When a president wants to talk to the people, the networks (whose stations are licensed by the federal government) often make available free prime time. Presidential news conferences are frequently televised live. People identify with a president they see so often on television; his style and personality help to shape the times and the national mood.

Modern presidents, to a greater extent than the public is aware, often tailor their daily activities to television, scheduling events in time to appear in a "sound bite" on the evening news. Presidents and their media affairs experts attempt to orchestrate and dominate the news to the advantage of the White House.

THE IMPOSSIBLE BURDEN: THE MANY ROLES OF THE CHIEF EXECUTIVE

During Bill Clinton's first week in office in 1993, he delivered his address at the Capitol on Inauguration Day; played the saxophone that night at the Arkansas inaugural ball in Washington; held an open house for thousands of people who came by to shake his hand; accepted the withdrawal of his nominee for attorney general, who had been opposed by several senators;

"Okay, bring in the new guy. . . ."
Cartoon by Auth © 1976 *The Philadelphia Inquirer*

presided over his first cabinet meeting; signed a series of executive orders to ease certain federal restrictions on abortions; received congratulatory messages from several world leaders; and was briefed on an attack by U.S. jet aircraft on a radar installation in Iraq. That was only a sample of his first week's calendar.

The president is one individual but fills many separate roles: chief of state, chief executive, commander in chief, chief diplomat, chief legislator, chief of party, and popular leader. All but the last two are required of him by the Constitution; in addition, as one scholar of the presidency suggested, he is expected to be the voice of the people, protector of the peace, manager of prosperity, and world leader.[16] A modern president is presumed to be all these things and more. But of course, no human being can live up to such expectations.

Moreover, it would be simplistic and misleading to think of the president as rapidly "changing hats" as he goes about filling these roles. Many of the presidential roles blend and overlap; some may collide. Being a vigorous party leader, for example, will often conflict with playing the role of chief of state, of being president of all the people. For a president's roles, as Cronin has noted, "are not compartmentalized, unrelated functions, but rather a dynamic, seamless assortment of tasks and responsibilities."[17]

For purposes of analysis, however, it is possible to separate out the principal roles of the president. When we do so, we see that the "awesome burden" has identifiable parts.

Chief of State

The president of the United States is the ceremonial and symbolic *head of state*. In another role, he is also *head of government*, the official who presides over the machinery of the executive branch.

In many countries, the two jobs are distinct: a figurehead king, queen, or president is head of state, but the premier or prime minister is head of government and exercises the real power. It is because the two functions are combined in the person of the American pres-

As the train bearing the body of Franklin D. Roosevelt left Warm Springs, a tearful Chief Petty Officer Graham Jackson played "Going Home."
Clark/*Life* Magazine, Inc. © Time, Inc.

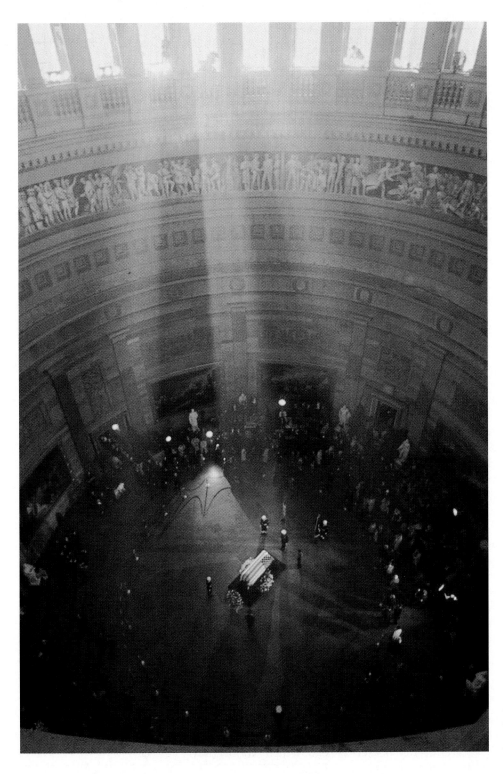

November 1963: President John F. Kennedy lies in state in the Capitol rotunda.
Copyright © CORBIS UPI/Bettmann

ident that he finds himself declaring National Codfish Week or toasting the grand duchess of Luxembourg at a state dinner on the same day that he makes a vital foreign policy decision or vetoes a major bill sent to him by Congress.

The distinction between head of state and head of government may seem trivial—of interest only to protocol officers and society columnists—but it is not. Much of the mystique and aura of power that have surrounded the institution of the presidency are due to the fact that the president is more than a prime minister; he is a symbol of nationhood as well as a custodian of the people's power. In Theodore Roosevelt's famous phrase, he is both "a king and a prime minister."[18]

 for more information about Theodore Roosevelt, see: *memory.loc.gov/ammem/trfhtml*

As noted earlier in this chapter, some critics of presidential power have argued that presidents lose their perspective and their ability to make sound judgments

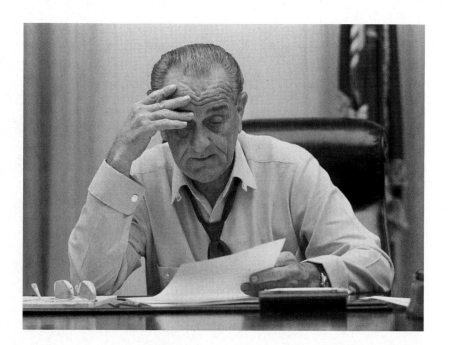

President Johnson working late as he prepared
an address on the war in Vietnam
Copyright © CORBIS/Bettmann

because they are treated too much like monarchs and are isolated from the problems faced by ordinary citizens. In part, this may happen because a president is surrounded by the trappings of power—large staffs, private aircraft, and the Secret Service.

Because the chief executive is such a symbolic and familiar figure, when a president dies in office people often react as though they have suffered a great personal loss. Even the radio announcers wept in 1945 as they told of Franklin Roosevelt's death. After President Kennedy's assassination in 1963, the nation went through a period of mourning; 250,000 people braved cold weather to line up to pass his bier in the Capitol rotunda; 100 million people watched the funeral on television. Social scientists studying the impact of the assassination on children and adults found definite physical and psychological effects.[*]

Chief Executive

"The executive Power shall be vested in a President of the United States of America." So reads Article II of the Constitution, which also states: "He shall take Care that the Laws be faithfully executed."

Under this simply worded but powerful grant of executive authority, the president runs the executive branch of the government. As of fiscal 2001, the president headed a federal establishment with an estimated total payroll of

$120 billion. No executive in private industry has responsibilities that match the president's. The president receives a salary of $400,000 a year plus $50,000 in nontaxable expenses and up to $100,000 in travel expenses, also tax-free, as well as handsome retirement benefits, including a lifetime pension of $157,000 a year.[19]

There are few legal qualifications for the office. The Constitution requires only that the president be a "natural-born" citizen, at least 35 years old, and 14 years a resident of the United States.[†]

Obviously, there would be more than enough work in the president's in-basket to keep him busy if he did nothing else but administer the government. And, in fact, presidents do find themselves bogged down under a mountain of paper. Most presidents work at night to try to keep up; the sight of Franklin Roosevelt, a polio victim, being wheeled to his office at night, preceded by wire baskets full of paperwork, was a familiar one to White House aides during the New Deal era. President Eisenhower tried to solve the paperwork problem by ordering his staff to prepare memos no more than one page long. Lyndon Johnson took a swim and nap each afternoon, then began a second working day at 4 P.M., often summoning weary aides for conferences at the end of *their* working day.

 for more information about Franklin Roosevelt, see:
www.fdrlibrary.marist.edu

Because administering the government is only one of seven major presidential roles, the president cannot

---

[*]For example, among adults, one study found that "the assassination generally evoked feelings similar to those felt at the death of a close friend or relative." Of a sample of the adult population, 43 percent said they did not feel like eating, 29 percent smoked more than usual, 53 percent cried, 48 percent had trouble sleeping, and 68 percent felt nervous and tense. Source: Paul B. Sheatsley and Jacob J. Feldman, "A National Survey on Public Reactions and Behavior," in Bradley S. Greenberg and Edwin B. Parker, eds., *The Kennedy Assassination and the American Public* (Stanford: Stanford University Press, 1965), pp. 158, 168.

[†]A citizen born abroad of American parents might well be regarded as "natural-born." The question arose in 1968 because George Romney, a Republican hopeful, had been born in Mexico. The requirement of 14 years' residence apparently does not mean that a president must have resided in the United States for 14 successive years immediately prior to the election, because Herbert Hoover had not.

spend all of his time running the executive branch. He has a White House staff, other agencies in the Executive Office of the President, and his cabinet to help him. He tries to confine himself to *presidential* decisions, such as resolving major conflicts within the bureaucracy, or among his own advisers, and initiating and approving major programs and policies.

Beneath the president in the executive branch are the 14 cabinet departments (as of January 2001) and about 60 major independent agencies, boards, and commissions. (See Figure 14-3 in the next chapter.) These agencies are of two main types: executive agencies and independent regulatory agencies. The **executive agencies** are independent agencies of government under the president within the executive branch, but not part of a cabinet department. They report to the president in the same manner as departments, even though they are not within any cabinet department. They are, therefore, independent of the departments, but not of the president. The **independent regulatory agencies** exercise quasi-judicial and quasi-legislative powers and are administratively independent of both the president and Congress (although politically independent of neither). The members of the major regulatory agencies are appointed by the president from both major parties to staggered, fixed terms but do not report to him.

The neat organizational charts do not show the overlapping and intricate real-life relationships among the three branches of government. Nor do they give any hint of the difficulties a president faces in controlling his own executive branch and in making the bureaucracy carry out his decisions.

President Truman understood the problems that Eisenhower would have as an Army general elected president: "He'll sit here," Truman would remark (tapping his desk for emphasis), "and he'll say, 'Do this! Do that!' *And nothing will happen.* Poor Ike—it won't be a bit like the army. He'll find it very frustrating."[20]

 for more information about President Truman, see: www.trumanlibrary.org

Despite their vast constitutional and extraconstitutional powers, presidents are sometimes as much a victim of bureaucratic inertia as anyone else. "I sit here all day," Truman said, "trying to persuade people to do the things they ought to have sense enough to do without my persuading them. . . . That's all the powers of the President amount to."[21]

Richard Neustadt agreed with Truman that "Presidential power is the power to persuade."[22] In persuading people, however, the president can draw upon formidable resources, not the least of which is his power to appoint and remove officials. Under the Constitution, the president, "with the advice and consent of the Senate," appoints ambassadors, Supreme Court justices, other federal judges, the heads of regulatory agencies, and other senior officials. Under present law, the president names about 3,000 upper-level federal officials who

are political appointees. (The great bulk of the 2.7 million federal civilian employees are appointed by department heads through the civil service system.)

The Constitution does not specifically give the president the power to remove government officials, but the Supreme Court has ruled that Congress cannot interfere with the president's right to fire officials whom he has appointed with Senate approval.[23] In this instance, and in many others, decisions of the Supreme Court have increased the growth of presidential power.

During Franklin Roosevelt's administration, on the other hand, the Court held that the president did not have the right to remove officials serving in administratively independent "quasi-legislative or quasi-judicial agencies."[24] Even though commissioners of regulatory agencies are thus theoretically immune from removal by presidential power, in practice they may not be. When scandal touched the chairman of the Federal Communications Commission in 1960, the incident embarrassed President Eisenhower; within a week the official resigned.

To the task of bureaucrat in chief, therefore, the president brings powers of persuasion that go beyond his formal, constitutional, and legal authority. By the

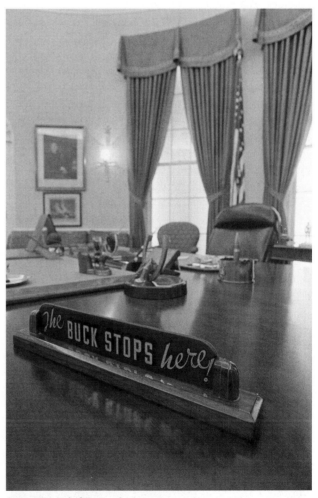

Harry Truman's famous sign
Copyright © CORBIS/Bettmann

nature of his job, he is the final decision maker in the executive branch. As the sign on Harry Truman's desk said: "The buck stops here."

The president also has the power to grant "reprieves and pardons for offenses against the United States," a power that seemed relatively unimportant in modern times until President Ford granted a pardon to his predecessor, Richard Nixon (who had appointed Ford vice president). Ford noted that in the Watergate affair, the former president had "become liable to possible indictment and trial for offenses against the United States." Ford said that such a trial would divide the country, and he pardoned Nixon for all crimes that he "has committed or may have committed" as president. Ford later testified under oath that, prior to taking office, he had not entered into any arrangement with Nixon to grant the pardon.

Commander in Chief

When President Kennedy died at Parkland Hospital in Dallas on November 22, 1963, an Army warrant officer named Ira D. Gearhart, armed but dressed in civilian clothes, picked up a locked briefcase known as the "football," or "black box," and walked down a hospital corridor to a small room where Vice President Lyndon Johnson was being guarded by Secret Service agents.

Lieutenant Commander Vivian Crea, United States Coast Guard, first woman to serve as military aide to the president, carries the "football."
Copyright © CORBIS
UPI/Bettmann

The officer who carries the "football" must be near whoever is the president, to guard "a national security portfolio of cryptographic orders the president would send his military chiefs to authorize the launching of nuclear missiles. The orders can be dispatched by telephone, teletype, or microwave radio."[25]

In effect, the warrant officer has custody of the "nuclear button," which is not a button but a set of coded orders. That such a person and such machinery exist is a reminder of the fact that, regardless of his other duties, the president is at all times commander in chief of the armed forces of the United States.

Although a president normally delegates most of this authority to his generals and admirals, he is not required to do so. During the Whiskey Rebellion of 1794, President Washington personally led his troops into Pennsylvania. During the Civil War, Lincoln often visited the Army of the Potomac to instruct his generals. Franklin Roosevelt and Prime Minister Winston Churchill conferred on the major strategic decisions of the Second World War. Truman made the decisions to drop the atomic bomb on Japan in 1945 and to intervene in Korea in 1950. Kennedy authorized the Bay of Pigs invasion of Cuba by Cuban exiles armed and trained by the Central Intelligence Agency. Johnson personally approved bombing targets in Vietnam. Nixon made the decision to send U.S. troops into Cambodia in 1970, to bomb North Vietnam, and to bomb Cambodia in 1973. Reagan made the decision to send troops to invade Grenada in 1983 and to bomb Libya in 1986. Bush dispatched 27,000 troops to invade Panama in

1989 and sent more than half a million men and women to the Persian Gulf in 1990. Clinton sent armed forces into Haiti and Bosnia, bombed Iraq, and authorized American warplanes to lead NATO's bombing campaign against Yugoslavia.

 for more information about Abraham Lincoln, see: lcweb2.loc.gov/ammem/alhtml

Civilian supremacy, the principle of civilian control of the military, is based on the clear constitutional power of the president as supreme commander of the armed forces. In many other countries, particularly in the Third World, military commanders often topple civilian leaders and seize power for themselves.

In the United States, the principle of civilian supremacy was put to a severe test during the Korean War when General Douglas MacArthur repeatedly defied President Truman's orders. The hero of the Pacific theater during the Second World War, MacArthur enjoyed personal prestige to rival the president's and had a substantial political following of his own. Truman finally dismissed MacArthur in April 1951. In the most dramatic conflict in modern times between the military and the president, the president prevailed.

The Constitution declares that "Congress shall have Power . . . to declare War," but Congress has not done so since December 1941, when it declared war against Japan, following the Japanese attack on Pearl Harbor, and later against Germany.* In the intervening years presidents have made the decision to go to war, although twice—in Vietnam and the Persian Gulf—they had congressional approval. By 1970, Congress was trying to regain some of its control over the war power. Congress repealed the Tonkin Gulf Resolution, which it had passed in 1964 to support President Johnson's Vietnam policy, and it restricted President Nixon's future use of U.S. troops in Cambodia. Sentiment continued to grow in Congress to curb the president's power to wage undeclared war.

*Congress has declared war five times: in the War of 1812, the U.S.-Mexican War, the Spanish-American War, the First World War, and the Second World War. It did not declare war in Korea, Vietnam, or the Persian Gulf. However, it authorized military action in Vietnam with the Tonkin Gulf Resolution in 1964, and in the Persian Gulf with the Authorization for Use of Military Force against Iraq Resolution in 1991.

Then, in 1973, Congress passed legislation to attempt to limit presidential war-making power. President Nixon vetoed the measure as an unconstitutional restraint on his power as commander in chief. Congress overrode the president's veto, however, and the War Powers Resolution became law. The measure provided that the president must report to Congress within 48 hours after sending armed forces into combat abroad, and that their use would have to end in 60 days unless Congress authorized a longer period. Within the authorized period, Congress could order an immediate withdrawal of U.S. forces.

Under five presidents, however, the War Powers Resolution had not effectively restricted presidential military power. Presidents Ford, Carter, Reagan, Bush, and Clinton all took military actions that they did not report to Congress under the War Powers Resolution. In some instances, they did report military actions to Congress, but either stated or implied that they had authority as president to deploy American forces, adding that these reports were a matter of courtesy rather than a legal requirement.

In September 1983, after President Reagan sent marines to Lebanon, Congress invoked the War Powers Resolution for the first time since its passage 10 years earlier. It enacted legislation declaring that the law applied to the conflict in Lebanon and authorizing continued deployment of the marines there for 18 months. President Reagan signed the bill, but said this did not mean he accepted the principle that the War Powers Resolution applied in Lebanon.

Other presidents followed this pattern; they informed Congress of military actions but maintained they did so, in effect, as a courtesy, not as a legal requirement.

The War Powers Resolution, or at least that portion giving Congress authority to order a withdrawal of American forces, is a form of legislative veto, a device ruled unconstitutional by the Supreme Court in 1983.[26]

The **military-industrial complex**—the term often used to describe the ties between the military establishment and the defense-aerospace industry—is another limit on the president's power as commander in chief. For example, a president may find it difficult to cancel production of a fighter plane, a bomber, an aircraft

The 22nd New York State militia answers Lincoln's call.
Copyright © Medford Historical Society Collection/CORBIS

carrier, or some other weapons system that enjoys the strong support of the Joint Chiefs of Staff, Congress, and private industry.

Politics may also narrow a president's options. President Reagan proposed a space-based missile defense program, popularly known as "Star Wars," to protect against Soviet ICBMs. The project cost $60 billion and produced nothing. President Clinton felt it necessary to support a more modest, land-based missile shield against smaller countries. Aside from the fact that defense contractors had a huge stake in building the system, Clinton had to weigh the political costs of killing the program. To do so would open the Democrats to Republican charges they were "soft on defense." In the end, Clinton postponed a decision and left it to his successor.

Despite these limits, presidents have claimed and exercised formidable war powers during emergencies. In the 10 weeks after the fall of Fort Sumter, South Carolina, in April 1861, Lincoln called out the militia, spent $2 million without authorization by Congress, blockaded Southern ports, and suspended the writ of habeas corpus in certain areas. Lincoln declared: "I felt that measures otherwise unconstitutional might become lawful by becoming indispensable to the preservation of the Constitution through the preservation of the nation. Right or wrong, I assumed this ground and now avow it."[27]

During the Second World War, Franklin Roosevelt exercised extraordinary powers over food rationing and the economy, only partly with congressional authorization. And in 1942, with the consent of Congress, he permitted the forced removal of 112,000 persons of Japanese descent—most of them native-born citizens of the United States—from their homes in California and other western states to internment camps called "relocation centers."

During the Korean War, Truman seized the steel mills in the face of a strike threat, but the Supreme Court ruled he had no constitutional right to do so, even as commander in chief.[28] President Johnson expanded American forces in Vietnam after Congress passed the Tonkin Gulf Resolution, empowering the president to take "all necessary measures" in Southeast Asia. The president contended, however, that he did not need congressional approval to fight the war in Vietnam.

 for more information about Lyndon Johnson, see: www.lbjlib.utexas.edu

Chief Diplomat

"I make American foreign policy," President Truman declared in 1948. By and large, presidents do make foreign policy; that is, they direct the relations of the United States with the other nations of the world. The Constitution does not specifically confer this power on the president, but it does so indirectly. It authorizes him to receive foreign ambassadors, to appoint ambassadors, and to make treaties with the consent of two-thirds of the Senate. Because it requires that the president share some foreign policy powers with Congress, the Constitution has been characterized as "an invitation to struggle for the privilege of directing American foreign policy."[29]

In this struggle the president usually enjoys the advantage. Because the State Department, the Pentagon, and the CIA report to him as part of the executive branch, the president—or so it is often assumed—has more information about foreign affairs available to him than do members of Congress. But senators and representatives also have sources of information—official briefings,

1942: Japanese Americans lining up in California before being sent to internment camps
Copyright © CORBIS

President Clinton discusses Bosnia with members of the National Security Council.
Dana Walker/TimePix copyright © Time, Inc.

background memoranda from the Library of Congress, data from the Congressional Budget Office, unofficial "leaks" from within the bureaucracy, and friends in the press and the universities. A president, therefore, does not have a monopoly on information. Much of the information he does receive is conflicting, because it represents different viewpoints within the bureaucracy; even with the best intelligence reports, a president may make decisions that prove to be misguided. Nevertheless, the information that flows in daily is a substantial source of power for the president.

Those who lack the information that the president has, or is presumed to have, including senators and representatives, find it difficult to challenge the president's actions. Often, at least in the short run, a foreign policy crisis may increase the public's support of the president's actions. (Refer again to Figure 13-1.) Over time, however, public opinion can change and Congress can chip away at a president's power in foreign affairs.

The president has sole power to negotiate and sign treaties. That power was reaffirmed by the Supreme Court in 1936.[30] The Senate may block a treaty by refusing to approve it, but it seldom does so. In 1920, however, it did refuse to ratify the Treaty of Versailles and its provision for U.S. membership in the League of Nations. Sometimes a president does not submit a treaty to the Senate because he knows it will not be approved, or he may modify the treaty to meet Senate opposition. In 1977 President Carter submitted two treaties to the Senate that turned over the Panama Canal to Panama in the year 2000. After months of controversy, the Senate finally approved the treaties the following year, but with a reservation sponsored by Senator Dennis DeConcini, a Democrat from Arizona, asserting the right of the United States to send troops into Panama to keep the canal open.

Executive agreements are international agreements between the president and foreign heads of state that, unlike treaties, do not require Senate approval. Today, these are employed by the president in the conduct of foreign affairs more often than treaties. Some executive agreements are made by the president with the prior approval of Congress. For example, in the Trade Act of 1974, Congress restored the president's power to negotiate tariff agreements with other countries. And sometimes, to gain political support, a president will submit an executive agreement to Congress after it is signed, although he is not legally required to do so.

Because a president can sign an executive agreement with another nation without the constitutional necessity of going to the Senate, the use of this device has increased enormously. This has been particularly true since the Second World War, as the U.S. role in international affairs has expanded. Today, in a single year, a president may sign several hundred executive agreements.

The president also has sole power to recognize or not recognize foreign governments. The United States did not recognize the Soviet Union until November 1933, some 16 years after the Russian Revolution. Since Woodrow Wilson's day, presidents have used diplomatic recognition as an instrument of foreign policy. President Nixon's historic journey to Beijing early in 1972 marked the start of diplomatic contacts between the United States and the People's Republic of China. President Carter recognized China in 1979, and the two countries opened full diplomatic relations. In 1991, President Bush recognized the Baltic nations—Lithuania, Latvia, and Estonia—after they gained independence from the Soviet Union, and he established diplomatic relations with Russia and with the other former republics of the Soviet Union.

 for more information about Jimmy Carter, see: *carterlibrary.peachnet.edu*

Online **for more information about George Bush, see:** *ww.csdl.tamu.edu/bushlib*

Presidents do make foreign policy: British Prime Minister Winston Churchill, President Truman, and Soviet Premier Stalin at Potsdam, 1945.
Copyright © CORBIS/Bettmann

In acting as chief diplomat, the president, as commander in chief, can back up his diplomacy with military power. Both the arrows and the olive branch depicted in the presidential seal are available to him, a good example of how presidential roles overlap.

Chief Legislator

"He shall from time to time give to the Congress Information of the State of the Union, and recommend to their Consideration such Measures as he shall judge necessary and expedient." With this statement in Article II, "the Constitution puts the President right square into the legislative business," as President Eisenhower once observed.

Today, presidents often use their televised State of the Union address, usually delivered to a joint session of Congress in January, as a public platform to unveil their annual legislative program. The details of proposed legislation are then filled in through a series of special presidential messages sent to Capitol Hill in the months that follow.

This was not always the case. Active presidential participation in the legislative process is a 20th-century phenomenon, and the practice of presidents sending a comprehensive legislative package to Congress developed only after the Second World War during the Truman Administration.[31]

The success of the president's role as chief legislator depends on the cooperation of Congress. A president faced with a Congress controlled by the opposition party, as was the case during the four years following Bush's election in 1988, and from midterm after Clinton's election in 1992, may find his role as chief legislator frustrating. President Kennedy, a Democrat whose legislative program was blocked by a coalition of Republicans and southern Democrats, felt a similar frustration. As Kennedy observed ruefully: "It is very easy to defeat a bill in the Congress. It is much more difficult to pass one. . . . They are two separate offices and two separate powers, the Congress and the Presidency. There is bound to be conflict."[32]

That conflict reached extraordinary levels during the budget battle of 1995–1996, when the government shut down twice because the Republican Congress and the Democratic chief executive were unable to agree on spending programs to achieve a balanced budget.

As one scholar, Charles O. Jones, has concluded, the president is often less influential in the legislative process than the public thinks. "Few, if any, major policy proposals are likely to pass both houses unchanged. Presidents rarely expect that to happen, and if they do, they are inevitably disappointed."[33]

The conflict between the president and Congress at times revolves around the doctrine of **executive privilege,** the claim by presidents of an inherent right to withhold information from Congress and the judiciary. This doctrine is nowhere explicitly stated in the Constitution but rests on the separation of powers of the three branches of government. Although presidents may invoke executive privilege, Congress in turn has argued that its legislative powers include the right to make inquiries and investigations of the executive branch, and to obtain all necessary information from the president and his administration. Usually conflicts over executive privilege arise when a congressional committee demands documents from, or testimony by, presidential assistants.

As the Watergate scandal unfolded during the Nixon administration, the president was accused by his former counsel of participating in an illegal plot to cover up the break-in and bugging at the Democratic Party headquarters in the Watergate office building in Washington. Nixon's tapes of his own White House conversations became the crucial evidence, although an 18½-minute segment of a key tape had apparently been erased. Eventually, the Watergate special prosecutor demanded the tapes for use in the trial of several high-ranking officials accused of covering up the break-in and the issue went to the U.S. Supreme Court. In ruling 8–0 that Nixon must surrender his tapes, the Court for the first time recognized the doctrine of executive privilege, but it also declared that the right of the president to keep some matters confidential must yield to the need for evidence in a criminal trial.[34]

Every president has staff assistants in charge of legislative liaison. Their job is to pressure Congress to pass the president's program. The senators or representatives who want the administration to approve a new federal building, or dam, or public works project in their state or district may discover that the price is their vote on a bill that the president wants passed. There are other,

more subtle pressures. A senator who opposes a president's foreign policies may no longer be invited to White House social functions. Often, on an important measure, the president himself takes charge of the "arm twisting"—telephoning members of Congress in their offices or inviting them to the White House for a chat about the merits of his program.

On the other hand, political scientist George C. Edwards, III, has argued, "while legislative skills may at times gain support for presidential policies, this is not typical." Examining the various resources available to a president, Edwards concluded that a chief executive "has relatively little influence to wield over Congress."[35]

As chief legislator, however, the president is not limited entirely to the art of persuasion. He has an important constitutional weapon in the **veto,** the constitutional power of the president to disapprove a bill and return it with his objections to the branch of Congress in which it originated. By a vote of two-thirds of each house, Congress may pass the bill over the president's veto. If he approves a bill, he may sign it—often in front of news photographers and with much fanfare and handing out of pens.

If the president does not either sign or veto a bill within 10 working days after he receives it, the measure becomes law without his signature. If Congress adjourns during the 10-day period after the president receives a bill, he can exercise his **pocket veto,** the power of a president to kill a bill by taking no action when Congress has adjourned.

But the Constitution is unclear on whether a president can pocket-veto a bill when Congress is in recess. During the 1970s, Senator Edward M. Kennedy successfully challenged in court three pocket vetoes by Presidents Nixon and Ford. The court rulings suggested that a president may not pocket-veto legislation when

President Clinton signs the bill overhauling the nation's welfare system.
AP/Wide World

Congress is in recess but only when it adjourns for good at the end of the second session of a Congress.

Except for joint resolutions, which are the same as bills, resolutions of Congress do not require presidential action because they are expressions of sentiment, not law.

Because Congress normally finds it difficult to override a presidential veto, merely the threat of a veto is often enough to force Congress to tailor a bill to conform to administration wishes. Only about 4 percent of presidential vetoes have been overridden by Congress. (See Table 13-1.)

President Clinton briefly enjoyed a **line-item veto,** the power of the president—struck down by the Supreme Court in 1998—to veto specific parts of appropriations bills. Most state governors have this power. In 1996 Congress passed and President Clinton signed a law to give the president such power for the first time, for a period of eight years. Clinton used that power to veto parts of 11 bills, eliminating money to dredge a lake in Indiana, build a truck and tank wash for the Army in California, and provide a tax break for Idaho potato growers.[36] The line-item veto was first voided by a federal judge in 1997 and then ruled unconstitutional in a 6–3 decision by the Supreme Court in 1998.[37]

In the words of Justice John Paul Stevens, who wrote the Supreme Court's opinion, "The Line-Item Veto Act authorizes the president himself to effect the repeal of

TABLE 13-1

Presidential Vetoes, 1789–2000

	Regular Vetoes	Pocket Vetoes	Total Vetoes	Vetoes Overridden
Washington	2	—	2	—
Madison	5	2	7	—
Monroe	1	—	1	—
Jackson	5	7	12	—
Tyler	6	3	9	1
Polk	2	1	3	—
Pierce	9	—	9	5
Buchanan	4	3	7	—
Lincoln	2	4	6	—
A. Johnson	21	8	29	15
Grant	45	49	94	4
Hayes	12	1	13	1
Arthur	4	8	12	1
Cleveland	304	109	413	2
B. Harrison	19	25	44	1
Cleveland	43	127	170	5
McKinley	6	36	42	—
T. Roosevelt	42	40	82	1
Taft	30	9	39	1
Wilson	33	11	44	6
Harding	5	1	6	—
Coolidge	20	30	50	4
Hoover	21	16	37	3
F. Roosevelt	372	261	633	9
Truman	180	70	250	12
Eisenhower	73	108	181	2
Kennedy	12	9	21	—
L. Johnson	16	14	30	—
Nixon	24	19	43	5
Ford	44	22	66	12
Carter	13	18	31	2
Reagan	39	39	78	9
Bush	29	15	44	1
Clinton	31	—	31	3
Total	1,474	1,065	2,539	105

SOURCES: Senate Library; *Congressional Quarterly;* the White House. Data for Clinton as of May 2, 2000.

laws, for his own policy reasons, without observing the procedures set out in Article I" of the Constitution.[38] The Court thus held that Congress cannot, simply by passing a law, modify a power granted by the Constitution; to do so would require a constitutional amendment.

Presidents Reagan, Bush, and Clinton had repeatedly asked Congress to enact a constitutional amendment to give the president a line-item veto. One reason is that Congress often passes **riders,** provisions tacked on to a piece of legislation that are not relevant to the bill. The president may find the rider objectionable, but must swallow the legislation whole or veto the entire bill—he cannot veto the rider alone.

As chief legislator, the president may call Congress back into session. He also may adjourn Congress if the House and the Senate should disagree about when to adjourn, although no president has exercised this constitutional power.

The Supreme Court has held that Congress may not delegate legislative authority to the president, but Congress has in some cases passed legislation setting broad guidelines within which the president may act. For example, under such laws the president may be authorized to reduce tariffs. And since 1939 Congress has periodically passed a series of Reorganization Acts that permit the president to restructure federal agencies under plans that he must submit to Congress. Unless Congress disapproves the plans within 60 days, they go into effect.

The president's real ability to persuade Congress often rests on his personal popularity rather than on his formal or informal powers. The veto, "arm twisting," threats to withhold funds for a public works project, and social ostracism of a representative or senator are, over the long run, less important than the ability of a president to enlist public support for his programs and the extent of his prestige with both Congress and the electorate.

Chief of Party

"No President, it seems to me, can escape politics," John Kennedy said in 1960 when he sought the presidency. "He has not only been chosen by the Nation—he has been chosen by his party."[39]

Not every president has filled the role of party chief with the same enthusiasm that Kennedy brought to it. President Eisenhower, a career Army officer for most of his life, displayed a reluctance to engage in the rough-and-tumble of politics. As he told a press conference in 1955: "In the general derogatory sense . . . I do not like politics . . . the word 'politics' as you use it, I think the answer to that one, would be, no. I have no great liking for that."[40]

For many months in 1980, President Carter declined to campaign actively for reelection, claiming that the hostage crisis in Iran took precedence over his political duties and made it necessary for him to remain in the White House. "I am not going to resume business as usual as a partisan campaigner out on the campaign trail until our hostages are back here, free and at home," Carter declared.[41] Carter thus attempted to adopt a presidential "above politics" stance. But two and a half months later, when Carter announced that the country's foreign and domestic problems "are manageable enough now for me to leave the White House," his statement brought hoots of disbelief from his critics.[42] He lost the election to Ronald Reagan.

Whether or not a president enjoys his partisan role, he is the chief of his party. The machinery of the national committee reports to him; he can install his choice as national chairperson; he can usually demand his party's renomination and can stage-manage the convention that acclaims him. Since success as chief legislator depends to a considerable degree on the political makeup of Congress, the president may find it advantageous to campaign for congressional candidates in off-year elections. Given the decentralized nature of American political parties, however, a president's influence may not extend to state and local party organizations in every case.

Nor does the president always prevail with members of his party in Congress. The nature of the American political system is such that a basic weakness is built into the president's role as party leader: His own leaders in Congress may not bow to his political wisdom or policy wishes in every case. A president may be hobbled in achieving his domestic policy goals, and even his foreign policy objectives, by the fact that he cannot always count on the support of his own party's members in Congress. By contrast, a British prime minister can generally depend on the disciplined support of the members of the majority party in Parliament.

When a president makes decisions, he is, in the broadest sense, engaging in politics. A successful president must lead and gauge public opinion, must be sensitive to change, and must have a sure sense of the limits of the possible. All of these are political skills. As chief of party, the president is also the nation's number one professional politician. And, as Richard Neustadt has suggested, "The Presidency is no place for amateurs."[43]

Popular Leader

The president also plays a vital role as the popular leader of the nation, the one person who speaks—in theory at least—for all of America. The president, aside from all of his more formal, constitutional, and political roles, is also expected to act as the national leader. In times of crisis, the people tend to look to the president for reassurance. For example, when the president addresses the nation on television from the Oval Office to explain why he is sending U.S. forces to some remote corner of the globe, as has often happened, he is technically acting as commander in chief, but in a larger sense he is acting as

MAKING A DIFFERENCE
THE UNFINISHED PRESIDENCY

What to do on the miserable January morning when you wake up and find you are no longer the most powerful man in the world?

Theodore Roosevelt mounted a grand, year-long safari to East Africa—where, nearsighted as Mr. Magoo, he fired off an astonishing amount of ammunition at every species in God's creation, to be stuffed for the American Museum of Natural History. Lyndon Johnson returned to his Texas ranch to drink and smoke and grow his hair long like a hippie and wait to die. Richard Nixon did brooding penance beside the Pacific, then went back East to reinvent himself as an elder statesman.

Perhaps a president's life after the White House is the real manifestation of his character. Consider the interesting case of Jimmy Carter. Buried, after one term, in the Ronald Reagan landslide of 1980, widely scorned as the micromanager of malaise, held hostage by the Ayatollah, Carter in his post–White House incarnation performed a cunning reversal. An engineer by training, he did not so much reinvent himself as reconstruct, in another dimension, the job from which the American people had fired him.

When Carter left the White House in 1981 at the relatively young age of 56, logic dictated that he continue to be politically active, although he promised he would never try to regain the presidency. The question was how he wanted to spend the rest of his life. He knew he wanted to do a lot more than build a museum-library in tribute to himself and give a lot of after-dinner speeches. What Carter really wanted was to find some way to continue the unfinished business of his presidency. In *Keeping Faith*, the memoir Carter wrote at home in Plains, Georgia, during his first 18 months out of office, he set forth the goals of "alleviating tension in the troubled areas of the world, promoting human rights, enhancing environmental quality. . . . These were hazy ideas at best, but they gave us something to anticipate which could be exciting and challenging during the years ahead." These "hazy ideas" evolved into a grand design: the Carter Center in Atlanta, which has become his lasting institutional legacy to peace, democracy, health, and human rights.

Since leaving office Carter had been involved in mediating an impressive list of foreign disputes, civil wars, and political transitions.

Some observers have suggested that Carter used the White House as a stepping-stone to the status of elder statesman. It is more accurate to say that instead of abandoning his agenda when he lost badly to Ronald Reagan in 1980, he chose to continue working toward programs and policies he believed in, in office or out of it. That he has tried to complete his unfinished agenda with such vigor and such success is a testament to his stubborn will and tenacious refusal ever to throw in the towel. Jimmy Carter may be many things, but a quitter is not among them.

—Adapted from *Time* magazine and *The Unfinished Presidency: Jimmy Carter's Journey beyond the White House*

national leader, the powerful figure to whom the voters turn, perhaps as much for psychological support as for factual explanations.

To this role of popular leader, the president normally brings an ideology and a philosophy. Franklin D. Roosevelt was identified with the social-welfare programs of the New Deal, Lyndon Johnson with their echo in the Great Society of the 1960s. Ronald Reagan, by contrast, was identified with limited government. To some extent, his successor, George Bush, shared that view, often contending that individuals could accomplish more than government programs. Clinton portrayed himself as a New Democrat, somewhat more conservative than his party's New Deal tradition.

As national leader, the president does more, of course, than expound a philosophy. The policies of his administration, the legislative agenda he sends to Congress, and the actions of his bureaucrats often reflect his point of view. He may hope, although he may often be disappointed, that the justices he appoints to the Supreme Court will also march to his tune. In fact, Supreme Court decisions sometimes cause troubles for a president. The 1954 *Brown* decision, requiring desegregation of public schools, resulted in turmoil for Presidents Eisenhower and Kennedy. The *Roe* v. *Wade* decision legalizing abortion in 1973 crystallized an emotional issue that still divides the nation nearly three decades later.

Today, presidential rhetoric—a chief executive's skills as an orator and persuader—powerfully affects his ability to govern. Indeed, "rhetorical leadership," in the view of presidential scholar Jeffrey K. Tulis, "is the essence of the modern presidency."[44] He adds: "Since the presidencies of Theodore Roosevelt and Woodrow Wilson, popular or mass rhetoric has become a principal tool of presidential governance. Presidents regularly 'go over the heads' of Congress to the people at large in support of legislation and other initiatives. . . . The doctrine that a president ought to be a popular leader has become an unquestioned premise of our political culture."[45] Presidents now are expected to inspire the public, Tulis notes. "And for many, this presidential 'function' is not one duty among many, but rather the heart of the presidency—its essential task."[46] President Reagan's "stunning string of partisan successes," including budget cuts and a military buildup, were due in no small measure to his skills as a popular leader, a "great communicator."[47]

But the president's role as popular leader is not without its perils. Modern presidents, Theodore J. Lowi has argued, are doomed to failure. Because of the "exalted rhetoric and high expectations surrounding the presidency," even a degree of success is considered a failure by the mass public, Lowi contends.[48] The presidency is thus a no-win situation, in Lowi's view, because for a successful presidential candidate, victory in November is the beginning of the end: "His political career is finished before he can fully enjoy the prize."[49]

In this view, as soon as a president wins, he loses. This paradox is a direct result of the enormous attention focused on modern presidents in the American political system.

As Lowi puts it: "Since the president has become the embodiment of government, it seems perfectly normal for millions upon millions of Americans to concentrate their hopes and fears directly and personally upon him. It is no wonder that [the] United States has developed such a tremendous stake in the 'personal president' and his personal capacity to govern."[50]

The president, it must be emphasized again, fills all of these various presidential roles at once. The powers and duties of the office are not divisible. The roles conflict and overlap; in performing one role, the president may incur political costs that make it more difficult for him to perform another. In short, the presidency is a balancing act.

In addition to these basic roles, Americans expect the president to take on many other roles. In the event of a major civil disturbance, he is expected to act as a police officer and restore domestic tranquility. As the manager of the economy, he is expected to prevent recession, ensure prosperity, and hold down the cost of butter and eggs. He is expected to set an example in his personal life—which is why accusations of marital infidelity became a campaign issue when Bill Clinton ran for president in 1992, and why his later sexual affair with a young intern cast a long shadow over his legacy.

A president is expected to be a teacher, to educate the people about great public issues. In some mysterious way, the president is expected to speak for all the people and to give voice to their deepest aspirations and ideals. "The Presidency," Franklin Roosevelt said, "is not merely an administrative office. That is the least of it. It is preeminently a place of moral leadership."[51]

THE TOOLS OF PRESIDENTIAL POWER

In the exercise of power, the president of the United States has available a formidable array of tools, money, and people. In ever widening circles, this last category includes the White House staff (secretaries and advisers), the Executive Office of the President (a conglomerate of presidential substaffs), the vice president, the cabinet, the 14 cabinet departments, the many other agencies of the executive branch, and the more than 5 million employees of the federal bureaucracy and the military.

He has almost unlimited personal resources as well. When President Johnson had reviewed the marines in California on one occasion and was walking back to a helicopter, he was stopped by an officer who pointed to another helicopter and said, "That's your helicopter over there, sir." Johnson replied, "Son, they are all my helicopters."[52]

When the president travels, he has at his disposal not only helicopters, but a fleet of jets; aboard Air Force One, he can communicate with his aides or with the military

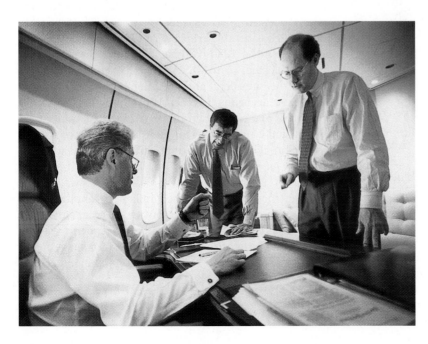

President Clinton confers with aides aboard Air Force One.
Copyright © Wally McNamee/Sygma

The Tools of Presidential Power   **429**

anywhere in the world. If he flies to Kansas City to deliver a speech, a special Pentagon communications unit that travels with the president links him to the White House.

In addition to the formal machinery of government at the president's command, he has other, informal resources—his reputation, personality and style, ability to arouse public opinion, political party, and informal advisers and friends.

As one leading presidential scholar, Thomas Cronin, has warned, however, listing the president's cabinet and all the other panels, staffs, and informal advisers that serve him might create the impression that a president "must have just about all the inside information and good advice anyone could want." As Cronin points out, one might even erroneously conclude that a president "can both set and shape the directions of public policy and can see to it that these policies work as intended."[53] Yet, that is often not the case. As we have already seen, there are limitations on presidential power at almost every turn. Indeed, one of the measures of a president's power is how well he can use the tools at his command.

The Cabinet

The president, the vice president, the heads of the major executive departments of the government, and certain other senior officials who may hold "cabinet rank" constitute the cabinet. (See Table 13-2.) But the cabinet is an informal institution. The Constitution speaks of "the principal Officer in each of the executive Departments" and of "Heads of Departments." The Twenty-fifth Amendment, ratified in 1967, allows for the possibility of the department heads acting as a group in case of presidential disability. But the cabinet as an organized body is nowhere specifically provided for by law or in the Constitution.

The president, Richard F. Fenno points out, "is not required by law to form a Cabinet or to keep one," and the cabinet has become "institutionalized by usage alone."[54] Perhaps because the cabinet is entirely a creature of custom, it is a relatively weak institution. The weakness of the cabinet under a strong president is often illustrated by the story of how Lincoln counted the votes when the entire cabinet was opposed to him: "Seven nays, one aye—the ayes have it."

In any case, a cabinet member may not be competent to discuss problems of a general nature, for "beyond his immediate bailiwick, he may not be capable of adding anything to the group conference."[55] For this reason, President Kennedy thought that cabinet meetings were "a waste of time."[56]

Modern presidents have made varied use of the cabinet. Lyndon Johnson met regularly with his cabinet, but the conduct of the war in Vietnam was normally discussed not in the cabinet, but at regular Tuesday luncheon meetings of the president and selected officials. Nixon sought, only briefly, to revitalize the cabinet as a formal advisory body, but seldom held cabinet meetings in his second term. Carter met with his cabinet more fre-

TABLE 13-2

The President's Cabinet

The Executive Departments, in Order of Formation*	
State	1789
Treasury	1789
Interior	1849
Justice†	1870
Agriculture‡	1889
Commerce§	1913
Labor§	1913
Defense¶	1947
Housing and Urban Development	1965
Transportation	1966
Energy	1977
Education	1979
Health and Human Services#	1979
Veterans Affairs	1989
Homeland Security	2002

*As of 2002. The office of postmaster general, created in 1789, received cabinet rank in 1829 and was made a cabinet department in 1872. In 1970 Congress abolished the Post Office as a cabinet department and replaced it with the U.S. Postal Service, an independent federal agency.

†The office of attorney general, created in 1789, became the Department of Justice in 1870.

‡Created in 1862 and elevated to a cabinet department in 1889.

§The Department of Commerce and Labor, created in 1903, was divided into two departments in 1913.

¶The Department of War (the Army), created in 1789, and the Department of the Navy, created in 1798, were consolidated with the Air Force into the Department of Defense in 1947.

#Created as the Department of Health, Education, and Welfare in 1953, it was divided into two cabinet departments in 1979.

quently than any president since Eisenhower. However, in one tumultuous week in 1979, he fired or accepted the resignations of five cabinet members. The shake-up brought considerable criticism of the president.

During the 1980 campaign, Ronald Reagan promised, if elected, to institute a "cabinet government," in which the president and the members of his cabinet arrived at decisions together. But in practice, it was the president and a small group of White House staff aides who usually made the real decisions. "Cabinet government is an illusion," one administration official acknowledged.[57] As one account put it, "Full Cabinet meetings, scornfully referred to as 'dog-and-pony shows' by one Cabinet member and as 'pep rallies' by another, were largely informational. The busier Cabinet members and White House staff members alike tended to regard them as a waste of time. 'I can't think of a single major decision that has been made at the full Cabinet meeting,' said one secretary."[58]

 for more information about Ronald Reagan, see: www.ronaldreagan.com

Several members of President Clinton's cabinet caused him political problems. Agriculture Secretary Mike Espy resigned amid charges that he had committed ethical lapses, Commerce Secretary Ronald H. Brown was under investigation for his business dealings when he was killed in a plane crash, Housing and Urban Development Secretary Henry Cisneros was investigated for payments to his mistress, and Hazel O'Leary, the secretary of energy, was criticized in Congress and by the press for her lavish travel style.[*]

On the other hand, cabinet members can sometimes serve as useful "lightning rods" to divert blame from a president.[59] In April 1993, for example, 85 persons died in the federal siege of the Branch Davidian religious sect at Waco, Texas. Attorney General Janet Reno, who had ordered the FBI to attack the compound, took full responsibility afterward. As a result, in the immediate aftermath of Waco, President Clinton escaped some of the public outrage over the government's handling of the matter. Later, Reno's repeated refusal to appoint an independent counsel to investigate financial abuses by the Clinton-Gore ticket during the 1996 election campaign subjected her to repeated Republican attacks. Again, Clinton let Reno take most of the criticism.

Although the cabinet is often considered to be a device to assist the president, it also limits his power to some extent. "The members of the Cabinet," Vice President (under Calvin Coolidge) Charles G. Dawes said, "are a President's natural enemies."[60] In part, this is because cabinet members after a time tend to adopt the parochial view of their own departments. They may

President Coolidge and his cabinet pose for photographers in 1924.
Copyright © CORBIS

become narrow advocates of the programs and needs of their bureaucracies, competing with other cabinet members for bigger budgets and presidential favor. As Fenno has noted, a cabinet member's "formal responsibilities extend both upward toward the President and downward toward his own department."[61]

The White House Staff

When President Clinton moved into the White House in January 1993, his staff at first was young, inexperienced in the ways of Washington, and still operating in the informal, chaotic fashion of the political campaign organization that had elected him.

For his chief of staff, Clinton appointed a boyhood friend, Thomas F. "Mack" McLarty, an Arkansas businessman with no Washington experience. It proved a mistake; McLarty ran an undisciplined White House prone to errors. A year and a half later, Clinton replaced McLarty with budget director Leon E. Panetta, a former congressman from northern California, wise in the ways

---

[*]Espy was tried and acquitted of all charges, Cisneros pleaded guilty to a single count of lying to the FBI about the amount of the payments and was fined $10,000, and Attorney General Janet Reno declined to appoint an independent counsel to investigate O'Leary.

RONALD REAGAN ON THE IRAN-CONTRA SCANDAL

As the Iran-contra scandal began to unfold in 1986, President Reagan offered shifting interpretations of what had occurred:

November 13, 1986:
"We did not—repeat—we did not trade weapons or anything else for hostages."

November 19, 1986:
"I don't think a mistake was made."

November 24, 1986:
"I'm not going to lie about that. I didn't make a mistake."

December 6, 1986:
"It's obvious that the execution of these policies was flawed, and mistakes were made."

March 4, 1987:
"I told the American people I did not trade arms for hostages. My heart and my best intentions still tell me that's true. But the facts and the evidence tell me it is not. . . . What began as a strategic opening to Iran deteriorated in its implementation into trading arms for hostages."

—*Washington Post*

of the capital. Panetta imposed order and discipline on the White House staff and emerged as a key player and presidential spokesman in 1995 during the budget negotiations with the Republican leaders of Congress. Panetta had proved once again the power that can be wielded by the president's chief of staff. His successors, Erskine B. Bowles, a millionaire North Carolina investment banker, and John D. Podesta, a lawyer and former congressional committee staff counsel, also exercised considerable power in the capital.

Presidents do not always choose wisely in making this key appointment. Soon after the 1988 election, George Bush appointed John H. Sununu chief of staff at the White House. As governor of New Hampshire, Sununu had helped Bush win the presidential primary in that state, a crucial victory in Bush's drive for the nomination. Now he was being rewarded. The announcement signaled to official Washington that Sununu would probably become one of the most powerful individuals in the capital during the Bush administration. Indeed he did, but Sununu's abrasive manner grated on his colleagues and members of Congress, and his high-living style caught the attention of the press. Stories appeared about Sununu using official limousines and military aircraft on personal trips, including ski trips and a visit to his dentist; soon the television networks were talking about "Air Sununu." At first, the combative chief of staff weathered the storm, but by December 1991 the criticism had become too intense to withstand; Sununu resigned.

The affair oddly echoed the fate of one of Sununu's predecessors during the Reagan administration. In his second term, Reagan named Donald T. Regan, a Wall Street broker who had been secretary of the treasury, to be the new White House chief of staff. Regan, too, was known for his take-charge, aggressive manner. But after the Iran-contra scandal broke, a presidential panel named to investigate the matter found that Regan "must bear primary responsibility for the chaos that descended upon the White House"[62] following the disclosure of the affair. Regan's days were numbered even before the report was made public. Behind the scenes he had feuded with Nancy Reagan, the president's wife, who led the campaign that resulted in Regan's ouster.

Modern presidents depend on large staffs. And great power is often wielded by those who surround the president, some of whom rise from relative obscurity to great influence. Wilson had his Colonel House, Franklin Roosevelt his Harry Hopkins, Eisenhower his Sherman Adams,* Johnson his Bill Moyers, and Nixon his H. R. (Bob) Haldeman and John D. Ehrlichman—both of whom went to prison in the Watergate scandal. Carter's aide, Hamilton Jordan, became a powerful figure in the White House. All modern presidents have come to rely on their advisers, and in every case, some aides have emerged as more influential than others.

The power of the president's assistants, however, flows from their position as extensions of the president. Seldom possessing any political prestige or constituency of their own, they depend entirely on staying in the president's good graces for their survival. Their power is derivative, though nonetheless real—it is not uncommon in the White House to see a cabinet member waiting to confer with a member of the president's staff.

In recent administrations, the president's assistant for national security affairs has often taken a central role in foreign policy formation and crisis management. With access to the president and the White House Situation Room, the downstairs office into which all military, intelligence, and diplomatic information flows, the national security adviser may emerge as a powerful rival to the secretary of state. Henry A. Kissinger, for example, took the post in the Nixon Administration and quickly emerged as the most powerful White House adviser in the field of foreign affairs, overshadowing Secretary of State William P. Rogers. Eventually, Kissinger himself was named secretary of state by Nixon.[63]

The members of the president's staff fill a variety of functions that are essential to presidential decision making. Some act as gatekeepers and guardians of the president's time. Others deal almost exclusively with Congress. Still others serve as links with the executive departments and agencies, channeling problems and conflicts among the departments to the president. Some advise the president on political questions, patronage, and appointments. Others may write his speeches. The press secretary issues presidential announcements on matters large and small and fences with correspondents at press briefings.

Presidents use their staffs differently. Eisenhower had a tight, formal system, with Sherman Adams, his chief of staff, screening all problems and deciding what the president should see. Kennedy favored a less structured arrangement, regarding his staff as "a wheel and a series of spokes" with himself in the center.[64] In his first term, Reagan relied on three senior advisers who seemed roughly equal in power. Bush returned to a more traditional White House staff system, with a single chief of staff. And after Leon Panetta took over, the Clinton White House also operated along traditional lines.

The Office of Personnel Management in the year 2000 listed almost 400 persons under "The White House Office," with a payroll of more than $30 million. Of these presidential staff members, perhaps fewer than a dozen occupied top-ranking positions of policy influence. Inevitably, the chief executive's vision, to a degree, is filtered through the eyes of his assistants. An Eisenhower or a Nixon, with a rigid staff system, may become isolated in the White House. A Lyndon Johnson, with an overpowering, demanding personality, may surround himself with deferential aides. In short, the president's staff may not let him hear enough, or it may tell him only what he wants to hear.

---

*Much to Eisenhower's distress, Adams was forced to resign in 1958 for accepting a vicuña coat and other gifts from Bernard Goldfine, a Boston textile manufacturer for whom Adams had interceded with federal regulatory agencies.

President Nixon and Secretary of State Henry Kissinger
Copyright © CORBIS

The Executive Office of the President

The White House staff is only a small part of the huge presidential establishment that has burgeoned since Franklin D. Roosevelt's day. Under the umbrella of the Executive Office of the President, there are more than half a dozen key agencies serving the president directly, with a combined payroll in the year 2000 of $142 million and a total staff of 1,600. (See Figure 13-2.) Many of these employees have offices in the Executive Office Building just west of the White House.

Roosevelt established the Executive Office of the President in 1939 by executive order, after a committee of scholars had reported to him: "The President needs help." Since that time, the office has grown substantially. As the Executive Office of the President existed in 2000, its major components included the following:

National Security Council When the United States emerged as a major power after the Second World War, no central machinery existed to assist the president in conducting foreign and military affairs. The **National Security Council (NSC)** is a White House office created under the National Security Act of 1947 to advise the president and help coordinate American military and foreign policy. By statute, its four members are the president, the vice president, and the secretaries of state and

defense. The president's assistant for national security directs the NSC staff.

Like the cabinet, the NSC has been put to vastly different uses by different presidents. Eisenhower used the NSC extensively, and during his administration a substructure of boards and committees mushroomed beneath it. During the Cuban Missile Crisis in 1962, Kennedy established an informal body known as the Executive Committee of the National Security Council. Much larger than the statutory membership of the NSC, it consisted of some 16 top officials and advisers in the foreign policy, military, and intelligence fields whom the president felt it appropriate to consult.

Nixon, an NSC member during the Eisenhower Administration, sought as president to restore the NSC and its staff to its former place in the White House policy machinery. During the Nixon Administration the NSC under Kissinger generated a steady flow of voluminous memoranda on foreign policy problems, all of which helped to increase Kissinger's great influence and power in foreign affairs.

Under Reagan, the NSC played a central role in the events that became known as the Iran-contra scandal. A major covert operation—the arms sales to Iran and diversion of money to the contra rebels in Nicaragua—was run out of the White House by the National Security Council staff, an operational role that Congress had not

Executive Office of the President, 2000

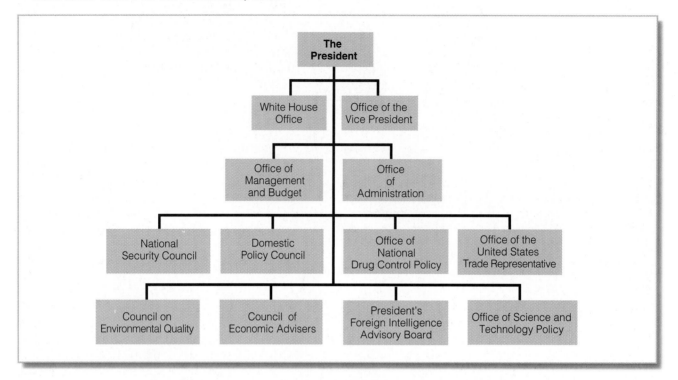

intended for the NSC. Under Presidents Bush and Clinton, the national security adviser and the NSC returned to their more traditional roles.

In 1990, retired Admiral John M. Poindexter, who had been Reagan's national security adviser, was convicted of felonies in the Iran-contra affair and sentenced to six months in prison. His conviction was overturned by a federal appeals court, which ruled that Poindexter's testimony to a congressional investigating committee had been unfairly used against him in court. Poindexter had admitted to Congress, however, that he had destroyed a secret and highly classified presidential finding about trading arms for hostages in Iran because he thought the document might be "politically embarrassing" to Reagan. The entire episode illustrated that the president's national security adviser may wield great power, not only in foreign affairs, but in domestic politics as well.

Domestic Policy Council   All recent presidents have had a staff to assist them in formulating domestic policy. Creation of a formal staff for this purpose began under Lyndon Johnson in the 1960s. Although the name of the unit has changed several times, later presidents continued to rely on a domestic policy staff. Under President Clinton, the staff of the Domestic Policy Council specialized in such policy fields as energy, education, agriculture, natural resources, economic affairs, health and human resources, welfare reform, commerce and trade, senior citizens' and veterans' affairs, and drug abuse and crime.

Office of Management and Budget   The Office of Management and Budget (OMB) was created in 1970. The office was designed to tighten presidential control over the federal bureaucracy and improve its performance.

The OMB has two overlapping functions: preparing the federal budget and serving as a management tool for the chief executive. The director of the office advises the president on the allocation of federal funds, and attempts to resolve the competing claims of the departments and agencies for a larger share of the federal budget. The task of preparing and administering the annual budget gives OMB enormous power within the government.

National Economic Council   The National Economic Council, a relatively new body modeled on the National Security Council, was created by President Clinton in 1993 to coordinate all economic policy decisions at the presidential level. It deals with the budget, international trade, and other economic issues and programs.

Council of Economic Advisers   Since the Great Depression of the 1930s, the president has been expected to manage the nation's efforts to achieve prosperity. Because few presidents are economic experts, presidents since 1946 have relied on a Council of Economic Advisers to assist them in the formation of national economic policy.

The three members, one of whom is designated chairperson by the president, are subject to Senate confirmation. The council is expected to give impartial professional advice, but because its members are also part of the president's administration, they perform a difficult task.

Office of the United States Trade Representative The United States trade representative, who carries the rank of ambassador, represents the president in often difficult and complex international trade and tariff negotiations. The role of the trade representative has become increasingly influential in recent years because of the growing importance of trade issues. For example, the trade representative has sought to persuade Japan to accept more American products, including automobiles.

The Vice President "I am Vice President," said John Adams. "In this I am nothing, but I may be everything."[65] The remark remains apt today. Under the Constitution, the vice president's only formal duties are to preside over the Senate, to vote in that body in case of a tie, and (under the Twenty-fifth Amendment) to help decide whether the president is disabled, and, if so, to serve as acting president. If the president dies, resigns, or is removed from office, however, the vice president becomes president. As of the year 2000, this had occurred nine times as the result of the death or resignation of a president. In four of those cases, the president had been assassinated.

Often in the past, the candidate for vice president has been chosen by the presidential nominee to "balance the ticket," to add geographic or some other strength to the campaign. Thus, in 1984, Walter Mondale, the Democratic nominee, chose Geraldine Ferraro, the first woman ever to be nominated for vice president by a major party, to add drama and excitement to his campaign. In 1992, however, Governor Bill Clinton chose a fellow southerner, Senator Albert Gore, Jr., as his running mate. In this case, instead of seeking geographic balance, Clinton opted for a youthful image for the Democratic ticket by choosing a vice presidential candidate who, like himself, was in his mid-forties. Eight years later, Gore was the Democratic candidate for president. Apparently to distance himself from the Clinton scandal, he chose Senator Joseph I. Lieberman, who had criticized Clinton's affair with Monica Lewinsky.

In 1988, George Bush, the Republican presidential nominee, had selected Senator Dan Quayle of Indiana as his running mate in an effort to appeal to younger voters and conservatives. But Bush's choice was controversial from the start. As vice president, Quayle was regarded by many voters, and widely in the media, as a lightweight. He soon became the butt of jokes by stand-up comics on late-night television. During the 1992 campaign, Quayle took on an aggressive role as Bush's point man, but he quickly became embroiled in controversy by attacking Murphy Brown, a fictitious character in a popular television situation comedy, for her decision to become a single parent. Quayle's difficulties reached their peak later that spring when he encouraged an elementary school boy to spell *potato* with an unnecessary "e" at the end.

SOME VICE PRESIDENTS VIEW THEIR OFFICE

John Adams
My country has in its wisdom contrived for me the most insignificant office that ever the invention of man contrived or his imagination conceived.

Thomas Jefferson
The second office of this Government is honorable and easy, the first is but a splendid misery.

John Nance Garner
The vice presidency isn't worth a pitcher of warm spit.

Harry Truman
Look at all the Vice Presidents in history. Where are they? They were about as useful as a cow's fifth teat.

Thomas R. Marshall
Like a man in a cataleptic state [the vice president] cannot speak; he cannot move; he suffers no pain; and yet he is perfectly conscious of everything that is going on about him.

Spiro Agnew
Now I know what a turkey feels like before Thanksgiving.

Walter Mondale
They know who Amy [Carter] is, but they don't know me.

George Bush
If I fall out of favor at the White House, I might end up attending a lot of funerals in funny little countries.

Dan Quayle
The president gets the plums, and I get what's left.

Al Gore
If you close your left eye and turn your head . . . the great seal of the Vice President reads—"President of the United States."

—Adams, Jefferson, Garner, Truman, and Marshall quoted in Donald Young, *American Roulette;* Spiro Agnew quoted in the *Los Angeles Times West Magazine,* June 22, 1969; Walter Mondale quoted in the *Los Angeles Times,* January 13, 1978; George Bush quoted in the *Chicago Tribune,* August 18, 1981; Dan Quayle quoted in the *Washington Post,* August 17, 1992; and Al Gore appearing on the *Late Show with David Letterman,* September 6, 1993

Vice President Dan Quayle teaches William Figueroa, 12, to spell.
Mike Mancuso/Sygma

In 1968 Richard Nixon, the Republican presidential nominee, chose Spiro Agnew of Maryland, a relatively obscure governor, in an effort to strengthen the ticket's appeal in southern and border states.

Agnew quickly emerged as a controversial political figure. He attacked Vietnam War protest leaders and assailed network news commentators who had been critical of the president. In the midst of the Watergate crisis, however, at a time when Nixon was battling for his own political survival, a federal prosecutor in Baltimore gathered evidence that Agnew had asked for and accepted more than $100,000 in cash payments from highway engineering firms that were awarded state contracts while Agnew was governor of Maryland, and that one payoff was even made to Agnew in the office of the vice president. Agnew resigned, pleaded no-contest to income tax evasion, received a $10,000 fine, and was placed on probation for three years.

In the 20th century seven vice presidents succeeded to the presidency through the death or resignation of an incumbent president, or by election.* As a result, during that century a former vice president served as president almost 40 percent of the time. These statistics would suggest that vice presidents be carefully selected on merit rather than solely for political considerations.

Presidential Commissions From time to time, presidents appoint ad hoc "blue ribbon" commissions of prominent citizens to study special problems. Such panels can help a president by dealing with a crisis, by providing influential support for his programs, or by deflecting political pressure. But they also may cause

him headaches by criticizing his administration, by proposing remedies he does not favor, or in other ways.

For example, in 1986 President Reagan named a special review board headed by former Senator John Tower, a Texas Republican, to investigate the Iran-contra affair. The panel strongly criticized the president personally as well as his administration, and some of its language was harsh. It concluded that top officials had lied to each other and to the public, and had possibly broken the law.[66]

Similarly, in 1976 President Ford named the Rockefeller Commission to study published reports of spying within the United States by the CIA. But the commission also gathered information about CIA plots to assassinate foreign leaders, causing Ford political embarrassment.

After President Kennedy's assassination, the nation was torn by doubt and speculation over the facts of his death. President Johnson convinced Chief Justice Earl Warren to head an investigating commission. The Warren Commission concluded that Lee Harvey Oswald shot the president and had "acted alone." At first this conclusion seemed to reassure much of the public that no conspiracy existed, but later the Warren Commission's conclusions were widely attacked by many critics who refused to accept the shooting as the act of one person.

The Informal Tools of Power

Many factors affect a president's ability to achieve his objectives. The president is the chief actor on the Washington stage. He is carefully watched by bureaucrats, members of Congress, party leaders, and the press. The decisions he makes affect his professional reputation among these groups. In turn, his effectiveness as president depends on this professional reputation.[67]

---

*The vice presidents who succeeded to the presidency in the 20th century were Theodore Roosevelt, Calvin Coolidge, Harry S Truman, Lyndon B. Johnson, Gerald R. Ford, Richard M. Nixon, and George Bush. Nixon became president in 1969, eight years after serving as vice president.

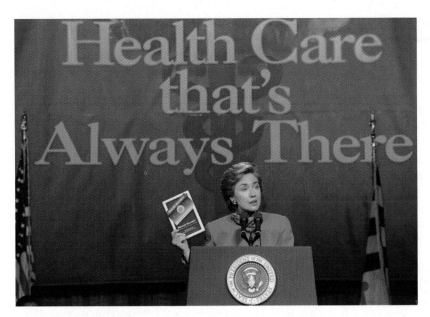

First Lady Hillary Rodham Clinton with a copy of the Clinton health care plan
AP/Wide World

In the exercise of presidential power, the president has available to him not only the formal tools of the office, but a broad range of informal techniques. Many presidents since Andrew Jackson have had a "kitchen cabinet" of informal advisers who hold no official position on the White House staff. Theodore Roosevelt had his "tennis cabinet," Warren Harding his "poker cabinet," and Herbert Hoover, who liked exercise, his "medicine ball cabinet." Lyndon Johnson often called on friends such as Washington attorneys Abe Fortas, James H. Rowe, Jr., and Clark Clifford for advice. Ronald Reagan, too, had a "kitchen cabinet" of old friends who were for the most part California businessmen.

Long before Bill and Hillary Clinton moved into the White House, it was apparent that a president's spouse is, in some cases at least, an important influence on both politics and policy. Both Eleanor Roosevelt and Lady Bird Johnson, for example, each in their own way had an impact on their husbands, Franklin Roosevelt and Lyndon Johnson. Hillary Rodham Clinton, a bright, successful lawyer, became a controversial figure in the Clinton White House. Breaking with precedent, President Clinton placed the First Lady in charge of his early efforts to reform the nation's health care system. That effort failed.

Thereafter, Hillary Clinton sought to adopt a lower profile and to become involved in issues, such as children's and women's rights, that were closer to the traditional concerns of previous presidential spouses. That strategy ran into difficulty when Mrs. Clinton was blamed for the dismissals of several employees of the White House travel office and when she became embroiled in the congressional investigation of the Whitewater affair. In January 1996, she was subpoenaed to answer questions about Whitewater before a federal grand jury—an embarrassment to the president, who was running for reelection that year.

Despite those problems, Hillary Clinton emerged as a powerful figure in the White House and an important, although unofficial, presidential adviser. She defended the president amid the sex scandal that threatened for a time to destroy his presidency, and in the year 2000 ran as the Democratic candidate for the U.S. Senate in New York. She won the election by a large margin.

Television is another powerful, informal tool of presidential power. With the development of electronic mass media, presidents can make direct appeals to the people. Franklin Roosevelt began the practice with his famous "fireside chats" over radio. Today, the president may schedule a live televised speech or press conference to publicize his policies. He may call a White House conference to dramatize a major issue.

A president can take advantage of other perquisites of power. He may flatter key members of Congress by telephoning them for advice on key issues or inviting them to ride with him on Air Force One. He bargains with congressional leaders who frequently call on him at the White House, an informal arrangement that pays presidential homage to the importance of the leaders and incidentally allows them to make statements for the television cameras as they emerge from the Executive Mansion.

The President and the Press   A president's ability to gain almost constant access to the news media, especially television, is a vital instrument of presidential power in the electronic age. When President Clinton took office in 1993, his communications director was George Stephanopoulos, a 31-year-old aide who had played a key role in Clinton's campaign. Stephanopoulos soon developed a high profile, appearing daily on television to speak for the president on a broad range of issues. But he did not achieve smooth relations with the Washington press corps, and soon Clinton brought in David Gergen, who had served under four Republican presidents, in an effort to improve Clinton's relations with the press and his public image. Gergen did not last long. Then the president's press secretary, Dee Dee Myers, was eased out of the White House and Clinton imported Michael McCurry from the State Department to replace her.

Under McCurry, a gentle man with a straightforward manner, Clinton's press relations seemed to reach a more stable level. He often leavened his news briefings with humor, even though it was his lot to deal with the press during the Lewinsky scandal and the impeachment trial. For example, he once told reporters, "I am double-parked in the no comment zone." In his final press briefing

he summed up his turbulent time in the White House: "I have been the chum in the feeding frenzy."[68]

Some press secretaries have more power than others. Several years earlier, Larry Speakes, a former public relations executive, left the White House after serving as press spokesman to President Reagan. Speakes wrote a book in which he disclosed that as press secretary, he had made up quotes and attributed them to President Reagan.[69] The disclosure caused a storm, forcing Speakes to resign his job on Wall Street.

The controversy focused attention on the crucial role of the White House press secretary. A president relies on a press secretary to speak for him in day-to-day dealings with the news media. Often, the press secretary acts as a buffer, standing between the president and the press and public, fielding questions that the president might prefer not to answer.

In recent years, most presidential press secretaries have held daily briefings for the White House press corps. The press secretary becomes a familiar personality to the public—but not always to the president's advantage. When the Watergate affair surfaced, President Nixon's press spokesman, Ronald L. Ziegler, repeatedly denied White House involvement and dismissed the break-in at Democratic headquarters as a "third-rate burglary attempt." After the truth began to emerge in April 1973, Ziegler announced that all previous White House denials were "inoperative," an explanation that did little to restore confidence in the administration's veracity—or Ziegler's. The White House had lied to the people, and the president found confidence in his administration shattered. After Nixon left the White House, he told television interviewer David Frost: "I want to say right here and now, I said things that were not true."[70]

The White House Office of Communications was created during the Nixon administration, in part to enable the White House to bypass the Washington

Nixon press secretary Ronald L. Ziegler briefs reporters in 1973.
AP/Wide World

THE PRESIDENT AND THE PRESS: "A SYMBIOTIC RELATIONSHIP"

A president and his top aides enjoy almost unchecked powers of communication to define and defend their policies and to attack their adversaries. They can shape the agenda of public discussion, commanding the airwaves and headlines with the slightest hint of crisis. They can bury their mistakes by sealing their files on the pretext of national security. The Washington press, in turn, feels so dependent on government information and so dutiful in disseminating official propaganda that it grows desperate to prove its mettle by also exposing error, hyperbole, hypocrisy, and abuses of power. Thus are government and press condemned to a symbiotic relationship, a precarious balance of collaborations and antagonisms.

—Max Frankel, *The Times of My Life and My Life with* The Times

---

press corps and reach the local news media directly. The office has often played a significant role in attempts at news management.[71] Administrations normally believe it to be in their self-interest to suppress embarrassing information. Mistakes, errors in judgment, or poorly conceived or badly executed policies are seldom brought to light unless discovered by the press or congressional investigators. Even then, White House spokespersons try to minimize unfavorable events. In describing military or intelligence operations, in particular, the government sometimes tends to conceal or distort. If the truth later becomes known, public confidence may be undermined.

Most presidents grant private interviews with a few syndicated columnists and influential Washington correspondents. They hope in that way to gain support for their views in the press and among readers. But the presidential press conference is a more direct device used by the chief executive to reach the public. (See Table 13-3.) Wilson began the practice by inviting reporters into his office. Harding, Coolidge, and Hoover accepted only written questions, and their press conferences were generally dull. Roosevelt held regular news conferences, canceled the requirement for written questions, and played the press like a virtuoso. Truman moved the press conference from his office to the Executive Office Building, establishing a more formal atmosphere.

Wilson established the policy that reporters could not quote the president directly without permission, but Eisenhower changed this, allowing his news conferences to be filmed and released to television after editing. Kennedy instituted "live," unedited TV press conferences in the modern auditorium of the State Department, and he dazzled the press with his skill in fielding questions. Johnson had some full-dress press conferences, but he

often preferred to answer questions from reporters while loping rapidly around the White House South Lawn. Nixon reverted to formal, televised press conferences, but he held very few. To an extent that exceeded any modern predecessors, the Nixon-Agnew administration considered the press a political target. Ford's amiable personality helped him maintain fairly good relations with the press. Carter also had reasonably good relations with the press during much of his presidency, although political cartoonists had a field day, invariably caricaturing him with "blubber lips."

President Reagan enjoyed the traditional "honeymoon" from intense press criticism normally afforded to any new chief executive. But as Fred I. Greenstein has noted, it does not take the press very long to begin criticizing a president: "Media coverage of the President-elect and the first few months of an administration tends to emphasize the endearing personal touches—Ford's preparation of his own English muffins, Carter's fireside chat in informal garb. No wonder both of these Presidents enjoyed high poll ratings during their initial months in office. But the trend can only go downward. . . . After idealizing Presidents, the media quickly search out their warts."[72]

And, in time, Reagan's relations with the press became somewhat less amicable. Reporters wrote stories pointing out that Reagan sometimes misstated facts and statistics. Other accounts suggested that Reagan napped, relaxed, or vacationed a good deal, leaving work to his aides, who hesitated to awaken him if a crisis developed in the middle of the night.

In his controversial book, Larry Speakes gave support to this image of Reagan. The president, he wrote, read few newspapers and preferred to "read the comics first."[73] Preparing Reagan for a news conference, the former press secretary added, was like "reinventing the wheel."[74] Despite some unfavorable news accounts during Reagan's

TABLE 13-3

Presidential Press Conferences

President	Number	Years in Office*	Average per Year[†]
Roosevelt	998	12	83
Truman	322	8	40
Eisenhower	193	8	24
Kennedy	64	3	21
Johnson	135	5	27
Nixon	37	5.5	7
Ford	39	2.5	16
Carter	59	4	15
Reagan	46	8	5.8
Bush	142	4	36
Clinton	192	8[†]	24

*Figures rounded.
[†]As of August 30, 2000.

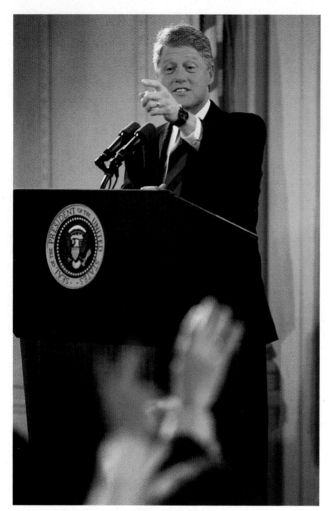
President Clinton answers a reporter's question.
Copyright © B. Markel/Liaison

of Nicaragua. But some Reagan critics voiced suspicions that the dispatch of the troops was an obvious attempt to divert attention from, and overshadow, the unwelcome news of the indictments of the president's men.

THE WATERGATE SCANDAL: A PRESIDENT RESIGNS

It had begun shortly after 1 A.M. on the morning of June 17, 1972, when Frank Wills, a 24-year-old, $80-a-week security guard at the Watergate office building, had pulled a piece of masking tape from the edge of a garage-level door. The tape presumably had been placed there to keep the door from latching shut. He left, but returned in a few minutes. To his astonishment, he found the door had been taped again—apparently by a persistent but foolish burglar. He called the police.

When Wills pulled the tape off the door of the Watergate, it was as though one tiny strand of thread had unraveled a whole skein of corruption and criminal activity planned and condoned in what—until then—had seemed the least likely of places, the White House.

At first, however, the press treated the break-in as little more than a routine crime story. Five men had been arrested inside the headquarters of the Democratic National Committee in the Watergate office building, part of a high-rise complex along the Potomac River. But one of the men turned out to be James W. McCord, Jr., director of security for the Committee for the Reelection of the President (CREEP). Later two other suspects were arrested, E. Howard Hunt, Jr., and G. Gordon Liddy, both former White House aides. Liddy, like McCord, was an official of CREEP. Several of the burglars had worked for the CIA.

It soon developed that the break-in had been ordered by high officials of the administration and of President Nixon's 1972 election campaign, and financed by money contributed to the campaign. Two young reporters from the *Washington Post*, Bob Woodward and Carl Bernstein, pursued the story.

As the scandal unfolded, it was disclosed that the burglars had bugged the Democratic headquarters and that telephone conversations of Democratic Party officials had been broadcast by a concealed transmitter to a motel across the street.

In the White House, Nixon's advisers took steps to cover up the links between the burglars and the president's campaign. Nixon was overwhelmingly reelected in November. Watergate seemed to have been "contained."

In January 1973, however, five of the defendants pleaded guilty and two others who chose to stand trial were convicted by a federal jury. In March, McCord, facing a long prison term from U.S. District Judge John J. Sirica, suggested that White House and other officials had advance knowledge of the Watergate bugging. President Nixon denied prior knowledge of the Watergate bugging or the subsequent cover-up by his staff. He accepted the

first term, criticism of his policies or the errors of his subordinates did not seem to stick to him personally, so much so that Reagan's stewardship was frequently referred to in the press as "the Teflon presidency."[*]

In Chapter 10, we discussed the advantages that a president normally enjoys as a political candidate, including the ability to dominate the news. But a president can wield that power day in and day out, even when no political campaign is under way. On the afternoon of March 16, 1988, the Iran-contra independent counsel, Lawrence E. Walsh, announced the indictments of President Reagan's former national security adviser, retired Admiral John M. Poindexter; Marine Lt. Col. Oliver L. North, the former NSC aide; and two other key participants in the Iran-contra scandal. A few hours later, the president announced he was sending 3,200 troops to Honduras on a "training exercise." The president's action was undoubtedly designed to place pressure on the left-wing government

---
[*]The phrase was coined by Representative Patricia Schroeder, a Colorado Democrat, in a speech to the House in August 1983, in which she said that Reagan was "perfecting the Teflon-coated presidency. He sees to it that nothing sticks to him." *Washington Post*, April 15, 1984, p. 1.

On March 21, 1973, President Nixon, White House counsel John Dean III, and H. R. Haldeman, Nixon's chief of staff, met in the Oval Office to discuss payoffs to buy the silence of the Watergate burglars. Their conversation, recorded by the President's secret taping system, became a crucial part of the evidence in the House Judiciary Committee's impeachment investigation of President Nixon. Following are excerpts from the March 21 conversation:

NIXON: How much money do you need?

DEAN: I would say these people are going to cost a million dollars over the next two years.

John W. Dean III
Copyright © Fred Ward/
Black Star

NIXON: We could get that. . . . You could get a million dollars. You could get it in cash. I know where it could be gotten. It is not easy, but it could be done. But the question is who the hell would handle it? Any ideas on that?

HALDEMAN: . . . We thought [Former Attorney General John] Mitchell ought to be able to know how to find somebody who would know how to do all that sort of thing, because none of us know how to.

DEAN: That's right. You have to wash the money. You can get $100,000 out of a bank, and it all comes in serialized bills.

NIXON: I understand.

DEAN: And that means you have to go to Vegas with it or a bookmaker in New York City. I have learned all these things after the fact. I will be in great shape for the next time around.

HALDEMAN: (Expletive deleted).

—From the White House transcripts,
released April 30, 1974

---

resignations of his two principal aides, H. R. Haldeman and John Ehrlichman, and of his attorney general, Richard Kleindienst, and authorized the new attorney general to appoint a special prosecutor to investigate the Watergate case. But the storm did not abate.

Nixon admitted that he had established a special investigative unit, known as "the Plumbers," to find the source of national security news leaks. The Plumbers had been headed by Howard Hunt and G. Gordon Liddy.

In the weeks that followed the break-in, the daily headlines brought one startling disclosure after another: In 1970 Nixon approved a plan for burglary and electronic surveillance of persons suspected of endangering national security, although he was warned, in writing, that burglary was "clearly illegal"; Nixon had ordered the secret wiretapping of 17 persons, including a number of his own assistants and several journalists; the president's personal attorney raised and secretly distributed funds totaling $220,000 to the Watergate burglars and their attorneys; the acting director of the Federal Bureau of Investigation had destroyed vital Watergate evidence; the attorney general of the United States, John Mitchell, was present during a discussion of proposals for bugging the Democratic Party's Watergate headquarters and for kidnapping American citizens and taking them to Mexico, and the president's assistants compiled an "enemies list" and requested tax audits of political opponents.

In May 1973 a Senate select committee under chairman Sam J. Ervin, Jr., a North Carolina Democrat, began holding televised hearings into Watergate and the 1972 campaign. The hearings revealed that Nixon had concealed microphones in his offices in the White House to record conversations on tape, in most cases without the knowledge of the persons being recorded. The tapes became key evidence in the scandal.

Within a few months, all seven of the Watergate burglars had been given jail sentences by Judge Sirica. In October Nixon dismissed the Watergate special prosecutor, but was forced by the tremendous public outcry to appoint another. The House of Representatives began its impeachment investigation. Nixon agreed to surrender some of the tapes of his conversations about Watergate.

Then came the climactic events of the summer of 1974. The Supreme Court ordered Nixon to surrender more tapes to the new Watergate special prosecutor, and the House Judiciary Committee voted to impeach the president. The committee approved three articles of impeachment and sent them to the full House. In addition, one of the newly released tapes showed that Nixon had lied when he denied he had participated in the cover-up of the Watergate burglary. On June 23, 1972, the tapes revealed, Nixon had ordered the CIA to try to confine the FBI investigation of the break-in, and he now admitted he knew that he would gain political advantage from that order.

Senator Sam J. Ervin, Jr., presides over
Senate Watergate hearings in 1973.
Copyright © Laffont/Sygma

Nixon's support in Congress within his own Republican Party crumbled. He did not have enough votes in Congress to avoid impeachment and removal from office.

Richard Nixon resigned on August 9, 1974, the first president in the nation's history to do so. A month later, he accepted a pardon from his successor, President Ford, and thus could not be prosecuted for acts committed while president. Many of Nixon's high advisers were less fortunate. In 1975 John Ehrlichman, H. R. Haldeman, and John Mitchell were convicted of covering up the Watergate break-in. All three went to prison.

A total of 19 persons were convicted or pleaded guilty in connection with Watergate-related crimes, including 10 Nixon aides and 3 CREEP officials. All 19 served prison sentences.

PRESIDENTIAL IMPEACHMENT, DISABILITY, AND SUCCESSION

Despite the enormous power of the president, under the Constitution he may be impeached by Congress and, if convicted of "Treason, Bribery or other high Crimes and Misdemeanors," removed from office.* Only the House can bring impeachment proceedings against a presi-

dent, by majority vote. The president is then tried by the Senate with the chief justice presiding. A two-thirds vote of the Senate is required to convict a president and remove him from office, a fate that Andrew Johnson escaped by one vote in 1868.

The unsuccessful attempt to remove Johnson from office grew out of the turmoil following the Civil War. The president hoped to carry out Lincoln's conciliatory Reconstruction policies toward the South after the war. This placed him in direct conflict with the Radical Republicans in Congress, who favored much harsher policies. When Johnson dismissed his secretary of war, the House charged he had violated the Tenure of Office Act and brought impeachment proceedings. The trial and balloting in the Senate went on for more than two months.

Historically, Congress has hesitated to impeach and remove a president, for several reasons. First, there has been an understandable reluctance to act against the highest official in the land, who—unless he succeeds to his office—is elected by all the people. Second, there has been a fear that impeachment, as a political remedy, might become a partisan weapon to remove a president whenever he displeases a Congress controlled by the opposition political party or by political opponents in his own party.

Third, the language of the Constitution dealing with impeachment, scattered in four places, leaves many unanswered questions. For example, can officials be indicted before they are impeached, or in place of impeachment? Many legal scholars believe the answer is yes, for judges and officials up to and including the vice president. But they also contend that a president must first be impeached and removed before prosecution. Otherwise the country might find itself in the untenable position of having its national leader behind bars while still holding office.

Yet another difficult problem is whether the "high crimes and misdemeanors" required as grounds for an impeachment conviction must literally be crimes in the legal sense—the breaking of specific laws—or whether that constitutional language encompasses serious abuses of the office of the president that might fall short of actual, indictable crimes. During the controversy leading up to the impeachment of President Clinton, his lawyers and other supporters argued that the actions he had committed did not rise to the level of an impeachable offense.

The Nixon Impeachment Proceedings and Resignation

Before 1973 it seemed most unlikely that any modern president could be impeached, but the Watergate scandal and the Clinton scandal changed all that. A resolution to impeach President Nixon was introduced in the House on July 31, 1973, by Robert F. Drinan, a Massachusetts Democrat who was also a Roman Catholic priest. Some

---

*Not only the president, but also the vice president and other federal officials and federal judges—as the Constitution puts it, all "civil officers of the United States"—are subject to impeachment. From 1789 through 1999, a total of 16 federal officials were impeached and tried by the Senate. Seven were convicted and removed from office, seven were acquitted, and in two cases the charges were dismissed. Members of Congress are subject to discipline and expulsion by their respective houses, but it is not clear whether they are "civil officers" subject to impeachment. At least some scholars believe that members of Congress are not exempt from removal by impeachment. See, for example, Raoul Berger, *Impeachment: The Constitutional Problems* (Cambridge: Harvard University Press, 1973), pp. 214–223.

of those who might otherwise have favored such a course were dismayed at the prospect of the succession of Vice President Agnew to the presidency in the event of Nixon's removal from office. But Agnew resigned the following October on the day he was convicted of criminal charges, and that same month the House Judiciary Committee began an inquiry into the possible impeachment of Nixon. It was the first time since 1868 that Congress had taken steps to consider whether a president of the United States should be impeached.

The formal proceedings of the committee, under chairman Peter W. Rodino, Jr., began in February 1974. The committee staff amassed 38 volumes of evidence dealing with the Watergate break-in, Nixon's wiretapping of 17 aides and news reporters, the White House enemies list, and other abuses. The committee members, earphones clamped to their heads, listened for hours to the White House tapes. They also heard presentations by the president's attorney, James D. St. Clair, and by the committee's special counsel, John Doar. They heard witnesses in closed session, and then on July 24 began six historic days of public deliberation. The sessions were televised and watched by millions of Americans.

The Judiciary Committee voted three articles of impeachment. Article I accused Nixon of obstruction of justice by "using the powers of his high office" to "delay, impede, and obstruct" the investigation of the break-in at Democratic headquarters. The article specifically charged that Nixon had made false public statements "for the purpose of deceiving the people of the United States" into believing that the president's campaign organization had not been involved. Article II accused the president of violating the constitutional rights of citizens by misusing the FBI, the CIA, the Internal Revenue Service, and other agencies, and by establishing a secret investigative unit, the Plumbers, in the White House itself. Article III charged that Nixon had defied the committee by failing to produce subpoenaed tapes and documents.

On July 24, 1974, the Supreme Court ruled 8–0 that Nixon had to yield 64 tapes of his White House conversations to the Watergate special prosecutor. His support in Congress collapsed when the tapes were released soon afterward and showed that Nixon had participated in the Watergate cover-up. As these climactic events unfolded, the full House had no opportunity to vote on the articles of impeachment nor was there a Senate trial, as occurred in the case of Andrew Johnson. On August 9, 1974, just 10 days after the last of the articles had been approved by the Judiciary Committee, Nixon resigned.

The Clinton Scandal and Impeachment

Bill Clinton was only the second president to be impeached. Like the first, Andrew Johnson, he was not convicted and removed from office.

Clinton's troubles began with an Arkansas land deal in which he and his wife had invested in 1978 with the owners of a local savings and loan association that later failed. The deal envisioned a real estate development called Whitewater on 230 acres in the Ozark Mountains in northern Arkansas, at the juncture of Crooked Creek and the White River. The plan was to sell the lots for vacation homes. The Whitewater venture was unsuccessful, and it led to charges of fraud and allegations that Clinton, as governor, had helped the bank's owners obtain federally insured loans, which Clinton denied.

The clamor over Whitewater had become so loud by early in 1994 that Clinton's attorney general, Janet Reno, appointed a special prosecutor to investigate. Five months later, a new problem surfaced for the president when Paula Jones, a clerk in the Arkansas state government, filed a lawsuit claiming that Clinton, while governor, solicited oral sex from her in a hotel room in Little Rock. In August, Kenneth W. Starr, who had been solicitor general in President Bush's administration, took over as independent counsel investigating the president.

In 1995, Monica S. Lewinsky, a dark-haired, 21-year-old intern from Beverly Hills, California, began working for the White House; by November they had begun a sexual relationship that began when Lewinsky showed the president her thong underwear. The following year, Clinton broke off but later resumed his affair, but that spring Lewinsky was transferred to a Pentagon job after the president's aides realized she seemed to be spending too much time in the West Wing of the White House. At the Pentagon, Lewinsky became friendly with Linda Tripp, another ex–White House employee.

In 1997, Tripp began secretly taping her conversations with Lewinsky, in which the young intern confided details of her affair with the president. In December, Lewinsky was subpoenaed to give a deposition in the Paula Jones case. Coached by the president, she signed a false affidavit saying she had no "sexual relationship" with Clinton.

In the meantime, the president's friend, Vernon Jordan, a powerful Washington attorney, was arranging a job interview for Lewinsky in New York.

In January 1998, in a famous finger-wagging denial for the TV cameras, Clinton said, "I did not have sexual relations with that woman, Miss Lewinsky." Earlier that same month, the president also testified in the Jones lawsuit.

What he did not know was that Linda Tripp had secretly tipped off Paula Jones's attorneys, and Kenneth Starr, about Clinton's affair with Lewinsky. During his testimony, Clinton was presumably caught off guard when it became apparent that Jones's lawyers possessed detailed information about his affair with Lewinsky and began questioning him about the intern. At the deposition, he denied under oath that he had had "sexual relations," as defined by Jones's lawyers, with Lewinsky.

A week earlier, Tripp had turned over to Starr 20 hours of tape recordings of Lewinsky's conversations

Monica Lewinsky is sworn in for the Senate impeachment trial of President Clinton.
APTN/Wide World

with her, and the next day at Starr's request, she wore a hidden microphone while having lunch with Lewinsky at a hotel in Arlington, Virginia.

Kenneth Starr opened a grand jury inquiry into the Lewinsky matter. Under a grant of immunity, Lewinsky admitted the affair to the grand jury. In August 1998, Clinton testified before the grand jury in the White House, now admitting an "improper relationship" with the young intern, and insisting that "sexual relations," as defined by Jones's lawyers, meant intercourse only, not oral sex. Afterwards, in a brief nationally televised speech, Clinton conceded, "I did have a relationship with Miss Lewinsky that was not appropriate."

In September, 1998, Starr delivered to Congress a lengthy, 445-page report. The document recited in minute and explicit detail the president's ten sexual encounters with Lewinsky in rooms next to the Oval Office. The report accused the president of perjury, obstruction of justice, witness tampering, and other acts that he claimed constituted grounds for impeachment. It said nothing about Whitewater, the original purpose of the investigation.

That same month, Henry J. Hyde, the House Judiciary Committee chairman, proposed a resolution for the impeachment of the president, and in October, the House voted 258–176 to begin impeachment proceedings. The following month, Clinton agreed to settle the Paula Jones lawsuit with a payment of $850,000.

In December, the Judiciary Committee approved four articles of impeachment. The articles charged that Clinton had committed perjury to the federal grand jury, and in his testimony in the Jones case; had obstructed justice by influencing Lewinsky and Clinton's personal secretary to conceal evidence and testify falsely; and had

abused the powers of his office by lying to Congress in his answers to questions sent to him by the committee.

On December 19, the full House voted for two of the articles, alleging that Clinton "willfully provided perjurious, false and misleading testimony to the grand jury" and "prevented, obstructed, and impeded the administration of justice." The House rejected the other two articles of impeachment. The vote came at the end of an extraordinary week in which the United States and Britain bombed Iraq, and the House speaker-designate, Bob Livingston, a Louisiana Republican, withdrew his candidacy after admitting past adulterous affairs of his own.

The trial of President Clinton in the Senate began on January 9, 1999, with Chief Justice William H. Rehnquist presiding in a black robe oddly festooned with gold stripes. Thirteen House "managers," Republican representatives acting as prosecutors, presented the case against Clinton, who was defended by the White House counsel, Charles F. C. Ruff. No witnesses were called, but the Senators viewed videotaped depositions from Lewinsky, Vernon Jordan, and a White House aide, Sidney Blumenthal.

From the start, public opinion polls showed a solid majority of Americans were opposed to the removal of the president from office. The senators and the public knew that there was little chance Clinton would be convicted. To a considerable extent, therefore, the senators were going through the motions, acting out a story with a predictable ending. Knowing the likely outcome, the senators wanted to get the trial over with as soon as possible. The numbers were in the president's favor; even if all 55 Senate Republicans voted to convict, 12 Democrats would have to cross party lines to vote against the president to achieve the two-thirds needed to remove him from office.

On February 12, 1999, the Senate found the president not guilty. Article I, alleging perjury to the grand jury, failed, with 45 senators voting in favor, and 55 against. Article II, alleging obstruction of justice, failed by a vote of 50 for and 50 against.

The first impeachment trial of a president of the United States in 131 years was over.

Disability and Succession

Twice in American history, presidents were incapacitated for long periods. Garfield lived for 80 days after he was shot in 1881. Wilson never fully recovered from the stroke that he suffered in September 1919, yet he remained in office until March 1921. To a considerable extent, his wife Edith Wilson was president. President Eisenhower suffered three serious illnesses, includ-

We arrived at Love Field in Dallas, as I remember, just shortly after 11:30 A.M. . . . The President and Mrs. Kennedy walked along the fence, shaking hands with people in the crowd that had assembled. . . .

Mrs. Johnson, Senator Ralph Yarborough, and I then entered the car which had been provided for us in the motorcade. . . . We were the second car behind the President's automobile. . . .

After we had proceeded a short way down Elm Street, I heard a sharp report. . . .

I was startled by the sharp report or explosion, but I had no time to speculate as to its origin because Agent Youngblood . . . shouted to all of us in the back seat to get down. . . . He vaulted over the back seat and sat on me. I was bent over under the weight of Agent Youngblood's body. . . .

When we arrived at the hospital, Agent Youngblood told me to get out of the car, go into the building, not

to stop, and to stay close to him and the other agents. . . .

In the hospital room to which Mrs. Johnson and I were taken, the shades were drawn—I think by Agent Youngblood. . . .

It was Ken O'Donnell who, at about 1:20 P.M., told us that the President had died. I think his precise words were "He's gone." . . .

I found it hard to believe that this had happened. The whole thing seemed unreal—unbelievable. A few hours earlier, I had breakfast with John Kennedy; he was alive, strong, vigorous. I could not believe now that he was dead. I was shocked and sickened.

—Statement of President Lyndon B. Johnson
to the Warren Commission, July 10, 1964

ing a heart attack in 1955 that incapacitated him for four days and curtailed his workload for 16 weeks. Sherman Adams, the White House chief of staff, and Press Secretary James Hagerty ran the executive branch machinery during this period.

Eisenhower's heart attack raised anew the question of presidential disability. The Constitution was exceedingly vague on the subject. It spoke of presidential "inability" and "disability," but it left it up to Congress to define those terms and to decide when and how the vice president would take over when a president was unable to exercise his powers and duties. If a president became physically or mentally ill, or disappeared, or was captured in a military operation, or was under anesthesia in a hospital, what was the vice president's proper role? Did he become president or merely assume the "powers and duties" of the office? And for how long? Eisenhower and Nixon sought to cover these contingencies with an unofficial written agreement, a practice followed by Kennedy and Johnson, and Johnson and Humphrey.

But suppose a president were unable or unwilling to declare that he was disabled? Who would then decide whether he was disabled or when he might resume his duties? Could a scheming vice president, with the help of psychiatrists, somehow have a perhaps temporarily unstable president permanently removed from office?

The Twenty-fifth Amendment, ratified in 1967, sought to settle these questions. It pro-

vides that the vice president becomes acting president if the president informs Congress in writing that he is unable to perform his duties. Or, the vice president may become acting president if the vice president and a majority of the cabinet, or of some "other body" created by Congress, decide that the president is disabled. The president can reclaim his office at any time unless the vice president and a majority of the cabinet or

Dallas, November 22, 1963: President Lyndon Johnson takes the oath of office.
Copyright © CORBIS/UPI/ Bettmann

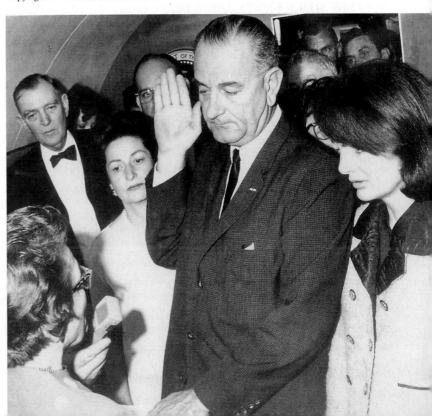

other body contend that he has not recovered. Congress would then decide the issue. But it would take a two-thirds vote of both houses within three weeks to support the vice president; anything less and the president would resume office.

Until the Twenty-fifth Amendment was ratified, there was no constitutional provision for replacing a vice president when that office became vacant.* So the amendment also provided that the president shall nominate a vice president, subject to the approval of a majority of both houses of Congress, whenever that office becomes vacant. The provision reduces the possibility of presidential succession by the House speaker or the Senate President Pro Tempore, or by cabinet members, unless the president and vice president die simultaneously, or unless a president dies, resigns, or is impeached while the vice presidency is vacant and before Congress has acted to approve a new vice president. (See Table 13-4.)

The Twenty-fifth Amendment was used for the first time in October 1973 when President Nixon nominated Gerald Ford to succeed Agnew. Congress approved his choice, 92–3 in the Senate and 387–35 in the House. Until Ford was sworn in that December, the office of vice president was vacant for 57 days. During that period, if Nixon had ceased to be president, his successor would have been House speaker Carl Albert.

The Twenty-fifth Amendment was used for the second time to fill a vice presidential vacancy after Nixon resigned and Ford succeeded him as president. In August 1974 Ford nominated former New York governor Nelson A. Rockefeller to be vice president. After lengthy hearings and approval by the House and Senate, Rockefeller took the oath of office in December.†

THE SPLENDID MISERY: PERSONALITY AND STYLE IN THE WHITE HOUSE

Thomas Jefferson described the presidency as "a splendid misery." Others, like Franklin Roosevelt and John Kennedy, brought great vigor and vitality to the job; they seemed to enjoy being president. The personality, style, and concept of the office that each president brings with him to the White House affect the nature of his presidency. William Howard Taft expressed the classic restrictive view of the presidency:

"The President can exercise no power which cannot be fairly and reasonably traced to some specific grant of power."[75] Theodore Roosevelt adhered to the "stewardship" theory. He saw the chief executive as "a steward of the people" and believed that "it was not only his right but his duty to do anything that the needs of the Nation demanded unless such action was forbidden by the Constitution or by the laws."[76] Abraham Lincoln and Franklin Roosevelt went even further, contending that in great emergencies the president could exercise almost unlimited power to preserve the nation. (See Figure 13-3.)

 for more information about William Taft, see: www.ipl.org/ref/POTUS/whtaft.html

Louis W. Koenig has classified presidents as "literalist" (Madison, Buchanan, Taft, and, to a degree, Eisenhower) or "effective" (Washington, Jackson, Lincoln, Wilson, and the Roosevelts), adding that many chief executives fall somewhere in the middle. A literalist president, as defined by Koenig, closely obeys the letter of the Constitution; an effective president, who generally flourishes in times of crisis and change, interprets his constitutional powers as broadly as possible.[77]

A president's personality and approach to the office may leave a more lasting impression than his substantive accomplishments or failures. We think of Teddy Roosevelt shouting "Bully!"; Wilson, austere and idealistic, in the end shattered by events; Franklin Roosevelt in a wheelchair, cigarette holder tilted at a jaunty angle, conquer-

---

*As of the year 2000, the nation had been without a vice president 18 times for a total of 37 years. Below the level of vice president, the order in which other officials might succeed to the presidency is spelled out in the Presidential Succession Act of 1947. The order of succession begins with the House speaker, followed by the President Pro Tempore of the Senate, and then members of the cabinet, starting with the secretary of state.

†Because of the extraordinary circumstances of a president and a vice president resigning during the same term, the United States had four vice presidents in a period of less than four years from 1973 to 1977: Spiro T. Agnew, Gerald R. Ford, Nelson A. Rockefeller, and Walter F. Mondale.

ing paralysis with élan. We think of Eisenhower's golf, Kennedy's glamour, Johnson's cowpuncher image, Nixon's isolation, Bush at the helm of his speedboat as it churned across the waters at Kennebunkport, Maine, and Clinton's living on the edge.

James David Barber has attempted to systematize the study of presidential behavior by analyzing how childhood and other experiences may have molded a president's character and style. Barber has proposed four broad character types into which presidents may be grouped, and he has suggested that from such an analysis it might ultimately be possible to theorize about future presidential behavior.[78] Barber contended, for instance, that Eisenhower reluctantly ran for president because he was "a sucker for duty" as a result of his background, that Johnson ruled through "manipulative maneuvering," and that Nixon "isolated himself."[79]

In an accurate prediction of Watergate and Nixon's downfall, Barber warned in 1972 that Nixon's character "could lead the President on to disaster. . . . The danger is that crisis will be transformed into tragedy. . . . The loss of power to forces beyond his control would constitute a severe threat. That would be a time to go down, if go down one must, in flames."[80]

Some observers contend that because of the many variables affecting human behavior, presidents may not act in ways that psychological analysis of their lives might suggest.* But because of the work of Barber and others, this approach has gained increasing attention.

Lyndon Johnson issues orders to a doubtful steer on his Texas ranch.
AP/Wide World

John F. Kennedy viewed the presidency as a "vital center of action."
Copyright © CORBIS/UPI/ Bettmann

Theodore Roosevelt strikes a typically exuberant pose.
Brown Brothers

William Howard Taft, who weighed 332 pounds, displays a graceful follow-through.
Brown Brothers

THE AMERICAN PRESIDENCY: TRIUMPH AND TRAGEDY

Running for president in 1980, Ronald Reagan said he wanted to "bring our government back under control and make it acceptable to the people."[81] He would, he declared, eliminate "extravagance and fat in government."[82] Twenty years earlier, John F. Kennedy, seeking the presidency in 1960, viewed it as "the vital center of action in our whole scheme of government." The problems of America, he said, "demand a vigorous proponent of the national interest—not a passive broker for conflicting private interests," a president who will "place himself in the very thick of the fight."[83]

---

*It is interesting to note in this connection that before President Kennedy met with Soviet Premier Khrushchev in Vienna in 1961, he had access to an assessment of Khrushchev's character prepared for the CIA by a panel of psychiatrists and psychologists. See Bryant Wedge, "Khrushchev at a Distance—A Study of Public Personality," *Trans-Action,* October 1968.

Presidential Greatness

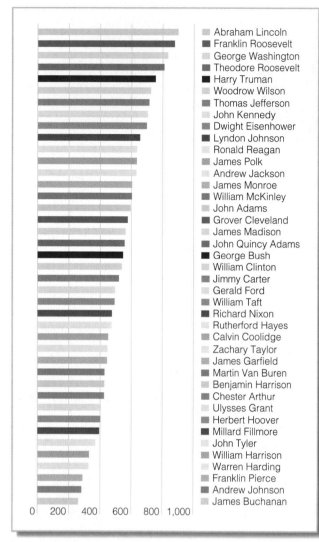

Abraham Lincoln
Franklin Roosevelt
George Washington
Theodore Roosevelt
Harry Truman
Woodrow Wilson
Thomas Jefferson
John Kennedy
Dwight Eisenhower
Lyndon Johnson
Ronald Reagan
James Polk
Andrew Jackson
James Monroe
William McKinley
John Adams
Grover Cleveland
James Madison
John Quincy Adams
George Bush
William Clinton
Jimmy Carter
Gerald Ford
William Taft
Richard Nixon
Rutherford Hayes
Calvin Coolidge
Zachary Taylor
James Garfield
Martin Van Buren
Benjamin Harrison
Chester Arthur
Ulysses Grant
Herbert Hoover
Millard Fillmore
John Tyler
William Harrison
Warren Harding
Franklin Pierce
Andrew Johnson
James Buchanan

0   200   400   600   800   1,000

NOTE: Points earned from ratings by fifty-eight historians based on the following categories: Public Persuasion, Crisis Leadership, Economic Management, Moral Authority, International Relations, Administrative Skills, Relations with Congress, Vision/Setting Agenda, Pursued Equal Justice for All, and Performance within Context of Times.
SOURCE: C-Span survey, February 21, 2000.

Whether a president takes an activist approach, like Kennedy, or a more conservative approach, like Reagan, the voters tend to look to the White House for solutions to major problems. Yet the president may not be able to solve the worst national problems that confront him. He may be hobbled by divided government if Congress is controlled by the opposition party. He cannot single-handedly end environmental pollution, nor control economic problems such as inflation, budget deficits, and unemployment. Nor can he easily use the nation's nuclear power in foreign policy crises—to prevent the seizure of American hostages, for example, or bring

peace to Bosnia. Koenig has suggested the concept of "the imagined Presidency," which is "vested in our minds with more power than the Presidency really has." The difference between the real and the imagined presidency, he contends, may lead to public frustration over presidential performance.

Although the great power of the presidency tends to overshadow its limitations, we have seen how, in many spheres, that power is circumscribed. As chief executive, the president faces an often intractable bureaucracy. As chief legislator, under the constitutional separation of powers, he faces an independent and often hostile Congress. As military and foreign policy leader, his powers are enormous, but he must, at least to some extent, consider sentiment in Congress and the bureaucracy. The Twenty-second Amendment limits the president to two terms and thereby weakens his power in the second term (since everyone knows he will not be president again). Federal law may restrict his options. The Supreme Court may strike down his programs. The press may expose corruption in the bureaucracy or in the White House itself. Public opinion may turn against him. The necessities of politics may occasionally force him to weigh his actions in terms of their effect on his party. Finally, he may be impeached and removed from office.

Whether the presidency is too powerful, or not powerful enough, depends, then, to some extent not only on how a president uses his power but also on what he hopes to accomplish. Presidents have different goals. Many Democratic presidents have tried to press forward with energetic programs of social reform. Other presidents, such as Eisenhower and Ford, have tried to act with restraint. President Reagan cut back on government social programs.

The answer to the question of whether presidents have too much power depends ultimately on what one expects of the office and of the American political system. In the domestic arena, those who regard the presidency as an essential instrument to meet the social challenges and problems of the nation today do not necessarily tend to regard that office as too powerful. Others, alarmed at the size of the federal bureaucracy and opposed to social-welfare programs, take a different view. They argue that the federal government intrudes too much into the lives of citizens.

In any event, presidential power fluctuates, depending in part on the situation in which it is being exercised. Franklin Roosevelt was able to wield extensive economic power during the early years of the New Deal because the nation was in the throes of an acute depression. By 1938 he was encountering substantial domestic opposition. When the Second World War came along, he was able once more to exercise great powers; people expected it.

The power a president exercises not only depends on the times and the circumstances but also on the

Once sworn into office, a president is free to push the most godawful songs in the world, or invite any performer to the White House, and there's nothing anybody can do about it.

So . . . it's irresponsible—no it's sheer insanity—to debate tax policy without also asking a basic question: What do these candidates listen to?

The answer matters, not just because we'll get an earful of the next president's favorite songs, whether we like it or not. . . . The presidential candidates participated in this mini-survey.

George W. Bush

Favorite artists: Van Morrison, the Everly Brothers, the Neville Brothers.

Favorite albums: Aaron Neville's *Warm Your Heart,* Van Morrison's *Moondance,* Travis Tritt's *No More Looking over My Shoulder,* Mark Chesnutt's *Too Cold at Home.*

Favorite song: John Fogerty's "Centerfield."

Favorite show: Mark Chesnutt at the governor's inaugural ball.

He's a bit country and a little bit rock-and-soul. Bush gets huge marks for tapping Van Morrison and his masterpiece *Moondance,* an album of Irish-flavored and jazz-influenced R&B numbers that has been widely imitated since its 1970 release. The Everly Brothers,

masters of close harmonies from rock's early days, add a nostalgic note to Bush's list and should help reassure the 60-and-over crowd. . . .

On the campaign trail, Bush has been playing "La Bamba" by Los Lobos, "Respect" by Aretha Franklin and "Signed Sealed Delivered" by Stevie Wonder.

Al Gore

Favorite albums: Bob Dylan's *Highway 61 Revisited,* Ray Charles's *Modern Sounds in Country and Western Music,* The Beatles' *Rubber Soul.*

Favorite song: The Beatles' "All You Need Is Love."

Favorite concert: Bruce Springsteen at MCI Center, 8/31/99.

Gore's list seems a bit like Gore himself: solid, impressive and slightly redolent of market-testing. The suspicions of cynics might be aroused by the choice of Charles's *Modern Sounds,* a 1962 opener in which the Genius of Soul discovered his inner hayseed and took on some country classics.

On the trail, Gore has been playing Shania Twain's "Rock This Country" and "Love Train" by the O'Jays, which doubled as intro music during the vice president's "Tonight Show" appearance.

—Adapted from *Washington Post,* March 7, 2000

policy area involved. Until the relatively ineffective War Powers Resolution of 1973, for several decades there had been few serious attempts to curb the president's

THE PRESIDENT IS NOT ABOVE THE LAW

After the Watergate scandal, a Senate intelligence committee under Senator Frank Church, Democrat of Idaho, investigated abuses by the FBI, CIA, and other federal intelligence and police agencies. Former President Nixon, responding to written questions from the committee, attempted to argue that a President was in some way above the law: "It is quite obvious," he said, "that there are certain inherently governmental actions which if undertaken by the sovereign in protection of the interest of the nation's security are lawful but which if undertaken by private persons are not." The committee emphatically rejected this concept of the President as "sovereign," and noted in its final report: "There is no inherent constitutional authority for the President or any intelligence agency to violate the law."

—Excerpt from the final report of the Senate Select Committee on Intelligence, Book IV, 1976

power to commit military forces abroad. In the field of domestic legislation, however, presidential powers may not be strong enough. For example, both Nixon and Carter were unable to get Congress to approve their welfare-reform programs. Reagan could not persuade Congress to shift responsibility for the welfare and Food Stamp programs from the federal government to the states, although later Clinton succeeded in doing so. And Bush was unable to get Congress to approve his "enterprise zones" for investment incentives in inner cities until after the riots in Los Angeles; he then vetoed the bill because it included new taxes. Clinton's major effort to revamp the nation's health care system fizzled in 1994.

The president (along with the vice president) is the only official of the U.S. government elected by all the people. The presidency, therefore, would seem to be the branch of government best situated to view and act on national problems in the interest of a national constituency. In a diverse democracy of conflicting interests and competing groups, the president is the one official who represents all the people and who can symbolize their aspirations. He is the custodian of the future. Despite the limits on his powers, he can be the greatest force for national unity—or disunity. He can recognize the demands of minorities for social justice, or he can repress or ignore their rights. He can protect constitutional liberties or turn loose federal police power to wiretap, eavesdrop, and burglarize. He can lead the nation into war or preserve the peace.

Such is his power that he leaves his indelible mark on the times, with the result that the triumph or tragedy of each presidency is, in some measure at least, also our own.

"A SMALL, SELECT CLUB"

Jumbo shrimp and canapes on silver trays were being offered by the serenely silent staff. . . . It was eight P.M., June 23, 1993, and summer light was still filtering into the parlor by the Lincoln Bedroom. . . . But this wasn't a social evening at the White House. President Clinton was about to order air strikes in defense of the president he had defeated.

Two months earlier, Kuwaiti authorities had arrested fourteen men for planning to place a 175-pound car bomb in the path of former President Bush as he received an award in Kuwait City. Immediately after the arrest, Clinton ordered the FBI and CIA to determine if this assassination attempt was authorized by Saddam Hussein. . . . The investigation had established a link between the bombing suspects and the Iraqi Intelligence Service. . . .

Yes, as Clinton would later tell the world, the plot against Bush was "an attack against our country and against all Americans." But it was also an attack against one man. I can only imagine what President Bush was thinking at 4:40 P.M. that Saturday afternoon when Clinton gave him the news: "We completed our investigation. Both the CIA and FBI did an excellent job. It's clear it was directed against you. I've ordered a cruise-missile attack."

"It's clear it was directed against you. I've ordered a cruise missile attack." The paradox of presidential power distilled into two sentences. Few people live as precarious a life as an American president. Every day, someone, somewhere, is plotting an assassination scheme—and the scary truth is that even the most effective Secret Service is no guarantee against a killer willing to die. But along with the vulnerability comes an awesome power: the ability to move global markets with a single statement, to obliterate an entire country by ordering the turn of two keys. . . .

It's a small, select club, a peerage, the few men alive at any one time who have served as president. What unites them, ultimately, overwhelms partisan differences or even the bitter memories of past political battles. Only they know what it's like to be president—to order troops into battle; to hate the press; to sacrifice privacy in return for power; to face the nation from the West Front of the Capitol and swear to defend the Constitution against all foes, foreign and domestic, so help you, God; to sit alone in the Oval Office late at night and contemplate the imperfect choices that are the stuff of history.

—George Stephanopoulos, *All Too Human: A Political Education*

Five former United States presidents: George Bush, Ronald Reagan, Jimmy Carter, Gerald Ford, and Richard Nixon
AP/Wide World

KEY TERMS

War Powers Resolution, p. 410

executive agencies, p. 414

independent regulatory agencies, p. 419

Cold War, p. 419

civilian supremacy, p. 421

military-industrial complex, p. 421

executive agreements, p. 423

executive privilege, p. 424

veto, p. 425

pocket veto, p. 425

line-item veto, p. 426

riders, p. 427

National Security Council (NSC), p. 433

CHAPTER HIGHLIGHTS

✦ The American presidency is an office of enormous contrasts, of great power and great limits. Although once viewed as extraordinarily powerful, the presidency more recently has seemed an institution of uncertain power.

✦ The presidency is both an institution and a person. The institution is the office created by the Constitution, custom, federal laws since 1789, and the gradual growth of various tools of presidential power. The person is a human being who brings a particular personality and style to the White House. The presidency, then, is both highly institutionalized and highly personal.

✦ Under the Twenty-second Amendment, in normal circumstances the incumbent must change at least once every eight years.

✦ There are few legal qualifications for the office; the Constitution requires only that the president be a "natural-born" citizen, at least 35 years old, and 14 years a resident of the United States.

✦ The president is one individual but fills many separate roles: chief of state, chief executive, commander in chief, chief diplomat, chief legislator, chief of party, and popular leader. All but the last two are required of him by the Constitution. Many of the presidential roles blend and overlap.

✦ The president of the United States is the ceremonial and symbolic head of state. In another role, he is also head of government, the official who presides over the machinery of the executive branch.

✦ The president runs the executive branch of government with the aid of a White House staff, various other agencies in the Executive Office of the President, and the cabinet.

✦ The president is commander in chief of the armed forces of the United States. The Constitution declares that "Congress shall have Power . . . to declare War," but Congress has not done so since 1941. In the intervening years the president has made the decision to go to war. The War Powers Resolution was a law passed by Congress in 1973 in an effort to set a time limit on the use of combat forces abroad by a president. The resolution has not effectively restricted presidential military power, however.

✦ Civilian supremacy, the principle of civilian control of the military, is based on the clear constitutional power of the president as supreme commander of the armed forces.

✦ Presidents make foreign policy; they direct the relations of the United States with other nations of the world. The Constitution does not specifically confer this power on the president, but it does so indirectly. The president has sole power to make treaties with the consent of two-thirds of the Senate. The president also can sign executive agreements with other nations that do not require Senate approval.

✦ Beneath the president in the executive branch are the 14 cabinet departments (as of January 2001) and about 60 major independent agencies, boards, and commissions. These agencies are of two main types: executive agencies and independent regulatory agencies.

✦ The conflict between the president and Congress at times revolves around the doctrine of executive privilege, the claim by presidents of an inherent right to withhold information from Congress and the judiciary. This doctrine is nowhere explicitly stated in the Constitution but rests on the separation of powers of the three branches of government.

✦ As chief legislator, the president has an important weapon in the veto, the constitutional power of the president to disapprove a bill and return it with his objections to the branch of Congress in which it originated.

✦ Because of the Watergate scandal, Richard Nixon resigned on August 9, 1974, the first president in the nation's history to do so.

✦ Only the House can bring impeachment proceedings against a president, by majority vote. The president is then tried by the Senate with the chief justice of the United States presiding. A two-thirds vote of the Senate is required to convict a president and remove him from office.

✦ Andrew Johnson was the first president to be impeached, in 1868. At his Senate trial, he escaped being removed from office by one vote. In 1998, Bill Clinton became the second president to be impeached. Like Andrew Johnson, he was not convicted and removed from office.

✦ If the president dies, resigns, or is removed from office, the vice president becomes president. The Twenty-fifth Amendment sets forth the procedures under which the vice president becomes acting president if the president is unable to perform his duties.

SUGGESTED WEB SITES

www.whitehouse.gov

The White House

The official Web site for the White House. Offers presidential speeches, press conferences, interviews, and other documents. Provides links to the personal home pages of the president, the First Lady, and the vice president. Also contains links to the Web sites of departments that make up the cabinet, independent agencies that report to the president, and special presidential commissions.

www.thepresidency.org
The Center for the Study of the Presidency
A nonpartisan, nonprofit organization dedicated to the study of the presidency. The Reference Center provides access to the center's publication, *Presidential Studies Quarterly,* and to special reports produced by the center.

SUGGESTED READING

Barber, James David. *The Presidential Character: Predicting Performance in the White House,* 4th edition* (Prentice-Hall, 1992). An important analysis of why presidents act as they do. Based on research on presidents from Taft to Carter, Barber's study explores the relationships between each president's personality type and his performance in office.

Burns, James MacGregor. *Roosevelt: The Lion and the Fox* (Harcourt Brace Jovanovich, 1963). (Originally published in 1956.) A political biography of Franklin D. Roosevelt, one of the foremost practitioners of the art of presidential leadership. Focuses primarily on Roosevelt's first two terms in office.

Corwin, Edward S. *The President: Office and Powers,* 5th revised edition* (New York University Press, 1984). A classic analysis of the American presidency. Stresses the historical development and the legal powers of the office.

Donald, David Herbert. *Lincoln* (Simon & Schuster, 1995). An absorbing, revealing, and superbly written biography of one of the greatest American presidents. The book emphasizes Lincoln's remarkable skills as a political leader.

Fenno, Richard F., Jr. *The President's Cabinet: An Analysis in the Period from Wilson to Eisenhower* (Harvard University Press, 1959). A thoughtful study of the development of the cabinet and its role as a distinct political institution. Examines the dual role of cabinet members as presidential advisers and department heads and the place of the cabinet in the larger political system.

Goodwin, Doris Kearns. *Lyndon Johnson and the American Dream* (St. Martin's Press, 1991). A revealing examination of one of our most colorful presidents. The author assesses his public and private life, his early career, his years in the Senate, and his presidency.

Greenstein, Fred I. *The Hidden-Hand Presidency: Eisenhower as Leader* (Basic Books, 1982). A study of the presidency of Dwight D. Eisenhower. Argues that Eisenhower exercised effective leadership behind the scenes while cultivating the appearance of being above the fray. Maintains that few observers recognized this "hidden-hand" technique.

Greenstein, Fred I. *The Presidential Difference: Leadership Style from Roosevelt to Clinton* (Free Press, 2000). An informative examination of the differing approaches to presidential leadership, by a leading presidential scholar.

Jones, Charles O. *The Presidency in a Separated System* (The Brookings Institution, 1994). A thoughtful analysis of factors that may limit and check "presidential leadership" in a system in which power is divided among separate branches of government. It argues that—over time—the role, the resources, and the relative power of the president vary greatly in such a system.

Koenig, Louis W. *The Chief Executive,* 5th edition (Harcourt Brace Jovanovich, 1986). An excellent, readable, and comprehensive study of the many facets of the presidency.

Light, Paul C. *The President's Agenda: Domestic Policy Choice from Kennedy to Clinton,* 3rd revised edition (Johns Hopkins University Press, 1999). An analysis of how specific policy proposals get on the agenda as part of the president's domestic program.

Lowi, Theodore J. *The Personal President: Power Invested, Promise Unfulfilled* (Cornell University Press, 1985). An analysis of the modern presidency that concludes that the president has become the personal embodiment of government in the United States. Argues that the high expectations surrounding today's presidents doom them to failure.

McCulloch, David. *Truman* (Touchstone, 1993). A warm, engaging biography of the plain-speaking president.

Nelson, Michael, editor. *The Presidency and the Political System* (Congressional Quarterly Press, 2000). A collection of interesting essays on some central aspects of the presidential office. Includes useful analyses of both the legal and political sources of presidential powers.

National Journal (Government Research Corporation). An excellent weekly report on American politics and government. Provides comprehensive detailed stories about current policy issues in many areas, and analyzes how Congress, the executive branch, and various interest groups interact.

Neustadt, Richard E. *Presidential Power: The Politics of Leadership from FDR to Carter* (Wiley, 1980). (Originally published in 1960.) A knowledgeable exploration of the problems faced by a modern president in seeking to exercise his power. The first edition of this book was influential in the Kennedy Administration, in which its author served for a time as a special consultant.

Schlesinger, Arthur M., Jr. *A Thousand Days* (Houghton Mifflin, 1965.) A well-written, detailed account of the Kennedy years by a scholar and former presidential aide. Although Schlesinger was not at the center of power in the Kennedy White House, he had the advantage of viewing events with the eye of a trained historian.

Skowronek, Stephen. *The Politics Presidents Make: Leadership from John Adams to Bill Clinton* (Belknap Press of Harvard University Press, 1997). A study, rich in historical detail, of the varying leadership strategies that American presidents have pursued. Emphasizes the differences in the impact that presidents have had on the politics of their time.

Tulis, Jeffrey K. *The Rhetorical Presidency** (Princeton University Press, 1987) An important analysis suggesting that a president's skills as an orator and communicator, and as a popular leader, are directly related to his success. The development of the "rhetorical presidency," the author argues, has fundamentally transformed American politics in the 20th century.

Walch, Timothy, ed. *At the President's Side: The Vice Presidency in the Twentieth Century* (University of Missouri Press, 1997). A useful collection of essays on an often neglected political office.

Wise, David. *The Politics of Lying: Government Deception, Secrecy, and Power* (Random House, 1973). An analysis, with detailed examples from several presidential administrations, of how government deception and official secrecy led to an erosion of confidence in the government during the late 1960s and early 1970s. Explores the relationship between the government and the press.

_____

*Available in paperback edition.

 Visit http://politicalscience.wadsworth.com/cummings9/update/ for current InfoTrac articles and other student resources related to this chapter.

CHAPTER 14
The Bureaucracy

During the 2000 presidential campaign, Texas Governor George W. Bush, the Republican opponent of Vice President Al Gore, attacked the government in Washington.

"Today, when Americans look to Washington, they see a government slow to respond," Bush told an audience in Philadelphia. "Slow to reform. And ignoring all the changes going on around it. At times the government is irrational, running things without any standard of what is necessary, or even what was intended.

"When an elderly patient is denied Medicare reimbursement for a simple procedure, it takes almost two years to process an appeal. Part of the reason may be that there are 132,000 pages of Medicare regulations, making decisions for provider and patient alike.

"Federal education policy can be even more bewildering. It is so complicated that there are 788 programs to carry it out. And there's actually a federal committee trying to figure out who's doing what in these 788 programs. The committee's been at work for 17 years now. Maybe it's become an example of the problem it set out to solve.

"The federal government is also responsible for the safety of our nation's food supply. The way things work now, there's one agency that inspects cheese pizza. There's another that inspects pepperoni pizza. There is one agency that inspects food grown outside the United States. Another that inspects food grown here inside the United States. Apparently, the revolutionary idea that maybe these functions could be combined hasn't dawned on anyone yet.

"Americans hear examples like this and conclude, quite reasonably, that government is out of touch, that it is too big and it spends too much."[1]

Bush had adopted the classic stance of the outsider campaigning against the government in Washington. In his speech, Bush added: "You may recall that the present administration came to Washington promising to change all this, to clear away the clutter of bureaucracy and streamline the system. They called their idea a National Performance Review to 'reinvent' government." But, Bush added, "They haven't reinvented government bureaucracy—they've just reshuffled it."[2]

By contrast, Bush's Democratic opponent, Vice President Al Gore, defended the programs and record of the Clinton Administration in which he had been the number two official for almost eight years. It was Gore who had promised to "reinvent government" by holding it to better performance, the effort that Bush had directly attacked in his Philadelphia speech.

BUREAUCRACY: HOW TO BREAK AN ASHTRAY

At the General Services Administration, the current "federal specification" for a glass or metal ashtray runs nine pages, including two pages of drawings. . . .

In making his point that the federal government has been burdened with unnecessary regulations, [Vice President] Gore appears to relish the part of the ashtray rules that govern "breakage, type I glass." To test for potential defects, paragraph 4.5.2 states:

> The test shall be made by placing the specimen on its base upon a solid support (1³/₄-inch, 44.5 mm, maple plank), placing a steel center punch (point ground to a 60-degree included angle) in contact with the center of the inside surface of the bottom and striking with a hammer in successive blows of increasing severity until breakage occurs.

> The specimen should break into a small number of irregular shaped pieces not greater in number than 35, and it must not dice. Any piece ¹/₄ inch (6.4 mm) or more on any three of its adjacent edges (excluding the thickness dimension) shall be included in the number counted. Smaller fragments shall not be counted (see 3.4.1).

Time will be needed to determine whether the Gore ashtray example assumes the legendary status accorded the 1985 discovery that the military was paying $640 each for toilet seats.

—*Washington Post*, August 17, 1993

Vice President Gore shows David Letterman how to break an ashtray.
Courtesy Alan Singer/CBS

In response to Bush's darts, the Gore campaign observed that the Texas government had grown in size by 36 percent after Bush became governor, compared to a 21 percent increase in the size of the federal bureaucracy during the same period.[3] Gore headquarters added: "The [federal] bureaucracy is smaller, spending is way down, and we've balanced the budget—while increasing investments in our public schools, putting more cops on the street and doubling the Head Start program for children. That's reform with results. Governor Bush hasn't followed through on reform promises he made in Texas. He needs some more experience on the job there before asking for a promotion to the biggest job in the land."[4]

The Bush presidential campaign in 2000 echoed past campaigns by Ronald Reagan and Bill Clinton, in which, as challengers to incumbents, they portrayed themselves as outsiders ready to do battle against the bureaucratic fortress in Washington.

Of course, when outsiders are elected, they immediately become insiders, responsible for the very bureaucracy they attacked so readily on the campaign trail.

Sometimes the importance of "the bureaucrats in Washington" is brought home dramatically by unexpected events—a budget crisis, a hurricane, floods in the Midwest, or the 1995 bombing of the federal building in Oklahoma City. Then the public may form a different view of the men and women who run the federal government.

When the people are deprived of government services they tend to take for granted, they may also form a different view. For example, twice in late 1995 and continuing into early 1996 the federal government shut down for days and weeks because President Clinton and leaders of the Republican-controlled Congress were locked in a battle over the budget. Hundreds of thousands of federal workers were thrown off the job temporarily.

Visitors to the nation's capital and to popular national parks such as Yellowstone were turned away. The Park Service was shut down. Washington's museums and monuments were closed to tourists, as were the Statue of Liberty and Ellis Island in New York. Americans planning to travel abroad could not get passports, because the State Department office that issues them was closed. Business executives and citizens who needed to deal with government agencies, such as the Commerce Department, were frustrated, for there was no one to call. Many voters voiced their disgust with both sides in the squabble in Washington. The shutdown caused great inconvenience to many people. But it also brought home the fact that perhaps the "bureaucrats in Washington"—so often the target of political brickbats—were necessary, after all.

In the 2000 presidential campaign, Vice President Al Gore, as the Democratic candidate, defended his record. By doing so, he was in effect praising the achievements of the federal bureaucracy. The record of the Clinton-Gore administration, after all, was largely the result of what bureaucrats had accomplished.

BUTTERING UP THE FARMERS: THE FEDERAL POPCORN BOARD

WASHINGTON—Since taking control of Congress, Republicans have repeatedly vowed to shrink the Government and its role in the nation's economy. But some matters are just too important to be left alone.

Popcorn, for example. The Senate this month passed a far-reaching farm bill that would scale back Federal subsidies for farmers. A little-noticed provision would establish a Federal Popcorn Board. . . .

The Popcorn Board got strong support from the chairman of the Senate Agriculture Committee, Richard G. Lugar of Indiana (a state that grows lots of popcorn), and from the Popcorn Institute, a trade association.

Andy Fisher, a spokesman for Mr. Lugar, a Republican Presidential candidate, said the board would operate "at no cost to the taxpayer" because it could levy assessments on popcorn processors. But the board could issue regulations, and violators would be subject to civil fines up to $1,000.

—*New York Times*, February 25, 1996

As the presidential race illustrated, bureaucracy—and bureaucrats—are often handy political targets to blame for society's ills. By one dictionary definition, "bureaucrat" is a neutral word—it simply means "an administrator"—but its connotations are far from complimentary. "Bureaucrat" and "bureaucracy" are words that, to some people, conjure up an image of self-important but inefficient petty officials wallowing in red tape. It has been wryly suggested, and is widely believed, that once established, bureaucracies tend to mushroom under "Parkinson's Law": "Work expands so as to fill the time available for its completion."[5] The political theorist Hannah Arendt has described bureaucracy as "rule by Nobody," that is, "an intricate system of bureaus in which no men, neither one nor the best, neither the few nor the many, can be held responsible."[6]

There are checks on bureaucratic power, however, including the news media and congressional scrutiny. And government at every level—federal, state, and local—could not function without people to run it. Many government programs are highly complex and require experts and professional people to administer them. **Public administration** is the term preferred by most political scientists to describe the bureaucratic process—the business of making government work—and bureaucrats are public administrators. The same bureaucrats who are blamed for red tape have also accomplished some remarkable tasks: The National Aeronautics and Space Administration (NASA) put men on the moon, and the Tennessee Valley Authority (TVA) brought about the greening of a large area of America.

Courtesy NASA

Today, Americans may turn to the federal government to solve or alleviate problems of the economy, of the cities, of mass transportation, and of poverty, pollution, public health, and energy. In all of these fields, public administrators—bureaucrats—make important decisions and bear great responsibilities.

The millions of persons who receive Social Security checks every month would not be getting them unless the Social Security Administration were part of the federal bureaucracy. The same "faceless bureaucrats" who are attacked in political campaigns process the Social Security checks. There is waste and red tape and inefficiency in the federal government, but, as in any large organization outside government, there are also thousands of honest, competent people.

Americans tend to be against "Big Government" in the abstract, but they also demand all kinds of government services. The "bureaucracy in Washington" did not grow overnight, but developed gradually, largely in response to public needs. Most government departments and agencies have been created as a result of pressure from some segment of the population. And the same citizens who complain about "the bureaucracy" may protest the loudest if Washington proposes to close a defense installation that provides jobs in their local community.

Criticism of bureaucracy is not limited to attacks on the government in Washington. The student in a large university may feel like a statistic, crushed by an impersonal bureaucracy. So may an employee of a big corporation. The growth of computer technology and the tendency to assign numbers to individuals (credit cards, bank accounts, Social Security) has made many people feel that they are mere cogs in a vast bureaucratic machine. Voice mail, e-mail, and answering machines have replaced human beings. Once, callers to companies, banks, or other institutions could talk to other people; today, as often as not, they must push buttons and leave messages—and hope for a reply.

But the fattest bureaucratic target of all is the federal government. Some of the sentiment directed

Officials of the Federal Emergency Management Agency (FEMA) meet with flood victims in Cuero, Texas, 1998.
Copyright © Bob Daemmrich/Stock, Boston
PictureQuest

DONALD DUCK GOES TO WASHINGTON

WASHINGTON—The General Accounting Office disclosed Thursday that it put Donald Duck's name on the payroll of the Department of Housing and Urban Development, and gave him a salary of $99,999 a year—without being challenged.

The department's computer, which is supposed to head off such shenanigans, not only failed to detect the "hiring" of the cartoon character, it raised no objections to a salary more than twice the legal limit, $47,500, for civil service pay.

It was not revealed what, if any, task the loquacious duck was supposed to perform at HUD, where 16,000 employees are charged with "providing for sound development of the nation's communities and metropolitan areas."

Officials of the GAO, Congress' watchdog over federal spending, disclosed the incident in testimony before the subcommittee on compensation and employee benefits of the House Post Office and Civil Service Committee. The subcommittee is looking into abuses of federal overtime pay.

—*Los Angeles Times*, October 27, 1978

"99,999 bucks! I've been working here in Washington for 30 years, and I only make 72,000!"

Editorial cartoon by Paul Conrad copyright © 1978 *Los Angeles Times*. Reprinted by permission.

against the federal bureaucracy can be traced to the social-welfare programs of the New Deal, which vastly expanded the role of government in the lives of individual citizens. For three decades much of the criticism of the bureaucracy came from Republicans and conservatives opposed to the welfare state and the concentration of power in Washington. Yet, during eight years of Republican rule under President Eisenhower, the federal government increased in size. In the late 1960s Democratic liberals began to voice similar thoughts. Ideological disenchantment with the federal bureaucracy had come full circle; conservatives and liberals joined in an antibureaucratic alliance of sorts.

The antigovernment sentiment reached a peak in the aftermath of the 1994 congressional elections, when Republicans captured both houses of Congress for the

"I'm sorry, dear, but you knew I was a bureaucrat when you married me."

Copyright © The New Yorker Collection 1980 Weber from cartoonbank.com. All rights reserved.

George Washington (Boss) Plunkitt, a 19th-century political boss in Tammany Hall, New York City's Democratic machine, had a low opinion of civil service:

> I know that the civil service humbug is stuck into the constitution . . . but, as Tim Campbell said: "What's the constitution among friends?" . . .
>
> The people's voice is smothered by the cursed civil service law; it is the root of all evil in our government. . . . Let me tell of one case. After the battle of San Juan Hill [in the Spanish-American War of 1898], the Americans found a dead man with a light complexion, red hair and blue eyes. They could see he wasn't a Spaniard, although he had on a Spanish uniform. . . . A private of the Seventy-first Regiment saw him and yelled, "Good Lord, that's Flaherty." That man grew up in my district, and he was once the most patriotic American boy on the West Side. He couldn't see a flag without yellin' himself hoarse.
>
> Now, how did he come to be lying dead with a Spanish uniform on? . . . Well, in the municipal campaign of 1897, that young man, chockful of patriotism, worked day and night for the Tammany ticket. Tammany won, and the young man determined to devote his life to the service of the city. He picked out a place that would suit him, and sent in his application to the head of department. He got a reply that he must take a civil service examination to get the place. . . . He read the questions about the mummies, the bird on the iron, and all the other fool questions—and he left that office an enemy of the country that he had loved so well. The mummies and the bird blasted his patriotism. He went to Cuba, enlisted in the Spanish army at the breakin' out of the war, and died fightin' his country. . . .
>
> If that young man had not run up against the civil examination, but had been allowed to serve his country as he wished, he would be in a good office today, drawin' a good salary.

—Boss Plunkitt, in William L. Riordon, *Plunkitt of Tammany Hall*

first time in 40 years and Newt Gingrich was elected speaker of the House. With Gingrich as the point man, the Republicans set out to dismantle or slow down major social programs, cut back the regulation of business, and greatly reduce the size and reach of the federal government. As noted in Chapter 13, even President Clinton—adopting some of his opponents' rhetoric—announced in his January 1996 State of the Union message: "The era of big government is over."[7]

Some critics, such as Peter F. Drucker, have gone so far as to conclude that "modern government has become ungovernable." Drucker contends that because of bureaucratic inertia and "administrative incompetence," government is unable to perform the tasks assigned to it. He adds: "There is no government today that can still claim control of its bureaucracy and of its various agencies. Government agencies are all becoming autonomous, ends in themselves, and directed by their own desire for power, their own rationale, their own narrow vision rather than by national policy."[8]

Even if such criticisms are overstated, they raise important, valid questions about the role of bureaucracy in modern society. But as long as people demand more and more services from their government—Social Security, health care, aid to education, housing, and the like—some form of bureaucracy is inevitable.

The classic concept of the bureaucracy was developed by the pioneering German sociologist Max Weber, who saw it as a secretive, strict hierarchy, with authority flowing from the top down within a fixed framework of rigid rules and regulations. In Weber's view, the bureaucracy draws its power from its expertise. Political rulers are in no position to argue with the technical knowledge of the trained bureaucrat: "The absolute monarch is powerless opposite the superior knowledge of the bureaucratic expert."[9] Even the Russian czar of old, Weber noted, could seldom act against the wishes of his bureaucracy.

Government in the United States today, of course, does not in every respect fit Weber's classic view of bureaucracy. Court decisions, probing by the press, the Freedom of Information Act, and congressional investigations place pressure on the bureaucracy to operate in public view. Bureaucrats may prefer to operate in secrecy, but they also know they risk embarrassing public disclosure if they cover up incompetence, lavish spending, or corruption. And the expertise of the bureaucracy, while still a formidable source of power, has been balanced in part by the fact that both the president and Congress are able to access other sources of expert opinion in framing national policies. For example, the Executive Office of the President has advisers in every important policy area. Similarly, Congress has the Congressional Budget Office, the General Accounting Office, and professional committee and office staffs to provide it and its members with expert advice.

"*Among the most familiar creatures of the political seas is the Bloated Bureaucracy . . . it cannot be hurried; it swims at its own pace.*"
Drawing by Jeff MacNelly from *A Political Bestiary* by Eugene J. McCarthy and James J. Kilpatrick, McGraw-Hill Book Company, 1979.

In the 19th century, elected officials in the United States customarily rewarded their supporters with government jobs. Selection of bureaucrats on the basis of merit rather than politics was the goal of the civil service reform movement of the late 19th century.

One result was that in the first third of the 20th century, classic theories of public administration emerged that were rooted in the civil service reform movement. As Dwight Waldo noted, early theorists in the field of public administration concluded that "politics and administration are distinct" and that "politics in any 'bad' sense ought not to intrude upon administration."[10] Today, however, political scientists recognize that politics and bureaucracy are inseparable, and that bureaucratic decision making involves political as well as policy choices.

Since bureaucrats have great discretion in the decisions they make, a central problem is how to make bureaucracy accountable to popular control[11]—in short, how to reconcile bureaucracy and democracy.

Because civil servants are not elected and are free of direct control by the voters, the bureaucracy is semipermanent in character and, at times, an independent center of power. Moreover, a government agency may yield to pressure from an interest group or from some

narrow segment of society rather than respond to broader public interests.

There is another danger. The executive branch may abuse its power and seek to misuse the bureaucracy—particularly police and intelligence agencies—against its political opponents. So, at the same time that it is responsive, bureaucracy, particularly in its law enforcement and regulatory functions, must also, in some degree, be independent. If it is too responsive, it may yield to improper political pressures.

The bureaucracy also must be effective if government is to solve the social problems that face it. A poverty program that creates jobs for bureaucrats but fails to meet the needs of the poor, or a pollution program that issues regulations but fails to eliminate smog, adds to the taxpayers' burden without alleviating social ills. Today, many students of public administration contend that bureaucracy should be designed to serve people and to be sensitive to human needs and social inequality. They argue that the first goal of bureaucracy should not be efficiency and economy, but influencing and carrying out public policies "which more generally improve the quality of life for all."[12]

In this chapter we will explore a key question: Should the bureaucracy be reduced in size; and, if so, can it still meet social needs in a democratic system? A number of other complex questions arise in assessing the role of public administration in a democracy: Can government really be "too big" if people demand increased services? Should the federal bureaucracy be broken up and decentralized, and power shifted to the states?

Closely tied to these questions is the important issue of whether the bureaucracy has been captured by industry or other interest groups, whether government regulators are tools of the regulated. In other words, to whom is the bureaucracy responsive? Does the bureaucracy make public policy solely by its own decisions? Can the president or Congress control it? In a democracy this is a serious question, for democratic institutions should be responsive to the people. How effective are the checks on bureaucratic power?

BUREAUCRACY AND THE POLICY PROCESS

In theory, bureaucrats are simply public servants who administer policy decisions made by the accountable officials of the government—the president, his principal appointees, and Congress. In fact, government administrators by their actions—or inaction—often make policy. That is, they play an important role in choosing among alternative goals and selecting the programs to achieve those goals. As Francis E. Rourke has noted, "Bureaucrats themselves have now become a central factor in the policy process: in the initiation of proposals, the weighing of alternatives, and the resolution of conflict."[13]

Moreover, there is no single bureaucracy in America, and the term is not limited to the federal government: Bureaucrats administer programs at every level, down to the smallest units of state and local government. Public administration in the United States is fragmented by the system of federalism. And at each level of government there are hundreds of bureaus and divisions.

Bureaucrats have great discretionary powers; what they decide to do, or not to do, constitutes a policy output of the political system. A bureaucrat has discretion when the power he exercises leaves him "free to make a choice among possible courses of action or inaction."[14]

Bureaucrats also help to shape policy through the advice they give to elected officials. The elected officials have the final say on decisions, but their choices may be limited by the options presented to them by the bureaucrats. As a practical matter, elected officials are confined to choosing policies and programs that the bureaucracies are capable of carrying out.

Bureaucracy and Client Groups

The American bureaucracy is deeply involved in politics as well as policy. As in the case of the president and members of Congress, government agencies also have **constituencies**—interest groups, or client groups, either directly regulated by the bureaucracy or vitally affected by its decisions.

Sometimes, through close political and personal association between a government agency and its client group, the regulating agency becomes a captive of the industry it is supposed to regulate. "In its most developed form," Rourke observes, "the relationship between an interest group and an administrative agency is so close that it is difficult to know where the group leaves off and the agency begins."[15] One reason for this close relationship is that a bureaucracy is often able to increase its political strength by building a constituency. As Rourke notes: "The groups an agency provides tangible benefits to are the most natural basis of . . . political support, and it is with these interest groups that agencies ordinarily establish the firmest alliances. Such groups have often been responsible for the establishment of the agency in the first place. Thereafter, the agency and the group are bound together by deeply rooted ties that may be economic, political, or social in character."[16]

Viewed in this light, the behavior of the bureaucracy becomes somewhat predictable. Thus, the Agriculture Department is a natural representative for farmers; the Commerce Department is friendly toward business; and the Pentagon is allied with defense contractors. These close relationships illustrate how some government agencies have mobilized the support of client groups.

Client groups do not always dominate, however. Although a government bureau may be influenced by its clients, it may at the same time be sensitive to, and responsive to, pressures from the public, Congress, and other actors in the political system. For example, often bureaucrats are particularly sensitive to the wishes of the congressional committees that monitor their activities and control their appropriations. At the same time, many senior bureaucrats complain that they are subject to so many pressures and controls that they are unable to do the work that the law requires their agency to perform.

The bureaucracy acts and reacts in a political way. It responds to a variety of pressures because it is at once accountable to several groups—its clients, the public at large, the press, Congress, and the president. Public administrators, in short, play a major role in the American political system, and their decisions are of crucial importance to government and society as a whole.

Bureaucracy and Congress

In addition to client groups, another source of bureaucratic power stems from the political support that an agency may enjoy in Congress, particularly among influential committee chairpersons. For a long time, the military services were able to count on the friendly support of powerful Democrats who chaired the House and Senate Armed Services Committees. Similarly, the FBI and the CIA have enjoyed the protection of a small group of influential representatives and senators.

But not always. In the mid-1970s Congress investigated and exposed illegal or questionable operations by both the FBI and the CIA. In the mid-1990s, both agencies were severely criticized in Congress. The CIA was taken to task over the disclosure that Aldrich H. Ames, a CIA officer, had betrayed the agency's secrets to Moscow, costing the lives of 10 Soviets serving as CIA agents and causing the imprisonment of several others.[17] The FBI was criticized for mishandling a con-

Aldrich Ames
Copyright © Win McNamee/Reuters

frontation at Ruby Ridge, Idaho, in 1992 in which the wife and son of white supremacist Randall Weaver were shot and killed by government agents.

Agencies that do not have cordial relations with important members of the legislative branch may find their power diminished. The Department of Energy was battered by congressional critics in the year 2000 after a series of security lapses at the Los Alamos National Laboratory in New Mexico, including the disappearance for a time of computer hard drives containing secrets of the nation's nuclear weapons program.

Other agencies have fared better. The United States Corps of Engineers is a classic example of a federal agency that won virtually independent status by mobilizing political support in the legislative branch. Its river-and-harbor, navigation, and flood-control projects brought important benefits to local communities—and to members of Congress in those districts.[18]

Government agencies exert considerable effort to maintain cordial diplomatic relations with Capitol Hill. That task has become more complex in recent years because congressional reforms have resulted in the creation of many new subcommittees, and the agencies must deal with them. The cabinet departments employ hundreds of persons to engage in liaison with Congress. Liaison officers watch over legislation concerning their agencies; they also field requests made by members of Congress on behalf of constituents who have business pending before their agency. The government prosecuted one scientist at the laboratory, Wen Ho Lee, for downloading nuclear secrets onto computer tapes, but it bungled the case. Lee pleaded guilty to one charge of mishandling classified information. The judge denounced the government for its harsh treatment of the scientist who had been kept in solitary confinement for months.

Political scientist Morris P. Fiorina has formulated an intriguing theory about the symbiotic relationship between Congress and the bureaucracy. He suggested that "the Washington System" follows a cycle: First, members of Congress earn credit from their constituents by establishing federal programs. Second, the legislation is drafted in very general terms, so that some government agency must create rules and regulations—which means "the trampling of numerous toes. At the next stage, aggrieved and/or hopeful constituents petition their members of Congress to intervene in the complex (or at least obscure) decision processes of the bureaucracy. The cycle closes when the congressman lends a sympathetic ear, piously denounces the evils of bureaucracy, intervenes in the latter's decisions, and rides a grateful electorate to ever more impressive electoral showings. Congressmen take credit coming and going. They are the alpha and the omega."[19]

Few members of Congress have ever served in the bureaucracy, a factor that adds to the tensions between legislators and bureaucrats. By contrast, in Britain, with its parliamentary system, many members of Parliament have been, or hope to be, cabinet ministers or junior ministers. As a result, the gulf between lawmakers and bureaucrats in Britain is much narrower.

Of course, in the relationship between Congress and the bureaucracy, the bureaucracy is not without powerful resources. Members of Congress, for example, are particularly sensitive to any plans by the Defense Department to close military bases in their districts. And when some members of Congress talked about

Wen Ho Lee
Courtesy and copyright © KOAT-TV, Albuquerque

reducing the subsidies for rail lines, Amtrak countered by revealing plans for reduced operations. "Just coincidentally, lines to be eliminated seemed to run through the districts of critical members of the Appropriations and Commerce committees."[20]

Bureaucracy, Triangles, and Subgovernments

The bureaucracy, interest groups, and congressional committees interact. In some areas, such as agriculture and defense, the relationship among the three actors is so close that it is often referred to as a **triangle,** an **iron triangle,** or a **subgovernment.** (See Figure 14-1.) Although the terms may vary, they refer essentially to the same phenomenon: a powerful alliance of mutual benefit among an agency or unit of the government, an interest group, and a committee or subcommittee of Congress.

As Robert L. Lineberry has suggested, in such a situation, policymaking is a result of "close cooperation and interaction among these triads of power." Lineberry adds: "When a group becomes strong enough, it gets a part of the government, its own piece of the action. The measure of an interest group's strength is how many 'shares' of the government it controls. 'Little' interests, such as the fisheries or tobacco growers, may have only an agency or two within a cabinet department and only a subcommittee of Congress. 'Big' interests, such as business and labor, have whole cabinet departments."[21]

There are numerous examples of triangles or subgovernments. In many cases the movement of people among the three corners of the triangle is also an important element; a Pentagon general may, after a required waiting period, end up as lobbyist for a missile manufacturer, or a staff member of the House Armed Services Committee may go to work for a defense contractor. Typically, in such triangles, many of the participants know one another and play "musical chairs," changing jobs within the triangle.

The existence of such triangles or subgovernments raises questions about the nature of the pluralist system. Instead of competing with one another, some analysts argue, interest groups merely capture a segment of the bureaucracy and call it their own.[22]

For most government agencies today, however, Francis Rourke has argued, the "highly exclusionary" closed system of iron triangles "is long gone."[23] In Rourke's view, this is the result of greater openness in the bureaucracy enforced by Congress, the increase in the number of competing interest groups attempting to influence agency policies, and the increased power of the news media.[24] Moreover, client groups today, Rourke has observed, are "less supportive and considerably less deferential toward their administrative patrons than was once the case."[25]

Issue Networks: The Policy Activists

While the concept of iron triangles and subgovernments is helpful, it may not tell the whole story. Political scientist Hugh Heclo has suggested that **issue networks,** a loose grouping of people and organizations who seek to influence policy formation, play an important role in the shaping of public policy. As Heclo has defined it, "An issue network is a shared-knowledge group having to do with some aspect . . . of public policy."[26] As the term implies, issue networks are made up of "policy activists, those who care deeply about a set of issues and are determined to shape the fabric of public policy accordingly."[27]

In Heclo's model, an issue network is rather fluid, a loose grouping of people and organizations who seek to influence policy formation. Thus, an issue network is not as easily identifiable or as neatly categorized as an iron triangle or subgovernment: "Looking for the closed triangles of control, we tend to miss the fairly open networks of people that increasingly impinge upon government."[28]

These loose networks of policy activists not only help to shape the programs that the government adopts, Heclo contends, but increasingly they influence the appointment of the bureaucrats who administer those programs. Presidents today may be somewhat less likely than in the past to appoint party politicians to fill cabinet and subcabinet posts. Instead, they tend to choose executives whose reputations have been established by word of mouth in the various issue networks that swirl and merge around the policy process in Washington.

THE POLITICS OF BUREAUCRACY

A new cabinet secretary in Washington often discovers that a title does not assure actual authority over his or her department. "I was like a sea captain who finds

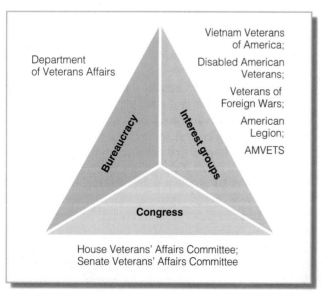

■ FIGURE 14-1

The Veterans' Affairs "Triangle"

Department of Veterans Affairs

Bureaucracy

Interest groups

Vietnam Veterans of America;
Disabled American Veterans;
Veterans of Foreign Wars;
American Legion;
AMVETS

Congress

House Veterans' Affairs Committee;
Senate Veterans' Affairs Committee

FIGHTING THE STATE DEPARTMENT WITH A TEASPOON

The State Department instructed me to survey Prague staffing needs, following the Communist seizure of the country, at which time the American staff, which I inherited, numbered 80. Six months after my recommendation, approved by the State Department, that personnel be reduced to 40, I had managed to get rid of two persons—two only. . . .

Today, a decade and a half later, it exhausts me to remember the struggle with Washington required to obtain that reduction from 80 to 78 persons. If I had started to dig the projected Nicaraguan Canal with a teaspoon, those 6 months might have shown a more impressive achievement. . . .

"Go cut the heads off somebody else's dandelions," was the gist of successive representations lodged in Foggy Bottom.

It was at that point that the Communists got into the act. Far as I know, they had no idea of the personnel war I was fighting—and losing—with Washington. They possi-

bly thought they were dealing the American Ambassador the most painful blow imaginable when they suddenly declared five-sixths of my staff persona non grata. They gave the Embassy two weeks to get 66 American employees and all their families over the border.

For 30 months thereafter, I ran the American Embassy in Prague with 12 individuals—13, counting the Ambassador. No propaganda establishment. No country team. No Peace Corps. No Minister Counselor of Embassy for Administration.

The staff . . . included a deputy who acted as chargé d'affaires in the absence of the Ambassador, an extremely competent man who used to drive the Communists crazy by talking Eskimo over the telephone on a tapped line. . . .

It was the most efficient Embassy I ever had.

—Former Ambassador Ellis O. Briggs, testimony to Senate Subcommittee on National Security Staffing and Operations in Administration of National Security

himself on the deck of a ship that he has never seen before," wrote one. "I did not know the mechanism of my ship; I did not know my officers—even by sight—and I had no acquaintance with the crew."[29]

As the cabinet member had quickly realized, the bureaucracy has its own sources of power that enable it to resist political authority. Cabinet secretaries come and go; the civil service remains. The expert technician in charge of a bureau within a department may have carved out considerable independence over the years and may resent the efforts of a political appointee to take control of the bureau.

This was precisely the problem faced by Bill Richardson, when President Clinton appointed him

Secretary of Energy in 1998. In attempting to improve security at Los Alamos and the other DOE weapons laboratories, Richardson discovered that the scientists at the labs resisted rules and regulations designed to protect secrets. Scientists by nature and training are used to a free exchange of ideas, a culture that ran counter to the secretary's efforts to tighten security.

In Francis Rourke's study of the politics of bureaucracy, he developed three central themes: the bureaucracy exercises an *impact on policy;* it does so by *mobilizing political support* and *applying its expertise.*[30] As Rourke points out, the growth of the civil service and the removal of much of the appointment power from politics does not mean that politics has been

Energy Secretary Bill Richardson testifies about security problems at Los Alamos.
Copyright © Reuters NewMedia Inc./CORBIS

removed from the bureaucracy. Quite the contrary: Federal departments and bureaus are extremely sensitive to the winds of politics. A request or inquiry from a member of Congress usually brings speedy action by a government agency—the officials in that agency know where appropriations come from.

Furthermore, in mobilizing support, the bureaucracy practices politics, often in expert fashion. The bureaucracy draws support from three areas—the public, Congress, and the executive branch.[31]

Bureaucracy and Public Opinion

A government agency that enjoys wide public support has an advantage over agencies that do not. The president and Congress are both sensitive to public opinion, and a popular, prestigious agency may receive more appropriations and achieve greater independence than others. In the mid-1970s it was disclosed that the FBI under J. Edgar Hoover had committed burglaries to search for evidence or to gather intelligence, and in other ways had violated the constitutional rights of Americans.[32] But for more than four decades, the FBI had managed to build such a favorable image with the general public that, until Hoover's death in 1972, both the bureau and its chief enjoyed a status of virtual independence. No president of the United States dared to fire J. Edgar Hoover.*

During the 1960s the National Aeronautics and Space Administration (NASA) and its Apollo astronauts captured the public imagination. To enable it to place men on the moon in 1969, NASA received massive appropriations at a time when some Americans were demanding a reordering of national priorities to meet social needs on earth.

In order to improve their image and enlist public support for their programs, many federal agencies employ substantial numbers of public relations people and information officials. These information specialists issue news releases and answer questions from members of the press and the general public. One study by CBS News, which the network dubbed its "Flack Census," estimated that the executive branch employed 10,858 people in public relations activities.[33] In one year, the Department of Defense alone listed 1,066 civilian and military public relations officials worldwide at a cost of $44.3 million.[34] And the actual cost and number of people performing public relations activities in the federal government are probably much higher than the "official" figures.

Bureaucracy and the President

The image of the department head as a sea captain aboard a strange ship with an unknown crew may be applied as well to a president seeking control over the bureaucracy. President Kennedy was particularly exasperated by vacillation and delay in the foreign policy bureaucracy. "The State Department is a bowl of jelly," he once declared. "It's got all those people over there who are constantly smiling. I think we need to smile less and be tougher."[35]

Other presidents have voiced similar complaints. Franklin Roosevelt complained that it was "almost impossible" to get results from the Treasury Department. Then he added:

> But the Treasury is not to be compared with the State Department. You should go through the experience of trying to get any changes in the thinking, policy, and action of the career diplomats. . . . But the Treasury and the State Department put together are nothing compared with the Na-a-vy. The admirals are really something to cope with—and I should know. To change anything in the Na-a-vy is like punching a feather bed. You punch it with your right and you punch it with your left until you are finally exhausted, and then you find the damn bed just as it was before you started punching.[36]

Often, presidents attempt to gain tighter control of the bureaucracy by reorganizing its structure. Postwar efforts toward administrative reform led in 1947 to creation of the first of two Hoover Commissions. Formally designated the Commission on Organization of the Executive Branch of the Government, the study panel was headed by former President Herbert Hoover. It first reported in 1949, and of its nearly 300 recommendations for streamlining the federal government, about half were adopted. Most of the commission's proposals emphasized centralization of authority and the need to simplify the organization of government.[37]

Since 1918 Congress has from time to time given presidents the right to restructure the executive branch. Presidents have made extensive use of this power under a series of reorganization acts passed since 1939; this power was increased by the Reorganization Act of 1949 and granted to later presidents for varying lengths of time.

The creation in 1970 of the Office of Management and Budget (OMB) was designed to shift to the president and his budget officials tighter control over management of the federal bureaucracy. OMB absorbed the old Bureau of the Budget, which had been created in 1921 as part of a law that for the first time required the president to submit to Congress an annual budget for the federal government. OMB is a unit of the Executive Office of the President. (See Chapter 13.)

The budget process, which OMB manages, can be a major tool of presidential control over the executive branch. The federal government runs on a fiscal year that starts October 1 and ends the following September 30. Each spring, agencies and departments begin planning their requests for the fiscal year starting 17 months later. Matching these requests against economic forecasts and revenue estimates from his advisers, the president estab-

---

*Hoover's confidential files, in which he squirreled away potentially embarrassing information about political leaders, was another significant source of his extraordinary power.

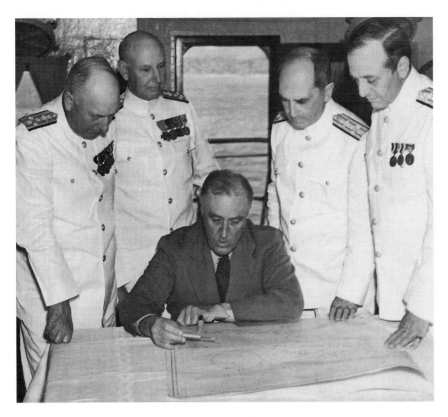

Franklin Delano Roosevelt: "But the Treasury and the State Department . . . are nothing compared with the Na-a-vy."
Culver Pictures

lishes budget guidelines; within this framework individual agency requests are studied by OMB and presented to the president for decision. Unless there is a political deadlock between the president and Congress, as has sometimes occurred, the budget then goes to Capitol Hill in January.

The in-fighting and competition among government agencies for a slice of the budget pie give the president, through OMB, an important lever for bureaucratic control. Indeed, as Aaron Wildavsky observed, "the budget lies at the heart of the political process."[38] Moreover, the

bureaucrat "whose requests are continually turned down in Congress finds that he tends to be rejected in the Budget Bureau and in his own department as well. . . . The Bureau finds itself treating agencies it dislikes much better than those it may like better but who cannot help themselves nearly as much in Congress."[39]

Bureaucracy and Policymaking

In theory, presidents make policy and bureaucrats carry it out. In fact, officials often play a major role in policy formation. In large part, this is because presidents rely on bureaucratic expertise in making their policy decisions. Frederick C. Mosher has noted the tendency of professionals with "specialized knowledge, science, and rationality" to dominate many areas of the bureaucracy.[40] On the other hand, that kind of expertise is a less reliable source of bureaucratic power today. As Francis Rourke has observed, "the private sector now abounds with think tanks, consulting firms, and watchdog groups that are widely regarded as more reliable sources of information and advice than the government itself."[41]

Other factors have combined to reduce the influence of bureaucrats in setting policy agendas. For example, the "divided government" that has often characterized the American political system during recent administrations has reduced the influence of the bureaucracy. During the Reagan years, for example, Republicans controlled the White House and competed with the Democrats who controlled the House of Representatives and, for two years, the Senate. In these circumstances, the White House sought to centralize executive power in

---

PRESIDENT KENNEDY'S STRUGGLE TO CONTROL THE BUREAUCRACY

Kennedy . . . was determined to . . . recover presidential control over the sprawling feudalism of government. This became a central theme of his administration and, in some respects, a central frustration. The presidential government, coming to Washington aglow with new ideas and a euphoric sense that it could not go wrong, promptly collided with the feudal barons of the permanent government, entrenched in their domains and fortified by their sense of proprietorship; and the permanent government, confronted by this invasion, began almost to function . . . as a resistance movement, scattering to the *maquis* in order to pick off the intruders. This was especially true in foreign affairs.

—Arthur M. Schlesinger, Jr., *A Thousand Days*

Iran rescue mission, 1980: the advisers . . .
CORBIS/UPI/Bettmann

. . . the result
J.T. Atlan/Sygma

the president's hands, while Congress tried to "micromanage" the bureaucrats. The result in each case was less power and discretion for the administrators.[42]

But presidents who rely too much on such expertise may get into trouble. For example, in April 1980, President Carter ordered a military force to attempt to rescue the American hostages being held in the United States embassy in Iran. Although the secretary of defense, Harold Brown, and the Joint Chiefs of Staff had apparently assured the president the mission would have a reasonable chance of success, it failed. It also cost the lives of eight American servicemen who died when a helicopter and a transport plane crashed into each other on the ground in a remote desert staging area. Of course, Carter was not only relying on his military experts. He undoubtedly felt that a successful rescue mission would be of enormous political benefit to him in an election year.

Other administrations have suffered similar setbacks. In 1961 President Kennedy approved a CIA plan to invade Cuba and topple Premier Fidel Castro. After the invasion of the Bay of Pigs proved a disaster, Kennedy publicly took responsibility for the mess, although privately he complained: "All my life I've known better than to depend on the experts. How could I have been so stupid, to let them go ahead?"[43] Of the Joint Chiefs of Staff, who had approved the CIA plan, Kennedy bitterly told a visitor: "They don't know any more about it than anyone else."[44]

Just as federal officials can promote policies that get the nation into trouble, they also can be instrumental in changing those policies. In 1968, during the war in Vietnam, several high-level Pentagon officials privately urged Clark M. Clifford, the secretary of defense, to try to bring about a reversal of President Johnson's Vietnam policy. As Clifford studied administration policy in Vietnam—and a request by the military for 206,000 more troops—he gradually became convinced of the folly of further escalation. Although his warm friendship with

the president "grew suddenly formal and cool," Clifford and an advisory group of prestigious civilians were apparently instrumental in persuading the president to reverse his policies.[45]

A PROFILE OF THE AMERICAN BUREAUCRACY

Who Are the Administrators?

In 1792 the federal government had 780 employees. Today there are 2,789,500 civilian employees of the federal government.[46] A study of this total reveals some surprising facts. In the first place, "the bureaucracy in Washington" is not in Washington—at least most of it is not.

One recent statistical breakdown, for example, showed that only 323,400 government employees—less than 12 percent of the federal total—worked in the metropolitan Washington area. The rest were scattered throughout the 50 states and overseas. California alone had 152,868 federal workers, and 104,200 employees worked overseas.[47]

In addition to workers on the federal payroll, however, there are several million persons working indirectly for the federal government. These are people working for defense contractors, as outside consultants, or in other programs funded by the government. Some of this outside consulting work has been criticized as wasteful or as a way of expanding the bureaucracy without seeming to do so.

In 1999 more than one-third (38.6 percent) of the civilian employees of the federal government worked for the Department of Defense. The 684,592 civilian workers in the Pentagon and other military installations, added to the 918,566 employees of the Postal Service, and the 218,379 in the Department of Veterans Affairs, comprised two-thirds of the entire federal bureaucracy. In contrast, the State Department employed only 31,085 persons.[48]

The federal civilian bureaucracy of 2,789,500 persons is unquestionably large compared to private industry; General Motors, the biggest corporation in America, had about 594,000 employees in the year 2000. Yet federal civilian workers comprise only 16 percent of total government employment—federal, state, and local—in the United States. More than five times as many people work for state and local governments as for the federal government. In the year 2000 local governments had 10,505,295 employees (including 261,228 firefighters) and state governments employed about 4,758,427 persons.[49] A comparison of federal, state, and local bureaucracies is shown in Figure 14-2.

A rough portrait can be drawn of the "average" man or woman in the federal service: He or she is 45.9 years old, has worked for the government for 16.9 years, and earns an annual salary of $48,764.[50] The president receives $400,000 a year, the vice president $181,400, and members of the cabinet $157,000. The great majority of federal workers are members of the career civil service, with their salaries in most cases fixed on a General Schedule that ranges from a starting salary of $12,960 for

Less than 12 percent of federal employees work in Washington. Here, Internal Revenue Service employees process income tax returns in Covington, Kentucky.
AP/Wide World

clerks (GS-1) to $94,287 for a relative handful of top civil servants (GS-15).[51] However, members of the **Senior Executive Service (SES),** a group of high-level administrators and managers at the top of the government bureaucracy, can earn salaries ranging up to $118,400.[52]

THE PAPER CHASE

The sheer volume of paper generated by the federal bureaucracy has long been the target of criticism. In one year, according to the government's own figures, it took Americans 913 million hours to fill out 4,900 different kinds of government forms. Congress, responding to public complaints about the amount of paperwork demanded by the government, established the Commission on Federal Paperwork. The task of the commission was to reduce the flood of official paper.

The commission acquired a staff of some three dozen people and issued 36 reports and 770 recommendations before it went out of business in 1977. Its major recommendation was that a new cabinet-level Department of Administration be created to manage federal paperwork.

Congress was less than enthusiastic over the idea of creating yet another bureaucracy to manage the bureaucracy. Representative Peter H. Kostmayer, a Pennsylvania Democrat, declared: "We can encourage each department to tighten up its operations without hiring thousands of more bureaucrats who, as we know, have an unsurpassed ability to produce paperwork." Congress did not establish the new department.

—Adapted from Congressional Quarterly, *Weekly Report*, December 10, 1977; and *New York Times*, December 1, 1979

FIGURE 14-2

Government Employment—Federal, State, and Local

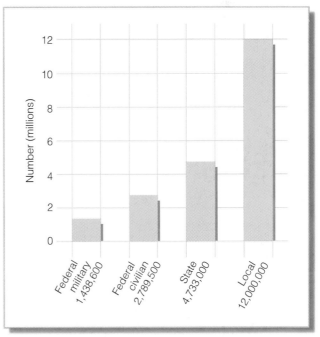

SOURCES: Data for military, U.S. Department of Defense, 1997; for civilian workforce, U.S. Office of Personnel Management, 1999; for local and state governments, U.S. Bureau of the Census, 1997.

FIGURE 14-3

Executive Branch of Government

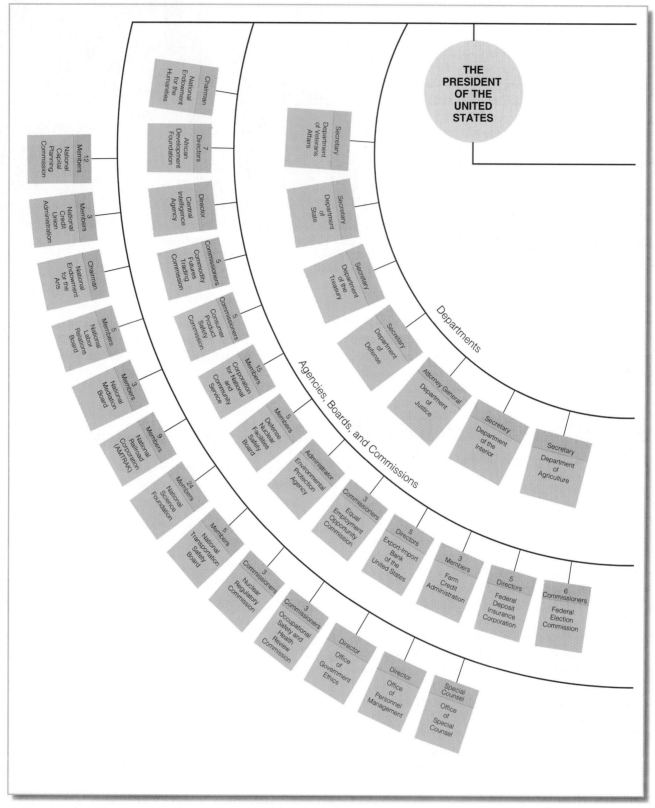

SOURCE: Adapted from the White House Web site, online at <www.whitehouse.gov/WH/Independent_Agencies/html/independent_links.html>.

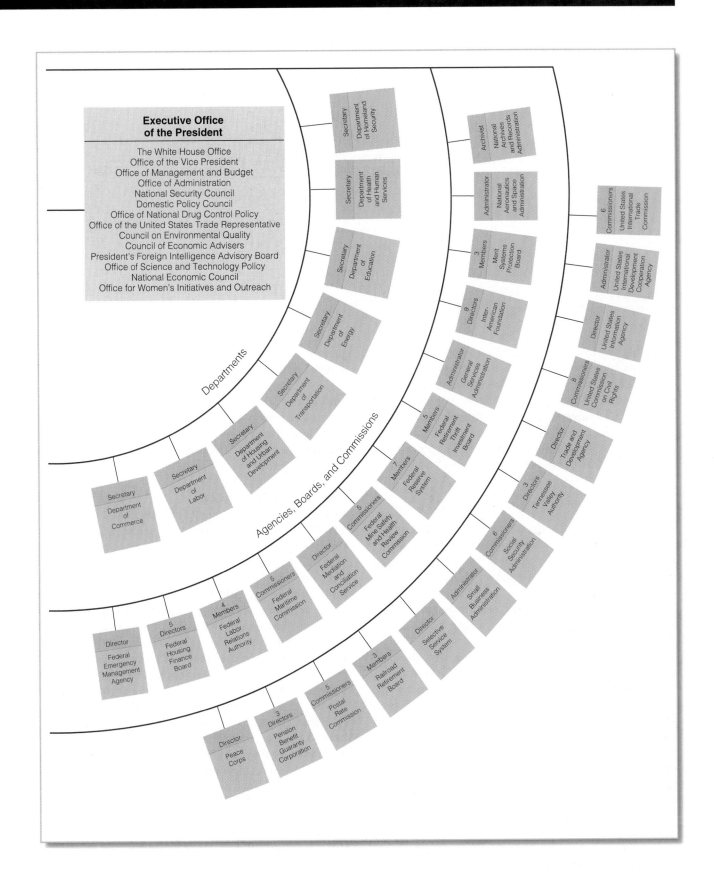

**Executive Office
of the President**

The White House Office
Office of the Vice President
Office of Management and Budget
Office of Administration
National Security Council
Domestic Policy Council
Office of National Drug Control Policy
Office of the United States Trade Representative
Council on Environmental Quality
Council of Economic Advisers
President's Foreign Intelligence Advisory Board
Office of Science and Technology Policy
National Economic Council
Office for Women's Initiatives and Outreach

Departments

Agencies, Boards, and Commissions

Secretary
Department of Homeland Security

Secretary
Department of Health and Human Services

Secretary
Department of Education

Secretary
Department of Energy

Secretary
Department of Transportation

Secretary
Department of Housing and Urban Development

Secretary
Department of Labor

Secretary
Department of Commerce

Archivist
National Archives and Records Administration

Administrator
National Aeronautics and Space Administration

3 Members
Merit Systems Protection Board

9 Directors
Inter-American Foundation

Administrator
General Services Administration

5 Members
Federal Retirement Thrift Investment Board

7 Members
Federal Reserve System

5 Commissioners
Federal Mine Safety and Health Review Commission

Director
Federal Mediation and Conciliation Service

5 Commissioners
Federal Maritime Commission

4 Members
Federal Labor Relations Authority

5 Directors
Federal Housing Finance Board

Director
Federal Emergency Management Agency

6 Commissioners
United States International Trade Commission

Administrator
United States International Development Cooperation Agency

Director
United States Information Agency

8 Commissioners
United States Commission on Civil Rights

Director
Trade and Development Agency

3 Directors
Tennessee Valley Authority

6 Commissioners
Social Security Administration

Administrator
Small Business Administration

Director
Selective Service System

Director
Railroad Retirement Board

3 Members
Railroad Retirement Board

5 Commissioners
Postal Rate Commission

3 Directors
Pension Benefit Guaranty Corporation

Director
Peace Corps

What kinds of workers make up the bureaucracy? Although almost half a million fit the conventional image of bureaucrats—general administrative and clerical employees—the government also employs 16,220 electronic engineers; 54,089 computer specialists; 37,459 nurses; 23,888 air traffic controllers; and 34,768 criminal investigators. Among federal white-collar workers, 764,712 (48 percent) are women.[53]

The Structure of the Bureaucracy

As noted in Chapter 13, the federal bureaucracy consists of three basic types of agencies: the cabinet departments, the executive agencies, and the independent regulatory agencies. Figure 14-3 shows the major executive branch agencies as of the year 2000, but approximately 100 smaller independent units of government existed, some even too small to warrant a line in the *United States Government Manual.*

As Richard E. Neustadt once emphasized, the executive branch is not a monolith: "Like our governmental structure as a whole, the executive establishment consists of separated institutions sharing powers. The president heads one of these; cabinet officers, agency administrators, and military commanders head others. Below the department level, virtually independent bureau chiefs head many more."[54] Fewer bureau chiefs have such freewheeling independence today, however; scrutiny by the news media, citizen groups, and Congress has reduced the autonomy that some units of government enjoyed when Neustadt wrote those words more than 40 years ago.

A president attempts to control the bureaucracy through his White House staff and other units of the Executive Office of the President—particularly the Office of Management and Budget—and through his department heads. Because of the sheer size of the federal government, however, no president can really hope to supervise all the activities of the administrators. And the effort to control the bureaucracy has led to the growth of the White House staff—creating a new bureaucracy at the presidential level. Thus, attempts to control bureaucracy may create new layers of bureaucracy.

The Cabinet Departments   The 15 cabinet departments are major components of the federal bureaucracy. Some idea of the structure of the executive branch and the problem of presidential control can be grasped by studying the organizational chart of a cabinet department. At first glance, it might appear to be a tightly organized agency, with lines of authority flowing upward to the secretary, who in turn reports to the president. In fact, the chart masks entrenched bureaus and key civil servants, some of whom enjoy close outside ties with interest groups and congressional committees—relationships that give them power independent of the cabinet secretary and the president. The sheer size of most departments would seem to defy presidential control. To take one example, the Department of Transportation, formed in 1966, had nearly 100,000 employees in the year 2000. As shown in Figure 14-4, the department was headed by a secretary, a deputy secretary, and five assistant secretaries, each of whom had responsibility for several offices down the line.

In addition, several major agencies—with sometimes competitive client groups—were loosely grouped under the Department of Transportation, including the United States Coast Guard, the Federal Aviation Administration (FAA), the Federal Railroad Administration, the Federal Highway Administration, and the Maritime Administration. Although the organizational chart does not show it,

President Clinton's Attorney General Janet Reno and aides
Copyright © Reuters NewMedia Inc./CORBIS

FIGURE 14-4

Department of Transportation

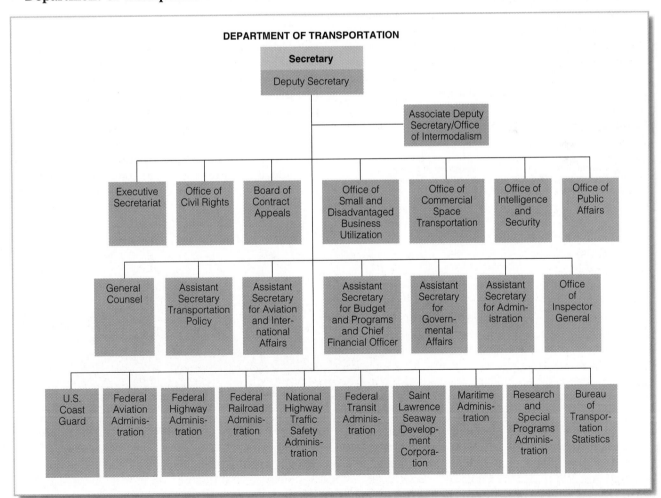

DEPARTMENT OF TRANSPORTATION

- Secretary
  - Deputy Secretary
    - Associate Deputy Secretary/Office of Intermodalism
      - Executive Secretariat
      - Office of Civil Rights
      - Board of Contract Appeals
      - Office of Small and Disadvantaged Business Utilization
      - Office of Commercial Space Transportation
      - Office of Intelligence and Security
      - Office of Public Affairs
      - General Counsel
      - Assistant Secretary Transportation Policy
      - Assistant Secretary for Aviation and International Affairs
      - Assistant Secretary for Budget and Programs and Chief Financial Officer
      - Assistant Secretary for Governmental Affairs
      - Assistant Secretary for Administration
      - Office of Inspector General
      - U.S. Coast Guard
      - Federal Aviation Administration
      - Federal Highway Administration
      - Federal Railroad Administration
      - National Highway Traffic Safety Administration
      - Federal Transit Administration
      - Saint Lawrence Seaway Development Corporation
      - Maritime Administration
      - Research and Special Programs Administration
      - Bureau of Transportation Statistics

SOURCE: *The United States Government Manual: 1999/2000* (Washington, D.C.: U.S. Government Printing Office, 1999), p. 409.

the Department of Transportation, like the other cabinet departments, is dispersed geographically. The air traffic controllers of the FAA operate airport towers across the United States; the Coast Guard and the Federal Highway Administration have field offices in several cities.

The creation of the cabinet departments parallels the growth of the American nation. Only three departments—State, War, and Treasury—were created in 1789. But new areas of concern have required the establishment of executive departments to meet new problems. This fact is reflected in the names of some of the departments created in past decades—Housing and Urban Development in 1965, Transportation in 1966, Energy in 1977, Education in 1979, and Health and Human Services, also in 1979.*

The Executive Agencies   The **executive agencies** are units of government under the president, within the executive branch, that are not part of a cabinet department. They do, however, report to the president in the same manner as departments and therefore are not independent of the president. Their heads are appointed by the president and may be dismissed by him. The executive agencies include several powerful units of the bureaucracy, such as NASA, the CIA, and the Environmental Protection Agency, to name a few.

Grouped with the executive agencies but somewhat different in status are **government corporations,** agencies that were at one time semiautonomous, but through legislation since 1945 have been placed under presidential control. In 1970 Congress abolished the Post Office as a cabinet department and established the U.S. Postal Service as an independent, government-owned corporation. The hope, at least, was to increase efficiency, remove

*The Department of Education and the Department of Health and Human Services replaced the Department of Health, Education, and Welfare, which had been created in 1953.

postal employees from politics, and give the new service power to raise rates to meet expenses. But new forms of organization do not automatically solve bureaucratic problems. Although the Postal Service made efforts to streamline its operations, many citizens have complained that under the new system postal rates have increased but the mail seems slower than ever in reaching its destination. As one result, several private delivery services, such as Federal Express, were soon competing actively with the government.

Some other examples of government corporations are the Federal Deposit Insurance Corporation (FDIC), which protects bank deposits, and the Tennessee Valley Authority (TVA), which has built dams and provided hydroelectric power and other economic benefits to an area covering eight states.

The Independent Regulatory Agencies   The **independent regulatory agencies** exercise quasi-judicial and quasi-legislative powers and are administratively independent of the president, Congress, and the courts. These agencies thus occupy a special status in the bureaucracy. In fact, however, as has been made abundantly clear over the years, the regulatory agencies and commissions are sometimes susceptible to pressures from the White House, Congress, and the industries they regulate.

The regulatory agencies decide such questions as who shall receive a license to operate a television station or build a natural gas pipeline to serve a large city. These licenses and franchises are worth millions of dollars, and the competition for them is fierce. As a result, the regulatory agencies are the target of intense pressures, including, at times, approaches by skillful and well-paid Washington lawyers who go in the "back door" to argue their clients' cases in private meetings with agency officials. Such ex parte (one-sided) contacts could become less useful, however; the Government-in-the-Sunshine

"All those in favor of establishing government regulatory agencies say 'Aye.'"

Act (1976) opened up most agency meetings to the public and also prohibited secret contacts.

In addition, a 1977 federal appeals court ruling in a case dealing with pay/cable television barred secret contacts with regulatory commission members when they were engaged in rule making in key cases. However, the Supreme Court, in another case, appeared to permit such backdoor approaches.[55]

The regulatory agencies were created because of the need for rule making and regulation in highly complex, technical areas involving the interests of the public. In awarding licenses, they also exercise a quasi-judicial function. Despite the separation of powers provided for in the Constitution, regulatory agencies combine aspects of all three branches of government—legislative, executive, and judicial.

Commission members are appointed by the president with the consent of the Senate, but, unlike cabinet members, they do not report to the president. Although members of the regulatory commissions cannot, by law, all be drawn from the same political party, the president designates the chairperson. Through his appointive powers a president may in time gain political control of the commissions.

More than four decades ago, a House inquiry into regulatory agencies demonstrated during a dramatic series of hearings that the agencies had, in many cases, become servants of industry instead of regulating in the interest of the larger public. The hearings, and subsequent disclosures, revealed a pattern of fraternization by commissioners and regulated industries.

Some regulatory agency members have accepted free transportation, lecture fees, hotel rooms, and gifts from businesses subject to their authority.[56] Others have left the government for well-paying jobs in the regulated industry. Many have seemed more concerned with protecting pipeline companies, airlines, railroads, and television networks than with making sure the industries are serving the public satisfactorily. On the other hand, at times, the regulatory agencies have been defenders of the public interest; for example, the Securities and Exchange Commission has protected investors from stock frauds, and the Federal Trade Commission has attempted to curtail false television advertising.

The major regulatory agencies, in order of their creation, are:

1. *The Federal Trade Commission* (1914): five members, seven-year terms; regulates industry; responsible for preventing unfair competition, price fixing, deceptive advertising, mislabeling of textile and fur products, false packaging, and similar abuses.
2. *The Federal Communications Commission* (1934): five members, five-year terms; licenses and regulates all television and radio stations in the United States; regulates frequencies used by police, aviation, taxicabs, citizens' band and "ham" operators, and others; fixes rates for telephone and telegraph companies in interstate commerce.
3. *The Securities and Exchange Commission* (1934): five members, five-year terms; created to protect the public from investing in securities on the basis of false or misleading claims; requires companies offering securities for sale to file an accurate registration statement and prospectus; registers brokers; regulates stock exchanges.
4. *The Federal Energy Regulatory Commission* (1978): five members, five-year terms; although within the Department of Energy, is an independent regulatory commission; fixes rates and has jurisdiction over natural gas companies, electric utilities, and interstate oil pipelines.

Many other government agencies have regulatory functions in whole or in part. For example, the Federal Maritime Commission regulates shipping; the National Labor Relations Board (NLRB) prohibits unfair labor practices; and the Board of Governors of the Federal Reserve System regulates the money supply, interest rates, and the banking industry. Many units of the regular cabinet departments also have regulatory functions. Examples include the Food and Drug Administration (FDA) in the Department of Health and Human Services; the Occupational Safety and Health Administration (OSHA) in the Labor Department; and the Antitrust Division of the Justice Department.

Deregulation: The Pattern Changes

The government regulation of industry, which blossomed during the New Deal administration of Franklin D. Roosevelt, had, by the 1970s, become a target of criticism by many Republicans and Democrats alike. President

Carter, for example, called for deregulation of airlines, banking, trucking, railroads, and telecommunications.

Even before Carter took office in 1977, Congress had begun exploring deregulation of the airline and other industries. The rising tide of sentiment in Congress reflected complaints by business of excessive and costly government regulation, red tape, delay, and paperwork. In 1978 Congress enacted the Airline Deregulation Act, which phased out and in 1985 abolished the Civil Aeronautics Board (CAB), the regulatory agency that had granted domestic and overseas airline routes, set air fares, and approved airline mergers. A decade later, in 1995, the oldest regulatory agency, the Interstate Commerce Commission (ICC), also went out of business. The ICC, created in 1887, had regulated railroads, trucking companies, and bus lines. When it closed its doors, its powers and duties were reassigned to the Department of Transportation.

In 1980 Congress passed the Motor Carrier Act to deregulate the trucking industry. Also in 1980, Congress passed the Staggers Rail Act, substantially deregulating the railroads. The new law gave the railroads much more freedom to set the prices they charge their customers. That same year, Congress reduced the power of the Federal Trade Commission (FTC) to regulate certain industries.

Pressures to deregulate continued after President Reagan was elected in 1980. In 1987, the Federal Communications Commission (FCC) abolished the fairness doctrine, which had required that broadcasters present all sides of important public issues.

In the rush to deregulate, some observers felt, the government may have gone too far. The airline industry is a case in point. After airlines were deregulated in 1978, they could, with some exceptions, fly anywhere they pleased on domestic routes. As a result, major carriers dropped all service to 132 cities.[57] A number of smaller communities suffered severely because of these changes. New carriers sprang up to compete with the

giants, and price wars broke out on transcontinental and other routes. The public sometimes benefited through lower air fares, and some airlines had a sharp increase in business at first. But after an initial surge of profits, the industry, beginning in 1981, operated at a loss for three years in a row. Eventually, Braniff, Pan Am, and Eastern airlines all went out of business. Thousands of airline workers lost their jobs.

By the summer of 2000, flight delays and cancellations had become worse than ever, with some hapless passengers trapped for hours on planes sitting on runways, waiting to take off. Travelers in economy class were often jammed into seats that provided little legroom, because the airlines tried to squeeze as many people as possible into each plane. Many passengers complained of being treated like cattle. In the airline industry, at least, deregulation had proved a mixed blessing.

The Growth of Social Regulation

Although considerable deregulation of transportation, communications, and financial institutions has taken place in recent years, social regulation by the federal government increased during the 1970s and 1980s. Laws and rules to protect the employment rights of blacks, other minorities, and women; legislation to preserve the natural environment and to protect the public from air or water pollution; and laws and rules to guard the health and safety of employees in the workplace are all forms of social regulation.

Although the authority of the federal government has been narrowed in such fields as transportation and communications, during the 1970s and 1980s the power of the Environmental Protection Agency (EPA), the Equal Employment Opportunity Commission (EEOC), and the Occupational Safety and Health Administration (OSHA) was strengthened.

But the Republican capture of Congress in 1994 coincided with a backlash against what some voters and

"Flight delays and cancellations had become worse than ever."
AP/Wide World

political leaders perceived as excessive government regulation in these very areas. The Republican Congress in 1995 attempted to reduce or remove altogether a broad range of regulations designed to protect the environment. Although Congress did not achieve all of these goals, it was able to weaken the Clean Water Act and the Endangered Species Act, and it cut back funding for the EPA.

Those opposed to government rules designed to protect the environment argued that they placed burdensome requirements on businesses. Environmental groups, by contrast, contended that only the federal government could crack down on corporate polluters.

Inevitably, the relatively recent growth of federal intervention in such fields as safety and the environment was accompanied by a political struggle over the proper scope of these kinds of regulations. And underlying that conflict over specific policy issues was the larger gulf between liberals and conservatives over the role of government itself.

As Michael D. Reagan has observed, "Traditional economic regulation and the alphabet soup of New Deal regulatory commissions" were designed to control "abuses of private economic power. . . . There was . . . almost no concept of what we now call social regulation: programs designed to achieve positive social benefits in such areas as protection of health, safety, and individual rights."[58]

A Firestone tire from a sport utility vehicle involved in a two-car accident in Arizona, June 2000
AP/Wide World

And public attitudes toward government regulation can vary dramatically with circumstances. By the fall of the year 2000, Firestone had recalled 6.5 million defective tires, after more than 100 deaths were caused in accidents, most involving Ford Explorers, in which the tire treads had separated causing drivers to lose control. In the wake of the recall and resulting controversy, there were demands by the public, by members of Congress, and by the Department of Transportation for more stringent laws that would require manufacturers to notify the government of tire safety defects.[59]

Those at the Top

When the new president of the United States took office in January 2001, he was viewed as the leader, not only of the nation, but also of his "administration." But what, exactly, did that mean? Although no formal definition of the term exists, in general a president's administration consists of the president, the heads of the 14 cabinet departments, 425 subcabinet officials and agency heads, 165 ambassadors, and 2,800 aides, assistants, and confidential secretaries. In all, an incoming president makes approximately 4,000 key appointments, for the most part exempt from civil service requirements. Of this total, perhaps 1,200 are important policy advisory posts.

Most of the 2,789,500 federal civilian workers are civil servants, not "the president's men" or women. They are not appointed by him to the key policy jobs in the bureaucracy.

In presidential election years, the House Government Reform and Oversight Committee or the Senate Governmental Affairs Committee has obligingly published something known affectionately in Washington as "the plum book" (as in "political plum"), a listing of the non–civil service jobs that the incoming president may fill.[60] For White House aides who screen patronage appointees for the new administration, the plum book is an indispensable reference guide. Job-seekers in the Clinton Administration who studied the new edition published after the 1996 presidential election found more than 8,000 positions listed in the 265-page book.

The Civil Service

Today the majority of government jobs are filled through the competitive civil service system. Yet presidents have always rewarded their political supporters and friends with government jobs. (In many cases, of course, presidents appoint persons recommended by powerful senators or House members.) Although George Washington declared that he appointed officials on the basis of "fitness of character," he favored members of his own party, the Federalists. Jefferson dismissed hundreds of Federalists when he became president, replacing them with members of his own party.

"The plum book"

Chester A. Arthur
Copyright © CORBIS/Bettmann

The Spoils System   After Andrew Jackson was elected in 1828, he dismissed more than a third of the 612 presidentially appointed officeholders and 10 to 20 percent of the 10,000 lesser government officials. Although Jackson thereby continued a practice started by Jefferson, he is generally credited with introducing to the national government the **spoils system,** the practice, known more often today as **political patronage,** under which victorious politicians reward their followers with jobs. (Jackson preferred to call it "rotation in office.")

In 1832 Senator William Learned Marcy of New York, defending a Jackson ambassadorial appointment, declared: "To the victor belong the spoils." The phrase became a classic statement of the right of victorious politicians to reward their followers with jobs. Political workers expected such rewards; when Lincoln became president, office-seekers prowled the White House stairways and hallways.

The Road to Reform   Inefficiency and corruption in the federal government led to the first efforts at reform in the 1850s. After the Civil War the reform movement gathered momentum. Although President Grant's administration was riddled by corruption, it was Grant who persuaded Congress in 1871 to set up the first Civil Service Commission. But the reform efforts had faltered by 1875, partly because Congress declined to appropriate new funds for the commission.

In 1880 the Republican Party was divided into two factions, for and against civil service reform. James A. Garfield, the Republican presidential candidate, ran on a reform platform. To appease the "Stalwarts," or antireform faction, Chester A. Arthur was chosen for vice president.

After Garfield's election, Charles J. Guiteau, an eccentric evangelist and lawyer, decided he deserved the post of ambassador to Austria or at least the job of Paris consul. In 1881 it was easy to get into the White House, and Guiteau actually had an unsuccessful interview with President Garfield. Brooding over his failure to join the diplomatic service, Guiteau purchased a revolver. On July 2, he approached Garfield at the railroad station in Washington and shot him in the back, crying, "I am a Stalwart and now Arthur is President!" Garfield died 80 days later, and his assassin was hanged.

To the dismay of his political cronies, Chester Arthur—who as collector of the Port of New York had been a major dispenser of political patronage—now became a champion of civil service reform. In the wake of public indignation over the assassination, Congress passed the Civil Service Reform Act of 1883 (the Pendleton Act). It established a bipartisan Civil Service Commission under which about 10 percent of federal employees were chosen through competitive examinations.

The basic purpose of the 1883 act was to transfer the power of appointment from politicians to a bipartisan commission that would select federal employees on merit. In recent decades Congress has placed more and more government workers under the protective umbrella of civil service. Today most of the federal bureaucracy is appointed under the merit system. During the Carter Administration, Congress enacted the Civil Service Reform Act of 1978, which replaced the Civil Service Commission with the Office of Personnel Management (OPM) and two other agencies.

To a degree, the removal of civil service appointments from politics has done the president a favor. No matter whom a president selects for a government post, he may antagonize others. William Howard Taft complained that every time he made an appointment he created "nine enemies and one ingrate."[61]

In 1995—the only year that OPM compiled the data—1.3 million government jobs were exempt from the civil service system. But many of these were in agencies such as the Postal Service, the Foreign Service of the Department of State, and the FBI, which have their own merit systems.

Recruiting the Bureaucrats   The OPM acts as an employment agency for the bureaucracy. It does so through Federal Job Information Centers, which are in kiosks located in federal buildings in many states, as well as a through a Web site and a telephone system. Through the kiosks, the Internet, or by telephone, people interested in federal employment can find out what jobs are available. Applicants contact OPM or apply directly to the agency that has the job openings and fill out the necessary forms. In some cases, examinations for various kinds of positions are held by OPM boards located in major population areas.

Online   *for more information about OPM, see:*
www.usajobs

When a job opens up in a federal agency, OPM may refer a list of names of eligible persons to the agency, which selects an applicant from among the three names at the top of the list. Or the agency may fill the job itself from its own resources and lists.

Under a system of "veteran preference," many military veterans who pass an exam and served during certain years or in specific campaigns—including the Vietnam War, the Persian Gulf War, or in Somalia or Bosnia, for example—receive extra points on their exam scores. Disabled veterans and certain members of their families also receive extra points on their exams.

Before being accepted for government employment, applicants are told that an investigation will be made of their reputation, character, and loyalty to the United States. OPM conducts most of these investigations, but if the job is in the national security area, in which the applicant has access to classified material, the FBI may conduct the background check. New government employees must swear or affirm that they will support and defend the Constitution. Employees must also swear that they will not participate in a strike against the government or any agency of the government. Within that framework, they are free to join one of the numerous unions and employee organizations that represent federal workers.

Unions of government workers at the federal, state, and local levels have in recent years advocated a national law to give full collective-bargaining rights to their members. But in a number of cases, the courts have ruled against the position favored by the unions.

Government workers receive annual vacations that increase from two to five weeks with length of service, and liberal sick leave and fringe benefits. Under the merit system, they almost certainly will be promoted if they remain in the career service.

Federal employees may express political opinions, contribute to political parties, vote, badger their representatives in Congress, wear a campaign button, display a bumper sticker on their cars, and attend political rallies. But they are limited by law from certain other forms of political participation. The **Hatch Act** is a federal law passed by Congress in 1939 to restrict political activities by federal workers. Under the law, federal employees are protected from political pressure to make campaign contributions or to work in political campaigns. Until 1993, the law barred federal workers from taking an active part in party politics or campaigns. In that year, Congress amended the Hatch Act to make it less restrictive by allowing federal workers to take an active part in political activities while off duty.*

But federal employees may not run for public office as the candidate of a political party. Many federal workers have considered the law a violation of their rights of free speech. In 1973, however, the Supreme Court upheld the constitutionality of the Hatch Act; the Court noted that Congress had passed the law because of the danger that a political party might use federal workers in campaigns and that promotions and job security might depend on party loyalty.[62]

There is no mandatory retirement age for federal employees, but they can voluntarily retire with a pension on reaching the age range of 55 to 62, depending on length of service. Retired government workers drawing a pension receive from 7 percent to 80 percent of their salaries for the rest of their lives, depending on length of service and their job. On average, federal employees retire after 30 years at age 58.

Federal workers hired after 1983 must usually join the Federal Employees' Retirement System (FERS), a pension program that combines Social Security, an annuity, and a savings plan. For most of the bureaucracy below the level of political appointees, a government career has offered a relatively high degree of security. It is true that federal employees may be fired for cause (such as misconduct or inefficiency) or if they are adjudged a security risk. Or employees may be given little to do, or dull work, or be transferred to the bureaucratic equivalent of Siberia if they offend a superior. But, by and large, they are protected from arbitrary dismissal. Firing most

---

*Some federal employees, such as those at the FBI, the CIA, and the Justice Department, are not permitted to take an active part in political activities even while off duty.

career federal workers is difficult because it still entails a complex and lengthy series of hearings and appeals. On the other hand, Congress may end a government program or cut the appropriation, resulting in a "reduction in force" in the bureaucracy. Workers who are thus "riffed" may be transferred to another job in their agency or to some other government unit, or they may be fired. About 26 percent of federal employees leave or retire each year, representing a turnover of more than 583,018 employees annually.[63]

The Carter Reforms

"We want a government that can be trusted," President Carter said in a speech in 1978, ". . . that will be efficient, not mired in its own red tape." Carter went on to propose major changes in the civil service system, designed, he said, to reward merit and penalize incompetence. Before the year was out, Congress had passed, and the president had signed, the Civil Service Reform Act of 1978.

This new law, the first major overhaul of the government civil service system in almost a century, established three new agencies: the Office of Personnel Management, to act as the president's personnel arm, handling recruitment, examinations, pay policy, job classification, and retirement; the Merit Systems Protection Board, to hear appeals and conduct investigations, including inquiries into complaints by **whistle-blowers,** government employees who publicly expose evidence of official waste or corruption that they have learned about in the course of their duties; and the Federal Labor Relations Authority, to oversee labor-management relations and arbitrate labor disputes between federal agencies and employee unions.

Under the law, federal officials were given somewhat more flexibility in firing employees for incompetence, although not nearly as much as Carter had requested. The appeals process still gave employees substantial job protection. For the first time, a system of merit pay increases, rather than entirely automatic raises, was established at the upper-middle levels of the bureaucracy.

The Senior Executive Service Perhaps the most important feature of the reform act was the establishment of the Senior Executive Service (SES), a corps of about 7,300 high-level administrators and managers at the top of the government bureaucracy. Those senior executives who chose to join the SES knew they would have less job tenure and could be transferred more easily within an agency or to another agency. At the same time, they became eligible for substantial cash bonuses for merit. Well over 90 percent of eligible government executives joined the SES.

The idea behind the creation of the SES was to establish a nucleus of top executives in the government in a way that would balance career risk-taking against rewards for high performance, and at the same time

would emphasize mobility, managerial discretion in assignments, and accountability.[64]

The senior executives receive substantially higher pay than other officials who are not in the SES. In enacting the reform law, Congress sought to apply the carrot-and-stick incentives of private industry to the massive federal bureaucracy. To an extent, at least, the experiment succeeded.

Bureaucracy and Society

During President Carter's administration Congress at his request established the Department of Energy. It also created the Department of Education and the Department of Health and Human Services, largely by splitting the old Department of Health, Education, and Welfare. And, the Carter Administration reorganized some other parts of the bureaucracy, including agencies dealing with civil rights, civil defense, and international communications.

Ronald Reagan promised during the 1980 campaign to abolish the Department of Energy and the Department of Education if elected. But as president, he found it easier said than done. Twenty years later, the two cabinet departments still existed.

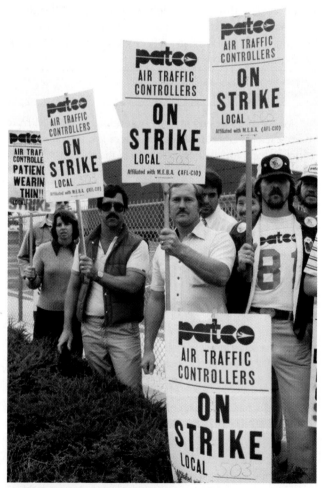

Air traffic controllers picketing in 1981
Copyright © Roger Ressmeyer/CORBIS

Reagan had campaigned against the bureaucracy, however, and as president he moved to try to control the bureaucracy and to reduce its power. When the nation's air traffic controllers went on strike in August 1981, Reagan fired 12,000 of them. The strikers were members of the Professional Air Traffic Controllers Organization (PATCO), ironically one of the few unions to have endorsed Reagan in the 1980 presidential campaign. Supervisory personnel of the Federal Aviation Administration and military air controllers manned the radar screens, and many flights were curtailed. In time, the strike was broken. Reagan emphasized that the walkout was illegal, since the strikers had defied a court order to return to their jobs, but his tough stance was a message to the bureaucracy as a whole.

Rational Decision Making

One of the criticisms of bureaucracy is that its decision making tends to be "incremental"—that is, what was decided yesterday limits the scope of choice today. New policies, instead of replacing old ones, tend to be "added on" to existing programs because government officials are usually wary of sweeping change or policy innovations.

Peter Drucker has suggested: "Certain things are inherently difficult for government. Being by design a protective institution, it is not good at innovation. It cannot really abandon anything. The moment government undertakes anything it becomes entrenched and permanent."[65]

Because of the obstacles to innovation, bureaucracy may overlook problems that do not fit into established forms. A former surgeon general of the United States, Dr. William H. Stewart, once told a Senate subcommittee on poverty that the federal government did not know the extent of hunger and malnutrition in America. "We just don't know," he said. "It hasn't been anybody's job."

On the other hand, bureaucracy is sometimes able to use its resources to attack the problems of society. For example, earlier than many private employers, the federal government was active in helping minorities, women, and the disadvantaged through affirmative action hiring policies and programs. Although these programs came under sharp political attack in the mid-1990s, for the most part they remained in place.

Often, when government is confronted with a new task, a new agency is established to handle it. For example, during the Kennedy Administration, the Peace Corps was made independent of the State Department, and during the Johnson Administration, the poverty program was created as a separate agency. The tendency to start new agencies for new programs to some

---

THE CLOCK-WATCHERS

The request from an Upper West Side restaurant to erect a large clock on a Broadway sidewalk had proceeded smoothly through the city's complicated approval process.

Only one defect marred the project's otherwise orderly flow through the city bureaucracy: The black, 19-foot-high clock has been standing in front of the Ancora Restaurant at Broadway and 85th Street off and on for more than a year. When city officials discovered that last month, they issued an ultimatum to the restaurant's owners. If you want permission to erect the clock, you must first remove it.

But discussions produced a less severe solution. The restaurant's owners agreed to donate to a community cause the $5,000 it would have cost to tear down and then reinstall the clock. In addition, they agreed to remove the restaurant's name from above the clock.

Vic DeLucia/NYT Pictures

"You would think 18 months would be enough to finish the normal planning process," [Douglas] Griebel [one of the partners in the restaurant] said. "I'm not putting up Trump Tower, after all."

—Adapted from the *New York Times*, August 5, 1986

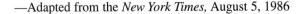

extent reflects resistance to change on the part of existing old-line agencies.

In an attempt to break through traditional forms of bureaucratic decision making, the federal government—beginning in the 1960s during the Kennedy Administration—tried to apply newer techniques of management technology to policy problems. The goal of the "rationalists," as advocates of the new techniques were sometimes called, was to arrive at decisions on the basis of systematic analysis, rather than on the basis of guesswork or custom. Presidents Johnson, Nixon, Ford, and Carter also sought to apply such management systems to control the federal budget.

Efforts to apply the tools and techniques of rational decision making and computer analysis to reform the management of the executive branch have been both praised and criticized. The system works best for areas in which goals can be "quantified"—expressed in dollar amounts. Thus, within limits, the Pentagon can use this technique to measure the relative merits and cost of weapons systems and military hardware. But in areas like welfare, education, and foreign policy, correct choices cannot so easily be arrived at by measuring benefits against costs. The long-range benefits to American society from an improved educational system, for example, cannot be evaluated wholly by a computer.

Checks on Bureaucratic Power

Bureaucracy is big and powerful. There are, however, some visible checks on that power. First, government agencies must share power with other elites in the political system, not only competing agencies in the executive branch, but also Congress, the courts, and groups and leaders outside the government. When government agencies mobilize political support among private industry or other client groups, they give up some of their independence and power in the process.

Congress exercises checks on bureaucratic power in several ways—through congressional oversight of departments and agencies of the executive branch, for instance, and through committee hearings and investigations. In addition, congressional staff members may intervene with government agencies to help citizens who feel the bureaucracy is unresponsive to their problems.

The courts and the legal system also play a role in controlling bureaucracy. Court rulings may narrow or overturn regulations issued by federal agencies. The courts may reject claims of executive privilege and require the production of documents that the bureaucracy would rather keep secret.

Or the courts may punish bureaucrats who break the law. Ten officials of the Nixon Administration were convicted and jailed in the Watergate scandal. In 1980 two former high-ranking FBI officials were tried in federal court on charges of violating the constitutional rights of citizens by authorizing FBI break-ins in the search for radical fugitives in the early 1970s. They were convicted,

TRUE GRITS: A PRESIDENT VERSUS THE BUREAUCRACY

President Clinton said good riddance to 16,000 pages of federal regulations yesterday and took special satisfaction in saying goodbye to a rule on how to test the consistency of southern grits. . . .

Of the 39 pounds of pages of regulations being eliminated, Clinton said one of the best examples of unnecessary rules was one governing how to test a southern dish, corn grits, for proper consistency. He proceeded to read the lengthy passage.

"Grits, corn grits, hominy grits, is the food prepared by so grinding and sifting clean white corn with removal of corn bran and germ that on a moisture-free basis its crude fiber content is not more than 1.2 percent and its fat content is not more than 2.25 percent," he said.

The crowd roared as he read on, then he cited as a "real sacrifice" a 2,700-word regulation on french fries.

—*Washington Post*, June 13, 1995

but were later pardoned by President Reagan. Several high-level officials of the Reagan Administration and other individuals were charged with crimes as a result of the Iran-contra scandal; some were convicted.

More than 100 officials of the Reagan Administration were accused of illegal or unethical conduct, forced to resign, indicted, or convicted.[66] The unusual number of aides involved in improprieties of one sort or another gave the Democrats a "sleaze factor" issue that they sought to exploit in the 1988 presidential campaign. Despite that effort, the Democrats lost. In the 2000 presidential campaign, the Republicans were able to remind voters of the various scandals of the Clinton Administration.

In addition to sharing power with other parts of government and with interest groups, officials are held in check to some degree by the press. Fear of adverse publicity is a powerful factor in decision making in Washington, as well as in state and local government. Moreover, some government employees have become whistle-blowers, publicly exposing evidence of waste or corruption that they discover in the course of their duties.

Whistle-Blowers Whistle-blowing can sometimes turn out to be a significant factor within the bureaucracy. For example, in 1968, A. Ernest Fitzgerald, a Pentagon official, exposed a $2 billion cost overrun in the C-5A aircraft program. After this, Fitzgerald was forced out of his job; he was not reinstated for five years. Later it was revealed that President Nixon had personally ordered Fitzgerald fired.

Whistle-blowers often pay a high price for their actions. Others, less well known, also have been fired.

In August of the year 2000, *NBC Nightly News* revealed that federal bureaucrats were actually proposing to measure and regulate something that—well—isn't there.

BOB FAW reporting: Imagine Uncle Sam, spending billions to defend us, making sure the air we breathe and the water we drink are safe, is also busily engaged in regulating—are you ready for this—the size of the holes in Swiss cheese. . . . The United States Department of Agriculture has now proposed, in 15 dense pages of regulation, that the holes in Swiss cheese—the industry calls them "eyes"—be made smaller, from the size of a nickel now—$^{11}/_{16}$ of an inch—to about the size of a dime—$^3/_8$ of an inch.

JOHN UMHOEFER (Wisconsin Cheesemakers Association): We've decided, as an industry, that we need a little more flexibility.

FAW: For cheesemakers, it is really a matter of economics. If the holes are bigger, there is more trim, more waste, and less profit. After all, when's the last time you've seen cheeseheads manning barricades demanding smaller holes in their Swiss?

UNIDENTIFIED WOMAN: It could be a pinhole, I don't care. As long as the taste is there.

FAW: There is, however, some dismay that your government is cracking down on those holes in your Swiss cheese.

JOHN FRYDENLUND (Citizens against Government Waste): They really are doing something that is completely pointless, irrelevant, and—and unnecessary.

FAW: His taxpayer watchdog group asks, "Doesn't Uncle Sam have better things to do?" The USDA, which spends $40 million a year setting prices for milk and standards for cheese, says taxpayers don't foot the bill for those regulatory changes—that the industry does. And that when it comes to the size of holes, the USDA is only doing what cheesemakers want. That, say critics, is part of the problem.

RUTH REICHL (*Gourmet Magazine*): I mean, that's—it's emblematic of how we think about food. It's not about flavor, it's not about its deliciousness. It's about, you know, "Oh, my God! The holes may be too big!"

—Adapted from *NBC Nightly News,* in cooperation with the *Washington Post,* August 8, 2000

A. Ernest Fitzgerald, cost-minded Pentagon employee
Copyright © CORBIS/UPI/Bettmann

Consider, for example, the case of Dr. J. Anthony Morris, a government virologist. In 1976 a soldier at Fort Dix, New Jersey, died of swine flu. Fearing a nationwide epidemic, federal authorities began a massive inoculation program. Alone within the government, Morris opposed the program; he had been questioning the value of flu shots for several years. He vigorously protested that there was no evidence the swine flu would cause an epidemic like the flu epidemic that had occurred in 1918 and killed millions of people worldwide. And, he warned, the vaccine was dangerous. At age 58, Morris was fired from his research job by the head of the Food and Drug Administration, who found him guilty of "insubordination and inefficiency."[67]

Inoculations started in October 1976, were suspended for a time, and then cut off entirely in February 1977. Fifty million Americans were given swine flu vaccine, but the program was halted after several persons became seriously ill with Guillain-Barré syndrome, a rare paralytic disease.[68] By January 1988, some 4,178 claims totaling $3.2 billion had been filed against the government. The lawsuits also claimed that at least 360 deaths and more than 1,600 cases of Guillain-Barré disease had resulted from the flu shots.[69]

There have been many similar stories. When John Kartak, an Army recruiter in Minneapolis, discovered his office had forged high school diplomas and concealed

MAKING A DIFFERENCE
WHISTLE-BLOWING: "UNDERSTAND THE RISKS"

The kingpin of Washington whistle-blowers may be Casey Ruud.

Ruud put himself in the public hot seat in 1986 after his inspection audits at the Hanford nuclear reservation contended the plutonium production plants in southeast Washington were unsafe and needed to be shut down.

His reports initially were ignored, then minimized by Hanford authorities. However, Ruud's conclusions were later deemed accurate, and led to his congressional testimony and an end to bomb making at Hanford.

Still, Ruud was laid off from Hanford in 1988 and shunned at another weapons site before resigning. He fought in court, claiming unlawful retaliation for whistle-blowing, and eventually got a job back at Hanford

with the state Department of Ecology, where he now works.

Along the way, Ruud has been lauded by former Energy Secretary Hazel O'Leary as a model whistle-blower and received a $10,000 Cavallo Foundation award in 1996 for moral courage in government.

Last month, a judge ruled the Westinghouse Corp. owes Ruud "front pay" for the rest of his working life—the difference between his state salary and the money he would have been making if he hadn't been canned at Hanford a decade ago.

Meanwhile, Ruud . . . still blows the whistle. During the past two years, he and Hanford scientist John Broeder proved that radioactive fluids leaking from massive storage tanks

have spread much further than Hanford authorities conceded.

Ruud says his recent efforts to expose that problem further alienated him at Hanford. "I am absolutely resented in every way by my superiors," he says.

Ruud estimates that he has counseled more than 200 Hanford employees on whistle-blowing. "The majority of the people who come to me only come to me because they are desperate," he says. His advice? He tells them to make sure their spouses and relatives understand the risks. And he discourages them from thinking like victims.

"That's the key. The public doesn't want to deal with victims."

—Seattle Times, January 3, 1999

---

criminal records to meet recruiting quotas, he called the Army whistle-blower hot line. The Army responded by ordering two psychological evaluations of Kartak, whose superior said he had been filing a lot of complaints lately and was "highly unstable." But Kartak was vindicated when the Army eventually determined his charges were true and found 58 people in the office guilty of engaging in illegal acts.[70] Less fortunate was Joseph Setepani of the Food and Drug Administration, who protested the use of

carcinogens and mutagens in food supplies. Setepani was "reassigned to long-term research in a trailer on an experimental farm."[71]

In 1989, after an earlier version proved ineffective, Congress reenacted the Whistleblower Protection Act, and President Bush signed it into law. Although whistle-blowers may still pay a high price, despite the law, the possibility of exposure from within the bureaucracy sometimes acts to curb potential abuses.

Fifty million Americans were given swine flu vaccine, despite the risks.
Copyright © CORBIS/Bettmann

Auth/*Philadelphia Inquirer,* United
Feature Syndicate. Reprinted by
permission.

Other Checks on Bureaucracy In addition, there
are certain "inner checks" on the bureaucracy. To some
extent, bureaucrats may be inhibited from abusing their
power by the social and political system in which they
operate. Like other citizens, bureaucrats have been
politically socialized, and in many cases they may tend
to adhere to standards of fair play and respect for individual rights. But relying on individual conscience is
rather uncertain, and the search continues for institutionalized methods of control. The device of the
ombudsman, for example, has proved popular in
Sweden and in some other countries. The ombudsman
is an official complaint-taker who tries to help citizens
wronged by the actions of government agencies.

In broader terms, public opinion and the political
culture may also serve as a check on bureaucratic
power. Because the public tends to be suspicious of

bureaucracy, bureaucrats may act more cautiously than
they would otherwise.

Despite these checks, the problems posed by
bureaucracy remain. Yet as long as government has
responsibility for allocating things of value, for deciding who gets what in American society, there will be
bureaucrats to help make and carry out those decisions. The size of the bureaucracy at any particular
time, then, depends on the demands made on the political system by the voters.

Bureaucrats are convenient political targets, vulnerable to attack, and their shortcomings will no doubt
continue to be criticized. Nevertheless, the government
could not function without bureaucrats. At the same
time, the problem of controlling bureaucracy and making it serve the people is a continuing challenge to the
American system.

KEY TERMS

CHAPTER HIGHLIGHTS

✦ Bureaucracy and bureaucrats are often handy political targets to blame for society's ills. Yet, government at every level—federal, state, and local—could not function without people to run it. Many government programs are highly complex and require experts and professional people to administer them.

✦ "Public administration" is the term preferred by most political scientists to describe the bureaucratic process—the business of making government work—and bureaucrats are public administrators.

✦ Americans tend to be against "Big Government" in the abstract, but they also demand all kinds of government services. The "bureaucracy in Washington" did not grow overnight, but developed gradually, largely in response to public needs. Most government departments and agencies have been created as a result of pressure from some segment of the population.

✦ Because civil servants are not elected and are free of direct control by the voters, the bureaucracy is semi-permanent in character and, at times, an independent center of power. A central problem is how to make bureaucracy accountable to popular control—in short, how to reconcile bureaucracy and democracy.

✦ In theory, bureaucrats are simply public servants who administer policy decisions made by the account-able officials of the government—the president, his principal appointees, and Congress. In fact, government administrators by their actions—or inaction—often make policy.

✦ There is no single bureaucracy in America, and the term is not limited to the federal government. Bureaucrats administer programs at every level, down to the smallest units of state and local government. Public administration in the United States is fragmented by the system of federalism.

✦ The American bureaucracy is deeply involved in politics as well as policy. As in the case of the president and members of Congress, government agencies also have constituencies—interest groups, or client groups, either directly regulated by the bureaucracy or vitally affected by its decisions.

✦ The bureaucracy, interest groups, and congressional committees interact. In some areas the relationship among the three actors is so close that it is often referred to as a triangle, an iron triangle, or a subgovernment.

✦ Issue networks, a loose grouping of people and organizations who seek to influence policy formation, play an important role in the shaping of public policy.

✦ The great majority of federal workers are members of the career civil service.

✦ The executive agencies are units of government under the president, within the executive branch, that are not part of a cabinet department.

✦ The independent regulatory agencies exercise quasi-judicial and quasi-legislative powers and are administratively independent of the president, Congress, and the courts.

✦ Andrew Jackson is generally credited with introducing to the national government the spoils system, the practice, known more often today as political patronage, under which victorious politicians reward their followers with jobs.

✦ Whistle-blowers are government employees who publicly expose evidence of official waste or corruption that they have learned about in the course of their duties.

SUGGESTED WEB SITES

www.opm.gov
Office of Personnel Management
The Office of Personnel Management (OPM), the federal government's human resources agency, contains general information for current and prospective federal employees and statistics about federal government workers.

www.usajobs.opm.gov
USAJobs
USAJobs is the federal government's official site for jobs and employment information. Current job openings, online applications for jobs, and information about working for the government are available.

www.pogo.org
Project on Government Oversight
The Project on Government Oversight (POGO) is a nonpartisan, nonprofit organization that investigates, exposes, and attempts to remedy abuses of power within the government. The site includes POGO Alerts, which are brief reports about the project's investigations, and legal resources for those who are considering becoming a whistle-blower.

www.whistleblower.org
Government Accountability Project
The Government Accountability Project (GAP) is a nonpartisan, nonprofit organization that promotes government and corporate accountability and assists whistle-blowers. The organization offers advice and

referrals for whistle-blowers. GAP also does its own research on government programs and offices. The reports of its investigations are available on the Web site.

SUGGESTED READING

Heclo, Hugh. *A Government of Strangers** (The Brookings Institution, 1977). An important analysis of the relations between political leaders and the bureaucracy. Heclo identifies weaknesses in the nation's political leaders and the bureaucracy as well as weaknesses in the nation's political structure and suggests reforms to bring about more effective executive leadership.

Kaufman, Herbert. *Are Government Organizations Immortal?* (The Brookings Institution, 1976). A thought-provoking exploration of the factors that work for or against the survival of governmental agencies once they have been established.

Meier, Kenneth J. *Politics and the Bureaucracy: Policymaking in the Fourth Branch of Government** (Harcourt Brace, 1993). A broad overview of the federal bureaucracy and its growing role in the policymaking process.

Mosher, Frederick C. *Democracy and the Public Service,* 2nd edition (Oxford University Press, 1982). An excellent and readable discussion of various trends in the public service, including professionalization, unionization, and the merit system. Discusses their implications for democratic government.

Osborne, David, and Plastrik, Peter. *Banishing Bureaucracy: The Five Strategies for Reinventing Government** (Penguin, 1998). An influential set of prescriptions, drawing upon numerous case studies, for making government more efficient through the reform of public management.

Rourke, Francis E. *Bureaucracy, Politics, and Public Policy,* 3rd edition* (Little, Brown, 1984). A concise general introduction to the role of the bureaucracy in the making of public policy. Among other topics, the book analyzes the sources of power of government bureaucracies, and new approaches to policymaking in bureaucratic agencies.

Salamon, Lester M. *Partners in Public Service* (Johns Hopkins University Press, 1995). A thorough account of the emergence of nonprofit organizations as major instruments for the delivery of public services.

Seidman, Harold, and Gilmour, Robert S. *Politics, Position, and Power: From the Positive to the Regulatory State,* 4th edition (Oxford University Press, 1986). An enlightening discussion of the operations of government agencies and the political realities affecting proposals for their reorganization.

Simon, Herbert A. *Administrative Behavior: A Study of Decision-Making Processes in Administrative Organizations,* 4th edition* (Free Press, 1997). A classic theoretical and empirical analysis of decision making in government bureaucracies. This book, first published in 1947, has influenced modern scholarly work on bureaucratic organizations.

Skowronek, Stephen. *Building a New American State: The Expansion of National Administrative Capacities, 1877–1920** (Cambridge University Press, 1982). A valuable study of the factors that led to the emergence and development of bureaucratic institutions as an integral part of the national government of the United States.

White, Leonard D. *The Federalists* (Macmillan, 1948); *The Jeffersonians, 1801–1829* (Macmillan, 1951); *The Jacksonians, 1829–1861* (Macmillan, 1954); and *The Republican Era, 1869–1901* (Macmillan, 1958). A notable study, in four volumes, of the historical development of the American public service from 1789 to the turn of the 20th century.

Wildavsky, Aaron. *The New Politics of the Budgetary Process,* 3rd edition (New York: HarperCollins, 1999). A revealing analysis of the nature of the federal budgetary process and its relationship to the making of public policy. Discusses and summarizes the important changes in the 1990 budget reconciliation act.

Wilson, James Q. *The Politics of Regulation* (Basic Books, 1980). A collection of nine case studies on public policymaking and the relationship between the public and private sectors in Washington regulatory agencies. Includes a discussion of the political and historical origins of a wide range of agencies—from state public utility commissions to the Federal Trade Commission.

Wilson James Q. *Bureaucracy: What Government Agencies Do and Why They Do It** (Basic Books, 1989). A comprehensive survey of why government agencies in the United States behave in the ways they do. Stresses the important differences that can be found among various agencies.

Wood, B. Dan, and Waterman, Richard W. *Bureaucratic Dynamics: The Role of Bureaucracy in a Democracy** (Westview Press, 1994). Argues that executive bureaucracies, contrary to the belief of many of their critics, do respond to election results and alter the policies of their agencies accordingly.

*Available in paperback edition.

 Visit http://politicalscience.wadsworth.com/cummings9/update/ for current InfoTrac articles and other student resources related to this chapter.

CHAPTER 15
Justice

In the high-ceilinged marble chamber of the Supreme Court late in June 2000, the marshal of the Court rapped his gavel on a wooden block and cried: "The honorable, the chief justice and the associate justices of the Supreme Court of the United States. Oyez, oyez, oyez. All persons having business before the honorable, the Supreme Court of the United States, are admonished to draw near."

As the marshal spoke, Chief Justice William H. Rehnquist and the associate justices, wearing their black robes, filed in through the red velvet curtains behind the bench. It was the last day of the Court's term before the summer adjournment, and decisions were announced in a number of important cases.

The Court ruled 5–4 that states cannot ban late-term abortions, a procedure called "partial-birth abortion" by its critics. The Court struck down a Nebraska law because it did not contain an exception to allow the procedure when necessary to protect the health of a pregnant woman. The decision had the effect of invalidating similar laws in 30 other states.[1] In a second abortion-related case, the Court upheld, 6–3, a Colorado law that required demonstrators to stay at least eight feet away from persons entering abortion clinics.[2]

On this final day of the term, the Court also ruled, 5–4, that the Boy Scouts of America had a constitutional right to ban gay members. Chief Justice Rehnquist wrote that the organization believed gay conduct was "inconsistent with the values it seeks to instill in its youth members."[3] The case had been brought by James Dale, a scoutmaster in New Jersey who had been expelled by the Boy Scouts.

The Supreme Court also ruled that a federal program that placed computers and other "instructional equipment" in parochial schools did not violate the separation of church and state.[4]

Two days before, in an historic decision, the Supreme Court had upheld its 1966 *Miranda* decision, ruling by a vote of 7–2 that the warnings police must give to criminal defendants are required by the Constitution.[5]

These decisions struck a neat balance between conservative and liberal values; the abortion and *Miranda* rulings tended to please liberals, but the opinions on the Scouts and parochial schools were more likely to satisfy conservatives. On the whole, however, although the Rehnquist Court was unpredictable, it tended to be a somewhat conservative body ideologically, and one that favored judicial caution in many of its decisions. The trend reflected appointments to the Court by two Republican presidents, Ronald Reagan and George Bush. Although President Clinton was able to name two justices to the high court during his first two years in the White House, those appointments did not change the usually cautious, moderate-to-conservative mood of the Court.

By the year 2000 many of the Court's key decisions were decided by a vote of 5–4. The narrow margin meant that a change of even one justice in the makeup of the high court could alter the ideological trend of its decisions. With the passage of time, as justices grow older, vacancies occur on the Court. As a result, the Republican and Democratic presidential candidates in 2000, George W. Bush and Al Gore reminded voters that the makeup of the Supreme Court, might depend on the outcome of the election, perhaps for years to come.

For example, Ronald Reagan, elected in 1980 as a conservative Republican, was able, over two terms, to place his imprint on the Court. During his first term, he filled only one vacancy, in 1981, choosing Sandra Day O'Connor, 51, a state appeals court judge in Arizona, to become the first woman to serve on the Supreme Court.

But in Reagan's second term, two more vacancies occurred. First, in 1986, Chief Justice Warren E. Burger retired. That allowed Reagan to promote Justice Rehnquist, then 61, to chief justice and to appoint Antonin Scalia, 50, like Rehnquist a conservative, and the first Italian American to serve on the Supreme Court. The following year, Justice Lewis F. Powell, Jr., retired, and Reagan named Anthony M. Kennedy, 52, a federal appeals court judge in San Francisco, to the Court.

Kennedy was confirmed by the Senate in 1988, ending a bitter seven-month battle over the vacant seat.

Reagan's successor, George Bush, had additional opportunities to attempt to shape the Court's conservative majority. When Justice William J. Brennan, Jr., one of the two remaining liberals on the Court, retired in July 1990, Bush nominated David H. Souter, 51, a little-known federal appeals court judge from New Hampshire. A year later, Justice Thurgood Marshall, a giant of the civil rights movement before he was named to the high court by President Lyndon Johnson, stepped down at the age of 82, citing his advanced years and health problems. Bush named Clarence Thomas, a conservative federal appeals court judge, to succeed him.

Thomas, a 43-year-old African American born in rural Georgia and raised in poverty, was on his way to Senate confirmation when Anita Hill, an Oklahoma law professor, accused him of sexual harassment. Hill's charges, aired on television for days by the Senate Judiciary Committee, erupted into a major political controversy and an extraordinary drama. Hill said that when she worked with Thomas at two government agencies, he had repeatedly asked her for dates and engaged in explicit sexual conversations with her about pornographic movies and his own sexual abilities.

Thomas categorically denied Hill's charges and accused the committee of a "high-tech lynching for uppity blacks."[6] The committee, unable to resolve the conflicting stories, approved the Thomas nomination, and he was narrowly confirmed by the full Senate, 52–48.

In 1993, President Clinton nominated Ruth Bader Ginsburg, a judge of the federal Court of Appeals in Washington, D.C., to the Supreme Court. Justice Ginsburg, 60, whose first job out of law school was as a legal secretary, was known as a strong advocate for women's rights. She joined Sandra Day O'Connor as the second woman to serve on the high court. Ginsburg was considered a moderate.

The following year, Clinton named Stephen G. Breyer, the chief judge of the federal Court of Appeals in Boston, to the Supreme Court. Breyer, 55 years old, was also known as a moderate and a pragmatist.

The Supreme Court and the lower federal courts comprise one of the three independent, constitutionally coequal branches of the federal government. But the Supreme Court is only one part of the fragmented, decentralized system of justice in America, a system that encompasses a network of federal courts, state and local courts and prosecutors, the United States Department of Justice, state and local police, the Federal Bureau of Investigation, prisons and jails, probation and parole officers, and parole boards.

Against this background, we will explore a two-part key question: What is the role of the Supreme Court in the American political system, and how well does the criminal justice system work?

Many related questions also arise. Since the Constitution created three separate branches of the federal government, can the Supreme Court, as head of the judicial branch, overrule the other two branches—the president and Congress? Because its members are appointed and not accountable to the voters, should the Supreme Court "legislate" and make social policy? Should the Supreme Court adhere closely to what it perceives as the "original intent" of the framers, or should it interpret the Constitution broadly and infer new constitutional principles to meet changed conditions?

The Supreme Court stands at the pinnacle of the judicial system. But is the system of criminal justice stacked against African Americans and other minorities? Do the rich have a better chance under the system than the poor? Should America continue to have capital punishment? What steps can be taken to protect the public against corrupt officials at the highest level of the government? Who can investigate impartially, if a president, other White House officials, or cabinet members are potential targets of a criminal investigation?

THE SYSTEM OF JUSTICE

Crime, Politics, and the Public

During a time of political activism, as in the 1960s and early 1970s—the era of protests against the Vietnam War—the police and the courts became the cutting edge and the enforcement arm of the "Establishment" in the eyes of dissident groups. To most Americans, however, the police and courts represent the forces of "law and order."

In a society plagued by crime and violence, most citizens look to government, to law enforcement authorities, to keep them safe on the streets and in their homes. Others seek more direct means to protect themselves; they buy guns and keep them in their homes or carry them.

Today, crime and its prevention influence American life in a variety of ways. Closed-circuit television guards stores and the lobbies of apartment and office buildings. Airline passengers must pass through metal detectors and submit their baggage to be X-rayed in order to prevent highjackers from taking weapons aboard a plane, or terrorists from planting a bomb. Many private homes, especially in affluent areas, have burglar alarms. Some drivers have remote-control key fobs to open or lock their car doors. Armed, uniformed guards are commonplace in shopping malls and office buildings. Gas station cashiers and tellers in some banks sit behind protective glass windows, talking to customers through microphones. These practices, many almost unheard of even two decades ago, grew so gradually that we now tend to accept them as a normal part of the landscape. Today, they are symbols of how crime affects the quality of life.

In recent years, the nature of justice in America, the crime rate, and the actions of the police have sometimes themselves become political issues. During the 1960s, when the Supreme Court was headed by Chief Justice Earl Warren, the Court handed down a series of decisions favoring the rights of criminal defendants. The resulting backlash from conservatives played a major part in making crime a political issue.

The political system has also been troubled in recent decades by wrongdoing and criminal investigations at the highest level—the presidency. In 1973 the extraordinary developments in the Watergate scandal led to the appointment of a special prosecutor, operating outside regular Justice Department channels, to handle the case. The appointment symbolized public skepticism over whether the normal machinery of justice could be relied on in a case involving the highest officials of the government. The special prosecutor demanded tape recordings that President Richard Nixon had secretly made of his White House conversations. Instead of complying, the president fired the prosecutor. The strong public reaction forced Nixon to name another special prosecutor. For months, Nixon and his attorneys resisted the courts; the president yielded his tapes only after the Supreme Court ruled 8–0 that he was required to produce them, and then only in the face of the growing sentiment in the House of Representatives for his impeachment.[7]

In time, Attorney General John Mitchell and several high officials of the White House went to prison. The president himself was named by a federal grand jury as an unindicted coconspirator in the cover-up of the Watergate burglary and eventually resigned and received a presidential pardon. It was clear that the president and his aides had tried to block the investigation of a crime. The Watergate controversy intensified the doubts sometimes raised about the system of justice in America.

In 1986 and afterward, the Iran-contra scandal cast a shadow over the final years of the Reagan presidency and led to the indictment and trial of senior presidential aides and other participants.

Beginning in 1994, President Clinton and his wife, Hillary Rodham Clinton, were scrutinized by an independent counsel investigating the Whitewater affair, a

Comparing Governments

CRIME AND PUNISHMENT AROUND THE WORLD

Differing historical and cultural traditions have produced strikingly divergent approaches to crime and punishment around the world. For example, the death penalty, which is widely accepted in the United States, has been rejected by most countries, and its use has been condemned by the European Parliament as inhumane. According to Amnesty International, 108 nations have abolished the death penalty, and 87 still retain it. (About 60 percent of all executions in the world each year are conducted in China.)

Differences in the system of justice go well beyond the use of capital punishment. Singapore imposes caning for vandalism and other offenses, such as illegal immigration. Jaywalking, littering, spitting, and the importation and sale of chewing gum carry stiff penalties as well. In the Netherlands, by contrast, the use of marijuana is permitted, and prostitution is legal.

In Saudi Arabia, the Mutawwa (religious police) enforce strict Islamic law. Public music and dancing are prohibited, as are "immodest" dress, pornography, and public interaction between a male and female who are not close relatives. Non-Muslim public religious services are forbidden, as are the display of Bibles, crucifixes, and other non-Islamic religious artifacts. Possession of alcohol may result in a jail sentence, fine, or public flogging, and drug trafficking carries a mandatory death sentence. Those convicted of homosexuality are subject to impris-onment, lashing, or death. Stealing is punished—in accord with Islamic law—by the cutting off of a hand.

A Pakistani soccer team learned firsthand about the differences among countries in the summer of 2000, on a sports trip to Afghanistan. When the athletes showed up for their match wearing soccer shorts, they were arrested for violating the ruling Taliban's strict Islamic dress code, which requires men to wear long shirts and trousers and women to be covered from head to toe. The visiting Pakistanis had their heads shaved, and were expelled from the country.

—Adapted from Amnesty International, U.S. State Department; and the *New York Times*, July 18, 2000

probe that shifted to Clinton's sexual relationship with Monica Lewinsky, the White House intern, and led to his impeachment, trial, and acquittal. Not until September 2000 did the independent counsel close the Whitewater investigation, concluding there was "insufficient" evidence to charge the Clintons with any crime.

The emergence of crime and "law and order" as a political issue; the increasing reliance on independent prosecutors to investigate political scandals; the furor over the deadly siege of a religious cult in Waco, Texas, in 1993 and the shootout between federal agents and a group of white supremacists at Ruby

Waco, 1993: The attorney general took responsibility.
Jerry Hoefer/*Fort Worth Star Telegram*/SIPA

492   CHAPTER 15   JUSTICE

Ridge, Idaho, in 1992; the terrorist attacks on targets in New York City, Oklahoma City, and in Atlanta during the 1996 summer Olympic games—all were indications of the pressures on the system of justice in America. It is a system, of course, that rests on a foundation of law.

THE LAW

In a political sense, law is the body of rules made by government for society, interpreted by the courts, and backed by the power of the state. While this is a simple, dictionary-type definition, there are conflicting theories of law and little agreement on precisely how it should be defined.

If law were limited to what can be established and enforced by the state, then Louis XIV would have been correct in saying, "It is legal because I wish it." The founders of the American nation were influenced by another tradition, rooted in the philosophy of John Locke and in the principle of **natural rights,** the belief that all people possess certain basic rights that may not be abridged by government. Under this theory, human beings, living in a state of nature, possessed

Dr. Martin Luther King, Jr., in jail in Birmingham, Alabama, 1967
Copyright © CORBIS/Bettmann

certain fundamental rights that they brought with them into organized society. The tradition of natural rights was used by the American revolutionaries of 1776 to justify their revolt against England. In modern times, the principle was embraced by Dr. Martin Luther King, Jr., and by others who practiced "civil disobedience" against laws they believed to be unjust, unconstitutional, or immoral.

Still another approach to law is sociological. In this view, law is seen as the gradual growth of rules and customs that reconcile conflict among people in societies; it is as much a product of culture, religion, and morality as of politics. There is always a problem of incorporating majority morality into criminal law; if enough people decide to break a law, it becomes difficult to enforce. One example was Prohibition, which was widely ignored and finally repealed.

Much American law is based on English **common law,** the cumulative body of judicial decisions, custom, and precedent, rather than law created by statute. In 12th-century medieval England, judges began to dispense law, and their decisions came to be called common law, or judge-made law, as opposed to written law passed by legislatures. In deciding cases, judges have often relied on the principle of *stare decisis,* the Latin phrase meaning "stand by past decisions." In other words, judges generally attempt to find a precedent for a decision in an earlier case involving similar principles. Most law that governs the actions of Americans is **statutory law,** law enacted by Congress, or by state legislatures or local legislative bodies, but many statutes embody principles of English common law.

Laws do not always ensure fairness. If a man discovers that his apple trees are gradually being cut down by a neighbor, he can sue for damages, but by the time the case is decided the trees may all be felled. Instead, he may seek help through **equity,** a legal principle of fair dealing, which may provide preventive measures and legal remedies that are unavailable under existing common law and statutory law. The man, for example, might ask a court for an immediate injunction to prevent any further tree chopping.

Cases considered by federal and state courts are either civil or criminal. **Civil cases** concern relations between individuals or organizations, such as a divorce action, or a suit for damages arising from an automobile accident, or for violation of a business contract. The government is often party to a civil action—when the Justice Department files a civil antitrust suit against a corporation, for example. It is in the civil courts that ordinary citizens are most likely to experience the system of justice, whether paying a speeding or a parking ticket, defending against some other misdemeanor, suing a neighbor, or filing for divorce. The majority of citizens, in other words, are not defendants in serious criminal cases. **Criminal cases** concern crimes committed against the public order. Most crimes are defined by local, state, and federal statutes, which set forth a range of penalties as well.

In 1954 the U.S. Supreme Court, in an historic decision, *Brown* v. *Board of Education of Topeka, Kansas,* voted unanimously to end racial segregation in the nation's public schools. The Court's opinion was written by Chief Justice Earl Warren:

In approaching this problem, we cannot turn the clock back to 1868 when the [Fourteenth] Amendment was adopted, or even to 1896 when *Plessy* v. *Ferguson* was written. We must consider public education in the light of its full development and its present place in American life throughout the Nation. . . .

Today, education is perhaps the most important function of state and local governments. . . . It is the very foundation of good citizenship. Today it is a principal instrument in awakening the child to cultural values, in preparing him for later professional training, and in helping him to adjust normally to his environment. In these days, it is doubtful that any child may reasonably be expected to succeed in life if he is denied the opportunity of an education. . . . We come then to the question presented: Does segregation of children in public schools solely on the basis of race, even though the physical facilities and other "tangible" factors may be equal, deprive the children of the minority group of equal educational opportunities? We believe that it does. . . .

We conclude that in the field of public education the doctrine of "separate but equal" has no place. Separate educational facilities are inherently unequal. . . . The plaintiffs and others similarly situated . . . are, by reason of the segregation complained of, deprived of the equal protection of the laws guaranteed by the Fourteenth Amendment.

—*Brown* v. *Board of Education of Topeka, Kansas,* 347 U.S. 483 (1954)

A growing body of cases in federal courts concerns questions of **administrative law,** the rules and regulations made and applied by federal regulatory agencies and commissions. Corporations and individuals can go into federal court to challenge the rulings of these agencies.

Supreme Court Justice Robert Jackson once observed that people are governed either by the will of one person, or group of persons—or by law. He added, "Law, as the expression of the ultimate will and wisdom of a people, has so far proven the safest guardian of liberty yet devised."[8]

THE SUPREME COURT

The Supreme Court is a political institution that makes both policy and law. Although insulated by tradition and judicial tenure from the turmoil of everyday politics, the Supreme Court lies at the heart of the ongoing struggle in the American political system. "We are very quiet there," said Justice Oliver Wendell Holmes, Jr., "but it is the quiet of a storm centre."

 Online *for more information about the Supreme Court, see:* www.supremecourtus.gov

In giving the Constitution contemporary meaning, the Supreme Court inevitably makes political and policy choices. "To consider the Supreme Court of the United States strictly as a legal institution," Robert A. Dahl has suggested, "is to underestimate its significance in the American political system. For it is also a political institution, an institution, that is to say, for arriving at decisions on controversial questions of national policy."[9]

The Supreme Court: Politics, Policy, and Public Opinion

A basic reason for the political controversy surrounding the Supreme Court is that its precise role in the American political system was left ambiguous by the framers of the Constitution. The Supreme Court is at the apex of the judicial branch, one of the three independent, constitutionally coequal branches of the federal government. But does it have the constitutional right to resolve conflicts among the three branches?

The Court may be seen, on the one hand, as one of three "coordinate" branches of the federal government, or it may be viewed as the final arbiter of constitutional questions. As Robert G. McCloskey noted, "The fact that the Constitution is supreme does not settle the question of who decides what the Constitution means."[10]

This was dramatically illustrated during the 1974 court battle over the Nixon tapes. When the Watergate special prosecutor subpoenaed tape recordings of the president's conversations for use in the criminal trial of Nixon's former subordinates, the president invoked executive privilege and refused to comply. Nixon claimed that because the Constitution established three independent branches of government, the Supreme Court could not compel the president to release the tapes. The Court held otherwise; it recognized the existence of executive privilege, but ruled that the president could not hold back evidence needed for the criminal trial of his subordinates.[11] Nixon yielded to the Supreme Court and surrendered the tapes.

Judicial Review

Since the era of Chief Justice John Marshall (1801–1835), the Supreme Court has exercised the right of **judicial review,** the power to declare acts of Congress or actions by the executive branch—or laws and actions at any level of local, state, and federal government—unconstitutional. Lower federal courts and state courts may exercise the same power, but the Supreme Court normally has the last word in deciding constitutional questions. "We are under a Constitution," Charles Evans Hughes declared, "but the Constitution is what the judges say it is."*

Yet why, it is often asked, should nine justices who are appointed for life and not elected by the people have the power in a democratic system to strike down the laws and decisions of popularly elected legislatures and leaders? The question is asked most often by people who disapprove of what the Supreme Court is doing at a particular time. Those who approve of the philosophy of a given Court seldom complain that it is overstepping its power.

And judicial review is in effect a coin with two sides. Although the Supreme Court may exercise judicial review and strike down a law as unconstitutional, it may also affirm that a law or executive act is constitutional.

*Alpheus T. Mason, *The Supreme Court: Palladium of Freedom* (Ann Arbor: University of Michigan Press, 1962), p. 143. Hughes, later chief justice of the United States, made this comment in 1907 as governor of New York.

To date, only a little more than 100 acts have been declared unconstitutional; thousands more have been sustained by the Court.

One view of the Supreme Court holds that, because the justices are not popularly elected, the Court should move cautiously and avoid "legislating" social change. Popular democracy and the principle of majority rule are more consistent, in this view, with legislative supremacy.

An opposite view holds that the Court is the cornerstone of a system of checks and balances and restraints on majority rule provided by the Constitution. In this view, the Supreme Court often may be the only place in the political system where minorities are protected from the majority.

The debate over the role of the Supreme Court in the American system is sharpened by the fact that the Constitution is written in broad and sometimes ambiguous language. As a result, the Supreme Court has interpreted the meaning of the Constitution very differently at different times. Justice Felix Frankfurter once observed:

> The meaning of "due process" and the content of terms like "liberty" are not revealed by the Constitution. It is the justices who make the meaning. They read into the neutral language of the Constitution their own economic and social views. . . . Let us face the fact that five Justices of the Supreme Court are the molders of policy rather than the impersonal vehicles of revealed truth.[12]

The Supreme Court must, however, operate within the bounds of public opinion, and, in the long run, within the political mainstream of the times. The Court possesses no armies, and it must finally rely on the executive branch to enforce many of its rulings. It was

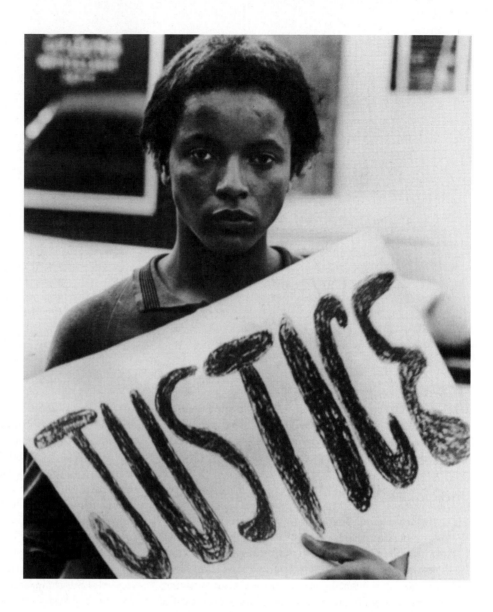

this truth that supposedly led President Andrew Jackson to declare of his chief justice, "John Marshall has made his decision—*now let him enforce it.*"[13] The Court cannot completely ignore the reactions to its decisions in Congress and in the nation because, as a political institution, its power ultimately rests on public opinion.

The Road to Judicial Review   The Constitution gives the Supreme Court power to consider "all Cases . . . arising under this Constitution." The principle of judicial review traces back to English common law, although the Constitution nowhere explicitly gives this power to the Court. The question of the framers' intent is still debated, but in 1788 Alexander Hamilton argued in *The Federalist* that the judicial branch did in fact have the right to judge whether laws passed by Congress were constitutional.[14] James Madison made the same point during the debate in Congress over the Bill of Rights. Later, so did James Wilson, another influential framer of the Constitution. And, according to political scientist Henry J. Abraham, "a vast majority" of the delegates to the constitutional con-

vention favored the idea of judicial review.[15] The principle of judicial review was largely taken for granted in the debates of the convention and in the state conventions that ratified the Constitution.

During the colonial period, the British Privy Council in London exercised judicial review over laws passed by the colonial legislatures. And during the first decade of the nation's existence, the Supreme Court, in a few cases, ruled on whether federal laws were constitutional. It invalidated one federal statute, for example, and at least twice struck down minor state laws.[16]

The power of judicial review, however—although it had already been exercised—was not firmly enunciated and established by the Supreme Court until 1803 in the case of ***Marbury* v. *Madison,*** which declared a portion of an act of Congress unconstitutional.[17]

When Jefferson became president in 1801 he was angered to find that his Federalist predecessor, John Adams, had appointed a number of federal judges just before leaving office, among them one William Marbury as a justice of the peace in the District of Columbia.

When Jefferson discovered that Marbury's commission had not actually been delivered to him, he ordered Secretary of State James Madison to hold it up. Under a provision of the Judiciary Act of 1789, Marbury sued in the Supreme Court for a writ of mandamus compelling the delivery of his commission. The Supreme Court under Chief Justice John Marshall dismissed the case, saying it lacked jurisdiction to issue such a writ. The Court held that the section of the Judiciary Act under which Marbury had sued was unconstitutional, since the Constitution did not empower the Court to issue a writ of mandamus, as the act provided. The ruling thus avoided an open political confrontation with the executive branch over Marbury's commission but at the same time established the power of the Court to void acts of Congress. "The Constitution is superior to any ordinary act of the legislature," Marshall wrote, and "a law repugnant to the Constitution is void."[18]

Although the Court's power of judicial review was thus established, the question of how the Court should apply its great power has remained a subject of controversy up to the present day. The debate has centered on whether the Court should practice judicial activism or judicial restraint. **Judicial activism** is the philosophy that Supreme Court justices and other judges should boldly apply the Constitution to social and political questions. **Judicial restraint** is the philosophy that the Supreme Court should avoid constitutional questions when possible and uphold acts of Congress unless they clearly violate a specific section of the Constitution.

As one scholar has posed the central questions: "Should the Court play an active, creative role in shaping our destiny, equally with the executive and legislative branches? Or should it be characterized by self-restraint, deferring to the legislative branch whenever there is room for policy judgment and leaving new departures to the initiative of others?"[19]

The philosophy of judicial activism was embraced on many issues by a majority of the members of the Warren Court, which vigorously applied the Constitution to social and political questions. For example, in protecting the rights of criminal defendants and in its reapportionment decisions, the Court moved into controversial areas that earlier Supreme Court justices had avoided.

The philosophy of judicial restraint is associated with Justices Felix Frankfurter, Louis D. Brandeis, and Oliver Wendell Holmes, Jr. Frankfurter, for example, held that the Court should avoid deciding "political questions" that could involve it in conflicts with other branches of the federal government.

The Changing Role of the Supreme Court

Although John Marshall had set forth the right of judicial review in 1803, the Supreme Court did not declare another act of Congress unconstitutional until the *Dred Scott* decision in 1857. Under Marshall's successor,

Roger B. Taney (1836–1864), the Court protected states' rights and stressed the power of the states over that of the federal government.

After the Civil War, the Court refused to apply the Fourteenth Amendment to protect the rights of black Americans, even though Congress had passed the amendment for this specific purpose (see Chapter 5). Instead, the Court used the amendment's due process clause to protect business from state regulation. The Fourteenth Amendment provides that no state shall "deprive any person of life, liberty, or property, without due process of law." The Court accepted the argument that a corporation was a "person" within the meaning of the amendment. In a series of cases, it used the Fourteenth and Fifth Amendments to protect industry, banking, and public utilities from social regulation. In the 1890s the Supreme Court struck down the federal income tax[*] and emasculated the federal antitrust laws. In general, the Court during this era served as a powerful guardian of the "robber barons"—the businessmen who amassed great fortunes in the late 19th century—as well as a champion of **laissez-faire** capitalism, a philosophy that government should interfere as little as possible in economic affairs.

The Court continued to expound a conservative philosophy under Chief Justice William Howard Taft in the 1920s. The election of Franklin D. Roosevelt in 1932 was followed by vast social change in America, but a majority of the Supreme Court was not in sympathy with the programs of the New Deal. Between 1933 and 1937 the Court struck down one after another of Roosevelt's programs. In 1936 the average age of members of the Court was 71, and the justices were dubbed the "nine old men."[†] Reelected by a landslide that year, Roosevelt risked his prestige in 1937 when he proposed his famous "court-packing" plan. His objective was to put on the Court younger justices who would be more sympathetic to the New Deal. Roosevelt's plan to bring the Supreme Court out of what he termed "the horse and buggy age" provided that whenever a justice refused to retire at age 70, the president could appoint an additional justice. Under the plan, the Court could have been expanded to a maximum of 15 members.

The debate raged in and out of Congress all that spring, but in less than six months the proposal was dead. Although Roosevelt's plan failed, by the time the Court recessed that summer it had already begun to shift to a more liberal position and to uphold New Deal programs. As a result, 1937 is regarded as a watershed year in the history of the Supreme Court. From that date on, the Court for many years often emerged as the protector not of big business but of the individual.

---

[*]The Sixteenth Amendment to the Constitution, ratified in 1913, allowed Congress to restore the federal income tax, which it did that year.
[†]A phrase popularized by columnists Drew Pearson and Robert S. Allen. See William Safire, *Safire's New Political Dictionary* (New York: Random House, 1993), pp. 499–500.

Chief Justice Earl Warren
Copyright © Fred Ward/Black Star

The Warren Court

During Earl Warren's 16 years as chief justice (1953–1969), the Supreme Court had a profound impact on politics and government in America. The Warren Court was an extraordinarily activist, innovative tribunal that wrought far-reaching change in the meaning of the Constitution.

Among its major decisions, the Warren Court outlawed official racial segregation in public schools, set strict national standards to protect the rights of criminal defendants, required the equal apportionment of state legislatures and the House of Representatives, and ruled that prayers and Bible reading in the public schools were unconstitutional. And it handed down other dramatic decisions that won it both high praise and sharp criticism—and engulfed it in great controversy.

Riding the crest of the tidal wave of social change that swept through America in the 1950s and 1960s, the Court became a natural target of those who felt it was moving too fast and too far. The political reaction to its bold decisions was symbolized by automobile bumper stickers and roadside billboards that read "Impeach Earl Warren."

Before he retired as chief justice in 1969, Warren was asked to name the most important decisions of the Warren Court.[20] He singled out those dealing with reapportionment, school desegregation, and the right to counsel, in that order.[21] Each of these cases symbolized one of three broad fields in which the Warren Court brought about far-reaching changes in America: the political process itself, civil rights, and the rights of the accused.

In its reapportionment decisions, the Warren Court required that each citizen's vote count as much as another's. If the quality of a democracy can be gauged, certainly the individual's vote is a basic unit of meas-

urement. Until the reapportionment revolution of the Warren Court, voters were often powerless to correct basic distortions in the system of representation itself.

The Warren Court's *Brown* decision has not eliminated racial segregation in American schools or American society. But by striking down the officially enforced dual school system in the South, the Court implied that "all racial discrimination sponsored, supported, or encouraged by government is unconstitutional."[22] Thus the decision foreshadowed a social upheaval. The civil rights movement, the civil rights legislation of the 1960s, and the continuing controversy over the busing of public school children all followed in the Supreme Court's wake.

By the 1980s, the goal of "integration" appeared to be less important to many African Americans than freedom, dignity, and a full share of the economic opportunities of American society. Nevertheless, the *Brown* decision remains a judicial milestone; by its action at a time when much of white America was complacent and satisfied with the existing social order, the Supreme Court provided moral as well as political leadership—it reminded the nation that the Constitution applies to all Americans.

The third broad area of decision by the Warren Court—the protection of the rights of criminal defendants—was discussed in Chapter 4. In a series of controversial decisions, including *Miranda, Escobedo, Gideon,* and *Mapp,* the Court, bit by bit, threw the mantle of the Bill of Rights around persons accused by state authorities of crimes. In so doing, the Court collided directly with the electorate's rising fear of crime; it was accused of "coddling criminals" and "handcuffing the police." Under the Burger Court the pendulum swung back substantially, in favor of the police and prosecutors.

The Warren Court moved aggressively in several other areas as well—banning prayers in the public schools, curbing the anti-Communist legislation of the 1950s, and easing the laws dealing with obscenity. All this activity provided ample ammunition to the Warren Court's conservative critics: The Court, they charged, had tinkered with legislative apportionment, forced school integration, overprotected the rights of criminals, banished prayer from the classroom, tolerated Communists, and encouraged pornography. Moreover, as many of the Court's critics frequently pointed out, it decided many important cases by a one-vote margin. The Burger Court and the Rehnquist Court moved more cautiously in the 1970s and thereafter and narrowed the sweep of some of the Warren Court's decisions, particularly in the areas of criminal justice and pornography. The Supreme Court might do so even more dramatically in the future. Yet one leading scholar predicted that

the doctrines of equality, freedom, and respect for human dignity laid down in the numerous decisions of the Warren Court cannot be warped back to their original dimensions. . . . Generations hence it may well appear that what is supposedly the most

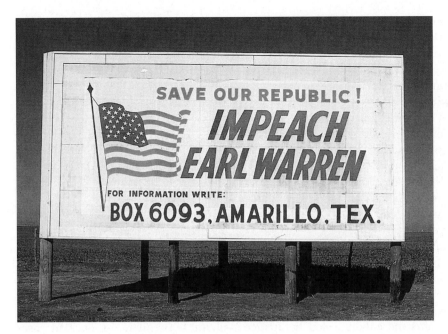

conservative of American political institutions, the Supreme Court, was the institution that did the most to help the nation adjust to the needs and demands of a free society.[23]

The Burger Court

During the 1968 presidential campaign, Richard M. Nixon promised to appoint to the Supreme Court "strict constructionists who saw their duty as interpreting law and not making law. They would see themselves as care-takers of the Constitution and servants of the people, not super-legislators with a free hand to impose their social and political viewpoints upon the American people."[24]

Nixon's comments clearly reflected one side of the historical argument over the "proper" role of the Supreme Court. Although the argument was as old as the republic itself, it had, by 1968, taken on new polit-ical meaning; the Warren Court had become linked in the minds of many voters with black militancy, urban riots, rising crime, and the volatile issue of "law and order" and justice. By contrast, others viewed the Warren Court as a humanitarian force that had revi-talized American democracy.

Then in 1969, Chief Justice Earl Warren, a liberal, retired, and Nixon named Warren E. Burger to succeed him. In Chief Justice Burger, Nixon made it clear, he believed he had found a "strict constructionist" who would fit his political and philosophical requirements. Over the next three years, Nixon appointed three more justices to the Court, and in 1975 President Gerald Ford chose one justice. Thus by 1976 a majority of the nine-member Court had been appointed since Earl Warren's retirement.

The more conservative trend represented a sea change from the Warren Court era. For example, the Burger Court handed down a number of decisions more favorable to police than to defendants. It narrowed the reach of the Fourth Amendment's protections against unreasonable search and seizure, making it easier for state and local prosecutors to use illegally seized evi-dence to convict defendants. (See Chapter 4.) And the Burger Court restored the death penalty.

The Court's decisions in these cases were hailed by conservatives, who argued that police should be given latitude in dealing with crime. In addition, the Court ruled that journalists had no First Amendment privi-lege to protect confidential sources and that journalists must answer questions about what they were thinking when they prepared reports resulting in libel suits. (See Chapter 8.)

After appointing Burger, Nixon sought to change the political balance on the Court further by nominat-ing a conservative as an associate justice. Twice, Nixon's nominees were rejected by the Senate. Finally, Nixon nominated Harry A. Blackmun, a Minnesota Republican and federal appeals court judge. Blackmun, a moderate, was confirmed. Over time, Blackmun often voted with the Court's liberal bloc; he was the chief architect of the Court's 1973 decision in *Roe* v. *Wade*, legalizing abortion.

In 1971 Nixon nominated two more Supreme Court justices said to share his "conservative" philosophy. They were Lewis F. Powell, Jr., a prominent Richmond, Virginia, attorney, and William Rehnquist, then an assis-tant United States attorney general. Both were con-firmed, giving President Nixon four appointees on the highest court. Because Byron R. White, a Kennedy appointee, and Potter Stewart, an Eisenhower appointee, voted in a number of important cases with the four new justices, from that point forward, in some decisions, Nixon had an effective majority in the highest tribunal. Later, however, Powell emerged as the important swing vote on the Supreme Court, sometimes siding with conservatives, sometimes with liberals. In a number of important cases, Powell's vote was decisive.

And in some policy areas such as desegregation and privacy, the Burger Court gave little comfort to conservatives and even broadened the decisions of the Warren Court. For example, the Burger Court legalized abortion, declined to stop the publication of the Pentagon Papers, extended the right to counsel to poor defendants even in misdemeanor cases, outlawed wiretapping of domestic groups without a court warrant, limited the power of local communities to ban pornography, and ruled that even the president must yield evidence to the courts. In the field of civil rights, the Burger Court banned racial discrimination in private schools and upheld affirmative action in education, jobs, and in federal contracts. And it held that all-male groups can be compelled to admit women—a ruling that the Rehnquist Court extended to include private clubs.[25]

In 1975 Justice William O. Douglas, an outspoken champion of individual liberties, retired after more than 36 years on the Court. President Ford named a moderate, John Paul Stevens, to replace him. In 1981, President Reagan named the first woman to serve on the Supreme Court, Judge Sandra Day O'Connor of the Arizona Court of Appeals. With the O'Connor appointment, the associate justices of the Supreme Court found it necessary to drop the traditional title of "Mr. Justice." From then on, their title became "Justice."

As a member of the Supreme Court, O'Connor at first generally allied herself with the Court's conservative wing, often voting with Chief Justice Burger, Justice Rehnquist, and Justice Powell. Even as the Supreme Court shifted to the right, many of its decisions still protected individual liberties and minority groups. But, clearly, the Burger Court had developed its own philosophy as it carried out its task of interpreting the Constitution. And this became even more apparent in the Rehnquist era.

The Rehnquist Court

After Warren Burger retired in 1986, President Reagan elevated William Rehnquist to chief justice and appointed Antonin Scalia, another conservative, to the Supreme Court. The appointment of Anthony Kennedy in 1987, and President Bush's appointments of Justices David Souter in 1990 and Clarence Thomas in 1991, meant that for a time, eight of the nine members of the Court had been appointed by Republican presidents. In the space of a relatively few years, the members and political philosophy of one of the three branches of the federal government had changed measurably.

When William Rehnquist was sworn in as chief justice of the United States in September 1986, many political observers expected that his appointment would usher in an era of conservative decisions by the highest court. In time the Court did become more conservative,

Chief Justice William H. Rehnquist, wearing a special robe with gold stripes, presided over the Senate impeachment trial and acquittal of President Clinton in 1999.
APTN/Wide World

but that was not the case initially. During the Rehnquist Court's first term, the liberals won all but two of the major cases and the conservatives prevailed only in the area of criminal law. A moderate-liberal coalition, led by Justice William J. Brennan, Jr., decided cases on affirmative action, teaching creationism in the public schools, protection for pregnant workers, and political asylum for illegal aliens.

Moreover, the Court, by a vote of 8–0, threw out the Reverend Jerry Falwell's suit against *Hustler* magazine.[26] In so doing, the Court declined to curb criticism of public figures.

But by 1988 the Rehnquist Court shifted in a more conservative direction, giving public school officials the right to censor school newspapers and plays, for example.[27] And after the appointment of Justice Anthony Kennedy, the Court in several decisions made it more difficult for workers to sue employers for discrimination.* The Court's action alarmed liberals and led to speculation that a conservative majority had finally emerged. In May 1988, in another decision that to some analysts seemed to reflect a more conservative trend, the Court ruled 6–2 that police may, without a warrant, search through trash that people leave outside their home to be collected.[28]

But, as always, the decisions varied; the Court in 1990 struck down the federal law that sought to ban flag-burning.[29] And in 1991, it invalidated New York's "Son of Sam" law, which had barred criminals from earning money from books about their crimes; the Court said the state law violated the First Amendment's provisions of free press and free speech.[30]

As these opinions demonstrated, the decisions of the Supreme Court are often unpredictable, and the Court's direction not always easily categorized. Although by the year 2000 the Court's conservative bloc was often a dominant force, it did not always prevail.

---

*Among the cases were *Patterson* v. *McLean Credit Union*, 491 U.S. 164 (1988), and *Wards Cove Packing Co., Inc.* v. *Atonio*, 490 U.S. 642 (1988). The series of decisions was overturned by the civil rights bill passed by Congress in 1991.

The President and the Court

Historically, presidents have picked Supreme Court justices for their politics more than for their judicial talents. By nominating justices whose political views appear compatible with their own, they try to gain political control of the Supreme Court. (Table 15-1 lists the current justices and the presidents who appointed them.)

When Franklin Roosevelt unsuccessfully attempted to pack the Supreme Court, he was aiming not so much at the age of its members as at their political views. As Justice Hugo Black put it, "Presidents have always appointed people who believed a great deal in the same things that the President who appoints them believes in."[31]

This practice is not necessarily bad if it does not lead to the appointment of mediocre judges. In fact, it is one important way in which the Supreme Court is at least indirectly responsive to the electorate. Along with the power of public opinion and the power of the Senate to confirm or reject the president's nominee, the presidential appointment power to some degree links the Court to the voters and the rest of the political system.

Approximately 90 percent of all Supreme Court justices in American history have belonged to the appointing president's political party; some have been selected from the president's inner circle of political advisers. In 1965, for example, President Johnson named Washington attorney Abe Fortas—a Democrat who had been his lawyer and political confidant for many years—to the Supreme Court.* The requirement that a majority of the Senate approve a Supreme Court nominee

---

*In 1968 the Senate declined to approve Johnson's elevation of Fortas to be chief justice. In 1969 Fortas resigned from the Court when it became known that three years earlier he had accepted a $20,000-a-year retainer from a foundation controlled by Louis E. Wolfson, a financier who went to prison for his stock dealings shortly before the Fortas resignation.

TABLE 15-1

The Supreme Court, 2000

Justices	Appointed by	Date
William H. Rehnquist[a]	Nixon	1971
John Paul Stevens	Ford	1975
Sandra Day O'Connor	Reagan	1981
Antonin Scalia	Reagan	1986
Anthony M. Kennedy	Reagan	1988
David H. Souter	Bush	1990
Clarence Thomas	Bush	1991
Ruth Bader Ginsburg	Clinton	1993
Stephen G. Breyer	Clinton	1994

[a]Chief justice of the United States. Rehnquist was elevated to chief justice by President Reagan on June 17, 1986. Members of the Court as of August 2000.

restricts the president's ability to shape the Court completely to his political liking. Up to the year 2000, the Senate had refused to approve 28, or almost 20 percent, of the 141 Supreme Court nominations sent to it.

Nor do justices always act as presidents expect. Supreme Court justices have a way of becoming surprisingly independent once they are on the bench; more than one president has been disappointed to find that he misjudged his appointee. As governor of California, Earl Warren helped to elect President Dwight Eisenhower. There was nothing in Warren's background as a moderate Republican to make the president think his chief justice would preside over a social upheaval. Later, Eisenhower reportedly called the Warren appointment "the biggest damn-fool mistake I ever made."[32] And President Nixon was bitterly disappointed when Chief Justice Burger, joined by two other Nixon appointees, voted with the rest of the Court to require the president to yield his crucial tape recordings, a decision that set the stage for Nixon's resignation.†

At times, presidential nominations of Supreme Court justices touch off memorable political battles. Such was the case in 1991, when President Bush nominated Clarence Thomas, and in 1987, when President Reagan nominated Robert Bork. A coalition of liberal and moderate forces sought to block the nomination of Bork, a former Yale University law professor who had opposed the Supreme Court's landmark 1973 ruling permitting abortions and who had taken other outspoken conservative positions. Opponents charged that Bork would attempt to undo rulings favoring women's rights, civil rights, privacy, and other individual rights. After televised Senate hearings and acrimonious debate, the Senate rejected Bork, by a vote of 58–42.

President Reagan then nominated another conservative, Douglas H. Ginsburg, to the Court vacancy. But his nomination went up in a puff of smoke when it was disclosed that he had used marijuana both as a student and as a professor at Harvard Law School. For an administration pledged to a war against drugs, it was too much; within two days Ginsburg asked the president to withdraw his nomination.

Congress and the Court

As Supreme Court Justice Robert Jackson once suggested, conflict among the branches of the federal government is always latent, "ready to break out again whenever the provocation becomes sufficient."[33] The Supreme Court, in deciding cases, must worry not only about public opinion, but about how Congress may react. Walter F. Murphy has suggested that the Court's

---

†J. Anthony Lukas, *Nightmare: The Underside of the Nixon Years* (New York: Viking Press, 1976), p. 518. Associate Justice William H. Rehnquist disqualified himself and did not participate in the tapes decision, since he had served in the Justice Department under Nixon.

conflicts with Congress ebb and flow in a three-step pattern: First, the Court makes decisions on important aspects of public policy. Second, the Court receives severe criticism coupled with threats of remedial or retaliatory action by Congress. The third step, according to Murphy, has generally been "judicial retreat."[34]

Robert A. Dahl has concluded that the dominant policy views of the Court "are never for long out of line" with the dominant views of the legislative majority.[35] Or, as humorist Finley Peter Dunne's "Mr. Dooley" put it, "the Supreme Court follows the election returns."

Under the Constitution, Congress can control the Supreme Court's **jurisdiction,** the kinds of cases that a court has the authority to decide. Congress can also control the size of the Supreme Court. In its early history, the Court had 5, 6, 7, and 10 justices. Congress did not fix the number at 9 until 1869.

After the Civil War, Congress blocked the Court from reviewing Reconstruction laws. During the late 1950s, a coalition in Congress of southern Democrats and conservative Republicans mounted a legislative assault to curb the power of the Supreme Court and limit its jurisdiction. That effort failed, but the threat of congressional retaliation is always present.

Indeed, in the 1980s, conservatives in Congress led by Senator Jesse Helms, a North Carolina Republican, introduced "court-stripping" bills designed to restrict the Supreme Court's jurisdiction and remove its power over cases dealing with abortion and school prayer. These attempts were defeated and did not become law.

Congress (in conjunction with the states) also possesses the power to overturn Supreme Court decisions by amending the Constitution.* The Sixteenth Amendment, establishing the federal income tax, passed by Congress in 1909 and ratified in 1913, was adopted as a direct result of a Supreme Court decision; in 1895 the Court had ruled unconstitutional an attempt by Congress to levy a national income tax.[36] And the Twenty-sixth Amendment, giving persons aged 18 and over the right to vote in all elections, was passed by Congress in 1971 and ratified that year because the Supreme Court had ruled that Congress could lower the voting age only in federal, not in state and local, elections.

Finally, Congress may attempt to overturn specific Supreme Court rulings by legislation. For example, in 1988, Congress reinstated civil rights protections that had been narrowed by the Supreme Court's 1984 decision in the *Grove City* case.[37] Congress did so by passing the Civil Rights Restoration Act that expanded civil rights for women, minorities, the elderly, and the disabled. The new law stated that federal antidiscrimination laws apply to an entire institution even if it accepts federal aid for only one program. The law directly overturned the Supreme Court decision in *Grove City.*

The Supreme Court in Action

Unlike Congress and the presidency, institutions that are the subject of continual scrutiny by the press, the Supreme Court has usually operated in secrecy. One result is that the public knows relatively little about the high court. In one poll, for example, 59 percent of respondents could name the Three Stooges, but only 17 percent could name three of the court's nine justices.[†]

Until relatively recently, the internal workings and deliberations of the Supreme Court have gone largely unreported, although oral arguments and decisions in major cases are given wide publicity.

In 1993, the papers of the late Justice Thurgood Marshall were made public by the Library of Congress. They contained a treasure trove of detail about the inner workings of the Court, the backstage dealings between the justices, and their very human concerns. In a controversial Missouri abortion case, the papers revealed, Justice John Paul Stevens complained about a first draft of Chief Justice Rehnquist's majority opinion. The Court's ruling in *Roe* v. *Wade,* Stevens wrote, should be given "a decent burial instead of tossing it out the window of a fast-moving caboose."[‡]

The justices refer to each other by first names or even nicknames in Marshall's papers. Scalia was called "Nino," and Anthony M. Kennedy was "Tony." Rehnquist was known as "Chief" or "CJ." When, in anticipation that women would be appointed to their ranks, the justices in 1980 dropped the "Mr." from their formal titles, at least two justices, Blackmun and Powell, objected. They preferred to wait until a woman was actually named. If the change was adopted, Blackmun pointed out, the Court would have "to remove and replace the brass plates that are on the backs of the chairs at the bench" and on the doors of their chambers. In a "Dear Chief" letter to Rehnquist, Blackmun strongly implied that he was not about to let anyone strip the brass plate off his chair.[38]

Even earlier, in 1979, much of the Court's traditional secrecy had been stripped away with the publication of *The Brethren,* a controversial book by two investigative reporters about the operations of the Supreme Court.[39] The book, which covered the years 1969 through 1975, published internal memoranda of the justices and reported in great detail on the private weekly conferences in which justices discuss pending cases. A number of scholars criticized the book because the sources of its material were not identified, and some lawyers and

---

*The Eleventh, Fourteenth, Sixteenth, and Twenty-sixth Amendments to the Constitution reversed specific Supreme Court rulings.

†The Three Stooges, a slapstick comedy team popular in films of the 1930s through the 1950s, were, for more than a decade, Larry, Moe, and Curly. An earlier Stooge, Shemp, dropped out of the team for a time and upon his death was replaced, in succession, by two actors named Joe. The 1995 poll of 1,200 persons by Luntz Research of Arlington, Virginia, did not require respondents to provide the last names of the comedians or the first names of the Supreme Court justices. Nor were the respondents required to name Joe or Shemp.

‡*New York Times,* May 24, 1993, p. A10. In the case, *Webster* v. *Reproductive Health Services,* the Court ruled 5–4 that states may impose sharp restrictions on abortions.

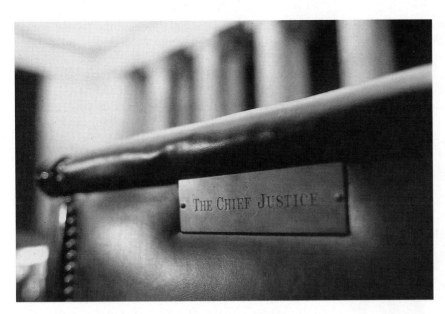

judges argued that the judicial process was not served by exposing the Court's internal deliberations.[40]

Nevertheless, in one area, *The Brethren* seemed persuasive—it revealed a degree of conflict and intense competition among the justices that previously had been suggested but not reported in such great detail.[41] As already noted, the Supreme Court is a political institution. According to the book, the justices engage in trade-offs and deals, and form shifting alliances, much as do political participants in the executive and legislative branches. This conclusion was later confirmed by the release of the Marshall papers.

Nor should it have been surprising that in the period from 1969 to 1975 there was sharp conflict and controversy inside the Court. It was precisely during those years that a Republican president was appointing justices with a very different philosophy from that of the Supreme Court's liberals, some of whom had been on the Court since the administration of Franklin D. Roosevelt.

The Brethren was particularly harsh on Chief Justice Warren Burger, whom it portrayed as a jurist of distinguished bearing, but a man of personal pomposity and shallow intellect. It quoted Justice William J. Brennan, Jr., as calling Burger a "dummy," and quoted Justice Lewis F. Powell, Jr., as saying of Burger's draft in a busing case: "If an associate in my law firm had done this . . . I'd fire him."[42]

The book's gossipy style and its emphasis on personalities are of less value to the scholar and student than the light it sheds on the ways that justices determine which cases reach the Court's docket and how those cases are decided.

In more recent years, Supreme Court justices have been less reluctant to speak out about the Court's operations and on public issues. Chief Justice Rehnquist even wrote a book about the history and procedures of the Court.[43]

How Cases Reach the Court Most cases never get to the Supreme Court. Those that do usually reach the Court in one of two ways. The Court has **original jurisdiction,** the right under the Constitution to hear certain kinds of cases directly, such as cases involving foreign diplomats, or cases in which one of the 50 states is a party. But the Court rarely exercises original jurisdiction. Rather, the overwhelming majority of cases presented to the Court come in the form of petitions for a **writ of certiorari.** The Court can choose which of the cases it wants to hear by denying or granting certiorari, a Latin term meaning "made more certain." The votes of four justices are needed to grant "cert." Between 90 and 95 percent of all such applications are denied.[44]

Cases may reach the Supreme Court for review either from state or federal courts. The cases come from a state court of last resort (usually a state supreme court), or from federal courts of appeals, United States district courts, or special-purpose federal courts.

Of the more than 10 million cases tried annually in American courts, only some 7,000 are taken to the Supreme Court. Of this total, the Court customarily hears argument on fewer than 100. The rest of the cases on the Court's docket are denied, affirmed, or reversed by written "memorandum orders." In choosing whether even to consider a case, the Supreme Court makes law (because, usually, the Supreme Court's refusal to take a case means that a lower court decision stands).

Court Tradition The Court normally sits from October through June. The Court building on Capitol Hill is a majestic structure of white marble, completed in 1935 and modeled after the Greek Temple of Diana at Ephesus, one of the seven wonders of the ancient world. The great bronze doors weigh six and a half tons each; the courtroom seats 300 and has a ceiling 44 feet high. Tradition is observed; federal government grandiose setting of the building and the formal atmosphere are designed to preserve the dignity of the nation's highest tribunal, but they also provide some comfort to its critics, particularly political cartoonists, who find it easy to lampoon the Court's elaborate Grecian setting.

Lawyers arguing before the Court usually have one-half hour to make their case. Five minutes before their time expires a white light comes on; when a red light flashes on they must stop. But the justices often use up some of the precious time by interrupting to question the attorneys, a procedure that can be totally unnerving for lawyers making their initial appearance before the Supreme Court.

On Fridays when the Court is sitting, the justices meet in conference to discuss and vote on pending cases and petitions for certiorari. The justices, by a tradition established in 1888, shake hands as they file into the oak-paneled conference room. The meetings are secret and presided over by the chief justice. Beneath a portrait of Chief Justice John Marshall, which hangs over the marble fireplace, the members of the Court gather around a conference table. Behind each justice is a cart on which law clerks have placed all the legal documents the justices may need to expound their positions on the various cases. During these discussions, no one other than the nine justices is allowed in the conference room, not even a clerk. The chief justice and the other justices take notes during their deliberations.

The Chief Justice Although theoretically equal to the other eight justices, "the Chief" has four important advantages: prestige, the power to influence the Court's selection of cases, the power to chair the conference, and the power to assign the writing of opinions by the justices. The chief justice, therefore, may play a very important role as "Court unifier."[45] Or the chief justice may be a source of disunity.

The Supreme Court
Copyright © Mark Gibson/CORBIS

lawyers appearing for oral argument still wear morning clothes—a formal cutaway coat with tails and striped pants—as do a few private attorneys, although rarely. Most private attorneys simply wear dark suits. The rather

The interior of the Supreme Court
AP/Wide World

THE CHIEF JUSTICES OF THE UNITED STATES

John Jay (1789–1795)	Edward D. White (1910–1921)
John Rutledge (1795)	William Howard Taft (1921–1930)
Oliver Ellsworth (1796–1800)	Charles Evans Hughes (1930–1941)
John Marshall (1801–1835)	Harlan F. Stone (1941–1946)
Roger B. Taney (1836–1864)	Fred M. Vinson (1946–1953)
Salmon P. Chase (1864–1873)	Earl Warren (1953–1969)
Morrison R. Waite (1874–1888)	Warren E. Burger (1969–1986)
Melville W. Fuller (1888–1910)	William H. Rehnquist (1986–)

Leadership styles among chief justices differ. Charles Evans Hughes, chief justice during the 1930s, was popular among the justices on the Court even though he ran the conference with a firm hand. His successor, Harlan Fiske Stone, was much less reserved and delighted in joining the debate. "'Jackson,' he would say, 'that's damned nonsense.' 'Douglas, you know better than that.'"[46]

The chief justice, if in the majority, decides who will write the Court's opinion; otherwise, the ranking justice among the majority assigns the writing of the opinion. According to *The Brethren*, Chief Justice Burger often maneuvered in conference to assign opinions (and thus perhaps influence their content) even when he was not in the majority on a case. In one such instance, the authors reported, Justice William O. Douglas threatened to make public a 1972 memo in which he complained that Burger should not have assigned a group of major abortion cases to Justice Harry A. Blackmun:

> When . . . the minority seeks to control the assignment, there is a destructive force at work in the Court. When a Chief Justice tries to bend the Court to his will by manipulating assignments, the integrity of the institution is imperiled.
>
> Historically, this institution has been composed of fiercely independent men with fiercely opposed views. . . . But up to now the Conference, though deeply disagreeing on legal and constitutional issues, has been a group marked by goodwill. . . . Perhaps the purpose of the Chief Justice, a member of the minority in the Abortion Cases, in assigning the opinions was to try to keep control of the merits. If that was the aim, he was unsuccessful.[47]

As related in *The Brethren*, Douglas eventually withdrew his threat to publish the explosive memo. But clearly, the interaction among the justices on the Court is a political process, in which votes are sometimes traded and positions compromised.

Shortly after Justice Lewis F. Powell, Jr., retired in 1987, he granted an interview in which he talked frankly about this process. "Whenever you're assigned to write a 5-to-4 decision, you know that you cannot afford to lose a vote," he said. "And sometimes you end up on the short end of a case when you started out with five votes, and that makes you more than a little unhappy."[48] He added: "You receive memos from other Justices, saying 'Dear Lewis, I'm inclined to join your opinion but it would help me if you changed so and so.' And sometimes a Justice will suggest language."[49]

The justices, Powell added, call uninteresting cases "dogs." "A dog is a case that you wish the Chief Justice had assigned to some other justice," he said—a deadly dull case, "a tax case, for example."[50]

Dissenting Opinions   Once an opinion is assigned, justices are free to write dissenting opinions if they disagree with the majority, or concurring opinions if they reach the same conclusion as the majority, often for different reasons. Important bargaining takes place backstage among the justices as the opinions are written and circulated informally, and justices may trade their votes to influence the shape of an opinion. Some legal experts believe that dissents, because they publicly reveal disunity, weaken the prestige of the Court—the large number of 5–4 decisions by the Warren Court, for example, provided fuel for its enemies. But many of the most eloquent arguments of the Supreme Court have been voiced in dissents by justices including the first John Marshall Harlan (of Kentucky), as well as Holmes, Brandeis, Stone, Black, and Douglas. Today's dissent may become tomorrow's majority opinion when the Court, as it has frequently done, overrules past decisions to meet new problems.

When it is in session, the Court usually hands down its opinions in the first part of each week. The justices read or summarize their opinions in the courtroom, sometimes adding informal comments. The words that echo through the marble chamber, often with enormous consequences for society, become the law of the land and renew the meaning of constitutional government.

THE AMERICAN COURT SYSTEM

Because the United States encompasses both a federal government and 50 state governments, it has a dual court system. "In effect, this means that there exist, side by side, two major court systems—one could even say fifty-one—which are wholly distinct."[51]

At the top of the system is the U.S. Supreme Court. But as we have seen, relatively few cases get there. The average citizen has neither the time nor the money to fight a case all the way to the highest tribunal. In any event, the Court only considers cases involving a substantial federal question or constitutional issue, and normally after all remedies in the state courts have been exhausted.

The Federal Courts

The bulk of the cases that come before the judicial branch of the federal government are handled in the "inferior" courts created by Congress under the Constitution. Immediately below the Supreme Court are the U.S. courts of appeals, also known as circuit courts. The nation is divided geographically into 12 judicial circuits, each with a court of appeals. Every state and territory falls within the jurisdiction of one of these circuit courts. Each court of appeals has from 4 to 23 judges, but usually 3 judges hear a case. The circuit courts hear appeals from lower federal courts and review the decisions of federal regulatory agencies. Each year about 55,000 cases reach the circuit courts.

Online *for more information about the federal courts, see:* www.uscourts.gov

---

Below the circuit courts are the federal district courts. In 1999 there were 89 district courts in the 50 states, plus one each for the District of Columbia, Puerto Rico, the Virgin Islands, Guam, and the Mariana Islands, making a total of 94. Each district has from 1 to 30 judges, making a total of 655 district judgeships.[52]

More than half of the federal judicial districts coincide with state lines, but some populous states, such as California, Texas, and New York, are divided into multiple districts. The federal district courts are trial courts; they handle cases involving disputes between citizens of different states, and violations of federal law—for example, of civil rights, patent and copyright, bankruptcy, immigration, counterfeiting, antitrust, and postal laws.

Special Federal Courts

Congress has created special-purpose courts to deal with certain kinds of cases. These include the U.S. Court of Federal Claims, which has jurisdiction over such cases as claims for compensation for property taken by the government, claims for income tax refunds, or claims by government workers for back pay; the U.S. Court of Appeals for the Federal Circuit, which hears copyright, trademark, and patent cases; the U.S. Tax Court, which hears a variety of tax cases; and the U.S. Court of Appeals for the Armed Forces, often termed the "GI Supreme Court."

This court, whose three judges are civilians, is the final appellate tribunal in court-martial convictions. It

was established by Congress in 1950, along with a Uniform Code of Military Justice. The code represented the first major overhaul of the system of military justice since the early 19th century.

The Vietnam War focused new attention on the process of military justice. The most controversial case growing out of that war was the murder conviction of 1st Lt. William L. Calley, Jr. In 1968 American soldiers swept through the South Vietnamese hamlet of My Lai and killed somewhere between 100 and more than 300 men, women, and children, all civilians. The tragedy was covered up for more than a year, until journalist Seymour M. Hersh publicized the story, for which he won a Pulitzer Prize. The government brought charges in connection with the massacre and its cover-up against 25 officers and enlisted men, including the general who commanded the division at the time of the murders. But only Lieutenant Calley, who led his platoon through My Lai, was convicted. In 1971 an Army court found Calley guilty of the premeditated murder of at least 22 South Vietnamese civilians at My Lai. He was sentenced to life imprisonment, but the Army later reduced the sentence to 10 years. Calley was paroled by the Army after he had served one-third of his sentence.

Lt. William Calley, Jr.
Copyright © CORBIS/UPI/Bettmann

The cases occurring in Vietnam dramatized the fact that many Americans—about 1.6 million in the year 2000—were subject to military courts and therefore were at least temporarily outside the civilian system of justice as it has evolved under the Constitution. Moreover, there is always the danger that military trials will be swayed by command influence—that is, that the decisions of prosecutors, and officers who serve on military juries, may be affected by the views of their commanding officers.

In 1983, Congress empowered the Supreme Court to review certain decisions of the Court of Appeals for the Armed Forces. Even before that, the Supreme Court had asserted a limited right to review some military cases.[53] Moreover, in recent years, the Court of Appeals for the Armed Forces itself has moved to broaden the legal rights of servicemen and women. For example, it held that the Supreme Court's *Miranda* decision, ruling out involuntary confessions, must also apply in military cases.[54]

Although defendants charged under military law have a right to counsel, they do not have a right to trial by a jury of 12 persons. And except in cases that carry the death penalty, juries in military courts do not have to be unanimous to convict.

In 1969 the Supreme Court ruled that military personnel must be tried in civilian courts for crimes not connected with the service and committed in peacetime while on leave or off duty.[55] However, in 1987 the Supreme Court, reversing itself, ruled that military personnel suspected of a crime of any type may be tried in military courts, whether or not the crime was committed at a military installation.[56] As a result, military defendants may be tried in either state or military courts for crimes unrelated to the service.

In 1974 the Supreme Court upheld the controversial Article 134, the "general article" of the Uniform Code of Military Justice, which permitted the military to impose criminal penalties for any offense that imperiled "good order and discipline" in the armed forces.[57] Although the Supreme Court thus declined to do away with the "general article," reforms were gradually taking place in the system of military justice. Beginning in 1980, for example, by presidential order, the rules of evidence used in federal criminal trials also apply to military courts-martial.

The State Court System

State and local courts, not the federal courts, handle most cases in the United States. The quality and structure of the state court systems vary tremendously, but most states have several layers of courts:

1. *Magistrates' courts* are courts in which justices of the peace, or magistrates, handle **misdemeanors,** minor criminal offenses such as speeding, and perform civil marriages. Most "JPs" do not have law degrees, but what they may lack in legal training they make up for in their well-known zeal for convictions, which average 80 percent in criminal cases.[58]

2. *Municipal courts* are known variously as police courts, city courts, traffic courts, and night courts. These courts, generally one step up from the magistrates' courts, usually hear civil and lesser criminal cases.

3. *County courts,* also called superior courts, try **felonies,** serious crimes, such as murder, arson, or rape. These courts also try major civil cases. At this level, jury trials are held in some cases.

4. *Special jurisdiction courts* are sometimes created at the county level to handle domestic relations, juveniles, probate of wills and estates, and other specialized tasks.

5. *Intermediate courts of appeals,* or appellate divisions, exist in some states to hear appeals from the county and municipal courts.

6. *Courts of appeals,* often called state supreme courts, are the final judicial tribunals in the states.

The Judges

Federal Court Judges All federal court judges are appointed by the president, subject to Senate approval. Historically, federal judges have been selected under a Senate patronage system that has often drawn criticism. The system changed briefly under President Jimmy Carter, but traditionally it has worked this way: Senators present the president with the names of three candidates for federal judgeships; from these, the president selects one; the Justice Department and the FBI check the background of the person selected; the American Bar Association files a report; and the name is submitted to the Senate for confirmation.

During the 1976 presidential campaign, however, Carter promised to appoint all federal judges "strictly on the basis of merit without any consideration of political aspect or influence." As president, Carter issued two executive orders, one creating merit commissions to recommend circuit court judges, and another encouraging the creation of such commissions in the states to recommend candidates for federal district courts.

Commissions were established in about half the states. Despite the loose, partly voluntary nature of the merit system, Carter's orders had an impact; more women and members of minority groups were appointed to the federal bench. President Reagan canceled both Carter orders and returned to the Senate patronage system. Fewer women and minority judges were named by Reagan and his successor, President George Bush, although their numbers increased during the Clinton years.

State and Local Judges A majority of the 28,793 state judges in the United States are elected, as are many local judges.[59] Judges are elected in 29 states, appointed

in 9, and selected by both methods in 3 states (Kansas, Missouri, and North Carolina). Eight states and the District of Columbia employ the merit system for the selection of judges, patterned after the "Missouri plan."[60] The basic elements of that plan, which went into effect in Missouri in 1940, are as follows:

1. Nomination of the judges by a nonpartisan commission made up of lawyers, a judge, and citizens.
2. Appointment by the governor.
3. Approval by the voters after an initial term on the bench.

Despite the efforts to bring about judicial reform, in most cases "it is the politicians who select the judges. The voters only ratify their choices."[61] Political parties sometimes do not run competing candidates for the judiciary; rather, political leaders of both major parties get together and carve up the available judgeships. The nominees then run with the endorsement of both parties. In the process, political hacks are sometimes elevated to the bench.

But a presidential commission has warned: "The quality of the judiciary in large measure determines the quality of justice."[62] Bad judges do more than administer bad law; in the process they erode public respect for the entire system of criminal justice and the political system of which it is a vital part.

CRIMINAL JUSTICE IN AMERICA

A presidential commission has observed that "the poor—like the rich—can go to court. Whether they find satisfaction there is another matter. . . . Too frequently courts . . . serve the poor less well than their creditors. . . . The poor are discouraged from initiating civil actions against their exploiters. Litigation is expensive; so are experienced lawyers."[63]

The commission that issued this critical report included a mixture of liberals, moderates, and conservatives. The report went on to criticize the nation's criminal justice system in words that were often harsh. In fact, the commission said, there is no real *system* of criminal justice:

> There is, instead, a reasonably well-defined criminal *process* . . . through which each accused offender may pass: from the hands of the police, to the jurisdiction of the courts, behind the walls of a prison, then back onto the street. . . . Criminal courts themselves are often poorly managed and . . . seriously backlogged. . . . Prisons . . . are . . . schools in crime. . . . The typical prison experience is degrading . . . and the outlook of most ex-convicts is bleak.[64]

Most criticism of the administration of justice in the United States is directed not at the principles of the system—the presumption that a defendant is innocent

THE CRIMINAL JUSTICE TREADMILL

- Half of all major crimes are never reported to police.
- Of those that are, fewer than 25 percent are solved by arrests.
- Half of these arrests result in dismissal of charges.
- Ninety percent of the rest are resolved by a plea of guilty.
- The fraction of cases that do go to trial represent fewer than 1 percent of all crimes committed.
- About 25 percent of those convicted are sent to prison; the rest are released on probation.
- Nearly everyone who goes to prison is eventually released.
- Between half and two-thirds of those released are arrested and convicted again; they become repeat criminals known as recidivists.

—Adapted from *To Establish Justice, To Insure Domestic Tranquility*, Final Report of the National Commission on the Causes and Prevention of Violence, 1969

until proven guilty and the protections of the Bill of Rights—but at the failure of the system to work the way it is supposed to work.

Americans, Edward L. Barrett, Jr., has noted, tend to think that the procedure of the criminal courts protects the dignity of the individual against the power of the government:

> Such is the general image we have of the administration of criminal justice. But if one enters the courthouse in any sizable city and walks from courtroom to courtroom, what does he see? One judge, in a single morning, is accepting pleas of guilty from and sentencing a hundred or more persons charged with drunkenness. Another judge is adjusting traffic cases with an average time of no more than a minute per case. A third is disposing of a hundred or more other misdemeanor offenses in a morning. . . .
>
> Suddenly it becomes clear that for most defendants in the criminal process, there is scant regard for them as individuals. They are numbers on dockets, faceless ones to be processed and sent on their way. The gap between the theory and the reality is enormous.[65]

A Profile of Crime in America

In 1998 there were an estimated 12.5 million violent and property crimes reported to law enforcement agencies in the United States, of which 1,531,044, or 12 percent, fell into the category of crimes that people fear the

Crime in the United States, 1998

Crime Offenses	Estimated Number of Crimes	Rate per 100,000 Inhabitants
Total	12,500,000	4,616
Violent	1,500,000	566
Property	11,000,000	4,049
Murder	16,914	6
Forcible rape	93,103	67
Robbery	446,625	165
Aggravated assault	974,402	360
Burglary	2,329,950	862
Larceny-Theft	7,400,000	2,728
Auto theft	1,200,000	459
Arson	78,094	39

SOURCE: Adapted from *Crime in the United States 1998*, Uniform Crime Reports, Federal Bureau of Investigation (Washington, D.C.: U.S. Government Printing Office, 1999), pp. 6–54.

most: murder, forcible rape, robbery, and aggravated assault.* (See Table 15-2.)

In the United States in 1998, a total of 16,914 persons were murdered, a decrease of 28 percent in four years. There were more than 2.3 million burglaries reported, 66.6 percent of these in homes. More than 1.2 million cars were stolen. Put another way, on the average a violent crime was committed every 21 seconds, a murder every 31 minutes, a rape every 6 minutes, a robbery every minute, a burglary every 14 seconds, and a car stolen every 25 seconds.[66] (See Figure 15-1.)

These figures, compiled annually by the FBI from reports received by law enforcement agencies, indicate a decrease in recent years in the rate of violent and major crime. Various factors have been cited to explain the apparent lower crime rates, including a booming economy, the decline of the crack cocaine epidemic that had gripped the inner cities in the mid-1980s, tougher police tactics, and new gun laws. According to an FBI study, for example, a 7 percent decrease in homicides in 1999 was entirely due to a decline in the number of murders committed with guns.[67]

However, there is no broad agreement among experts even that crime has really declined, let alone a consensus on the possible causes of any decrease. For example, in 1999 an update of the landmark 1969 study

*In 1998, guns were the weapon of choice in 7 out of 10 murders. The highest number of murders occurred in the month of August, the lowest number in February, and 75 percent of all victims were males. Among the geographic regions of the country, the South had the greatest number of murders. Forty percent of all victims were related to or acquainted with their assailants. Among female victims, 32 percent were killed by husbands or boyfriends. See *Crime in the United States 1998*, Uniform Crime Reports, Federal Bureau of Investigation (Washington, D.C.: U.S. Government Printing Office, 1999), pp. 13–22.

Crime Clocks, 1998

SOURCE: Adapted from *Crime in the United States 1998*, Uniform Crime Reports, Federal Bureau of Investigation (Washington, D.C.: U.S. Government Printing Office, 1999), p. 4.

of the National Commission on the Causes and Prevention of Violence found that despite a short-term drop in crime from a peak in the early 1990s, there had been an increase of 40 percent over 30 years in the overall level of violence in major cities, as well as a sharp increase in the fear of crime.[68]

Moreover, the annual crime statistics may not reflect the full magnitude of lawbreaking in the United States. A presidential commission has estimated, based on population sampling, that the actual amount of crime committed is "several times" greater than the amount of crime reported to the authorities.[69] People fail to report crime for a variety of reasons, including a reluctance to "get involved," doubt that police can do anything about it, or fear of reprisal by the criminal.[70]

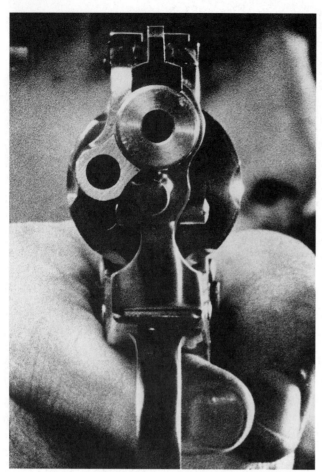

Larry Morris/*Washington Post*

There are some popular misconceptions about crime. As the president's commission noted, "the risks of personal harm are spread very unevenly," because they are much higher for residents of the inner city than for most other Americans.[71] Author Richard Harris reported, for example, that for a black resident of Chicago's inner city, "the chance of being physically assaulted, on the basis of reported crimes, was one in seventy-seven, whereas for the white resident of a nearby suburb the chance was one in ten thousand."[72] But even people who live in relatively "safe" areas have either been victims of crime or know someone who has been a crime victim.

Crime by youths accounts for a substantial share of all crime. In 1998, for example, 38 percent of the arrests for violent and property crimes were of persons under age 18.[73] Drug addiction is another source of crime. Estimates vary greatly as to how much crime is committed by drug addicts in order to get money to support their habit. Some estimates have attributed as much as three-quarters of all serious crime in New York City and Washington, D.C., to drug addicts.[74]

In 1998 the rate of violent and property crimes in America fell. The rate of violent crimes in 1998 was 21 percent lower than the 1994 rate and 15 percent lower than the 1989 rate.[75] Property crimes also decreased,

with the 1998 rate 13 percent lower than the 1994 rate and 20 percent lower than the 1989 rate.[76]

Because the population is increasing, however, the actual number of such crimes remained disturbingly high. Even if the crime rate remained level, there would be more crime because of population growth.

One approach in the effort to reduce crime is gun control, legislation designed to restrict criminals from acquiring handguns or assault weapons. It is an approach strongly opposed by many gun owners and their powerful lobby, the National Rifle Association. In 1993, President Clinton signed the Brady Bill, which requires the buyer of a handgun to wait five days while authorities check to see if the purchaser has a criminal record or a history of drug addiction or mental problems. The law was named after James Brady, the White House press secretary severely injured when he was shot in the head during an assassination attempt against President Reagan in 1981.

In a study of the first four years of the law's operation, the Justice Department reported that of 12.7 million background checks, 312,000 would-be gun buyers were rejected.[77] In 1998, under the Brady law, the Justice Department began a program of instant background checks of potential gun buyers; in the first year of operation, 160,000 of 8.7 million people who attempted to buy guns were turned down.[78] The Brady law continued to draw criticism and one study reported that the background checks had not reduced homicide rates.[79] However, other analyses showed that the law had reduced interstate gun trafficking, and a California study reported that state laws requiring background checks had reduced crimes committed with guns by 25 to 30 percent.[80]

In 1994, as part of a crime bill enacted into law and signed by President Clinton, 19 types of semiautomatic assault-style weapons were banned after law enforcement authorities said they were used primarily to com-

TABLE 15-3

Death and Guns: A Look around the World

The high rate of deaths from guns in the United States is not reflected in many other countries, as these numbers show. The statistics are for gun deaths in one year.

Gun Deaths	Country	Population
2	New Zealand	3,547,983
15	Japan	125,449,703
30	Great Britain	58,489,975
106	Canada	28,820,671
213	Germany	83,536,115
9,390	United States	265,562,845

SOURCE: Center to Prevent Handgun Violence, "Handgun Control," online at <www.handguncontrol.org/research/progun/firefacts.asp>. Data for 1996.

The evolution of ecstasy from an underground urban drug to middle-class life in the United States is a new phenomenon. Ecstasy—or "e"—came out of European clubs and peaked in popularity in the early 1990s. In the United States, ecstasy remained common only on the margins of society. But in the past year or so, ecstasy has come to the American heartland. In May, authorities seized half a million pills at San Francisco's airport—the biggest American e bust ever. Each pill costs pennies to make but sells for between $20 and $40.

Ecstasy use in the United States is growing: 8 percent of U.S. high school seniors say they have tried it at least once, up from 5.8 percent in 1997. Ecstasy pills are (or at least they are supposed to be) made of a compound called methylenedioxymethamphetamine, or MDMA.

Broadly speaking, there are two dangers: First, a pill you assume to be MDMA could actually contain something else. Anecdotal evidence suggests that most serious short-term medical problems that arise from "ecstasy" are caused by pills adulterated with other, more harmful substances. Second, MDMA itself might do harm. MDMA resculpts the brain cells that release the chemical. The changes to these cells could be permanent.

In 1998, emergency rooms participating in the Drug Abuse Warning Network reported receiving 1,135 mentions of ecstasy during admissions, compared with just 626 in 1997. The two most common short-term side effects of MDMA are overheating and psychological trauma.

A few users have mentally broken down on ecstasy, unprepared for its powerful psychological effects. A schoolteacher in San Francisco who took ecstasy a year ago began to recall, in horrible detail, an episode of sexual abuse. She became severely depressed for three months and had to seek psychiatric treatment.

Ecstasy's aftermath can also include a depressive hangover, a down day that users sometimes call Terrible Tuesdays. Another downside: Because users feel empathetic, ecstasy can lower sexual inhibitions. Dr. Robert Klitzman, a psychiatrist at Columbia University, has found that men in New York City who use ecstasy are 2.8 times more likely to have unprotected sex.

Still, the majority of people who end up in the E.R. after taking ecstasy are almost certainly not taking MDMA but something masquerading under its name. No one knows for sure what they're taking, since emergency rooms don't always test blood to confirm the drug identified by users.

In the United States, an organization called DanceSafe, which tests pills for anonymous users who send in samples from around the nation, found that 40 percent of those pills are fake.

—Adapted from *Time*, International Edition, July 17, 2000

---

mit crimes. Polls showed that 70 percent or more of the public supported the ban on assault weapons.[81] The crime bill also provided funds to help communities hire 100,000 more police officers and to help the states build more prisons.

In recent years there have been a number of school shootings, including the carnage at Columbine High School in Littleton, Colorado, in the spring of 1999. Then in February 2000, a 6-year-old boy took a handgun to school and shot and killed Kayla Rolland, his first-grade classmate in Flint, Michigan. In response to these tragedies, thousands of people gathered on the mall in Washington, D.C., in May of 2000 in a "Million Mom March" for gun control and an end to violence.

Despite the shocking school shootings, and repeated workplace killings by disgruntled or mentally disturbed current or former employees, and the mass protest in Washington, Congress by the year 2000 had not passed more stringent gun control legislation.

The Prisons

The Department of Justice reported in the year 2000 that there were a record 2,026,596 persons in prisons and jails in the United States, in federal, state, and local institutions.[82] Of the total, 135,246 persons were inmates of federal prisons.[83] The bulk of prisoners are in the state prison systems, where uprisings, often violent, and the seizure of hostages have become familiar occurrences in recent years.

Prison overcrowding is recognized as a serious problem in America, which has the highest incarceration rate in the world. Many states have passed laws providing for early release of prisoners when overcrowding reaches certain levels. In a number of states, prisoners sleep on floors, or two and three prisoners are

Kayla Rolland, 6, the first-grade Michigan student shot and killed at school by a 6-year-old classmate
AP/Wide World

WASHINGTON, May 14—With a rallying cry of "enough is enough," hundreds of thousands of mothers and other gun control advocates marched on the nation's capital and in several cities around the country today, demanding "sensible gun laws," mourning the loss of children to gun violence and vowing to transform the politics of gun control.

Under a clear spring sky, the Million Mom March crowded the grassy expanse of the National Mall, cheering one speaker after another who assailed the National Rifle Association and its power over Congress. Many of the demonstrators wept at the stories of mothers who had lost their children, listening transfixed to the families shattered by shootings from Columbine High School, in Littleton, Colorado, where 15 died last year to the Michigan elementary school where a 6-year-old girl was killed by a classmate on Feb. 29.

"I come to you today, two days after what would have been her seventh birthday," said Veronica McQueen, the Michigan girl's mother. "I am a mom with a terrible tragedy, and I hope it never, ever happens again."

It was a Mother's Day of high emotion and powerful imagery, both here and in more than 60 other demonstrations scheduled around the country this weekend. Many in the crowd on the Mall today wore T-shirts with the photographs of family members killed by guns. Judi Ellis of Toledo, Ohio, carried a placard that declared, "I march today to save a child tomorrow," with a picture of her son, who was killed in 1995, before he left for college. "You're not supposed to bury your son," she said.

—Robin Toner, *New York Times,* May 15, 2000

AP/Wide World

jammed into cells built for one. Overpopulation is a major factor in the outbreaks of riots and cases of hostage-taking in the prisons.

Yet the U.S. Supreme Court has ruled 8–1 that prison overcrowding is not forbidden by the Constitution. In a 1981 decision, the Burger Court held that "harsh" prison conditions are the price of crime, "part of the penalty that criminal offenders pay for their offenses against society." Although prison conditions may not be "grossly disproportionate to the severity of the crime . . . persons convicted of serious crimes cannot be free of discomfort."[84] The case challenged the housing of two men in cells of 63 square feet in an Ohio prison. In 1984 the Court held that the Constitution protected prisoners far less than other citizens.[85]

In 1992, the Supreme Court ruled that federal courts are no longer obliged to hear appeals by state prison inmates.[86] In the same year, however, the Court decided an important case strengthening prisoners' rights when it ruled that beatings or other excessive use of force by guards may violate the Constitution even when there is no serious injury to the prisoner.[87]

The nation's prisons, instead of rehabilitating offenders, may contribute to the crime rate by serving in many instances as "human warehouses" for the custody of convicts. Close to half of felons released from prison commit new crimes. In many cases little is done to prepare prisoners for their return to the outside world. More than half of all state prisons have no vocational training programs. A presidential study commission concluded that "for a great many offenders . . . corrections does not correct."[88] Moreover, state parole systems are badly overburdened. As a result, the decision on when to release prisoners is often arbitrary and unfair, creating further bitterness among those who must remain behind bars.

As noted earlier, tensions in America's prisons sometimes run so high that they explode into prison riots, in which guards or other hostages are seized and inmates demand better conditions. One of the most dramatic and tragic outbreaks occurred in 1971 at Attica, a maximum-security state prison in New York State. The dismal conditions at Attica were typical of many state prison systems: old and overcrowded buildings, with guards who were often poorly trained and sometimes brutal. Racial tensions ran high at Attica, as at other prisons where many inmates are African American and most of the guards white.

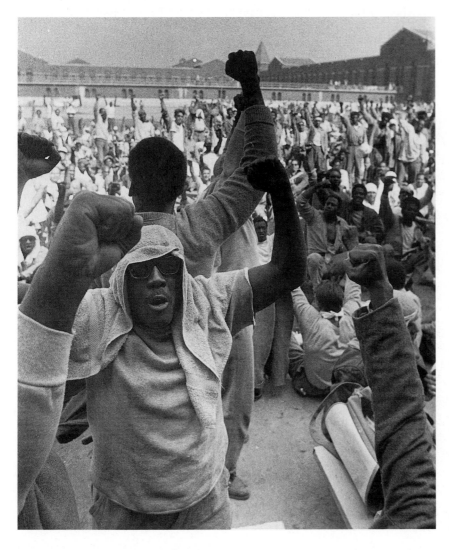

Attica, 1971
AP/Wide World

For four days, convicts took control of the courtyard of a cell block and held hostages. Governor Nelson Rockefeller ordered 200 state troopers to storm the prison. Thirty-two inmates and 11 hostages died. Almost all of them had been killed in the hail of troopers' bullets. A special New York State commission that investigated the bloodshed at Attica concluded that the conditions that sparked the revolt were, in a sense, universal: "Attica is every prison; and every prison is Attica."[89]

The Police

Police in the United States walk a tightrope; often underpaid, with inadequate personnel and resources, they are expected to fight crime, enforce the law, keep the peace, and provide a wide variety of social and community services.

Police must spend much of their time performing community services—from directing traffic to rescuing stray cats. These duties greatly reduce the amount of time police can spend fighting crime. As the armed embodiment of the law, police are sometimes caught between the established order and dissident or minority groups seeking change; for instance, mutual hostility between police and militant minorities or political protesters erupted in tragic violence and bloodshed in the 1960s. And police face violence in fighting crime. From 1970 through 1999, there were 3,102 police officers in the United States slain in the line of duty.[90]

"The policeman," in the words of a task force report to one presidential commission, "lives on the grinding edge of social conflict, without a well-defined, well-understood notion of what he is supposed to be doing there."[91] And differences in the social and cultural background of police and minorities or dissidents may contribute to tension between them.

Many Americans strongly support and defend the police. Even when police employed violence against young antiwar demonstrators at the 1968 Democratic National Convention in Chicago, 56 percent of the public approved of the way the police had acted.* Later, a staff study of a presidential commission adjudged the events at Chicago "a police riot."[92] But in times of turmoil and fear of violence, many Americans appear to regard "law and order" as a requirement that takes precedence over all other considerations, including the constitutional right of peaceful dissent.†

---

*Gallup poll, September 17, 1968. The question asked of 1,507 persons was, "Do you approve or disapprove of the way the Chicago police dealt with the young people who were registering their protest against the Vietnam war at the time of the Chicago Convention?" The nationwide findings were: approve, 56 percent; disapprove, 31 percent; no opinion, 13 percent.
†For example, 76 percent of the people questioned in a telephone survey by the Columbia Broadcasting System said extremist groups should not be allowed to "organize protests" against the government; 55 percent said news media should not report stories that the government considers harmful to the national interest; and 58 percent thought that a suspect in a serious crime should be held in jail by police until they can get enough evidence to charge him with the crime. See *The CBS News Poll*, Survey Operations Department, CBS News Election Unit, March 20, 1970, pp. 1–6.

Wally Skalij/*Daily Breeze*/Zuma

On the other hand, when a state jury acquitted four white Los Angeles police officers in the beating of black motorist Rodney King, 77 percent of respondents thought that the jury verdict was "not justified."[93] In this instance, the beating had been videotaped by a citizen and shown repeatedly on television. The acquittal touched off the devastating riots in Los Angeles in April 1992. In 1993, two of the police officers, Stacey C. Koon and Laurence Powell, were convicted in federal court of violating King's civil rights, and sent to prison. The two other officers were acquitted of the federal charges. Because so many Americans had viewed the brutal beating on TV, the episode, the trials, and the riots focused new attention on the controversial question of how far police may go in enforcing the law before they themselves become lawbreakers.

And police do break the law. In New York, in the year 2000, three officers were convicted and given substantial prison terms in the brutalization of a Haitian immigrant, Abner Louima, in the bathroom of a police station in Brooklyn. A year earlier, four New York City plainclothes officers fired 41 shots at Amadou Diallo, an immigrant from Guinea, who had been standing, unarmed, outside his house in the Bronx. Diallo's death—he had been hit by 19 bullets—led to widespread protests in the city, but the four officers were acquitted of all charges.

During the O. J. Simpson murder trial it was revealed that a star witness, Los Angeles Detective Mark Fuhrman, had given interviews to a film writer in which he talked of planting evidence in other cases and abusing minorities. In Philadelphia, several police officers pleaded guilty to charges ranging from creating false evidence to implicate innocent people, to selling drugs, lying under oath, and beating up victims, mostly poor blacks. In a typical case, James Morris, a restaurant owner, was convicted of drug trafficking and sentenced to three years in prison on completely false evidence given by a police officer, who claimed he witnessed a drug buy that never took place. As a result of the Philadelphia police scandal, 116 criminal convictions were overturned, and more were expected; a total of 1,800 cases were under review.[94]

More recently, in Los Angeles a similar police scandal erupted. It was disclosed that some L.A.P.D. officers had planted guns, drugs, or other evidence on persons they arrested. More than 100 cases may have been tainted in this manner, many in a gang-infested inner-city neighborhood. Police planted a gun on one unarmed man, Javier Francisco Ovando, after he was shot by officers, leaving him paralyzed for life. He was sentenced in 1997 to 23 years in prison but freed by a judge two years later when the truth emerged.[95]

The controversy over the role of the police in responding to social protest has to some extent tended

Los Angeles, March 2000: The police scandal led to this protest by demonstrators.
AP/Wide World

FIGURE 15-2

Crime and Law Enforcement

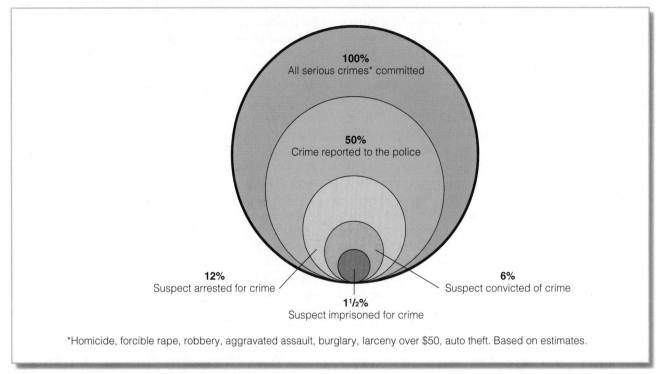

100%
All serious crimes* committed

50%
Crime reported to the police

12%
Suspect arrested for crime

6%
Suspect convicted of crime

1¹/₂%
Suspect imprisoned for crime

*Homicide, forcible rape, robbery, aggravated assault, burglary, larceny over $50, auto theft. Based on estimates.

SOURCE: *To Establish Justice, To Insure Domestic Tranquility,* Final Report of the National Commission on the Causes and Prevention of Violence (Washington, D.C.: U.S. Government Printing Office, December 1969), p. xviii.

to obscure the conventional role of the police officer in the system of criminal justice. Police officers are, after all, highly visible and important public officials. As "the cop on the beat" dealing with everyday social conflict and crime, they exercise great discretionary powers.[96] Should a fight be broken up, a speeding car stopped, a street-corner crowd dispersed? The police officer must decide. To a great extent, law enforcement policy is made by the police.

Police do not capture most lawbreakers, however. There is a huge gap between the number of crimes reported and the number of criminals arrested. Crime can be viewed as a series of concentric circles, in which the smallest, innermost circle represents persons actually convicted and sent to prison. (See Figure 15-2.)

The Department of Justice

Although criminal justice and law enforcement are primarily the responsibility of state and local authorities, the federal government wields substantial power in this field. The Department of Justice in recent years has emerged as a major policy-making agency in relation to a broad range of political, legal, and social issues. The department is headed by the attorney general, who is both a cabinet officer and the president's chief legal adviser.

 for more information about the Department of Justice, see: www.usdoj.gov

One of the Justice Department's basic responsibilities is to conduct criminal prosecutions in the federal courts. This means that the attorney general has tremendous power to make political as well as legal decisions about who will be prosecuted and who will not.

Sometimes the attorney general can deflect public criticism from the president. In 1993, for example, after 85 persons died in the FBI siege of a religious cult's compound in Waco, Texas, Attorney General Janet Reno took responsibility. As a result, much of the criticism of the attack was focused on Reno and the FBI rather than on President Clinton and the White House.

The attorney general is sometimes a controversial political figure in Washington. This was dramatically illustrated by the turmoil that enveloped Attorney General Edwin Meese III during the twilight of the Reagan administration. For months, Meese's finances were under investigation. An independent counsel was appointed to probe the allegations. The news media focused heavily on the Meese case, and the nation was treated to the spectacle of an attorney general spending the bulk of his time testifying before grand juries, answering questions by investigators, and defending his record. By the spring of 1988, Meese had clearly become a liability to Vice President George Bush, who was already assured of the Republican presidential nomination. Finally, Meese resigned in midsummer, to the relief of the Bush camp.

Similarly, during the Clinton years, Attorney General Reno was the target of a constant drumbeat of Republican criticism, much of it centered on her refusal to name an independent counsel to investigate charges of fund-raising abuses by the Democrats in the 1996 presidential campaign. Republican lawmakers accused Reno of protecting Vice President Al Gore, the party's presidential nominee in 2000.

As noted earlier, during the Watergate inquiries more than a decade before, there was deep public suspicion about the willingness of the Justice Department to prosecute high officials of the Nixon administration who had participated in wrongdoing or helped to cover it up. Against this background, a special prosecutor, Harvard law professor Archibald Cox, was named to pursue the Watergate case and related cases. When Cox sought presidential tape recordings to learn whether Nixon himself had participated in covering up the burglary of Democratic headquarters and in obstructing justice, Nixon dismissed him. Attorney General Elliot L. Richardson then resigned, along with the deputy attorney general.* There were immediate demands for the appointment of a new special prosecutor. Responding to these pressures, Nixon named Texas attorney Leon Jaworski to the post. The appointment, dismissal, and replacement of the special Watergate prosecutor was a dramatic illustration of the politically sensitive nature of the Justice Department.

In the wake of Watergate, Congress in 1978 passed the Ethics in Government Act, providing for appointment of an independent counsel in cases involving possible crimes by high officials. The law proved controversial, in part because of independent counsel Kenneth Starr's relentless pursuit of President Clinton in what had begun as the Whitewater investigation. Congress allowed the law to expire in 1999, except for investigations already in progress. As a result, Robert W. Ray, Starr's successor, continued his inquiry into whether the Clinton Administration or the president had broken the law. As noted earlier, the independent counsel closed the Whitewater inquiry in September 2000. However, Ray continued to weigh whether to indict Clinton after the president's term ended.

An attorney general might publicly disclaim any suggestion that the decisions of that office were political. But the attorney general is a cabinet officer responsible to the president. As a result, both the attorney general and the Justice Department play a significant political role. The attorney general's political viewpoint is normally an important factor weighed by the presi-

dent in selecting an individual for that post. In exercising discretion about whom to prosecute, the attorney general may also reflect personal ideology and outlook. Should an antitrust suit be brought against a major American corporation, such as Microsoft? Should the vice president of the United States be brought to trial on criminal charges? Should the department increase its efforts to combat organized crime? The attorney general may decide.

The Justice Department prosecutes persons accused of federal crimes through its U.S. attorneys in each of the federal judicial districts. Although U.S. attorneys are appointed by the president, subject to Senate approval, they serve under the attorney general. Under the supervision of the department's criminal division, the U.S. attorney in each district initiates investigations and decides whether to prosecute or to seek a grand jury indictment in criminal cases.

Separate divisions of the Justice Department deal with criminal, civil, antitrust, tax, civil rights, and environment and natural resources cases. A special unit in the criminal division handles cases involving organized crime. The Justice Department also includes the Immigration and Naturalization Service, the Drug Enforcement Administration, and the Bureau of Prisons, which is in charge of federal prisons and youth centers.

The FBI

Best known of all the arms of the Justice Department is the Federal Bureau of Investigation. In 1999 the FBI had a budget of $3.1 billion and employed 27,800 people (about 23 percent of all the Justice Department's employees). Of the total, 11,400 were FBI special agents; most of the rest were laboratory technicians, clerks, and secretaries.[97] The FBI is the investigative arm of the Justice Department, and its jurisdiction is limited to suspected violations of federal law. It has 56 field offices and 37 offices abroad for liaison with foreign police and intelligence services.[98] In its files are 226 million fingerprint cards, representing approximately 79 million individuals.[99]

Online *for more information about the FBI, see: www.fbi.gov*

Senate and House investigations of the FBI in the 1970s, in the wake of the Watergate scandal, revealed that for years—while the FBI enjoyed a highly favorable public image—the bureau had systematically engaged in illegal activities that violated the constitutional rights of American citizens. FBI agents, for example, engaged in hundreds of burglaries of individuals and groups to plant microphones or to photograph documents. From 1956 to 1971, the bureau, through its counterintelligence program (COINTELPRO), harassed American citizens and disrupted their organizations through a wide variety of clandestine techniques, some of which broke up marriages or endangered lives.

---

*A separate confrontation over Nixon's tapes in 1974 resulted in the Supreme Court ruling requiring him to surrender additional tape recordings.

Moreover, it was disclosed that since the administration of Franklin D. Roosevelt, the FBI had gathered intelligence on domestic groups and individuals with only the shakiest legal authority to do so. It had files on entertainers such as John Lennon, Elvis Presley, and Lucille Ball; on movie stars, including Marilyn Monroe; and on a wide range of other persons, from Eleanor Roosevelt, Pablo Picasso, and Albert Einstein to Al Capone and Walt Disney—even on justices of the U.S. Supreme Court.[100] For years the bureau compiled various indexes or lists of politically unreliable persons to be rounded up in an emergency. And as the congressional investigations also disclosed, the FBI opened first-class mail in violation of the law.[101] All of these disclosures of FBI abuses surfaced several years after the death of the bureau's longtime chief, J. Edgar Hoover, but many of the illegal practices had taken place under his leadership.

For 48 years, until his death in 1972 at the age of 77, Hoover was director of the FBI. Under eight presidents, Hoover and the FBI acquired an unprecedented degree of power and independence. One major source of Hoover's power was the secret dossiers and files of the FBI. A member of Congress who had a drinking problem, or who had accepted a campaign contribution from someone rumored to have connections with organized crime, or who was having an extramarital affair, might have good reason to fear the contents of the FBI's file on him or her.

Even presidents respected Hoover's power, and under his reign the FBI, although an arm of the Justice Department, became largely independent of the attorney general. With a masterful gift for publicity, Hoover invented the "Ten Most Wanted" list and helped to project the image of the "G-man" as square-jawed, clean-cut, and infallible. Through movies, a television series, and guided tours of its headquarters for the millions of tourists who visit Washington each year, the FBI became the most publicized agency of the federal government. During Hoover's years, it was able to obtain almost anything it wanted from Congress, including a new $126 million headquarters building named for Hoover that opened in 1975.

Even before Hoover's death, the FBI had become controversial. The majority of Americans traditionally thought of it in favorable terms, as an agency adept at catching bank robbers and spies. But other Americans worried about the concentration of power in the hands of the FBI, and they feared that its wiretaps and dossiers might be used for political ends, or to enhance the power of the director. Because Hoover's political views were generally conservative, liberals feared that the FBI was more concerned about pursuing domestic radicals than organized crime.

In addition, events during the Vietnam War focused widespread public attention on the American system of justice and raised important questions about its operations, adequacy, and fairness. For example, in prosecuting antiwar protesters, the government sometimes

J. Edgar Hoover
Copyright © Okomoto/Photo Researchers

relied on informers who encouraged or committed the same acts for which their associates were later tried. During the same period, federal grand juries were used to gather intelligence against the peace movement and to suppress political dissent. And as mentioned earlier, through COINTELPRO, its domestic counterintelligence program, the FBI secretly harassed American citizens and in some cases even endangered lives.

The FBI's reputation suffered after President Nixon named an old political associate, L. Patrick Gray, as acting director to succeed Hoover. According to evidence published by congressional investigating committees, Gray—at Nixon's request, relayed through the Central Intelligence Agency—slowed down and restricted the FBI investigation of the Watergate burglary. And Gray admitted that he had burned key files in the Watergate case.

In 1976 Congress enacted a law that limits the director of the FBI to one 10-year term of office. President Carter named a federal judge, William Webster of Missouri, as head of the FBI in 1978. The FBI's image improved substantially under Webster, who remained director until 1987, when President Reagan named him to head the CIA. Reagan appointed another federal judge, William S. Sessions of Texas, as the new director of the FBI. Sessions was praised for bringing more women and minorities into the FBI but was forced to resign in 1993 after questions were raised about his personal travel and other alleged infractions of bureau rules. To replace him, President Clinton appointed Louis J. Freeh, a federal judge in New York and a former prosecutor. President George W. Bush named Robert S. Mueller, III, as FBI director.

The FBI's entanglement in the Watergate case had raised a question exactly opposite of that posed by

Rex Babin/*Times Union*

Hoover's independence. Patrick Gray's actions had illustrated the danger of an FBI chief who was too responsive to political control. In the early 1980s, some critics questioned whether the FBI had improperly entrapped members of Congress in its "Abscam" investigation, in which seven lawmakers were indicted and convicted for taking bribes from agents posing as wealthy Arabs. Clearly the role and power of a secretive police agency raises disturbing problems in a democracy.

At the same time, the FBI is expected to take the lead in protecting the nation from terrorism. In 2002, a joint congressional committee investigating the 9/11 terrorist attacks criticized both the FBI and the CIA for failing to predict or prevent the attacks on the World Trade Center and the Pentagon. Some of the criticism centered on an unheeded warning by an FBI agent in Phoenix that potential terrorists might be training in flight schools in the United States—as the 9/11 hijackers had done.

In addition, the FBI drew criticism for its handling of the case of Zacarias Moussaoui, a man suspected of close links to the 19 9/11 hijackers. An agent in the Minneapolis office of the FBI complained that efforts to obtain permission to search the suspect's laptop were rejected by officials at FBI headquarters in Washington.

Less than a month after the 9/11 attacks, letters containing deadly anthrax spores were mailed to media offices and two United States senators, Patrick J. Leahy, Democrat of Vermont, and Tom Daschle, Democrat of South Dakota, causing the death of five persons, including two postal workers, and infecting twenty-two others.

The FBI had the responsibility of trying to identify and arrest the anonymous mailer of the anthrax letters. It was not immediately clear whether the murders-by-

mail were the work of home-grown or foreign terrorists, but the authorities believed that the letters were most likely mailed by a scientist or laboratory worker, perhaps someone who had been employed in a government lab that conducted research on biological weapons. The FBI questioned and gave polygraph tests to dozens of scientists who had access to anthrax in their laboratories, and searched the homes of some of them in an effort to find the person or persons responsible.

The Criminal Courts

Americans who have never had a brush with the law may tend to think of the system of criminal justice in terms of "due process of law," trial by jury, and the right to counsel—in short, the adversary system of justice, in which the power of the state is balanced by the defendant's constitutional rights and by the presumption, not specifically written in the Constitution, but deeply rooted in Anglo-Saxon law, that a person is innocent until proven guilty beyond a reasonable doubt.*

Plea Bargaining   These protections may prevail when a case goes to trial. But in fact, the great majority of cases never go to trial. According to one report, "Most defendants who are convicted—as many as 90 percent in some jurisdictions—are not tried. They plead guilty, often as the result of negotiations about the charge or

---

*The Supreme Court has held that the due process clause of the Constitution requires the presumption that a criminal defendant is innocent until proven guilty beyond a reasonable doubt. See *Davis* v. *United States*, 160 U.S. 469 (1895); *Coffin* v. *United States*, 156 U.S. 432 (1895); and *In the Matter of Samuel Winship*, 396 U.S. 885 (1970).

the sentence."[102] In other words, the machinery of the adversary system of justice exists—but it may not be used. Most guilty pleas are the result of backstage discussions between the prosecutor and defense counsel. The practice is commonly known as plea bargaining, or, less elegantly, as "copping a plea."

The practice sometimes serves everyone's needs but the defendant's. The government is saved the time and expense of a public prosecution; the defense attorney can collect a fee and move on to the next client; the judge can keep the business of the court moving along. But the guilt or innocence of the accused person is not proven.

Usually, the plea bargaining process works this way: A defendant agrees to plead guilty to a less serious charge than might be proven at a trial, and often to cooperate as a witness for the prosecution; in return the prosecutor agrees to reduce the charges or recommend leniency. Often, the accused person will get a lighter sentence this way than if the case went to trial and resulted in a conviction. There is no guarantee, however, that the judge will act as the prosecutor has promised. And, an innocent person may be persuaded to plead guilty to a crime he or she did not commit.

In 1970 the Supreme Court upheld the practice of plea bargaining.[103] The Court ruled that a guilty plea, entered voluntarily and intelligently with the advice of counsel, was constitutional.

Sometimes an accused person will simply plead guilty without plea bargaining, perhaps in the hope of receiving a lighter sentence. If the accused pleads not guilty, a trial date is set.

Court Delay   American courts do not have enough judges to handle the volume of cases that come before them. In a single year the courts may dispose of more than 3 million cases.[104]

The high caseload, the lack of judges, and poor administration of the courts all result in major delays in the criminal process. The courts are badly backlogged; in many large cities the average delay between arrest and trial is close to a year. In Great Britain the period from arrest to final appeal frequently takes four months, but the same process in many states in America averages 10 to 18 months.

Bail Reform   During the long wait for their trials, accused persons may be free on bail or detained. Bail is a system designed to ensure that defendants will appear in court when their cases are called; typically, arrested persons go before a judge or magistrate who fixes an amount of money to be "posted" with the court as security in exchange for the defendant's freedom. If defendants do not have the money, a bondsman may post bail for them, but the defendants must pay the bondsman a premium of 5 to 20 percent. If the accused persons cannot raise bail either way, they may have to remain in jail until their case comes up. If they go free on bail but fail to appear for their trial, the bail is forfeited.

The rights of the individual and the community conflict during the pretrial period. The accused person may have a job and a family to support, and he or she needs to be free in order to prepare a defense. On the other hand, the community demands that the accused appear for trial; that, after all, is the rationale of the bail system.

Such a system obviously discriminates against the poor, who may not be able to buy their way out of jail. "Millions of men and women are, through the American bail system, held each year in 'ransom' in American jails, committed to prison cells often for prolonged periods before trial," Ronald Goldfarb has written. "Because they are poor or friendless, they may spend days, weeks, or months in confinement, often to be acquitted of wrongdoing in the end."[105]

Until the Bail Reform Act of 1966, federal judges had often deliberately set a high bail for defendants they considered dangerous, in the hope that the bail could not be paid; the practice was an illegal but widespread system of pretrial detention. Under the 1966 act this subterfuge was no longer possible. Federal judges were required to release defendants before trial except in capital cases—in which death was the possible punishment—and unless there were good reasons to believe that the defendant would flee if released. A federal judge might still set bail, but defendants could no longer be held because they did not have the money. The reform legislation does not apply to state or local courts, however, where the amount of bail remains up to the judge. And in those courts, many defendants are still imprisoned because they lack bail money.

The Trial   Under the Fifth Amendment, a person charged with a serious federal crime must first be accused in an **indictment,** a finding by a grand jury that there is enough evidence against an individual to warrant a criminal trial. The Supreme Court has not applied this requirement to the states, where defendants are more often brought to trial on a **criminal information,** a formal accusation by a prosecutor, made under oath before a court, charging a person with a crime. The grand jury, so named because it is larger than the trial jury, does not determine guilt or innocence. It does seek to establish whether there is enough evidence to justify a criminal trial.

Within the states, although procedures vary in different jurisdictions, in general, arrested persons are brought before a magistrate for a preliminary hearing at which they are either held or released on bail. They may be assigned counsel if they cannot afford a private attorney. The district attorney or prosecutor next may seek a grand jury indictment or may present an information to a judge. In two-thirds of the states, however, most grand juries have been eliminated in recent years. Many people are reluctant to serve, sometimes for months, on a grand jury. And, because of police corruption in some localities and skepticism by the public about police testimony, prosecutors can no longer depend on grand juries to issue indictments. For that reason, district attorneys often prefer to go before a judge to present an information.

Once formally accused, either by an indictment or information, defendants are brought into court for **arraignment,** the proceeding before a judge in which the formal charges of an indictment or information are read to an accused person, who may plead guilty or not guilty. (In some cases they may plead "no-contest" and put themselves at the mercy of the court.) At every critical stage, a criminal suspect is entitled to have the advice of a lawyer, and defendants too poor to hire one must be offered or assigned counsel in all criminal cases where conviction might mean imprisonment.

Jury trials are required in federal courts in all criminal cases and in all common-law civil suits where the sum involved is larger than $20. Under a 1968 Supreme Court decision, states must also provide jury trials in "serious" criminal cases,[106] which the Supreme Court defined in 1970 as all cases in which the penalty for conviction could exceed six months' imprisonment.[107] However, in 1971 the Supreme Court held 6–3 that juveniles do not have a constitutional right to a trial by jury in state courts.[108] (In a federal court, if a defendant wishes to waive the right to a jury trial and have the judge try the case, it is usually possible, but many states do not permit this practice.)

Federal juries must render a unanimous verdict in all criminal and civil cases, but more than two-thirds of the states permit a less-than-unanimous verdict (usually by three-fourths of the jurors) in civil cases. In 1972 the Supreme Court ruled that unanimous jury verdicts were not required even in state criminal cases.[109]

In a number of states, juries may consist of fewer than the traditional number of 12 persons; the Supreme Court in 1970 upheld the constitutionality of such juries.[110] Federal criminal juries contain 12 members.

But most federal civil cases may be tried with juries of six persons.[111]

Although courtroom procedures vary on the federal, state, and local levels, in general the pattern is the same. First, the jury is chosen, with the prosecution and the defense each having the right to challenge and replace prospective jurors. Then the prosecution presents its case, and the defense cross-examines the witnesses for the prosecution. After that, the defense presents its own witnesses, who are cross-examined in turn by the prosecutor. A defendant does not have to take the stand to testify on his or her own behalf. A trial may be over in a few hours or drag on for months. Finally, the judge delivers a charge to the jury, explaining the law and emphasizing that the defendant's guilt must be proven beyond a reasonable doubt. The jury deliberates, then renders its verdict.

After the trial, of course, comes sentencing if the defendant is convicted. In federal courts, judges have relatively little discretion, because since 1987 they have been required to mete out prison terms under guidelines resulting from the Sentencing Reform Act of 1984. The law created a commission that wrote guidelines for sentencing persons convicted of federal crimes. The purpose of the law was to ensure uniform sentencing so that defendants in different parts of the country convicted of the same type of crime received similar sentences. The guidelines take into account both the seriousness of the crime and the prior convictions of the person to be sentenced. But some critics argue that the law has reduced the power of judges to take into account special circumstances that might apply in some cases. The law also eliminated parole in the federal prison system.

Congress, in addition, has set mandatory minimum penalties for certain federal crimes. One of the most controversial, enacted in 1988, imposed a five-year mandatory sentence for anyone convicted of possession of 5 grams of crack cocaine with intent to distribute. But

"Of course everybody is looking at you accusingly. You are, after all, the accused."

Criminal Justice in America **521**

"We find the defendant not guilty but not all that innocent, either."

a person must be convicted of possessing 100 times that amount of powdered cocaine with intent to distribute to receive the same sentence. In the mid-1980s, crack cocaine, an inexpensive drug, was widely used, often by African Americans, in the inner city. Powdered cocaine, by contrast, was often the drug of choice for many affluent white-collar addicts. The disparity meant that many low-income blacks were crowded into federal prisons for crack possession, compared to a much lower proportion of whites convicted on cocaine charges.

In California and almost half the states, public reaction to increased crime resulted in passage of "three strikes and you're out" laws. In California, for example, persons convicted of a third felony were required to serve a minimum of 25 years in prison. In 1996, however, the California Supreme Court ruled that judges could ignore the law and give felons lighter sentences. Several other states have adopted some version of these "three strikes" laws. And the crime bill passed by Congress in 1994 contained a "three strikes" provision mandating life in prison for a third violent federal offense.* Critics contend that the laws have little impact, because most states already provide long prison terms for habitual offenders. Others argue that the laws may eventually result in a prison population of older offenders who are no longer a likely threat to society. Crime, however, is a popular political issue, and many political leaders, particularly in election campaigns, try to outdo one another in portraying themselves as public servants who will "get tough" on crime.

Capital Punishment

In January of the year 2000 the Republican governor of Illinois, George Ryan, halted all executions in the state because of a "shameful record of convicting innocent people and putting them on death row."

---

*Under the "three strikes" provision, the first two violent felony convictions may be for state or federal crimes, but the third must be a federal offense other than a drug conviction.

It was the first time the governor of a state had declared a halt to executions. Although Ryan supported the death penalty in principle, he noted that 13 men had been sentenced to death in Illinois since 1977 for crimes they did not commit, but were later found innocent and set free by the courts. "I cannot support a system, which in its administration, has proven so fraught with error," he said "and has come so close to the ultimate nightmare, the state's taking of innocent life."[112]

Governor Ryan's action reflected increasing concern by many Americans that the death penalty in some cases may have resulted in the execution of persons who were not guilty of the crimes for which they were convicted. In addition, there was growing concern over racial disparity in sentencing; many opponents of capital punishment argued that a disproportionate number of African Americans were awaiting execution, compared to the nation's total black population. For example, 36 percent of death row inmates were black, although African Americans constitute only 12 percent of the U.S. population.[113] And support for capital punishment, although still high, had fallen to 66 percent, its lowest level in 19 years. (See Table 15-4.)

The death penalty even became embroiled in the 2000 presidential election, because George W. Bush, the Republican nominee, was the governor of Texas, the state that led the nation in executions. "As far as I'm concerned," Bush declared in June 2000, "there has not been one innocent person executed since I've been governor."[114] He made this statement, a standard reply to critics, shortly before the controversial execution in Texas of Gary Graham, who was convicted on the testimony of one woman who said she had glimpsed his face for a few seconds in a parking lot. During the campaign, both Bush and his Democratic opponent, Al Gore, supported the death penalty.

By the year 2000, there were more than 3,500 convicts on death row in the United States, not only the largest number in U.S. history, but the largest in any country in the world.[115]

MAKING A DIFFERENCE

JOURNALISM 101: FREEING PRISONERS ON DEATH ROW

David Protess, a journalism professor at Northwestern University, examines death row cases, assigning them to his students, and teaching them to pore over documents, reenact crimes, and interview witnesses.

In 1996, Protess and three students helped prove the innocence of four men who had spent 18 years in prison for a double murder in Ford Heights, Illinois.

Last month, an investigation by Protess and six students led to the release of Anthony Porter, 43, who had spent 16 years on death row for the murder of a Chicago couple.

Protess's pursuit of cases, his enthusiastic style, and the skills he teaches have earned him admirers among students, journalists, and professors. Still, he gets questions about his passion in these cases.

"Do I bring a passion to my work?" he asked. "Yeah, I do. Some believe that the higher calling of journalism is that after you find the truth, you can in fact right the wrong."

He added: "In some cases, the truth was the guy was guilty, and those students got an A."

Protess now gets three to four requests a day from inmates and lawyers around the country.

He looks for cases with no incriminating physical evidence like blood or semen, no credible witness, no reliable confession, and other "viable suspects." He emphasizes that his investigations are collaborative efforts.

David Protess wants his students to learn investigative skills, but he also wants to solve cases.

—Adapted from the *New York Times*, March 3, 1999

For a brief period of four years, between 1972 and 1976, the U.S. Supreme Court had suspended the death penalty. In 1972, in a 5–4 decision, it had ruled out executions under any law then in effect, holding that capital punishment, as then administered, was unconstitutional.[116] At that time, 38 states, the federal government, and the District of Columbia had laws authorizing the death penalty for various crimes, although no one had been executed in the United States since 1967.

In the years following the 1972 decision, 38 states and the federal government passed new laws providing for capital punishment and designed to satisfy the standards set forth by the Supreme Court. Most of the state laws prescribed death sentences for such crimes as mass murder; killing a police officer, firefighter, or prison guard; and murder while committing rape, kidnapping, arson, or hijacking. Federal law provided the death penalty for crimes including air hijacking resulting in death, and for murder linked to drug trafficking.

On July 2, 1976, the Court ruled 7–2 that the death penalty was constitutional.[117] Specifically, the majority held that capital punishment, if administered under adequate guidelines, did not violate the Eighth Amendment's prohibition against "cruel and unusual punishments." The Supreme Court ruled that judges and juries could impose the death sentence as long as they had sufficient information to determine whether the sentence was appropriate in each case. The Court upheld state laws providing for capital punishment in Georgia, Florida, and Texas, but it struck down two other state statutes requiring automatic death sentences for murder.[118]

"We now hold that the punishment of death does not invariably violate the Constitution," the Supreme Court declared. And it noted that the framers of the Constitution accepted capital punishment: "At the time the Eighth Amendment was ratified, capital punishment was a common sanction in every state. Indeed, the first Congress of the United States enacted legislation providing death as the penalty for specified crimes."

In upholding the new capital punishment laws in 1976, the Court concluded: "It is an extreme sanction, suitable to the most extreme of crimes." Approximately half of the 611 inmates then on death row faced possible execution as a result of the Court's decision; they were imprisoned either in the three states whose laws were upheld or in states with similar statutes. In 1977

TABLE 15-4

Public Support for the Death Penalty, 1960–2000

Year	Favor	Opposed
1960	53%	36%
1971	49	40
1978	62	27
1981	66	25
1985	75	17
1988	79	16
1991	76	18
1995	77	13
2000	66	28

SOURCE: The Gallup Organization, *Gallup Social and Economic Indicators*, "Death Penalty," February 14–15, 2000, online at <www.gallup.com/poll/indicators/inddeath_pen.asp>.

Howard has just served us four plates of the best chocolate chip cookies I've ever eaten when Warden Burl Cain tells us that Howard killed a man and is going to die an old man in prison for it. It's as blunt as that, but it exposes the intimate, relevant detail of Howard's life. "I don't know how Howard killed somebody, and I don't care," says Cain about his favorite prisoner. "I care about how he is now." Even though Louisiana offers no hope for parole, Cain says he believes Howard is rehabilitated and should be freed if he can meet the family of the man he killed and receive its forgiveness. Howard nods in agreement, because justice is as simple and brutal as that, even if he is going to die here in Angola prison.

Here in Angola, heaven and hell and sin and redemption aren't philosophy. They are answers to why you're here and who you are and where you are going to end up.

There are 88 men on death row, and Burl Cain has killed more people than most of them. He has set five down by lethal injection, and he has held each of their hands as they died. The table has five straps on the gurney—two leg manacles, two wristbands and one chest belt.

At 18,000 acres, it's the largest prison in the United States, with the lowest-paid guards, few of whom have graduated from high school. It's a place that *Collier's* magazine once called "the worst prison in America," where in 1951, in an effort to protest the brutal conditions, 31 prisoners sliced their Achilles tendons so they wouldn't be sent to work.

At the prison museum Cain has built, where all the T-shirts, coffee mugs and videos have the name ANGOLA printed in big letters, Cain points his thick

fingers at the pictures of men he has executed. "They're special people to me."

There are 88 more men waiting to be made special. Everyone spends all day on his bed, silent, reading the Bible or playing chess against a neighbor he can't see except for the hand that reaches through the bars into the hall to move pieces. Jenny Jones is on the TV, and she is looking good, but no one looks. Instead the inmates study the Bible, which they know better than some preachers.

These men, like most prisoners, don't get many visitors. So Cain says his main job is to give the 5,018 hopeless men on this former slave-breeding farm hope, even though 86 percent of them will stay here for "life and one dark day." The dark day is the one after they die, when their body gets embalmed and waits to go home and get buried, although the truth is that when they die, no one comes, and they get buried right here on the Farm. Cain thinks he can summon hope through a four-year Bible college, or the amateur rodeo the prisoners put on every year, or having them pick cotton by hand in the fields that were once a real plantation, and still really are, for 4 cents an hour.

A few months ago, though, some prisoners lost it, lost the hope, and one of them took a guard hostage. Burl Cain couldn't talk the hope back into him, and they had a shootout. "He got one of ours, and we got one of theirs," he says. "It all worked out in the end." And wrong as that sounds, in Angola that's how it is.

—Adapted from Joel Stein, "The Lessons of Cain", *Time*, July 10, 2000

Gary Gilmore, a killer who had demanded to die, was shot by a Utah firing squad in the first execution in America in a decade. And on November 2, 1984, Margie Velma Barfield, age 51, became the first woman to be executed in the United States in 22 years. As the executions continued, the Supreme Court set a minimum age for capital punishment; in 1988, it declared unconstitutional the death penalty for juveniles who are under age 16 when they commit murder.[119]

Among the states with laws providing for the death penalty, lethal injection is the most common method, employed by 36 states, then electrocution, the gas chamber, hanging, and the firing squad. Since the federal government began keeping statistics on executions in 1930, some 3,859 persons had been executed by civil authority in the United States prior to the Supreme Court's ruling in 1972. After the death penalty was restored in 1976, there were an additional 657 executions by mid-2000, some 225 in Texas alone, bringing the total since 1930 to 4,516.[120]

At the time the U.S. Supreme Court faced the constitutional issue in 1972, at least 37 nations worldwide

had abolished imposition of the death penalty in peacetime. In western Europe, for example, only France and Spain retained capital punishment. Increasingly in the United States as well, the death penalty has come under attack, and intense legal battles have been fought to save some of the condemned men. In Texas, James D. Autry was scheduled to die in 1983: "Already strapped to the execution table, with the intravenous needles stuck in place and only 24 minutes before the poison was to flow at midnight, Autry was rescued by a stay order from Associate Justice Byron R. White."[121] The reprieve was only temporary, however; Autry was executed on March 14, 1984.

Proponents of capital punishment argue that it is appropriate punishment by society for terrible, brutal crimes, including serial murders. They argue as well that capital punishment brings a measure of justice to the families of the victims of homicides. Moreover, the proponents contend, the death penalty may deter other murders. They also note that persons convicted of murder may in time be released from prison and may kill again.

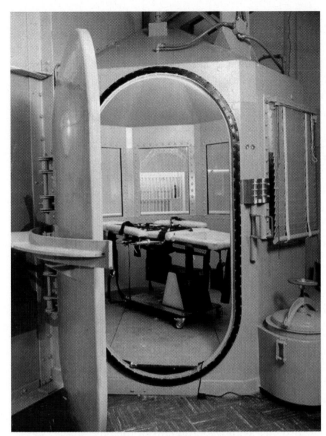

The death chamber at San Quentin prison in California
AP/California Dept. of Corrections/Wide World

John Gotti
Copyright © Robin Graubard/Sygma

A number of studies, however, have concluded that capital punishment is not necessarily an effective deterrent—there have been more than 300,000 slayings in the United States since the death penalty was restored—and opponents also argue that there is always the possibility that innocent persons will be executed if justice miscarries. One study of hundreds of capital cases between 1900 and 1985 concluded that in 350 of these cases an innocent person had been convicted, and that 23 of these prisoners were executed.[122] Since 1972, the study found, 24 innocent persons had been sentenced to death; one was executed but the others were eventually released from prison.[123]

In 1996, Congress passed an antiterrorism law that included a provision designed to make it much more difficult for prisoners on death row to file successive appeals in federal courts to delay their executions. The Supreme Court upheld the law, but ruled that prisoners awaiting execution could still appeal directly to the Supreme Court in extraordinary circumstances.

ORGANIZED CRIME

In April 1992, John Gotti, the head of the Gambino crime family based in New York City, was convicted in federal court on murder and racketeering charges.

Gotti was found guilty of arranging the slaying of Paul Castellano, his predecessor as crime boss of the Gambinos, who was gunned down on the streets of Manhattan seven years earlier. He was sentenced to life in prison without parole.[*]

With his $1,000 double-breasted suits, his smile, and his mobster's swagger, Gotti had become a sort of media celebrity, a real-life "godfather." Previously acquitted in three other trials, Gotti had seemed so immune to prosecution that he had earned the sobriquet "the Teflon don." But this time, his underboss, Salvatore ("Sammy the Bull") Gravano testified against his chief. Gotti's conviction symbolized both the government's increased success in fighting organized crime and the gradual deterioration of crime families in many cities across the country. In Los Angeles, New Jersey, New England, New Orleans, Detroit, and St. Louis, the conviction of top crime bosses had weakened but not destroyed the mob.

One important tool the federal government employed in fighting the mob was the 1970 Racketeer Influenced and Corrupt Organizations Act (RICO). In addition, the FBI had used electronic surveillance to penetrate the crime families, and it relied on the federal witness-protection program to provide safety and new identities for mobsters willing to testify.

Many years before the conviction of John Gotti, a flurry of federal indictments, along with tape recordings of "bugged" conversations made public by the FBI, suggested that mobsters virtually dominated the government of Newark, New Jersey. Much of the power in Newark, at least according to these documents, was wielded not by

---

*Gotti died in a federal prison hospital in June 2002.

the elected mayor, Hugh Addonizio, but by the local crime chieftain, Anthony ("Tony Boy") Boiardo, heir to a crime empire built by his father, Ruggiero ("Richie the Boot") Boiardo.[124]

The FBI transcripts included this conversation between Angelo ("Gyp") De Carlo, identified as "Ray," and an associate named "Joe":

Joe: You know . . . it's going to take three weeks but we'll own this Hughie [Addonizio]. This guy here, I'll guarantee we'll own him. I'll use that term—in three or four weeks. . . .

Ray: Hughie [Addonizio] helped us along. He give us the city.[125]

According to another tape-recorded conversation, two of the mobsters discussed an important question—who should be appointed police director of Newark. "Tony Boy" said the decision was up to De Carlo.[126] Addonizio was later convicted of extortion and sentenced to 10 years in prison.

There is still argument over whether organized crime in America should be called the Mafia, the mob, or the syndicate, but there is little doubt that it has existed on a major scale. (Some Italian American groups have objected to the term "Mafia" on the grounds that if reflects unfairly on the majority of law-abiding Italian Americans.) Organized crime controls illegal gambling, loan sharking, narcotics, and other unlawful activities. It also owns legitimate businesses and infiltrates labor unions. In some instances it corrupts public officials by paying them to permit the mob to operate.

A presidential commission estimated some years ago that the mob operated in 80 percent of all cities of more than a million residents.[127] According to the commission, each mob "family" is organized to resemble the structure of the Mafia that has operated for more than a century in Sicily: a "boss" at the top; an underboss; a counselor; several lieutenants; beneath them, the "soldiers" or "button men"; an "enforcer" whose job is "the maiming and killing of recalcitrant members"; and a "corrupter" who buys off public officials. "The highest ruling body of the twenty-four families is the 'commission,'" a combination supreme court and board of directors composed of 9 to 12 of the most powerful bosses.[128]

"All available data indicate that organized crime flourishes only where it has corrupted local officials," the presidential commission emphasized.[129] Donald R. Cressey, an expert on organized crime, reports that in one instance a congressman resigned when ordered to do so by a crime boss. In this district, the crime syndicate "also 'owns' both judges and the officials who assign criminal cases to judges. About 90 percent of the organized crime defendants appear before the same few judges."[130]

The Justice Department's Organized Crime and Racketeering Section is the government unit in charge of attempts to curb the power of the crime syndicate. In recent years the department and the FBI have had considerable success in infiltrating and prosecuting organized crime, particularly in New York City. Despite the diminishing power of the mob there and in many cities, and the conviction of hundreds of organized crime figures, the problem has not been eradicated.

Organized crime could not thrive if some segments of the public did not demand the services it provides, including illegal drugs. Corruption of the political system is the most disturbing threat posed by the mob. "The extraordinary thing about organized crime," the presidential commission concluded, "is that America has tolerated it for so long."[131]

JUSTICE AND THE AMERICAN POLITICAL SYSTEM

Although the Supreme Court and the Constitution may seem remote from the lives of most citizens, the decisions of the Court—the ultimate outputs of the system of justice—have direct, immediate relevance for the individuals involved and much broader meaning for the political system as a whole. As Chief Justice Earl Warren noted in his last words from the bench, "The Court develops the eternal principles of our Constitution in accordance with the problems of the day."[132]

Although each specific case decided by the Supreme Court may affect only one person directly, the Court's rulings often affect society as a whole. For example, the decision of the Court in favor of the heirs of Rose Cipollone, who had smoked cigarettes for 42 years, meant that the families of persons who died of lung cancer after smoking could sue the tobacco companies on grounds that the industry knew the hazards of smoking but had conspired to cover up the risks.[133]

The decisions of the Supreme Court have great political significance as well. In the field of civil rights, for example, the Warren Court was well ahead of the executive branch or Congress. Because its power rests on public opinion, the Court cannot get too far ahead of the country, but it can, in the words of Archibald Cox, attempt to respond to the "dominant needs of the time."[134] And it can also serve as the conscience of the nation and a guardian of minorities, the poor, and the forgotten.[135]

There are serious inequalities and flaws in the American system of justice, as we have seen—backlogged criminal courts and a bail system that often penalizes poor defendants; plea bargaining in the place of trial by jury; some judges and officials who are puppets of organized crime; prisons that are overcrowded and do not rehabilitate. Some of these problems can, of course, be solved by specific reforms—bringing defendants to trial more rapidly by appointing more judges, strengthening law enforcement, improving facilities for handling juvenile offenders, and so forth.

BOSTON—For generations, maybe forever, parents have been telling their children to settle their differences with words, not fists. But usually those words didn't include phrases like "subpoena, "restraining order" or "temporary injunction."

That was before the sandbox case, pitting a 3-year-old girl, and her mother, against a 3-year-old boy, and his mother. In a possible index of the soaring litigiousness of American society, a literal sandbox squabble has turned into a full-blown legal case between statutory grown-ups, their lawyers and the state Supreme Court. . . .

The daughter of Anne Pevnev was playing with the son of Margareth Inge. The two families are neighbors, and both 3-year-olds go to the same preschool. Neither has a criminal record. . . .

Said Pevnev in her official complaint about the incident: "My daughter came to me and told me that a boy was kicking her. . . . I ran up and shouted at him to stop kicking her in the head. . . . The mother took exceptional offense at this and started screaming at me and yelling at the top of her lungs at both myself and my daughter." . . .

Judge Charles Spurlock issued a temporary restraining order to keep Jonathan away from Stacey, then summoned the parties to court. . . . After learning in court that the parties were still in diapers, he modified his order somewhat.

Attorney Howard Speicher, who represents the 3-year-old boy, said the entire affair has gotten out of hand. . . . "This is something that really never should have left the playground. . . . It's an incident that happens in every sandbox in the country, and somehow people manage to deal with it every day."

—*Washington Post*, March 9, 1996

At the same time, as one report concluded: "The most significant action that can be taken against crime is action designed to eliminate slums and ghettos, to improve education, to provide jobs. . . . We will not have dealt effectively with crime until we have alleviated the conditions that stimulate it."[136]

Ultimately, as Justice Robert Jackson observed, the third branch of government, the judiciary, maintains "the great system of balances upon which our free government is based"—the balances among the various parts of the federal system, between authority and liberty, and between the rule of the majority and the rights of the individual.[137] Chief Justice Earl Warren confessed on the day he retired that performing this task is extremely difficult, "because we have no constituency. . . . We serve only the public interest as we see it, guided only by the Constitution and our own conscience."[138]

The resolution of conflict in American society through law, rather than through force, depends on public confidence in the courts and in the process of justice. And confidence in the system of justice requires that the words "Equal Justice Under Law," carved in marble over the entrance to the Supreme Court, be translated into reality at every level of the system.

KEY TERMS

CHAPTER HIGHLIGHTS

✦ The Supreme Court and the lower federal courts comprise one of the three independent, constitutionally coequal branches of the federal government.

✦ The Supreme Court is only one part of the fragmented, decentralized system of justice in America, a system that encompasses a network of federal courts, state and local courts and prosecutors, the U.S. Department of Justice, state and local police, the Federal Bureau of Investigation, prisons and jails, probation and parole officers, and parole boards.

✦ Law is the body of rules made by government for society, interpreted by the courts, and backed by the power of the state.

✦ Much American law is based on English common law, the cumulative body of judicial decisions, custom, and precedent, rather than law created by statute.

✦ Most law that governs the actions of Americans is statutory law, law enacted by Congress, or by state legislatures or local legislative bodies; but many statutes embody principles of English common law.

✦ Civil cases concern relations between individuals or organizations, such as a divorce action, or a suit for damages arising from an automobile accident, or for violation of a business contract.

✦ Criminal cases concern crimes committed against the public order.

✦ The Supreme Court has exercised the right of judicial review, the power to declare acts of Congress or actions by the executive branch—or laws and actions at any level of local, state, and federal government—unconstitutional.

✦ Judicial activism is the philosophy that Supreme Court justices and other judges should boldly apply the Constitution to social and political questions.

✦ Judicial restraint is the philosophy that the Supreme Court should avoid constitutional questions when possible and uphold acts of Congress unless they clearly violate a specific section of the Constitution.

✦ Congress (in conjunction with the states) also possesses the power to overturn Supreme Court decisions by amending the Constitution. And Congress may attempt to overturn specific Supreme Court rulings by legislation.

✦ The Supreme Court has original jurisdiction, the right under the Constitution to hear certain kinds of cases directly, such as cases involving foreign diplomats, or cases in which one of the 50 states is a party. But the overwhelming majority of cases presented to the Court come in the form of petitions for a writ of certiorari.

✦ Under the Fifth Amendment of the Constitution, a person charged with a serious federal crime must first be accused in an indictment, a finding by a grand jury that there is enough evidence against an individual to warrant a criminal trial. In state courts, defendants are more often brought to trial on a criminal information, a formal accusation by a prosecutor, made under oath before a court, charging a person with a crime.

✦ Although the Supreme Court and the Constitution may seem remote from the lives of most citizens, the decisions of the Court—the ultimate outputs of the system of justice—have direct, immediate relevance for the individuals involved and much broader meaning for the political system as a whole.

SUGGESTED WEB SITES

http://www.supremecourtus.gov
The Supreme Court
The official Web site of the Supreme Court. Offers recent opinions, biographies of the current and past justices, and the history of the Court.

http://www.law.cornell.edu/supct
Cornell Law School—Legal Information Institute
Contains material about cases presented to the U.S. Supreme Court, and whenever possible the full text of decisions, including concurring and dissenting opinions.

http://www.oyez.nwu.edu
The Oyez Project—Northwestern University
Offers synopses and texts of U.S. Supreme Court decisions. Some arguments and decisions are available in Real Audio. Also has a "tour" of the Supreme Court and biographies of current and past justices.

http://www.findlaw.com
FindLaw
FindLaw is a Web portal focused on law and government, providing access to a comprehensive and fast-growing online library of legal resources for anyone with an interest in the law.

www.fbi.gov
Federal Bureau of Investigation
The official Web site of the FBI. The site offers crime reports, history of the FBI, and information about job opportunities.

www.sentencingproject.org
The Sentencing Project
The Sentencing Project is a nonprofit organization focusing on the problems in the U.S. prison system. Offers fact sheet and policy reports about the penal system.

www.deathpenaltyinfo.org
Death Penalty Information Center
The Death Penalty Information Center is a nonprofit organization that examines the death penalty. Contains state-by-state analysis, including the number of executions, and issues concerning the death penalty.

http://www.uscourts.gov
Federal Judiciary Homepage
The Web site for federal courts, not including the Supreme Court.

SUGGESTED READING

Abraham, Henry J. *The Judicial Process*, 7th edition* (Oxford University Press, 1998). A useful general introduction to the American judicial process. Explains the operations of local, state, and federal courts and the legal system, and compares the U.S. judicial system with that of other countries.

Baum, Lawrence. *The Supreme Court*, 6th edition (Congressional Quarterly Press, Inc., 1998). A useful general overview of the Supreme Court, its personalities, the way it conducts its business, and the Court's impact upon American politics and society.

Canon, Bradley, and Johnson, Charles. *Judicial Policies*, 2nd edition* (Congressional Quarterly Press, Inc., 1999). An insightful study of the practical consequences of Supreme Court decisions. Examines the range of persons and organizations responsible for interpreting and applying the Supreme Court's rulings—including bureaucrats, local groups, Congress, and the media. The authors also suggest that implementation of the Court's decisions can be influenced as much by politics as by legal doctrine.

Cooper, Phillip. *Battles on the Bench: Conflict on the Supreme Court* (University of Kansas Press, 1995). A revealing examination of conflict and competition among the Supreme Court justices.

Cressey, Donald R. *Theft of the Nation* (Harper & Row, 1969). A comprehensive study of organized crime in the United States by a sociologist who served as consultant to the President's Crime Commission. Describes the corruption of law enforcement and government by organized crime.

Ewick, Patricia, and Silbey, Susan. *The Common Place of Law: Stories from Everyday Life** (University of Chicago Press, 1998). A thoughtful analysis, drawing upon more than 400 interviews, of the varying ways in which citizens perceive the law. The authors explore why some people are willing to use legal institutions for dispute resolution, while others view the law with suspicion and distrust.

Friedman, Lawrence M. *American Law: An Introduction*, 2nd edition* (W.W. Norton, 1998). An excellent survey of the American legal system by a respected authority.

Howard, J. Woodford, Jr. *Courts of Appeals in the Federal Judicial System* (Princeton University Press, 1981). An innovative study of three U.S. courts of appeals. Analyzes the political values, role perceptions, and judicial opinions of the judges and examines the flow of litigation to and from the courts of appeals.

Irons, Peter, and Guitton, Stephanie, eds. *May It Please the Court** (New Press, 1993). Transcripts and audiotapes of 23 landmark cases as argued before the Supreme Court after 1955.

McCloskey, Robert G. *The American Supreme Court*, 2nd edition, edited by Sanford Levinson* (University of Chicago Press, 1994). A lucid and penetrating analysis of the role of the Supreme Court in the American system of government.

Neubauer, David W. *Judicial Process: Law, Courts, and Politics in the United States*, 2nd edition* (Harcourt Brace, 1997). A comprehensive overview of the American judicial system.

O'Brien, David. *Storm Center: The Supreme Court in American Politics*, 5th edition (W.W. Norton, 2000). A lively introduction to the Supreme Court. The author, a noted legal scholar, examines the place of the Court in American society and politics, and concludes that it has become increasingly politicized in recent years.

Perry, H. W. *Deciding to Decide: Agenda Setting in the U.S. Supreme Court** (Harvard University Press, 1991). A scholarly and award-winning book exploring the internal dynamics of the Supreme Court. Analyzes how the justices select the cases they consider.

The Supreme Court, Justice, and the Law, 3rd edition (Congressional Quarterly, 1983). A study of the Supreme Court and federal judiciary from 1969 to 1983. Includes summaries of the Court's major decisions and biographical sketches of the justices who served on the Court during those years.

Ungar, Sanford J. *FBI* (Atlantic-Little, Brown, 1976). A detailed analysis of the Federal Bureau of Investigation—its history and development, and its personnel, procedures, and power. Examines

J. Edgar Hoover's 48-year reign as director, as well as events since his death, including the Watergate investigation.

Walker, Samuel. *Police in America*, 3rd edition* (McGraw Hill, 1999). A readable introduction to police and policing practices in the United States.

Wilson, James Q., ed. *Crime and Public Policy* (Institute for Contemporary Studies, 1983). A collection of 13 articles examining crime control policies in America. Proposes a number of initiatives that might be used in the effort to combat crime.

Wise, David. *The American Police State* (Random House, 1976). Details and summarizes the abuse of power and violation of constitutional rights of individuals by the federal intelligence agencies, including the FBI, CIA, and others. Includes the major findings of the Senate and House select committees on intelligence, and additional case studies.

*Available in paperback edition.

 Visit http://politicalscience.wadsworth.com/cummings9/update/ for current InfoTrac articles and other student resources related to this chapter.

PART FOUR

Government in Operation

CHAPTER 16
Foreign Policy and National Security

On September 20, 2001, nine days after the attack on the World Trade Center in New York and the Pentagon in Washington, President Bush stood before a joint session of Congress and pledged a global war against terrorism.

He demanded that the Taliban rulers of Afghanistan hand over Osama bin Laden, the terrorist responsible for the attack on America. Beyond that, he warned that any nation that harbors terrorists would be regarded as an enemy. "Americans should not expect one battle, but a lengthy campaign, unlike any other we have seen," he said.

In less than three weeks, the U.S. began bombing Taliban targets in Afghanistan, and later that month American troops began ground assaults in that country. In the fighting, the U.S. supported the forces of the Northern Alliance, a loose grouping of tribal leaders opposed to the ruling Taliban. By mid-November, Kabul, the capital, fell. In December, most of bin Laden's Al Qaeda forces had retreated to a complex of caves in the mountains near Tora Bora in eastern Afghanistan. U.S. bombers pounded the caves, and by January, the war was over. But bin Laden was nowhere to be seen, and many of his men had escaped over the border into Pakistan.

Even so, the success of the short-lived war in Afghanistan was not only a foreign policy victory for President Bush, it was also a political triumph. The president's approval rating soared to 90 percent* in the immediate aftermath of the attacks and it was months before opposition Democrats dared to question his policies.

But in the spring of 2002, it was revealed that on August 6 of the previous year, a month before the terrorist attack, Bush had received an intelligence briefing warning that bin Laden was planning to bring his terrorist fight to America, and might even hijack airliners. The report touched off a political firestorm, because it raised the question of whether the administration might have done more to avoid the attack. And Congress was investigating why the nation's intelligence agencies—the CIA and the FBI in particular—had failed to warn of the attacks.

In addition, opponents of the administration criticized the way in which Attorney General John Ashcroft and the Justice Department had rounded up more than 1,200 persons, most of them foreign nationals, in the aftermath of the attack, detaining them for months on immigration and other charges and refusing to release their names. Critics maintained that in the effort to combat terrorism, the government was infringing on civil liberties and constitutional rights.

President Bush, however, buoyed by the administration's success in Afghanistan, said that the U.S. might launch a preemptive strike against another country if it believed America was in danger of being attacked. "If we wait for threats to fully materialize, we will have waited too long," he said in an address to graduates of the United States Military Academy at West Point.† And elsewhere he called for the removal of Saddam Hussein, the brutal leader of Iraq, who was reported to be developing weapons of mass destruction. Some Democrats and even some Republican congressional leaders warned against any unprovoked attack by the U.S. against Iraq. Such a preemptive attack, the critics argued, would mark a sharp, historic departure from the way that the United States had conducted itself in the world.

The political debate over military action against Iraq, the rumblings over what the government had known prior to September 11, and the question of why the intelligence agencies had not provided advance warning of the terrorist attacks reflected the fact that foreign policy and national security are closely related to, and interwoven with, domestic politics.

Indeed, Karl Rove, Bush's chief political adviser told a meeting of the Republican National Committee that the party should make the president's handling of the war on terror the central theme of the effort to win back the Senate and keep control of the House in the midterm elections of 2002. "We can go to the country on this issue because they trust the Republican Party to do a better job of protecting and strengthening

---

*Gallup/USA Today/CNN Poll, reported in *The New York Times*, September 24, 2001, p. B6. A lagging economy and corporate scandals may have contributed to a later drop in Bush's approval rating, which was down to 52% in a new Gallup poll in July 2002.

†*The New York Times*, June 2, 2002, p. 1.

American troops in Afghanistan, March 2002.
AP/Wide World

Vietnam: *The costs were high.*
Copyright © Bill Strode/Woodfin Camp & Associates

America's military might and thereby protecting America," Rove said.*

Presidents may be reluctant to admit that their foreign policy is affected by domestic political considerations. They usually prefer to describe their actions in terms of national security and global complexities. But they are always well aware of the impact of foreign policy on politics at home. Often, they consider how a particular defense or foreign policy may affect their chances for reelection.

In an uncertain era of nuclear proliferation, terrorism, regional conflicts, assassinations, famine, and genocide, American foreign policy often plays an important role when the voters, every four years, choose their president. Who has more experience in foreign affairs? Which candidate will be most likely to protect the nation from further terrorist attacks? To keep America out of war? To maintain its military strength? Whose policies seem best in trouble spots such as the Middle East?

Events in other countries often affect public opinion in the United States. Domestic issues, bread-and-butter concerns, may mean more to American voters than foreign policy, but that is not always the case. President Lyndon Johnson, for example, chose not even to run in 1968, because the Vietnam War—and therefore Johnson—had become unpopular.

As the **Cold War**—the period of intense East-West rivalry after the Second World War—faded into history, new global issues came to the fore, centering on challenges that transcended national boundaries. Increasingly, political leaders and economists spoke of **globalization**, a world economy characterized by the free movement of goods, capital, labor, and information across national borders. It was a process that opponents argued benefited giant multinational corporations and other industries but harmed the environment, American labor unions, and poor workers in less developed countries.

Nuclear proliferation—the spread of weapons of mass destruction to other nations—threatened the world. The nuclear threat, the global environment, over-population, famine, disease (including the AIDS epidemic), a rising tide of nationalism, and ethnic and religious conflicts—all were issues that, in a global context, were broader than the old rivalry of competing political systems. They were also issues that in many cases involved the future of humanity and the survival of the planet.

In this chapter we will explore a key question: What is foreign policy, and how is it formulated in a democratic political system such as the United States? Many related questions arise. Who makes foreign policy? What role should the president play? The Congress? And how, in a democratic society, can people make their views felt and influence foreign policy? What should America's objectives be in its relations with the rest of the world? Should it attempt to be the world's police force, intervening in conflicts around the globe? When should the United States intervene? Do circumstances ever justify a preemptive attack on another country? How much of the nation's resources should go into mili-

---

Washington Post, January 19, 2002, p. A2.

The AMERICAN PAST

TRUMAN FIRES GENERAL MacARTHUR

On April 11, 1951, in the midst of the Korean War, President Harry S Truman fired General of the Army Douglas MacArthur for insubordination. MacArthur had consistently defied the president's orders. Truman describes what led to his decision in his memoirs:

On March 24 General MacArthur released a statement that was . . . entirely at cross-purposes with the one I was to have delivered. . . . This was a most extraordinary statement for a military commander of the United Nations to issue on his own responsibility. It was an act totally disregarding all directives to abstain from any declarations on foreign policy. It was in open defiance of my orders as President and as Commander in Chief. This was a challenge to the authority of the President under the Constitution. It also flouted the policy of the United Nations.

By this act MacArthur left me no choice—I could no longer tolerate his insubordination. In effect, what MacArthur was doing was to threaten the enemy with an ultimatum—intimating that the full preponderance of Allied power might be brought to bear against Red China. . . .

If there is one basic element in our Constitution, it is civilian control of the military. Policies are to be made by the elected political officials, not by generals or admirals. . . .

That is why our Constitution embodies the principle of civilian control of the military. This was the principle that General MacArthur threatened. I do not believe that he purposefully decided to challenge civilian control of the military, but the result of his behavior was that this fundamental principle of free government was in danger.

It was my duty to act. . . . I felt compelled to have Joseph Short, my press secretary, call a special news conference for 1 A.M., April 11. . . . The reporters were handed a series of papers, the first being my announcement of General MacArthur's relief. . . .

—Memoirs by Harry S Truman: Years of Trial and Hope 1946–1952

tary spending? What dangers are posed to American institutions by a multibillion-dollar defense budget? What are the responsibilities of richer nations toward less developed nations?

THE UNITED STATES AND WORLD AFFAIRS

American Foreign Policy

Foreign policy is the sum of the goals, decisions, and actions that govern a nation's relations with the rest of the world. But the world changes, and so does foreign policy. A president may adopt one policy only to discard it later; a new president may reverse the policies of his predecessor. Alliances shift; the Soviet Union, America's ally against Nazi Germany in the Second World War, became its principal adversary in the Cold War that began soon afterward and lasted more than four decades. Japan, which had been America's wartime enemy, became its peacetime ally, as did West Germany.

So "foreign policy" is a changing and elusive concept. Roger Hilsman, a former assistant secretary of state, has suggested that the problem of foreign policy is

President Kennedy, standing, right, leaning forward, meets with advisers, including his brother, Attorney General Robert F. Kennedy, standing at left, during the Cuban missile crisis, October 1962.
Copyright © CORBIS

not so much one of relating decisions to a single set of goals as it is "precisely one of choosing goals" in the midst of onrushing events and crises and of reconciling the advocates of competing goals and policies. "The making of foreign policy," he concluded, "is a political process."[1]

The preservation of **national security** is a fundamental consideration in the formulation of foreign policy. National security is a broad concept that may be defined in many ways, but the term is generally used to refer to the basic protection and defense of the nation. But "national security" is so broad and vague a term that it can be used to justify almost any action that a nation or a president takes. President Nixon, for example, invoked it to attempt to justify a broad range of abuses of power that eventually led to his resignation.

After the Second World War, there were two approaches to the question of national security and American foreign policy. One view emphasized threats to United States security posed by the power of Communist or unfriendly nations. Another regarded U.S. security as dependent on some form of world order "compatible with our values and interests."[2] This second view holds that there can be no real security for the United States without world peace and security for all people.

Yet national security proved a relative term in the thermonuclear age. During the Cuban Missile Crisis of 1962, President Kennedy's advisers knew that their decisions, if wrong, "could mean the destruction of the human race."[3] So any description of national security and foreign policy must take into account the changed nature of the world since the beginning of the atomic age.

In Korea and Vietnam, the United States fought a protracted war against Communist power in Asia. Faced with often hostile, armed Communist nations, the United States sought to maintain a high level of military strength. American policymakers argued that this costly arms burden was necessary to protect the national security, American liberties at home, and the freedom of other nations. Only the shield of American power, they contended, prevented Communist expansion to a degree that would threaten American security.

Critics of this view maintained that the United States often used its vast power to support military governments in Asia, Latin America, and elsewhere in the world, including some that violated human rights and civil liberties, and tortured or killed political opponents. For example, the United States supported the government of El Salvador despite the operations of right-wing "death squads" that murdered thousands of persons with the apparent approval of high-ranking Salvadoran military and civilian officials. In Guatemala, the army, supported by millions of dollars from Washington, murdered an estimated 100,000 persons in four decades of guerrilla warfare. A presidential panel concluded in 1996 that the Central Intelligence Agency had recruited

NATIONAL SECURITY: A PRESIDENT'S VIEW

Together we shall save our planet, or together we shall perish in its flames.

—John F. Kennedy, Address to the General Assembly of the United Nations, September 25, 1961

and paid as sources of information Guatemalan military officers who engaged in assassinations, torture, kidnappings, murder, and widespread violations of human rights.[4]

A major foreign policy issue often debated, but unresolved, is: when should the United States intervene militarily abroad? One view maintains that it should do so only when its vital interests are clearly at stake and it can act with the broad support of the American public and the nation's allies. Another view argues that the nation's humanitarian values may also sometimes require armed intervention. In Africa in 1998, for example, at least 500,000 Tutsis were massacred by Rwanda's Hutu majority. The United Nations was unable to halt the genocide and the United States stood by and did nothing.

The creation of a "national security state" at times threatened liberties at home. During the Watergate scandal, President Nixon argued that the wiretapping of his own aides and of journalists, the formation of a special White House investigative unit known as "the Plumbers" to plug news leaks, and a plan to open first-class mail and burglarize the homes or offices of suspected persons were all justified by "national security."

Globalization has focused attention on another major foreign policy issue—the powerful multinational corporations, many of them based in the United States, whose activities cut across national borders. Richard J. Barnet and Ronald E. Muller argue that these giant corporations are primarily concerned with profits, ignoring the social or environmental effects of their activities. They ask: "By what right do a self-selected group of druggists, biscuit makers, and computer designers become the architects of the new world?"[5]

All of these issues and conflicts provide a challenge to the policymakers seeking to manage America's foreign policy.

The Historical Setting

A nation's foreign policy is rooted in its politics and in its past. In discussing the history of American foreign policy, we can identify some recurring strands and major themes that are relevant to today's changed world.

One fundamental characteristic of America's early foreign policy was **isolationism,** a policy of avoiding foreign involvement. President George Washington declared that it was the nation's policy "to steer clear of permanent alliance," and Thomas Jefferson said that America wanted peace with all nations, "entangling alliances with none."

During the 19th century, the diplomats of Europe maneuvered to preserve the "balance of power" in the Old World; America, protected by the broad Atlantic, could afford to remain relatively aloof from the problems of Europe. The **Monroe Doctrine,** a declaration by President James Monroe in 1823, warned European powers to keep out of the Western Hemisphere and pledged that the United States would not intervene in the internal affairs of Europe. American isolation, of course, was only relative. The United States fought a war with Great Britain in 1812; it annexed Texas, which led to a war with Mexico in 1846; and it took possession of Puerto Rico, Guam, and the Philippines under the treaty ending the Spanish-American War in 1898. (The Philippines gained independence in 1946.) However, the United States did not become a major colonial power, with vast overseas territories, on a scale comparable with Great Britain or some of the nations of Europe.

By the end of the 19th century, an opposite strand of American foreign policy was visible—**interventionism,** or military involvement by the United States in various parts of the world. In the early 20th century,

the United States practiced "gunboat diplomacy," intervening militarily in Mexico, the Caribbean, and Latin America. The First World War brought major U.S. military involvement in Europe for the first time. After the war, however, the United States declined to join with other countries in the League of Nations. President Woodrow Wilson's dream of world order was shattered, and America retreated "back to normalcy" and isolationism.

But during the Second World War, the United States and its allies defeated Nazi Germany and Japan, and America emerged in the position of a great world power. The United States traded its former position of isolationism for one of **internationalism,** the policy that America must take an active leadership role in world affairs.

A world weary of war and destruction centered its hopes for peace on the United Nations (UN), created in 1945. It quickly became clear, however, that the future of the postwar world would be shaped not in the UN but in the relations between the two major powers, the United States and the Soviet Union.

The Era of the Cold War

In a speech at Westminster College in Fulton, Missouri, in March 1946, Britain's great wartime Prime Minister, Winston Churchill, declared that from the Baltic to the Adriatic seas, "an iron curtain has descended across the

President Truman and Secretary of State George C. Marshall
U.S. Army Photo

continent." In retrospect, it became clear that the Cold War had begun.

During this period, the United States adopted a policy of **containment** of the power of the Soviet Union. That policy was first elaborated in the quarterly *Foreign Affairs* by George F. Kennan, a senior American diplomat who later became ambassador to the Soviet Union. Kennan, who was a State Department official in 1947 when the article was published, signed his name "Mr. X" to preserve his anonymity. The article set forth a doctrine that became "the Bible of Western foreign policy" in the mid-20th century.[6] Kennan argued that the Soviet Union would expand its power wherever it could to challenge Western institutions. He advocated that U.S. policy toward the Soviet Union be one of "firm and vigilant containment of Russian expansive tendencies."[7]

In the immediate aftermath of the Second World War, the United States moved to counterbalance Soviet power. Under the Truman Doctrine, Washington began a program of military aid to Greece, which was fighting Communist guerrillas, and Turkey, which was under pressure to cede military bases to the Soviet Union. As enunciated by President Harry S Truman, the doctrine declared that American security and world peace depended on U.S. protection for the "free peoples of the world."[8]

In the summer of 1947, the United States launched the **Marshall Plan** (named for its creator, Secretary of State George C. Marshall) and poured more than $13 billion in four years into Western Europe to speed its postwar economic and social recovery. The Soviet Union and other East European nations declined to join the Marshall Plan.

In 1949 the United States and many of the nations of Western Europe formed the North Atlantic Treaty Organization (NATO), whose members were pledged to defend each other against attack. NATO was the first and most important of a series of postwar collective security pacts signed by the United States. These arrangements were greatly expanded during the Eisenhower administration. In 1996 the United States was pledged under security pacts to defend 48 nations. (See Figure 16-1.)

Although America was preoccupied with European recovery and collective security, and with containing Soviet expansion, it was in the Pacific that a new war broke out only five years after the end of the Second World War. During the Korean War (1950–1953), the United States became involved for the first time in a land war in Asia. After North Korea invaded South Korea in June of 1950, U.S. forces were sent to Korea in a conflict that eventually cost the lives of 33,667 Americans killed in combat.

New forces, sometimes obscured by the rhetoric of the Cold War, were loose in the world. The United States, the sole nuclear power at the end of the Second World War, lost that advantage when the Soviet Union acquired atomic weapons in 1949. About the same time, however, world Communist unity began to come apart. As early as 1948, Yugoslavia's President Tito had broken with the Soviet Union. In 1956 Soviet tanks crushed a revolt against Communist rule in Hungary.

By 1961 Russia and its former ally, Communist China, were open and bitter adversaries. In 1968 Soviet and Warsaw Pact troops invaded Czechoslovakia in order to put down a movement toward democratic reforms in that country.

FIGURE 16-1

U.S. Security Pacts

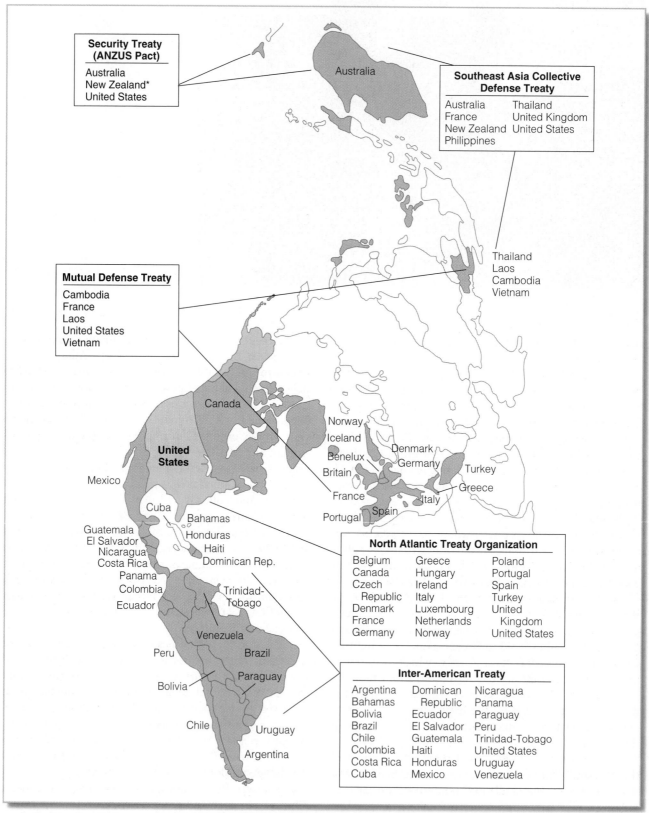

Security Treaty (ANZUS Pact)
Australia
New Zealand*
United States

Southeast Asia Collective Defense Treaty

Australia	Thailand
France	United Kingdom
New Zealand	United States
Philippines	

Thailand
Laos
Cambodia
Vietnam

Mutual Defense Treaty
Cambodia
France
Laos
United States
Vietnam

Australia

Canada

United States

Mexico

Norway
Iceland
Denmark
Benelux
Germany
Britain
Turkey
France
Greece
Italy
Portugal   Spain

Cuba
Bahamas
Guatemala   Honduras
El Salvador   Haiti
Nicaragua   Dominican Rep.
Costa Rica
Panama
Colombia
Ecuador   Trinidad-Tobago

Venezuela

Peru   Brazil

Bolivia   Paraguay

Chile   Uruguay

Argentina

North Atlantic Treaty Organization

Belgium	Greece	Poland
Canada	Hungary	Portugal
Czech	Ireland	Spain
Republic	Italy	Turkey
Denmark	Luxembourg	United
France	Netherlands	Kingdom
Germany	Norway	United States

Inter-American Treaty

Argentina	Dominican	Nicaragua
Bahamas	Republic	Panama
Bolivia	Ecuador	Paraguay
Brazil	El Salvador	Peru
Chile	Guatemala	Trinidad-Tobago
Colombia	Haiti	United States
Costa Rica	Honduras	Uruguay
Cuba	Mexico	Venezuela

*As of September 1, 1986, the United States suspended its obligations with New Zealand
SOURCE: United States Department of State, *Treaties In Force: A List of Treaties and Other Agreements of the United States in Force on January 1, 1999*, pp. 363–366; 422–426. Data as of 1999.

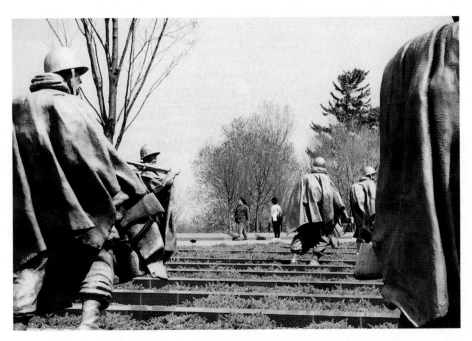

The Korean War Memorial in Washington, D.C.
Copyright © Kristin Kenney Williams

During the same postwar period, a rising tide of nationalism brought independence to various nations in Africa, Asia, and the Middle East and stirred political currents in Latin America. Like the term "national security," **nationalism** can be defined in different ways. In its best sense it is a love of country and a desire for independence. But it can also mean an excessive form of patriotism that unscrupulous political leaders may exploit to whip up one group against another, leading to civil war and bloody "ethnic cleansing," such as occurred in the former Yugoslavia under the Serbian dictator Slobodan Milosevic.

In 1947 India and Pakistan gained their independence from Britain, and in 1949 Indonesia became free of Dutch control. The 1960s saw a second wave of nationalism, this time in Africa. As European powers withdrew from what remained of their 19th-century colonial empires, the Third World became a new battleground in which the United States, the Soviet Union, and Communist China competed for influence and power. In the 1970s the United States and the Soviet Union vied for power in the Middle East and Africa. In many of these areas of the globe, poverty, hunger, disease, illiteracy, and political instability were combined in a volatile mixture.

Not all relationships that cut across national boundaries are controlled by governments. Modern scholars have also focused on transnationalism, which includes such global activities as trade, personal contacts, communications between private groups, and business relationships. Transnational relations may be defined as "contacts, coalitions, and interactions across state boundaries that are not controlled by the central foreign-policy organs of governments."[9] Today, that concept is more often described as part of the process of globalization, in which multilateral trade and lending institutions are deeply involved.

In addition, foreign policy analysts often speak of interdependence, or mutual dependence among nations. Sometimes this mutual dependence is cooperative, as when several nations agree to combat an environmental problem. Or it can be involuntary, as was the case of the United States and the Soviet Union, whose strategic interdependence derived "from the mutual threat of nuclear destruction."[10]

Vietnam and Its Aftermath

In Vietnam, the United States gradually moved into the power vacuum created when the French withdrew from Indochina following their defeat in 1954 by Ho Chi Minh. Presidents Eisenhower and Kennedy supported the government of South Vietnam, and Kennedy sent 16,000 troops there as "advisers." But it was President Johnson who, in 1965, committed the United States to a full-scale war against Communist North Vietnam and the National Liberation Front, or Vietcong. Eventually, Johnson sent more than 500,000 combat troops to Vietnam. The war proved divisive and increasingly unpopular at home, and it was a major factor in Johnson's decision to announce, in March 1968, that he would not seek the presidency again.*

---

*Polls indicated that a majority of Americans considered the U.S. involvement in Vietnam to have been an error. For example, a Gallup poll of June 1970 reported that 56 percent of the public considered that the United States had made "a mistake" in sending troops to Vietnam. The percentage of people who answered "yes" when asked "Do you think the United States made a mistake sending troops to fight in Vietnam?" rose above 50 percent for the first time in August 1968 and remained above 50 percent thereafter.

"Thanks a lot."
Dan Wright/The *Miami News*

Paris, January 1973: The Vietnam peace accords are signed in Paris.
AP/Wide World

Richard Nixon's promise to end the war helped to bring about his election in November 1968. Yet it took Nixon four years to redeem his pledge. By the time the peace agreement was signed in Paris in January 1973, more than 47,000 Americans had died in combat in eight years, and more than 303,000 had been wounded. Perhaps a million Vietnamese soldiers, North and South, were killed. At least 415,000 civilians died in South Vietnam. The United States dropped more than 7 million tons of bombs in Southeast Asia in eight years, three times the total bomb tonnage dropped in the Second World War. In money, even excluding billions in veterans' benefits, the cost of the war was more than $140 billion.

The Vietnam War illustrated the limits of American world power, and in its wake much of the crusading zeal that had marked the nation's foreign policy gave way to a more cautious, pragmatic approach. One of the legacies of Vietnam, therefore, was a reluctance on the part of many Americans and their political leaders to undertake another foreign venture that might embroil the United States in a war.

For almost a decade the Vietnam issue divided the nation and cast a shadow over the quality of American life. The lengthy war caused many Americans to become disillusioned with the workings of the political system itself. For that reason alone, the cost of the Vietnam War may continue to be felt for many years to come.

From Détente to the End of the Cold War

Even before the United States had disengaged from Vietnam, a period of **détente,** or relaxation of tensions, between the two superpowers had begun in May 1972, when President Richard Nixon held a summit meeting in Moscow with Soviet party chief Leonid Brezhnev. In Moscow, Nixon signed the SALT (Strategic Arms Limitation Talks) agreement placing a measure of control over nuclear weapons, and a separate **Antiballistic Missile (ABM) Treaty** limiting the number of defensive missiles each country could build. The meeting followed Nixon's historic trip to China, the first by an American president. President Nixon was able to open doors to Moscow and Beijing because, in both America and the Soviet Union, there was gradual recognition that the arms race not only threatened the survival of humanity, but also was distorting the economies of both nations and diverting energies and resources into military hardware that might better be used to serve people. Secretary of State Henry A. Kissinger was the architect of the new policy of détente.

The spirit of cooperation continued, as President Jimmy Carter, elected in 1976, achieved an important foreign policy breakthrough in the Middle East. In March 1979, Carter brought about the signing of a peace treaty between Israel and Egypt after a generation of hostility between those two nations. The agreement followed a summit meeting between the leaders of Egypt and Israel that had taken place six months earlier at Camp David, the presidential retreat near Washington. The treaty provided for the withdrawal of Israeli troops from the Sinai Peninsula and for talks on autonomy for Palestinians on the West Bank of the Jordan River and in the Gaza Strip.

The same year that the Camp David peace accords were signed, the United States under President Carter entered into full diplomatic relations with the People's Republic of China and ended diplomatic relations with the Republic of China (Taiwan). But the pro-democracy movement that swept through Eastern Europe and ended with the collapse of the Soviet Union in 1991 had much more difficulty taking root in China, whose leaders continued to practice police-state repression against those who challenged the Communist leadership. In May and June of 1989, hundreds of thousands of Chinese students and other citizens demonstrated for democracy in Beijing's Tiananmen Square. The students erected a replica of the Statue of Liberty. The army opened fire on the demonstrators, and tanks crushed some of them. Thousands were killed or injured, and there were mass arrests in the wake of the demonstrations. For the moment, at least, democracy had been crushed in China.

Beijing's Tiananmen Square, 1989: A lone protester defies the tanks.
AP/Wide World

A decade earlier, in 1979, Soviet troops invaded Afghanistan and established a pro-Soviet government there. Through the Central Intelligence Agency, the United States provided money and arms in support of the Afghan rebels fighting the more than 100,000 Soviet troops in that country. By 1992, the United States had spent more than $2 billion to arm the rebels.[11] The war in Afghanistan proved to be costly and unpopular for the Soviets, evoking parallels to the U.S. experience in Vietnam. In 1988, the Soviets began pulling their armed forces out of Afghanistan. Within four years, the rebels marched into Kabul, the capital. The civil war in Afghanistan continued unabated in the mid-1990s, however, as the various rebel factions fought for control. The Taliban, a fundamentalist Islamic movement, imposed its harsh rule over most of the country.

In November 1979, Iranian militants forced their way into the American embassy in Teheran and seized more than 60 Americans as hostages. The militants demanded that the deposed shah of Iran, then in New York, be returned to Iran by the United States. Their demands were backed by the Ayatollah Khomeini, leader of Iran's Islamic revolution.

In April 1980 President Carter approved a military rescue mission to Iran that turned into a disaster in the desert, leaving eight American servicemen dead and the hostages still imprisoned. Election Day 1980—the first anniversary of the seizure of the Americans—came and went with the hostages still in Iran. Carter lost to Ronald Reagan. Finally, on Inauguration Day 1981, only moments after Reagan had taken the oath of office, all 52 remaining hostages were flown out of Iran, ending their 444 days in captivity.

President Reagan had promised to strengthen the nation's diplomacy and its military power. True to his word, Reagan presided over a major buildup of military strength.

Early in his presidency, Reagan denounced the Soviet Union as an "evil empire."[12] But later in the Reagan years, after initial tensions, relations with the Soviet Union improved substantially. In 1987 Reagan and Gorbachev signed the first treaty in history reducing the size of their nations' nuclear arsenals.

After Israel invaded Lebanon in 1982, President Reagan dispatched 1,200 Marines to serve as part of a multinational peacekeeping force in Beirut, the Lebanese capital. In 1983, a terrorist drove a truck laden with explosives into the U.S. Marine barracks in a suicide attack that killed 241 servicemen. After the bombing, criticism of the administration increased at home. An independent Defense Department commission blamed the tragedy on failures in the chain of command from top to bottom.[13] In the face of eroding public support for the Marine mission, Reagan in February 1984 pulled the troops out.

During the 1980s, the United States pursued policies in Central America aimed at defeating forces in Nicaragua and El Salvador that were supported, President Reagan charged, by the Soviet Union and Cuba. In El Salvador, the administration poured in millions of dollars to shore up the government against pressure from left-wing guerrillas. In Nicaragua, through the Central Intelligence Agency, Reagan supported a covert war against that country's leftist Sandinista rulers.

Reagan soon found himself caught in a scandal growing out of crises in Iran and Nicaragua. Other

American hostages are seized at the United States embassy in Teheran, November, 1979.
Copyright © CORBIS/UPI/Bettmann

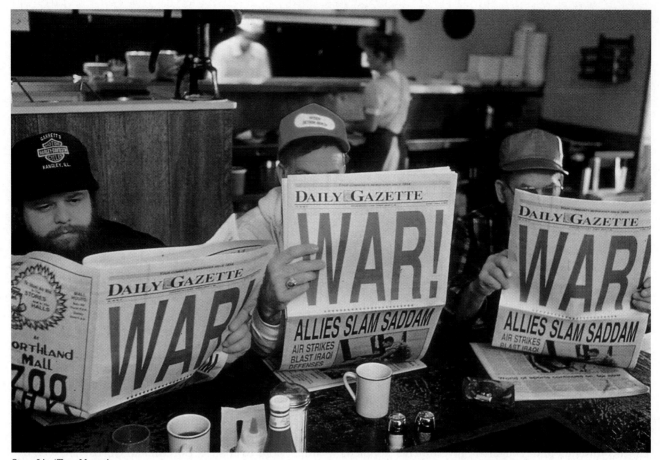

Steve Liss/*Time* Magazine

American hostages had been seized in Lebanon, and President Reagan wanted them out. As a result, under Reagan, the staff of the National Security Council, operating from within the White House itself, conducted a secret foreign policy. Arms were sold to Iran to try to persuade the Iranian government to pressure the groups holding the hostages seized in Lebanon to free them. Millions of dollars in profits from those arms sales were diverted to support the contra rebels in Nicaragua, at a time when Congress had banned such aid. Even larger sums ended up in the Swiss bank accounts of the private individuals who ran the secret operations for Marine Lt. Col. Oliver L. North, a staff member of the National Security Council. By turning to private citizens to conduct such operations, the White House attempted to circumvent the constitutional requirement that Congress as well as the president play a role in the conduct of foreign policy.

The Iran-contra scandal eventually created a dilemma for Reagan's vice president, George Bush, who was elected president in 1988. When he ran for reelection in 1992, his role in the scandal became a major campaign issue. As vice president, Bush had emphasized his importance within the Reagan White House. He had presented himself as an official who was completely informed on the great affairs of state. Yet he professed to have only marginal knowledge of the Iran-contra affair, claiming he was "out of the loop," a position that seemed contradictory and opened him to attack by his Democratic opponent, Bill Clinton.

Only a year earlier, in 1991, President George Bush had faced a crisis in the Middle East. The United States and its West European allies depended on the oil fields of the Persian Gulf region to fuel their economies. In 1990, Iraq's Saddam Hussein invaded Kuwait, threatening Saudi Arabia, a major oil supplier. President Bush deployed American forces to the area as part of a coalition of allied nations opposed to Saddam. In 1991, in the Persian Gulf War, U.S. military forces drove Iraq out of Kuwait.

The Cold War Ends

For more than 40 years, the United States and the Soviet Union had been locked in a seemingly insoluble era of conflict, somewhere between peace and war. With both sides possessing unimaginably destructive nuclear missiles and bombs, the possibility of Armageddon was never far in the background. Indeed, in the Cuban Missile Crisis of 1962, the world went to the brink of nuclear war.

But in the fall of 1989, the tide of history once more swept across Eastern Europe. In one country after another, democratic forces were able to break the grip

*Taking down the Berlin Wall,
November 1989*
Christopher J. Wise

of the Communist dictatorships, closely allied with Moscow, that had come to power in the aftermath of the Second World War. In Hungary, Poland, East Germany, Czechoslovakia, and Bulgaria, governments toppled, often after mass demonstrations by citizens. In Romania, the revolt was bloody as security forces fired into the crowds, and dictator Nicolae Ceausescu and his wife, who attempted to flee by helicopter, were caught and shot.

In November, East Germany opened its borders to the West, and on television the world watched the memorable scene of crowds dancing in celebration atop the Berlin Wall, the symbol of divided Germany. Soon afterward, the wall itself came down, and chunks of its stones became souvenirs of a vanished and unla-mented era. A year later, in October 1990, East and West Germany were united.

Still, the mighty Soviet Union stood, seemingly impervious to change. But Mikhail Gorbachev, who had come to power in 1985, had unleashed *glasnost,* or change, and *perestroika,* the restructuring of Soviet society, which had become much more open in just a few years. But the new policies had some unexpected results. On May Day of 1990, something extraordinary happened in Red Square—the crowds jeered President Gorbachev and the Kremlin leaders atop Lenin's tomb. As the loudspeakers blared out martial music, demonstrators marched across the cobblestones carrying banners that said "Down with the Politburo! Resign!" and calling for freedom for Lithuania.

*After the collapse of the Soviet Union, the
toppled statue of dictator Josef Stalin makes
a pleasant perch for Russian children in a
Moscow park.*
AP/Wide World

In August 1991, a cabal of hardliners led by Vladimir A. Kryuchkov, the chairman of the KGB, the Soviet secret police, briefly held Gorbachev prisoner at his dacha on the Black Sea. As demonstrators in Moscow rallied in support of Gorbachev, Boris Yeltsin, the president of Russia, climbed onto a tank and defied the coup plotters. The tide turned, the plotters were arrested, and a weakened Gorbachev returned briefly to power. But within four months, the republics of the Soviet Union declared their independence of central control, Gorbachev resigned, and Yeltsin, as president of Russia, emerged as the most important leader in the former Soviet empire, which had broken up into 15 independent states.

At 7:32 P.M. on December 25, 1991, the red flag of the Soviet Union with hammer-and-sickle fluttered in the wind for the last time as it was slowly lowered over the Kremlin in Moscow, marking the formal end to the Soviet Union. The breakup of the Communist empire had seemed inconceivable only a few years earlier.

The superpower conflict that had most threatened the survival of humanity was history. On February 1, 1992, President Bush and President Yeltsin of Russia met at Camp David, Maryland, and formally declared what was already apparent to the world: The Cold War was over.

The Post–Cold War World

The end of the Cold War did not mean an end to conflict around the globe. Ethnic and religious strife—in the Balkans, Africa, Asia, and the Middle East—demonstrated that the world was still not a peaceful place.

There was progress in some areas, however. In South Africa, for example, where blacks had been repressed for decades by a policy of apartheid, or forced separation of the races, the transition to democracy took place rapidly despite sporadic violence. In 1990, the white government lifted its ban on the African National Congress, and the congress's leader, Nelson Mandela, was freed after more than 27 years in prison. Apartheid laws were ended and a new constitution was written. In 1994, Mandela was elected president.

And in 1994, a major breakthrough—which at the time appeared to hold at least a promise of peace—occurred in the Middle East. Israel and the Palestinians reached a peace agreement ending their 48-year state of war. The accords were signed at the White House in September, and in a ceremony on the south lawn, Prime Minister Yitzhak Rabin of Israel and Palestinian leader Yasir Arafat reached across President Clinton in an historic handshake. Under this and related agreements, the Palestinians would gradually gain self-rule in Gaza and the West Bank of the Jordan. But in November 1995, Rabin was assassinated and his successor, Benjamin Netanyahu had campaigned in favor of a much tougher policy toward Arafat and the Arab countries. He was defeated in 1999 in a landslide by Ehud Barak, the

President Nelson Mandela of South Africa
Copyright © Brooks Kraft/Sygma

Labor Party candidate. Although Barak sought to continue the peace process, as noted earlier, fighting broke out in Jerusalem, the West Bank, and the Gaza Strip in the midst of the 2000 presidential election in the United States. President Clinton journeyed to Egypt during the crisis to meet with Barak and Arafat to try to end the violence and restart the peace process. But the clashes continued and tensions in the area remained high.

With the collapse of communism, new global issues emerged. As more countries attempted to acquire nuclear weapons, for example, it was possible that the world might actually become more unstable than it was during the Cold War years when the superpowers faced off against each other.

The Clinton Administration based its foreign policy, in part, on the goal of global democratization. The administration's hope was that more countries would gradually adopt democracy as their form of government. Under this policy, the administration supported democratization of the former Soviet republics and of countries in Asia, Latin America, and Africa. Clinton and his foreign policy advisers viewed their support for wider democracy as a replacement for the Cold War policy of containment.

To some extent this doctrine influenced the administration's support of United Nations peacekeeping missions. In 1994, Clinton sent U.S. forces to restore the democratically elected president of Haiti; later the United Nations peacekeepers took over that mission. The Clinton administration also proposed that NATO be expanded to include limited membership for former communist adversaries in the Warsaw Pact. President Boris Yeltsin of Russia opposed NATO expansion eastward as a threat to Moscow's security, but in 1997 Russia agreed to NATO's expansion, and the Czech Republic, Poland, and Hungary became members in 1999.

The dispatch of American troops under the flag of the United Nations and under NATO in the post–Cold War era revived the familiar debate between the internationalist and isolationist strains in America. Some conservatives objected strongly to placing American troops in harm's way except under the control of U.S. commanders. To do otherwise, they argued, was to give up American sovereignty.

Yeltsin himself faced substantial obstacles as he struggled to impose a free market economy on the rubble of the Soviet system. Although reelected president of Russia in 1996, his health had seriously deteriorated. In addition, Yeltsin was bogged down by the war in Chechnya, a southern region that had rebelled against Russian rule. And the emergence of a class of economic buccaneers in Russia had only increased the gap between the newly rich and the rural poor. In the aftermath of the collapse of the Soviet Union, there was a Wild West quality to life in Moscow, with bankers, journalists, and members of parliament gunned down by powerful criminal elements. The Russians, once America's adversaries, were seeking billions of dollars in aid from the United States. Both sides drastically reduced their nuclear arsenals. All of these changes—political, military, economic, and social—had come so fast as to be breathtaking.

Then at the end of 1999, Boris Yeltsin unexpectedly resigned as president before his term had ended. He was succeeded, as acting president, by Vladimir Putin, a former KGB officer in East Germany and a Yeltsin protégé. In March of 2000, Putin was elected president of Russia.

The long war in the former Yugoslavia posed another challenge to Clinton's foreign policy. UN peacekeeping forces and NATO air strikes had proved unable to stop the intense fighting among Serbs, Muslims, and Croats. The administration finally brought the warring parties to the peace table in 1995 in Dayton, Ohio. After the peace accords were signed there, Clinton dispatched American troops to Bosnia in December as part of a NATO peacekeeping force.

But four years later, new trouble erupted in the Balkans. In 1999, Serbia's military invaded Kosovo, a province in southern Yugoslavia, forcing an estimated 700,000 ethnic Albanians to flee—mostly into neigh-boring Albania—and creating an enormous refugee crisis. Acting through the NATO alliance, U.S. warplanes bombed Yugoslavia repeatedly for more than two months. Under pressure of the bombing, Slobodan Milosevic, then Yugoslavia's president, finally signed a peace agreement and allowed international peacekeeping forces, including American troops, to enter Kosovo. The residents of Kosovo, mostly Muslims, returned to what was left of their homes.

Terrorism, too, continued to afflict the post–Cold War world. The 1983 bombing of the Marine barracks in Lebanon by terrorists had its echo in 1996 when terrorists set off a huge truck bomb outside a U.S. Air Force barracks in Dhahran, Saudi Arabia, killing 19 American airmen and wounding more than 400 others.

The bombings; the murder or kidnapping of diplomats, businesspersons, educators, or others; embassy takeovers and kidnapping of hostages; aircraft hijackings; and other forms of terror were becoming increasingly familiar. These violent actions have been carried out by a wide range of political groups for a variety of reasons. By 1999, some 14,660 persons had been killed in 14,419 terrorist incidents since 1968.[14]

On August 7, 1998, almost simultaneous terrorist bombings of the U.S. embassies in Kenya and Tanzania killed at least 220 people, including 12 Americans, and injured 4,000 persons. Two years later, in October 2000, Ali Mohamed, a former U.S. army sergeant and a naturalized American citizen, pleaded guilty to conspiracy in the embassy bombings. He linked the attack to Osama bin Laden, the wealthy Saudi terrorist who had been indicted by a federal grand jury in New York, but remained in Afghanistan committed to a war of terror against the United States. Then on September 11, 2001, bin Laden's attack on America triggered the war that drove his troops from Afghanistan. But that success by the U.S. military did not end the threat of further terrorist attacks on targets at home.

Not only terrorism, but also international drug trafficking had an increasing impact on foreign policy. In 1988 the federal government indicted General Manuel Antonio Noriega, the military dictator of Panama, for drug dealing. In 1989, President Bush sent troops into Panama. They toppled Noriega, who was arrested, brought back to Miami, placed on trial, convicted of drug trafficking, and sentenced to 40 years in prison.

The drug overlords had gained extraordinary power in some countries, such as Colombia, a major cocaine producer. Even though several leaders of the Colombian cartels had been captured or killed, these actions and the best efforts of American authorities had done relatively little to stem the flow of illegal drugs into the United States.

By the year 2000, Americans had become increasingly aware that the United States, while still a superpower—indeed, the only surviving superpower—was but one nation in an increasingly interdependent, multi-

It was just past midnight as Stanislav Petrov settled into the commander's chair inside the secret bunker at Serpukhov-15, the installation where the Soviet Union monitored its early-warning satellites over the United States.

Then the alarms went off. On the panel in front of him was a red pulsating button. One word flashed: "Start."

It was September 26, 1983, and Petrov was playing a principal role in one of the most harrowing incidents of the nuclear age: a false alarm signaling a U.S. missile attack.

The episode resonates today because Russia's early-warning system has fewer than half the satellites it did back then, raising the specter of more such dangerous incidents.

As Petrov described it, one of the Soviet satellites sent a signal to the bunker that a nuclear missile attack was under way. The warning system's computer concluded that a missile had been launched from a base in the United States.

The responsibility fell to Petrov, then a 44-year-old lieutenant colonel, to make a decision: Was it for real?

Petrov was situated at a critical point in the chain of command. He reported to superiors at warning system headquarters; they reported to the general staff, which would consult with Soviet leader Yuri Andropov on the possibility of launching a retaliatory attack.

Petrov's role was to evaluate the incoming data. At first, the satellite reported that one missile had been launched—then another, and another. Soon, the system was "roaring," he recalled—five Minuteman intercontinental ballistic missiles had been launched, it reported.

Less than five minutes after the alert began, however, Petrov decided the launch reports must be false. He recalled making the tense decision under enormous stress—electronic maps and consoles were flashing as he held a phone in one hand and juggled an intercom in the other, trying to take in all the information at once. Another officer at the early-warning facility was shouting into the phone to him to remain calm and do his job.

Petrov's decision was based partly on a guess. He had been told many times that a nuclear attack would be massive—an onslaught designed to overwhelm Soviet defenses at a single stroke. But the monitors showed only five missiles. "When people start a war, they don't start it with only five missiles," he remembered thinking at the time. "You can do little damage with just five missiles." Another factor, he said, was that Soviet ground-based radar installations showed no evidence of an attack.

Thus, Petrov decided—and advised the others—that the satellite alert was a false alarm, a call that may have averted a nuclear holocaust. But he was relentlessly interrogated afterward and was never rewarded for his decision. According to Petrov and other sources, the false alarm was eventually traced to the satellite, which picked up the sun's reflection off the tops of clouds and mistook it for a missile launch. The computer program that was supposed to filter out such information was rewritten. Today Petrov is a long-forgotten pensioner living in a town outside Moscow.

SOURCE: Adapted from the *Washington Post*, February 10, 1999

---

polar world, that is, a world in which there are many competing centers of power. The American who watches television on a Sony, uses a Toshiba laptop computer, and drives a Volkswagen could hardly fail to understand the reality of globalization. Nor was it possible to separate military and diplomatic policies from domestic economic policies. Economic factors affected the strength of the dollar abroad and the balance of trade.

Despite the collapse of the Soviet Union, the threat of nuclear war remained, even if substantially diminished. The United States, Britain, France, Russia, and China still retained nuclear weapons, and several Third World nations were attempting to acquire such weapons. In May 1998 both India and Pakistan, two countries often in conflict, conducted underground tests of nuclear weapons. The threat of nuclear proliferation continued. Even small wars carry the potential of growing out of control into nuclear war. Although political candidates and leaders debate about America's military strength and the best way to ensure "national security," it is also possible to ask whether nations and people can ever really achieve security in the nuclear age.

HOW FOREIGN POLICY IS MADE

The President and Foreign Policy

In the field of foreign affairs, as President Kennedy once remarked, "the President bears the burden of the responsibility. . . . The advisers may move on to new advice."[15]

As noted in Chapter 13, the president is both chief diplomat and commander in chief. The two roles overlap; national security, foreign policy, and domestic programs are closely related because the president must decide how much money to allocate for each area within the overall framework of his annual budget.

A large defense budget means less money for meeting priorities at home, and the level of defense expenditures affects the economy. As a Senate subcommittee on national security put it: "The boundary between foreign and domestic policy has almost been erased."[16]

The president has the responsibility of deciding whether to use nuclear weapons. The collapse of the Soviet system has diminished, but not eliminated, that terrible responsibility. During the Cold War, Richard

JFK: A STRATEGY OF PEACE

What kind of peace do I mean? What kind of peace do we seek? Not a Pax Americana enforced on the world by American weapons of war. . . . I am talking about genuine peace, the kind of peace that makes life on earth worth living, the kind that enables men and nations to grow and to hope and to build a better life for their children—not merely peace for Americans but peace for all men and women—not merely peace in our time but peace for all time. . . . Total war makes no sense . . . in an age when the deadly poisons produced by a nuclear exchange would be carried by wind and water and soil and seed to the far corners of the globe and to generations yet unborn. . . .

First: Let us examine our attitude toward peace itself. Too many of us think it is impossible. . . .

We need not accept that view. Our problems are manmade—therefore, they can be solved by man. . . . No problem of human destiny is beyond human beings. . . . And if we cannot end now our differences, at least we can help make the world safe for diversity. For, in the final analysis, our . . . common link is that we all inhabit this small planet. We all breathe the same air. We all cherish our children's future. And we are all mortal.

—John F. Kennedy, Commencement Address at American University in Washington, June 10, 1963

LBJ AND FOREIGN POLICY: WRONG COLLEGE?

The Eastern intellectuals still bothered him. . . . He was serious one afternoon when he said very early in his Presidency, "I'm not sure whether I can lead this country and keep it together, with my background." He paused during one of those soul-cleansings after the day's work was done and looked far off and in a very subdued voice said, "I do not think that I will ever get credit for anything I do in foreign policy, no matter how successful, because I did not go to Harvard."

—Hugh Sidey, *A Very Personal Presidency: Lyndon Johnson in the White House*

Neustadt could write that the president "lives daily with the knowledge that at any time he, personally, may have to make a human judgment . . . which puts half the world in jeopardy."[17] Although this fear eased after the breakup of the Soviet Union, several nations still possess the bomb, and others are trying to acquire nuclear weapons. As a result, the president's finger remains on the nuclear "button." The vast power of the president in the realm of foreign policy carries with it great risks—risks that a president will exercise his judgment unwisely or that he will act without public or congressional support.

In conducting the nation's foreign and military policies, the president must often choose among conflicting advice as he makes his decisions. "The State Department wants to solve everything with words, and the generals, with guns," President Johnson was quoted as saying.[18] A president's background, experience, and beliefs may strongly influence his attitude toward foreign affairs. President Nixon, for example, had long been identified with international affairs as vice president; as president he put great emphasis on foreign policy and negotiations. In time, however, a domestic event—Watergate—beclouded his diplomatic initiatives and ended his presidency.

President Reagan's strong anti-Communist philosophy colored his early rhetoric against the Soviet Union, but his views appeared to have softened substantially by

the time of his fourth summit meeting with Mikhail Gorbachev in the spring of 1988. Reagan also took a strong stance against dealing with terrorists. Yet he secretly sold arms to Iran to try to persuade terrorists who had seized American hostages to release them. The Iran-contra disclosures in the latter years of his presidency lessened public confidence in his leadership.

Like both Reagan and Nixon, President Bush also appeared more confident dealing with foreign rather than domestic issues. President Clinton, by contrast, was slow at first to exercise leadership in foreign affairs. By the end of his two terms in office, however, his efforts to secure peace in the Middle East and Northern Ireland, his commitment of U.S. troops in Bosnia, and the U.S. intervention in Kosovo had enhanced his image as a world leader.

Congress and Foreign Policy

Under the Constitution, power to conduct foreign and military affairs is divided between Congress and the president. While the Constitution gave the president power to appoint ambassadors and command the armed forces, Congress was given power to declare war, raise and support armies, and appropriate money for defense; and the Senate was granted power to approve or disapprove treaties and ambassadorial nominations made by the president.

But the Constitution does not spell out the boundaries of the power that each branch shall exercise. The result has been intermittent conflict between the president and Congress over foreign policy. The war in Vietnam and the Persian Gulf War illustrated the central role of the president in the conduct of foreign relations. Although the Constitution gives Congress the power to declare war, it never did so in either Vietnam or the Gulf. In both instances a president made the decision to go to war.

In the struggle between Congress and the president, at various times in history one branch has dominated.

On September 1, 1970, the U.S. Senate rejected an amendment sponsored by Senators George McGovern, Democrat of South Dakota, and Mark O. Hatfield, Republican of Oregon, to withdraw U.S. troops from Vietnam. Just before the vote, Senator McGovern arose on the Senate floor to plead for an end to a war that Congress had never declared:

> Every senator in this chamber is partly responsible for sending 50,000 young Americans to an early grave. This chamber reeks of blood. Every senator here is partly responsible for the human wreckage at Walter Reed and Bethesda Naval and all across our land— young boys without legs, or arms, or genitals, or faces, or hopes. There aren't very many of these blasted and broken boys who think this war is a glorious venture. Don't talk to them about bugging out, or national honor, or courage. It doesn't take courage at all for a congressman, or a senator, or a President to wrap himself in the flag and say we're staying in Vietnam. Because it isn't our blood that is being shed. But we are responsible for those young men and their lives and their hopes. And if we don't end this foolish, damnable war, those young men will someday curse us for our pitiful willingness to let the Executive carry the burden the Constitution puts on us.

—Quoted in Robert Sam Anson, *McGovern: A Biography*

After the Second World War, however, Congress lost to the president much of its war power and control over foreign policy. In the late 1960s and early 1970s, as a result of the increasing unpopularity of the war in Vietnam, a movement began in Congress to try to restore some of the war power to the legislative branch. (These efforts are traced in Chapter 12.)

It was not until 1973 that Congress succeeded in placing any significant restrictions on presidential power to wage war. The first congressional victory was a bill barring any combat in, or bombing of, Cambodia after August 15, 1973. That same year, Congress passed the **War Powers Resolution,** designed to limit to 60 or 90 days the president's ability to commit American troops to combat without congressional authorization. The bill became law over President Nixon's veto. The War Powers Resolution failed to restrict presidential use of military power, however. It was clear as America moved into the 21st century that the president remained the dominant partner in the conduct of foreign policy.

Meanwhile, Congress made efforts to gain greater control over secret intelligence operations. Beginning in 1974, Congress required that before a covert operation can take place the president must issue a "finding" that the proposed operation is important to the national security. Congress also provided that the Central Intelligence Agency (CIA) could not spend money on covert operations without reporting them to six (later eight) congressional committees "in timely fashion." In 1980 Congress reduced to two the number of committees to which the CIA must report, but required prior notice of most secret operations.

President Reagan circumvented this provision in 1986, however, when he ordered his CIA director, William J. Casey, to conceal the arms sales to Iran from Congress. As a result, Congress in 1991 enacted a law tightening the provisions requiring the president to notify the congressional committees of covert actions, including those operations carried out through other countries or private citizens.

Early each morning, officials meet at the CIA to prepare the president's daily intelligence briefing on world developments.
Copyright © CORBIS/Roger Ressmeyer/Starlight

Between 1950 and 2000, nine American presidents committed U.S. troops to foreign soil (in Korea, Lebanon, the Dominican Republic, Vietnam, Cambodia, Iran, Grenada, Honduras, Panama, the Persian Gulf, Somalia, Haiti, Rwanda, Bosnia, and Kosovo) without any declaration of war by Congress. In several instances, however, Congress had passed resolutions broadly supporting presidential action in various geographic areas: the Formosa Resolution (1954); the Middle East Resolution (1957); the Cuba Resolution (1962); the Tonkin Gulf Resolution (1964); the Multinational Force in Lebanon Resolution (1983); and the Authorization for Use of Military Force against Iraq Resolution (1991).

But, because the president has substantial control over the channels of information about military actions—the news that the Pentagon releases to the public and to Congress—he may be able to shape the congressional response. Congress passed the Tonkin Gulf Resolution after President Johnson announced on nationwide television on August 4, 1964, that two U.S. destroyers, the *Maddox* and the *Turner Joy*, had been attacked in the Gulf of Tonkin off Vietnam. Secretary of Defense Robert S. McNamara declared that the two ships had been under "continuous torpedo attack." Up to this point 163 Americans had died in Vietnam and there were 16,000 troops there as "advisers." After passage of the Tonkin Gulf Resolution, President Johnson—beginning early in 1965—vastly expanded the war.

It developed, however, that reports of the attack in the Tonkin Gulf had been considerably exaggerated. For example, the captain of the *Maddox*, Commander Herbert L. Ogier, later said he thought that two torpedoes were fired but that subsequent reports of torpedoes were actually sonar readings caused by the destroyer's own propellers.[19] Indeed, as the task force commander warned Washington: "Freak weather effects and an over-eager sonarman may have accounted for many reports."[20] At a Senate hearing four years later, Senator Albert Gore, Democrat, of Tennessee (whose son and namesake was elected vice president in 1992 and 1996 and ran for president in 2000), told Secretary McNamara to his face: "I feel that I have been misled, and that the American people have been misled."[21]

As the Tonkin Gulf episode illustrates, one major reason Congress has lost to the president so much of its power over foreign affairs is that diplomatic, military, and intelligence information flows directly to the president. As a result, Congress and the public have tended to assume that the president "has the facts" and is acting on the basis of expert advice. Second, foreign policy decisions are often made in crisis situations, in "an atmosphere of real or contrived urgency."[22]

This, too, puts pressure on Congress to defer to presumed presidential wisdom. More recently, however, there has been an increasing realization that the extensive flow of information to the president does not guarantee that his foreign policy decisions will necessarily prove correct or wise.

The Machinery

Today the president of the United States has powerful tools available for the conduct of foreign policy, including a personal staff and that of the National Security Council, the State Department, the Pentagon, the CIA, and other agencies.

The existence of this machinery does not mean, however, that the United States can always influence, let alone control, the course of international events. American policymakers may not be able to affect the price of OPEC oil, stop the seizure of American diplomats by Islamic revolutionaries, or prevent terrorist attacks on U.S. installations or military forces.

Until 1947 no formal centralized machinery existed to aid the president in his foreign policy tasks. In that year, Congress attempted to give the president the tools to match his responsibilities.

The National Security Council   The National Security Act of 1947 created the **National Security Council (NSC),** a White House panel designed to help coordinate American military and foreign policy. The NSC, in the language of the statute, advises the president on "the integration of domestic, foreign, and military policies relating to the national security." In one sense the act, amended and expanded in 1949, was an effort to institutionalize the power that had been wielded over military-diplomatic affairs by President Roosevelt in the Second World War. It was also an effort to provide continuity from one administration to the next in the conduct of national security affairs. The NSC, however, has been used very differently by a succession of presidents.

> **Online**   *for more information about the National Security Council, see:*
> *www.whitehouse.gov/WH/EOP/NSC/html/nschome.html*

Eisenhower, who had spent most of his career in the military, relied upon it frequently. During both the Kennedy and Johnson administrations, the NSC was occasionally used for "window dressing" during a crisis to give the appearance of somber decisions being made by the president with his highest national security advisers. Real decisions were sometimes reached in less formal meetings. During the Cuban Missile Crisis of 1962, however, Kennedy expanded the NSC, creating an executive committee, or Ex Comm, that met almost continuously to deal with the threat of Soviet nuclear missiles that had been sent to Cuba.

President Nixon directed that the NSC "be reestablished as the principal forum for presidential consideration of foreign-policy issues."[23] Various interagency groups, special panels, and review committees began to flourish once again under Nixon and his adviser for national security, Henry Kissinger. During the Reagan Administration, it was a member of the NSC staff, Marine Lt. Col. Oliver North, who, with help from the CIA, coordinated the secret operations that burgeoned into the Iran-contra scandal. The president's national security adviser, Vice Adm. John M. Poindexter, worked closely with North in carrying out and concealing the Iran arms sales and the diversion of profits to the contras in Nicaragua.

After an investigation by an independent counsel, North, Poindexter, and others were indicted for conspiring to defraud the government and then covering up their actions. North was convicted in 1989 of falsifying and destroying documents, but his conviction was overturned by a federal appeals court, which questioned whether his testimony to congressional investigators had been unfairly used against him. The independent counsel then dropped all charges. But in North's testimony to Congress he had admitted shredding documents sought by investigators.

Poindexter was convicted of deceiving Congress and lying to Congress, but the appeals court also overturned his conviction on similar grounds. At the congressional hearings into the scandal, however, Admiral Poindexter, calmly puffing on his pipe, admitted that he had destroyed a presidential "finding," a statement permitting the covert arms-for-hostages sales. He also asserted that he had never informed Reagan of the diversion of millions of dollars to the contras. Thus, under Reagan, the NSC and the post of national security adviser fell, for a time, into disrepute.

After George Bush was elected president in 1988, he named former Air Force General Brent Scowcroft to head the NSC staff. Clinton appointed Anthony Lake, and then Samuel R. "Sandy" Berger to the post.

The State Department   George F. Kennan has described the American State Department in a less turbulent era: "The Department of State . . . in the 1920s when I entered it, was a quaint old place, with its law-office atmosphere, its cool dark corridors, its swinging doors, its brass cuspidors, its black leather rocking chairs, and the grandfather's clock in the Secretary of State's office."[24]

Today the State Department is huge; it occupies a large, antiseptically modern building that houses about a third of its 23,000 employees. Department couriers hand-carry diplomatic documents 10 million miles a year in travels between Washington and the 177 U.S. embassies abroad. High-speed coded communications link the secretary of state to American embassies overseas, handling more than 300,000 words daily. In the Operations Center on the seventh floor, behind a locked door that is opened by a buzzer, the secretary can monitor a developing crisis. A device flashes incoming cables on a screen; the center can reach any U.S. post abroad in two minutes.

Online   *for more information about the State Department, see:*
www.state.gov

Despite all this, the State Department's level of efficiency has been the target of periodic criticism. As the United States became a world power, the size of the department increased vastly; bureaus and assistant secretaries proliferated. One reason that the State Department is slow to form policy is the "clearance factor"—the tendency of each branch of the department to check and clear matters with other branches and bureaus and other agencies of government. The department's snail-like replies to President Kennedy's requests were a constant source of frustration in the White House, where McGeorge Bundy was the national security adviser. By one account Kennedy would say, "Damn it, Bundy and I get more done in one day in the White House than they do in six months at the State Department. . . . They never have any ideas over there . . . never come up with anything new."[25]

The role of the secretary of state varies greatly according to the secretary's personal relationship with the president. In theory the principal foreign policy adviser and the ranking officer of the cabinet, the secretary in practice may be overshadowed by the president's national security assistant or the secretary of defense. For example, as national security adviser, Henry Kissinger was far more powerful than Secretary of State William P. Rogers during the first Nixon administration. Rogers was often kept in the dark about major foreign policy decisions, which were concealed from him by Kissinger and Nixon.[26] Later Nixon appointed Kissinger secretary of state. Toward the end of the Clinton Administration, Sandy Berger, the national security adviser, appeared to some analysts to have become more influential in dealing with foreign policy than Secretary of State Madeleine K. Albright.[27]

To help administer the State Department and its annual budget of about $3.2 billion, the secretary of state has the Executive Secretariat, which controls the flow of paperwork and tries to keep the secretary from being drowned in a sea of words. There are six geographic bureaus: African Affairs, East Asian and Pacific Affairs, European Affairs, South Asian Affairs, Near Eastern Affairs, and Western Hemisphere Affairs. Within the geographic bureaus are more than a hundred country desks. In addition, there are functional bureaus dealing with subjects such as economic and business affairs; arms control; nonproliferation; political-military affairs; verification and compliance; educational and cultural affairs; public affairs; international information programs; diplomatic security; the Foreign Service Institute; consular affairs; finance and management policy; democracy, human rights, and labor; international narcotics and law enforcement; population, refugee, and migration; and international organizations (the bureau that manages U.S. policy at the United Nations).[28]

The U.S. Foreign Service consists of the professional diplomats who represent the United States overseas and staff key policy posts in the State Department in Washington. Most foreign service officers are stationed abroad as ambassadors, ministers, and political and consular officials. Posts are normally rotated, and members of the foreign service periodically return to Washington between tours of duty overseas. In the year 2000, the Foreign Service numbered 8,190 men and women; of whom 3,215 were foreign service "officers"—the nation's professional diplomats.

Overseas, the ambassador is the president's personal representative to the chief of state and government to which he or she is accredited. Appointed by the president and subject to Senate confirmation, the ambassador is formally in charge of the entire U.S. mission in a foreign capital. The mission may include representatives of the Agency for International Development (AID), as well as the military service attachés, military assistance advisory groups, and officers of the CIA, all of whom make up the so-called "country team." Often it is a team in name only, however, with each element reporting back to its own headquarters in Washington and some officials working at cross-purposes to the ambassador. "To a degree," a Senate subcommittee concluded, "the primacy of the ambassador is a polite fiction."[29]

In addition to problems of coordination with other agencies of government, the State Department also faces competition from those agencies. In the past it has competed for the president's attention, not only with the White House national security adviser but with other agencies involved in foreign policy—the Office of International Security Affairs in the Defense Department, for example, and the CIA. To some extent the State Department must also compete with outside sources of advice in foreign policy—defense research firms, universities, presidential task forces, private organizations interested in foreign policy, and former government officials who may be called in and consulted by the president.

Information and Arms Control   In 1999, under a reorganization enacted by Congress, the U.S. Information Agency (USIA) and the Arms Control and Disarmament Agency (ACDA), formerly independent entities, were merged into the State Department, along with the 7,000 employees of the two agencies. The goal of the international information program, although absorbed into the State Department, remained unchanged: to present information about America to people overseas in the best possible light and to try to gain support for U.S. policies.

The arms control component of the State Department prepares and manages U.S. participation in international arms control and disarmament negotiations, and it also has important responsibilities in conducting long-range research on techniques of arms control. In the past, as an independent agency, ACDA played an active role in negotiations between the United States and the Soviet Union to reduce the number of nuclear arms in the two countries.

The State Department must share the foreign policy field with dozens of other agencies of the federal government involved in various aspects of foreign affairs. These include not only the Department of Defense and the CIA, but the departments of Agriculture, Labor, Commerce, Justice, Treasury, and Transportation, all which have some foreign responsibilities.

Intelligence and Foreign Policy: The CIA, the National Security Agency, and the National Reconnaissance Office   In February 1994, FBI agents arrested Aldrich H. Ames, an officer of the Central Intelligence Agency, and his wife, Rosario, touching off a spy scandal that shook public and congressional confidence in the CIA. Ames had acted as a Soviet mole for nine years, betraying to the KGB, Moscow's intelligence service, the names of Soviet intelligence officers and other Russians who were secretly working for the CIA. Ten were executed and many others imprisoned. Ames was paid or promised a total of $4.6 million by the Russians, making him the highest-paid spy in history. He was convicted and sentenced to life in prison with no possibility of parole. His wife received a prison sentence of five years. Investigations by the CIA and the Senate and House intelligence committees criticized the intelligence agency for its failure to detect the spy inside its own ranks.[30]

All major powers, and many smaller countries, have intelligence services. In the United States, the CIA gathers information from human spies, satellites, and open sources, and the agency's analysts prepare reports for the president to assist him in making foreign policy decisions. But the CIA has also engaged in covert operations—secret political action in other countries, usually conducted with presidential approval, that have sometimes caused the United States embarrassment.

---

 for more information about the CIA, see: www.cia.gov

During the 1992 presidential campaign, as noted earlier, President Bush was questioned about the extent of his knowledge of the Iran-contra affair, which had its roots in a CIA covert operation. The controversy had begun in the Reagan Administration, in which Bush served as vice president. Under Reagan, the CIA had supported what eventually grew into an army of 15,000 "contras," exiles dedicated to overthrowing the leftist Sandinista government of Nicaragua.

President Reagan, concerned over what he saw as Communist expansion in Central America, vigorously pursued what had begun as a secret war but soon became widely discussed and debated. Disturbed over the secret war in Nicaragua, Congress passed restrictions on CIA participation—the "Boland amendments."

It was in an effort to circumvent these laws that the Reagan White House, through the NSC staff, took control of the contra operation. But CIA director William Casey worked closely with Marine Lt. Col. Oliver North in the resupply effort, and some CIA personnel took part despite the congressional ban. In an effort to free American hostages seized in the Middle East, the administration sold arms to Iran and diverted the profits to aid the contras. The chief of covert operations retired in the wake of the Iran-contra scandal and the new CIA director, former FBI chief William Webster, disciplined seven CIA officers for their roles.[31]

During the 1970s Senate and House investigating committees disclosed a series of startling actions by the Central Intelligence Agency: The CIA had hired two underworld figures, Sam Giancana and Johnny Rosselli (both of whom were later murdered), to assassinate Cuban Premier Fidel Castro with poison. During four presidential administrations, the CIA had also plotted the assassination of, or coups against, seven other foreign leaders.* The congressional committees also disclosed abuses by the FBI, the National Security Agency (NSA), and other branches of the intelligence community.

The congressional inquiries were launched after Seymour M. Hersh, an investigative reporter for the *New York Times,* disclosed that for several years, beginning in the late 1960s, the CIA had, in violation of its charter, spied on American citizens at home and infiltrated antiwar and other dissident groups.[32] These charges were later documented in a report of a presidential commission headed by Vice President Nelson A. Rockefeller, which found that some of the CIA's actions were "plainly unlawful."[33]

The Rockefeller report and the congressional committees disclosed that the CIA had photographed and followed American citizens; engaged in break-ins, wiretapping, and bugging of Americans; and for 20 years had opened, read, and photographed first-class mail in violation of federal law. The agency had also experimented with mind-altering drugs; one subject, an army civilian researcher, committed suicide several days after the CIA had laced his after-dinner drink with LSD. He was not told about the drug until 20 minutes after it was administered.

Activities of this sort were not mentioned in the law passed by Congress in 1947 establishing the CIA. The law said that the agency was to advise the National Security Council and to acquire and analyze political, military, and economic knowledge about other countries on which the president could base his decisions about foreign affairs.

The 1947 law makes no specific reference to covert operations abroad, although the statute does permit the CIA to perform such "other functions and duties" as the National Security Council may direct. Presidents have authorized covert operations under this loophole in the law. But as the Senate Intelligence Committee concluded: "Authority for covert action cannot be found in the National Security Act."[34] Yet the committee reported that the CIA had carried out 900 major covert operations between 1961 and 1975. In 1984, the CIA was reported to be conducting 50 covert operations around the globe.[35] And the Senate panel found that the CIA's widespread domestic spying, to which it gave the code name Operation CHAOS, violated the provisions of the 1947 act designed to prohibit the agency from acting as a domestic police force.

Prior to the Japanese attack on Pearl Harbor in 1941, the United States had no central intelligence-gathering agency. After Pearl Harbor, President Roosevelt created the Office of Strategic Services (OSS) to gather intelligence, conduct secret political warfare, and carry out sabotage operations behind enemy lines during the Second World War.

*See U.S. Senate, Select Committee to Study Governmental Operations with Respect to Intelligence Activities, 94th Cong., 1st sess., *Alleged Assassination Plots Involving Foreign Leaders, Interim Report,* (Washington, D.C.: U.S. Government Printing Office, 1975). In addition to describing the efforts to assassinate Castro, the report also details CIA plots against Patrice Lumumba of the Congo, Rafael Trujillo of the Dominican Republic, President Salvador Allende and General René Schneider of Chile, President Ngo Dinh Diem of South Vietnam, President François Duvalier of Haiti, and President Achmed Sukarno of Indonesia.

The CIA was the direct descendant of the wartime OSS. The director of the CIA wears one hat as head of the agency and principal intelligence adviser to the president. But the director simultaneously is responsible for coordinating the work of the other government intelligence agencies, including the National Security Agency (NSA), the code-making and code-breaking arm of the Pentagon; the National Reconnaissance Office (NRO), which manages spy satellites; the Defense Intelligence Agency (DIA), the military rival to the CIA; the FBI; and the State Department's Bureau of Intelligence and Research (INR). Together, these agencies spend an estimated $30 billion a year.[36]

The CIA has two principal divisions. An Intelligence Directorate engages in overt collection, research, and analysis of foreign intelligence. Most of the criticism of the CIA has been directed at its Operations Directorate, which engages in the secret collection of intelligence (espionage) and in secret political action (covert operations). On occasion this directorate has helped to overthrow governments—in Iran in 1953 and Guatemala in 1954, for example. It was this clandestine arm of the CIA that plotted the assassination of such leaders as Cuba's Fidel Castro and Patrice Lumumba in the Congo (now Zaire), launched the invasion of Cuba at the Bay

of Pigs in 1961, and supported a secret army of 30,000 persons in Laos.

Although, unlike the FBI, the CIA has no police power within the United States, in 1967 it was disclosed that the CIA was subsidizing the National Student Association and dozens of foundations and private groups within the country. President Johnson ordered that most of the secret funding be ended.

In 1972 the CIA again became enmeshed in domestic activities. Most of the burglars caught in the Watergate break-in had CIA backgrounds, and one was on the intelligence agency's payroll at the time of the break-in. A year earlier, at the request of the White House, the CIA had secretly assisted E. Howard Hunt, Jr., a former CIA operative and White House "plumber," and one of the men eventually convicted in the Watergate burglary. And President Nixon tried to use the CIA to block the FBI from probing the burglary of Democratic headquarters.

The CIA's size and budget are secret, but it has been unofficially estimated that the agency spends about $3.1 billion a year and employs some 17,000 people.[37] The CIA has its headquarters in a secluded, wooded area of Langley, Virginia, just across the Potomac River from Washington.

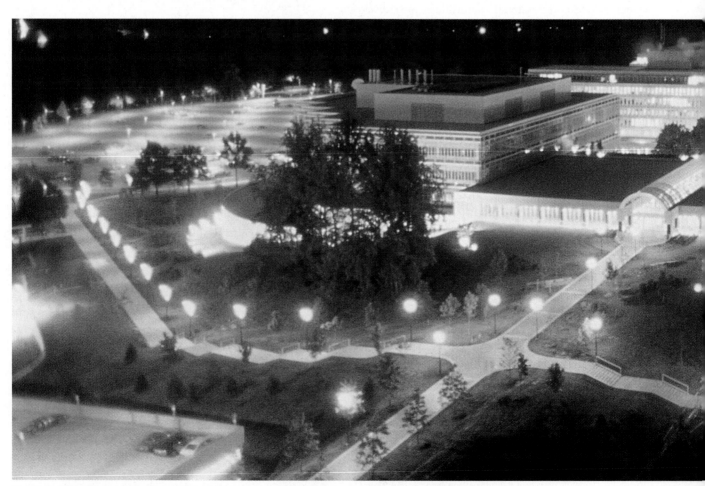

The Central Intelligence Agency, Langley, Virginia
Copyright © CORBIS/Roger Ressmeyer/Starlight

But the CIA is only one of a dozen U.S. intelligence agencies that together make up what is sometimes called the "intelligence community." The CIA, in fact, has a much smaller annual budget than the National Reconnaissance Office (NRO), which spends $6.2 billion, or the National Security Agency (NSA), which has a reported budget of $3.7 billion and 38,000 employees—much larger than the CIA or any of the other intelligence agencies.[38]

The ability of the NSA to intercept all forms of communication, including telephone conversations and e-mail, has raised privacy concerns both at home, and abroad, where the agency has been criticized for its mysterious and supersecret Echelon program that gathers communications intelligence in foreign countries. France and other European nations have investigated the program. From what is known, Echelon grew out of an agreement among the United States, Britain, Canada, Australia, and New Zealand to share intelligence.

As one account described it, "At its core, Echelon is a network of ground stations with dishes aimed at the dozen or so satellites that now shepherd much of the world's television, fax, Internet and voice data. High-capacity computers allow millions of signals per hour to be intercepted and scanned for keywords of interest to each country's intelligence community."[39]

The NSA is prohibited from intercepting strictly domestic conversations or communications in the United States without a court order. But at the same time that the agency has been criticized in Europe for listening in to traffic overseas, it has been criticized in Congress for failing to keep up with new technology. For example, data encryption, widely available commercially, fiber-optic cables, and the overwhelming number of e-mails criss-crossing the globe have made it more difficult for the NSA to do its job.

Until the 1960s, the American public knew little about the activities of the intelligence agencies. During the 1950s, the CIA, under its director, Allen W. Dulles, toiled largely out of the limelight. The loss of a U-2, a CIA spy plane, on a flight over the Soviet Union in 1960 and the disaster at the Bay of Pigs in 1961 thrust the CIA into the headlines and focused attention on its activities. By 1964 critics charged that the CIA stood at the center of what had become "an invisible government."[40] Former Assistant Secretary of State Roger Hilsman wrote: "The root fear was that the CIA represented . . . a state within a state, and certainly the basis for fear was there."[41]

On the other hand, because the CIA is a secret agency and usually does not make any public comment, it is sometimes blamed for things it does not do. Defenders of the CIA argue that it operates under sufficient control and does not carry out any covert operations abroad "without appropriate approval at a high political level in our government outside the CIA."[42] This approval usually comes from an interagency board that has responsibility for authorizing covert operations. However, in the mid-1970s the Senate Intelligence Committee (known at the time as the Church Committee for its chairman at the time, Senator Frank Church, Democrat of Idaho) reported that the interagency board seldom met. And former CIA director Richard Helms conceded in testimony to the committee that the board has acted as a "circuit breaker" to insulate the president from responsibility for covert CIA operations.[43] Nor has the interagency board always been advised of CIA covert operations.

The CIA's defenders have argued that despite the agency's mistakes, it is an essential arm of the government. Allen Dulles wrote, for example, that an intelligence service "is the best insurance we can take out against surprise." As for covert CIA operations inside other countries, Dulles contended that the United States could not limit its activities "to those cases where we are invited in."[44]

In the wake of the various investigations of the CIA and the FBI, Congress finally moved to strengthen its control over the intelligence establishment. The Senate and the House each created a permanent Select Committee on Intelligence with authority over the CIA and the other intelligence agencies. Congress declined to enact detailed reform bills to control the intelligence agencies, but it did pass a law requiring the president to furnish information to the intelligence committees and to notify them in advance of covert operations in most circumstances.

When President Reagan appointed William J. Casey, a millionaire New York lawyer, as director of the CIA, the choice proved controversial, in part because Casey had managed Reagan's 1980 presidential campaign, and there was concern over a political figure directing the intelligence agency. The CIA director was also criticized for certain stock market transactions and other business dealings.

Casey died in May 1987, before he could be fully questioned by Congress about his role in the Iran-contra scandal. After Casey's death, it was revealed that he had gone outside normal CIA channels and arranged with the Saudi Arabian intelligence service to undertake covert operations; one such operation, an assassination attempt, mistakenly killed 80 innocent people when a car bomb exploded in Beirut in 1985.[45] When William Webster retired as CIA director in 1991, President Bush named Robert M. Gates to succeed him. Because Gates had worked closely with William Casey during the time of the Iran-contra operation, his nomination was contro-

versial. Additional controversy revolved around charges by CIA analysts that Gates had slanted intelligence estimates to please his superiors. After protracted hearings, Gates was confirmed by the Senate.

Clinton appointed R. James Woolsey as CIA director. But Woolsey, criticized in Congress for his handling of the Ames spy case, resigned at the end of 1994, and Clinton named John M. Deutch, the deputy secretary of defense, as his successor. In 1996, published reports claimed that drug dealers had sold crack cocaine to street gangs in South Central Los Angeles to finance the CIA-supported contra rebels in Nicaragua. Deutch asserted there was, "no substance" to the charges, and later investigations found no evidence to support the allegations. President Clinton replaced Deutch in 1995 with the CIA's deputy director, George J. Tenet. In 2000, Deutch was investigated by the Justice Department for mishandling classified information in his home computers, both while at the Pentagon and later at the CIA.

However necessary it may be to protect American security, the existence of a clandestine intelligence and espionage establishment creates special problems in a free society. The operations of the CIA and the other U.S. intelligence agencies pose the continuing dilemma of how secret intelligence machinery can be made compatible with democratic government.[46]

Other Instruments: AID, the Peace Corps, and the Voice of America

The State Department must compete in the foreign policy field with the president's NSC staff, the CIA, and the Pentagon. Several other agencies and units of the federal government also are involved in foreign policy.

One of the agencies with foreign policy responsibilities both in Washington and in the field is the Agency for International Development (AID). AID, as its initials imply, is responsible for carrying out programs of financial and technical assistance to less economically developed nations.

Since the initiation of the Marshall Plan, the United States has spent more than $200 billion on foreign aid, contributions to international organizations, and military assistance. For fiscal 2001, for example, the president's budget request for foreign aid totaled $10.7 billion and included economic assistance for about 80 countries in Latin America, Asia, Africa, the Middle East, Eastern Europe, and the former republics of the Soviet Union. In recent years, the United States has placed greater emphasis on channeling aid through multilateral financial institutions, and it has increased its participation in the International Bank for Reconstruction and Development (World Bank), which makes loans to and promotes foreign investments in underdeveloped nations.

AID is politically unpopular because many Americans regard it as a "give-away" program with little visible benefit to the taxpayers. But the aid program can be defended both on humanitarian grounds and, more narrowly, on political grounds. As the richest nation in the

MAKING A DIFFERENCE

INSPIRING HOPE: MIDDLE EAST TEENAGERS WORKING FOR PEACE IN MAINE

OTISFIELD, MAINE—This pine-scented camp on the shore of Pleasant Lake, Maine, may hold hope for the tormented Holy Land. It is the site of "Seeds of Peace," a program that brings together Arab and Israeli teenagers for a month of fun and serious discussions.

The camp is part of a private program launched in 1993 by John Wallach, former foreign editor of the Hearst newspapers, to bring together children from troubled lands. Wallach says that he was tired of "being a fly on the wall of history" and wanted to "inspire hope."

Aside from swimming and other summer camp activities, the heart of "Seeds of Peace" is a daily, 90-minute discussion known in camp shorthand as "coexistence." Many of the sessions center on fear. Israeli teenagers tell of being afraid that someone—anyone—standing next to them might be a suicide bomber. They talk a lot about the Holocaust, which many of their co-campers know little about because it is not taught in most Arab schools.

Sara Jabari, a 15-year-old Palestinian, said her father, a gas station owner in Hebron, was warned by Hamas, the extremist Palestinian group responsible for the suicide bombings, not to send her to the peace camp. He ignored the warning "because he believes in peace, and I believe in peace," Jabari said.

Jabari said she was wary of the Israeli campers at first. "I thought all Israelis were like the [Israeli] settlers, and the settlers are always killing our people." Then she met Dana Naor. "She is my friend. She is so nice and I know [among] the Israelis, there is good and there is bad from them. And from the Palestinians, there is good and there is bad too. I really had a new idea of the Israelis from Dana."

"Seeds of Peace" takes no government money, and Wallach said he raises the necessary funds each year from individuals and corporations.

"The whole point of it is to let people recognize that the differences are wide, that they are deep, but that it's up to them to find a way to resolve it," said Wallach. "This may seem like a simple thing, but you have to understand that many of these boys and girls have never heard the other side."

Wallach says it is nearly impossible to do the same with adults because, in his words, "They have too much baggage." That is why Wallach founded this program centered on young people who would return to their homelands as "ambassadors of peace."

This program has so impressed agencies in other countries that Wallach has been asked to create similar pilot programs for Greek and Turkish Cypriot youths and one for youngsters from Serbia, Croatia, and Bosnia.

The teens leave camp full of hope. Then they return home. There most will face criticism from those, including friends, who say they have been brainwashed.

They will keep in touch with their newfound friends via e-mail and will try to visit each other. For some, that will mean traveling in secret.

Adi Fassler, an Israeli, says now she knows why building peace is so difficult. She believes if adults and government leaders went through the same camp experience, they would learn to accept each other.

—Adapted from the *Boston Globe, USA Today,* and the *Washington Post*

---

world, the United States has felt a moral obligation to try to alleviate poverty, disease, and malnutrition in other nations. At the same time, supporters of the aid program contend, peace and stability are unlikely to be achieved for the United States or the world as a whole as long as such conditions exist in the poorer nations.

Despite some popular misconceptions, most foreign aid is not given to other countries in the form of cash. Most AID dollars are spent in the United States to buy commodities and to hire technical experts for projects overseas. AID provides technical assistance by sending abroad specialists in such fields as health, economic growth, environment, and democracy. Through development loans, repayable in dollars, AID offers other countries long-term, low-interest financing for such projects as highways, dams, schools, and hospitals. In addition, the United States donates and sells agricultural commodities at low cost to other countries.

Many poorer countries have been burdened by debt as a result of loans by industrial nations and multilateral organizations. In the year 2000, many diverse world figures, including Pope John Paul II, and well-known entertainment figures, urged that the wealthier nations forgive the debt of the world's poorest nations. In October of that year, congressional leaders agreed to allot $435 million for the U.S. share of a $90 billion global debt relief initiative.[47]

The Peace Corps was created under President Kennedy in 1961 to provide a trained corps of highly motivated American volunteers, many of them young, to help people in developing nations. By the year 2000, some 7,000 Peace Corps volunteers were in training or serving abroad in 76 countries as teachers, agricultural aides, doctors, and in many other capacities. In 1990, after democratic governments emerged in the former Soviet Union and Eastern Europe, the Peace

Corps sent volunteers for the first time to many of those countries, including Czechoslovakia, Hungary, Poland, Russia, and Ukraine.

Peace Corps volunteers, who must be U.S. citizens and at least 18 years old, serve abroad for two years and receive a monthly allowance for food, clothing, housing, and other living expenses. Upon completing a tour, Peace Corps volunteers receive an additional $225 for each month served. By 2000, some 161,000 persons had served in the Peace Corps.

The Voice of America became an independent government agency in 1999. As the government's official radio, it beams news broadcasts, music, and feature programs in 53 languages to some 90 million listeners around the globe. Although its purpose is to promote American democracy abroad, its staff attempts to report the news objectively in order to maintain credibility with its foreign audience. A bipartisan Broadcasting Board of Governors, an independent agency of the executive branch, oversees the VOA.

The United Nations

The **United Nations (UN)** was founded in San Francisco in 1945 to fulfill the dream of a community of nations, a world body that could take collective action to keep the peace and work for the betterment of humanity. The opening words of the UN charter declared: "We the peoples of the United Nations determined to save succeeding generations from the scourge of war, which twice in our lifetime has brought untold sorrow to mankind."

Online for more information about the United Nations, see: www.un.org

During the Cold War years, however, the United Nations was generally unable to keep the peace on issues that divided the major world powers. Decisions affecting world peace were made in Washington, Moscow, Beijing, and other capitals, but less often at UN headquarters in New York City. In part, this was predictable from the structure of the UN and the nature of international relations.

The UN Security Council, with 15 members, cannot act over the veto of any of the five permanent members—as of 2000, the United States, Russia, Britain, France, and China. Other countries, including Germany and Japan, have been pressing to become permanent members of the Security Council. Because the former Soviet Union frequently exercised a veto in the Security Council, UN members sought a way to circumvent the council. In November 1950, the UN General Assembly decided that it could act to meet threats to peace when the Security Council failed to do so because the permanent members lacked unanimity. There is no veto power in the General Assembly, to which all member nations belong. Although the General Assembly has thus increased somewhat in importance, it, too, has proved

unable to cope with many major conflicts. The United States is represented in the UN by an ambassador who heads a U.S. mission in New York.

The UN has acted with varying success in several world crises: in Korea in 1950, Suez in 1956, the Congo in 1961, and Cyprus in 1964. And in the Arab-Israeli War of October 1973, the UN played a significant role in reducing tensions and avoiding a military confrontation between the United States and the Soviet Union. But the UN was not able to end the tragic war in Nigeria nor the fighting in Vietnam, and it had scant success in the Middle East during the Arab-Israeli Six-Day War in 1967. The UN failed in its efforts to mediate in the dispute between Argentina and Britain over the Falkland Islands in 1982, and its attempt to end Israel's invasion of Lebanon that year was also unsuccessful.

On the other hand, the UN played a role in bringing about the Soviet withdrawal from Afghanistan and in halting the long war between Iran and Iraq in the 1980s. And it provided the umbrella for the coalition of nations, led by the United States, that forced Iraq to withdraw from Kuwait in 1991. The following year UN teams, at great risk and with casualties, brought relief supplies by air and land to beleaguered Sarajevo in the civil war that followed the breakup of Communist Yugoslavia. The UN also voted trade sanctions against Yugoslavia in an effort to promote peace among the warring factions. But the UN was unable to stop the slaughter in that conflict, or to end the siege of Sarajevo and attacks on other Muslim cities in Bosnia by the Bosnian Serbs.

At the start of the 21st century, despite some setbacks, the United Nations was playing a more active role as world peacekeeper. To some extent, this change reflected the fact that the Security Council often had the unanimity it needed to act, in contrast to the past, when the Soviet Union had frequently exercised its veto. In the year 2000, there were more than 47,794 UN peacekeepers deployed around the world. (These are detailed in Table 16-1.)

The United States provides one-quarter of the UN's $1 billion annual budget, plus several hundred million dollars more each year as its share of the UN's peacekeeping costs. However, the United States lost much of its influence in the United Nations in the 1960s as the UN shifted from a pro-Western to a neutralist stand. As many of the former colonial territories of Africa and Asia gained independence, they joined the UN, and the United States could no longer count on winning its political battles in that body.

With the loss of American leadership in the UN, criticism of the world body increased in the United States, particularly during the 1980s among conservatives associated with the Reagan Administration. At the same time, public support for the UN diminished.

In 1984, discontented with anti-American and anti-Western sentiments in the United Nations Educational, Scientific, and Cultural Organization (UNESCO), the

United Nations Peacekeeping Forces, 2000

Member states of the United Nations provide troops and officers for UN peacekeeping forces that are periodically sent to crisis areas around the world. In the year 2000, there were more than 47,000 UN military personnel in the field.

UN Force (year created)	Location	Troops
UN Truce Supervision Organization (1948)	Israel	143
UN Military Observer Group in India and Pakistan (1949)	India and Pakistan	46
UN Peacekeeping Force in Cyprus (1964)	Cyprus	1,253
UN Disengagement Observer Force (1974)	Golan Heights (Syria-Israel border)	1,040
UN Interim Force in Lebanon (1978)	Southern Lebanon	5,643
UN Iraq-Kuwait Observation Mission (1991)	Iraq-Kuwait	1,104
UN Mission for the Referendum in Western Sahara (1991)	Western Sahara	1,309
UN Protection Force in Bosnia and Herzegovina (1992)	Bosnia-Herzegovina	8,566
UN Observer Mission in Georgia (1993)	Georgia	102
UN Confidence Restoration Operation in Croatia (1996)	Prevlaka peninsula	27
UN Interim Administration Mission in Kosovo (1999)	Kosovo	1,870
UN Mission in Sierra Leone (1999)	Freetown, Sierra Leone	13,000
UN Transitional Administration in East Timor (1999)	Dili, East Timor	9,229
UN Organization Mission in the Democratic Republic of the Congo (1999)	Democratic Republic of the Congo and the subregion, including Namibia, Rwanda, Uganda, Zambia, and Zimbabwe	262
UN Mission in Ethiopia and Eritrea (2000)	Ethiopia and Eritrea	4,200
		Total 47,794

SOURCE: Data provided by the United Nations, "Current Peacekeeping Operations," online at <www.un.org/Depts/dpko/dpko/cu_mission/body.htm>.

United States withdrew from the body. In Washington's view, UNESCO had become a forum to blame Israel and the West for many of the problems of the developing world. The United States was also opposed to a UNESCO plan backed by Third World nations to place tighter government controls over journalists.

By 2000 the UN had expanded from its original 50 to 189 members, with a biennial budget of $2.16 billion and a staff of 52,100 around the world.[48] The UN is administered by a secretariat, staffed by the member nations, and headed by a secretary-general, who in 1999 was Kofi Annan of Ghana.

In recent years, public support in the United States for the UN has been high. A 1999 poll, for example, found that 70 percent of Americans had a favorable opinion of the United Nations.[49] Some segments of the public, however, have seen the world organization as a threat to American sovereignty. Some militia groups even imagined that "black United Nations helicopters" were coming to invade America.[50]

Although the UN has had limited success as a peacekeeping agency, it has served several other constructive purposes. It provides a forum for discussion, a place where new and small nations can be heard. It sometimes helps to defuse world crises by allowing nations to talk instead of fight. And its economic, social, and health agencies have made significant contributions in improving the lives of millions of people all over the world. The UN was also having some success in dealing with such international environmental issues as the peaceful use of outer space and seabeds, pollution of the oceans, and overpopulation. Finally, the UN, for all its inadequacies, still remains a symbol of hope, the tangible embodiment of humanity's fragile dream of peace.

The Politics of Foreign Policymaking

Over a period of time, widespread or intense domestic reaction to foreign policy may have an impact on government. During the late 1960s, there was domestic protest against the war in Vietnam by students, professors, and many other citizens. Some Americans reacted against the protesters, but others were undoubtedly favorably influenced by the peace movement. Eventually, a majority of Americans felt the war was a mistake, and a climate developed in which President Johnson felt it prudent not to run for reelection. The growing opposition to the war provided the political backdrop for President Nixon's decision in 1969 to begin the withdrawal of American troops and for the lengthy peace negotiations, conducted initially in secret, that finally brought an end to U.S. participation in the war in 1973.

The Role of the Public   Despite public awareness of highly publicized issues like Vietnam or the seizure of American diplomats in Iran, some political scientists have argued that on most foreign policy issues, the public is both uninterested and uninformed. Gabriel A. Almond has observed that "Americans tend to exhaust their emotional and intellectual energies in private pursuits." While members of the public may develop well-defined views on domestic questions that affect them directly, he has argued, on questions of foreign policy they tend to react in changeable, "formless and plastic moods."[51] Almond has suggested that relatively small leadership groups play the major role in the making of most specific foreign policy decisions, and that the public's role is largely confined to the expression of mass attitudes that provide a framework within which officials may work.[52]

James N. Rosenau has also differentiated between public response to domestic issues and foreign policy issues, but he emphasizes that when a foreign policy question becomes so big that it involves "a society's resources and relationships," it quickly turns into a domestic political issue—and he cites the war in Vietnam as an example.[53]

Copyright © Burt Glinn/Magnum

Nevertheless, a president has wide latitude in conducting foreign policy. Kenneth N. Waltz has suggested that as a rule: "The first effect of an international crisis is to increase the president's popular standing." But, Waltz points out, a president sometimes risks political unpopularity in a foreign policy crisis no matter what he does.[54] And a president who responds too readily to public opinion may be pushed into dangerous choices if public sentiment is running high for quick or simple solutions. Just as the public may demand peace, at other times it may demand retaliation that risks war.

Domestic influence on foreign policy is not limited to mass public opinion as reflected in polls, e-mail, letters, or protest demonstrations. Congress, individual legislators or committee chairpersons, interest groups, private organizations concerned with foreign policy, opinion leaders, the press, TV commentators, and proximity to an election all may have some effect on policy outcomes. Some foreign policy questions are of special importance to particular groups. A president who is interested in carrying New York, California, and Illinois, for example, in his reelection campaign may frame U.S. policy toward Israel with some thought to the likely reaction among the many Jewish voters in those states. On Polish patriotic days, members of Congress from heavily Polish areas such as Buffalo or Chicago stand in the House and Senate and carefully pay homage to the contribution of Polish heroes to the nation's heritage.

Presidential Credibility   A president's conduct of foreign policy depends in large measure on whether he is able to carry the public along with him on big decisions. Without public trust in his leadership, he may fail.

President Reagan's approval rating plummeted after the disclosure in 1986 that—despite his stated public policy of never dealing with terrorists—he had secretly sold arms to Iran to try to extricate American hostages seized by terrorists in Lebanon.

Other presidents have encountered credibility problems. Since the Second World War, the government has on more than one occasion told official lies designed to protect secret intelligence operations. Under President Eisenhower, for example, the administration claimed at first that the U-2 spy plane shot down 1,200 miles inside the Soviet Union was a "weather research" aircraft that had strayed off course. Under President Kennedy, the government initially denied, but later admitted, that it was responsible for the CIA-backed invasion of Cuba at the Bay of Pigs.

President Johnson suffered from a "credibility gap" that seriously hampered his presidency. The Tonkin Gulf episode, discussed earlier in this chapter, was one example of an event during his presidency that took on a far different coloration after the fact. During the Watergate scandal, President Nixon claimed he had concealed certain information for "national security" reasons, but he later admitted political motivation as well; "national security" had been used as a pretext to cover up a crime.[55] Official statements about foreign policy and national security, in short, have contributed to an erosion of public confidence in government honesty.

Political Parties, Campaigns, and Foreign Policy

The two-party system tends to push both major parties toward the center on foreign policy issues. Kenneth N. Waltz explains that "failure to do so will give a third party the chance to wedge itself in between its two larger competitors. . . . The policy positions of two competing parties begin to approach one another, and the candidates even begin to look and talk very much alike."[56]

Nevertheless, foreign policy questions often become campaign issues. In 2000, for example, Vice President Gore sought to emphasize his own experience in foreign affairs, and to contrast that with his Republican opponent's inexperience in foreign policy, since George W. Bush was a state governor.

Advocates of bipartisanship in foreign policy contend that both major political parties should broadly support the president, and that foreign policy issues should not be sharply debated in political campaigns. They argue that it is in the nation's interest to appear united to the rest of the world. Opponents of bipartisanship have argued that foreign policy issues must be discussed in political campaigns precisely because those issues are so important. Bipartisanship flourished particularly in the period shortly after the Second World War. It was symbolized by the phrase "Politics stops at the water's edge," a concept popularized in 1950 by Senator Arthur H. Vandenberg, a Michigan Republican who had served as chairman of the Senate Foreign Relations Committee under a Democratic president, Harry Truman.

The Economics of Foreign Policymaking

In a world in which the American economy is so directly affected by trade, foreign policy cannot be concerned with political and military power alone. As the nation moved further into the 21st century, foreign policy increasingly involved major economic questions, such as trade restrictions, import quotas, the balance of trade, and interest rates. The impact of economic policy and globalization on foreign affairs is discussed in Chapter 17.

THE DEFENSE ESTABLISHMENT

On August 2, 1990, Iraqi troops invaded the desert sheikdom of Kuwait, seizing control of the capital and its oilfields. For President Bush, the surprise invasion posed a major dilemma. To respond with military force risked a war in which there might be many thousands of American casualties. To do nothing, the policymakers in Washington reasoned, might encourage Iraq's dictator, Saddam Hussein, to move farther south into Saudi Arabia, jeopardizing a major source of oil supplies for the United States and the West.

Bush ordered American forces into the Persian Gulf. With the backing of the United Nations and a coalition of 28 countries, Washington went to war, eventually sending 527,000 men and women to the Gulf. When Iraq did not back down, on January 16, 1991, Bush launched Operation Desert Storm with massive air and missile attacks on targets in Iraq and Kuwait. Saddam Hussein responded: "The mother of all battles has begun."[57]

Iraq began firing Scud missiles at Saudi Arabia and Israel, and the United States destroyed a number of them with Patriot missiles. When repeated bombing failed to dislodge Iraqi forces from Kuwait, Bush ordered a ground war to begin on February 23. Four days later, the war was over, with Iraqi forces in full retreat.

U.S. casualties were remarkably light. A total of 146 Americans were killed in action and 467 were wounded. It was a war that Americans at home watched on television. CNN correspondent Peter Arnett reported from Baghdad even as the bombs were dropping around him. Viewers watched Scud missiles arcing into Israel and videotapes of American "smart bombs" literally dropping into the smokestacks of enemy targets. The commander of Desert Storm, General H. Norman Schwarzkopf, became an instant celebrity (and after he retired, a millionaire from his memoirs). President Bush's popularity soared.

A year later, the war had to a large extent faded from public memory. Bush, facing voters worried about their jobs and futures, saw his approval rating plummet. And in the aftermath of war, the public learned that some of what had occurred had been concealed and that some of the information that was released had been misleading. For example, almost 24 percent of American battle deaths were from so-called "friendly fire." Only 6 percent of all bombs dropped in the war were "smart," that is, guided to their targets by lasers, and most of the rest missed their targets.[58]

Leading scientists testified to Congress that the Patriot missiles may have caused more damage from explosive debris than if they had never been fired. This was true, the scientists said, because when a Patriot antimissile intercepted a Scud, the broken pieces from both missiles inflicted great damage when they fell to the ground. And because the Patriot system fired more than one interceptor missile at each incoming Scud, the number of explosive warheads that fell to earth in Israel was larger than if the defensive system had not been deployed.[59] One study found that Patriot missiles had intercepted Iraqi Scud missiles only 9 percent of the time.[60] And the war had cost the taxpayers at least $7.3 billion.*

---

*The total initial cost to the United States of the Persian Gulf War was $61.3 billion. However, allied countries, including Kuwait, Saudi Arabia, Japan, and Germany, reimbursed the United States almost $54 billion, so that the final cost to American taxpayers was reduced to $7.3 billion. See Department of Defense, *Conduct of the Persian Gulf War: Final Report to Congress*, April 1992, pp. P-2–P-3.

American soldiers in Kuwait, 1991
Copyright © Bruno Barbey/Magnum

Nevertheless, as a purely military exercise, it was an impressive performance. More than half a million men and women had been moved across the ocean to the Middle East, along with hundreds of planes, tanks, missiles, bombs, and other military equipment. The United States had rolled up Iraq's army, considered the best in the region, in four days, with relatively low casualties.

To an extent, the success of American forces on the battlefield was a reflection of the enormous expenditures for defense by the United States in recent decades. Since the Second World War the United States has spent more than $3 trillion on national defense; in fiscal 2001 the Defense Department's budget request was $286.4 billion. Because of expanding technology, however, some weapons systems become obsolete even as they are deployed. And during the years when the Soviet Union stood as a rival superpower, a strong argument could be made that, because of the threat of nuclear war, as spending for armaments increased, national security actually diminished.

Aside from this paradox, the existence of a multi-billion-dollar military machine has created numerous problems for American society. Within the military-industrial complex, whole industries depend on government defense contracts; aerospace industry lobbyists attempt to guard their clients' interests in Washington; and some universities compete for classified military research contracts. A society that devotes some 16 percent of the its national budget to defense-related spending cannot allocate as much as it otherwise might to eliminate poverty, or improve health, schools, and the natural environment. The "cost" of a defense economy cannot be measured simply in terms of the size of the annual Pentagon budget.

Up to now, America's nuclear weapons have remained in their underground silos and beneath the sea in submarines. With the end of the Cold War, their use seems even less likely. But since the Second World War, the United States has fought a series of "limited" or conventional wars in Korea, Vietnam, and the Persian Gulf. Despite its vast weaponry, manpower, and technology, the United States learned in Vietnam that superior size and resources were of little advantage against an elusive and politically dedicated enemy skilled in guerrilla warfare.

The United States could not employ nuclear weapons against a smaller nation without being morally condemned by most of the rest of the world as well as by millions of citizens at home. The use of such weapons

"Put simply, the mission is to discover a potential enemy who could justify our three-hundred-billion-dollar defense budget."

has been considered, however. During the Korean War, for example, President Eisenhower discussed with his advisers the possible employment of nuclear arms.[61] But the use of tactical or strategic nuclear weapons in a conventional "limited war" may carry with it the threat of escalation into a larger war. To an extent, therefore, the "usable power" of the United States has been limited. Furthermore, domestic opposition to U.S. involvement in Southeast Asia, the Middle East, Central America, and the Persian Gulf has demonstrated the potential political risks and limitations for American leaders pursuing military solutions to foreign policy problems.

Foreign policy and defense policy are intimately linked. Ideally, as Burton M. Sapin notes: "Foreign policy establishes the broad outlines within which the defense establishment must do its work."[62] A modern president must contend with the problems of controlling a huge, powerful military establishment with its friends and protectors in Congress and its clients in private industry. The president must see that the generals serve his foreign policy goals, rather than the other way around.

The Department of Defense

The principle of civilian control over the American military establishment is deeply rooted in the Constitution and the nation's tradition. The president is commander

The Pentagon

in chief of all the armed forces, and the secretary of defense, by law, must be a civilian. Yet the effectiveness of civilian control of the military has sometimes been open to question.

Across the Potomac River from Washington, in Arlington, Virginia, lies the Pentagon. Completed in 1943 at a cost of $83 million, the Pentagon houses some 23,000 civilian and military employees. In its concourse is a shopping center large enough for most suburban cities. The Pentagon has its own bank, post office, barbershop, department stores, florist—even an optometrist and medical and dental clinics. The secretary of defense is the Western world's biggest employer, in charge of 703,000 civilians and 1,370,000 members of the armed forces as of 1999. Indirectly, the Pentagon is also the biggest private employer in America; in 1999, for example, the Defense Department's contracts were running at a level of $118 billion a year.[63]

The National Security Act of 1947, as amended in 1949, unified the armed forces under the control of a single secretary of defense. The Army, Navy, and Air Force continue to exist as separate entities within the Defense Department, each with its own secretary. The secretaries of the armed services do not control their military operations, however; that is the responsibility of the president, acting through the secretary of defense and the Joint Chiefs of Staff. The Pentagon has its own "little State Department," the Office of International Security Affairs (ISA), which serves both as the Defense Department's link with the State Department and as a competing source of foreign policy formulation. The Pentagon also has its own intelligence organization, the Defense Intelligence Agency (DIA), created in 1961, as well as the supersecret National Security Agency (NSA), discussed earlier in this chapter, which intercepts the coded messages of other nations and conducts electronic espionage.

The Joint Chiefs of Staff

The members of the **Joint Chiefs of Staff** are the chairman, the chiefs of staff of the three armed services, and, when Marine Corps matters are under consideration, the commandant of the Marines. By law the chairman, whose powers were greatly strengthened by the Defense Reorganization Act of 1986, advises the president and the secretary of defense.

The chairman and other members of the Joint Chiefs are appointed by the president. Sometimes the president may skip over senior officers to appoint a more dynamic, younger service chief. The chairman of the Joint Chiefs outranks the other members. Together, the Joint Chiefs are responsible for day-to-day conduct of military operations as well as long-range strategic planning. They are assisted by a Joint Staff of 1,300 officers from the three services. Although the president relies on the chairman of the Joint Chiefs for military advice, he may choose to disregard the chairman's views. The president has the

responsibility to weigh military risks against the nation's total foreign policy objectives.

Robert Kennedy related that during the Cuban Missile Crisis in 1962, one member of the Joint Chiefs advocated the use of nuclear weapons: "I thought, as I listened, of the many times that I had heard the military take positions which, if wrong, had the advantage that no one would be around at the end to know."[64]

But not every military officer is a "hawk." A series of leading military figures in recent decades—generals like George Marshall, Omar Bradley, Matthew Ridgway, James Gavin, and Maxwell Taylor—clearly demonstrated that they could view foreign policy in its broadest context, not merely in narrow, military terms. Another career military man, President Eisenhower, resisted the advice of some of his military advisers and refused, for example, to intervene in Southeast Asia in 1954. And some high-ranking military officers and ex-officers criticized the war in Vietnam.

Selective Service

Although in peacetime the United States has usually relied on a volunteer army, the government has registered or drafted men for military service during times of international tension or war. During the Second World War, the Korean War, and the Vietnam War, for example, men were conscripted for military duty.

Early in 1980, in response to events in Iran and Afghanistan, President Carter asked Congress to resume draft registration. Congress approved the legislation, and registration at 34,000 post offices began that summer. The Selective Service System did not issue draft cards or classify those who registered. There could not be an actual draft unless Congress approved a call-up. Although Carter had asked for authority to register both men and women, Congress refused to approve draft registration for women. In 1981, the Supreme Court ruled that a draft of men only was constitutional.[65] Draft registration of men continued under Presidents Reagan, Bush, and Clinton.

Strategic Arms: The Balance of Terror

With the collapse in 1991 of the Soviet Union, the chief adversary of the United States, the threat of a nuclear world war seemed much less likely. But both the United States and Russia in the year 2000 still possessed intercontinental nuclear missiles, as did China and several other nations; and a number of smaller countries were attempting to obtain nuclear weapons. The *New York Times* reminded its readers of this reality with a report on an ICBM base 60 feet below a windswept prairie in Wyoming: "It is easy to forget that the United States military still spends about $28 billion a year to keep about 7,500 nuclear warheads ready for use. This is roughly the equivalent of 145,000 Hiroshima bombs."[66]

FIGURE 16-2

Potential Destruction from Nuclear Weapons

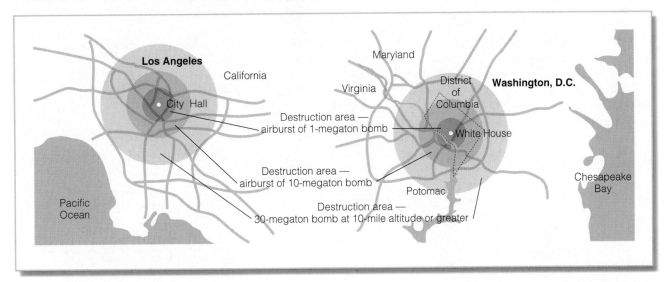

In the decades after the 1950s, the world lived with the knowledge that it was less than 30 minutes away from nuclear disaster. Even now, with the end of the Cold War and major cutbacks in strategic arms, a nuclear war—even one started by accident—while much less likely, is not an impossibility. (Figure 16-2 illustrates the potential destruction of two major U.S. cities.)

The American nuclear monopoly was broken when the Soviet Union exploded an atomic bomb in 1949. In 1957 the Soviet Union launched the first Sputnik, or earth satellite. The military implications were clear: If Russia possessed the technology to boost a satellite into outer space, it had long-range missiles that could be targeted on American cities. In October 1964 Communist China exploded its first nuclear bomb, and the "nuclear club" then had five members—the United States, the Soviet Union, Britain, France, and China. India became the sixth member when it exploded a nuclear device in May 1974. Both India and Pakistan held underground tests of nuclear weapons in 1998. Israel has nuclear weapons. South Africa has said it built six nuclear bombs and then destroyed them.

After the Second World War, the United States adopted a policy of **strategic deterrence.** The theory of deterrence, developed in the Pentagon with the assistance of defense "think tanks" such as the Rand Corporation and the Institute of Defense Analyses (IDA), involved deploying enough nuclear weapons so that an enemy would not, in theory, attack the United States, for fear of being attacked in retaliation.

But how, if it relied on nuclear arms alone, could the United States respond to nonnuclear military challenges? President Kennedy believed it was necessary for the United States to supplement its nuclear power by expanding its capacity to fight "conventional" wars. During the 1960s, the policy of massive nuclear retaliation changed to one of "limited" or "flexible" response, and the Pentagon trained its Special Forces (the Green Berets) in guerrilla warfare and "counterinsurgency." In Vietnam, at least, the new theory and techniques did not prove to be very successful.

Henry A. Kissinger argued in 1957 that the United States must be able to fight a "limited nuclear war,"[67] a position from which he later retreated.[68]

Some defense intellectuals shocked many people by their attempts at rational analysis of an essentially irrational process—thermonuclear war. For example, Herman Kahn wrote in 1961 that a nuclear war "would not preclude normal and happy lives for the majority of survivors and their descendants."[69] The picture of nuclear survivors living joyful lives amid the charred, radioactive debris did not convince everyone. Other analysts, such as Ralph E. Lapp, argued that the nation's arsenal of weapons had grown into "a monstrous stockpile which could not only kill, but overkill, any possible enemy."[70]

The strategy of deterrence had a language all its own. Military theorists spoke of "first-strike capability" and "second-strike capability," "stable deterrent," or "counterforce." By the late 1960s the jargon included ominous new acronyms: MIRV (multiple independently targetable reentry vehicle), MAD (mutual assured destruction), and ABM (antiballistic missile). Whatever parity had been achieved in the "balance of terror" was threatened by new technology—the simultaneous development of the ABM as a defense against ballistic missiles, and the MIRV, designed to overwhelm the ABM system by firing from one missile a cluster of real and dummy warheads to confuse radar defenses.

A United States Air Force underground control center
Copyright © Herman Kokojan/Black Star

The spiraling arms race, in short, threatened to go out of control. The history of U.S. development of the ABM illustrates the problem: In 1967 the Johnson Administration disclosed that the Soviet Union had deployed an antiballistic missile system around Moscow. The administration opposed deployment of the ABM by the United States, arguing that Soviet countermeasures would leave both countries with no net increase in security.

But the Joint Chiefs of Staff and powerful members of Congress favored an ABM program. So the United States in 1969 embarked on a round of strategic spending for the Safeguard ABM system, which would cost the taxpayers many billions of dollars.

On October 1, 1975, the enormous complex of radars, missiles, and computers, located in the wheat fields near Grand Forks, North Dakota, was completed, at a cost of $5.7 billion. The Pentagon announced that Safeguard was fully operational. By an irony of history, the next day the House of Representatives voted to dismantle the project. The Senate concurred and the missile facilities were shut down. Even before its completion, the ABM had become obsolete when the Soviets developed MIRV—multiple independently targetable warheads that could overwhelm the antimissile defense system.[71] This was precisely the argument that critics

of the ABM had used during a Senate debate over the ABM in 1968.

The 1972 SALT agreements limited ABM deployment by the United States and the Soviet Union and included a five-year freeze on production and testing of offensive nuclear weapons. At the time of the agreement, however, the United States had 1,054 intercontinental ballistic missiles (ICBMs) and 656 submarine-launched missiles; the Soviet Union had 1,618 ICBMs and 650 submarine-launched missiles.[72] Both sides, in other words, continued to possess immense destructive power despite the 1972 agreement and later accords.

American strategic deterrence has long rested on a "triad" of nuclear weapons—land-based missiles, submarines armed with nuclear missiles, and the Strategic Air Command's bombers. But the theories of how these deadly weapons should be used have changed over the years. For example, in 1983, President Reagan announced the new Strategic Defense Initiative (SDI), better known as "Star Wars." The $60 billion program was designed to develop and test components for tracking and shooting down Soviet nuclear missiles in space. SDI assumed the development of such advanced technology as lasers or particle beams that could intercept

"General Hoskins, I don't care if you are in charge of our star-wars defense. You must wear a regulation uniform."

incoming missiles. The Reagan strategy thus meant a shift from the traditional doctrine of "massive retaliation" to a defensive posture.

Critics of the program said it would be overwhelmed by countermeasures, would cost vast sums of money, and, most of all, might encourage an enemy to attack first, before such a defensive net could be deployed. With the end of the Cold War, the program was scaled down. Proponents argued that it was still necessary because more nations were acquiring nuclear weapons and ballistic missiles, increasing the chance of accidental or intentional use. Star Wars was never built.

During the 1990s, a scaled-down version of Star Wars was pursued by the Pentagon during the Clinton administration, despite a series of failed tests in which an "exoatmospheric kill vehicle" mounted atop a rocket was supposed to intercept a missile and destroy it by colliding with it. The Clinton plan, although termed a national missile defense system, was not designed to counter an all-out attack, but to ward off missiles that might be launched by so-called "rogue" nations. Although the administration pledged $6.6 billion over five years to begin building the system, Clinton in September 2000 deferred the decision on deployment, leaving it to his successor. He acted after a second failed test of the kill vehicle in July. Russia strongly objected to the planned missile defense system, arguing that it violated the 1972 ABM treaty limiting the deployment of antiballistic missiles.

Even as the arms race spiraled, scientists raised new questions about whether a nation that launched a nuclear attack, even a "successful" attack, might destroy itself and the planet. Some experts questioned whether any nuclear strategy could provide true security for any nation. In 1984, for example, the chief of staff of the U.S. Air Force, General Charles A. Gabriel, declared: "I don't think anyone in his right mind would argue that nuclear war is winnable."[73]

Arms Control and Disarmament

For years, leaders of both the United States and the Soviet Union realized that the arms race and the strategy of deterrence, however "logical," could lead to disaster. One obvious but elusive alternative was arms control and disarmament, the subject of intermittent negotiations between Moscow and Washington since the Second World War. But progress was slow, until the global political framework changed so suddenly and surprisingly.

The march toward disarmament began in 1963 when the United States, the Soviet Union, and Great Britain reached agreement on a limited nuclear test-ban treaty. The treaty, banning tests in the air, underwater, and in outer space—but not underground—was signed in Moscow and ratified by the U.S. Senate. More than a hundred nations signed the treaty, but two atomic powers—France and China—refused to do so.

Despite progress between Washington and Moscow, nuclear proliferation, the spread of atomic weapons to more countries, continued as a threat to the world. Even as the superpowers were cutting back, other nations were busily attempting to acquire nuclear weapons and join the "nuclear club." As that has happened, some analysts believe, global stability may be threatened even more than it had been during the Cold War era.

In 1968 the United Nations General Assembly voted approval of a draft treaty banning the spread of nuclear weapons to states not already possessing them. The United States, the Soviet Union, and 60 other nations signed the Nonproliferation Treaty, and the Senate ratified it in 1969. But Israel, India, Japan, France, and China did not sign. The treaty was extended indefinitely in 1995.

In 1972 the United States and the Soviet Union signed the SALT treaty to limit strategic arms, and in 1979, a second agreement, known as SALT II, was reached, although never ratified by the U.S. Senate.

In the summer of 1982, a new round of arms control talks began in Geneva. SALT was renamed START (Strategic Arms Reduction Talks) by the Reagan administration. Finally in 1987, the United States and the Soviet Union agreed to dismantle all of their intermediate- and shorter-range missiles, and Soviet leader Gorbachev journeyed to Washington to sign the treaty in December. The agreement, sometimes known as the INF (Intermediate-range Nuclear Forces) treaty, was historic because it marked the first time that the two countries had agreed to reduce their nuclear arsenals. Under it, the United States pledged to destroy the nuclear missiles it had deployed in Western Europe as well as all other intermediate- and shorter-range weapons, and the Soviets in turn promised to destroy their intermediate- and shorter-range missiles. And in 1991, both sides signed the START I agreement to reduce strategic, long-range missiles.

In January 1993, President Bush and President Yeltsin of Russia met in Moscow and signed a far-reaching treaty to destroy three-quarters of their nuclear warheads over 10 years. The treaty, known as START II, also called for the elimination of all land-based intercontinental ballistic missiles with multiple warheads. The agreement required each country to reduce its total of missiles, to 3,500 for the United States and 3,000 for Russia, by the year 2003 or sooner. The Senate ratified the pact in 1996.

That same year, the United States, Russia, and most of the nations of the world signed the Comprehensive Test Ban Treaty (CTBT), banning all underground nuclear weapons tests and explosions, just as testing in the atmosphere is already banned. It was rejected by the Republican-controlled Senate in 1999 as a result of opposition by Majority Leader Trent Lott and other Republicans, who did not want to approve the treaty unless the White House moved forward with a missile defense system.

During the war in the Persian Gulf, Israel and the UN allies feared that Iraq might arm its missiles with chemical weapons. That did not occur, but the world still faced the threat of chemical and biological warfare. In 1969 President Nixon announced that the United States was renouncing germ warfare and would no longer stockpile biological weapons. But he said the United States would continue to engage in "defensive research" in biological weapons. At that time the United States did not renounce chemical warfare, including the production of deadly nerve gases like sarin or VX—a tiny drop of which can kill instantly.

In 1970, however, President Nixon submitted to the Senate the Geneva Protocol outlawing chemical and biological warfare among nations. The United States had signed the treaty in 1925, but the Senate had never ratified it. It finally did so in 1974. In 1972 the United States, the Soviet Union, and some 70 other nations signed an international agreement to outlaw biological weapons. This treaty, too, was ratified by the Senate in 1974. Thus, today, the United States is formally pledged not to use chemical or biological weapons.

But the treaties did not prohibit the production or stockpiling of chemical weapons. In April 1984, Reagan proposed a new international treaty to ban the use, production, or stockpiling of chemical weapons. In 1992 disarmament negotiators in Geneva reached agreement on a Chemical Weapons Convention to ban the production, sale, and use of nerve gas and other chemical weapons. By 1995, a total of 159 nations, including the United States and Russia, had signed the treaty. It was ratified by the Senate in 1997 and went into effect that same year.

THE MILITARY-INDUSTRIAL COMPLEX

In his final speech to the nation, President Eisenhower warned against what he called "unwarranted influence" by the **military-industrial complex.**[74] The term has often been used since that time to describe the economic and political ties between the military establishment and the defense-aerospace industry. Eisenhower thus focused attention on the consequences for America of a vast military establishment linked to a huge arms industry. In the years after Eisenhower's 1961 warning, the concept of the military-industrial complex was expanded to encompass universities conducting defense research, scientists, laboratories, aerospace industry contractors, and research firms.

Entire communities in some areas were dependent on defense industries or military installations. In fiscal 1999 the Lockheed Martin Corporation received $12.67 billion in defense contracts from the government, heading the list of the hundred largest defense contractors in the United States.[75] The top 10 defense contractors in America are shown in Table 16-2.

Defense spending fattens the congressional "pork barrel." Powerful individual legislators can, and do, obtain multimillion-dollar contracts for their states and districts. Another example of the interrelationships within the military-industrial complex is the fact that retired military officers are frequently hired by aerospace industry contractors.

The effect of the military-industrial complex is pervasive and difficult to measure. But with many billions of dollars at stake, the scramble for contracts, the pressure on Congress and the Pentagon, and the politi-

TABLE 16-2

The Top 10 Defense Contractors

Rank	Company	Amount of Defense Contracts (in billions)
1	Lockheed Martin Corp.	$12.67
2	Boeing Company, Inc.	11.56
3	Raytheon Company, Inc.	6.40
4	General Dynamics	4.56
5	Northrop Grumman	3.19
6	United Technologies	2.36
7	Litton Industries, Inc.	2.09
8	General Electric	1.71
9	TRW, Inc.	1.43
10	Textron, Inc.	1.42

SOURCE: Figures are rounded. Data from the Center for Defense Information, Fact Sheet, "Top 15 U.S. Defense Contractors of FY '99," online at <www.cdi.org/issues/usmi/complex/top15FY99.html>.

cal and economic rewards involved have given some Americans a substantial interest in an economy geared to defense production.

A military-industrial complex spawned to protect American security has created numerous problems for American society. America faced, and still faces, the problem of how to balance its military needs against social needs at home. Billions of dollars that might, in part at least, have been used for education, housing, transportation, and similar programs were siphoned off into arms. Even when the United States lost its main adversary, with the disintegration of the Soviet Union, the questions remained of whether, and to what extent, the vast defense and aerospace industries would retool for peace, and how much money previously earmarked for the military would find its way into education, health care, or other social programs.

Professor Paul Kennedy has also argued: "If . . . too large a proportion of the state's resources is diverted from wealth creation and allocated instead to military purposes, then that is likely to lead to a weakening of national power over the longer term."[76]

Huge military expenditures are often the result of intense political battles and pressures. The debate over the controversial B-1 and B-2 bombers provided an example of the enormous economic stakes in a new weapons system. For years the Air Force, backed by the aerospace industry and influential members of Congress, had pushed for production of the supersonic missile-firing B-1 bomber. Killed by President Carter, it took wing again under President Reagan, who announced plans to produce 100 of the supersonic aircraft at a cost of billions. The bomber was the most expensive weapons system in the federal budget. Moreover, the B-1 was produced only as an interim plane until the B-2, or Stealth bomber, which was designed to evade enemy radar, was developed for the 1990s.

The first B-1 rolled off the production line in October 1986. But accidents and serious flaws in its performance raised questions about whether the costly plane really worked. As author Nick Kotz wrote in 1988, "By now the B-1 is more than a bomber. It has become a cause. . . . Decisions about the American defense arsenal are influenced as much by psychological, political, and economic factors as by military analysis."[77] Whether a weapons system gets built may depend as much on political factors as on military necessity, Kotz argued. The result may be "billions wasted on weapons and military facilities we don't need," and an arms program "totally out of control."[78] A total of 97 B-1 bombers were built, but the aircraft was never used in the war in the Persian Gulf; the Air Force depended on older, more reliable aircraft.

A B-2 stealth bomber
Antelope Valley Press/AP/Wide World

DUBAI, UNITED ARAB EMIRATES—Sleek fighter jets made in the USA glimmer on a desert tarmac while American top-gun pilots hover like car salesmen.

Courting oil-rich sheiks and princes, the pilots enthrall the royalty with war stories from Desert Storm.

This is the Dubai Air Show, where the glitter of marketing meets the drab-green reality of war. It is a six-day extravaganza that is the Third World's largest showcase of the latest high-tech weaponry.

"These things can fight, we found that out," Gulf war hero Eric Dodson boasts to a group of Emirates' royalty viewing the merchandise. With $5 billion to spend, they are in the market for 80 fighter jets. . . .

In this climate of the hard sell, America's arms industry—backed by President Clinton and his Defense and Commerce departments—has gone from 13 percent of the pre–Cold War global market to about 70 percent today. In the seven years since the collapse of the Soviet Union, America has emerged as the world's leading exporter of conventional weapons. . . .

But it's not traditional foreign policy that's made America dominant in exports, rather it is a domestic economic strategy by the Clinton administration.

Washington has funneled subsidies to the industry to facilitate exports, arguing that foreign sales keep U.S. procurement costs down and jobs at home. . . . Critics argue that U.S. arms export policy is misguided and dangerous, eroding the industrial base of the economy, spreading advanced weapons technology and generally making the world a more dangerous place.

—*Boston Globe*, February 11, 1996

Next, Congress funded the B-2, the Stealth bomber, and production began on 21 of the planes, which cost $2 billion each, at a total cost of $44.7 billion. The aircraft experienced a series of technical problems during years of flight tests, including faulty radar, and the General Accounting Office reported in 1997 that the plane's skin was so sensitive it had to be sheltered from heat and rain. The B-2 was finally used in combat for the first time in 1999 during the NATO bombing of Yugoslavia. One of the planes mistakenly bombed the Chinese embassy in Belgrade because the CIA had relied upon inaccurate maps.

One result of the military-industrial complex is that the United States has become arms merchant to the world. In just one year, for example, American contractors sold almost $11.8 billion in weapons to other nations in 1999, making the United States by far the world's biggest arms merchant. The total was larger than arms sales by all European countries combined.[79] In addition, the United States ships war matériel, ranging from rifles to jet fighter planes, to other nations under a military assistance program.

The military-industrial complex also has had social and political effects. Demographically, it has been partly responsible for increased population in states such as California, Texas, and Florida, with large defense or aerospace industries. This, in turn, has increased the political power of those states. Influential committee chairmen in Congress have channeled huge defense expenditures to their states, bringing economic benefits to those states and political benefits to the legislators. Conversely, in the early 1990s, cutbacks in defense spending caused by the end of the Cold War led to increased unemployment among defense workers in these states.

Finally, the huge amounts of money flowing into defense contracts can lead to fraud and bribery in the Pentagon's procurement of military weapons. In 1988, for example, it was disclosed that billions of dollars in contracts had been awarded to companies improperly and that some Pentagon officials had been bribed.

EISENHOWER'S WARNING: THE MILITARY-INDUSTRIAL COMPLEX

This conjunction of an immense military establishment and a large arms industry is new in the American experience. The total influence—economic, political, even spiritual—is felt in every city, every statehouse, every office of the federal government. We recognize the imperative need for this development. Yet we must not fail to comprehend its grave implications. Our toil, resources, and livelihood are all involved; so is the very structure of our society.

In the councils of government, we must guard against the acquisition of unwarranted influence, whether sought or unsought, by the military-industrial complex.

The potential for the disastrous rise of misplaced power exists and will persist.

We must never let the weight of this combination endanger our liberties or democratic processes. We should take nothing for granted. Only an alert and knowledgeable citizenry can compel the proper meshing of the huge industrial and military machinery of defense with our peaceful methods and goals, so that security and liberty may prosper together.

—Dwight D. Eisenhower, Farewell Radio and Television Address to the American People, January 17, 1961

Rina Castelnuovo/NYT Pictures

AMERICA'S WORLD ROLE IN THE 21ST CENTURY

By the year 2000, as we have seen, foreign policy issues had arisen in many new forms. They tended, perhaps even more than in the past, to involve economic issues—world trade, import restrictions, oil reserves and prices—and other issues such as the international environment and the ocean bed, hunger, overpopulation, nuclear proliferation, genocide, and disease, including the AIDS epidemic.

THIS ENDANGERED PLANET

The scale of modern technology is overflowing every political boundary. Whether it is a matter of radioactive fallout, carbon monoxide, or other poison effluents, multinational corporations, computer technology, satellite broadcasting, or air and space travel, we constantly witness a drive toward operations on a planetary scale. And yet most political behavior continues to be dominated by the territorial state. States compete with one another for power, wealth, and prestige, and jealously guard their sovereign prerogatives. This competitive pattern generates conflict, waste, and distrust. Huge amounts of resources are devoted to national defense, collective violence is persistent and pervasive, and wars occur at many points of the planet. . . . Governments at all levels have not demonstrated a great capacity to solve the most urgent problems of human society. Violence and misery persist in most national societies of the world.

—Richard A. Falk, *This Endangered Planet*

In the environmental area alone, the United States and other countries faced the daunting challenges of global warming, acid rain, depletion of the ozone layer, oil spills, controlling pesticides, preserving the rain forests that help to provide oxygen, and ensuring biodiversity, that is, maintaining the diversity of animals and plants in a world that humans share with other species.

These global problems suggest a new definition of the term "national security." As one study concluded, "the new concept of security in terms of common global threats, including threats to the environment, now presents an alternative to the traditional definition."[80]

Yet the old tensions among nations continued to exist, even if their shape had changed. The United States emerged from the Second World War as a major power, and it could wish away its power and global responsibility. At the same time, it faced the challenge of redefining its foreign policy goals and reordering its priorities in a world where tensions had been reduced by the end of superpower rivalry.

As the nation moved into the 21st century, many changes had taken place in the relations among nations. In the 1970s, American forces had come back from Vietnam, an American president had opened the door to the People's Republic of China, and Congress had at least tried to reassert its voice in the conduct of foreign policy. In the 1980s, the United States and the Soviet Union had moved part of the way down the road to limiting nuclear armaments. In the 1990s, both sides, now with Russia as the new player on the world stage, pledged drastic cuts in their nuclear arsenals. Democracy had come to Eastern Europe. But the collapse of communism had created new ethnic strife, for example, among nationalities in the former Soviet republics and in the former Yugoslavia. The Middle East remained volatile.

In the immediate aftermath of the Vietnam War, the conviction grew among many Americans that the nation should exercise great caution in intervening in armed conflicts beyond its borders. There was concern over the danger of U.S. involvement in "another Vietnam." By the time of the Persian Gulf War, however, these concerns had diminished substantially.

At the same time, domestic issues increased the pressures on the policymakers in Washington to weigh the legitimate concerns of American national security against needs at home. And it was increasingly clear that in addition to military power alone, a strong domestic economy—and with it, an increased ability to compete in world markets—would be the true measure of the nation's strength and its position in the world. It was no longer really possible to separate economic and foreign policies.

America in the new millennium remained a major international power. U.S. relations with the rest of the world were both broad-ranging and highly complex. And the formation of American foreign policy continued to be a major challenge to the nation's political leadership. The survival of the planet might depend on the decisions made in America.

KEY TERMS

globalization, p. 534
nuclear proliferation,
   p. 534
foreign policy, p. 535
national security, p. 535
Cold War, p. 537
isolationism, p. 538
Monroe Doctrine, p. 538
interventionism, p. 538
internationalism, p. 538
containment, p. 539
Marshall Plan, p. 539
nationalism, p. 541
détente, p. 543

Antiballistic Missile (ABM)
   Treaty, p. 543
War Powers Resolution,
   p. 551
National Security Council
   (NSC), p. 552
United Nations (UN),
   p. 560
Joint Chiefs of Staff,
   p. 566
strategic deterrence,
   p. 567
military-industrial
   complex, p. 570

CHAPTER HIGHLIGHTS

✦ Foreign policy is the sum of the goals, decisions, and actions that govern a nation's relations with the rest of the world.

✦ National security is a broad concept that may be defined in many ways, but the term is generally used to refer to the basic protection and defense of the nation.

✦ One fundamental historical characteristic of American foreign policy was that of isolationism, a policy of avoiding foreign involvement.

✦ An opposite strand of American foreign policy is interventionism, or military involvement by the United States in various parts of the world.

✦ The United States traded its former position of isolationism for one of internationalism, the policy that America must take an active leadership role in world affairs.

✦ Congress passed the War Powers Resolution, designed to limit to 60 or 90 days the president's ability to commit American troops to combat without congressional authorization. The law proved ineffective, however.

✦ Today the president of the United States has powerful tools available for the conduct of foreign policy, including a personal staff and that of the National Security Council, the State Department, the Pentagon, the CIA, and other agencies.

✦ The role of the secretary of state varies greatly according to the secretary's personal relationship with the president. In theory the principal foreign policy adviser and the ranking officer of the cabinet, the secretary in practice may be overshadowed by the president's national security assistant or the secretary of defense.

✦ The Peace Corps was created under President Kennedy in 1961 to provide a trained corps of highly motivated American volunteers, many of them young, to help people in developing nations.

✦ The United Nations was founded in San Francisco in 1945 to fulfill the dream of a community of nations, a world body that could take collective action to keep the peace and work for the betterment of humanity.

✦ The principle of civilian control over the American military establishment is deeply rooted in the Constitution and the nation's tradition. The president is commander in chief of all the armed forces, and the secretary of defense, by law, must be a civilian.

✦ Members of the Joint Chiefs of Staff are the chairman, the chiefs of staff of the three armed services, and, when Marine Corps matters are under consideration, the commandant of the Marines. By law the chairman, whose powers were greatly strengthened by the Defense Reorganization Act of 1986, advises the president and the secretary of defense.

✦ The term "military-industrial complex" has often been used to describe the economic and political ties between the military establishment and the defense-aerospace industry.

SUGGESTED WEB SITES

www.state.gov
State Department
The official Web site for the U.S. State Department. Offers advice for those traveling or living abroad, information about careers with the State Department, and "Background Notes," a detailed description of the geography, government, and politics of foreign countries.

www.cia.gov
Central Intelligence Agency
The Central Intelligence Agency's Web site describes its work and contains information about world affairs in its two publications, *The World Factbook*, and *Factbook on Intelligence*. Information is also available about careers in the CIA.

www.voa.gov
Voice of America
Voice of America is the U.S. government's official radio station. The Web site includes short-wave frequencies for the Voice of America, schedules of its programs, and a link that enables visitors to listen to its broadcasts over the Internet.

www.defenselink.mil
DefenseLink—The Official Web Site of the U.S. Department of Defense
DefenseLink offers links to the branches of the armed forces, news about the military, a virtual tour of the Pentagon, job listings for civilians, and the

Defense Almanac, a comprehensive book containing information and statistics about the Department of Defense.

www.peacecorps.org
The Peace Corps
The Peace Corps Web site offers information on joining, volunteer stories, and facts and news about the Peace Corps.

SUGGESTED READING

Allison, Graham, and Treverton, Gregory F., eds. *Rethinking America's Security: Beyond Cold War to New World Order** (New York: Norton, 1992). A valuable collection of essays on foreign policy after the end of the Cold War. The editors and some of the authors argue that responding to the nation's social problems is the first priority in preserving America's national security.

Almond, Gabriel A. *The American People and Foreign Policy,* 2nd edition (Greenwood Press, 1977). (Originally published in 1950.) An influential study of public opinion and how it relates to the formation and conduct of American policy.

Bush, George Herbert Walker, and Scowcroft, Brent. *A World Transformed** (Knopf, 1998). An account of the end of the Cold War by the former president and his national security adviser. They argue for continued internationalism, and against isolationism, in the post–Cold War era.

Halberstam, David. *The Best and the Brightest** (Random House, 1972). A detailed account of the men and the policies that led the United States into the costly war in Vietnam. Written in a highly readable, anecdotal style by a leading journalist who was one of the first to challenge the optimistic official reports on the progress of the war.

Huntington, Samuel P. *The Third Wave: Democratization in the Late Twentieth Century** (University of Oklahoma Press, 1993). A study of countries seeking to achieve a democratic form of government after the breakup of the Soviet Union and the demise of formerly Communist regimes in Eastern Europe. The author argues that a variety of factors may affect the success or failure of transitions to democracy.

Johnson, Loch K. *Secret Agencies: U.S. Intelligence in a Hostile World** (Yale University Press, 1998). A valuable and wide-ranging examination of the activities of the U.S. intelligence community.

Kennedy, Paul. *The Rise and Fall of the Great Powers: Economic Change and Military Conflict from 1500 to 2000** (Random House, 1987). An analysis of the shifts in global power over the past five centuries and how historical patterns are reflected in modern times. The author argues that nations actually lose power by "overextending" militarily and not allocating enough resources to the creation of wealth.

Kennedy, Robert F. *Thirteen Days** (Norton, 1999). (Originally published in 1969.) A short, fascinating account of the Cuban Missile Crisis of 1962 as it appeared to a key participant in the crucial decisions made by the Kennedy Administration. Reflects the great tension during the world's first nuclear confrontation.

Kissinger, Henry A. *Diplomacy** (Diane Publishing, 1998). A sweeping history of relations between nations by a prominent figure in 20th-century diplomacy. Kissinger, who was President Nixon's secretary of state, recounts his own experiences in foreign affairs.

Kotz, Nick. *Wild Blue Yonder: Money, Politics and the B-1 Bomber* (Random House, 1988). An excellent, detailed case study of the development of the B-1 bomber over 30 years. The author argues that the country's defense programs depend less on military merit than on the demands of dozens of interlocking special interests.

Maynes, Charles William, and Williamson, Richard S., eds. *U.S. Foreign Policy and the United Nations System* (Norton, 1996). A useful collection of essays on the role the United Nations can play in managing global problems and advancing U.S. foreign policy interests. The contributors discuss proposals for reforming the UN, as well as a number of major foreign policy issues.

Ohmae, Kenichi. *The End of the Nation State* (Diane Publishing, 1998). A provocative study on the transformation of the global economy. The author argues that nation-states have lost their key role in the management of economies, and are being supplanted by private corporations and by regional economic units.

Porter, Gareth, and Brown, Janet Welsh. *Global Environmental Politics,* 3rd edition (Westview Press, 1999). A brief but useful exploration of global environmental issues, such as acid rain and depletion of the ozone layer, that transcend national boundaries. The authors argue that threats to the global environment are replacing traditional definitions of national security.

Richelson, Jeffrey T. *The U.S. Intelligence Community,* 4th edition* (Westview Press, 1999). A detailed look at the American intelligence community, including its organization, operations, and structure. The author also examines the challenges that the intelligence community faces in the 21st century.

Rosenau, James N., ed. *Domestic Sources of Foreign Policy* (Free Press, 1967). A series of essays on the relationship between American domestic politics and foreign policy, written by a number of specialists in the field.

Woodward, Susan L. *Balkan Tragedy: Chaos and Dissolution after the Cold War* (The Brookings Institution, 1996). A detailed examination of the forces that led to political disintegration and war in the former Yugoslavia. Argues that differences among the Western powers prolonged the conflict and led to crises and frustration in the United Nations and in NATO.

---

*Available in paperback edition.

 Visit http://politicalscience.wadsworth.com/cummings9/update/ for current InfoTrac articles and other student resources related to this chapter.

CHAPTER 17

Government and the Economy

On March 29, 1999, the Dow Jones Industrial Average of 30 leading stocks rose above the 10,000 mark for the first time in history. On Wall Street, brokers and traders celebrated and uncorked the champagne.

Three years later, by the early fall of 2002, the champagne had gone flat. The Dow had fallen to below 7,500, and the NASDAQ index, which tracks high-technology stocks, had plunged as well. Millions of investors had lost an estimated $8.4 trillion in stock market value. Corporate fraud, the collapse of Enron—the giant energy trading company—and the indictment of top executives of major firms had shaken the faith of many ordinary citizens in the nation's business establishment. Only a strong housing market and substantial consumer spending buoyed an otherwise sluggish economy.

Along with Enron, the problems of WorldCom, a major telecommunications company, symbolized the corporate and accounting scandals. The firm, the nation's second-largest long-distance telephone company, had concealed more than $7 billion in expenses in order to show a profit on its books. The Securities and Exchange Commission charged WorldCom with defrauding its investors, and the company filed for bankruptcy.

A year earlier, a panel of economic experts declared that an economic recession had officially begun in March 2001. By the spring of 2002, Alan Greenspan, the chairman of the Federal Reserve Board, expressed optimism that the nation was recovering from the recession. Nevertheless, unemployment remained high, and the market continued its downward trend for many months.

The market slide directly affected Americans who had counted on their 401(k) and other pension plans to support them during their retirement years. Many workers were remaining on the job longer than they had expected; others who had already retired were forced to return to work to make ends meet.

The sharp fluctuations in the stock market, and the huge losses, hit people on Main Street as hard as in the skyscraper canyons of downtown Manhattan. In 2000, before the market declined, more than half of Americans had invested in stocks, a substantial increase from one-third only a decade earlier.* Millions of ordinary Americans, from auto mechanics to bank presidents, had bought stocks, bonds, or mutual funds. About 80 million Americans were shareholders, as individuals or through their company or union pension funds. In the aftermath of the terrorist attacks of September 11, 2001, however, and as the market continued to slide, investors withdrew billions from mutual funds.

Much of the earlier growth in the stock market had been driven by high-technology stocks such as Microsoft, the computer giant, and Intel, the chip maker, both among the components of the Dow. But many of the high-tech stocks on the NASDAQ exchange did poorly in 2000, as a large number of so-called "dot-com" companies fell by the wayside.† Many, even some of the most glamorous, had failed to turn a profit. It began to dawn on people that they had invested their savings in companies that had not made any money. Much of the initial excitement over the Internet firms faded.

By the summer of 2000 stocks were fluctuating wildly. Many small first-time investors worried whether the bubble would burst. Older Americans remembered the market crash of 1929 that led to the Great Depression of the 1930s.

The nation's economy had a measurable impact on the political system. For example, the Republican presidential candidate in 2000, Texas Governor George W. Bush, proposed a plan to allow workers to invest a por-

tion of their Social Security taxes in the stock market. The plan appealed to many younger workers, who had seen the market take wing, but worried some older Americans with longer memories. What if the market failed to perform as expected? Would the government then have to step in and shore up Social Security from general tax revenues? Only two years later, as the Dow dropped to new lows, less was heard about privatizing Social Security.

By the mid-term congressional election campaigns of 2002, Democrats sought to emphasize the faltering economy as their strongest issue. But the Republicans, led by President Bush, warned of the danger to the world posed by Iraq, which the administration said had acquired and might use weapons of mass destruction. Bush called repeatedly for the disarmament of Iraq and the ouster of its dictator, Saddam Hussein, and he sought and received authority from Congress to go to war in Iraq. Democrats in turn accused the Republicans of beating the war drums to divert attention from the nation's economic troubles.

But Iraq remained in the forefront as President Bush campaigned vigorously for Republican candidates in the 2002 midterm elections. The Republicans maintained their majority in the House of Representatives and regained control of the Senate. And, under pressure from the administration, the United Nations Security Council voted uanimously to require Iraq to rid itself of weapons of mass destruction or face "serious consequences," a term that President Bush made clear would mean a war with Iraq led by the United States.

The economic downturn also had a dramatic impact on the federal budget. A major tax cut proposed by President Bush and approved by Congress in the spring of 2001, combined with the faltering economy, turned the federal government's budget surpluses into deficits. For decades, the government had incurred multibillion-dollar deficits. But by the late 1990s, during the Clinton administration, there were substantial budget surpluses.

For a time, the surplus and projections that such bonanzas would continue resulted in an entirely new kind of political debate—how to spend the money. Differing answers to that question were at the heart of the 2000 presidential campaign. Within two years, and in the wake of 9/11, however, all that had changed. New questions were raised about how the government could fight a war in Iraq and still find money to meet needs at home, such as education and health care.

In this chapter, we will explore a key question: How well does government manage the economy? Several related questions also may be asked. For example: What are the politics of economic policy? To what extent should the government be involved in economic policy? What tools are available to the government in attempting to manage the economy, to maintain full employment, and control inflation?

---

*In May 2000, 54 percent of adult Americans reported that individually, or with a spouse, they had money invested in the stock market. See The Gallup Organization, *Gallup Poll Topics*, "Stock Market," May 2000, online at www.gallup.com/oll/indicators/indstock_mkt.asp; data for 1989 from the Denver *Rocky Mountain News*, October 15, 2000, p. 1G. For more information about the Dow Jones Industrial Average, see: http://averages.dowjones.com/abtdja.html

†For more information about the NASDAQ, see: www.nasdaq.com

The floor of the New York Stock Exchange
AP/Wide World

MANAGING THE ECONOMY

The Political Context of Economic Policy

During the 2000 presidential campaign, George W. Bush, the Republican candidate, offered the voters an across-the-board tax cut for everyone. "If you pay taxes, you ought to get tax relief," he said. "I believe the people who pay the bills ought to get some money back. . . . I trust you with your own money."[1] Bush proposed to cut taxes by $1.3 trillion over 10 years.

Al Gore, his Democratic opponent, advocated more limited, targeted tax cuts to help the middle class, leaving more money available for such programs as a prescription drug benefit through Medicare, support for education, and protecting the environment.

It was no accident that during Bill Clinton's successful campaign for the presidency in 1992, the sign on the wall of his headquarters in Little Rock, Arkansas, said: "It's the economy, stupid!" The sign was there to remind campaign workers that the biggest issue on the minds of the voters that year was the economy. When Clinton took office in 1993, he inherited a deficit of $290 billion; five years later, in 1998, he was able to announce a surplus of $70 billion, the first surplus in 29 years. By 2000, the surplus had grown to $237 billion.[2]

Voters may be concerned about foreign policy, education, abortion, guns, and a host of other issues, but often they think first about how well off they are, the so-called "bread-and-butter" or "pocketbook" issues. They are interested in whether they can afford to buy a home, or fix the leaky roof, or pay for quality health care—

"Well, if the economic boom benefits everyone, what good is it?!"
Copyright © Jim Borgman/*Cincinnati Inquirer*

Washington University, St. Louis, October 17, 2000: a televised town hall debate between the Republican and Democratic candidates for president
AFP POOL/AP/Wide World

including health insurance and prescription drugs—or, even more basically, whether they can feed and clothe their children.

Sometimes, a major foreign policy issue such as the Vietnam War or Iraq will preoccupy the public. But often, the voters' personal financial situation may be of primary concern. Hence the sign on the wall in Little Rock.

And in 1992, poll data supported the Clinton campaign's view. For example, more than half of respondents to a Gallup poll taken in August of that year thought that economic conditions in the country were "poor." That did not help George Bush, the Republican president, who lost his bid for reelection. When people were asked in 1996 to choose one issue from a list as "most important" to their vote, 33 percent—by far the largest group—singled out "Jobs and the economy."[3] And clearly the economy, the battle over how to spend the surplus, Social Security, and taxes were central to the campaign four years later.

Although America is a nation that prides itself on its system of free enterprise, most voters, whether conservative or liberal, look to the government in Washington to provide remedies to the country's economic problems. Those problems vary with the times, but whether they concern health care, inflation, unemployment, interest rates, or foreign competition, the president and his advisers are expected to provide solutions. Today most people expect the federal government to exercise a major responsibility for the health, stability, and growth of the national economy.

Since political leaders are normally interested in winning reelection, they realize it is in their self-interest, as well as in the interest of millions of Americans, to try to promote a strong, healthy economy. How to accomplish that goal, of course, is the subject of wide disagreement among politicians, political parties, and economists.

The Historical Context

The federal government took a major role in economic affairs with the coming of Franklin D. Roosevelt's New Deal. When Roosevelt was inaugurated in 1933, at the

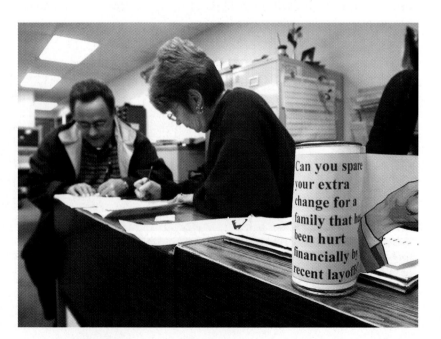

A textile worker laid off in Virginia signs up for computer training, 2001.
AP/Wide World

The AMERICAN PAST
THE CRASH OF 1929

In October 1929, the stock market crashed, touching off the Great Depression of the 1930s. Economist John Kenneth Galbraith describes what did—and did not—happen:

> Dr. Julius Klein, Assistant Secretary of Commerce, friend of President Hoover, and the senior apostle of the official economic view, took to the radio to remind the country that President Hoover had said that the "fundamental business of the country" was sound. . . .
>
> Most important, perhaps, from Pocantico Hills came the first public statement by John D. Rockefeller in several decades. So far as the record shows, it was spontaneous. However, someone in Wall Street— perhaps someone who knew that

another appeal to President Hoover to say something specifically encouraging about stocks would be useless—may have realized that a statement from Rockefeller would, if anything, be better. The statement ran: "Believing that fundamental conditions of the country are sound . . . my son and I have for some days been purchasing sound common stocks."

> The statement was widely applauded, although [entertainer] Eddie Cantor . . . said later, "Sure, who else had any money left?" . . .
>
> In the week or so following Black Thursday, the London penny press told delightedly of the scenes in downtown New York. Speculators were hurling themselves from windows; pedestrians

picked their way delicately between the bodies of fallen financiers. . . . In the United States the suicide wave that followed the stock market crash is also a part of the legend of 1929. In fact, there was none. . . .

> Since the market crash took place late in the year, there could have been a substantial increase in suicides in late October. . . . However . . . the number of suicides in October and November was comparatively low. . . . During the summer months, when the market was doing beautifully, the number of suicides was substantially higher.

—John Kenneth Galbraith, *The Great Crash, 1929*

height of the Great Depression, 13 million people—25 percent of the labor force—were unemployed.

The New Deal marked a dramatic shift from what had gone before. Although the government had invested in canals and railroad development in the 19th century, in the 1930s the government for the first time committed itself not simply to repairing problems in the economy, but to assuming a key role in the nation's

economic system. It did so in a variety of ways, including regulation of business; economic support for the unemployed, the poor, and retired persons; and using the government's taxing and spending powers to try to control the business cycle—the level of unemployment and inflation.

Despite these measures, unemployment remained high until the rapid recovery of the economy during the

A MODERN-DAY HERO: "I FEEL THAT I AM A SYMBOL"

LAWRENCE, MASS.—Six months after a fire nearly destroyed his textile company, Malden Mills Industries, Aaron M. Feuerstein has set himself up as a hero of corporate responsibility, insisting that his loyalty to his workers should be the model for all chief executives.

But in playing the role of model chief executive— lionized in the media for promising to re-employ all his workers once he rebuilt and for paying most of them in the interim—he is risking his company and his reputation. And therein, his wife worries, lies the potential for a modern-day tragedy.

There were certainly safer alternatives. He could have closed and walked away with tens of millions of dollars in fire insurance, giving up to rivals his company's flagship product, Polartec, a synthetic fabric much in demand for sporty outerwear. Or he could have reduced

the risk by being far more parsimonious in his payments to his workers and less ambitious in rebuilding.

Mr. Feuerstein will have none of that. He is rebuilding in the grand style, installing huge quantities of the best machinery and restoring the fine details of 19th-century factory buildings—spending in two years what he normally invests in a decade. By relying on insurance to pay the entire bill and on the efficiency and inventiveness of loyal workers to make the investment pay off, he is gambling the solvency of his company. . . .

"I feel that I am a symbol of the movement against downsizing and layoffs that will ultimately produce an answer. People see me as a turning of the tide."

—Adapted from the *New York Times*, July 4, 1996

Monday, October 19, 1987: The Dow Jones Industrial average plunged more than 500 points for the biggest one-day percentage loss in history.
AP/Wide World

Second World War. In the postwar world, with the nation still concerned about avoiding another economic depression, national growth with full employment and low inflation became a major goal.

The Employment Act of 1946 spelled out in law the responsibility of the federal government for the economy and its obligation "to promote maximum employment, production, and purchasing power." The law directed the president to submit an annual economic report to Congress; it created a three-member Council of Economic Advisers to assist the president; and it established a Joint Economic Committee, made up of members of the House and Senate, to study the president's report and the economy.

Most U.S. economists believe that a stock market crash and a depression as severe as that which began in 1929 are unlikely to happen again because there "are more built-in economic stabilizers today. Even so, the sharp dip in the stock market in October 1987, and the sharp decline in the Dow in 2001 and 2002, caused great alarm on Wall Street, in Washington, and in the country, and had repercussions in markets around the world.

Theories of Economic Policy

The United States operates predominantly under an economic system of free enterprise, or **capitalism.** Under capitalism, there is private ownership of the means of production. In such a system, in its purest form, there is little room for government; people own private property, either directly or as shareholders; and as consumers they participate in a free marketplace that responds to the laws of supply and demand. In practice, however, the United States has a mixed, or modified, free enterprise system in which both private industry and government play important roles.

The individual's economic freedom is sharply limited by federal, state, and local economic policies. To begin with, the higher the federal, state, and local taxes a person pays, the less money he or she will have to spend on consumer goods. If government fails to prevent a recession, the person may be out of work. If government fails to prevent inflation, the dollar buys less and retired people living on pensions and savings may find their fixed incomes inadequate.

There is, obviously, an interaction between government policies and the economy. What the government does influences economic conditions; in turn the state of the economy affects government actions and policies.

In general, Democrats have favored a larger role for government in regulating the welfare of society and the individual, and Republicans generally have favored less government intervention. But the basic responsibility of government for economic policy is now well established.

That said, there are great differences among political leaders and economists about how to exercise that responsibility. There is conflict, as well, not only about the proper extent of government action, but also about the underlying economic theory. Economists have different views about how to prevent cycles of recession and unemployment, about growth and productivity, about government taxing and spending. They may belong to one "school" or another that has different perspectives on economic policy. There is, in short, a good deal of crystal-ball gazing involved, for no one economist or school has all the answers. If they did, there would never be periods of recession, high unemployment, layoffs, downsizing, or hardship.

Because there is so much difference among economists about economic theory, politicians can choose the economic advice—and advisers—that suit their own brands of politics. As a result, a change in the presidency often means a change in economic policy; the occupant of the White House does not normally appoint economic advisers who are in sharp disagreement with him.

Laissez-Faire Economics In French, **laissez-faire** means to "leave alone."* It describes a theory that an economic system works best when free of government interference. Although the principles were first developed in France, laissez-faire is associated with Adam Smith, the Scottish economist and founder of the classical school of economics, and his book *Wealth of Nations,* published in 1776.

---

*The words literally mean "to allow" (people) "to do" (what they please).

There are echoes of laissez-faire philosophy in modern politics—for example, when House Republicans in 1995 sought to roll back government regulation of the workplace and the environment. They believed that government had become too intrusive and burdensome to business.

Keynesian Economics   John Maynard Keynes, later Baron Keynes of Tilton, died in 1946, but he was perhaps the most influential economist of the 20th century. Keynes's views were just the opposite of laissez-faire. He advocated government intervention in the marketplace. The English economist argued that when people did not consume and invest enough to maintain national income at full employment levels, government must step in and regulate the economy, primarily through **fiscal policy**—by cutting taxes or increasing spending in the public sector, or both. In Keynes's view, during an economic downturn if the government spent more than it took in from taxes and other revenues, the deficit that resulted was not bad, it was good. Thus, Keynes argued that deficit spending by the government was necessary to combat a recession.

Keynesian economics provided the underpinning of economic policy for President Franklin Roosevelt's New Deal administration in the 1930s and 1940s. Since that time, many government economists have been influenced by the thinking of Keynes.

Today, however, the political framework has changed. In the mid-1990s, a Democratic president, Bill Clinton, and the leaders of a Republican-controlled Congress agreed publicly on the need to balance the budget. Their arguments were over how to do so and how soon.

Keynesian economists and their modern successors place major emphasis on fiscal policy to guide the economy, although they also recognize the role of **monetary policy,** the control of the supply of money and the supply of credit through the actions of the Federal Reserve Board.

Supply-Side Economics   In 1981, when President Reagan took office, the United States was experiencing severe inflation. Reagan and his advisers advocated economic policies that were a sharp departure from the past.

They called for a program of federal tax and spending cuts to try to assure growth without inflation and to end recessions. The theory was that inflation could be controlled by increasing the supply of goods. The concept was called **supply-side economics,** an economic philosophy that advocates both tax and budget cuts to increase incentives to produce, in order to expand the total supply of the nation's goods and services.

The money moving into the economy because of tax reductions, it was hoped, would be used by industry to build new factories and machinery to provide jobs and growth. The benefits would thus flow to the public, in

John Maynard Keynes
Copyright © CORBIS/ UPI/Bettmann

theory. Supply-side economists attacked the Keynesian model of the economy for Keynes's view that inflation is the result of too much demand—too many dollars chasing after too few goods. The supply-siders argued that inflation is caused by a lack of supply—not enough goods on the market. Thus, their solution is to cut taxes to encourage greater production.

Congress went along with Reagan's program, enacting extensive tax and spending cuts. Journalists dubbed the program Reaganomics. The Reagan cutbacks had an immediate impact on millions of Americans: Government social services were cut or their projected rate of increase reduced.

At first, economic conditions worsened. Unemployment reached 10.7 percent at one point in 1982, the highest figure since the Second World War, and 12 million people were jobless. The government's budget deficits soared to unprecedented multibillion-dollar levels, in part because the Reagan Administration increased defense spending.

Taken together, the Reagan budget and tax cuts reduced the income of the poor and increased the income of the rich.[4] The percentage and number of poor people increased substantially under Reagan.[5]

Monetarism   Some economists argue that the money supply—the quantity of money in circulation—is the key to government regulation of the economy. Monetarists contend that the government should confine its role in economic affairs to ensuring that the money supply expands fast enough to accommodate economic growth. These theories are identified with the "Chicago school" of economists, led by Milton Friedman of the University of Chicago. Friedman argued that interest rates, which are one aspect of monetary policy, and fiscal policy—taxes and spending—have little effect or importance. He also argued that the money supply should be increased at a constant rate. Friedman received the Nobel Prize in 1976.

His views won increasing, but by no means universal, acceptance in the United States and abroad. For example, during the Clinton years, which saw dramatic economic expansion, low unemployment, and low inflation, the government closely and successfully regulated interest rates through the Federal Reserve Board to act as a brake on inflation.

In sum, in the more than six decades since the New Deal, sharply differing economic theories have been advocated and carried out by the government. But during this period, complex fiscal and monetary policies—even direct economic controls—have not always avoided the twin evils of recession and inflation.

THE MACHINERY

In making economic policy, the president has a number of tools and advisers available to him—the Council of Economic Advisers, the National Economic Council, the Office of Management and Budget, the secretary of the treasury, the Department of Labor, and the economists and experts who staff these government agencies. He can invoke his power to delay major strikes under the Taft-Hartley Act. Various presidents have had power to negotiate and alter U.S. tariffs.

for more information about the National Economic Council and the Council of Economic Advisers, see:
www.whitehouse.gov/WH/EOP/nec/html/index.html and
www.whitehouse.gov/WH/EOP/CEA/html/index.html

Through his appointment power, the president can influence the makeup of the Federal Reserve Board. And, of course, the president is free to consult outside economists and experts in the private sector, including the universities. The president can also impose economic controls or voluntary guidelines on prices and wages. He may call upon all of these resources in shaping the fiscal and monetary policies of the federal government. Yet, despite the boom times of the 1990s, presidents in recent decades often have not been successful in controlling inflation, recession, or high unemployment. In part, this may be due to world economic conditions—factors that are beyond any president's control. But it also may stem from the nature of the American economic system, in which there are limits on the government's ability to manage the economy.

The Tools of Economic Policy

Usually, the federal government has attempted to influence the total shape of the economy through two sets of tools: *fiscal policy* and *monetary policy*. The fiscal tools of the government, as noted, are primarily spending and taxation. The monetary tools are control of the supply of money and control of the supply of credit through the Federal Reserve System.

Fiscal Policy

The Budget   The federal budget reflects an allocation of resources by the national government. It spells out the programs and purposes for which the government will spend money and it estimates the source of federal revenues. (See Figure 17-1.) But the budget is also an important tool of fiscal policy. During a time of inflation, the president may cut spending and ask for higher taxes to cool down the economy. In a recession he may propose a bigger budget, more public works spending, and lower taxes. Or, as Reagan did in 1981, a president may call for both lower taxes and less domestic spending. In the 2000 presidential campaign, as noted earlier, George W. Bush, the Republican candidate, proposed a tax cut for everyone as the centerpiece of his economic program. Bush's proposal would cut taxes by $1.3 trillion over 10 years.

By planning a budget surplus or deficit, the federal government attempts to pump money into or out of the economy, to stimulate it or slow it down. In the 1980s and early 1990s, however, repeated federal deficits were perceived by both major political parties as an economic, or at least a political, problem rather than a tool to stabilize the economy.

The president must share with Congress his fiscal control over the economy. Only Congress can vote to spend federal funds. It does so in a three-step process. First, it passes **budget resolutions** to set overall spending targets. Second, it passes **authorizations** to spend federal money. Third, it passes **appropriations bills** to pay for the spending it has authorized. The budget process is described in more detail in Chapter 14.

Under this system, legislative committees deal with the substance of programs and, by authorizing funds, set forth their view of what ought to be spent. Within that framework, the appropriations committees decide what actually may be spent.

The idea behind this system is that appropriations committees have an overview of expenditures by Congress—something that legislative or "program" committees do not have—and are therefore in a better position to allocate funds. Because an authorization without an appropriation is meaningless, the system places great power in the hands of the House and Senate appropriations committees and subcommittees. Congress may increase or cut the president's appropriations requests.

Once money is appropriated, Congress has its own accountant—the comptroller general of the United States, who heads the General Accounting Office (GAO)—to check up on how it is spent.

When the federal government spends more than it receives in taxes and other revenues, the budget is said to operate at a **deficit,** the gap between the government's income and outlays.

In the 1980s and early 1990s, the deficit became a hot political issue. When the Republicans were out of power in the 1960s, they assailed the "deficit spending"

FIGURE 17-1

The Federal Government Dollar

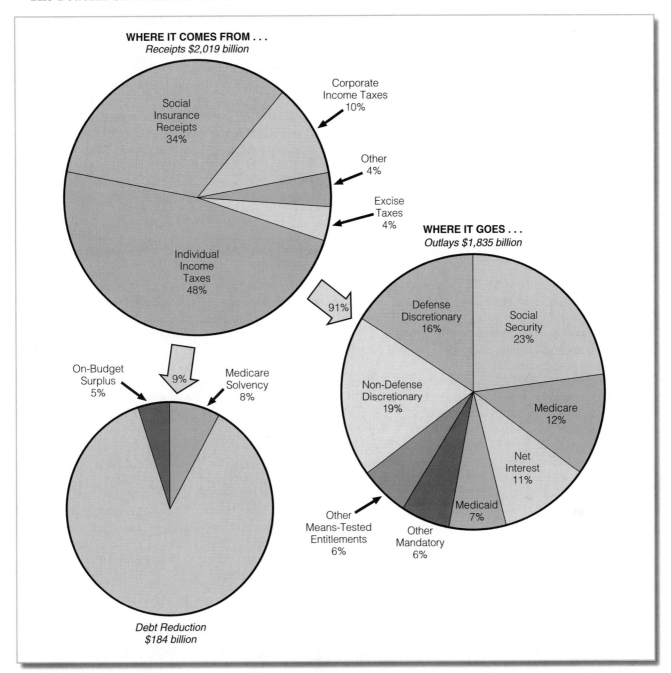

WHERE IT COMES FROM . . .
Receipts $2,019 billion

Social Insurance Receipts 34%

Corporate Income Taxes 10%

Other 4%

Excise Taxes 4%

Individual Income Taxes 48%

91%

9%

On-Budget Surplus 5%

Medicare Solvency 8%

Debt Reduction $184 billion

WHERE IT GOES . . .
Outlays $1,835 billion

Defense Discretionary 16%

Social Security 23%

Non-Defense Discretionary 19%

Medicare 12%

Net Interest 11%

Other Means-Tested Entitlements 6%

Other Mandatory 6%

Medicaid 7%

NOTE: Fiscal year 2001, estimated.
SOURCE: *Budget of the United States Government, Fiscal Year 2001,* (Washington, D.C.: U.S. Government Printing Office, 2001), p. 2.

of the Democrats, whom they labeled the party of "tax and spend." But when two Republicans, Ronald Reagan and his successor George Bush, served as president from 1981 until 1993, the deficit more than doubled. When Reagan took office, the deficit stood at a little over $100 billion. By the time his successor, George Bush, left office, the deficit had soared to $290 billion.

Mounting deficits led both major political parties to call for a balanced budget. But the battle over just how to balance the budget led to the struggle between President Clinton and the Republican Congress and caused the two government shutdowns in 1995 and 1996.

Congress passed a series of laws in an attempt to come to grips with the budget process and the federal deficit. Budget, tax, and spending policies were uncoordinated, and sometimes seemed to be moving in different directions; Congress sought to impose a structure and coherence on the budget process. The Congressional

The government's tea party is over.

President Clinton, without fanfare, signed legislation Tuesday abolishing the federal Board of Tea Experts. . . .

The tempest over the teapots has steamed along since the early 1970s, when the Nixon administration tried to dump the board. Clinton brought the issue back to a boil in 1993 as part of his budget review of federal advisory panels, and a Congress intent on downsizing the government finally passed legislation last month.

Congressional opponents of the board argued the government did not need tea tasters on its payroll, but hanging up the kettles probably won't make a dent in the deficit. . . .

The 99-year-old law created the tea board, mandating it meet for two days every year to set minimum quality standards for whole-leaf tea imported into the United States. In most years, the board selected one tea from each tea category—the black, oolong and green—to serve as the standard. . . . Some tea experts suggested Washington's willingness to throw the tea tasters overboard has more to do with political posturing than with saving money.

"It's the silliest cost-cutting measure that I can think of," said John Frederick Walter, author of "Coffee and Tea" and a contributing editor at *Food & Wine* magazine.

"Somehow this image of people sitting around a table with their pinkies raised galled a lot of people who don't understand it serves a valid function," Walter said.

—*Washington Post*, April 11, 1996

Budget and Impoundment Act of 1974 established the budget committees in the House and Senate and created a framework for Congress to use in dealing with the president's budget. The Gramm-Rudman Acts of 1985 and 1987 were congressional attempts to control spending and eliminate the deficit.

The complicated Budget Enforcement Act of 1990 set limits on appropriations for domestic, international, and defense programs. It put mandatory spending programs such as Medicare on a "pay-as-you-go" basis. Under the act, as discussed in Chapter 12, the president submits his budget request on the first Monday of each February. Congress is required to adopt a budget resolution by April 15, and the fiscal year begins on October 1.

These laws did not make much of a dent on the annual federal deficit, which, as just mentioned, had reached $290 billion by 1992. By fiscal 1996, however, with both the Democratic president and the Republican-controlled Congress publicly agreed on the goal of balancing the budget within six years, the deficit had dropped dramatically. (See Figure 17-2.)

The deficit was not only an economic problem; it had also become a major political issue. The government closings in 1995 and early 1996 were the result of an impasse over the federal budget and over how to balance the budget by 2002.

But the goal of a balanced budget was reached earlier than expected. President Clinton was able to announce a $70 billion surplus in 1998, a surplus of $123 billion in 1999, and a surplus of $237 billion in 2000. Within two years, however, the surplus had vanished.

Why does a balanced budget or a budget surplus matter? A budget deficit means the government has to borrow more and pay more interest than it would otherwise. Some economists believe that eliminating deficits helped to keep interest rates down during the Clinton years, which in turn stimulated the stock market. And finally, a surplus makes large amounts of money available for social programs to improve American society, for tax cuts, or both.

New York, May 11, 2000: the National Debt clock in New York City
AP/Wide World

FIGURE 17-2

Federal Budget Deficit and Surplus, 1940–2010

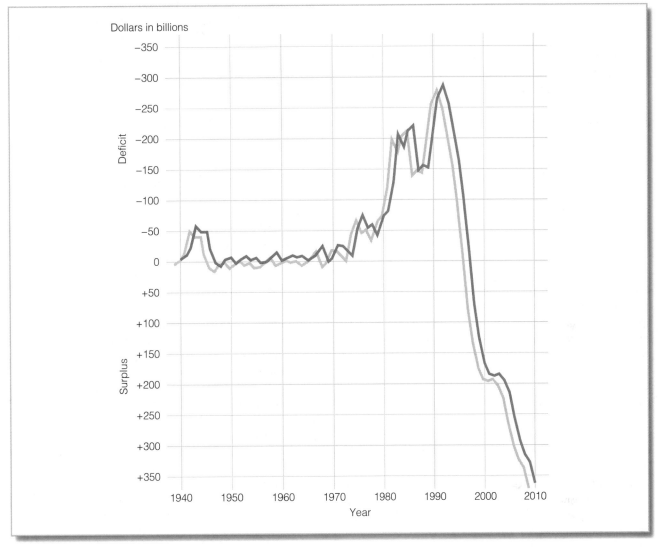

NOTE: Data after 1999 are projections.
SOURCE: *Budget of the United States Government, Fiscal Year 2001*, (Washington, D.C.: U.S. Government Printing Office, 2001), p. 24.

Borrowing   Just as individuals do, governments may spend more than their income. When that happens, governments—like individuals—borrow to make up the difference. The United States, for example, borrows money by selling federal securities. It issues interest-bearing Treasury bills, long-term Treasury bonds, and other notes, which are purchased by institutions, corporations, and individuals.

When the government runs at a deficit for many years, the amount of money it owes piles up. The **national debt** is exactly what it sounds like—the total amount of money that the United States owes to its creditors. The national debt stood at $16.2 billion in 1930. By 2000, the national debt stood at more than $5.6 trillion.[6]

In 1917 Congress passed a statutory debt limit, or ceiling, on government borrowing, which limits the

amount of debt the nation may incur—but the limit has been revised upward many times. Borrowing costs money; in fiscal 2001 the government expected to spend $184 billion, or some 10 percent of the federal budget, on interest payments.

Taxes   "The Congress shall have Power to lay and collect Taxes." And Congress, as every taxpayer knows, exercises this constitutional authority. Under the budget for fiscal 2001 the federal government planned to spend $1,835 billion, most of it raised from taxes. Of every dollar the government expected to take in during fiscal 2001, 48 cents came from individual income taxes, 34 cents from social-insurance taxes, 10 cents from corporate income taxes, 4 cents from excise taxes (taxes on commodities), and another 4 cents from other revenue sources.[7]

The Federal Budget: Where the Money Comes From

Source	2001 estimate (in billions)	Percent
Individual income taxes	$ 969.12	48%
Social-insurance taxes and contributions	686.46	34
Corporation income taxes	201.90	10
Excise taxes	80.76	4
All other receipts	80.76	4
Total budget receipts	$2,019.00	100%

SOURCE: Adapted from *Budget of the United States Government, Fiscal Year 2001* (Washington, D.C.: U.S. Government Printing Office, 2000), p. 2.

Estimated tax receipts for 2001 appear in Table 17-1. As these figures show, individual income taxes are the federal government's largest single source of revenue. The federal income tax is graduated—although less sharply since passage of the 1986 tax reform law—on the theory that persons with higher incomes should be taxed at a higher rate. But taxpayers at all levels grumble about the tax squeeze; not many people enjoy paying their taxes or consider them low.

Until the 20th century, the Constitution required the federal government to collect income taxes in proportion to state population. The Sixteenth Amendment, ratified in 1913, permitted the government to levy a general income tax. Since that time, however, various interest groups have lobbied Congress and won special tax advantages. Until 1975 the major oil producers had a "depletion allowance," which reduced their taxes. Business executives and many other persons still enjoy certain "expense account" deductions. There are also other loopholes in the tax law. Rich persons can afford to hire high-priced tax attorneys to find them. People in high-income brackets may set up foundations, invest in tax-free municipal bonds or various types of "tax shelters" (businesses or other activities that receive special tax breaks), or take business losses that enable them to avoid high taxes.

By the end of the 1960s, growing public awareness of inequalities in the federal tax laws led to talk of "a taxpayers' revolt." Congress responded by passing several tax reform laws over two decades.

The 1986 tax reform measure, passed during the Reagan administration, was the most extensive revision in the nation's tax laws in 40 years. The Tax Reform Act of 1986 cut individual and corporate tax rates. The measure for a time ended the preferential treatment for capital gains, and ended or modified a wide variety of taxpayer deductions.

The politics of taxation results in intense pressures on Congress from interest groups when changes in the structure of the tax laws are under consideration. And Congress and the president often fight political battles over how tax policy should be used as a fiscal tool to slow down or stimulate the economy. The use of fiscal policy to control the economy depends, in theory, on delicate timing; but Congress tends to move very slowly in passing tax legislation.

And tax and spending policies are often at the center of the nation's political debate. As already noted, the size and nature of proposed tax cuts was a central issue in the 2000 presidential race. After George W. Bush was elected, he proposed and Congress passed the largest tax cut in twenty years, reducing personal income tax rates over a period of five years.

The Internal Revenue Service (IRS), the agency responsible for collecting federal taxes, is not the most popular agency in Washington. Most citizens regard tax forms as far too complicated. Political leaders do not hesitate to tap into this frustration with both the tax code and the IRS.

In 1997, Senate hearings revealed that the IRS had harassed taxpayers for money they did not owe, or had paid or tried to pay. The agency suspended a number of midlevel employees after it was disclosed that field agents had been rated on the number of seizures, levies, and liens they imposed on taxpayers.

Although Americans complain about high taxes, compared with other democratic countries the United States stands near the bottom of the ladder in terms of how much it taxes its citizens. As a percentage of the **gross domestic product (GDP),**[*] the yearly value of goods and services produced within a country, the United States, at 34.4 percent, ranks much lower than Sweden, with a tax burden of 63 percent, Denmark at 56.1 percent, or France at 50.9 percent.[8] (See Figure 17-3.)

Monetary Policy

Government also attempts to regulate the economy by monetary policy—controlling the supply of money and the cost and availability of credit. It does this through the operations of the Federal Reserve System. "The Fed," as the system is often called, was established in 1913. Prior to that time, the United States had no way to expand and contract the money supply according to the needs of the economy. To provide such an elastic system, Congress created the Federal Reserve.

During the year 2000, and for many years before that, the chairman of the Fed, Alan Greenspan, emerged as one of the nation's best-known and most powerful figures. A bespectacled economist with a studious, sober manner, Greenspan started out as a saxophone player

---

[*]From 1941 until 1991, economists used the term *gross national product (GNP)* as a measure of the nation's total output of goods and services. The GNP included production by American companies or individuals anywhere in the world. The GDP covers output within the borders of the United States.

with a 1940s swing band. That may have helped to form a bond with his fellow saxophonist, President Clinton, who reappointed him to two terms as Fed chairman.[*]

In December 1996, when Greenspan remarked that the stock market might be exhibiting "irrational exuberance" and used the word "bubble" in the same speech, the Dow plunged and markets shook in Japan and Germany.

Wall Street listened carefully to Greenspan, because it was within his and the board's power to raise interest rates to stem inflation. The Fed, to Wall Street's relief, did so during this period only in small increments. A big increase in interest rates can have an adverse effect on the stock market, because investors then fear that corporations in which they hold shares will not be able to borrow as much at higher rates in order to expand their factories, production, and profits.

Higher interest rates affect more than the stock market. For example, higher rates mean college loans cost

more. Mortgage loans cost more as well, and that may influence young couples to put off buying a home, which in turn affects the construction industry and many other parts of the economy.

The Fed is headed by a Board of Governors. Although the board's seven members are appointed by the president with the approval of the Senate, they serve overlapping 14-year terms and are largely independent of both Congress and the White House.

Alan Greenspan
Justin Lane/NYT Pictures

The Fed's chair, appointed by the president for a term of four years, can, and sometimes does, oppose the policies of the administration. During the Reagan administration, for example, there was frequent tension between the president and the chairman of the Fed.

---

[*]Greenspan, who served as an adviser to Richard Nixon's 1968 presidential campaign, was first named chairman in 1987 by President Reagan to fill an unexpired term, reappointed as chairman by President George Bush in 1992 and to a full 14-year term on the board, and named to a third and fourth term as chairman by President Clinton in 1996 and 2000.

FIGURE 17-3

Tax Burdens of Selected Countries

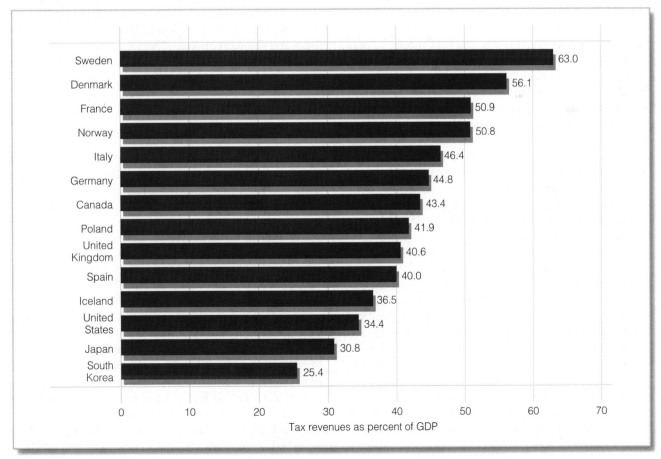

Country	Tax revenues as percent of GDP
Sweden	63.0
Denmark	56.1
France	50.9
Norway	50.8
Italy	46.4
Germany	44.8
Canada	43.4
Poland	41.9
United Kingdom	40.6
Spain	40.0
Iceland	36.5
United States	34.4
Japan	30.8
South Korea	25.4

NOTE: Data for 1998.
SOURCE: Adapted from *Statistical Abstract of the United States: 1999*, p. 847.

The Federal Reserve is the central banking system of the United States; it operates through 12 Federal Reserve Banks and 24 branches across the nation. All national banks and about 10 percent of state banks are members of the system.

When individuals or corporations need money, they normally borrow from a bank. When banks need money, they may borrow from the Federal Reserve System. The Federal Reserve is, therefore, a banker's bank. When it lends to the banks, it can, in effect, create money.

Through its control of the flow of money and credit within the United States, the Fed attempts to pump more money into the economy when a recession threatens. In a time of rising prices and excessive spending, the Fed normally tries to tighten the supply of money and credit so that people will have less to spend.

When the Fed raises interest rates, in other words, it does so in the hope of slowing down the economy. To take one example, millions of Americans have credit cards, and the interest they pay every month is a major source of income for the nation's banks. If the Fed raises interest rates, then the rate charged by credit card companies goes up, and consumers—or so the Fed hopes—may spend less money in order to save on finance charges. When the Fed cuts interest rates, as it did repeatedly in 2001 and 2002, it hopes to stimulate the economy.

As one chairman remarked, the Fed tries "to lean against the prevailing economic winds." It does so chiefly in four ways:

1. *Open market operations.* Banks lend money to people in relation to the amount of reserves the banks have on deposit with the Federal Reserve. When the Fed sells government bonds on the open market, they are purchased by individuals and commercial banks. When people take money out of the bank to buy bonds, or when the banks pay for the securities, the banks have fewer dollars on hand. The effect is to reduce bank reserves and tighten credit; banks then have less money to lend to people. Or, the Federal Reserve can buy government securities and expand credit. When the Fed buys government securities, banks have more cash to lend, and interest rates go down, which should encourage people to borrow money.

2. *The discount rate.* The Fed can raise or lower the discount rate that it charges member banks for loans. This affects interest rates in the economy generally. If the rate is lowered, banks borrow more from the Fed and have more money to lend to their customers.

3. *Reserve requirements.* It can raise or lower the size of the reserves that member banks must keep in the Federal Reserve banks against their deposits and thus tighten or expand credit. For example, if the Fed wants to speed up the growth of the economy, it can lower the reserve requirement, which gives the banks access to more of their money to lend to customers.

4. *Margin requirements.* It can raise or lower the margin requirements for persons buying securities. The margin requirement defines how much money people can borrow to purchase stocks.

The Fed's actions can influence the federal funds rate, which banks charge each other for the overnight sale of federal funds. A lower federal funds rate encourages banks to lend more money; a higher rate makes it more difficult for people and businesses to borrow money.

As discussed earlier, economists and politicians disagree over the best way to maintain price stability, full employment, and economic growth. Some measures are politically safer to take than others; for example, it is easier for government to spend money on public works to combat recession than it is to impose wage-price controls to fight inflation.

Whatever steps an administration takes carry great political risks if they fail. Normally both the president and Congress try to steer a safe course between the twin reefs of recession and inflation. Prosperity and bread-and-butter concerns are often key election issues.

At times, although rarely, when fiscal policy and monetary policy prove unable to control inflation, the government has imposed direct economic controls—on wages and prices, for example. Most presidents have been reluctant to take such a drastic step, although President Richard Nixon did so in 1971. There was precedent for Nixon's actions; economic controls were imposed during the First World War, the Second World War, and the Korean War. There was also some peacetime precedent, since for a time controls were kept on prices and rents during the Truman Administration.

International Trade Policy

When members of the World Trade Organization (WTO) met in Seattle in December 1999, they were not prepared for what happened. Thousands of protesters surrounded the convention hall, blocked delegates from leaving their hotels, and braved the tear gas, pepper spray, and rubber pellets of the city's police, who moved about in armored personnel carriers.

 for more information about the World Trade Organization, see: www.wto.org

As a few delegates managed to gather to meet in the hall, the demonstrators outside chanted: "Whose world? Our world! Whose streets? Our streets!"[9]

Downtown Seattle was in turmoil, the area was placed under curfew, and the governor called in the National Guard to try to keep order. More than 600 persons were arrested. The majority of the protestors were peaceful, but a small group, most wearing masks, smashed store windows. The United Nations secretary general, Kofi Annan, was unable to deliver his speech to the delegates.[10]

Seattle, Washington, November 30, 1999: Anti–World Trade Organization protesters stage a demonstration downtown.
AP/Wide World

THE SEATTLE PROTESTS: TEAR GAS AND PONYTAILS

SEATTLE, Dec. 2—If there is any clear message coming through the clouds of tear gas and the broken glass in Seattle this week, it is that the terms of debate about free trade have changed in the United States.

It is no longer a debate about trade at all, but rather a debate about globalization, a process that many now understand affects not only traditional economic factors such as jobs and incomes but also the food people eat, the air they breathe, the quality of medical care, and the social and cultural milieu in which they live.

The demonstrators in Seattle this week were a thoroughly mixed bunch, from anarchistic hooligans at one extreme to pacifist nuns at the other. Some were aging hippies, their gray hair now pulled back in ponytails. Others were kids with nose rings cruising the streets on skateboards. Both were outnumbered by the thousands of union workers in baseball caps and nylon jackets. And not surprisingly, there was a large contingent of Washington wonks on hand from policy shops on Capitol Hill.

By and large, these are the people who have never bought into the New Economy, either because it has left them behind or because they never embraced its values. They are folks who don't check each day to see how their 401(k) is doing or hang out with people who have become millionaires after their companies went public. Their perspective on globalization is less economic than it is cultural and political.

What they all seem to agree on is that giant corporations have gone too far in gaining control over their lives and defining the values of their culture, and that the WTO has become a handmaiden to those corporate interests.

—Adapted from the *Washington Post,* December 3, 1999

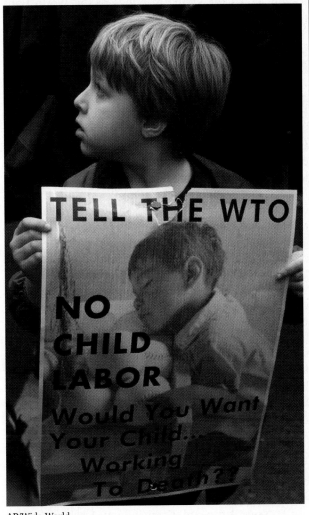

AP/Wide World

The WTO was created in 1995 and had 135 nations as members by the time of the Seattle protests. Its task was to act as a global referee to resolve international trade disputes. The organization, with headquarters in Geneva, Switzerland, was also given the authority to reduce international tariffs by 38 percent.

But the WTO acted largely in secret, and it soon became a symbol of globalization, and the target of a diverse group of environmentalists, human rights activists, labor unions, and others.

President Clinton, in Seattle for the meeting, denounced the violence but sided with the peaceful protesters. He pleaded with the member nations to shape trade agreements that would protect workers and the environment, and he attacked the WTO for operating in secrecy. "What they are telling us in the streets is that this is an issue we've been silent on," Clinton said. "And we won't be silent any more."[11]

But the trade talks collapsed as a result of the protests, and the failure shattered Clinton's hopes of beginning a new round of trade negotiations, one of the major foreign policy goals of his second administration.

In April 2000, the Seattle protests had a more peaceful echo in Washington, D.C., as protesters attempted to shut down the spring meetings of the World Bank and the International Monetary Fund. This time, police were ready, and although the capital was disrupted the protesters were allowed to march and chant, and the demonstrations ended with voluntary arrests.

But, as in Seattle, the message of the protesters was clear—that the policies of the two lending institutions had harmed the environment, and actually led to cuts in spending for health and education in poor countries. Critics charged that the IMF imposed rigid economic conditions on Third World countries in exchange for its loans and ignored humanitarian concerns.

The protests and demands for reform of international organizations such as the WTO and the IMF underscored the fact that globalization, and international trade policies—once the province of bankers, economists, and specialists meeting in quiet anonymity—have become a volatile political issue both at home and abroad.

But trade and tariff policies have often been caught up in domestic politics throughout U.S. history. In the United States, a **tariff** is a federal tax on imports. A high tariff discourages other nations from sending goods to U.S. markets and is therefore "protective" of American manufacturers. When American corporations are hurt by foreign competition, it often creates pressures to protect industries at home by setting high tariffs. That makes the price of foreign products higher and may encourage people to buy domestically manufactured products instead.

But a tariff wall can work two ways. Other countries can and do retaliate by setting up trade barriers of their own; they raise their tariffs on imports from the United States. As a result, most presidents favor free trade.

Pressure from American industry seeking foreign markets for its products, and from consumers wanting lower prices for imported goods, has resulted in a gradual reduction of U.S. tariff barriers since the 1930s.

In 1947 the United States and 22 other nations signed the General Agreement on Tariffs and Trade (GATT)—the predecessor of the WTO—which provided a formal framework for international tariff reductions. More trade barriers fell during the 1960s.

During the same period, however, industry in Japan and the creation of the European Community in western Europe threatened the competitive advantage previously enjoyed at home by American business.[*] Protectionist sentiment succeeded in placing many restrictions on tariff reductions—for example, by imposing quotas on certain categories of imports. In 1988 Congress passed and the president signed a trade bill that provided protection for industries seriously injured by imports.

In 1992, the United States, Mexico, and Canada completed negotiations on an agreement to create a free-trade area for the three countries. President Bush submitted the North American Free Trade Agreement (NAFTA) to Congress. But in an election year, many members of Congress were cautious about the pact, fearing that some U.S. companies would move their plants to Mexico, where labor is cheaper. Ross Perot, an independent candidate for president that year, repeatedly voiced this argument. Although business generally supported the pact, the agreement was bitterly opposed by organized labor, which feared job losses. Opponents of NAFTA also worried that the pact would lead to expanded competition from Mexico, since products manufactured there could now enter the United States more freely. Despite strong opposition by organized labor and by many Democrats, President Clinton supported the pact, Congress approved the agreement in 1993, and it went into effect on January 1, 1994.

NAFTA greatly bolstered Mexico's economy. Trade between the United States and Mexico, which totaled $81.5 billion before the agreement, was expected to reach $240 billion in 2000, and Mexico became the second-largest buyer of U.S. goods and services. Although opponents of NAFTA said it had cost 200,000 U.S. jobs, economists estimated that the total expansion of the American economy had created 15 million jobs, far more than went south of the border.[12]

It was in 1994 that Congress approved a new international trade agreement that created the WTO, which officially came into being on January 1, 1995. But well before the protests in Seattle, various groups were opposed to the WTO; in the United States, some unions feared loss of jobs; and textile manufacturers and other businesses worried about foreign competition.

For example, a coalition of labor unions, environmentalists, religious groups, and veterans opposed China's

---

[*]In 1958, the European Economic Community, known as the Common Market, was established to integrate the nations of western Europe by the gradual removal of trade and tariff barriers. This led in 1967 to the formation of the European Community (EC), which Great Britain joined in 1973. In 1994, the EC became known as the European Union (EU).

Workers at an American-owned electric plant in Juarez, Mexico. NAFTA raised fears that American jobs would move south of the border.
Copyright © William Campbell/Sygma

entry into the WTO. The unions feared that American industry would move high-paying jobs to China; others objected to rewarding a Communist government that threatened its neighbors and harshly repressed all dissent. But business organizations, eager to open China's vast market to American industry, lobbied hard for eliminating trade restrictions against China. In 2000, Congress approved normal trade relations with Beijing.

Then in 2002, Congress enacted legislation granting President Bush "fast track" authority to negotiate trade agreements with other countries, pacts that Congress could approve or reject but not change. Most Democrats voted against the bill, warning that it might cost jobs for American workers. Previous presidents, beginning with Gerald Ford, had been granted such authority, but it had expired in 1994 under President Clinton.

International economics has a direct effect on the relations among nations and on the economy at home. Across the industrial heartland of America, many workers lost their jobs to foreign competition in the 1980s and 1990s. During those years, layoffs, plant closings, and unemployment became all too familiar in what some called "the rust belt." (See Figure 17-4.)

FIGURE 17-4

Annual Rate of Unemployment in the United States, 1980–1999

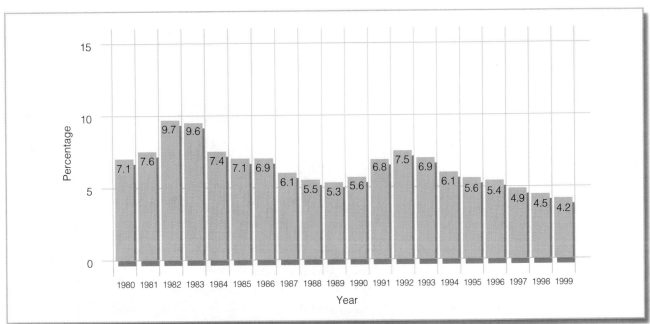

SOURCE: U.S. Bureau of Labor Statistics.

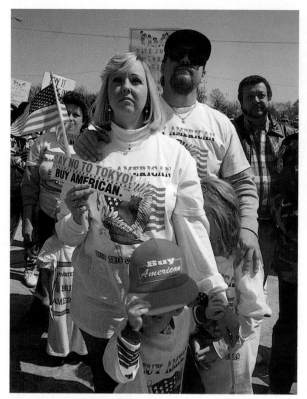

Copyright © Rob Nelson/Black Star

In Japan, South Korea, Taiwan, and other countries, industry, often heavily subsidized by government, has been turning out products that are sometimes better and often cheaper than those produced in California, Ohio, or Pennsylvania. And Americans are buying those products.

Europe, dependent on America for foreign assistance after the destruction of the Second World War, has also emerged as a powerful economic rival. The 15-nation European Union (EU) has eliminated most tariffs among its member states. In 1999, 11 of the EU countries began using a common currency, the euro, for some purposes.

The American auto industry can be studied as an example of how the nation has had to adjust to globalization. For many years after the Second World War, Detroit did not have to worry about significant competition from foreign auto manufacturers. General Motors, Ford, and Chrysler could compete at home for the domestic auto market.

Gradually, however, German Volkswagens and then Japanese small cars began appearing on U.S. highways. In 1998, some 6.7 million American-made passenger cars were sold in the United States, but another 1.4 million foreign cars were imported, including almost 700,000 from Japan and 367,000 from Germany. In other words, 16.9 percent of cars sold in the United States that year were foreign.[13]

To the extent that Americans buy cars made in Japan, for example, some American autoworkers lose jobs, which in turn creates protectionist pressures on the American government to erect trade barriers against imports. By the mid-1990s, however, the American auto industry was increasing domestic sales and expanding its markets overseas, including Japan.

At the same time, the flow of dollars to Japan and other nations adversely affects the U.S. **balance of trade,** the relationship between the total cost of foreign goods imported to this country and sales of U.S. products overseas. In 1999, for example, the United States spent $329

That happened in part because the United States had become less competitive with the rest of the world. Not only are the wages of its workers higher, thanks to strong unions, but the salaries and benefits of its executives have skyrocketed. It is not unusual for CEOs of major U.S. corporations to earn salaries and stock options in the millions of dollars a year.

Many American companies, attracted by cheaper labor in less developed countries, have moved their manufacturing operations overseas. Look closely at the running shoes you buy and chances are the label will say "Made in Taiwan" or "Made in China."

Doug Marlette/*New York Newsday*

In recent decades, there has been a shift from manufacturing to service industries. Here, chefs are trained at a culinary institute in New England.
Copyright © George Zimbel

Ironically, Barnum's and Bailey's respective kids—Sid and Marty—both ran away one night to join corporate America.
Copyright © Gary Larson/The Far Side, United Press Syndicate. Reprinted by permission.

billion more to buy foreign goods than it earned from sales abroad, an increase of $99 billion over the previous year.[14]

The deficit in the balance of trade with Japan increased somewhat in 1999, from $64 billion in 1998 to $73 billion in 1999.[15] Japan accounted for about 22 percent of the total U.S. trade deficit. The deficit with China in 1999 was $69 billion, or about 20 percent of the total trade imbalance.[16]

Foreign policy and economic policy also are concerned with the **balance of payments,** the net balance or relationship between total income and total expenditures by the nation in its dealings with the rest of the world.

So complex is the trade picture, however, that even citizens who want to "buy American" to support the economy at home may find themselves frustrated. Globalization has meant that some Japanese car manufacturers have opened plants in the United States, employing American workers. Is a Japanese auto made in Kentucky a "foreign" car?

Because some foreign manufacturers enjoy help from their governments, Congress has legislated against "dumping," a term that means selling goods in the United States at prices below their cost of production, usually because of subsidies by a foreign government to its own industries. Brazil, for example, subsidizes its steel industry, and American steelmakers complained that this gives Brazilian steel an unfair advantage over the U.S. steel industry.

In 1988, Representative Richard A. Gephardt, Democrat of Missouri, sponsored what became known as the "Gephardt amendment" to a trade bill then pending in Congress. The amendment would have opened the way to retaliation by Washington against countries that had a trade surplus with the United States. Congress rejected the amendment but passed a major trade bill to stiffen the

Dilbert copyright © 1992 reprinted with permission of United Features Syndicate, Inc.

MAKING A DIFFERENCE
HOW TWO GRADUATE STUDENTS CREATED YAHOO!

David Filo and Jerry Yang were friends at Stanford University pursuing their Ph.D. degrees in electrical engineering, when in April 1994 they started making lists of Internet sites that interested them.

Soon, as their lists grew and became too unwieldy, Filo and Yang started to spend more time on the project. Eventually, they created a customized database, so that other users could search for information.

They called their brainchild Yahoo! Legend has it that the name Yahoo! is supposed to stand for "Yet Another Hierarchical Officious Oracle." However, Yang and Filo still insist, self-mockingly, that they selected the name Yahoo! because that was how they saw themselves—as yahoos, the loutish creatures in Jonathan Swift's *Gulliver's Travels*. (The dictionary defines the term more broadly as anyone who is uneducated and anti-intellectual.)

All of Yahoo!'s information resided on Yang's student workstation, "akebonon," while the search engine was on Filo's computer, "konishiki." The computers were named after famous Hawaiian sumo wrestlers.

Even as Yahoo! was growing, the friends still considered it a hobby. Both David and Jerry were looking around for another startup idea because they didn't think Yahoo! had a chance for success.

Soon, however, as they began spending 20 hours a day maintaining Yahoo!, they realized their hobby had grown beyond their own expectations. Not only was the Web site taking up all their time, but it needed more computer servers, bandwidth, and more people to help manage it. Either they had to shut it down or find a corporate sponsor to help them.

Early in 1995, Marc Andreessen, cofounder of Netscape Communications, invited them to move their information files to Netscape. Additionally, Yang and Filo were being approached by venture capitalists interested in investing in Yahoo!.

As Yahoo! moved from hobby to job, Yang and Filo realized that while they had a passion for Yahoo!, they didn't have the business background to make it succeed. They hired a CEO and a president but stayed on to help guide the company. To reflect this change, they each took on the title of Chief Yahoo.

Today Yahoo! has grown far beyond its original intent, and is one of the most popular search engines on the Internet. Now, in addition, users can get free e-mail accounts, check the stock market, search for jobs, pay their bills, chat with their friends in real time, and read the current news headlines.

Jerry Yang did not complete his Ph.D. In an article he later wrote, he said: "At the time, we didn't realize the thing we'd been working on for fun was going to be the one that succeeded. But we finally realized that if we stopped, then all those people using Yahoo! would go away and they wouldn't have anything. . . . It was really, really hard to leave the Ph.D. program at Stanford. I'm not a quitter. We—David Filo and I—could have put Yahoo! off for six months, finished our dissertations. . . . It still bothers me. It's a personal goal that I never finished.

"But on the other hand, had I finished my thesis, what impact would I have had? Maybe 100 people in the world would have read it. And understood it? Maybe 5. And I probably wouldn't use the thesis much because I would go out and work on something completely different. . . . The attraction to Yahoo! was that millions of people were going to read what we produced."

—Adapted from *Forbes, Sunday Today, Fortune,* and the Yahoo! Company History online at <docs.yahoo.com/info/misc/history.html>

U.S. response to unfair trading practices by other countries. It was signed into law by President Reagan.

Economic policy affects U.S. foreign policy in various ways. Even interest rates in the United States have an impact overseas. For more than two decades, for example, Third World nations sought some relief from repayment of loans to American banks. Interest rates in America, which at times have been high, have made it difficult for the poorer nations to repay their debts. As discussed in Chapter 16, growing concern by many prominent figures, including Pope John Paul II, over the plight of poor countries burdened by debt led Congress in the year 2000 to agree to provide $435 million for the U.S. share of a $90 billion global debt relief program.

Other factors that have little to do with foreign competition have markedly reshaped the American economy. In recent decades, for example, there has been a shift from manufacturing into high-tech and service industries in the United States. Inevitably, this has led to dislocation and loss of jobs by many blue-collar workers.

THE AMERICAN ECONOMY IN THE 21ST CENTURY

Economic indicators, the various guideposts that the government uses to measure the health of the economy, were good in 2000, a presidential election year. Unemployment was extraordinarily low, home sales were up, and hundreds of thousands of new jobs had been created. Inflation was relatively low.

Although the economy generally appeared to be healthy, among many Americans there was optimism mixed with a sense of uncertainty over the future. Within

A ticker on the New York Stock Exchange
AP/Wide World

two years, the economic picture was less rosy. The stock market had soared to unprecedented heights as many small investors put their savings into mutual funds and stocks. But Wall Street no less than ordinary investors worried that the market was overheated and could just as easily drop, as indeed it did after the election. Baby boomers were concerned that Social Security would not be there for them when they retired. Some corporate profits were up, but so were the enormous salaries of corporate chief executive officers. (See Table 17-2.)

Economic policies have important and far-reaching social and political consequences. Americans expect the government to maintain prosperity, and to protect their economic security, both now and in the future, in a rapidly changing world.

Nevertheless, there is little agreement over what precise steps the government should take to meet the goals of full employment, low inflation, and economic stability. There is a contradiction in all this, for Americans philosophically want as little interference as possible in their lives by government. At the same time, they expect their political leaders to preserve a healthy, growing economy for the nation and its citizens. Whether a president or a political party remains in power may depend on how well that challenge is met.

Copyright © Steve Kelley/Copley News Service. Reprinted with permission.

TABLE 17-2

Top 10 Chief Executive Officer Salaries

CEO	Company	Pay
Charles Wang	Computer Associates International	$655,424,000
L. Dennis Kozlowski	Tyco International	169,996,000
David Pottruck	Charles Schwab	127,900,000
John Chambers	Cisco Systems	121,700,000
Stephen Case	America Online	117,085,000
Louis Gerstner	IBM	102,250,000
Jack Welch	General Electric	93,138,000
Sanford Weill	Citigroup	90,230,000
Peter Karmanos, Jr.	Compuware	87,521,000
Reuben Mark	Colgate-Palmolive	85,318,000

*Includes 1999 salary, bonuses, and long-term compensation.
SOURCE: *Business Week,* April 17, 2000, no. 3677, p. 100.

KEY TERMS

capitalism, p. 584
laissez-faire, p. 584
fiscal policy, p. 585
monetary policy, p. 585
supply-side economics,
    p. 585
budget resolutions, p. 586
authorizations, p. 586
appropriations bills, p. 586

deficit, p. 586
national debt, p. 589
gross domestic product
    (GDP), p. 590
tariff, p. 594
balance of trade, p. 596
balance of payments,
    p. 597

CHAPTER HIGHLIGHTS

✦ The United States operates predominantly under an economic system of free enterprise, or capitalism. Under capitalism, there is private ownership of the means of production.

✦ In practice, however, the United States has a mixed, or modified, free enterprise system in which both private industry and government play important roles.

✦ Keynesian economists and their modern successors place major emphasis on fiscal policy to guide the economy, although they recognize the role of monetary policy—the control of the supply of money and the supply of credit through the actions of the Federal Reserve Board.

✦ Supply-side economics is an economic philosophy that advocates both tax and budget cuts to increase incentives to produce, in order to expand the total supply of the nation's goods and services. It was a policy adopted by the Reagan Administration in the 1980s.

✦ The federal government, which for decades had incurred multibillion-dollar deficits, was, by the late 1990s, producing substantial budget surpluses. By 2002, however, the surplus had vanished. A budget surplus is the amount of money available when the government's income is greater than what it spends in a fiscal year.

✦ When the federal government spends more than it receives in taxes and other revenues, the budget is said to operate at a deficit, the gap between the government's income and outlays.

✦ When the government runs at a deficit for many years, the amount of money it owes piles up. The national debt is the total amount of money that the United States owes to its creditors.

✦ Government also attempts to regulate the economy by monetary policy—controlling the supply of money and the cost and availability of credit. It does this through the operations of the Federal Reserve System.

✦ When individuals or corporations need money, they normally borrow from a bank. When banks need money, they may borrow from the Federal Reserve System. The Fed is, therefore, a banker's bank. When it lends to the banks, it can, in effect, create money.

✦ In the United States, a tariff is a federal tax on imports. A high tariff discourages other nations from sending goods to U.S. markets and is therefore "protective" of American manufacturers.

✦ The balance of trade is the relationship between the total cost of foreign goods imported to this country and sales of U.S. products overseas.

✦ Foreign policy and economic policy also are concerned with the balance of payments, the net balance or relationship between total income and total expenditures by the nation in its dealings with the rest of the world.

✦ In the 21st century, globalization has become the target of a diverse group of environmentalists, human rights activists, labor unions, and others. These groups protested against the policies of the World Trade Organization when the WTO met in Seattle in 1999.

SUGGESTED WEB SITES

www.federalreserve.gov
Board of Governors of the Federal Reserve
Contains background information on the work of the Federal Reserve Board and biographies of current members. The *Beige Book,* an informal review conducted by the Federal Reserve Banks that summarizes current economic conditions in their districts, and the *Monetary Policy Report to Congress* are both available online.

www.whitehouse.gov/OMB
Office of Management and Budget
The Office of Management and Budget's Web site offers the current federal budget, along with previous recent budgets.

www.gao.gov
Government Accounting Office
The Web site of the Government Accounting Office, the investigative arm of Congress, contains daily reports about the GAO's latest findings. The GAO site also includes FRAUDNet, a section that encourages and allows people to report fraud, waste, abuse, or mismanagement of federal government funds.

www.whitehouse.gov/WH/EOP/CEA/html/index.html
Council of Economic Advisers
The Council of Economic Advertisers site contains the council's current economic report to the president and other economic data.

SUGGESTED READING

Axelrod, Donald. *Budgeting for Modern Government,*
    2nd edition (St. Martin's, 1995). A comprehensive
    examination of the budget process. Includes suggestions for reforms.

Collender, Stanley. *The Guide to the Federal Budget 2000** (The Brookings Institution, 1999). A useful overview of federal budget making. The author examines the economic and political forces driving the budgetary process, and analyzes the budget in detail.

Destler, I. M., and Balint, Peter. *The New Politics of U.S. Trade Policy** (Institute for International Economics, 1999). A concise examination of the politics of foreign trade in an increasingly global economy.

Galbraith, John Kenneth. *The Affluent Society** (Houghton Mifflin, 1957); and *The Industrial State** (New American Library, 1968). Two well-known works by an influential American economist. In both, Galbraith examines the economic structure of the United States.

Heilbroner, Robert, and Milberg, William. *The Crisis of Vision in Modern Economic Thought** (Cambridge University Press, 1996). A thorough historical analysis of the events that shaped the various schools of economic thought. Examines the divisions among economists in the post-Keynesian era.

Krugman, Paul. *The Age of Diminished Expectations** (MIT Press, 1997). A lively examination of major economic issues. Krugman argues that although for a time American voters were content to let economic policy drift, as the Baby Boom generation moves into retirement this will no longer be possible.

Morris, Irwin. *Congress, the President, and the Federal Reserve: The Politics of American Monetary Policy-Making* (University of Michigan Press, 2000). A comprehensive overview of the politics of monetary policy in the United States.

Peters, B. Guy. *The Politics of Taxation: A Comparative Approach* (Basil Blackwell, 1991). An informative study of how various governments raise revenue.

Includes data about spending policies, taxation, and revenue sources.

Rivlin, Alice M. *Reviving the American Dream: The Economy, the States, and the Federal Government** (The Brookings Institution, 1992). A thoughtful and perceptive account of the state of the American economy. The author later became a former key economic adviser to President Clinton.

Sampson, Anthony. *Company Man: The Rise and Fall of Corporate Life* (Times Books/Random House, 1995). A lively account by a British author detailing the history of corporations in the United States and England.

Smith, Hedrick. *Rethinking America** (Random House, 1995). An examination of the modern American economy by a distinguished journalist. Smith proposes reforms to cope with a changed world order.

Schick, Allen. *The Federal Budget: Politics, Policy and Process** (The Brookings Institution, 2000). A revealing analysis, including detailed case studies and an array of statistical data, of how the federal budget is formulated.

Stein, Herbert. *The Illustrated Guide to the American Economy,* 3rd revised edition* (American Enterprise Institute for Public Policy Research, 1999). A concise overview, with numerous charts and graphs, of the state of the American economy.

Stein, Herbert. *Presidential Economics: The Making of Economic Policy from Roosevelt to Clinton,* 3rd revised edition* (American Enterprise Institute for Public Policy Research, 1994). A stimulating analysis of how economists participate in making federal economic policy. The author served as chief economic adviser to President Nixon.

*Available in paperback edition.

 Visit http://politicalscience.wadsworth.com/cummings9/update/ for current InfoTrac articles and other student resources related to this chapter.

CHAPTER 18
Promoting the General Welfare

During the presidential campaign of 2000, the candidates of both major parties talked repeatedly about the public's growing concern over the fate of Social Security. Many Americans worried that the money to fund the program would not be there when the Baby Boom generation—Americans in their forties and fifties—retired.

The managers of the Social Security program had warned that by 2015, payroll taxes would no longer be large enough to cover Social Security's payments to retirees; and by 2037, unless changes were made in the system, Social Security would be broke.[1] One survey had found that more young people believed in UFOs than believed Social Security would be solvent when they reached retirement age.[2]

The candidates of the two major parties proposed two very different approaches to rescuing the Social Security system. Their disagreement reflected long-standing philosophical differences between the Democratic and Republican parties. Al Gore, the Democratic nominee, insisted that the structure of the program should remain basically unchanged. His plan called for using anticipated annual budget surpluses to pay off the national debt within 13 years. Then, money saved from interest payments on the debt would be used to bolster the Social Security trust funds.

George W. Bush, the Republican candidate, proposed a more sweeping overhaul of the Social Security system. Bush called for partially privatizing Social Security. Under his plan, Social Security taxes would be reduced by up to one-sixth, and workers could invest that amount in the stock market, creating personal retirement accounts. Bush pointed out that from 1926 to 1997, stocks rose in value, after inflation, by an average of 7.2 percent each year. Americans presently entering the workforce, however, could only expect a return of about 2 percent on their Social Security contributions.[3]

Critics of Gore's plan, including a prominent Democratic senator, Daniel Patrick Moynihan of New York, argued that it would not resolve the basic problem facing the system, which was the growing imbalance between revenues and promised benefits.

Critics of Bush's approach claimed that his reforms would undermine the basic principle of the Social Security system, which was created as a "pay-as-you-go" public safety net, in which the contributions of people currently working are used to pay the benefits of those who have retired. They saw Bush's proposal as the first step in transforming Social Security from a social-welfare program into a private pension system. Others expressed concern that, even in a rising stock market, many would lose money. If millions of Americans lost money in stocks, wouldn't there be public pressure on the government to bail them out with tax money? How would the government make sure that individuals invested their retirement account funds prudently, and would that mean an expanded role for Washington in administering and regulating the stock market? Many such questions about the future of Social Security remained unanswered.

Well before the 2000 presidential campaign, the large social programs begun by President Franklin D. Roosevelt during the New Deal and expanded by John F. Kennedy and Lyndon B. Johnson had come under increasing scrutiny. One observer, Anthony King, pointed to what he called "the decline of the ideas of the New Deal as the principal organizing themes of American political life. The central idea of the New Deal was a simple one: that the federal government could, and should, solve the country's economic and social problems."[4]

By contrast, during the 1980s the Reagan and Bush administrations sought to restrict the government to a more limited role; where possible, social programs were eliminated or cut back. Conservatives argued that government programs had not worked and that the federal bureaucracy, and the rules and regulations spawned by these programs, had proved burdensome to individuals. To the Reagan conservatives, government was not the solution; it was the problem. These views were embraced again after the Republicans took control of Congress in

1994 and chose Newt Gingrich as speaker of the House and Bob Dole as Senate majority leader.

Al Gore, in contrast to George W. Bush, advocated the view that government should intervene more often to manage the economy and to provide social programs for people. Gore also believed, however, that too much emphasis on such social programs had cost the Democrats politically in previous elections. Like his predecessor Bill Clinton, he sought to avoid the "liberal" label and to move closer to the political center than had Democrats in the recent past. Gore was repositioning himself, but at the same time he was still the defender of much of the legacy of the New Deal.

Although the presidential candidates in 2000 battled over such diverse issues as tax cuts, health care, and the environment, at the heart of the campaign was a philosophical debate over the proper role of government.

But the heated rhetoric of a presidential campaign does not always match the reality. Although views about the role of government vary greatly, no modern president would propose to shut down a program like Social Security, on which millions of retired persons depend. The responsibility of the national government to make social policy was recognized at the beginning of the American nation, for the Constitution was established, among other purposes, to "promote the general welfare."

To take one example of the need for federal intervention, it would be difficult, if not impossible, for individuals, or even groups of people, to compel American industry to reduce pollution of the environment. But government, supported by public opinion and public demands, possesses the power to accomplish that task.

Whether government can be expected to exercise that power, however, and intervene to regulate corporate power on behalf of consumers and individuals is not always clear. Government regulation, no matter how desirable and necessary, is a source of potential and actual tension in a mostly free-enterprise capitalist economy such as that of the United States. Many of the conflicts of American politics concern the degree to which government should intervene in the private sector.

Some political theorists have even contended that political liberty exists only where there is a free market system and private enterprise, with a minimum of government intervention. In the view of Charles E. Lindblom, for example, "much of the fuller development of personal liberty that men have sought is freedom to engage in trade . . . freedom also to move about, to keep one's earnings and assets."[5]

On the other hand, E. E. Schattschneider has suggested that "the struggle for power is largely a confrontation of two major power systems, government and business." The function of democracy, he argues, has been "to provide the public with a second power system, an alternative power system, which can be used to counterbalance the economic power."[6]

FDR ON SOCIAL SECURITY: "A LAW THAT WILL TAKE CARE OF HUMAN NEEDS"

On August 14, 1935, President Franklin D. Roosevelt signed the Social Security Act into law with a ringing statement:

Today a hope of many years' standing is in large part fulfilled. The civilization of the past hundred years, with its startling industrial changes, has tended more and more to make life insecure. Young people have come to wonder what would be their lot when they came to old age. The man with a job has wondered how long the job would last.

This social security measure gives at least some protection to thirty millions of our citizens who will reap direct benefits through unemployment compensation, through old-age pensions and through increased services for the protection of children and the prevention of ill health.

We can never insure one hundred percent of the population against one hundred percent of the hazards and vicissitudes of life, but we have tried to frame a law which will give some measure of protection to the average citizen and to his family against the loss of a job and against poverty-ridden old age. . . .

If the Senate and the House of Representatives in this long and arduous session had done nothing more than pass this Bill, the session would be regarded as historic for all time.

—The Public Papers and Addresses of Franklin D. Roosevelt

To "promote the general welfare," the federal government fills several major roles. It is regulator, promoter, manager, and protector. It performs these roles in a wide variety of ways and with a degree of zeal that varies with the political climate and the administration in power. It regulates business and labor. But it also promotes business and labor. It assists farmers. It runs such agencies as the Food and Drug Administration and the Tennessee Valley Authority. It tries to manage the economy through fiscal and monetary policies. It acts, to some extent—and with varying success—as protector in consumer affairs, health, education, welfare, science, poverty, hunger, and the environment.

The government does not necessarily perform all of its roles well. By the 2000 election, during an economic boom of historic proportions, there were still more than 35 million people struggling below the poverty level, and large numbers of homeless persons were living on the streets of the nation's cities in rain, snow, heat, and cold. Although economic conditions had greatly improved, two-income households had become the norm, as families—often uncertain about their economic future—struggled to make ends meet. As a result, many Americans took a rather dim view of the ability of the government to manage the economy.

As noted throughout this book, there are many areas in which American government and society have failed to live up to American expectations. So in discussing government in operation, a careful distinction must be made between the various roles of the government and its actual performance.

A government like that of the United States, which exercises responsibility for the welfare of its citizens in such areas as social security, housing, and education, is sometimes described as a welfare state. The term is often used as one of criticism. But the role of the federal government in making social policy has been well established in this century, particularly since the days of the New Deal. As one study suggested, "social welfare programs substantially improve the well-being of most beneficiaries and . . . retrenchment does have serious repercussions. . . . There is no reason to abandon the aim of providing a minimal level of support for all who remain in need."[7]

Despite the cutbacks in government social programs under President Reagan, and the sharply differing philosophy of his administration from that of Democratic administrations in the past, Washington did not ignore its domestic role during the Reagan-Bush years. Programs such as Social Security, public assistance, and Medicare continued to aid millions of Americans.

Today, regardless of who occupies the White House, the terms of the argument usually concern the proper extent of government intervention in domestic problems, as well as how government should respond to national needs. Government services require government spending, and the size of government programs is directly related to the level of taxes. The level of government taxing and spending for welfare and social programs is a volatile political issue, directly affecting votes. That is why the question of how much the government should spend on such programs is often an important issue in presidential campaigns.

Where people stand on social-welfare issues may be related to their economic, social, and political background. The homeowner in a comfortable suburb may have less sympathy for federal welfare-assistance programs than would the mother of four children living in a rat-infested Harlem tenement.

In this chapter we will explore a key question: How and to what extent should the federal government "promote the general welfare"? Many other questions also

A soup kitchen in the nation's capital
Copyright © J.L. Atlan/Sygma

arise. How efficiently does government regulate corporate power on behalf of the consumer? How well has it performed in the field of social welfare, in eliminating poverty and hunger, in coping with rising medical costs, including the high price of prescription drugs, in meeting educational needs, and in protecting the environment?

GOVERNMENT AS REGULATOR AND PROMOTER

Government and Business

The Constitution, as Justice Oliver Wendell Holmes, Jr., once wrote, "is not intended to embody a particular economic theory."[8] But the Supreme Court, which interprets the meaning of the Constitution, has often embodied the particular economic theory of its time. For half a century, from the late 1880s until 1937, during Franklin Roosevelt's New Deal, the Court generally interpreted the Constitution in such a way as to prevent government from regulating industry. It adopted the prevailing **laissez-faire** philosophy, which held that government should intervene as little as possible in economic affairs.

During the late 19th century, economic power was concentrated in the "trusts" and in the hands of the "robber barons." But a rising tide of populism created public demands that led to the passage of state and federal laws regulating industry. Nevertheless, the Supreme Court, as was noted in Chapter 15, interpreted the Fourteenth Amendment to protect business from social regulation by the states and by Congress.

Justice Holmes made the comment quoted at the beginning of this section in his famous dissent in the *Lochner* case. In that 1905 decision the majority of the Supreme Court struck down a New York State law that had limited bakery employment to "sixty hours in any one week" and "ten hours in any one day." Today it might seem incredible that the Supreme Court would permit a bakery owner to work his employees more than 60 hours a week. But in 1905 the Supreme Court refused to approve the use of the power of the state to regulate private property—in this case a bakery.

The Great Depression and the New Deal brought about a reversal of Supreme Court thinking. Since 1937 the Court has upheld laws policing business; the right of government to regulate wages, hours, and working conditions of employees is now firmly established. Indeed, some of the regulations of the Occupational Safety and

A garment factory in Los Angeles: Government regulates wages, hours, and working conditions.
Copyright © Michael Newman/PhotoEdit

Health Administration (OSHA) have been so detailed and stringent that they have brought a storm of protests from business and industry. And corporate power often counterbalances government power. As one scholar has suggested, the scope and effectiveness of the federal government's efforts "have been sharply limited by business's success in weakening the content and constraining the enforcement of the legislation."[9]

But business, even as it protests government regulation, asks for government protection. "A powerful campaign has been mounted [by industry] to contain government; reduce its size—or rate of growth—especially as regards social welfare functions; and diminish its regulatory encroachments. . . . On the other hand, business clamors for government protection, decisive efforts to control inflation. . . . This is a whipsaw treatment of government."[10]

Regulating Business: Antitrust Policy   In 1890 Congress passed the Sherman Antitrust Act, which was designed to encourage competition in business and prevent the growth of monopolies. The Supreme Court

severely limited the scope of the act, however, by ruling that it was up to the states to control industrial monopolies. Then in 1914 Congress passed the Clayton Act, which sought to put teeth into the federal antitrust law by defining illegal business practices, by providing the remedy of court injunctions, and by giving the Federal Trade Commission power to issue cease-and-desist orders. The same measure exempted labor unions from antitrust actions.

Subsequent legislation has strengthened the antitrust laws, and both the Federal Trade Commission and the antitrust division of the Justice Department have blocked many large corporate mergers. But the degree of enforcement of the antitrust laws varies with the attitudes of the administration in power in Washington.

Nevertheless, there have been a number of landmark cases in which the government has changed the shape of major industries. In a famous case in 1957, the Supreme Court, under the Clayton Act, forced du Pont to divest itself of 23 percent of the stock of General Motors.[11] In 1982, American Telephone and Telegraph Company, AT&T, was broken up into "Baby Bells." At the time, AT&T was the largest corporation in the world.

In 1998, the Justice Department filed an antitrust suit against the powerful Microsoft Corporation, led by its billionaire chairman, Bill Gates. The government charged that the computer software giant was using its monopoly in personal computer operating systems to gain competitive advantage in other software fields, such as Internet browsers. According to Attorney General Janet Reno, Microsoft had "restricted the choices available for consumers in America and around the world" with its practices.[12] In April 2000, after a fiercely contested legal battle, U.S. District Judge Thomas Penfield Jackson found Microsoft guilty of violating antitrust law, ruling that it had used the predominance of its Windows operating system to "quell incipient competition," and to pressure computer makers into using Microsoft's Web browser.[13] The judge ordered that Microsoft be broken up into two companies, one specializing in computer operating systems, and one dealing with other software applications. Microsoft promised to appeal the ruling.

Although government regulation has had some success at blocking **monopoly,** the control of a market by a single company, it has not been able to prevent **oligopoly,** the concentration of economic power in the hands of a relatively few large companies. Economist John Kenneth Galbraith has noted that "in the characteristic market of the industrial system, there are only a handful of sellers."[14] Even as the government was pursuing the breakup of Microsoft, for example, oil giants Exxon and Mobil announced plans to merge.[15] And in May 2000, FCC officials approved media giant Viacom's $30 billion acquisition of CBS, a merger that gave Viacom control of 35 percent of the American broadcasting market.[16] The 10 largest corporations in the United States are shown in Table 18-1.

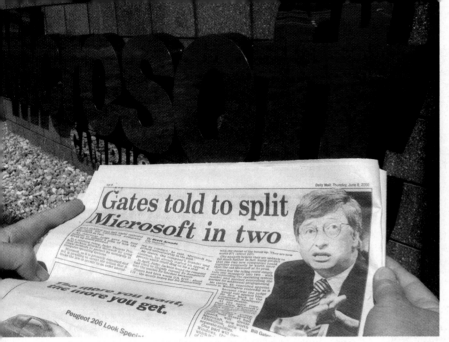

April, 2000: A federal judge rules against Microsoft in the government's antitrust suit.
AP/Wide World

Of the 100 largest economic units in the world in the year 2000, only 49 were countries; 51 were multinational corporations.[17] As ownership of industry becomes more and more impersonal and remote, it is increasingly difficult for the private citizen to fix responsibility for corporate actions. In some instances, individuals have turned to the courts to fight corporations.

But the issue of corporate responsibility extends beyond the individual to the larger question of the responsibility of corporations toward society as a whole. The consumer movement, public concern over pollution by industry, and similar pressures have led a number of corporations to take steps to improve their public image in the area of corporate responsibility.

In the year 2000, Firestone recalled 6.5 million tires after more than 100 people had been killed in accidents involving vehicles equipped with Firestone tires. Many of the accidents involved tread separation that caused the drivers to lose control of their vehicles. Most of the defective Firestone tires were on Ford Explorers that rolled over. After the recall, Congress and the Department of Transportation called for more stringent laws to prevent such avoidable and tragic loss of life.

Ralph Nader's crusade for auto safety brought federal legislation and prodded the automobile industry to produce safer cars and to recall those with suspected defects. Increasing awareness of the issue of corporate responsibility led in the 1960s and 1970s to the emergence of public interest law firms composed of young law school graduates. Instead of joining traditional, old-line law firms representing large corporations, the

Thus, despite government regulation, some American corporations have increased in both size and diversity. Nothing illustrates the trend better than the rise in recent years of conglomerates: large multi-interest, and often multinational, corporations that may, under one corporate roof, manufacture products ranging from missiles to baby bottles. Because conglomerates are formed by mergers of companies in unrelated fields, they have long been considered exempt from most antitrust regulation.

The ordinary consumer cannot keep up with the complexities of corporate ownership in what Galbraith has called "the new industrial state." Indeed, large corporations have become more powerful than many nations.

TABLE 18-1

The 10 Largest Corporations in the United States, 2000

Rank (by sales volume) (in billions)	Company	Profits (in billions)	Assets (in billions)
1	General Motors	$189.058	$273.921
2	Wal-Mart Stores	166.809	70.245
3	Exxon-Mobil	163.881	63.466
4	Ford Motor	162.558	276.229
5	General Electric	111.630	405.200
6	International Business Machines	87.548	87.495
7	Citigroup	82.005	716.900
8	AT&T	62.391	169.406
9	Philip Morris	61.751	61.381
10	Boeing	57.993	36.147

SOURCE: Data provided by FORTUNE.com, August 2000, online at <www.fortune.com/fortune/>.

graduates offered their skills to protect consumers, minorities, and the poor. Today, these public interest firms are much fewer in number, although some conventional law firms perform a limited amount of public interest work. A number of private organizations, such as environmental and consumer groups, also have staff attorneys who practice public interest law in representing their organizations.

The Regulatory Agencies Although the Justice Department has responsibility for fostering competition through the antitrust laws, much of the day-to-day contact between government and industry is carried on through federal regulatory agencies, including the major commissions discussed in Chapter 14. Thus the Securities and Exchange Commission (SEC) has responsibility for regulating the stock market; the Federal Communications Commission (FCC), the broadcast industry; the Federal Energy Regulatory Commission (FERC), power companies and pipelines; and the Federal Trade Commission (FTC), industry as a whole. Other federal agencies, such as the Food and Drug Administration, the Environmental Protection Agency, the Federal Maritime Commission, and the Consumer Product Safety Commission, have played an important role in regulating business.

As also noted in Chapter 14, many of the commissions have, to varying degrees, become captives of their client industries, and deregulation has reduced the authority of some of these agencies. Nor has regulation always been successful. A case in point is the railroad industry, which has long asserted that its passenger operations lose money while its freight operations make money. The great increase in air and highway travel in the past few decades was a major factor in reducing railroad revenues. Poor management by some railroads was certainly another factor.

But some would argue that the government was also partly responsible for the deterioration of the railroads. Although the Interstate Commerce Commission, abolished in 1995, was supposed to regulate the railroads in the public interest, it permitted passenger service to decline to a point approaching extinction. Americans visiting Japan or Europe found better rail service in cleaner, more modern trains than in many parts of their own country. On the other hand, the railroads have complained that government regulation forced the railways to continue service on unwanted passenger routes and in other ways made it difficult for them to compete with the airlines.

In 1970 Congress passed legislation to establish a federally subsidized national rail network of passenger trains. The law created a government-sponsored corporation to run many of the nation's intercity passenger trains (but not commuter lines). The National Railroad Passenger Corporation, better known as Amtrak, lost

Firestone tires may have caused the crash of this sport utility vehicle in June 2000.
Arizona Dept. of Public Safety/AP/Wide World

money. But the corporation expanded its Metroliner service between Washington, New York, and New Haven, providing comfortable high-speed train service at frequent intervals. Because the Metroliner was well run and competitive with the airlines in the heavily traveled northeast corridor, the Metroliner initially made a profit, even though Amtrak as a whole did not.[*] By 2000, Amtrak had only 0.3 percent of the nation's total passenger traffic.[18] In that year, in an effort to compete with low-fare air flights in the Northeast, it began operating a new generation of high-speed trains, the Acela, along the busy corridor between Boston and Washington, D.C., with plans to expand their use nationally.

Two decades earlier, in 1980, as part of a general trend toward deregulation, Congress passed the Staggers Rail Act, which substantially deregulated the nation's railroads, giving them more freedom to set rates and drop routes.

Aiding Business Related to the concept of government as regulator is that of government as promoter. Government promotes commerce by providing services and direct and indirect subsidies to producers and farmers. Many business firms and farmers benefit from government aid. Appropriations for highways are indirect subsidies to truckers, bus lines, and automobile manufacturers and users. The federal government pays the airlines and the railroads to carry the mail; it helps support the merchant marine through subsidies to shipbuilders and ship operators; and it finances airport construction.

In the "alphabet soup" of government agencies in Washington there are several service agencies for

---

[*]Amtrak's excellent safety record was marred by a series of accidents in the 1980s and 1990s that caused a number of deaths and hundreds of injuries.

Amtrak's high-speed Acela began service between Washington, New York, and Boston in 2000.
AMTRAK/AP/Wide World

industry—the Department of Commerce and the Small Business Administration (SBA), for example—as well as the Department of Agriculture, which serves farmers.

At times the government has even extended direct aid to large corporations in financial trouble. In 1979, for example, Congress authorized a massive $3.5 billion aid package for the ailing Chrysler Corporation, the nation's third-largest automobile manufacturer. Chrysler had underestimated the increased consumer demand for small cars that use less gasoline and started building them too late; by 1979 the company's losses had mounted to $1.1 billion for the year. Congress acted, and President Carter signed the bill, because of growing concern over the impact on the economy if the government permitted a major auto manufacturer to go under. By 1983, Chrysler had turned the corner, showing a profit of $927 million. In 1998, Chrysler merged with German automaker Daimler-Benz.

In addition to subsidies and services, the federal government assists industry through its trade and tariff policies, as discussed in Chapter 17.

Aiding Agriculture In 1996, Congress passed and President Clinton signed a major new law to assist farmers and replace the program adopted during Franklin D. Roosevelt's New Deal that paid farmers not to plant certain crops.

The new law ended the Depression-era subsidies that were paid to farmers when prices for farm products dropped below certain levels. Instead, the law guaranteed farmers fixed annual payments through fiscal 2002, regardless of prices. No longer did Washington have power to tell farmers what crops to plant, or to leave some land unplanted. Farmers themselves could decide what to plant. The legislation also phased out dairy price supports over four years.

The new farm law marked a victory for the Republican Congress elected in 1994, since it moved farming away from many government controls and toward a free market approach. At the same time, it provided an estimated $56 billion to farmers over seven years.[19]

Because the nation's 3 million farmers sometimes produce more than they can sell profitably and are often hostage to drought, or floods, or extreme cold, there were still enormous problems in agriculture. The government's programs over many decades to aid farmers reflect not only the political power of the farm belt, but also recognition by Washington of the responsibility of the federal government to promote and assist a vital segment of the nation's economic life.

Government and Labor

As in the case of business, labor is both regulated and helped by the federal government. Today organized labor wields great economic and political power in the United States. This was not always the case; the history of the labor movement in America is one of long struggle, intermittent violence, and only gradual recognition.

The industrialization of the 19th century brought American laborers job opportunities in factories but scant bargaining power with employers. As a result they worked long hours at low wages and under hazardous working conditions. In 1881 Samuel Gompers, a London-born cigarmaker, founded what became the American Federation of Labor (AFL). The AFL fought for "bread-and-butter" improvements—the eight-hour day, higher pay, fringe benefits, and restrictions on child labor. It was largely a federation of craft unions—groups of skilled workers organized by trades: construction, printing, mining, clothing manufacturing, and others.

The Great Depression, which threw millions of people out of work, and the liberal policies of the New Deal created a favorable climate for the labor movement. In the mid-1930s a group of labor leaders within the AFL began to organize industrial unions in the mass-production industries, thus bringing unskilled workers into a labor movement dominated until then by craft unions. Led by John L. Lewis, head of the United Mine Workers, the dissidents formed a new labor organization that became known in 1938 as the Congress of Industrial Organizations (CIO). The CIO rapidly won recognition from the automotive, steel, rubber, and other industries. In 1955 the AFL merged with the CIO. By 1999 there were 16.5 million union members in the United States, of which 13.2 million belonged to unions in the AFL-CIO.

In its early years the labor movement was unable to gain protection in the courts, so in the 1920s it turned to Congress for help. As early as 1926, the Railway Labor Act stated labor's right to organize and established the National Mediation Board to assist in settling rail strikes. The Norris-LaGuardia Act of 1932 sharply restricted the power of the courts to issue injunctions in labor disputes. Up to that time employers were frequently able to break strikes by obtaining court injunctions against the unions.

The National Labor Relations Act of 1935 was labor's great milestone. Sponsored by Senator Robert F. Wagner, Democrat of New York, it established labor's right to collective bargaining and barred employers from setting up "company unions" (unions controlled by the employer) or discriminating against any worker for union activity or membership. The act also established the National Labor Relations Board (NLRB), an independent regulatory agency that supervises union elections and determines unfair labor practices. The Fair Labor Standards Act of 1938 established a minimum wage for American workers, a maximum 40-hour workweek, and time-and-a-half for overtime. It also outlawed child labor. Over the years, the minimum-wage law has been amended by Congress and its coverage expanded. In 1996, Congress raised the federal minimum wage from $4.25 to $4.75 per hour and to $5.15 beginning September 1, 1997. The law covered more than 80 million workers, of whom 7.7 million earned less than $5.15 per hour.

The power gained by labor during the New Deal inevitably brought a political reaction. The National Labor Relations Act had placed restrictions on employers but none on unions. In 1947 Congress passed the Taft-Hartley Act, which sought to shift some of labor's newly won power back to management. The act prohibited the **closed shop,** under which only union members may be hired, but it did permit the **union shop,** under which any person may be hired provided he or she joins the union within a specified time. Under Section 14B of the Taft-Hartley Act, 21 states (10 in the South) passed state **right to work laws** to outlaw the union shop. The act also defined and prohibited unfair labor practices by unions; expanded the membership of the NLRB, an agency that employers had considered too favorable to labor; barred labor unions from making political contributions; and outlawed strikes by government employees. Finally, the law provided that in strikes creating a national emergency, the president can seek a court injunction against a union during an 80-day "cooling off period."

 for more information about the National Labor Relations Board, see:
www.nlrb.go

Big labor unions continued to prosper, despite the restrictions of the Taft-Hartley Act. And the legislation had one result that its Republican sponsors had not intended: Because passage of the law demonstrated to labor that legislation aimed at unions could win support in Congress, it had the effect of increasing the political activity of labor unions. Often that labor support went to Democrats.

In the late 1950s a Senate committee held a series of hearings to investigate labor racketeering. Two successive Teamsters Union presidents, Dave Beck and James R. Hoffa, eventually went to jail after the disclosures, and the AFL-CIO expelled the Teamsters. The televised hearings brought national recognition to the Senate committee's chief counsel, Robert F. Kennedy. It also led to demands for reform legislation.

The Labor Reform Act of 1959 (Landrum-Griffin Act) grew out of the hearings. The act (1) required unions to file elaborate financial reports, constitutions, and bylaws with the secretary of labor; (2) granted union members the right to elect officers by secret ballot; (3) barred ex-convicts from holding union office; and (4) tightened Taft-Hartley provisions against secondary boycotts, organizational picketing, and other labor practices that employers felt gave unions an unfair advantage.

Despite provisions for injunctions that sometimes avert or delay major strikes, the public is often unprotected against walkouts that may inconvenience millions of people—airline, rail, and garbage strikes, for example. Compulsory arbitration to settle major labor disputes has not won wide acceptance, and the problem of disruptive strikes in an industrial society remains.

Because unions have concentrated on bread-and-butter gains through collective bargaining, organized labor has made great economic progress in the United States. The extent of labor's political power is less clear. Unlike many industrial nations, the United States has never had a major, enduring "labor party." Rather than run its own candidates for political office, labor has usually worked through the two-party system. Since the New Deal era, labor has usually supported the national Democratic Party, but it carefully watches the records of members of Congress in both parties and supports those whom it considers friendly to labor.

Although labor support is vital to many political candidates, the concept of a deliverable "labor vote" is dubious because union members are also Republicans and Democrats as well as members of other groups. In the 2000 presidential campaign Al Gore enjoyed the support of organized labor, as has almost every modern Democratic presidential candidate.

As the nation has shifted away from manufacturing industries, shrinking labor's traditional blue-collar base, union membership in the United States has declined over the past generation. In the 1950s, 35 percent of the nation's nonagricultural workers were union members, but by the late 1990s, that figure had fallen to 13.9 percent. There are signs, however, that the decline may be slowing. In 1999, after an aggressive membership drive, unions organized 600,000 new workers, the largest increase since the 1970s. Nevertheless, the total percentage of the workforce that was unionized remained virtually unchanged from the previous year, as a result of layoffs of union members.[20]

The Department of Labor, which achieved cabinet status in 1913, administers and enforces laws relating to the welfare of wage earners in the United States. Its responsibilities include manpower and job-training programs, administering the wages and hours law, and enforcing the safety and health standards for workers set by various federal laws.

GOVERNMENT AS PROTECTOR

When Democrat Bill Clinton won the presidency in 1992, he appointed his wife, Hillary Rodham Clinton, to head a task force to draw up a plan to provide health insurance coverage for all Americans. The task force labored in secret and produced a complex plan calling for "managed competition" through "health alliances," which were described as large, regional insurance pools. But the plan seemed likely to push many people into health maintenance organizations (HMOs), where in most cases they would be forced to give up their own, familiar doctors. Public skepticism—and a coalition of conservatives, small business, and parts of the health care industry—not only doomed the plan to defeat in 1994 but also contributed to the Republican capture of Congress that year. At that time almost 40 million Americans lacked any health insurance.

Although the Clinton health plan was defeated, the goal of providing good, affordable health care to all Americans, including those too poor to pay for it, continued to be a key political issue. During the presiden-

tial election campaign of 2000, the candidates of both major parties expressed support for the general goal of providing health coverage for all Americans. Their proposed solutions reflected the differing political philosophies of the two parties. Al Gore, the Democratic candidate, favored the extension of existing government programs, such as the Children's Health Insurance Program, to cover more families. His Republican opponent, George W. Bush, called for tax credits for workers whose employers did not provide health insurance and who purchased it on their own.

Despite their widely differing approaches to the issue, the fact that neither candidate could explicitly reject any government role in providing health coverage for seniors or for the needy was an indication of how much public opinion had shifted over the past two generations. Helping people to obtain health care in an era of astronomical medical costs remained one of the most important tasks of government as protector of the public. Individuals do not have the power to reduce health costs or require insurance coverage for everyone. They look to the government to accomplish those objectives.

When Social Security was enacted in 1935, President Franklin D. Roosevelt's opponents criticized the expansion of government, and voiced fears of "creeping socialism." Times change. The government now spends hundreds of billions of dollars each year on social programs, ranging from school lunches to health care for the elderly. And while many Americans might criticize specific programs, by and large most Americans expect the government to act as protector of the general welfare. Proposing to abolish or modify established social programs that enjoy broad public support carries a high political risk.

In the rest of this chapter, we shall explore some of the important aspects of government as protector. It should be kept in mind, of course, that the government does not always successfully fulfill its role as protector of the public.

Despite screening by the Food and Drug Administration, dangerous prescription drugs have been sold to the public. Some 800 innocent people, without their knowledge, were deliberately exposed to radiation in government experiments conducted between the 1940s and the 1960s. In addition, thousands of people were exposed to radiation leaking from hundreds of underground nuclear tests conducted in Nevada without any notice to the public. Hazardous nuclear waste escaped into the atmosphere and into the ground for years from the government's plutonium plant in Rocky Flats, Colorado, until the plant was finally shut down for safety violations in 1988. Congress has passed laws to clean up the air we breathe, but the executive branch has sometimes enforced those laws in ways that favor the polluters, not the public. As always, in studying the operations of government we should remember that there is often a gap between the goal and the reality.

UNSAFE TO ATTACK GENERAL MOTORS

In 1965, Ralph Nader, then a 31-year-old Connecticut attorney, criticized the safety of American automobiles, particularly the General Motors Corvair, in his book *Unsafe at Any Speed.* General Motors, through an attorney in Washington, hired a "private eye" to investigate Nader. Senate investigators found that the New York detective agency, Vincent Gillen Associates, Inc., had issued the following instructions to its "gumshoes":

> [Nader] apparently is a freelance writer and attorney. Recently he published a book *Unsafe at Any Speed,* highly critical of the automotive industry's interest in safety. Since then our clients' client apparently made some cursory inquiries into Nader to ascertain his expertise, his interest, his background, his backers, etc.

They have found out relatively little about him, and that little is detailed below. Our job is to check his life and current activities to determine "what makes him tick," such as his real interest in safety, his supporters, if any, his politics, his marital status, his friends, his women, boys, etc., drinking, dope, jobs—in fact all facets of his life. This may entail surveillance which will be undertaken only upon the OK of Vince Gillen as transmitted by him to the personnel of Vincent Gillen Associates, Inc.

—Hearings before the Subcommittee on Executive Reorganization, Committee on Government Operations, U.S. Senate, *Federal Role in Traffic Safety,* March 22, 1966

Government and the Consumer

Today, most Americans would agree that government has a responsibility to protect ordinary consumers from the perils of the marketplace. Three decades ago few citizens were aware of consumer issues. That the picture changed dramatically was, to a considerable extent, the work of a single crusader for consumer protection: attorney Ralph Nader.

In his book, *Unsafe at Any Speed,* published in 1965, Nader charged that the automobile industry bore partial responsibility for many highway accidents and deaths by making cars that emphasized style over safety. Nader was then investigated by private detectives hired by attorneys for the General Motors Corporation (GM). A Senate subcommittee disclosed that the private detectives had put Nader under surveillance and had even checked into his sex life. As a result of the Senate investigation, James M. Roche, the president of GM, found it prudent to apologize publicly to Nader at a committee hearing.*

The congressional investigation of GM's flagrant action against a private citizen made Nader a national figure overnight. In the years that followed, he played a vital role in the passage of five major federal consumer laws (listed a little later in this section). GM removed the Corvair from production after Nader charged that the car was hazardous to drive under certain conditions. Today, major auto companies routinely recall cars from consumers to correct safety defects. Ralph Nader's crusades found a response among the public, the press, Congress, and the executive branch. In the 2000 election, Nader ran for president on the Green Party ticket.

The basic demand of the consumer movement is that government step in to protect buyers from hazardous products, shoddy merchandise, mislabeling, fraudulent sales techniques, consumer credit abuses, and other deceptive or dangerous practices. "Consumerism" holds that when business will not police itself, government must act.

The person who must return a coffeepot to the repair shop three times before it is fixed properly; the child playing with an inflammable toy; the inner-city resident talked into buying an overpriced bedroom suite for "only $899"; the family injured in an auto crash because of defective tires—all are victims of consumer abuses. Many products that Americans buy seem to have "built-in" obsolescence—that is, they are designed to wear out after a certain amount of time.

Consumer frauds victimize the most those who can afford it the least. Various studies have shown that "the poor pay more." Residents of the inner city often buy low-quality merchandise at high prices. Why? One reason is that neighborhood merchants extend "easy" credit terms to poor people who may not be able to buy on credit in major department stores. And, as David Caplovitz noted in his study of poverty areas in Manhattan, "neighborhood merchants . . . compensate for extending credit to poor risks by high markups."[21] The result is that poor families often end up paying higher prices for appliances such as television sets and washing machines than do more affluent families.[22] To deal with customers who cannot keep up the payments, the merchant can use the weapons of repossession and salary garnishment, backed by the power of the law.

During the 1960s and 1970s, legislation was passed to deal with consumer problems, and limited machinery to deal with those problems was established within the executive branch. Presidents Kennedy, Johnson, Nixon, Ford, Carter, Reagan, Bush, and Clinton all appointed staff assistants for consumer affairs. Several federal

---

*In 1970, four years after the Senate hearings, GM paid Nader $425,000 in an out-of-court settlement of his invasion-of-privacy suit. See *New York Times,* August 14, 1970, p. 1.

The gas gauge was nearing "empty" so the University of Arizona co-ed pulled off the freeway into the nearest service station. All went routinely enough until suddenly she noticed white smoke billowing out from under the open hood. The attendant, standing over it with a properly concerned expression, informed her that the car needed "a new accelerator in its generator" and that if she tried to drive out of the station without having it fixed, the car would be ruined.

One tank of gas and $119 later the student was back on the freeway, heading for the university campus. To confirm her growing suspicion, she took the car to her regular mechanic for a recheck. His verdict: Potassium powder had been used to simulate smoke, and she had been "conned" (a generator does not have an accelerator).

The case is not as exceptional as one might think. Despite stepped-up efforts by law-enforcement agencies and more widespread and vehement complaining on the part of car owners, deceptive auto-repair practices persist as a major consumer problem.

—*Christian Science Monitor*

agencies are involved in consumer matters, but the principal responsibility is in the hands of the Federal Trade Commission.

The principal consumer laws include the following:

1. *Auto safety* (1966). One law requires manufacturers to meet federal standards for automobile and tire safety, and another requires each state to establish federally approved highway safety programs or lose 10 percent of federal highway construction funds.
2. *Truth-in-packaging* (1966). To help shoppers make price comparisons, a law was passed requiring

manufacturers to label their products more clearly. But it does not require standard package sizes, which would aid shoppers in threading their way through the supermarket jungle of "jumbo," "family," and "large economy" sizes.
3. *Meat and poultry inspection* (1967 and 1968). Two laws were designed to tighten consumer protection against poor-quality meat and poultry. Prior to this legislation, these products were subject to federal inspection when shipped between states, but products consumed within a state were subject only to state inspection. Seven states had no meat inspection at all.
4. *Truth-in-lending* (1968). This legislation requires merchants and lenders to provide full, honest, and understandable information about credit terms. For example, a customer who agrees to pay "only 3 percent per month" must be told that the annual interest rate is actually 36 percent.
5. *Product safety* (1972). The law establishes the independent five-member Consumer Product Safety Commission. The commission has broad power to act against hazardous products that by 1996 caused an estimated 12 million consumer injuries each year.

In almost every case, industry has lobbied against consumer bills and has often weakened the final versions. There is some danger, therefore, that the passage of consumer legislation may create the appearance of government regulation without the reality. Consumer advocates now are increasingly focusing their attention on how consumer laws are put into effect and on their real impact once enacted. At the same time, the power of the consumer movement had diminished as Congress and the electorate became preoccupied with other issues.

The General Welfare

In 2000, some 48.4 million Americans—retired or disabled workers and their dependents—received about $333.4 billion in Social Security payments. Another 2.5 million families received public assistance (welfare) payments totaling about $16 billion, of which the federal government paid about half (with state and local governments paying the rest).

But the federal government no longer administers the welfare program. As the 1996 presidential campaign gathered momentum in midsummer of that year, President Clinton, who was seeking reelection, signed a bill that completely restructured the nation's welfare plan.

The new law, passed by the Republican-controlled Congress, dismantled the program established 60 years earlier during President Roosevelt's New Deal administration. The federal government no longer guarantees payments to poor families with children. Instead, the law provides that each state receives federal money to design and run its own welfare programs.

"Granted the public has a right to know what's in a hot dog, but does the public really want to know what's in a hot dog?"

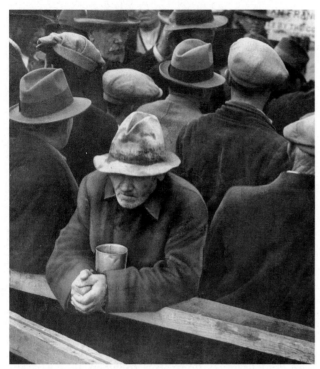

Dorothea Lange/Culver Pictures

People who receive assistance under the new welfare law are required to find work within two years, and lifetime benefits are limited to five years, although states are free to set even stricter limits. The law preserved the Medicaid program of health care for persons with low incomes but placed restrictions on the Food Stamp program.

Although some liberal Democrats and advocates for children sharply criticized the president's decision to sign the bill into law, the measure redeemed Clinton's pledge in the 1992 campaign to "end welfare as we know it." The law was strongly backed by Republicans and conservatives. It marked a fundamental change in social policy after six decades.

By the year 2000, another $26 billion a year in federal benefits went to 6.6 million persons under the Supplemental Security Income (SSI) program. In addition, it was estimated that a monthly average of 5.8 million jobless workers would collect $20.3 billion in unemployment insurance.[23]

Yet prior to 1935 these programs did not exist. The hardships of old age, ill health, poverty, unemployment, blindness, or disability were problems for individuals, their families, private charity, states, and local communities.

The Great Depression of the 1930s changed all that. Millions lost their jobs, and a blight of hunger and poverty descended on the land. "Brother, Can You Spare a Dime?" was a popular song of 1932. America realized that individuals needed help from the national government to maintain their income in hard times. In the midst of the Depression, Franklin D. Roosevelt proposed, and Congress passed, the landmark Social

Security Act of 1935. Although to some Americans it seemed a revolutionary step at the time, the United States was the last major industrial nation in the world to adopt a general system of social security.

There are two kinds of social-welfare programs, both designed to guarantee personal economic security to individuals. One is called *social insurance*. The Social Security program is, in effect, a compulsory national insurance program, in theory self-financed by taxes on employers and employees. The other kind of program, *public assistance*, had no pay-as-you-go features; until the 1996 welfare law changed the system and ended the federal guarantee, it simply distributed public funds to poor families. (Recipients were usually said to be "on welfare.") The distinction is important, because each approach has significant political consequences.

Social insurance is widely accepted because it is "earned." People assume that they have a "right" to retirement income after a lifetime of work. But "welfare" programs have not enjoyed the same acceptance by the public. Many Americans who have received welfare payments, and many others who have not, believe that society has a responsibility to care for those who are less fortunate. Some Americans, however, as Gilbert Y. Steiner points out, hold a different view:

> [They] resent supporting those who can't make their own way. . . . The idea of "toughening up" is forever popular. Toughening up, it is argued, will drive the cheaters out, the slackers to work, the unwed mothers into chastity; and it will save money. It is this clash between the ideas of public aid as a right and public aid as a matter of sufferance, to be granted with suspicion, with strings, and with restraints, that is reflected in public policy debates and political action.[24]

By the mid-1990s, politicians of both parties, relying on polling data and other information, realized that many voters, rightly or wrongly, had concluded that welfare was a program of "handouts" of their tax money to loafers. Both Republicans and Democrats agreed that welfare needed to be modified. And it was. By shifting responsibility for welfare programs to the states, however, the law meant that states and localities would be under new financial pressures to provide for poor families.

Social Security The Social Security Act of 1935 and its later amendments provide for both social insurance and public assistance programs. The insurance aspects fall into four categories: old-age and survivors insurance, disability insurance, Medicare, and unemployment insurance.

 for more information about Social Security, see:
www.ssa.gov

When people talk about receiving **Social Security,** they generally mean the monthly cash payments received by retired, older people through a compulsory national

SOMEDAY SON, NONE OF THIS WILL BE YOURS...

Drawing by Mike Peters for the *Dayton Daily News*. Reprinted by permission of United Features Syndicate, Inc.

insurance program financed by taxes on employers and employees. A man or woman who reaches the age of 62 may draw partial Social Security payments if he or she has worked enough years to qualify (10 years in 2000). Men and women who have worked long enough to qualify may receive Social Security at the full, higher rate beginning at age 65, a figure that will gradually rise to age 67 by 2027. The payments depend on a person's average earnings over a period of years. In December 2000 the average monthly benefit for a retired worker was $804 and about 44 million people were receiving checks. (Examples of Social Security payments are shown in Table 18-2.)

As originally passed, Social Security payments provided only retirement benefits. In 1939 the program was expanded to provide payments to dependents and survivors of workers covered by the system. And in 1956 it was expanded to include disabled workers.

Over the years, Congress has extended Social Security coverage to virtually all types of workers. The system is financed by a Social Security tax levied equally on employers and employees. Self-employed persons also must pay a Social Security tax. In 2000, employers and employees each paid 7.65 percent of an employee's income for Social Security and Medicare taxes (up to a ceiling of $72,600 for Social Security); self-employed persons paid 15.3 percent.[*]

Inflation hits hardest at persons living on fixed incomes, such as retired workers who depend on Social Security payments. Because of this, Congress has linked the benefits to the cost of living; increases in the amounts paid out under the program are now as a rule automatic.

Social Security is the largest of the various federal **entitlement programs,** which are programs mandated by law and not subject to annual review by Congress or the president. By fiscal 2000, these entitlement programs, including interest, accounted for more than two-thirds of the total federal budget.

Well before the year 2000, the Social Security program was in crisis. The expansion of the Social Security system, coupled with continuing inflation, had created enormous financial strain. To put it simply, Social Security was running out of money. Social Security taxes go into trust funds so that the program can be self-sustaining. But payments to recipients were outpacing the growth of the system's reserves. Part of the problem was demographic: Compared to when the program started, there were, proportionately, fewer people of working age to pay taxes and more people of retirement age to draw benefits, and this trend was expected to continue. Because people were living longer, further changes probably would have to be made in the system; for example, Congress might decide to reduce benefits for wealthier persons.

Certainly some measures would have to be taken if Social Security was to survive. As noted earlier, government officials estimated in 2000 that the program, without changes, would remain solvent only until 2037.[25]

Medicare In 1965 Congress created **Medicare,** a federal program of health insurance to provide hospital and medical services to persons aged 65 and over through the Social Security system.[†] Medicare helps to pay hospital bills, and for those who choose to pay an extra amount ($45.50 a month in 2000), it also pays part of doctor bills. In general, Medicare pays 80 percent of doctor bills, but less for some hospital outpatient services. In 2000 there were an estimated 39 million people on Medicare, most of whom had also enrolled in the voluntary insurance program for doctor bills. Those who could afford it purchased "medigap" policies from private insurance companies to make up the difference between the 80 percent the government pays and the full amount of the doctors' bills.

But Medicare was running out of money fast. In 2000, officials estimated that the trust fund that pays for hospital bills would run out of cash by 2023 unless changes were made in the program.

■ TABLE 18-2 ■

Examples of Average Monthly Cash Payments under Social Security

Retired worker, all ages	$ 804
Retired couple	$1,348
Disabled worker	$ 754
Disabled worker with spouse and child	$1,255
Widow(er)	$ 749
Young widow(er) with two children	$1,611

SOURCE: Data provided by the Social Security Administration, as of January 2000.

---

[*]The percentages were composed of the tax for Social Security and a smaller tax for the Medicare program for the elderly.
[†]In 1996 Medicare also covered 4.7 million disabled persons under age 65.

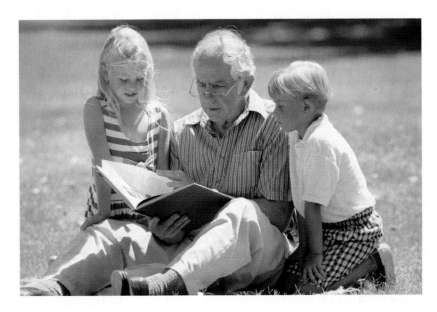

Medicare cost $213 billion in fiscal 1999, and as these projections indicated, it will undoubtedly cost more in the future, even if it is merged one day into a general program of national health insurance. As of the year 2000 about 44 million Americans had no health insurance. Some proposals to create a national health insurance system would keep Medicare; others would absorb Medicare into a general plan covering all persons.

In 1988, Congress passed a new law to pay for more of the costs of catastrophic illness for persons eligible for Medicare. It was immediately controversial. The expanded Medicare coverage was to pay for most hospital costs, doctors bills, and prescription drugs, although it did not cover nursing homes. The new law would have meant an extra tax for many older Americans, as much as $1,600 a year in the case of the wealthiest 5 percent. Highly vocal opposition led by this affluent minority killed the measure in little more than a year; Congress repealed the law in 1989 before it could go into effect.

Following the 1994 defeat of President Clinton's plan to provide health insurance for all Americans, politicians of both political parties largely avoided the issue of universal health coverage. One issue that did receive increasing attention, however, was the problem of rising prescription drug costs. This was partly a result of the political power of seniors: Although only 13 percent of Americans were over age 65, they comprised a quarter of all voters in the 1998 midterm elections. But the new attention to the issue also reflected a serious problem for many older Americans, who use an average of 29 prescriptions each year. From 1992 to 2000, the amount spent annually by older persons on prescription drugs doubled, from $559 to $1,205; and it was expected to double again by 2010. Because Medicare does not cover the cost of prescription drugs, many lower-income seniors and other Americans were forced to go without needed medications, or to choose between buying drugs or food.[26]

During the 2000 presidential race, Al Gore called for prescription drug coverage for all Medicare recipients. Under Gore's plan—projected to cost $255 billion over 10 years—Medicare would pay half the cost of prescription drugs, up to $5,000 a year. Gore criticized pharmaceutical companies for price-gouging, and compared drug costs in the United States with those in Canada and Mexico, which frequently cost less than half as much. George W. Bush proposed a plan that would cover prescription drug costs for low-income seniors. He also called for government subsidies to insurance companies, as incentives for providing affordable health plans that included drug coverage.

Unemployment Insurance The Social Security benefits discussed above are paid directly by the federal government. But the Social Security Act of 1935 also virtually forced the states to set up unemployment insurance programs to pay benefits to people out of work. The program is financed by federal and state taxes on employers. Every state has an unemployment insurance program, but the size of benefits and the amount of time they are granted vary greatly. Most, but by no means all, workers are covered. By 2000, the majority of states paid unemployment benefits of 26 weeks (up to 30 weeks in a few states). But a weekly payment in 1999 of $223.08—the national average—was scarcely enough to support a jobless worker with a family.

Welfare: Politics and Programs The Social Security Act of 1935 created three public assistance or "welfare" programs: old-age assistance; aid to the blind; and the largest program, known later as Aid to Families with Dependent Children (AFDC). The AFDC program was eliminated by the 1996 welfare law. It was replaced by Temporary Assistance for Needy Families (TANF), which set limits on cash benefits of five years, and allowed states to set their own shorter limits. TANF also required

GREENVILLE, MISS.—While President Clinton has flatly declared "the debate is over—we now know that welfare reform works," the hard-luck counties of the Mississippi Delta show the difficulties that can emerge when tough laws collide with a weak economy.

The welfare rolls have fallen sharply across this 200-mile stretch of cotton fields and catfish farms, as they have in most of the country. But with unemployment rates hovering at 10 percent or more, many of those leaving the rolls are failing to find jobs.

Across the Delta, mothers dropped from the welfare rolls are now turning to relatives, boyfriends or other Federal programs—most notably disability payments—or traveling long distances in search of work. Maggie Miller lost her benefits and moved in with her sister, raising the number of children in the two-bedroom house to 15. Patricia Watson worked a day at a distant catfish-processing plant but quit after returning home to discover that her baby-sitter could not find her 6-year-old daughter. . . .

It was scenarios like these, in places like this, that critics of last year's landmark law feared. The landmark measure ended a 61-year-old guarantee of Federal aid and transferred money and authority to the states. While some states might make good use of their autonomy, the critics said, others would prove unwilling or unable to construct safety nets of their own. Mindful of this state's last-place rankings on socioeconomic scales, they summarized their fears with a frequent refrain: "What about Mississippi?"

—*New York Times*, October 16, 1997

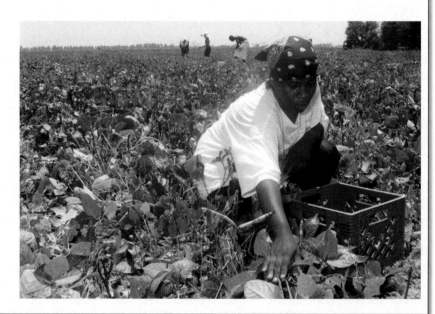

A farm worker in the Mississippi Delta picks peas under the broiling sun for $2.50 a box.
Delta Democrat Times/AP/Wide World

recipients to work after being on assistance for a maximum of two years, and gave bonuses to states that reduced the number of out-of-wedlock births.

In 1950 a fourth program was added—aid to the permanently and totally disabled. Then in 1974 the Supplemental Security Income (SSI) program was established to provide uniform federal benefits to needy aged, blind, or disabled persons.

As the system operated for many decades, the federal government provided most of the money for welfare in the form of grants to the states. In some states, local governments also assumed part of the cost. State and local welfare agencies ran the programs.

The welfare system came under attack on several grounds. First, its advocates argued, the program did not cover all the poor. Moreover, because the states control the programs, benefits varied sharply. Southern states paid lower welfare benefits than did the big industrial states of the North.

For many years, more than one-third of the states had some kind of rule barring welfare payments to families in which there was a "man in the house" who was not married to the mother. Welfare recipients objected strongly to this attempt by the states to regulate moral behavior. The U.S. Supreme Court has ruled that states may no longer restrict welfare payments to dependent children just because there is a "man in the house," unless it can be shown that he is actually contributing some of his income to the support of the children.[27]

The welfare system has frequently been criticized on the grounds that it degrades the people it is attempting to help. Welfare agencies regularly investigate those receiving payments, and poor people often regard welfare workers as unwelcome detectives. Behind all this is the public suspicion that many welfare recipients are "loafers" and "chiselers."

The welfare program that emerged from the New Deal had been criticized on the basis that it "creates a class of dependent persons and then sustains them in their dependency."[28] In 1972 Congress established for the first time a guaranteed minimum income program. This Supplemental Security Income program, which began in 1974, replaced a web of state and local programs and provided uniform federal payments to the needy, aged, blind, or disabled. SSI supplemented Social Security payments to such persons.

The Politics of Poverty

"This administration," President Lyndon B. Johnson declared in his first State of the Union message, "today here and now declares unconditional war on poverty in America."[29]

When President Johnson spoke these words in January 1964, many Americans might have wondered what he was talking about. Through the picture window of split-level suburbia, the poor could not be seen. Yet they were there, millions of people living in poverty in the mountains of Appalachia and in the inner cities. When the black urban neighborhoods exploded in flames during the second half of the decade, the poor became more visible.

The federal antipoverty program resulted in part from the publication in 1962 of Michael Harrington's *The Other America,* a book that forcefully described the extent of poverty in the United States and had a substantial impact among segments of the public and within the federal government. The poor, he noted, were "across the tracks," out of view of more comfortable Americans.[30] The poor lived, in Ben H. Bagdikian's words, "in the midst of plenty," occupying "a world inside our society in which the American dream is dying." Yet poor people "are not made so differently from their fellow Americans."[31]

Who are the poor? The federal government answers the question in terms of how many people have incomes below a certain "poverty" level. But to some extent poverty is a relative term; people may feel poor if they have a good deal less than most other people have. And with affluence no farther away than the commercials shown on television, the poor in American society are constantly reminded of their poverty.

In statistical terms the Census Bureau estimated that in 1999 there were more than 32 million poor people in the United States. The government defined poverty in that year as an income of less than $16,895 for a family of four.[32] The profile of the poor included these facts:

1. About 11.8 percent of the nation's population was poor.
2. There were more than twice as many poor white people as poor African Americans—21.9 million as

compared with 8.4 million. But a higher percentage of African Americans were poor—almost one in every four African Americans as opposed to about one in every ten whites.[33]

In response to President Johnson's "war on poverty," Congress in 1964 passed legislation creating the Office of Economic Opportunity (OEO). Community-action programs became a highly controversial aspect of the antipoverty agenda. They were designed to give federal grants to a wide range of programs organized and administered by local public or private groups, "with maximum feasible participation" of the poor. While successful in some areas, the community-action programs led in some other cases to what one critic, Daniel P. Moynihan, termed a "maximum feasible misunderstanding."[34]

Supporters of the antipoverty program argued that through community action the poor could be organized politically to express their grievances to the "power structure." But in some cases the strategy led to widely publicized confrontations between the poor and established political leaders. Big-city mayors and other critics charged that the federal government was funding community-action groups to march on City Hall and challenge the entrenched power of local political organizations. Conflict over the program was inevitable. Perhaps one of the problems as well was that President Johnson, by promising, in effect, to end poverty in the United States, had created public expectations that exceeded the ability of the program to achieve its goal.

President Nixon did not support the poverty program. He dissolved OEO and dispersed its functions to other government units. Then in 1994, Congress created the Corporation for National and Community Service, which administers AmeriCorps, a kind of domestic peace corps promoted by President Clinton. In exchange for one or two years of community service, those enrolled in the year 2000 received up to $4,725 a year to help finance their college education or vocational training, or to pay back student loans. AmeriCorps members tutored schoolchildren, assisted disabled persons, helped to restore national parks, and participated in recycling, poverty programs, and other activities to benefit communities.

The Politics of Hunger

In the summer of 2000, as the Republican Party held its national convention in Philadelphia, the *Philadelphia Enquirer* ran an editorial titled "In Gilded Times, Some Children Languish." In the midst of economic abundance, the editorial declared, millions of American children remained mired in poverty. "Leave no child behind. The failure to honor that phrase is bipartisan. It's always painfully clear at election time that children don't vote."[35]

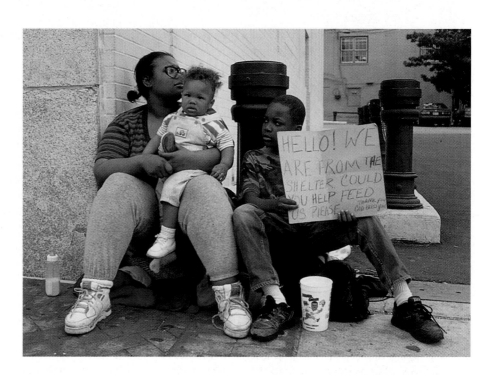

The statistics of hunger in America were indeed startling. According to one study, nearly 31 million Americans went hungry or lived in households with inadequate food supplies in the year 2000. Fourteen million were children. The antihunger organization Second Harvest reported that 26 million Americans had received food from food banks in 1999. Requests for emergency food assistance had risen 14 percent from the previous year, and nearly two-thirds were coming from families with children.[36]

Part of the problem had to do with wages. Although unemployment was low, having jobs did not necessarily mean that people had escaped poverty. The number of Americans who remained below the poverty level, despite holding full-time jobs, rose from 1.5 million in the 1970s to almost 3 million in 1998.[37]

In addition, to some extent the problem of hunger in America was related to what seemed to be a growing population of homeless people. Estimates of the size of that population varied, however. As far back as 1983, Margaret M. Heckler, the secretary of health and human services, said she was leading a campaign "to house and feed an estimated two million homeless Americans."[38] By 2000, even after the longest economic expansion in the nation's history, the problem had grown. A study by the Urban Institute concluded that the number of Americans who were homeless at least once in the course of the previous year had risen to 3.5 million. Of those, 1.2 million were children.[39] In an affluent society, these figures are shocking.

Despite government and private programs, hunger and homelessness have not been eliminated.

Many low-income Americans benefit from an extensive federal Food Stamp program. In 1961 President Kennedy, by executive order, initiated the Food Stamp program to increase the buying power of low-income families, and Congress established the system by law in 1964. Most recipients of food stamps have incomes well below the national poverty level.

From its modest beginnings, the Food Stamp program rapidly spiraled into one of the federal government's largest welfare programs. However, legislation passed as part of the 1996 welfare reform plan cut $24 billion from the program over six years, and barred most adults without children from receiving food stamps for more than three months. By 1999, $16 billion a year was budgeted for food stamps, down from $24 billion three years earlier. An average of 18 million persons received food stamps at any given time, down from 26.1 million. Monthly benefits averaged $72.28 per recipient.[40] In addition to food stamps, the federal government distributed surplus food crops to the poor through local welfare agencies, and it financed a school lunch program and a special milk program for children.

Health

In fiscal 1999 the federal government spent $347.9 billion, or 20 percent of the national budget, for health services.[41] The funds were allocated for research, training and education, hospital construction, Medicare and Medicaid, and prevention of disease.

The Medicare program, established in 1965 and discussed earlier in the chapter, provided hospital and medical services to older persons through the Social Security system. **Medicaid,** also established in 1965, is a public assistance program created to help pay hospital, doctor, and medical bills for persons with low incomes. It is financed through general federal, state, and local taxes. Washington pays 50 to 83 percent of the

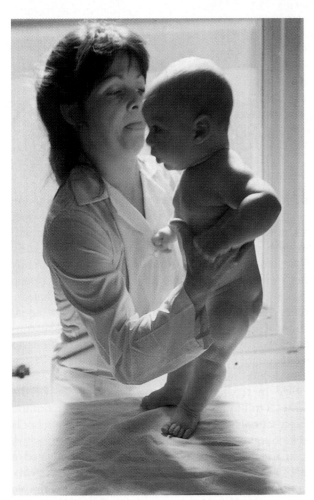

Copyright © George Zimbel

cost of state programs established under Medicaid.[42] By 1999, Medicaid served 41 million people at a cost of $181 billion in federal and state funds.[43]

The Medicaid program takes up 19 percent of the average state's budget, and it has been growing more costly. For that reason, by 1996 a dozen states had received permission from the federal government to design their own programs of medical aid to the poor. In Tennessee, and in other states that established their own programs, patients were funneled into "managed care" programs that cut costs by limiting the specialists, drugs, and treatments allowed. Because costs were controlled, Tennessee was also able to expand coverage to include many previously uninsured persons.[44]

There are signs, however, that the states have not always been able to carry the added burden. Between 1996 and 1999, a million low-income parents were dropped from the Medicaid roles of 15 states. In Georgia and Texas, the number of parents receiving Medicaid benefits was cut in half. In 2000, parents in 32 states who received the minimum wage earned too much to qualify for Medicaid.[45]

While federal programs have assisted the aged and the needy, they have not helped the majority of Americans to obtain adequate health care at a reasonable cost. The cost of hospital rooms, physicians' care, and other health services has increased at an alarming rate. Major illness could quickly wipe out the financial resources of the average American family, and private insurance plans often fail to cover the cost of prolonged hospitalization or medical treatment, or long-term care for older persons.

Comparing Governments

HEALTH CARE IN CANADA AND THE UNITED STATES

Although the United States and Canada are neighbors, they are, on many cultural and policy issues, far apart. One of the public policies on which they differ the most markedly is health care. In the United States, medical care is, like any other industry, profit-driven. In recent years, medicine has been increasingly dominated by for-profit health maintenance organizations (HMOs), corporations whose interest in health care is matched by their concern for the bottom line.

In Canada, where most industries are private and for-profit, health care is treated differently. Since the creation of a national health system in 1971, the Canadian government has used tax funds to pay for universal medical coverage, and sets the costs of medical services through negotiations with health care providers. Every citizen is guaranteed access to needed medical treatment.

Both systems have their advocates and their critics. The American health care system boasts many of the finest doctors and hospitals in the world, and the most advanced medical technology. As in other industries, the profit motive has been a spur to innovation. For those who are able to afford it, the best of American health care is the best available anywhere, and patients travel from all over the world to have complicated medical procedures performed by American doctors in American facilities. But for many Americans, access to basic medical care is unavailable. In the year 2000, there were about 44 million Americans who lacked health insurance.

Critics of the Canadian system point to delays in receiving specialized treatments, reduced availability of the most advanced technologies, and the rationing of certain expensive procedures, such as organ transplantation. They also warn that government involvement leads to greater inefficiency and bureaucratic red tape. They argue that the American health care system provides excellent care for a majority of those who need it.

It should. Per capita health care spending in the United States is nearly twice that of any other country. In 1997, Americans spent an average of $4,090 per person for health care, compared to $2,090 in Canada. But, according to a 2000 study by the Commonwealth Fund, 25 percent of Americans reported that they have difficulty getting health care when it is needed, compared with 21 percent of Canadians.

In 2000, the World Health Organization evaluated the health care systems of 191 nations. Canada was ranked 30th in the world. The American system was ranked 37th, positioned between Costa Rica and Slovenia.

SOURCES: The Commonwealth Fund, "Multinational Comparisons of Health Care Expenditures, Coverage, and Outcomes," October 1998, online at <www.cmwf.org>; and "Despite Big Spending, U.S. Ranks 37th in Study of Global Health Care," *Los Angeles Times*, June 21, 2000

As a result of spiraling health costs, pressure for a general federal program of health insurance grew in the 1980s, and emerged as a major issue in the 1990s. By the 2000 presidential election, 44 million Americans were without any health insurance, despite a booming economy. Neither candidate offered a comprehensive plan to deal with the problem. Much of the debate over national health insurance continued to center, as it had during President Clinton's failed effort to enact a universal health care plan, on the question of who would pay for such a multibillion-dollar program—to cover the cost of an estimated 29 million operations and more than 1 billion prescriptions a year.

Education

By the 2000 presidential election campaign, Americans of all political persuasions seemed to agree that the nation's educational system was in crisis. Many parents, students, and other citizens were concerned that America's public schools were not doing a good enough job of educating the nation's children in a world where the United States faced increasing economic competition with other countries. The recession in the early 1990s had compounded the problem, forcing many states—even large states like California—to make deep cuts in their education budgets. Across the nation, teachers were often underpaid, their status not equal to that of other important professions. Political candidates vied with one another in offering solutions to the challenge.

In 2000, more than 68 million students were enrolled in the nation's schools and colleges. Of the total, 14.8 million were enrolled in colleges, 14.6 million in high schools, and 38.5 million in elementary schools and kindergartens.[46]

In fiscal 2001 the federal government budgeted a total of $36.9 billion for various kinds of direct aid to education. (See Table 18-3.) This aid was channeled in two ways: to educational institutions and to individuals.

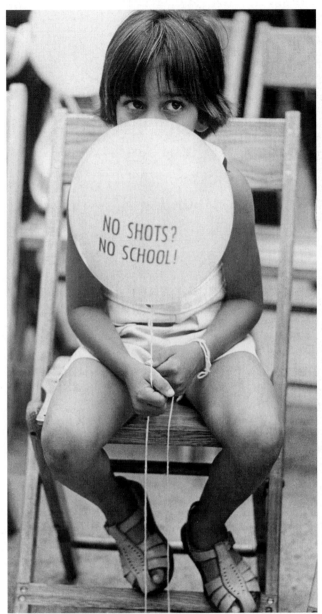

Boenzi/NYT Pictures

after the Soviet Union launched its Sputnik earth satellite, Congress enacted the National Defense Education Act to provide loans for college students in the fields of science, engineering, mathematics, and foreign languages. In 1963 Congress began appropriating funds for the construction of college classrooms.

Not until 1965, however, did Congress pass a law providing for general federal aid to education. In that year, the high-water mark of President Johnson's "Great Society," it enacted the Elementary and Secondary Education Act and the Higher Education Act. Until 1965 the church-state controversy had blocked passage of a general aid to education bill. (See the discussion of the establishment clause in Chapter 4.) The Elementary and Secondary Education Act bypassed that dispute by providing aid to children in both public and private (including religious-affiliated) schools on the basis of economic need. The bulk of the money was concentrated in urban and rural areas with a high percentage of children from poor families. Under the law, the federal government also provided general purpose grants, plus money for textbooks, library books, special programs for handicapped children, and teacher training.

The Higher Education Act of 1965 for the first time provided federal scholarships, called educational opportunity grants, for undergraduates. These were later revised and renamed Pell grants for their sponsor, Senator Claiborne Pell, Democrat of Rhode Island. The law also provided federally insured loans for college students, federal subsidies to pay the interest on student loans from private lenders, and a work-study program to help the colleges pay the wages of students with part-time jobs obtained through the schools. It channeled money to colleges to buy library books and created a program of fellowships for graduate students. It also established a Teacher Corps in which future teachers who received federal aid while studying agreed, after graduating, to teach in schools in inner cities and poor rural areas.

In 1992, Congress extended the Higher Education Act, providing $100 billion over a five-year period for student financial aid and making more middle-class students eligible for aid. For fiscal year 1997, the government budgeted more than $32 billion a year to assist 6 million college undergraduate and graduate students.

As far back as 1862, Congress had passed the Morrill Act to establish "land-grant" colleges. And millions of veterans of the Second World War went to college under the federally financed GI Bill of Rights. In 1958, the year

TABLE 18-3

Federal Outlays for Education, 1968–2001 (in billions of dollars)

	1968	1976	1979	1985	1989	1993	1998	2001
Elementary and secondary education	3.2	4.7	5.9	6.2	9.8	12.6	14.9	17.2
Higher education	4.4	2.6	4.5	7.2	9.6	14.1	15.9	17.9
Adult and other education	1.2	0.8	2.0	2.1	1.4	1.2	1.5	1.8
Total	$8.8	$8.1	$12.4	$15.5	$20.8	$27.9	$32.3	$36.9

SOURCE: Adapted from *Budget of the United States Government,* for fiscal years 1968–2001.

An overcrowded first-grade classroom in Texas: "Continuing problems in the nation's public schools . . ."
Copyright © Bob Daemmrich/Tony Stone

But federal spending has failed to avert continuing problems in the nation's public schools. The quality of education in many big-city public school systems has deteriorated. As large numbers of middle-class residents have moved to the suburbs, big cities have found their tax dollars dwindling; one result is that schools are often poorest where their services are needed most—in low-income, inner-city communities. In 1979 Congress created a new Department of Education at the cabinet level. The department, which was given responsibility for the entire federal educational effort, absorbed the education branches of the old Department of Health, Education, and Welfare, as well as units concerned with education in several other government departments. The department had long been advocated by the National Education Association, the influential teachers' lobby. Ronald Reagan opposed the new department, and during the 1980 campaign he called for its abolition. However, as president, Reagan in 1981 appointed a secretary of education to his cabinet, and the department survived his presidency.* In 1995, Republicans in Congress introduced legislation

to abolish the Department of Education, but the measure was not enacted into law.

By the election of 2000, the issue of school vouchers was gaining increasing national attention. The vouchers would be used by parents to help pay part of the cost of sending their children to private schools. Advocates of the vouchers argued that they would provide greater parental choice, and raise the quality of American education by bringing market competition to schools. Critics worried that vouchers would drain needed funds from the public school system. In the election campaign, Republican candidate George W. Bush supported school vouchers, and Democrat Al Gore opposed them.

Science

In an age of science and technology some people have come to feel that, more and more, decisions affecting their lives are being made not by elected political leaders, but by "faceless technocrats in long, white coats."[47]

Should American astronauts try to land on Mars? Should a new weapons system, such as a scaled-down version of the Strategic Defense Initiative, or "Star Wars," be developed? What should government medical researchers be doing about AIDS? For the answers to such questions, the president must turn to scientists.

---

*A cabinet department can be abolished only by Congress, and not solely by a president.

Government today has become far too complicated for political leaders to know all the scientific data they need to make policy decisions.

The federal government spends billions of dollars every year on scientific research and development. In fiscal 1999, more than $73 billion was budgeted for this purpose. Of the total, more than $38 billion went to military programs. The National Aeronautics and Space Administration (NASA) accounted for $9.2 billion. More than $14 billion was spent on basic research, most of it conducted in colleges and universities. This level of spending has raised questions about the relationship of science and government. For instance, what is the proper role of science within the political system? Today, some critics regard science as "something very close to an establishment . . . a set of institutions supported by tax funds, but largely on faith, and without direct responsibility to political control."[48] Another question is whether universities can accept government funds for research without restricting or losing their academic independence.

The president has a science adviser within the White House. The adviser heads the Office of Science and Technology Policy, which has broad responsibility for advising the president on scientific affairs. In addition, the National Science Foundation, a government agency established in 1950, supports basic and applied research.

In the years after 1957 the federal science effort in large part was geared to responding to Soviet space accomplishments, particularly the launching of Sputnik, the world's first earth satellite. American scientists were called on to solve scientific, military, and technological problems, and America soon surpassed the Soviet Union in outer space. In 1969 the Apollo 11 astronauts landed on the moon. In 1976 America's Viking robot spacecraft landed on Mars and transmitted photographs back to earth. And in 1980, Voyager 1 photographed the rings of Saturn, almost a billion miles away in outer space. But there have been disasters as well, notably the explosion that sent the space shuttle *Challenger* plunging into the ocean shortly after launch in 1986, killing all seven persons aboard. In 1996, NASA announced the design for a new, reusable space shuttle called Venture Star.

The government has also funded scientific research projects with more immediate, down-to-earth consequences. In 2000, scientists announced that the first stage of the Human Genome Project had been completed. The project was begun in 1990, with the goal of mapping the approximately 100,000 genes in the human genetic code. It would provide insights into genetic diseases, and lay the groundwork for treatments based on genetic engineering.

Meanwhile, the growing ability to manipulate the genetic characteristics of plants and animals—including cloning—was raising concerns over possible unforeseen consequences. Consumer groups in the United States protested against "Frankenfoods," and European nations threatened to prohibit the importation of bioengineered produce.

Protecting the Environment

During the 1992 presidential campaign, President Bush, seeking votes in the timber country of the Pacific Northwest, took aim at the spotted owl in a speech in Colville, Washington. "It is time," Bush declared, "to make people more important than owls."[49]

Bush was well aware that preserving the old-growth forests that are the habitat of the spotted owl,

"I don't see why all the fuss over dioxin. . . . Shoot, it didn't even kill the chickens. . . ."
Drawing by Schorr for the *Los Angeles Herald Examiner.* Reprinted by permission. Tribune Media Services, Inc.

THE POLLUTED LAND

Those of us who were born after 1900, or even after 1920, inherited a land that was generally pleasant, livable, and lovely to look at. To be sure, there were slums and tenements and soft coal soot, and quite a lot of mud mixed with the horse manure, but the quality of life, as measured in clean air, clean water, and verdant hills, was something to remember with wonder—and with dismay.

For the generations of this century have squandered that inheritance. Never was so great a trust so grossly violated. We turned our valleys into dust bowls and our rivers into sewers, killed the lakes, fouled the air, choked the cities. With the brute efficiency of systematic vandals, we combined stupidity and greed. Now we measure the quality of our life by the tons of litter we leave behind. The hallmark of our society is stamped on 10 million roadside bottles: No deposit, no return.

—James J. Kilpatrick, *Washington Star*, January 8, 1970

an endangered species, had cost thousands of jobs in Oregon and Washington. Calling the owl "that little furry, feathery guy,"[50] Bush said he would not sign an extension of the Endangered Species Act unless it were changed to balance economic costs against wildlife protection. Although he had promised four years earlier to serve as the "environmental president," Bush calculated in 1992 that owls don't vote. But in appealing to the economic self-interest of workers in the Northwest, he risked the wrath of pro-environment voters, also an important constituency in the western states, and particularly in California.

The owl itself is about 2 feet tall and weighs 22 ounces, its chocolate-colored plumage marked with white spots. There are perhaps 2,000 pairs left. Officials of the Bush Administration had estimated that saving the bird could cost 32,000 jobs in the Pacific Northwest by 1995.[51]

To try to resolve the controversy, the Bush Administration proposed in 1992 that logging be allowed on some acres of federal land in Oregon, but not on other tracts of land in dispute, action that would still cost thousands of timber jobs. Two years later, President Clinton announced a new timber policy that reduced the amount of logging permitted in forests controlled by the federal government and established reserves for the spotted owl where very limited amounts of logging could take place.

Despite the fact that protecting the owl cost jobs in Oregon, the state's economy was thriving by 1994. Over a five-year period, the state gained about 5,000 more jobs in high technology industries than it lost in the mills.

As recently as the 1970s, words and phrases like "pollution," "the environment," and "energy crisis" were unfamiliar. Within a few years, however, Americans were acutely aware of the danger to the environment posed by technology. At the same time, they wanted to enjoy the benefits of that technology. Americans wanted clean air and water—but they were also aware that cars that met clean-air standards would cost more money. They were concerned about oil spills polluting their beaches—but they wanted plenty of gasoline for their automobiles at the lowest possible price. There was a conflict, in other words, between the environment and energy.

In the winter of 1973–1974 the nation found itself facing a major energy crisis. The president appointed an "energy czar" to allocate oil supplies; gasoline stations were closed on Sundays; speed limits were lowered; the federal government ordered cutbacks in deliveries of heating oil to homes and offices; and airlines laid off thousands of pilots, flight attendants, and other employees as a shortage of jet fuel forced the cancellation of many flights. Other industries that depended on oil were adversely affected. The immediate shortages were the result of a cutoff of oil shipments by the Arab states after the Arab-Israeli War in October 1973. But the crisis forced the nation to reassess its entire approach to the use of energy; the long lines of cars at gas stations left little choice.

Americans in large numbers had begun to understand that humanity in the technological age was slowly destroying nature and the earth itself—and endangering its own survival. Scientists warned that economic growth combined with overpopulation might end in disaster for the world. In the United States, cities had become enveloped in smog, rivers clogged with human and industrial waste, sea birds and shorelines ravaged by oil spills and litter. Alarmed and concerned, the public focused on the science of ecology, which deals with the relationship between living organisms and their environment.

The upsurge of interest in the quality of the natural environment was soon reflected in the political environment. Political leaders of both major parties scrambled to stake out a position. Public pressure for a cleanup led rapidly to major legislation. First, the Clean Air Act amendments of 1970 set federal air quality standards to control automobile and industrial pollution. Legislation to clean up the nation's waterways followed two years later. A new government unit, the Environmental Protection Agency (EPA), began operating in 1970.

 for more information about the Environmental Protection Agency, see:
www.epa.gov

Pollution is a result of industrialization and increased consumption, combined with population growth. In 1804, after 100,000 years of human history, the earth's population reached 1 billion. By 1999, just 200 years later, as a result of advances in life expectancy made during the industrial revolution, there were 6 billion people living on the planet.[52] Scientists

MAKING A DIFFERENCE
SAVING THE REDWOODS: TWO YEARS IN A TREE

SACRAMENTO, CALIF.—When Julia Hill decided to leave Arkansas and travel the world, her reasons were simple enough. She was a mixed-up 23-year-old who had been dragged around America as a child by her father, a "preacher man," and then had been involved in a near-fatal car crash. Her plan was to follow the old hippie trail through the Far East in search of spiritual enlightenment.

In the end, Miss Hill only got as far as the Pacific Coast of Northern California. Without really planning to, she drifted into the ranks of environmental "guerrillas" determined to save the last remaining sequoias, or giant redwoods, the world's tallest and oldest trees, from commercial logging. She joined the cause, climbed into a tree—and stayed there.

For 738 days, her feet did not touch the ground. She lived on a plywood platform the size of a double bed, perched 180 feet high in the branches of one of the oldest trees of all, a "grandmother" that she named Luna, a 600-year-old redwood. Her supporters brought food and supplies to her every two days, hauled up by rope. She vowed that she would stay there until she won a promise that her tree would be saved.

Julia came down from Luna in December 1999, after she had reached an agreement with Pacific Lumber Company. The company agreed to spare Luna along with other trees in 2.9 acres near Stafford, California. Julia also gets to visit with the 200-foot-tall Luna regularly with company permission. Also as part of the agree-

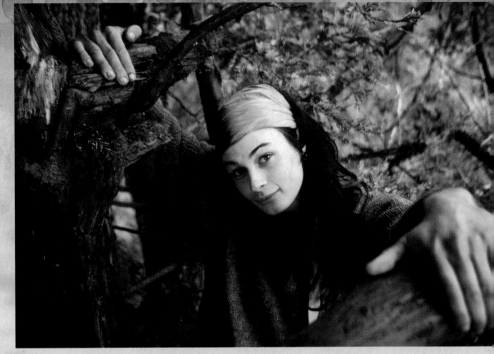

Julia Hill in her tree
AP/Wide World

ment, Hill and her supporters will pay the lumber company $50,000 for lost logging revenue. The company, in turn, will donate $50,000 to Humboldt State University for forestry studies. She had also picked up a "green" nom de guerre, and become Julia "Butterfly" Hill, all-time champion of the tree-hugging world and an international celebrity.

Now 25, she has—inevitably—secured a book deal and a huge advance payment for her story. Although she swears that everything was unplanned, she has unwittingly achieved the dream of her generation: instant

fame and fortune. However, as part of the agreement, HarperCollins, the publisher for her book, *The Legacy of Luna,* agreed to print it on special paper—30 percent recycled and 70 percent pulped from wood produced by a forestry group in Canada that employs American Indian loggers and specializes in preserving natural biodiversity.

"I was not about to use a forest just to make this book," she says.

—Adapted from *USA Today,*
December 20, 1999; and
Washington Times,
February 4, 2000

worried that the rapidly expanding "population bomb" was putting unsustainable demands upon the air, water, and natural resources. The National Academy of Sciences and 57 other scientific organizations issued a warning that mankind was "approaching a crisis point" in population growth.[53]

As with most major national problems, progress toward restoring the environment requires coopera-

tion by individuals, corporations, and institutions—but it also requires government action in the form of legislation and enforcement. For that reason, many organizations and individuals who supported environmental causes were concerned when the Reagan Administration came to power in 1981. They feared that protection of the environment would be given a lower priority than either the search for new energy sources or the effort to reduce government regulation of business.

Criticism of the Reagan Administration's environmental policies quickly focused on the person of James G. Watt, a conservative lawyer from Wyoming who fought for business against environmentalists and whom the president appointed secretary of the interior. Watt was eventually forced to resign from the cabinet because of indiscreet remarks about minorities. His departure followed by several months a major scandal at the Environmental Protection Agency over the government's handling of toxic wastes. After many years of concern over toxic waste dumps, especially the contamination of Love Canal near Buffalo, New York, Congress in 1980 had created a $1.6 billion "superfund" to clean up such sites. The dangers of hazardous industrial waste were underscored even more sharply early in 1983 when residents of the entire town of Times Beach, Missouri, had to be moved because of deadly dioxin contamination.

The dollar cost of a cleaner environment, the personal inconvenience caused by new laws and regulations, and the competing pressures for development of energy sources have combined to create many conflicts. Despite counterpressures, the environmental movement became firmly rooted in only a few years, with some visible results. In 1971, for example, Congress canceled plans to build an American supersonic jet transport (SST) in part because of the danger that the plane's exhaust would deplete the ozone layer in the stratosphere. The ozone layer filters out ultraviolet sunlight, and some studies concluded that because damage to the ozone layer would expose more people to ultraviolet radiation, the SST exhaust might lead to an increase in skin cancer in human beings. But environmentalists do not always win; the federal government permitted the British Concorde, a supersonic plane, as well as the French Concorde, to fly regular routes to the United States.

On the other hand, by 2000 Americans were much more aware of the need to preserve the environment, and some tried to do something about it in their daily lives. For example, many Americans voluntarily separated their trash for recycling, and in a number of cities the law began requiring it.

With the competing pressures in American society, environmentalists will inevitably lose many battles. Energy needs will often prevail over environmental concerns. Nevertheless, the political power of the environmental supporters is tangible. Millions of people belong to an estimated 2,000 to 3,000 environmental organizations across the country. Public interest in the environment has been followed by legislation and expansion of the government's role as environmental regulator. Clean air, clean water, land use, and other similar issues are significant factors in political campaigns. And a major new concern has been added to the government's policy agenda.

However, despite widespread public concern over the environment, critics complained about the effects of environmental laws. Many businesses and industries chafed under antipollution regulations. When the Republicans won both houses of Congress in 1994, they were determined at first to roll back many environmental laws.

Congress suspended the law protecting endangered species for more than a year, and the program was running out of money. Finally, in the spring of 1996, the Endangered Species Act went back into effect when Congress and President Clinton reached an agreement on spending. The federal government then complied with a court order and granted protection under the act to the California red-legged frog.[54]

By the late 1990s, some Republicans worried that a backlash had developed among voters against policies that weakened environmental laws. One Republican

Since 1985, Bobbie Lively-Diebold has worked at the Environmental Protection Agency mapping out a strategy to clean up the nation's most polluted industrial dump sites.

Now the pollution has hit closer to home. When she enters her office at EPA headquarters in Southwest Washington, Lively-Diebold might as well be knee deep in toxic waste. Her lips, ear canals, throat and eyes burn. Her vocal cords swell so that she cannot speak. The room seems to spin in slow motion as she strains for every breath, wheezing like an asthmatic.

Lively-Diebold and dozens of her colleagues are suffering from indoor pollution at the headquarters of the agency dedicated to clean air. . . .

The situation at EPA adds an ironic twist to a growing public health problem known as "sick build-ing syndrome," which is believed to account for millions of lost workdays each year through the exposure of a captive work force to insidious chemical gases and fibers. . . .

Unlike the factory smoke stacks and auto exhaust normally associated with air pollution, the indoor version is invisible and often odorless. It comes in the form of microscopic fungi and bacteria spun out of dirty ventilation systems; molecules of formaldehyde and other toxic substances that rise from new carpets and room partitions; ozone and hydrocarbons that seep from copying machines; asbestos fibers that flake off from damaged insulation, and cigarette smoke.

—*Washington Post*, May 25, 1988

---

poll-taker warned: "A large plurality would vote against a member of Congress who voted to cut back EPA spending by one third."[55] Faced with continuing public concern over protecting the environment, the Republicans began to pull back from their efforts to overturn or weaken environmental legislation, and worked to avoid the issue in the 2000 elections.

The Environmental Protection Agency   The environment is a major arena of conflict, with competing interest groups clashing over policy. The Environmental Protection Agency (EPA) was established in 1970 as an independent unit of the executive branch. The creation of the EPA pulled together under one roof various regulatory powers that had been scattered through a dozen bureaus and agencies. The EPA's administrator is often called on to make hard and controversial decisions— whether to grant the auto industry more time to manufacture cars with cleaner engines, for example.

In recent years Congress has passed major legislation dealing with the environment. The laws have dealt with clean air, clean water, and endangered species.

Air Pollution   The Clean Air Act amendments of 1970, steered through the Senate by Edmund Muskie, Democrat of Maine, set strict federal air quality standards governing major forms of pollution by industry, including automobile emissions. The law provides heavy fines for violators. Under the 1970 act, auto manufacturers were required by 1975 to reduce by 90 percent the levels of carbon monoxide, hydrocarbons, and nitrogen oxides in engine exhaust. When the big auto companies in Detroit claimed they needed more time to comply, Congress and the administrator of the EPA granted extensions. The act also required cities to meet

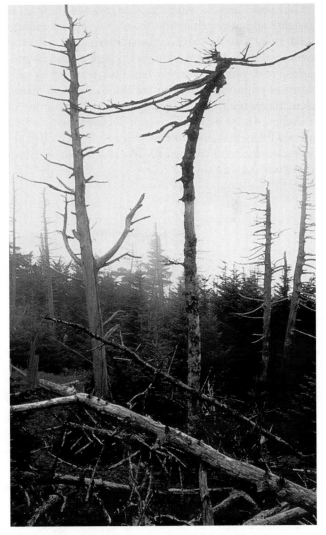

North Carolina: Acid rain knows no geographic boundaries.
Copyright © Judy Canty/Stock, Boston

national clean-air standards by 1982. These deadlines were also moved forward after many cities failed to meet the initial target dates.

In 1990, Congress passed major revisions to the Clean Air Act. The law was designed gradually to phase out the use of chlorofluorocarbons and the chemicals used in aerosol sprays that deplete the ozone layer and to reduce automobile emissions. It also set new rules to reduce urban smog, to curb the chemicals that produce acid rain, and to regulate toxic pollutants.

By the mid-1990s alarm over the depletion of the ozone layer had subsided somewhat. In Montreal, Canada, in 1987, 23 nations had signed an agreement to phase out the use of ozone-destroying chemicals. In the years following this pact, researchers concluded from test results that the amount of these chemicals in the atmosphere had declined. They predicted that beginning in the year 2000 the ozone layer should begin to improve, recovering fully in 5 or 10 years.[56]

Air pollution is a global, not merely a national, problem. For example, acid rain is an increasing concern that has caused friction between the United States and Canada, which has complained that sulfur dioxide and nitrogen oxides from U.S. factories cause acid rain that destroys lakes, forests, and fish and other wildlife. Acid rain knows no geographic boundaries, and similar damage has been caused by this form of pollution in the United States. In 1988, President Reagan agreed to freeze U.S. emission levels of nitrogen oxides at 1987 levels, a decision that cleared the way for the United States to join with 23 other nations in signing a treaty, in November 1988, aimed at controlling acid rain.

By the end of the 20th century there was widespread agreement among scientists that gases—such as carbon dioxide—that are emitted in the burning of fossil fuels were producing a "greenhouse effect," trapping heat in the atmosphere. In 2000, an international panel of scientists warned that global warming would raise the temperature of the Earth's surface by 2 to 9 degrees in the next hundred years.[57] By comparison, the world has warmed an estimated 5 to 9 degrees since the peak of the last ice age.[58] The rising temperature is expected to have major consequences for the global environment, including melting the polar icecaps, raising the sea level, causing coastal flooding and erosion, reducing soil moisture, and promoting deforestation.[59]

In 1992, at the first Earth Summit, the United States joined with 106 other countries in signing the Climate Change Treaty, which established nonbinding targets for reducing emissions. In 1997, the United States was the 60th nation to sign the Kyoto Protocol, an international agreement that set specific targets for six greenhouse gases. The target for the United States was a 7 percent reduction from 1990 levels by the year 2012. Implementation of the new standards, however, proved difficult to achieve. In 1999, scientists reported that the 1990s had been the warmest decade in recorded history.[60]

Water Pollution   On March 24, 1989, the 987-foot supertanker Exxon *Valdez* ran aground on a reef 25 miles south of Valdez, Alaska, spilling nearly 11 million gallons of crude oil into Prince William Sound. It was the largest oil spill from a tanker in U.S. history, and it had a devastating effect on fish, birds and other wildlife, and on the beaches of Alaska. The spill also caused great

Drawing by Borgman for the *Cincinnati Inquirer.* Copyright © 1989. Reprinted with special permission of King Features Syndicate.

April 1989: cleaning up the Exxon Valdez oil spill
AP/Wide World

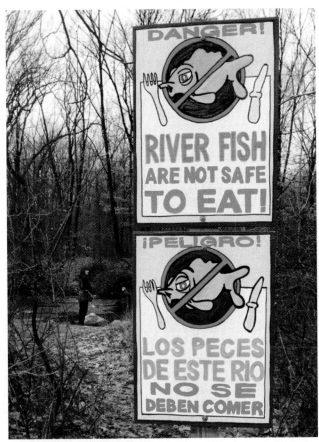

Rina Castelnuovo/NYT Pictures

hardship among those who lived in the area, especially the Alaska Natives and others who fished the sea or depended on its bounty for their livelihood. Exxon spent $2.5 billion to clean up the spill. Two years later, Exxon paid $1.1 billion as part of a plea bargain in which federal criminal and state charges were dropped. In 1994, a federal jury ordered Exxon to pay $5 billion in punitive damages to 14,000 commercial fishermen, Alaska Natives, businesses, and landowners who had sued the oil giant over the oil spill.

The Exxon *Valdez* episode was only the most dramatic example of a larger problem that had begun to cause concern some two decades earlier. By the start of the 1970s, all across America, rivers, lakes, and streams were getting dirtier. Cities and towns were dumping their waste into rivers. Industrial plants pumped chemical wastes and toxic compounds into once-clear waters. The result: fouled drinking water, polluted beaches unfit for swimming, dead fish, and algae-clogged streams.

Congress responded by passing the Water Pollution Control Act of 1972, which had as its goal the complete elimination of discharges of pollutants into the nation's waterways by 1985. The law allotted $18 billion to the states to build the waste treatment plants they needed to clean up the water. Within five years pollution began to diminish in at least some of the nation's waterways. According to one federal report, of 12 major rivers studied, five—including the Colorado

A confrontation on Guam between a tiny bird that does not fly and the United States Air Force found the Air Force backing off. . . .

Under a Strategic Air Command directive to bolster defenses against terrorists, Andersen Air Force Base on the island had moved to clear an area of heavy shrubbery near the flight line that attackers might use for cover . But when environmentalists protested that the shrubbery was the last known habitat of the small Guam rail, the United States Fish and Wildlife Service placed the bird on its emergency endangered-species list.

The action blocked the Air Force land-clearing for 240 days while the two sides considered the plight of the Guam rail, believed left with but 50 survivors after suffering thousands of losses since 1968.

Maj. James McGuire, a spokesman for the Strategic Air Command's headquarters near Omaha, says the command has temporarily waived its security order while it seeks to "develop a coordinated approach" with United States and Guam wildlife officials to protect the rail.

—*New York Times*, June 24, 1984

and the Ohio—showed significant reductions in bacterial counts.[61]

Oil spills from drilling rigs or tankers like the Exxon *Valdez* are also a major form of pollution that has fouled the nation's beaches and endangered wildlife. There have been several other major oil spills, such as those off Santa Barbara, California, in 1969, near Nantucket, Massachusetts, in 1976, and in the Gulf of Mexico in 1979. In the summer of 1988 many East Coast beaches were closed because of a new type of pollution—syringes, blood bags, and other forms of medical waste dumped by hospitals and laboratories.

Environmental Impact and Endangered Species
The National Environmental Policy Act of 1969 required the government to assess the impact on the environment of all new projects involving the federal government. The provision is important because it has since been adopted by many states and communities; in addition, it has provided the basis for environmental lawsuits. The 1969 act also established a three-member Council on Environmental Quality to advise the president, and required the president to submit an annual "state of the environment" report to Congress.

The Endangered Species Act was passed by Congress in 1973 to protect wildlife and plants that might otherwise vanish forever from the earth. The law helped to save the American bald eagle, the national symbol, and more than 700 other species.[62] But long before the

northern spotted owl became a presidential campaign issue, the law proved controversial.

The battle over the tiny snail darter, a rare fish in the Little Tennessee River, is a case in point. In 1973 David Etnier, a University of Tennessee zoologist, discovered the 3-inch fish in an area where the Tennessee Valley Authority (TVA) planned to build the Tellico Dam. The fish was placed on a list under the Endangered Species Act, entitling it to protection from actions of the government. Opponents of the dam took their case to the U.S. Supreme Court and won a ruling in 1978 requiring the TVA to halt the project. A special board created by Congress studied the problem and also sided with the fish. But in 1979 Congress voted to finish construction of the dam and also voted to allow exemptions to the Endangered Species Act in the future. Reluctantly, President Carter signed the bill. The snail darter had lost.

But the story had a happy ending after all. In 1976, some 710 snail darters had been transplanted to a tributary of the Little Tennessee, 10 miles downstream from the dam, and the species thrived there. In 1980, 14 baby snail darters were unexpectedly discovered 80 miles below the dam in the South Chickamauga Creek. And in July 1984, the tiny fish was removed from the endangered species list.

Energy Policy   Even before the 1990s, the nuclear power industry in America was in serious trouble. Five plants, including Seabrook in New Hampshire and another in Midland, Michigan, had shut down in one two-month period because of excessive cost or safety reasons. Orders for about 100 other reactors had been canceled, representing a loss of billions of dollars, and there had been no orders for new nuclear plants since 1978.

Drawing by Mike Peters for the *Dayton Daily News*. Reprinted by permission of United Features Syndicate, Inc.

A combination of skyrocketing costs and public opposition because of accidents, such as that in 1979 at the Three Mile Island nuclear power plant in Pennsylvania, had turned many of the nuclear construction projects into financial disasters. The problems besetting the nuclear power industry meant higher prices for consumers, but beyond that, disappointment for those who hoped that nuclear power would solve the nation's future energy needs.

Groups such as the Clamshell Alliance and other foes of nuclear power did not win every round, however: In 1984, after massive and prolonged protests, the Nuclear Regulatory Commission gave the Diablo Canyon nuclear plant near San Luis Obispo, California, permission to open. All told, there were 103 nuclear plants in operation in the United States in the year 2000, producing 20 percent of the nation's electricity. Nuclear plants have become the most important source of electric power after coal.

But the public continued to fear the release of deadly radiation in the event of an accident at a nuclear power plant. The Nuclear Regulatory Commission conceded in 1982 that 100,000 people could be killed in a worst-case accident at the Salem plant in New Jersey, assuming a total meltdown of the nuclear core and adverse weather conditions.[63]

Concerns about nuclear power did not pose the only problems for the nation's energy policy. When long lines formed at gas pumps across the nation during the energy crisis of 1973–1974, fuel prices spiraled. In the summer of 1979, the shortage recurred in many areas. In the 1980s, the war between Iraq and Iran had the potential of again reducing oil supplies to the West; even Americans who normally paid little attention to foreign policy were aware that their ability to take the family out for a Sunday drive might depend on what happened 6,000 miles away in the Persian Gulf. America's dependence on foreign oil from the Middle East was never more apparent than in 1990 and 1991 when the United States went to war against Iraq's Saddam Hussein, who had seized Kuwait and was then in a position to threaten Saudi Arabia and its vast oilfields.

For the ordinary citizen, the energy crisis that had emerged two decades earlier was difficult to understand. Some argued that there had been no shortage at all in the 1970s—that gas lines and the crisis were artificial, created by the actions of "Big Oil." Many Americans were reluctant to adjust their affluent lifestyles to the energy crisis—to commute to work in car pools or turn down their thermostats in winter. Energy legislation was extremely complex, and even concerned citizens were bewildered by the explanations.

Some of the basic facts were not all that complicated, however. The United States has abundant petroleum deposits in Texas, Louisiana, Oklahoma, California, Alaska, and offshore in the oceans and the Gulf of Mexico. Before the Second World War, domestic fields supplied about 95 percent of the oil used in this country. By 2000, however, the United States was using almost 19.5 million barrels of oil a day, and domestic sources were providing about 50 percent of the total. The other 50 percent was imported, about half of that amount from OPEC nations in the Middle East. Although the United States had only 4.6 percent of the world's population, it was consuming 26 percent of the world's energy.[64]

The dependence on foreign oil created problems at home. Rising fuel prices contributed to inflation. The billions of dollars paid annually to import oil accounted for a substantial share of U.S. trade and balance-of-payments deficits. And energy problems were directly linked to the nation's foreign policy, as the war in the Persian Gulf illustrated.

Over the years, the federal government and Congress attempted to deal with the energy problem. For example, President Carter proposed a number of measures, ranging from increased conservation to the use of alternative energy sources, such as synthetic fuels (called synfuels) and solar power. In 1977 Carter asked for and got a new cabinet-level Department of Energy. The creation by Congress of the new department underscored the importance of the energy issue and its continuing impact on the political system and the lives of individual Americans.

 for more information about the Department of Energy, see: www.doe.gov

By the mid-1980s, abundant supplies of oil on the world market and declining demand had led OPEC to cut its prices. Americans appeared much less worried about the prospect of gas shortages or energy problems in general. But the Persian Gulf War of 1991 was a dramatic reminder that events in the Middle East could quickly endanger the flow of oil to the rest of the world. Escalating oil prices in 2000 attested to the influence of OPEC on the American economy; gasoline prices soared to more than $2 a gallon that summer, and oil reserves became an issue in the presidential campaign.

Nuclear Power: Three Mile Island March 28, 1979, was a routine night in the control room of the nuclear power plant on Three Mile Island in the Susquehanna River, 11 miles southeast of Harrisburg, Pennsylvania. Inside the control room, a horseshoe-shaped panel stretched 40 feet along three walls. It was lined with dials, gauges, and 1,200 red and green warning lights.

Suddenly, at 4 A.M., a Klaxon sounded. A voice on the loudspeaker intoned: "Turbine trip in Unit 2." It was the beginning of the worst accident in the history of nuclear power production in the United States.

A valve had failed in the nuclear reactor's cooling system, and the nuclear core of the reactor was rapidly overheating, raising the possibility of a meltdown. If that

Pennsylvania Gov. Richard L. Thornburgh, in unusually forceful testimony, told the Nuclear Regulatory Commission yesterday that the health and safety of people living around the crippled Three Mile Island nuclear reactor will be at risk if the NRC allows a twin reactor on the island to resume operation.

The statement from Thornburgh, a Republican who was in office when the nation's worst commercial nuclear power accident occurred more than five years ago, intensified one of the most emotional nuclear-power debates—whether the NRC should restore the license of the undamaged reactor on Three Mile Island.

"I was there when the worst fear of modern man almost came to pass in central Pennsylvania," Thornburgh said. . . . "I saw anger and confusion on the faces of good and innocent people who realized, for the first time, that there was something out there powerful and strange and not entirely under control."

—*Washington Post*, August 16, 1984

happened, the nuclear core would burn through steel and concrete walls and would release lethal levels of radioactivity into the atmosphere. What opponents of nuclear power had always warned against—a nuclear disaster in a populated urban area—seemed close at hand.

The governor of Pennsylvania closed nearby schools and advised pregnant women and preschool children within 5 miles of the site to leave and people within 10 miles to stay indoors. An evacuation of up to 300,000 people was planned but not ordered. Many residents left on their own.

It took technicians and government experts seven days to bring the danger under control. Although the feared meltdown did not take place, some radiation was released. There were no reported injuries to the public, but the incident sowed fear and confusion among residents of the area and alerted millions of Americans to the dangers of nuclear power. A presidential commission studied the accident and recommended that new nuclear plants be built in areas remote from population centers.

Despite the dangers dramatized by the accident at Three Mile Island, advocates of nuclear power argued that nuclear plants were an important element in the nation's energy supply. Opponents maintained that the disaster averted at Three Mile Island would surely come, sooner or later.

In 1986, it did. The meltdown of a reactor in a Soviet nuclear plant at Chernobyl, near Kiev, released high levels of radiation into the air. At least 23 people were killed, hundreds were hospitalized, and 40,000 persons were evacuated from the area. European nations banned the import of food from eastern Europe

for fear of contamination. It was the worst nuclear power disaster in history.

By the end of the 20th century, the nuclear power industry was facing another challenge: a growing problem in disposing of its nuclear waste. With insufficient disposal facilities for the hazardous waste produced by nuclear power plants, by 1998 there were 37,000 tons of spent nuclear fuel—which remains radioactive for 10,000 years—stored in temporary containers on the grounds of the nation's nuclear plants.[65]

CAN GOVERNMENT MEET THE CHALLENGE?

This discussion of government in operation has examined a number of crucial areas in which government—and therefore American society—has attempted to solve urgent social and economic problems. The results have been mixed.

In some policy areas, the government has had only limited success. Economic stability has been endangered by soaring budget deficits, even as Congress and the president struggled to control them. Government has been slow to develop new and alternative sources of energy to meet the nation's future needs. In many cases, regulatory agencies have served corporate interests and have failed to protect the public. In America's free enterprise economy, it has not always been clear whether government has the will or the power to regulate industry on behalf of consumers.

In the field of social welfare, the federal government has promised much and delivered less. President Johnson declared his "war on poverty" in 1964, but more than three decades later more then 35 million Americans were still poor. The public assistance program has helped millions of people, but it has also been widely criticized. As a result, the 1996 federal law reshaping the welfare program shifted much of the burden to the states.

Despite government programs, in the early 21st century there remained a wide gap between rich and poor in the United States, and the number of persons living in poverty continued to increase steadily. Indeed, Benjamin I. Page, a political scientist, concluded that government welfare programs do little to redistribute wealth and have been largely offset by other government policies that favor the rich: "After all government actions are taken into account . . . after New Deals and Fair Deals and Wars on Poverty, the incomes of Americans remain very unequal. The welfare state may help establish a minimum level of existence for its citizens, but . . . it does not produce a substantial degree of equality."[66]

On the other hand, Congress has continued to fund a wide variety of programs to assist the people it represents. Environmental legislation and the creation of new federal agencies dealing with the environment are an example of government responding to public demands and societal needs. And the Social Security program provides benefits to more than 44 million Americans.

Achieving desirable social and economic ends requires money, however, and not all Americans want to or can afford to pay the price in higher taxes. How to deal with the complex social and economic problems confronting America is by no means clear. Not every problem may have an answer. But effective programs at any level of government—whether national, state, or local—may mean hard choices, high taxes, and other sacrifices. Better public schools, for example, require money for more teachers and classrooms, as well as higher standards. In the area of social policy, the real dilemma facing Americans today is whether they are willing to pay the costs of "promoting the general welfare" and attempting to build a better society.

KEY TERMS

laissez-faire, p. 606
monopoly, p. 607
oligopoly, p. 607
closed shop, p. 611
union shop, p. 611
right to work laws, p. 611

Social Security, p. 615
entitlement programs, p. 616
Medicare, p. 616
Medicaid, p. 620

CHAPTER HIGHLIGHTS

✦ To "promote the general welfare," the federal government fills several major roles. It is regulator, promoter, manager, and protector.

✦ For half a century, from the late 1880s until 1937, the Supreme Court generally interpreted the Constitution in such a way as to prevent government from regulating industry. It adopted the prevailing laissez-faire philosophy, which held that government should intervene as little as possible in economic affairs.

✦ Although government regulation has had some success at blocking monopoly, the control of a market by a single company, it has not been able to prevent oligopoly, the concentration of economic power in the hands of a relatively few large companies.

✦ As in the case of business, labor is both regulated and helped by the federal government. Today organized labor wields great economic and political power in the United States.

✦ The power gained by labor during the New Deal inevitably brought a political reaction. The National Labor Relations Act had placed restrictions on employers but none on unions. In 1947 Congress passed the Taft-Hartley Act. The act prohibited the closed shop, but it did permit the union shop. Under Section 14B of the Taft-Hartley Act, 21 states passed state right to work laws to outlaw the union shop.

✦ The Social Security Act of 1935 and its later amendments provide for both social insurance and public assistance programs. The insurance aspects fall into four categories: old-age and survivors insurance, disability insurance, Medicare, and unemployment insurance.

✦ When people talk about receiving Social Security, they generally mean the monthly cash payments received by retired, older people through a compulsory national insurance program financed by taxes on employers and employees.

✦ Social Security is the largest of the various federal entitlement programs, which are programs mandated by law and not subject to annual review by Congress or the president.

✦ In 1965 Congress created Medicare, a federal program of health insurance to provide hospital and medical services to persons aged 65 and over through the Social Security system.

✦ Medicaid, also established in 1965, is a public assistance program created to help pay hospital, doctor, and medical bills for persons with low incomes. It is financed through general federal, state, and local taxes.

✦ Public concern over environmental pollution in the 1970s led to the passage of laws to try to bring about clean air and water.

✦ The Environmental Protection Agency (EPA) was established in 1970 as an independent unit of the executive branch. The creation of the EPA pulled together under one roof various regulatory powers that had been scattered through a dozen bureaus and agencies.

SUGGESTED WEB SITES

http://www.census.gov/
The Census Bureau
The official Web site of the U.S. Census Bureau. Provides access to up-to-date national- and state-level demographic data.

http://www.epn.org/
Electronic Policy Network
Web site of the Electronic Policy Network, a useful source of information on a broad range of public policy issues.

http://www.lcweb.loc.gov/global/executive/fed.html
Official U.S. Executive Branch Web Sites
A service of the Library of Congress, this site provides a comprehensive listing of the Web sites of federal executive branch departments and agencies, with links to each.

http://www.secondharvest.org/
Second Harvest
Web site of the largest hunger-relief organization in the United States. Provides access to news stories about hunger and related issues, as well as links and other information to assist individuals who want to become involved in efforts to alleviate hunger.

http://www.ssa.gov/
Social Security Administration
Official Web site of the Social Security Administration. Contains useful information related to Social Security, including the most recent Trustees' reports.

http://www.urban.org/
The Urban Institute
Web site of the Urban Institute, a policy research organization concerned with social and economic issues.

SUGGESTED READING

Benedick, Richard Elliot. *Ozone Diplomacy: New Directions in Safeguarding the Planet** (Harvard University Press, 1998). A revealing account, written by a leading U.S. negotiator, of the delicate politics of an important global environmental treaty.

Browning, Robert X. *Politics and Social Welfare Policy in the United States** (University of Tennessee Press, 1986). A detailed analysis of the development of the federal government's social-welfare programs since the 1940s. Emphasizes the effects that various economic and political factors have had on the growth of these programs.

Bryner, Gary C. *Politics and Public Morality: The Great American Welfare Reform Debate** (Norton, 1998). A useful examination of the politics of welfare reform in the 1990s.

Derthick, Martha. *Policymaking of Social Security** (The Brookings Institution, 1979). A comprehensive study of policymaking for Social Security. Examines the basic policies that have shaped the program, the small group of people who influence decisions, and the future of the Social Security system.

Dubos, René. *Reason Awake: Science for Man* (Columbia University Press, 1970). A collection of essays by a distinguished microbiologist focusing on the threat to people and the environment caused by the technological and population explosions. Analyzes a range of problems—from nuclear weapons to urban sprawl—that have resulted from a constantly expanding technology.

Gore, Al. *Earth in the Balance* (Houghton Mifflin, 2000). A passionate polemic about mankind's effects upon the environment by the Democratic nominee for president in 2000. Gore makes several specific recommendations for policy reforms, including the gradual elimination of the internal-combustion engine.

Harrington, Michael. *The Other America** (Collier, 1994). (Originally published in 1962.) One of the most widely read introductory surveys of the nature and extent of poverty in the United States in the early 1960s.

Johnson, Haynes, and Broder, David S. *The System: The American Way of Politics at the Breaking Point* (Little, Brown, 1996). A revealing analysis of the failed effort to enact major new health care legislation in the 1993–1994 congressional session. The authors, each a Pulitzer Prize–winning political reporter, conducted extensive interviews with both supporters and opponents of President Clinton's health care proposals.

Levitan, Sar A., and Taggart, Robert. *The Promise of Greatness** (Harvard University Press, 1976). A careful, detailed examination of social-welfare programs, including Medicare, Medicaid, and the former Aid to Families with Dependent Children. The authors argue that the federal programs and policies of the 1960s moved the nation toward a better, more equitable society and urge renewed government efforts to achieve social reform.

Nader, Ralph; Green, Mark; and Seligman, Joel. *Taming the Giant Corporation* (Norton, 1977). A critical analysis of the political, economic, and social consequences of large corporations. Argues that big corporations should be chartered by the federal government and made to reveal far more information about their activities to the public.

Page, Benjamin I. *Who Gets What from Government** (University of California Press, 1983). An analysis of the redistributive effect of government economic and social programs. Concludes that significant inequality persists in the United States and that recent governmental policies have been making it worse.

Phillips, Kevin P. *The Politics of Rich and Poor: Wealth and the American Electorate in the Reagan Aftermath* (Random House, 1990). An analysis of the economic policies of the Reagan Administration and the consequences of those policies for American society. The author argues that the Reagan policies widened the income gap between the well-to-do and those with low incomes.

Price, Don K. *The Scientific Estate* (Belknap Press of Harvard University Press, 1965). A thoughtful and perceptive analysis of science and scientists, and their relation to public policymaking in the United States.

Rosenbaum, Walter A. *Environmental Politics and Policy** (Congressional Quarterly, 1998). A useful overview of the forces that work to shape American environmental policy.

Schlesinger, Arthur M., Jr. *The Coming of the New Deal** (Houghton Mifflin, 1959). A revealing and highly readable historical account of the inauguration of Franklin Roosevelt's New Deal, which established the basis for much of the nation's current economic welfare legislation. Part of Schlesinger's multivolume historical study of Roosevelt and New Deal politics.

Schwarz, John E. *America's Hidden Success: A Reassessment of Twenty Years of Public Policy* (Norton, 1984). An exploration of the impact and consequences of a number of government programs that were enacted in the 1960s and 1970s. The author gives special attention to the antipoverty and environmental programs, and argues that, on balance, those programs were successful.

Sundquist, James L. *Politics and Policy: The Eisenhower, Kennedy, and Johnson Years* (The Brookings Institution, 1968). An informative and valuable study of the battles in Congress and in the country to pass what became the new domestic social-welfare programs of the Johnson Administration.

Waldman, Steven. *The Bill* (Viking Press, 1995). A revealing analysis of how President Clinton's proposal to create a national service corps moved through Congress and—after some modifications—became law.

Wilson, William Julius. *When Work Disappears: The World of the New Urban Poor** (Vintage Books, 1997). An insightful examination of the decline in the number of manufacturing jobs in American cities, and how this decline has helped to shape urban culture. The author calls for a government program of jobs creation to restore economic vitality, and hope, to inner cities.

---

*Available in paperback edition.

 Visit http://politicalscience.wadsworth.com/cummings9/update/ for current InfoTrac articles and other student resources related to this chapter.

PART FIVE
The American Community

CHAPTER 19
State and Local Government

In the Washington suburb of Suitland, Maryland, 5 miles southeast of the Capitol dome and far from familiar paths trod by tourists, a complex of federal buildings houses a group of men and women whose business, in part, is to peer into the future.

The building is the headquarters of the U.S. Bureau of the Census, a division of the Commerce Department. Using computers, and by calculating birth and death rates and other factors, the Census Bureau is able to make population projections for the future. It cannot do so with precision, because there is a wide margin for error in such tabulations. Nevertheless, the Census Bureau is able to guess that the population of the United States, which was an estimated 275 million in 2000, may increase, by the year 2015, to 312 million.[1]

Although this projection is only an estimate, an increase of about 37 million people in 15 years would be like adding the populations of Australia, Denmark, Ireland, and Sweden to the United States. And, by 2050, the population of the United States may reach 404 million, according to Census Bureau estimates.[2] In other words, there is a possibility that the year 2000 population of 275 million will increase by about 130 million in 50 years.

Online *for more information about the U.S. Census, see:* *www.census.gov*

Today American society, although prosperous at the start of the new century, is burdened with multifold, interlocking problems—environmental pollution, inadequate public schools, limited energy resources, racial discrimination, crime, drug abuse, poverty, and homelessness. If, as seems possible, the population increases substantially in five decades, will the American political system and American society be able to cope with these problems? To take a random example—and assuming there is enough gasoline or alternative sources of power to go around—would anyone care to visualize what it might be like driving along the San Bernardino Freeway during the morning rush hour in 2050? It is bad enough now, as Los Angeles commuters can attest.

Not only the size of the population but also its geographic distribution affect the nature of a society. In the United States, more than 70 percent of the people are crowded into just over 10 percent of the land area. More than half of the population of the United States lives in just nine states.* Since 1920 the population of the United States has been more urban than rural. In 1990, when the population stood at 248.7 million, 192.7 million Americans, or 77 percent, lived in metropolitan areas. Of this total, 77.6 million lived in central cities and about 115 million lived outside the cities, mostly in the suburbs. About 56 million lived in rural or other nonmetropolitan areas.† (See Figure 19-1.)

In 1996 almost 149 million people, or more than half the population of the United States, lived in metropolitan areas of at least 1 million.[3] As America has become urbanized, many of the nation's difficult problems have developed in their most acute form in urban areas—in the central "core" cities and the surrounding suburbs. Obviously, the decisions and actions of state,

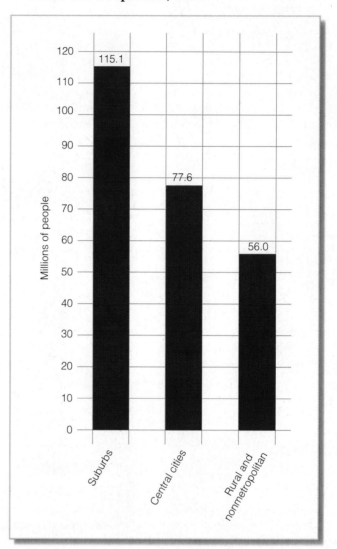

FIGURE 19-1

Where the People Are, 1990

SOURCE: Data provided by Statistical Information Office, Population Division, U.S. Bureau of the Census.

city, and other local governments have a direct impact on the quality of American life.

In turn, the national economy affects states and communities. By the year 2000, because of a long period of economic expansion, many states were enjoying budget surpluses. State legislatures, mirroring the debate in the presidential campaign, were arguing over how to spend the money.

The healthy economy had allowed states—many of which had faced a budget crunch a decade earlier—to pass tax cuts, estimated at $7 billion in 1999; 29 states had reduced taxes.[4] However, many state officials warned that the loss of billions of dollars in tax revenue in sales over the Internet and by mail could cause fiscal problems for the states in the future.

And if the economy faltered, states would be the first to be affected, because they depend heavily on

*California, Texas, New York, Florida, Illinois, Pennsylvania, Ohio, Michigan, and New Jersey. Together these large states, ranked here in order of population in 1998, comprised 51.3 percent of the population. See U.S. Bureau of the Census, *Statistical Abstract of the United States: 1999*, p. 33.

†Data provided by Statistical Information Office, Population Division, U.S. Bureau of the Census. The terms "urban," "rural," "metropolitan," and "suburban" are subject to varying definitions. The federal government in 1983 divided the nation into Metropolitan Statistical Areas (MSAs), each of which contains at least one city of 50,000 persons, or an urban area of that size and a total population of 100,000 (75,000 in New England). Suburbs are defined here as areas outside central cities but within the Census Bureau definition of a metropolitan area. Not all the millions of people in the suburbs, so defined, might feel that they live in suburbia; suburban population obviously depends on how one defines a "suburb."

income from sales taxes, which are the quickest type of tax to reflect a downturn in economic activity. Only a decade earlier, reduced revenues because of a lagging economy meant that one state after another had been forced to raise taxes and cut services drastically. Schools, libraries, health facilities, and other basic needs suffered as a result.

One of the most dramatic examples occurred in California in 1992. For 64 days, Governor Pete Wilson and state legislators were unable to agree on a budget, and the mighty state of California had to issue IOUs of uncertain worth to pay its own employees. The fiscal package finally approved meant increased fees for students at community colleges and universities, reduced hours for many public facilities, and the closing of trauma centers in hospitals in many counties.

Only a few years later, economic conditions in the country had improved and the states had rebounded. One survey found the states by fiscal 1999 were in solid financial condition. Over a 5-year period, the survey reported, the states had cut taxes by $22 billion, and almost every state reported a surplus for fiscal 1999.[5]

Despite the economic boom that began in the early 1990s, there was no assurance that the lean times would not return again, especially if Congress continued to shift programs to the states, as it did in 1996 when it ended the largest federal welfare program and turned over responsibility for public assistance to the states. Washington still gave block grants for welfare to the states, but the restrictions in the welfare law meant that state and local governments would end up paying a much larger portion of welfare costs.

Because the law restructuring the welfare system initially prohibited most aid—including welfare, food stamps, and Medicaid—to undocumented immigrants and legal immigrants who are not citizens, the law was expected to have a particularly severe impact in California. The state was home to about 40 percent of the nation's estimated 1.5 million legal immigrants. Officials predicted that the state's counties might have to pay $10.7 billion in medical and social services for noncitizens over a 6-year period.[6] One California welfare executive declared: "The counties have virtually no ability to raise general tax revenues, but they'll still have to care for these people. It's a disaster in the making."[7] In 1998, Congress restored welfare and Medicaid benefits for the nation's legal immigrants, but California and other states with a high percentage of undocumented immigrants were still faced with providing basic services for low-income residents.

Much of this book has focused on the national government and national politics, but at last count there were, in addition to the government in Washington, 87,504 units of state and local government in the United States.[8] The performance of these governments is often criticized for failure to keep pace with the complex problems they face—transportation, housing, schools, drugs, crime, pollution, welfare services—to name some of the major ones. This inability to keep pace is not always the fault of the state or community; many of the problems that exist have been compounded by urbanization and patterns of population migration in recent decades. These factors have interacted to place a serious strain on the federal system.

Since the Second World War, for a variety of reasons, large numbers of low-income African Americans and whites have migrated from rural areas to big cities. At the same time, many middle-class families and business firms have moved out to the suburbs, taking the city tax base with them. The newcomers to the inner city have required costly government services—schools, welfare, police and fire protection, for example—but

The AMERICAN PAST

MUNICIPAL CORRUPTION: BOSS TWEED LOOTS NEW YORK

For more than a decade after 1857, William Marcy Tweed ruled politics in New York City and state, enriching himself by at least $30 million through padded construction contracts and other skullduggery. This account captures the flavor of Tweed and an era:

On the night of October 27, 1870, it was raining hard and steadily. . . . Very early in the evening thousands of loyal Democrats had assembled outside their district political clubs. All these storm-defying citizens were wearing red shirts. This was a compliment to William Marcy Tweed, State Senator, Grand Sachem of Tammany and boss of the city. Tweed had begun his political career, twenty-two years earlier, by helping to organize the celebrated "Big Six" brigade of volunteer firemen whose engine, at his suggestion, was adorned with the emblem of a ferocious tiger. It was

the emblem of Tammany Hall, to which, under the driving rain, fifty thousand red-shirted citizens carrying flaring torches were marching in the largest political parade that New York had ever witnessed. . . .

For two years, in nearly every issue of *Harper's Weekly,* the great cartoonist Thomas Nast had been attacking Tweed as head of a ring that was systematically looting the city. . . . While the great torchlight parade was in progress, Tweed faced an enthusiastic audience in Tammany Hall. He was forty-seven years old, tall, heavily bearded, growing bald, a man of enormous bulk. His eyes glittered as coldly as the huge diamond adorning his shirt front, but his ruddy face wore a jovial expression.

Tweed received a frenzied ovation when he arose to speak, and his brief address was constantly interrupted by outbursts of cheers and applause. . . .

But a scandal of this magnitude could not be ignored. Eventually, Tweed was prosecuted. At Tweed's first trial, the jury disagreed. At a second, he was convicted. Tweed was confined in the debtors' prison, where he was accorded all the privileges to which so distinguished a citizen was entitled. That was how, on a visit to his home accompanied by a warden and a keeper, he managed to make his escape. After remaining in hiding near New York, he made his way to Florida in disguise, thence to Cuba, finally to Spain. On landing in Vigo, Tweed was recognized; a cartoon by Thomas Nast revealed his identity. The Spanish authorities delivered him to an American warship sent to bring him back to the United States. . . . Tweed died in jail in the Spring of 1878.

—Adapted from Lloyd Morris, *Incredible New York*

---

have not had sufficient taxable incomes and property to finance these services.

By the early 1970s the flow of African American migrants to the cities had declined sharply.[9] And by that time African Americans were also migrating to the suburbs. But many African Americans in the suburbs continued to live in highly segregated neighborhoods. Moreover, the percentage of African Americans living in the central cities was more than twice that of whites.[10]

For the most part, cities rely on the property tax to finance the bulk of municipal services. Suburban governments now collect the taxes on the property of families and industries that have left the cities—and suburban residents have little desire to "bail out" City Hall. Big-city mayors look to Washington and the statehouses for relief. But, the mayors maintain, what limited federal funds are available have been siphoned off in part by the states for use in the suburbs and in rural areas.

In this chapter we will explore a key question: How well are the state and local governments meeting their responsibilities? Many related questions arise. For example, in the federal system in the United States (discussed in Chapter 3), how should responsibilities be divided

among the federal, state, and local governments? How are state and local governments organized? What are the major problems of the cities and the suburbs? Given the politics and existing structure of state and local governments, can they hope to solve problems that are larger than their geographic boundaries and financial resources? What are the implications of these problems for America's future?

THE STATES

America is a nation of states. The political institutions of the 13 colonies foreshadowed the shape of the federal system created under the Constitution. The states, in short, were here before the American nation. They grew in number as the frontier was pushed westward to the Pacific. They are not mere administrative or geographic units established for the convenience of the central government. Rather, the states are key political institutions rooted in the nation's historical development, sharing power under the federal system with the national government in Washington. But the federal system was constructed when the United States was a small, rural nation. In today's predominantly urban America—a nation of congested cities, inner-city neighborhoods devastated by poverty and drugs, and sprawling suburbs—are the states any longer relevant? Can they meet the new demands placed on them by urbanization?

Moreover, states vary greatly in size and character. California has the ninth-largest economy in the world, and a huge influx of immigrants, both legal and undocumented, from south of the border. It is very different in many ways from a state such as Vermont or Delaware. Some states have several metropolitan areas; others have none.

Many critics of state government feel that the states are not doing as much as they should, particularly in the crucial area of urban problems. However, the states have been making an effort to meet their responsibilities. For example, in recent decades state and local spending has increased at an even faster rate than federal spending.

In addition, in recent years the staffs of the bureaucracies that run the state governments, and the staffs of the state legislatures, have become more professional; that is, they tend to be better educated, better trained, and to have a longer-term commitment to their government jobs than in the past. The states and localities do not, of course, spend as much as the federal government, but their level of spending for domestic programs often actually exceeds that of the federal government.

Although by 2000 a majority of states had cut taxes and were enjoying budget surpluses, in some years a serious imbalance, or income gap, has existed between the demands on state and local governments and the revenues they raise through taxes. One reason for this is that state and local governments rely heavily on consumer and property taxes, which do not reflect the general growth of the economy as rapidly as the federal income tax does. The federal government collects more than half of all taxes; the states and communities divide the remainder.

About half of state revenues come from taxes, about one-quarter from federal aid, and the rest from a variety of sources.[11] The general sales tax is the largest single category of state income, amounting to about 40 percent of all state revenues.[12] One rapidly growing revenue source for the states is the sales tax and gross receipts tax on the $30 billion-a-year gambling industry.[13]

Beginning in the late 1960s and through the early 1990s, in an effort to find new sources of revenue, states raised taxes and imposed new taxes on a massive scale. Between 1990 and 1991, for example, 37 states increased their taxes. As noted, that pattern changed within a few years, as boom times brought tax reductions in many states.

Two decades earlier, however, it was a very different picture. There had been a significant tax revolt in several states, most notably in California. In 1978 California voters approved by 2 to 1 a constitutional amendment that appeared on the ballot as Proposition 13. It limited real estate taxes in the state to 1 percent of previous property values and was approved by the electorate despite warnings that it would result in cuts in government services. In Washington, and across the nation, political leaders read the election returns as a general "taxpayers' revolt" and a demand for lower taxes.

One result of the passage of Proposition 13 was to increase the power of the state and the state legislature because "local governments in California . . . now have less political capacity, as well as less fiscal capacity, with which to shape the futures of their communities."[14]

At first, the impact of Proposition 13 was cushioned by a $5 billion state surplus that had accumulated in California. Two years later, in 1980, a new proposition, which would have cut the state's income tax in half, was offered to the voters. By now, however, the atmosphere in California had changed. People had begun to feel the pinch in government services brought about by the passage of Proposition 13. This time, the new tax-cutting initiative was defeated by a margin of 5 to 3.

In 1999 seven states still had no personal income tax, however, and many other states taxed incomes at relatively low rates.* States are cautious about raising taxes in part because they must compete with one another. They "must be wary of increasing taxes or redistributing income in a way that will enable neighboring states to attract away industry."[15]

The federal government provides some financial help. In fiscal 2001, federal aid to the states was budgeted at $305.6 billion, or more than 16 percent of the federal budget.

What do the states do? They have major responsibilities in the fields of education, welfare, transportation, the administration of justice, the prisons, housing, public health, and the environment. (See Figure 19-2.) States share with local governments the responsibility for delivery of these and many other vital public services. And this responsibility is the source of many of the difficulties faced by the states, as well as by local governments.

To provide these services, state and local governments employ more people than does the federal government—with all of the accompanying problems of labor negotiations, strikes, and control of bureaucracy. Even though states are spending more money on public services, they have not always been successful in attacking the urban problems they face. There is a wide variation in the performance and effectiveness of the 50 states, just as there are substantial differences in state politics and state political institutions.

As noted in Chapter 3, however, many states have adopted innovative programs in education and other areas that have later been copied by the federal government. Particularly during the 1980s, when Washington cut back on social programs, the states experimented with their own programs. Wisconsin introduced the first

---

*States with no income tax in 1999 were Alaska, Florida, Nevada, South Dakota, Texas, Washington, and Wyoming.

FIGURE 19-2

Major Expenditures of State and Local Governments (in millions of dollars)

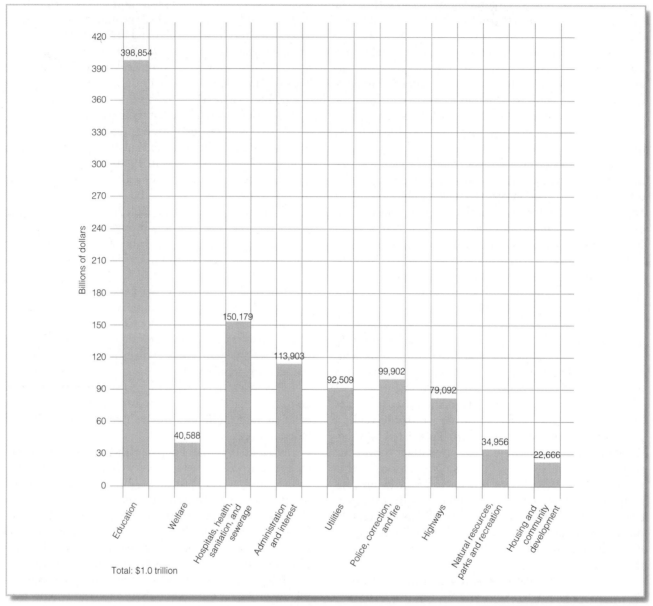

Total: $1.0 trillion

NOTE: Total is for all state and local expenditures, including items not shown.
SOURCE: U.S. Bureau of the Census, *Statistical Abstract of the United States: 1999*, p. 312. Data for 1996.

welfare plan linking payments to school attendance, and Wisconsin and other states experimented with new welfare programs in the 1990s; Illinois introduced self-management of public housing projects; Vermont proposed a system of universal access to health care; and Minnesota, the state of Washington, and Alaska established programs to target parents who evade child support by changing jobs frequently. Arkansas, Bill Clinton's home state, made its teachers accountable for their classroom performance.

Beyond providing services, states have a major impact on people's lives. It is the states, not the federal government, that regulate marriage, divorce, child custody, driver's licenses, auto inspection, transfer of property,

wills and estates, and many other matters. And it is the states, as well as the federal government, that determine the penalty for possession of marijuana, or whether capital punishment shall be applied for certain crimes. The federal courts may eventually review state cases that involve constitutional questions, but initially at least, in cases that do not involve federal laws, the states decide.

The State Constitutions

State constitutions spell out the basic structure of each state government. Every state constitution provides for an executive, legislative, and judicial branch. Although each includes a bill of rights, some state constitutions

INITIATIVES: "DEMOCRACY IN ITS PUREST FORM" OR "DEMOCRACY RUN AMOK"?

SCAPPOOSE, ORE., Oct. 24—Forgive Carolyn Knowles for feeling a bit "overwhelmed," as she put it, when Volume I of the Oregon voters' guide—all 376 pages of it, encompassing 26 ballot measures and 607 arguments for or against them—showed up in her mailbox a few days ago.

Make federal income taxes fully deductible on Oregon returns? Limit total state spending to 15 percent of taxpayers' personal income? Prohibit public school instruction "encouraging, promoting or sanctioning" homosexual or bisexual behaviors? Ban the use of all "body-gripping animal traps"?

"It's like a full-time job trying to figure all these out," said Ms. Knowles, who already has a full-time job as a cashier in a nearby casino. "It's totally confusing. Sometimes I'm not even sure if a yes vote really means yes or no. Unless you're a real intellectual, you can get mighty bogged down."

It may be democracy in its purest form, as proponents of Oregon's initiative process like to say, or democracy run amok, as critics contend. But no one disputes that voters here face a staggering number of policy decisions, or that the official voters' guide hardly helps cut through the fog for voters who mark their ballots at home in a state where almost all votes are mailed in.

"For most voters, it resembles something written in Greek as poorly translated from the original Urdu," said William M. Lunch, a political science professor at Oregon State University.

Some 102 years after South Dakota became the first state to allow citizens to vote directly on their laws, Oregon is sticking to its tradition of using the process more than any other state. Not since North Dakota did so in 1932 has a state put so many citizen-sponsored initiatives before its people in a single election. . . .

Oregon's crowded ballot this year also illustrates two broader themes in the initiative process around the nation: its ever-expanding use and the growing number of questions about whether it is such a wise method of making public policy. Critics say the initiative process is subject to exploitation, especially by those who have the wealth to pay professional signature gathers to get a measure on the ballot and finance an advertising blitz to get it passed.

"Whatever happened to representative government?" said Darryl Sykes, an operator in the local wastewater treatment plant here in this Portland suburb. "A lot of the stuff in the voters' guide is not written in layman's terms that the average guy can understand. I thought we elected people to figure this stuff out."

—*New York Times*, October 25, 2000

---

are more liberal than others. For example, the constitutions of the newest states, Alaska and Hawaii, have strong civil rights provisions.

State constitutions tend to be lists of what the state cannot do; they limit the power of the governor and of the legislature—to levy taxes and borrow money, for example. As a result, state constitutions are often condemned as restrictive, negative documents that impede the ability of states to meet modern problems.

In the late 1960s and early 1970s, many states streamlined their constitutions. But modernizing state constitutions does not in itself improve governmental performance unless there are also changes in the political climate in those states. In many areas of the nation, there is political resistance to major, costly undertakings by governments to solve urban problems.

The state constitutions, as Duane Lockard has pointed out, "have been amended more than 3,000 times and in some instances it is necessary to read the constitution backwards like a Chinese newspaper, in order to see what the last word is on an original provision."[16] Lockard also found a number of oddities; the California constitution, for example, limited the power of the legislature to regulate the length of wrestling matches, and the Georgia constitution provided a $250,000 reward for the first person to strike oil within the borders of the Peach State.[17]

The most common means of amending state constitutions is by a majority or two-thirds vote of the legislature and approval by a majority of the voters at the next election. In addition, 41 states permit constitutional conventions to amend their constitutions, with the changes subject to approval by the voters. In a few states, the legislature may appoint a commission to recommend constitutional changes, again subject to voter approval.[18]

And most states now either permit their constitutions to be amended, or laws enacted, by **initiative**.* Under this method, proposed constitutional amendments or legislation can be placed on the ballot if enough signatures are obtained on a petition. California's Proposition 13 was an example of a constitutional amendment approved by the voters in this fashion.

About half the states—mostly in the West and Midwest—permit voters to enact laws by initiative. For example, voters in these states have chosen to enact or repeal taxes, and have approved or rejected initiatives dealing with issues such as abortion, gay rights, state lotteries, banning trucks with triple trailers, requiring employers to provide health insurance, and outlawing the hunting of nursing mother bears.[19]

---

*As of 2000, there were 18 states that allowed their constitutions to be amended by some form of initiative. Data from Initiative and Referendum Institute, Washington, D.C., online at <www.iandrinstitute.org>.

By the 2000 election year, voters in 42 states faced a total of 204 initiatives. In Oregon, which uses the initiative more than any other state, voters faced 26 such issues on the ballot that year. Because many voters found it confusing to have to deal with so many choices, a backlash had developed in several states against the use of the initiative. Other voters liked the idea of direct control over laws or state constitutional amendments. Many state legislators, however, felt that the use of the initiative poached on their lawmaking authority. In the two years after 1998, seven states took steps to make it more difficult to get initiatives on the ballot.[20]

In addition to the initiative, every state has provisions for a **referendum**, a method that allows voters, in effect, to "veto" a bill passed by the legislature or to accept or reject a proposal, such as a bond issue, made by a government agency.

Sixteen states also allow the **recall**, a procedure that in certain circumstances permits voters to remove elected state officials from office before their terms have expired.[21] In many local units of government, citizens also may vote for the recall of local public officials.

The Governors

At first glance, it might appear as though the 50 states are federal governments in miniature. Each has the familiar three branches with checks and balances. The governors are usually prestigious figures, at least within their states; like the president, they head an executive branch. And, like the president, they have armed forces under their command in the form of the state police and the National Guard. Appearances are deceptive, however, for the position of governor in some states is generally much less powerful than may be imagined.

To begin with, the actions of a governor, and of other state officials, and the laws passed by state legislatures cannot conflict with federal law and are subject to judicial review by the U.S. Supreme Court. During the 1950s and 1960s, at Little Rock, Arkansas, and elsewhere in the South, federal power prevailed over that of state governors in confrontations over public school and university desegregation.

Beyond this, the position of governor has been weakened by historical and political factors. During the colonial period, the royal governors clashed with the elected legislatures. The state constitutions written at the time of the American Revolution reflected the prevailing distrust of executive power; in most states, the legislature chose the governor. During the 19th century, popular election of governors spread through the states, but the power of the governors remained relatively weak. Not until the 20th century were state governments reorganized and executive power increased in some states. But even today, the office of governor is weak in a number of states.

At the same time, political scientists have noted marked improvements in the abilities and stature of American governors in recent decades. Larry Sabato has suggested that the political hacks of the past have faded away: "The good-time Charlies are gone."[22] In their place, Sabato observes, there has arisen "a new breed of governor," more highly skilled, better trained, and better able to lead their states in the modern age.[23]

Variations in the power of state governors were shown in a study published by a federal commission. In only 10 states was the governor said to be "very strong."[24] Another study, by Thad L. Beyle, a political scientist, ranked the states on a scale according to the formal powers of the governors—including tenure, appointment, budget, veto powers, and party control—and concluded that nine governors had the most institutional power; 21 states ranked next, followed by a group of 17 states. Three states ranked at the low end of the scale.[25]

As Beyle also noted, the governors of the biggest states, such as California, New York, and Texas, "are important and powerful in political circles. They have greater influence in national political conventions and larger congressional delegations. They are often elevated to potential presidential candidacy just because they are the governors of these states. The national press covers them closely. . . . In short, these governors have national power because of the states they head."[26] This tendency was demonstrated once again in 2000 when the governor of Texas, George W. Bush, was nominated as the Republican candidate for president.

In recent years, a number of states have taken steps to strengthen the power of the governor. In 22 states, the governor has power to reorganize the executive branch by executive order, subject to veto by the legislature.[27] Several governors have been given broader power to appoint department heads and other state officials.[28]

In most states, the governor shares executive power with at least one other popularly elected official. Typically, the officials elected by the voters along with the governor may include the lieutenant governor, attorney general, secretary of state, treasurer, auditor, and superintendent of education. The governor's difficulties are increased if one or more of these elected executive branch officials belong to the opposing political party. The power of governors to appoint important officials (in states where they are not elected independently) varies from state to state; in some cases their choices are subject to approval by the state senate.

All states grant their governors the power to veto state legislation. By the year 2000, governors in 43 states could also exercise a **line-item veto,** the power to reject single parts of appropriations bills.[29]

As of 2000, 38 states limited the term of office of the governor, restricting the governor in almost every case to two four-year terms. (In Utah, the limit is three four-year terms and in Virginia the governor cannot serve more than one successive four-year term.) Ten states have four-year terms with unlimited succession; only two states, New Hampshire and Vermont, had two-year terms with unlimited succession.[30]

MAKING A DIFFERENCE

BRYANT HALL: WHEN HE SPEAKS THE LEGISLATORS LISTEN

On the agenda today in the Maryland General Assembly in Annapolis, there is a bill to limit the number of passengers a teenage driver can carry in a car, and Bryant Hall is there to fight it.

Bryant Hall is 15. He doesn't vote. He doesn't even drive. But he understands the workings of government better than most adults. . . . He represents a mammoth constituency: all the state's teenagers. So when Bryant speaks, leaders listen.

Bryant is a sophomore at Southern High School in rural Anne Arundel County. He plays varsity football and is a shot putter. He lives in a tiny house in Galesville, a bay town south of Annapolis, with his mother and their snaggletooth old poodle named Cody. He buses tables Sunday evenings and is learning how to drive.

He is also state legislative affairs coordinator for the Maryland Association of Student Council, which represents 250,000 kids, and vice president of the Chesapeake Region Association

of Student Councils, which represents 35,000, and for this his opinion matters in Annapolis. . . . He plans to get a poli-sci degree, and become a "politician or something." He's immensely charismatic and popular and not obnoxious at all—"he's what everyone hopes their politician to be," says Anne Arundel student council adviser Sue Barnes Hannahs.

If you ask them all, his advisers are divided between those who say he'll be president one day and those who say he might be "too nice a guy" for that.

He *is* nice and he is not a geek. Bryant may fall asleep to C-SPAN radio, but he gets dressed to MTV. He got the *Sports Illustrated* swimsuit calendar for Christmas, and he was homecoming prince this year.

The headline March 15, 2000 reads "Passengers Increase Teen Drivers' Risk," and it makes Bryant feel a little guilty about opposing the bill. But not too guilty. And it

apparently doesn't make the legislators feel too guilty either, because a week later they convert the bill from one that would limit the number of passengers into one that just requires them to wear seat belts.

"I guess this means my lobbying effort on this part was a success!!!!!!!!!!!" he e-mails when he reads about the conversion of the passenger bill to a seat belt requirement. "I am ecstatic right now. I guess the power of the student voice shouldn't be doubted!"

Later, Bryant contemplates the situation, and decides that what really matters is the end result and he shouldn't bother trying to figure out how much of the success was attributed to "the student voice"— attributable to *him*.

"Then," he says, "I would be like a politician."

—Adapted from the *Washington Post*, April 6, 2000

In general, a governor's power and ability to develop long-range policies are greater if the term in office is four years and he or she is permitted to seek reelection. Otherwise, to some extent, the governor becomes a "lame duck" as soon as the inauguration takes place.

The degree of the governor's control over the state budget is another index of power. In all but a few states, the governor prepares an executive budget and submits it to the legislature. Even though this usually serves to increase the governor's strength, much still depends on the skill a governor shows in managing the state bureaucracy and on other fiscal and political practices within the state.

Nevertheless, the fact that the governor develops the state's budget and presents it to the legislature is a major source of gubernatorial power. State legislatures may revise or change the details, but it is the governor who sets the agenda.

Because federal grants provide a substantial share of state revenues, the power of governors also varies with the degree of control they have over state participation in federal programs. Even so, the power of gov-

ernors to use federal grants is limited by the administrative "strings" attached to money flowing from Washington; states receiving grants must comply with federal laws—such requirements as affirmative action, for example—and with various federal reporting and record-keeping rules.

The Legislatures

When the American nation began, state legislatures were powerful and prestigious political institutions. Today, they are sometimes described in unflattering terms. During the 19th century, in the era of Jacksonian democracy and again after the Civil War, voters in many states wrote into the state constitutions various restrictions on legislative power—limiting state expenditures and borrowing power, for example. Many of these curbs are still in effect.

Public respect for state legislators and legislatures also has been eroded by occasional disclosures of bribes and corruption among the lawmakers. One result has been a suspicion that some state legislators manage to use their position for private gain. Closely tied to this

TABLE 19-1

The State Legislatures, 1999

	Senate Members	Length of Term	House Members	Length of Term	Years Sessions Are Held	Salary*
Alabama	35	4	105	4	annual	$ 10(d)
Alaska	20	4	40	2	annual	24,012
Arizona	30	2	60	2	annual	24,000
Arkansas	35	4	100	2	odd	12,500
California	40	4	80	2	annual	99,000
Colorado	35	4	65	2	annual	30,000
Connecticut	36	2	151	2	annual	21,788
Delaware	21	4	41	2	annual	29,574
Florida	40	4	120	2	annual	26,388
Georgia	56	2	180	2	annual	11,347.80
Hawaii	25	4	51	2	annual	32,000
Idaho	35	2	70	2	annual	14,760
Illinois	59	4†	118	2	annual	50,803
Indiana	50	4	100	2	annual	11,600
Iowa	50	4	100	2	annual	20,758
Kansas	40	4	125	2	annual	72.06(d)
Kentucky	38	4	100	2	even	151(d)
Louisiana	39	4	105	4	even	16,800
Maine	35	2	151	2	annual	10,500
Maryland	47	4	141	4	annual	30,591
Massachusetts	40	2	160	2	annual	46,410
Michigan	38	4	110	2	annual	55,054
Minnesota	67	4	134	2	biennial	31,140
Mississippi	52	4	122	4	annual	10,000
Missouri	34	4	163	2	annual	26,802.96
Montana	50	4	100	2	odd	59.67(l)
Nebraska	49	4	‡	‡	annual	12,000
Nevada	21	4	42	2	odd	130(d)
New Hampshire	24	2	400	2	annual	200

assumption is the belief that lobbyists and special interest groups can work their will at the statehouse more easily than in Washington. An industry, utility, or labor union that exercises great power within a state capital sometimes achieves its legislative aims more easily at the state level than in Congress, where its power may be diffused and it must compete with many other interest groups.

Finally, until the Supreme Court's reapportionment decisions of the 1960s, overrepresentation of rural areas in the state legislatures diminished legislative prestige in urban areas. City dwellers grumbled about state legislatures controlled by "appleknockers" and "farmers" who primarily served rural interests.

One of the most important and politically powerful jobs of the state legislators is to redraw the district lines for the U.S. House of Representatives every 10 years after the census. This task often leads to fierce political infighting, because the party in power in the legislature can draw the lines to favor its own members of Congress.

Because of population shifts, some states lose representatives after a census and others gain.

In the year 2000, both major parties spent millions on polls, television commercials, and consultants to try to sway a handful of state legislative races that might decide control of the U.S. House for the next 10 years. As described by Tom Hofeller, redistricting director for the Republican National Committee, "It's the hidden national election of 2000."[31]

In most states, the two branches of the legislature redraw the congressional district lines, but the governor has veto power. If one party controls both houses of the legislature and the governorship, then it can tailor districts to help its candidates. For example, a conservative Republican House member might benefit from a newly shaped district that excluded minority voters in an inner-city neighborhood. Conversely, a liberal Democrat might prefer a district that included exactly those areas. The stakes are high; for instance, in 2000 if the Republicans won just 17 key state legislative contests,

	Senate Members	Length of Term	House Members	Length of Term	Years Sessions Are Held	Salary*
New Jersey	40	4	80	2	annual	$35,000
New Mexico	42	4	70	2	annual	75(d)
New York	61	2	150	2	annual	79,500
North Carolina	50	2	120	2	odd	13,951
North Dakota	49	4	98	4	odd	111
Ohio	33	4	99	2	annual	42,426.90
Oklahoma	48	4	101	2	annual	38,400
Oregon	30	4	60	2	odd	14,496
Pennsylvania	50	4	203	2	annual	59,245.74
Rhode Island	50	2	100	2	annual	10,768
South Carolina	46	4	124	2	annual	10,400
South Dakota	35	2	70	2	annual	12,000
Tennessee	33	4	99	2	annual	16,500
Texas	31	4	150	2	odd	7,200
Utah	29	4	75	2	annual	100(d)
Vermont	30	2	150	2	annual	536(w)
Virginia	40	4	100	2	annual	18,000 (Senate)
						17,640 (House)
Washington	49	4	98	2	annual	28,300
West Virginia	34	4	100	2	annual	15,000
Wisconsin	33	4	99	2	annual	41,809
Wyoming	30	4	60	2	annual	125(d)

*Salaries as of March 1999. Amounts are annual unless otherwise noted as (d) per day, (l) per legislative day, (w) per week, (m) per month, (o) odd year, or (e) even year.
†Terms vary from two to four years.
‡Unicameral legislature.
SOURCE: *The Book of the States, 2000–2001 Edition,* vol. 33 (Lexington, Kentucky: Council of State Governments), pp. 66–67, 70, 83–84.

out of a total of 5,900, and two important governor's races, the Republican Party would have full control over redrawing 182 House seats.[32]

Although state legislatures are often criticized, there have been some signs of improvement. By the 1980s, a number of state legislatures had begun modernizing both their procedures and facilities—for example, strengthening their committee system, installing computers, and initiating other reforms. As noted, this has been accompanied by a trend toward greater professionalism in the staffing of state legislatures.

Every state has a two-house **bicameral legislature** except Nebraska, which has a **unicameral legislature.** The 7,424 state lawmakers serve in legislatures that range in size from 49 in Nebraska to 424 in New Hampshire. Typically, the upper house has about 40 members and the lower house about 100 members. Most state senators serve four-year terms; most state representatives in the lower house serve for two years. In 37 states the legislature meets annually. In most of the other states, the legislatures meet regularly only every two years, normally in January.[33] (See Table 19-1.)

For the majority of state legislators, public service is only a part-time job. In more than two-thirds of the states the length of regular legislative sessions is constitutionally limited, sometimes to 60 days. Even then, the legislators may spend only a few days in the capital each week, often ending the session with a great flurry of last-minute legislation. Sometimes the clock is literally stopped to permit the passage of bills within the time limit.

In 1999, California legislators were paid $99,000 a year, the highest state legislative salaries in the nation. Although seven states—California, Illinois, Massachusetts, Michigan, New York, Ohio, and Pennsylvania— paid legislators $40,000 or more annually, nine states paid only a per diem rate.[34]

Who are the legislators? State lawmakers tend to come from a higher-than-average social and economic background. As Samuel C. Patterson has noted:

The largest occupational group among state legislators is that of lawyers. . . . Few white- and blue-collar workers serve in the legislatures, even in the industrial states with large labor union memberships. . . . In the last decade women have been winning legislative seats in increasing numbers, but the percentages are not very large.[35]

However, this occupational profile is changing. In part because the federal government has given more responsibilities to the states, legislatures tend to meet more often for longer periods. As a result, people with careers who need to work cannot always afford to serve in the legislature. In some states, the number of lawmakers who are lawyers has declined, their place taken by retired persons.

By 2000, the number of state legislators who were women had increased from 10 percent in 1980 to 22.5 percent.[36] Of the 7,424 state legislators, 1,669 were women. In the state senates there were 392 women, or 19.8 percent of 1,984 state senate seats; and women held 1,277, or 23.5 percent, of the 5,440 House seats. Washington State, with 40.8 percent women in the legislature, led the nation, followed by Nevada, Arizona, and Colorado.[37]

Perhaps the most important aspect of state legislatures today is their changing nature as a result of the "reapportionment revolution" discussed in Chapter 11. In *Baker* v. *Carr* in 1962, the Supreme Court held that the voters of Tennessee did have the right to challenge unequal representation in the state's legislature.[38] And in *Reynolds* v. *Sims* in 1964, it ruled that apportionment of both houses of state legislatures must be based closely on population and the principle of "equal representation for equal numbers of people."[39]

The Court's decisions did not, despite popular expectations, shift the base of state political power from rural areas to the central cities. Instead, the main beneficiary has proved to be the suburbs. And suburban legislators have often proved to be just as conservative on many social-welfare and urban issues as lawmakers from a state's rural areas.

As a result of voter discontent with politicians, by the year 2000 a total of 18 states had amended their constitutions to limit the terms of elected officials and legislators; 11 states had already done so and the other 7 would have limits in effect by 2007.[40] California, Oklahoma, and Colorado led the way, adopting term limits in 1990. The movement to limit terms of office has had the most success in states that have the initiative; limiting the number of years that a legislator may serve has proved very popular with voters. The legislators, of course, do not like term limits, since it means they must give up their seats. Advocates argue that it keeps lawmakers from becoming entrenched and too powerful, and has opened the way for more women and minorities to serve.

In more than a dozen states, voters approved limits on the terms of members of the U.S. Congress, restricting senators to two terms and representatives to two or

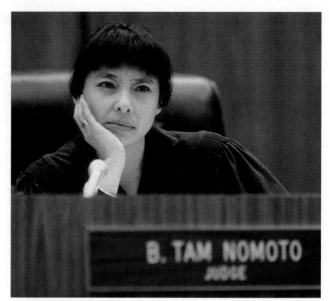

Spencer Grant/Photo Researchers

three terms. In 1995, however, the U.S. Supreme Court ruled that the states could not pass laws limiting the terms of members of Congress.[41] That meant that only an amendment to the U.S. Constitution could impose congressional term limits.

The Judges

Most Americans never see the inside of the U.S. Supreme Court, or even of a federal district court. But many have been to state and local courts—for example, traffic court to pay a fine, or divorce court—where most criminal and civil cases are handled. The quality of justice in America, therefore, depends to a great extent on the quality of justice in the states and communities. These courts, rather than federal courts, are most visible to the average citizen.

Just as the Supreme Court may strike down federal, state, or local laws that conflict with the U.S. Constitution, state courts often strike down state laws that conflict with their state constitutions. But the decisions of state and local courts must conform to the U.S. Constitution as interpreted by the Supreme Court.

State and local judgeships can be important political prizes. Young lawyers who "go into politics" may serve in the legislature or in a state or municipal administration. But often their hope is to be appointed a judge, as their safe, prestigious, and ultimate political reward. The power to appoint legislators as judges is used by many governors to enhance their ability to get bills through the legislature and reward their political allies.

The majority of state judges are elected, however, and the costs and intensity of many of these campaigns have increased. Election contests for judgeships in many states have begun to resemble other political campaigns, sometimes raising troublesome questions about the source of campaign contributions. For example, judges can accept contributions from law firms whose partners or associates may later appear before them in court.

The structure of the state and local judiciary and the problems of the nation's criminal justice system are discussed in detail in Chapter 15.

Politics and Parties

In Chapter 9 we examined the structure of state political party organizations, their relation to national parties, the geographic cleavage that exists between "upstate" and "downstate" urban-rural areas in many states, and the decline of big-city political machines. In Chapter 11 we mentioned the various national influences on state politics and the increasing effort of states to isolate themselves from the tides of presidential politics by scheduling elections for governor in the off-years. In the American federal system, state politics and state political parties cannot be separated from any discussion of politics and government at the national level.

In the seven presidential elections from 1976 through 2000, four former or incumbent governors were elected president: Jimmy Carter of Georgia in 1976, Ronald Reagan of California in 1980 and 1984, Bill Clinton of Arkansas in 1992 and 1996, and George W. Bush in 2000. Thirteen other presidents also had served as governors.

The states are the building blocks of the national political parties. But among the states, the pattern of party competition differs widely. For example, for many years in the one-party states of the Deep South, competition was largely within the Democratic Party. The real battles were fought for the Democratic nomination; the winner of the nomination was virtually assured of victory over a Republican opponent in the general election.

The emergence of Alabama Governor George Wallace's third party in the 1960s, combined with major Republican inroads in the "Solid South," changed the face of southern politics. In 1968 Richard Nixon, the Republican presidential candidate, carried five southern states, and in 1972 he won the entire South. Four years later a southerner, Jimmy Carter, headed the Democratic ticket and carried all but one southern state. But in 1980 the Republican candidate, Ronald Reagan, accomplished exactly the reverse, carrying the entire South except for Carter's home state of Georgia. And in 1984, Reagan carried every southern state, as George Bush did in 1988. In 1992, however, the Democratic ticket was headed by Bill Clinton, a southern governor, and Al Gore, a southern senator, and the Democrats captured 4 of the 11 states of the old Confederacy.

Some states have vigorous two-party competition. Other states have modified one-party competition—one party is on the average stronger than the other. But in both situations, control of the statehouse and the legis-

lature can swing back and forth. One study measuring party competition for state offices characterized 13 states as modified one-party Democratic, 31 as two-party, and 6 as modified one-party Republican.* (See Figure 19-3.) Since then, the pattern may have changed in some states, but not in most.

Within the states, political parties show considerable ideological variation. A Democrat from rural Florida may be much closer to a Republican in ideological hue than to a Wisconsin Democrat. The Republican Party in Mississippi bears little resemblance to the Republican Party in Massachusetts.

The rise of the direct primary for state political nominations (discussed in Chapter 11) has weakened control of state political machines by party leaders. The primary has at least partially shifted control over nominations to the voters, in those states where they care to exercise that power.

LOCAL GOVERNMENTS

A cartoon in the *New Yorker* showed a woman sitting at a table on her apartment terrace, calling to her husband: "Hurry, dear, your soup is getting dirty." For most city dwellers, air pollution is no joke. And a city's laws and regulations affect the battle for cleaner air. Whether a person lives in a skyscraper, a tenement, or a small town, the quality of local government is likely to have immediate impact on that person's life. In this sense, local government is "closer" to the citizen, even though the federal government may have a greater effect on one's life in the long run.

New York City is a case in point. Although the city has done better in recent years, its residents have lived through financial crises and strikes by sanitation workers, transit workers, and teachers. One way or another, these inconveniences involved the city government. If New Yorkers watched noxious trash piling up on the sidewalks, if they had to walk several miles to work because of a labor dispute, or if they could not send their children to school, they had ample reason to be aware of the impact of local government on their lives.

Although the connection is not always well understood, local governments are in actuality legal creatures of the states. The state constitutions vest power in the

---

*John F. Bibby and Thomas M. Holbrook, "Parties and Elections," in Gray and Jacob, eds., *Politics in the American States: A Comparative Analysis*, 6th ed. (Washington, D.C.: CQ Press), p. 105. The measure of interparty competition used in this study is based entirely on elections for state offices between 1989 and 1994. The authors point out that the states are more competitive in presidential and congressional elections. In addition, they note, the study gave more weight to partisan control of state legislatures than of governorships. As a result, the study does not reflect Republican successes in gubernatorial elections in such once reliably Democratic states as Florida, North Carolina, South Carolina, and Texas.

FIGURE 19-3

Party Competition in the States

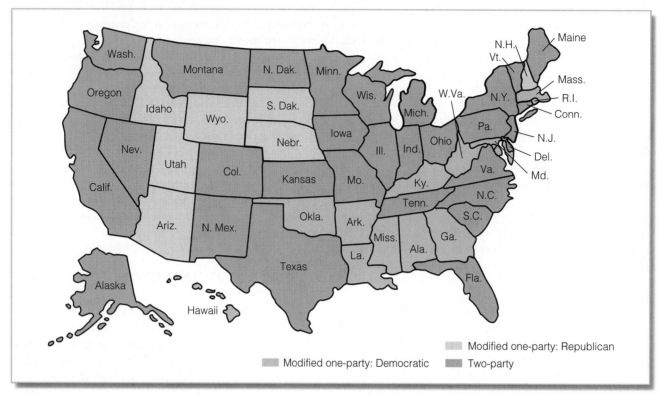

Modified one-party: Republican
Modified one-party: Democratic
Two-party

SOURCE: Adapted from data from John F. Bibby and Thomas M. Holbrook, "Parties and Elections," in Virginia Gray and Herbert Jacob, eds., *Politics in the American States: A Comparative Analysis,* 6th ed., p. 105. Data for states from 1989 through 1994.

state governments; local governments merely exercise the power that the state gives to them.

Cities

Cities are municipal corporations chartered by the states. The charters define the municipal powers. About half the states have widely varying provisions for local home rule. As the term implies, **home rule** empowers municipalities to modify their charters and run their affairs without approval by the legislature, subject to the constitution and laws of the state. While home rule may give municipalities more freedom in choosing their form of government, in most states their freedom is not much greater than that of other localities in such fields as education, police power, and other substantive areas. Home rule, in other words, may not help cities solve problems. At a time when so many urban problems cut across the boundaries of local government units, many urban specialists believe there is a need for greater

"You should have been here in the old days, before the budget cutbacks. . . . There were cops and fire engines and planes buzzing around . . ."
Mike Peters/*Dayton Daily News*

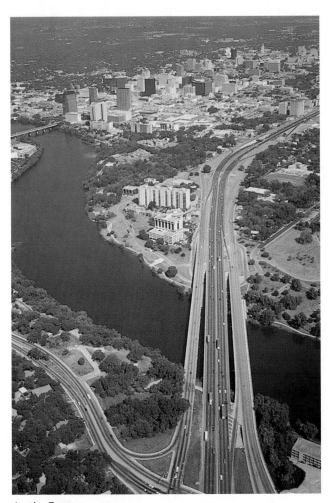

Austin, Texas
Ron Dorsey/Stock, Boston

interdependence and cooperation among local governments, not greater autonomy and independence.

There are three basic forms of city government: the mayor-council plan, the council-manager plan, and the commission plan.

The Mayor-Council Plan Under the **mayor-council plan,** power is divided between a mayor and an elected city council. Today, most of the nation's cities of half a million people or more employ a strong mayor-council form of government in which the mayor has substantial formal power over the executive agencies and in dealings with the council. In some cities, however, a weak mayor-council form is still in use. In these cases, the mayor is merely a figurehead and must share administrative power with the council and other elected officials. Some cities employ a mixture of the two systems. More than half the cities of 2,500 or more people use the mayor-council plan.

The Council-Manager Plan The council-manager form of government was first adopted before the First World War by the communities of Staunton, Virginia, and Sumter, South Carolina. Under the **council-manager plan,** a council, usually elected on a nonpartisan ticket, hires a professional city manager, who runs the city government and has power to hire and fire city officials. The council in turn has power to fire the city manager (although the city council is not supposed to interfere in the day-to-day administration of city affairs).

City managers often bring professional skills to the business of running a city and may frequently receive high salaries. Although city managers are nominally "nonpolitical," they may be dismissed as a result of a political battle within the community. Almost half of all cities with populations of 2,500 or more have city managers. The plan is employed all across the nation but is particularly popular in California and other western states. It is also used widely in Virginia and Ohio.

The Commission Plan When a hurricane and high waves smashed Galveston, Texas, in 1900, more than 5,000 people were killed and property damage was estimated to be in the millions. In the emergency, while the city government was paralyzed, the Texas state legislature appointed a commission of five local businessmen to run Galveston.

The plan caught on and for a time, at least, was extremely popular in American cities. Under the **commission plan,** a board of city commissioners, usually five, is popularly elected (on a nonpartisan ballot, in a majority of cities that use the system). The commissioners make policy as a city council, but they also run the city departments as administrators. One commissioner is usually designated mayor but often has no extra power. In time, the commission plan proved disappointing to reformers. Responsibility was diffused under the system, and commissioners frequently lacked the skills needed to administer city departments. More than 100 cities of 2,500 or more people still use this form of local government. But in 1960 it was abandoned by Galveston, which turned to the council-manager plan.

Counties

In rural areas the county is the most important geographic unit of local government. There are 3,043 counties in the United States.[42] Their size and power vary, but typically the elected officials include the sheriff, county prosecutor, coroner, clerk, and treasurer. These officials share governing power with elected county boards, most frequently called a "board of commissioners" or a "board of supervisors." Some large counties elect a county executive to act as chief administrator, and others appoint an administrator, much like city managers. The county courthouse is usually the local center of political power, the gathering place of those local officials, political leaders, and hangers-on referred to in some counties as "the courthouse gang." But county governments are changing. Of the total, about two-thirds were run by commissioners, and most of the rest by professional county administrators or elected county executives.

Towns and Townships

The New England town meeting has long stood as a symbol of direct participatory democracy. These meetings are still held in many New England towns: The townspeople come together for an annual meeting in the spring, at which they elect a board of selectmen and settle local policy questions. But today, urbanization and a vastly increased population have sapped the town meeting of much of its former strength.

In New England and New York, the "town" includes the village and the surrounding countryside. In the Middle Atlantic states and the Midwest, counties are often subdivided into townships. By order of Congress, many Midwest townships were laid out early in the nation's history in 6-by-6-mile checkerboard fashion. For this reason, many townships today are 36 square miles in area. Rural townships are declining in importance and number. But in a number of urban areas, townships perform the function of cities.

Special Districts

Special districts are established within states to deal with problems that cut across the boundary lines of local units of government or to spread the tax burden over a geographic area larger than that of the preexisting local units. They are created for such purposes as fire protection, sewage, water, schools, transportation, and parks. The number of special districts has been growing at a rapid rate.

The existence of so many kinds and layers of local government results in fragmentation and overlapping, contributing to the inability of local governments to respond effectively to their problems. For example, the existence in so many states of a separate system of government control for schools often makes it difficult for local governments to coordinate education with other programs. Special districts often mean that problems will be dealt with by experts and specialists. But such districts may also mean that local governments give up control over those programs. And the tax revenues raised by special districts cannot be used by other units of government to meet other needs.

CITIES AND SUBURBS: THE METROPOLITAN DILEMMA

For more than a decade, the suburbs, by Census Bureau estimates, have formed the largest segment of the American population. It was one day in 1970—no one knows the exact date—that the number of people living in suburbia exceeded the population living in the central cities or rural areas.*

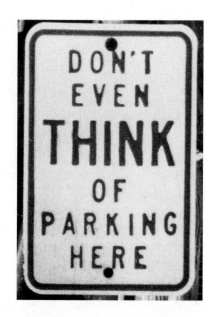

AP/Wide World

There were no ceremonies to mark the occasion, no presidential ribbon cutting, no television coverage. But the date was a milestone, nevertheless.

One political result can be measured in the increase in suburban representation in Congress and in state legislatures. Another result has been to sharpen the conflict between the suburbs and the cities on issues where their interests differ. Even before the suburbs outgrew the cities in population, the urban-suburban rift was clearly visible. In state after state, suburban legislators, sometimes in alliance with rural forces, defeated legislation to aid central cities.

At the turn of the 20th century, George Washington Plunkitt, the Tammany district leader, complained that rural legislators had imposed an unfair tax burden on New York City:

> This city is ruled entirely by the hayseed legislators at Albany. . . . In England . . . they make a pretense of givin' the Irish some self-government. In this state, the Republican government makes no pretense at all. It says right out in the open: "New York City is a nice big fat Goose. Come along with your carvin' knives and have a slice." They don't pretend to ask the Goose's consent.[43]

Today, the white suburban resident has largely replaced the "hayseeds" of yesteryear as the adversary of the city dweller. If Boss Plunkitt were around today, he probably would be complaining about the "commuters" in New York City's suburban Nassau and Westchester counties.

The picture of conflict between cities and suburbs might be even bleaker but for two emerging factors. First, the pattern of metropolitan growth has created an interdependence among all governments in the area, especially in such fields as air pollution, mass transit, and land use, where no single government's boundaries conform to the size of the problem. Suburbs and cities

---

*New York Times, June 21, 1970, p. 1. As noted in the footnote on p. 642, the "suburbs" are defined as areas outside central cities but within the Census Bureau definition of a metropolitan area.

can, and have, cooperated on problems in which their mutual benefit is at stake. Second, many of the problems of the cities—crime, overcrowding, welfare rolls, traffic, housing—exist in the suburbs as well. Suburban residents have discovered that, to some extent, they "took the city with them."

As a result, more and more suburbs and cities may come to realize that, on certain issues at least, they are in the same boat. This happened in Georgia; urban and suburban legislators, formerly political enemies, joined in an "Urban Caucus"—in part because the area around Atlanta, including Cobb County, began experiencing many of the same problems afflicting the core city. With the population shift to suburbia, the "urban crisis" in America has become the "urban-suburban crisis," or, more accurately, a "metropolitan crisis."

The Problems of the Cities

In Greece more than 2,000 years ago planners dreamed of a new city-state called Megalopolis. *Polis* was the Greek word for "city-state" (from which "politics" is derived), and *mega* comes from the word for "large," so Megalopolis meant a very large city. In 1961 Jean Gottmann used the word to describe "the unique cluster of metropolitan areas of the northeastern seaboard of the United States."[44]

Stretching 600 miles through 11 states and the District of Columbia, in a band ranging from 30 to 100 miles wide, this region contained more than 55 million people and included the cities of Boston, New York, Philadelphia, Baltimore, and Washington.[45] Driving through the area seemed almost like traveling in one continuous community. Some urban experts foresee the time when the United States will have three megalopolises, "Boswash" (the corridor from Boston to Washington), "Chipitts" (a strip from Chicago to Pittsburgh), and "San-San" (San Francisco to San Diego) along the West Coast.

But is this how people were meant to live? Since the beginning of civilization, people have clustered together in cities, which have served as magnets of communication, commerce, and culture. But critics of megalopolis have deplored the effect of the modern city on the quality of life. Lewis Mumford has asked: "Will the whole planet turn into a vast urban hive?"[46] Mumford argued that the modern metropolis has grown in "a continuous shapeless mass" and that its residents are subject to constant frustration and harassment in their daily lives while becoming increasingly removed from nature.[47]

On the other hand, Edward C. Banfield has argued that most city dwellers "live more comfortably and conveniently than ever before." In Banfield's view, many urban problems—congestion, for example—are overstated: "People come to the city . . . precisely because it is congested. If it were not congested, it would not be worth coming to." In defending the city, Banfield adds: "To a large extent, then, our urban problems are just like the mechanical rabbit at the racetrack, which is set to keep just ahead of the dogs no matter how fast they may run. Our performance is better and better but because we set our standards and expectations to keep ahead of performance, the problems are never any nearer to solution."[48] Despite Banfield's defense of urban life, a more general view is that the nation's cities are in difficulty and that problems such as poverty, crime, drugs, racial inequalities, housing, transportation, and the quality of public education are not being solved fast enough in what is often perceived as the world's richest society.

Part of the problem is that cities are no longer performing the same role they performed in the past. In the 19th and early 20th centuries, America's cities were great socializing engines, taking unskilled immigrants from Europe and, in a generation or two, turning many of them into middle-class or even affluent Americans. Some of this is still taking place; the Cubans who migrated to Miami and the Mexicans and other Hispanics who settled in Texas, California, and other areas have become a political force, and in the past two decades Asian immigrants have contributed significantly to the urban mix.

But to an extent, the socializing process has stopped. Many of the migrants to the cities in recent decades have been African Americans who historically, especially among those with lower incomes, have not been integrated into American society in the same way as the Irish, Italians, Jews, Poles, and other groups; African Americans have faced greater and more persistent discrimination.

"Help!"

Cities and Suburbs: The Metropolitan Dilemma　**657**

FIGURE 19-4

Distribution of White and African American Population, 1990

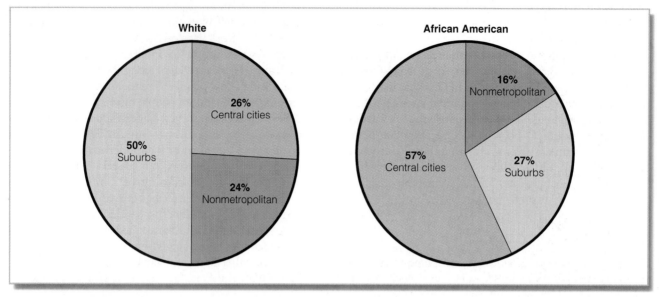

White

50%
Suburbs

26%
Central cities

24%
Nonmetropolitan

African American

16%
Nonmetropolitan

57%
Central cities

27%
Suburbs

SOURCE: Adapted from U.S. Bureau of the Census, 1990 Census of Population, "Race, Hispanic Origin, and Group Quarters Population: Metropolitan Areas, 1990," p. 4. Preliminary data, percentages rounded.

Who will pay for the cost of providing schools, housing, and other social services for residents of the inner city? That remains the core of the dilemma: The cities say they cannot do it, and many residents of the suburbs either have little desire to do so or feel they cannot afford higher taxes. City mayors complain that the federal government has simply not allocated enough money to bridge the gap. And many taxpayers—82 percent in one survey—either do not want an increase in services that would require higher taxes, or they favor a decrease in taxes and services.[49]

Despite the popular image of poor whites and African Americans pouring into the cities to go on welfare, one study of urban migration indicates that people come to the cities for jobs, not social services, and that, compared to the nonwhite population already living in the cities, the average nonwhite who comes to the city has a higher occupational and educational background.[50] But the newcomers face job and housing discrimination; they are not in the same position as whites moving to a pleasant suburban neighborhood. As one observer put it, "The Welcome Wagon rarely calls in the ghetto."[51] (See Figure 19-4.)

One approach to revitalizing the inner cities is the creation of **enterprise zones,** areas in which businesses are encouraged to locate because of tax breaks and other incentives. President Bush supported this concept, but in 1992 he vetoed a bill to create 50 such zones, saying the measure would have raised taxes. By then, however, 36 states and the District of Columbia had already established more than 1,000 such zones. Many local govern-

ments in these areas combined tax benefits to businesses in the zones with increased police and fire protection and street improvements.[52]

Urban problems are complex and often have resulted in physical deterioration of the cities. Some cities have attempted to reverse the trend by building attractive new commercial or residential complexes in the downtown area. Baltimore's impressive Inner Harbor complex of markets, restaurants, and museums, which opened in 1980, is one example, and similar projects have been developed in Boston and Philadelphia. But some critics have argued that expensive downtown centers, catering mainly to business executives, visitors, and the affluent, may only serve to mask the continuing and serious social and economic problems of the cities.

The challenges faced by America's cities were dramatically illustrated in New York City more than 25 years ago. On a bleak day in October 1975, the city stood literally only two hours away from financial default. The proud eastern metropolis, which considers itself America's cultural and business leader, the city that is the home of Wall Street and the great television networks, stood on the brink of insolvency. It was unable to meet its fiscal obligations to its bondholders.

At that perilous moment, Albert Shanker, the leader of the city's teachers' union, came forward and saved New York from default by investing $150 million from union pension funds in the bonds of the Municipal Assistance Corporation, known colloquially as "Big Mac."

There was widespread fear at the time that if New York went under, other cities facing similar financial

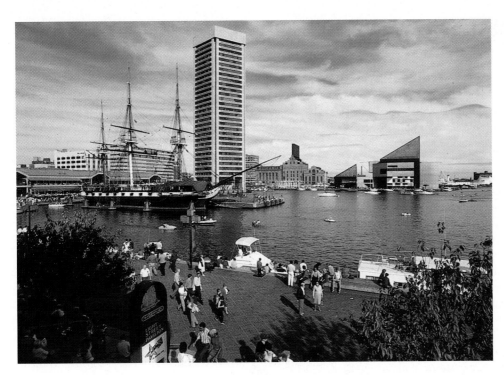

The Inner Harbor, Baltimore, Maryland
George Hall/Woodfin Camp & Associates

problems might find it impossible to sell their bonds to investors, which in turn could have serious effects on the national economy. The crisis faced by New York City had historical roots. For many years, the city, which has a liberal political tradition, spent billions for social services and welfare programs. At the same time, its expenditures were rising much faster than its revenues.[53]

But mounting city deficits—despite heavy borrowing—had shaken the municipal bond market. Put simply, the city found that no one wanted its bonds. New York State moved to help the city and also established an emergency financial control board to monitor city spending. That meant that the governor and a state-dominated board, rather than the city's mayor, were then in control of the city's finances.[54]

In the 1976 election year, President Ford, sensing a profitable political issue, campaigned for a time against New York City. "I am prepared to veto any bill that has as its purpose a federal bailout of New York City to prevent a default," he said.[55] By November the hostility toward New York had given way to fear; bankers, economists, and politicians worried that the snowballing effect of default by the city might cause a more general financial crisis. Ford reversed course and proposed a $2.3 billion package of aid to New York City, which Congress approved. The immediate crisis was over.

In Donald H. Haider's view, the city's troubles stemmed from "an insufficient tax base to carry out the range of services and redistributive programs to which it gradually had become wedded."[56] By 1987, however, New York City had paid off all of its loans and was considered one of the most stable economic regions in the country. But the crisis a decade earlier, the precarious

situation that had been faced by the nation's largest city and its more than 7 million residents, had served as a dramatic reminder of the serious nature of the problems confronting America's cities.

Housing, HUD, and Community Development

Officials of the federal government and others who have studied urban problems differ widely on how to break the circle of poverty in the inner city. Where should government begin in attempting to eliminate poverty? With housing? Schools? Jobs? All of those things at once? Nobody really knows the answer.

The difficulties of making progress in attacking the overall problem can be illustrated by a close look at just one aspect of urban needs: housing. Substandard housing exists in rural as well as urban areas. Nevertheless, deteriorating inner-city neighborhoods were and are a highly visible, urgent social problem.

How well has government coped with that problem? In the Housing Act of 1949, Congress proclaimed the goal of "a decent home and a suitable living environment for every American family." That goal, the law states, shall be met "as soon as feasible." Yet, more than four decades later, there were still 6.1 million dwellings listed as physically inadequate in the United States.[57]

The government has spent billions on housing, yet the federal effort has nowhere near kept pace with the need for better housing. And many public housing projects tend to be institutional-looking sterile places plagued by crime, drugs, and vandalism. In St. Louis, the government razed the Pruitt-Igoe housing project,

THE MYTH OF MONEY

There is a wistful myth that if only we had enough money to spend—the figure is usually put at a hundred billion dollars—we could wipe out all our slums in ten years, reverse decay in the great, dull, gray belts that were yesterday's and day-before-yesterday's suburbs, anchor the wandering middle class and its wandering tax money, and perhaps even solve the traffic problem.

But look what we have built with the first several billions: Low-income projects that become worse centers of delinquency, vandalism, and general social hopelessness than the slums they were supposed to replace. Middle-income housing projects which are truly marvels of dullness and regimentation, sealed against any buoyancy or vitality of city life. Luxury housing projects that mitigate their inanity, or try to, with a vapid vulgarity. Cultural centers that are unable to support a good bookstore. Civic centers that are avoided by everyone but bums, who have fewer choices of loitering place than others. Commercial centers that are lackluster imitations of standardized suburban chainstore shopping. Promenades that go from no place to nowhere and have no promenaders. Expressways that eviscerate great cities. That is not the rebuilding of cities. This is the sacking of cities.

—Jane Jacobs, *The Death and Life of Great American Cities*

which had been built with federal support, because vandals and the high crime rate had led to the abandonment of most of the apartments.

In many cities—most notably in St. Louis and the South Bronx in New York—whole neighborhoods have become wastelands of rubble-strewn streets, boarded-up and abandoned buildings, vacant lots, and stripped automobiles. Across the nation, tens of thousands of deteriorated housing units have been abandoned.

Sometimes federal programs appear to have conflicting goals. More than 800 communities and practically every large city in America participated in the federal urban renewal program that began in 1949. Under the program, the federal government defrayed two-thirds to three-fourths of the cost. In many cases, however, urban renewal merely added to inner-city tensions by forcing poor people from their homes to make way for middle- or upper-income housing and commercial centers. Fannie Lou Hamer, an outspoken African American civil rights leader in Mississippi, made this observation on the subject of urban renewal: "We're already living nowhere, and now they're going to move us out of that."[58]

The responsibility of the federal government for housing was given recognition at the cabinet level in 1965 when Congress established the Department of Housing and Urban Development (HUD). The same year, Congress passed a comprehensive housing bill, including for the first time a program of rent supplements for low-income families.

The Pruitt-Igoe housing project is dynamited in St. Louis.
AP/Wide World

President Nixon curtailed or ended a number of federal housing programs, arguing that federally aided public housing had often failed. "All across America, the federal government has become the biggest slumlord in history," Nixon said.[59]

As an alternative to public housing, the Nixon Administration started a program of rent subsidies in private housing for very low-income families. The program, known as Section 8, provides vouchers that people can present to participating landlords. Families that qualify pay about 30 percent of their income in rent, and the federal government makes up the rest. In the year 2000, Section 8 was the nation's major public housing program, providing help to 3.6 million poor persons.

Some middle-class voters have opposed spending tax money for low-income housing for the poor. Yet middle-income and more affluent homeowners receive what amounts to a federal housing subsidy because they can deduct the interest they pay on their mortgage loans in figuring their federal income taxes. Low- and middle-income homeowners benefit as well from the fact that the Federal Housing Administration (FHA) insures the mortgages of many homes.

Federal housing policy is closely related to civil rights issues. In 1977 the Supreme Court held that suburban communities could not be compelled to change their zoning to permit low- and middle-income housing unless the "intent" of the zoning was to keep out African Americans or other minorities.[60] As a result, suburbs had consider-

WELFARE IN THE LAND OF PLENTY

MARSHALLTOWN, IOWA—This city of 25,000 sits amid cornfields and factories in the center of a state that has been riding out the recession with one of the lowest unemployment levels in the country. Yet around 2,000 poor people here are getting help of some kind from the welfare system, from vouchers to heat a house to a regular welfare check.

This is not the South Bronx or Appalachia, where poverty often gets blamed on culture or behavior, on racism or reckless childbearing.

But Marshalltown shows with unusual clarity other powerful forces that make welfare and poverty hard to escape anywhere: the nation's proliferation of low-wage jobs and two decades of falling wages, especially for the least skilled, in terms of what they can buy. . . .

But no one can blame racism for poverty here. Ninety-eight percent of the 38,000 people of Marshall County, of which Marshalltown is the seat, are white, as are nearly all the families on welfare.

—New York Times, July 7, 1992

HOUSING PROGRAMS DON'T ALWAYS WORK

LOUISVILLE, OHIO—For two decades, the Federal Government's Section 8 housing subsidy program has helped poor working people like Wanda Schott get off welfare. After spending two years on a waiting list, Ms. Schott, a divorced mother of two boys, became eligible for one of those precious Section 8 vouchers and, in 1994 used it to rent a trailer in this suburb of Canton.

Not long after, she got off welfare, taking a 25-hour-a-week job in the bakery at the I.G.A. supermarket in the Buckeye Village shopping center. A few afternoons a week she works a second job, for a lawn care service.

Then, in April, the county housing authority determined that the trailer no longer met Federal housing standards. Ms. Schott had 90 days to find another apartment that would accept her Section 8 voucher.

She was not able to, though she searched frantically, visiting 20 apartments a month. "I looked everywhere," Ms. Schott said. . . .

For now, she has moved her two boys in with her mother, but there is no room for her. So Ms. Schott sleeps in her '72 Ford truck, which she keeps parked in her mother's driveway, filled with pillows and cushions and a windup alarm clock to wake her for work.

—New York Times, July 22, 1996

able power to exclude public housing. "For large numbers of suburbanites," Michael N. Danielson has observed, "subsidized housing is a threat, the incarnation of everything in urban society they have sought to insulate themselves from in politically autonomous communities."[61] Danielson suggests that racial prejudice is an important factor in such suburban resistance to housing projects, but he argues that many suburbanites are also concerned about the socioeconomic impact in their communities of low-income families; they fear lower property values, increased crime, and higher taxes for social services.[62]

In the 1980s, a goal of President Reagan's administration was to end construction of low-cost public housing. Although Congress funded some public housing during the eight Reagan years, total outlays for new public housing dropped by 80 percent.[63]

In fiscal 2001 the federal government had budgeted $32.4 billion for housing programs, including funds designed to allow persons with low incomes to buy their own homes, and block grants to help state and local governments to assist low-income families. About 4.3 million households were receiving assistance from HUD. But the number of people living in substandard housing was much greater than the number receiving help from the federal government.

Taken as a whole, the federal housing program illustrates the difficulties confronting the nation in meeting the urban crisis. Although housing has been recognized as a cabinet-level problem, the provision of decent housing for all Americans remains a goal rather than a reality.

Urban Transportation

The reporter in the traffic helicopter seldom broadcasts good news; getting in and out of the nation's cities during morning and evening rush hours, or getting to work within the city limits, is often an ordeal. Americans spend a substantial part of their lives commuting to and from their jobs; and time spent in a crowded subway, as Lewis Mumford has suggested, takes its toll: "Emerson said that life was a matter of having good days, but it is a matter of having good minutes too. Who shall say what compensations are not necessary to the metropolitan worker to make up for the strain and depression of the twenty, forty, sixty, or more minutes he spends each night and morning passing through these metropolitan man-sewers?"[64]

Metropolitan transportation in the United States has been dominated by the automobile and the highway. Commuter railroads and other forms of mass transit were permitted to decline during the 1950s and 1960s. Federal policy has to some extent influenced the dominance of highways over rails. The federal government pays 90 percent of the cost of the huge interstate highway program, a massive incentive for states and cities to build roads rather than transit lines. The federal funds come from highway user taxes on trucks and buses, tires, and gasoline; the program, passed by Congress in 1956, was designed to link the nation's cities with 41,000 miles of superhighways, almost all of them four-lane. Powerful interest groups have major stakes in

highway politics. But the nation has been slow to develop an overall transportation policy, one that would balance highways and rapid transit, and ease congestion in metropolitan centers. The nation's dependence on the

Neal Boenzi/NYT Pictures

automobile became painfully obvious when Americans were confronted in 1973 and 1979 with a shortage of oil and gasoline, and more recently, when gasoline prices soared to more than $2 a gallon in some parts of the country during the summer of 2000.

The Urban Mass Transportation Act of 1970 authorized a 10-year, $12 billion program to enable cities to build or improve rapid rail, subway, and bus commuter lines. Congress in 1973 for the first time approved the use of millions of dollars in the Highway Trust Fund for urban transit needs. In the years since then, Congress has provided more billions for urban mass transit and highways, including bridge repairs and highway construction, financed in part from an increase in the tax on gasoline.

San Francisco's gleaming BART subway system, the Metro subway in Washington, D.C., and Atlanta's MARTA and Dallas's DART are examples of both the benefits and limitations of mass transit. BART has provided modern transportation for many residents of the San Francisco Bay area, but it has not—as its sponsors hoped—substantially reduced traffic jams on the highways or the bridges over the bay. The commuters who now use BART instead of cars to get to work appear to have been replaced by other drivers.

 for more information about San Francisco's BART, Washington's Metro, Atlanta's MARTA, and Dallas's DART, see: www.bart.org; www.wmata.com; www.marta.com; and www.dart.org

The first segment of Washington's Metro opened in 1976 and provided fast, comfortable, and esthetically pleasing downtown transportation for the nation's capital. In 2001, the 103-mile system that was originally planned had been completed. Metro's construction costs had soared to $10 billion, but the system had proved an enormous benefit to the area's commuters and visitors to the nation's capital. And additional lines were under consideration, including one to Dulles Airport in Virginia.

Urban rapid transit systems are often affected by local politics. In Dallas, for example, the two branches of the first section of DART served mostly black and Hispanic neighborhoods south of the downtown area. Political leaders from these neighborhoods had successfully fought earlier plans to build the first part of the system in white areas north of downtown. Lines to serve the communities to the north and west were to open later.

As attractive as these urban rail systems are, they are unsuitable for many cities, which cannot afford them. Because commuters travel to widely scattered destinations, rail lines do not take most people where they want to go. As a result, urban rail links are often difficult to justify in economic terms. And for most people the automobile still offers the most convenient form of transportation.

Problems interlock. The dominance of the automobile and the highway is directly related both to the energy crisis and to the problem of pollution, since automobiles produce at least 60 percent of total air pollution in the United States (electric power plants and industry account for most of the rest).

Poverty

Poverty remains a pervasive problem in American cities, overshadowing or underlying almost all other problems. According to the Census Bureau, in 1990 about 73 percent of all persons with low incomes lived in metropolitan areas. Of these, more than 48 percent of poor whites lived in the central cities, but for African Americans the total was more than 76 percent.[65]

This does not mean that urban and racial problems are synonymous. However, the African American, Mexican American, or Puerto Rican child in the inner city is often caught up in a cycle of poverty from which there is often no exit. Education may be one key to eliminating poverty, but inner-city schools often occupy the oldest buildings and have the least experienced teachers, since many teachers with seniority shun assignments to those classrooms. African Americans and other minorities face discrimination in employment and housing as well. Unlike such physical problems as transportation or air pollution, racial bias involves social attitudes that work against certain minority groups. Many of the problems of the nation's cities, therefore, are bound up with the larger problem of ensuring full equality for all Americans.

Urban Politics: Governing the Cities

The term **power structure** was popularized in the 1950s by Floyd Hunter, a sociologist who studied community leadership in Atlanta, Georgia.[66] Hunter concluded that a group of about 40 people, mostly top businessmen, determined policy in Atlanta and used the machinery of government to attain their own goals.

But in a study of New Haven, Connecticut, Robert A. Dahl concluded that the city was not run by a single power elite of economic or social notables, and that policy decisions were made by changing coalitions of leaders drawn from different segments of the community.[67] As noted in Chapter 6, scholars have provided diverse answers to the question of "Who governs?" Some scholars argue that power elites make public policy, but other political scientists see American society as pluralistic, with many—although not all—groups sharing in the decision making.

Edward C. Banfield and James Q. Wilson have contended that, regardless of how decisions are made in various American cities, all cities have one thing in common: "Persons not elected to office play very considerable parts in the making of many important decisions."[68] Banfield and Wilson have suggested the term "influentials" for powerful citizens who hold no official position.

When most people think of city government, however, they usually think of decisions being made by officials elected to political office by the voters. As on the national and state levels, parties, politics, and the ballot box play a central role in the decisions made at the city level that affect people's lives.

But cities are not nations. Paul E. Peterson has argued that cities "cannot make war or peace; they cannot issue passports or forbid outsiders from entering their territory" and as a result are limited in the policies they can adopt.[69]

Moreover, cities are limited in size and geographical jurisdiction and they must compete with each other for new industry. As a result, Peterson maintains, cities tend to favor policies that "enhance the economic position of a community in its competition with others."[70] They do not favor policies that benefit the poor but cost money and create economic risks for the cities. If cities attempt to redistribute income—to raise taxes to finance large-scale social programs—they face the danger that businesses and employees will leave. Given these constraints, Peterson concludes, the cities are, for the most part, unable to redistribute income effectively to help the disadvantaged.[71]

Population trends, as well as economic factors, affect city government. One result of the migration of many whites to the suburbs has been that more cities with a large African American electorate have chosen African American officials. There were black mayors in many large cities, including Detroit, San Francisco, Dallas, St. Louis, Memphis, Denver, and Washington, D.C.[72] In several of these cities the African American population exceeded the white population. In all, there were 445 American cities with African American mayors.[73]

Historically, the big-city political machine has characterized urban politics. The political machines traded jobs and social services for the votes of immigrants. But with the changing nature of American society, urban political machines have declined. The power of Tammany

Mayor Richard J. Daley of Chicago
Dennis Brack/Black Star

Hall was broken in New York City in the early 1960s by a Democratic reform movement. In Chicago the reign of Chicago's powerful political leader, Mayor Richard J. Daley, often described as the last of the big-city bosses, ended with his death in 1976.

As the tightly structured, old-style political machines have faded away, mayors of large cities have found it more difficult to govern. Their power has become diffused. One reason for this is the growth of "functional fiefdoms," specialized government agencies that operate specific programs, such as urban renewal or highway construction.[74] As these agencies have increased in number, they have often made independent decisions, bypassing mayors and city councils.

Just as public administrators exercise great power in the federal government, on the local level bureaucracies influence and limit the power of a big-city mayor, as do other factors. One study of urban politics noted that the mayor of New York must share his power with party leaders, appointed and elected public officials, the bureaucracy, nongovernmental associations, the media, and officials and agencies of governments outside New York City. Since no one group dominates, decisions are actually the result of "mutual accommodation."[75] In short, the business of governing a metropolis usually means that mayors are constantly striving to build and maintain workable coalitions of interest groups; their power is limited and they are handy targets when things go wrong. Another study of how mayors govern found at least five distinct mayoral styles and concluded that no one approach was necessarily the "best." And the study noted that mayors, because of the difficulties and frustrations of their jobs, may not ever achieve any higher political office.[76]

The Face of the Suburbs

The 1990 census figures confirmed the existence of a trend that urban specialists had begun to suspect several years earlier—some suburbs closest to central cities were actually losing population.

"This is a national phenomenon," Dr. George Sternlieb of Rutgers University said. "It is a pattern that is occurring within every large metropolitan area." Blue- and white-collar workers, he said, are "leapfrogging" farther out into "exurbia" to find housing they can afford.[77]

The changing population pattern in the suburbs was in marked contrast to the massive migration to the closer-in suburbs after the Second World War. One of the phenomena of that migration was the construction of whole new communities by a single builder. In 1958 Herbert J. Gans, a young sociologist, moved with his family into one such instant suburb, Levittown, New Jersey. His purpose was to study the community as a participant and observer. In recording the quality of social life in this suburb of Philadelphia, Gans quoted one woman describing her next-door neighbor: "We see eye to eye on things, about raising kids, doing things together with your husband, living the same way; we have practically the same identical background."[78]

Although most suburbs are not modeled on Levittown, the quote summarizes both sides of the argument about suburbia. In an impersonal society, where people toil on assembly lines or in beehive offices of large corporations, many Americans long for a sense of identity and belonging. In part, people have moved to the suburbs in "a search for community." To some extent, the migration to the suburbs may be seen as a turning back to the grass-roots, a yearning for the small-town America celebrated by Booth Tarkington and Mark Twain. On the other hand, the suburbs have been assailed as centers of conformity and homogeneity, in which community pressures tend to produce narrow social and political attitudes among suburbanites and massive unconcern for urban and national problems.

Why do people move to the suburbs in the first place? According to Peter H. Rossi, they are both "pushed" and "pulled."[79] The "push" reasons are often emphasized: crime in the cities, bad schools, deteriorating housing. But the "pull" reasons are also highly important: the desire for more space and to "own our own home" and the attraction of suburban schools, for example. The automobile and FHA mortgage guarantees, allowing lower- and middle-income families to purchase their own homes, have been powerful factors as well.

The move to suburbia has brought change to the center of America's cities. A number of cities have revitalized their downtown districts. In many metropolitan areas, however, not only people, but also jobs and industry, have moved to the suburbs. Suburban residents no longer need to go to the city to shop; the department stores have moved to suburban shopping malls to be near them. Or people can shop on the Internet. There is still a need for downtown business areas, but often less as centers of retail trade than as places for the conduct of businesses that require face-to-face contact—banking, finance, and communications, for example.

Rafael Maldonado/*Santa Barbara News-Press*

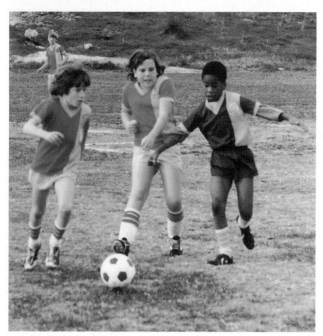

David Wise

Not all suburbs are alike. Some of the older, more affluent suburbs have been able to preserve their residential character. But the newer suburbs have mammoth retail shopping centers, office buildings, industrial parks, and other hallmarks of cities. As Louis H. Masotti has noted, suburbia is "becoming increasingly less suburban and more urban."[80]

In the popular image, however, life in the suburbs tends to be centered around home and family. And the stereotype of the suburban father happily barbecuing steaks on his outdoor grill or fussing with his lawn sometimes reflects the reality. But what about his less fortunate fellow citizens back in the city? Gans suggests that the Levittowners "deceive themselves into thinking that the community, or rather the home, is the single most influential unit in their lives. . . . The real problem is that the Levittowners have not yet become aware of how much they are a part of the national society and economy."[81]

Today, however, the suburbs face many of the same problems that are faced by cities. The suburbanites who take pride in their shrubs, homes, and communities are also part of a larger American community with many unpleasant problems that cannot be wished away. Particularly the older suburbs, closest to the central cities, are experiencing difficulties, including rising welfare costs, crime, and physical deterioration. The quality of life in the nation as a whole is to a great extent reflected in the suburbs. For example, it might surprise most Americans to know that the majority of welfare recipients live in suburbs, small towns, and rural areas—not in the inner cities.[82]

Although social problems such as inferior education, poor housing, crime, and inadequate health care have greatest impact in the cities, "they are not unknown to the suburbs and are increasingly being found there. . . . More and more suburban communities have city-like characteristics and all the problems associated with those characteristics."[83] There is, in short, no place to hide from the problems faced by American society as a whole.

The Politics of Suburbia

The fact that more Americans live in what could be termed "the suburbs" might be expected to have a major impact on the political system. A closely related question is whether people who live in the suburbs really hold different political views from residents of other

HOW ONE WOMAN MOVED A PIPELINE

CLINTON CORNERS, N.Y., May 28—In the tradition of ordinary people who wage crusades against big business, Anne Marie Mueser may set a new standard of stubbornness. To fight a pipeline, she put aside just about everything for 10 years, including, she says, cleaning her rickety farmhouse and painting her dilapidated barn.

Her target was a company that built one of the largest utility projects in the Northeast in years, the Iroquois Pipeline, which brings Canadian natural gas through New York State and Connecticut to Long Island.

She was vindicated on May 23, when the Iroquois Pipeline Operating Company, its former president and three other former executives pleaded guilty to violating Federal environmental laws by failing to install required erosion-control devices. The company agreed to pay $22 million in fines in what prosecutors said was the biggest environmental settlement since the Exxon *Valdez* case.

The battle she started in 1987 and, for some reason, refused to give up, is one of those David-and-Goliath yarns that include dozens of boxes of evidence, angry farmers and suggestions about which actors to cast in the movie. The most dramatic scene would undoubtedly be the one in which just about everyone acknowledges that she is largely responsible for the humiliation of a big company. . . . She quickly defeated a plan to put [the pipeline] through her . . . property here. . . .

In a baggy T-shirt, with long gray hair, she chortled about the buttoned-down types she had tied in knots. "It was kind of interesting," she said, "being in a room full of $300-an-hour-plus suits and beating them at their own game."

—*New York Times*, June 4, 1996

Kim Kulish/NYT Pictures

areas, or whether the suburbs are merely experiencing the first stages of urbanization—growing into cities, as it were.

One way to measure the political impact of the population shift to suburbia is to study the reflection of that growth in the Congress. Richard Lehne has noted that in 1974, following the redistricting in Congress after the 1970 census, the 132 representatives from suburban areas for the first time composed the largest single group in Congress. In other words, there were more legislators from the suburbs than from the cities or from rural areas. That trend has continued.

"The election of large and increasing numbers of suburban representatives to Congress means that, today and in the future, Congress must come to grips with the policy positions and reform preferences of suburbanites," Richard Lehne has suggested.[84] Analyzing ratings of representatives by interest groups, Lehne concluded that central-city legislators take liberal policy positions, rural representatives favor conservative policies, and men and women who represent suburban constituents "strike a moderate balance between the other two groups."[85]

But Lehne also discovered that members of Congress from older, established suburbs tend to take more liberal positions on most issues than representatives from the newer suburbs. These findings, Lehne concluded, support those who contend that the process of urbanization has extended to the suburbs. The members of Congress from older suburbs tended to vote much like their city cousins.[86]

Another study of emerging suburban political power, by Thomas P. Murphy and John Rehfuss, found great diversity among the suburbs and their representatives in Congress. "Despite the increase in the number of congressmen representing suburban districts," the authors said, "a strong suburban bloc has not emerged." One reason they cite is that "different types of suburbs have different needs." The study concluded: "'Suburban power' remains a paper tiger, but it has the potential to exert great influence."[87]

EXPLODING METROPOLIS AND AMERICA'S FUTURE

Metropolitan Solutions

Two overriding conclusions may be drawn from a number of studies of state and local problems:

1. Many of the problems are larger than the boundaries of the governmental units that are attempting to deal with them. Smog, for example, respects no city lines, and the issue of commuter transportation in a metropolitan area may involve as many as two dozen local communities.
2. The solutions frequently cost more than the governmental units have available or are willing to spend. A suburban area cannot possibly afford, for example, to build a mass-transit line to carry its residents to downtown offices, nor can the central cities raise the tax revenues to provide adequate social services for those inner-city residents who need them most.

If metropolitan problems are larger than the boundary lines of local governments, why not create larger political units to solve these problems? The approach might seem logical, but there are many obstacles to metropolitan government. Not the least of these is the

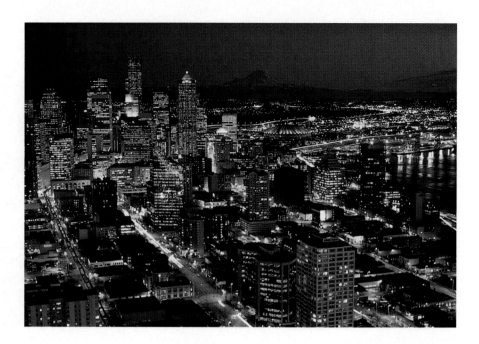

Seattle, Washington
Copyright © M. Sulik/Image Works

reluctance of suburban areas to give up their political independence and to pay for services for residents of the central cities. And African American residents of the cities, having finally achieved greater political power—and with African American mayors elected in several major cities—are equally reluctant to lose that hard-won power to a metropolitan government.

Some efforts at "metro" solutions are being made, however, including the creation of special districts to handle specific functions, interstate compacts, areawide planning agencies, consolidated school and library systems, and various informal intergovernmental arrangements. Annexation of outlying areas by the central city and the consolidation of cities and surrounding counties have all been tried; in many cases, they have been found wanting. Another approach has been the plan adopted in Los Angeles, under which the county has assumed responsibility for many areawide functions, but local communities have retained their political autonomy.

Some urban experts have advocated metropolitan federalism as the best solution. Toronto, Canada, and its suburbs have operated under this system since 1953. Mass transit, planning, highways, and many other functions are run by a council made up of elected officials from the central city and surrounding suburbs.

In Florida, Miami and Dade County narrowly opted for "Metro" government in 1957. Under the plan, Miami and 27 suburban cities retain control of local functions, but have ceded to "Metro" many areawide functions such as fire and police protection and transportation. Political control is vested in an elected board of commissioners, which appoints a county manager.

Varying degrees of areawide consolidation have been established in Nashville, Tennessee; Jacksonville, Florida; Baton Rouge, Louisiana; Indianapolis, Indiana;

Columbus and Athens, Georgia; Lexington, Kentucky; and Butte, Montana. By 1996 there had been 27 consolidations.[88]

Despite steps toward consolidation and metropolitan government in many areas of the country, some scholars have strongly disputed the "reformist" belief that a single metropolitan government, by eliminating overlapping jurisdictions, will promote greater efficiency. For example, one study has concluded that because individuals have different preferences in government services, "a system of government composed of many different units will be more responsive to the interests of citizens than a single government for any one urban region."[89]

As urban growth continues, however, old concepts of metropolitan areas may change. The cities of the industrial Northeast, for example, may indeed come closer to the concept of "Boswash." One scholar has suggested that tomorrow's metropolis may look less like a fried egg, with a clearly defined center and outer ring, and more like "a thin layer of scrambled eggs over much of the platter."[90]

Intergovernmental Relations

Although this chapter has focused on state and local problems, any real solution to metropolitan ills depends in large measure on the relationship among federal, state, and local governments.

Although the states were doing relatively well financially in 2000, state and local governments often do not have enough revenues to meet the social demands of both urban and rural areas. The confusing, overlapping programs of federal grants have been widely criticized. At the same time, state and local revenues have frequently lagged behind national economic growth. The federal system, insofar as intergovernmental fiscal relations are concerned, has become rather creaky at the joints.

The American Challenge

The problems discussed in this chapter involve the question of what kind of nation America wants to be. How people live in their local communities reflects the quality of American life.

Do Americans have a sense of national community? Will comfortable or affluent Americans be willing to have their taxes used to provide better schools and other social services for those with lower incomes? There is no constitutional requirement that an affluent majority take such steps on behalf of a less affluent minority. But the future of the nation's democratic institutions may be affected by the answer. John Gardner, a former cabinet member, has suggested:

> If Americans continue on their present path their epitaph might well be that they were a potentially great people—a marvelously dynamic people—who forgot their obligations to one another, who forgot how much they owed one another.[91]

A further question is whether political institutions created when America was a rural nation can respond to, and cope with, the demands and problems of a highly urbanized, changing society. American democracy is under pressure; its institutions are being tested. Yet, the problems of American society—education, affordable health care, environmental pollution, racial discrimination, periodic economic ills, crime, drugs, poverty, homelessness, political corruption, energy resources, and all the rest—are not necessarily beyond solution if Americans, acting through the political process, insist on change. To a great extent, the America of tomorrow can be what the American people make it.

More than 100 years ago, the English philosopher John Stuart Mill voiced much the same thought in his essay *On Liberty:* "The worth of a State, in the long run, is the worth of the individuals composing it."

KEY TERMS

initiative, p. 647
referendum, p. 648
recall, p. 648
line-item veto, p. 648
bicameral legislature,
   p. 651
unicameral legislature,
   p. 651

home rule, p. 654
mayor-council plan,
   p. 655
council-manager plan,
   p. 655
commission plan, p. 655
enterprise zones, p. 658
power structure, p. 663

CHAPTER HIGHLIGHTS

✦ America is a nation of states. The political institutions of the 13 colonies foreshadowed the shape of the federal system created under the Constitution. The states, in short, were here before the American nation.

✦ The states have major responsibilities in the fields of education, welfare, transportation, the administration of justice, the prisons, housing, public health, and the environment.

✦ State constitutions spell out the basic structure of each state government. Every state constitution provides for an executive, legislative, and judicial branch. Although each includes a bill of rights, some state constitutions are more liberal than others.

✦ The most common means of amending state constitutions is by a majority or two-thirds vote of the legislature and approval by a majority of the voters at the next election.

✦ Forty-one states permit constitutional conventions to amend their constitutions, with the changes subject to approval by the voters.

✦ Most states now either permit their constitutions to be amended, or laws enacted, by initiative.

✦ Every state has provisions for the referendum, a method that allows voters, in effect, to "veto" a bill passed by the legislature or to accept or reject a proposal, such as a bond issue, made by a government agency.

✦ Sixteen states also allow the recall, a procedure that in certain circumstances permits voters to remove elected state officials from office before their terms have expired.

✦ About half the states have widely varying provisions for local home rule. As the term implies, home rule empowers municipalities to modify their charters and run their affairs without approval by the legislature, subject to the constitution and laws of the state.

✦ One of the most important and politically powerful jobs of the state legislatures is to redraw the district lines for the U.S. House of Representatives every 10 years after the national census. This task often leads to fierce political infighting, because the party in power in the legislature can draw the lines to favor their own members of Congress.

✦ Under the mayor-council form of government, power is divided between a mayor and an elected city council.

✦ The council-manager form of government has a council, usually elected on a nonpartisan ticket, that hires a professional city manager who runs the city government and has power to hire and fire city officials. The council in turn has power to fire the city manager (although the city council is not supposed to interfere in the day-to-day administration of city affairs).

✦ The commission plan has a board of city commissioners, usually five, that is popularly elected. The commissioners make policy as a city council, but they also run the city departments as administrators.

✦ One approach to revitalizing the inner cities is the creation of enterprise zones, areas in which businesses are encouraged to locate because of tax breaks and other incentives.

SUGGESTED WEB SITES

www.stateline.org
Stateline
Contains the latest news about the states, in-depth information about each state, and background on important issues.

www.ncsl.org
National Conference of State Legislators
Offers information about state lawmakers. Click on "Public User" to find information about state legislators, federal-state relations, a description of the initiatives and referendums on the ballots, and information about various policy issues.

www.iandrinstitute.org
Initiative and Referendum Institute
A nonprofit, nonpartisan organization that focuses on the different types of initiatives and referendums at the local, state, and international levels.

SUGGESTED READING

Banfield, Edward C., and Wilson, James Q. *City Politics* (Harvard University Press, 1963). A comprehensive examination of politics in American cities.

Beyle, Thad L., and Muchmore, Lynn, eds. *Being Governor: The View from the Office* (Duke University Press, 1983). A valuable and revealing collection of articles on the way governors view their office and responsibilities. Based on surveys of governors, former governors, and their staffs.

Book of the States, 2000–2001 (Council of State Governments, 2000). A useful, up-to-date compilation of statistics summarizing social, economic and political indicators for each of the American states.

Gottmann, Jean. *Megalopolis Revisited* (University of Maryland Press, 1987). An update of a pioneering study of the geographical, economic, social, and cultural characteristics of America's northeastern urban corridor.

Gray, Virginia, and Jacob, Herbert, eds. *Politics in the American States: A Comparative Analysis*, 7th edition* (CQ Press, l999). A useful collection of essays on various aspects of the political systems in the states, written by a number of leading authorities in the field.

Harrigan, John J. *Political Change in the Metropolis*, 6th edition (Addison-Wesley, 1999). A detailed assessment of political change in urban America. Harrigan focuses on the decline of the old-style political machine and on the growth of specialized government agencies that often bypass the power of elected officials.

Kotter, John P., and Lawrence, Paul R. *Mayors in Action: Five Approaches to Urban Governance* (Wiley, 1974). A study of how mayors govern in urban areas. The authors found at least five distinct types of mayoral styles; they concluded that no one approach to the job is necessarily the best.

Mollenkopf, John H. *The Contested City** (Princeton University Press, 1983). A detailed analysis of the ways the federal government has tried to aid American cities since the New Deal. Discusses the consequences of these policies for urban development in the United States.

Peirce, Neal R. *The Megastates of America* (Norton, 1972); *The Pacific States of America* (Norton, 1972); *The Mountain States of America* (Norton, 1972); *The Great Plains States of America* (Norton, 1973); *The Deep South States of America* (Norton, 1974); *The Border South States* (Norton, 1975); *The New England States* (Norton, 1976); *The Mid-Atlantic States of America* (Norton, 1977); *The Great Lake States of America* (Norton, 1980); and *The Book of America: Inside Fifty States Today* (Warner Books, 1984). An unusually comprehensive and richly detailed sociopolitical guide to America, state by state.

Peterson, Paul E. *City Limits** (University of Chicago Press, 1997). An important analysis of city government and politics. Argues that a city will tend to favor policies that strengthen its own economic position in its competition with other cities, counties, and states.

Rosenthal, Alan. *The Third House: Lobbyists and Lobbying in the States* (Congressional Quarterly, 1992). A revealing account, including a number of readable case studies, of the varied policy goals of those lobbying state legislators, and the techniques they employ.

Sabato, Larry. *Goodbye to Good-Time Charlie: The American Governorship Transformed*, 2nd edition (CQ Press, 1983). A lively study of modern American governors. Concludes that the political hacks who sometimes served as governors in the past have departed, their place taken by a new breed of better-prepared, better-trained governors.

State Policy Reports. (McConnellsburg, PA: Brizius & Foster and State Policy Research, Inc.) A biweekly review of politics, government, and policies in the states.

Van Horn, Carl. *State of the States*, 3rd edition* (CQ Press, 1996). A survey of developments and trends in the American states.

Weber, Ronald E., and Brace, Paul, eds. *American State and Local Politics: Directions for the Twenty-First Century** (Chatham House, 1999). A useful overview of the politics of state and local policymaking.

Wilson, James Q. *Thinking about Crime*, revised edition (Random House, 1985). A discussion of the problems of crime and law enforcement faced by many urban and suburban areas. Includes an analysis of the ways local communities attempt to deal with crime and offers some suggestions for improving public policies in this area.

---

*Available in paperback edition.

 Visit http://politicalscience.wadsworth.com/cummings9/update/ for current InfoTrac articles and other student resources related to this chapter.

The Declaration of Independence

In Congress, July 4, 1776.
A DECLARATION
By the Representatives of the
United States of America,
In General Congress Assembled.

When in the Course of human Events, it becomes necessary for one People to dissolve the Political Bands which have connected them with another, and to assume among the Powers of the Earth, the separate and equal Station to which the Laws of Nature and of Nature's God entitle them, a decent Respect to the Opinions of Mankind requires that they should declare the causes which impel them to the Separation.

We hold these Truths to be self-evident, that all Men are created equal, that they are endowed by their Creator with certain unalienable Rights, that among these are Life, Liberty, and the Pursuit of Happiness—That to secure these Rights, Governments are instituted among Men, deriving their just Powers from the Consent of the Governed, that whenever any Form of Government becomes destructive of these Ends, it is the Right of the People to alter or to abolish it, and to institute new Government, laying its Foundation on such Principles, and organizing its Powers in such Form, as to them shall seem most likely to effect their Safety and Happiness. Prudence, indeed, will dictate that Governments long established should not be changed for light and transient Causes; and accordingly all Experience hath shewn, that Mankind are more disposed to suffer, while Evils are sufferable, than to right themselves by abolishing the Forms to which they are accustomed. But when a long Train of Abuses and Usurpations, pursuing invariably the same Object, evinces a Design to reduce them under absolute Despotism, it is their Right, it is their Duty, to throw off such Government, and to provide new Guards for their future Security. Such has been the patient Sufferance of these Colonies; and such is now the Necessity which constrains them to alter their former Systems of Government. The History of the present king of Great-Britain is a History of repeated Injuries and Usurpations, all having in direct Object the Establishment of an absolute Tyranny over these States. To prove this, let Facts be submitted to a candid World.

He has refused his Assent to Laws, the most wholesome and necessary for the public good.

He has forbidden his Governors to pass Laws of immediate and pressing Importance, unless suspended in their

Operation till his Assent should be obtained; and when so suspended, he has utterly neglected to attend to them.

He has refused to pass other Laws for the Accommodation of large Districts of People, unless those People would relinquish the Right of Representation in the Legislature, a Right inestimable to them, and formidable to Tyrants only.

He has called together Legislative Bodies at Places unusual, uncomfortable, and distant from the Depository of their public Records, for the sole Purpose of fatiguing them into Compliance with his Measures.

He has dissolved Representative Houses repeatedly, for opposing with manly Firmness his Invasions on the Rights of the People.

He has refused for a long Time, after such Dissolutions, to cause others to be elected; whereby the Legislative Powers, incapable of Annihilation, have returned to the People at large for their exercise; the State remaining in the mean time exposed to all the Dangers of Invasion from without, and Convulsions within.

He has endeavoured to prevent the Population of these States; for that Purpose obstructing the Laws for Naturalization of Foreigners; refusing to pass others to encourage their Migrations hither, and raising the Conditions of new Appropriations of Lands.

He has obstructed the Administration of Justice, by refusing his Assent to Laws for establishing Judiciary Powers.

He has made Judges dependent on his Will alone, for the Tenure of their Offices, and the Amount and Payment of their Salaries.

He has erected a Multitude of new Offices, and sent hither Swarms of Officers to harrass our People, and eat out their Substance.

He has kept among us, in Times of Peace, Standing Armies, without the consent of our Legislatures.

He has affected to render the Military independent of and superior to the Civil Power.

He has combined with others to subject us to a Jurisdiction foreign to our Constitution, and unacknowledged by our Laws; giving his Assent to their Acts of pretended Legislation:

For quartering large Bodies of Armed Troops among us:

For protecting them, by a mock Trial, from Punishment for any Murders which they should commit on the Inhabitants of these States:

For cutting off our Trade with all Parts of the World:

For imposing Taxes on us without our Consent:

For depriving us, in many Cases, of the Benefits of Trial by Jury:

For transporting us beyond Seas to be tried for pretended Offences:

For abolishing the free System of English Laws in a neighbouring Province, establishing therein an arbitrary Government, and enlarging its Boundaries, so as to render it at once an Example and fit Instrument for introducing the same absolute Rule into these Colonies:

For taking away our Charters, abolishing our most valuable Laws, and altering fundamentally the Forms of our Governments:

For suspending our own Legislatures, and declaring themselves invested with Power to legislate for us in all Cases whatsoever.

He has abdicated Government here, by declaring us out of his Protection and waging War against us.

He has plundered our Seas, ravaged our Coasts, burnt our Towns, and destroyed the Lives of our People.

He is, at this Time, transporting large Armies of foreign Mercenaries to compleat the Works of Death, Desolation, and Tyranny, already begun with circumstances of Cruelty and Perfidy, scarcely paralleled in the most barbarous Ages, and totally unworthy the Head of a civilized Nation.

He has constrained our fellow Citizens taken Captive on the high Seas to bear Arms against their Country, to become the Executioners of their Friends and Brethren, or to fall themselves by their Hands.

He has excited domestic Insurrections amongst us, and has endeavoured to bring on the Inhabitants of our Frontiers, the merciless Indian Savages, whose known Rule of Warfare, is an undistinguished Destruction, of all Ages, Sexes and Conditions.

In every stage of these Oppressions we have Petitioned for Redress in the most humble Terms: Our repeated Petitions have been answered only by repeated Injury. A Prince, whose Character is thus marked by every act which may define a Tyrant, is unfit to be the Ruler of a free People.

Nor have we been wanting in Attentions to our British Brethren. We have warned them from Time to Time of Attempts by their Legislature to extend an unwarrantable Jurisdiction over us. We have reminded them of the Circumstances of our Emigration and Settlement here. We have appealed to their native Justice and Magnanimity, and we have conjured them by the Ties of our common Kindred to disavow these Usurpations, which, would inevitably interrupt our Connections and Correspondence. They too have been deaf to the Voice of Justice and of Consanguinity. We must, therefore, acquiesce in the Necessity, which denounces our Separation, and hold them, as we hold the rest of Mankind, Enemies in War, in Peace, Friends.

We, therefore, the Representatives of the UNITED STATES OF AMERICA, in GENERAL CONGRESS, Assembled, appealing to the Supreme Judge of the World for the Rectitude of our Intentions, do, in the Name, and by Authority of the good People of these Colonies, solemnly Publish and Declare, That these United Colonies, are, and of Right ought to be, FREE AND INDEPENDENT STATES; that they are absolved from all Allegiance to the British Crown, and that all political Connection between them and the State of Great-Britain, is and ought to be totally dissolved; and that as FREE AND INDEPENDENT STATES, they have full Power to levy War, conclude Peace, contract Alliances, establish Commerce, and to do all other Acts and Things which INDEPENDENT STATES may of right do. And for the support of this Declaration, with a firm Reliance on the Protection of divine Providence, we mutually pledge to each other our Lives, our Fortunes, and our sacred Honor.

Signed by ORDER *and in* BEHALF *of the* CONGRESS, JOHN HANCOCK, PRESIDENT.
ATTEST.
CHARLES THOMSON, SECRETARY.
PHILADELPHIA: PRINTED BY JOHN DUNLAP.

Signers of the Declaration of Independence
According to the Authenticated List Printed by Order of Congress of January 18, 1777[*]

John Hancock.

New-Hampshire.
Josiah Bartlett,
W^m. Whipple,
Matthew Thornton.[†]

Massachusetts-Bay.
Saml. Adams,
John Adams,
Robt. Treat Paine,
Elbridge Gerry.

Rhode-Island and
Providence, &c.
Step. Hopkins,
William Ellery.

Connecticut.
Roger Sherman,
Saml. Huntington,
W^m. Williams,
Oliver Wolcott.

New-York.
W^m. Floyd,
Phil. Livingston,
Fran^s. Lewis,
Lewis Morris.

New-Jersey.
Rich^d. Stockton,
Jno. Witherspoon,
Fra^s. Hopkinson,
John Hart,
Abra. Clark.

Pennsylvania.
Robt. Morris,
Benjamin Rush,
Benja. Franklin,
John Morton,
Geo. Clymer,
Ja^s. Smith,

Geo. Taylor,
James Wilson,
Geo. Ross.

Delaware.
Caesar Rodney,
Geo. Read,
(Tho. M:Kean.)[‡]

Maryland.
Samuel Chase,
W^m. Paca,
Thos. Stone,
Charles Carroll,
  of Carrollton.

Virginia.
George Wythe,
Richard Henry Lee,
Th^s. Jefferson,
Benj^a. Harrison,

Thos. Nelson, J^r.
Francis Lightfoot Lee,
Carter Braxton.

North-Carolina.
W^m. Hooper,
Joseph Hewes,
John Penn.

South-Carolina.
Edward Rutledge,
Thos. Heyward, jun^r
Thomas Lynch, jun^r
Arthur Middleton.

Georgia.
Button Gwinnett,
Lyman Hall,
Geo. Walton.

---

[*]Spelling and abbreviation of names conform to original printed list.

[†]Matthew Thornton's name was signed on the engrossed copy following the Connecticut members, but was transferred in the printed copy to its proper place with the other New Hampshire members.

[‡]Thomas McKean's name was not included in the list of signers printed by order of Congress on January 18, 1777, as he did not sign the engrossed copy until some time thereafter, probably in 1781.

The Constitution of the United States of America*

We the people of the United States, in Order to form a more perfect Union, establish Justice, insure domestic Tranquility, provide for the common defence, promote the general Welfare, and secure the Blessings of Liberty to ourselves and our Posterity, do ordain and establish this Constitution for the United States of America.

Article I

Section 1. All legislative Powers herein granted shall be vested in a Congress of the United States, which shall consist of a Senate and House of Representatives.

Section 2. The House of Representatives shall be composed of Members chosen every second Year by the people of the several States, and the Electors in each State shall have the Qualifications requisite for Electors of the most numerous Branch of the State Legislature.

No Person shall be a Representative who shall not have attained to the Age of twenty-five Years, and been seven Years a Citizen of the United States, and who shall not, when elected, be an Inhabitant of that state in which he shall be chosen.

[Representatives and direct Taxes shall be apportioned among the several States which may be included within this Union, according to their respective Numbers, which shall be determined by adding to the whole Number of free persons, including those bound to Service for a Term of Years, and excluding Indians not taxed, three fifths of all other Persons.][1] The actual Enumeration shall be made within three Years after the first Meeting of the Congress of the United States, and within every subsequent Term of ten Years, in such Manner as they shall by Law direct. The Number of Representatives shall not exceed one for every thirty Thousand, but each State shall have at Least one Representative; and until such enumeration shall be made, the State of New Hampshire shall be entitled to chuse three, Massachusetts eight, Rhode-Island and Providence Plantations one, Connecticut five, New-York six, New Jersey four, Pennsylvania eight, Delaware one, Maryland six, Virginia ten, North Carolina five, South Carolina five, and Georgia three.

When vacancies happen in the Representation from any State, the Executive Authority thereof shall issue Writs of Election to fill such Vacancies.

The House of Representatives shall chuse their Speaker and other Officers; and shall have the sole Power of Impeachment.

---

*The Constitution and all amendments are shown in their original form. Parts that have been amended or superseded are bracketed and explained in the footnotes.

Section 3. The Senate of the United States shall be composed of two Senators from each State, [chosen by the Legislature thereof,]² for six Years; and each Senator shall have one Vote.

Immediately after they shall be assembled in Consequence of the first Election, they shall be divided as equally as may be into three Classes. The Seats of the Senators of the first Class shall be vacated at the Expiration of the second Year, of the second Class at the Expiration of the fourth Year, and of the third Class at the Expiration of the sixth Year, so that one-third may be chosen every second year; [and if Vacancies happen by Resignation, or otherwise, during the Recess of the Legislature of any State, the Executive thereof may make temporary Appointments until the next Meeting of the Legislature, which shall then fill such Vacancies].³

No Person shall be a Senator who shall not have attained to the Age of thirty Years, and been nine Years a Citizen of the United States, and who shall not, when elected, be an Inhabitant of that State in which he shall be chosen.

The Vice-President of the United States shall be President of the Senate, but shall have no vote, unless they be equally divided.

The Senate shall chuse their other Officers, and also a President pro tempore, in the absence of the Vice-President, or when he shall exercise the Office of the President of the United States.

The Senate shall have the sole Power to try all Impeachments. When sitting for that purpose, they shall be on Oath or Affirmation. When the President of the United States is tried, the Chief Justice shall preside: And no person shall be convicted without the Concurrence of two thirds of the Members present.

Judgment in Cases of Impeachment shall not extend further than to removal from Office, and disqualification to hold and enjoy any Office of honor, Trust, or profit under the United States: but the Party convicted shall nevertheless be liable and subject to Indictment, Trial, Judgment, and punishment, according to Law.

Section 4. The Times, Places and Manner of holding Elections for Senators and Representatives, shall be prescribed in each state by the Legislature thereof; but the Congress may at any time by Law make or alter such Regulations, except as to the Places of Chusing Senators.

The Congress shall assemble at least once in every Year, and such Meeting shall [be on the first Monday in December,]⁴ unless they shall by Law appoint a different Day.

Section 5. Each House shall be the Judge of the Elections, Returns and Qualifications of its own Members, and a Majority of each shall constitute a Quorum to do Business; but a smaller number may adjourn from day to day, and may be authorized, to compel the Attendance of absent Members, in such Manner, and under such Penalties, as each House may provide.

Each House may determine the Rules of its Proceedings, punish its Members for disorderly Behavior, and, with the Concurrence of two thirds, expel a Member.

Each House shall keep a Journal of its Proceedings, and from time to time publish the same, excepting such Parts as may in their Judgment require Secrecy; and the Yeas and Nays of the Members of either House on any question shall, at the Desire of one fifth of those present, be entered on the journal.

Neither House, during the Session of Congress, shall, without the Consent of the other, adjourn for more than three days, nor to any other Place than that in which the two Houses shall be sitting.

Section 6. The Senators and Representatives shall receive a Compensation for their Services, to be ascertained by Law, and paid out of the Treasury of the United States. They shall in all Cases, except Treason, Felony, and Breach of the Peace, be privileged from Arrest during their Attendance at the Session of their respective Houses, and in going to and returning from the same; and for any Speech or Debate in either House, they shall not be questioned in any other place.

No Senator or Representative shall, during the Time for which he was elected, be appointed to any civil Office under the Authority of the United States, which shall have been created, or the Emoluments whereof shall have been increased, during such time; and no person holding any Office under the United States shall be a Member of either House during his continuance in Office.

Section 7. All Bills for raising Revenue shall originate in the House of Representatives; but the Senate may propose or concur with Amendments as on other bills.

Every Bill which shall have passed the House of Representatives and the Senate, shall, before it become a Law, be presented to the President of the United States; If he approve he shall sign it, but if not he shall return it, with his Objections, to that House in which it shall have originated, who shall enter the Objections at large on their Journal, and proceed to reconsider it. If after such Reconsideration two thirds of that House shall agree to pass the bill, it shall be sent, together with the objections, to the other House, by which it shall likewise be reconsidered, and if approved by two thirds of that House, it shall become a Law. But in all such Cases the Votes of both Houses shall be determined by Yeas and Nays, and the Names of the Persons voting for and against the Bill shall be entered on the Journal of each House respectively. If any Bill shall not be returned by the President within ten Days (Sundays excepted) after it shall have been presented to him, the Same shall be a Law, in like Manner as if he had signed it, unless the Congress by their Adjournment prevent its Return, in which Case it shall not be a Law.

Every Order, Resolution, or Vote to which the Concurrence of the Senate and House of Representatives may be necessary (except on a question of Adjournment) shall be presented to the President of the United States; and before the Same shall take Effect, shall be approved by him, or being disapproved by him, shall be repassed by two thirds of the Senate and House of Representatives, according to the Rules and Limitations prescribed in the Case of a Bill.

Section 8. The Congress shall have Power to lay and collect Taxes, Duties, Imposts and Excises, to pay the Debts and provide for the common Defence and general Welfare of the United States; but all Duties, Imposts and Excises shall be uniform throughout the United States;

To borrow money on the credit of the United States;

To regulate Commerce with foreign Nations, and among the several States, and with the Indian Tribes;

To establish an uniform Rule of Naturalization, and uniform Laws on the subject of Bankruptcies throughout the United States;

To coin Money, regulate the Value thereof, and of foreign Coin, and fix the Standard of Weights and Measures;

To provide for the Punishment of counterfeiting the Securities and current Coin of the United States;

To establish Post Offices and Post Roads;

To promote the Progress of Science and useful Arts, by securing for limited times to Authors and Inventors the exclusive Right to their respective Writings and Discoveries;

To constitute Tribunals inferior to the Supreme Court;

To define and punish Piracies and Felonies committed on the high Seas, and Offenses against the Law of Nations;

To declare War, grant Letters of Marque and Reprisal, and make Rules concerning Captures on Land and Water;

To raise and support Armies, but no Appropriation of Money to that Use shall be for a longer Term than two Years;

To provide and maintain a Navy;

To make Rules for the Government and Regulation of the land and naval forces;

To provide for calling forth the Militia to execute the Laws of the Union, suppress Insurrections and repel Invasions;

To provide for organizing, arming, and disciplining the Militia, and for governing such part of them as may be employed in the Service of the United States, reserving to the States respectively, the Appointment of the Officers, and the Authority of training the Militia according to the discipline prescribed by Congress;

To exercise exclusive Legislation in all Cases whatsoever, over such District (not exceeding ten Miles square) as may, by Cession of particular States, and the acceptance of Congress, become the Seat of the Government of the United States, and to exercise like Authority over all places purchased by the Consent of the Legislature of the State in which the Same shall be, for the Erection of Forts, Magazines, Arsenals, dock-Yards, and other needful Buildings;—And

To make all Laws which shall be necessary and proper for carrying into Execution the foregoing Powers, and all other Powers vested by this Constitution in the Government of the United States, or in any Department or Officer thereof.

Section 9. The Migration or Importation of such Persons as any of the States now existing shall think proper to admit shall not be prohibited by the Congress prior to the Year one thousand eight hundred and eight, but a tax or duty may be imposed on such Importation, not exceeding ten dollars for each person.

The privilege of the Writ of Habeas Corpus shall not be suspended, unless when in Cases of Rebellion or Invasion the public Safety may require it.

No Bill of Attainder or ex post facto Law shall be passed.

[No capitation, or other direct, Tax shall be laid unless in proportion to the Census or Enumeration herein before directed to be taken.][5]

No Tax or Duty shall be laid on Articles exported from any State.

No Preference shall be given by any Regulation of Revenue to the ports of one State over those of another: nor shall Vessels bound to, or from, one State, be obliged to enter, clear, or pay Duties in another.

No Money shall be drawn from the Treasury, but in Consequence of Appropriations made by Law; and a regular Statement and Account of the Receipts and Expenditures of all public Money shall be published from time to time.

No Title of Nobility shall be granted by the United States: And no Person holding any Office of profit or Trust under them, shall, without the Consent of the Congress, accept of any present, Emolument, Office, or Title, of any kind whatever, from any King, Prince, or foreign State.

Section 10. No State shall enter into any Treaty, Alliance, or Confederation; grant Letters of Marque and Reprisal; coin Money; emit Bills of Credit; make any Thing but gold and silver Coin a Tender in payment of Debts; pass any Bill of Attainder, ex post facto Law, or Law impairing the Obligation of Contracts, or grant any Title of Nobility.

No State shall, without the Consent of the Congress, lay any Imposts or Duties on Imports or Exports, except what may be absolutely necessary for executing its inspection Laws: and the net Produce of all Duties and Imposts, laid by any State on Imports or Exports, shall be for the Use of the Treasury of the United States; and all such Laws shall be Subject to the Revision and Control of the Congress.

No State shall, without the Consent of Congress, lay any duty of Tonnage, keep Troops, or Ships of War in time of peace, enter into any Agreement or Compact with another State, or with a foreign power, or engage in War, unless actually invaded, or in such imminent Danger as will not admit of delay.

Article II

Section 1. The executive Power shall be vested in a President of the United States of America. He shall hold his Office during the Term of four years, and, together with the Vice-President, chosen for the same Term, be elected, as follows:

Each State shall appoint, in such Manner as the Legislature thereof may direct, a Number of Electors, equal to the whole Number of Senators and Representatives to which the State may be entitled in the Congress: but no Senator or Representative, or person holding an Office of Trust or profit under the United States, shall be appointed an Elector.

[The Electors shall meet in their respective States, and vote by Ballot for two persons, of whom one at least shall not be an Inhabitant of the same State with themselves. And they shall make a List of all the Persons voted for, and of the Number of Votes for each; which List they shall sign and certify, and transmit sealed to the Seat of the Government of the United States, directed to the President of the Senate. The President of the Senate shall, in the Presence of the Senate and House of Representatives, open all the Certificates, and the Votes shall then be counted. The person having the greatest Number of Votes shall be the President, if such Number be a Majority of the whole Number of Electors appointed; and if there be more than one who have such Majority, and have an equal Number of Votes, then the House of Representatives shall immediately chuse by Ballot one of them for president; and if no person have a Majority, then from the five highest on the List the said House shall in like Manner chuse the President. But in chusing the President, the Votes shall be taken by States, the Representation from each State having one Vote; a quorum for this Purpose shall consist of a Member or Members from two-thirds of the States, and a Majority of all the States shall be necessary to a Choice. In every Case, after the Choice of the President, the Person having the greatest Number of Votes of the Electors shall be the Vice-President. But if there should remain two or more who have equal votes, the Senate shall chuse from them by Ballot the Vice-President.][6]

The Congress may determine the Time of chusing the Electors, and the Day on which they shall give their Votes; which Day shall be the same throughout the United States.

No person except a natural-born Citizen, or a Citizen of the United States, at the time of the Adoption of this Constitution, shall be eligible to the Office of President; neither shall any person be eligible to that Office who shall not have attained to the Age of thirty-five years, and been fourteen Years a Resident within the United States.

[In Case of the Removal of the President from Office, or of his Death, Resignation, or Inability to discharge the powers and Duties of the said Office, the same shall devolve on the Vice-President, and the Congress may by Law provide for the Case of Removal, Death, Resignation, or Inability, both of the President and Vice-President, declaring what Officer shall then act as President, and such Officer shall act accordingly, until the disability be removed, or a President shall be elected.][7]

The President shall, at stated Times, receive for his Services a Compensation, which shall neither be increased nor diminished during the period for which he shall have been elected, and he shall not receive within that Period any other Emolument from the United States, or any of them.

Before he enter on the execution of his Office, he shall take the following Oath or Affirmation:—"I do solemnly swear (or affirm) that I will faithfully execute the Office of President of the United States, and will, to the best of my Ability, preserve, protect, and defend the Constitution of the United States."

Section 2. The president shall be Commander in Chief of the Army and Navy of the United States, and of the Militia of the several States, when called into the actual Service of the United States; he may require the Opinion, in writing, of the principal Officer in each of the executive Departments, upon any subject relating to the Duties of their respective Offices, and he shall have Power to Grant Reprieves and Pardons for Offenses against the United States, except in Cases of Impeachment.

He shall have Power, by and with the Advice and Consent of the Senate, to make Treaties, provided two thirds of the Senators present concur; and he shall nominate, and by and with the Advice and Consent of the Senate, shall appoint Ambassadors, other public Ministers and Consuls, Judges of the supreme Court, and all other Officers of the United States, whose Appointments are not herein otherwise provided for, and which shall be established by Law: but the Congress may by Law vest the Appointment of such inferior Officers, as they think proper, in the President alone, in the Courts of Law, or in the Heads of Departments.

The President shall have Power to fill up all Vacancies that may happen during the Recess of the Senate, by granting Commissions which shall expire at the End of their next Session.

Section 3. He shall from time to time give to the Congress Information of the State of the Union, and recommend to their Consideration such Measures as he shall judge necessary and expedient; he may, on extraordinary occasions, convene both Houses, or either of them, and in Case of Disagreement between them, with respect to the Time of Adjournment, he may adjourn them to such Time as he shall think proper; he shall receive Ambassadors and other public Ministers; he shall take Care that the Laws be faithfully executed, and shall Commission all the Officers of the United States.

Section 4. The President, Vice-President and all civil Officers of the United States, shall be removed from Office on Impeachment for, and Conviction of, Treason, Bribery, or other high Crimes and Misdemeanors.

Article III

Section 1. The judicial power of the United States, shall be vested in one supreme Court, and in such inferior Courts as the Congress may from time to time ordain and establish. The Judges, both of the supreme and inferior Courts, shall hold their Offices during good Behaviour, and shall, at stated Times, receive for their Services, a Compensation, which shall not be diminished during their Continuance in Office.

Section 2. The judicial Power shall extend to all Cases, in Law and Equity, arising under this Constitution, the Laws of the United States, and treaties made, or which shall be made, under their Authority;—to all Cases affecting ambassadors, other public ministers and consuls;—to all cases of admiralty and maritime Jurisdiction;—to Controversies to which the United States shall be a Party;—to Controversies between two or more States;—[between a State and Citizens of Another State;][8]—between Citizens of different States,—between Citizens of the same State claiming Lands under Grants of different States, and between a State, or the Citizens thereof, and foreign States, Citizens or Subjects.

In all Cases affecting Ambassadors, other public Ministers and Consuls, and those in which a State shall be Party, the supreme Court shall have original Jurisdiction. In all the other Cases before mentioned, the supreme Court shall have appellate Jurisdiction, both as to Law and Fact, with such Exceptions, and under such Regulations as the Congress shall make.

The trial of all Crimes, except in Cases of Impeachment, shall be by Jury; and such Trial shall be held in the State where the said Crimes shall have been committed; but when not committed within any State, the Trial shall be at such Place or Places as the Congress may by Law have directed.

Section 3. Treason against the United States, shall consist only in levying War against them, or in adhering to their Enemies, giving them Aid and Comfort. No person shall be convicted of Treason unless on the Testimony of two Witnesses to the same overt Act, or on Confession in open Court.

The Congress shall have power to declare the Punishment of Treason, but no Attainder of Treason shall work Corruption of Blood, or Forfeiture except during the Life of the Person attainted.

Article IV

Section 1. Full Faith and Credit shall be given in each State to the public Acts, Records, and judicial Proceedings of every other State. And the Congress may by general Laws prescribe the Manner in which such Acts, Records and Proceedings shall be proved, and the Effect thereof.

Section 2. The Citizens of each State shall be entitled to all Privileges and Immunities of Citizens in the several States.

A Person charged in any State with Treason, Felony, or other Crime, who shall flee from Justice, and be found in another State, shall on demand of the executive Authority of the State from which he fled, be delivered up, to be removed to the State having Jurisdiction of the crime.

[No person held to Service or Labour in one State, under the Laws thereof, escaping into another, shall, in Consequence of any Law or Regulation therein, be discharged from such Service or Labour, but shall be delivered up on Claim of the party to whom such Service or Labour may be due.][9]

Section 3. New States may be admitted by the Congress into this Union; but no new State shall be formed or erected within the Jurisdiction of any other State; nor any State be formed by the Junction of two or more States, or parts of States, without the Consent of the Legislatures of the States concerned as well as of the Congress.

The Congress shall have power to dispose of and make all needful Rules and Regulations respecting the Territory or other property belonging to the United States; and nothing in this Constitution shall be so construed as to prejudice any Claims of the United States, or of any particular State.

Section 4. The United States shall guarantee to every State in this Union a Republican Form of Government, and shall protect each of them against Invasion; and on Application of the Legislature, or of the Executive (when the Legislature cannot be convened) against domestic Violence.

Article V

The Congress, whenever two-thirds of both Houses shall deem it necessary, shall propose Amendments to this Constitution, or, on the Application of the Legislatures of two-thirds of the several States, shall call a Convention for proposing Amendments, which, in either Case, shall be valid to all Intents and Purposes, as part of this Constitution, when ratified by the Legislatures of three-fourths of the several States, or by Conventions in three-fourths thereof, as the one or the other Mode of Ratification may be proposed by the Congress; provided that no Amendment which may be made prior to the Year One thousand eight hundred and eight shall in any Manner affect the first and fourth Clauses in the Ninth Section of the first Article; and that no State, without its Consent, shall be deprived of its equal Suffrage in the Senate.

Article VI

All Debts contracted and Engagements entered into, before the Adoption of this Constitution, shall be as valid against the United States under this Constitution, as under the Confederation.

This Constitution, and the Laws of the United States which shall be made in Pursuance thereof; and all Treaties made, or which shall be made, under the Authority of the United States, shall be the supreme Law of the Land; and the Judges in every State shall be bound thereby, any Thing in the Constitution or Laws of any State to the Contrary notwithstanding.

The Senators and Representatives before mentioned, and the Members of the several State Legislatures, and all executive and judicial Officers, both of the United States and of the several States, shall be bound by Oath or Affirmation to support this Constitution; but no religious Test shall ever be required as a qualification to any Office or public Trust under the United States.

Article VII

The Ratification of the Conventions of nine States shall be sufficient for the Establishment of this Constitution between the States so ratifying the same.

Done in Convention by the Unanimous Consent of the States present the Seventeenth Day of September in the Year of our Lord one thousand seven hundred and Eighty seven, and of the Independence of the United States of America the Twelfth. In Witness thereof We have hereunto subscribed our Names.

Articles in Addition to, and Amendment of, the Constitution of the United States of America, Proposed by Congress, and Ratified by the Legislatures of the Several States, Pursuant to the Fifth Article of the Original Constitution.

Amendment I[10]

Congress shall make no law respecting an establishment of religion, or prohibiting the free exercise thereof; or abridging the freedom of speech, or of the press; or the right of the people peaceably to assemble, and to petition the Government for a redress of grievances.

Amendment II

A well regulated Militia, being necessary to the security of a free State, the right of the people to keep and bear Arms shall not be infringed.

Amendment III

No Soldier shall, in time of peace, be quartered in any house, without the consent of the Owner, nor in time of war, but in a manner to be prescribed by law.

Amendment IV

The right of the people to be secure in their persons, houses, papers, and effects, against unreasonable searches and seizures, shall not be violated, and no Warrants shall issue, but upon probable cause, supported by Oath or affirmation, and particularly describing the place to be searched, and the persons or things to be seized.

Amendment V

No person shall be held to answer for a capital, or otherwise infamous crime, unless on a presentment or indictment of a Grand Jury, except in cases arising in the land or naval forces, or in the Militia, when in actual service in time of War or public danger; nor shall any person be subject for the same offence to be twice put in jeopardy of life or limb; nor shall be compelled in any criminal case to be a witness against himself, nor be deprived of life, liberty, or property, without due process of law; nor shall private property be taken for public use without just compensation.

Amendment VI

In all criminal prosecutions, the accused shall enjoy the right to a speedy and public trial, by an impartial jury of the State and district wherein the crime shall have been committed, which district shall have been previously ascertained by law, and to be informed of the nature and cause of the accusation; to be confronted with the witnesses against him; to have compulsory process for obtaining witnesses in his favor, and to have the Assistance of Counsel for his defence.

Amendment VII

In suits at common law, where the value in controversy shall exceed twenty dollars, the right of trial by jury shall be preserved, and no fact tried by a jury, shall be otherwise reexamined in any Court of the United States, than according to the rules of the common law.

Amendment VIII

Excessive bail shall not be required, nor excessive fines imposed, nor cruel and unusual punishments inflicted.

Amendment IX

The enumeration in the Constitution, of certain rights, shall not be construed to deny or disparage others retained by the people.

Amendment X

The powers not delegated to the United States by the Constitution, nor prohibited by it to the States, are reserved to the States respectively, or to the people.

Amendment XI (1795)[11]

The Judicial power of the United States shall not be construed to extend to any suit in law or equity, commenced or prosecuted against one of the United States by Citizens of another State, or by Citizens or Subjects of any Foreign State.

Amendment XII (1804)

The Electors shall meet in their respective States and vote by ballot for President and Vice-President, one of whom, at least, shall not be an inhabitant of the same State with themselves; they shall name in their ballots the person voted for as President, and in distinct ballots the person voted for as Vice-President, and they shall make distinct lists of all persons voted for as President, and of all persons voted for as Vice-President, and of the number of votes for each, which lists they shall sign and certify, and transmit sealed to the seat of the government of the United States, directed to the President of the Senate;—The President of the Senate shall, in the presence of the Senate and House of Representatives, open all the certificates and the votes shall then be counted;—The person having the greatest number of votes for President, shall be the President, if such number be a majority of the whole number of Electors appointed; and if no person have such majority, then from the persons having the highest numbers not exceeding three on the list of those voted for as President, the House of Representatives shall choose immediately, by ballot, the President. But in choosing the President, the votes shall be taken by states, the representation from each state having one vote; a quorum for this purpose shall consist of a member or members from two-thirds of the states, and a majority of all the states shall be necessary to a choice. [And if the House of Representatives shall not choose a President whenever the right of choice shall devolve upon them, before the fourth day of March next following, then the Vice-President shall act as President, as in the case of the death or other constitutional disability of the President.][12]—The person having the greatest number of votes as Vice-President, shall be the Vice-President, if such number be a majority of the whole number of Electors appointed, and if no person have a majority, then from the two highest numbers on the list, the Senate shall choose the Vice-President; a quorum for the purpose shall consist of two-thirds of the whole number of Senators, and a majority of the whole number shall be necessary to a choice. But no person constitutionally ineligible to the Office of President shall be eligible to that of Vice-President of the United States.

Amendment XIII (1865)

Section 1. Neither slavery nor involuntary servitude, except as a punishment for crime whereof the party shall have been duly convicted, shall exist within the United States, or any place subject to their jurisdiction.

Section 2. Congress shall have power to enforce this article by appropriate legislation.

Amendment XIV (1868)

Section 1. All persons born or naturalized in the United States, and subject to the jurisdiction thereof, are citizens of the United States and of the State wherein they reside. No State shall make or enforce any law which shall abridge the privileges or immunities of citizens of the United States; nor shall any State deprive any person of life, liberty, or property, without due process of law; nor deny to any person within its jurisdiction the equal protection of the laws.

Section 2. Representatives shall be apportioned among the several States according to their respective numbers, counting the whole number of persons in each State, excluding Indians not taxed. But when the right to vote at any election for the choice of electors for President and Vice-President of the United States, Representatives in Congress, the Executive and Judicial Officers of a State, or the members of the Legislature thereof, is denied to any of the male inhabitants of such State, being twenty-one years of age, and citizens of the United States, or in any way abridged, except for participation in rebellion, or other crime, the basis of representation therein shall be reduced in the proportion which the number of such male citizens shall bear to the whole number of male citizens twenty-one years of age in such State.

Section 3. No person shall be a senator or Representative in Congress, or elector of President and Vice-President, or hold any Office, civil or military, under the United States, or under any State, who, having previously taken an oath, as a member of Congress, or as an Officer of the United States, or as a member of any State legislature, or as an executive or judicial Officer of any State, to support the Constitution of the United States, shall have engaged in insurrection or rebellion against the same, or given aid or comfort to the enemies thereof. But Congress may by a vote of two-thirds of each House, remove such disability.

Section 4. The validity of the public debt of the United States, authorized by law, including debts incurred for payment of pensions and bounties for services in suppressing insurrection or rebellion, shall not be questioned. But neither the United States nor any State shall assume or pay any debt or obligation incurred in aid of insurrection or rebellion against the United States, or any claim for the loss or emancipation of any slave; but all such debts, obligations, and claims shall be held illegal and void.

Section 5. The Congress shall have the power to enforce, by appropriate legislation, the provisions of this article.

Amendment XV (1870)

Section 1. The right of citizens of the United States to vote shall not be denied or abridged by the United States or by any State on account of race, color, or previous condition of servitude—

Section 2. The Congress shall have power to enforce this article by appropriate legislation.

Amendment XVI (1913)

The Congress shall have power to lay and collect taxes on incomes, from whatever source derived, without apportionment among the several States, and without regard to any census or enumeration.

Amendment XVII (1913)

The Senate of the United States shall be composed of two Senators from each State, elected by the people thereof, for six years; and each Senator shall have one vote. The electors in each State shall have the qualifications requisite for electors of the most numerous branch of the State legislatures.

When vacancies happen in the representation of any State in the Senate, the executive authority of such State shall issue writs of election to fill such vacancies: *Provided,* That the legislature of any State may empower the executive thereof to make temporary appointments until the people fill the vacancies by election as the legislature may direct.

This amendment shall not be so construed as to affect the election or term of any Senator chosen before it becomes valid as part of the Constitution.

Amendment XVIII (1919)[13]

Section 1. After one year from the ratification of this article the manufacture, sale, or transportation of intoxicating liquors within, the importation thereof into, or the exportation thereof from the United States and all territory subject to the jurisdiction thereof for beverage purposes is hereby prohibited.

Section 2. The Congress and the several States shall have concurrent power to enforce this article by appropriate legislation.

Section 3. This article shall be inoperative unless it shall have been ratified as an amendment to the Constitution by the legislatures of the several States, as provided in the Constitution, within seven years from the date of the submission hereof to the States by the Congress.

Amendment XIX (1920)

The right of citizens of the United States to vote shall not be denied or abridged by the United States or by any State on account of sex.

Congress shall have power to enforce this article by appropriate legislation.

Amendment XX (1933)

Section 1. The terms of the President and Vice-President shall end at noon on the 20th day of January, and the terms of Senators and Representatives at noon on the 3d day of January, of the years in which such terms would have ended if this article had not been ratified; and the terms of their successors shall then begin.

Section 2. The Congress shall assemble at least once in every year, and such meeting shall begin at noon on the 3d day of January, unless they shall by law appoint a different day.

Section 3. If, at the time fixed for the beginning of the term of the President, the President elect shall have died, the Vice-President elect shall become President. If a President shall not have been chosen before the time fixed for the beginning of his term, or if the President elect shall have failed to qualify, then the Vice-President elect shall act as President until a President shall have qualified; and the Congress may by law provide for the case wherein neither a President elect nor a Vice-President elect shall have qualified, declaring who shall then act as President, or the manner in which one who is to act shall be selected, and such person shall act accordingly until a President or Vice-President shall have qualified.

Section 4. The Congress may by law provide for the case of the death of any of the persons from whom the House of Representatives may choose a President whenever the right of choice shall have devolved upon them, and for the case of the death of any of the persons from whom the Senate may choose a Vice-President whenever the right of choice shall have devolved upon them.

Section 5. Sections 1 and 2 shall take effect on the 15th day of October following the ratification of this article.

Section 6. This article shall be inoperative unless it shall have been ratified as an amendment to the Constitution by the legislatures of three-fourths of the several States within seven years from the date of its submission.

Amendment XXI (1933)

Section 1. The eighteenth article of amendment to the Constitution of the United States is hereby repealed.

Section 2. The transportation or importation into any State, Territory, or possession of the United States for delivery or use therein of intoxicating liquors, in violation of the laws thereof, is hereby prohibited.

Section 3. This article shall be inoperative unless it shall have been ratified as an amendment of the Constitution by conventions in the several States, as provided by the Constitution, within seven years from the date of the submission hereof to the States by the Congress.

Amendment XXII (1951)

No person shall be elected to the Office of the President more than twice, and no person who has held the Office of President, or acted as President, for more than two years of a term to which some other person was elected President shall be elected to the Office of the President more than once.

But this Article shall not apply to any person holding the Office of President when this Article was proposed by the Congress, and shall not prevent any person who may be holding the Office of President, or acting as President, during the term within which this Article becomes operative from holding the Office of President or acting as President during the remainder of such term.

Amendment XXIII (1961)

Section 1. The District constituting the seat of Government of the United States shall appoint in such manner as the Congress may direct:

A number of electors of President and Vice-President equal to the whole number of Senators and Representatives in Congress to which the District would be entitled if it were a State, but in no event more than the least populous State; they shall be in addition to those appointed by the States, but they shall be considered, for the purposes of the election of President and Vice-President, to be electors appointed by a State; and they shall meet in the District and perform such duties as provided by the twelfth article of amendment.

Section 2. The Congress shall have power to enforce this article by appropriate legislation.

Amendment XXIV (1964)

Section 1. The right of citizens of the United States to vote in any primary or other election for President or Vice-President, for electors for President or Vice-President, or for Senator or Representative in Congress, shall not be denied or abridged by the United States or any State by reason of failure to pay any poll tax or other tax.

Section 2. The Congress shall have power to enforce this article by appropriate legislation.

Amendment XXV (1967)

Section 1. In case of the removal of the President from Office or of his death or resignation, the Vice-President shall become President.

Section 2. Whenever there is a vacancy in the Office of the Vice-President, the President shall nominate a Vice-President who shall take Office upon confirmation by a majority vote of both Houses of Congress.

Section 3. Whenever the President transmits to the President pro tempore of the Senate and the Speaker of the House of Representatives his written declaration that he is unable to discharge the powers and duties of his Office, and until he transmits to them a written declaration to the contrary, such powers and duties shall be discharged by the Vice-President as Acting President.

Section 4. Whenever the Vice-President and a majority of either the principal Officers of the executive department or of such other body as Congress may by law provide, transmit to the President pro tempore of the Senate and the Speaker of the House of Representatives their written declaration that the President is unable to discharge the powers and duties of his Office, the Vice-President shall immediately assume the powers and duties of the Office as Acting President.

Thereafter, when the President transmits to the President pro tempore of the Senate and the Speaker of the House of Representatives his written declaration that no inability exists, he shall resume the powers and duties of his Office unless the Vice-President and a majority of either the principal Officers of the executive department or of such other body as Congress may by law provide, transmit within four days to the President pro tempore of the Senate and the Speaker of the House of Representatives their written declaration that the President is unable to discharge the powers and duties of his Office. Thereupon Congress shall decide the issue, assembling within forty-eight hours for that purpose if not in session. If the Congress, within twenty-one days after receipt of the latter written declaration, or, if Congress is not in session, within twenty-one days after Congress is required to assemble, determines by two-thirds vote of both Houses that the President is unable to discharge the powers and duties of his Office, the Vice-President shall continue to discharge the same as Acting President; otherwise, the President shall resume the powers and duties of his Office.

Amendment XXVI (1971)

Section 1. The right of citizens of the United States, who are eighteen years of age or older, to vote shall not be denied or abridged by the United States or by any State on account of age.

Section 2. The Congress shall have power to enforce this article by appropriate legislation.

Amendment XXVII (1992)

No law varying the compensation for the services of the Senators and Representatives shall take effect, until an election of Representatives shall have intervened.

Presidents of the United States

Year	President	Party	Votes Received	Electoral Vote	Percentage of Popular Vote
1789	George Washington	no designation	Unknown	69	Unknown
1792	George Washington	no designation	Unknown	132	Unknown
1796	John Adams	Federalist	Unknown	71	Unknown
1800	Thomas Jefferson	Democratic-Republican	Unknown	73	Unknown
1804	Thomas Jefferson	Democratic-Republican	Unknown	162	Unknown
1808	James Madison	Democratic-Republican	Unknown	122	Unknown
1812	James Madison	Democratic-Republican	Unknown	128	Unknown
1816	James Monroe	Democratic-Republican	Unknown	183	Unknown
1820	James Monroe	Democratic-Republican	Unknown	231	Unknown
1824	John Quincy Adams	Democratic-Republican	108,740	84	30.5
1828	Andrew Jackson	Democratic	647,286	178	56.0
1832	Andrew Jackson	Democratic	687,502	219	55.0
1836	Martin Van Buren	Democratic	765,483	170	50.9
1840	William H. Harrison	Whig	1,274,624	234	53.1
1841	John Tyler*	Whig			
1844	James K. Polk	Democratic	1,338,464	170	49.6
1848	Zachary Taylor	Whig	1,360,967	163	47.4
1850	Millard Fillmore*	Whig			
1852	Franklin Pierce	Democratic	1,601,117	254	50.9
1856	James Buchanan	Democratic	1,832,955	174	45.3
1860	Abraham Lincoln	Republican	1,865,593	180	39.8
1864	Abraham Lincoln	Republican	2,206,938	212	55.0
1865	Andrew Johnson*	Democratic			
1868	Ulysses S. Grant	Republican	3,013,421	214	52.7
1872	Ulysses S. Grant	Republican	3,596,745	286	55.6
1876	Rutherford B. Hayes	Republican	4,036,572	185	48.0
1880	James A. Garfield	Republican	4,453,295	214	48.5
1881	Chester A. Arthur*	Republican			
1884	Grover Cleveland	Democratic	4,879,507	219	48.5
1888	Benjamin Harrison	Republican	5,447,129	233	47.9
1892	Grover Cleveland	Democratic	5,555,426	277	46.1
1896	William McKinley	Republican	7,102,246	271	51.1
1900	William McKinley	Republican	7,218,491	292	51.7
1901	Theodore Roosevelt*	Republican			
1904	Theodore Roosevelt	Republican	7,628,461	336	57.4
1908	William H. Taft	Republican	7,675,320	321	51.6
1912	Woodrow Wilson	Democratic	6,296,547	435	41.9
1916	Woodrow Wilson	Democratic	9,127,695	277	49.4
1920	Warren G. Harding	Republican	16,143,407	404	60.4
1923	Calvin Coolidge*	Republican			
1924	Calvin Coolidge	Republican	15,718,211	382	54.0
1928	Herbert C. Hoover	Republican	21,391,993	444	58.2
1932	Franklin D. Roosevelt	Democratic	22,809,638	472	57.4
1936	Franklin D. Roosevelt	Democratic	27,752,869	523	60.8
1940	Franklin D. Roosevelt	Democratic	27,307,819	449	54.8
1944	Franklin D. Roosevelt	Democratic	25,606,585	432	53.5
1945	Harry S Truman*	Democratic			
1948	Harry S Truman	Democratic	24,105,812	303	49.5
1952	Dwight D. Eisenhower	Republican	33,936,234	442	55.1
1956	Dwight D. Eisenhower	Republican	35,590,472	457	57.6

(continued)

Presidents of the United States *(continued)*

Year	President	Party	Votes Received	Electoral Vote	Percentage of Popular Vote
1960	John F. Kennedy	Democratic	34,227,096	303	49.9
1963	Lyndon B. Johnson*	Democratic			
1964	Lyndon B. Johnson	Democratic	43,126,506	486	61.1
1968	Richard M. Nixon	Republican	31,785,480	301	43.4
1972	Richard M. Nixon	Republican	47,169,905	520	60.7
1974	Gerald R. Ford†	Republican			
1976	Jimmy Carter	Democratic	40,827,394	297	50.0
1980	Ronald Reagan	Republican	43,899,248	489	50.8
1984	Ronald Reagan	Republican	54,450,603	525	58.8
1988	George Bush	Republican	47,946,422	426	53.9
1992	Bill Clinton	Democratic	43,728,375	370	43.2
1996	Bill Clinton	Democratic	45,628,667	379	49.2
2000	George W. Bush	Republican	50,456,169	271	47.9

*Succeeded to presidency upon death of the incumbent.
†Succeeded to presidency upon resignation of the incumbent.

Selections from the Federalist Papers

The Federalist No. 10

James Madison
November 23, 1787

TO THE PEOPLE OF THE STATE OF NEW YORK

Among the numerous advantages promised by a well-constructed Union, none deserves to be more accurately developed than its tendency to break and control the violence of faction. The friend of popular governments never finds himself so much alarmed for their character and fate, as when he contemplates their propensity to this dangerous vice. He will not fail, therefore, to set a due value on any plan which, without violating the principles to which he is attached, provides a proper cure for it. The instability, injustice, and confusion introduced into the public councils, have, in truth, been the mortal diseases under which popular governments have everywhere perished; as they continue to be the favorite and fruitful topics from which the adversaries to liberty derive their most specious declamations. The valuable improvements made by the American constitutions on the popular models, both ancient and modern, cannot certainly be too much admired; but it would be an unwarrantable partiality, to contend that they have as effectually obviated the danger on this side, as was wished and expected. Complaints are everywhere heard from our most considerate and virtuous citizens, equally the friends of public and private faith, and of public and personal liberty, that our governments are too unstable, that the public good is disregarded in the conflicts of rival parties, and that measures are too often decided, not according to the rules of justice and the rights of the minor party, but by the superior force of an interested and overbearing majority. However anxiously we may wish that these complaints had no foundation, the evidence of known facts will not permit us to deny that they are in some degree true. It will be found, indeed, on a candid review of our situation, that some of the distresses under which we labor have been erroneously charged on the operation of our governments; but it will be found, at the same time, that other causes will not alone account for many of our heaviest misfortunes; and, particularly, for that prevailing and increasing distrust of public engagements, and alarm for private rights, which are echoed from one end of the continent to the other. These must be chiefly, if not wholly, effects of the unsteadiness and injustice with which a factious spirit has tainted our public administrations.

By a faction, I understand a number of citizens, whether amounting to a majority or a minority of the whole, who are united and actuated by some common impulse of passion, or of interest, adversed to the rights of other citizens, or to the permanent and aggregate interests of the community.

There are two methods of curing the mischiefs of faction: the one, by removing its causes; the other, by controlling its effects.

There are again two methods of removing the causes of faction: the one, by destroying the liberty which is essential to its existence; the other, by giving to every citizen the same opinions, the same passions, and the same interests.

It could never be more truly said than of the first remedy, that it was worse than the disease. Liberty is to faction what air is to fire, an aliment without which it instantly expires. But it could not be less folly to abolish liberty, which is essential to political life, because it nourishes faction, than it would be to wish the annihilation of air, which is essential to animal life, because it imparts to fire its destructive agency.

The second expedient is as impracticable as the first would be unwise. As long as the reason of man continues fallible, and he is at liberty to exercise it, different opinions will be formed. As long as the connection subsists between his reason and his self-love, his opinions and his passions will have a reciprocal influence on each other; and the former will be objects to which the latter will attach themselves. The diversity in the faculties of men, from which the rights of property originate, is not less an insuperable obstacle to a uniformity of interests. The protection of these faculties is the first object of government. From the protection of different and unequal faculties of acquiring property, the possession of different degrees and kinds of property immediately results; and from the influence of these on the sentiments and views of the respective proprietors, ensues a division of the society into different interests and parties.

The latent causes of faction are thus sown in the nature of man; and we see them everywhere brought into different degrees of activity, according to the different circumstances of civil society. A zeal for different opinions concerning religion, concerning government, and many other points, as well of speculation as of practice; an attachment to different leaders ambitiously contending for pre-eminence and power; or to persons of other descriptions whose fortunes have been interesting to the human passions, have, in turn, divided mankind into parties, inflamed them with mutual animosity, and rendered them much more disposed to vex and oppress each other than to co-operate for their common good. So strong is this propensity of mankind to fall into mutual animosities, that where no substantial occasion presents itself, the most frivolous and fanciful distinctions have been sufficient to kindle their unfriendly passions and excite their most violent conflicts. But the most common and durable source of factions has been the various and unequal distribution of property. Those who hold and those who are without property have ever formed distinct interests in society. Those who are creditors, and those who are debtors, fall under a like discrimination. A landed interest, a manufacturing interest, a mercantile interest, a moneyed interest, with many lesser interests, grow up of necessity in civilized nations, and divide them into different classes, actuated by different sentiments and views. The regulation of these various and interfering interests forms the principal task of modern legislation, and involves the spirit of party and faction in the necessary and ordinary operations of the government.

No man is allowed to be a judge in his own cause, because his interest would certainly bias his judgment, and, not improbably, corrupt his integrity. With equal, nay with greater reason, a body of men are unfit to be both judges and parties at the same time; yet what are many of the most important acts of legislation, but so many judicial determinations, not indeed concerning the rights of single persons, but concerning the rights of large bodies of citizens? And what are the different classes of legislators but advocates and parties to the causes which they determine? Is a law proposed concerning private debts? It is a question to which the creditors are parties on one side and the debtors on the other. Justice ought to hold the balance between them. Yet the parties are, and must be, themselves the judges; and the most numerous party, or, in other words, the most powerful faction must be expected to prevail. Shall domestic manufactures be encouraged, and in what degree, by restrictions on foreign manufactures? are questions which would be differently decided by the landed and the manufacturing classes, and probably by neither with a sole regard to justice and the public good. The apportionment of taxes on the various descriptions of property is an act which seems to require the most exact impartiality; yet there is, perhaps, no legislative act in which greater opportunity and temptation are given to a predominant party to trample on the rules of justice. Every shilling with which they overburden the inferior number, is a shilling saved to their own pockets.

It is in vain to say that enlightened statesmen will be able to adjust these clashing interests, and render them all subservient to the public good. Enlightened statesmen will not always be at the helm. Nor, in many cases, can such an adjustment be made at all without taking into view indirect and remote considerations, which will rarely prevail over the immediate interest which one party may find in disregarding the rights of another or the good of the whole.

The inference to which we are brought is, that the *causes* of faction cannot be removed, and that relief is only to be sought in the means of controlling its *effects*.

If a faction consists of less than a majority, relief is supplied by the republican principle, which enables the majority to defeat its sinister views by regular vote. It may clog the administration, it may convulse the society; but it will be unable to execute and mask its violence under the forms of the Constitution. When a majority is included in a faction, the form of popular government, on the other hand, enables it to sacrifice to its ruling passion or interest both the public good and the rights of other citizens. To secure the public good and private rights against the danger of such a faction, and at the same time to preserve the spirit and the form of popular government, is then the great object to which our inquiries are directed. Let me add that it is the great desideratum by which this form of government can be rescued from the opprobrium under which it has so long labored, and be recommended to the esteem and adoption of mankind.

By what means is this object attainable? Evidently by one of two only. Either the existence of the same passion or interest in a majority at the same time must be prevented, or the majority, having such coexistent passion or interest, must be rendered, by their number and local situation, unable to concert and carry into effect schemes of oppression. If the impulse and the opportunity be suffered to coincide, we well know that neither moral nor religious motives can be relied on as an adequate control. They are not found to be such on the injustice and violence of individuals, and lose their efficacy in proportion to the number combined together, that is, in proportion as their efficacy becomes needful.

From this view of the subject it may be concluded that a pure democracy, by which I mean a society consisting of a small number of citizens, who assemble and administer the government in person, can admit of no cure for the mischiefs of faction. A common passion or interest will, in almost every case, be felt by a majority of the whole; a communication and concert result from the form of government itself; and there is nothing to check the inducements to sacrifice the weaker party or an obnoxious individual. Hence it is that such democracies have ever been spectacles of turbulence and contention; have ever been found incompatible with personal security or the rights of property; and have in general been as short in their lives as they have been violent in their deaths. Theoretic politicians, who have patronized this species of government, have erroneously supposed that by reducing mankind to a perfect equality in their political rights, they would, at the same time, be perfectly equalized and assimilated in their possessions, their opinions, and their passions.

A republic, by which I mean a government in which the scheme of representation takes place, opens a different prospect, and promises the cure for which we are seeking. Let us examine the points in which it varies from pure democracy, and we shall comprehend both the nature of the cure and the efficacy which it must derive from the Union.

The two great points of difference between a democracy and a republic are: first, the delegation of the government, in the latter, to a small number of citizens elected by the rest; secondly, the greater number of citizens, and greater sphere of country, over which the latter may be extended.

The effect of the first difference is, on the one hand, to refine and enlarge the public views, by passing them through the medium of a chosen body of citizens, whose wisdom may best discern the true interest of their country, and whose patriotism and love of justice will be least likely to sacrifice it to temporary or partial considerations. Under such a regulation, it may well happen that the public voice, pronounced by the representatives of the people, will be more consonant to the public good than if pronounced by the people themselves, convened for the purpose. On the other hand, the effect may be inverted. Men of factious tempers, of local prejudices, or of sinister designs, may, by intrigue, by corruption, or by other means, first obtain the suffrages, and then betray the interests, of the people. The question resulting is, whether small or extensive republics are more favorable to the election of proper guardians of the public weal; and it is clearly decided in favor of the latter by two obvious considerations:

In the first place, it is to be remarked that, however small the republic may be, the representatives must be raised to a certain number, in order to guard against the cabals of a few; and that, however large it may be, they must be limited to a certain number, in order to guard against the confusion of a multitude. Hence, the number of representatives in the two cases not being in proportion to that of the two constituents, and being proportionally greater in the small republic, it follows that, if the proportion of fit characters be not less in the large than in the small republic, the former will present a greater option, and consequently a greater probability of a fit choice.

In the next place, as each representative will be chosen by a greater number of citizens in the large than in the small republic, it will be more difficult for unworthy candidates to practice with success the vicious arts by which elections are too often carried; and the suffrages of the people being more free, will be more likely to centre in men who possess the most attractive merit and the most diffusive and established characters.

It must be confessed that in this, as in most other cases, there is a mean, on both sides of which inconveniences will be found to lie. By enlarging too much the number of electors, you render the representatives too little acquainted with all their local circumstances and lesser interests; as by reducing it too much, you render him unduly attached to these, and too little fit to comprehend and pursue great and national objects. The federal Constitution forms a happy combination in this respect; the great and aggregate interests being referred to the national, the local and particular to the State legislatures.

The other point of difference is, the greater number of citizens and extent of territory which may be brought within the compass of republican than of democratic government; and it is this circumstance principally which renders factious combinations less to be dreaded in the former than in the latter. The smaller the society, the fewer probably will be the distinct parties and interests composing it; the fewer the distinct parties and interests, the more frequently will a majority be found of the same party; and the smaller the number of individuals composing a majority, and the smaller the compass within which they are placed, the more easily will they concert and execute their plans of oppression. Extend the sphere, and you take in a greater variety of parties and interests; you make it less probable that a majority of the whole will have a common motive to invade the rights of other citizens; or if such a common motive exists, it will be more difficult for all who feel it to discover their own strength, and to act in unison with each other. Besides other impediments, it may be remarked that, where there is a consciousness of unjust or dishonorable purposes, communication is always checked by distrust in proportion to the number whose concurrence is necessary.

Hence, it clearly appears, that the same advantage which a republic has over a democracy, in controlling the effects of faction, is enjoyed by a large over a small republic,—is enjoyed by the Union over the States composing it. Does the advantage consist in the substitution of representatives whose enlightened views and virtuous sentiments render them superior to local prejudices and schemes of injustice? It will not be denied that the representation of the Union will be most likely to possess these requisite endowments. Does it consist in the greater security afforded by a greater variety of parties, against the event of any one party being able to outnumber and oppress the rest? In an equal degree does the increased variety of parties comprised within the Union, increase this security. Does it, in fine, consist in the greater obstacles opposed to the concert and accomplishment of the secret wishes of an unjust and interested majority? Here, again, the extent of the Union gives it the most palpable advantage.

The influence of factious leaders may kindle a flame within their particular States, but will be unable to spread a general conflagration through the other States. A religious sect may degenerate into a political faction in a part of the Confederacy; but the variety of sects dispersed over the entire face of it must secure the national councils against any danger from that source. A rage for paper money, for an abolition of debts, for an equal division of property, or for any other improper or wicked project, will be less apt to pervade the whole body of the Union than a particular member of it; in the same proportion as such a malady is more likely to taint a particular county or district, than an entire State.

In the extent and proper structure of the Union, therefore, we behold a republican remedy for the diseases most incident to republican government. And according to the degree of pleasure and pride we feel in being republicans, ought to be our zeal in cherishing the spirit and supporting the character of Federalists.

PUBLIUS

The Federalist No. 51
James Madison
February 8, 1788

TO THE PEOPLE OF THE STATE OF NEW YORK

To what expedient, then, shall we finally resort, for maintaining in practice the necessary partition of power among the several departments, as laid down in the Constitution? The only answer that can be given is, that as all these exterior provisions are found to be inadequate, the defect must be supplied, by so contriving the interior structure of the government as that its several constituent parts may, by their mutual relations, be the means of keeping each other in their proper places. Without presuming to undertake a full development of this important idea, I will hazard a few general observations, which may perhaps place it in a clearer light, and enable us to form a more correct judgment of the principles and structure of the government planned by the convention.

In order to lay a due foundation for that separate and distinct exercise of the different powers of government, which to a certain extent is admitted on all hands to be essential to the preservation of liberty, it is evident that each department should have a will of its own; and consequently should be so constituted that the members of each should have as little agency as possible in the appointment of the members of the others. Were this principle rigorously adhered to, it would require that all the appointments for the supreme executive, legislative, and judiciary magistracies should be drawn from the same fountain of authority, the people, through channels having no communication whatever with one another. Perhaps such a plan of constructing the several departments would be less difficult in practice than it may in contemplation appear. Some difficulties, however, and some additional expense would attend the execution of it. Some deviations, therefore, from the principle must be admitted. In the constitution of the judiciary department in particular, it might be inexpedient to insist rigorously on the principle: first, because peculiar qualifications being essential in the members, the primary consideration ought to be to select that mode of choice which best secures these qualifications; secondly, because the permanent tenure by which the appointments are held in that department, must soon destroy all sense of dependence on the authority conferring them.

It is equally evident, that the members of each department should be as little dependent as possible on those of the others, for the emoluments annexed to their offices. Were the executive magistrate, or the judges, not independent of the legislature in this particular, their independence in every other would be merely nominal.

But the great security against a gradual concentration of the several powers in the same department, consists in giving to those who administer each department the necessary constitutional means and personal motives to resist encroachments of the others. The provision for defense must in this, as in all other cases, be made commensurate to the danger of attack. Ambition must be made to counteract ambition. The interest of the man must be connected with the constitutional rights of the place. It may be a reflection on human nature, that such devices should be necessary to control the abuses of government. But what is government itself, but the greatest of all reflections on human nature? If men were angels, no government would be necessary. If angels were to govern men, neither external nor internal controls on government would be necessary. In framing a government which is to be administered by men over men, the great difficulty lies in this: you must first enable the government to control the governed; and in the next place oblige it to control itself. A dependence on the people is, no doubt, the primary control on the government; but experience has taught mankind the necessity of auxiliary precautions.

This policy of supplying, by opposite and rival interests, the defect of better motives, might be traced through the whole system of human affairs, private as well as public. We see it particularly displayed in all the subordinate distributions of power, where the constant aim is to divide and arrange the several offices in such a manner as that each may be a check on the other—that the private interest of every individual may be a sentinel over the public rights. These inventions of prudence cannot be less requisite in the distribution of the supreme powers of the State.

But it is not possible to give to each department an equal power of self-defense. In republican government, the legislative authority necessarily predominates. The remedy for this inconveniency is to divide the legislature into different branches; and to render them, by different modes of election and different principles of action, as little connected with each other as the nature of their common functions and their common dependence on the society will admit. It may even be necessary to guard against dangerous encroachments by still further precautions. As the weight of the legislative authority requires that it should be thus divided, the weakness of the executive may require, on the other hand, that it should be fortified. An absolute negative on the legislature appears, at first view, to be the natural defense with which the executive magistrate should be armed. But perhaps it would be neither altogether safe nor alone sufficient. On ordinary occasions it might not be exerted with the requisite firmness, and on extraordinary occasions it might be perfidiously abused. May not this defect of an absolute negative be supplied by some qualified connection between this weaker department and the weaker branch of the stronger department, by which the latter may be led to support the constitutional rights of the former, without being too much detached from the rights of its own department?

If the principles on which these observations are founded be just, as I persuade myself they are, and they be applied as a criterion to the several State constitutions, and to the federal Constitution it will be found that if the latter does not perfectly correspond with them, the former are infinitely less able to bear such a test.

There are, moreover, two considerations particularly applicable to the federal system of America, which place that system in a very interesting point of view.

First. In a single republic, all the power surrendered by the people is submitted to the administration of a single government; and the usurpations are guarded against by a division of the government into distinct and separate departments. In the compound republic of America, the power surrendered by the people is first divided between two distinct governments, and then the portion allotted to each subdivided among distinct and separate departments. Hence a double security arises to the rights of the people. The different governments will control each other, at the same time that each will be controlled by itself.

Second. It is of great importance in a republic not only to guard the society against the oppression of its rulers, but to guard one part of the society against the injustice of the other part. Different interests necessarily exist in different classes of citizens. If a majority be united by a common interest, the rights of the minority will be insecure. There are but two methods of providing against this evil: the one by creating a will in the community independent of the majority that is, of the society itself; the other, by comprehending in the society so many separate descriptions of citizens as will render an unjust combination of a majority of the whole very improbable, if not impracticable. The first method prevails in all governments possessing an hereditary or self-appointed authority. This, at best, is but a precarious security; because a power independent of the society may as well espouse the unjust views of the major as the rightful interests of the minor party, and may possibly be turned against both parties. The second method will be exemplified in the federal republic of the United States. Whilst all authority in it will be derived from and dependent on the society, the society itself will be broken into so many parts, interests, and classes of citizens, that the rights of individuals, or of the minority, will be in little danger from interested combinations of the majority. In a free government the security for civil rights must be the same as that for religious rights. It consists in the one case in the multiplicity of interests, and in the other in the multiplicity of sects. The degree of security in both cases will depend on the number of interests and sects; and this may be presumed to depend on the extent of country and number of people comprehended under the same government. This view of the subject must particularly recommend a proper federal system to all the sincere and considerate friends of republican government, since it shows that in exact proportion as the territory of the Union may be formed into more circumscribed Confederacies, or States oppressive combinations of a majority will be facilitated: the best security, under the republican forms, for the rights of every class of citizens, will be diminished; and consequently the stability and independence of some member of the government, the only other security, must be proportionately increased. Justice is the end of government. It is the end of civil society. It ever has been and ever will be pursued until it be obtained, or until liberty be lost in the pursuit. In a society under the forms of which the stronger faction can readily unite and oppress the weaker, anarchy may as truly be said to reign as in a state of nature, where the weaker individual is not secured against the violence of the stronger; and as, in the latter state, even the stronger individuals are prompted, by the uncertainty of their condition, to submit to a government which may protect the weak as well as themselves; so, in the former state, will the more powerful factions or parties be gradually induced, by a like motive, to wish for a government which will protect all parties, the weaker as well as the more powerful. It can be little doubted that if the State of Rhode Island was separated from the Confederacy and left to itself, the insecurity of rights under the popular form of government within such narrow limits would be displayed by such reiterated oppressions of factious majorities that some power altogether independent of the people would soon be called for by the voice of the very factions whose misrule had proved the necessity of it. In the extended republic of the United States, and among the great variety of interests, parties, and sects which it embraces, a coalition of a majority of the whole society could seldom take place on any other principles than those of justice and the general good; whilst there being thus less danger to a minor from the will of a major party, there must be less pretext, also, to provide for the security of the former, by introducing into the government a will not dependent on the latter, or, in other words, a will independent of the society itself. It is no less certain than it is important, notwithstanding the contrary opinions which have been entertained, that the larger the society, provided it lie within a practical sphere, the more duly capable it will be of self-government. And happily for the *republican cause*, the practicable sphere may be carried to a very great extent, by a judicious modification and mixture of the *federal principle*.

PUBLIUS

Chapter 1

[1]Remarks by Governor Bush in Dayton, Ohio, *NBC Nightly News,* July 31, 2000.

[2]*New York Times,* August 4, 2000, p. A20.

[3]Ibid.

[4]*New York Times,* August 18, 2000, p. A1.

[5]*Motor Vehicle Safety Standards* 104 (1991).

[6]The National Center for Education Statistics, *Digest of Education Statistics, 1999,* Table 322; and *Statistical Abstract of the United States: 1999,* p. 198.

[7]V. O. Key, Jr., *Politics, Parties, and Pressure Groups,* 5th ed. (New York: Crowell, 1964), p. 3.

[8]David Easton, *The Political System: An Inquiry into the State of Political Science* (New York: Knopf, 1953), pp. 136–137.

[9]Key, *Politics, Parties, and Pressure Groups,* p. 2.

[10]*Observer* (London), November 29, 1964, p. 2.

[11]Key, *Politics, Parties, and Pressure Groups,* p. 2.

[12]"Remarks of Senator John F. Kennedy, Street Rally, Waterbury, Connecticut, November 6, 1960," in *The Speeches of Senator John F. Kennedy, Presidential Campaign of 1960* (Washington, D.C.: U.S. Government Printing Office, 1961), p. 912.

[13]Robert L. Lineberry, *American Public Policy: What Government Does and What Difference It Makes* (New York: Harper & Row, 1977), p. 3.

[14]Ibid., p. 24.

[15]Ibid., p. 69.

[16]Ibid., p. 71.

[17]For 2000 estimate, U.S. Census Bureau, POPClock as of August 22, 2000. For 2010 and 2015, U.S. Bureau of the Census, Current Population Reports, *Population Projections of the United States by Age, Sex, Race, and Hispanic Origin: 1995 to 2050,* series P25-1130, January 2000, p. 1; figures rounded.

[18]Ben J. Wattenberg, in collaboration with Richard M. Scammon, *This U.S.A.* (New York: Doubleday, 1965), p. 18. Population projections have been lowered since this study was published.

[19]Data provided by U.S. Bureau of the Census.

[20]See Wattenberg and Scammon, *This U.S.A.,* pp. 45–46.

[21]U.S. Bureau of the Census, Population Projections Program, *Projections of the Resident Population by Race, Hispanic Origin, and Nativity: Middle Series, 2050 to 2070,* series NP-T5-G, January 13, 2000.

[22]U.S. Bureau of the Census, Current Population Reports, *Residents of Farms and Rural Areas: 1991,* series P20-472, August 1993, p. 1.

[23]John Kenneth Galbraith, *The New Industrial State* (Boston: Houghton Mifflin, 1967), pp. 7–9, 392–393.

[24]See Rachel Carson, *Silent Spring* (Boston: Houghton Mifflin, 1962).

[25]John F. Kennedy, "Remarks at Amherst College," October 26, 1963, in *Public Papers of the Presidents of the United States, John F. Kennedy, 1963* (Washington, D.C.: U.S. Government Printing Office, 1964), p. 816.

[26]*Parliamentary Debates, House of Commons, Fifth Series,* vol. 444 (London: His Majesty's Stationery Office, 1947), pp. 206–207.

Chapter 2

[1]Daniel J. Boorstin, *The Americans: The National Experience* (New York: Random House, 1965), pp. 325ff.

[2]Ralph Ketcham, *Framed for Posterity: The Enduring Philosophy of the Constitution* (Lawrence: University Press of Kansas, 1993), p. 11.

[3]*Board of Regents of the University of Wisconsin v. Southworth,* 120 S. Ct. 1346 (2000).

[4]*Los Angeles Times,* November 1, 1999, p. A1; *The Washington Post,* November 7, 1999, p. A2; *The New York Times,* November 10, 1999, p. A20; and online at <www.news.wisc.edu./misc/fees/summary/html>.

[5]*Abood v. Detroit Board of Education,* 431 U.S. 209 (1977); *Keller v. State Bar of California,* 496 U.S. 1 (1990).

[6]*Rosenberger v. Rector and Visitors of University of Virginia,* 515 U.S. 819 (1995).

[7]Ibid.

[8]*Brown v. Board of Education of Topeka et al.,* 347 U.S. 483 (1954).

[9]*Roe v. Wade,* 410 U.S. 113 (1973); *Doe v. Bolton,* 410 U.S. 179 (1973).

[10]Carl L. Becker, *The Declaration of Independence* (New York: Vintage Books, 1942), p. 5.

[11]David Hawke, *A Transaction of Free Men* (New York: Scribner's, 1964), p. 209.

[12]Ibid.

[13]Peter Laslett, ed., *Locke's Two Treatises of Government* (Cambridge: Cambridge University Press, 1960), p. 348.

[14]Samuel Eliot Morison, "The Mayflower Compact," in Daniel J. Boorstin, ed., *An American Primer* (Chicago: University of Chicago Press, 1966), p. 19.

[15]Clinton Rossiter, *Seedtime of the Republic* (New York: Harcourt Brace Jovanovich, 1953), p. 35.

[16]Ibid., p. 87.

[17]Ibid., p. 88.

[18]Nat Hentoff, *The First Freedom: The Tumultuous History of Free Speech in America* (New York: Delacorte Press, 1980), pp. 160–161.

[19]The newspaper was published in Boston on September 25, 1690.

[20]In Charles Francis Adams, ed., *The Works of John Adams,* vol. 10 (Boston: Little, Brown, 1856), p. 282.

[21]Gordon S. Wood, *The Radicalism of the American Revolution* (New York: Knopf, 1992), p. 6.

[22]Alpheus T. Mason, "America's Political Heritage: Revolution and Free Government—A Bicentennial Tribute," in M. Judd Harmon, ed., *Essays on the Constitution of the United States* (Port Washington, N.Y.: Kennikat Press, 1978), p. 17.

[23]Merrill Jensen, *The New Nation* (New York: Knopf, 1950), pp. 347, 348.

[24]William H. Riker, *Federalism: Origin, Operation, Significance* (Boston: Little, Brown, 1964), pp. 18, 20.

[25]Letter to James Duane, in Clinton Rossiter, *1787: The Grand Convention* (New York: Macmillan, 1966), p. 53.

[26]Catherine Drinker Bowen, *Miracle at Philadelphia* (Boston: Little, Brown, 1966).

[27]Charles Warren, *The Making of the Constitution* (New York: Barnes & Noble, 1967), pp. 55–60.

[28]Bowen, *Miracle at Philadelphia,* p. 23.

[29]John P. Roche, "The Founding Fathers: A Reform Caucus in Action," *American Political Science Review,* vol. 55, no. 4 (December 1961), p. 803.

[30]Fred Barbash, *The Founding: A Dramatic Account of the Writing of the Constitution* (New York: Linden Press/Simon & Schuster, 1987), p. 58.

[31]Ibid., p. 69.

[32]Bowen, *Miracle at Philadelphia,* p. 186.

[33]James MacGregor Burns, *The Vineyard of Liberty: The American Experiment* (New York: Knopf, 1982), p. 40.

[34]Barbash, *The Founding,* p. 149.

[35]In Carl Van Doren, *The Great Rehearsal* (New York: Viking Press, 1948), p. 153.

[36]Warren, *The Making of the Constitution,* pp. 687–688.

[37]In Van Doren, *The Great Rehearsal,* p. 174.

[38]Baron de Montesquieu, *The Spirit of the Laws,* vol. 1 (New York: Hafner, 1949), p. 151.

[39]Edward S. Corwin, Harold W. Chase, and Craig R. Ducat, *The Constitution and What It Means Today* (Princeton: Princeton University Press, 1978), p. 5.

[40]The War Powers Resolution is discussed in detail in Chapter 13.

[41]Alpheus T. Mason, *The Supreme Court: Palladium of Freedom* (Ann Arbor: University of Michigan Press, 1962), p. 8.

[42]Archibald Cox, *The Court and the Constitution* (Boston: Houghton Mifflin, 1987), p. 42.

[43]*Marbury v. Madison*, 1 Cranch 137 (1803). Judicial review is discussed in Chapter 15.

[44]Richard F. Fenno, Jr., *The President's Cabinet* (Cambridge: Harvard University Press, 1959), pp. 19–20.

[45]Charles A. Beard, *An Economic Interpretation of the Constitution of the United States* (New York: Macmillan, 1935), p. 188. Originally published in 1913.

[46]Forrest McDonald, *We the People* (Chicago: University of Chicago Press, 1958), pp. vii, 350, 415.

[47]Robert E. Brown, *Charles Beard and the Constitution* (Princeton: Princeton University Press, 1956), p. 198.

[48]Charles Francis Adams, ed., *The Works of John Adams*, vol. 6 (Boston: Little, Brown, 1851), p. 484.

[49]Ketcham, *Framed for Posterity: The Enduring Philosophy of the Constitution*, p. 27.

[50]James Madison, "The Federalist, No. 40," in Edward Mead Earle, ed., *The Federalist* (New York: Random House, Modern Library), p. 257.

[51]Alexander Hamilton, "The Federalist, No. 84," in Earle, ed., *The Federalist*, p. 561.

[52]Seymour Martin Lipset, *The First New Nation* (New York: Basic Books, 1963), p. 2.

[53]Ibid, p. 16.

[54]*McCulloch v. Maryland*, 4 Wheaton 316 (1819).

[55]Alexander Hamilton, "The Federalist, No. 68," in Earle, ed., *The Federalist*, pp. 441–442.

[56]Year after each amendment refers to year of ratification.

[57]*U.S. Term Limits v. Thornton*, 115 S. Ct. 1842 (1995).

[58]*Clinton v. City of New York*, 524 U.S. 417 (1998).

[59]"Letter to Samuel Kercheval, 1816," in Saul K. Padover, ed., *The Complete Jefferson* (New York: Duell, Sloan & Pearce, 1943), p. 291.

Chapter 3

[1]Data as of May 1, 1996, provided by Office of Highway Safety, Federal Highway Administration; and data for the year 2000 provided by "Maximum Speed Limits in Each State," online at web.missouri.edu/~c669885/ncasl/limits.html.

[2]*Washington Post*, November 19, 1995, p. A16; and *New York Times*, November 19, 1995, p. A24.

[3]William H. Riker, *Federalism: Origin, Operation, Significance* (Boston: Little, Brown, 1964), p. 1.

[4]Riker, *Federalism: Origin, Operation, Significance*, pp. 152–153.

[5]Adapted from U.S. Department of Commerce, Bureau of Economic Analysis, online at <www.bea.doc.gov/bea/regional/spi/pcpi.htm>.

[6]Morton Grodzins, *The American System* (Chicago: Rand McNally, 1966), pp. 3–4.

[7]U.S. Bureau of the Census, *Statistical Abstract of the United States: 1999*, p. 309.

[8]Morton Grodzins, "Centralization and Decentralization in the American Federal System," in Robert A. Goldwin, ed., *A Nation of States* (Chicago: Rand McNally, 1963), pp. 1–4.

[9]Grodzins, *The American System*; Daniel J. Elazar, *American Federalism: A View from the States* (New York: Crowell, 1966); Daniel J. Elazar, *The American Partnership* (Chicago: University of Chicago Press, 1962).

[10]Michael D. Reagan, *The New Federalism* (New York: Oxford University Press, 1972), pp. 4, 145.

[11]*Regulatory Federalism: Policy, Process, Impact and Reform* (Washington, D.C.: Advisory Commission on Intergovernmental Relations, 1984), p. 9.

[12]Donald F. Kettl, *The Regulation of American Federalism* (Baltimore: Johns Hopkins University Press, 1987), p. 174.

[13]James L. Sundquist with David W. Davis, *Making Federalism Work* (Washington, D.C.: The Brookings Institution, 1969), p. 12.

[14]"Letter to George Washington, April 16, 1787," in Saul K. Padover, ed., *The Complete Madison* (New York: Harper & Brothers, 1953), p. 184.

[15]Riker, *Federalism: Origin, Operation, Significance*, pp. 4–5.

[16]*McCulloch v. Maryland*, 4 Wheaton 316 (1819).

[17]*United States v. Curtiss-Wright Export Corp.*, 299 U.S. 304 (1936).

[18]*McCulloch v. Maryland* (1819).

[19]Alfred H. Kelly and Winfred A. Harbison, *The American Constitution* (New York: Norton, 1955), p. 176.

[20]In Walter Berns, "The Meaning of the Tenth Amendment," in Goldwin, ed., *A Nation of States*, p. 138. For a spirited defense of the opposite view, see "The Case for 'States' Rights'" by James J. Kilpatrick in the same volume.

[21]*Collector v. Day*, 11 Wallace 113 (1871). This decision was overruled by the Supreme Court in 1939 in *Graves v. O'Keefe*, 306 U.S. 466 (1939).

[22]*Schechter Poultry Corporation v. United States*, 295 U.S. 495 (1935).

[23]*Steward Machine Co. v. Davis*, 301 U.S. 548 (1937); *National Labor Relations Board v. Jones & Laughlin Steel Corp.*, 301 U.S. 1 (1937).

[24]*United States v. Darby*, 312 U.S. 100 (1941).

[25]*The National League of Cities v. Usery*, 426 U.S. 833 (1976).

[26]*Equal Employment Opportunity Commission v. Wyoming*, 460 U.S. 226 (1983).

[27]*Garcia v. San Antonio Metropolitan Transit Authority*, 469 U.S. 528 (1985).

[28]*United States v. Lopez*, 514 U.S. 549 (1995).

[29]*Seminole Tribe of Florida v. Florida*, 517 U.S. 44 (1996).

[30]*Printz v. United States* and *Mack v. United States*, 521 U.S. 98 (1997).

[31]*Alden v. Maine*, 527 U.S. 706 (1999).

[32]*Kimel v. Florida Board*, 528 U.S. 62 (2000).

[33]*United States v. Morrison*, 120 S. Ct. 1740 (2000).

[34]*Federal Maritime Commission v. South Carolina Ports Authority*, No. 01-46, 2002.

[35]Elazar, *American Federalism: A View from the States*, p. 164.

[36]*Williams v. North Carolina*, 317 U.S. 287 (1942), 325 U.S. 226 (1945).

[37]*Powell v. Alabama*, 287 U.S. 45 (1932).

[38]*Norris v. Alabama*, 294 U.S. 587 (1935).

[39]*New York Times*, August 8, 1965, section 4, p. 2.

[40]Testimony of David A. Stockman, director, Office of Management and Budget, to House Budget Committee, February 22, 1984, p. 12.

[41]John W. Ellwood, "Introduction," in John William Ellwood, ed., *Reductions in U.S. Domestic Spending: How They Affect State and Local Governments* (New Brunswick, N.J.: Transaction Books, 1982), p. 3.

[42]*New York Times*, February 16, 1988, p. D19.

[43]*National Journal*, December 8, 1990, p. 2957.

[44]*Budget of the United States Government, Fiscal Year 2001* (Washington, D.C: U.S. Government Printing Office, 2000), p. 2.

[45]V. O. Key, Jr., *Southern Politics in State and Nation* (New York: Knopf, 1949), p. 307.

[46]Richard E. Dawson and James A. Robinson, "Inter-Party Competition, Economic Variables and Welfare Policies in the American States," *Journal of Politics*, vol. 25 (1963), pp. 265–289; Thomas R. Dye, *Politics, Economics, and the Public: Policy Outcomes in the American States* (Chicago: Rand McNally, 1966), p. 293; Thomas R. Dye, *Understanding Public Policy*, 2nd ed. (Englewood Cliffs, N.J.: Prentice Hall, 1975), p. 304.

[47]Brian R. Fry and Richard F. Winters, "The Politics of Redistribution," *American Political Science Review*, vol. 64 (June 1970), pp. 508–522.

[48]Virginia H. Gray, "The Determinants of Public Policy: A Reappraisal," in Thomas R. Dye and Virginia Gray, eds., *The Determinants of Public Policy* (Lexington, Mass.: D. C. Heath, 1980), p. 217.

[49]Analytical Perspectives, *Budget of the United States Government, Fiscal Year 2001* (Washington, D.C: U.S. Government Printing Office, 2000), p. 241.

[50]Advisory Commission on Intergovernmental Relations, *Fiscal Balance in the American Federal System*, vol. 1 (Washington, D.C.: U.S. Government Printing Office, 1967), p. 137.

[51]Advisory Commission on Intergovernmental Relations, *Summary and Concluding Observations: The Intergovernmental Grant System* (Washington, D.C.: U.S. Government Printing Office, 1978), p. 3.

[52]*Budget of the United States Government, Fiscal Year 2001*, p.2. Of every dollar the federal government collected in fiscal 2001, approximately 58 cents came from the federal income tax. The total includes both

individual income taxes (48 percent) and corporate income taxes (10 percent).

53David R. Beam, "Washington's Regulation of States and Localities: Origins and Issues," *Intergovernmental Perspective,* published by the Advisory Commission on Intergovernmental Relations, vol. 7, no. 3 (Summer 1981), p. 10. For a discussion of some of the complex issues related to regulatory federalism, see Mel Dubnick and Alan Gitelson, "Nationalizing State Policies," in *The Nationalization of State Government,* Jerome J. Hanus, ed. (Lexington, Mass.: D. C. Heath, 1981), pp. 39–74.

54Nelson A. Rockefeller, *The Future of Federalism* (Cambridge: Harvard University Press, 1962), p. 15.

55*New York Times,* December 31, 1998, p. A11.

Chapter 4

1*Reno v. American Civil Liberties Union,* 521 U.S. 844 (1997).

2*New York Times,* June 27, 1997, p. A20.

3John Stuart Mill, *On Liberty* (New York: Appleton-Century-Crofts, 1947), p. 52.

4As noted in Chapter 2, some scholars regard only the first eight or nine amendments as the Bill of Rights.

5Earl Warren, "The Law and the Future," *Fortune,* November 1955, p. 107.

6Alpheus T. Mason, *The Supreme Court: Palladium of Freedom* (Ann Arbor: University of Michigan Press, 1962), p. 58.

7*Palko v. Connecticut,* 302 U.S. 319 (1937).

8*Feiner v. New York,* 340 U.S. 315 (1951).

9*Schenck v. United States,* 249 U.S. 47 (1919).

10*United States v. O'Brien,* 391 U.S. 367 (1968).

11*Texas v. Johnson,* 491 U.S. 397 (1989).

12*United States v. Eichman* and *United States v. Haggerty,* both 496 U.S. 310 (1990).

13*Smith v. Goguen,* 415 U.S. 566 (1974).

14*Rankin v. McPherson,* 483 U.S. 378 (1987).

15*Simon & Schuster v. New York State Crime Victims Board,* 502 U.S. 105 (1991).

16*Hill v. City of Houston,* 483 U.S. 1001 (1987).

17*Ward v. Rock Against Racism,* 491 U.S. 781 (1989).

18*R. A. V. v. St. Paul,* 505 U.S. 377 (1992).

19*Washington Post,* September 12, 1992, p. A1.

20Ibid.

21*Wisconsin v. Mitchell,* 508 U.S. 476 (1993).

22*Tinker v. Des Moines School District et al.,* 393 U.S. 503 (1969).

23*Bethel School District No. 403 v. Fraser,* 478 U.S. 675 (1986).

24*Hazelwood School District v. Kuhlmeier,* 484 U.S. 260 (1988).

25Ibid.

26*Board of Education, Island Trees Union Free School District v. Pico,* 457 U.S. 853 (1982).

27*Washington Post,* May 10, 1982, p. A2.

28Hugo L. Black, "The Bill of Rights," *New York University Law Review,* vol. 35 (April 1960), p. 867.

29*United States v. Carolene Products Co.,* 304 U.S. 144 (1938).

30*Roth v. United States* and *Alberts v. California,* both 354 U.S. 476 (1957).

31D. H. Lawrence, "Pornography and Obscenity," in Diana Trilling, ed., *The Portable D. H. Lawrence* (New York: Viking Press, 1947), p. 646.

32*Jacobellis v. Ohio,* 378 U.S. 184 (1964).

33*Miller v. California,* 413 U.S. 15 (1973).

34Ibid.

35*Pope v. Illinois,* 481 U.S. 497 (1987).

36*Jenkins v. Georgia,* 418 U.S. 153 (1974).

37*Barnes v. Glen Theatre,* 501 U.S. 560 (1991).

38*City of Erie v. Pap's* A.M. 529 U.S. 277 (2000).

39*Sable Communications of California, Inc. v. Federal Communications Commission,* 492 U.S. 115 (1989).

40*Hamling v. United States,* 418 U.S. 87 (1974).

41*New York v. Ferber,* 458 U.S. 747 (1982).

42*National Endowment for the Arts v. Finley,* 524 U.S. 569 (1998).

43*Olmstead v. United States,* 277 U.S. 438 (1928).

44*Griswold v. Connecticut,* 381 U.S. 479 (1965).

45*Roe v. Wade,* 410 U.S. 113 (1973).

46*Stanley v. Georgia,* 394 U.S. 557 (1969).

47*Cantrell v. Forest City Publishing Co.,* 419 U.S. 245 (1974).

48*Cox Broadcasting Corp. v. Cohn,* 420 U.S. 469 (1975).

49*De Jonge v. Oregon,* 299 U.S. 353 (1937).

50*Davis v. Massachusetts,* 167 U.S. 43 (1897).

51*Hague v. C. I. O.,* 307 U.S. 496 (1939).

52*Collin v. Smith,* 439 U.S. 916 (1978); see also *National Socialist Party v. Village of Skokie,* 432 U.S. 43 (1977).

53*Hurley v. Irish-American Gay, Lesbian, and Bisexual Group of Boston,* 515 U.S. 557 (1995).

54*United States v. Grace,* 461 U.S. 171 (1983).

55*United States v. Seeger,* 380 U.S. 163 (1965).

56*Welsh v. United States,* 398 U.S. 333 (1970).

57Ibid.

58*Gillette v. United States* and *Negre v. Larsen,* 401 U.S. 437 (1971).

59*Minersville School District v. Gobitis,* 310 U.S. 586 (1940).

60The Jehovah's Witnesses won their fight in *West Virginia Board of Education v. Barnette,* 319 U.S. 624 (1943). (Walter Barnett's name was misspelled in court records.)

61The Amish prevailed in *Wisconsin v. Yoder,* 406 U.S. 205 (1972).

62A member of the Seventh-Day Adventist church won her case in *Sherbert v. Verner,* 374 U.S. 398 (1963).

63William Cohen, Murray Schwartz, and DeAnne Sobul, *The Bill of Rights: A Source Book* (New York: Benziger Brothers, 1968), pp. 267–268.

64*Oregon v. Smith,* 494 U.S. 872 (1990).

65*Reynolds v. United States,* 98 U.S. 145 (1878); *Davis v. Beason,* 133 U.S. 333 (1890).

66*Church of the Lukumi Babalu Aye Inc. v. City of Hialeah,* 508 U.S. 520 (1993).

67*Bob Jones University v. United States* and *Goldsboro Christian Schools, Inc. v. United States,* 461 U.S. 574 (1983).

68*City of Boerne v. Flores,* 521 U.S. 507 (1997).

69*Everson v. Board of Education,* 330 U.S. 1 (1947).

70*Lynch v. Donnelly,* 465 U.S. 471 (1984).

71*Engel v. Vitale,* 370 U.S. 421 (1962).

72"Almighty God, we acknowledge our dependence upon Thee, and we beg Thy blessings upon us, our parents, our teachers, and our country."

73*Engel v. Vitale* (1962).

74*Abington School District v. Schempp* and *Murray v. Curlett,* both 374 U.S. 203 (1963).

75Data provided by the National Center for Educational Statistics, the Department of Education, and the National Catholic Education Association.

76*Everson v. Board of Education* (1947).

77*Zorach v. Clauson,* 343 U.S. 306 (1952).

78*Agostini v. Felton,* 521 U.S. 203 (1997), which overruled the Supreme Court's decision in *Aguilar v. Felton,* 473 U.S. 402 (1985), and *Grand Rapids v. Ball,* 473 U.S. 373 (1985).

79*Mitchell v. Helms,* 120 S. Ct. 2530 (2000).

80*Washington Post,* June 29, 2000, p. A. 13.

81*Board of Education of Westside Community Schools v. Mergens,* 496 U.S. 226 (1990).

82*Zobrest v. Catalina Foothills School District,* 508 U.S. 1 (1993).

83*Lee v. Weisman,* 505 U.S. 577 (1992).

84*Santa Fe Independent School District v. Doe,* 120 S. Ct. 2266 (2000).

85Ibid.

86*Tilton v. Richardson,* 403 U.S. 672 (1971).

[87]*Dennis v. United States,* 341 U.S. 494 (1951).

[88]*Yates v. United States,* 354 U.S. 298 (1957); *Scales v. United States,* 367 U.S. 203 (1961); *Noto v. United States,* 367 U.S. 290 (1961); *Elfbrandt v. Russell,* 384 U.S. 11 (1966).

[89]*Communist Party v. Subversive Activities Control Board,* 367 U.S. 1 (1961).

[90]*Albertson v. Subversive Activities Control Board,* 382 U.S. 70 (1965).

[91]*McNabb v. United States,* 318 U.S. 332 (1943).

[92]*Wilson v. Layne,* 526 U.S. 603 (1999), and *Hanlon v. Berger,* 526 U.S. 808 (1999).

[93]*Wilson v. Layne* (1999).

[94]*Hanlon v. Berger* (1999).

[95]*Payton v. New York,* 445 U.S. 573 (1980).

[96]Ibid.

[97]*Wilson v. Arkansas,* 514 U.S. 927 (1995).

[98]*Chimel v. California,* 395 U.S. 752 (1969).

[99]*New York Times,* July 1, 1973, section 4, p. 6.

[100]*New York Times,* September 26, 1975, p. 1.

[101]*New Jersey v. T. L. O.,* 469 U.S. 325 (1985).

[102]*Vernonia School District v. Acton,* 515 U.S. 646 (1995).

[103]*Carroll v. United States,* 267 U.S. 132 (1925); *Texas v. White,* 423 U.S. 67 (1976); *United States v. Ross,* 456 U.S. 305 (1982).

[104]*United States v. Ross* (1982).

[105]*Wyoming v. Houghton,* 526 U.S. 295 (1999).

[106]*Pennsylvania v. Mimms,* 434 U.S. 106 (1977).

[107]*New York v. Belton,* 453 U.S. 454 (1981).

[108]Ibid.

[109]*Knowles v. Iowa,* 525 U.S. 113 (1998).

[110]*Michigan v. Sitz,* 496 U.S. 444 (1990).

[111]*Terry v. Ohio,* 392 U.S. 1 (1968).

[112]*Adams v. Williams,* 407 U.S. 143 (1972).

[113]*United States v. Watson,* 423 U.S. 411 (1976).

[114]*Illinois v. Wardlow,* 528 U.S. 119 (2000).

[115]*Florida v. J.L.* 120 S. Ct. 1375 (2000).

[116]*Mapp v. Ohio,* 367 U.S. 643 (1961).

[117]*Weeks v. United States,* 232 U.S. 383 (1914).

[118]*United States v. Calandra,* 414 U.S. 338 (1974).

[119]*United States v. Peltier,* 422 U.S. 531 (1975).

[120]*Stone v. Powell* and *Wolff v. Rice,* both 429 U.S. 874 (1976).

[121]*Illinois v. Gates,* 462 U.S. 213 (1983).

[122]*Nix v. Williams,* 464 U.S. 417 (1984).

[123]*United States v. Leon,* 468 U.S. 897 (1984).

[124]*Massachusetts v. Sheppard,* 468 U.S. 981 (1984).

[125]*Maryland v. Garrison,* 480 U.S. 79 (1987).

[126]*Zurcher v. Stanford Daily,* 436 U.S. 547 (1978).

[127]Alan F. Westin, *Privacy and Freedom* (New York: Atheneum, 1967), pp. 70, 87.

[128]*Olmstead v. United States* (1928).

[129]*Nardone v. United States,* 302 U.S. 379 (1937); *Benanti v. United States,* 355 U.S. 96 (1957).

[130]*Katz v. United States,* 389 U.S. 347 (1967). *Katz* overruled the *Olmstead* decision. In a related case, *Berger v. New York,* 388 U.S. 41 (1967), the Supreme Court invalidated a New York State law that permitted police to engage in electronic surveillance with a court warrant; the Court held that the state law was too broad in setting standards for electronic eavesdropping.

[131]*Tyler v. Berodt,* 493 U.S. 1022 (1990).

[132]Data provided by Steven Aftergood, the Federation of American Scientists, and the Department of Justice Web site, online at <www.usdoj.gov/04foia/readingrooms/oipr_records.htm>.

[133]*Dalia v. United States,* 441 U.S. 238 (1979).

[134]*Mallory v. United States,* 354 U.S. 449 (1957).

[135]*Escobedo v. Illinois,* 378 U.S. 478 (1964).

[136]*United States v. Henry,* 447 U.S. 264 (1980); *Illinois v. Perkins,* 496 U.S. 292 (1990).

[137]*Miranda v. Arizona,* 384 U.S. 436 (1966).

[138]*Lego v. Twomey,* 404 U.S. 477 (1972); *Dutton v. Evans,* 400 U.S. 74 (1970); *Kastigar v. United States,* 406 U.S. 441 (1972); *Michigan v. Tucker,* 417 U.S. 433 (1974); *Oregon v. Hass,* 420 U.S. 714 (1975).

[139]*Michigan v. Mosley,* 423 U.S. 96 (1975).

[140]*Doyle v. Ohio* and *Wood v. Ohio,* both 426 U.S. 610 (1976).

[141]*Jenkins v. Anderson,* 447 U.S. 231 (1980).

[142]The Supreme Court reversed Williams's conviction in *Brewer v. Williams,* 430 U.S. 387 (1977). His conviction at the second trial was upheld by the Court in *Nix v. Williams* (1984).

[143]*Rhode Island v. Innis,* 446 U.S. 291 (1980).

[144]*New York v. Quarles,* 467 U.S. 649 (1984).

[145]*Washington Post,* August 26, 1985, p. A6.

[146]*New York Times,* May 31, 1987, section 4, p. 1.

[147]*Dickerson v. United States* 120 S. Ct. 2326 (2000).

[148]*Gideon v. Wainwright,* 372 U.S. 335 (1963).

[149]*Betts v. Brady,* 316 U.S. 455 (1942).

[150]*Argersinger v. Hamlin,* 407 U.S. 25 (1972).

[151]Chief Justice John Marshall, in *Barron v. Baltimore,* 7 Peters 243 (1833).

[152]*Gitlow v. New York,* 268 U.S. 652 (1925).

[153]*Fiske v. Kansas,* 274 U.S. 380 (1927).

[154]*Near v. Minnesota* (1931).

[155]*Powell v. Alabama,* 287 U.S. 45 (1932).

[156]*Hamilton v. Regents of the University of California,* 293 U.S. 245 (1934).

[157]*De Jonge v. Oregon* (1937).

[158]*Palko v. Connecticut* (1937).

[159]*Robinson v. California,* 370 U.S. 660 (1962); *Furman v. Georgia,* 408 U.S. 238 (1972).

[160]*Malloy v. Hogan,* 378 U.S. 1 (1964).

[161]*Gideon v. Wainwright* (1963); *Argersinger v. Hamlin* (1972).

[162]*Klopfer v. North Carolina,* 386 U.S. 213 (1967).

[163]*Pointer v. Texas,* 380 U.S. 400 (1965).

[164]*Washington v. Texas,* 388 U.S. 14 (1967).

[165]*Duncan v. Louisiana,* 391 U.S. 145 (1968).

[166]*Benton v. Maryland,* 395 U.S. 784 (1969).

[167]*West Virginia Board of Education v. Barnette* (1943).

[168]In Mason, *The Supreme Court: Palladium of Freedom,* p. 171n.

[169]*Trop v. Dulles,* 356 U.S. 86 (1958).

[170]*Kennedy v. Mendoza-Martinez,* 372 U.S. 144 (1963).

[171]*Schneider v. Rusk,* 377 U.S. 163 (1964).

[172]*Afroyim v. Rusk,* 387 U.S. 253 (1967).

[173]Data provided by U.S. Immigration and Naturalization Service for October 1996.

[174]*Sale v. Haitian Centers Council,* 509 U.S. 155 (1993).

[175]Data for November 1996 from U.S. Immigration and Naturalization Service, online at <www.ins.usdoj.gov>.

[176]*Graham v. Richardson,* 403 U.S. 365 (1971); *In re Griffiths,* 413 U.S. 717 (1973); *Foley v. Connelie,* 435 U.S. 291 (1978); *Ambach v. Norwick,* 441 U.S. 68 (1979).

[177]*Plyler v. Doe,* 457 U.S. 202 (1982).

[178]*The San Antonio Independent School District v. Rodriguez,* 411 U.S. 1 (1973).

[179]*New York Times,* October 4, 1989, p. B9.

[180]Data provided by Education Commission of the States.

[181]Ibid.

Chapter 5

[1]U.S. Bureau of the Census, Current Population Reports, Population Characteristics, *The Black Population in the United States: March 1997 (Update),* series P20-508, June 1998, p. 1.

[2]The Centers for Disease Control and Prevention, *National Vital Statistics Report*, vol. 47, no. 4, table 14, October 7, 1998, p. 28.

[3]The Centers for Disease Control and Prevention, *National Vital Statistics Reports*, vol. 47, no. 19, table 8, June 20, 1999, p. 35.

[4]The Sentencing Project, Briefing/Fact Sheets, online at <www.sentencingproject.org>.

[5]Ibid. Data for 1997.

[6]Data from Bureau of Labor Statistics, U.S. Department of Labor, for January 2000.

[7]U.S. Bureau of the Census, Current Population Reports, *Consumer Income, Money Income in the United States: 1998*, series P60-206, September 1999, p. viii.

[8]William Julius Wilson, *The Truly Disadvantaged: The Inner City, the Underclass and Public Policy* (Chicago: University of Chicago Press, 1987).

[9]Data from U.S. Bureau of the Census.

[10]U.S. Bureau of the Census, Current Population Reports, *The Hispanic Population in the United States: March 1997 (Update)*, series P20-511, July 1998, p. 1

[11]U.S. Bureau of the Census, Population Projections Program, *Projections of the Resident Population by Race, Hispanic Origin and Nativity: Middle Series, 1999 and 2000*, NP-T5-A, January 13, 2000.

[12]U.S. Bureau of the Census, Current Population Reports, Consumer Income, *Money Income in the United States: 1998*, series P60-206, September 1999, p. x.

[13]U.S. Bureau of the Census, Population Projections Program, *Projections of the Resident Population by Race, Hispanic Origin and Nativity: Middle Series, 2050 to 2070*, NP-T5-G, January 13, 2000.

[14]U.S. Bureau of the Census, *Census Facts for Native American Month*, November 1997.

[15]Data provided by Bureau of Indian Affairs, U.S. Department of the Interior.

[16]The federal budget for fiscal 2001 included a totaled $9.4 billion for programs to assist Native Americans. Data provided by the White House.

[17]U.S. Bureau of the Census, Economic and Statistics Administration, *We the . . . First Americans*, September 1993, p. 6.

[18]Bureau of Indian Affairs, U.S. Department of the Interior, *1997 Labor Market Information on the Indian Labor Force: A National Report*, 1998.

[19]U.S. Bureau of the Census, *1997 Trends in Indian Health, Part 6— Community Health Statistics*, 1998, p. 177.

[20]Indian Health Service, U.S. Department of Health and Human Services, *Trends in Indian Health 1995*, p. 30.

[21]Ibid., pp. 62–63.

[22]Ibid., p. 68.

[23]*United States v. Sioux Nation of Indians*, 448 U.S. 371 (1980).

[24]Dee Brown, *Bury My Heart at Wounded Knee* (New York: Holt, Rinehart and Winston, 1970).

[25]Adapted from U.S. Bureau of the Census, *Median Income by Sex, Race, Age, and Education 1997–98*.

[26]U.S. Bureau of the Census, Current Population Reports, *The Hispanic Population in the United States: March 1997 (Update)*, series P20-511, July 1998, p. 1.

[27]*1999 National Directory of Latino Elected Officials* (Washington, D.C.: National Association of Latino Elected and Appointed Officials Educational Fund, 1999).

[28]There were 93 Hispanic state legislators in these eight states in 1984, and 146 in 1999. Data provided by the National Association of Latino Elected and Appointed Officials Educational Fund.

[29]*Washington Post*, March 29, 1978, p. A6.

[30]*New York Times*, April 21, 1978, p. 14.

[31]Data provided by U.S. Immigration and Naturalization Service for October 1996.

[32]U.S. Bureau of the Census, March 1997 Current Population Survey, *Foreign-Born and Citizenship by Race-Ethnicity: Both Sexes— Values/Percents*, table 10.7, August 7, 1998, p. 1.

[33]*DeCanas v. Bica*, 424 U.S. 351 (1976).

[34]*Plyler v. Doe*, 457 U.S. 202 (1982).

[35]Current Population Reports, table 1.1, March 1997 *CPS: Age by Race-Ethnicity: Both Sexes-Values*.

[36]Data on Asian population distribution from U.S. Bureau of the Census, 1990 *Census of Population*

[37]In the year 2000, there were 58 women in the House and 9 in the Senate.

[38]Department of Defense, *Defense Issues*, vol. 11, no. 31, September 13, 1999, p.1

[39]Data provided by the Center for American Women and Politics, Eagleton Institute of Politics, Rutgers University online at <www.cawp.rutgers.edu>. Total for female mayors is for cities of more than 30,000 population.

[40]Ibid.

[41]Data provided by National Center for Education Statistics, U.S. Department of Education. Of the 1997 total, 6,450 women were graduates of medical schools and 17,531 earned law degrees.

[42]Bureau of Labor Statistics, U.S. Department of Labor, *Employment Situation*, table A-1, January 18, 2000, p. 1.

[43]Carol A. Whitehurst, *Women in America: The Oppressed Majority* (Santa Monica: Goodyear Publishing, 1977), p. 69.

[44]*Grove City v. Bell*, 465 U.S. 555 (1984).

[45]Joyce Gelb and Marian Lief Palley, *Women and Public Policies* (Princeton: Princeton University Press, 1982), p. 4.

[46]Ibid., p. 5.

[47]*Rostker v. Goldberg*, 453 U.S. 57 (1981).

[48]*New York Times*, January 25, 1980, p. 1.

[49]Data provided by the Center for American Women and Politics, Eagleton Institute of Politics, Rutgers University. Of the 197 women who have served in Congress, 22 were elected to the Senate and 170 to the House, and five served in both the House and Senate. In addition, three women have served as delegates to the House.

[50]Center for American Women and Politics, Eagleton Institute of Politics, Rutgers University, *Fact Sheet: Women in Elective Office 2000*, pp. 1–2.

[51]*New York Times*, October 11, 1991, p. A1.

[52]*Harris v. Forklift Systems, Inc.*, 510 U.S. 17 (1993).

[53]Ibid.

[54]The Gallup Organization, Poll Releases, "Many Women Cite Spousal Abuse, Job Performance Affected," October 25, 1997, pp. 1–2, online at <www.gallup.com/poll/releases/pr971025.asp>.

[55]*Akron v. Akron Center for Reproductive Health, Inc.*, 462 U.S. 416 (1983).

[56]*Thornburgh v. American College of Obstetricians and Gynecologists*, 476 U.S. 747 (1986).

[57]*Hartigan v. Zbaraz*, 484 U.S. 171 (1987).

[58]*Webster v. Reproductive Health Services*, 492 U.S. 990 (1989).

[59]*Washington Post*, July 4, 1989, p. A1.

[60]*Hodgson v. Minnesota*, 497 U.S. 417 (1990), and *Ohio v. Akron Center for Reproductive Health*, 497 U.S. 502 (1990).

[61]*Planned Parenthood of Southeastern Pennsylvania v. Casey*, 505 U.S. 833 (1992).

[62]Ibid.

[63]Ibid.

[64]*Stenberg v. Carhart* No. 99-830.

[65]*Harris v. McRae*, 448 U.S. 297 (1980).

[66]*Washington Post*, December 21, 1999, p. A1.

[67]*New York Times*, December 21, 1999, p. A1.

[68]*Washington Post*, October 7, 1994, p. A1.

[69]Robert E. Fay, Charles F. Turner, Albert D. Klassen, and John H. Gagnon, "Prevalence and Patterns of Same-Gender Sexual Contact among Men," *Science*, vol. 243, January 20, 1989, pp. 338–348. The conclusions of the authors were based on their interpretation of a Kinsey survey taken in 1970.

[70]Gallup poll, June 1998, in the *New York Times*, August 2, 1998, section 4, p. 3.

[71]Ibid.

[72]The Gallup Organization, Gallup Social and Economic Indicators: Homosexual Relations, p. 1, online at <www.gallup.com/poll/indicators/indhomosexual.asp>.

[73]Ibid, pp. 1–2.

[74]Gallup Opinion Index, *Report No. 160*, November 1978, p. 26.

[75]Lambda Legal Defense and Education Fund, "Summary of States, Cities, and Counties Which Prohibit Discrimination Based on Sexual Orientation," October 25, 1999, pp. 1–12, online at <www.lldef.org/cgi-bin/pages/documents/record?record=217>.

[76]*Bowers v. Hardwick*, 478 U.S. 186 (1986).

[77]*Romer v. Evans*, 116 S.Ct. 1620 (1996).

[78]*Boy Scouts of America v. Dale*, No. 99–699.

[79]Ibid.

[80]*Washington Post*, June 9, 2000, p. A1.

[81]Data provided by the National Organization on Disability.

[82]*Washington Post*, May 2, 1992, p. A15.

[83]*Los Angeles Times*, October 4, 1995, p. A1. Data from an ABC News poll released the week prior to the October 3 verdict.

[84]James Baldwin, *The Fire Next Time* (New York: Dial Press, 1963), p. 40.

[85]Ralph Ellison, *Invisible Man* (New York: Random House, 1952), p. 3.

[86]Gunnar Myrdal, *An American Dilemma: The Negro Problem and Modern Democracy* (New York: Harper & Row, 1962). (Originally published in 1944.)

[87]Ibid., p. lxxi.

[88]Charles E. Silberman, *Crisis in Black and White* (New York: Random House, 1964), p. 10.

[89]William Julius Wilson, *The Declining Significance of Race: Blacks and Changing American Institutions* (Chicago: University of Chicago Press, 1978), p. 22.

[90]Lucius J. Barker and Jesse J. McCorry, Jr., *Black Americans and the Political System*, 2nd ed. (Boston: Little, Brown, 1980), p. 342.

[91]Silberman, *Crisis in Black and White*, pp. 43–44.

[92]Myrdal, *An American Dilemma: The Negro Problem and Modern Democracy*, p. 33.

[93]John Hope Franklin, *From Slavery to Freedom* (New York: Knopf, 1967), p. 128.

[94]*Dred Scott v. Sandford*, 19 Howard 393 (1857).

[95]*Plessy v. Ferguson*, 163 U.S. 537 (1896).

[96]*Brown v. Board of Education of Topeka, Kansas*, 347 U.S. 483 (1954).

[97]In Robert H. Jackson, *The Supreme Court in the American System of Government* (Cambridge: Harvard University Press, 1955), p. 11.

[98]*Brown v. Board of Education of Topeka, Kansas*, 349 U.S. 294 (1955). John Marshall Harlan, grandson of the justice who dissented in *Plessy v. Ferguson*, was by this time a member of the Supreme Court and participated in the second *Brown* decision.

[99]*Alexander v. Holmes County Board of Education*, 396 U.S. 19 (1969).

[100]*National Journal*, September 18, 1999, p. 2615.

[101]*Swann v. Charlotte-Mecklenburg County Board of Education*, 402 U.S. 1 (1971).

[102]Diane Ravitch, "Busing: The Solution That Has Failed to Solve," *New York Times*, December 21, 1975, section 4, p. 3.

[103]*Keyes v. School District No. 1*, 413 U.S. 189 (1973).

[104]*Board of Education v. Dowell*, 498 U.S. 237 (1991).

[105]*Washington Post*, June 12, 1999, p. A12.

[106]The Supreme Court had barred segregation on interstate transportation in a series of decisions: on buses in *Morgan v. Commonwealth of Virginia*, 328 U.S. 373 (1946); on trains in *Henderson v. United States*, 339 U.S. 816 (1950), which held that an interstate railroad could not segregate a dining car; and in other cases.

[107]*The Negro in American History, Vol. I: Black Americans 1928–1968*, with an introduction by Saunders Redding (Chicago: Encyclopedia Britannica Educational Corp., 1969), pp. 175–176.

[108]Southern Regional Council data in 1965 *Congressional Quarterly Almanac*, p. 537.

[109]United States Commission on Civil Rights, *Political Participation*, May 1968, pp. 171, 222.

[110]U.S. Bureau of the Census, Current Population Reports, *Voting and Registration in the Election of November 1988*, series P20-440, October 1989, p. 17; and "Voting and Registration: November 1988," Internet release date, October 17, 1997.

[111]U.S. Bureau of the Census, Current Population Reports, Population Characteristics, *Voting and Registration in the Election of November 1996*, series P20-504, July 1998, table 4, p. 23.

[112]*Shaw v. Reno*, 509 U.S. 630 (1993).

[113]*Miller v. Johnson*, 115 S.Ct. 2475 (1995).

[114]See *Shaw v. Hunt*, 517 U.S. 899 (1996), which invalidated the same North Carolina district that the Supreme Court had reviewed in 1993, when the case was called *Shaw v. Reno;* and *Bush v. Vera*, 517 U.S. 952 (1996).

[115]*Report of the National Advisory Commission on Civil Disorders* (New York: Bantam Books, 1968), pp. 1, 10.

[116]Stokely Carmichael and Charles V. Hamilton, *Black Power* (New York: Random House, 1967), p. 44.

[117]*New York Times*, May 23, 1970, p. 12.

[118]*Regents of the University of California v. Allan Bakke*, 438 U.S. 265 (1978).

[119]*United Steelworkers of America v. Weber*, 443 U.S. 193 (1979).

[120]*Fullilove v. Klutznick*, 448 U.S. 448 (1980).

[121]*Johnson v. Transportation Agency, Santa Clara County*, 480 U.S. 616 (1987).

[122]*Adarand Constructors v. Pena*, 115 S. Ct. 2097 (1995).

[123]Ibid.

[124]*New York Times*, April 2, 1996, p. A23.

[125]In July 2000, the African Americans in Clinton's cabinet were Secretary of Labor Alexis M. Herman, Secretary of Transportation Rodney Slater, and Secretary of Veterans Affairs Togo D. West, Jr.

[126]Data for 1998 provided by Joint Center for Political and Economic Studies.

[127]Arthur M. Schlesinger, Jr., *The Disuniting of America: Reflections on a Multicultural Society* (New York: Norton, 1992), p.15.

[128]"Radio and Television Report to the American People on Civil Rights," June 11, 1963, *Public Papers of the Presidents of the United States, John F. Kennedy 1963* (Washington, D.C.: U.S. Government Printing Office, 1964), p. 469.

Chapter 6

[1]Gallup poll, February 28–March 3, 1991.

[2]Gallup/*USA Today*/CNN poll, February 19–20, 1992.

[3]Gallup poll, "Presidential Impeachment Crisis," January 22–24, 1999.

[4]James Bryce, *The American Commonwealth*, vol. 1 (New York: Putnam, Capricorn Books, 1959), p. 296.

[5]V. O. Key, Jr., *Public Opinion and American Democracy* (New York: Knopf, 1961), p. 10.

[6]Ibid., p. 14.

[7]Floyd H. Allport, "Toward a Science of Public Opinion," *Public Opinion Quarterly*, vol. 1 (January 1937), p. 23.

[8]W. Lance Bennett, *Public Opinion in American Politics* (New York: Harcourt Brace Jovanovich, 1980), pp. 12–13.

[9]Allport, "Toward a Science of Public Opinion," p. 15.

[10]Walter Lippmann, *Public Opinion* (New York: Free Press, 1965), pp. 18–19. (Originally published in 1922.)

[11]Robert E. Lane, *Political Life* (New York: Free Press, 1959), p. 204.

[12]Fred I. Greenstein, *Children and Politics* (New Haven: Yale University Press, 1965), p. 1.

[13]Ibid., pp. 71–73.

[14]Key, *Public Opinion and American Democracy*, pp. 301, 305.

[15]Bennett, *Public Opinion in American Politics*, pp. 165–166, citing Theodore M. Newcomb's study in Theodore M. Newcomb, *Personality and Social Change* (New York: Dryden Press, 1943).

[16]M. Kent Jennings and Richard G. Niemi, *The Political Character of Adolescence* (Princeton: Princeton University Press, 1974), p. 319.

[17]Ibid., p. 328.

[18]Gallup poll, April–May 1999.

[19]*The Gallup Poll Monthly*, April 1993, p. 43. Respondents were asked, "Do you think abortions should be legal under any circumstances, legal only under certain circumstances, or illegal in all circumstances?"

[20]Lloyd A. Free and Hadley Cantril, *The Political Beliefs of Americans* (New Brunswick: Rutgers University Press, 1967), p. 216. See also extensive data of the Survey Research Center (University of Michigan,

1956), quoted in Key, *Public Opinion and American Democracy*, chapter 6.

²¹Samuel A. Stouffer, *Communism, Conformity, and Civil Liberties* (Gloucester, Mass.: Peter Smith, 1963).

²²*The Gallup Poll Monthly*, April 1992, p. 6.

²³Greenstein, *Children and Politics*, pp. 155–156.

²⁴Gallup poll, "Vote by Groups, 1992–1996," p. 1, online at <www.gallup.com/poll/trends/ptgrp9296.asp>.

²⁵Free and Cantril, *The Political Beliefs of Americans*, p. 148.

²⁶Mark Twain, *The Autobiography of Mark Twain*, ed. Charles Neider (New York: Harper & Row, 1959), p. 386.

²⁷Elisabeth Noelle-Neumann, "The Spiral of Silence: A Theory of Public Opinion," *Journal of Communication*, vol. 24 (Spring 1974), p. 43.

²⁸Ibid., p. 45.

²⁹Angus Campbell, Philip E. Converse, Warren E. Miller, and Donald E. Stokes, Survey Research Center, University of Michigan, *The American Voter* (New York: Wiley, 1960).

³⁰The Gallup Organization, *Poll Releases*, "Americans Oppose General Legalization of Marijuana", March 19–21, 1999, p. 3, online at <www.gallup.com/poll/releases/pr990409b.asp>.

³¹The Gallup Organization, *Poll Releases*, "More Americans Approve of House Vote to Impeach Clinton Now than a Year Ago", December 19–20, 1998, p. 1, online at <www.gallup.com/poll/releases/pr991221.asp>. Forty percent of independents favored the impeachment decision.

³²*New York Times*, February 23, 2000, p. A14. Data based on Voter News Service exit polls. All Michigan voters, regardless of party affiliation, were free to vote in the Republican primary.

³³Key, *Public Opinion and American Democracy*, p. 11.

³⁴Robert E. Lane and David O. Sears, *Public Opinion* (Englewood Cliffs, N.J.: Prentice Hall, 1964), p. 106.

³⁵Harry S. Truman, *Memoirs by Harry S. Truman: Years of Trial and Hope*, vol. 2 (Garden City, N.Y.: Doubleday, 1956), p. 177.

³⁶"New Hampshire Confounded Most Pollsters," *Washington Post*, February 8, 1988, p. A1.

³⁷*Dallas Morning News*, February 1, 2000, p. 1A.

³⁸Elizabeth Drew, *Showdown: The Struggle between the Gingrich Congress and the Clinton White House* (New York: Simon & Schuster, 1996), p. 103.

³⁹Herbert F. Weisberg and Bruce D. Bowen, *An Introduction to Survey Research and Data Analysis* (San Francisco: Freeman, 1977), p. 24.

⁴⁰For a discussion of the pitfalls and problems of public opinion polling, see Michael Wheeler, *Lies, Damn Lies, and Statistics: The Manipulation of Public Opinion in America* (New York: Liveright, 1976).

⁴¹The Gallup Organization, *Poll Trends*, "The 1996 Presidential Election," November 2–3, 1996, p. 1, online at <www.gallup.com/poll/trends/ptpreselec.asp>.

⁴²"Polling's Dirty Little Secret: No Response," *New York Times*, November 21, 1999, section 4, p. 1.

⁴³*New York Times*, November 3, 1992, p. A13; and *National Journal*, November 7, 1992, p. 2539.

⁴⁴Bernard Hennessy, *Essentials of Public Opinion* (North Scituate, Mass.: Duxbury Press, 1975), pp. 70–71.

⁴⁵Elisabeth Noelle-Neumann, "Turbulences in the Climate of Opinion: Methodological Applications of the Spiral of Silence Theory," *Public Opinion Quarterly*, vol. 41, no. 2 (Summer 1977), p. 144.

⁴⁶*New York Times*, February 23, 2000, p. A16.

⁴⁷Free and Cantril, *The Political Beliefs of Americans*, p. 13.

⁴⁸Ibid., p. 30.

⁴⁹See Bennett, *Public Opinion in American Politics*, pp. 141–150.

⁵⁰Norman H. Nie, Sidney Verba, and John R. Petrocik, *The Changing American Voter*, enlarged ed. (Cambridge: Harvard University Press, 1979), p. 348.

⁵¹Ibid.

⁵²Ibid., p. 156.

⁵³U.S. Bureau of the Census, *Statistical Abstract of the United States*, 1999, p. 301.

⁵⁴Ibid.

⁵⁵Ibid.

⁵⁶E. E. Schattschneider, *The Semisovereign People* (New York: Holt, Rinehart and Winston, 1960), p. 99. By 1994 the number of nonvoters totaled about 105 million.

⁵⁷Free and Cantril, *The Political Beliefs of Americans*, p. 61.

⁵⁸Gallup poll, January 29, 2000.

⁵⁹*Washington Times*, September 16, 1997, p. A3. Survey taken by the National Constitution Center.

⁶⁰*Washington Post*, the Kaiser Family Foundation, and Harvard University survey, *Washington Post*, January 29, 1996, p. A1.

⁶¹Gallup poll conducted for the National Endowment for the Humanities, Boulder (Colorado) *Daily Camera*, October 9, 1989, p. 1.

⁶²Schattschneider, *The Semisovereign People*, p. 132.

⁶³See David Wise, *The Politics of Lying: Government Deception, Secrecy, and Power* (New York: Random House, 1973).

⁶⁴Richard G. Niemi and Herbert F. Weisberg, *Controversies in American Voting Behavior* (San Francisco: Freeman, 1976), p. 168. See also Bennett, *Public Opinion in American Politics*, pp. 27–30, 43–48, and 90–91.

⁶⁵"Assassination," in *To Establish Justice, To Insure Domestic Tranquility: Final Report of the National Commission on the Causes and Prevention of Violence* (Washington, D.C.: U.S. Government Printing Office, 1969), p. 120.

⁶⁶Perot interview with Dan Rather, *CBS Evening News*, June 3, 1991.

⁶⁷Dan Nimmo, *Political Communication and Public Opinion in America* (Santa Monica: Goodyear Publishing, 1978), p. 98.

⁶⁸Walter Lippmann, *Essays in the Public Philosophy* (Boston: Little, Brown, 1955), p. 14.

⁶⁹Schattschneider, *The Semisovereign People*, p. 136.

⁷⁰Ibid., p. 133.

⁷¹Key, *Public Opinion and American Democracy*, p. 7.

Chapter 7

¹Report of a study by Public Citizen, a Ralph Nader group, quoted in the *Washington Post*, December 20, 1997, p. A2. Nader's group was opposed to the tobacco settlement.

²Report of a study by Common Cause of tobacco company political contributions, quoted in the *Washington Post*, December 20, 1997, p. A2.

³C. Wright Mills, *The Power Elite* (New York: Oxford University Press, 1959), pp. 8, 13.

⁴See, for example, Peter Bachrach, *The Theory of Democratic Elitism* (Boston: Little, Brown, 1966); G. William Domhoff, *Who Rules America?* (Englewood Cliffs, N.J.: Prentice Hall, 1967); and Domhoff, *The Higher Circles* (New York: Vintage Books, 1970).

⁵Richard H. Rovere, *The American Establishment* (New York: Harcourt Brace Jovanovich, 1962), p. 6.

⁶Robert A. Dahl, *Who Governs?* (New Haven: Yale University Press, 1961), p. 86.

⁷See Peter Bachrach and Morton S. Baratz, "Two Faces of Power," *American Political Science Review*, vol. 56, no. 4 (December 1962), pp. 947–952.

⁸David B. Truman, *The Governmental Process* (New York: Knopf, 1951), p. 37.

⁹James Madison, "The Federalist, No. 10," in Edward Mead Earle, ed., *The Federalist* (New York: Random House, Modern Library), p. 56.

¹⁰Quoted in William Safire, *Safire's New Political Dictionary: The Definitive Guide to the New Language of Politics* (New York: Random House, 1993), p. 841.

¹¹Ibid., p. 612.

¹²Alexis de Tocqueville, *Democracy in America*, vol. 1, ed. Phillips Bradley (New York: Vintage Books, 1945), p. 198.

¹³Robert H. Salisbury, *Governing America: Public Choice and Political Action* (New York: Appleton-Century-Crofts, 1973), p. 90.

¹⁴Ibid.

¹⁵Robert E. Lane, *Political Life* (New York: Free Press, 1959), p. 75.

¹⁶*New York Times*, May 27, 1982, p. 1. Data on contributions from Congress Watch.

¹⁷Ibid. Mikulski was elected to the Senate in 1986.

[18]David Bollier, *Citizen Action and Other Big Ideas: A History of Ralph Nader and the Modern Consumer Movement* (Washington, D.C.: Center for Study of Responsive Law, 1991), p. 14.

[19]Lester W. Milbrath, *The Washington Lobbyists* (Chicago: Rand McNally, 1963), pp. 212–213.

[20]Quoted in William Safire, *Safire's New Political Dictionary*, p. 418.

[21]*New York Times*, September 29, 1998, pp. A22–23.

[22]Connally was indicted by the federal government but acquitted in 1975 on charges that he had accepted a total of $10,000 from AMPI in return for urging Nixon to raise milk price supports.

[23]For more detailed accounts of the milk producers' lobbying, see Carol S. Greenwald, *Group Power* (New York: Praeger, 1977), pp. 3–8; and U.S. Senate, 93rd Cong., 2nd sess., *The Final Report of the Select Committee on Presidential Campaign Activities*, pp. 579–929.

[24]*New York Times*, September 29, 1998, pp. A22.

[25]Data for 1999 from The Center for Responsive Politics, online at <www.opensecrets.org/2000elect/select/AllCands.htm>.

[26]*New York Times*, December 14, 1999, p. A25.

[27]V. O. Key, Jr., *Politics, Parties, and Pressure Groups*, 5th ed. (New York: Crowell, 1964), p. 130.

[28]The AAA mounted its successful campaign in 1968, but the automobile association's victory was only temporary. In 1975 a bill became law permitting larger trucks on the roads.

[29]NRA membership and staff size as of the year 2000; budget for fiscal 1999. Data provided by the National Rifle Association. Total for NRA contributions to congressional candidates provided by the Federal Election Commission.

[30]Donald Devine, *The Attentive Public* (Chicago: Rand McNally, 1969), p. 119. Data from 1964.

[31]*National Journal*, March 4, 1995, p. 552; and *Washington Post*, July 6, 1995, p. C2.

[32]Joseph C. Goulden, *The Superlawyers: The Small and Powerful World of the Great Washington Law Firms* (New York: Weybright & Talley, 1972), p. 6.

[33]Ibid., p. 70. In the early 1990s, however, Clifford's reputation was tarnished by his involvement in a scandal surrounding the Arab-owned Bank of Commerce and Credit International (BCCI). He was indicted on federal and New York State charges of alleged fraud and bribery for his role. But the federal charges were dropped and the state decided not to prosecute because of his ill health. See the *Washington Post*, April 8, 1993, p. A1; and December 1, 1993, p. A1. Clark Clifford died in 1998 at the age of 91.

[34]*USA Today*, March 20, 2000, p. 24A; and *New York Times*, March 14, 2000, p. 19.

[35]NRA Fact Sheet, March 20, 2000, online at <www.nraila.org>.

[36]*Buckley* v. *Valeo*, 424 U.S. 1 (1976). The federal campaign spending laws and the impact of Supreme Court decisions are discussed in detail in Chapter 10.

[37]Data provided by Federal Election Commission, June 1999.

[38]*First National Bank of Boston* v. *Bellotti*, 435 U.S. 765 (1978).

[39]*Consolidated Edison* v. *Public Service Commission*, 447 U.S. 530 (1980).

[40]Institute of Politics, John F. Kennedy School of Government, Harvard University, "An Analysis of the Impact of the Federal Election Campaign Act, 1972–78," prepared for the Committee on House Administration, U.S. House of Representatives (Washington, D.C.: U.S. Government Printing Office, 1979), p. 4.

[41]Ibid.

[42]Data provided by Center for Responsive Politics.

[43]Fred Wertheimer, "Of Mountains: The PAC Movement in American Politics" (Paper written for the Conference on Parties, Interest Groups, and Campaign Finance Laws, Washington, D.C., September 1979), pp. 5–8.

[44]The remaining 12 percent of PAC contributions in 1998 went to candidates for seats where no incumbent was seeking reelection. Data provided by Federal Election Commission, June 8, 1999.

[45]Data provided by Federal Election Commission, January 2000. The number of PACs is constantly changing; during the 1998 congressional elections, for example, there were 4,599 PACs.

[46]*United States* v. *Harris*, 347 U.S. 612 (1954).

[47]*Washington Post*, July 17, 1991, p. A21.

[48]Ibid.

[49]Milbrath, *The Washington Lobbyists*, p. 358.

[50]Theodore J. Lowi, *The End of Liberalism: Ideology, Policy, and the Crisis of Public Authority*, 2nd ed. (New York: Norton, 1979).

[51]Ibid., p. xvi.

[52]E. E. Schattschneider, *The Semisovereign People* (New York: Holt, Rinehart and Winston, 1960), p. 35.

[53]Mancur Olson, Jr., *The Logic of Collective Action: Public Goods and the Theory of Groups*, rev. ed. (Cambridge: Harvard University Press, 1971), p. 2.

Chapter 8

[1]*New York Times Co.* v. *United States*, 403 U.S. 713 (1971).

[2]W. A. Swanberg, *Citizen Hearst: A Biography of William Randolph Hearst* (New York: Scribner's, 1961), pp. 107–108.

[3]Data from Jerry Yang, cofounder of Yahoo!, quoted in the *Washington Post*, April 12, 2000, p. A26.

[4]Data provided by the Newspaper Association of America.

[5]Magazine circulation figures from Audit Bureau of Circulations, 1999.

[6]Data provided by CNN.

[7]Data for 1999 provided by Mediavest.

[8]Data provided by Mediavest.

[9]It was Newton Minow, President Kennedy's chairman of the Federal Communications Commission, who called television a "vast wasteland" in a speech to broadcasters in 1961. See Arthur M. Schlesinger, Jr., *A Thousand Days* (Boston: Houghton Mifflin, 1965), p. 736.

[10]*Washington Post*, March 5, 1998, p. A1.

[11]*National Broadcasting Co.* v. *United States*, 319 U.S. 190 (1943).

[12]See Norman Dorsen, Paul Bender, and Burt Neuborne, *Political and Civil Rights in the United States*, 4th ed., vol. 1 (Boston: Little, Brown, 1976), pp. 774–777.

[13]*Turner Broadcasting Corp.* v. *Federal Communications Commission*, 114 S.Ct. 2445 (1994).

[14]David Wise, *The Politics of Lying: Government Deception, Secrecy, and Power* (New York: Random House, 1973), p. 273.

[15]*Red Lion Broadcasting Co., Inc.* v. *Federal Communications Commission*, 395 U.S. 367 (1969).

[16]*Rosenbloom* v. *Metromedia*, 403 U.S. 29 (1971).

[17]*Federal Communications Commission* v. *Pacifica Foundation*, 438 U.S. 726 (1978).

[18]*Near* v. *Minnesota*, 283 U.S. 697 (1931).

[19]Ibid.

[20]*New York Times Co.* v. *United States*, 403 U.S. 713 (1971).

[21]Ibid.

[22]*Cable News Network, Inc.* v. *Noriega*, 498 U.S. 976 (1990).

[23]*New York Times*, March 10, 1979, p. 1.

[24]Howard Morland, "The H-Bomb Secret: How We Got It—Why We're Telling It," *The Progressive*, November 1979, p. 14.

[25]*Miami Herald Publishing Co.* v. *Tornillo*, 418 U.S. 241 (1974).

[26]*New York Times*, March 30, 1996, p. 24. Justice Souter made this comment in testimony before a House Appropriations subcommittee two days earlier.

[27]*Sheppard* v. *Maxwell*, 384 U.S. 333 (1966).

[28]*Richmond Newspapers, Inc.* v. *Virginia*, 448 U.S. 555 (1980).

[29]*United States* v. *Caldwell*, *Branzburg* v. *Hayes*, *In the Matter of Paul Pappas*, all 408 U.S. 665 (1972).

[30]Robert H. Phelps and E. Douglas Hamilton, *Libel* (New York: Macmillan, 1966), p. 62.

[31]*New York Times Co.* v. *Sullivan*, 376 U.S. 254 (1964).

[32]*Curtis Publishing Co.* v. *Butts* and *Associated Press* v. *Walker*, 388 U.S. 130 (1967); *Rosenbloom* v. *Metromedia* (1971).

[33]*Time* v. *Firestone*, 424 U.S. 448 (1976).

[34]*Hutchinson* v. *Proxmire*, 443 U.S. 111 (1979).

[35]*Wolston* v. *Reader's Digest*, 443 U.S. 157 (1979).

[36]*Mitchell* v. *Bindrim* and *Doubleday* v. *Bindrim*, 444 U.S. 984 (1979).

[37]*Hustler Magazine, Inc.* v. *Falwell*, 485 U.S. 46 (1988).

[38]*Milkovich* v. *Lorain Journal Co.*, 497 U.S. 1 (1990).

[39]*Masson* v. *New Yorker Magazine*, 501 U.S. 496 (1991). In 1993, a federal jury in San Francisco ruled that Malcolm had fabricated quotes and libeled Masson, but the jury could not agree on monetary damages.

[40]*Brill's Content*, July–August 1998, p. 132.

[41]Thomas B. Ross, then chief of the *Chicago Sun-Times* Washington bureau, quoted in Wise, *The Politics of Lying*, pp. 287, 394.

[42]Ibid., pp. 105–106.

[43]*Gallup Report*, January 1982, no. 196, p. 31.

[44]*The People, the Press & Their Leaders, 1995* (Washington, D.C.: The Times Mirror Center for the People and the Press, 1995), p. 9.

[45]Ibid.

[46]Ibid.

[47]U.S. Congress, House of Representatives, Committee on Government Operations, *Administration of the Freedom of Information Act*, 92nd Cong., 2nd sess., *Twenty-first Report* (Washington, D.C.: U.S. Government Printing Office, 1972), p. 8.

[48]*Snepp* v. *United States*, 444 U.S. 507 (1980).

[49]*New York Times*, November 14, 1969, p. 1.

[50]James Fallows, *Breaking the News: How the Media Undermine American Democracy* (New York: Pantheon, 1996), p. 37.

[51]Ibid., p. 88.

[52]Ibid., p. 103.

[53]Harris poll, March 3–6, 2000, Roper Center at University of Connecticut, Public Opinion Online at <www.ropercenter.uconn.edu>.

[54]History Channel, Roper poll, January 27–30, 2000, Roper Center at University of Connecticut, Public Opinion Online at <www.ropercenter.uconn.edu>.

[55]Freedom Forum poll, quoted in *USA Today*, July 2, 1999, p. 3A.

[56]Harris poll, January 6–10, 2000, Roper Center at University of Connecticut, Public Opinion Online at <www.ropercenter.uconn.edu>.

[57]Pew Research Center, January 12–16, 2000, Roper Center at University of Connecticut, Public Opinion Online at <www.ropercenter.uconn.edu>.

[58]Gallup poll, February 19, 1999.

[59]*The People, the Press & Their Leaders*, 1995, pp. 36–37.

[60]*New York Times*, November 18, 1992, p. A20. The survey, by the Freedom Forum, a nonpartisan organization that studies media issues, was based on a telephone poll of 1,400 reporters nationwide.

[61]Wise, *The Politics of Lying*, p. 367.

[62]W. Lance Bennett and David L. Paletz, *Taken by Storm: The Media, Public Opinion, and U.S. Foreign Policy in the Gulf War* (Chicago: University of Chicago Press, 1994), pp. 282–283.

Chapter 9

[1]Frank J. Sorauf, *Political Parties in the American System* (Boston: Little, Brown, 1964), p. 1.

[2]Ibid.

[3]V. O. Key, Jr., *Politics, Parties, and Pressure Groups*, 5th ed. (New York: Crowell, 1964), p. 9.

[4]Key, *Politics, Parties, and Pressure Groups*, p. 167.

[5]Wilfred E. Binkley, *American Political Parties* (New York: Knopf, 1963), p. 19.

[6]Clinton Rossiter, *Parties and Politics in America* (Ithaca, N.Y.: Cornell University Press, 1960), pp. 73–74.

[7]Ibid., p.7.

[8]Allan P. Sindler, *Political Parties in the United States* (New York: St. Martin's, 1966), p. 15.

[9]Herbert McCloskey, Paul J. Hoffmann, and Rosemary O'Hara, "Issue Conflict and Consensus among Party Leaders and Followers," *American Political Science Review*, vol. 54, no. 2 (June 1960), pp. 415–426. The study was based on interviews with delegates who attended the 1956 Democratic and Republican National Conventions.

[10]*New York Times*, August 14, 2000, p. A17.

[11]Ibid.

[12]*Gallup Opinion Index*, Report no. 131, June 1976, p. 11; *Gallup Opinion Index*, Report no. 180, August 1980, p. 31; *Gallup Report*, no. 255, December 1986, pp. 27–28; and The Gallup Organization, *Poll Releases*, April 1999, online at <www.gallup.com/poll/releases/pr990409c.asp>.

[13]Everett Carll Ladd, Jr., "The 1994 Congressional Elections: The Realignment Continues," in *Political Science Quarterly*, vol. 10, no. 1 (Spring 1995), p. 19.

[14]Everett Carll Ladd, Jr., with Charles D. Hadley, *Transformations of the American Party System: Political Coalitions from the New Deal to the 1970s*, 2nd ed. (New York: Norton, 1978), p. 329.

[15]Martin P. Wattenberg, *The Decline of American Political Parties, 1952–1980* (Cambridge: Harvard University Press, 1984), p. xv.

[16]Austin Ranney, "The Political Parties: Reform and Decline," in Anthony King, ed., *The New American Political System* (Washington, D.C.: American Enterprise Institute for Public Policy Research, 1979), p. 245.

[17]Ladd with Hadley, *Transformations of the American Party System: Political Coalitions from the New Deal to the 1970s*, pp. 329–333.

[18]Frank J. Sorauf, *Party Politics in America*, 5th ed. (Boston: Little, Brown, 1984), p. 420.

[19]Ibid.

[20]Ladd with Hadley, *Transformations of the American Party System: Political Coalitions from the New Deal to the 1970s*, pp. 258, 268.

[21]Sorauf, *Party Politics in America*, p. 148.

[22]Everett Carll Ladd, Jr., "The 1992 Vote for President Clinton: Another Brittle Mandate?" in *Political Science Quarterly*, vol. 108, no. 1 (Spring 1993), p. 5.

[23]Ibid.

[24]Ibid.

[25]Voter News Service exit polls for 1996 in *National Journal*, November 9, 1996, p. 2407.

[26]Jo Freeman, "The Political Culture of the Democratic and Republican Parties," *Political Science Quarterly*, vol. 101, no. 3 (Fall 1986), p. 337.

[27]Quoted in Andrew Hacker, "Is the Party Over?" *New York Times Book Review*, November 26, 1978, p. 12.

[28]Rossiter, *Parties and Politics in America*, p. 117.

[29]Theodore H. White, *The Making of the President, 1968* (New York: Atheneum, 1969), p. 33.

[30]Data provided by Center for Responsive Politics, as of September 1, 2000.

[31]Rossiter, *Parties and Politics in America*, p. 131.

[32]Jerome L. Himmelstein, "The New Right," in Robert C. Liebman and Robert Wuthnow, eds., *The New Christian Right: Mobilization and Legitimation* (New York: Aldine, 1983), p. 16.

[33]Key, *Politics, Parties, and Pressure Groups*, p. 255.

[34]Rossiter, *Parties and Politics in America*, pp. 5–6.

[35]Key, *Politics, Parties, and Pressure Groups*, p. 316.

[36]Robert J. Huckshorn, *Party Leadership in the States* (Boston: University of Massachusetts Press, 1976), pp. 69–95.

[37]David R. Mayhew, *Placing Parties in American Politics* (Princeton: Princeton University Press, 1986), pp. 17–77, 78.

[38]Sorauf, *Political Parties in the American System*, p. 53.

[39]David Halberstam, "Daley of Chicago," in William J. Crotty, Donald M. Freeman, and Douglas S. Gatlin, *Political Parties and Political Behavior* (Boston: Allyn and Bacon, 1971), p. 286. Reprinted from *Harper's*, August 1968.

[40]Raymond E. Wolfinger, "Why Political Machines Have Not Withered Away and Other Revisionist Thoughts," *The Journal of Politics*, vol. 34 (1972), p. 384.

[41]Ibid., pp. 384–386.

[42]For general discussions of political participation, see Chapters 6 and 11.

[43]Nelson W. Polsby and Aaron B. Wildavsky, *Presidential Elections*, 9th ed. (Chatham, N.J.: Chatham House, 1996), pp. 165, 285.

[44]Michael Kelly, "Glasshouse Conventions: How the Parties Built Their Pretty Facades—and Why They're So Fragile," *New Yorker*, September 9, 1996, p. 39.

[45]Ibid., p.40.

[46]Nelson W. Polsby, *Consequences of Party Reform* (New York: Oxford University Press, 1983), p. 77.

[47]*USA Today*, August 14, 2000, p. 8A.

[48]Michael G. Hagen, "Press Treatment of Front-Runners," in William G. Mayer, ed., *In Pursuit of the White House: How We Choose Our Presidential Nominees* (Chatham, N.J.: Chatham House, 1996), p. 191.

[49]Austin Ranney, "Turnout and Representation in Presidential Primary Elections," *American Political Science Review*, vol. 66 (March 1972), p. 27.

[50]For a discussion of the pros and cons of a national presidential primary, see Judith H. Parris, *The Convention Problem* (Washington, D.C.: The Brookings Institution, 1972), pp. 172–177.

[51]Austin Ranney, *The Federalization of Presidential Primaries* (Washington, D.C.: American Enterprise Institute for Public Policy Research, 1978), pp. 33–38.

[52]Polsby, *Consequences of Party Reform*, p. 182.

[53]Ibid.

[54]Rossiter, *Parties and Politics in America*, p. 34.

[55]Gerald M. Pomper with Susan S. Lederman, *Elections in America: Control and Influence in Democratic Politics*, 2nd ed. (New York: Longman, 1980), p. 152.

[56]Ibid., pp. 161, 164. See also Paul T. David, "Party Platforms as National Plans," *Public Administration Review*, vol. 31, no. 3 (May–June 1971), pp. 303–315.

[57]Max Lerner, *America as a Civilization*, vol. 1 (New York: Simon & Schuster, 1967), pp. 389–390.

[58]See, for example, Report of the Committee on Political Parties of the American Political Science Association, *Toward a More Responsible Two-Party System* (New York: Holt, Rinehart and Winston, 1950).

[59]Paul T. David, Ralph M. Goldman, and Richard C. Bain, *The Politics of National Party Conventions*, rev. ed. (Lanham, MD: University Press of America, 1984), p. 344.

[60]Public Papers of the President, *Lyndon B. Johnson, 1963–64*, book 2 (Washington, D.C.: U.S. Government Printing Office, 1965), p. 1391.

Chapter 10

[1]*New York Times*, September 16, 2000, p. A10.

[2]*New York Times*, September 22, 2000, p. A1.

[3]*New York Times*, January 23, 2000, section 4, p. 1.

[4]Nelson W. Polsby and Aaron B. Wildavsky, *Presidential Elections*, 9th ed. (Chatham, N.J.: Chatham House, 1996), p. 181.

[5]William H. Flanigan and Nancy H. Zingale, *Political Behavior of the American Electorate*, 8th ed. (Washington, D.C.: CQ Press, 1994), pp. 162–163.

[6]Dan Nimmo and Robert L. Savage, *Candidates and Their Images: Concepts, Methods, and Findings* (Pacific Palisades, Calif.: Goodyear Publishing, 1976), p. 208.

[7]Ibid., pp. 136–137.

[8]Ibid., p. 143.

[9]Dan Nimmo, *Political Communication and Public Opinion in America* (Santa Monica: Goodyear Publishing, 1978), pp. 361–372. See also David L. Swanson, "Political Communication: A Revisionist View Emerges," *The Quarterly Journal of Speech*, vol. 64 (1978), pp. 211–222.

[10]Norman H. Nie, Sidney Verba, and John R. Petrocik, *The Changing American Voter*, enlarged edition, A Twentieth Century Fund Study (Cambridge: Harvard University Press, 1979), p. 319.

[11]Walter DeVries and Lance Tarrance, Jr., *The Ticket-Splitter: A New Force in American Politics* (Grand Rapids: Eerdmans, 1972), p. 37.

[12]Ibid., p. 111.

[13]Theodore H. White, *The Making of the President, 1968* (New York: Atheneum, 1969), pp. 326–333.

[14]"Assassination," in *To Establish Justice, To Insure Domestic Tranquility: Final Report of the National Commission on the Causes and Prevention of Violence* (Washington, D.C.: U.S. Government Printing Office, 1969), p. 132.

[15]*CBS Evening News*, October 1, 1996.

[16]V. O. Key, Jr., *Politics, Parties, and Pressure Groups*, 5th ed. (New York: Crowell, 1964), p. 471.

[17]Polsby and Wildavsky, *Presidential Elections*, 2nd ed. (New York: Scribner's, 1968), p. 129.

[18]Polsby and Wildavsky, *Presidential Elections*, 9th ed. (Chatham, N.J.: Chatham House, 1996), p. 99.

[19]*New York Times*, September 16, 2000, p. A10.

[20]*New York Times*, March 21, 2000, p. A20.

[21]President Bush, quoted on *NBC Nightly News*, January 15, 1992.

[22]*Washington Post*, August 14, 1984, p. A6; and October 12, 1984, p. A10.

[23]*Washington Post*, March 6, 1998, p. A18.

[24]*New York Times*, October 27, 1992, p. A1.

[25]*Washington Post*, September 5, 2000, p. A4.

[26]Ibid.

[27]*USA Today*, September 20, 2000, p. 13A.

[28]*Washington Post*, September 24, 2000, p. A14.

[29]"Decision 2000," September 12, 2000, online at <www.msnbc.com/news>.

[30]Theodore H. White, *The Making of the President, 1964* (New York: Atheneum, 1965), p. 322.

[31]Theodore H. White, *The Making of the President, 1960* (New York: Atheneum, 1961), p. 289.

[32]*New York Times*, October 30, 1980, p. B19.

[33]*Washington Post*, October 6, 1988, p. A1.

[34]*Washington Post*, October 7, 1988, p. A14.

[35]*Washington Post*, October 12, 1992, p. A18.

[36]Sidney Kraus and Dennis Davis, *The Effects of Mass Communication on Political Behavior* (University Park: The Pennsylvania State University Press, 1976), p. 59.

[37]Ibid.

[38]Herbert E. Alexander and Anthony Corrado, *Financing the 1992 Election* (Armonk, N.Y.: Sharpe, 1995), p. 233.

[39]The 1996 data and estimate for 2000 provided by the Television Bureau of Advertising, online at <www.tvb.org/tvfacts/politics/ad_spending.html>. Of the estimate for 2000, about $15 million was spent on network commercials and the rest on local television.

[40]*Washington Post*, October 21, 1980, p. B4.

[41]*Washington Post*, October 30, 1982, p. 1.

[42]Reported in *Washington Post*, October 5, 1988, p. 1.

[43]John F. Bibby, *Politics, Parties, and Elections in America*, 3rd edition (Chicago, IL: Nelson-Hall, 1996), p. 233.

[44]Thomas E. Patterson and Robert D. McClure, *The Unseeing Eye: The Myth of Television Power in National Politics* (New York: Putnam, 1976), pp. 22–23.

[45]Harold Mendelsohn and Garrett J. O'Keefe, *The People Choose a President: Influences on Voter Decision Making* (New York: Praeger, 1976), p. 171.

[46]*New York Times*, July 16, 1992, p. A11.

[47]*New York Times*, September 19, 1980, p. B1.

[48]Ibid.

[49]Larry J. Sabato, *The Rise of Political Consultants: New Ways of Winning Elections* (New York: Basic Books, 1981), p. 15.

[50]Ibid., pp. 310–311.

[51]Ibid., p. 337.

[52]James M. Perry, *The New Politics* (New York: Potter, 1968), pp. 25–26.

[53]Stanley Kelley, Jr., *Professional Public Relations and Political Power* (Baltimore: Johns Hopkins Press, 1956), p. 212.

[54]Dan Nimmo, *The Political Persuaders* (Englewood Cliffs, N.J.: Prentice Hall, 1970), pp. 197–198.

[55]*Time*, September 15, 1980.

[56]*Washington Post*, October 18, 1988, p. 1.

[57]Ibid.

[58]Bush statement while campaigning in South Carolina, October 20, 1992, broadcast by NBC News on the *Today* show, October 21, 1992.

[59]Earl Mazo and Stephen Hess, *Nixon: A Political Portrait* (New York: Harper & Row, 1968), p. 282.

[60]See White, *The Making of the President, 1960*, pp. 336–338; and White, *The Making of the President, 1968*, p. 327.

[61]Polsby and Wildavsky, *Presidential Elections*, 9th ed., p. 201.

[62]Quoted in Carl Sandburg, *Abraham Lincoln: The Prairie Years*, vol. 1 (New York: Harcourt Brace, 1926), p. 344.

[63]Herbert E. Alexander and Monica Bauer, *Financing the 1988 Election* (Boulder: Westview Press, 1991), p. 4; Alexander and Corrado, *Financing the 1992 Election*, p. 3; and John C. Green, ed., *Financing the 1996 Election* (Armonk, N.Y.: Sharpe, 1999), p. 13. Estimate for 2000 provided by Herbert E. Alexander.

[64]*New York Times*, July 10, 1992, p. A18.

[65]Federal Election Commission data in *The Washington Times*, August 16, 2000, p. A9.

[66]*Washington Post*, July 8, 1996, p. A1.

[67]*Washington Post*, July 27, 1988, p. A4.

[68]*Buckley v. Valeo*, 424 U.S. 1 (1976).

[69]Elizabeth Drew, *Politics and Money: The New Road to Corruption* (New York: Macmillan, 1983), pp. 1, 2.

[70]*Colorado Republican Federal Campaign Committee v. Federal Election Commission*, 116 S. Ct. 2309 (1996).

[71]*New York Times*, January 18, 1979, p. 19.

[72]Larry Makinson, *The Price of Admission: Campaign Spending in the 1990 Election* (Washington, D.C.: Center for Responsive Politics, 1991), p. 35.

[73]Data for 1992 and 1994 from the Federal Election Commission.

[74]Data from Center for Responsive Politics, online at <www.opensecrets.org/2000elect/storysofar/topraces.asp>.

[75]Alexander and Bauer, *Financing the 1988 Election*, p. 53.

[76]Makinson, *The Price of Admission: Campaign Spending in the 1990 Election*, p. 22.

[77]Norman J. Ornstein, Thomas E. Mann, and Michael J. Malbin, *Vital Statistics on Congress 1995–1996* (Washington, D.C.: Congressional Quarterly, 1996), p. 76.

[78]Ibid, p. 77

[79]Data from Center for Responsive Politics, online at <www.opensecrets.org/2000elect/storysofar/topraces.asp>.

[80]Ibid.

[81]*Washington Post*, November 30, 1980, p. A1.

[82]Carl E. Van Horn, *The State of the States*, 3rd ed. (Washington, D.C.: CQ Press, 1996), p. 58.

[83]Herbert E. Alexander, *Financing Politics: Money, Elections, and Political Reform*, 4th ed. (Washington, D.C.: CQ Press, 1992), pp. 5–6.

[84]Presidential campaign costs for 1980 to 1992 in Alexander and Corrado, *Financing the 1992 Election*, p. 21.

[85]Green, *Financing the 1996 Election*, p.13.

[86]Estimate for the year 2000 provided by Herbert E. Alexander.

[87]Alexander, *Financing Politics: Money, Elections, and Political Reform*, pp. 66–67.

[88]Drew, *Politics and Money: The New Road to Corruption*, pp. 14–18.

[89]Alexander Heard, *The Costs of Democracy* (Chapel Hill: University of North Carolina Press, 1960), pp. 14, 35.

[90]Ibid., p. 394.

[91]Data provided by the Federal Election Commission. Figures rounded. Total expenditures by PACS in those years was much higher, but included their staff salaries and other overhead.

[92]Alexander and Bauer, *Financing the 1988 Election*, pp. 68–69.

[93]Data provided by Federal Election Commission.

[94]*Buckley v. Valeo* (1976).

[95]Drew, *Politics and Money: The New Road to Corruption*, p. 1.

[96]For a discussion of the complex motives for campaign giving, see Heard, *The Costs of Democracy*, chapter 4.

[97]Heard, *The Costs of Democracy*, p. 163.

[98]*New York Times*, January 15, 1981, p. B10.

Chapter 11

[1]See Lester W. Milbrath and M. L. Goel, *Political Participation*, 2nd ed. (Chicago: Rand McNally, 1977), for detailed citations of studies of political participation.

[2]U.S. Bureau of the Census, *Statistical Abstract of the United States: 1999*, p. 300.

[3]Milbrath and Goel, *Political Participation*, p. 114; and Raymond E. Wolfinger and Steven J. Rosenstone, *Who Votes?* (New Haven: Yale University Press, 1980), pp. 37–38. However, Wolfinger and Rosenstone add that "the decline in turnout among people over sixty . . . is explained not by their greater age but by differences in education, marital status, and sex," p. 47.

[4]U.S. Bureau of the Census, *Statistical Abstract of the United States: 1999*, p. 300.

[5]Sandra Baxter and Marjorie Lansing, *Women and Politics: The Invisible Majority* (Ann Arbor: University of Michigan Press, 1980), p. 1.

[6]U.S. Bureau of the Census, *Statistical Abstract of the United States: 1999*, p. 300.

[7]For a discussion of the "very strong relationship between rates of voting and years of education," see Wolfinger and Rosenstone, *Who Votes?* pp. 17–20, 34–36.

[8]Angus Campbell, Philip E. Converse, Warren E. Miller, and Donald E. Stokes, *The American Voter* (New York: Wiley, 1960), pp. 96–101. Our discussion of voter attitudes is based in part on chapter 5 of this landmark study of voting conducted at the Survey Research Center, University of Michigan.

[9]Ibid., p. 111.

[10]Adapted from the *New York Times*/CBS News poll taken November 10–16, 1988. The total number of responses is smaller than the 91 million nonvoters in 1988.

[11]Milbrath and Goel, *Political Participation*, p. 143.

[12]Paul F. Lazarsfeld, Bernard Berelson, and Hazel Gaudet, *The People's Choice* (New York: Columbia University Press, 1968). (Originally published in 1944.)

[13]Ibid., p. 21.

[14]Bernard R. Berelson, Paul F. Lazarsfeld, and William N. McPhee, *Voting* (Chicago: University of Chicago Press, 1966). (Originally published in 1954.)

[15]Gallup poll, July 1992.

[16]Angus Campbell, Philip E. Converse, Warren E. Miller, and Donald E. Stokes, "Stability and Change in 1960: A Reinstating Election," *American Political Science Review*, vol. 55, no. 2 (June 1961), pp. 269–280. Actual votes were obtained by applying percentages to the 1960 total two-party vote.

[17]See Ithiel de Sola Pool, Robert P. Abelson, and Samuel L. Popkin, *Candidates, Issues, and Strategies* (Cambridge: MIT Press, 1964), pp. 68, 117–118.

[18]Voter News Service exit polls for 1996, *National Journal*, November 9, 1996, p. 2407.

[19]Congressional Quarterly, *Weekly Report*, February 10, 1973, p. 308; Congressional Quarterly, *Weekly Report*, November 6, 1976, p. 3118; *New York Times*, January 6, 1981, p. A14; and *New York Times*, December 22, 1984, p. 10. Vote totals are for the 11 states of the Old Confederacy: Alabama, Arkansas, Florida, Georgia, Louisiana, Mississippi, North Carolina, South Carolina, Tennessee, Texas, and Virginia.

[20]For a comparison of voting between men and women in the Eisenhower era, see Campbell, Converse, Miller, and Stokes, *The American Voter*, p. 493.

[21]Baxter and Lansing, *Women and Politics: The Invisible Majority*, p. 57.

[22]Voter Research and Surveys exit polls for 1992, in *National Journal*, November 7, 1992, p. 2543.

[23]Voter News Service exit polls for 1996, *National Journal*, November 9, 1996, p. 2407.

[24]Campbell, Converse, Miller, and Stokes, *The American Voter*, p. 17.

[25]Arthur H. Miller, Warren E. Miller, Alden S. Raine, and Thad A. Brown, "A Majority Party in Disarray: Policy Polarization in the 1972 Election," *American Political Science Review*, vol. 70, no. 3 (September 1976), p. 770.

[26]Campbell, Converse, Miller, and Stokes, *The American Voter*, pp. 171–172.

[27]Ibid., p. 180.

[28]Norman H. Nie, Sidney Verba, and John R. Petrocik, *The Changing American Voter*, enlarged edition (Cambridge: Harvard University Press, 1979), pp. 96–109, 156–173.

[29]See Gregory B. Markus, "Political Attitudes during an Election Year: A Report on the 1980 NES Panel Study," *American Political Science Review*, vol. 76, no. 3 (September 1982), pp. 538–560, especially p. 560.

[30]Voter News Service exit polls for 1996, *National Journal*, November 9, 1996, p. 2408.

[31]Morris P. Fiorina, *Retrospective Voting in American National Elections* (New Haven: Yale University Press, 1981), pp. 5–6.

[32]*New York Times*, February 26, 2000, p. A15.

[33]Angus Campbell, "Surge and Decline: A Study of Electoral Change," in Angus Campbell, Philip E. Converse, Warren E. Miller, and Donald E. Stokes, *Elections and the Political Order* (New York: Wiley, 1966), pp. 44–45, 59, 61–62.

[34]Barbara Hinckley, "Interpreting House Midterm Elections: Toward a Measurement of the In-Party's 'Expected' Loss of Seats," *American Political Science Review*, vol. 61, no. 3 (September 1967), p. 699.

[35]Edward R. Tufte, "Determinants of the Outcomes of Midterm Congressional Elections," *American Political Science Review*, vol. 69, no. 3 (September 1975), p. 824.

[36]Thomas Mann and Norman Ornstein, "Election '82: The Voters Send a Message," *Public Opinion*, December/January 1983, p. 8.

[37]For an additional discussion of the coattail phenomenon, see Warren E. Miller, "Presidential Coattails: A Study in Political Myth and Methodology," *Public Opinion Quarterly*, vol. 19, no. 1 (Spring 1955), pp. 353–368.

[38]V. O. Key, Jr., *Politics, Parties, and Pressure Groups*, 5th ed. (New York: Crowell, 1964), p. 304.

[39]*Los Angeles Times*, March 10, 2000, p. 1.

[40]*New York Times*, January 2, 2000, p. 22.

[41]*Washington Post*, February 3, 2000, p. A10.

[42]*Los Angeles Times*, March 10, 2000, p. 1.

[43]*New York Times*, August 8, 2000, p. 22.

[44]*Newsweek*, November 20, 2000, pp. 89–90.

[45]*New York Times*, October 19, 2000, p. A22.

[46]*Newsweek*, November 20, 2000, p. 102.

[47]Ibid.

[48]*Newsweek*, November 20, 2000, pp. 18–19.

[49]Ibid.

[50]Ibid.

[51]Congressional Quarterly, *Weekly Report*, November 11, 2000, pp. 2650, 2652.

[52]Responses to the question: "Do you approve or disapprove of the way George W. Bush is handling his job as president?" Data from The Gallup Organization, November 7, 2002, online at <www.gallup.com/poll/releases/pr021018.asp>.

[53]*New York Times*, November 7, 2002, p. B4.

[54]Data from The Gallup Organization, October 9, 2002, online at <www.gallup.com/poll/releases/pr021009.asp>.

[55]*New York Times*, November 5, 2002, p. A22.

[56]Ibid.

[57]Gallup poll taken October 31–November 3, 2002, The Gallup Organization, November 7, 2002, online at <www.gallup.com/poll/releases/pr021104.asp>.

[58]*New York Times*, November 3, 2002, Section 4, p. 1.

[59]As of November 15, 2002, one Senate contest and one race for governor were still undecided.

[60]*Washington Post*, November 8, 2002, p. A10

[61]*Washington Post*, November 10, 2002, p. B6.

[62]*Washington Post*, November 7, 2002, p. A39.

[63]*Dunn v. Blumstein*, 405 U.S. 330 (1972).

[64]*Marston v. Mandt*, 410 U.S. 679 (1973); and *Burns v. Fortson*, 410 U.S. 686 (1973).

[65]Elizabeth Yadlosky, *Election Laws of the Fifty States and the District of Columbia*, Legislative Reference Service of the Library of Congress, June 5, 1968, p. 305.

[66]*Oregon v. Mitchell*, 400 U.S. 112 (1970).

[67]U.S. Bureau of the Census, *Current Population Reports, Population Characteristics*, series P-20, no. 244, December 1972, p. 3.

[68]Adapted from Voter News Service exit polls for 1996, *National Journal*, November 9, 1996, p. 2407.

[69]*Washington Post*, June 27, 2000, p. A1.

[70]*Report of the President's Commission on Registration and Voting Participation*, p. 32.

[71]*Washington Post*, May 12, 1993, p. A1.

[72]*Washington Post*, January 23, 1996, p. A1.

[73]Ibid.

[74]Campbell, Converse, Miller, and Stokes, *The American Voter*, p. 285.

[75]*Washington Post*, November 29, 1998, p. A6.

[76]Congressional Quarterly, *Weekly Report*, February 3, 1996, p. 310.

[77]Ibid.

[78]*Washington Post*, November 29, 1998, p. A6.

[79]*New York Times*, November 6, 1996, p. B7.

[80]Richard M. Nixon, *Six Crises* (New York: Doubleday, 1962), p. 413.

[81]Neal R. Peirce, *The People's President* (New York: Simon & Schuster, 1968), p. 41.

[82]See, for example, Irving Kristol and Paul Weaver, "A Bad Idea Whose Time Has Come," *New York Times Magazine*, November 23, 1969.

[83]*Colgrove v. Green*, 328 U.S. 549 (1946).

[84]*Baker v. Carr*, 369 U.S. 186 (1962).

[85]*Reynolds v. Sims*, 377 U.S. 533 (1964).

[86]*Wesberry v. Sanders*, 376 U.S. 1 (1964).

[87]*Kirkpatrick v. Preisler*, 394 U.S. 526 (1969); *Mahon v. Howell, City of Virginia Beach v. Howell*, and *Weinberg v. Prichard*, all 410 U.S. 315 (1973); *Gaffney v. Cummings*, 412 U.S. 735 (1973); and *White v. Regester*, 412 U.S. 755 (1973).

[88]William J. D. Boyd, in Congressional Quarterly, *Weekly Report*, November 21, 1969, p. 2342.

[89]Gerald M. Pomper, "Census '70: Power to the Suburbs," *Washington Monthly*, May 1970, p. 23.

[90]C-SPAN, "Capitol Questions," online at <www.cspan.org/questions/weekly69.htm>.

[91]*New York Times*, June 14, 1996, p. A1.

[92]Ibid.

[93]Ibid.

[94]Ibid.

[95]*Washington Post*, November 23, 1996, p. A1.

[96]Key, *Politics, Parties, and Pressure Groups*, pp. 520–536.

[97]V. O. Key, Jr., "A Theory of Critical Elections," *Journal of Politics*, vol. 17 (February 1955), pp. 3–18.

[98]Campbell, Converse, Miller, and Stokes, *The American Voter*, pp. 531–538.

[99]Key, *Politics, Parties, and Pressure Groups*, pp. 522–523.

Chapter 12

[1]*New York Times*, September 30, 2000, p. A14.

[2]U.S. Bureau of the Census, *Statistical Abstract of the United States: 1969*, p. 279.

[3]Peter A. Corning, *The Evolution of Medicare*, U.S. Department of Health, Education, and Welfare (Washington, D.C.: U.S. Government Printing Office, 1969), p. 93.

[4]Data from the *New York Times*, April 3, 1992, p. 1; Handgun Control, Inc.; and the Centers for Disease Control and Prevention, *National Vital Statistics Report*, vol. 48, no. 11, table 18, July 24, 2000, p. 71.

[5]Ralph K. Huitt, "Congress, the Durable Partner," in Ralph K. Huitt and Robert L. Peabody, eds., *Congress: Two Decades of Analysis* (New York: Harper & Row, 1969), p. 219.

[6]Data from C-SPAN, online at <www.cspan.org/questions>.

[7]Ibid.

[8]Ibid.

[9]Ibid.

[10]Roger H. Davidson, *The Role of the Congressman* (New York: Pegasus, 1969), p. 69.

[11]Data from C-SPAN, online at <www.cspan.org/questions>.

[12]Charles L. Clapp, *The Congressman: His Work as He Sees It* (Washington, D.C.: The Brookings Institution, 1963), p. 61.

[13]Luther Patrick, "What Is a Congressman?" *Congressional Record*, May 13, 1963, p. A2978.

[14]David Burnham, "Computer Is Leaving a Wide Imprint on Congress," *New York Times*, April 13, 1984, p. B10.

[15]Roger H. Davidson and Walter J. Oleszek, *Congress and Its Members*, 6th ed. (Washington, D.C.: CQ Press, 1998), p. 147.

[16]Ibid., p. 148.

[17]In John F. Kennedy, *Profiles in Courage* (New York: Harper & Row, 1956), p. 30.

[18]Davidson and Oleszek, *Congress and Its Members*, p. 130, citing survey by Joint Committee on the Organization of Congress.

[19]Davidson, *The Role of the Congressman*, pp. 98–99.

[20]Davidson and Oleszek, *Congress and Its Members*, pp. 129, 131.

[21]Louis Harris, "Public Gives Congress Mixed Rating for Year's Work," *Philadelphia Inquirer*, January 13, 1969. Respondents were asked: "How would you rate the job Congress did this past year . . . excellent, pretty good, only fair, or poor?"

[22]The Gallup Organization, *Gallup Poll Topics*, "Confidence in Institutions," online at <www.gallup.com/poll/indicators/indconfidence.asp>.

[23]*U.S. Term Limits, Inc. v. Thornton*, 514 U.S. 779 (1995).

[24]CBS News poll, July 1992, in *New York Times*, August 9, 1992, p. E5.

[25]Davidson and Oleszek, *Congress and Its Members*, p. 402.

[26]Richard F. Fenno, Jr., "If, As Ralph Nader Says, Congress Is 'The Broken Branch,' How Come We Love Our Congressmen So Much?", in *Congress in Change*, Norman J. Ornstein, ed. (New York: Praeger, 1975), pp. 277–287.

[27]Edmund Burke, *The Works of the Right Honourable Edmund Burke*, vol. 2 (London: Oxford University Press, 1930), pp. 164–165.

[28]V. O. Key, Jr., *Public Opinion and American Democracy* (New York: Knopf, 1961), pp. 492–493.

[29]Davidson, *The Role of the Congressman*, p. 119.

[30]Ibid., pp. 117–119.

[31]Davidson and Oleszek, *Congress and Its Members*, p. 4.

[32]David R. Mayhew, *The Electoral Connection* (New Haven: Yale University Press, 1974), pp. 13, 49.

[33]Richard F. Fenno, Jr., *Home Style: House Members in Their Districts* (Boston: Little, Brown, 1978).

[34]Aage R. Clausen, *How Congressmen Decide: A Policy Focus* (New York: St. Martin's, 1973), pp. 9, 53.

[35]Donald R. Matthews and James A. Stimson, *Yeas and Nays: Normal Decision-Making in the U.S. House of Representatives* (New York: Wiley, 1975), p. 45.

[36]Warren E. Miller and Donald E. Stokes, "Constituency Influence in Congress," *American Political Science Review*, vol. 57 (March 1963), pp. 53–54.

[37]Ibid.

[38]Virginia F. Depew, ed., *The Social List of Washington, D.C., and Social Precedence in Washington* (Kensington, MD: Jean Shaw Murray, 1980).

[39]*Atlanta Constitution*, September 24, 2000, p. 6A. The survey was sponsored by National Public Radio, the Kaiser Family Foundation, and the Kennedy School of Government, Harvard University.

[40]Thomas E. Mann, *Unsafe at Any Margin: Interpreting Congressional Elections* (Washington, D.C.: American Enterprise Institute for Public Policy Research, 1978), p. 30.

[41]In Robert A. Dahl, *Pluralist Democracy in the United States: Conflict and Consent* (Chicago: Rand McNally, 1967), p. 35.

[42]David R. Mayhew, "Congressional Elections: The Case of the Vanishing Marginals," *Polity*, vol. 6 (Spring 1974), pp. 295–317.

[43]Morris P. Fiorina, *Congress: Keystone of the Washington Establishment* (New Haven: Yale University Press, 1977), p. 50.

[44]Lewis A. Froman, Jr., *Congressmen and Their Constituencies* (Chicago: Rand McNally, 1963), pp. 69–84.

[45]Davidson and Oleszek, *Congress and Its Members*, p. 115.

[46]Neil MacNeil, *Forge of Democracy: The House of Representatives* (New York: David McKay, 1964), pp. 82–83.

[47]Walter J. Oleszek, *Congressional Procedures and the Policy Process*, 4th ed. (Washington, D.C.: CQ Press, 1996), pp. 327–328.

[48]For a detailed study of the complex rules and procedures of the House and Senate, see Oleszek, *Congressional Procedures and the Policy Process;* and text of the Legislative Reorganization Act of 1970.

[49]Milton C. Cummings, Jr., and Robert L. Peabody, "The Decision to Enlarge the Committee on Rules: An Analysis of the 1961 Vote," in

Robert L. Peabody and Nelson W. Polsby, eds., *New Perspectives on the House of Representatives* (Chicago: Rand McNally, 1963), p. 193.

[50]Davidson and Oleszek, *Congress and Its Members*, p. 228.

[51]Congressional Quarterly, *Weekly Report*, March 15, 1980, p. 735.

[52]Boris Weintraub, "TV in Congress—Measuring the Impact," *Washington Star*, March 19, 1980, p. C5.

[53]*USA Today*, June 8, 2000, p. 6A.

[54]William S. White, *Citadel* (New York: Harper & Row, 1957), pp. 2, 82–84.

[55]Donald R. Matthews, *U.S. Senators and Their World* (Chapel Hill: University of North Carolina Press, 1960), pp. 92–117.

[56]Nelson W. Polsby, "Goodbye to the Inner Club," *Washington Monthly*, August 1969, pp. 30–34.

[57]Ralph K. Huitt, "The Outsider in the Senate: An Alternative Role," in Huitt and Peabody, *Congress: Two Decades of Analysis*, pp. 159–178.

[58]Barbara Sinclair, *The Transformation of the U.S. Senate* (Baltimore: Johns Hopkins University Press, 1989), p. 79.

[59]Ibid., p. 94.

[60]Ibid., p. 101.

[61]Ibid., p. 99.

[62]Ibid.

[63]Robert L. Peabody, Norman J. Ornstein, and David W. Rohde, "The United States Senate as Presidential Incubator: Many Are Called but Few Are Chosen," *Political Science Quarterly*, vol. 91, no. 2 (Summer 1976), pp. 252–253.

[64]Ibid., pp. 253–256.

[65]Charles O. Jones, "The New, New Senate," in Ellis Sandoz and Cecil V. Crabb, Jr., eds., *A Tide of Discontent: The 1980 Elections and Their Meaning* (Washington, D.C.: Congressional Quarterly, 1981), p. 100.

[66]Ralph K. Huitt, "Democratic Party Leadership in the Senate," in Huitt and Peabody, *Congress: Two Decades of Analysis*, p. 147.

[67]*Congressional Record*, November 27, 1963, p. 22862.

[68]Mark Green, with Michael Calabrese et al. and Ralph Nader Congress Watch, *Who Runs Congress*, 3rd ed. (New York: Bantam Books, 1979), pp. 100–101.

[69]*New York Times*, February 25, 1988, p. A26.

[70]Norman J. Ornstein, Thomas E. Mann, and Michael J. Malbin, *Vital Statistics on Congress 1999–2000* (Washington, D.C.: AEI Press, 2000) table 6-7, p. 164.

[71]*Washington Post*, February 25, 1988, p. A4.

[72]Ibid., p. A1.

[73]Woodrow Wilson, *Congressional Government* (New York: World, Meridian Books, 1956), pp. 69, 82–83. (Originally published in 1885.)

[74]Anthony King, "Introduction," in King, ed., *The New American Political System*, p. 2.

[75]Samuel C. Patterson, "The Semi-Sovereign Congress," in King, ed., *The New American Political System*, p. 160.

[76]Richard F. Fenno, Jr., *Congressmen in Committees* (Boston: Little, Brown, 1973). The names of many of the Senate and House committees cited in Fenno's work have changed; the committee names as of 2000 have been substituted by the authors.

[77]*New York Times*, August 4, 1987, p. 1.

[78]*Watkins v. United States*, 354 U.S. 178 (1957).

[79]*Barenblatt v. United States*, 360 U.S. 109 (1959).

[80]Data from C-SPAN, online at <www.cspan.org/questions/weekly35.htm>.

[81]Harrison W. Fox, Jr., and Susan Webb Hammond, *Congressional Staffs* (New York: Free Press, 1977), p. 2.

[82]Ibid., p. 27.

[83]Richard F. Fenno, Jr., "The Internal Distribution of Influence: The House," in David B. Truman, ed., *The Congress and America's Future*, prepared for the American Assembly, Columbia University (Englewood Cliffs, N.J.: Prentice Hall, 1965), p. 53.

[84]Samuel C. Patterson, "The Semi-Sovereign Congress," in King, ed., *The New American Political System*, pp. 158–159.

[85]Fenno, "The Internal Distribution of Influence: The House," p. 70.

[86]Allen Schick, *Congress and Money: Budgeting, Spending and Taxing* (Washington, D.C.: The Urban Institute, 1980), p. 42.

[87]Joel Havemann, *Congress and the Budget* (Bloomington: Indiana University Press, 1978), p. 205.

[88]Allen Schick, *Congress and Money: Budgeting, Spending and Taxing,* pp. 566–579.

[89]Allen Schick, *Reconciliation and the Congressional Budget Process* (Washington, D.C.: American Enterprise Institute for Public Policy Research, 1981), p. 37.

[90]*Immigration and Naturalization Service v. Chadha,* 462 U.S. 919 (1983).

[91]Patterson, "The Semi-Sovereign Congress," in King, *The New American Political System,* p. 163.

[92]Havemann, *Congress and the Budget,* p. 205.

[93]E. E. Schattschneider, *The Semisovereign People* (New York: Holt, Rinehart and Winston, 1960), p. 102.

Chapter 13

[1]Arthur M. Schlesinger, Jr., *The Imperial Presidency* (Boston: Houghton Mifflin, 1973).

[2]Louis W. Koenig, *The Chief Executive,* 4th ed. (New York: Harcourt Brace Jovanovich, 1981), p. 11.

[3]Schlesinger, *The Imperial Presidency,* p. 410.

[4]Thomas E. Cronin, *The State of the Presidency,* 2nd ed. (Boston: Little, Brown, 1980), pp. 76, 90.

[5]Arthur Schlesinger, Jr., "So Much for the Imperial Presidency," *New York Times,* September 3, 1998, p. A23.

[6]Schlesinger, *The Imperial Presidency,* p. x.

[7]From a television and radio interview: "After Two Years—A Conversation with the President," December 17, 1962, in *Public Papers of the Presidents of the United States, John F. Kennedy, 1962* (Washington, D.C.: U.S. Government Printing Office, 1963), p. 890.

[8]White House press release (Remarks by the president, Democratic National Committee dinner, New York City), April 24, 2000.

[9]White House press release (Remarks by the president, PBS screening of *American Presidents,*), April 7, 2000.

[10]Carl Van Doren, *The Great Rehearsal* (New York: Viking Press, 1948), p. 145.

[11]Thomas E. Cronin, in Thomas E. Cronin, ed., *Inventing the American Presidency* (Lawrence: University Press of Kansas, 1989), p. ix.

[12]In Richard F. Fenno, Jr., *The President's Cabinet* (Cambridge: Harvard University Press, 1959), p. 217.

[13]Clinton Rossiter, *The American Presidency,* rev. ed. (New York: Harcourt Brace Jovanovich, 1960), p. 25.

[14]Edward S. Corwin, *The President, Office and Powers 1787–1957* (New York: New York University Press, 1957), p. 311.

[15]*New York Times,* January 24, 1996, p. 1.

[16]Rossiter, *The American Presidency,* pp. 16–41.

[17]Cronin, *The State of the Presidency,* p. 156.

[18]Letter to Lady Delamere, March 7, 1911.

[19]Data provided by Office of Management and Budget and the Office of Administration, the White House.

[20]In Richard E. Neustadt, *Presidential Power* (New York: Wiley, 1980), p. 9.

[21]Ibid., p. 9.

[22]Ibid., p. 10.

[23]*Myers v. United States,* 272 U.S. 52 (1926).

[24]*Humphrey's Executor v. United States,* 295 U.S. 602 (1935).

[25]Bob Horton, Associated Press staff writer, "The Job of Guarding the President's Code Box," *Washington Star,* November 21, 1965. See also William Manchester, *The Death of a President* (New York: Harper & Row, 1967), pp. 62, 321.

[26]*Immigration and Naturalization Service v. Chadha,* 462 U.S. 919 (1983).

[27]In Arthur Bernon Tourtellot, *The Presidents on the Presidency* (Garden City, N.Y.: Doubleday, 1964), p. 311

[28]*Youngstown Sheet and Tube Co.* v. *Sawyer,* 343 U.S. 579 (1952).

[29]Corwin, *The President, Office and Powers 1787–1957,* p. 171.

[30]*United States v. Curtiss-Wright Export Corp.,* 299 U.S. 304 (1936).

[31]Richard E. Neustadt, "Presidency and Legislation: Planning the President's Program," *American Political Science Review,* vol. 49 (December 1955), p. 981.

[32]"After Two Years—A Conversation with the President," p. 894.

[33]Charles O. Jones, *The Presidency in a Separated System* (Washington, D.C.: The Brookings Institution, 1994), p. 182.

[34]*United States* v. *Nixon,* 418 U.S. 683 (1974).

[35]George C. Edwards, III, *Presidential Influence in Congress* (San Francisco: Freeman, 1980), pp. 10, 205.

[36]*New York Times,* June 26, 1998, p. A1; *Washington Post,* October 7, 1997, p. A1, and October 18, 1997, p. A4.

[37]*Clinton v. City of New York,* 524 U.S. 417 (1998).

[38]*New York Times,* June 26, 1998, p. A1.

[39]*Congressional Record,* January 18, 1960, pp. 710–712.

[40]Neustadt, *Presidential Power,* p. 166.

[41]*Weekly Compilation of Presidential Documents,* February 13, 1980, p. 310.

[42]See Dom Bonafede, "Who's He Trying to Kid?" *National Journal,* May 10, 1980, p. 781.

[43]Neustadt, *Presidential Power,* p. 180.

[44]Jeffrey K. Tulis, *The Rhetorical Presidency* (Princeton: Princeton University Press, 1987) p. 4.

[45]Ibid.

[46]Ibid.

[47]Ibid.

[48]Theodore J. Lowi, *The Personal President: Power Invested, Promise Unfulfilled* (Ithaca, N.Y.: Cornell University Press, 1985), p. 11.

[49]Ibid., p. 10.

[50]Ibid., p. 96.

[51]Rossiter, *The American Presidency,* p. 148.

[52]Hugh Sidey, *A Very Personal Presidency* (New York: Atheneum, 1968), p. 98.

[53]Cronin, *The State of the Presidency,* p. 80.

[54]Fenno, *The President's Cabinet,* p. 19.

[55]Ibid., p. 137.

[56]"Conversation between President Kennedy and NBC Correspondent Ray Scherer," broadcast over NBC television network, April 11, 1961 (stenographic transcript), p. 17.

[57]*Washington Post,* July 18, 1982, p. 1.

[58]*Washington Post,* July 19, 1982, pp. 1, A8.

[59]See Richard J. Ellis, *Presidential Lightning Rods: The Politics of Blame Avoidance* (Lawrence: University Press of Kansas, 1994). As Ellis points out, some presidential advisers may attract blame toward a president, serving as a liability rather than a lightning rod.

[60]Neustadt, *Presidential Power,* p. 39.

[61]Fenno, *The President's Cabinet,* p. 218.

[62]*Report of the President's Special Review Board* (Washington, D.C.: U.S. Government Printing Office, February 26, 1987), p. IV-11. The panel was generally known as the Tower Commission, after its chairman, Senator John Tower, a Texas Republican.

[63]In a new departure, Nixon also permitted Kissinger to keep his title as assistant to the president for national security.

[64]"Conversation between President Kennedy and NBC Correspondent Ray Scherer," p. 3.

[65]Donald Young, *American Roulette: The History and Dilemma of the Vice Presidency* (New York: Holt, Rinehart and Winston, 1965), p. 10.

[66]*Report of the President's Special Review Board* (Washington, D.C.: U.S. Government Printing Office, February 26, 1987).

[67]Neustadt, *Presidential Power,* chapter 4.

[68]*Washington Times,* October 2, 1998, p. A2.

[69]Larry Speakes, *Speaking Out* (New York: Macmillan, 1988).

[70]*New York Times,* May 5, 1977, p. 33.

[71]See John Anthony Maltese, *Spin Control: The White House Office of Communications and the Management of Presidential News* (Chapel Hill: University of North Carolina Press, 1992).

[72]Fred I. Greenstein, "Change and Continuity in the Modern Presidency," in Anthony King, ed., *The New American Political System* (Washington, D.C.: American Enterprise Institute for Public Policy Research, 1978), pp. 74–75.

[73]Speakes, *Speaking Out,* p. 111.

[74]Ibid., p. 113.

[75]Tourtellot, *The Presidents on the Presidency*, p. 426.

[76]Ibid., pp. 55–56.

[77]Koenig, *The Chief Executive*, pp. 16–19.

[78]James David Barber, *The Presidential Character: Predicting Performance in the White House*, 2nd ed. (Englewood Cliffs, N.J.: Prentice Hall, 1977). The four types that Barber identified are active-positive, active-negative, passive-positive, and passive-negative.

[79]Ibid., pp. 94, 159, 423–424, 441.

[80]Ibid., pp. 441–442.

[81]Congressional Quarterly, *Weekly Report*, July 19, 1980, p. 2064.

[82]Congressional Quarterly, *Weekly Report*, November 1, 1980, p. 3282.

[83]*Congressional Record*, January 18, 1960, p. 711. Louis W. Koenig, *The Chief Executive*, 3rd ed. (New York: Harcourt Brace Jovanovich, 1975), p. 11.

Chapter 14

[1]Governor George W. Bush, "Getting Results from Government," Philadelphia, Penn., June 9, 2000, online at <georgewbush.com>.

[2]Ibid.

[3]*New York Times*, June 10, 2000, p. 11.

[4]*U.S. Newswire*, June 9, 2000.

[5]C. Northcote Parkinson, *Parkinson's Law* (Boston: Houghton Mifflin, 1957), p. 2.

[6]Hannah Arendt, *Crises of the Republic* (New York: Harcourt Brace Jovanovich, 1972), p. 137.

[7]*New York Times*, January 24, 1996, p. 1.

[8]Peter F. Drucker, *The Age of Discontinuity* (New York: Harper & Row, 1969), p. 220.

[9]In H. H. Gerth and C. Wright Mills, *From Max Weber: Essays in Sociology* (New York: Oxford University Press, 1953), p. 234.

[10]Dwight Waldo, "Public Administration," *Journal of Politics*, vol. 30, no. 2 (May 1968), p. 448.

[11]Wallace Sayre, "Premises of Public Administration: Past and Emerging," *Public Administration Review*, vol. 18, no. 2 (Spring 1958), p. 105.

[12]H. George Frederickson, "Toward a New Public Administration," in Frank Marini, ed., *Toward a New Public Administration: The Minnowbrook Perspective* (Scranton: Chandler, 1971), p. 314.

[13]Francis E. Rourke, ed., *Bureaucratic Power in National Politics* (Boston: Little, Brown, 1978), p. vii.

[14]Kenneth Culp Davis, *Discretionary Justice* (Baton Rouge: Louisiana State University Press, 1969), p. 4.

[15]Francis E. Rourke, *Bureaucracy, Politics, and Public Policy*, 2nd ed. (Boston: Little, Brown, 1976), p. 46.

[16]Ibid.

[17]David Wise, *Nightmover: How Aldrich Ames Sold the CIA to the KGB for $4.6 Million* (New York: HarperCollins, 1995).

[18]See Arthur Maass, *Muddy Waters* (Cambridge: Harvard University Press, 1951); and "Congress and Water Resources," in Rourke, ed., *Bureaucratic Power in National Politics*.

[19]Morris P. Fiorina, *Congress: Keystone of the Washington Establishment* (New Haven: Yale University Press, 1977), pp. 48–49. After the Republicans gained control of Congress in 1994, however, Congress sought to eliminate federal programs rather than create new ones. The cycle described by Fiorina seemed more applicable to the decades when the Democrats controlled Congress and enacted many new programs.

[20]Ibid., p. 78.

[21]Robert L. Lineberry, *American Public Policy: What Government Does and What Difference It Makes* (New York: Harper & Row, 1977), p. 55.

[22]See Theodore J. Lowi, *The End of Liberalism: Ideology, Policy, and the Crisis of Public Authority* (New York: Norton, 1969), chapter 3.

[23]Francis E. Rourke, "American Bureaucracy in a Changing Political Setting," *Journal of Public Administration Research and Theory*, vol. 1, no. 2 (April 1991), p. 119.

[24]Ibid.

[25]Ibid., p. 112.

[26]Hugh Heclo, "Issue Networks and the Executive Establishment," in Anthony King, ed., *The New American Political System* (Washington, D.C.: American Enterprise Institute for Public Policy Research, 1978), p. 103.

[27]Ibid.

[28]Ibid., p. 88.

[29]In Richard F. Fenno, Jr., *The President's Cabinet* (Cambridge: Harvard University Press, 1959), p. 225. The cabinet secretary who voiced this nautical complaint was William Gibbs McAdoo, Wilson's secretary of the treasury.

[30]Rourke, *Bureaucracy, Politics, and Public Policy*, chapter 3.

[31]Ibid.

[32]Frank J. Donner, *The Age of Surveillance: The Aims and Methods of America's Political Intelligence System* (New York: Knopf, 1980).

[33]CBS News survey, on *CBS Evening News*, September 7, 1993.

[34]Data provided by Department of Defense for 1987.

[35]Arthur M. Schlesinger, Jr., *A Thousand Days* (Boston: Houghton Mifflin, 1965), p. 406.

[36]Richard E. Neustadt, *Presidential Power* (New York: Wiley, 1960), p. 42.

[37]Commission on Organization of the Executive Branch of the Government, *Reports to Congress and Task Force Reports* (Washington, D.C.: U.S. Government Printing Office, 1949). The second Hoover Commission was established in 1953 and reported in 1955. Because it urged the government to eliminate many activities that competed with private enterprise, its proposals were more politically controversial. The second Hoover Commission report had little impact. See Commission on Organization of the Executive Branch of the Government, *Reports to Congress and Task Force Reports* (Washington, D.C.: U.S. Government Printing Office, 1955).

[38]Aaron Wildavsky, *The Politics of the Budgetary Process* (Boston: Little, Brown, 1964), p. 5.

[39]Ibid., pp. 41–42.

[40]Frederick C. Mosher, *Democracy and the Public Service* (New York: Oxford University Press, 1968), pp. 21, 109.

[41]Rourke, "American Bureaucracy in a Changing Political Setting," *Journal of Public Administration Research and Theory*, p. 120.

[42]Ibid., pp. 113–114.

[43]Theodore C. Sorensen, *Kennedy* (New York: Harper & Row, 1965), p. 309.

[44]David Wise and Thomas B. Ross, *The Invisible Government* (New York: Random House, 1964), p. 185.

[45]Townsend Hoopes, *The Limits of Intervention* (New York: David McKay, 1969), p. 181, chapters 8–10.

[46]U.S. Office of Personnel Management, *The Fact Book: Federal Civilian Workforce Statistics 1999 Edition*, p. 8.

[47]Ibid., pp. 8, 18.

[48]U.S. Office of Personnel Management, Federal Civilian Workforce Statistics, *Employment and Trends as of January 2000*, pp. 10, 13, and 16; and United States Office of Personnel Management, *Profile of Federal Civilian Non-Postal Employees*, September 30, 1999, p. 2.

[49]U.S. Bureau of the Census, online at <www.census.gov/govs/apes.html>.

[50]U.S. Office of Personnel Management, *Profile of Federal Civilian Non-Postal Employees*, September 30, 1999, pp. 1–2.

[51]U.S. Office of Personnel Management, Federal Civilian Workforce Statistics, *Pay Structure of the Federal Civil Service*, March 31, 1998, p. 51.

[52]Ibid.

[53]Data provided by U.S. Office of Personnel Management, as of 1999.

[54]Neustadt, *Presidential Power*, p. 39.

[55]*Vermont Yankee Nuclear Power Corporation v. Natural Resources Defense Council, Inc.*, 435 U.S. 519 (1978).

[56]Bernard Schwartz, *The Professor and the Commissions* (New York: Knopf, 1959), p. 48.

[57]*National Journal*, March 6, 1982, p. 405.

[58]Michael D. Reagan, *Regulation: The Politics of Policy* (Boston: Little, Brown, 1987), p. v.

[59]*Washington Post*, September 20, 2000, p. E1.

[60]U.S. Congress, House Committee on Government Reform and Oversight, *United States Government Policy and Supporting Positions*, 104th Cong., 2nd sess. (Washington, D.C.: U.S. Government Printing Office, 1996).

[61]In Louis W. Koenig, *The Chief Executive*, 4th ed. (New York: Harcourt Brace Jovanovich, 1981), p. 132.

[62]*Civil Service Commission* v. *National Association of Letter Carriers, AFL-CIO*, 413 U.S. 548 (1973).

[63]U.S. Office of Personnel Management, Federal Civilian Work Force Statistics, *Employment and Trends as of January 2000*, p. 47.

[64]James P. McGrath, *Civil Service Reform Act: Implementation* (Washington, D.C.: Library of Congress, Congressional Research Service, 1980), p. 9.

[65]Drucker, *The Age of Discontinuity*, p. 226.

[66]*Washington Post*, February 9, 1988, p. E7.

[67]Helen Dudar, "The Price of Blowing the Whistle," *New York Times Magazine*, October 30, 1977, pp. 48–49.

[68]See Richard E. Neustadt and Harvey V. Fineberg, M.D., *The Swine Flu Affair* (Washington, D.C.: U.S. Department of Health, Education, and Welfare, 1978).

[69]Data provided by Torts Division, Department of Justice; and *New York Times*, June 10, 1979, p. 1.

[70]*Washington Post*, August 25, 1989, p. A19.

[71]Ibid.

Chapter 15

[1]*Stenberg* v. *Carhart*, 120 S. Ct. 2597 (2000).

[2]*Hill* v. *Colorado*, 120 S. Ct. 2480 (2000).

[3]*Boy Scouts of America* v. *Dale*, 120 S. Ct. 2446 (2000).

[4]*Mitchell* v. *Helms*, 120 S. Ct. 2530 (2000).

[5]*Dickerson* v. *United States*, 120 S. Ct. 2326 (2000).

[6]*Chicago Tribune*, October 13, 1991, p. A1.

[7]*United States* v. *Nixon*, 418 U.S. 683 (1974).

[8]Robert H. Jackson, *The Supreme Court in the American System of Government* (Cambridge: Harvard University Press, 1955), p. 27.

[9]Robert A. Dahl, "Decision-Making in a Democracy: The Role of the Supreme Court as a National Policy-Maker," in Raymond E. Wolfinger, ed., *Readings in American Political Behavior* (Englewood Cliffs, N.J.: Prentice Hall, 1966), p. 166.

[10]Robert G. McCloskey, *The American Supreme Court* (Chicago: University of Chicago Press, 1960), p. 8.

[11]*United States* v. *Nixon* (1974).

[12]Felix Frankfurter, "The Supreme Court and the Public," *Forum*, vol. 83 (June 1930), pp. 332–334.

[13]Quoted in Robert H. Jackson, *The Supreme Court in the American System of Government*, p. 11.

[14]Edward Mead Earle, ed., *The Federalist, No. 78* (New York: Modern Library), p. 506.

[15]Henry J. Abraham, *The Judicial Process*, 4th ed. (New York: Oxford University Press, 1980), p. 322.

[16]Ibid., pp. 324–336.

[17]*Marbury* v. *Madison*, 1 Cranch 137 (1803).

[18]Ibid.

[19]Archibald Cox, *The Warren Court* (Cambridge: Harvard University Press, 1968), p. 2.

[20]*1968 Congressional Quarterly Almanac*, p. 539.

[21]*Baker* v. *Carr*, 369 U.S. 186 (1962); *Brown* v. *Board of Education of Topeka, Kansas*, 347 U.S. 483 (1954); *Gideon* v. *Wainwright*, 372 U.S. 335 (1963), respectively.

[22]Robert L. Carter, "The Warren Court and Desegregation," *Michigan Law Review*, vol. 67, no. 2 (December 1968), p. 246.

[23]William M. Beaney, "The Warren Court and the Political Process," *Michigan Law Review*, vol. 67, no. 2 (December 1968), p. 352.

[24]Campaign speech, November 2, 1968, quoted in Congressional Quarterly, *Weekly Report*, May 23, 1969, p. 798.

[25]*Roberts* v. *U.S. Jaycees*, 468 U.S. 609 (1984); *New York State Club Association* v. *New York City*, 487 U.S. 1 (1988).

[26]*Hustler Magazine, Inc.* v. *Rev. Jerry Falwell*, 485 U.S. 46 (1988).

[27]*Hazelwood School District* v. *Kuhlmeier*, 484 U.S. 260 (1988).

[28]*California* v. *Greenwood*, 486 U.S. 35 (1988).

[29]*United States* v. *Eichman* and *United States* v. *Haggerty*, both 496 U.S. 310 (1990).

[30]*Simon & Schuster* v. *New York State Crime Victims Board*, 502 U.S. 105 (1991).

[31]"Justice Black and the Bill of Rights," interview broadcast over CBS television network, December 3, 1968, transcript in Congressional Quarterly, *Weekly Report*, January 3, 1969, p. 9.

[32]In Joseph W. Bishop, Jr., "The Warren Court Is Not Likely to Be Overruled," *New York Times Magazine*, September 7, 1969, p. 31.

[33]Jackson, *The Supreme Court in the American System of Government*, p. 9.

[34]Walter F. Murphy, *Congress and the Court* (Chicago: University of Chicago Press, 1962), pp. 246–247.

[35]Dahl, "Decision-Making in a Democracy: The Role of the Supreme Court as a National Policy-Maker," pp. 171, 180.

[36]*Pollock* v. *Farmers' Loan and Trust Co.*, 158 U.S. 601 (1895).

[37]*Grove City* v. *Bell*, 465 U.S. 555 (1984).

[38]*Washington Post*, May 23, 1993, pp. A1, A20.

[39]Bob Woodward and Scott Armstrong, *The Brethren: Inside the Supreme Court* (New York: Simon & Schuster, 1979).

[40]See, for example, Alpheus Thomas Mason, "Eavesdropping on Justice," in *Political Science Quarterly*, vol. 95, no. 2 (Summer 1980), pp. 295–304.

[41]For two earlier analyses of conflict and decision making in the Supreme Court, see J. Woodford Howard, Jr., *Mr. Justice Murphy: A Political Biography* (Princeton: Princeton University Press, 1968); and Walter F. Murphy, *Elements of Judicial Strategy* (Chicago: University of Chicago Press, 1964).

[42]Woodward and Armstrong, *The Brethren: Inside the Supreme Court*, p. 284.

[43]William H. Rehnquist, *The Supreme Court: How It Was, How It Is* (New York: Morrow, 1988).

[44]Abraham, *The Judicial Process*, p. 187.

[45]David J. Danelski, "The Influence of the Chief Justice in the Decisional Process," in Walter F. Murphy and C. Herman Pritchett, eds., *Courts, Judges and Politics: An Introduction to the Judicial Process*, 3rd ed. (New York: Random House, 1979), pp. 695–703.

[46]In Danelski, "The Influence of the Chief Justice in the Decisional Process," p. 698.

[47]Woodward and Armstrong, *The Brethren: Inside the Supreme Court*, pp. 187–188.

[48]*New York Times*, July 11, 1987, p. 18.

[49]Ibid.

[50]Ibid.

[51]Abraham, *The Judicial Process*, p. 146.

[52]Data provided by the Public Affairs Office, Administrative Office of the United States Courts.

[53]*Burns* v. *Wilson*, 346 U.S. 137 (1953).

[54]*United States* v. *Tempia*, 16 USCMA 629 (1967).

[55]*O'Callahan* v. *Parker*, 395 U.S. 258 (1969).

[56]*Solorio* v. *United States*, 483 U.S. 435 (1987).

[57]*Parker* v. *Levy*, 417 U.S. 733 (1974); *Secretary of the Navy* v. *Avrech*, 418 U.S. 676 (1974).

[58]Abraham, *The Judicial Process*, p. 148.

[59]Brian J. Ostrom and Neal B. Kauder, *Examining the Work of State Courts, 1998: A National Perspective from the Court Statistics Project* (Williamsburg, VA: National Center for State Courts, 1999), p. 12. Only one state, Montana, combines elections and the Missouri method.

[60]U.S. Department of Justice, Office of Justice Programs, Bureau of Justice Statistics, *State Court Organization 1998*, pp. 34–49.

[61]Glenn R. Winters and Robert E. Allard, "Judicial Selection and Tenure in the United States," in Harry W. Jones, ed., *The Courts, the Public, and the Law Explosion*, prepared for the American Assembly, Columbia University (Englewood Cliffs, N.J.: Prentice Hall, 1965), p. 157.

[62]*The Challenge of Crime in a Free Society*, report by the President's Commission on Law Enforcement and Administration of Justice (Washington, D.C.: U.S. Government Printing Office, 1967), p. 146.

[63]"Violence and Law Enforcement," in *To Establish Justice, To Insure Domestic Tranquility, Final Report of the National Commission on the Causes and Prevention of Violence* (Washington, D.C.: U.S. Government Printing Office, December 1969), pp. 143–144.

[64]Ibid., pp. 149–152, 155.

[65]Edward L. Barrett, Jr., "Criminal Justice: The Problem of Mass Production," in Jones, *The Courts, the Public, and the Law Explosion,* pp. 86–87.

[66]*Crime in the United States 1998,* Uniform Crime Reports, Federal Bureau of Investigation (Washington, D.C.: U.S. Government Printing Office, 1999), p. 4.

[67]*New York Times,* October 18, 1999, p. A18.

[68]*Washington Post,* December 5, 1999, p. A3.

[69]*The Challenge of Crime in a Free Society,* pp. 21–22

[70]*Task Force Report: Crime and Its Impact—An Assessment,* The President's Commission on Law Enforcement and Administration of Justice (Washington, D.C.: U.S. Government Printing Office, 1967), pp. 93–94.

[71]*The Challenge of Crime in a Free Society,* p. 19.

[72]Richard Harris, *Justice: The Crisis of Law, Order, and Freedom in America* (New York: Dutton, 1970), pp. 27–28.

[73]*Crime in the United States 1998,* pp. 11, 36.

[74]Harris, *Justice: The Crisis of Law, Order, and Freedom in America,* p. 44.

[75]*Crime in the United States 1998,* Uniform Crime Reports, Federal Bureau of Investigation, (Washington, D.C.: U.S. Government Printing Office, 1999), p. 11.

[76]Ibid, p. 36.

[77]U.S. Department of Justice, Bureau of Justice Statistics, *Bulletin* (June 1999), p. 1.

[78]*USA Today,* December 1, 1999, p. 23A.

[79]*New York Times,* August 2, 2000, p. A11.

[80]Ibid.

[81]*Washington Post,* March 22, 1995, pp. A1, A4.

[82]U.S. Department of Justice, Office of Justice Programs, Bureau of Justice Statistics, *Bulletin: Prisoners in 1999* (August 2000), p.1. Online at <www.ojp.usdoj.gov/bjs/pub/pdf/p99.pdf>.

[83]Ibid.

[84]*Rhodes v. Chapman,* 452 U.S. 337 (1981).

[85]*Hudson v. Palmer,* 468 U.S. 517 (1984); *Block v. Rutherford,* 468 U.S. 576 (1984).

[86]*Keeney v. Tamayo-Reyes,* 504 U.S. 1 (1992).

[87]*Hudson v. McMillian,* 503 U.S. 1 (1992).

[88]*The Challenge of Crime in a Free Society,* p. 159.

[89]*Attica: The Official Report of the New York State Special Commission on Attica* (New York: Bantam Books, 1972), p. xii.

[90]The Officer Down Memorial Page, online at <www.odmp.org>.

[91]James S. Campbell, Joseph R. Sahid, and David P. Stang, *Law and Order Reconsidered,* Report of the Task Force on Law and Law Enforcement to the National Commission on the Causes and Prevention of Violence (Washington, D.C.: U.S. Government Printing Office, 1969), p. 290.

[92]Daniel Walker, *Rights in Conflict,* Report of the Chicago Study Team to the National Commission on the Causes and Prevention of Violence (New York: Bantam Books, 1968), p. 5.

[93]Gallup poll, April 30–May 1, 1992.

[94]*Time,* September 11, 1995, pp. 38–41; and *New York Times,* March 24, 1996, p. 35.

[95]*Time,* September 27, 1999, p. 44.

[96]See, for example, James Q. Wilson, *Varieties of Police Behavior* (Cambridge: Harvard University Press, 1968), pp. 7, 278.

[97]Federal Bureau of Investigation, "Frequently Asked Questions about the FBI," online at <www.fbi.gov/yourfbi/faq/faqover.htm>.

[98]Federal Bureau of Investigation, "FBI Mission, History, and Organization," online at <www.fbi.gov/yourfbi/facts/fbimission.htm#structure>.

[99]Federal Bureau of Investigation, "Frequently Asked Questions about the FBI: FBI Law Enforcement Services," online at <www.fbi.gov/yourfbi/faq/faqlaw.htm>.

[100]David Wise, "The FBI's Greatest Hits," *Washington Post Magazine,* October 27, 1996, p. 15.

[101]For details of these and other abuses by the intelligence agencies, see U.S. Congress, Senate Select Committee to Study Governmental Operations with Respect to Intelligence Activities, *Intelligence Activities and the Rights of Americans, Book II,* 94th Cong., 2nd sess., Final Report (Washington, D.C.: U.S. Government Printing Office, 1976).

[102]*The Challenge of Crime in a Free Society,* p. 134.

[103]*Brady v. United States,* 396 U.S. 809 (1970).

[104]*Attica: The Official Report of the New York State Special Commission on Attica,* p. xiii.

[105]Ronald Goldfarb, *Ransom* (New York: Harper & Row, 1965), p. 1.

[106]*Duncan v. Louisiana,* 391 U.S. 145 (1968).

[107]*Baldwin v. New York,* 399 U.S. 66 (1970).

[108]*McKeiver v. Pennsylvania,* 403 U.S. 528 (1971).

[109]*Johnson v. Louisiana,* 406 U.S. 356 (1972); *Apodaca v. Oregon,* 406 U.S. 404 (1972).

[110]*Williams v. Florida,* 399 U.S. 78 (1970).

[111]*Colgrove v. Battin,* 413 U.S. 149 (1973).

[112]*New York Times,* February 1, 2000, p. A1.

[113]American Civil Liberties Union, "Execution Watch," online at <www.aclu.org/executionwatch.html>.

[114]*Washington Post,* June 22, 2000, p. A3.

[115]American Civil Liberties Union, "Execution Watch," online at <www.aclu.org/executionwatch.html>.

[116]*Furman v. Georgia,* 408 U.S. 238 (1972).

[117]*Gregg v. Georgia,* 428 U.S. 153 (1976).

[118]*Woodson v. North Carolina,* 428 U.S. 280 (1976); *Roberts v. Louisiana,* 428 U.S. 325 (1976).

[119]*Thompson v. Oklahoma,* 487 U.S. 815 (1988).

[120]Death Penalty Information Center, online at <www.deathpenaltyinfo.org/dpicexec.html> and <www.deathpenaltyinfo.org/texas.html>.

[121]Robert Sherrill, "Death Row on Trial," the *New York Times Magazine,* November 13, 1983, p. 80.

[122]The study, by Michael L. Radelet and Hugo Adam Bedau, was published in *Stanford Law Review* of November 1987.

[123]Ibid. Source: *New York Times,* May 3, 1989, p. A18.

[124]Fred J. Cook, "The People v. The Mob; or, Who Rules New Jersey?" the *New York Times Magazine,* February 1, 1970, p. 36.

[125]*New York Times,* January 7, 1970, p. 28.

[126]Cook, "The People v. The Mob; or, Who Rules New Jersey?" p. 36.

[127]*The Challenge of Crime in a Free Society,* p. 191.

[128]Ibid., pp. 193–194.

[129]Ibid., p. 191.

[130]Donald R. Cressey, *Theft of the Nation* (New York: Harper & Row, 1969), pp. 252–253.

[131]*The Challenge of Crime in a Free Society,* p. 209.

[132]Woodward and Armstrong, *The Brethren: Inside the Supreme Court,* p. 26.

[133]*Cipollone v. Liggett Group,* 505 U.S. 504 (1992).

[134]Cox, *The Warren Court,* p. 5.

[135]See, for example, Justice Black's opinion in *Chambers v. Florida,* 309 U.S. 227 (1940).

[136]*The Challenge of Crime in a Free Society,* p. 15.

[137]Jackson, *The Supreme Court in the American System of Government,* p. 61.

[138]*New York Times,* June 24, 1969, p. C24.

Chapter 16

[1]Roger Hilsman, *To Move a Nation* (Garden City, N.Y.: Doubleday, 1967), pp. 12–13, 541.

[2]Paul H. Nitze, "The Secretary and the Execution of Foreign Policy," in Don K. Price, ed., *The Secretary of State,* prepared for the American Assembly, Columbia University (Englewood Cliffs, N.J.: Prentice Hall, 1960), pp. 6–7.

[3]Robert F. Kennedy, *Thirteen Days* (New York: Norton, 1969), p. 44.

[4]*Washington Post,* June 29, 1996, p. A1. The Guatemala study was conducted by the president's Intelligence Oversight Board.

[5]Richard J. Barnet and Ronald E. Muller, *Global Reach: The Power of the Multinational Corporations* (New York: Simon & Schuster, 1974), p. 25.

[6]H. Bradford Westerfield, *The Instruments of America's Foreign Policy* (New York: Crowell, 1963), p. 165.

[7]Mr. X, "The Sources of Soviet Conduct," *Foreign Affairs*, July 1947, pp. 566–582.

[8]Harry S. Truman, *Memoirs by Harry S. Truman*, vol. 2, *Years of Trial and Hope* (Garden City, N.Y.: Doubleday, 1958), p. 106.

[9]Joseph S. Nye, Jr., and Robert O. Keohane, eds., *Transnational Relations and World Politics* (Cambridge: Harvard University Press, 1972), pp. x–xi.

[10]Robert O. Keohane and Joseph S. Nye, *Power and Interdependence: World Politics in Transition* (Boston: Little, Brown, 1977), p. 9.

[11]*Washington Post*, July 19, 1992, p. A24.

[12]*Weekly Compilation of Presidential Documents*, March 14, 1983, p. 369.

[13]*New York Times*, December 29, 1983, p. 1.

[14]U.S. State Department, "Patterns of Global Terrorism," online at <www.state.gov/www/global/terrorism/annual-reports.html>.

[15]Television and radio interview: "After Two Years—A Conversation with the President," December 17, 1962, in *Public Papers of the Presidents of the United States: John F. Kennedy, 1962* (Washington, D.C.: U.S. Government Printing Office, 1963), p. 889.

[16]U.S. Senate, Subcommittee on National Security Staffing and Operations, Committee on Government Operations, "Basic Issues," in *Administration of National Security* (Washington, D.C.: U.S. Government Printing Office, 1965), p. 7.

[17]Richard E. Neustadt, testimony to U.S. Senate, Subcommittee on National Security Staffing and Operations, Committee on Government Operations, March 25, 1963, in *Administration of National Security*, p. 76.

[18]Eric F. Goldman, *The Tragedy of Lyndon Johnson* (New York: Knopf, 1969), p. 383.

[19]David Wise, "Remember the Maddox!" *Esquire*, April 1968, p. 126. See also, Joseph C. Goulden, *Truth Is the First Casualty* (New York: Rand McNally, 1969).

[20]U.S. Senate, Committee on Foreign Relations, 90th Cong., 2nd sess., *Hearings, The Gulf of Tonkin: The 1964 Incidents* (Washington, D.C.: U.S. Government Printing Office, 1968), p. 54.

[21]Ibid., p. 91.

[22]U.S. Senate, Committee on Foreign Relations, 90th Cong., 1st sess., *Report on National Commitments* (Washington, D.C.: U.S. Government Printing Office, 1967), p. 14.

[23]Congressional Quarterly, *Weekly Report*, February 20, 1970, p. 518.

[24]George F. Kennan, *American Diplomacy* (Chicago: University of Chicago Press, 1951), pp. 91–92.

[25]Arthur M. Schlesinger, Jr., *A Thousand Days* (Boston: Houghton Mifflin, 1965), p. 406.

[26]For details of this and other aspects of Kissinger's role, see Seymour M. Hersh, *The Price of Power: Kissinger in the Nixon White House* (New York: Summit, 1983); and Walter Isaacson, *Kissinger: A Biography* (New York: Simon & Schuster, 1992).

[27]*New York Times*, December 14, 1999, p. A12.

[28]U.S. State Department, "Department of State Organization Chart," online at <www.state.gov/www/dept/org_chart.html>.

[29]U.S. Senate, Subcommittee on National Security Staffing and Operations, Committee on Government Operations, "Basic Issues," in *Administration of National Security*, p.16.

[30]David Wise, *Nightmover: How Aldrich Ames Sold the CIA to the KGB for $4.6 Million* (New York: HarperCollins, 1995).

[31]*Washington Post*, December 18, 1987, p. A12.

[32]*New York Times*, December 22, 1974, p. 1.

[33]*Report to the President by the Commission on CIA Activities within the United States* (Washington, D.C.: U.S. Government Printing Office, 1975), p. 10.

[34]U.S. Senate, Select Committee to Study Governmental Operations with Respect to Intelligence Activities, 95th Cong., 2nd sess., *Foreign and Military Intelligence, Final Report* (Washington, D.C.: U.S. Government Printing Office, 1976), book 1, p. 128.

[35]*New York Times*, June 11, 1984, p. 1.

[36]*Washington Post*, July 8, 1996, p. A13.

[37]*Washington Post*, March 12, 1996, p. A11. Data based on an analysis by Steven Aftergood, Federation of American Scientists.

[38]Ibid.

[39]*New York Times*, July 16, 2000, section 4, p. 16.

[40]David Wise and Thomas B. Ross, *The Invisible Government* (New York: Random House, 1964), p. 3.

[41]Hilsman, *To Move a Nation*, pp. 64–65.

[42]Allen Dulles, *The Craft of Intelligence* (New York: Harper & Row, 1963), p. 189.

[43]U.S. Senate, Select Committee to Study Governmental Operations with Respect to Intelligence Activities, *Foreign and Military Intelligence, Final Report*, p. 46.

[44]Dulles, *The Craft of Intelligence*, pp. 48–51, 235–236.

[45]Bob Woodward, *Veil: The Secret Wars of the CIA 1981–1987* (New York: Simon & Schuster, 1987), pp. 395–398.

[46]See David Wise, *The American Police State* (New York: Random House, 1976).

[47]*New York Times*, October 18, 2000, p. A1.

[48]"Facts about the United Nations," online at <www.un.org/News/facts/setting.htm>; "List of Member States," online at <www.un.org/Overview/unmember.html>; budget information from the UN Press Hotline, United Nations, New York.

[49]Zogby International poll, April 1999, cited in "What Do Americans Really Think of the UN?" online at <www.un.org/News/facts/think.htm>.

[50]*New York Times*, June 25, 1995, p. 6.

[51]Gabriel A. Almond, *The American People and Foreign Policy* (New York: Praeger, 1950), p. 53.

[52]Ibid., pp. 4–6.

[53]James N. Rosenau, "Foreign Policy as an Issue-Area," in James N. Rosenau, ed., *Domestic Sources of Foreign Policy* (New York: Free Press, 1967), p. 49.

[54]Kenneth N. Waltz, "Electoral Punishment and Foreign Policy Crises," in Rosenau, ed., *Domestic Sources of Foreign Policy*, pp. 273, 283.

[55]"President Nixon's August 5, 1974 Statement" and "The June 23, 1972 Nixon-Haldeman Transcripts" in the *New York Times, The End of a Presidency* (New York: Bantam Books, 1974), pp. 324–353.

[56]Kenneth N. Waltz, *Foreign Policy and Democratic Politics* (Boston: Little, Brown, 1967), p. 86.

[57]*Washington Post*, January 17, 1991, p. A1.

[58]Barton Gellman, "One Year Later: War's Faded Triumph," *Washington Post*, January 16, 1992, p. A10.

[59]*New York Times*, April 17, 1991, p. A11.

[60]The study was conducted for Congress by the General Accounting Office. See the *Washington Post*, September 30, 1992, p. A4.

[61]*New York Times*, June 8, 1984, p. 8.

[62]Burton M. Sapin, *The Making of United States Foreign Policy* (New York: Praeger, for The Brookings Institution, 1966), p. 136.

[63]See "The Department of Defense Almanac," online at <www.defenselink.mil/pubs/almanac>; and Center for Defense Information, Fact Sheet, "Top 15 U.S. Defense Contractors of FY '99," online at <www.cdi.org/issues/usmi/complex/top15FY99.html>.

[64]Kennedy, *Thirteen Days*, p. 48.

[65]*Rostker v. Goldberg*, 453 U.S. 57 (1981).

[66]*New York Times*, December 15, 1997, p. A14.

[67]Henry A. Kissinger, *Nuclear Weapons and Foreign Policy* (New York: Harper & Row, 1957), pp. 174–202. Published for the Council on Foreign Relations.

[68]Henry A. Kissinger, *The Necessity for Choice* (New York: Harper & Row, 1961), p. 81.

[69]Herman Kahn, *On Thermonuclear War* (Princeton: Princeton University Press, 1961), p. 21.

[70]Ralph E. Lapp, *Kill and Overkill* (New York: Basic Books, 1962), p. 10.

[71]*Washington Post*, November 20, 1975, p. 1; and *New York Times*, November 25, 1975, p. 1.

[72]*New York Times*, May 27, 1972, p. 1.

[73]*Seattle Times*, August 26, 1984, p. B2.

[74]Dwight D. Eisenhower, *The White House Years, Waging Peace 1956–1961* (New York: Doubleday, 1965), p. 616.

[75]Data provided by the Center for Defense Information, "Top 15 U.S. Defense Contractors of FY '99", online at <www.cdi.org/issues/usmi/complex/top15FY99.html>.

[76]Paul Kennedy, *The Rise and Fall of the Great Powers: Economic Change and Military Conflict from 1500 to 2000* (New York: Random House, 1987), p. xvi.

[77]Nick Kotz, *Wild Blue Yonder: Money, Politics, and the B-1 Bomber* (New York: Pantheon, 1988), p. 234.

[78]Ibid., p. 235.

[79]*New York Times*, August 21, 2000, p. A8.

[80]Gareth Porter and Janet Welsh Brown, *Global Environmental Politics* (Boulder: Westview Press, 1991), p. 141.

Chapter 17

[1]The Commission on Presidential Debates, excerpt from the debate between Governor George W. Bush and Vice President Al Gore, St. Louis, Missouri, October 17, 2000.

[2]*New York Times*, October 1, 1998, p. A.1.

[3]*National Journal*, April 13, 1996, p. 842. Peter D. Hart and Robert M. Teeter for NBC News/*Wall Street Journal*. Respondents were asked: "Please tell me which one of the following issues will be most important to you personally in your voting for Congress and President this year."

[4]Congressional Budget Office, "The Combined Effects of Major Changes in Federal Taxes and Spending Programs since 1981," *Staff Memorandum*, April 1984, table 5; and the *Washington Post*, July 26, 1984, p. A7.

[5]U.S. Bureau of the Census, Current Population Reports, *Money Income and Poverty Status of Families and Persons in the United States: 1983*, August 1984, p. 1; and the *New York Times*, July 26, 1984, p. A19.

[6]Debt total as of October 25, 2000, from The Public Debt online, Bureau of Public Debt, "The Public Debt to the Penny," online at <www.savingsbonds.gov/opd/opdpenny.htm>.

[7]Budget of the United States Government, *The Budget for Fiscal Year 2001* (Washington, D.C.: U.S. Government Printing Office, 2000), p. 2.

[8]Adapted from U.S. Bureau of the Census, *Statistical Abstract of the United States: 1999*, p. 847. Data for 1998.

[9]*New York Times*, December 1, 1999, p. A1.

[10]Ibid.

[11]*New York Times*, December 2, 1999, p. A1.

[12]*USA Today*, August 28, 2000, p. 1B.

[13]Data provided by U.S. Bureau of Economic Analysis, Department of Commerce.

[14]International Trade Administration, U. S. Department of Commerce, Office of Trade and Economic Analysis, U.S. Foreign Trade Data, "U.S. International Trade Summary 1998–2000," online at <www.ita.doc.gov/td/industry/otea/usftd/>.

[15]Ibid.

[16]Ibid.

Chapter 18

[1]*New York Times*, May 19, 2000, p. A21.

[2]*Time*, March 20, 1995, p. 24.

[3]*New York Times*, May 19, 2000, p. A21.

[4]Anthony King, "The American Polity in the Late 1970s: Building Coalitions in the Sand," in Anthony King, ed., *The New American Political System* (Washington, D.C.: American Enterprise Institute for Public Policy Research, 1978), p. 371.

[5]Charles E. Lindblom, *Politics and Markets: The World's Political-Economic Systems* (New York: Basic Books, 1977), pp. 163–164.

[6]E. E. Schattschneider, *The Semisovereign People* (New York: Holt, Rinehart and Winston, 1960), pp. 118, 121.

[7]Sar A. Levitan and Robert Taggart, *The Promise of Greatness* (Cambridge: Harvard University Press, 1976), pp. 283, 293.

[8]*Lochner* v. *New York*, 198 U.S. 45 (1905).

[9]Edward S. Herman, *Corporate Control, Corporate Power: A Twentieth Century Fund Study* (New York: Cambridge University Press, 1981), p. 177.

[10]Ibid., p. 185.

[11]*United States* v. *E. I. du Pont de Nemours and Co.*, 353 U.S. 586 (1957).

[12]*New York Times*, May 19, 1998, p. A1.

[13]*New York Times*, April 4, 2000, p. A1.

[14]John Kenneth Galbraith, *The New Industrial State* (Boston: Houghton Mifflin, 1967), p. 179.

[15]*New York Times*, December 2, 1998, p. A1.

[16]*New York Times*, May 4, 2000, p. C1.

[17]Global Policy Forum, "Corporate Watch 2000," June 2000, online at <www.igc.org/globalpolicy/socecon/tncs/top200.htm>.

[18]*New York Times*, April 4, 1999, p. Tr3.

[19]Congressional Quarterly, *Weekly Report*, May 4, 1996, p. 1243.

[20]*New York Times*, January 20, 2000, p. A10.

[21]David Caplovitz, *The Poor Pay More* (New York: Free Press of Glencoe, 1963), p. 85.

[22]Ibid., p. 84.

[23]Data provided by the Social Security Administration; Office of Family Assistance, U.S. Department of Health and Human Services; and Unemployment Insurance Claims Office, U.S. Department of Labor.

[24]Gilbert Y. Steiner, *Social Insecurity: The Politics of Welfare* (Chicago: Rand McNally, 1966), pp. 7–8.

[25]*New York Times*, May 19, 2000, p. A21.

[26]Data from Families USA, "Cost Overdose: Growth in Drug Spending for the Elderly, 1992–2010," July 2000, online at <www.familiesusa.org/pubs/drugod.htm>.

[27]*King* v. *Smith*, 392 U.S. 309 (1968); *Lewis* v. *Martin*, 397 U.S. 552 (1970).

[28]Daniel P. Moynihan, "One Step We Must Take," *Saturday Review of Literature*, May 23, 1970, p. 22.

[29]*1964 Congressional Quarterly Almanac*, p. 862.

[30]Michael Harrington, *The Other America* (New York: Macmillan, 1962), p. 4.

[31]Ben H. Bagdikian, *In the Midst of Plenty* (Boston: Beacon, 1964), pp. 6–7.

[32]U.S. Bureau of the Census, *Poverty: 1999 Highlights*, online at <www.census.gov/hhes/poverty99/pov99hi.html> and *Poverty 1999* at <www.census.gov/hhes/poverty/threshld/thresh99.html>.

[33]U.S. Bureau of the Census, Current Population Reports, September 2000, series P60–210, *Poverty in the United States*, 1999, Table A, p. 6.

[34]Daniel P. Moynihan, *Maximum Feasible Misunderstanding: Community Action in the War on Poverty* (New York: Free Press, 1969).

[35]*Philadelphia Enquirer*, July 31, 2000.

[36]Second Harvest, "Hunger in the Era of Welfare Reform," April 2000, online at <www.secondharvest.org/whoshungry/hunger_welfare.html>.

[37]*Christian Science Monitor*, June 30, 2000, p. 1.

[38]*New York Times*, May 2, 1984, p. 1.

[39]The Urban Institute, online at <www.urban.org>.

[40]Data provided by the Food and Consumer Service, Department of Agriculture.

[41]Adapted from *Budget Supplement, Budget of the United States Government, Fiscal Year 1997* (Washington, D.C.: U.S. Government Printing Office, 1996), p. 168.

[42]*A Citizen's Guide to the Federal Budget, Budget of the United States Government, Fiscal Year 1997* (Washington, D.C.: U.S. Government Printing Office, 1996), p. 10.

[43]Data provided by the Health Care Financing Administration.

[44]Ibid.

[45]*New York Times*, June 20, 2000, p. A1.

[46]U.S. Bureau of the Census, *Statistical Abstract of the United States: 1999*, p. 163.

[47]Senator E. L. Bartlett, Democrat of Alaska, in Don K. Price, *The Scientific Estate* (Cambridge: Belknap Press of Harvard University Press, 1965), p. 57.

[48]Price, *The Scientific Estate*, p. 12.

[49]*Washington Post*, September 15, 1992, p. A8.

[50]Ibid.

[51]*New York Times*, April 2, 1993, p. A22.

[52]*USA Today*, October 11, 1999, p. D5.

[53]Ibid.

[54]*New York Times*, May 21, 1996, p. A1.

[55]*Washington Post*, January 24, 1996, p. A6.

[56]*Washington Post*, May 31, 1996, p. A3.

[57]*Washington Post*, April 18, 2000, p. A2.

[58]*New York Times*, December 19, 1999, p. A1.

[59]*Washington Post*, November 12, 1997, p. A1.

[60]*New York Times*, December 19, 1999, p. A1.

[61]Council on Environmental Quality, *Seventh Annual Report* (Washington, D.C.: U.S. Government Printing Office, 1976), p. 272.

[62]*New York Times*, May 26, 1992, p. A1.

[63]*USA Today*, November 2, 1982, p. A3.

[64]Data provided by the Energy Information Administration, Department of Energy. Data for world energy consumption for 1994.

[65]*USA Today*, December 31, 1998, p. A6.

[66]Benjamin I. Page, *Who Gets What from Government* (Berkeley: University of California Press, 1983), p. 19.

Chapter 19

[1]U.S. Bureau of the Census, Population Projections Program, *Projections of the Resident Population by Race, Hispanic Origin, and Nativity: Middle Series, 1999 and 2000*, NP-T5-A; and *Projections of the Resident Population by Race, Hispanic Origin, and Nativity: Middle Series, 2011 to 2015*, NP-T5-D, January 13, 2000. Figures rounded.

[2]*Projections of the Resident Population by Race, Hispanic Origin, and Nativity: Middle Series, 2050 to 2070*, NP-T5-G.

[3]U.S. Bureau of the Census, *Statistical Abstract of the United States: 1999*, p. 39.

[4]*New York Times*, December 31, 1998, p. A11, citing a survey by the National Governors' Association and the National Association of State Budget Officers.

[5]Ibid.

[6]*Washington Post*, August 2, 1996, p. A9.

[7]Ibid., quoting Frank Mecca, executive director of the California Welfare Directors Association.

[8]U.S. Bureau of the Census, *Statistical Abstract of the United States: 1999*, p. 309.

[9]Karl E. Taeuber, "Racial Segregation: The Persisting Dilemma," *Annals of the American Academy of Political and Social Science* (November 1975), p. 93.

[10]U.S. Bureau of the Census, *1990 Census of Population*, "Race, Hispanic Origin, and Group Quarters Population: Metropolitan Areas, 1990," p. 4. Preliminary data; percentage rounded.

[11]*The Book of the States, 2000–2001 Edition*, vol. 33 (Lexington, Ky.: The Council of State Governments, 1996), p. 276.

[12]*New York Times*, December 31, 1998, p. A11.

[13]Richard F. Winters, "The Politics of Taxing and Spending," in Virginia Gray and Herbert Jacob, eds., *Politics in the American States: A Comparative Analysis*, 6th ed. (Washington, D.C.: CQ Press, 1996), p. 336.

[14]John J. Kirlin, *The Political Economy of Fiscal Limits* (Lexington, Mass.: Lexington Books, D. C. Heath, 1982), p. 4.

[15]James Q. Wilson, "Urban Problems in Perspective," in James Q. Wilson, ed., *The Metropolitan Enigma* (Washington, D.C.: U.S. Chamber of Commerce, 1967), p. 395.

[16]Duane Lockard, *The Politics of State and Local Government*, 2nd ed. (New York: Macmillan, 1969), p. 85.

[17]Duane Lockard, *The Politics of State and Local Government*, 3rd ed. (New York: Macmillan, 1983), p. 94.

[18]*The Book of the States, 2000–2001 Edition*, p. 8.

[19]*New York Times*, October 16, 1992, p. A10.

[20]*New York Times*, October 25, 2000, p. A1.

[21]Joseph F. Zimmerman, *The Recall: Tribunal of the People* (Westport, Conn.: Praeger, 1997), pp. 52–53.

[22]Larry Sabato, *Goodbye to Good-Time Charlie: The American Governorship Transformed*, 2nd ed. (Washington, D.C.: CQ Press, 1983), p. 201.

[23]Ibid.

[24]Advisory Commission on Intergovernmental Relations, *Fiscal Balance in the American System*, vol. 1 (Washington, D.C.: U.S. Government Printing Office, October 1967), pp. 233–234.

[25]Thad L. Beyle, "Governors: The Middlemen and Women in Our Political System," in Gray and Jacob, eds., *Politics in the American States: A Comparative Analysis*, 6th ed., pp. 228–237.

[26]Ibid., p. 221.

[27]*The Book of the States, 1996–97 Edition*, pp. 22–23.

[28]Beyle, "Governors: The Middlemen and Women in Our Political System," in Gray and Jacob, eds., *Politics in the American States: A Comparative Analysis*, 6th ed., p. 231.

[29]*The Book of the States, 2000–2001 Edition*, pp. 20–21.

[30]Data provided by National Governors' Association.

[31]Quoted in the *Washington Post*, October 30, 2000, p. A2.

[32]Ibid.

[33]*The Book of the States, 2000–2001 Edition*, pp. 66–67,70.

[34]Ibid., pp. 83–84.

[35]Samuel C. Patterson, "State Legislators and Legislatures" in Gray, Jacob, and Albritton, eds., *Politics in the American States*, 5th ed., p. 176.

[36]Data provided by the Center for American Women and Politics, Eagleton Institute of Politics, Rutgers University, online at <www.cawp.rutgers.edu>.

[37]Ibid.

[38]*Baker* v. *Carr*, 369 U.S. 186 (1962).

[39]*Reynolds* v. *Sims*, 377 U.S. 533 (1964).

[40]*New York Times*, February 14, 2000, p. A1.

[41]*U.S. Term Limits* v. *Thornton*, 115 S. Ct. 1842 (1995).

[42]U.S. Bureau of the Census, *Statistical Abstract of the United States: 1999*, p. 309.

[43]In William L. Riordon, *Plunkitt of Tammany Hall* (New York: Dutton, 1963), p. 21. (Originally published in 1905.)

[44]Jean Gottmann, *Megalopolis* (New York: Twentieth Century Fund, 1961), p. 4.

[45]Adapted from U.S. Bureau of the Census, *1990 Census of Population*.

[46]Lewis Mumford, *The City in History: Its Origins, Its Transformations, and Its Prospects* (New York: Harcourt Brace Jovanovich, 1961), p. 3.

[47]Ibid., pp. 543–548.

[48]Edward C. Banfield, *The Unheavenly City* (Boston: Little, Brown, 1970), p. 5.

[49]Advisory Commission on Intergovernmental Relations, *Changing Public Attitudes on Governments and Taxes 1988*, table 38, p. 60. Data for 1986. The poll showed that 51 percent of respondents wanted governments to "keep taxes and services about where they are," while 31 percent favored a decrease, for a total of 82 percent; 9 percent favored increased services and taxes, and 9 percent had no opinion.

[50]Charles Tilly, "Race and Migration to the American City," in Wilson, ed., *The Metropolitan Enigma*, pp. 129–131.

[51]Ibid., p. 142.

[52]Congressional Quarterly, *Weekly Report*, August 8, 1992, p. 2354.

[53]Donald H. Haider, "Fiscal Scarcity: A New Urban Perspective," in Louis H. Masotti and Robert L. Lineberry, *The New Urban Politics* (Cambridge: Ballinger, 1976), p. 187.

[54]Ibid., p. 202.

[55]Ibid., p. 204.

[56]Ibid., p. 187.

[57]Data provided by Office of Economic Affairs, U.S. Department of Housing and Urban Development.

[58]Speech, Robert F. Kennedy Memorial Journalism Awards dinner, Washington, D.C., June 19, 1969.

[59]President Nixon's message to Congress on community development, September 19, 1973, quoted in Congressional Quarterly, *Weekly Report*, September 22, 1973, p. 2522.

[60]*Village of Arlington Heights* v. *Metropolitan Development Corporation*, 429 U.S. 252 (1977).

[61]Michael N. Danielson, *The Politics of Exclusion* (New York: Columbia University Press, 1976), p. 83.

[62]Ibid., pp. 83–92.

[63]*National Journal*, April 9, 1988, p. 977.

[64]Mumford, *The City in History: Its Origins, Its Transformations, and Its Prospects*, pp. 549–550.

[65]U.S. Bureau of the Census, Current Population Reports, *Poverty in the United States: 1990*, series P-60, no. 175, August 1991, p. 6.

[66]Floyd Hunter, *Community Power Structure* (Chapel Hill: University of North Carolina Press, 1953).

[67]Robert A. Dahl, *Who Governs?* (New Haven: Yale University Press, 1961).

[68]Edward C. Banfield and James Q. Wilson, *City Politics* (Cambridge: Harvard University Press, 1963), pp. 244–245.

[69]Paul E. Peterson, *City Limits* (Chicago: University of Chicago Press, 1981), p. 4.

[70]Ibid., p. 41.

[71]Ibid., pp. 167–183.

[72]Data for 1998, provided by Joint Center for Political and Economic Studies.

[73]Ibid.

[74]John J. Harrigan, *Political Change in the Metropolis* (Boston: Little, Brown, 1976), pp. 139–146.

[75]Wallace S. Sayre and Herbert Kaufman, *Governing New York City: Politics in the Metropolis* (New York: Norton, 1965), pp. 710–712.

[76]John P. Kotter and Paul R. Lawrence, *Mayors in Action: Five Approaches to Urban Governance* (New York: Wiley, 1974).

[77]*New York Times*, October 7, 1980, p. 1.

[78]Herbert J. Gans, *The Levittowners* (New York: Pantheon, 1967), p. 155.

[79]Peter H. Rossi, *Why Families Move* (New York: Free Press of Glencoe, 1955).

[80]Louis H. Masotti and Jeffrey K. Hadden, eds., *The Urbanization of the Suburbs* (Beverly Hills: Sage, 1973), p. 17.

[81]Gans, *The Levittowners*, p. 418.

[82]*New York Times*, July 7, 1992, p. A1.

[83]Alan K. Campbell and Donna E. Shalala, "Problems Unsolved, Solutions Untried: The Urban Crisis," in Alan K. Campbell, ed., *The States and the Urban Crisis* (Englewood Cliffs, N.J.: Prentice Hall, 1970), p. 21.

[84]Richard Lehne, "Suburban Foundations of the New Congress," *Annals of the American Academy of Political and Social Science* (November 1975), p. 143.

[85]Ibid., p. 144.

[86]Ibid., p. 150.

[87]Thomas P. Murphy and John Rehfuss, *Urban Politics in the Suburban Era* (Homewood, Ill.: Dorsey, 1976), pp. 29, 40, 42.

[88]Data provided by Geography Division, U.S. Bureau of the Census.

[89]Robert L. Bish and Vincent Ostrom, *Understanding Urban Government: Metropolitan Reform Reconsidered* (Washington, D.C.: American Enterprise Institute for Public Policy Research, 1973), p. 73.

[90]York Willbern, *The Withering Away of the City* (Tuscaloosa: University of Alabama Press, 1964), p. 33.

[91]Text of speech prepared for delivery to the Illinois Constitutional Convention, Springfield, Ill., May 13, 1970.

Appendix

[1]Modified by the Fourteenth and Sixteenth amendments.

[2]Superseded by the Seventeenth Amendment.

[3]Modified by the Seventeenth Amendment.

[4]Superseded by the Twentieth Amendment.

[5]Modified by the Sixteenth Amendment.

[6]Superseded by the Twelfth Amendment.

[7]Modified by the Twenty-fifth Amendment.

[8]Modified by the Eleventh Amendment.

[9]Superseded by the Thirteenth Amendment.

[10]The first ten amendments were passed by Congress September 25, 1789. They were ratified by three-fourths of the states December 15, 1791.

[11]Date of ratification.

[12]Superseded by the Twentieth Amendment.

[13]Repealed by the Twenty-first Amendment.

"absolute" position The view advocated by Supreme Court Justices Hugo Black and William O. Douglas that there are provisions of the Bill of Rights that cannot be diluted by judicial decisions.

administrative law The rules and regulations made and applied by federal regulatory agencies and commissions.

adversary system of justice A judicial system in which the power of the state is balanced by the defendant's constitutional rights and by the presumption that a person is innocent until proven guilty beyond a reasonable doubt.

affirmative action Programs of government, universities, and businesses designed to favor minorities and remedy past discrimination.

agenda setting The power to determine which public policy questions will be debated or considered.

Antiballistic Missile (ABM) Treaty A 1972 treaty between the United States and the Soviet Union limiting the number of defensive missiles each country could build.

Antifederalists Those who opposed ratification of the Constitution.

appropriations Bills passed by Congress to pay for the spending it has authorized.

arraignment The proceeding before a judge in which the formal charges of an indictment or information are read to an accused person, who may plead guilty or not guilty.

Articles of Confederation (1781–1789) The written framework for the government of the original 13 states before the Constitution was adopted. Under the Articles of Confederation, the national government was weak and dominated by the states. There was a unicameral legislature, but no national executive or judiciary.

assignment committees See steering committees.

authorizations Laws passed by Congress that recommend levels of funding for federal programs. See appropriations.

backgrounder A meeting in which government officials discuss policies and plans with reporters with the mutual understanding that the information can be attributed only to unnamed "officials" or sometimes not attributed to any source.

bail An amount of money "posted" with the courts as security in exchange for a defendant's freedom until the case comes to trial.

balance of payments The net balance or relationship between total income and total expenditures by the nation in its dealings with the rest of the world.

balance of trade The relationship between the total cost of foreign goods imported to this country and sales of U.S. products overseas.

balancing test The view of the majority of the Supreme Court that First Amendment rights must be weighed against the competing needs of the community to preserve order.

bandwagon effect The possible tendency of some voters or convention delegates to support the candidate who is leading in the polls and seems likely to win.

bicameral legislature A two-house legislature.

bill of attainder A law aimed at a particular individual. Prohibited by the Constitution.

Bill of Rights The first ten amendments to the Constitution, which set forth basic protections for individuals.

(Some scholars define the Bill of Rights as only the first eight or nine amendments.)

bipartisanship A view that both major political parties should support the president on foreign policy issues.

blanket primary A primary in which any registered voters are able to vote for candidates from more than one party. A voter, for example, may vote for a Democrat for U.S. senator, and for a Republican for governor. In 2000, the Supreme Court struck down the blanket primary in California, Washington State, and Alaska, but left intact Louisiana's somewhat different "nonpartisan" version of the blanket primary.

block grants Federal grants to states and local communities that are for general use in a broad area, such as community development.

Brown v. Board of Education of Topeka, Kansas Ruling by the Supreme Court in 1954 that racial segregation in public schools violates the Fourteenth Amendment's requirement of equal protection of the laws for all persons.

budget resolutions Overall spending targets set by the Congress.

budget surplus The amount of money available when the government's income is greater than what it spends in a fiscal year.

bureaucrats Public administrators.

cabinet The president, the vice president, the heads of the major executive departments of the government, and certain other senior officials who may hold "cabinet rank."

capitalism An economic system of free enterprise with private ownership of the means of production.

categorical grants Federal grants to states and local communities earmarked for specific purposes, such as pollution control, schools, or hospitals. Also known as grants-in-aid.

caucus A group or a meeting of a group of a political party or organization in which such matters as selection of candidates, leaders, or positions on issues are decided.

certiorari, writ of A writ that, if granted by the Supreme Court, means the Court agrees to hear a case. Most cases reach the Supreme Court this way.

charter colonies Colonies in which freely elected legislatures chose the governors, and laws could not be vetoed by the king.

checks and balances The provisions of the Constitution that divide power among three constitutionally equal and independent branches of government—legislative, executive, and judicial—in the hope of preventing any single branch from becoming too powerful.

civil cases Court cases that involve relations between individuals and organizations, such as a divorce action, or a suit for damages arising from an automobile accident or for violation of a business contract.

civil disobedience The conscious refusal to obey laws that are believed to be unjust, unconstitutional, or immoral.

civilian supremacy The principle of civilian control of the military, based on the clear constitutional power of the president as supreme commander of the armed forces.

civil liberties The fundamental rights of a free society that are protected by the Bill of Rights against the power of the government, such as freedom of speech, religion, press, and assembly.

civil rights The constitutional rights of all individuals, and especially of African Americans and other minorities, to enjoy full equality and equal protection of the laws.

civil service The civilian employees of the government and the administrative system in which they work.

clear and present danger test A test established by Supreme Court Justice Oliver Wendell Holmes in 1919 to define the point at which speech loses the protection of the First Amendment.

closed primary A form of primary election in which only registered members of a political party or persons declaring their affiliation with a party can vote.

closed shop A place of work in which only union members may be hired.

cloture A Senate procedure to cut off a filibuster by a vote of three-fifths (sixty members) of the entire Senate.

cluster sampling A technique used by polling organizations in which several people from the same neighborhood are interviewed.

coalitions Alliances of segments of the electorate, interest groups, and unorganized masses of voters who coalesce behind a political candidate or party.

coattail effect The ability of a major candidate, such as a presidential or gubernatorial candidate, to help carry into office lesser candidates from the same party who are also on the ballot.

COINTELPRO The "counterintelligence program" of the FBI that harassed American citizens and disrupted their organizations from 1956 to 1971 through a wide variety of clandestine techniques.

Cold War (1945–1991) the period after the Second World War marked by rivalry and tension between the two nuclear superpowers, the United States and the communist government of the Soviet Union. The Cold War ended with the collapse of the Soviet government in 1991.

collective security A principle embraced by the United States during the Truman and Eisenhower administrations, under which the nation attempted to "contain" communism and entered into a series of military alliances with other countries for this purpose.

commission plan A form of city government under which a board of city commissioners is popularly elected (often on a nonpartisan ballot). The commissioners make policy as a city council, but they also run city departments as administrators.

Committee of the Whole A device that allows the House of Representatives to conduct its business with fewer restrictions on debate and a quorum of only 100 members.

Committees of Correspondence A political communications network established in 1772 by Samuel Adams to unite the colonists in their fight against British rule.

common law The cumulative body of judicial decisions, custom, and precedent, rather than law created by statute.

concurrent powers Powers of government exercised independently by both the federal and state governments, such as the power to tax.

confederation A group of independent states or nations that come together for a common purpose and whose central authority is usually limited to defense and foreign relations.

conference committee A committee composed of members of the House and Senate that tries to reconcile disagreements between the two branches of Congress over differing versions of a bill.

conglomerates Multi-interest and often multinational corporations that, under one corporate roof, may manufacture a wide variety of products.

Connecticut Compromise The plan adopted during the Constitutional Convention of 1787 providing for a House of Representatives based on population and a Senate with two members from each state. (Also known as the Great Compromise.)

constituencies Voters in a political district, or supporters of an elected official; or interest groups or client groups that are either directly regulated by the bureaucracy or vitally affected by its decisions.

Constitution The written framework for the United States government that establishes a strong national government of three branches—legislative, executive, and judicial—and provides for the control and operation of that government.

constitutional amendment A change to the Constitution proposed by a two-thirds vote of both houses of Congress or a constitutional convention, and ratified by legislatures or ratifying conventions in three-fourths of the states.

containment The foreign policy of the United States in the period after the Second World War, designed to contain the expansion of Soviet power.

cooperative federalism A view that the various levels of government in America are related parts of a single governmental system, characterized by cooperation and shared functions.

council-manager plan A form of city government under which a council, usually elected on a nonpartisan ticket, hires a professional city manager, who runs the city government and has power to hire and fire officials.

court-packing plan A plan proposed by President Franklin D. Roosevelt in 1937, which Congress rejected, to appoint additional, younger justices to the Supreme Court who would be more sympathetic to the New Deal.

covert operations Secret political action within other countries.

creative federalism A term coined by President Lyndon B. Johnson to describe his own view of the relationship between Washington and the states.

credentials committee The body of a political convention that decides which delegates should be seated, subject to approval of the entire convention.

criminal cases Court cases that concern crimes committed against the public order.

criminal information A formal accusation by a prosecutor, made under oath before a court, charging a person with a crime. Used in most state cases in place of a grand jury indictment to bring a person to trial.

dark horse A political candidate who is thought to have only an outside chance of gaining the nomination.

deficit The gap between the government's income and outlays.

delegates The men and women formally entitled to select the presidential nominees of the two major parties at their party's presidential nominating convention.

demands What people and groups want from the political system.

democracy Rule by the people.

deregulation The elimination or reduction of government regulation of industry.

desegregation The process of ending separation of persons by race.

détente A relaxation of international tensions.

deviating elections Elections in which the majority party (according to party identification) is defeated in a temporary reversal.

direct mail fund raising A technique to raise money directly from the public with the aid of computerized mailing lists.

distribution What occurs when government adopts a public policy that provides, or distributes, benefits to people or groups.

distributive policy A public policy that is meant to benefit everyone.

double jeopardy More than one prosecution for the same offense. Prohibited by the Constitution.

downsizing Corporate action to cut costs by the layoff or dismissal of large numbers of employees and executives.

Dred Scott decision A ruling by the Supreme Court in 1857—reversed by the Fourteenth Amendment in 1868—that black Americans were not citizens under the Constitution.

dual federalism The concept—accepted until 1937—of the federal government and the states as competing power centers, with the Supreme Court as referee.

due process of law A phrase, contained in the Fifth and Fourteenth amendments, that protects the individual against the arbitrary power of the state. Substantive due process means that laws must be reasonable. Procedural due process means that laws must be administered in a fair manner.

elastic clause Article I, Section 8, of the Constitution, which allows Congress to make all laws that are "necessary and proper" to carry out the powers of the Constitution.

elections The procedure by which voters choose, usually among competing candidates, to determine who shall hold public office. See also deviating elections, maintaining elections, and realigning elections.

electoral college The body composed of electors from the 50 states, who formally have the power to elect the president and vice president of the United States. Each state has a number of electors equal to its number of senators and representatives in Congress.

elite theory The view that power in America is held by the few, not by the masses of people.

enabling act A congressional act that allows the people of a territory desiring statehood to frame a state constitution.

enterprise zones Urban or rural areas in which businesses are encouraged to locate because of tax breaks and other incentives.

entitlement programs Programs mandated by law and not subject to annual review by Congress or the president.

enumerated powers Powers of government that are specifically granted to the three branches of the federal government under the Constitution.

equality A concept that all people are of equal worth, even if not of equal ability.

equal protection clause The provision of the Fourteenth Amendment that seeks to guarantee equal treatment for all persons.

Equal Rights Amendment (ERA) A proposed amendment to the Constitution, aimed at ending discrimination against women, that stated: "Equality of rights under the law shall not be denied or abridged by the United States or by any state on account of sex." The proposal was defeated in 1982.

equal time provision A provision of the Federal Communications Act that requires broadcasters to provide "equal time" to all legally qualified political candidates.

equity A legal principle of fair dealing, which may provide preventive measures and legal remedies that are unavailable under existing common law and statutory law.

"establishment clause" The First Amendment provision that "Congress shall make no law respecting an establishment of religion."

exclusionary rule A doctrine established by the Supreme Court that, with some exceptions, bars the federal government from using illegally seized evidence in court.

executive agencies Units of government under the president, within the executive branch, that are not part of a cabinet department.

executive agreements International agreements between the president and foreign heads of state that, unlike treaties, do not require Senate approval.

executive privilege The claim by presidents of an inherent right to withhold information from Congress and the judiciary.

exit polls Polls taken as people leave the voting booths. Sometimes have been used by the television networks to predict election outcomes before the polls close.

ex parte contacts One-sided contacts, such as an approach to a regulatory agency by a lawyer representing one side in a case.

ex post facto laws Laws that punish an act that was not illegal at the time it was committed. Prohibited by the Constitution.

extradition A constitutional provision allowing a state to request another state to return fugitives.

fairness doctrine A requirement by the Federal Communications Commission, abolished in 1987, that radio and television broadcasters present all sides of important public issues.

Federal Election Campaign Act amendments of 1974 An act that attempted to regulate campaign finance by providing for public funding of presidential elections and by placing limits on campaign contributions.

Federal Election Commission A six-member commission created in 1974 to enforce campaign finance laws and administer public financing of presidential elections.

federalism A system of government characterized by a constitutional sharing of power between a national government and regional units of government.

Federalist, The A series of letters published in the late 1780s by Alexander Hamilton, James Madison, and John Jay to explain and help bring about ratification of the Constitution.

Federalists Those who supported the Constitution during the struggle over its ratification following the Constitutional Convention of 1787.

federal system (see federalism, above).

feedback The response of the rest of society to decisions made by the authorities of a political system.

felonies Serious crimes, such as murder, arson, or rape.

filibuster The process by which a single senator, or a group of senators, can sometimes talk a bill to death and prevent it from coming to a vote.

First Amendment of the Constitution protects freedom of speech, freedom of the press, freedom of religion, and freedom of assembly.

fiscal policy Government regulation of the economy through its control over taxes and government spending.

flexible construction The principle, established by Chief Justice John Marshall in 1819 in the case of *McCulloch* v. *Maryland*, that the Constitution must be interpreted flexibly to meet changing conditions.

foreign policy The sum of the goals, decisions, and actions that govern a nation's relations with the rest of the world.

franking privilege A system entitling members of Congress to send mail to constituents without charge by putting their frank, or mark, on the envelope. The law forbids this privilege for soliciting money or votes, or for mass mailings 60 days before an election.

Freedom of Information Act A law passed in 1966 that requires federal executive branch and regulatory agencies to make information available to journalists, scholars, and the public unless it falls into one of several confidential categories.

"free exercise clause" The First Amendment provision that Congress shall make no law "prohibiting the free exercise" of religion. The clause protects the right of individuals to worship or believe as they wish, or to hold no religious beliefs.

full faith and credit A clause in Article IV of the Constitution, requiring each state to respect the laws, records, and court decisions of another state.

gender gap A difference, such as that in the 1992 elections, in the voting behavior of men and women.

general purpose grants Federal aid that may be used by states and localities mostly as they wish.

general revenue sharing A controversial program that lasted from 1972 to 1986 with the federal government turning over billions in federal tax monies to state and local governments to spend at will.

gerrymandering The drawing of the lines of congressional districts, or of any other political district, in order to favor one political party or group over another.

globalization A world economy characterized by the free movement of goods, capital, labor, and information across national borders.

government The individuals, institutions, and processes that make the rules for society and possess the power to enforce them.

government corporations Agencies that were at one time semiautonomous, but that through legislation have been placed under presidential control since 1945.

gross domestic product (GDP) The yearly value of goods and services produced within a country.

guaranteed annual income A proposed alternate approach to welfare that would guarantee everyone a minimum income.

habeas corpus, writ of A writ designed to protect against illegal imprisonment by requiring that a person who is detained be brought before a judge for investigation.

Hatch Act A federal law passed by Congress in 1939 to restrict political activities by federal workers. The law prevents federal employees while on duty from taking an active part in party politics or campaigns and also bars federal employees from running for public office as a candidate of a political party.

"hold" The practice that allows senators to delay or even kill floor action on legislation, a nomination, or other matters by asking their party leaders not to schedule them.

home rule The power of some municipalities to modify their charters and run their affairs without approval by the state legislature.

impeachment Under the Constitution, the formal proceedings against the president or other federal officials or federal judges, who may be removed from office if convicted of "Treason, Bribery or other high Crimes and Misdemeanors."

implementation The action, or actions, taken by government to carry out a policy.

implied powers Powers of the national government that flow from its enumerated powers and the "elastic clause" of the Constitution.

independent counsel A special federal prosecutor appointed under the 1978 Ethics in Government Act in cases involving possible crimes by high officials. The law providing for independent counsels expired in 1999.

independent expenditures Funds spent for or against a candidate by committees not formally connected to the candidate's campaign and without coordination with the campaign.

independent regulatory agencies Government agencies that exercise quasi-judicial and quasi-legislative powers and are administratively independent of both the president and Congress (although politically independent of neither).

Indiana ballot Also known as the party-column ballot. Used in a majority of states, it lists the candidates of each party in a row or column, beside or under the party emblem. Allows for and encourages straight-ticket voting.

indictment A finding by a grand jury that there is enough evidence against an individual to warrant a criminal trial.

information *See* **criminal information.**

inherent powers Powers of government that the national government may exercise simply because it exists as a government, such as the right to conduct foreign relations.

initiative A method of amending state constitutions, used in 18 states under which proposed constitutional amendments can be placed on the ballot if enough signatures are obtained on a petition. Almost half the states also employ the initiative on the ballot to allow voters to enact or repeal laws.

injunction An order from a court to prevent or require an action.

inputs The demands upon, and supports for, a political system.

internationalism The policy established after the Second World War that America must take an active leadership role in world affairs.

instructed delegate A legislator who automatically mirrors the will of the majority of his or her constituents.

interest groups Private groups that attempt to influence the government to respond to the shared attitudes of their members.

interstate compacts Agreements between or among states made with the approval of Congress.

interventionism A strand of American foreign policy that was visible by the end of the 19th century; it included "gunboat diplomacy" and other forms of military involvement by the United States in various parts of the world.

Iran-contra scandal The attempt by President Reagan's White House to trade arms for American hostages in the Middle East.

iron triangle A powerful alliance of mutual benefit among an agency or unit of the government, an interest group, and a committee or subcommittee of Congress. Also called a triangle or a subgovernment.

isolationism A policy of avoiding foreign involvement.

issue networks A loose grouping of people and organizations who seek to influence policy formation.

Jim Crow laws Laws that were designed to segregate black and white Americans and give legal recognition to discrimination.

Joint Chiefs of Staff The chairman, the chiefs of staff of the three armed services, and, when Marine Corps matters are under consideration, the commandant of the marines. By law, the Joint Chiefs of Staff advise the president and the secretary of defense and are the chiefs of their respective military services.

joint committees Committees of Congress composed of both representatives and senators.

judicial activism A philosophy that Supreme Court justices and other judges should boldly apply the Constitution to social and political questions.

judicial restraint A philosophy that the Supreme Court should avoid constitutional questions when possible and uphold acts of Congress unless they clearly violate a specific section of the Constitution.

judicial review The power of the Supreme Court to declare acts of Congress or actions by the executive branch—or laws and actions at any level of local, state, and federal government—unconstitutional.

jurisdiction The kinds of cases that a court has the authority to decide.

jus sanguinis Right of blood. Under this principle, the citizenship of a child is determined by that of the parents.

jus soli Right of soil. Under this principle, citizenship is conferred by place of birth.

kitchen cabinet Informal advisers to the president who hold no official position on the White House staff.

laissez-faire The philosophy that government should intervene as little as possible in economic affairs.

"lame duck" A legislator or other official whose term of office extends beyond an election at which he or she has been defeated or did not run.

legislative veto A provision of law in which Congress asserts the power to nullify actions of the executive branch. In 1983 the Supreme Court ruled that the "legislative veto" was unconstitutional, but Congress continued to pass laws containing such provisions.

liaison officers Employees of government agencies whose job is to maintain good relations with Congress.

line item veto The power of the president, struck down by the Supreme Court in 1998, to veto parts of appropriations bills. Most state governors have this power.

literacy tests Tests of a voter's ability to read and write, which were often used to keep recent immigrants and blacks from voting.

lobbying Communication with legislators or other government officials to try to influence their decisions.

magistrates' courts Courts in which justices of the peace, or magistrates, handle misdemeanors, minor offenses such as speeding, and perform civil marriages.

Magna Carta An historic British document, signed by King John in 1215, in which the nobles confirmed that the power of the king was not absolute.

maintaining elections Elections that reflect the basic party identification of the voters.

majority leader A leader elected by the majority party in a legislative house.

majority rule A concept of government by the people in which everyone is free to vote, but normally whoever gets the most votes wins the election and represents all the people (including those who voted for the losing candidate).

Mallory rule A rule established by the Supreme Court in *Mallory* v. *United States* (1957) requiring that a suspect in a federal case be arraigned without unnecessary delay.

Marbury v. Madison The 1803 case in which the Supreme Court, by declaring a portion of an act of Congress unconstitutional, first firmly set forth and established the power of judicial review.

marginal district A congressional district in which the winning candidate receives less than 55 percent of the vote.

Marshall Plan A plan named for its creator, Secretary of State George C. Marshall, to provide billions of dollars of American aid to Western Europe to speed its economic and social recovery after the Second World War.

Massachusetts ballot Also known as the office-column ballot. This ballot groups candidates according to the office for which they are running.

matching requirements The federal government's requirement that state or local governments put up some of their own funds in order to be eligible for federal aid for a program.

mayor-council plan A form of city government under which power is divided between a mayor and an elected city council.

McCulloch v. Maryland An important decision of the Supreme Court in 1819 that established the key concepts of implied powers, broad construction of the Constitution, and supremacy of the national government.

Medicaid A public assistance program established in 1965 to help pay hospital, doctor, and medical bills for persons with low incomes.

Medicare A federal program established in 1965 to provide hospital and medical services to older persons through the social security system.

megalopolis By definition, a very large city. The term has also been used to describe the cluster of metropolitan areas of the northeastern seaboard of the United States.

merit commissions Commissions set up to recommend candidates for federal district and circuit courts on the basis of merit.

military-industrial complex A term often used to describe the economic and political ties between the military establishment and the defense-aerospace industry.

minority leader A leader elected by the minority party in a legislative house.

minor party A political party other than one of the major parties; also known as a third party.

Miranda warnings Warnings that police must give suspects to advise them of their constitutional rights. Under the Supreme Court decision in *Miranda* v. *Arizona* (1966), before suspects are questioned they must be warned that they have the right to remain silent, that any statements they make may be used against them, and that they have the right to a lawyer.

misdemeanors Minor criminal offenses, such as speeding.

mixed (or modified) free enterprise system An economic system, such as that of the United States, in which both private industry and government play important roles.

monetary policy Government regulation of the economy through its control over the supply of money and the cost and availability of credit.

money supply The quantity of money in circulation.

monopoly Control of a market by a single company.

Monroe Doctrine A declaration by President James Monroe in 1823 that warned European powers to keep out of the Western Hemisphere and pledged that the United States would not intervene in the internal affairs of Europe.

muckrakers A group of writers, journalists, and critics who exposed corporate malfeasance and political corruption in the first decade of the 20th century.

national chairperson The head of a national political party.

national committee Between conventions, the governing body of a major political party. Members of the national committee are chosen in the states and formally elected by the party's national convention.

national convention The formal source of all authority in each major political party. It nominates the party candidates for president and vice president, writes a platform, settles disputes, writes rules, and elects the members of the national committee.

national debt The total amount of money that the United States owes to its creditors.

nationalism Love of country and a desire for independence; it can also mean an excessive form of patriotism exploited by political leaders.

national presidential primary A proposed new form of primary in which voters could directly choose the presidential candidates of the major parties.

national security A broad concept that may be defined in many ways, but the term is generally used to refer to the basic protection and defense of the nation.

National Security Council (NSC) A White House council created under the National Security Act of 1947 to advise the president and help coordinate American military and foreign policy.

natural rights The belief that all people possess certain basic rights that may not be abridged by government.

negative advertising Political commercials that strongly attack a rival candidate.

negative campaigning Political campaigning in which the candidates appear to spend more time attacking each other than discussing policies and programs.

new federalism President Richard Nixon's effort to return federal tax money to state and local governments. The term was also adopted by President Ronald Reagan.

New Jersey Plan A plan offered at the Constitutional Convention of 1787 by William Paterson of New Jersey, and favored by the small states, which called for one vote for each state in the legislature, an executive of more than one person to be elected by Congress, and a Supreme Court to be appointed by the executive.

New York Times rule A rule established by the Supreme Court in the case of *New York Times Company* v. *Sullivan* (1964), which makes it almost impossible to libel a public official unless the statement is made with "actual malice"—that is, unless it is deliberately or recklessly false.

nuclear proliferation The spread of nuclear weapons of mass destruction to other nations.

oligopoly The concentration of economic power in the hands of a relatively few large companies.

ombudsman An official complaint taker who tries to help citizens who have been wronged by the actions of government agencies.

open primary A form of primary election in which any voter may participate and vote for a slate of candidates of one political party.

original jurisdiction The right of the Supreme Court, under the Constitution, to hear certain kinds of cases directly, such as cases involving foreign diplomats, or cases in which one of the 50 states is a party.

out party A major political party that functions as an opposition party because it does not control the presidency.

outputs The binding decisions that a political system makes, whether in the form of laws, regulations, or judicial decisions.

party identification Attraction to one political party by a voter.

patronage The practice by which victorious politicians reward their followers with political jobs.

Pentagon Papers A 47 volume study of the Vietnam War compiled by the Defense Department and leaked to the press by a former Pentagon official in 1971.

periodic registration A system of voter registration in which the voter must register every year or at other stated intervals.

permanent registration A system of voter registration in which voters must register only once in their district.

plea bargaining A bargain in which a defendant in a criminal case agrees to plead guilty to a less serious charge than might be proven at a trial. In return, the prosecutor agrees to reduce the charges or recommend leniency.

plum book A listing of the non-civil-service jobs that an incoming president may fill.

pluralism A system in which many conflicting groups within the community have access to government officials and compete with one another in an effort to influence policy decisions.

pocket veto A power of the president to kill a bill by taking no action (if Congress adjourns during the 10-day period after the president receives the bill). Some court rulings have suggested that a president may exercise a pocket veto only when Congress adjourns for good at the end of a second session, and not during a recess.

policy A course of action decided upon by a government—or by any organization, group, or individual—that usually involves a choice among competing alternatives.

political action committees (PACs) Independent organizations, but more often the political arms of corporations, labor unions, or interest groups, established to contribute to candidates or to work for general political goals.

political culture A nation's set of fundamental beliefs about how government and politics should be conducted.

political opinion Opinions on political issues, such as a choice among candidates or parties.

political participation The involvement of citizens in the political process of a nation.

political party, major A broadly based coalition that attempts to gain control of the government by winning elections, in order to exercise power and reward its members.

political socialization The process through which an individual acquires a set of political attitudes and forms opinions about political and social issues.

politics The pursuit and exercise of power.

poll tax A tax on voting repealed by the Twenty-fourth Amendment in 1964, long used by southern states to keep blacks (and, in some cases, poor whites) from participating in elections.

pork-barrel legislation Bills that benefit legislators' home districts, or powerful corporate contributors, with sometimes wasteful or unnecessary public works or other projects.

power The possession of control over others.

power structure A term popularized by sociologist Floyd Hunter to describe the community leaders who he said determined policy in Atlanta, Georgia. More broadly, the term is used to describe "power elites" generally.

precedent An earlier court case that serves as a justification for a decision in a later case. Also known as stare decisis.

presidential primary Method used by about three-quarters of the states in which voters in one or both parties express their preference for a presidential nominee and choose all or some convention delegates.

primary groups Groups that a person comes into face-to-face contact with in everyday life; for example, friends, office associates, or a local social club.

prior restraint The censoring of news stories by the government prior to publication.

proportional representation A system of multimember election districts that encourages the existence of many parties by allotting legislative seats to competing parties according to the percentage of votes that they win.

Proposition 13 A constitutional amendment approved by California voters in 1978 that limits real estate taxes in the state to 1 percent of previous property values.

proprietary colonies Colonies in which the proprietors (who had obtained their patents from the king) named the governors, subject to the king's approval.

psychological method An approach in studying how voters decide that attempts to find out what is going on inside the minds of the voters and to measure their perceptions of parties, candidates, and issues.

public administration The term preferred by most political scientists to describe the bureaucratic process—the business of making government work.

public assistance A welfare program that distributes public funds to people who are poor.

public interest law firms Law firms, often staffed by young lawyers, that represent consumers, minorities, and the poor.

public opinion The expression of attitudes about government and politics.

public policy A course of action chosen by government officials.

quota sample A method of polling, considered less reliable than a random sample, in which interviewers are instructed to question members of a particular group in proportion to their percentage in the population as a whole.

random sample A group of people, chosen by poll-takers, that is representative of the universe that is being polled.

realigning elections Elections that may lead to a basic shift in the party identification of the electorate.

recall A procedure that in certain circumstances permits voters to remove elected state or local officials from office before their terms have expired.

recorded votes Votes in the House of Representatives in which the position of each member is noted and published in the *Congressional Record*.

redistributive policy A public policy that takes something away from one person or group and gives it to another person or group.

redistricting The drawing of new boundary lines for legislative districts based on the results of a census of the population.

reference groups Groups whose views serve as guidelines to an individual's opinion. See also primary groups and secondary groups.

referendum A method available in most states that allows voters, in effect, to "veto" a bill passed by the legislature or to accept or reject a proposal, such as a bond issue, made by a government agency.

regulatory federalism The emergence of federal programs that set standards and requirements for the states through federal laws and regulations. The federal programs are then implemented by state and local governments.

representative democracy A democracy in which leaders are elected to speak for and represent the people. Also called a republic.

republic A form of government in which the people are sovereign but their power is exercised by their elected representatives. Also called a representative democracy.

retrospective voting Voting based upon looking back and making judgments about the way things have gone and the kind of government experienced during a political leader's time in office.

riders Provisions tacked on to a piece of legislation that are not relevant to the bill.

right to work laws State legislation designed to outlaw the union shop, passed by 21 states acting under Section 14B of the federal Taft-Hartley Act.

Roe* v. *Wade A 1973 Supreme Court decision affirming that no state may interfere with a woman's right to have an abortion during the first three months of pregnancy.

roll-call vote A method of voting in a legislature in which the positions of the members become a matter of public record.

royal colonies Colonies controlled by the British king through governors appointed by him and through the king's veto power over colonial laws.

safe congressional district As usually defined, a district in which the winner receives 55 percent or more of the vote.

secondary groups Organizations or groups, such as labor unions or fraternal, professional, or religious groups, that may influence an individual's opinion.

Secret Service The government agency that guards the president, the vice president, the major presidential and vice-presidential candidates, and their spouses.

segregation The separation of persons by race.

select committees Committees created by Congress to conduct special investigations. Although normally temporary, some select committees become, in effect, permanent.

selective incorporation The process under which the Supreme Court has applied most of the provisions of the Bill of Rights to the states under the Fourteenth Amendment.

senatorial courtesy An unwritten custom by which individual senators who belong to the same political party as the president exercise an informal veto power over presidential appointments in their states.

Senior Executive Service (SES) A group of high-level administrators and managers at the top of the government bureaucracy. SES members have less job tenure but are eligible for substantial cash bonuses for merit.

seniority system A system, until modified and reformed in the 1970s, that automatically resulted in the selection as committee chair of those members of the majority party in Congress who had the longest continuous service on a committee.

separate but equal A doctrine established by the Supreme Court in 1896 under which "Jim Crow" segregation laws were held to be constitutional. Overruled by the Supreme Court in 1954 in *Brown* v. *Board of Education of Topeka, Kansas*.

separation of powers The principle that each of the three branches of government is constitutionally equal to and independent of the others.

shared powers The fusing or overlapping of powers and functions among the separate branches of government.

shield laws Laws passed by state legislatures that are designed to protect reporters from being forced to reveal their news sources.

smoke-filled room A phrase that grew out of the 1920 Republican Convention in Chicago, symbolizing the selection of a candidate by political bosses operating in secret.

social security A compulsory national insurance program, financed by taxes on employers and employees. The insurance falls into four categories: old-age and survivors insurance, disability insurance, Medicare, and unemployment insurance.

sociological method An approach in studying how the voters decide that focuses on the social and economic background of the voters, their income, social class, ethnic group, education, and similar factors.

soft money Unregulated campaign funds not subject to the limits of federal law until 2002. A campaign finance law passed that year banned contributions of soft money to national political parties.

speaker of the House The presiding officer and most powerful member of the House of Representatives. The speaker is technically elected by the full House but in practice is chosen by the majority party.

special committees Committees created by Congress to conduct special investigations.

special prosecutor An independent federal prosecutor appointed under the 1978 Ethics in Government Act in cases involving possible crimes by high officials. Later known formally as an "independent counsel." The law expired in 1999.

special publics A concept developed by political scientists to describe those segments of the public with views about particular issues.

special rule A rule from the House Rules Committee that limits the time to be allowed for floor discussion of a bill and the extent to which it may be amended.

spoils system The practice under which victorious politicians reward their followers with jobs.

standing committees The permanent committees of a legislature that consider bills and conduct hearings and investigations.

stare decisis A Latin phrase meaning "stand by past decisions," a principle that is often used by judges in deciding cases.

statutory law Law enacted by Congress, or by state legislatures or local legislative bodies.

steering committees Committees that appoint House members and Democratic senators to standing committees. (The Republican Committee on Committees appoints Republican senators.) Also known as assignment committees.

straight-ticket voting Voting for all candidates of a single party for all offices.

Strategic Arms Limitation Talks (SALT) Negotiations between the United States and the Soviet Union that resulted in the signing of two nuclear arms agreements in 1972 SALT I and the Anti-Ballistic Missile (ABM) Treaty, and the SALT II agreement in 1979. SALT II was not ratified by the U.S. Senate.

Strategic Arms Reduction Treaty (START) A treaty to reduce strategic nuclear arms, signed by the United States and the Soviet Union in 1991.

strategic deterrence A policy adopted by the United States after the Second World War that assumed that if enough nuclear weapons were deployed by the United States, an enemy would not attack for fear of being destroyed in retaliation.

subcommittees Small committees formed from the members of a larger committee.

subgovernment A powerful alliance of mutual benefit among an agency or unit of the government, an interest group, and a committee or subcommittee of Congress. Also called a triangle or iron triangle.

subpoena A written document issued by a court that orders a person to appear in court or to produce evidence.

subsidy A government grant of money.

suffrage The right to vote.

supply-side economics An economic philosophy that advocates both tax and budget cuts to increase incentives to produce in order to expand the total supply of the nation's goods and services.

supports The attitudes and actions of people that sustain and buttress the political system at all levels and allow it to continue to work.

supremacy clause Article VI, Paragraph 2, of the Constitution, which declares that the Constitution, and the laws and treaties of the United States made under it, are "the supreme Law of the Land" and prevail over any conflicting state constitutions or laws.

suspension of the rules A procedure permitted two days each week under the rules of the House of Representatives that allows many noncontroversial bills to be debated and passed by two-thirds of the members who are voting.

system maintenance The process of keeping a diverse, unwieldy institution, such as the House of Representatives, functioning.

tariff A federal tax on imports.

third party A minor party that is an alternative to the two major parties; for example, the Know-Nothings of the 1850s, a party that exploited fear of Irish immigrants and other "foreigners," or the Populists of the 1890s, a protest party of Western farmers favoring "free silver."

ticket-splitter A voter who votes for candidates of more than one party in the same election.

tombstone voters Deceased voters whose names are fraudulently recorded as voting in an election.

town meeting An annual meeting held in the spring in many New England towns, at which the townspeople come together to elect a board of selectmen and to discuss local policy questions. The town meeting has become a symbol of participatory democracy.

transnational relations Contacts, coalitions, and interactions across national boundaries—such as personal contacts or business relationships—that are not controlled by the central foreign-policy organs of governments.

triangle A powerful alliance of mutual benefit among an agency or unit of the government, an interest group, and a committee or subcommittee of Congress. Also called an iron triangle or a subgovernment.

Truman Doctrine As enunciated by President Truman, a doctrine declaring that American security and world peace depend on United States protection for the "free peoples of the world."

trustee Concept of the British statesman Edmund Burke that legislators should act according to their own consciences.

unanimous consent A time-saving procedure under which bills may be called up for consideration in the Senate unless one or more members object.

unfunded mandates Federal laws that require states to meet certain standards, but often provide no money to help the states comply. The practice was restricted by a law passed in 1995.

unicameral legislature A legislature with only one house.

union shop A place of work in which any person may be hired provided he or she joins the union within a specified time.

unitary system of government A centralized system of government, such as that of France, where most of the important policy decisions are made by a central government.

United Nations A world organization founded in 1945 for the purpose of collectively keeping the peace and working for the betterment of humanity.

universe The total group from which poll-takers may select a random sample in order to measure public opinion.

unreasonable searches and seizures Searches prohibited by the Fourth Amendment, often because they take place without a search warrant issued by a court.

vanishing marginals An electoral trend in which the number of unsafe, marginal districts in House elections appears to be declining.

veto Disapproval of a bill by a chief executive, such as the president or a governor.

Virginia Plan A plan offered at the Constitutional Convention of 1787, and favored by the large states, that called for a two-house legislature, the lower house chosen by the people and the upper house chosen by the lower; and a national executive and a national judiciary chosen by the legislature.

War Powers Resolution A law passed by Congress in 1973 in an effort to set a time limit on the use of combat forces abroad by a president.

Watergate scandal The 1972 break-in at Democratic Party headquarters in the Watergate office building in Washington, D.C., by burglars working for the Republican president's reelection campaign. The scandal led to the resignation and pardon of President Richard Nixon in 1974.

welfare state A government like that of the United States that exercises responsibility for the welfare of its citizens in such areas as social security, housing, and education.

whips Legislative leaders of each party who are responsible for rounding up party members for important votes.

whistle-blowers Government employees who publicly expose evidence of official waste or corruption that they have learned about in the course of their duties.

winner-take-all primaries Presidential primaries in which the victorious candidate could win all of a state's convention delegates, no matter how slim the margin of victory. The Democratic Party abandoned this type of primary in 1976. The Republican Party has continued to use winner-take-all primaries in many states.

Chapter Opening Photos

Chapter 1: AP/Wide World; **Chapter 2:** Copyright © Dennis Brack/Black Star Publishing/PictureQuest; **Chapter 3:** Nevada Appeal/AP/Wide World; **Chapter 4:** Copyright © 2000 Susan Holtz; **Chapter 5:** AP/Wide World; **Chapter 6:** AP/Wide World; **Chapter 7:** AP/Wide World; **Chapter 8:** AP/Wide World; **Chapter 9:** Michael Smith/Newsmakers; **Chapter 10:** AP/Wide World; **Chapter 11:** Copyright © Steve Liss/Time Inc.; **Chapter 12:** AP/Topeka Capital-Journal/Wide World; **Chapter 13:** AP/Wide World; **Chapter 14:** Copyright © Bohdan Hrynewych/Stock, Boston/PictureQuest; **Chapter 15:** AP/Supreme Court/Wide World; **Chapter 16:** AP/Wide World; **Chapter 17:** Copyright © Doug Armand/Tony Stone; **Chapter 18:** Copyright © Ramey/Stock, Boston; and **Chapter 19:** Copyright © Jeff Greenberg/Photo Researchers.

Part Opening Photos

Part One: AP/Wide World; **Part Two:** Copyright © Mark T. Osler/Copley News Service; **Part Three:** Copyright © Paul Conklin; **Part Four:** NASA TV/AP/Wide World; and **Part Five:** Copyright © Dan McCoy/RAINBOW/PictureQuest

May 22, Monday
Foreign Desk

Referendum on 2-Party Plan in Italy Fizzles

By Alessandra Stanley

An ambitious referendum aimed at reducing the instability in Italy's electoral system was invalidated tonight because too few Italians turned out for the vote to be accepted.

Only about 32 percent of voters cast ballots today, far less than the 50.1 percent quorum needed. The referendum was supposed to make Italians decide seven questions, covering a broad range of political, economic, and social issues.

But the most contested item was an effort to move Italy closer to a two-party system by ridding it of the parliamentary seats that are allotted proportionally. That measure, fiercely opposed by small parties who feared that they would be wiped out in the new system, was also opposed by Silvio Berlusconi, leader of the center-right party Forza Italia. An exit poll by the Abacus agency showed that 82 percent of the people who bothered to vote wanted to get rid of the old system.

The low turnout was a blow to the embattled government of Giuliano Amato, which had hoped that a favorable vote would give it strong public backing for electoral reforms that previous center-left governments had not been able to pass in the badly divided Italian Parliament. A similar referendum on changing the electoral system narrowly failed to reach a quorum last year.

This year the government passed a decree to purge electoral lists of deceased voters and some nonresidents, hoping that the decree would make it easier to reach a quorum. Even Sophia Loren, who does not reside in Italy, was removed from the lists of her native town of Potzzuoli, near Naples. After the voter rolls were cleaned up, just over 49 million Italians were registered.

But the failure to win voter approval for a change in the electoral system means that it is likely that Italy's political instability will continue. The current center-left coalition is Italy's 58th government since World War II.

The low turnout was a short-term political victory for Mr. Berlusconi, who leads the center-right opposition and is already campaigning to become prime minister in the next election. But the current system, which often forces the ruling majority to make ill-matched alliances with small parties that can easily balk and bring down a government, has inherent problems for any candidate. Mr. Berlusconi was prime minister in 1994 for less than a year, but lost office when a coalition partner defected and forced his center-right government to collapse.

The low turnout did not necessarily mean that most Italians favor their current electoral system or disagreed with the referendum's other questions, like whether to loosen laws protecting employees from dismissal, or whether prosecutors can also serve as trial judges.

The low attendance mainly reflected most Italians' disgust with politics as usual and widespread referendum fatigue. Voters have been summoned to vote in referendums seven times since 1990.

The measure, once reserved for weighty social matters like abolishing the monarchy in 1946, or legalizing divorce in 1974, became a kind of political crutch for settling issues that Parliament was unable to resolve. (In 1990, a referendum on hunting regulations and the use of pesticides also failed to reach a quorum.)

"People who are coming to vote are very confused, the issues are so diverse and complicated," said Laura Bianchi, 43, after she voted in Rome. She said that with Italy's chronic revolving governments, "the legislatures are so short that they can't pass any laws."

April 28, 1999, Wednesday
Editorial Desk

The Internet vs. the First Amendment
By Laurence H. Tribe

As we try to make sense of the school massacre in Littleton, Colo., we suddenly find ourselves swept up in a national debate about whether the Internet, with its dazzling array of interactive mayhem and violence, is partly to blame.

Should the Internet be available to anyone, of any age, with a computer and a telephone connection? Many who have long wanted to muzzle the Internet are making symbols of Eric Harris and Dylan Klebold, who used the Internet to play violent computer games and promote their racist views.

How much protection should Internet "speech" receive under the First Amendment? And, under the Fourth Amendment's search and seizure provisions, may the Government browse Web sites without a warrant in order to nip mass murder plots in the bud? While nearly every possible view has its champions, most of the opinions expressed reflect more confusion than clarity.

The point to remember is that basic constitutional principles do not arise and disappear as each new technology comes on the scene. We have come to this conclusion rather slowly. Early in the 20th century, the Supreme Court expressed doubt that free-speech principles had any application at all to motion pictures, and in 1981, Justice Byron White introduced his analysis of a law regulating outdoor billboard advertising by saying, "We deal here with the law of billboards."

Only in recent years has the Court recognized that new technology doesn't affect basic constitutional principles. The Court has found that technological details, however, can be relevant to certain applications of the law, especially because, in principle, speech may not be restricted any more than necessary.

For instance, the Supreme Court struck down provisions in 1997 of the Communications Decency Act because they blocked pornographic materials from being transmitted over the Internet, when technology already existed that allowed parents to selectively censor such materials.

Even though the Internet allows nearly anyone to obtain or transmit information instantaneously to and from anywhere on the planet, it does not deserve more—or less—free-speech protection than older media.

A Web page simulating, or even glorifying, violence and hatred is not outside the First Amendment's protection any more than are disgusting board games, magazines or political tracts. The same First Amendment that safeguards the right of Nazis to march through Skokie protects the right of an adult to put virtual machine guns aimed at lifelike human targets on his or her computer screen.

At the same time, Internet speech doesn't have more constitutional protection than speech disseminated in a more old-fashioned and limited manner. In particular, direct threats or their messages that by their very utterance cause harm receive no more protection on the Internet than anyplace else. Releasing a computer virus through E-mail deserves no greater immunity than crying "Fire" in a crowded theater.

What about someone who posts a Web page with detailed, step-by-step instructions on how to assemble an explosive device from readily available materials? Such instructional materials are not quite like yelling "Fire" in a theater; they do not cause harm in a purely reflexive or automatic manner. Instead, they change the mix of ideas and information in the heads o the speaker's audience.

Speech disseminating such instructions on the Internet, however reprehensible, is thus entitled to a degree of First Amendment protection. But it is not entitled to the same level of protection to which speech advocating ideas is entitled because it is rarely part of any dialogue about what is true or what ought to e done. Distributing such materials doesn't try to persuade anyone to take a course of action, but instead provides the means for committing a crime.

Thus, the United State Courts of Appeals have held that distributing pamphlets on how to evade taxes, make illegal drugs or kill someone can amount to aiding and abetting a crime and may be punished as such, depending, of course, on the particular facts.

The First Amendment, therefore, should shoulder none of the guilt in the Littleton killings. In truth, the First Amendment leaves considerable room for government to exert control, and the advent of the Internet neither broadens nor narrows government's options.

Nor, for that matter, is the Fourth Amendment protection against unreasonable searches and seizures among the culprits here. Those who launch murderous plots by posting their deranged plans on a Web site are exposing their schemes in a public space, one that Government agencies may freely browse without a warrant despite the fanciful argument that all talk on the World Wide Web is as private as E-mail messages might be.

At the same time, it would be a grave mistake to assume that either government surveillance or control can play an important role in prevent violent crimes. Doing more to keep lethal weapons out of youthful hands—something the Second Amendment, under any reading, does not prevent—and trying to diagnose all forms of rage before they erupt into violence, are likely to be far more effective than anything government could do either by spying on the Internet's users or by suppressing their speech.

March 6, 1999, Saturday
National Desk

Death Row Lessons and One Professor's Mission

By Pam Belluck

David Protess believes his career was shaped at age 7, growing up near Sheepshead Bay in Brooklyn. In that year, 1953, Julius and Ethel Rosenberg were executed.

"I saw the headline, 'Rosenbergs Fried,' " Mr. Protess said, recalling that he was the same age as one of the Rosenbergs' sons. "It seemed so unjust, and I'm not taking a position about whether they were guilty or not. What was unjust was that the state orphaned two young boys."

Now 52, Mr. Protess, a journalism professor at Northwestern University, examines death row cases, assigning them to his students and teaching them to pore over documents, re-enact crimes and interview witnesses.

It has brought him and a handful of students remarkable success.

In 1996, Mr. Protess and three students helped prove the innocence of four men who had spent 18 years in prison for a double murder in Ford Heights. Today, the men agreed to a $36 million settlement in a civil suit they filed against Cook County.

Last month, an investigation by Mr. Protess and six students led to the release of Anthony Porter, 43, who had spent 16 years on death row in the murder of a Chicago couple.

The state's principal witness recanted statements incriminating Mr. Porter. A woman implicated her estranged husband, Alstory Simon, a Milwaukee laborer. And Mr. Simon, interviewed by a private investigator working with Mr. Protess, confessed to the killings.

Mr. Porter, although not officially exonerated, is free while the authorities investigate the new findings.

Mr. Protess's pursuit of cases, his enthusiastic style, and the skills he teaches have earned him admirers among students, journalists and professors. Still, he gets questions about his passion in these cases.

"Do I bring a passion to my work?" he asked. "Yeah, I do. Sometimes that is controversial. I just believe that the higher calling of journalism is that after you find the truth, you can in fact right the wrong."

He added: "In some cases, the truth was they guy was guilty, and those students got an A."

Mr. Protess has tempered his approach somewhat since 1995, when he and 10 students tried to overturn the murder conviction of Gervies Davis. They testified at Mr. Davis's clemency hearing. On the day of the execution, Mr. Protess gathered students at his home with a grief counselor on standby for what he said "was really a wake." Mr. Davis called from prison and "I put him on the speaker phone so we could all hear him." Mr. Protess said.

After that execution, some people accused Mr. Protess of being more advocate than journalist.

He believes he should have done things differently. For example, instead of testifying, he should have required defense lawyers subpoena his research so he would not appear to be working for the defense.

"I think we became too personally involved," he said.

Mr. Protess, who has a doctorate in public policy, investigated cases for the Better Government Association, a private watchdog group, in the 1970s. Afterward, while teaching at Northwestern, he investigated wrongful convictions for *Chicago Lawyer* magazine, asking his students to help with the legwork. He now gets three to four requests a day from inmates and lawyers around the country.

He looks for cases with no incriminating physical evidence like blood or semen, no credible eyewitness, no reliable confession, and other "viable suspects."

In the Porter case there was no physical evidence and a shaky witness. One victim was in Mr. Porter's gang, which cast doubt on motive. The other victim's mother believed Mr. Porter was innocent because she last saw her daughter with Mr. Simon and his wife.

Mr. Protess emphasizes that his investigations are collaborative efforts.

Early on in Mr. Protess's course, the private investigator, Paul Ciolino, teaches about dicey neighborhoods. Mr. Protess makes students act out all interviews in advance.

"We rehearse everything, so that if there's a person in prison who hasn't talked about his crime for years, we practice how to get him talk," said Shawn Armbrust, a student on the Porter case.

Mr. Protess wants his students to learn investigative skills, but he also wants to solve cases. Sometimes he speaks to witnesses before students do. Sometimes he suggests a certain interview team, knowing students appear less threatening than a professional reporter or an investigator. On crucial interviews, he or Mr. Ciolino go along, because "the credibility of college students would be in question," he said.

Mr. Protess sat in a car while Ms. Armbrust and Cara Rubinsky, another student, went into Mr. Simon's home in Milwaukee. The students were to play "good cops" while Mr. Protess would come in later as the "bad cop."

When students found Mr. Simon's estranged wife, Inez Jackson, in Milwaukee, they told her there was a message from a relative in prison that their professor wanted to deliver personally. They did not reveal the relative's name because Mr. Protess feared that would prompt a detailed conversation in which he should take part.

Mr. Protess knows private investigators like Mr. Ciolino may use techniques that journalists would not. Mr. Ciolino tried to elicit Mr. Simon's confession by showing a videotape of a man who said he saw Mr. Simon commit the murders. The man, who worked for Mr. Ciolino, was only pretending to be an eyewitness.

Prosecutors have delayed exonerating Mr. Porter, saying they need to investigate the impact of the fake tape. Mr. Simon's lawyer is not saying his client did not kill the couple, only that it was self-defense.

Mr. Protess said he considered a tactic like Mr. Ciolino's tape inappropriate for journalists unless it was the only way to get

(continued)

information "in a story with life and death stakes." He said other methods were available in the Porter case.

Mr. Protess also involves members of the news media to get the story out. He allowed a CBS producer to follow the Porter investigation. And he often consults with a columnist at the *Chicago Tribune.*

Sometimes, Mr. Protess's approach spawns the criticism that he is controlling or didactic.

"There were some issues that we did not agree with him on, how to handle the case, and we would have to do it his way,"

said Laura Sullivan, a student on the Ford Heights case.

Ms. Sullivan, now a reporter with *The Sun* in Baltimore, added, "It's like your greatest defects are also your best assets. It's all those negative attributes that make him so good at what he does."

After the Ford Heights case, Mr. Protess had a well-publicized spat with his students over a movie deal. Ms. Sullivan said the students felt that he pressured them to sign a contract. Mr. Protess said he was angry that the students pocketed their movie fees. He gave his to the wrongly convicted

men. In retrospect, Mr. Protess, who is rejecting movie deals on the Porter case, said he could have been "more understanding' in conveying his views.

Mr. Protess has also learned to alter his dealings with prosecutors and defense lawyers, requiring both to subpoena information. When prosecutors interviewed them about Inez Jackson, Mr. Protess refused to disclose her address.

"I didn't want to have a bunch of cops running up there and interrogating her," he said. "They said, 'We're going to find her anyway.' We said, 'We don't think so.'"

Glossary terms appear in bold type. Page references to captions are italicized. Suffixes to page references are t (table), f (figure), and n (notes).

American Institute of Public Opinion. *See* Gallup Poll

American Medical Association (AMA)
    as interest group, 200
    Medicare and, 376

American Nazi Party, freedom of assembly for, 98–99

American Psychiatric Association, gays classified by, 144

American Revolution, 36–38
    African Americans during, 149

Americans with Disabilities Act (1990), 145, 391

America Online, 221, 222

AmeriCorps, 619

Ames, Aldrich H., *463*, 558
    and Rosario, 554

Amestoy, Jeffrey, 142

Amish church, 100

Amtrak, 609

Ancestry, of U.S. population, 19

Anderson, John B., 254, 263, 308–9

Andreessen, Marc, 598

Andropov, Yuri, 549

Animal sacrifice, 100–101

Annan, Kofi, 592

Annapolis conference, 38–39

Annexations, by U.S., 538

Anthony, Susan B., 329

Anthrax, 519

Antiballistic Missile (ABM) Treaty, 543

Antifederalists, 46

Anti-Masons, 261

Antipoverty program, 619

Antitrust Division, of Justice Department, 475

Antitrust policy, 607–9

Antitrust suit, against Microsoft, 517

Antiwar demonstrators, search warrant and, 108

AOL. *See* America Online

Apartheid, end of, 547

Apollo 11 astronauts, 625

Appellate courts. *See* Courts of appeals

Appropriations bills, 399, 586

Arab Americans, 126

Arab-Israeli Six-Day War (1967), UN and, 560

Arab-Israeli War (1973), 626
    UN and, 560

Arab world. *See also* Islam; Middle East
    energy crisis and, 626
    peace accords of 1994 and, 547

Arafat, Yasir, 295, 547

Arendt, Hannah, 457

Argersinger, John Richard, 112

Arizona, female legislators in, 652

Arkansas, 646

Armed forces. *See also* Military; Wars and warfare; specific wars
    African Americans in Union Army, *149*, 150
    homosexuals in, 144
    in Korean War, 539

Arms. *See* Arms control; Weapons

Arms control
    disarmament and, 569–70
    foreign policy and, 554
    SALT and, 568

Arms Control and Disarmament Agency (ACDA), 554

Arms race, 567–69, *568*

Armstrong, Scott, 502n39, 503n42, 505n47, 526n132

Army, 566

Arnett, Peter, *223*, 563

ARPANET, 219

Arraignment, 521

Arthur, Chester A., 478, *478*

Articles of Confederation (1781–1789), 37–38, *38*
    amendment process for, 46
    dissatisfaction with, 38–39
    state power in, 68

Articles of Constitution
    Article I, 48
    Article II, 48–49
    Article III, 49
    Article IV, 49, 72
    Article V, 49
    Article VI, 49, 72
    Article VII, 46, 49

Ashcroft, John, 534

Asia
    Communism in, 536
    Korean War in, 539

Asian Americans, 125, 134–35, 134t
    in House and Senate, 379

Assassinations
    attempt on Reagan, 186, *187*, 293, 510
    attempt on Truman, 134
    CIA and, 555, 556
    conspiracy theories about, 187
    of Garfield, 186
    of Kennedy, John F., 9, *52*, 186, 187, 418
    of Kennedy, Robert F., 9
    of King, Martin Luther, Jr., 9, 159
    of Lincoln, 186, 187
    of McKinley, William, 186
    political violence and, 186–87

Assembly, freedom of, *98*, 98–99

Associated Milk Producers, Inc. (AMPI), lobbying and, 199

Associated Press (AP), 359
    My Lai massacre coverage by, 220

Associate justices. *See* Supreme Court

Associations, 196

AT&T, breakup of, 607

Atlanta, Georgia
    city-suburban cooperation in, 657
    study of, 663
    subway in (MARTA), 663

Atlanta Journal-Constitution, 236

Atlanta Olympics, bombing at, 236, *237*

Atomic bomb. *See also* H-bomb; Nuclear power
    Chinese, 567
    Russian, 567
    testing of, 10, *10*
    Truman and, 420

Attica, *513*, 513–14

Attorney General, 516–17
    office of, 430n

Attorneys. *See* Lawyers

Attucks, Crispus, 149

Audiotapes (Nixon), 443. *See also* Watergate scandal
    court battle over, 494–95, 501n, 517

Austin, Texas, *655*

Australian ballot, 360

Authorization for Use of Military Force against Iraq Resolution (1991), 552

Authorizations, 399, 586

Automobile industry
    foreign manufacturers and, 596–97
    fuel-powered cars and, 23
    pollution and, *24*, 25
    regulation of, 608–9, *609*

Automobiles, search and seizure of, 105–6, *107*

Auto safety law (1966), 614

Autry, James D., 524

Axelrod, Donald, 600

Baby Bells, 607

Baby boomers
    Social Security and, 603
    stock market and, 599

Bachrach, Peter, 194n4, 194n7

"Backgrounder," 233–34

Bail, 520

Bailey, Michael A., 323

Bail Reform Act (1966), 520

Bailyn, Bernard, 56

Bain, Richard C., 276n59, 279

Baker, Bobby, 390

Baker, Charles W., 364

Baker, James A., 242

Baker, Jim, 377

Baker v. *Carr,* 652

Bakke, Allan Paul, 160

Bakke case, 160

Balanced budget, 588

Balance of payments, 597

Balance of power, 537
    big government and, 74–76

Balance of trade, 596–97

Balancing test, 94

Baldwin, James, 147–49, 165

Baldwin, Tammy, 143

Balint, Peter, 601

Balkan region, conflict in, 548

Ballots, 358–59
    butterfly, 348, *352*

Bandwagon effect, 181

Banfield, Edward C., 657, 663, 670

Banks and banking, Federal Reserve and, 592

Banning, Lance, 56

Barak, Ehud, 547

Baratz, Morton S., 194n7

Barbash, Fred, 41n30, 41n31, 42n34

Barber, James David, 244, 322, 447, 452

Barfield, Margie Velma, 524

Barker, Lucius J., 148n90, 165

Barnburners, 261

Barnes v. *Glen Theatre,* 95

Barnet, Richard J., 537

Barnett, Walter, 100n60

Barone, Michael, 404

Barrett, Edward L., Jr., 508

Barron v. *Baltimore,* 113

Barry, Frank J., 171

Bartels, Larry M., 279

Bartlett, E. L., 624n47

BART subway system (San Francisco), 663

Bauer, Monica, 313n63, 317n80, 319n97

Campbell, Ben Nighthorse, 379
Campbell, Bill, 160
Campbell, James S., 514n91
Camp David peace accords, 543
Canada
    health care in, 622
    NAFTA and, 594
Candidate, The (movie), 309
Candidates. *See* Political candidates
Canon, Bradley, 529
Cantril, Albert H., 190
Cantril, Hadley, 173n20, 175n25, 183n47,
    183n48, 183n57
Cantril, Susan Davis, 190
Capitalism, 584
    laissez-faire, 497
Capital punishment, 522–25
    deterrence value of, 524
Caplovitz, David, 613
Cardozo, Benjamin N., 90, 113
Carlin, George, 225
Carmichael, Stokely, 159, 165
Carmines, Edward G., 166
Carnahan, Jean, 355
Carnahan, Mel, 347
Carpenter, John, *222*
Carr, Joe C., 364
Carson, Rachel, 24n24, 26
Carter, Jimmy, 50, 254, 259, 289, 367n,
    632, 653
    campaign finances of, 313, 314–15
    Civil Service reforms and, 480
    deregulation and, 476
    draft and, 566
    election of 1976 and, 295
    energy crisis and, 633
    impression made by, 335
    Iran hostage crisis and, 468, 544
    media endorsement of, 313
    Middle East breakthrough and, 543
    on PACs, 321
    pardon of draft evaders by, 114
    on presidency, 412
    on president as chief of party, 427
    presidential debates and, 303
    Puerto Ricans freed by, 134
    treaties and, 423
    voter gender and, 334
    voters for, 333
Carter, Robert L., 498n22
Carville, James, 289, 308
Case, Steve, 221
Casey, William J., 551, 554, 558
Casper, Gerhard, 56
Cassell, Paul, 111–12
Castellanos, Alex, 301
Castro, Fidel, 468
    CIA and, 555, 556
    González, Elián, and, 215–16
Casualties
    in Persian Gulf War, 563
    in Vietnam War, 541–42
    among women in Persian Gulf war, 135
Categorical grants, 79–80
Catholics. *See* Roman Catholic Church
Caucus, in House, 385
CBS, 221, 222
    libel suit against, 230
    merger of, 607

Censorship
    of Internet, 88
    of library materials, 94
    of school materials, 93–94
Census, 18
Census Bureau, 19
    projected U.S. population and, 641–42
Center for Auto Safety, 204
Center for Public Integrity, 209
Center for Study of Responsive Law, 204
Central America, foreign policy toward,
    544–45
Central High School, Little Rock, 151–52
Central Intelligence Agency (CIA), 474,
    519, *551, 556*
    abuses by, 555
    Afghanistan and, 544
    Bay of Pigs invasion and, 468
    Castro, Fidel, and, 555, 556
    Congress and, 462–63, 551
    defenses of, 558
    FBI and, 518
    foreign policy and, 554–58
    governments overthrown by, 556
    Guatemala and, 537
    misinformation from, 241
    origins of, 556
Certiorari, Writ of, 503
Chad, 348
    dimpled, 348
    hanging, 348
Chadha case, 400
Challenger space shuttle, 137, 625
Changing American Voter, The (Nie, Verba,
    and Petrocik), 183, 291
Character tests, for voting, 355–56
Charbonneau, Toussaint, 129
Charlotte, North Carolina, school busing
    in, 152
Charter colonies, 35
Chase, Harold W., 44n39, 56
Chase, Salmon P., 505
Chavez, Cesar, 131–32, *132*
Chechnya, 548
"Checkers" speech, of Nixon, 298–99, *299*
"Checkoff law," 316
Checks and balances, 43–44
Check scandal, in House, 401
Chemical warfare, 570
Chemical Weapons Convention (1992),
    570
Cheney, Dick, 305, 344, 391
Chernobyl, nuclear accident and, 634
Chicago, Illinois
    Black Panther raid in, 159
    Daley, Richard J., in, 265, 664, *664*
    Democratic National Convention (1968)
        in, 514
Chief diplomat, president as, 422–24
Chief executive. *See* President of the U.S.
Chief executive officers, top 10 salaries,
    599t
Chief Justice, 489, *503*
    listing of, 505
    role of, 504–5
Chief legislator, president as, 424–27
Chief of party, President as, 427
Chief of state, president as, *416*, 416–18,
    417

Child labor, *70*
Chimel, Ted Steven, 105
China
    competition for power by, 541
    nuclear bomb of, 567
    recognition of, 423, 543
    Tiananmen Square riot in, *543*
Chinese Americans, 134
Chipitts, 657
Chiquita Brands International, law suit
    brought by, 231
Chisholm v. *Georgia*, 50
Chlorofluorocarbons, 630
Christian Coalition, 261
Christians
    evangelical, 202, *202*
    political affiliation of religious right,
        261
Christopher, George, 309
Chrysler Corporation, aid package for, 610
Church(es). *See also* Freedom(s);
        Religion(s)
    colonial, 36
Church, Frank, 449, 558
Churchill, Winston S., 25, 420
    "iron curtain" speech of, 538
Church-state separation, school prayer,
        school aid, and, 101–2
CIA. *See* Central Intelligence Agency (CIA)
Cigler, Allan J., 212
Cincinnati Enquirer, law suit settled by, 231
CIO. *See* Congress of Industrial Organiza-
        tions (CIO)
"Circuit breaker" system, of property tax
        relief, 83
Circuit courts, 506
Cisneros, Henry, 431
Cities, *656. See also* Housing projects;
        Urban areas
    African American migration to,
        643–44
    deterioration of, 658, 660
    governments of, *654*, 654–55, 656–67
    housing and community development
        in, 659–62
    inner-city schools and, 624
    political machines in, 265
    politics in, 663–64
    power structure in, 663
    problems of, *657*, 657–63
    residential patterns in, 21
    suburbs and, 656–57, 665
Citizens and citizenship
    citizen action, dissent, and, 117–18
    composition of U.S. population and,
        115–17
    freed slaves and, 150
    government relationship with, 11–13
    loss of citizenship, 114–15
    qualifications for citizenship, 114
    and voting requirements, 358
City of Erie v. *Pap's A.M.*, 95
Civil Action, A (movie), 218
Civil Aeronautics Board (CAB), 476
Civil cases, 493
Civil disobedience, 13
    by King, Martin Luther, Jr., 493, *493*
Civilian supremacy, 421
    over military, 566

Committee on Political Education (COPE), of AFL-CIO, 200
Committees of Correspondence, 37
Committee system (congressional), 393–97
  chairs and, 394, 398
  procedures, 395–96, 397–98
Common Cause, 203, 209
Common law, 34, 493
Common Market, 594n
Common Sense (Paine), 32
Commonwealth of Independent States, as federal system, 61n
Communication, Internet and, 87–88
Communications Decency Act (1996), 88
Communications director, in White House, 437–39
Communism, national security and, 537
Communist Party, Smith Act and, 104
Community-action programs, antipoverty program and, 619
Community development, 659–62
Community standards yardstick, for obscenity, 96–97
Commuter railroads, 662
Company unions, 611
Compensation, for Indians, 130
Comprehensive Test Ban Treaty (CTBT), 570
Computer technology, 23. *See also* Internet; Technology
Concurrent powers, 68
Confederation, 38
Conference committee, 400
Confidentiality, of reporters and sources, 228–29
Conflict, in post-Cold War world, 547–48
Conglomerates. *See* Corporations; Multinational corporations
Congò, UN and, 560
Congress. *See also* Central Intelligence Agency (CIA)
  African Americans in, 365, 379
  American Indians in, 379
  bills passed in, 399–400
  budget and, 581n, 586
  bureaucracy and, 462–64
  Clinton and, 373–75, 424
  deficit and, 587–88
  domestic affairs and, 415
  ethics in, 400–402, *401*
  fiscal policy and, 586
  foreign policy and, 402, 550–52
  Hispanic Americans in, 365
  laws passed in, 386–87
  Select Committees on Intelligence and, 558
  suburban growth and, 667
  taxes and, 589–90
Congressional Budget and Impoundment Control Act (1974), 398, 402, 587–88
Congressional Budget Office, 397, 399
Congressional committees, 263–64
Congressional districts
  black and Hispanic majorities in, 365
  gerrymandering and, 398
  irregular, 366f
  one person, one vote principle and, 364

suburban, central city, and rural, in U.S. House of Representatives, 365t
  Supreme Court on, 364–65
Congressional investigations, 396–97, *397*
  federal intelligence agencies and, 398
Congressional Record, votes in, 387
Congressional Research Service, of Library of Congress, 397
Congress of Industrial Organizations (CIO), 611
Congress Watch, *204,* 204–5
  Nader, Ralph, and, 196
Conlan, Timothy, 85
Connally, John, 199
Connecticut Compromise, 41
Connor, Eugene "Bull," 154
Conscientious objectors, 99–100
Conscription. *See* Draft (military)
Conservation bill, 373–74
Conservatism
  Bush, George W., and, 5
  of press, 239–40
  Rudman on, 374
  social programs and, 604
Conservative (Tory) Party (Britain), 36
Conservative Party, in New York, 263
Conspiracy theories, about assassinations, 187
Constituencies, 462
  of legislators, 380, 382–83
Constitution
  British, 36
  Fundamental Orders of Connecticut as, 35
Constitution (U.S.), 29, 30, 42. *See also* Articles of Constitution; Constitutional Amendments; Constitutional Convention; Specific amendments
  adaptability of, 54
  amendment process, 49–50, 49f
  amendments, A8–A11
  Bill of Rights and, 29, 46–47, 50
  on citizenship, 114
  completion of, 42–43
  content of, 48–49
  document, A4–A8
  electoral college and, 362
  on equal rights for women, 137–38
  federal system and, 43, 68–74
  Great Compromise and, 40–41
  on House of Representatives, 384
  issues not addressed in, 44–45
  Marshall, Thurgood, on, 46
  motives of framers, 45
  national government in, 43–44
  popular democracy and, 45–46
  press and, 225–32
  ratification of, 46–47, 47t
  requirements for president in, 418
  on right to declare war, 421
  slavery and, 42
  Supreme Court and, 30, 494
  as supreme law of the land, 72
  today, 30–31
  200th anniversary of, 54, *54*
  voting rights under, 356
Constitutional Amendments, 48, A8–A11. *See also* Bill of Rights (U.S.); Constitution (U.S.); specific amendments

amendment process, 49–50, 49f
  Bill of Rights as, 50, 90–114
  later amendments, 50–53
  proposed, 53
  voting rights and, 356
Constitutional Convention, 39–40
  compromises during, 41–42
  federal system and, 68
  presidential title and, 7
Constitutional Union Party, 252
Constitutions, state, 646–48
Consumer, government and, 613–14
Consumer Product Safety Commission, 609, 614
Consumer protection, 196
  interest-group representation and, 210
  regulation and, 477, *477*
Consumers, principal laws protecting, 614, *614*
Containment policy, 415, 538–39
Continental Congress, 32
  First and Second, 37
Contract with America, 53
  unfunded mandates and, 67
Conventions. *See* National convention
Converse, Philip E., 177n29, 329n8, 329n9, 332n16, 334n20, 335n24, 336n26, 336n27, 341n33, 361n74, 367n98, 370
Conway, M. Margaret, 370
Cook, Fred J., 526n124, 526n126
Coolidge, Calvin, 253, 272, 335
Coons, John E., 117
Cooper, Phillip, 529
Cooperative federalism, 65
Corning, Peter A., 376n3
Corporate culture, 7
Corporate PACs, 208t
Corporation for National and Community Service, 619
Corporations. *See also* Business; Industry; Regulation
  governmental, 474
  ten largest U.S., 608t
Corrado, Anthony, 307n38, 313n, 313n63, 318n89
Corrections Calendar, in House, 387
Corrupt Practices Act (1925), 316
Corwin, Edward S., 44n39, 56, 73n, 415, 422n29, 452
Corzine, Jon S., 318
Costain, Anne M., 212
Cost-of-living index, for public financing of candidates, 317n
Costs, of television advertising, 306, 307
Council-manager plan, 655
Council of Economic Advisers, 434–35, 584, 586
Council on Environmental Quality, 632
Counsel, rights to, 111
Counterintelligence, FBI and, 517
Counties, government of, 655
County courts, 507
Coups, in Soviet Union, 15
Court of Appeals for the Armed Forces, 506, 507
Court of Appeals for the Federal Circuit, 506

Federalism (continued)
constitutional basis of, 68–74
cooperative, 65
creative, 65–66
division of federal and state power under, 69–74
dual, 65
in emerging nations, 68
federal aid distribution and, 81–82
future of, 83
historical basis of, 67–68
jurisdictional conflicts and, 64
metropolitan, 668
new, 66
politics and, 76–79
pros and cons of, 61–63
regulatory, 66, 66–67, 82–83
revenue sharing and, 80–81
Supreme Court and, 68–69
Federalist, The, 47
judicial branch and, 496
No. 10, 195, 250, A14–A17
No. 51, A17–A18
No. 84, 91
Federalist Party, 250–51
Federalists, 46
Federal Job Information Centers, 479
Federal Maritime Commission, 71, 475, 609
Federal Regulation of Lobbying Act (1946), 208
Federal Reserve Board, 580, 591
interest rates and, 586
Federal Reserve System ("The Fed"), 475
credit and, 586
monetary policy and, 590–93
Federal system, 43. *See also* Federalism
advantages and disadvantages of, 62–63, 62t
cooperation and tensions within, 64–65
environmental regulation and, 66, 66
interstate agreements and, 74
speed limits and, 58, 59–60
vs. unitary system, 60f
Federal Trade Commission (FTC), 475, 476, 607, 609
consumer protection and, 196
Feedback, in political system, 17
Feingold, Russell D., 315
Feinstein, Dianne, 317, 379
Feldman, Jacob J., 418n
Felonies, 507
Feminism, 138
Fenno, Richard F., Jr., 45, 382, 383, 395, 396n76, 398, 404, 411, 413n12, 452, 465n29
Ferraro, Geraldine, 10, 135, 435
news media and, 311–12
Feuerstein, Aaron M., 583
Fifteenth Amendment, 51, 150
black voting rights and, 356
restrictions on states and, 72
voting rights and, 156
Fifth Amendment, 50
applied to states, 113
Communist registration and, 104
congressional investigations and, 397
due process of law and, 104
rights of accused and, 109

right to indictment by grand jury, 113
self-incrimination and, 110
trials and, 520
Figueroa, William, 300
Filibuster, 392
cloture and, 392–93
against gas deregulation bill, 392
group, 392
in Senate, 391–93
Filipino Americans, 134
Fillmore, Millard, 251n, 263
Films. *See* Movies
Filo, David, 598
Finances. *See also* Economy
campaign, 313–21
as political issue, 296–97
Fineberg, Harvey V., 483n69
Finer, S. E., 26
Finkel, Brian, 141
Finley, Karen, 96, 97
Fiorina, Carleton, 136
Fiorina, Morris P., 279, 337, 370, 384, 404, 463, 464n20
Fire Next Time, The (Baldwin), 147–48
Fireside chats, of Roosevelt, Franklin D., 437
Firestone, Russell A. (Mrs.), 229–30
Firestone tires, defects in, 477, 477, 608
First Amendment, 30–31, 50, 90, 90–94.
See also Press
balancing test and, 94
campus speech codes and, 92–93
congressional investigations and, 397
establishment clause of, 101–3
freedom of assembly and, 98, 98–99
freedom of religion and, 99–103
freedom of speech and, 90–94
freedom of the press and, 94–95, 216
free exercise clause of, 99–101
hate crime laws and, 92
individual vs. societal rights, 88–90, 114
Internet and, 87–88
loyalty and security issue, 103–4
national security vs. individual freedom of expression, 103–4
obscenity and, 95–97
privacy and, 97–98
rights to verbal opposition of police, 92
searches for criminal evidence and, 108
student rights and, 93–94
Supreme Court and, 499, 500
television protected by, 224, 224–25
First Continental Congress (1774), 37
First Lady, role of, 437
First World War, 538
Fiscal issues, federal system and, 81–82
Fiscal policy, 585, 586–90
borrowing and, 589
budget and, 586–88
taxes and, 589–90
Fisher, Andy, 457
Fishing industry, oil spills and, 630, 630–31, 631
Fiss, Owen M., 120
Fitzgerald, A. Ernest, 482, 483
Flag
burning of, 90, 91–92, 92
saluting of, 100
wearing of, 92

Flanigan, William H., 266t, 290n5, 370
Flexible construction, of Constitution, 48
"Flexible" response, 567
Florida
court and political battle over 2000 results in, 348–51
Metro government in, 668
Flowers, Gennifer, 223–24, 300
Flu inoculations, 483, 484
Flynn, Edward J., 265
Foley, Thomas S., 386
Food. *See* Hunger
Food and Drug Administration (FDA), 475, 609
protection by, 612
Food Lion libel suit, 231
Food Stamp program, 80, 615, 620
Forbes, Steve, 224
Forced termination policy, 129
Ford, Gerald R., 64, 254, 261, 289, 367–68, 446n
assassination attempts against, 293
assumption of vice presidency by, 446
campaign finances of, 313
election of 1976 and, 295
New York City and, 659
Nixon pardon by, 419
pocket vetoes of, 425
presidential debates and, 303
press and, 439
primary elections and, 292
Rockefeller Commission and, 436
Supreme Court and, 499, 500
Twenty-fifth Amendment and, 52n
Ford Motor Company
defects in Explorer tires, 477, 608
hybrid car of, 23
Foreign Affairs, 538
Foreign Agents Registration Act, 208
Foreign aid, 558–60
Foreign governments, recognition of, 423
Foreign Intelligence Surveillance Act (FISA, 1978), 109
Foreign policy, 535–37, 536. *See also* Defense establishment; Military-industrial complex
Agency for International Development (AID) and, 558–59
aid to poorer countries and, 558–60
big government and, 75–76
as campaign issue, 297–98
Congress and, 402, 550–52
containment and, 538–39
critics of, 537
defense establishment and, 565
détente and, 543
drug trafficking and, 548
economics and, 563, 598
end of Cold War and, 545–47
executive agreements and, 423–24
future world role and, 573–74
humanitarian interventions and, 537
intelligence operations and, 554–58
internationalism and, 538
interventionism and, 538
isolationist period of, 537–38
toward Latin America, 536–37
machinery of, 552–60
mutual dependence and, 541

MDMA, 511
Meat and poultry inspection laws (1967, 1968), 614
Mecca, Frank, 643n7
Media. *See* Mass media
Medicaid, 80, 615, 620–21
    abortions funded by, 141
Medicare, 588, 615, 616–17
    Congress and, 375–76
Meese, Edwin, III, 111, 516–17
Megalopolis, 657
Meier, August, 165
Meier, Kenneth J., 487
Men. *See* Gender
Mendelsohn, Harold, 307
Meredith, James H., 64, 152
Mergens, Bridget, 102
Mergers
    of Daimler-Benz-Chrysler, 610
    regulation and, 607
Merit system, for appointing judges, 507
Merit Systems Protection Board, 480
Metro (Washington, D.C.), 663
Metropolitan areas. *See also* Cities; Suburbs
    consolidations in, 668
    defined, 642n
    federal funding to, 83
    government of, 656–67
    population of, 642
    solutions for problems of, 667–69
Metzenbaum, Howard M., 392
Mexican Americans, 125
Mexico
    NAFTA and, 594, *595*
    oil in, 633
Miami, Metro government in, 668
Michigan, legislative salaries in, 651
Microsoft Corporation, 580
    antitrust suit against, 517
    breakup of ordered by court, 607, *608*
Middle Atlantic states, townships in, 656
Middle East, 9, 533–34
    Clinton, 1996 campaign, and, 295
    peace accords for (1994), 547
    peace treaty in (1979), 543
    Persian Gulf War in, 545
    power struggles in, 541
    "Seeds of Peace" program and, 559
Middle East Resolution (1957), 552
Midwest
    megalopolis in, 657
    townships in, 656
Migrant labor, Mexican American farm workers as, 130–32
Migration. *See also* Immigrants and immigration
    of blacks to North, 148–49
Mikulski, Barbara A., 196, 379
Milberg, William, 601
Milbrath, Lester W., 196, 197, 209, 327n1, 328n3, 330n11
Milgram, Stanley, 175–76
Military. *See also* Armed forces; Commander in chief; Defense Department
    conscientious objectors and, 99–100
    costs of, 564
    courts for, 506–7

homosexuals in, 144
jargon of, 567
presidential power over, 411
press and, 241–42, *242*
Reagan and, 544
satellites and, 567
Selective Service System and, 566
troops on foreign soil, 552
women in, 135
Military assistance, 539
Military governments, U.S. support of, 536–37
Military-industrial complex, 22, 421–22, 570–72
Military policy, president and, 550
Military spending, 75–76
Militia, Lincoln and, *421*
Mill, John Stuart, 89, 121, 669
Miller, Arthur H., 335n25
Miller, Warren E., 177n29, 329n8, 329n9, 332n16, 334n20, 335n24, 335n25, 336n26, 336n27, 341n33, 341n37, 361n74, 367n98, 370, 383n36, 383n37
Miller v. *California*, 95–96, 97
Million Man March, 159
Million Mom March, 13, 511, *512*
Mills, C. Wright, 194, 212, 460n9
Milosevic, Slobodan, 9, 541
    presidential power and, 411
Mineta, Norman Y., 134
Minimum income, guaranteed, 619
Minimum-wage provisions, 70
Minnesota, 646
    federal funding and, 83
    political parties in, 255n
Minorities. *See also* specific groups
    in cities, 663
    equal rights for, 123–24
    gays as, 142–45
    income of, 124, 124f
    populations of, by group, 134
    protecting through redistricting, 158–59
    Voting Rights Acts and, 157
    whites as, 127
Minority leader, in House, 386
Minor political parties, 261–63. *See also* Third parties
    voting for (1880–1996), 262f
Minow, Newton, 222n9
Miranda, Ernesto, 110, *110*, 111
Miranda warnings, 110–12, *111*, 490, 498, 507
MIRV (multiple independently targetable reentry vehicle), 567, 568
Misdemeanors, 507
Misinformation, from government, 241
Missiles. *See also* Nuclear proliferation
    arms race and, 567–68, *568*
    false alarm for attack, 549
    in Persian Gulf War, 563
    presidential support of, 422
    strategic arms and, 566–69
Mississippi Delta, welfare system and, 618, *618*
Mitchell, Andrea, *240*
Mitchell, George J., *199*, 200, 297, 390
Mitchell, John, 441, 442, 491

Mixed (or modified) free enterprise system, 584
Mob. *See* Organized crime
Mobil, merger of, 607
Moffett, Toby, 196
Mollenkopf, John H., 671
Monarchy, in Britain, 36
Mondale, Walter F., 135, 259, 300, 354–55, 435, 446n
    Ferraro and, 435
    presidential debates and, 304
    primary elections and, 292
    voter geography and, 338
Monetarism, 585–86
Monetary policy, 585, 586, 590–92
Money. *See also* Finances
    city deterioration and, 660
    Congress and, *69*
    lobbyists' uses of, 198–99
Monopoly, 607
    regulation of, 607–8
Monroe, James, 251
Monroe Doctrine, 538
Montesquieu, Baron de, 15, 44
Montgomery, Alabama
    bus boycott in, 153–54
    civil rights march to, 156–57, *157*
Moore, Robert, 78
Morison, Samuel Eliot, 35
Morland, Howard, 226
Morrill Act (1862), 623
Morris, Dick, 268, 308
Morris, Gouverneur, 39, *40*, 42, 384
Morris, Irwin, 601
Morris, J. Anthony, 483
Mortality, infant, 124
Moseley-Braun, Carol, 365
Mosher, Frederick C., 467, 487
Moss, John E., 236
Motor Carrier Act (1980), 476
Motor Voter Act, 67, 360, 432
Mott, Lucretia, 135
Moussaoui, Zacarias, 519
Movies. *See also* specific movies
    filibuster in, 391
    political culture and, 218
Movie stars, FBI intelligence gathering and, 518
Moyers, Bill, 432
Moynihan, Daniel Patrick, 389, 604, 619, 619n28
Muchmore, Lynn, 670
Muckrakers, 217
Mueller, Robert S., III, 518
Mueser, Anne Marie, 666
Muller, Ronald E., 537
Multiculturalism, 123–24, 127
Multinational corporations, 608
Multinational Force in Lebanon Resolution (1983), 552
Mumford, Lewis, 657, 662
Municipal Assistance Corporation, 658
Municipal courts, 507
Muñoz Marin, Luis, 134
Murders, gun control and, 206
Murphy, Thomas P., 667
Murphy, Walter F., 501–2, 503n41, 504n45
Murrah federal building bombing, 7, *228*, 493

Murray, Patty, 379
Music, during political campaigns, 285
Muskie, Edmund, 629
Muslims. *See also* Islam; Middle East
   fighting by, 548
Mutual dependence, 541
Myers, Dee Dee, 438
My Lai massacre, 506
   press coverage of, 220, *220*
Myrdal, Gunnar, 148, 149n92, 165

NAACP
   Brown decision and, 151
   civil rights movement and, 153–54
   opposition to Million Man March,
      159
Nader, Ralph, 193n1, 209, 255, 344–45,
      347, 637
   auto industry and, 608–9
   Congress Watch of, 196, 203–4, *204*
   election of 2000 and, 5, *12*, 284, *284*,
      344–45, 347, 613
   public interest groups affiliated with,
      203, 203–5
   Unsafe at Any Speed and General
      Motors, 612
NAFTA. *See* North American Free Trade
      Agreement (NAFTA)
Napolitano, Grace Flores, 132
NASA. *See* National Aeronautics and
      Space Administration (NASA)
NASDAQ, 6, 579–80, *580*
National Aeronautics and Space Adminis-
      tration (NASA), 457, *458*, 474, 625
   public opinion of, 466
National Archives, *28, 29*
National Association for the Advancement
      of Colored People. *See* NAACP
National Automobile Dealers Association,
      196
National Bank of the United States,
      McCulloch v. *Maryland* and, 69
National chairperson, 263
National Commission on the Causes and
      Prevention of Violence, 509
National committee, 263
National convention, 263, *264,* 266–74,
      267, 269, 270, 275, 276, 277
   delegates to, 270–71
   Democratic, in 1996, 268
   development of presidential nominating
      system and, 273t
   evolution of, 271–74
   future of, 274
   historic role of, 267
   nominating process and, 356–57
   nomination of presidential candidate
      at, 268–70
   Republican convention of 1860, 250
   in 2000, *246,* 247–48, 256
National debt, 589. *See also* Budget;
      Debt; Deficit; Economy; Surplus
National Debt clock, *588*
National defense, budget for, 75–76
National Defense Education Act (1958),
      623
National Economic Council, 434, 586
National Education Association, 624
National Endowment for the Arts, decency
      standards and, 97

National government, 43–44. *See also*
      Constitution (U.S.); Government
      (U.S.)
   growth of, 74–76
   powers of, 44–45
National health system, in Canada, 622
National Industrial Recovery Act, uncon-
      stitutionality of, 70
Nationalism, 539–41
National Labor Relations Act (1935), 611
   Supreme Court on, 70
National Labor Relations Board (NLRB),
      475, 611
National Liberation Front (Vietcong), 541
National Mediation Board, 611
National Organization for Women (NOW),
      138, 139, *139*
National origins system of quotas, 115, 116
National presidential primaries. *See*
      Primary elections
National Public Radio (NPR), 221
National Railroad Passenger Corporation.
      See Amtrak
National Reconnaissance Office (NRO), 557
   CIA and, 556
National Rifle Association (NRA), *70*
   gun control and, 510
   lobbying and, *194,* 202, 205–6
National Right to Life Committee, 205
National Science Foundation, 625
National security, *532,* 535–37
   foreign policy and, 533–35
   global issues and, 573
   individual freedom of expression and,
      103–4
   security pacts of U.S., 540f
   wiretapping, bugs, and, 109
National Security Act (1947), 433, 552,
      555
   amended 1949, 566
National security adviser, 554
National Security Agency (NSA), 557, 566
   abuses by, 555
   CIA and, 556
National Security Council (NSC), 423,
      433–34, 552–53
   CIA and, 555
   Iran-contra and, 545
National security state, 537
National Student Association, CIA and,
      556
National supremacy, 69
National Women's Political Caucus, 138,
      139
Native American Party. *See* Know-Nothings
Native Americans. *See also* American
      Indians
   use of term, 127
Nativity, in cities, 101
NATO (North Atlantic Treaty Organization),
      539, 540f
   expansion of, 548
   Kosovo conflict and, 548
   Yugoslavia bombing and, 8
"Natural-born citizen," defined, 418n
Naturalized citizens, 114, *115*
Natural resources. *See* Environment;
      Pollution
Natural rights, 33, 493
Navajo Indians, 100

Navy, 566
Navy, Department of the, 430n
NBC, 221, 222
Nebraska, 651
   late-term vs. partial-birth abortion in,
      141
"Necessary and proper" clause, 48
Negative advertising, 306–7
Negative campaigning, 296
Nelson, Candice J., 323
Nelson, Michael, 370, 452
Nelson, Robert L., 212
Nerve gas, 570
Netanyahu, Benjamin, 295, 547
Netscape Communications, 598
Networks, issue, 464
Neubauer, David W., 529
Neuborne, Burt, 224n12
Neustadt, Richard E., 419, 424n31, 427,
      431n60, 436n67, 452, 466n36, 472,
      483n69, 549–50
Neutralist policy, UN and, 560
Nevada, female legislators in, 652
Newark, New Jersey, organized crime and,
      525–26
Newcomb, Theodore M., 172n15
New Deal, 258, 415
   economy during, 583–84
   federal bureaucracy and, 459
   federalism during, 65
   government regulation and, 606–7
   labor and, 611
   Supreme Court and, 497
"New Democrats," 258
New Economy, 593
New federalism, 66
New Frontier, 253, 258
New Hampshire, 648, 651
New Haven, Connecticut, 663
New Jersey Plan, 41
New Orleans, river pilot regulation and, 66
New Right, 261
News, biased reporting of, 240
News leaks, 232–34
News media. *See* Mass media
Newspapers, 220–21
   Internet and, 219
   top 10, 221
News programs. *See* Magazine-style news
      programs; Press; Television
New York (state), legislative salaries in,
      651
New York City
   Criminal Court in, 519
   deterioration of, 660
   financial default of, 658–59
   government of, 653, 664
   police lawbreaking in, 515
   Tammany in, 644, 664
   Tweed in, 644
New Yorker magazine, 231
New York Journal, 217
New York Stock Exchange, *599*
New York Times
   confidentiality of reporters' sources
      and, 228–29
   coverage of Clintons by, 240
   libel and, 229
   prior restraint and, 225–26

New York Times rule, 229
New York World, 217
Nicaragua, 411
    CIA and, 558
    Iran-contra scandal and, 433, 544–45, 553
Nicholas, H. G., 26
Nichols, Terry, 8
Nicholson, Henry, 171
Nie, Norman H., 183n50, 183n51, 183n52, 291, 336, 337n28, 370
Niemi, Richard G., 172, 186n64
Nightline (television program), 237
Nimmo, Dan, 188, 290–91, 310
Nineteenth Amendment, 51, *52*, 135, 356
Ninth Amendment, 50
Nitze, Paul H., 537n2
Nixon, Richard
    economic controls of, 592
    Geneva Protocol, 570
    housing programs and, 661
    poverty program dissolved by, 619
    southern politics and, 653
Nixon, Richard M., 30, 253, 254. *See also* Watergate scandal
    Agnew and, 436
    campaigning by, 293
    candidate TV statements and, *312*
    charges of election fraud by, 362
    "Checkers" speech of, 298–99, *299*
    China and, 543
    CIA and, 556
    as commander in chief, 420
    credibility of, 562
    education of voters and, 331
    Executive Office of the President and, 433, *433*
    foreign policy and, 297, 550
    illegal searches under, 105
    impeachment and, 48, 442–43
    impression made by, 335
    justice system and, 491
    lobbying and, 199
    media attacks and, 236–37
    misinformation from administration of, 241
    national security and, 537
    on news media, 311
    NSC and, 433, 552
    officials jailed under, 482
    pardon of, 419
    personality of, 447
    pocket vetoes of, 425
    presidential debates and, 302–3, *303*
    press and, 439
    public opinion and, 169
    resignation of, 9, *300*, 396, *396*, 442
    rights of accused and, 110
    Supreme Court and, 499, 501
    Twenty-fifth Amendment and, 52n, 446
    Vietnam and, 541, 561
    war powers and, 411
    Watergate scandal and, 9, 316, 367, 396, 440–42
    wiretapping, bugs, and, 109
Noelle-Neumann, Elisabeth, 176n27, 176n28, 181
Nominating convention, *272*
Nominating process, voting and, 356–57

Nomination, of presidential candidate, 268–70
Nonpartisan blanket primary, 358
Nonproliferation Treaty, 570
Nonviolence. *See* King, Martin Luther, Jr.
Nonvoters, characteristics of, 329–30
Noriega, Manuel Antonio, 411, 548
    broadcasting of tapes made by, 226, 227
"Normalcy," 538
Norris, Clarence, *73*
Norris-LaGuardia Act (1932), 611
North
    black migration to, 148–49
    Constitution and, 42
North, Oliver L., 317, 396, 409, 440, 545, 552–53, 554
North American Free Trade Agreement (NAFTA), 594, *595*
North Atlantic Treaty Organization. *See* NATO (North Atlantic Treaty Organization)
Northeast, megalopolis in, 657
North Korea. *See* Korean War
North Vietnam. *See* Vietnam War
Novak, Robert, 390n
NOW. *See* National Organization for Women (NOW)
NRA. *See* National Rifle Association (NRA)
NSA. *See* National Security Agency (NSA)
NSC. *See* National Security Council (NSC)
Nuclear age, presidency and, 414–15
Nuclear power, 10, *10. See also* Atomic bomb; H-bomb
    accidents at power plants, 633–34
    environment and, 632–34
Nuclear weapons
    after Cold War, 10
    countries with bombs, 567
    jargon of, 567
    potential destruction from, 567f
    presidential authority and, 420
    presidential support of, 422
    strategic arms and, 566–69
    weapons after Cold War, 564–65
Nuclear proliferation, 535. *See also* Missiles
    reduction of weaponry and, 548
    SALT and, 543
    threat of, 549
Nuclear Regulatory Commission, 633, 634
Nude dancing, 95, 97
Nunn, Sam, 144
Nye, Joseph S., Jr., 541n10, 541n11

Obedience, Milgram's studies of, 175–76
O'Brien, David P., 91, 529
Obscenity, 95–97, *96*
    laws regarding, 498
Obst, David, 220
Occupation
    public opinion and, 173
    voter decision making by, 331
Occupational Safety and Health Act (1970), 82
Occupational Safety and Health Administration (OSHA), 475, 476, 607
O'Connor, Karen, 165

O'Connor, Sandra Day, 78, 136, 158, 490, 500, 501t
    congressional districts and, 366
Office-column ballot, 360
Office of Economic Opportunity (OEO), 619
Office of Homeland Security, 4
Office of International Security Affairs (ISA), 554, 566
Office of Management and Budget (OMB), 434, 466–67, 586
Office of Personnel Management (OPM), 432, 479
Office of Science and Technology Policy, 625
Office of Strategic Services (OSS), 555–56
Office of the U.S. Trade Representative, 435
Ogier, Herbert L., 552
O'Hara, Rosemary, 256n9
Ohio, legislative salaries in, 651
Ohmae, Kenichi, 576
Oil
    crisis, 626
    deposits in U.S., 633
    embargo, 60
    gasoline prices and, 663
    lobbying by industry, 200–201
    Middle East conflicts and, 633
    monopoly regulation and, 607
    spills, 24, 630–31, *631*, 632
O'Keefe, Garrett J., 307
Oklahoma, term limits in, 652
Oklahoma City
    bombing in, *7*, 8, *228*, 231, 492
    busing in, 153
Old-age and survivors insurance, 615–16
O'Leary, Hazel, 431, 484
Oleszek, Walter J., 380n15, 380n16, 380n18, 380n20, 382n25, 383, 385n45, 386n47, 386n48, 386n50, 404
Oligopoly, 607
Olson, Mancur, Jr., 210, 212
Olympic Games. *See* Atlanta Olympics
OMB. *See* Office of Management and Budget (OMB)
O'Neill, Thomas P. "Tip," 385
One-party system, in states, 653
One person, one vote principle, 362–65
On Liberty (Mill), 89, 669
OPEC, 633
Open housing law, 156
Open market operations, of Fed, 592
Open primary, 358
Operation CHAOS, 555
Operation Desert Storm. *See* Persian Gulf War
Operation Rescue, 140n, 141
Operations Directorate, of CIA, 556
Opinion. *See* public opinion
Oppenheimer, Bruce I., 404
Oregon
    environment and, 625–26
    initiative in, 648
Organized crime, 525–26
    Prohibition and, 51
Organized Crime and Racketeering Section, of Justice Department, 526
Original jurisdiction, 503

as popular leader, 428
power of, 448
press and, 438
regulation of industry under, 475–76
social programs of, 604
Social Security and, 612, 615
style of, 446–47
Supreme Court and, 497, 501
Twenty-second Amendment and, 51
voter coalition of, 338
workday of, 418
Roosevelt, Theodore, 253, 261
assassination attempt against, 186
campaigning by, *293*
on presidency, 446
on president as head of state, 417
press and, 438
style of, 447
"tennis cabinet" of, 437
Rosales, Francisco A., 166
Rosenau, James N., 576–77
Rosenbaum, Walter A., 637
Rosenberger, Ronald W., 31
Rosenbloom, Myra, 621
Rosenstone, Steven J., 328n3, 328n7
Rosenthal, Alan, 671
Ross, Alexander Coffman, 285
Ross, Thomas B., 233n41, 468n44, 557n41
Rosselli, Johnny, CIA and, 555
Rossi, Marie, 135
Rossi, Peter H., 665
Rossiter, Clinton, 36n15, 36n16, 36n17,
38n25, 56–57, 196, 251, 254n7, 260,
261n31, 263n34, 274, 414, 416n16,
429n51
Rostenkowski, Dan, 401
Rother, John, 204
Roth v. *United States*, 95
Rourke, Francis E., 462, 463n18, 464, 465,
466n31, 467, 468n42, 487
Rove, Karl, 534–35
Rovere, Richard H., 194
Rowley, James J., 171
Royal colonies, 35
Roybal-Allard, Lucille, 132
Ruby, Jack, 228
Ruby Ridge, Idaho, confrontation at, 463,
491–92
Rudman, Warren B., 374
Rudwick, Elliott M., 165
Ruff, Charles F. C., 444
Rule of law, intelligence agencies and, 555
Rules Committee, in House, 386
Rural areas
defined, 642n
political power of, 364
population of, 642, 642f
Rush, Benjamin, 33
Russert, Tim, 347
Russia. *See also* Soviet Union
after Cold War, 548
nuclear power of, 10, 566
"Rust belt," 595–96
Rutherford, William, 621
Rutland, Robert A., 57
Rutledge, John, 39, 505
Ruud, Casey, 484
Rwanda, 537, 552
Ryan, George, 522

Sabato, Larry J., 245, 309, 314, 323, 648,
671
Sacagawea, 129, *129*
Saenz v. *Roe*, 78
Safe congressional districts, 384, 385
Safe Drinking Water Act, 67
Safeguard, military complex, 568
Safety, in automobile industry, 608, *609*
Safire, William, 195n10, 196n11, 198n20,
232, 273, 391n, 497n
Sahid, Joseph R., 514n91
St. Clair, James D., 443
St. Louis, Pruitt-Igoe in, 659–60, *660*
Salamon, Lester M., 487
Salaries
of federal civil service workers, 469–70
of federal legislators, 380
of president, 418
of state legislators, 650t, 651
of vice president, 469
Sales tax, 643, 645
Salisbury, Robert H., 196n13, 196n14, 212
Salon, Web page of, 219
SALT (Strategic Arms Limitation Talks),
543
SALT I (1972) and, 568, 570
SALT II (1979) and, 570
Sampling, in political polls, 179–81
Sampson, Anthony, 601
Sanchez, Loretta, 132
Sandbox case, in Boston, 526
Sandburg, Carl, 313n62
Sandler, Marion, 136n
Sandoz, Ellis, 389n65
Sanford, Bruce, 245
Sanford, Terry, 62
San Francisco
gay political power, 145
rapid transit in (BART), 663
San Quentin prison, death chamber at, *524*
San-San, 657
Santaniello, Tom, 271
Santeria, animal sacrifice in, *100,* 100–101
Sanzone, John G., 85
Sapin, Burton M., 565
Sasser, Jim, 306
Satellites, Sputnik as, 567
Saudi Arabia
oilfields in, 633
terrorist bombing in, 548
Savage, Robert L., 290–91
Sayre, Wallace S., 461n11, 664n75
Scalia, Antonin, 95, 490, 500, 501t
press bias and, 240
Scammon, Richard M., 19n18, 20n20,
259n, 368n, 370
Scandals. *See also* specific scandals
in Congress, 401
political campaigns and, 298, 299–300
Schantz, Harvey L., 338n, 370
Schattschneider, Elmer E., 26, 184–85,
188–89, 210, 402, 604
Schendel, William, 92
Scherer, Ray, 430n56, 432n64
Schick, Allen, 399, 601
Schlesinger, Arthur M., Jr., 162, 166,
222n9, 409, 410, 452–53, 466n35,
467, 553n26, 637
Schlozman, Kay Lehman, 212

Schmitz, John G., 261
Schneider, René, 555n
Schneiderman, Jill S., 26
School prayer, 53, 101, *101,* 102, *103,* 498
School records, parental rights to, 98n
Schools. *See also* Education; School
prayer; Universities and colleges
Brown decision and, 151
busing controversy and, 152–53
Central High School, Little Rock, and,
151–52
discrimination and financing of, 117–18
financial aid to religious schools, 101–3
Fourth Amendment search/seizure pro-
tections and, 105
government support of, 622–24
inoculations and, *623*
integration of, 64, *64,* 151–52, *152*
overcrowding in, *624*
Pledge of Allegiance in, 89
political socialization in, 172–73
vouchers for, 624
Schott, Wanda, 661
Schroeder, Patricia, 440n
Schwartz, Bernard, 475n56
Schwartz, Murray, 100n63
Schwarz, John E., 637
Schwarzkopf, H. Norman, *241,* 563
Science. *See also* Technology
government support of, 624–25
Scott, Dred, 150, *150*
Scottsboro case, 73, *74*
Scowcroft, Brent, 553, 576
Scud missiles, 563
Searches and seizures, 89, *89,* 104–8, *105,*
107
Search warrants, 105, *105,* 106, 108, 500
Sears, David O., 178
Seattle, Washington, *668*
WTO meeting in, 592, 593, *593*
Secessionist parties, 263
Second Amendment, 50
states and, 113n
Secondary groups, 176
Second Continental Congress (1775), 37
Second Harvest, 620
Second World War, 538
Secretary of defense, 566
Secretary of state, role of, 553
Secretary of the treasury, 586
Secret Service
for political candidates, 294
Reagan assassination attempt and, *187*
Section 8 housing subsidy program, 661
Securities and Exchange Commission
(SEC), 475, 609
Security Council (UN), 560
Security pacts, U.S., 540f
Sedition Act (1798), 48
"Seeds of Peace" program, for Middle East,
559
Segregation, 151, 644
Brown decision and, 151, 494, 498
de facto, 153
on interstate transportation, 154
Supreme Court and, 31
Seidman, Harold, 487
Selective incorporation, 113

Index **I-29**

collapse of, 6, 8, 10, 15, 47, 75, 103, 409, 414, 537, 545–47
end of Cold War and, 6, 10, 414, 545–47
as federal system, 61n
Khrushchev and, 15
U.S. recognition of, 423
world politics and, 10
Space program
funding of, 625
future colonization and, 23
women in, 136–37
Spanish-American War, 538
Speaker, 385
assistants of, 386
Speakes, Larry, 438, 439–40
Special districts, 656
Special Forces, 567
Special interests. *See also* Interest groups; Political parties
federal system and, 63
Special investigations, 385
Special jurisdiction courts, 507
Special prosecutors, 517
Speech
broadcasting of indecent, 225
freedom of, 87–88, 90–94
of public employees, 92
Speech code, on college campuses, 92–93
Speedy trial, 109
Speicher, Howard, 527
Spencer, Stuart, 309
Spencer-Roberts political management firm, 309–10
Spending. *See also* Budget; Defense budget
big government and, 75
congressional approach to, 402
federal, 79–82
mandatory spending programs and, 588
state and local, 645
spending, taxation and, 586
Spin
government misinformation and, 241
use of term, 233
Spin doctors
after presidential debates, 304
use of term, 233
Spirit of the Laws, The (Montesquieu), 15, 44
Split-ticket voting, 257
Spoils system, 478
Sport utility vehicles (SUVs), environment and, *24*, 25
Spotted owl, 625–26
Spurlock, Charles, 527
Sputnik, 567
science education and, 623
Spy scandal, Ames and, 554
Stability, of public opinion, 178
Staffs, congressional, 397
Staggers Rail Act (1980), 476, 609
Stahl, Lesley, 267
"Stalwarts," 478
Standard Oil Company, 201
muckrakers and, 217
Standing committees, 393
of 106th Congress, 394t
Stanford case, 108
Stang, David P., 514n91
Stanley, Robert Eli, 97–98

Stanton, Elizabeth Cady, 135
Stare decisis principle, 493
Starr, Kenneth W., 170, 240–41, 409, 443–44, 517
news leaks by, 233
START (Strategic Arms Reduction Talks), 570
START I (1991) and, 570
START II (1993) and, 570
"Star Wars." *See* Strategic Defense Initiative (SDI, "Star Wars")
State(s). *See also* Federal system; Grants
admission to Union, 72
big government and, 74–76
Bill of Rights and, 50, 90, 112–13
character tests for voting in, 355–56
court system in, 507
division of power with federal government, 69–74
election of governors in, 342t
employees of, 469, 469f
federal grants to, 81f, 81t
federal juries in, 521
federal obligations to, 72
federal system and, 68
judges in, 507–8
most populous, 21
political parties in, 76–77, 255n, 264–66
politics in, 76–79
power of, 71–72
restrictions on, 72
speed limits in, 59–60
State Department, 474
Bureau of Intelligence and Research (INR), 556
employees of, 469
federal agencies and, 554
foreign policy and, 553–54
management of, 553
State legislatures, one person, one vote principle in, 364
State of the Union address, 424
States
bicameral and unicameral legislatures in, 651
constitutions of, 646–48
economy and, 642–43
government responsibilities of, 644–53
governors of, 648–49
initiatives in, 647
intergovernmental relations and, 668–69
judges in, *652*, 652–53
legislatures in, 649–52, 650t–651t
most-populous, 642n
party competition in, 653, 654f
political parties in, 653
politics in, 653
regulation by, 646
responsibilities of, 645
revenues of, 645
solutions for problems of, 667–69
welfare shifted to, 618, 643, *643*
State sovereignty, federal system and, 63
States' rights, 71
Supreme Court and, 497
Statutory law, 493
Stealth bomber, *571*, 571–72
Steering Committee, 393

Steffens, Lincoln, 196
Stein, Herbert, 601
Steiner, Gilbert Y., 615
Stephanopoulos, George, 289, 437, 450
Sternlieb, George, 665
Stevens, John Paul, 78, 105, 351, 426–27, 500, 501t, 502
Stevenson, Adlai, 269n
voter identification with, 335
Stewart, Joseph, Jr., 165
Stewart, Potter, 95, 108, 499
Stewart, William H., 481
Stimpson, George, 51n
Stimson, James A., 191, 383
Stock exchange, *581*, *599*
Stockman, David A., 75n40
Stock market, 6, *578*, 579–80, 599
plunge of (1987), 584, *584*
Stokes, Donald E., 177n29, 329n8, 329n9, 332n16, 334n20, 335n24, 336n26, 336n27, 341n33, 361n74, 367n98, 370, 383n36, 383n37
Stone, Harlan Fiske, 70, 94, 505
Stone, Oliver, 218
Stop-and-frisk search, 106, *107*
Storing, Herbert J., 57
Stouffer, Samuel A., 173n21
Stout, David, 197
Strategic Air Command, 568
Strategic arms, 566–69
Strategic Arms Limitation Talks (SALT). *See* SALT (Strategic Arms Limited Talks)
Strategic Arms Reduction Treaty (START). *See* START (Strategic Arms Reduction Talks)
Strategic Defense Initiative (SDI, "Star Wars"), 422, 568–69, *569*
Strategic deterrence, 567
Strikes, 586
by air traffic controllers, *480*, 481
courts and, 611
Student rights, 30–31
First Amendment and, 93–94
Students. *See also* Schools; Universities and colleges
Fourth Amendment and, 105
political socialization of, 172
Subcommittees, in Congress, 393, 395
Subgovernment, 464
Subsidy, Section 8 housing program as, 661
Substantive due process, 104
Suburbs, 21, *665*, 665–66. *See also* Cities
characteristics of, 666
cities and, 656–57
defined, 642n
housing in, *667*
housing policy and, 661
political power of, 364
politics of, 666–67
population of, 642, 642f
taxes and, 644
voter affiliations in, 333
Subway systems, 663
Succession, to presidency, 444–46, 446t
Succession to power, political parties and, 248
Suez crisis, UN and, 560

Verba, Sidney, 183n50, 183n51, 183n52, 291, 336, 337n28, 370
Vermont, 646, 648
Verner, Liipfert, Bernhard, McPherson and Hand, 198–99
"Veteran preference" system, in bureaucratic recruitment, 479
Veterans Affairs Department, employees of, 468
Veto, 425–27
    legislative, 400
    line-item, 426–27, 648
    pocket, 425
    between 1789 and 2000, 426t
Viacom, 221
    merger of, 607
Vice president
    Ford as, 446
    order of succession and, 446n
    as political heir, 295–96
    role of, 435–36
    salary of, 469
    selecting nominee for, 269–70
    separate election of, 49
    television debates by, 305
    tips for hopefuls, 294
    Twenty-fifth Amendment and, 52
    Twenty-second Amendment and, 412n
Vietcong. *See* National Liberation Front (Vietcong)
Vietnam, boat people from, 116
Vietnam Veterans Memorial (Washington, D.C.), *11*
Vietnam War, *9*, 535, *542*, 552. *See also* Congressional districts; House of Representatives; Legislators; Senate
    Congress and, 398, 551, 552
    conscientious objectors to, 99–100
    court cases and, 506–7
    foreign policy during, 541–43
    Johnson and, 367n, 420, 535
    loss of citizenship and, 114
    McGovern on, 551
    My Lai massacre and, 220
    opposition to, 561
    peace accords after, *542*
    policymaking and, 468
    presidential power and, 410
    press and, 241–42
    protests against, 491
    public opinion about, 541n, 542–43
Violence Against Women Act, 71
Violent crime
    death penalty and, 523–25
    frequency of commission, 509, 509f
Virginia, 648
Virginia Plan, 40–41
Virginia Resolutions, 40
Virtual assistant (VA), 23
Voice of America, 560
Vote-projection systems, 359–60
Voter(s), *330*, *336*. *See also* specific issues and characteristics
    attitudes of, 173t, 328–29
    characteristics of, 327–29
    decision-making by, 330–37
    Hispanic, 132
    impact of campaigns on, 290–91
    influence of polls on, 310

nonvoter characteristics and, 329–30
    opinion of Congress, 380–82, 382t
    participation by, 327
    participation in other countries, 328t
    participation in presidential and House elections, 1960–2000, 326f
    participation in presidential elections, 1880–1996, 327f
    political party accountability to, 276–77
    registration of, 359
    studies of, 331
    targeting of, 291–92
    as ticket-splitters, 291
    timing of picking candidate, 291t
    turnout by group and region, 1996, 329t
    votes by groups in presidential elections, 1960–1996, 332t–333t
Voter News Service (VNS), 181, 361
Voting, 183–84, *184*, *324*, 325–27. *See also* Elections; Electoral system; Political parties; Voter(s); Voting rights; specific parties
    age for, 358
    coalitions and, 338
    coattail effect and, 338–42
    for Congress, 338
    in congressional districts, 363–65
    control of presidency and, 338
    counting of votes, 359–60
    fraud in, 362, *362*
    in House, 387
    House vote, 1928–1996, 339f
    by labor, 612
    literacy and character tests for, 355–56
    for minor and independent parties (1880–1996), 262f
    nominating process for, 356–57
    patterns of, 337–42
    power of, 12
    presidential vote, 1928–1996, 339f
    residency requirements for, 356
    retrospective, 337
    in state legislatures, 364
    by young Americans, 358
Voting machines, 361
Voting rights, 117. *See also* Civil Rights Act; Women's suffrage
    in District of Columbia, 51
    and Fifteenth Amendment, 51
    for former slaves, 150
    for people over 18, 52–53, 502
    poll tax and, 51
    reapportionment and, 498
    suffrage and, 354–55
    of women, 51, *52*, 135
Voting Rights Act (1965), 156–59, 156t, 158f, 356, 365
    amendments to, 355–56
    black registered voters and, 328
    extension of, 157
    poll taxes and, 356n
Voucher programs, religious freedom and, 102
Vouchers, school, 624

Waco, Texas, siege in, *492*, 492–93, 516
Wages. *See* Income
Wagner, Robert F., 611

Wagner Act. *See* National Labor Relations Act (1935)
Waite, Morrison R., 505
Walch, Timothy, 453
Waldman, Steven, 638
Waldo, Dwight, 461
Walker, Daniel, 514n92
Walker, David B., 85
Walker, Jack L., 213
Walker, Samuel, 530
Wallace, George C.
    American Independent Party and, 254, 259n, 261
    assassination attempt against, 293
    campaigning by, 293
    integration and, 64, *65*, 152
    politics and, 653
Wallach, John, 559
Wall Street, *578*, 579, 599
Walsh, Lawrence E., 440
Walt Disney Company, 221
Walter, John Frederick, 588
Waltz, Kenneth N., 562, 563
Walz v. *Tax Commission of the City of New York,* 102n
War Department, 430n, 474
Wards Cove Packing Co., Inc. v. *Atonio,* 500n
War on Poverty, 17, 619, 634
War on Terrorism, 4, 222
War powers, of U.S. government, 68
War Powers Resolution (1973), 44, 402, 410, 412, 421, 551
    Congress and, 398
    legislative vetoes and, 400
Warren, Charles, 40n27, 42n36
Warren, Earl, and Warren Court, 91, 113, 491, *498*, 498–99, 501, 505
    civil rights and, 526
    on justice, 526
    rights of accused and, 109–10
    role of Court and, 527
    school segregation and, 151, 494, 498
Warren, Robert W., 226
Warren Commission, 187, 436
Wars and warfare. *See also* specific wars
    African American soldiers in, 149, *149*
    armed conflicts in 1992 and 1996, 534
    congressional power over, 411
    conscientious objectors and, 99–100
    in 19th century, 538
    nuclear weapons and, 10
    presidency and Congress during, 414–15
    presidential responsibility for, 414, *414*
    television coverage of, 222–23
Warsaw Pact, 548
Washington, D.C.
    lobbyists in, 197, 198
    Metro in, 663
    top 10 interest groups in, 204
Washington, George, 38, *39*, 41, 47, 68n14
    African American soldiers and, 149
    appointments by, 477
    as commander in chief, 420
    at Philadelphia Convention, 39
    political buttons of, *251*
    on political parties, 250
    on presidency, 412
    title of, 7

1972

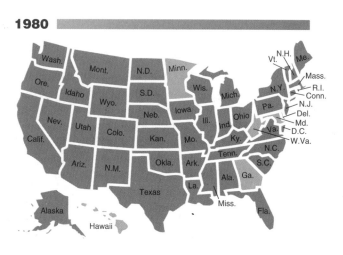

Electoral votes*

McGovern (D) 17
Nixon (R) 521

*A Virginia Republican elector cast his vote for Libertarian Party
candidate John Hospers, making the official count: Nixon, 520; McGovern, 17;
Hospers, 1.

1976

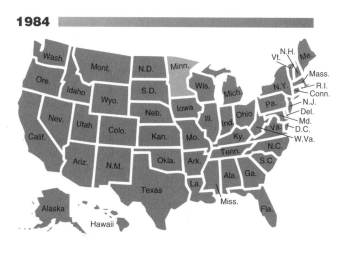

Electoral votes†

Carter (D) 297
Ford (R) 241

†A Republican elector from the state of Washington cast his vote for
Ronald Reagan, making the official count: Carter, 297; Ford, 240;
Reagan, 1.

1980

Electoral votes

Carter (D) 49
Reagan (R) 489

1984

Electoral votes

Mondale (D) 13
Reagan (R) 525